SOURCEBOOK ON ENVIRONMENTAL LAW

Second Edition

Cavendish
Publishing
Limited

London • Sydney

SOURCEBOOK ON ENVIRONMENTAL LAW

Second Edition

Maurice Sunkin, Chief Editor, LLM, Barrister,
Professor of Law,
David M Ong, LLB, LLM, Senior Lecturer in Law,
and Robert Wight, LLB, M Phil, CAS, Lecturer in Law,
all at the University of Essex

Cavendish
Publishing
Limited

London • Sydney

Second edition first published in Great Britain 2002 by Cavendish Publishing Limited
The Glass House, Wharton Street, London WC1X 9PX, United Kingdom

Telephone: +44 (0)20 7278 8000   Facsimile: +44 (0)20 7278 8080

Email: info@cavendishpublishing.com

Website: www.cavendishpublishing.com

Sunkin, Maurice
Sourcebook on environmental law – (Cavendish publishing sourcebook series)
1 Environmental law 2 Environmental law – Great Britain
I Title II Ong, David M III Wight, Robert IV Environmental law
344.4'1'046

ISBN 1 85941 586 5   1 0 0 25 4 1 2 0 7

Printed and bound in Great Britain

PREFACE TO THE SECOND EDITION

The aim of the second edition of *Sourcebook on Environmental Law* is to provide ready access to the principal international, European and domestic sources of environmental law together with an extended commentary and references to secondary materials. In the period since the first edition environmental law has continued to develop in scope and complexity. Against this background we have endeavoured to provide a comprehensive selection of key materials in a single, albeit enlarged, volume.

We have taken the opportunity to fully revise the text and include reference and commentary to key developments, including the Kyoto Protocol 1997, the Aarhus Convention 1998, the Basel Protocol 1999 and the Biosafety Protocol 2000. At the European level there is coverage of the changes introduced by the Amsterdam Treaty 1997; the Water Framework Directive 2000; the new Air Quality Directives; and the EC White Paper on Environmental Liability. There is also discussion of the proposed Sixth Environmental Action Programme. The domestic coverage now includes consideration of the Pollution Prevention and Control Act 1999, the Countryside and Rights of Way Act 2000, the implementation of the contaminated land regime, together with coverage of the new UK Waste Strategy. This edition also includes extensive consideration of the impact of the Human Rights Act 1998 on environmental law.

At the time of writing this Preface the future of the Kyoto Protocol looks a little rosier following the relative success of the Bonn Conference of Parties in the face of US intransigence. Looking ahead, we can anticipate continued developments at the EC level including adoption of the Sixth Environmental Action Programme, a new Directive on Strategic Environmental Assessment, further responses to air and water pollution, as well as the prospect of a new environmental liability regime. We await the UK responses to these developments. In this context we should note that following the 2001 General Election most of the environmental functions of the Department of the Environment, Transport and the Regions (DETR) were transferred to a new Department, the Department for Environment, Food and Rural Affairs (Defra). References to DETR throughout this book should be read with this in mind. Clearly there is much to occupy the attention of environmental lawyers and students of this subject. We trust that this book will make a useful contribution.

The decision of the High Court in *Marcic v Thames Water Utilities Ltd*, was reported shortly after finalisation of proofs (see [2001] 3 All ER 698), but nonetheless deserves a mention. Here it was held that although at common law a statutory undertaker was not liable to a person in its area for failing, negligently or otherwise, to fulfil its statutory duty of drainage by carrying out works necessary to prevent repetition of a nuisance which it had not caused or created, it could be liable under the Human Rights Act 1998. Here, a failure to carry out works to bring an end to flooding of Marcic's property constituted a breach of Art 8(1) of the European Convention on Human Rights (ECHR) (right to a home). There had also been a breach of Art 1 of the First Protocol (peaceful enjoyment of property). The case provides an indication of the way the Human Rights Act 1998 may be used to complement nuisance law as a tool for environmental protection.

Special thanks are owed to Lorna Woods, Reader in Law at Essex, for drawing our attention to European materials that we might otherwise have missed, our students and the reviewers of the first edition for their valuable feedback. Finally we thank Cara Annett of Cavendish Publishing for her continued support and encouragement. We have endeavoured to incorporate developments up to 1 August 2001.

Maurice Sunkin

David M Ong

Robert Wight

October 2001

PREFACE TO THE FIRST EDITION

The aim of this book is to provide convenient access to the primary sources of international, European Community and domestic environmental law. There is now a considerable body of legislation and case law on this subject and we have tried to maintain a balance between the competing needs of comprehensive coverage on the one hand and space and cost on the other. Although we have not included extracts from secondary material we have thought it important to provide a full commentary to each of the chapters as well as more specific commentary to the instruments themselves. A special feature of this book is its inclusion of source materials from across the three jurisdictional dimensions of international, European and domestic law. In this way we hope that the book will be a useful text for students as well as a single source of material which is difficult to find elsewhere.

All authors and editors of legal texts have to cope with change and the habit of judges and legislators to generate important law after texts have been written or sources compiled. Those working in the context of environmental law will be particularly aware of the problems this causes. Although the text of this book was completed during the early autumn of 1997, we have been able to include reference to some of the more significant developments which have occurred since then. In particular the publishers have allowed us to include commentary to, and the relevant extracts of, the Amsterdam Treaty as an Appendix. This Treaty has important implications for European environmental law and we are pleased to have been able to incorporate it.

Unfortunately the Kyoto (Third) Conference of Parties to the Framework Convention on Climate Change which took place during 1–10 December 1997, is too recent for us to give it detailed consideration within the book. However, it is too significant to ignore here.

The Conference of Parties was able to agree a programme of measures aimed at reducing the concentration of greenhouse gases in the atmosphere in order to address the problem of global warming and consequential adverse climatic changes. These measures are notable in moving away from a focus upon setting strict emissions targets as the preferred method for securing reductions in overall greenhouse gas concentrations. A legally-binding reduction target for carbon dioxide (the main greenhouse gas) of at least 5% (below 1990 levels) between 2008 and 2010 has been imposed on most industrialised countries in the Kyoto Protocol (Art 3(1)). However, a system of differentiated targets within the rolling time scale have also been agreed between the main industrialised actors, namely the EU, the US and Japan. Their targets are 8%, 7% and 6%, respectively (Annex B). More important is the inclusion, after insistence by the US, of a provision for the possible establishment of an economic mechanism for the trading of so-called 'emission reduction units' (Art 6(1)). This has raised concerns that richer countries such as the US may be able to purchase such units from countries such as Russia whose emissions have been much reduced of late due to the restructuring of its industries, thereby allowing the richer country to maintain or even increase its own greenhouse gas emissions but nevertheless maintain that it has achieved its target. Provision has also been made for the achievement of these targets not merely by emissions reductions but also through the implementation of forestry projects as 'sinks' to remove these gases from the atmosphere. The success (or otherwise) of these various alternative methods for securing the reduction of greenhouse gas concentrations may open the way for their possible introduction within other international environmental agreements.

Finally, there are a number of people who have helped us in the production of this book. We owe a special debt of gratitude to Elaine Kelly and Alison Smith for so efficiently helping with the typing; to our colleagues at Essex, Nick Bernard, Geoff Gilbert and Steve Peers for guiding us to international and European Community materials which we might have otherwise have missed; to our publishers, and especially Jo Reddy, for their patience and encouragement. We alone are responsible for the content.

Every effort has been made to trace all the copyright holders but if any have been inadvertently overlooked the publishers will be pleased to make the necessary arrangement at the first opportunity.

Maurice Sunkin
David Ong
Robert Wight
University of Essex
December 1997

NOTE ON TERMINOLOGY

The Maastricht Treaty (in force 1 November 1993) created the European Union which rests on three foundations: (1) a common foreign and security policy; (2) the development of home affairs and justice policy; and (3) issues covered by the European Community. Each element has different policy-making processes, but basically the powers of the Commission and Parliament are greater in relation to (3) than (1) or (2). All matters falling within (1) and (2) are exclusively European Union policies and should be referred to as such. Legislation under the amended Treaty of Rome (including all environmental matters) can either be called EC law or EU law because the European Community is also part of the European Union. For the sake of consistency this text endeavours to refer throughout to EC law and policy, where the context dictates otherwise.

It is also worth noting that the Maastricht Treaty amended the Treaty of Rome by replacing the term 'European Economic Community' with European Community. It is now incorrect to use the former term when referring to legislation which has come into force since the Maastricht Treaty.

CONTENTS

Contents

Contents

TABLE OF CASES

TABLE OF STATUTORY INSTRUMENTS

TABLE OF EU LEGISLATION

TABLE OF OTHER LEGISLATION

STANDARD TEXTS AND REFERENCES

TEXTS REFERRED TO THROUGHOUT THIS BOOK

Alder, J and Wilkinson, D, *Environmental Law and Ethics*, 1999, London: Macmillan

Bell, S and McGillivray, D, *Environmental Law*, 5th edn, 2000, London: Blackstone

Birnie, P and Boyle, A, *Basic Documents on International Law and the Environment*, 1995, Oxford: OUP

Birnie, P and Boyle, A, *International Law and the Environment*, 1992, Oxford: OUP

Elworthy, S and Holder, J, *Environmental Protection Text and Materials*, 1997, London: Butterworths

Garner, JF, *Garner's Environmental Law*, updated quarterly, London: Butterworths (loose leaf)

Grant, M and Tromans, S, *Encyclopaedia of Environmental Law*, updated quarterly, London: Sweet & Maxwell (loose leaf)

Gillies, A, *Guide to EC Environmental Law*, 1999, London: Earthscan

Haigh, N, *Manual of Environmental Policy: The EC and Britain*, London: Longman (loose leaf)

Hughes, D, *Environmental Law*, 3rd edn, 1996, London: Butterworths

Jans, J, *European Environmental Law*, 2nd edn, 2000, Groningen: Europa

Kiss, A and Shelton, D, *Manual of European Environmental Law*, 2nd edn, 1997, Cambridge: Grotius

Krämer, L, *EC Environmental Law*, 4th edn, 1999, London: Sweet & Maxwell

Krämer, L, *Focus on European Environmental Law*, 1992 and 1997, London: Sweet & Maxwell

Lyster, S, *International Wildlife Law: An Analysis of International Treaties Concerned With the Conservation of Wildlife*, 1985, Cambridge: Grotius

Malcolm, R, *A Guide to Environmental Law*, 1994, London: Sweet & Maxwell

McEldowney, JF and McEldowney, S, *Environment and the Law: An Introduction for Environmental Scientists and Lawyers*, 1996, Harlow, Essex: Addison Wesley Longman

McEldowney, JF and McEldowney, S, *Environmental Law and Regulation*, 2001, London: Blackstone

Sands, P, *Principles of International Environmental Law, Vol 1: Frameworks, Standards and Implementation*, 1995, Manchester: Manchester UP

Scott, J, *EC Environmental Law*, 1998, London: Longman

Somsen, H (ed), *Protecting the European Environment: Enforcing EC Environmental Law,* 1996, London: Blackstone

Tromans, S, Encyclopaedia of Environmental Law, 1995, London: Sweet & Maxwell (looseleaf)

Tromans, S, Nash, M and Poustie, M, *Current Law Statute Annotations on the Environment Act 1995,* 1995, London: Sweet & Maxwell

Wolf, S and White, AH, *Principles of Environmental Law,* 2nd edn, 1997, London: Cavendish Publishing

Ziegler, AR, *Trade and Environmental Law in the European Community,* 1996, Oxford: Clarendon

FURTHER READING

Each chapter will end with a list of further reading. General reference, however, should be made to the periodical literature contained in:

The Journal of Planning and Environment Law (Sweet & Maxwell); *Environmental Liability* (Law Text); *The Journal of Environmental Law* (OUP); *Water Law* (John Wiley); *Environmental Data Services (ENDS) Reports* (Environmental Data Services); *European Environmental Law Review* (Kluwer); *Review of European Community & International Environmental Law; Environmental Law Review* (Blackstone); *Yearbook of International Environmental Law* (OUP); *The Yearbook of European Environmental Law* (OUP).

LIST OF USEFUL ENVIRONMENTAL WEBSITES

International Organisations

United Nations: www.un.org

United Nations Environment Programme (UNEP): www.unep.org

International Court of Justice (ICJ): www.icj-cij.org

Global Environment Facility: www.gefweb.org

Law of the Sea Office at the UN: www.un.org/Depts/los

International Maritime Organisation (IMO): www.imo.org/home_noflash.html

Joint Website of the Biodiversity-related Conventions: http://216.95.224.234/rio-conv/websites.html

European and UK Government Organisations

Environmental Agency: www.environment-agency.gov.uk

English Nature: www.english-nature.org.uk

European Union On-Line: http://europa.eu.int/index_en.htm#

European Court of Justice: www.curia.eu.int

European Environment Agency: www.eea.eu.int

European Court of Human Rights: www.echr.coe.int

UK Government: www.open.gov.uk

Department for the Environment, Food and Rural Affairs: www.defra.gov.uk/environment/index.htm

Department of Transport, Local Government and Regions:
www.local-regions.detr.gov.uk

Department of Trade and Industry: www.dti.gov.uk

Environment, Food and Rural Affairs Select Committee: www.parliament.uk/commons/selcom/efrahome.htm

Transport, Local Government and Regions Select Committee: www.parliament.uk/commons/selcom/tlrhome.htm

Royal Commission on Environment Protection: www.rcep.org.uk

Non-Governmental Organisations and Research Institutes

Directory of Environmental Monitoring Organisations and Institutes: www.gsf.de/UNEP/contents.html

Environmental Treaty and Resource Indicators: www.sedac.ciesin.org/entri

European Environmental Law: www.asser.nl/EEL

Friends of the Earth International: www.foei.org

Friends of the Earth (UK): www.foe.org.uk

Greenpeace International: www.greenpeace.org/index.shtml

Greenpeace (UK): www.greenpeace.org.uk

International Union for the Conservation of Nature: www.iucn.org

Project on International Courts and Tribunals (PICT):
www.pict-pcti.org/news/news.html

TRAFFIC – the Wildlife Trade Monitoring Programme of the WWF and IUCN: www.traffic.org

UK Environmental Law Association: www.ukela.org

World Wide Fund for Nature (WWF) Global Network: www.panda.org

PRINCIPAL CITATIONS

AJIL	American Journal of International Law
Cm	Command Paper
Cmnd	Command Paper
CMLR	Common Market Law Reports
CML Rev	Common Market Law Review
D & R	Decisions and Reports of the European Commission on Human Rights
ECR	European Community Law Reports
EELR	European Environmental Law Review
EGCS	Estates Gazette Current Survey
EHRR	European Human Rights Reports
ELM	Environmental Law Monthly
ENDS	Environmental Data Services
Env Liability	Environmental Liability
Env LR	Environmental Law Reports
EPL	Environmental Policy and Law
HC	House of Commons
HUDOC	Human Rights Documents (European Court of Human Rights)
ICJ Rep	Reports of the International Court of Justice
ICLQ	International and Comparative Law Quarterly
ILM	International Legal Materials
ILR	International Law Reports
JEL	Journal of Environmental Law
J Leg Studies	Journal of Legal Studies
JPL	Journal of Planning and Environmental Law
LMELR	Land Management and Environment Law Reports
MLR	Modern Law Review

OJ	Official Journal of the European Communities
OJLS	Oxford Journal of Legal Studies
PLR	Planning Law Reports
UKTS	UK Treaty Series
UNTS	UN Treaty Series

CHAPTER 1

SOURCES AND PRINCIPLES OF ENVIRONMENTAL LAW

INTRODUCTION

Environmental problems may be local, regional or global. The effects of global warming, ozone depletion, and contamination of the high seas do not recognise territorial or jurisdictional boundaries. For this reason global, regional and local responses are often necessary to establish standards, to co-ordinate actions and to cajole States, industry and us as individuals to work to improve and protect our environment. One consequence is that lawyers handling environmental issues have to work with legal materials which span international, regional and domestic systems of law. This sourcebook, therefore, presents the principal sources of environmental law to be found in international law, European law and UK domestic law.

Environmental law is increasingly relevant across an ever-widening range of activities affecting industry and commerce, land use planning, health and safety at work, as well as the way we organise our domestic lives. This means that while much of the law is very specialised, it is increasingly likely to impinge upon the work of those who do not regard themselves as environmental lawyers.

While this book presents the principal sources of law, those studying environmental law will quickly discover that this area of law is developing extremely rapidly. Lawyers must keep on their toes and must be aware of where the law is to be found at any given time. This book will provide guidance to these sources, critical commentary and pointers to future developments. Also, the law cannot be understood in isolation from economic, moral and scientific considerations. For instance, it has been emphasised that the rules of nature are basic to environmental law and that '[E]nvironmental law depends on science to assess and predict the environmental impact of many human activities' (McEldowney and McEldowney (1996) 8).

Throughout the book we shall see situations where it is difficult to identify the precise point at which policy and principle become law. This will be clearly seen when we consider declarations, resolutions and other instruments produced by international conferences such as the Rio Declaration (see p 69, below) which set out principles in aspirational rather than legal terms. Such instruments are often described as 'soft law' because they seem to sit somewhere between law properly so-called and expressions of policy and hope. We shall also see that the line between policy and law becomes blurred when legal regulation is mediated through the discretion conferred on bodies such as the Environment Agency which is required to exercise its powers having regard to guidance issued by the Secretary of State (s 4(4) of the Environment Act 1995). This contributes to the extreme complexity of environmental law.

This chapter introduces the main sources of law which are of particular relevance to environmental lawyers, the key principles of environmental law and presents extracts of the key instruments containing these principles with a brief commentary. It also contains a section on liability for environmental damage.

THE SOURCES OF ENVIRONMENTAL LAW

Environmental law: the international perspective

At the international level, the primary actors recognised by public international law are States, although it is now widely accepted that States are no longer the only subjects of international law and that international law governs the activities of bodies which are not States such as international or inter-governmental organisations, non-governmental organisations (NGOs), multinational or transnational corporations and individuals (Sands (1992) 103). Despite this expansion in the number and types of subjects of international law, international legal rules are generally framed in terms of obligations entered into by States and the international legal framework regulating, for example, pollution and nature conservation is in practice based on State-to-State relations, either at the bilateral or multilateral levels. A short description of the generally accepted sources of international environmental law follows. However, before this discussion is entered into, it is important to stress that in principle States incur obligations under international law, including international environmental law, only when they have consented to such obligations.

Since the end of the Second World War, and especially following the establishment of newly independent States, the development of international law has been governed by one abiding principle: all States recognised under international law are regarded as both sovereign and equal in their relations with each other. International law is therefore a body of rules which these sovereign and equal States have explicitly or implicitly consented to. For example, with respect to treaties or conventions, which as we shall see are an especially important part of international environmental law, such consent is formally acquired through the signature and ratification process. In terms of general or customary international legal obligations, however, it has been argued that the requirement of consent need not be expressly provided for in order to hold that a State is bound by such obligations. Indeed, the increasing amount of State practice, in the form of domestic legislation and national institutions for environmental protection in similar issue areas to those that have received international attention, would appear to support the notion that most States are bound by certain general rules of customary international law regarding the environment without the need for formal evidence of their consent. Nevertheless, it is imperative to note that the consent of States is an essential element to the operation of international law and international environmental law.

International environmental law is a relatively new branch of international law. It is generally accepted that a truly international environmental movement, in global terms, only began in 1972 on the occasion of the Stockholm Conference on the Human Environment, which yielded the now famous Stockholm Declaration (see p 61, below). Aside from such global instruments, much of the law is found in the burgeoning number of environmental treaty regimes that either have been, or are being, established to respond to particular environmental problems. Some of these problems have been with us for a while, others are of more recent pedigree. All now require prompt action.

Another important aspect of international environmental law is the specific nature of many modern environmental threats. These require both detailed regulation as opposed to broad guidelines to combat them effectively and explicit rules, which are nevertheless susceptible to simple amendment procedures when new scientific information, for example, is available. In many cases there is also need for international co-operation in the identification, monitoring and prevention or control of the environmental problem concerned. These factors mean that negotiation of new treaty regimes is likely to be a more effective technique for legal change than reliance on the usually slower accretion of *opinio juris* and State practice giving rise to new rules of customary international law. The result is that codified rather than accumulated rules prevail.

The sources of international environmental law

The key sources of international environmental law are the same as those which are traditionally recognised by general international law, namely: (1) international treaties or conventions; (2) customary international law; (3) general principles of law; and, as secondary sources (4) judicial decisions and the writings of eminent publicists. These sources are referred to in Art 38(1) of the 1945 Statute of the International Court of Justice (ICJ) as those sources which will be applied by the ICJ in cases that come before it. Questions, however, remain as to whether these traditional sources of international law are exhaustive in respect of new subject areas such as international environmental law. As Sands notes, '(T)he list of sources identified in Art 38(1) does not wholly reflect the sources of obligation, broadly understood, which have arisen in international environmental law' (Sands (1992) 103). In particular, as we shall see, many developing principles of international environmental law are also to be found set out in declarations and resolutions which are not themselves binding sources of law. These are often referred to as international 'soft law' by commentators. Each of the main sources of international environmental law will be considered briefly.

International conventions or treaties

Establishing rules expressly recognised by the States concerned, international conventions or treaties represent the clearest form of legal obligations between States. Accordingly, it has been suggested that the existence of a treaty relating to any particular matter will usually provide a clear and conclusive statement of the rights and duties of the States parties to it in their relations with each other. Treaties often require, in addition to signature at the conclusion of negotiations, ratification by parties. In the case of multilateral treaties, ratification by a minimum number of States parties is often required before they come into force (and then only between those ratifying States). Rules concerning the conclusion, application, interpretation, reservation, amendment, invalidation, suspension, and termination of treaties are set down in the 1969 Vienna Convention on the Law of Treaties, which codified and in certain respects added to the customary international law on the subject.

Treaties are only binding upon States that are parties to them, although the provisions of certain 'law-making' treaties may become binding upon other States if they are adjudged to reflect or to have passed into customary international law (for example, the UN Convention on the Law of the Sea 1992, see Chapter 3, p 214, below). Factors which are relevant in assessing the law-making authority of a particular treaty's provisions include: whether it was concluded for the purpose of laying down general rules of conduct among a large number of States; the subject matter it addresses; the number of States participating in its negotiation; the number signing it or becoming parties to it; the commitments it establishes; and State practice prior to and following its entry into force (Sands (1995) 105).

Customary international law

While being a significant source of international legal obligations between States generally, customary international law fulfils a less significant role in international environmental law. This is because customary rules generally take time to evolve and rarely fulfil the specific requirements of international environmental law. It is widely accepted that two main elements are required to be present in the establishment of any particular rule of customary international law. These are, first, the physical element as evidenced by a general and consistent pattern of State practice and secondly, the psychological element of acceptance by these States that such practice is either required or allowed by law, the so-called criterion of *opinio juris*. The presence of these two elements, of State practice and *opinio juris*, is sufficient to prove the existence of a binding rule of customary international law.

Once it has been determined that a rule of customary international law exists, then in principle it is binding upon all States. However, the essential role of consent in the formation of customary international law, as in all international law, has two important consequences. If a State persistently objects to an emerging rule of customary international law, it may not be regarded as being bound by that rule. Secondly, as a corollary to the requirement of consent, it is unnecessary to have recourse to the *general* practice of States in order to create the presumption that a particular State is bound by a rule if it can be proved that the State in question has in fact consented to the rule by its *own* practice.

General principles of international law

Unlike treaties and custom, general principles do not usually play a major role as a primary source of international law. Nonetheless these principles are important to the current development of international environmental law (Birnie and Boyle (1992) 21). There are two views as to the nature and application of general principles of international law. The traditional view is that these principles amount to no more than generally accepted procedural rules that are present and accepted by most national or domestic legal systems. Among these, for example, are the principles of good faith between States in their diplomatic relations and the provision of a fair and equitable legal process for the settlement of disputes. This type of general principle designed to ensure procedural fairness has been acknowledged by the ICJ but is rarely relied upon to settle disputes that come before it.

On the other hand, it has been argued that international law includes principles which have been recognised by the States themselves as governing relations between them, either generally or specifically. Such substantive principles include the prohibition against use of force, basic principles of human rights, the freedom of the seas, and the prevention of harm to another State's territory. The recognition of these substantive principles of international law, in addition to the more commonly accepted procedural ones, enhances the general body of applicable international law, especially international environmental law. As has been noted, '(S)uch an approach could be helpful in developing international environmental law, perhaps eventually leading to the acceptance of principles of precautionary action, sustainable development, equitable utilisation of shared resources, etc' (Birnie and Boyle (1992) 22). These principles, however, are often enunciated in the form of inter-governmental declarations which are codified but without the usual signature and ratification process to confirm the consent of States as in a treaty. There now exists an increasing number of these so-called 'soft' law instruments, two of which – the Rio and Stockholm Declarations – are set out later in this chapter (pp 69 and 63, below). There is considerable uncertainty as to the validity of such declarations as a source of international law. One argument is that the general principles laid down in these declarations are secondary sources of international law, which will only become sources of law when applied or enunciated by the ICJ or other international adjudicatory bodies (Birnie and Boyle (1992) 22).

It has been argued that even if 'soft' law rules are not binding *per se*, they play an important role in the field of international environmental law. They do so in at least three ways: by pointing to the likely future direction of formally binding obligations; by informally establishing acceptable norms of behaviour; and by codifying or possibly reflecting rules of customary international law (Sands (1995) 103).

Judicial decisions and the writings of eminent publicists

These are explicitly stated in the Statute of the ICJ to be subsidiary or secondary means for the determination of international law. There have been very few international law cases concerning the environment[1] and at least one of the major commentaries on international environmental law has suggested that the impact of cases on the progressive development of the law has been over-emphasised (Birnie and Boyle (1992) 24–25 and 145–46).

By contrast the literature on the subject has burgeoned of late. In international law generally, the published works of some academic writers and reports of international codification bodies, such as the International Law Commission, have been recognised by national and international adjudicative bodies as indicating the law as well as the way the law is developing. Their impact on the development of international environmental law however has yet to be felt.

United Nations General Assembly Resolutions

United Nations General Assembly Resolutions on environmental subjects (as well as in other fields of international law) have also been proposed as a source of international law, imputating international legal obligations upon States voting in favour of such Resolutions. Since membership of the UN now comprises most States constituting the international community, resolutions of the General Assembly may be argued to be generally representative of world opinion and cited as evidence of the *opinio juris* of States

---

1   The principal cases include: *Trail Smelter Arbitration Case (US v Canada)* (1938 and 1941) 3 RIAA 1905; *Corfu Channel Case (Merits) (UK v Albania)* (1949) ICJ Rep 4; *Lake Lanoux Arbitration (Spain v France)* (1957) 24 ILR 101; *Nuclear Test Cases (Australia v France, New Zealand v France)* (1974) ICJ Rep 253, p 457.

(Birnie and Boyle (1992) 19). In principle, there is no reason why support for United Nations resolutions should not evidence such consent, but in fact most States do not intend – which is the crucial test – their support to be taken as consent to any rule of law which the resolution may purport to lay down, and in the absence of such intention an affirmative vote for a resolution is merely a declaration of political intent and not an assumption of legal obligation (Churchill and Lowe (1999) 9). Despite this and other reservations, it has been argued that although resolutions are not *per se* binding upon States, even those that have supported them, they may become so in the light of the subsequent conduct of these States (Birnie and Boyle (1992) 19).

Environmental law: European Community perspective

European Community (EC) law is to be found in the various treaties from which the European Union (EU) is derived;[2] in numerous pieces of legislation passed by Community institutions; in international treaties to which the EU is party and which become binding on Member States; and in the judgments and principles of the European Court of Justice (ECJ) (see Note on Terminology, p ix).

The treaties

Although it is convenient to refer to EC law, today's EU is based on three founding treaties. The 1951 Paris Treaty which established the European Coal and Steel Community; the 1957 European Atomic Energy Community Agreement (EURATOM); and the 1957 Treaty of Rome creating the European Economic Community. The first two agreements related to particular sectors of the economy and are not relevant to our discussion. The EEC dealt with all sectors of the economy not covered by the other two agreements and was joined by the UK in 1973. The Rome Treaty has since been amended on a number of occasions, notably by the inter-governmental conference which resulted in the Single European Act 1986 establishing the single market; by the Treaty of European Union signed at Maastricht in 1991 which aimed at economic and monetary union and greater inter-governmental co-operation; and the treaty of Amsterdam signed in 1997.[3]

The original task of the EC as formulated in Art 2 of the Treaty of Rome was to 'promote ... a harmonious development of economic activities, a continuous and balanced expansion, an increase in stability and accelerated raising of the standard of living and closer relations between the states belonging to it'. The emphasis then was on the need to promote peace in Western Europe through economic co-operation and by raising the living standards of ordinary people. Environmental issues were not addressed by the Treaty and indeed the term 'environment' did not appear. This is hardly surprising when one recalls that the environmental problems so familiar today were simply not recognised in the 1950s in the context of war-damaged economies and the need to reorganise industries and promote self-sufficiency in food supplies. However, during the course of

---

2   Paris Treaty establishing the European Coal and Steel Community Treaty 1951; European Atomic Energy Community Agreement 1957; Treaty of Rome 1957 creating the European Economic Community Treaty; the 1986 Single European Act; Maastricht Treaty 1992 (amending the Treaty of Rome); Treaty of Amsterdam 1997 (further amending the Treaty of Rome).

3   Also the Treaty of Nice aimed primarily at preparing EC Institutions for further enlargement. It was signed December 2000 and is yet to be ratified.

the more affluent 1960s and 1970s it became apparent that the achievement of the Treaty's aims could no longer 'be imagined in the absence of an effective campaign to combat pollution ... or of an improvement in the quality of life and the protection of the environment'.[4]

To quote from the 1972 Declaration of Heads of State and Government: '... [e]conomic expansion is not an end in itself. Its firm aim should be to enable disparities in living conditions to be reduced ... It should result in an improvement in the quality of life as well as in standards of living. As befits the genius of Europe, particular attention will be given to intangible values and to protecting the environment, so that progress may really be put at the service of mankind.' (Commission Sixth General Report (1972) 8.)

Although this makes formal recognition of a link between economic growth and environmental degradation it is too simplistic to say that all European environmental law appeared after this date. To further the goal of a common market, the Treaty required the dismantling of all barriers to the free movement of 'goods, persons, services and capital'. This necessitated the development of common policies in various sectors of the economy, notably agriculture, fisheries, transport and energy (Arts 2 and 3). This, in turn, saw the promulgation of 'quasi-environmental instruments' such as the Directive on Noise from Motor Vehicles 70/157 (since amended) which *inter alia* set noise levels for different categories of cars, buses and lorries. Although the Directive has an obvious environmental effect, its purpose was not expressed to be a reduction in noise pollution *per se*, but rather to place an obligation upon States not to obstruct the free market by prohibiting the entry of vehicles which did not comply with their national noise standards.

This tacit acceptance of the need to harmonise national environmental standards to promote the common market together with the need to promote quality of life, led to the promulgation of what became the first of five Community Programmes of Action on the Environment in 1973 (see p 28, below).[5] It is important to note that these programmes do not constitute a legal basis for Community law-making. They can best be described as political declarations of intent. However, numerous environmental measures did appear prior to the insertion of the environment title into the Treaty in 1986 and two Articles of the Treaty were used to permit the enactment of environmental measures.

Article 94 (formerly Art 100) enables directives to be made that seek to harmonise the laws and administrative practices of Member States which directly affect the establishment or functioning of the Common Market. The use of this Article again tends to suggest a close link between environmental standards and economic policy. It again recognises that if the law regulating producers in one Member State imposes stricter limits on pollution than those in a neighbouring Member State, then this will distort trade and competition and would amount to a disguised subsidy in the latter case. It is possible to describe many of the European environmental measures discussed in this book as attempts to ensure a level playing field for producers within the Community.[6]

---

4   Declaration of the Council of Ministers on the Programme of Action of the European Communities on the Environment, 22 November 1973.
5   The sixth Programme of Action on the Environment is currently under consultation, see p 30, below.
6   *Commission v Italy* [1981] CMLR 331 – environmental matters do fall within Art 100.

The other Article used to justify environmental measures was Art 235 (now Art 308) which allows the institutions of the EC to take appropriate measures to attain any of the objectives of the EC that cannot be achieved through other powers. This Article has been used to justify purely environmental measures such as the Wild Birds Directive 79/409.

If there was a blurring of economic and environmental objectives in legislation appearing in the 1970s and early 1980s, the EC had demonstrated a clear commitment to pure environmental law by 1986 when a firm legal basis for environmental provisions was provided by the Single European Act 1986.[7] This basis now exists even where the legislation has no direct link to the economic aims of the EU. The EU's commitment to environmental protection has since been strengthened by changes wrought by the Maastricht and Amsterdam Treaties (see pp 18 *et seq*, below).

The institutions of the EC

The European Commission is the main executive body of the EC, (see Arts 211–19). There are 20 commissioners nominated by Member States who are required to be 'completely independent'[8] in the performance of their duties, that is, they do not represent their own country's interests but must act in the general interests of the Community. The larger Member States (Germany, France, Italy, Spain, and the UK) have two members, the other countries provide one Commissioner each. The current Environment Commissioner is Margot Wallstrom from Sweden. The Amsterdam Treaty (Art 214) has introduced a requirement that the appointment of the President of the Commission must be approved by the European Parliament. The Commission is divided into 30 Directorates-General each with its own portfolio. DG XI has specific responsibility for environmental matters.

The role of the Commission within the EC is crucial and indeed it has been described as the guardian of the treaties. In our context it can: (a) set the agenda for environmental protection by proposing environmental policy; (b) play a major role in law-making by formulating proposals for legislation which are then passed to the Council. Under Protocol No 9 of the Amsterdam Treaty, the Commission is required to provide all consultation documents and proposals for legislation to national Parliaments. This is intended to ensure greater involvement by national parliaments in the activities of the EC and to enhance their ability to (c) express their views on matters which may be of particular interest to them; and (c) it also has wide enforcement powers to ensure that Community law is not breached.[9] Article 226 of the Treaty provides that if the European Commission considers that a Member State has failed to fulfil its obligations under the Treaty, it shall deliver a reasoned opinion on the matter after giving the State concerned the opportunity to submit its observations. Most cases would be settled by negotiation at this stage but if the State does not comply with the opinion within a period set by the Commission, then the latter may bring the matter before the European Court.

---

7 Originally Title VII, now Title XIX under the Amsterdam Treaty, see p 23, below.
8 Merger Treaty 1967, Art 10(2).
9 In June 2000 the Commission published its 7th Annual Report, *Monitoring the Application of Community Law* (COM (00) 92) covering the period 1 January to 31 December 1999. The Report shows that environmentally related infringements continue to dominate.

The Council of Ministers is a political body made up of one representative of each Member State. States are usually represented by their foreign ministers unless specialist subject areas are under discussion in which case, for example, the environment ministers of each State would meet as the Council. Because of its law-making power, the Council's voting procedure is of crucial importance and very complex. There are four ways in which environmental legislation may be enacted:

- The bulk of existing environmental legislation has been adopted under Art 100 (now Art 94) and Art 235 (now Art 308). Today, this procedure, which also requires consultation with the Economic and Social Committee and the Committee if the Regions, only operates in limited areas referred to in Art 175(2) of the EC Treaty, that is, provisions primarily of a fiscal nature, town and country planning and energy. Here the opinion of Parliament is advisory only.

- More significantly, Art 175(1) allows for the use of qualified majority voting (QMV) for all measures to be taken to achieve the objectives set out in Art 175. QMV is a system whereby the votes of Member States are weighted according to size (Art 205). Sixty two votes cast by at least 10 Member States constitutes the majority. This procedure is to be conducted by way of co-decision with the European Parliament (Art 251) and is now the general method for enacting environmental measures.

- Under Art 95, which deals with measures aimed at establishing the internal market (Art 14), QMV will be combined with the system of co-decision with Parliament (Art 251). Art 95(3) provides that where the Commission makes proposals concerning environmental protection under Art 95 it 'will take as a base a high level of protection, taking account in particular of any new development based on scientific facts'. Article 95 goes on to provide that if a Member State deems it necessary to maintain (Art 95(4)) or adopt (Art 95(5)) national provisions relating to the protection of the environment after a harmonisation measure has been adopted, then it must notify the Commission of these provisions together with the grounds for maintaining/introducing them. Art 95(5)) will only allow States to introduce such measures if they are based on new scientific evidence and they must refer to a problem ' specific to that Member State' arising after the adoption of the harmonisation measure. The Commission then has six months to approve or reject the national provisions having verified whether they constitute an obstacle to the functioning of the internal market (Art 95(5). If a Member State is authorised to maintain or introduce national provisions derogating from a harmonisation measure the Commission must examine whether to propose an adaptation to that measure.

- Finally, QMV in Council together with co-decision with Parliament applies in the case of general action programmes (Art 175(3)). General Action also require there to be consultation with the Economic and Social Committee and the Committee of the Regions. The increased use of QMV to cover most environmental law-making could speed up Council decision-making and arguably make higher environmental standards easier to agree.

The European Parliament (see Arts 189–201) is made up of 626 members who are directly elected by the electorates of Member States (Art 190). Originally, the Parliament's role was purely advisory. However, the powers of Parliament have gradually been extended by the Single European Act 1986, the Maastricht Treaty, and most significantly the Amsterdam Treaty. As mentioned above, the usual method of law-making within the EU is now QMV in Council combined with the co-decision of Parliament (in which Parliament acts on an equal basis with Council in legislative matters). The co-operation procedure formerly used is now restricted to decisions on economic and monetary policy.

Briefly the co-decision procedure under Art 251 increases the involvement of Parliament as follows:

(1) The Commission submits a proposal for new legislation.

(2) The European Parliament gives its opinion on the proposal to the Council, acting by an absolute majority of the votes cast in Parliament (Art 198):

    (a) If Parliament accepts the proposal, the Council will apply QMV when considering whether to adopt the proposal.

    (b) If Parliament rejects the proposal it will not become law.

    (c) If Parliament makes amendments, the Council and Commission must consider those amendments. If the Commission accepts the amendments, the Council will vote (using QMV) upon whether to accept the amended proposal. If the Commission rejects the amendments made by Parliament, the Council will need a unanimous vote in order to adopt the amended proposal. If the Council refuses to accept the amended text the matter is passed to the Conciliation Committee (consisting of an equal number drawn from Council and Parliament) who will debate and vote on the proposal. If the Conciliation Committee rejects the amended text the proposal will not be adopted.

Whereas the influence of the European Parliament in the legislative process has undoubtedly been increased, the consequences for environmental law-making have yet to be identified.

The European Court of Justice (Arts 220–45) consists of 15 judges appointed by common accord of the Member States. It has the final say on matters of EC law and it has the ultimate power to interpret the Treaties and any legislation made by the other Community institutions. It may also declare whether Member States are implementing EC law properly. The Court of First Instance, created by the Single European Act, was formed to hear cases from individuals – mainly employment and competitiveness issues – and so reduce pressure on the ECJ. A significant incentive to Member States to implement EC law properly has been given by Art 228, relating to the enforcement of judgments by the European Court. This now provides that if the Commission considers that a Member State has not complied with a judgment of the Court within the time-limit specified by the Commission, it may refer the matter back to the Court with a recommendation that the Member State should pay a specified lump sum or penalty payment. The Court will then decide whether to impose a fine and how much it is to be. On 4 July 2000 the ECJ (for the first time) imposed a financial penalty of 20,000 ECUs per day (£12,650) upon Greece for failing to comply with its 1992 ruling that Greece was in breach of the Waste Framework and Hazardous Waste Directives (Case 387/97). The level of the fine was based on a number of criteria, including the duration of the infringement, its degree of seriousness and the ability of the Member State to pay.

One significant feature of the ECJ is the extent to which its decision-making is based on policy; that policy being to promote European integration by upholding European law above conflicting national law. An example of the ECJ's policy-making has been the concept of 'direct effect' (see pp 12 *et seq*, below).[10]

The Economic and Social Committee (Arts 257–62) is an advisory body comprising 222 members drawn from Member States and is composed of representatives of employers, employees, the professions and the general public. It advises the Council and the Commission on various matters, including the environment.

The Committee of the Regions (Arts 263–65) is an advisory body comprising 222 members representing regional and local bodies. It advises the Commission and the Council on regional matters, including the environment.

The European Environment Agency, was established under Council Regulation 1210/90 and began life as a legal entity on 30 October 1993 when the seat of the new Agency was announced to be in Copenhagen. The Agency's aim (Art 1(2)) is to provide EC institutions and Member States with 'objective, reliable and comparable' information to enable them to protect the environment, to 'assess the results of such measures' and to disseminate information to the public'. Amongst a list of tasks set out in Art 2 aimed at achieving these objectives is the requirement to establish an Environmental Information and Observation Network so as to collect data on a comparable basis; to ensure broad dissemination of reliable environmental information; to stimulate environmental forecasting techniques and to stimulate the exchange of information on the best available technology available for preventing or reducing damage to the environment.

Clearly, the main role of the Agency is currently to collect and provide information for decision-makers in the environmental field. Article 20 states that eventually the Agency will be expected to assist in monitoring the implementation of Community environmental legislation, establishing criteria for assessing the environmental impact of projects and in furthering the EU's eco-labelling scheme (see below).

Law-making by Community institutions

Regulations, directives and decisions

Article 249 (formerly Art 189) lists three types of measure made by Community institutions and which have binding force:[11] regulations, directives and decisions. A regulation is binding in its entirety and is directly applicable in all Member States. Not only do regulations take immediate legal effect in Member States without the need for enactment by national legislators,[12] but they also take precedence over national law in the event of a conflict.[13] It is relatively unusual for regulations to be used in the context of

---

10 The *Van Gend en Loos* case [1963] 1 ECR 1.
11 Unlike recommendations and opinions which have no binding effect but which seek to encourage good practice within the Community, Resolutions establish fundamental principles upon which EC action should be taken.
12 European Communities Act 1972, s 2(1).
13 *Simmenthal* [1978] ECR 628.

environmental matters.[14] Directives are binding as to the result to be achieved 'but shall leave to the national authorities the choice of form and methods'; thus the Member States are given the choice of how to implement directives. In the UK, for example, a directive could be implemented by means of secondary legislation made under s 2(3) of the European Communities Act 1972. Alternatively, delegated legislation may be made under other enabling legislation, or directives may be implemented by a new Act of Parliament. Perhaps the most important point to stress is that directives are not directly applicable and do require Member States to take implementing measures within a set period specified in the directive. A decision is an instrument binding in its entirety, but only upon those to whom it is addressed.

Voluntary agreements

In addition to the 'hard law' referred to above, the use of voluntary agreements between the Commission and industry is becoming more common. An example of this form of 'soft law' is the agreement with the ACEA (European Automobile Manufacturers Association) to cut average new car CO_2 emissions. This agreement is backed by the threat to introduce a legally binding instrument to force CO_2 cuts if the agreement fails (see further Chapter 2); see also the agreement between the Commission and industry on detergents in relation to water pollution (see further Chapter 3).

Direct effect and enforcement

The bulk of EC environmental legislation takes the form of directives. Unlike regulations, which are directly applicable in all Member States, directives do not usually affect the national laws of Member States until actually implemented. As outlined above, directives create or impose legal obligations upon Member States to act (that is, implement and enforce) in order to achieve specified objectives. The primary obligation is therefore owed by the State to the Community and logically it is for the Community via the Commission under Art 226 to take infringement proceedings in the event of a failure by the State to implement directives. However, it is now well established through the case law of the ECJ that directives can in some circumstances have an effect on the national laws of Member States which have either not transposed the directive into national law or whose implementing measures are deemed to be insufficient. The ECJ has developed various devices by which directives can be held to have such an effect. The first such device is the concept of 'direct effect'.

This concept is one which was not derived from the treaties but is rather a creation of the ECJ. It is not restricted to directives but can apply to all EC activities, including treaty provisions and decisions. It was first established in the 1963 seminal judgment in the case of *Van Gend en Loos*.[15] Here the court decided that provisions of EC law may confer rights on individuals which must be recognised by national courts, that is, individual rights may be created by EC law independently of the laws of Member States; and where they do arise individuals must be able to invoke them before national courts. To date there

---

14   But not unknown. See, eg, Council Regulation 2037/00/94 on Substances that Deplete the Ozone Layer.
15   [1963] 1 ECR 1.

have been few court rulings on the direct effect of environmental directives and it may be that the concept has only limited effect in this area (see below).

Not all provisions of EC law have direct effect. The ECJ has developed various conditions which must be fulfilled before EC law can be directly effective. These can be listed as follows:

- the provision must impose a clear and unambiguous obligation upon Member States;

- the obligation must be unconditional;

- the obligation must not be dependent upon further implementing measures being taken either by the Community or by Member States;

- Member States must not be left with any discretion as to the implementation of the obligation;

- the provision must confer a legally enforceable right upon an individual.

Application of direct effect

The doctrine is always described as having 'vertical' rather than 'horizontal' effect. This means that directly effective provisions provided by EC law can only be invoked against State entities and not horizontally by one person against another.[16] Two points can be made here. The first is that the term 'State entity' should be interpreted broadly to include any body, whatever its legal form, which assumes responsibility pursuant to a directive.[17] In the UK context, this would probably embrace all the privatised utilities (gas, electric, water companies) including the waste disposal companies. Secondly, the concept of direct effect only operates in one direction in that State entities cannot force individuals to act in accordance with the terms of a directive which has not been implemented into the national law. This is because directives impose obligations upon Member States, not individual citizens, a feature which underlies the lack of horizontal effect.

It is apparent that not all the provisions contained in the 200 or so pieces of Community environmental law have direct effect. The protection of the environment is primarily perceived as the responsibility of national authorities and the majority of directives are not drafted in such a way as to confer legally enforceable rights upon individuals. Still, the Commission in its communication dated 22 October 1996, *Implementing Community Environmental Law* (Com (96) 500), has acknowledged the importance of court actions by individuals in environmental protection:

> ... actions by non-governmental organisations and/or citizens in relation to the application and enforcement of environmental laws ... would assist in the protection of the environment.

It is therefore appropriate to consider which categories of environmental directives are capable of having direct effect.

---

16 *Marshall v Southampton Area Health Authority* [1986] 2 All ER 584; [1986] QB 401.

17 *Foster v British Gas plc* [1990] 3 All ER 897; [1991] 1 QB 405.

Environmental directives with direct effect

It is possible to identify three categories of environmental provision contained in EC law which satisfy the criteria for direct effect.[18]

- Directives which specify limits or maximum concentration values for permissible discharges that are precise, unconditional and not dependant on further action by the Council or Member States. A prime example was the framework Directive 76/464 on pollution caused by certain dangerous substances discharged into the aquatic environment together with the daughter directives made thereunder (see now the Water Framework Directive 2000 (00/60), Chapter 3). These directives set maximum concentration values *inter alia* for discharges of mercury[19] carbon tetrachloride, DDT and pentachlorophenol,[20] which are Community standards applicable even where the State has not taken implementing measures. The same framework directive allows[21] Member States in limited circumstances to set water quality values which must not be exceeded, rather than impose discharge limit values. Such quality values laid down under daughter directives are clear and unconditional and may have direct effect.[22] The approach taken in the Drinking Water Directives of 1980 and 1998[23] is to establish maximum admissible concentrations for substances in water. Commentators[24] have no doubt that such provisions also have direct effect. The quality limit values for air pollution (sulphur dioxide, suspended particulates, lead, nitrogen dioxide) also fall within this category.[25]

- Directives prohibiting the use of substances or their discharge into the environment are expressed as absolute obligations and clearly have direct effect. An example is the Groundwater Directive 80/68 which requires Member States to prohibit 'all direct discharge of substances in List 1 into groundwater'. Similarly, directives which establish precise and detailed conditions to which products deemed harmful to the environment must conform before being placed on the market have direct effect. The *Ratti Case*[26] is an example of such a provision having direct effect.

  Kramer has argued[27] that provisions which prohibit certain activities, such as the disposal of hazardous waste, which endanger human health or the environment were sufficiently precise and clear as to have direct effect, for example, Art 5, Directive 78/319 on toxic and dangerous waste. This, however, was not the view of the ECJ in *Comitato di Coordina per la Difesa Della Cava v Regions Lombardia*[28] which examined the

---

18 See Kramer, *Focus on European Environmental Law*, 1992, pp 160–67.
19 Directives 82/176 on Mercury discharges from chlor-alkali electrolysis industry. Directive 84/156 on Other Mercury Discharges.
20 Directive 86/280.
21 Art 6(3).
22 But see *Luciano Arcaro* [1997] All ER (EC) 82 (ECJ).
23 Directive 80/778 on the quality of water for human consumption and 98/83 of the same name.
24 *Op cit*, Kramer, fn 18, p 160.
25 Directive 80/779 on Air Quality Limit Values for Sulphur Dioxide and Suspended Particulates; Directive 82/884 on a Limit Value for Lead in Air; Directive 85/203 on Air Quality Standards for Nitrogen Dioxide.
26 [1980] CMLR 96.
27 *Op cit*, Kramer, fn 18, p 163.
28 Case C-236/92 [1994] 1 ECR 488.

Waste Directive 75/442, Art 5. This required Member States to take the necessary measures to ensure that waste is recovered or disposed of without endangering human health and without using processes or methods which could harm the environment. The court took the view that this was not capable of having direct effect. It concluded:

> the provision at issue must be regarded as defining the framework for the action to be taken by the Member States regarding the treatment of waste and not as requiring, in itself, the adoption of specific measures or a particular method of waste disposal. It is therefore neither unconditional nor sufficiently precise and thus is not capable of conferring rights which individuals may rely on as against the State.

Such general framework provisions are frequently encountered in EC environmental law (for example, the Birds Directive 79/409, see p 632, below). The fact that they leave a wide margin of discretion in their manner of performance probably prevents them having direct effect.

- Directives which impose a clear obligation *upon Member States to act* will have direct effect. A directive which has occupied the British courts recently, and falls within this category, is the Environmental Impact Assessment Directive 85/337.[29] Article 3 provides, for example, that an environmental impact assessment must be carried out for certain public or private projects. As far as projects listed in Annex 1 of the Directive are concerned, this obligation is clear, concise and unconditional; and so has direct effect.

A common category of obligations found in environmental directives are those which require Member States to classify areas which then become subject to special protection measures. Examples include the Birds Directive 79/409, the Habitats Directive 92/43, the Bathing Water Directive 76/160 and the Shellfish Waters Directive 1978.

Article 4(1) of the Birds Directive 79/409 requires States to:

> ... classify in particular the most suitable territories in number and size as special protection areas for the conservation of those species [protected under the Directive] taking into account their protection requirements in the geographical sea and land area where this directive applies.

There is no doubt that the directive does require Member States to classify Special Protection Areas (SPAs) when specific species of birds occur in their territories. What is more contentious is whether the directive creates an enforceable obligation to classify a particular defined area as an SPA just because of the presence of 'directive' birds. It is generally accepted that these types of obligation require further implementing measures and therefore lack direct effect. In the *Leybucht* case[30] the ECJ noted that '[M]ember States do have a certain discretion with regard to the choice of territories which are most suitable for classification as special protection areas pursuant to Art 4(1)'. Because States have a discretion under the directive, it would appear that an obligation to classify particular areas could not be established.

---

29   *R v Swale BC ex p RSPB* [1991] JPL 39; *R v Poole Borough Council ex p Beebee* [1991] 2 PLR 27, [1991] JPL 643; *Twyford Parish Council v Secretary of State for the Environment* [1991] 3 LMELR 89. But see also Tromans, S, 'Environmental Impact Assessment: Recent Cases and Practical Issues' [2001] 1 Env Liability 18.

30   Case C-57/89 *Commission v Germany* [1991] 3 LMELR 97.

However, *Commission v Spain*[31] involved a finding by the ECJ that Spain had breached the directive by failing to classify a particular area, the Marismas de Santoña, as a special protection area. Again, the UK in *EC Commission v UK*[32] was found not to have implemented its obligations under the Bathing Water Directive 76/160 to ensure that the quality of bathing waters at Blackpool, Southport and Formby conform to the limit values set by the directive. At the time set for implementation, none of these resorts had been designated as having bathing waters within the meaning of the Directive. The ECJ found this failure to designate unacceptable because the presence of changing huts and lifeguards showed that the beaches were clearly intended for bathing. The UK was therefore required to ensure that these waters satisfied the bathing water quality objectives.

One might argue that the closer an area comes to the criteria set in the various directives, the more likely it will be that the ECJ will impose a concrete obligation to classify that area. There can, however, be no direct effect when the circumstances surrounding a particular area give the Member State a broad discretion whether to classify it or not.

Enforcement by individuals

The question whether individuals can use provisions contained in a directive to force State authorities to take steps to achieve the objectives of that directive cannot be answered merely by concluding that the provision has direct effect. For example, Directive 76/464 on discharges of certain dangerous substances into the aquatic environment set maximum concentration values which had direct effect (see now Water Framework Directive 2000, Chapter 3). However, neither an individual nor an environmental organisation concerned about the impact upon fish-life when such limits are exceeded could have a right of action because they would both lack *locus standi* (see p 828, below).

If, however, an EC environmental rule aims to protect individuals or their rights, then they will be able to enforce these rights through the courts. The Drinking Water Directive 80/778, for example, imposes maximum concentration limits which must not be exceeded and which are intended to protect the life and health of individuals. These would not be effective if individuals did not have an enforceable right to drinking water which conforms to community standards. Similarly, Directive 85/337 on Environmental Impact Assessment gives members of the public concerned by a project subject to the directive a right to be consulted during the assessment procedure. This is a right to consultation protected by the directive which can be enforced by the courts.[33]

To be given a positive right of action by a provision of EC law an individual must establish three things: (a) that the provision is capable of having direct effect; (b) that the provision is such as to provide a right of action; and (c) that the individual satisfies the requirements of *locus standi* before the national courts. On these criteria it is relatively

---

31 Case C-355/90 [1993] ECR I-4221.
32 Case C-56/90 [1993] Env LR 472; ECR I-4109 (ECJ).
33 See fn 29, above.

unusual for directly effective provisions of EC law to grant rights to individuals capable of enforcement in the courts. The Commission[34] has recently commented on this in the context of implementing community environmental law. Whilst recognising the desirability of allowing actions by non-governmental organisations and/or citizens in order to improve enforcement, the Commission recognises two main obstacles restricting access to the courts. One is the issue of *locus standi* which frequently involves some kind of economic interest which individuals or environmental interest groups might not be able to satisfy. The other is the costs of enforcement actions which may prove to be prohibitive (see Chapter 7).

Rather than tackle divergent national notions of *locus standi* of individuals, the approach of the Commission is to examine ways of ensuring that environmental NGOs recognised by Member States are given standing to bring judicial review actions against public authorities alleged to be in breach of directly effective EC provisions.

Even if a provision of EC environmental law deemed to have direct effect does not give individuals a right capable of being enforced in the courts, it still has a major impact upon national systems of law. Any directly effective Community law prevails over conflicting national legislation[35] and so national courts must apply the Community provision even if this conflicts with inconsistent national law.[36] This principle may be used by individuals to found a defence to criminal prosecutions.[37] Directly effective EC provisions may also be used to withhold payment of illegal charges. An example of this occurred in the *Becker* case[38] where a credit broker refused to respond to a notice of assessment issued by the tax authorities on the grounds that the legal basis for requiring payment had become invalid due to the entry into force of a directive.

Civil liability of the State for infringing Community law

Having established that the concept of direct effect provides individuals with the possibility of redress against Member States for breach of their directly effective rights, the next question is whether an aggrieved individual is entitled to compensation from the State in those circumstances. The ECJ decision in *Francovich v Italian Republic*[39] stated that a failure by a Member State to take all necessary steps to achieve the result required by a directive as required by Art 249 could give rise to a right to damages based directly on Community law. The individual's right to compensation for losses incurred due to a Member State's breach of community law was further elucidated in the joined cases of *Brasserie du Pêcheur v Germany* and *R v Secretary of State for Transport ex p Factortame Ltd.*[40] The ECJ has circumscribed this right to damages by imposing three conditions:

- The rule of law infringed must be intended to confer rights on individuals.

---

34   COM (96) 500.
35   *Costa v ENEL* [1964] ECR 585.
36   European Communities Act 1972, s 2(1) and (4).
37   Case C-148/78 *Ratti Case* [1980] CMLR 96.
38   Case C-8/81 *Becker v Finanzamt Munster-Innenstadt* [1982] 1 CMLR 499.
39   [1991] ECR I-5357; [1993] 2 CMLR 66.
40   [1996] All ER (EC) 301.

- The breach must be sufficiently serious. This would be so where the Member State had manifestly and gravely disregarded the limits on its discretion imposed by Community law.
- There must be a direct causal link between the breach of the obligation and the damage sustained by the injured party.

The impact of these decisions within the context of EC environmental law is not apparent as yet. However, they may have a profound effect whenever provisions are intended to confer upon individuals positive rights, rather than impose more general obligations upon States to protect the environment.

The duty to interpret national law in the light of a directive: 'indirect effect'

EC directives may also have what is referred to as 'indirect effect'. This is a result of comments made by the ECJ in a number of decisions, that national courts should interpret national law so that directive objectives are brought about. In *Marleasing SA v La Comercial*[41] the ECJ held that if there is a conflict between national provisions and a directive, national courts must interpret national law so as to accord with a directive so far as this is possible. This is sometimes referred to as 'sympathetic interpretation'.[42] The '*Marleasing* principle' exists to prevent national courts passing judgments which conflict with EC law. In *R v Secretary of State for the Environment ex p Greenpeace,*[43] for example, Potts J decided that he would read words into a UK statute so as to ensure consistency with EC law, provided he did not thereby alter its plain meaning. The obligation applies both **vertically** where proceedings involve State entities as well as **horizontally** in proceedings between private persons. The result is that the *spirit* of all EC environmental directives must be taken into account when interpreting national environmental statutes.

The bases of European environmental law

Article 2 of the Treaty provides that one of the basic tasks of the Community is to promote 'a high level of protection and improvement of the quality of the environment' and for this purpose Art 3(k) requires the Community to develop 'a policy in the sphere of the environment'. Interestingly, there was no attempt to define the concept of the 'environment' in either the Single European Act 1986 (which introduced for the first time an Environment Title VII), the Maastricht Treaty or the Treaty of Amsterdam.

Since 1986 the Treaty has contained express provisions setting out the commitment of the EC to environmental protection and improvement, currently to be found in Title XIX (Arts 174–76). What is clear from an examination of the various issues mentioned in Title X1X is that the concept of the environment is an all-embracing one, so that 'environmental' action by the Community could include measures to protect the man-made as well as the natural environment.[44]

---

41 [1990] ECR I-4135; [1992] 1 CMLR 305.
42 See Case C-168/95 *Luciano Arcaro* [1997] All ER (EC) 82 (ECJ).
43 [1994] 6 Env Law Mats 82.
44 See, eg, measures concerning Town and Country Planning referred to in Art 175(2).

Article 174 sets out the objectives of the Community environmental policy. Whereas environmental protection is now accorded equal status with the traditional economic concerns of the Community, there is no suggestion that the environment is given any priority in the case of conflict with other objectives (See Kramer (2000) 6). The EC Commission is charged with ensuring that the environmental protection provisions in Art 174 are applied.[45]

Four specific objectives for Community policy on the environment are listed by Art 174(1):

- Preserving, protecting and improving the quality of the environment

    Clearly, this objective is very broad in scope and would permit virtually any environmental measure to be taken by the Community. Measures aimed at protecting animal habitats whether on land or sea (for example, banning the dumping of waste at sea) would be covered as would the whole range of pollution control provisions which either attempt to clean up existing pollution or prevent pollution occurring in the first place.

- Protecting human health

    Measures taken under this second objective could generally be subsumed under Objective 1 as they would usually serve to protect human health. However, it does establish that Community measures aimed at protecting public health, for example, drinking water regulations or consumer protection issues can, and in the latter case did, fall under Art 130r.[46]

- Prudent and rational utilisation of natural resources

    Although there is again no definition of what is meant by 'natural resources', it no doubt includes all economic assets to be found in the natural environment, that is, timber, minerals, natural energy sources, water, and fauna and flora. Although the term 'sustainable growth' does not appear in Art 174, it is presumed that prudent and rational utilisation of natural resources would respect that concept which is mentioned in Art 2.

- Promoting measures at international level to deal with regional or worldwide environmental problems

    Although this objective was only inserted by the Maastricht Treaty it is questionable whether it constitutes a significant extension of Community competence. The environment does not recognise frontiers, national or regional, and the Community has frequently adopted measures aimed at environmental protection outside the physical boundaries of the EU, for example, the Community is party to international conventions of global significance, such as the Vienna Convention for the Protection of the Ozone Layer 1985 and the Montreal Protocol on Substances that Deplete the Ozone Layer 1987 as well as regional measures such as the Barcelona Convention for

---

45 See Art 155, 'In order to ensure the proper functioning and development of the common market, the Commission shall: ensure that the provisions of this Treaty and the measures taken by the institutions pursuant thereto are applied ...'.

46 Council Regulation 1992 concerning the export from and import into the Community of certain dangerous chemicals, for example.

the Protection of the Mediterranean Sea against Pollution 1976 and the Bonn Convention for the Protection of the Rhine against Chemical Pollution 1976. The Community is also party to the Rio de Janeiro Conventions on Biological Diversity and Climate Change 1992. As such, this fourth objective seems little more than express recognition of existing practice.

Article 174(2) states that Community policy on the environment shall aim at a high level of protection taking into account the diversity of situations in the various regions of the Community.

A similar provision first appeared in Art 100a(3) of the Single European Act 1986 (now Art 95(3)) as follows:

> The Commission, in its proposals [which have as their object the establishment and functioning of the internal market] ... concerning health, safety, environmental protection and consumer protection, will take as a base a high level of protection, taking account in particular of any new development based on scientific facts. Within the respective powers the European Parliament and the Council will also seek to achieve this objective.

The combined effect of these two Articles is to ensure that Community proposals on the environment (including Commission proposals and Council decision-making) should all be based on a high level of environmental protection and policy should aim to achieve this goal.

A major difficulty exists in trying to establish what is meant by a 'high level' of protection. The two Articles do not refer to the highest possible level of protection but neither would they permit environmental policy to be based on the lowest common denominator to be found within the Community, leaving it up to the Member States to adopt a higher national level under Art 176. Kramer suggests (2000, 8) that a 'high level' can probably best be determined by looking at environmental standards which Member States that normally have a high standard of environmental protection (Denmark, the Netherlands, Sweden, Finland, Austria, Germany) have set'. It is perhaps disheartening that the UK cannot yet be held up as a model for a high level of environmental protection.

The force of Art 174(2) is limited by the qualification that a high level of protection should take into account 'the diversity of situations in the various regions of the Community'. It is by no means clear what is intended here. Whereas it is obvious that standards of environmental protection vary markedly between Member States, there would seem to be no reason why all States should not aspire to a single 'high' standard of protection. As stated the qualification seems to rule out an environmental policy based on the objective of achieving the highest level of protection.

Having listed the goals of environmental policy, Art 174(2) then proceeds to outline the principles used to achieve that policy. Every environmental measure passed under this Article has to satisfy these principles and may be subject to challenge. It should be noted that the Article refers specifically to environmental *policy* being based on the principles rather than environmental *action*. To the extent that environmental action is taken to implement the requirements of policy, the principles undoubtedly have an indirect effect on law-making, but it is at best dubious whether Art 174(2) could be used to mount a legal challenge to a Directive.[47] The principles are as follows: the precautionary principle (see p 49, below); the preventive principle (see p 49, below); rectification of damage at source principle (see p 51, below); the polluter pays principle (see p 52, below); the integration principle (see p 54, below).

The subsidiarity principle

Although the competence of Community institutions to legislate in the field of environmental protection is drawn very widely, in practice the extent to which they intervene is limited by the 'principle of subsidiarity' introduced by the Single European Act 1986, which was originally restricted to environmental policy.[48] Article 5 of the Treaty of Amsterdam extends the principle to all areas of Community action: 'In areas which do not fall within its exclusive competence, the Community shall take action, in accordance with the principle of subsidiarity, only if and in so far as the objectives of the proposed action cannot be sufficiently achieved by the Member States and can, therefore, by reason of the scale or effects of the proposed action, be better achieved by the Community.'

Although this principle has underpinned European environmental legislation for nearly a decade it does not appear to figure largely within the deliberations of the Council (but cf Kramer (2000) 11). It is also very difficult to establish clear lines of demarcation between environmental policy objectives which can be better attained at Community level. Environmental protection is one area where action needs to be taken on at least a regional level if it is to be effective, for example, protecting migrating wildlife or avoiding the creation of pollution havens. Bearing in mind that the perception of the need for environmental regulation tends to vary widely within the Community – some States view it as a barrier to economic development – it would be at best inappropriate to allow industrial pollution standards to be set at national level. To do so would distort the single market and endanger the whole rationale of the Community. It is to be hoped that environmental protection measures will not be unduly affected by this principle.

TREATY ESTABLISHING THE EUROPEAN COMMUNITY (AMSTERDAM CONSOLIDATED VERSION)

PART 1

PRINCIPLES

Article 2

The Community shall have as its task, by establishing a common market and an economic and monetary union and by implementing common policies or activities referred to in Articles 3 and 4, to promote throughout the Community a harmonious, balanced and sustainable development of economic activities, a high level of employment and of social protection, equality between men and women, sustainable and non-inflationary growth, a high degree of competitiveness and convergence of economic performance, a high level of

---

47 See *op cit*, Kramer, fn 18, p 62 *et seq*.
48 Art 130r(4) inserted by Maastricht, now dropped.

protection and improvement of the quality of the environment, the raising of the standard of living and quality of life, and economic and social cohesion and solidarity among Member States.

Article 3

For the purposes set out in Article 2, the activities of the Community shall include, as provided in this Treaty and in accordance with the timetable set out therein:

... (k) a policy in the sphere of the environment; ...

Article 6

Environmental protection requirements must be integrated into the definition and implementation of the Community policies and activities referred to in Article 3, in particular with a view to promoting sustainable development.

CHAPTER 3

APPROXIMATION OF LAWS

Article 94

The Council shall, acting unanimously on a proposal from the Commission and after consulting the European Parliament and the Economic and Social Committee, issue directives for the approximation of such laws, regulations or administrative provisions of the Member States as directly affect the establishment or functioning of the common market.

Article 95

1   By way of derogation from Article 94 and save where otherwise provided in this Treaty, the following provisions shall apply for the achievement of the objectives set out in Article 14. The Council shall, acting in accordance with the procedure referred to in Article 251 and after consulting the Economic and Social Committee, adopt the measures for the approximation of the provisions laid down by law, regulation or administrative action in Member States which have as their object the establishment and functioning of the internal market.

2   Paragraph 1 shall not apply to fiscal provisions, to those relating to the free movement of persons nor to those relating to the rights and interests of employed persons.

3   The Commission, in its proposals envisaged in paragraph 1 concerning health, safety, environmental protection and consumer protection, will take as a base a high level of protection, taking account in particular of any new development based on scientific facts. Within their respective powers, the European Parliament and the Council will also seek to achieve this objective.

4   If, after the adoption by the Council or by the Commission of a harmonisation measure, a Member State deems it necessary to maintain national provisions on grounds of major needs referred to in Article 30, or relating to the protection of the environment or the working environment, it shall notify the Commission of these provisions as well as the grounds for maintaining them.

5   Moreover, without prejudice to paragraph 4, if, after the adoption by the Council or by the Commission of a harmonisation measure, a Member State deems it necessary to

introduce national provisions based on new scientific evidence relating to the protection of the environment or the working environment on grounds of a problem specific to that Member State arising after the adoption of the harmonisation measure, it shall notify the Commission of the envisaged provisions as well as the grounds for introducing them.

6   The Commission shall, within six months of the notifications as referred to in paragraphs 4 and 5, approve or reject the national provisions involved after having verified whether or not they are a means of arbitrary discrimination or a disguised restriction on trade between Member States and whether or not they shall constitute an obstacle to the functioning of the internal market.

In the absence of a decision by the Commission within this period the national provisions referred to in paragraphs 4 and 5 shall be deemed to have been approved.

When justified by the complexity of the matter and in the absence of danger for human health, the Commission may notify the Member State concerned that the period referred to in this paragraph may be extended for a further period of up to six months.

7   When, pursuant to paragraph 6, a Member State is authorised to maintain or introduce national provisions derogating from a harmonisation measure, the Commission shall immediately examine whether to propose an adaptation to that measure.

8   When a Member State raises a specific problem on public health in a field which has been the subject of prior harmonisation measures, it shall bring it to the attention of the Commission which shall immediately examine whether to propose appropriate measures to the Council.

9   By way of derogation from the procedure laid down in Articles 226 and 227, the Commission and any Member State may bring the matter directly before the Court of Justice if it considers that another Member State is making improper use of the powers provided for in this Article.

10 The harmonisation measures referred to above shall, in appropriate cases, include a safeguard clause authorising the Member States to take, for one or more of the non-economic reasons referred to in Article 30, provisional measures subject to a Community control procedure.

TITLE XIX

ENVIRONMENT

Article 174

1   Community policy on the environment shall contribute to pursuit of the following objectives:
    –   preserving, protecting and improving the quality of the environment;
    –   protecting human health;
    –   prudent and rational utilisation of natural resources;
    –   promoting measures at international level to deal with regional or worldwide environmental problems.

2   Community policy on the environment shall aim at a high level of protection taking into account the diversity of situations in the various regions of the Community. It shall be based on the precautionary principle and on the principles that preventive action

should be taken, that environmental damage should as a priority be rectified at source and that the polluter should pay.

In this context, harmonisation measures answering environmental protection requirements shall include, where appropriate, a safeguard clause allowing Member States to take provisional measures, for non-economic environmental reasons, subject to a Community inspection procedure.

3   In preparing its policy on the environment, the Community shall take account of:

- available scientific and technical data;
- environmental conditions in the various regions of the Community;
- the potential benefits and costs of action or lack of action;
- the economic and social development of the Community as a whole and the balanced development of its regions.

4   Within their respective spheres of competence, the Community and the Member States shall co-operate with third countries and with the competent international organisations. The arrangements for Community co-operation may be the subject of agreements between the Community and the third parties concerned, which shall be negotiated and concluded in accordance with Article 300.

The previous sub-paragraph shall be without prejudice to Member States' competence to negotiate in international bodies and to conclude international agreements.

Article 175

1   The Council, acting in accordance with the procedure referred to in Article 251 and after consulting the Economic and Social Committee and the Committee of the Regions, shall decide what action is to be taken by the Community in order to achieve the objectives referred to in Article 174.

2   By way of derogation from the decision-making procedure provided for in paragraph 1 and without prejudice to Article 95, the Council, acting unanimously on a proposal from the Commission and after consulting the European Parliament, the Economic and Social Committee and the Committee of the Regions, shall adopt:

- provisions primarily of a fiscal nature;
- measures concerning town and country planning, land use with the exception of waste management and measures of a general nature, and management of water resources;
- measures significantly affecting a Member State's choice between different energy sources and the general structure of its energy supply.

The Council may, under the conditions laid down in the preceding sub-paragraph, define those matters referred to in this paragraph on which decisions are to be taken by a qualified majority.

3   In other areas, general action programmes setting out priority objectives to be attained shall be adopted by the Council, acting in accordance with the procedure referred to in Article 251 and after consulting the Economic and Social Committee and the Committee of the Regions.

The Council, acting under the terms of paragraph 1 or paragraph 2 according to the case, shall adopt the measures necessary for the implementation of these programmes.

4   Without prejudice to certain measures of a Community nature, the Member States shall finance and implement the environment policy.

5   Without prejudice to the principle that the polluter should pay, if a measure based on the provisions of paragraph 1 involves costs deemed disproportionate for the public authorities of a Member State, the Council shall, in the act adopting that measure, lay down appropriate provisions in the form of:

   –   temporary derogations; and/or

   –   financial support from the Cohesion Fund set up pursuant to Article 161.

Article 176

The protective measures adopted pursuant to Article 175 shall not prevent any Member State from maintaining or introducing more stringent protective measures. Such measures must be compatible with this Treaty. They shall be notified to the Commission.

CHAPTER 2

PROVISIONS COMMON TO SEVERAL INSTITUTIONS

Article 249

In order to carry out their task and in accordance with the provisions of this Treaty, the European Parliament acting jointly with the Council, the Council and the Commission shall make regulations and issue directives, take decisions, make recommendations or deliver opinions.

A regulation shall have general application. It shall be binding in its entirety and directly applicable in all Member States.

A directive shall be binding, as to the result to be achieved, upon each Member State to which it is addressed, but shall leave to the national authorities the choice of form and methods.

A decision shall be binding in its entirety upon those to whom it is addressed.

Recommendations and opinions shall have no binding force.

Article 250

1   Where, in pursuance of this Treaty, the Council acts on a proposal from the Commission, unanimity shall be required for an act constituting an amendment to that proposal, subject to Article 251(4) and (5).

2   As long as the Council has not acted, the Commission may alter its proposal at any time during the procedures leading to the adoption of a Community act.

Article 251

1   Where reference is made in this Treaty to this Article for the adoption of an act, the following procedure shall apply.

2   The Commission shall submit a proposal to the European Parliament and the Council.

The Council, acting by a qualified majority after obtaining the opinion of the European Parliament,

- if it approves all the amendments contained in the European Parliament's opinion, may adopt the proposed act thus amended;

- if the European Parliament does not propose any amendments, may adopt the proposed act;

- shall otherwise adopt a common position and communicate it to the European Parliament. The Council shall inform the European Parliament fully of the reasons which led it to adopt its common position. The Commission shall inform the European Parliament fully of its position.

If, within three months of such communication, the European Parliament:

(a) approves the common position or has not taken a decision, the act in question shall be deemed to have been adopted in accordance with that common position;

(b) rejects, by an absolute majority of its component members, the common position, the proposed act shall be deemed not to have been adopted;

(c) proposes amendments to the common position by an absolute majority of its component members, the amended text shall be forwarded to the Council and to the Commission, which shall deliver an opinion on those amendments.

3   If, within three months of the matter being referred to it, the Council, acting by a qualified majority, approves all the amendments of the European Parliament, the act in question shall be deemed to have been adopted in the form of the common position thus amended; however, the Council shall act unanimously on the amendments on which the Commission has delivered a negative opinion. If the Council does not approve all the amendments, the President of the Council, in agreement with the President of the European Parliament, shall within six weeks convene a meeting of the Conciliation Committee.

4   The Conciliation Committee, which shall be composed of the members of the Council or their representatives and an equal number of representatives of the European Parliament, shall have the task of reaching agreement on a joint text, by a qualified majority of the members of the Council or their representatives and by a majority of the representatives of the European Parliament. The Commission shall take part in the Conciliation Committee's proceedings and shall take all the necessary initiatives with a view to reconciling the positions of the European Parliament and the Council. In fulfilling this task, the Conciliation Committee shall address the common position on the basis of the amendments proposed by the European Parliament.

5   If, within six weeks of its being convened, the Conciliation Committee approves a joint text, the European Parliament, acting by an absolute majority of the votes cast, and the Council, acting by a qualified majority, shall each have a period of six weeks from that approval in which to adopt the act in question in accordance with the joint text. If either of the two institutions fails to approve the proposed act within that period, it shall be deemed not to have been adopted.

6   Where the Conciliation Committee does not approve a joint text, the proposed act shall be deemed not to have been adopted.

7   The periods of three months and six weeks referred to in this Article shall be extended by a maximum of one month and two weeks respectively at the initiative of the European Parliament or the Council.

Article 252

Where reference is made in this Treaty to this Article for the adoption of an act, the following procedure shall apply:

(a) The Council, acting by a qualified majority on a proposal from the Commission and after obtaining the opinion of the European Parliament, shall adopt a common position.

(b) The Council's common position shall be communicated to the European Parliament. The Council and the Commission shall inform the European Parliament fully of the reasons which led the Council to adopt its common position and also of the Commission's position.

   If, within three months of such communication, the European Parliament approves this common position or has not taken a decision within that period, the Council shall definitively adopt the act in question in accordance with the common position.

(c) The European Parliament may, within the period of three months referred to in point (b), by an absolute majority of its component Members, propose amendments to the Council's common position. The European Parliament may also, by the same majority, reject the Council's common position. The result of the proceedings shall be transmitted to the Council and the Commission.

   If the European Parliament has rejected the Council's common position, unanimity shall be required for the Council to act on a second reading.

(d) The Commission shall, within a period of one month, re-examine the proposal on the basis of which the Council adopted its common position, by taking into account the amendments proposed by the European Parliament.

   The Commission shall forward to the Council, at the same time as its re-examined proposal, the amendments of the European Parliament which it has not accepted, and shall express its opinion on them. The Council may adopt these amendments unanimously.

(e) The Council, acting by a qualified majority, shall adopt the proposal as re-examined by the Commission.

   Unanimity shall be required for the Council to amend the proposal as re-examined by the Commission.

(f) In the cases referred to in points (c), (d) and (e), the Council shall be required to act within a period of three months. If no decision is taken within this period, the Commission proposal shall be deemed not to have been adopted.

(g) The periods referred to in points (b) and (f) may be extended by a maximum of one month by common accord between the Council and the European Parliament.

The EC's Environmental Action Programmes

As a source of environmental law, the EC has developed two main aspects. Firstly, as previously discussed, it produces secondary legislation mainly in the form of directives which impose legal obligations upon States. Secondly, and very significantly, since 1972 it has had in place a Europe-wide environmental policy in the form of Action Programmes which set various proposals for action in the field to be achieved over a prescribed timescale, usually about five years. The Action Programmes take the form of resolutions by the Council of the European Communities and the representatives of the governments of Member States. Although not legally enforceable, a Member State which has agreed to the Action Programme cannot deny the need for action in the area concerned.

To date, there have been five Action Programmes which together combine measures which respond to existing perceived environmental problems and those which endeavour to deal with future problems before they occur. The EC's first Action Programme was for the period 1973–76 and *inter alia* and most significantly laid the basis for what has become the principle of preventive action (see below) by stating its first general principles as follows:

... the best environmental policy consists in preventing the creation of pollution and nuisances at source, rather than subsequently trying to counteract their effects.

The second programme (1977–81) was divided into two titles. Title I sets out detailed measures to combat existing pollution, for example, by setting standards for certain pollutants. Title II sets out measures to improve and protect the environment. The third programme (1982–86) highlighted the preventative aspect of environmental policy by providing *inter alia* for the environmental dimension to be incorporated into other Community policies and for the establishment of an environmental impact assessment procedure.

In terms of content, the fourth Action Programme represented a departure from the earlier programmes. While the principles appearing in those programmes were reiterated the programme introduced three main new ideas or themes. The first was a response to pressure both from the public and from Community industry, to establish a set of environmental standards which were sufficiently strict. It was at least questionable whether this had been the case prior to the programme. Secondly, the importance of both implementation (formal and practical) of EC environmental legislation and its enforcement (see below) was highlighted. Thirdly, to augment the then current regulatory approach the Programme envisaged the implementation of an environmental education and information policy. In short, there was express recognition of the need to clarify substantive environmental law and to develop coherence ensuring prompt implementation and strict enforcement.

The fifth Environmental Action Programme, 'A European Community Programme of Policy and Action in relation to the Environment and Sustainable Development' was due to cover the period 1993–2000 and then to be replaced by the sixth Programme. However, although that programme was forwarded to the Council on 26 January 2001, it is yet to be formally adopted. The central theme running through the fifth Programme has been sustainable development and is discussed in detail below at p 46. That theme is taken up by the proposed sixth Environmental Action Programme.

The proposed sixth Environmental Action Programme, entitled 'Environment 2010: Our Future, Our Choice' (COM (01) 0031) sets out a Community strategy for sustainable development over the next 10 years.[49] An Executive summary is set out below at p 30. In addition to the list of priority areas for action, the proposal reflects the concerns of Environment Commissioner Wallström by stressing the importance of implementing existing environmental laws, not only by way of 'vigorous legal action through the European Court', but also indirectly, through a policy of providing the public with information in order to 'name, fame and shame' polluters (for an early example, see *The Times*' front page headline, 19 March 2001: 'Britain Tops EU's Dirty Cities Charts'). The importance of integrating environmental concerns into other EC policies has also been highlighted.

The particular priority areas set out in the proposal are as follows:

- Tackling climate change. The proposal makes it a key priority for the Sixth Programme to ratify and implement the Kyoto Protocol to cut greenhouse gas emissions by 8% over 1990 levels by 2008–12.

- The protection and restoration of nature and biodiversity using the Community's Natura 2000 Programme with particular reference being paid to the marine environment.

- Under the sub-heading 'Environment and health' there is a commitment to ensure that man-made contaminants in the environment do not pose significant risks to human health. The principles of precaution and prevention of risk are to be central in implementing this commitment.

- There is a renewed commitment to the sustainable use of natural resources and management of wastes, with particular emphasis on waste prevention as the key element of an integrated approach.

- There is recognition that the implementation of the sixth Programme over the coming decade will take place within an enlarged EU. This will involve a substantial input of Community funds to enable candidate States to implement EC environment legislation.

- Finally, environmental policy, its implementation and evaluation should be based on sound scientific knowledge and economic assessment.

---

49 The proposed Programme has gone to the Council and the European Parliament under the co-decision procedure. This procedure is expected to last into 2002. Environment Ministers debated the Programme in March 2001, when the proposal was given a 'cool reception' [2001] 2 Env Liability CS 26.

COMMUNICATION FROM THE COMMISSION TO THE COUNCIL, THE EUROPEAN PARLIAMENT, THE ECONOMIC AND SOCIAL COMMITTEE AND THE COMMITTEE OF THE REGIONS

on the sixth environment action programme of the European Community 'Environment 2010: our future, our choice'

(COM (01) 0031)

(Presented by the Commission) Executive Summary

Context for the new programme

A healthy environment is essential to long term prosperity and quality of life and citizens in Europe demand a high level of environmental protection. Future economic development and increasing prosperity will put pressure on the planet's capacity to sustain demands for resources or to absorb pollution. At the same time, high environmental standards are an engine for innovation and business opportunities. Overall, society must work to de-couple environmental impacts and degradation from economic growth. Business must operate in a more eco-efficient way, in other words producing the same or more products with less input and less waste, and consumption patterns have to become more sustainable. In the European Union, thirty years of environment policy has led to a comprehensive system of environmental controls. The fifth Environment Action Programme (1992–99), 'Towards Sustainability', took new measures and a broader commitment to integration of environmental concerns into other policies. The Global Assessment of the programme concluded that while progress was being made in cutting pollution levels in some areas, problems remained and the environment would continue to deteriorate unless: – more progress was made in the implementation of environmental legislation in Member States; – integration of environment into the economic and social policies driving the pressures on the environment was improved and deepened; – stakeholders and citizens took more ownership of efforts to protect the environment; – new impetus to measures aimed at addressing a number of serious and persistent environmental problems as well as a number of emerging concerns. This context has guided the strategic focus of the sixth Environmental Action Programme, which effectively sets the environmental objectives and priorities that will be an integral part of the European Community's strategy for sustainable development. The programme sets out the major priorities and objectives for environment policy over the next five to ten years and details the measures to be taken.

A strategic approach to meeting our environmental objectives

Environment policy must be innovative in its approach and seek new ways of working with a wide cross-section of society. Implementation of existing environmental legislation needs to be improved. Vigorous legal action through the European Court of Justice should be combined with support for best practices and a policy of public information to 'name, fame and shame'. Integration of environmental concerns into other policies must be deepened, for example all Commission policy initiatives should be fully assessed in this light. Progress should be measured through indicators and benchmarking.

Working with the market through business and consumer interests will contribute to more sustainable production and consumption patterns. Business should not simply be penalised for failure but schemes should be introduced to reward good performance. Consumers need useful information to allow them to choose environmentally benevolent products, thus driving the market. Public subsidies should promote environmentally friendly practices. Business must be encouraged to innovate, for example seizing the opportunities offered by the use, development and spread of clean technologies. Individual citizens make daily decisions that directly or indirectly impact the environment. Better quality and easily accessible information on the environment and on practical matters will help shape opinions and thus decisions.

Land use planning and management decisions in the Member States can have a major influence on the environment, leading to fragmentation of the countryside and pressures in urban areas and the coast. The Community can provide support by promoting best practice and through the Structural Funds.

These approaches will apply across the spectrum of environmental issues. In addition, special attention will be paid to four priority areas for action.

Tackling climate change

Objective – to stabilise the atmospheric concentrations of greenhouse gases at a level that will not cause unnatural variations of the earth's climate. The scientific consensus is that climate change is happening and that human activity is causing the increases in concentrations of greenhouse gases that are the cause of the problem. The key priority for the sixth Programme will be the ratification and implementation of the Kyoto Protocol to cut greenhouse gas emissions by 8% over 1990 levels by 2008–12. This must be considered as a first step to the long term target of a 70% cut.

Nature and biodiversity – protecting a unique resource

Objective – to protect and restore the functioning of natural systems and halt the loss of biodiversity in the European Union and globally. To protect soils against erosion and pollution. Healthy and balanced natural systems are essential to supporting life and the functioning of society. Pressures from pollution, unsustainable use of the land and sea and risks to biodiversity need to be redressed. Full implementation of environmental legislation is the key to the pollution threat. Valuable environmental areas should be protected by the Community's Natura 2000 programme and this must be implemented fully. Extending protection to the wider countryside requires a deeper and effective integration of environment and biodiversity into agriculture, landscape, forestry and marine policies, coupled with new initiatives, for example to develop a soil strategy for Europe. More attention will be given to protecting the marine environment.

Environment and health

Objective – to achieve a quality of the environment where the levels of man-made contaminants, including different types of radiation, do not give rise to significant impacts on or risks to human health. There is increasing realisation, and evidence, that human health is affected by environmental problems related to air and water pollution, dangerous chemicals and noise. A holistic and comprehensive approach to environment and health is needed, with precaution and prevention of risk being central to this policy and taking account of particularly vulnerable groups such as children and the elderly. Implementation of existing legislation and further actions will be needed in the individual policy areas.

Sustainable use of natural resources and management of wastes

Objective – to ensure the consumption of renewable and non-renewable resources does not exceed the carrying capacity of the environment. To achieve a de-coupling of resource use from economic growth through significantly improved resource efficiency, dematerialisation of the economy, and waste prevention. The planet's resources, especially renewable resources like soil, water, air and timber, are under severe pressure from human society. A strategy is needed aimed at measures, such as taxes and incentives, to ensure a more sustainable use of resources. Waste volumes are predicted to continue rising unless remedial action is taken. Waste prevention will be a key element of an integrated product policy approach. Further measures are needed to encourage recycling and recovery of wastes.

The European Union in the wider world

The implementation of the sixth Programme will be undertaken in a context of an enlarged European Union and subsequent measures will need to take this broader perspective into account. The implementation of the Community's environmental legislation will of course be the main task for the candidate countries, supported by Community funding programmes. The Candidate Countries have the opportunity to make progress towards an economic development that is sustainable and avoids the type or scale of environmental problems now faced in Western Europe.

Internationally, it will be essential that environmental concerns are fully and properly integrated into all aspects of the Community's external relations. Environment must be taken seriously by international organisations and properly resourced. International conventions, notably on climate change, biodiversity, chemicals and desertification need to be supported and implemented. Policy-making based on participation and sound knowledge and broad involvement of stake-holders will be central to the successful implementation of the sixth Programme in every stage of the policy process from agreeing targets to putting measures into practice. Sound scientific knowledge and economic assessments, reliable and up-to-date environmental data and information and the use of indicators will underpin the drawing-up, implementation and evaluation of environmental policy.

The proposed decision on a sixth Environment Action Programme will give an enlarged European Union the direction, impetus and tools we need to create a clean and safe environment. It will involve citizens and business in this endeavour and will contribute to sustainable development.

European Convention on Human Rights

Recent jurisprudence before the European Court of Human Rights has confirmed that the European Convention on Human Rights may prove to be a valuable source of environmental law (see further Chapter 7). And this is now of particular importance to domestic law, given the effective incorporation of the Convention by the Human Rights Act 1998. Article 8 of the Convention, for example, protects an individual's rights to respect for his or her home, private and family life. In *López Ostra v Spain*[50] the applicant's flat in Lorca was situated within 12 metres of the perimeter of a waste disposal plant. She alleged that the plant emitted fumes, noise and smell that 'made her family's living conditions intolerable and caused her and her family serious health problems'. Expert evidence stated that hydrogen sulphide emissions from the plant exceeded the permitted limit and could endanger the health of those living nearby and supported the contention that there could be a causal link between these emissions and the applicant's daughter's illness. The European Court of Human Rights held that Spain was in breach of Art 8 by

---

50   (1995) 20 EHRR 277; (1994) EHRR A 303-C.

not 'striking a fair balance between the interest of the town's economic well-being – that of having a waste-treatment plant – and the applicant's effective enjoyment' of her Art 8 rights. The applicant was awarded four million pesetas in damages and her costs.

Although this is the first example of the European Convention on Human Rights being used successfully in an environmental case, Art 8 has been invoked against the UK in two earlier cases involving alleged noise pollution. In *Arrondelle v UK*,[51] the applicant complained under Art 8 about nuisance caused by the development of Gatwick airport and the construction of a motorway near her home. The case was settled out of court when the UK paid the applicant £7,500. In *Powell and Rayner v UK*,[52] Art 8 was invoked unsuccessfully before the European Court of Human Rights. The case arose out of aircraft noise affecting persons living near Heathrow airport. The European Court of Human Rights decided that the UK had struck a fair balance between the need for international airports in urban areas for the country's economic well-being and the applicant's rights under Art 8 to private life and home (see also *Guerra and others v Italy* (1998) 26 EHRR 357 and other cases discussed in Chapter 7, p 857).

Environmental law: the UK perspective

Sources of UK environmental law

The common law

Much of the modern UK law on the environment is the product of legislative enactment, often in response to European Directives. However, the common law has provided a rudimentary system for enforcing obligations to protect the environment for several centuries.[53] Common law principles are still potentially valuable both in the private law sphere and in the public law sphere where judicial review is of growing importance to those seeking to challenge action or inaction on the part of regulatory bodies or ministers.

The common law, however, is limited in a number of important ways. First, potential litigants may face problems of access to the courts, including those associated with funding. In order to use tort it is necessary to bring a claim within the requirements of an established cause of action and each of these have particular characteristics that may or may not be appropriate to a particular plaintiff. Moreover, taken together, tortious principles do not provide a comprehensive scheme of environmental protection.[54] For example, those sustaining personal injuries may use negligence, but only if the plaintiff can establish that a duty of care is owed by a defendant who has been at fault; there must also be a causal link between that fault and the injury sustained. Establishing fault and causation may be extremely difficult. To succeed in nuisance does not require establishing fault, but nuisance is only available to protect legal interests in land and will therefore be of no avail either to those who have sustained personal injuries or who do

---

51   (1993) 5 EHRR 118.

52   (1990) EHRR A 172.

53   See further Maclaren, JPS, 'Nuisance and the Industrial Revolution' 3(2) OJLS 221.

54   The principal torts relevant to environmental protection are nuisances; the rule in *Rylands v Fletcher*, negligence and trespass. They are discussed at various points throughout this book. For a more general treatment of the principles in the context of environmental law, see Bell, S and McGillivray, D, *Environmental Law*, 5th edn, 2000, London: Blackstone, Chapter 10.

not have the requisite legal interest. In *Hunter v Canary Wharf* [1997] 2 All ER 426, for example, the House of Lords held that a mere licensee or occupier of land could not rely on nuisance. More generally, the common law has limitations as a vehicle for environmental protection because cases tend to focus on incidents rather than on, for example, industry-wide practices. Cases also tend to arise after environmental damage has been caused so that judges are concerned with what happened rather than with what should be done in the future to minimise or prevent environmental harm. Finally, tortious principles are ill-equipped to impose liability for damage to biodiversity and the environment in general (cf the liability regimes discussed below, p 76).

Statutes

Modern UK environmental law can be traced back to the 19th century, in particular to the establishment by the Alkali Act 1863 of the Alkali Inspectorate to regulate atmospheric emissions from factories such as those producing caustic soda,[55] the Rivers Pollution Prevention Act 1876, and the Public Health Act 1875. This latter legislation was the precursor to the Public Health Acts 1936 and 1961. The Public Health Acts were an attempt to improve the horrendous conditions in which the urban poor lived during and following the Industrial Revolution. In the 20th century, regulation of the built environment was through the Town and Country Planning Acts (see now the Town and Country Planning Act 1990). The Health and Safety at Work etc Act 1974 is also important in the context of the safety of the environment at work. Legislation also exists to regulate specific contexts such as the Radioactive Substances Act 1993 and the Planning (Hazardous Substances) Act 1990. The Food and Environment Protection Act 1985, *inter alia*, concerns dumping of waste at sea and the protection of marine ecosystems. The Wildlife and Countryside Act 1981 (as amended) seeks to protect wildlife by providing protection of their habitats by establishing Sites of Special Scientific Interest (thereby implementing international law and EC directives (see further Chapter 6)).

Two key statutes are concerned with environmental matters more generally and will be referred to at various places in the book: the Environmental Protection Act (EPA) 1990 and the Environment Act (EA) 1995.

Delegated legislation

While it is important, primary legislation is only the tip of a huge iceberg of law. As with much primary legislation today, Acts of Parliament concerned with environmental matters tend to provide little more than a general framework of institutions and powers leaving the detailed rules to be enacted by government in the form of statutory instruments. For example, while the Pollution Prevention and Control Act 1999 establishes a new regime of integrated pollution prevention and control, the details of the regime are contained in regulations made under the Act (see Chapter 5). This approach is typical.

Codes of Practice

As well as power to enact regulations, the Secretary of State is often authorised to issue Codes of Practice, designed to assist relevant authorities in the carrying out of their

---

55   See further Chapter 2.

functions. The EPA, for example, introduced a new concept to English law, the duty of care in relation to waste (s 34, on which see further Chapter 4). In order to assist in applying the duty of care the Secretary of State is required to issue and keep revised a Code of Practice on the Duty of Care (s 34(7)). The first Code of Practice was issued in 1991 and this was revised in 1996. The Code, which gives advice on such matters as the steps to be taken to ensure that waste is kept safe, is not legally binding but may be admitted as evidence to assist in determining whether the duty of care has been complied with.

Ministerial guidance

Likewise, although strictly not law, ministerial guidance on how powers and discretions are to be exercised under the relevant legislation may also be of considerable practical importance. For example, s 4(1) of the EA 1995 requires the Environment Agency to discharge its functions to protect or enhance the environment 'so as to make the contribution towards attaining the objective of achieving sustainable development'. The section goes on to provide in s 4(2) that 'Ministers shall from time to time give guidance to the Agency with respect to objectives which they consider it appropriate for the Agency to pursue in the discharge of its functions'. Such guidance 'must include guidance with respect to the contribution which, having regard to the Agency's responsibilities and resources, the Ministers consider it appropriate for the Agency to make, by the discharge of its functions, towards attaining the objective of achieving sustainable development' (s 3). The Agency is under a duty to 'have regard to' such guidance. In guidance issued under this section the Minister accepts that 'sustainable development entails reconciling the need for economic development and the needs of environmental protection'.

Government White Papers

White Papers set out firm proposals for legislation and policy (Green Papers are consultation documents setting out tentative proposals for legislation). While they are not sources of law (and for this reason are strictly beyond the scope of this book), environmental lawyers need to be aware of the contents of government White Papers. White Papers such as *This Common Inheritance* (Cm 1200) and *Sustainable Development: The UK Strategy* (Cm 2426) explain government thinking on policy issues. These documents often also throw light on the government's understanding and interpretation of principles of environmental law, such as the 'polluter pays' principle and the meaning of sustainable development.

Reports of the Royal Commission on Environmental Pollution

Lawyers also need to be aware of the reports of The Royal Commission on Environmental Pollution. Unlike other Royal Commissions this is a permanent body which reports to Parliament.[56] It is composed of experts from a range of disciplines and is able to investigate and research issues on its own initiative. Its influence on policy is said to be subtle rather than overt (Hughes (1996) 79). Nonetheless it has produced important

---

56 The Royal Commission on Environmental Protection has a homepage at www.rcep.org.uk.

reports which are widely referred to. For example its 5th, 10th, 11th and 12th reports (Cm 6371, Cm 9149, Cm 9675 and Cm 310) developed the principle known as 'best practicable environmental option' (BPEO) (see p 55, below).

Select Committee reports

The reports of the House of Commons Departmental Select Committees also provide valuable and often influential coverage of environmental issues. The Select Committee on Environment, Transport and Regional Affairs, for example, has recently produced reports on *The UK Climate Change Programme* (Department of Environment, Transport and Regional Affairs, Select Committee Report, Session 1999–2000, 5th Report, HC 194-I); and on the work of the Environment Agency (Department of Environment, Transport and Regional Affairs, Select Committee Report, Session 1999–2000, 6th Report, HC 34-I).

The Environment Agency

The Environment Agency was established on the 1 April 1996 (s 1 of the Environment Act 1995). The need for an agency with overall responsibility for safeguarding the environment had been strenuously argued for several years, in particular by the Select Committee on the Environment (see in particular that Committee's report on *Toxic Waste*, Session 1988–89, 2nd Report of the Environment Committee, HC 22, Toxic Waste, para 9). At that time the government said that such a body was 'neither necessary nor desirable' (*Government Response to the Second Report of the Environment Committee, Session 1988–89, on Toxic Waste*: Cm 679). Nonetheless, following sustained pressure from the Select Committee and elsewhere, the government eventually accepted the need for such a body (see, for example, the following reports: *Contaminated Land* (1990), Session 1989–90, 1st Report of the Environment Committee, HC 170; *Pollution of Beaches* (1990), Session 1989–90, 4th Report of the Environment Committee, HC 12; *Environmental Issues in Northern Ireland* (1990); *Indoor Pollution* (1991), Session 1990–91, 6th Report of the Environment Committee, HC 61; and *On the EC Draft Directive on the Landfill of Waste* (1991), Session 1990–91, 7th Report of the Environment Committee, HC 263.

When finally established the Environment Agency took over all the functions of the former National Rivers Authority, Her Majesty's Inspectorate of Pollution, and 83 local authority waste regulation authorities, as well as some new functions relating to, for example, contaminated land and air pollution.

The Agency employs about 10,000 people and currently spends around £600 million each year on a wide range of tasks including:

- air quality and the control of industrial emissions;
- regulating waste and dealing with contaminated land;
- water quality, water resources, flood management, fisheries and water-based recreation;
- habitat protection and conservation.

Its principal aim in discharging its functions as defined in the Environment Act is: '... so to protect or enhance the environment, taken as a whole, as to make the contribution that

Ministers consider appropriate towards attaining the objective of achieving sustainable development.' (Section 4(1), (2) and (3).)

In May 2000 the Department of the Environment, Trade and Regions Select Committee issued a report on the work of the Environment Agency during the first years of its operation (Session 1999–2000, 6th Report, HC 34-I). In this, the Committee commented that 'while the principle of the Agency continues to enjoy broad support and ... there is recognition of the positive steps which it has taken since its establishment':

> ... [t]he overall perception has been that progress in creating an effective, coherent and confident new body has not been as rapid in the three years since the Agency was formed as it ought to have been. This perception was confirmed during our inquiry. Comments such as 'the planned one-stop-shop for integrated environmental management in England and Wales is not working effectively for waste'; 'it is now three years since the Agency was formed and many fundamental problems do not seem to have been addressed'; 'the Agency still has many improvements to make before it can be considered to be an effective, fair and independent regulator'; and 'trying hard, but could do better' were typical of the kinds of things said by witnesses from across the spectrum of the Agency's partners, regulated industry, NGOs and others [paras10–11, notes omitted].

The principal powers and duties of the Environment Agency are set out in the following provisions of Pt 1, Chapter 1 of the Environment Act 1995.

Section 1: The Environment Agency

(1) There shall be a body corporate to be known as the Environment Agency or, in Welsh, Asiantaeth yr Amgylchedd (in this Act referred to as 'the Agency'), for the purpose of carrying out the functions transferred or assigned to it by or under this Act.

(2) The Agency shall consist of not less than eight nor more than fifteen members of whom–

    (a) three shall be appointed by the Minister; and

    (b) the others shall be appointed by the Secretary of State.

(3) The Secretary of State shall designate–

    (a) one of the members as the chairman of the Agency; and

    (b) another of them as the deputy chairman of the Agency.

(4) In appointing a person to be a member of the Agency, the Secretary of State or, as the case may be, the Minister shall have regard to the desirability of appointing a person who has experience of and has shown capacity in, some matter relevant to the functions of the Agency.

(5) Subject to the provisions of section 38 below, the Agency shall not be regarded–

    (a) as the servant or agent of the Crown, or as enjoying any status, immunity or privilege of the Crown; or

    (b) by virtue of any connection with the Crown, as exempt from any tax, duty, rate, levy or other charge whatsoever, whether general or local;

and the Agency's property shall not be regarded as property of or property held on behalf of the Crown.

(6) The provisions of Schedule 1 to this Act shall have effect with respect to the Agency.

Section 2: Transfer of functions to the Agency

(1) On the transfer date there shall by virtue of this section be transferred to the Agency–

    (a) the functions of the National Rivers Authority [...];

    (b) the functions of waste regulation authorities, that is to say, the functions conferred or imposed on them by or under–

        (i) the Control of Pollution (Amendment) Act 1989; or

        (ii) Part II of the Environmental Protection Act 1990 (in this Part referred to as 'the 1990 Act');

    or assigned to them by or under any other enactment, apart from this Act;

    (c) the functions of disposal authorities under or by virtue of the waste regulation provisions of the Control of Pollution Act 1974;

    (d) the functions of the chief inspector for England and Wales constituted under section 16(3) of the 1990 Act [...];

    (e) the functions of the chief inspector for England and Wales appointed under section 4(2)(a) of the Radioactive Substances Act 1993 [...];

    (f) the functions conferred or imposed by or under the Alkali, etc, Works Regulation Act 1906 (in this section referred to as 'the 1906 Act') on the chief, or any other, inspector (within the meaning of that Act), so far as exercisable in relation to England and Wales;

    (g) so far as exercisable in relation to England and Wales, the functions in relation to improvement notices and prohibition notices under Part I of the Health and Safety at Work etc Act 1974 (in this section referred to as 'the 1974 Act') of inspectors appointed under section 19 of that Act by the Secretary of State in his capacity as the enforcing authority responsible in relation to England and Wales for the enforcement of the 1906 Act and section 5 of the 1974 Act; and

    (h) the functions of the Secretary of State specified in sub-section (2) below.

(2) The functions of the Secretary of State mentioned in sub-section (1)(h) above are the following, that is to say–

    (a) so far as exercisable in relation to England and Wales, his functions under section 30(1) of the Radioactive Substances Act 1993 (power to dispose of radioactive waste);

    (b) his functions under Chapter III of Part IV of the Water Industry Act 1991 in relation to special category effluent, within the meaning of that Chapter, other than any function of making regulations or of making orders under section 139 of that Act;

    (c) so far as exercisable in relation to England and Wales, the functions conferred or imposed on him by virtue of his being, for the purposes of Part I of the 1974 Act, the authority which is by any of the relevant statutory provisions made responsible for the enforcement of the 1906 Act and section 5 of the 1974 Act;

    (d) so far as exercisable in relation to England and Wales, his functions under, or under regulations made by virtue, of section 9 of the 1906 Act (registration of works), other than any functions of his as an appellate authority or any function of making regulations;

    (e) so far as exercisable in relation to England and Wales, his functions under regulations 7(1) and 8(2) of and paragraph 2(2)(c) of Schedule 2 to, the Sludge (Use in Agriculture) Regulations 1989 (which relate to the provision of information and the testing of soil).

(3) The National Rivers Authority and the London Waste Regulation Authority are hereby abolished.

Section 4: Principal aim and objectives of the Agency

(1) It shall be the principal aim of the Agency (subject to and in accordance with the provisions of this Act or any other enactment and taking into account any likely costs) in discharging its functions so to protect or enhance the environment, taken as a whole, as to make the contribution towards attaining the objective of achieving sustainable development mentioned in sub-section (3) below.

(2) The Ministers shall from time to time give guidance to the Agency with respect to objectives which they consider it appropriate for the Agency to pursue in the discharge of its functions.

(3) The guidance given under sub-section (2) above must include guidance with respect to the contribution which, having regard to the Agency's responsibilities and resources, the Ministers consider it appropriate for the Agency to make, by the discharge of its functions, towards attaining the objective of achieving sustainable development.

(4) In discharging its functions, the Agency shall have regard to guidance given under this section.

(5) The power to give guidance to the Agency under this section shall only be exercisable after consultation with the Agency and such other bodies or persons as the Ministers consider it appropriate to consult in relation to the guidance in question.

[Sub-sections (6)–(9) omitted.]

Section 5: General functions with respect to pollution control

(1) The Agency's pollution control powers shall be exercisable for the purpose of preventing or minimising, or remedying or mitigating the effects of, pollution of the environment.

(2) The Agency shall, for the purpose–

    (a) of facilitating the carrying out of its pollution control functions; or

    (b) of enabling it to form an opinion of the general state of pollution of the environment,

compile information relating to such pollution (whether the information is acquired by the Agency carrying out observations or is obtained in any other way).

(3) If required by either of the Ministers to do so, the Agency shall–

    (a) carry out assessments (whether generally or for such particular purpose as may be specified in the requirement) of the effect, or likely effect, on the environment of existing or potential levels of pollution of the environment and report its findings to that Minister; or

    (b) prepare and send to that Minister a report identifying–

        (i) the options which the Agency considers to be available for preventing or minimising, or remedying or mitigating the effects of, pollution of the environment, whether generally or in cases or circumstances specified in the requirement; and

        (ii) the costs and benefits of such options as are identified by the Agency pursuant to sub-paragraph (i) above.

(4) The Agency shall follow developments in technology and techniques for preventing or minimising, or remedying or mitigating the effects of, pollution of the environment.

(5) In this section, 'pollution control powers' and 'pollution control functions', in relation to the Agency, mean respectively its powers or its functions under or by virtue of the following enactments, that is to say–

    (a) the Alkali, etc, Works Regulation Act 1906;

    (b) Part I of the Health and Safety at Work etc Act 1974;

    (c) Part I of the Control of Pollution Act 1974;

    (d) the Control of Pollution (Amendment) Act 1989;

    (e) Parts I, II and IIA of the 1990 Act (integrated pollution control etc, waste on land and contaminated land);

    (f) Chapter III of Part IV of the Water Industry Act 1991 (special category effluent);

    (g) Part III and sections 161 to 161D of the 1991 Act (control of pollution of water resources);

    (h) the Radioactive Substances Act 1993;

    (i) regulations under section 2 of the Pollution Prevention and Control Act 1999;

    (j) regulations made by virtue of section 2(2) of the European Communities Act 1972, to the extent that the regulations relate to pollution.

Notes:

Sub-s (5): in para (e) reference to 'I', underlined repealed by the Pollution Prevention and Control Act 1999, s 6(2), Sched 3.

Date in force: to be appointed: see the Pollution Prevention and Control Act 1999, s 7(3).

Sub-s (5): para (i) inserted by the Pollution Prevention and Control Act 1999, s 6(1), Sched 2, paras 14, 15.

Date in force (in relation to England and Wales): 21 March 2000: see SI 2000/800, Art 2.

Date in force (in relation to Scotland): to be appointed: see the Pollution Prevention and Control Act 1999, s 7(3).

Functions of the Ministers, so far as exercisable in relation to Wales, transferred to the National Assembly for Wales, by the National Assembly for Wales (Transfer of Functions) Order 1999 SI 1999/672, Art 2, Sched 1.

Section: 6 General provisions with respect to water

(1) It shall be the duty of the Agency, to such extent as it considers desirable, generally to promote–

    (a) the conservation and enhancement of the natural beauty and amenity of inland and coastal waters and of land associated with such waters;

    (b) the conservation of flora and fauna which are dependent on an aquatic environment; and

    (c) the use of such waters and land for recreational purposes,

and it shall be the duty of the Agency, in determining what steps to take in performance of the duty imposed by virtue of paragraph (c) above, to take into account the needs of persons who are chronically sick or disabled.

This sub-section is without prejudice to the duties of the Agency under section 7 below.

(2) It shall be the duty of the Agency to take all such action as it may from time to time consider, in accordance with any directions given under section 40 below, to be necessary or expedient for the purpose–

(a) of conserving, redistributing or otherwise augmenting water resources in England and Wales; and

(b) of securing the proper use of water resources in England and Wales;

but nothing in this subsection shall be construed as relieving any water undertaker of the obligation to develop water resources for the purpose of performing any duty imposed on it by virtue of section 37 of the Water Industry Act 1991 (general duty to maintain water supply system).

(3) The provisions of the 1991 Act relating to the functions of the Agency under Chapter II of Part II of that Act and the related water resources provisions so far as they relate to other functions of the Agency shall not apply to so much of any inland waters as–

(a) are part of the River Tweed;

(b) are part of the River Esk or River Sark at a point where either of the banks of the river is in Scotland; or

(c) are part of any tributary stream of the River Esk or the River Sark at a point where either of the banks of the tributary stream is in Scotland.

(4) Subject to section 106 of the 1991 Act (obligation to carry out flood defence functions through committees), the Agency shall in relation to England and Wales exercise a general supervision over all matters relating to flood defence.

(5) The Agency's flood defence functions shall extend to the territorial sea adjacent to England and Wales in so far as–

(a) the area of any regional flood defence committee includes any area of that territorial sea; or

(b) section 165(2) or (3) of the 1991 Act (drainage works for the purpose of defence against sea water or tidal water, and works etc to secure an adequate outfall for a main river) provides for the exercise of any power in the territorial sea.

(6) It shall be the duty of the Agency to maintain, improve and develop salmon fisheries, trout fisheries, freshwater fisheries and eel fisheries.

(7) The area in respect of which the Agency shall carry out its functions relating to fisheries shall be the whole of England and Wales, together with–

(a) such part of the territorial sea adjacent to England and Wales as extends for six miles from the baselines from which the breadth of that sea is measured ...

[The remaining parts of s 6(7) and s 6(8) omitted.]

Section 7: General environmental and recreational duties

(1) It shall be the duty of each of the Ministers and of the Agency, in formulating or considering–

(a) any proposals relating to any functions of the Agency other than its pollution control functions, so far as may be consistent–

(i) with the purposes of any enactment relating to the functions of the Agency,

(ii) in the case of each of the Ministers, with the objective of achieving sustainable development,

(iii) in the case of the Agency, with any guidance under section 4 above,

(iv) in the case of the Secretary of State, with his duties under section 2 of the Water Industry Act 1991,

so to exercise any power conferred on him or it with respect to the proposals as to further the conservation and enhancement of natural beauty and the conservation of flora, fauna and geological or physiographical features of special interest;

(b) any proposals relating to pollution control functions of the Agency, to have regard to the desirability of conserving and enhancing natural beauty and of conserving flora, fauna and geological or physiographical features of special interest;

(c) any proposal relating to any functions of the Agency–

(i) to have regard to the desirability of protecting and conserving buildings, sites and objects of archaeological, architectural, engineering or historic interest;

(ii) to take into account any effect which the proposals would have on the beauty or amenity of any rural or urban area or on any such flora, fauna, features, buildings, sites or objects; and

(iii) to have regard to any effect which the proposals would have on the economic and social well-being of local communities in rural areas.

(2) Subject to sub-section (1) above, it shall be the duty of each of the Ministers and of the Agency, in formulating or considering any proposals relating to any functions of the Agency–

(a) to have regard to the desirability of preserving for the public any freedom of access to areas of woodland, mountains, moor, heath, down, cliff or foreshore and other places of natural beauty;

(b) to have regard to the desirability of maintaining the availability to the public of any facility for visiting or inspecting any building, site or object of archaeological, architectural, engineering or historic interest; and

(c) to take into account any effect which the proposals would have on any such freedom of access or on the availability of any such facility.

(3) Sub-sections (1) and (2) above shall apply so as to impose duties on the Agency in relation to–

(a) any proposals relating to the functions of a water undertaker or sewerage undertaker,

(b) any proposals relating to the management, by the company holding an appointment as such an undertaker, of any land for the time being held by that company for any purpose whatever (whether or not connected with the carrying out of the functions of a water undertaker or sewerage undertaker), and

(c) any proposal which by virtue of section 156(7) of the Water Industry Act 1991 (disposals of protected land) falls to be treated for the purposes of section 3 of that Act as a proposal relating to the functions of a water undertaker or sewerage undertaker,

as they apply in relation to proposals relating to the Agency's own functions, other than its pollution control functions.

(4) Subject to obtaining the consent of any navigation authority, harbour authority or conservancy authority before doing anything which causes obstruction of, or other

interference with, navigation which is subject to the control of that authority, it shall be the duty of the Agency to take such steps as are–

(a) reasonably practicable, and

(b) consistent with the purposes of the enactments relating to the functions of the Agency,

for securing, so long as the Agency has rights to the use of water or land associated with water, that those rights are exercised so as to ensure that the water or land is made available for recreational purposes and is so made available in the best manner.

(5) It shall be the duty of the Agency, in determining what steps to take in performance of any duty imposed by virtue of sub-section (4) above, to take into account the needs of persons who are chronically sick or disabled.

(6) Nothing in this section, the following provisions of this Act or the 1991 Act shall require recreational facilities made available by the Agency to be made available free of charge.

(7) In this section–

'building' includes structure;

'pollution control functions', in relation to the Agency, has the same meaning as in section 5 above.

Section 8: Environmental duties with respect to sites of special interest

(1) Where English Nature or the Countryside Council for Wales is of the opinion that any area of land in England or, as the case may be, in Wales–

(a) is of special interest by reason of its flora, fauna or geological or physiographical features; and

(b) may at any time be affected by schemes, works, operations or activities of the Agency or by an authorisation given by the Agency,

that Council shall notify the fact that the land is of special interest for that reason to the Agency.

(2) Where a National Park authority or the Broads Authority is of the opinion that any area of land in a National Park or in the Broads–

(a) is land in relation to which the matters for the purposes of which sections 6(1) and 7 above (other than section 7(1)(c)(iii) above) have effect are of particular importance; and

(b) may at any time be affected by schemes, works, operations or activities of the Agency or by an authorisation given by the Agency,

the National Park authority or Broads Authority shall notify the Agency of the fact that the land is such land, and of the reasons why those matters are of particular importance in relation to the land.

(3) Where the Agency has received a notification under sub-section (1) or (2) above with respect to any land, it shall consult the notifying body before carrying out or authorising any works, operations or activities which appear to the Agency to be likely–

(a) to destroy or damage any of the flora, fauna, or geological or physiographical features by reason of which the land is of special interest; or

(b) significantly to prejudice anything the importance of which is one of the reasons why the matters mentioned in sub-section (2) above are of particular importance in relation to that land.

(4) Subsection (3) above shall not apply in relation to anything done in an emergency where particulars of what is done and of the emergency are notified to English Nature, the Countryside Council for Wales, the National Park authority in question or, as the case may be, the Broads Authority as soon as practicable after that thing is done.

(5) In this section–

'authorisation' includes any consent or licence;

'the Broads' has the same meaning as in the Norfolk and Suffolk Broads Act 1988; and

'National Park authority' means a National Park authority established under section 63 below which has become the local planning authority for the National Park in question.

Section 9: Codes of practice with respect to environmental and recreational duties

(1) Each of the Ministers shall have power by order to approve any code of practice issued (whether by him or by another person) for the purpose of–

(a) giving practical guidance to the Agency with respect to any of the matters for the purposes of which sections 6(1), 7 and 8 above have effect; and

(b) promoting what appear to him to be desirable practices by the Agency with respect to those matters,

and may at any time by such an order approve a modification of such a code or withdraw his approval of such a code or modification.

(2) In discharging its duties under section 6(1), 7 or 8 above, the Agency shall have regard to any code of practice, and any modifications of a code of practice, for the time being approved under this section.

(3) Neither of the Ministers shall make an order under this section unless he has first consulted–

(a) the Agency;

(b) the [Countryside Agency], English Nature and the Countryside Council for Wales;

(c) the Historic Buildings and Monuments Commission for England;

(d) the Sports Council and the Sports Council for Wales; and

(e) such other persons as he considers it appropriate to consult.

(4) The power of each of the Ministers to make an order under this section shall be exercisable by statutory instrument; and any statutory instrument containing such an order shall be subject to annulment in pursuance of a resolution of either House of Parliament.

Notes:

Commencement order: SI 1995/1983.

Sub-s (3): in para (b) words 'Countryside Agency' in square brackets substituted by SI 1999 /416, Art 3(d), Sched 1, para 17(1), (2).

Date in force: 20 February 1999 (with effect from 1 April 1999): see SI 1999/416, Arts 1, 2.

PRINCIPLES OF ENVIRONMENTAL LAW

This part of the chapter examines the evolution and progressive development of general principles of law intrinsic to environmental protection, at the international, European and domestic levels.

It may be argued that the development of environmental law reflects the practical application of underlying general principles of law which have evolved in tandem with rising concern over environmental degradation, and the real and potential threats of such degradation for the survival of humankind. Hughes, for example, notes that a simplistic description of this relationship would view it as existing on three levels: the application of specific *rules* based on accepted *general principles*, which in turn reflect certain *ethical values* deemed important enough to be protected. He argues, however, that a better view is that there exists a dynamic relationship between rules, principles and ethics both as to the formulation of the law and as to its implementation and enforcement (Hughes (1996) 15).

The relationship between principles

Broadly speaking, the principles fall into three categories: those concerned with the relationship between environmental controls and the need for socio-economic development; those concerned with preventing or reducing likely pollution; those concerned with allocating liability for pollution when it has occurred (polluter pays principle).

These principles, often vague in content and uncertain in application, are not necessarily binding rules of law. This is illustrated in the UK context by *Ex p Duddridge* [1995] 7 JEL 224; [1996] Env LR 325 (see p 55, below). The relationship between these principles is as yet unclear. According to Hughes, 'if any hierarchy exists in them it must be that sustainable development must be the first and greatest principle and that all others should serve that end' (Hughes (1996) 23–24).

Sustainable development

Defined simply, 'sustainable development' is the general principle that human development and use of natural resources must take place in a sustainable manner (Sands (1995) 198). At the international level, the 1987 Brundtland Report of the *World Commission on Environment and Development* (WCED), widely accepted as a precursor to the 1992 UN Conference on Environment and Development (UNCED) in Rio de Janeiro, defined 'sustainable development' as 'development that meets the needs of the present without compromising the ability of future generations to meet their own needs'. (For the Rio Declaration 1992, see p 69, below.) As Sands has noted, there are at least four main elements or principles in their own right that are encompassed by the general principle of 'sustainable development': first, the conservation of natural resources for the benefit of future generations (the principle of inter-generational equity); second, the exploitation of natural resources in a manner which is 'sustainable' or 'prudent' (the principle of sustainable use); third, the 'equitable use' of natural resources, which implies that the use by one State must take account of the needs of other States (the principle of equitable use, or intra-generational equity); and fourth, the integration of environmental considerations into economic and other development plans, programmes and projects (the principle of integration of environment and development needs) (Sands (1995) 199).

'Sustainable development' is arguably the most important general principle of environmental law. Indeed 'sustainable development' may be seen as the guiding principle in the evolution of environmental law at all three levels of international, European and domestic UK law (see, for example, s 4(1) of the EA 1995, p 39, above). It is also the principle which best illustrates Hughes' point (above) about the dynamic nature of rules, principles and the ethical values they represent. This is because in its broadest sense, the principle encompasses not merely the legal, but also the economic and political fields. The successful application of this principle would require not merely legal measures, but also economic and policy instruments in order to bring it about. Perhaps even more importantly, any human activity deemed useful, but which affects the environment in which we all live in a detrimental manner, may be required to fulfil the criterion of sustainability in the sense that such activity may not be allowed to reduce the capacity of the environment to ensure its continued usefulness for that and other human activities.

This recognition of the broad nature and application of the principle of 'sustainable development', in terms of the various disciplines it covers, does raise questions concerning its progressive development as a general legal principle of environmental law. For example, at the international level, can it be said that it is specific enough in its formulation to be capable of creating legal obligations between States? One might want to argue that the function of general legal principles does not necessarily include the formulation of legal rights and duties but is merely to guide the policies and actions of the authorities involved. Nevertheless, it may be important to know exactly how far individuals and other entities are legally required to implement the principle of sustainable development in their daily activities.

Turning to the EC, the primary theme of the EC's fifth Environmental Action Programme, taken up by the proposed sixth Environmental Action Programme, is to achieved:

> ... sustainable development which is defined as a policy and strategy for continued economic and social development without detriment to the environment and the natural resources on the quality of which continued activity and further development depend.

The definition of sustainable development provided by the Brundtland Report is quoted with approval (see above).

The approach adopted to implement the fifth Programme differs from that in the previous four programmes in the following respects.

- It focuses on the agents and activities which deplete natural resources and otherwise damage the environment, rather than waiting for problems to emerge.
- It endeavours to initiate changes in current trends and practices which are detrimental to the environment, so as to provide optimal conditions for socio-economic well-being and growth for the present and future generations.

These two approaches have been used to target five sectors specifically chosen because of the significant impact they have on the environment and their crucial role in achieving sustainable development. These are:

(a) *Industry* – an environment/industry relationship is to be built up based on:

(i) improved resource management with a view to achieving both a more economical use of resources and an improvement in other competitiveness;

(ii) the use of information for the promotion of better consumer choice and to increase public confidence in industrial activities and their control and in the quality of their products (eco-labelling, see p 825, below);

(iii) the development of Community standards for production process and products.

(b) *Energy* – the aim is to improve energy efficiency and develop what are described as 'strategic technology programmes' which move towards an energy structure which is less dependent on fossil fuels and promotes renewable energy options. Various specific measures are proposed to achieve these ends, including, *inter alia*, increasing awareness by education and training; the use of economic and fiscal instruments and by developing and applying energy efficient norms.

(c) *Transport* – the programme refers to 'a strategy for sustainable mobility' which will include improving land use/economic development planning at local, regional, national and transnational levels; incorporating the real costs of both infrastructure and environment when considering investment policies and making decisions; developing public transport; continuing the technical improvement of vehicles and fuels and encouraging the use of less polluting fuels; and promoting a more environmentally rational use of the private car. Various specific measures have been agreed including the imposition of taxes on driving, a reduction in parking facilities and the use of speed limits and other physical constraints.

(d) *Agriculture* – the programme notes that (Community-led) changes in farming practices within the Community have led to over-exploitation and degradation of the natural resources on which agriculture ultimately depends, viz soil, water and air. However, in addition to environmental degradation, serious problems have also emerged in the case of commodity overproduction and storage, rural depopulation, the Community budget and international trade. It is therefore a combination of these factors which lie behind the various measures to be taken to strike a more sustainable balance between agricultural activity, other forms of rural development and the natural resources of the environment. These measures would include reducing the nitrate content of surface and underground water; achieving a reduction in the use of pesticides in cultivated soil by imposing controls on sale and use; maintaining biodiversity and natural habitat; and by the extension of reafforestation to agricultural land.

(e) *Tourism* – although the European Community supports tourism through its investment in necessary infrastructures it recognises that it is mainly at levels other than that of the Community that the real work of reconciling tourism activity and development and the guardianship of natural and cultural assets must be brought into a sustainable balance in States, regional and local authorities, the tourism industry itself and individual tourists. This can be seen as a practical reflection of the principles of subsidiarity. The three main lines of action indicated in the programme deal with diversification of tourist activities to include the better management of tourist activities; improving the quality of tourist services; and taking action to influence tourist behaviour, including media campaigns, codes of conduct and choices of transport.

- It aims to achieve changes in society's patterns of behaviour through the optimum involvement of all sectors of society in a spirit of shared responsibility, including public administration, public and private enterprise, and the general public (as both individual citizens and consumers). Whilst recognising that it will take some considerable time to turn current patterns of consumption and behaviour in the direction of sustainability the Programme requires the following three *ad hoc* dialogue groups to be consulted by the Commission: a General Consultative Forum comprising representatives of firms, consumers, trade unions, non-governmental organisations and local and regional authorities; an Implementation Network comprising representatives of relevant national authorities and of the Commission involved in the practical implementation of Community measures, the main function of which will be to ensure the exchange and pooling of information so as to make it possible to develop common approaches at a practical level, under the supervision of the Commission; and an Environmental Policy Review Group comprising representatives of the Commission and the Member States at Director-General level to develop mutual understanding and to promote an exchange of views on environmental policy and measures. The overall aim of these dialogue groups is to complement the legislative (top-down) existing approach to environmental protection by involving all economic and social partners in the task.

- Responsibility will be shared through a significant broadening of the range of instruments to be applied contemporaneously to the resolution of particular issues or problems.

The previous Action Programmes relied almost entirely on legislative measures to achieve their aims. The fifth Programme seeks to involve all sectors of society in a full sharing of responsibility and as such, a broader mix of instruments is needed. These can be categorised under four headings:

- legislative instruments designed to set fundamental levels of protection for public health and the environment, to implement wider international commitments and to provide Community-wide rules and standards necessary to preserve the integrity of the internal market;

- market-based instruments such as fiscal and economic measures designed to reflect the true environmental costs in the prices of goods and services;

- horizontal supporting instruments including improvements in statistical data, the encouragement of research and development, the provision of public/consumer information and education and professional and vocational education and training;

- financial support mechanisms – bearing in mind that Art 6 provides that environmental policy must be integrated into the definition and implementation of other Community policies, it will be necessary to ensure that all Community funding operations, particularly those involving the Structural Funds, will be as sensitive as possible to environmental considerations and in conformity with environmental legislation.

The principle of sustainable growth, as well as sustainable development, is referred in Art 2 of the Treaty. There is some doubt as to whether there is a distinction between these two principles, but any distinction appears more semantic than real, it being accepted that sustainable development implies a commitment to sustainable growth (Bell and McGillivray (2000) 16).

Subsidiarity: underlying this new strategy for the Environment and Sustainability is the principle of subsidiarity (Art 5b).[57] This principle is used to ensure that the various objectives, targets and actions are implemented by the appropriate national, regional and local efforts and initiatives. This is said to ensure that full account is taken of the traditions and sensitivities of different regions within the Community and to improve the choice of actions and appropriate mixes of instruments at Community and/or other levels. Regard should be had to Protocol No 30 to the Treaty of Amsterdam which stresses that the exclusive powers of the Community institutions set out in the Treaty and interpreted by the Court are not affected by the subsidiarity principle, which only applies where the Community has shared competence with Member States. The Protocol also reminds Member States that they are required to take all appropriate measures to fulfill their Treaty obligations and not to obstruct the attainment of Treaty objectives

Preventive and precautionary principles

The preventive principle has a longer history and a greater record of acceptance and implementation by States, both on the international plane as well as in their domestic legislation, and is more precise in terms of its obligatory character than the principle of sustainable development (discussed above) and the precautionary principle (below). Broadly stated, this principle requires that activity which does or will cause environmental pollution or damage is to be prohibited. The preventive principle therefore seeks to minimise environmental damage by requiring that action be taken at an early stage of the process, where possible before such damage has actually occurred. As Sands notes, the preventive principle is now supported by an extensive body of domestic environmental protection legislation and many international conventions (Sands (1995) 195). At the international level, this is especially significant because the acceptance of this principle means that States are actively constrained against allowing polluting activities within their own national jurisdictions, in addition to their international obligation not to allow activities which cause damage to territories of other States and areas beyond national jurisdiction. (See Principle 21 of the Stockholm Declaration 1972 (p 66, below) and Principle 2 of the Rio Declaration 1992 (p 69, below).) A notable example of this general prohibition against polluting activities is Art 194 of the 1982 UN Convention on the Law of the Sea (UNCLOS), which enjoins all States to prevent, reduce and control pollution of the marine environment as a whole, both within and without their national maritime zone jurisdictions.

---

57   See p 21, above.

The precautionary principle has a much shorter history than the preventive principle. It has only recently appeared in binding international treaty law, as opposed to Declarations and other international instruments of a non-binding character. However, its potential impact on the development of environmental law is immense. In its most progressive (some might argue extreme) formulation, the precautionary principle may be utilised to overturn the traditional burden of proof which is presently weighted in favour of polluters, in the sense that any activity has to be proven to cause pollution before action may be taken to prevent, reduce or control such pollution. The precautionary principle would act to reverse the burden of proof and require any potential polluter to ensure that the activity would not cause pollution before it is allowed to commence. Such an unambiguous approach has been deemed too costly in the short term.

Therefore legal formulations of the principle have tended to include a cost-benefit element. For example, Principle 15 of the Rio Declaration 1992 (see p 73, below) provides that 'where there are threats of serious or irreversible damage lack of full scientific certainty shall not be used as a reason for postponing cost-effective measures to prevent environmental degradation'. The Climate Change Convention 1992 incorporates a similar formulation of the precautionary principle (see Art 3(3), p 104, below). On the other hand, the 1992 Paris Convention for the Protection of the Marine Environment of the North East Atlantic introduces a different formulation of the principle, linking it with the preventive principle: preventive measures are to be taken when there are 'reasonable grounds for concern ... even when there is no conclusive relationship between inputs and their alleged effects' (see Art 2(2)(a); Sands (1995) 211). The different emphases within these formulations of the precautionary and preventive principles, especially with respect to the level of threat to the environment that is required before precautionary action should be taken and the introduction of a cost-benefit element to such action, means that there is no uniform understanding of the legal content of the principles.

The EC's first Action Programme laid the basis for what has become the principle of preventive action within EC law, stating that:

> ... the best environmental policy consists in preventing the creation of pollution and nuisances at source, rather than subsequently trying to counteract their effects.

Also included for the first time in the Maastricht amendments to the Treaty of Rome is a requirement that the Community's environmental policy 'shall be based on the precautionary principle' (see now Art 174(2)). In the absence of any definition it is unclear as to how this principle should be differentiated from the need to take preventive action. Wilkinson (1992) suggests that it could be used to justify protective environmental measures before a specific environmental hazard has been identified and to place the onus of proof that environmental damage would not occur upon the 'polluter'. However, since the Community is bound to take 'available scientific and technical data' into account (Art 174(3)) and because such measures could be politically sensitive, it is hard to support the view that this principle could be used to justify new policy initiatives not previously sanctioned. Whether this insertion is little more than a strengthening of the principle that preventive action should be taken is questionable.

The precautionary principle achieved prominence in the context of the BSE crisis. In its judgment on the validity of the Commission's decision banning the export of beef from the UK to reduce the risk of BSE transmission (Cases C-157/96 and C-180/96), the ECJ said that:

> Where there is uncertainty as to the existence or extent of risk to human health, the institutions may take protective measures without having to wait until the reality and seriousness of those risks become fully apparent. (Grounds 63) [see also Judgment of the Court of First Instance 16 July 1998 (Case T-199/96)].

The President of the Court of First Instance referring to the precautionary principle, affirmed that 'requirements linked to the protection of public health should undoubtedly be given greater weight than economic considerations' (Order of 30 June 1999 (Case T-70/99)).[58]

The European Commission has recently issued a communication on the precautionary principle (COM (00) 1). This communication outlines, *inter alia*, the Commission's approach to using the precautionary principle and establishes guidelines for applying the principle. The Commission notes that reliance on the precautionary principle 'constitutes an essential plank of its [the Community's] policy' (p 11):

> The Community has consistently endeavoured to achieve a high level of protection, among others in environment and human, animal or plant health. In most cases, measures making it possible to achieve this high level of protection can be determined on a satisfactory scientific basis. However, when there are reasonable grounds for concern that potential hazards may affect the environment or human, animal or plant health, and when at the same time the available data preclude a detailed risk evaluation, the precautionary principle has been politically accepted as a risk management strategy in several fields. (Paragraph 3.)

The Commission identifies two distinct aspects of the precautionary principle: (1) the political decision to act or not to act; and (2) decisions concerning how to act, that is, the measures resulting from application of the precautionary principle. In relation to the factors that trigger application of the precautionary principle, the Commission says that the principle is relevant only in the event of a potential risk of harm. Existence of a risk requires evaluation of the scientific data (accepting that the data may make it impossible to determine with sufficient certainty the risk in question). This evaluation should be followed by an assessment of the potential consequences of inaction. This assessment should involve 'all interested parties' to the 'fullest possible extent' and the procedure should be as 'transparent as possible' (p 16). The measures adopted presuppose examination of the benefits and costs of action or inaction. The Commission notes that in undertaking such a cost-benefit analysis the decision-maker may, in certain circumstances, be guided by non economic considerations such as the protection of health (para 6.3.4).

Bearing in mind that some environmental pollution can never be cleaned up, or at least not without incurring substantial costs, it is clearly appropriate for environmental policy to focus upon avoiding environmental damage before it occurs. To date, various Community measures have been taken to prevent damage, for example, environmental impact assessment requirements for major projects, measures restricting the transport of waste both within and outside the Community.

---

58   See also Case C-6/99 *Greenpeace France v Ministère de l'Agriculture*, in relation to GM crops.

An associated principle is that environmental damage should as a priority be rectified at source. Whereas this principle is fairly clear in itself, and was inserted into the Treaty by the Single European Act 1986, it is questionable whether it has been used 'as a priority'. For example, the source of a great deal of pollution within the Community is the motor car and indeed emission standards have been applied to car exhaust gases. However, far from prioritising sources of pollution and imposing strict limits on their polluting activities, the Community has given equal weight to tackling pollution by imposing quality objectives. This approach focuses upon the consequences of pollution rather than its source, and therefore tends to negate the usefulness of this principle.

The UK government's understanding of these principles is explained in *This Common Inheritance* ((1990) Cm 1200):

> We must act on facts, and on the most accurate interpretation of them, using the best scientific and economic information ... That does not mean we must sit back until we have 100% evidence about everything. Where the state of our planet is at stake, the risks can be so high and the costs of corrective action so great, that prevention is better and cheaper than cure. We must analyse the possible benefits and costs both of action and of inaction. Where there are significant risks of damage to the environment, the government will be prepared to take precautionary action to limit the use of potentially dangerous materials or the spread of potentially dangerous pollutants, even where scientific knowledge is not conclusive. This precautionary principle applies particularly where there are good grounds for judging that action taken promptly at comparatively low cost may avoid more costly damage later, or that irreversible effects may follow if action is delayed' (paras 1.17–1.18, p 11. See also '*Sustainable Development: The UK Strategy*' ((1994) Cm 2426).

In *R v Secretary of State for Trade and Industry ex p Duddridge*[59] it was argued that the Secretary of State should take precautionary action to prevent risks of childhood leukaemia arising from exposure to electromagnetic fields generated by power cables. The scientific evidence of a link between power cables and childhood leukaemia was found to be unclear and not to establish a causal link. At first instance Smith J said that the mere possibility of serious harm to the environment or to human health is not enough to justify imposing an obligation on government to take precautionary action (see the judgment of the Court of Appeal, pp 55–61, below). See also in relation to GM Crops, *R v Secretary of State for the Environment ex p Watson* (1998) *The Times*, 31 August, EGCS (2) 122.

Polluter pays principle

This principle provides that the costs of environmental pollution should be borne by those whose activities were responsible for causing the pollution. It is possible to consider the application of this principle at both the general and specific levels. At the specific level, it has been held that identified polluters should be required to pay the full costs of the rectification of any environmental degradation that has occurred as a result of their activities. The application of the polluter pays principle in this manner is manifest in the rules governing civil and State liability for environmental damage due to hazardous activities. Examples at the international level include the 1992 Conventions on Civil

---

59   [1995] 7 JEL 224; [1996] Env LR 325.

Liability for Oil Pollution Damage and Establishment of an International Fund for Compensation for Oil Pollution Damage (replacing the 1969 and 1971 Conventions of the same names) (see p 207, below) and the 1960 Convention on Third Party Liability in the Field of Nuclear Energy (Paris), with 1963 Supplementary Convention (Brussels). Examples in domestic law include 'causing water pollution' (s 85, Water Resources Act 1991); 'unlawful keeping, depositing or treating of waste' (s 33 of the EPA 1990). For a recent proposal seeking to implement the polluter pays principle see the European Commission's White Paper on *Environmental Liability*, pp 84–86, below; for a discussion of the principle in the context of marine oil pollution, see pp 207–12, below.

At the more general level, the polluter pays principle may be seen to act in such a way that all human economic activity which impinges upon the environment should be fully accounted for in the economic pricing system of the goods and services produced by such activity. In economic terms, this process is called 'the internalisation of environmental costs' and is potentially much more far-reaching in its impact on our daily lives than the mere provision of full compensation for environmental damage as a result of defined polluting activities. It is significant therefore that it is this version of the polluter pays principle that is included within Principle 16 of the Rio Declaration 1992 (see p 73, below).

Perhaps because of the uncertainty in the level of application of the polluter pays principle to be preferred and the obvious economic implications of its application, 'the polluter pays principle has not received the broad geographic and subject matter support over the long term accorded to the principle of preventive action, or the attention accorded to the precautionary principle in recent years' (Sands (1995) 213). Thus, 'it is doubtful whether it has achieved the status of a generally applicable rule of customary international law, except perhaps in relation to States in the EC, the UN/ECE (Economic Commission for Europe) and the OECD (Organisation for Economic Co-operation and Development)' (Sands (1995) 213).

The UK government's understanding of the polluter pays principle is summarised in *This Common Inheritance* (Cm 1200) as being 'to make those who cause environmental damage face the costs of control in full, without subsidy' (para 1.25, p 13; see also *Sustainable Development: The UK Strategy* ((1994) Cm 2426)). Although easy to state in the abstract this principle is very difficult to apply in practice. For example, if a polluter is a large manufacturer, should it be able to pass the costs of its pollution on to its customers in the form of extra charges? Identifying the polluter may also be a problem. Cars cause pollution, but is the polluter the car manufacturer, the car driver, the fuel supplier, the car seller, the road builder? Further problems relate to pollution which has been caused in the past (historic pollution). In such a situation it may be impossible to identify the polluter, or the polluter may have gone out of business.

The principle of citizen participation and the right to a healthy environment

This principle is based on the premise that in order to ensure the effective implementation of environmental laws at all levels, individuals should be able to participate in environmental decision-making. There are several aspects of this principle that need to be considered (see further Chapter 7).

It is important to note the extent to which such a principle may be utilised to ensure participation. At one end of the spectrum participation may amount to little more than procedural rights such as the right to seek information, to be consulted before decisions are taken, or to gain access to the courts to challenge decisions. To this extent participation rights are enshrined in Principle 10 of the Rio Declaration 1992 (see p 71, below), in the requirement that EC institutions should be transparent in their decision-taking (see the *WWF* case, p 806, below), in the need to ensure access to justice (see *Implementing Community Environmental Law*, p 828, below), and in the recent liberalisation of standing in the context of UK judicial review proceedings (see, for example, *Greenpeace* case, p 842, below).

At the other end of the spectrum is the argument that the principle of citizen participation extends beyond procedural matters and demands nothing short of legally enforceable environmental rights. In this respect, it is interesting to note that Principle 1 of the Stockholm Declaration 1972 appears to provide an early basis for such environmental rights (see p 63, below). Such rights have now received concrete recognition in the UN/ECE Convention on Access to Information, Public Participation in Decision-making and Access to Justice in Environmental Matters (the Aarhus Convention, June 1998) This is the first binding international treaty to recognise 'the right of every person of present and future generations to live in an environment adequate to his or her health and well-being' (Art 1, see further Chapter 7).

The principle of integration

Article 6 of the Treaty states that '[e]nvironmental protection requirements must be integrated into the definition and implementation of Community policies'. Although expressed rather more robustly than the original provision inserted by the Single European Act (environmental protection requirements shall be a component of the Community's other policies) it is debatable whether the effect has been to reinforce a commitment to integration. The current provision appears to envisage future action without specifying how integration is to be achieved. Nor does it specify any particular penalty for non-compliance. Still, it reflects the strong emphasis placed on the need to integrate environmental protection in all policies and Art 218 imposes an obligation upon the Commission to 'adapt its rules of procedure so as to ensure that both it and its departments operate in accordance with the provisions of this Treaty'. The integration principle now requires that environmental protection requirements (as set out in Art 175) must be incorporated into other Community policies, such as agriculture and industry, although the practical effect of this requirement is uncertain.

The need to integrate the environment into other policy sectors was stressed by EU Leaders at the Cardiff Summit in June 1998 and at Vienna in 1999. They instructed all meetings of the Council of Ministers to establish strategies aimed at achieving environmental integration in their respective policy areas. In addition to requiring the Commission to review all existing policies it was suggested that the Commission should prepare a detailed environmental assessment of all key proposals likely to result in important environmental impacts and show how the results of the assessment have been incorporated into the proposal.

Integrated pollution control

The need to adopt an integrated approach was also recognised within UK environmental regulation in the context of what was called 'integrated pollution control' and is now Integrated Pollution, Prevention and Control (see Chapter 5). Integrated pollution control (IPC) recognised that pollution prevention or reduction strategies must treat the environment as a whole and cannot be focused on the specific sectors of: land, water and, air. Tromans has explained that IPC recognised two basic concepts:

(a) that pollutants have effects in media other than those into which they have been released; and

(b) that reducing opportunities to dispose of waste to one medium often increases the need to dispose of the waste ... into one of the other media ...

(Tromans (1990) 8–9).

IPC was introduced into UK domestic law by the EPA 1990 as the basis for regulating prescribed industrial processes. It, and the new regime, is dealt with in more detail in Chapter 5. Suffice to say for the present that in applying IPC the following standards are used:

Best practicable environmental option (BPEO)

The concept of the BPEO was developed by the Royal Commission on Environmental Pollution. In its eleventh report (1985, Cm 9675), it explained:

A BPEO is the outcome of a systematic consultative and decision-making procedure which emphasises the protection and conservation of the environment across land, air, and water. The BPEO procedure establishes, for a given set of objectives, the option that provides the most benefit or the least damage to the environment as a whole, at acceptable cost, in the long term as well as in the short term.

Best available techniques not entailing excessive costs (BATNEEC)

The BPEO is used in conjunction with the principle that industry use the best available techniques not entailing excessive costs (BATNEEC). BATNEEC has now largely replaced the older notion that the best practicable means (BPM) must be adopted to prevent pollution, although reference to BPM is still found in the law relating to statutory nuisances where it is a defence to show that the best practicable means have been taken to prevent or minimise the effects of a nuisance. On the meaning of BPM in this context see s 79(9) of the Environmental Protection Act 1990. BATNEEC itself is soon to be superceded by Best Available Techniques (BAT) by virtue of the Pollution Prevention and Control Act 1999 (see further Chapter 5).

On the precautionary principle in UK law

R v Secretary of State for Trade and Industry ex p Duddridge and Others [1996] Env LR 325

Sir Iain Glidewell: This is an application made on behalf of three children – Lloyd Duddridge, Danielle Bye and Naomi Holliday – by their fathers for leave to appeal against the decision of the Queen's Bench Divisional Court, Farquharson LJ and Smith J, given on 3

October 1994 refusing an application for judicial review of a decision of the President of the Board of Trade.

At the conclusion of the hearing on 3 October 1995 Kennedy LJ announced that this court refused the application for leave. I now give my reasons for being party to that decision. The leading judgment in the Divisional Court was given by Smith J with whom Farquharson LJ concurred. She set out the background to the application and the order sought by the applicants so clearly that I cannot do better than incorporate what she said into this judgment:

> This is an application for judicial review of the decision of the Secretary of State for Trade and Industry whereby he declined to issue regulations to the National Grid Company plc and or other licence holders under the Electricity Act 1989 so as to restrict the electromagnetic fields from electric cables which are being laid or are to be laid as part of the national grid. The application is brought on behalf of three children who live in South Woodford, an area of North East London where the National Grid Company is presently laying a new high voltage underground cable between Tottenham and Redbridge. The applicants allege that the non-ionising radiation which will be emitted from these new cables when commissioned, which will enter their homes and schools, will be of such a level as will or might expose them to a risk of developing leukaemia. They say that the Secretary of State should issue regulations which would remove any such risk.
>
> By their application they seek an order to compel him to issue regulations, guidelines or some other directive to licence holders so as to be laid as part of the national grid do not exceed (i) 0.2 micro-teslas at the nearest point of houses adjoining the cables; or (ii) some other level at which on current research, there is no evidence to suggest or otherwise hypothesise any possible risk to the health of those exposed to such fields. Alternatively, they seek an order of mandamus to oblige the Secretary of State to advise the Crown to issue such regulations, guidelines or other form of directive. In the further alternative, they seek a declaration that, in refusing to issue such regulations, guidelines or directive, the Secretary of State has failed to comply with his duty under s 3 of the Electricity Act 1989.
>
> Leave to move for judicial review was granted by Schiemann J who also made an order for expedition. Also before the Court is the National Grid Company plc, who appear as a Party Directly Affected. Behind this application lies the concern of residents of South Woodford, particularly those who are the parents of young children, who saw a BBC Panorama television programme transmitted on 31 January 1994. The programme discussed a number of epidemiological studies which examine the possible connection between exposure to high levels of non-ionising radiation in the electromagnetic fields (EMFs) created by high voltage electric cables and the incidence of childhood leukaemia. To the non-expert, some of these studies might appear to suggest that children who have substantial exposure to EMFs from high voltage cables passing near their homes face a three to fourfold (or even possibly six-fold) increased risk of developing leukaemia. However, as has been readily accepted by counsel appearing for the applicants, the study of the effects of EMFs by epidemiology is fraught with difficulty and the results of these studies, when expertly evaluated, do not allow, let alone require, any such positive or alarming conclusions to be drawn.
>
> Understandably, the programme caused anxiety in the minds of the residents and parents of South Woodford. Some of them formed an action group and on 15 February 1994 wrote to the National Grid Company seeking information, inter alia, about the levels of radiation which would be emitted from the cables when energised. On 27

February, the National Grid Company provided the information requested from which the action group perceived that their children would indeed be exposed to levels of non-ionising radiation well in excess of the average domestic level. The action group took the view that their children might be at risk of leukaemia if the cables were commissioned in the manner intended.

The action group had by this time taken legal advice and on 15 March 1994 their solicitor wrote to the Secretary of State asking him to lay down regulations to cover the alleged danger to health arising from the installation of these cables. They urged him to take a precautionary view of the risk of damage to health. They warned him that, if he refused, they would commence an application for judicial review. On the same day their solicitor wrote to the National Grid Company, asking it to take voluntary measures to reduce the levels of EMF exposure or alternatively to stop work until the issue had been resolved. No reply was received from the company. On 28 April, the Secretary of State replied to his letter saying that he had never regarded it as necessary or appropriate to take specific measures to limit EMFs to protect the public from the possibility of a very small risk of cancer. He had reconsidered the matter in the light of the group's recent letter and application for judicial review. He adhered to his previous opinion and would oppose the application. Hence this application comes before the court.

The judge also said:

The only issue before the court is whether the Secretary of State, in declining to take specific measures to limit the level of EMFs, has acted unlawfully.

And that was the only issue before this court. The statutory regime so far as English legislation is concerned is to be found in the Electricity Act 1989. By s 3(3):

Subject to subsections (1) and (2) above, the Secretary of State ... shall ... have a duty to exercise the functions assigned to him by this Part in the manner in which he considers is best calculated;

...

(d) to protect the public from dangers arising from the generation, transmission or supply of electricity.

By s 29(1):

The Secretary of State may make such regulations as he thinks fit for the purpose of–

(b) protecting the public from dangers arising from the generation, transmission or supply of electricity, from the use of electricity supplied or from the installation, maintenance or use of any electric line or electrical plant; and

(c) without prejudice to the generality of (b) above, eliminating or reducing the risks of personal injury, or damage to property or interference with its use, arising as mentioned in that paragraph.

Clearly, the making of such regulations under that power is a function assigned to the Secretary of State. The regulations which the Secretary of State has made, namely the Electricity Regulations 1988 which were continued in force by the 1989 Act and which have been subsequently amended, do not contain specific provisions limiting ... electromagnetic fields.

It is clear from the provisions of the Act that if there is a risk of personal injury, or damage to property, arising from the transmission of electricity through the new cables, that is, the use of those lines, the Secretary of State is under a duty to use his powers to protect the public from that risk. He would do so by exercising his power to make appropriate regulations: and an order that he shall do so is the primary remedy which the applicants seek.

However, it is common ground that the expert evidence which was before the Divisional Court does not establish that there is such a risk. The furthest the evidence for the applicants went – and I am now quoting from the evidence of Dr Dennis, a former member of the NRBP (National Radiological Board of Protection) – was:

> The totality of the scientific evidence points to the weak possibility that prolonged exposure to power frequency magnetic fields, while not a direct causal factor in inducing human leukaemias, may enhance the risk of these cancers especially in young children when acting in conjunction with other social and environmental factors. The degree of this enhancement for prolonged exposure to fields in excess of 100 to 300 nanoteslas may be about 1.5 to 4.

Professor Scott Davis, the other expert relied on by the applicants, said:

> Thus on balance it is my judgment that at present it is not possible to conclude with certainty that residential EMF exposure causes leukaemia in childhood. In other words, I do not believe that a causal relationship has yet been established. Nevertheless it is also my judgment that the most important criteria of causation ... have largely been met: strength of association, temporality, biological gradient and to a fair degree consistency. Thus, in my judgment, that such exposure may increase the risk of childhood leukaemia cannot be dismissed, given the current evidence.

In essence, the scientific opinion relied upon by the Secretary of State does not differ markedly from the evidence of the two experts for the applicants. The Secretary of State's case is that that evidence is not sufficient to prove that there is a risk to health such as to impose on him a duty to make regulations limiting the emission of EMFs. Whether that threshold has been passed and where the threshold should be are the issues between the Secretary of State and the applicants. They claim that he set the threshold too high. Their case is that if there is evidence of a possible risk, the Secretary of State is under a duty to use his powers to obviate it. They argue that he is under this duty as a matter of domestic law because, they submit, the standard was that adopted as government policy in a White Paper of 1990, entitled 'This Common Inheritance'.

Alternatively, they submit that the Secretary of State is required to adopt this approach by the provisions of European Community law. The application of the test for which the applicants argue – that is to say that evidence of a possible risk imposes a duty on the Secretary of State to make appropriate regulations – is referred to as the adoption of the 'precautionary principle'.

Smith J summarised the evidence of which only some short extracts have been given here. She said at page 18G in her judgment:

> I am prepared to accept that, if the Secretary of State is shown to be under a legal obligation to apply the precautionary principle to legislation concerned with health in the environment, the possibility of harm raised by the existing state of scientific knowledge is such that would oblige him to apply it in considering whether to issue regulations to restrict exposure to EMFs. He would at least in my view be obliged to conduct the cost-benefit analysis necessary for the proper application of the principle. The Secretary of State accepts that he has not considered the precautionary principle, except to the limited extent required by the policy set out in the 1990 White Paper. If he

were to be under an obligation to apply the principle, I would be in favour of granting relief limited to requiring the Secretary of State to reconsider the need for the regulation of EMFs in the light of that principle.

However, the learned judge then concluded at page 21 of her judgment:

If the government announces a policy which it intends to adopt without being under any obligation to do so, it must be entitled to define the limits of that policy in any way it wishes. If the government says it will apply a precautionary policy when it perceives a significant risk of harm, it must, in my view, be entitled to apply that threshold for action. The Secretary of State says that he has considered the need for regulations in the light of this policy and has concluded such are neither necessary nor appropriate. In my judgment, on the basis of the advice he has received, his conclusion that there is no significant risk of developing cancer from exposure to EMFs cannot be impugned as wholly unreasonable or perverse.

She also rejected an alternative argument relating to the application of the precautionary principle as a matter of domestic law. Although the applicants' Notice of Appeal seeks to challenge these conclusions, Mr Beloff QC for the applicants makes it clear that he does not persist in that challenge.

The intended appeal, if we had granted leave, would therefore have been limited to the argument that, in not adopting the precautionary principle, the Secretary of State has failed to comply with the relevant provisions of European Community law. The appeal, however, is now coupled with an application to refer the issues raised in the argument about the applicability of Community law to the European Court of Justice.

I turn to consider these provisions. They are to be found in the Treaty establishing the European Community, The Treaty of Rome, as subsequently amended notably by the Treaty on European Union, the Treaty of Maastricht, and incorporated into English law by the European Communities Act 1972 as amended by the Act of 1993 ... [the judge then set out extracts from Articles 130r, 130s, 130t. [Now Art 174. See pp 23–24, above].

Mr Beloff's argument, on behalf of the applicants, advanced before the Divisional Court, and repeated before us, is that Article 130r imposes a duty on the Secretary of State to adopt and apply the precautionary principle when deciding whether to exercise his power to make regulations under s 29 of the Electricity Act 1989. The application of that principle, Mr Beloff submits, would require the Secretary of State to make regulations controlling the limit of emission of an electromagnetic field.

Shortly, the issue is thus whether Article 130r does impose a duty on the Secretary of State to apply the precautionary principle. The Divisional Court held that the Article does not have that effect. Mr Beloff submits that this issue is one which should be decided by the European Court of Justice on a reference for that purpose. He therefore urges us to grant leave to appeal and then ourselves order a reference of the issue to the European Court. Alternatively, we could grant leave to appeal and leave it to the full court to decide whether to make such a reference.

I am, of course, aware that if leave to appeal be not granted, there can be no reference. Thus we should not, in my view, refuse leave unless this court 'can with complete confidence resolve the matter itself' to quote Sir Thomas Bingham MR in *R v the Stock Exchange ex p Else and Another* [1993] QB 534; [1993] 1 All ER 420 at 545E of the former report.

I say at once that I have such confidence. It is my clear opinion that the Divisional Court were correct to reject Mr Beloff's submissions on this issue.

In my judgment Article 130r sets out the aims which the Community policy shall be designed to achieve and the principles to which such a policy shall adhere. The Article does not of itself place any obligation on any organ of a national government. The repeated use of the future tense makes it clear that the Article itself does not contain or create such a policy. The procedures which are to be followed to bring Community policy into being are set out in Article 130s. If the particular aspect of policy is one of those defined in Article 130s(2) the procedure is contained in that sub-article. For a policy relating to some other aspect, the procedure is contained in Article 189c. Whichever procedure is followed, the creation of a policy on the environment requires an election by organs of the Community such as the promulgation of a directive and it may be decisions or actions by the Commission, the Council or the European Parliament.

Thus if measures relating to the control of emission of EMFs significantly affected the general structure of a Member State's electricity supply, the relevant procedure would be that contained in Article 130s(2), that is, a proposal from the Commission after consultation with the European Parliament and the Economic and Social Committee followed by a measure adopted by the Council. The Secretary of State will be under whatever obligation it imposes. At present he is under no such obligation ...

My view about the effect of Article 139r is reinforced by the decision of the European Court of Justice in *Peralta*, Case C379/92. I adopt Smith's J summary of the facts of that case at page 39 of the judgment:

> Mr Peralta, an Italian national and Master of a ship flying the Italian flag, had been prosecuted for discharging caustic soda into the sea outside Italian territorial waters. The relevant provision of Italian law prohibited the discharge of such substances within territorial waters by ships of any flag and also prohibited such discharges by Italian ships on the high seas. Mr Peralta sought to argue that the relevant provision of Italian law was inconsistent with the principles of prevention referred to in Article 130r and could therefore be challenged.

In para 57 of its judgment, the court said:

> Secondly, Article 130r is confined to defining the general objectives of the Community in the matter of the environment. Responsibility for deciding what action is to be taken is conferred on the Council by Article 130s. Moreover, Article 130t states that the protective measures adopted pursuant to Article130s are not to prevent any Member State from maintaining or introducing more stringent protective measure compatible with the Treaty.

I note also that in paras 32 and 34 of his opinion, the Advocate General said in relation to Articles 84 and 130r:

> 32 These provisions lay down rules for action by the Council in the field of sea and air transport (Article 84(2) and the environment (Article 130r).

and –

> 34 More generally, the Italian legislation does not encroach upon the competence which is reserved to the Council in the sphere of sea transport or the environment.

Mr Beloff seeks to argue that *Peralta* did not decide that Member States had no obligations under Article 130r. Nevertheless, the passages to which I have referred in the opinion and judgment are essential parts of the reasoning of the court, and are thus authority on the effect of Article 130r.

It is for those reasons that I concurred in refusing the application for leave ...

Peter Gibson and Kennedy LJJ agreed.

ENVIRONMENTAL PRINCIPLES: THE KEY INSTRUMENTS

Defining the 'environment' and 'pollution of the environment'

Section 1 of the Environmental Protection Act 1990 provides a convenient starting point. This Act contains the following definitions:

(2) The 'environment' consists of all, or any, of the following media, namely, the air, water and land; and the medium of air includes the air within buildings and the air within other natural or man-made structures above or below ground.

(3) 'Pollution of the environment' means pollution of the environment due to the release (into any environmental medium) from any process of substances which are capable of causing harm to man or any other living organisms supported by the environment.

(4) 'Harm' means harm to the health of living organisms or other interference with the ecological systems of which they form part and, in the case of man, includes offence caused to any of his senses or harm to his property; and 'harmless' has a corresponding meaning.

Stockholm Declaration on the Human Environment 1972

The 1972 UN Conference on the Human Environment, which yielded, *inter alia*, the now famous set of principles known as the Stockholm Declaration represents the first formal sign of increasing international concern for environmental degradation on a global scale. Previous to this there had been bilateral, regional and even global instruments agreed between States addressing specific environmental problems, but none of these had highlighted both the universal (as opposed to specific) nature of environmental degradation and the global (as opposed to localised) effects of such degradation.

The Conference adopted three non-binding instruments: a Declaration of 26 principles, an Action Plan containing 109 recommendations and a Resolution on institutional and financial arrangements. Of these, the most significant from a legal perspective was the adoption of the general guiding principles, set out in the Declaration of Principles (for the Preservation and Enhancement of the Human Environment) (see p 63, below). The 26 principles in the Stockholm Declaration reflected a compromise between those States which sought only to indicate their recognition and concern over the mounting problems affecting the global environment, and those that wanted the adoption of the Declaration to act as a catalyst for specific international and domestic action, along the lines set down by the principles within it (Sands (1995) 36). Here we see another reason why international environmental 'soft' law, with its inherently non-binding character, is useful for the progressive development of the law on this subject. Although it is possible to State that none of the principles in the Stockholm Declaration create legally binding obligations, nevertheless these principles set down general guidelines for the behaviour of States in this field (see discussion, pp 4 and 5, above). The passage of time has seen many of these principles incorporated into international agreements addressing specific environmental problems, and re-affirmed in global, regional and national policy statements, if not actual legislation. This crystallisation process from 'soft' to 'hard' rules of international environmental law could not have occurred had the initial negotiation process that yielded the Declaration attempted to come up with a legally binding document, because the broad differences between the negotiating stances of various groups of States would have prevented such an agreement. The successful brokering of a compromise between these different stances was dependent upon the non-binding nature of the resulting Declaration.

The Declaration therefore fulfils an inspirational purpose, even though it is not in itself a legalistic document, nor can its provisions be held to be binding upon States. It does however represent a formalisation in UN practice which is used only when principles of special importance are being laid down and 'the general tone is one of a strong sense of dedication to the idea of trying to establish the basic rules of international environmental law' (Sohn (1973)). As Birnie and Boyle note further, 'few of the principles are expressed in the obligatory "shall" form; most use "should" or "must", and there is evident reluctance to couch all principles in the form of clear duties of States. Thus, only a handful are of special legal significance' (Birnie and Boyle (1995) 1).

From a legal perspective, the most immediately relevant provisions are Principles 21, 22, 23, and 24. The other principles are generally couched in non-legal language, but here again it may be seen that recent history has shown their relevance in the progressive development of international environmental law. The Stockholm Declaration's Principles, however, are weak on techniques for implementing environmental standards, such as environmental impact assessment, prior notification and consultation procedures, access to environmental information, participation in the formulation of environmental policies and the availability of administrative and judicial remedies (Sands (1995) 36). Subsequent developments in these areas of environmental law, at the international, EC, and national levels, will be covered later in this book.

The most important of the Stockholm Declaration's Principles, is that enunciated by Principle 21. This is in many respects the 'golden' rule of international law for the protection of the environment, and may be described as the starting point for the sub-discipline of *international environmental law*. It has been called the fundamental principle of State responsibility for transboundary environmental harm, enshrining as it does the principle of national sovereignty while imposing limits on a State's activities where these inflict environmental damage to other States and to areas beyond national jurisdiction. As Pallemaerts notes, '(A)lthough worded in a general, even vague way, Principle 21 is clearly formulated as a legal principle which could be interpreted and applied in concrete situations through international mechanisms for dispute settlement' ((1993) 5). It is held by many writers to reflect international law and has subsequently been referred to as such in a number of multilateral environmental treaties. It also appears, although in a modified version, in Principle 2 of the Rio Declaration 1992 (see p 69, below).

DECLARATION OF THE UNITED NATIONS CONFERENCE ON THE HUMAN ENVIRONMENT, STOCKHOLM (1972)

The United Nations Conference on the Human Environment,

Having met at Stockholm from 5 to 16 June 1972,

Having considered the need for a common outlook and for common principles to inspire and guide the peoples of the world in the preservation and enhancement of the human environment,

...

States the common conviction that:

Principle 1

Man has the fundamental right to freedom, equality and adequate conditions of life, in an environment of a quality that permits a life of dignity and well-being, and he bears a solemn responsibility to protect and improve the environment for present and future generations. In this respect, policies promoting or perpetuating apartheid, racial segregation, discrimination, colonial and other forms of oppression and foreign domination stand condemned and must be eliminated.

Notes:

1   This principle arguably incorporates two different though related principles of international environmental law which are recognised more widely nowadays. The first appears to be the right to a healthy environment, framed as a fundamental human right presumably to be protected by international law. The second seems to be the principle of inter-generational equity (see also Principle 2 of the Stockholm Declaration), by which is meant that the present generation of humankind owes a duty to future generations to ensure that the state of the global environment that they will be born into is no worse than that which presently exists.

2   The former right has had some very limited influence on the development of legal protection of environmental rights, mainly in domestic legal systems. It has however been reformulated in Principle 1 of the Rio Declaration 1992, eschewing the concept of an environmental 'right' for the more legally neutral 'entitlement' to a healthy environment. The consequent reduction in emphasis of the human rights element under Rio not only reduced the scope for progress on legal protection of the environment through an extension of human rights law, but also appeared to reduce human beings to the status of legal 'objects' rather than 'subjects' of the law. Thus, they would appear not to have recognised legally enforceable rights and obligations in this area of the law (Pallemaerts (1993) 8–9). But, see now Art 1, Aarhus Convention, Chapter 7, p 766, below).

Principle 2

The natural resources of the earth, including the air, water, land, flora and fauna and especially representative samples of natural eco-systems, must be safeguarded for the benefit of present and future generations through careful planning or management, as appropriate.

Principle 3

The capacity of the earth to produce vital renewable resources must be maintained and, wherever practicable, restored or improved.

Principle 4

Man has a special responsibility to safeguard and wisely manage the heritage of wildlife and its habitat, which are now gravely imperilled by a combination of adverse factors. Nature conservation, including wildlife, must therefore receive importance in planning for economic development.

Principle 5

The non-renewable resources of the earth must be employed in such a way as to guard against the danger of their future exhaustion and to ensure that benefits from such employment are shared by all mankind.

Principle 6

The discharge of toxic substances or of other substances and the release of heat, in such quantities or concentrations as to exceed the capacity of the environment to render them harmless, must be halted in order to ensure that serious or irreversible damage is not inflicted upon eco-systems. The just struggle of the peoples of all countries against pollution should be supported.

Principle 7

States shall take all possible steps to prevent pollution of the seas by substances that are liable to create hazards to human health, to harm living resources and marine life, to damage amenities or to interfere with other legitimate uses of the sea.

Notes:

1   Principle 6 alludes to the notion of an assimilative capacity of the environment, suggesting that pollution levels should not be allowed to exceed the capacity of the environment to assimilate The 'preventive' Principle (7) above, was significant too as one of the first attempts at setting down an obligation among states to prevent polluting activities, especially in the maritime sphere. This principle was later re-iterated in a more comprehensive fashion in Article 194 of the 1982 UN Convention on the Law of the Sea (UNCLOS), incorporating all measures necessary to 'prevent, reduce and control pollution of the marine environment'.

2   Both the above principles however have been superceded somewhat by the gradual emergence and acceptance by states in various fora of the precautionary principle, albeit with less agreement as to its precise meaning and the exact nature of its implementation. The precautionary principle argues that measures to control environmentally-threatening activities should be undertaken, even when there is a lack of scientific certainty as to the true extent of any environmental damage resulting from such activities. This principle is now enunciated in Principle 15 of the Rio Declaration, as well as several other treaty regimes such as the 1972 London Convention on the Prevention of Marine Pollution by Dumping, the 1985 Vienna Convention for the Protection of the Ozone Layer, and the 1992 Framework Convention on Climate Change.

Principle 8

Economic and social development is essential for ensuring a favourable living and working environment for man and for creating conditions on earth that are necessary for the improvement of the quality of life.

Principle 9

Environmental deficiencies generated by the conditions of under-development and natural disasters pose grave problems and can best be remedied by accelerated development through the transfer of substantial quantities of financial and technological assistance as a supplement to the domestic effort of the developing countries and such timely assistance as may be required.

Principle 10

For the developing countries, stability of prices and adequate earnings for primary commodities and raw materials are essential to environmental management since economic factors as well as ecological processes must be taken into account.

Principle 11

The environmental policies of all states should enhance and not adversely affect the present or future development potential of developing countries, nor should they hamper the attainment of better living conditions for all, and appropriate steps should be taken by states and international organisations with a view to reaching agreement on meeting the possible national and international economic consequences resulting from the application of environmental measures.

Principle 12

Resources should be made available to preserve and improve the environment, taking into account the circumstances and particular requirements of developing countries and any costs which may emanate from their incorporating environmental safeguards into their development planning and the need for making available to them, upon their request, additional international technical and financial assistance for this purpose.

Principle 13

In order to achieve a more rational management of resources and thus to improve the environment, states should adopt an integrated and co-ordinated approach to their development planning so as to ensure that development is compatible with the need to protect and improve environment for the benefit of their population.

Principle 14

Rational planning constitutes an essential tool for reconciling any conflict between the needs of development and the need to protect and improve the environment.

Principle 15

Planning must be applied to human settlements and urbanisation with a view to avoiding adverse effects on the environment and obtaining maximum social, economic and environmental benefits for all. In this respect, projects which are designed for colonialist and racist domination must be abandoned.

Principle 16

Demographic policies which are without prejudice to basic human rights and which are deemed appropriate by governments concerned should be applied in those regions where the rate of population growth or excessive population concentrations are likely to have adverse effects on the environment of the human environment and impede development.

Principle 17

Appropriate national institutions must be entrusted with the task of planning, managing or controlling the environmental resources of states with a view to enhancing environmental quality.

Principle 18

Science and technology, as part of their contribution to economic and social development, must be applied to the identification, avoidance and control of environmental risks and the solution of environmental problems and for the common good of mankind.

Principle 19

Education in environmental matters, for the younger generation as well as adults, giving due consideration to the underprivileged, is essential in order to broaden the basis for an enlightened opinion and responsible conduct by individuals, enterprises and communities in protecting and improving the environment in its full human dimension. It is also essential that mass media of communications avoid contributing to the deterioration of the environment, but, on the contrary, disseminate information of an educational nature on the need to protect and improve the environment in order to enable man to develop in every respect.

Principle 20

Scientific research and development in the context of environmental problems, both national and multinational, must be promoted in all countries, especially the developing countries. In this connection, the free flow of up-to-date scientific information and transfer of experience must be supported and assisted, to facilitate the solution of environmental problems; environmental technologies should be made available to developing countries on terms which would encourage their wide dissemination without constituting an economic burden on the developing countries.

Principle 21

States have, in accordance with the Charter of the United Nations and the principles of international law, the sovereign right to exploit their own resources pursuant to their own environmental policies, and the responsibility to ensure that activities within their jurisdiction or control do not cause damage to the environment of other states or of areas beyond the limits of national jurisdiction.

Notes:

1   This was the most important contribution of the Stockholm Conference and Declaration to the progressive development of international environmental law. It is the first principle of this sub-discipline of public international law which has transcended its initial 'soft' law status to become a recognised and widely accepted rule of customary international law governing the relations between states in matters concerning the environment. As such it has been re-affirmed in a number of global, regional and bilateral instruments, as well as the Rio Declaration, albeit with certain potentially significant changes to its wording.

2   The principle is clearly formulated as a legal principle which describes limits to national sovereignty and therefore imposes limits to state activities, even where these are within the state's territory, should the environmental damage from them be transboundary in nature (Pallemaerts (1993) 5). But it is important to note that the first sentence of this principle affirms the national sovereignty of states before juxtaposing and balancing this with the principle of state responsibility for transboundary environmental damage.

3   The legal significance of the extension of state responsibility over activities within its jurisdiction or control which cause damage to the environment beyond the jurisdictional limits of other states should also be noted. This represents the progressive development of the principle applied in several landmark cases, which was confined to damage to the environment of another State; see the *Trail Smelter Arbitration* case (*US v Canada*) (1938 and 1941) 3 RIAA 1905, discussed below, p 94). This extension of state responsibility to cover damage to areas beyond national jurisdiction, the so-called 'international commons areas' of the world, namely, the high seas, atmosphere and outer space, is also recognised and well-accepted among many states. However, it does raise the problem of how and by whom a claim for such damage occurring wholly within an international commons area beyond the national jurisdiction of all states can be mounted.

Principle 22

States shall co-operate to develop further the international law regarding liability and compensation for the victims of pollution and other environmental damage caused by activities within the jurisdiction or control of such states to areas beyond their jurisdiction.

Principle 23

Without prejudice to such criteria as may be agreed upon by the international community, or to standards which will have to be determined nationally, it will be essential in all cases to consider the systems of values prevailing in each country, and the extent of the applicability of standards which are valid for the most advanced countries but which may be inappropriate and of unwarranted social cost for the developing countries.

Principle 24

International matters concerning the protection and improvement of the environment should be handled in a co-operative spirit by all countries, big and small, on an equal footing. Co-operation through multilateral or bilateral arrangements or other appropriate means is essential to effectively control, prevent, reduce and eliminate adverse environmental effects resulting from activities conducted in all spheres, in such a way that due account is taken of the sovereignty and interests of all states.

Principle 25

States shall ensure that international organisations play a co-ordinated, efficient and dynamic role for the protection and improvement of the environment.

Principle 26

Man and his environment must be spared the effects of nuclear weapons and all other means of mass destruction. States must strive to reach prompt agreement, in the relevant international organs, on the elimination and complete destruction of such weapons.

21st plenary meeting 16 June 1972.

Rio Declaration on Environment and Development 1992

The post-Stockholm period leading up to the 1992 UN Conference on Environment and Development (UNCED), the so-called 'Earth Summit', in Rio de Janeiro was a particularly productive one in terms of the number of international environmental instruments agreed during that time. These agreements covered a wide range of issues, of both a general and specific nature, as well as being global, regional and bilateral in their application. Examples of these agreements which will be examined further in this volume are the 1979 Geneva Convention on Long-Range Trans-boundary Air Pollution (p 132), the 1973 Convention for the Prevention of Pollution from Ships, as modified by the 1978 Protocol (MARPOL 73/78) (p 212), the 1973 Convention on International Trade in Endangered Species of Wild Fauna and Flora (CITES) (p 570), the 1989 Basel Convention on the Control of Trans-boundary Movements of Hazardous Wastes and their Disposal (p 352) and the 1991 Espoo Convention on Environmental Impact Assessment in a Trans-boundary Context (p 752).

As Sands points out, this period was also marked by 'a proliferation of international environmental organisations (including those established by treaty) and greater efforts by existing institutions to address environmental issues; the development of new sources of international environmental obligation from acts of such organisations; new environmental norms established by treaty; the development of new techniques for implementing environmental standards, including environmental impact assessment and access to information; and the formal integration of environment and development particularly in relation to international trade and development assistance' (Sands (1995 38). In this context, it is important to note too the rise of environmental non-governmental organisations (NGOs) such as Greenpeace, Friends of the Earth and the World Wide Fund for Nature (WWF), and the consequent part they have played in raising public consciousness over environmental issues at the international, national and local levels.

Even though many new instruments were agreed and organisations set up, concern over continuing environmental degradation mounted. This concern began to focus less on specific, sectoral or regional environmental issues, and more on the overall impact of increasing human activity, and the capacity of the environment to sustain such activity. Acting on this concern, the UN General Assembly convened the World Commission on Environment and Development in 1983, chaired by the then Prime Minister of Norway Gro Harlem Brundtland. One of the Brundtland Commission's main objectives was to re examine critical environment and development issues and formulate realistic proposals for dealing with them. The Brundtland Report was a catalyst for the 1992 UN Conference on Environment and Development and the five instruments there adopted: the Framework Convention on Climate Change 1992 (see p 101, below), the Biodiversity Convention 1992 (see p 586, below), the Rio Declaration 1992 (see below), Agenda 21, and the Non-binding Principles on Sustainable Development of Forests (Sands (1995) 45). The Brundtland Report was also the first major attempt to bring together the seemingly divergent concerns on development and the environment, through the use of the sustainable development concept.

The UN Conference on Environment and Development (UNCED) was held in June 1992 in Rio de Janeiro, Brazil. The Conference was attended by 176 States, more than 50 inter-governmental organisations and several thousand non-governmental organisations

Two treaties, the Climate Change and Biodiversity Conventions were opened for signature, and three other non-legally binding instruments were adopted (see below). The most significant of these non-binding instruments, in terms of the principles of international environmental law which it purports to set down, is the 1992 Rio Declaration on Environment and Development. The Rio Declaration represents an important step in the process begun by the Brundtland Commission towards the legal recognition of the concept of sustainable development, representing as it does 'a series of compromises between developed and developing countries and a balance between the objectives of environmental protection and economic development' (Sands (1995) 49).

DECLARATION OF THE UNITED NATIONS CONFERENCE ON ENVIRONMENT AND DEVELOPMENT, RIO DE JANEIRO (1992)

Preamble

The United Nations Conference on Environment and Development,

Having met at Rio de Janeiro from 3 to 14 June 1992,

Reaffirming the Declaration of the United Nations Conference on the Human Environment, adopted at Stockholm on 16 June 1972, and seeking to build upon it,

With the goal of establishing a new and equitable global partnership through the creation of new levels of co-operation among states, key sectors of societies and people,

Working towards international agreements which respect the interests of all and protect the integrity of the global environmental and developmental system,

Recognising the integral and inter-dependent nature of the Earth, our home,

Proclaims that

Principle 1

Human beings are at the centre of concerns for sustainable development. They are entitled to a healthy and productive life in harmony with nature.

Note:

1   Unlike Principle 1 of the Stockholm Declaration, which acknowledged that environmental problems could also be approached from a human rights perspective, Principle 1 of Rio contains no clear affirmation of a human right to a healthy environment. Indeed, it has been argued (see p 63, above) that the legal status of human beings has moved from being subjects of law, that is, autonomous actors who have certain rights and obligations in relation to other subjects, to objects of law, who are dependent upon States' conception and implementation of the sustainable development theme.

Principle 2

States have, in accordance with the Charter of the United Nations and the principles of international law, the sovereign right to exploit their own resources pursuant to their own environmental and developmental policies, and the responsibility to ensure that activities within their jurisdiction or control do not cause damage to the environment of other states or of areas beyond the limits of national jurisdiction.

Notes:

1   This is a re-statement of the principle of state responsibility for transboundary environmental damage previously enunciated by Principle 21 of the Stockholm Declaration, albeit with certain possibly significant additions. On the face of it, the position of this principle as Principle 2 within the Rio Declaration itself, at a much earlier point in the document than Principle 21 in the Stockholm Declaration, may give cause for optimism.

2   On the other hand, the inclusion of the words 'and developmental' to describe the range of areas that fall within a State's sovereign rights is arguably detrimental to the delicate balance achieved between a State's sovereign rights and its responsibility for any environmental damage as a result of the exercise of these sovereign rights (Pallemaerts (1993) 5). The expansion of 'environmental policies' to include 'environmental and developmental policies' may be explained, however, by placing this phrase within the context of the overall UNCED (UN Conference on Environment and Development) process, which was centred around the 'sustainable development' theme, that was in turn very much concerned with the integration of socio-economic development and environmental protection.

Principle 3

The right to development must be fulfilled so as to equitably meet developmental and environmental needs of present and future generations.

Notes:

1   This principle reiterates the one established at Stockholm in Principle 1, concerning the need to achieve inter-generational equity, with the important addition of 'developmental' as well as 'environmental' needs.

2   The intra-generational aspect of this principle is also much more to the fore in this (Rio) Declaration, providing that not only future members of the human race but also present members in diverse areas of the world are able to benefit from a healthy environment.

Principle 4

In order to achieve sustainable development, environmental protection shall constitute an integral part of the development process and cannot be considered in isolation from it.

Note:

1   This principle reflects the elements of compromise between, and integration of, protection of the natural environment and economic growth that is inherent to the concept of sustainable development. These in turn are the main reasons why 'sustainable development' was an important objective of the Rio 'Earth Summit' (UNCED). It was intended to serve not simply the needs of the environment, but also entail a much more far-reaching re-orientation of the world's economic system in which the burdens of environmental protection will fall more heavily on the developed northern States and the economic benefits will accrue more significantly to the underdeveloped south (Boyle (1994) 175–77) (see also Principles 5–7).

Principle 5

All states and all people shall co-operate in the essential task of eradicating poverty as an indispensable requirement for sustainable development, in order to decrease the disparities in standards of living and better meet the needs of the majority of the people of the world.

Principle 6

The special situation and needs of developing countries, particularly the least developed and those most environmentally vulnerable, shall be given special priority. International actions in the field of environment and development should also address the interests and needs of all countries.

Principle 7

States shall co-operate in a spirit of global partnership to conserve, protect and restore the health and integrity of the Earth's eco-system. In view of the different contributions to global environmental degradation, states have common but differentiated responsibilities. The developed countries acknowledge the responsibility that they bear in the international pursuit of sustainable development in view of the pressures their societies place on the global environment and of the technologies and financial resources they command.

Note:

1   The roots of the above two principles may be found in two related sources: First, the notion of intra-generational equity, as an important aspect of the principle of inter-generational equity espoused in Principle 3 of Rio Declaration 1992 and Principle 1 of the Stockholm Declaration 1972, means that developing countries need to be given priority as they invariably contain populations most at risk from environmental degradation. Secondly, in order to achieve the objective of a New International Economic Order (NIEO) between developed and developing States, developed countries are expected to shoulder more of the burden of reversing global environmental degradation, on the understanding that they bear most of the initial responsibility for such degradation.

Principle 8

To achieve sustainable development and a higher quality of life for all people, states should reduce and eliminate unsustainable patterns of production and consumption and promote appropriate demographic policies.

Principle 9

States should co-operate to strengthen endogenous capacity-building for sustainable development by improving scientific understanding through exchanges of scientific and technological knowledge, and by enhancing the development, adaptation, diffusion and transfer of technologies, including new and innovative technologies.

Principle 10

Environmental issues are best handled with the participation of all concerned citizens, at the relevant level. At the national level, each individual shall have appropriate access to information concerning the environment that is held by public authorities, including information on hazardous materials and activities in their communities, and the opportunity to participate in decision-making processes. States shall facilitate and encourage public awareness and participation by making information widely available.

Effective access to judicial and administrative proceedings, including redress and remedy, shall be provided.

Notes:

1   This principle, although formulated in vague terms, is important for two reasons: first, because its call for better citizen participation in environmental decision-making and rights of access to environmental information can help to ensure greater compliance by States of international environmental standards, through the domestic political accountability of their governments. In this manner, another dimension of accountability is achieved, complementary to the usual method of ensuring compliance of international law by way of inter-State pressure; secondly, these concepts of citizen participation and access to information did not feature in the Stockholm Declaration and, therefore, their inclusion here may be seen as an example of the progressive development of legal mechanisms for ensuring environmental protection.

2   On the other hand, it has been argued while this principle is the only one in the Rio Declaration which uses individual human rights discourse in an environmental context, it is formulated in manifestly non-judicial language (Pallemaerts (1993) 11).

Principle 11

States shall enact effective environmental legislation. Environmental standards, management objectives and priorities should reflect the environmental and developmental context to which they apply. Standards applied by some countries may be inappropriate and of unwarranted economic and social cost to other countries, in particular developing countries.

Principle 12

States should co-operate to promote a supportive and open international economic system that would lead to economic growth and sustainable development in all countries, to better address the problems of environmental degradation. Trade policy measures for environmental purposes should not constitute a means of arbitrary or unjustifiable discrimination or a disguised restriction on international trade. Unilateral actions to deal with environmental challenges outside the jurisdiction of the importing country should be avoided. Environmental measures addressing transboundary or global environmental problems should, as far as possible, be based on an international consensus.

Principle 13

States shall develop national law regarding liability and compensation for the victims of pollution and other environmental damage. States shall also co-operate in an expeditious and more determined manner to develop further international law regarding liability and compensation for adverse effects of environmental damage caused by activities within their jurisdiction or control to areas beyond their jurisdiction.

Notes:

1   The second sentence of this principle represents an attempt to reaffirm the recommendation contained in Principle 22 of the Stockholm Declaration, calling for further development of the international law regarding liability and compensation for pollution victims and other environmental damage caused by a State's activities. Little progressive development in this issue can be discerned in the present sentence which merely calls for further co-operation.

2   The first sentence of this principle, however, may be seen as progressive. The requirement that States develop national laws regarding liability and compensation can be used to circumvent the lack of movement on this issue at the international level, provided that access to such national schemes is made available to victims of transboundary damage that may not be of the same nationality (cf Pallemaerts (1993) 8).

Principle 14

States should effectively co-operate to discourage or prevent the relocation and transfer to other states of any activities and substances that cause severe environmental degradation or are found to be harmful to human health.

Principle 15

In order to protect the environment, the precautionary approach shall be widely applied by states according to their capabilities. Where there are threats of serious or irreversible damage, lack of full scientific certainty shall not be used as a reason for postponing cost-effective measures to prevent environmental degradation.

Notes:

1   The precautionary principle adopted here represents one of the most important new principles of the international environmental law sub-discipline within public international law. Like the polluter pays principle discussed below (Principle 16), the precautionary principle has the potential of bringing about significant innovation in the law. It represents a progressive shift from the preventive principle that was obtained previously (see Principles 6 and 7 of the Stockholm Declaration 1972), which was predicated upon the notion that only when pollution threatens to exceed the assimilative capacity of the environment to render it harmless, should it be prevented from entering the environment. The precautionary principle acts to reverse this assumption, arguing that when pollution is discerned, uncertainty as to whether the assimilative capacity of the environment has been reached should not prevent measures to reduce such pollution from entering the environment.

2   Should the precautionary principle be implemented to its fullest extent, for example it may be construed as reversing the burden of proof required so that it will be would-be polluters who have to show that any pollution from their activities is below the minimum requirements set down by legislation, rather than the regulatory authorities having to prove that they have exceeded such limits and pollution has resulted, as is presently the case.

Principle 16

National authorities should endeavour to promote the internalisation of environmental costs and the use of economic instruments, taking into account the approach that the polluter should, in principle, bear the cost of pollution, with due regard to the public interest and without distorting international trade and investment.

Notes:

1   The polluter pays principle is another very important principle of international environmental law. Along with the precautionary principle discussed above (Principle 15), it represents a significant development in the evolution of international environmental law as a discrete sub-discipline of public international law. Like the

precautionary principle however there is some uncertainty as to the extent of its application in practice.

2   In particular, it is unclear whether the internalisation of environmental costs for all polluting activities through various economic instruments envisaged by the application of this principle can be achieved without a complete overhaul of the present system for the allocation of the cost of natural resources utilisation by such activities.

3   For the above reason, as well as the more practical ones of defining the 'polluter', and gauging the extent of the pollution to be paid for, the application of this principle under international environmental law has been limited to the liability incurred by the perpetrators of polluting acts, such as increasing the amount of compensation for tanker oil spills and allowing more heads under which to claim such compensation (see International Convention on Civil Liability for Oil Pollution Damage 1969 (Civil Liability Convention), and the Oil Pollution Compensation Fund Convention 1971 (Fund Convention) and related Protocols in Part D: Judicial Remedies and Liability). For further discussion, see pp 77 and 211, below).

Principle 17

Environmental impact assessment, as a national instrument, shall be undertaken for proposed activities that are likely to have a significant adverse impact on the environment and are subject to a decision of a competent national authority.

Notes:

1   This principle requiring the undertaking of environmental impact assessment exercises for proposed activities which may have adverse environmental effects is a procedural rule designed to facilitate the preventive (Principles 6 and 7 of the Stockholm Declaration 1972) and precautionary principles (Principle 15 of Rio) already mentioned above.

2   An environmental impact assessment exercise can identify the potential environmental threats of a proposed activity or project. This information can then be used to modify the proposed activity in order to take these threats into account. Remedial measures can also be introduced in order to mitigate or reduce any perceived detrimental environmental impacts of the project. In this sense, therefore, an EIA (environmental impact assessment) exercise can be instrumental in establishing exactly which areas of a proposed project or activity require precautionary or preventive measures in order to ensure the overall environmental viability of the project.

Principle 18

States shall immediately notify other states of any natural disasters or other emergencies that are likely to produce sudden harmful effects on the environment of those States. Every effort shall be made by the international community to help States so afflicted.

Principle 19

States shall provide prior and timely notification and relevant information to potentially affected States on activities that may have a significant adverse trans-boundary environmental effect and shall consult with those states at an early stage and in good faith.

Notes:

1   The requirement of prior notification and consultation on the possible adverse trans-boundary environmental effects of either anthropocentric/ man-made activities or natural disasters is a well established principle which has many further references in

other international environmental instruments. Chief among these are the Convention on Early Notification of a Nuclear Accident 1986 (see Chapter 7), Article 206 of the UN Convention on the Law of the Sea 1982 (UNCLOS), and Articles 5 and 8(b) of the Geneva Convention on Long Range Trans-boundary Air Pollution 1979 (see Chapters 3 and 2 respectively).

2   Article 5 of the regional 1974 Nordic Environmental Protection Convention carries the duty of information a step further by requiring that the national authorities responsible for the licensing or authorisation of environmentally hazardous activities supply information regarding such activities to potentially affected States (Francioni (1991) 206). See also the 1992 Paris Convention for the Protection of the Marine Environment of the NE Atlantic (OSPAR). Ireland has recently sought arbitration under Art 32 OSPAR in relation to the Sellafield plant. This is the first example of one State taking another State (the UK) to an international tribunal for violating freedom of information rules, *The Guardian*, 14 June 2001. See Chapter 7, below.

Principle 20

Women have a vital role in environmental management and development. Their full participation is therefore essential to achieve sustainable development.

Principle 21

The creativity, ideals and courage of the youth of the world should be mobilised to forge a global partnership in order to achieve sustainable development and ensure a better future for all.

Principle 22

Indigenous people and their communities, and other local communities, have a vital role in environmental management and development because of their knowledge and traditional practices. States should recognise and duly support their identity, culture and interests and enable their effective participation in the achievement of sustainable development.

Principle 23

The environment and natural resources of people under oppression, domination and occupation shall be protected.

Principle 24

Warfare is inherently destructive of sustainable development. States shall therefore respect international law providing protection for the environment in times of armed conflict and co-operate in its further development, as necessary.

Principle 25

Peace, development and environmental protection are interdependent and indivisible.

Principle 26

States shall resolve all their environmental disputes peacefully and by appropriate means in accordance with the Charter of the United Nations.

Principle 27

States and people shall co-operate in good faith and in a spirit of partnership in the fulfilment of the principles embodied in this Declaration and in the further development of international law in the field of sustainable development.

LIABILITY FOR ENVIRONMENTAL DAMAGE

International liability for environmental damage

A significant aspect of international environmental law where agreement between States has not been forthcoming is the question of liability for environmental damage.[60] While the principle of State responsibility and liability for environmental damage to other States is undeniable (see Principle 21 of the Stockholm Declaration 1972, p 66, above), a settled international legal regime has yet to emerge.[61] The general lack of provision for international environmental liability is reflected in the conspicuous failure to include provisions for such liability in most of the major multilateral environmental agreements between States.[62]

Some mitigation of this general problem is nevertheless effected through the provision of specific international civil liability regimes for certain activities deemed extra or ultrahazardous due to their extremely pernicious and lasting effects, such as radioactive fall-out from nuclear accidents and marine oil pollution damage from supertanker spills. These two types of ultrahazardous activities have provoked the establishment of international civil liability and compensation regimes by the international community of States.[63] The aim of these schemes is to allow individual victims of pollution to claim compensation from funds established by the industries. A third category of activity is now subject to an international liability regime, namely the transboundary movement of hazardous wastes (see Chapter 4, below, for text and commentary on Basel Protocol on Liability and Compensation 1999).

In the case of environmental damage caused by nuclear industry accidents, Birnie and Boyle note that, '(C)ivil liability proceedings are the preferred method employed by the majority of nuclear States for reallocating the costs for transboundary nuclear accidents'.[64] A number of conventions exist providing for the strict, though not unlimited

---

60 See, eg, Kiss, A, 'Present limits to the enforcement of State responsibility for environmental damage', in Francioni and Scovazzi (eds), *International Responsibility for Environmental Harm*, 1991, London/Dordrecht: Graham and Trotman/Martinus Nijhoff, pp 3–14.

61 Note the continuing efforts of the International Law Commission (ILC) on this subject in the form of the work of the Special Rapporteur, Julio Barboza. See Barboza, J, 'The ILC and State responsibility for environmental damage', in Wetterstein, R (ed) (1997). See also Tomuschat, C, 'International liability for injurious consequences arising out of acts not prohibited by international law: the work of the International Law Commission', in *op cit*, Francioni and Scovazzi, 1991, fn 60, pp 37–72.

For an analysis of the continuing relevance of the doctrine of State responsibility and liability in respect of environmental damage incurred by private persons within their jurisdiction and control, see Handl, G, 'State liability for accidental transnational environmental damage by private persons', (1980) 74 AJIL 525–65. See also Handl, G, 'Paying the piper for transboundary nuclear damage: State liability in a system of transnational compensation', in Magraw, DB, (ed), *International Law and Pollution*, 1991, Philadelphia: University of Pennsylvania Press, pp 150–74, for a similar perspective in respect of State responsibility and liability for transboundary nuclear damage in the aftermath of the Chernobyl disaster.

62 Examples include the 1987 Montreal Protocol to the 1985 Vienna Convention on Substances that Deplete the Ozone Layer, amended in 1990; the UN Framework Convention on Climate Change, 1992; and the UNEP Convention on the Conservation of Biological Diversity, 1992. One exception is the Convention on International Liability for Damage Caused by Space Objects 1972, 961 UNTS 187, UKTS 16 (1974), Cmnd 5551. In force on 1 September 1972.

63 Note also the Convention on Civil Liability for Damage caused during Carriage of Dangerous Goods by Road, Rail and Inland Navigation Vessels (CRTD) UN, New York, 1990. See Chapter 3, below, on oil pollution.

64 Birnie, P and Boyle, A, *International Law and the Environment*, 1992, Oxford: Clarendon, p 371.

liability of operators. These include the following: the 1960 Paris Convention on Third Party Liability in the Field of Nuclear Energy,[65] and the 1963 Vienna Convention on Civil Liability for Environmental Damage.[66] However, only the 1960 Paris Convention and its 1963 (Brussels) Supplementary Agreement, which was drafted by the OECD and applies to nuclear incidents within Western European Member States, has attracted significant support among nuclear States. These conventions harmonise the international law on (civil) liability for nuclear accidents, providing for strict liability of the operators of nuclear facilities but within defined upper limits for total compensation claims, thus protecting the nuclear industry from unpredictable and unlimited exposure.[67] As Birnie and Boyle note, '(T)he nuclear liability conventions thus reflect on the one hand an early recognition of the need for a stronger, more equitable system of loss distribution, appropriate to the serious risks of nuclear accidents, and on the other a desire to encourage the (then) infant nuclear industry'.[68]

In the case of oil tanker spills, the 1969 Civil Liability and 1971 Fund Conventions as amended in 1992 by two Protocols[69] govern the liability of ship and cargo owners for oil pollution damage. They laid down the principle of strict liability and established a system of compulsory liability insurance. The provision of strict liability is subject to limits, which are in turn linked to the tonnage of the ship.[70] The implications of such definitive external controls on corporate decision-making processes within the oil industry are clear: The preventive approach (see p 49, above) becomes not merely a legal but also an economic imperative for companies in this industrial sector. Moreover, the polluter pays principle is being applied directly at the international level, thus bypassing the usual systemic requirement for national or domestic implementation of internationally agreed rules.[71] However, despite the continuing success of these relatively comprehensive civil

---

65 In force: 1 April, 1968. Amended by 1964 Additional Protocol, UKTS 69 (1968), Cmnd 3755, in force on 1 April 1968. See also Brussels Convention Supplementary to the Paris Convention (1963 2 ILM (1963) 685), in force on 4 December 1974. Both Conventions were further amended by 1982 Protocols, UKTS 23 (1983), Cmnd 9052, in force on 1 August 1991.

66 2 ILM (1963) 727, in force on 12 November 1977. 1983 Protocol, not in force. Two other treaties deal with nuclear-powered ships and maritime carriage of nuclear materials. These are the Brussels Convention on the Liability of Operators of Nuclear Ships 1962, 12 ICLQ (1963) 778, 57 AJIL (1963) 100, which is not in force; and the Brussels Convention Relating to Civil Liability in the Field of Maritime Carriage of Nuclear Material 1971, in force. See IAEA, *International Conventions on Civil Liability*, p 55.

67 See Boyle, AE, 'Nuclear energy and international law: an environmental perspective' (1990) British Yearbook of International Law 257–313, p 298.

68 *Op cit*, Birnie and Boyle, fn 64, p 372. See also Faure, MG and Skogh, G, 'Compensation for damages caused by nuclear accidents: a convention as insurance', in Faure, MG (ed) (1992) 17(65) The Geneva Papers on Risk and Insurance 499–513.

69 Convention on Civil Liability for Oil Pollution Damage 1969 (9 ILM (1970) 45), and Convention on the Establishment of an International Fund for Compensation of Oil Pollution Damage 1971 (11 ILM (1972) 284), as amended by 1992 Protocols and now collectively known as the Civil Liability and Fund Conventions for Oil Pollution Damage 1996.

70 *International Oil Pollution Compensation Funds*, Annual Report on the Activities of the IOPC Funds, 1997, p 11.

71 For a fuller discussion of these and other improvements in the legal regime for environmental protection and its implications for the oil industry in particular, see Ong, DM, 'International legal developments in environmental protection: implications for the oil industry', in Orszulik, ST (ed), *Environmental Technology in the Oil Industry*, 1997, London: Blackie, pp 16–72.

liability regimes, a recent appraisal concludes that '(T)here is substantial room for improvement in the international ship-source oil pollution compensation regimes'.[72]

Thus, both here at the international level and also below at the comparative domestic level, we can observe what Teubner notes is the development of a trend shifting liability away from the individual responsibility of single actors towards a new collective responsibility of industry-wide risk networks.[73] Francioni, for example, suggests that 'a clear preference industry wide has emerged toward shifting the focus to the tort liability of the operator, leaving the State immune'.[74] Choucri affirms that 'there has been increased evidence of corporate liability for environmental harm'.[75] He further notes the numerous and regular corporate pollution incidents such as the Exxon Valdez that are cumulatively serving as a 'hidden hand', placing corporate activities under increasing public scrutiny and global business as a whole on the defensive.[76] This pressure is in turn leading to the establishment of industry-based international civil liability schemes, as noted above.

On the other hand, the narrow ambit of current international civil liability regimes merely serves to emphasise their limited utility for ensuring corporate compliance with applicable environmental norms and standards. The veracity of the preceding statement may be illustrated by the continuing absence of any general international civil liability scheme providing for the compensation of corporate environmental damage beyond the narrow confines of recognised ultrahazardous activities such as nuclear power stations, crude oil-carrying supertankers and the transboundary movement of hazardous wastes. Even the European Community has been unable to agree upon a Community-wide legal regime providing for civil liability for general environmental damage.[77]

Moreover, the jurisdictional, evidentiary, causation and other litigation issues raised by claims for compensation for international or transnational environmental damage continue to dog efforts to provide for multinational corporate environmental liability. This is evidenced by the case law arising out of the 1976 Seveso (Hoffmann-La Roche),[78] 1984 Bhopal (Union Carbide),[79] and 1986 Rhine (Sandoz)[80] disasters. In the Bhopal litigation, for example, the question whether death and serious illness caused by the

---

72   Gauci, G, 'Protection of the marine environment through the international ship-source oil pollution compensation regimes' (1999) 8(1) Review of European Community & International Environmental Law 29–36, p 34.
73   Teubner, G, 'The invisible cupola: from causal to collective attribution in ecological liability', in Teubner, G, Farmer, L and Murphy, D (eds), Environmental Law and Ecological Responsibility: The Concept and Practice of Ecological Self-Organization, 1994, Chichester: John Wiley, p 18.
74   Op cit, Francioni, fn 60, p 276.
75   Choucri, N, 'Corporate strategies towards sustainability', in Long, W, Sustainable Development and International Law, 1995, London/Dordrecht, Graham and Trotman/Martinus, pp 189–201.
76   Ibid.
77   But see now, the White Paper on Civil Liability for Environmental Damage, below.
78   See Scovazzi, T, in op cit, Francioni and Scovazzi, fn 60, pp 397–403.
79   For a synopsis of litigation arising from the Bhopal incident, see Anderson, MR, 'State obligations in a transnational dispute', in Butler, WE (ed), Control over Compliance with International Law, 1991, Dordrecht: Martinus Nijhoff, pp 83–95, pp 84–85. See also Muchlinski, P, 'The Bhopal case: controlling ultrahazardous industrial activities undertaken by foreign investors' (1987) 50 MLR 545.
80   For a full discussion of the impact of the Sandoz disaster and the State and civil liability issues arising, see d'Oliveira, HUJ, 'The Sandoz Blaze: the damage and the public and private liabilities', in op cit, Francioni and Scovazzi, fn 60, pp 429–45.

accidental release of toxic fumes from a local factory owned by a subsidiary company could be visited upon the parent company in its 'home' jurisdiction was answered in the negative.[81] The overriding legal difficulty here was due to the United States courts' reliance on the principle of *forum non conveniens*, to deny jurisdiction to hear Indian liability claims against the parent Union Carbide company in the US for the damage incurred by its Indian subsidiary.[82]

On the other hand, the reliance on traditional company law notions of separation of individual corporate entities is not necessarily reflected in the municipal courts of certain countries. Recent developments in the English courts arguably herald a more progressive approach to tortious claims against a company from another jurisdiction. The House of Lords ruling allowing South African miners afflicted by asbestos-related diseases to sue the British mining company, Cape plc, in the English courts has potentially wide implications for multinational corporations based in this jurisdiction.[83] It means that English parent companies can be sued for negligence in the country where they are domiciled and not just in the countries where their subsidiaries operate.[84] It is important to note, however, that the principle of allowing workers of foreign subsidiaries to sue their parent companies for health and safety at work related torts will not necessarily extend to allow environmental pressure groups to claim for ecological damage occurring only in foreign countries.[85] US courts are also using more flexible criteria to determine corporate responsibility and liability.[86] For example, a claim for damages arising from environmental and human rights violations has recently been filed at a San Francisco federal court under the Alien Tort Claims Act 1789 on behalf of the people of Bougainville island in Papua New Guinea against Rio Tinto, the world's third largest mining conglomerate. The claimants' lawyers submit that the court should accept jurisdiction on

---

81 See Seward, AC, III, 'After Bhopal: implications for parent company liability', in Rubin SJ and Wallace, D (Jr) (eds), *Transnational Corporations and National Law*, 1994, UN Library on Transnational Corporations, London: Routledge, Vol 19, pp 300–12. First published in (1987) 21 International Lawyer 695–707.

82 For an in-depth discussion of the negative aspects of the US interpretation of this principle, see Prince, P, 'Bhopal, Bougainville and Ok Tedi: why Australian's *forum non conveniens* approach is better' (1998) 47(3) ICLQ 573–98, p 577, citing *In re Union Carbide Corp*, Gas Plant Disaster at Bhopal India in December, 1984, 634 FSupp 842 (1986).

83 See *Lubbe and Others v Cape plc and Related Appeals* (2000) The Times, 27 July (HL), p 31. See also Gibb, F, and Dynes, M, 'African asbestos miners win right to sue in Britain' (2000) The Times, 21 July, p 8.

84 For an analysis of the implications of the *Cape* plc cases for English-based Multinational Enterprises (MNEs) with foreign subsidiaries, see Muchlinski, PT, 'Corporations in international litigation: problems of jurisdiction and the United Kingdom asbestos cases' (2001) 50(1) ICLQ 1.

85 See below for a further discussion of *locus standi* problems for environmental non-governmental organisations (NGOs).

86 Bakst, DS, 'Piercing the corporate veil for environmental torts in the United States and the European Union: the case for the proposed civil liability directive' (1996) XIX(2) Boston College International and Comparative L Rev 323–51.

the basis that Rio Tinto has extensive mining interests in the US, including California.[87] These criteria more readily reflect the reality of the parent/subsidiary corporate relationship, and thus provide a way forward towards the achievement of a more equitable notion of corporate accountability to the diverse interests, including the environment, that are affected by business activities.

European Community law

Major environmental catastrophes over the years have highlighted the inadequacies of national laws for dealing with issues of liability for damage caused. For example, traditional English tort law only provides remedies for those who have suffered personal injury or damage to property. It does not attach liability for damage to aspects of the environment that are incapable of being owned, including the environment in general and biodiversity in particular. This, together with the technical requirements of much of the law of tort, often allows polluters to escape their responsibility. For these reasons tort law is widely regarded as failing to provide an adequate incentive to those engaged in potentially harmful activities to take steps to ensure that the environment is protected.

Recent initiatives have therefore been taken to harmonise and strengthen environmental liability regimes. Two major recent initiatives should be noted. In March 2001 the Commission presented a proposal for a Directive on the *Protection of the Environment through Criminal Law* (COM (01) 139, which is set out below). In the context of civil liability the European Commission has recently adopted a White Paper on *Environmental Liability* (COM (00) 66, February 2000).

The Proposed Directive on the Protection of the Environment through Criminal Law

As a part of a strategy to introduce more effective sanctions (sanctions that are likely to be more 'dissuasive') a new Directive on the protection of the environment through the criminal law has recently (March 2001) been proposed. At present there is no Community provision requiring States to impose criminal penalties for breaches of Community environmental law. As well as creating uncertainty regarding the obligations of Member States, it also means that there is no minimum standard with regard to environmental offences. The proposed directive is intended to meet the concern that 'in many cases, only criminal penalties will provide a sufficiently dissuasive effect' (explanatory memorandum).

> First, the imposition of criminal sanctions demonstrates a social disapproval of a qualitatively different nature compared to administrative sanctions or a compensation mechanism under civil law. It sends a strong signal, with a much greater dissuasive effect to offenders. For instance, administrative or other financial sanctions may not be dissuasive in cases where the offenders are impecunious or, on the contrary, financially very strong.
>
> Second, the means of criminal prosecution and investigation (and assistance between Member States) are more powerful than tools of administrative or civil law and can

---

87 See Pallister, D, 'Islanders sue in US over impact of Rio Tinto mine' (2000) *The Guardian*, 8 September, p 17.

enhance effectiveness of investigations. Furthermore, there is an additional guarantee of impartiality of investigating authorities because other authorities than those administrative authorities that have granted exploitation licences or authorisations to pollute will be involved in a criminal investigation [explanatory memorandum].

The legal basis providing the Community with competence to tackle environmental crime is Art 175 permitting measures 'aimed at protection of the environment' coupled with Art 10 which requires States to take, if necessary, effective dissuasive and proportionate sanctions in order to enforce Community law.[88] The key features of the proposed directive are as follows:

(1) It only applies to activities which are in breach of Community law protecting the environment.

(2) It will only apply to pollution which can be attributed to individuals or legal persons. It therefore does not cover pollution from diffuse sources.

(3) The proposal is intended to catch polluting activities which usually cause significant deterioration of, or substantial damage to, the environment.

(4) The activities must be committed intentionally or by serious negligence (Art 3).

(5) While Member States are to be under obligations to ensure that such activities are criminalised, they appear to be left with discretion as to whether to prosecute in particular circumstances, such as when a particular polluting activity has an insignificant environmental impact.

(6) The proposal draws a distinction between legal and natural persons. While natural persons are to be subject to 'effective, dissuasive and proportionate criminal penalties', legal persons may be subject to sanctions other than a criminal nature, such as non-criminal fines, judicial supervision, judicial winding up orders, or exclusion from entitlement to public benefits or aid. It appears paradoxical that individuals are to be subject to criminal sanctions, but companies and other legal persons may be excluded from criminal sanctions by a proposed directive whose *raison d'etre* is to impose such sanctions on the worst offenders.

---

88 However, it has been argued that this proposal should fall under the EU rather than the EC Treaty. This is significant because the role of the Commission and Parliament is more restricted under the EU pillar dealing with police and judicial co-operation in criminal matters.

2001/0076 (COD) Proposal for a

DIRECTIVE OF THE EUROPEAN PARLIAMENT AND OF THE COUNCIL

on the protection of the environment through criminal law

(2001) OJ C180E/238

THE EUROPEAN PARLIAMENT AND THE COUNCIL OF THE EUROPEAN UNION,

Whereas:

(1) Under Article 174(2) of the Treaty Community policy on the environment must aim at a high level of protection.

(2) The Community is concerned at the rise in environmental offences and their effects, which are increasingly extending beyond the borders of the States in which the offences are committed. Such offences pose a threat to the environment and therefore call for an appropriate response.

(3) Activities breaching Community law and/or rules adopted by Member States in order to comply with Community law should be subject to effective, dissuasive and proportionate sanctions at national level throughout the Community.

(4) Experience has shown that the existing systems of sanctions have not been sufficient to achieve complete compliance with Community law. Such compliance can and should be strengthened by the application of criminal sanctions, which demonstrate a social disapproval of a qualitatively different nature compared to administrative sanctions or a compensation mechanism under civil law.

(5) Common rules on criminal sanctions would make it possible to use methods of investigation and assistance within and between Member States, which are more effective than the tools available under administrative co-operation.

(6) Entrusting to judicial authorities, rather than administrative authorities the task of imposing sanctions, entails giving responsibility for investigating and enforcing the respect of environmental regulations to authorities which are independent of those which grant exploitation licences and discharge authorisations.

(7) In order to achieve effective protection of the environment, there is particular need for more dissuasive sanctions for polluting activities which typically cause or are likely to cause significant deterioration of the environment.

(8) Therefore, those activities should be considered criminal offences throughout in the Community, when they are committed intentionally or with serious negligence, and should be subject to criminal penalties, involving in serious cases deprivation of liberty.

(9) Participation in and instigation of such activities should also be considered a criminal offence, in order to achieve effective protection of the environment. This is also true for failures to comply with a legal duty to act, because such failures can have the same effects as active behaviour and should therefore be subject to corresponding sanctions.

(10) Legal persons should also be subject to effective, dissuasive and proportionate sanctions throughout the Community, because breaches of Community law to a large extent are committed in the interest of legal persons or for their benefit.

(11) Member States should provide information to the Commission on the implementation of this Directive, in order to enable it to evaluate the effect of this Directive.

(12) This act respects fundamental rights and principles as recognised notably in the Charter of fundamental rights of the European Union.

HAVE ADOPTED THIS DIRECTIVE:

Article 1 – Purpose

The purpose of this Directive is to ensure a more effective application of Community law on the protection of the environment by establishing throughout the Community a minimum set of criminal offences.

Article 2 – Definitions for the purpose of this Directive

(a) 'legal person' means any legal entity having such status under the applicable national law, except for States or other public bodies acting in the exercise of their sovereign rights and for public international organisations.

{b) 'activities' means active behaviour and failure to act, in so far as there is a legal duty to act.

Article 3 – Offences

Member States shall ensure that the following activities are criminal offences, when committed intentionally or with serious negligence, as far as they breach the rules of Community law protecting the environment as set out in the Annex and/or rules adopted by Member States in order to comply with such Community law:

(a) the discharge of hydrocarbons, waste oils or sewage sludge into water;

(b) the discharge, emission or introduction of a quantity of materials into air, soil or water and the treatment, disposal, storage, transport, export or import of hazardous waste;

(c) the discharge of waste on or into land or into water, including the operation of a landfill;

(d) the possession, taking, damaging, killing or trading of or in protected wild fauna and flora species or parts thereof;

(e) the significant deterioration of a protected habitat;

(f) trade in ozone-depleting substances;

(g) the operation of a plant in which a dangerous activity is carried out or in which dangerous substances or preparations are stored or used.

Article 4 – Sanctions

Member States shall ensure that the offences referred to in Article 3, and the participation in or instigation of such offences are punishable by effective, proportionate and dissuasive sanctions.

(a) As concerns natural persons, Member States shall provide for criminal penalties, involving in serious cases deprivation of liberty.

(b) As concerns natural and legal persons, where appropriate, Member States shall provide for fines, exclusion from entitlement to public benefits or aid, temporary or permanent disqualification from the practice of commercial activities, placing under judicial supervision or judicial winding up orders.

Article 5 – Reporting

Every three years, Member States shall transmit information to the Commission on the implementation of this Directive in the form of a report. Based on these reports, the Commission shall submit a Community report to the European Parliament and the Council.

[Articles 6–8 omitted.][89]

European Commission White Paper on Environmental Liability (COM (00) 66)

This White Paper was published on 9 February 2000. It proposes an EC-wide strict liability regime seeking to ensure that polluters pay for the costs of remedying the environmental damage that they have caused. The Paper seeks to ensure implementation of the main principles of environmental policy, above all the polluter pays principle, enshrined in Art 174(2) of the Treaty.

The White Paper can be traced back to the draft Directive on Damage caused by Waste (1989) which proposed retroactive strict liability for damage caused by deposits of waste. In the face of opposition by Member States the proposal was dropped and replaced by the 1993 Green Paper proposing liability in respect of damage caused through all environmental media and not just waste. Progress on this Green Paper was hampered by political problems with the Commission anxious to produce a proposal with some chance of being accepted by Member States.[90] The result is the present White Paper which proposes a framework directive which will fix objectives and desired results at the European level, leaving the method of implementation to Member States. Although Member States all have existing liability regimes the Commission feels that an EC framework is required for three reasons: (i) to implement the polluter pays and preventive principles; (ii) to address gaps in the laws of Member States; and (iii) to ensure the consistent enforcement of the basic principles set out in the White Paper.

The key proposals are as follows:

(1) The White Paper proposes liability for both 'traditional damage' (to persons or property) and 'environmental damage'. By environmental damage the White Paper means damage to biodiversity and 'damage in the form of contamination of sites'. This latter phrase is not clearly defined. The reference to biodiversity calls for liability in respect of living phenomena incapable of being owned and therefore beyond existing liability regimes. In the context of this White Paper the phrase is confined to birds, plants, animals and habitats mentioned in the Wild Birds Directive 79/409 and the Habitats Directive 92/43 (para 4.2.1; see also Chapter 6).

---

89 If adopted, Member States would have to apply the Directive by September 2003.

90 For a discussion of the EC's Green Paper, see Reid, D, 'Civil liability for environmental damage', in Swart, M (ed), *International Environmental Law and Regulations*, 1996, Chichester: John Wiley, Vol 1, 249–62; also, Grant, M, 'Environmental liability', in Winter, G (ed), *European Environmental Law: A Comparative Perspective*, 1996, Aldershot: Dartmouth, pp 219–37.

(2) The White Paper proposes strict liability, that is, there is no necessity to prove fault (but see (6), below, in relation to non-dangerous activities).

One reason for this is that it is very difficult for plaintiffs to establish fault of the defendant in environmental liability cases. Another reason is the view that someone who is carrying out an inherently hazardous activity should bear the risk if damage is caused by it, rather than the victim or society at large (para 4.3).

Dispensing with the requirement of fault only goes some way to overcoming liability problems. Even with strict liability causation must still be established. This requirement may also constitute a very significant hurdle to attaching liability. The White Paper recognises this, albeit rather vaguely, by suggesting that because it may be harder for the plaintiff than the defendant to establish facts concerning a causal link, the traditional rules concerning the burden of proof may require a 'form of alleviation'. This could mean imposing a lower burden of proof upon the plaintiff or it could indicate that the White Paper envisages that the burden of proof should pass to the defendant in some circumstances. The White Paper says that this must be precisely defined at a later stage (para 4.3).

(3) The proposal is for a strict liability regime rather than an absolute liability regime and therefore certain defences are to be permitted, namely Act of God, consent by the plaintiff, and intervention by a third party. The White Paper suggests that although operating within a permit would not amount to a defence, there are some circumstances where it would be 'inequitable' for the polluter to bear the full cost of the damage when a release was 'entirely and exclusively' within the scope of a permit. In these circumstances part of the compensation should be borne by the permitting authority (para 4.3).

(4) The liability regime envisaged by the White Paper should not be retroactive. Member States should be left to deal with 'pollution from the past' (see Pt IIA of the Environmental Protection Act 1990 in relation to the UK's contaminated land regime, Chapter 4). The White Paper notes that there is likely to be litigation and consequential significant costs associated with drawing the line between past pollution and pollution covered by the new regime (para 4.1).

(5) It is proposed that liability should be imposed on the 'operator', namely the person who 'exercises control over the activity'. Where companies are involved liability will rest on the company as a legal person and not on individual managers or employees. This also means that there will be no lender liability imposed upon those who finance the operations in the absence of their having operational control (para 4.4).

(6) The White Paper only deals with 'traditional damage' and contaminated sites where the damage is caused by 'dangerous activities', that is, activities regulated by EC law such as discharges and emissions of hazardous substances, waste management, and use of biotechnology. Specific provisions relate to biodiversity damage. Because these natural resources are vulnerable and so deserving of special protection, the White Paper proposes that liability be imposed for damage caused by activities which are not inherently dangerous (para 4.2). In this context, the White Paper proposes that liability should be fault-based, rather than strict.

(7) Concerning the level of damage that would trigger liability, the White Paper proposes a distinction between 'traditional damage' on the one hand and contaminated sites and biodiversity on the other. Regarding the latter, the liability regime should only be triggered in the event of 'significant' damage or contamination (paras 4.5.1 and 4.5.2). The notion of 'significant damage' would not apply in relation to 'traditional damage' (4.5.3).

(8) Moving to remedial action, the White Paper recommends that (in the context of biodiversity) the aim be to restore the natural resource to its original state. But given the difficulty and the likely costs of full restoration, it is recommended that account be taken of such factors as 'the function and the presumed future use of the damaged resources'. If restoration of the site is impossible the solution should be to establish natural resources equivalent to the destroyed natural resources (para 4.5.1). In the context of contaminated sites the main objectives should be 'removal of any serious threat to man and environment' (4.5.2).

(9) In the context of enforcement, the White Paper emphasises the importance of access to justice, particularly in relation to 'environmental damage' that does not fall within 'traditional' categories. The White Paper builds upon its *Communication on Implementing Community Environmental Law* (COM (96) 500, see page 828, below) and stresses the significance of the Aarhus Convention (see Chapter 7). A two tier approach is called for. Because the protection of the environment is a public interest the State should have a primary duty to protect the environment. If the State does not act, or does not act properly then 'public interests' groups should be able to take action on a subsidiary basis. It appears to be envisaged that this action may be against public bodies or against the actual polluter. In this context only those groups complying with 'objective qualitative criteria' will qualify. In urgent cases special provision is proposed for such interest groups to take immediate rather than subsidiary action in order to prevent significant damage or avoid further damage to the environment. They should, says the Paper, be allowed to seek injunctive relief against the alleged polluter without going to the State first. In such circumstances the interest groups would have the right to claim reimbursement of reasonable costs incurred, although the White Paper does not say against whom this claim is to be made (see para 4.7).

(10) Recognising that insurance provision in relation to environment risk is 'fragile' the Paper does not call for compulsory insurance or financial securities for those involved in dangerous activities. The Paper merely suggests that discussions should take place to 'stimulate' relevant sectors to provide appropriate 'financial guarantee instruments' (para 4.9).

While the thrust of the Paper is very positive, many key elements (including the role to be played by interest groups in litigation against polluters) are vague and ambiguous, as is its impact on UK tort law. For an argument against a specialist liability regime for environmental damage, see Cane, P, 'Are environmental harms special?' [2001] 13(1) JEL 3–20. See also Wilde, M, 'The EC Commission's White Paper on *Environmental Liability*' 13(1) JEL 21–37; Rice, P, 'From Lugano to Brussels via Aarhus – *Environmental Liability White Paper Published*' [2000] 2 Env Liability 39.

REFERENCES AND FURTHER READING

Baldock, D and Bennett, G, *Agriculture and the Polluter Pays Principle – A Study of Six EC Countries*, 1991, London: IEEP

Baldock, D et al, *The Integration of Environmental Protection Requirements into the Definition and Implementation of Other EC Policies*, 1992, London: IEEP

Bell, S and McGillivray, D, *Environmental Law*, 5th edn, 2000, London: Blackstone

Birnie, P, 'International environmental law: its adequacy for present and future needs', in Hurrell and Kingsbury (eds), *The International Politics of the Environment*, 1992, Oxford: Clarendon, pp 51–84

Birnie, P and Boyle, A, *Basic Documents on International Law and the Environment*, 1995, Oxford: Clarendon Press

Birnie, P and Boyle, A, *International Law and the Environment*, 1992, Oxford: Clarendon

Boyle, A, 'Economic growth and protection of the environment: the impact of international law and policy', in Boyle, A (ed), *Environmental Regulation and Economic Growth*, 1994, Oxford: Clarendon, pp 173–88

Boyle, A, 'Saving the world? Implementation and enforcement of international environmental law through international institutions' [1991] 3 JEL 229

Boyle, A and Freestone, D (eds), *International Law and Sustainable Development*, 2001, Oxford: OUP

Brown-Weiss, E, *Environmental Change and International Law*, 1992, New York: UN UP

Brown-Weiss, E, 'Agora: what does our generation owe to the next? An approach to global environmental responsibility' (1990) 84 AJIL 190

Campiglio, L, Pineschi, L, Siniscalco, D and Treves, T (eds), *The Environment after Rio: International Law and Economics*, 1994, London/Dordrecht: Graham and Trotman/Martinus Nijhoff

Cassese, A, *International Law*, 2nd edn, 2001, Oxford: Clarendon

Churchill, RR and Freestone, D (eds), *International Law and Global Climate Change*, 1991, London: Graham and Trotman

Churchill, RR and Lowe, AV, *The Law of the Sea*, 3rd edn, 1999, Manchester: Manchester UP

Churchill, RR, Warren, L and Gibson, J (eds), *Law, Policy and the Environment*, 1991, Oxford: Blackwell

Commission of the European Communities, *Communication on the Precautionary Principle*, 2000, COM (00) 1

Eckersley, R, *Environmentalism and Political Theory*, 1992, London: University College of London Press

Francioni, F, 'International co-operation for the protection of the environment: the procedural dimension', in Lang, W *et al* (eds), *Environmental Protection and International Law*, 1991, London: Graham and Trotman, pp 203–21

Freestone, D, 'The road from Rio' [1994] 6(2) JEL 193

Freestone, D and Hey, E (eds), *The Precautionary Principle and International Law: The Challenge of Implementation*, 1996, The Hague: Kluwer

Gillespie, A, *International Environmental Law, Policy and Ethics*, 1997, Oxford: Clarendon

Glasbergen, P and Blowers, A, *Environmental Policy in an International Context: Perspectives*, 1995, London: Arnold

Guruswamy, L, Palmer, G and Weston, B, *International Environmental Law and World Order: A Problem-Oriented Coursebook*, American Casebook Series, 1994, St Paul, Minn, USA: West Publishing

House of Lords Select Committee on the EC, *European Environment Agency*, Session 1994–95, 5th Report, HL Paper 29, 1995, London: HMSO

House of Lords Select Committee on the European Community's Implementation and Enforcement of Environmental Legislation, *Sustainable Development: The UK Strategy*, Session 1991–92, 9th Report, Cm 2426, 1994, London: HMSO

Hughes, D, *Environmental Law*, 3rd edn, 1996, London: Butterworths

Hurrell, A and Kingsbury, B, *The International Politics of the Environment*, 1992, Oxford: OUP

Kramer, L, *EC Environmental Law*, 4th edn, 2000, London: Sweet & Maxwell

Kramer, L, 'The open society, its lawyers and its environment' [1989] 1 JEL 1

Lafferty, W and Meadowcroft, J, *Implementing Sustainable Development*, 2000, Oxford: Clarendon

Lammers, J *et al*, *Environmental Protection and Sustainable Development: Legal Principles and Recommendations*, 1987, London: Graham and Trotman

Lang, W, Neuhold, H and Zemanek, K (eds), *Environmental Protection and International Law*, 1991, London/Dordrecht: Graham and Trotman/Martinus Nijhoff

Larsson, M-L, *The Law of Environmental Damage: Liability and Reparation*, 1999, The Hague: Kluwer

Lomborg, B, *The Skeptical Environmentalist: measuring the Real State of the World*, 2001, Cambridge: CUP

McIntyre, O and Mosedale, T, 'The precautionary principle as a norm of customary international law' [1997] 2 JEL 221–42

O'Riordan, T and Cameron, J (eds), *Interpreting the Precautionary Principle*, 1994, London: Earthscan

Ong, DM, 'The impact of environmental law on corporate governance: international and comparative perspectives' (2001) 12(4) EJIL 68–726

Pallemaerts, M, 'International environmental law from Stockholm to Rio: back to the future?', in Sands, P (ed), *Greening International Law*, 1993, London: Earthscan, pp 1–19

Pearce, D and Barbier, E, *Blueprint for a Sustainable Economy*, 2000, London: Earthscan

Pearce, D, Markandya, A and Barbier, E, *Blueprint for a Green Economy*, 1989, London: Earthscan

Pearce, D *et al*, *Blueprint 2: Greening the World Economy*, 1991, London: Earthscan

Sands, P, *Principles of International Environmental Law, Vol I: Frameworks, Standards and Implementation*, 1995, Manchester: Manchester UP

Sands, P (ed), *Greening International Law*, 1993, London: Earthscan

Sohn, L, 'The Stockholm Declaration on the Human Environment' (1973) 14 Harvard International Law Journal 423

Spector, B, Sjöstedt, G and Zartman, IW (eds), *Negotiating International Regimes: Lessons Learned from the United Nations Conference on Environment and Development (UNCED)*, 1994, London/Dordrecht: Graham and Trotman/Martinus Nijhoff

Stewart, R, Revesz, R and Sands, P, *Environmental Law – The Economy and Sustainable Development*, 2000, Cambridge: CUP

Tromans, S, *Environmental Protection Act 1990: Text and Commentary*, 1990, London: Sweet & Maxwell

Turner, RK, Pearce, D and Bateman, I, *Environmental Economics: An Elementary Introduction*, 1994, New York: Harvester

Werksman, J (ed), *Greening International Institutions*, 1996, London: Earthscan

Wilde, M, 'The law of tort and the precautionary principle – civil liability arising from trial plantings of GM crops' [1998] 6 Env Liability 163

Wilkinson, D, 'Maastricht and the environment: the implications for the EC's environmental policy of the treaty on European Union' [1992] 4 JEL 221

Wilkinson, D, *Greening the Treaty – Strengthening Environmental Protection in the Treaty of Rome*, 1990, London: IEEP

Wilson, ED, *The Diversity of Life*, 1992, Harmondsworth: Penguin

World Commission on Environment and Development, *Our Common Future*, 1987, Oxford: OUP

USEFUL WEBSITES

For a list of useful environmental websites, see pages l–li, above.

AIR AND ATMOSPHERIC POLLUTION

INTRODUCTION

It has long been recognised that the quality of the air we breathe is an essential element in the protection and promotion of human health. The link between poor air and poor health has been recognised since at least the early 19th century (see in particular Sir Edwin Chadwick's 1842 *Report on the Sanitary Condition of the Labouring Population of Great Britain*, ed MW Flinn, 1965, Edinburgh UP).

The effects of 19th century pollution are graphically described by the House of Lords Select Parliamentary Committee on Noxious Vapours (1862) (Parliamentary Papers, 14 Report iii-iv (McLaren (1983) 166)). In the following extract the Committee considers the rapid changes to the environment in the region of St Helens following the establishment in the area of alkali plants, copper foundries, glassworks and lead smelters. We are told that before 1835 St Helens was a small and attractive town in a district 'still well known for its orchards', with gardens 'well stocked with choice fruit trees' (Barker and Harris (1983) 178, cited by McLaren). During the next 30 years, however, St Helens was transformed as industry took hold. By 1862 the Committee reported that:[1]

> It is difficult to exaggerate the amount of injury to the adjoining district, which in some instances is caused by the neighbourhood of these works. The pungent vapour is perceptible, in certain states of the atmosphere, at the distance of five or six miles; and its effects, within a radius of one or two miles, are fearful. Trees appear to suffer the most: 'they lose their leaves; the top branches begin to decay; afterwards the bark becomes discoloured and hardened; when very much affected it adheres to the tree, and the tree is ultimately killed.' The same witness, describing the neighbourhood of St Helens, where there are numerous works of this description, says: 'It is one scene of desolation. You might look around for a mile, and not see a tree with any foliage on whatever ... Other witnesses speak to the destruction of trees, by hundreds, in successive years, from the effects of these vapours. Farms recently well wooded, and with hedges in good condition, have now neither tree nor hedge left alive; whole fields of corn are destroyed in a single night, especially when the vapour falls upon them while in bloom; orchards and gardens, of which there were great numbers in the neighbourhood of St Helens, have not a fruit tree left alive; pastures are so deteriorated that graziers refuse to place stock upon them; and some of the witnesses have attributed to the poisonous nature of the grass the fact that their sheep and cattle have cast their young in considerable numbers.'

Following the report the first system for regulating air pollution was enacted in 1863. This and later statutes were consolidated in the Alkali, etc Works Regulation Act 1906. These Acts established the Alkali inspectorate with responsibility for seeking to ensure that industrial processes used the best practicable means to prevent noxious gases and fumes polluting the air. Although ground-breaking in its day the approach established by this

---

1   See also *St Helen's Smelting Co v Tipping* (1865) 11 HL Cas 642, p 172, below.

early legislation was, from the perspective of protecting the general environment, limited in two fundamental ways. First, it concentrated on certain types of air pollution caused by particular industrial activities. It did not look at industry as a whole and nor was it concerned with pollution to land or water. Secondly, it focused on what came out of chimneys rather than on the industrial processes which generated the pollution to begin with. This sector-specific and reactive approach has only recently given way to a more integrated approach to industrial pollution in the form of IPC and IPPC controls (see Chapter 5).

The London smog of 1952, which caused an estimated 4,000 additional deaths of sick and mainly elderly people in just a few days, showed that air pollution continued to present a serious risk to health in the 20th century. It also showed that the problems were not localised in the traditional manufacturing areas of the country nor were they solely a consequence of industry. Here an important cause of the smog was identified as being smoke generated by domestic coal fires. The response was the introduction of the Clean Air Act 1956 which gave local authorities power to control emissions of dark smoke and to establish Smoke Control Areas. That legislation and later amendments were codified in the Clean Air Act 1993, extracts of which are given below (p 188–191).

This legislation combined with changes in methods of heating and in particular the now widespread use of central heating rather than coal fires, have led to reductions in this form of pollution. But the poor quality of urban air remains a serious problem, largely due to the massive increase in the past 40 years or so in the use of roads (for an analysis of this growth, see the 18th report of The Royal Commission on Environmental Pollution, *Transport and the Environment*, Chapter 2 (1994) Cm 2674).

In one particularly notorious instance covering four days during December 1991 traffic pollution in London, according to evidence produced by the Department of Health, led to a 10% increase in the death rate in London when 160 additional deaths were recorded. The 18th report of The Royal Commission on Environmental Pollution on Transport and the Environment (p 3) provides this summary of the episode:

> Over the period 12–15 December 1991, unusually high concentrations of nitrogen dioxide were recorded in London. An anticyclone over the Alps was affecting south east England and producing low wind speeds, low temperatures, mist and high stability. Nitrogen dioxide pollution reached its peak in the early hours of 13 December. This contrasted with previous episodes because there was no obvious correlation with peak traffic flow. Nevertheless, the correlation of concentrations of nitrogen oxides with concentrations of carbon monoxide, and the absence of a correlation with sulphur dioxide, strongly suggests that vehicle emissions were the dominant source of pollution. The highest concentrations of nitrogen dioxide were recorded at Bridge Place and Earls Court.

A report published in January 1998 by the independent expert Committee on the Medical Effects of Air Pollutants (COMEAP) for the Department of Health was the first official attempt to quantify the impact of short term air pollution on the health of people living in the UK (*Quantification of the Effects of Air Pollution on Health in the United Kingdom*, Committee on the Medical Effects of Air Pollutants, published by the Department of Health, January 1998.) It suggested that the deaths of between 12,000 and 24,000 vulnerable people may be brought forward each year and that between 14,000 and 24,000 hospital admissions and re-admissions may also result from poor air quality. These effects are attributed to three of the eight pollutants for which objectives have been set in the *National Air Quality Strategy* (discussed below): particulate matter (PM10), (which is estimated to bring forward 8,100 deaths annually); sulphur dioxide (3,500 deaths); and ozone (from 700 to 12,500 deaths). The Report only tried to quantify the short term effects of these three pollutants. It did not quantify the long term chronic impacts, nor cover the other emissions associated with transport such as benzene or 1,3 butadiene, which are known carcinogens, or lead which is associated with harming cognitive development in children, as it was considered inappropriate to quantify health effects of these pollutants in this way. (More information about the health effects of different pollutants can be found in the *National Air Quality Strategy*, see p 182, below.)

Air pollution does not respect national boundaries and it is for this reason that strategies to improve air quality have to approach the problem on an international and regional basis, as well as at national and local levels. The following extract from the government's consultation paper on the United Kingdom's 1996 *National Air Quality Strategy* (DoE, 1996) emphasises the international character of the problem (p 8, footnotes omitted):

> In general, the long-range movement of air masses across the Earth's surface means that pollution emitted in one country is, to a significant extent, shared with its neighbours. For some pollutants, such as sulphur dioxide (SO_2) or nitrogen oxides (NOx), emissions can travel much further than a country's immediate neighbours. The winter pattern for Northern Europe is for air masses to travel eastwards from the Atlantic, over the British Isles towards France, Germany, Benelux and Scandinavia. The UK therefore 'exports' a significant proportion of some of the pollutants emitted in this country. Recent estimates suggest that more than 75% of the UK's SO_2 emissions and as much as 90% of our NOx emissions are transboundary, leading to deposition either in other countries or in the sea ...

> There are flows in other directions ... Around 40% of the deposition ... of oxidised nitrogen in the UK originates from sources outside the UK, and up to one half of ambient ozone (O_3) levels in Southern Britain are of continental origin.

> The consequence ... is that ... there must be a sufficient degree of international co-operation ... For a strategic approach to controlling long-range transboundary pollution, such as acid rain or ozone, international co-operation is the only option.

The most fundamental implications of atmospheric pollution are those concerned with global climate change. This is recognised as one of the greatest environmental threats facing the world today. Broad consensus now exists amongst the world's foremost climate scientists on the Intergovernmental Panel on Climate Change (IPCC) that human activities are having a discernible effect on the climate. Certain gases, naturally present in the atmosphere, keep the Earth at a temperature suitable for life by trapping outgoing terrestrial radiation from the earth's surface. Levels of some of these so-called 'greenhouse gases' are increasing as a result of human activity and this, scientists believe, is leading to a gradual increase in the temperature of the atmosphere. Climate models predict that the global temperature will rise by between 1.5°C and 3.5°C by 2100. This will exceed any climate change experienced since the last Ice Age 10,000 years ago. These predictions have been reiterated in successive IPCC reports at recent conferences of parties to the Framework Convention on Climate Change 1992 (see p 112, below).

While it is still too early to predict accurately the size and timing of climate change in specific regions, the impact on the global environment is likely to be significant. Sea levels are expected to rise causing flooding to low lying areas. Storms and other extreme weather events could become more severe and frequent. Climatic zones could shift towards the poles. Many natural habitats could decline or fragment and individual species become extinct. Water resources will be affected, some regions may experience food shortages and economic activities and human settlements will experience many direct and indirect effects. Climate change is also likely to have wide-ranging and mostly adverse impacts on human health, with potentially significant loss of life. (More information about the impact of climate change and recent developments in climate change science is to be found in the Meterological Office publication, *Climate Change and its impacts* and the UK climate impacts programme publication, *Climate Change Screening for the United Kingdom*. See also useful websites, p 201, below.)

Structure of the chapter

This chapter considers the principal international sources of law on air and atmospheric pollution and in particular the 1992 Framework Convention on Climate Change and its 1997 Kyoto Protocol and the 1979 Convention on Long-range Transboundary Air Pollution (LRTAP) and Related Protocols. Reference is made to the Vienna Convention for the Protection of the Ozone Layer 1985 and the 1987 Montreal Protocol, although these instruments are not extracted. The Chapter also deals with EC law and domestic law, including responses to smoke pollution (The Clean Air Act 1993), road traffic pollution and the establishment of Air Quality Strategies in Pt IV of the Environment Act 1995.

AIR AND ATMOSPHERIC POLLUTION: THE INTERNATIONAL CONTEXT

Customary international law

In the *Trail Smelter* arbitration, to date still the only example of international adjudication on the subject of transboundary air pollution, the arbitral tribunal held that: '... no state has the right to use or permit the use of its territory in such a manner as to cause injury by fumes in or to the territory of another or the properties or persons therein, when the case is of serious consequence and the injury is established by clear and convincing evidence' (*American Journal of International Law* (1941) Vol 35, 716). In this seminal case, sulphur dioxide fumes emanating from a Canadian smelting company were carried across into the United States where they were allegedly causing considerable damage to land and other interests in the State of Washington. Apart from the above principle which is a precursor to Principle 21 of the Stockholm Declaration (see pp 66–67, above), the arbitral tribunal also held that in addition to liability for damage already caused, the smelting company was required to refrain from causing any further damage in the State of Washington, thus establishing a further precursor for the preventive principle already discussed in Chapter 1 (p 49, above).

The principle applied in *Trail Smelter* has been more generally recognised. Article 3(1) of the International Law Association (ILA) 1982 Montreal Draft Rules on Transboundary Pollution restates customary international law as requiring States to prevent transfrontier air pollution so that no substantial injury is caused in the territory of another State (International Law Association, 60th Report, 1982). On the basis of this provision, Sands suggests that, '(G)eneral principles of international environmental law, as reflected in State practice, treaties and other international instruments, provide strong support for the view that customary international law prohibits States from causing significant environmental damage from transboundary atmospheric pollution' (Sands (1995) 247). However, Birnie and Boyle point out that 'a rule of this generality, applicable only in inter-State claims, has proved to be of limited utility'. They go on to argue that a rule intended mainly to compensate for serious harm is unsuitable for determining the content of obligations of diligent control and prevention of air pollution. For this purpose 'more detailed standards are required to implement a fully preventive approach. These can only be created through negotiation and international co-operation' (Birnie and Boyle (1992) 394).

Framework Convention on Climate Change 1992

This treaty is perhaps the most forward looking (in terms of its global environmental objectives) and far-reaching (in terms of its implications for human economic activity) yet agreed. It was one of two (the other being the Biodiversity Convention) that were opened for signature at the Rio 'Earth Summit', UN Conference on Environment and Development (UNCED) in 1992. The treaty entered into force on 21 March 1994, and by 7 September 2000 there were 186 States' parties, and 52 ratifications.[2]

The problems of damaging climate change and the loss of plant and animal biodiversity are issues of common concern to the whole of humankind. They have the potential to affect all countries, wherever they are situated, either in a geographical sense or in terms of their relative level of socio-economic development. Both the Climate Change and Biodiversity Conventions represent attempts to construct international regimes designed to address these environmental issues of truly global import. Recent satellite data has been used to verify the greenhouse effect caused by the build-up of greenhouse gases in the atmosphere,[3] thus justifying measures introduced under the climate change treaty regime.

---

2   See www.unfccc.de/resource/convkp.html. Also 31 ILM (1992) 849. See also Grimeaud, DJE, 'An overview of the policy and legal aspects of the international climate change regime' [2001] 2 Env Liability 39–52, Pt 1; [2001] 3 Env Liability 95–126, Pt 2.

3   By comparing two sets of satellite data obtained 27 years apart between 1970 and 1997, it was found that in the parts of the spectrum absorbed by carbon dioxide, ozone and methane, the amount of longwave infra-red radiation from the sun that was reflecting back from the earth's surface had dropped sharply in this period. This is the radiation that causes the greenhouse effect when it is captured by the increasing levels of so-called greenhouse gases in the atmosphere. The sharp reduction in radiation leads to the conclusion that it has indeed been captured by these greenhouse gases and is causing the greenhouse effect on the earth's surface. This is therefore possibly the first direct evidence confirming the increase in the greenhouse effect over the past three decades. See 'Measuring the greenhouse effect' (2001) *The Economist*, 17–23 March, Science and Technology Report, p 120.

The specific problem of global climate change arising from the build-up of so-called 'greenhouse' gases such as carbon dioxide in the atmosphere obviously required the establishment of a new international regime extending beyond the limits of national jurisdictions. It was also clear that the Framework Convention on Climate Change had to provide a structure within which not only States but also multinational or transnational corporations (MNCs or TNCs) as well as other non-governmental organisations (NGOs) could act, in order to achieve its aims (Nilsson and Pitt (1994) 9).

The main outcomes of the entry into force of the Framework Convention were: (1) the establishment of a treaty-based regime designed to facilitate the accumulation of scientific knowledge and advice on the global warming phenomenon. This information is produced by the Inter-governmental Panel on Climate Change (IPCC); (2) the creation of an inter-governmental forum for discussion and elaboration of policies and measures addressing the problem of global warming (the annual Conference of Parties (COP)); and (3) the creation of a framework for the provision of technical and financial support to help alleviate the special problems faced by developing countries, small island States and countries with transitional economies when implementing policies and measures designed to mitigate environmentally damaging climate change.

A major thrust of the strategy within this new treaty regime is to control and reduce emissions of carbon dioxide from anthropogenic sources (Doos (1991) 14). Interestingly, the negotiating process of the Framework Convention did not address measures for the absorption of carbon dioxide (the main greenhouse gas emitted by human activities) until fairly late in the day, with the result that provisions for effecting and measuring this absorption were not fully addressed in the Convention (Read (1994) 4–5). An edited text of the Framework Convention is set out below.

Kyoto Protocol 1997

The Kyoto Protocol was adopted at the Third Conference of Parties (COP3) to the Framework Convention on Climate Change. This took place at the eponymous Japanese city during 1–10 December, 1997. The Kyoto Protocol was adopted by more than 160 States at COP3, although it is not yet in force at the time of writing. This is at least partly due to the fact that the Protocol not only requires ratification by 55 State Parties, but these States must also account for at least 55% of the carbon dioxide (CO_2 emitted in 1990 by the States listed in Annex 1 to the Framework Convention (see p 119, below). The participation of a relatively small number of major industrialised countries, namely the United States, Japan, Russia, and the European Union is vital for the entry into force of the Protocol. As at 9 May 2001 84 States have signed the Protocol and there have been 34 ratifications. To date no major industrialised country has ratified the Protocol, although several have said that they will do so in the near future.

COP3 was able to agree a programme of measures aimed at reducing the concentration of 'greenhouse' gases in the atmosphere in order to address the problem of global warming and consequential adverse climatic changes. These measures are notable in moving away from a focus upon setting strict emissions targets as the preferred method for securing reductions in overall greenhouse gas concentrations. A legally-binding reduction target[4] for carbon dioxide (the main greenhouse gas) of at least 5% (below 1990 levels) between 2008 and 2012 has been imposed on most industrialised countries in the Kyoto Protocol (Art 3(1)). However, a system of differentiated targets within the rolling time scale has also been agreed between the main industrialised actors, namely the EU, the USA and Japan. Their targets are 8%, 7% and 6%, respectively (Annex B, see p 129, below). More important still is the inclusion, after insistence by the USA, of a provision for the possible establishment of an economic mechanism for the trading of so-called 'emission reduction units' (ERUs) (Art 6(1)). This has raised concerns that richer countries such as the USA may be able to purchase ERUs from countries such as Russia whose emissions have been much reduced of late due to the re-structuring of its industries. This may allow the richer country to maintain or even increase its own greenhouse gas emissions, but nevertheless maintain that it has met its target. Provision has also been made for the achievement of these targets not merely by emissions reductions but also through the implementation of forestry projects as 'sinks' to remove these gases from the atmosphere. The success (or otherwise) of these various alternative methods for securing the reduction of greenhouse gas concentrations may open the way for their possible introduction within other international environmental agreements.

Apart from the measures described briefly above, the Protocol also includes provisions for the use of so-called flexible, market-based mechanisms by Parties to achieve their targets. These include Joint Implementation,[5] the Clean Development Mechanism,[6] and Emissions Trading.[7] Joint Implementation allows Annex I Parties only to trade among themselves emission reduction units (ERUs) obtained by implementing co-operative projects reducing their emissions or establishing greenhouse gas sinks. As it is cheaper at the margin for some countries to abate their greenhouse gases compared to other countries, such joint implementation projects are in theory at least a cost-effective mechanism for achieving global targets. The global cost of achieving the Kyoto Protocol targets are US$120 billion if each country satisfies its obligations entirely through domestic actions, but this cost drops to just US$11-54 billion if emissions trading and certified emissions reductions (CERs) under the Clean Development Mechanism (CDM) are allowed (Ellerman *et al* (2000)).

The Clean Development Mechanism (CDM) purports to assist Annex I Parties in complying with their targets while also helping non-Annex I Parties to achieve the overall objective of the Climate Change Convention and Kyoto Protocol. Under the CDM, Annex I countries receive credits for either financially sponsoring, or by technology transfer, providing for actual greenhouse gas emissions reduction projects in non-Annex I countries.[8] Thus, non-Annex I Parties will benefit from such projects even if they do not yield certified emissions reductions because they must first be initiated. Annex I Parties on the other hand can use any certified emissions reductions to contribute to their own emissions reduction targets provided there is an additional benefit to overall greenhouse gas emissions.

---

4   Incorporating a variety of measures, not limited solely to emissions.

5   Kyoto Protocol 1997, Art 6.

6   *Ibid*, Art 12.

7   *Ibid*, Art 17.

8   *Ibid*, Art 12(3)(b).

Finally, the establishment of an emissions trading market is proposed which would allow Annex I Parties to purchase emissions credits from other Annex I Parties that are able to cut their emissions below what is legally required by the Protocol. As Cameron notes, it is important to bear in mind that the modalities for such a market, and indeed all these mechanisms, will need to be elaborated in future COPs (Cameron (2000) 8–9).

These joint implementation projects and their attached emissions credit transfer and trading systems are subject to a number of conditions. Chief among these are as follows: first, these projects must result in additional reductions than would normally be expected to occur. Secondly, they must supplement, not replace domestic emissions reduction programmes (Cameron (2000) 7–8). The fear is that emissions reductions and potential sinks will be exaggerated for domestic political and economic reasons, especially as the 1990 baseline cannot be accurately measured. Carbon accounting systems must therefore have six features: they must be transparent, consistent, comparable, complete, accurate and verifiable (IPCC (2000)). For a global greenhouse gas emissions reduction to occur, sinks must become permanent. If land set aside for sinks is ploughed, then all the gains in the reduction of 'greenhouse' gas emissions are lost. This raises a core challenge for emissions trading systems, namely to guarantee that emissions reductions are not reneged upon. The reason is that there is no such thing as permanent emissions reduction units, nor a permanently sequestered tonne of carbon once it has been traded. Without guarantees, these can be reversed at any time (Pretty and Ball (2001) 19).

The Kyoto Protocol was successful in at least two aspects: first, by establishing specific greenhouse gas emissions targets to be achieved by nearly every industrialised nation although not including developing countries, as required by the application of the principle of common but differentiated responsibilities in favour of developing countries.[9] Secondly, by determining how these targets are to be met, albeit only in general terms. The Protocol does not introduce any new commitments for developing countries, although Art 10 re-affirms existing commitments in the Climate Change Convention on the part of both Annex I and non-Annex I countries. As such it includes the obligation to periodically update national inventories of greenhouse gases, to formulate and implement national programmes to reduce the effects of climate change, to co-operate on scientific and technical research, and to develop education and training programmes (Davies (1998) 456).

However, subsequent Conferences of Parties (COPs) to the Climate Change Convention, culminating in COP6 (2000) held in The Hague have until now focused with little success on the exact measures to implement the emissions reduction targets noted above. For example, the Buenos Aires Plan of Action, adopted at COP4 in late 1998, established a timetable for negotiations on several issues, including the international emissions trading scheme and the Clean Development Mechanism for joint projects between industrialised countries and developing countries, to be completed in time for the Hague COP6. Despite this lengthy negotiating period, these issues were still not

---

9   See Principle 7, Rio Declaration 1992, p 71, above. As French notes, only developed States were obliged to 'aim' to return their 'greenhouse' gas emissions to 1990 levels, citing Arts 4(1) and 4(2) of the 1992 Climate Change Convention (for text, see p 101, below); French, D, 'Developing State and international environmental law: the importance of differentiated responsibilities' (2000) 49(1) ICLQ 35–61, p 40). See also Rajamani, L, 'The principle of common but differentiated responsibilities and the balance of commitments under the climate regime' (2000) 9(2) Review of European Community and International Environmental Law 120–31.

resolved by the time of COP6. The Bonn COP5, held in late 1999, was also able to agree on several issues, notably guidelines for improved information from the industrialised countries on the policies and measures they are introducing to achieve their emissions targets. However, no consensus could be achieved on how to review the actual commitments of the Parties towards implementing the Kyoto targets.

The main cause for controversy is the reluctance of the United States to implement its required target in the manner assumed by the other Parties, although not exactly prescribed by the Protocol as such. These State Parties hold that the Protocol requires these targets to be met mainly by reducing emissions from identified sources. The US is attempting to exploit the ambiguity inherent in the Protocol over the exact *modus operandi* to be utilised for achieving its emissions reduction target. Thus, the US has proposed, so far unsuccessfully, that it should be allowed to meet its emissions target by instead funding forest planting to create so-called carbon dioxide (CO_2) sinks, thereby gaining emissions reduction units as credits to offset against its emissions target. Initially, the US proposed funding projects in developing countries under the joint implementation scheme provided in the Convention (Art 4(2)(a)) and elaborated in the Protocol (Arts 3, 5, 6, and 7). Latterly, the US has proposed planting more trees in its own territory. Both these proposals were rejected by the other Parties, notably the European Community, in the latest COP6.

This is notwithstanding the Community's own sleight of hand in creating an 'EC bubble' within which a few of its own Member States, for example, Greece, Portugal, and Spain can actually increase their 'greenhouse' gas emissions, these being offset by greater than expected reductions in other EC Member States, notably the UK.[10] As Davies notes, this burden-sharing process will allow the wealthier EC Member States to accept much of the burden of reaching the overall EC emissions reduction target (Davies (1998) 455). Such joint action is however allowed under Arts 4(1) and 4(2) of the Protocol.[11]

Finally, it should be noted the newly-elected US President, George W Bush has now indicated that he is abandoning a campaign pledge he made to curtail carbon dioxide emissions as required by the climate change regime.[12] Indeed, latest reports indicate that the President has requested the US State Department to explore ways to formally withdraw the US signature from the Kyoto Protocol.[13] This turn of events was predicted by von Seht, who notes that the EC, Japan, Russian Federation and Central and East European countries with economies in transition together amount to more than 55% of Annex I 1990 CO_2 emissions. This could bring the Protocol into force irrespective of US ratification (von Seht (2000) 232–33).

On the other hand, it should be reiterated that none of the major industrialised countries and thus major contributors of greenhouse gases have to date (March 2001)

---

10 Department of Environment, Transport and Regions (DETR) has reaffirmed the present UK Government's commitment to a 20% cut in carbon dioxide emissions. See DETR website for details.

11 For EC action in relation to Kyoto, see pp 143 and 148, below.

12 Pianin, P and Drozdiak, W, 'A setback is feared on global warming: environmental groups see Bush's turnaround as a bar to world pact' (2001) *International Herald Tribune*, 17–18 March, pp 1 and 4.

13 See McCarthy, M, 'Bush declares he won't sign Kyoto's landmark treaty on global warming' (2001) *The Independent*, 29 March, p 1.

ratified the Kyoto Protocol. Moreover the US is correct to point out that within the next couple of decades, the greenhouse gas emissions from several major rapidly industrialising, albeit still developing, countries like the People's Republic of China (PRC) and India will begin to catch up with those produced by the major industrialised countries. These rapidly industrialising countries do not as yet have any strict emissions reduction targets. Developing country commitments are currently restricted to certain general commitments under Art 10 of the Protocol and voluntary participation in the Clean Development Mechanism (CDM). However, as their industries and cars produce more greenhouse gases so will the pressure to require them to establish such targets and strive to meet them. It is not too much to conclude that their co-operation will become necessary in the near future to ensure the success of the climate change regime.

Following the failure of COP6 in The Hague, the Conference of Parties reconvened in Bonn in late July, 2001. Despite dire predictions of failure engendered by the US non-ratification of the Kyoto Protocol, the Parties were nevertheless able to reach a broad agreement on the operational rules for the implementation of the Kyoto Protocol. In doing so, however, significant concessions were made to certain countries that are high carbon emitters such as Japan, Russia, Canada and Australia, to secure their continued participation in the climate change regime. These concessions were necessary to ensure the Protocol could enter into force with not just 55 ratifying Parties but also at least 55% of global carbon emissions as required by Art 25(1) of the Protocol. The following issues were resolved at the Bonn meeting:

(1) provision for greater flexibility in allowing these States to offset their individual emission reduction requirements by using carbon sinks to absorb carbon from the atmosphere. Eligible activities include re-vegetation and management of forests, cropland and grazing lands;

(2) use of Joint Implementation (between Annex I countries) and the Clean Development Mechanism (CDM) between Annex I countries and non-Annex I, that is, developing countries, through which climate-friendly projects are initiated in return for some credit to the Annex I country for the emissions avoided by these projects. These include energy efficiency, renewable energy and forest sink projects but not nuclear energy facilities;

(3) establishment of a special climate change fund for developing countries generally and another fund for the least developed countries to assist them to adapt to climate change impacts, obtain clean technologies and limit their carbon emissions growth. A Kyoto Protocol Adaptation Fund will also be established to finance concrete climate change adaptation projects and programmes;

(4) establishment of a compliance mechanism to ensure Parties meet their emission targets. The Kyoto Protocol's compliance mechanism consists of a Compliance Committee with a facilitative branch and enforcement branch. For every tonne of gas

that a country emits over its target, it will be required to reduce its emissions by an additional 1.3 tonnes during the Protocol's second commitment period, which begins in 2013.

UNITED NATIONS FRAMEWORK CONVENTION ON CLIMATE CHANGE (1992)

Entered into force: 21 March 1994

THE PARTIES TO THIS CONVENTION,

Acknowledging that change in the Earth's climate and its adverse effects are a common concern of humankind,

Concerned that human activities have been substantially increasing the atmospheric concentrations of greenhouse gases, that these increases enhance the natural greenhouse effect, and that this will result on average in an additional warming of the Earth's surface and atmosphere and may adversely affect natural eco-systems and humankind,

Noting that the largest share of historical and current global emissions of greenhouse gases has originated in developed countries, that *per capita* emissions in developing countries are still relatively low and that the share of global emissions originating in developing countries will grow to meet their social and development needs,

Aware of the role and importance in terrestrial and marine eco-systems of sinks and reservoirs of greenhouse gases,

Noting that there are many uncertainties in predictions of climate change, particularly with regard to the timing, magnitude and regional patterns thereof,

Acknowledging that the global nature of climate change calls for the widest possible co-operation by all countries and their participation in an effective and appropriate international response, in accordance with their common but differentiated responsibilities and respective capabilities and their social and economic conditions,

Recalling the pertinent provisions of the Declaration of the United Nations Conference on the Human Environment, adopted at Stockholm on 16 June 1972,

...

Reaffirming the principle of sovereignty of states in international co-operation to address climate change,

Recognising that states should enact effective environmental legislation, that environmental standards, management objectives and priorities should reflect the environmental and developmental context to which they apply, and that standards applied by some countries may be inappropriate and of unwarranted economic and social cost to other countries, in particular developing countries,

Recalling the provisions of General Assembly Resolution 44/228 of 22 December 1989 on the United Nations Conference on Environment and Development, and Resolutions 43/53 of 6 December 1988, 44/207 of 22 December 1989, 45/212 of 21 December 1990 and 46/169 of 19 December 1991 on protection of global climate for present and future generations of mankind,

Recalling also the provisions of General Assembly Resolution 44/206 of 22 December 1989 on the possible adverse effects of sea level rise on islands and coastal areas, particularly low lying coastal areas and the pertinent provisions of General Assembly Resolution 44/172 of 19 December 1989 on the implementation of the Plan of Action to Combat Desertification,

Recalling further the Vienna Convention for the Protection of the Ozone Layer, 1985, and the Montreal Protocol on Substances that Deplete the Ozone Layer, 1987, as adjusted and amended on 29 June 1990,

Noting the Ministerial Declaration of the Second World Climate Conference adopted on 7 November 1990,

Conscious of the valuable analytical work being conducted by many states on climate change and of the important contributions of the World Meteorological Organisation, the United Nations Environment Programme and other organs, organisations and bodies of the United Nations system, as well as other international and inter-governmental bodies, to the exchange of results of scientific research and the co-ordination of research,

Recognising that steps required to understand and address climate change will be environmentally, socially and economically most effective if they are based on relevant scientific, technical and economic considerations and continually re-evaluated in the light of new findings in these areas,

Recognising that various actions to address climate change can be justified economically in their own right and can also help in solving other environmental problems,

Recognising also the need for developed countries to take immediate action in a flexible manner on the basis of clear priorities, as a first step towards comprehensive response strategies at the global, national and, where agreed, regional levels that take into account all greenhouse gases, with due consideration of their relative contributions to the enhancement of the greenhouse effect,

Recognising further that low lying and other small island countries, countries with low lying coastal, arid and semi-arid areas or areas liable to floods, drought and desertification, and developing countries with fragile mountainous eco-systems are particularly vulnerable to the adverse effects of climate change,

Recognising the special difficulties of those countries, especially developing countries, whose economies are particularly dependent on fossil fuel production, use and exportation, as a consequence of action taken on limiting greenhouse gas emissions,

Affirming that responses to climate change should be co-ordinated with social and economic development in an integrated manner with a view to avoiding adverse impacts on the latter, taking into full account the legitimate priority needs of developing countries for the achievement of sustained economic growth and the eradication of poverty,

Recognising that all countries, especially developing countries, need access to resources required to achieve sustainable social and economic development and that, in order for developing countries to progress towards that goal, their energy consumption will need to grow taking into account the possibilities for achieving greater energy efficiency and for controlling greenhouse gas emissions in general, including through the application of new technologies on terms which make such an application economically and socially beneficial,

Determined to protect the climate system for present and future generations,

HAVE AGREED AS FOLLOWS:

Article 1: Definitions*

[* Titles of Articles are included solely to assist the reader.]

For the purposes of this Convention:

1   'Adverse effects of climate change' means changes in the physical environment or biota resulting from climate change which have significant deleterious effects on the composition, resilience or productivity of natural and managed eco-systems or on the operation of socio-economic systems or on human health and welfare.

2   'Climate change' means a change of climate which is attributed directly or indirectly to human activity that alters the composition of the global atmosphere and which is in addition to natural climate variability observed over comparable time periods.

3   'Climate system' means the totality of the atmosphere, hydrosphere, biosphere and geosphere and their interactions.

4   'Emissions' means the release of greenhouse gases and/or their precursors into the atmosphere over a specified area and period of time.

5   'Greenhouse gases' means those gaseous constituents of the atmosphere, both natural and anthropogenic, that absorb and re-emit infra-red radiation.

6   'Regional economic integration organisation' means an organisation constituted by sovereign states of a given region which has competence in respect of matters governed by this Convention or its protocols and has been duly authorised, in accordance with its internal procedures, to sign, ratify, accept, approve or accede to the instruments concerned.

7   'Reservoir' means a component or components of the climate system where a greenhouse gas or a precursor of a greenhouse gas is stored.

8   'Sink' means any process, activity or mechanism which removes a greenhouse gas, an aerosol or a precursor of a greenhouse gas from the atmosphere.

9   'Source' means any process or activity which releases a greenhouse gas, an aerosol or a precursor of a greenhouse gas into the atmosphere.

Article 2: Objective

The ultimate objective of this Convention and any related legal instruments that the Conference of the Parties may adopt is to achieve, in accordance with the relevant provisions of the Convention, stabilisation of greenhouse gas concentrations in the atmosphere at a level that would prevent dangerous anthropogenic interference with the climate system. Such a level should be achieved within a time frame sufficient to allow eco-systems to adapt naturally to climate change, to ensure that food production is not threatened and to enable economic development to proceed in a sustainable manner.

Note:

1 The ultimate objective of 'stabilisation of greenhouse gas concentrations' is important for a couple of reasons: first, as mentioned above, this goal of stabilisation can be achieved both by reduction as well as absorption of greenhouse gas emissions. Thus, measures that contribute to either of these are acceptable under the Convention. Secondly, stabilisation is to be achieved 'at a level that would prevent dangerous anthropogenic interference with the climate system'. This takes into account the fact that some amount of greenhouse

gases in the atmosphere is not just acceptable but also required to help maintain a relatively stable world climate system.

Article 3: Principles

In their actions to achieve the objective of the Convention and to implement its provisions, the Parties shall be guided, *inter alia*, by the following:

1   The Parties should protect the climate system for the benefit of present and future generations of humankind, on the basis of equity and in accordance with their common but differentiated responsibilities and respective capabilities. Accordingly, the developed country Parties should take the lead in combating climate change and the adverse effects thereof.

2   The specific needs and special circumstances of developing country Parties, especially those that are particularly vulnerable to the adverse effects of climate change, and of those Parties, especially developing country Parties, that would have to bear a disproportionate or abnormal burden under the Convention, should be given full consideration.

3   The Parties should take precautionary measures to anticipate, prevent or minimise the causes of climate change and mitigate its adverse effects. Where there are threats of serious or irreversible damage, lack of full scientific certainty should not be used as a reason for postponing such measures, taking into account that policies and measures to deal with climate change should be cost-effective so as to ensure global benefits at the lowest possible cost. To achieve this, such policies and measures should take into account different socio-economic contexts, be comprehensive, cover all relevant sources, sinks and reservoirs of greenhouse gases and adaptation, and comprise all economic sectors. Efforts to address climate change may be carried out co-operatively by interested Parties.

4   The Parties have a right to, and should, promote sustainable development. Policies and measures to protect the climate system against human induced change should be appropriate for the specific conditions of each Party and should be integrated with national development programmes, taking into account that economic development is essential for adopting measures to address climate change.

5   The Parties should co-operate to promote a supportive and open international economic system that would lead to sustainable economic growth and development in all Parties, particularly developing country Parties, thus enabling them better to address the problems of climate change. Measures taken to combat climate change, including unilateral ones, should not constitute a means of arbitrary or unjustifiable discrimination or a disguised restriction on international trade.

Notes:

1   Several emerging and established principles of international environmental law are discernible here: Article 3(1) incorporates the now well established principle of intra- and inter-generational equity. (See Principles 1 and 3 of the Stockholm and Rio Declarations 1972 and 1992 respectively, Chapter 1, pp 63 and 70, above.) It also includes the relatively new principle, first articulated at the Earth Summit, of common but differentiated responsibilities for environmental protection, among developed and developing countries (see Principle 7 of the Rio Declaration 1992). The special concerns of developing country Parties that are particularly vulnerable to the adverse effects of climate change, such as the small island States of the South Pacific region are further highlighted in Art 3(2).

2   Article 3(3) lays down the precautionary principle (see p 49, above), whereby action is proposed to minimise the possible adverse effects of climate change due to global warming, even though the nature and extent of the phenomena is as yet uncertain. This new principle of international environmental law is to be applied in a cost-effective manner, as provided for in Principle 15 of the Rio Declaration on Environment and Development. However, even if the precautionary principle or approach is to be rendered cost-effective, and there are indications that it may be quite expensive in strictly economic terms, it has nevertheless been argued to be an appropriate response to the problem of global warming, because of our appreciation of the truly global scale of environmental damage due to climate change that may occur (Read (1994) 2).

Article 4: Commitments

1   All Parties, taking into account their common but differentiated responsibilities and their specific national and regional development priorities, objectives and circumstances, shall:

   (a) Develop, periodically update, publish and make available to the Conference of the Parties, in accordance with Article 12, national inventories of anthropogenic emissions by sources and removals by sinks of all greenhouse gases not controlled by the Montreal Protocol, using comparable methodologies to be agreed upon by the Conference of the Parties;

   (b) Formulate, implement, publish and regularly update national and, where appropriate, regional programmes containing measures to mitigate climate change by addressing anthropogenic emissions by sources and removals by sinks of all greenhouse gases not controlled by the Montreal Protocol, and measures to facilitate adequate adaptation to climate change;

   (c) Promote and co-operate in the development, application and diffusion, including transfer, of technologies, practices and processes that control, reduce or prevent anthropogenic emissions of greenhouse gases not controlled by the Montreal Protocol in all relevant sectors, including the energy, transport, industry, agriculture, forestry and waste management sectors;

   (d) Promote sustainable management, and promote and co-operate in the conservation and enhancement, as appropriate, of sinks and reservoirs of all greenhouse gases not controlled by the Montreal Protocol, including biomass, forests and oceans as well as other terrestrial, coastal and marine eco-systems;

   (e) Co-operate in preparing for adaptation to the impacts of climate change; develop and elaborate appropriate and integrated plans for coastal zone management, water resources and agriculture, and for the protection and rehabilitation of areas, particularly in Africa, affected by drought and desertification, as well as floods;

   (f) Take climate change considerations into account, to the extent feasible, in their relevant social, economic and environmental policies and actions, and employ appropriate methods, for example impact assessments, formulated and determined nationally, with a view to minimising adverse effects on the economy, on public health and on the quality of the environment, of projects or measures undertaken by them to mitigate or adapt to climate change;

   (g) Promote and co-operate in scientific, technological, technical, socio-economic and other research, systematic observation and development of data archives related to the climate system and intended to further the understanding and to reduce or eliminate the remaining uncertainties regarding the causes, effects, magnitude and timing of climate change and the economic and social consequences of various response strategies;

(h) Promote and co-operate in the full, open and prompt exchange of relevant scientific, technological, technical, socio-economic and legal information related to the climate system and climate change, and to the economic and social consequences of various response strategies;

(i) Promote and co-operate in education, training and public awareness related to climate change and encourage the widest participation in this process, including that of non-governmental organisations; and

(j) Communicate to the Conference of the Parties information related to implementation, in accordance with Article 12.

2   The developed country Parties and other Parties included in Annex I commit themselves specifically as provided for in the following:

(a) Each of these Parties shall adopt national policies and take corresponding measures on the mitigation of climate change, by limiting its anthropogenic emissions of greenhouse gases and protecting and enhancing its greenhouse gas sinks and reservoirs. These policies and measures will demonstrate that developed countries are taking the lead in modifying longer-term trends in anthropogenic emissions consistent with the objective of the Convention, recognising that the return by the end of the present decade to earlier levels of anthropogenic emissions of carbon dioxide and other greenhouse gases not controlled by the Montreal Protocol would contribute to such modification, and taking into account the differences in these Parties' starting points and approaches, economic structures and resource bases, the need to maintain strong and sustainable economic growth, available technologies and other individual circumstances, as well as the need for equitable and appropriate contributions by each of these Parties to the global effort regarding that objective. These Parties may implement such policies and measures jointly with other Parties and may assist other Parties in contributing to the achievement of the objective of the Convention and, in particular, that of this sub-paragraph;

(b) In order to promote progress to this end, each of these Parties shall communicate, within six months of the entry into force of the Convention for it and periodically thereafter, and in accordance with Article 12, detailed information on its policies and measures referred to in sub-paragraph (a) above, as well as on its resulting projected anthropogenic emissions by sources and removals by sinks of greenhouse gases not controlled by the Montreal Protocol for the period referred to in sub-paragraph (a), with the aim of returning individually or jointly to their 1990 levels these anthropogenic emissions of carbon dioxide and other greenhouse gases not controlled by the Montreal Protocol. This information will be reviewed by the Conference of the Parties, at its first session and periodically thereafter, in accordance with Article 7;

(c) Calculations of emissions by sources and removals by sinks of greenhouse gases for the purposes of sub-paragraph (b) above should take into account the best available scientific knowledge, including of the effective capacity of sinks and the respective contributions of such gases to climate change. The Conference of the Parties shall consider and agree on methodologies for these calculations at its first session and review them regularly thereafter;

(d) The Conference of the Parties shall, at its first session, review the adequacy of sub-paragraphs (a) and (b) above. Such review shall be carried out in the light of the best available scientific information and assessment on climate change and its impacts, as well as relevant technical, social and economic information. Based on this review, the Conference of the Parties shall take appropriate action, which may include the adoption of amendments to the commitments in sub-paragraphs (a) and (b) above. The Conference of the Parties, at its first session, shall also take decisions regarding criteria for joint implementation as indicated in sub-paragraph (a) above. A second review of sub-paragraphs (a) and (b) shall take place not later than 31 December 1998, and thereafter at regular intervals determined by the Conference of the Parties, until the objective of the Convention is met;

(e) Each of these Parties shall:

(i) co-ordinate as appropriate with other such Parties, relevant economic and administrative instruments developed to achieve the objective of the Convention; and

(ii) identify and periodically review its own policies and practices which encourage activities that lead to greater levels of anthropogenic emissions of greenhouse gases not controlled by the Montreal Protocol than would otherwise occur;

(f) The Conference of the Parties shall review, not later than 31 December 1998, available information with a view to taking decisions regarding such amendments to the lists in Annexes I and II as may be appropriate, with the approval of the Party concerned;

(g) Any Party not included in Annex I may, in its instrument of ratification, acceptance, approval or accession, or at any time thereafter, notify the Depositary that it intends to be bound by sub-paragraphs (a) and (b) above. The Depositary shall inform the other signatories and Parties of any such notification.

3   The developed country Parties and other developed Parties included in Annex II shall provide new and additional financial resources to meet the agreed full costs incurred by developing country Parties in complying with their obligations under Article 12, paragraph 1. They shall also provide such financial resources, including for the transfer of technology, needed by the developing country Parties to meet the agreed full incremental costs of implementing measures that are covered by paragraph 1 of this Article and that are agreed between a developing country Party and the international entity or entities referred to in Article 11, in accordance with that Article. The implementation of these commitments shall take into account the need for adequacy and predictability in the flow of funds and the importance of appropriate burden sharing among the developed country Parties.

4   The developed country Parties and other developed Parties included in Annex II shall also assist the developing country Parties that are particularly vulnerable to the adverse effects of climate change in meeting costs of adaptation to those adverse effects.

5   The developed country Parties and other developed Parties included in Annex II shall take all practicable steps to promote, facilitate and finance, as appropriate, the transfer of, or access to, environmentally sound technologies and know-how to other Parties, particularly developing country Parties, to enable them to implement the provisions of the Convention. In this process, the developed country Parties shall support the development and enhancement of endogenous capacities and technologies of

developing country Parties. Other Parties and organisations in a position to do so may also assist in facilitating the transfer of such technologies.

6   In the implementation of their commitments under paragraph 2 above, a certain degree of flexibility shall be allowed by the Conference of the Parties to the Parties included in Annex I undergoing the process of transition to a market economy, in order to enhance the ability of these Parties to address climate change, including with regard to the historical level of anthropogenic emissions of greenhouse gases not controlled by the Montreal Protocol chosen as a reference.

7   The extent to which developing country Parties will effectively implement their commitments under the Convention will depend on the effective implementation by developed country Parties of their commitments under the Convention related to financial resources and transfer of technology and will take fully into account that economic and social development and poverty eradication are the first and overriding priorities of the developing country Parties.

8   In the implementation of the commitments in this Article, the Parties shall give full consideration to what actions are necessary under the Convention, including actions related to funding, insurance and the transfer of technology, to meet the specific needs and concerns of developing country Parties arising from the adverse effects of climate change and / or the impact of the implementation of response measures, especially on:

   (a) Small island countries;

   (b) Countries with low lying coastal areas;

   (c) Countries with arid and semi-arid areas, forested areas and areas liable to forest decay;

   (d) Countries with areas prone to natural disasters;

   (e) Countries with areas liable to drought and desertification;

   (f) Countries with areas of high urban atmospheric pollution;

   (g) Countries with areas with fragile eco-systems, including mountainous eco-systems;

   (h) Countries whose economies are highly dependent on income generated from the production, processing and export, and / or on consumption of fossil fuels and associated energy-intensive products; and

   (i) Land-locked and transit countries.

   Further, the Conference of the Parties may take actions, as appropriate, with respect to this paragraph.

9   The Parties shall take full account of the specific needs and special situations of the least developed countries in their actions with regard to funding and transfer of technology.

10 The Parties shall, in accordance with Article 10, take into consideration in the implementation of the commitments of the Convention the situation of Parties, particularly developing country Parties, with economies that are vulnerable to the adverse effects of the implementation of measures to respond to climate change. This applies notably to Parties with economies that are highly dependent on income generated from the production, processing and export, and / or consumption of fossil fuels and associated energy-intensive products and / or the use of fossil fuels for which such Parties have serious difficulties in switching to alternatives.

Notes:

1   Under Art 4 (Commitments), the action to be taken is dual in nature. First, such action aims at improving knowledge of climate change and thus reducing remaining uncertainties regarding the phenomena itself. Secondly, it consists of the adoption of policies and measures aimed at preventing or mitigating climate change and its effects. Article 4.1 is concerned with the wide-ranging needs for all countries to prepare inventories of emissions, implement abatement measures that promote the sustainable development of sinks and reservoirs, prepare for the impact of climate change, protect vulnerable areas, and review and monitor programmes of mitigation as part of an international co-operative effort in the context of the widest possible promotion of communication, education, training and awareness (Nilsson and Pitt (1994) 24).

2   Article 4.2(a) requires each Party to adopt national policies and measures on the mitigation of climate change. Under Art 4.2(b), communication of progress towards this end shall be made within six months of the entry into force of the Convention and periodically thereafter, in accordance with Art 12 (see below). This information will be reviewed by the Conference of Parties, at its first session and periodically thereafter, in accordance with Art 7 (see below).

3   Although the obligations established in this regard must be complied with by all State Parties, including both developed and developing countries, the onus is placed on the developed countries (and other Parties included in Annex I) (Art 4.2). A specific, though non-binding, benchmark for the stabilisation of emissions by these Parties is provided, namely the 1990 emission levels (Art 4.2(b)). Developing countries therefore are not only actors but also beneficiaries of actions to be carried out in this field.

4   Article 4.3 further provides that the developed country Parties (and other Parties listed in Annex II) should meet the full costs of any obligations incumbent upon the developing country Parties under Art 12 (which deals with the communication of information related to the implementation of the substantive obligations of these parties under Art 4); as well as the agreed full incremental costs of implementing measures undertaken by developing country parties in accordance with their Art 4 commitments. However, it is still uncertain what this level of assistance will be or even what 'incremental' really means (Nilsson and Pitt (1994) 25).

5   In this context, the term 'joint implementation' becomes important as a means for enabling developed countries to carry out their additional and differentiated responsibilities in relation to developing countries. The third sentence of Art 4.2(a) provides that certain policies and measures may be implemented jointly. According to the treaty text, joint implementation is merely a policy option available to States, into which they may enter if they wish by special arrangement, and in accordance with criteria established by the Conference of Parties (Art 4.2(d)). However, this provision for joint implementation is widely understood as a prescription or recommendation addressed to industrialised countries to increase the efficiency of their actions to reduce the overall concentration of greenhouse gases within the atmosphere by carrying out such action in other less developed countries, where the return on investment naturally would be higher in terms of greater greenhouse gas emissions reduction per unit of investment, for example (Kuik *et al* (1994) 4).

6   The joint development issue was the subject of a heated debate at the Berlin (First) Conference of the Parties (COP) in 1995 where it was finally decided that a pilot phase would be set up, but involving Annex I countries only. The participating industrialised

countries are not to be credited for technology transferred and the ensuing emission reductions during the pilot phase (Cooke (1995) 243).

Article 5: Research and systematic observation

In carrying out their commitments under Article 4, paragraph 1(g), the Parties shall:

(a) support and further develop, as appropriate, international and inter-governmental programmes and networks or organisations aimed at defining, conducting, assessing and financing research, data collection and systematic observation, taking into account the need to minimise duplication of effort;

(b) support international and inter-governmental efforts to strengthen systematic observation and national scientific and technical research capacities and capabilities, particularly in developing countries, and to promote access to, and the exchange of, data and analyses thereof obtained from areas beyond national jurisdiction; and

(c) take into account the particular concerns and needs of developing countries and co-operate in improving their endogenous capacities and capabilities to participate in the efforts referred to in sub-paragraphs (a) and (b) above.

Article 6: Education, training and public awareness

In carrying out their commitments under Article 4, paragraph 1(i), the Parties shall:

(a) Promote and facilitate at the national and, as appropriate, sub-regional and regional levels, and in accordance with national laws and regulations, and within their respective capacities:

   (i) the development and implementation of educational and public awareness programmes on climate change and its effects;

   (ii) public access to information on climate change and its effects;

   (iii) public participation in addressing climate change and its effects and developing adequate responses; and

   (iv) training of scientific, technical and managerial personnel.

(b) Co-operate in and promote, at the international level, and, where appropriate, using existing bodies:

   (i) the development and exchange of educational and public awareness material on climate change and its effects; and

   (ii) the development and implementation of education and training programmes, including the strengthening of national institutions and the exchange or secondment of personnel to train experts in this field, in particular for developing countries.

Article 7: Conference of the Parties

1   A Conference of the Parties is hereby established.

2   The Conference of the Parties, as the supreme body of this Convention, shall keep under regular review the implementation of the Convention and any related legal instruments that the Conference of the Parties may adopt, and shall make, within its mandate, the decisions necessary to promote the effective implementation of the Convention. To this end, it shall:

(a) periodically examine the obligations of the Parties and the institutional arrangements under the Convention, in the light of the objective of the Convention, the experience gained in its implementation and the evolution of scientific and technological knowledge;

(b) promote and facilitate the exchange of information on measures adopted by the Parties to address climate change and its effects, taking into account the differing circumstances, responsibilities and capabilities of the Parties and their respective commitments under the Convention;

(c) facilitate, at the request of two or more Parties, the co-ordination of measures adopted by them to address climate change and its effects, taking into account the differing circumstances, responsibilities and capabilities of the Parties and their respective commitments under the Convention;

(d) promote and guide, in accordance with the objective and provisions of the Convention, the development and periodic refinement of comparable methodologies, to be agreed on by the Conference of the Parties, *inter alia*, for preparing inventories of greenhouse gas emissions by sources and removals by sinks, and for evaluating the effectiveness of measures to limit the emissions and enhance the removals of these gases;

(e) assess, on the basis of all information made available to it in accordance with the provisions of the Convention, the implementation of the Convention by the Parties, the overall effects of the measures taken pursuant to the Convention, in particular environmental, economic and social effects as well as their cumulative impacts and the extent to which progress towards the objective of the Convention is being achieved;

(f) consider and adopt regular reports on the implementation of the Convention and ensure their publication;

(g) make recommendations on any matters necessary for the implementation of the Convention;

(h) seek to mobilise financial resources in accordance with Article 4, paragraphs 3, 4 and 5, and Article 11;

(i) establish such subsidiary bodies as are deemed necessary for the implementation of the Convention;

(j) review reports submitted by its subsidiary bodies and provide guidance to them;

(k) agree upon and adopt, by consensus, rules of procedure and financial rules for itself and for any subsidiary bodies;

(l) seek and utilise, where appropriate, the services and co-operation of, and information provided by, competent international organisations and inter-governmental and non-governmental bodies; and

(m) exercise such other functions as are required for the achievement of the objective of the Convention as well as all other functions assigned to it under the Convention.

3 The Conference of the Parties shall, at its first session, adopt its own rules of procedure as well as those of the subsidiary bodies established by the Convention, which shall include decision-making procedures for matters not already covered by decision-making procedures stipulated in the Convention. Such procedures may include specified majorities required for the adoption of particular decisions.

4   The first session of the Conference of the Parties shall be convened by the interim secretariat referred to in Article 21 and shall take place not later than one year after the date of entry into force of the Convention. Thereafter, ordinary sessions of the Conference of the Parties shall be held every year unless otherwise decided by the Conference of the Parties.

5   Extraordinary sessions of the Conference of the Parties shall be held at such other times as may be deemed necessary by the Conference, or at the written request of any Party, provided that, within six months of the request being communicated to the Parties by the secretariat, it is supported by at least one-third of the Parties.

6   The United Nations, its specialised agencies and the International Atomic Energy Agency, as well as any State member thereof or observers thereto not Party to the Convention, may be represented at sessions of the Conference of the Parties as observers. Any body or agency, whether national or international, governmental or non-governmental, which is qualified in matters covered by the Convention, and which has informed the secretariat of its wish to be represented at a session of the Conference of the Parties as an observer, may be so admitted unless at least one-third of the Parties present object. The admission and participation of observers shall be subject to the rules of procedure adopted by the Conference of the Parties.

Notes:

1   The Berlin Conference of Parties (1995) (COP1) concluded that commitments currently delineated in the Convention are not adequate and agreed a mandate for the negotiation of a Protocol, designed to elaborate upon climate change abatement and in particular, emissions reduction strategies. However, setting up the time-frame for the new commitments was a major obstacle, with any new commitments being viewed as potentially limiting the capacity of developing countries such as the G-77 (see G77/china homepage: www.g77.org), and especially China and India, to carry on with their socio-economic development plans. Thus, no new commitments were introduced for non-Annex I Parties, although developing countries did agree to confirm existing agreements and give more attention to their execution. This reflects the underlying reality that increasing industrialisation means emissions from G-77 countries such as Brazil, India and China will account for the major proportion of emission increases in the next decade.

2   The Geneva Conference of Parties (1996) (COP2) was notable for two main reasons: first, there came further recognition by the inter-governmental Panel on Climate Change (IPCC) that global warming is not only occurring but is in fact due at least in part to humankind's activities. Secondly, and not unconnected with the first point, was the recognition by several hitherto sceptical governments, most notably the USA, that the problem of global warming needed to be addressed sooner rather than later. This change of policy stance was not, however, matched by more urgent efforts on its part to make commitments to specific emission reduction targets or shorten the time period of the schedule for such reductions. Specifically, the US rejected the proposal by the Alliance of Small Island States (AOSIS) for steep and immediate cuts in carbon dioxide emissions to 20% below 1990 levels by 2005. Rather the US-led group of developed or industrial nations favoured setting new, legally binding, targets on the reduction or mitigation of emissions beyond 2000 in the next annual meeting of the COP. The methods by which such mitigation should be achieved however are still the subject of some debate. Various proposals include, the setting up of a market in tradeable emission permits, joint implementation measures, carbon taxes on fossil fuel energy

consumption, energy efficiency measures, and the phasing out of subsidies to the fossil fuel industry.

3   It is also important to note here the contribution to the COP of arguably the most important body to the conception, evolution, establishment and continuing legitimation of the climate change regime and its proposed measures for mitigating global warming: the Inter-governmental Panel on Climate Change (IPCC). The IPCC is an international institution comprised of about 2,000 of the world's leading scientists on climate change, whose reports have been largely accepted by the Parties to the Convention as indicative of the current State of scientific understanding on this issue. The IPCC has established that there is now a discernible human influence on the global climate. This has enormous implications for the debate on climate change, moving the discussion over whether mankind is disrupting the climate to deciding what to do about it. The IPCC will continue to play an important role in the climate change regime under Art 21.2.

The Kyoto Protocol was adopted at COP3 (see p 120, below). For a discussion of the post-Kyoto Conferences of Parties, see p 98, above.

Article 8: Secretariat

1   A secretariat is hereby established.

2   The functions of the secretariat shall be:
   (a) to make arrangements for sessions of the Conference of the Parties and its subsidiary bodies established under the Convention and to provide them with services as required;
   (b) to compile and transmit reports submitted to it;
   (c) to facilitate assistance to the Parties, particularly developing country Parties, on request, in the compilation and communication of information required in accordance with the provisions of the Convention;
   (d) to prepare reports on its activities and present them to the Conference of the Parties;
   (e) to ensure the necessary co-ordination with the secretariats of other relevant international bodies;
   (f) to enter, under the overall guidance of the Conference of the Parties, into such administrative and contractual arrangements as may be required for the effective discharge of its functions; and
   (g) to perform the other secretariat functions specified in the Convention and in any of its protocols and such other functions as may be determined by the Conference of the Parties.

3   The Conference of the Parties, at its first session, shall designate a permanent secretariat and make arrangements for its functioning.

Article 9: Subsidiary body for scientific and technological advice

1   A subsidiary body for scientific and technological advice is hereby established to provide the Conference of the Parties and, as appropriate, its other subsidiary bodies with timely information and advice on scientific and technological matters relating to the Convention. This body shall be open to participation by all Parties and shall be multi-disciplinary. It shall comprise government representatives competent in the relevant field of expertise. It shall report regularly to the Conference of the Parties on all aspects of its work.

2   Under the guidance of the Conference of the Parties, and drawing upon existing competent international bodies, this body shall:

   (a) provide assessments of the state of scientific knowledge relating to climate change and its effects;

   (b) prepare scientific assessments on the effects of measures taken in the implementation of the Convention;

   (c) identify innovative, efficient and state of the art technologies and know-how and advise on the ways and means of promoting development and/or transferring such technologies;

   (d) provide advice on scientific programmes, international co-operation in research and development related to climate change, as well as on ways and means of supporting endogenous capacity building in developing countries; and

   (e) respond to scientific, technological and methodological questions that the Conference of the Parties and its subsidiary bodies may put to the body.

3   The functions and terms of reference of this body may be further elaborated by the Conference of the Parties.

Article 10: Subsidiary body for implementation

1   A subsidiary body for implementation is hereby established to assist the Conference of the Parties in the assessment and review of the effective implementation of the Convention. This body shall be open to participation by all Parties and comprise government representatives who are experts on matters related to climate change. It shall report regularly to the Conference of the Parties on all aspects of its work.

2   Under the guidance of the Conference of the Parties, this body shall:

   (a) consider the information communicated in accordance with Article 12, paragraph 1, to assess the overall aggregated effect of the steps taken by the Parties in the light of the latest scientific assessments concerning climate change;

   (b) consider the information communicated in accordance with Article 12, paragraph 2, in order to assist the Conference of the Parties in carrying out the reviews required by Article 4, paragraph 2(d); and

   (c) assist the Conference of the Parties, as appropriate, in the preparation and implementation of its decisions.

Article 11: Financial mechanism

1   A mechanism for the provision of financial resources on a grant or concessional basis, including for the transfer of technology, is hereby defined. It shall function under the guidance of and be accountable to the Conference of the Parties, which shall decide on its policies, programme priorities and eligibility criteria related to this Convention. Its operation shall be entrusted to one or more existing international entities.

2   The financial mechanism shall have an equitable and balanced representation of all Parties within a transparent system of governance.

3   The Conference of the Parties and the entity or entities entrusted with the operation of the financial mechanism shall agree upon arrangements to give effect to the above paragraphs, which shall include the following:

(a) modalities to ensure that the funded projects to address climate change are in conformity with the policies, programme priorities and eligibility criteria established by the Conference of the Parties;

(b) modalities by which a particular funding decision may be reconsidered in light of these policies, programme priorities and eligibility criteria;

(c) provision by the entity or entities of regular reports to the Conference of the Parties on its funding operations, which is consistent with the requirement for accountability set out in paragraph 1 above; and

(d) determination in a predictable and identifiable manner of the amount of funding necessary and available for the implementation of this Convention and the conditions under which that amount shall be periodically reviewed.

4   The Conference of the Parties shall make arrangements to implement the above mentioned provisions at its first session, reviewing and taking into account the interim arrangements referred to in Article 21, paragraph 3, and shall decide whether these interim arrangements shall be maintained. Within four years thereafter, the Conference of the Parties shall review the financial mechanism and take appropriate measures.

5   The developed country Parties may also provide and developing country Parties avail themselves of, financial resources related to the implementation of the Convention through bilateral, regional and other multi-lateral channels.

Article 12: Communication of information related to implementation

1   In accordance with Article 4, paragraph 1, each Party shall communicate to the Conference of the Parties, through the secretariat, the following elements of information:

(a) a national inventory of anthropogenic emissions by sources and removals by sinks of all greenhouse gases not controlled by the Montreal Protocol, to the extent its capacities permit, using comparable methodologies to be promoted and agreed upon by the Conference of the Parties;

(b) a general description of steps taken or envisaged by the Party to implement the Convention; and

(c) any other information that the Party considers relevant to the achievement of the objective of the Convention and suitable for inclusion in its communication, including, if feasible, material relevant for calculations of global emission trends.

2   Each developed country Party and each other Party included in Annex I shall incorporate in its communication the following elements of information:

(a) a detailed description of the policies and measures that it has adopted to implement its commitment under Article 4, paragraphs 2(a) and 2(b); and

(b) a specific estimate of the effects that the policies and measures referred to in sub-paragraph (a) immediately above will have on anthropogenic emissions by its sources and removals by its sinks of greenhouse gases during the period referred to in Article 4, paragraph 2(a).

3   In addition, each developed country Party and each other developed Party included in Annex II shall incorporate details of measures taken in accordance with Article 4, paragraphs 3, 4 and 5.

4   Developing country Parties may, on a voluntary basis, propose projects for financing, including specific technologies, materials, equipment, techniques or practices that would be needed to implement such projects, along with, if possible, an estimate of all incremental costs, of the reductions of emissions and increments of removals of greenhouse gases, as well as an estimate of the consequent benefits.

5   Each developed country Party and each other Party included in Annex I shall make its initial communication within six months of the entry into force of the Convention for that party. Each Party not so listed shall make its initial communication within three years of the entry into force of the Convention for that Party, or of the availability of financial resources in accordance with Article 4, paragraph 3. Parties that are least developed countries may make their initial communication at their discretion. The frequency of subsequent communications by all Parties shall be determined by the Conference of the Parties, taking into account the differentiated timetable set by this paragraph.

6   Information communicated by Parties under this Article shall be transmitted by the secretariat as soon as possible to the Conference of the Parties and to any subsidiary bodies concerned. If necessary, the procedures for the communication of information may be further considered by the Conference of the Parties.

7   From its first session, the Conference of the Parties shall arrange for the provision to developing country Parties of technical and financial support, on request, in compiling and communicating information under this Article, as well as in identifying the technical and financial needs associated with proposed projects and response measures under Article 4. Such support may be provided by other Parties, by competent international organisations and by the secretariat, as appropriate.

8   Any group of Parties may, subject to guidelines adopted by the Conference of the Parties, and to prior notification to the Conference of the Parties, make a joint communication in fulfilment of their obligations under this Article, provided that such a communication includes information on the fulfilment by each of these Parties of its individual obligations under the Convention.

9   Information received by the secretariat that is designated by a Party as confidential, in accordance with criteria to be established by the Conference of the Parties, shall be aggregated by the secretariat to protect its confidentiality before being made available to any of the bodies involved in the communication and review of information.

10   Subject to paragraph 9 above, and without prejudice to the ability of any Party to make public its communication at any time, the secretariat shall make communications by Parties under this Article publicly available at the time they are submitted to the Conference of the Parties.

Article 13: Resolution of questions regarding implementation

The Conference of the Parties shall, at its first session, consider the establishment of a multi-lateral consultative process, available to Parties on their request, for the resolution of questions regarding the implementation of the Convention.

Article 14: Settlement of disputes

1   In the event of a dispute between any two or more Parties concerning the interpretation or application of the Convention, the Parties concerned shall seek a settlement of the dispute through negotiation or any other peaceful means of their own choice.

2   When ratifying, accepting, approving or acceding to the Convention, or at any time thereafter, a Party which is not a regional economic integration organisation may declare in a written instrument submitted to the Depositary that, in respect of any dispute concerning the interpretation or application of the Convention, it recognises as compulsory *ipso facto* and without special agreement, in relation to any Party accepting the same obligation:

(a) submission of the dispute to the International Court of Justice; and/or

(b) arbitration in accordance with procedures to be adopted by the Conference of the Parties as soon as practicable, in an annex on arbitration.

A Party which is a regional economic integration organisation may make a declaration with like effect in relation to arbitration in accordance with the procedures referred to in sub-paragraph (b) above.

3   A declaration made under paragraph 2 above shall remain in force until it expires in accordance with its terms or until three months after written notice of its revocation has been deposited with the Depositary.

4   A new declaration, a notice of revocation or the expiry of a declaration shall not in any way affect proceedings pending before the International Court of Justice or the arbitral tribunal, unless the Parties to the dispute otherwise agree.

5   Subject to the operation of paragraph 2 above, if after 12 months following notification by one Party to another that a dispute exists between them, the Parties concerned have not been able to settle their dispute through the means mentioned in paragraph 1 above, the dispute shall be submitted, at the request of any of the parties to the dispute, to conciliation.

6   A conciliation commission shall be created upon the request of one of the parties to the dispute. The commission shall be composed of an equal number of members appointed by each Party concerned and a chairman chosen jointly by the members appointed by each Party. The commission shall render a recommendatory award, which the Parties shall consider in good faith.

7   Additional procedures relating to conciliation shall be adopted by the Conference of the Parties, as soon as practicable, in an annex on conciliation.

8   The provisions of this Article shall apply to any related legal instrument which the Conference of the Parties may adopt, unless the instrument provides otherwise.

Note:

1   The Convention provides a fairly comprehensive range of possible compulsory dispute settlement mechanisms in order to facilitate disputing Parties. These include negotiations or any other peaceful means of the Parties' choice such as submission to the International Court of Justice, arbitration in accordance with procedures adopted by the COP, or where the dispute is still unresolved after 12 months' conciliation. The recommendations of any conciliation commission are not binding, although the Parties are required to consider them in good faith.

Article 15: Amendments to the Convention

1   Any Party may propose amendments to the Convention.

2   Amendments to the Convention shall be adopted at an ordinary session of the Conference of the Parties. The text of any proposed amendment to the Convention shall

be communicated to the Parties by the secretariat at least six months before the meeting at which it is proposed for adoption. The secretariat shall also communicate proposed amendments to the signatories to the Convention and, for information, to the Depositary.

3   The Parties shall make every effort to reach agreement on any proposed amendment to the Convention by consensus. If all efforts at consensus have been exhausted, and no agreement reached, the amendment shall as a last resort be adopted by a three-fourths majority vote of the Parties present and voting at the meeting. The adopted amendment shall be communicated by the secretariat to the Depositary, who shall circulate it to all Parties for their acceptance.

4   Instruments of acceptance in respect of an amendment shall be deposited with the Depositary. An amendment adopted in accordance with paragraph 3 above shall enter into force for those Parties having accepted it on the ninetieth day after the date of receipt by the Depositary of an instrument of acceptance by at least three-quarters of the Parties to the Convention.

5   The amendment shall enter into force for any other Party on the ninetieth day after the date on which that Party deposits with the Depositary its instrument of acceptance of the said amendment.

6   For the purposes of this Article, 'Parties present and voting' means Parties present and casting an affirmative or negative vote.

Article 16: Adoption and amendment of annexes to the Convention

1   Annexes to the Convention shall form an integral part thereof and, unless otherwise expressly provided, a reference to the Convention constitutes at the same time a reference to any annexes thereto. Without prejudice to the provisions of Article 14, paragraphs 2(b) and 7, such annexes shall be restricted to lists, forms and any other material of a descriptive nature that is of a scientific, technical, procedural or administrative character.

2   Annexes to the Convention shall be proposed and adopted in accordance with the procedure set forth in Article 15, paragraphs 2, 3, and 4.

3   An annex that has been adopted in accordance with paragraph 2 above shall enter into force for all Parties to the Convention six months after the date of the communication by the Depositary to such Parties of the adoption of the annex, except for those Parties that have notified the Depositary, in writing, within that period of their non-acceptance of the annex. The annex shall enter into force for Parties which withdraw their notification of non-acceptance on the ninetieth day after the date on which withdrawal of such notification has been received by the Depositary.

4   The proposal, adoption and entry into force of amendments to annexes to the Convention shall be subject to the same procedure as that for the proposal, adoption and entry into force of annexes to the Convention in accordance with paragraphs 2 and 3 above.

5   If the adoption of an annex or an amendment to an annex involves an amendment to the Convention, that annex or amendment to an annex shall not enter into force until such time as the amendment to the Convention enters into force.

Article 17: Protocols

1   The Conference of the Parties may, at any ordinary session, adopt protocols to the Convention.

2   The text of any proposed protocol shall be communicated to the Parties by the secretariat at least six months before such a session.

3   The requirements for the entry into force of any protocol shall be established by that instrument.

4   Only Parties to the Convention may be Parties to a protocol.

5   Decisions under any protocol shall be taken only by the Parties to the protocol concerned.

Article 18: Right to vote

1   Each Party to the Convention shall have one vote, except as provided for in paragraph 2 below.

2   Regional economic integration organisations, in matters within their competence, shall exercise their right to vote with a number of votes equal to the number of their Member States that are Parties to the Convention. Such an organisation shall not exercise its right to vote if any of its Member States exercises its right, and vice versa.

[Articles 19 (on Depositary), 20 (on Signature), 21 (on Interim Arrangements), 22 (on Ratification, Acceptance, Approval or Accession) and 23 (on Entry into Force) omitted.]

Article 24: Reservations

No reservations may be made to the Convention.

[Article 25 (on Withdrawal) and Article 26 (on Authentic Texts) omitted.]

DONE at New York this ninth day of May one thousand nine hundred and ninety-two.

Annex I

Australia, Austria, Belarus a/, Belgium, Bulgaria a/, Canada, Czechoslovakia a/, Denmark, European Community, Estonia a/, Finland, France, Germany, Greece, Hungary a/, Iceland, Ireland, Italy, Japan, Latvia a/, Lithuania a/, Luxembourg, Netherlands, New Zealand, Norway, Poland a/, Portugal, Romania a/, Russian Federation a/, Spain, Sweden, Switzerland, Turkey, Ukraine a/, United Kingdom of Great Britain and Northern Ireland, United States of America.

a/ Countries that are undergoing the process of transition to a market economy.

Annex II

Australia, Austria, Belgium, Canada, Denmark, European Community, Finland, France, Germany, Greece, Iceland, Ireland, Italy, Japan, Luxembourg, Netherlands, New Zealand, Norway, Portugal, Spain, Sweden, Switzerland, Turkey, United Kingdom of Great Britain and Northern Ireland, United States of America.

KYOTO PROTOCOL TO THE UNITED NATIONS FRAMEWORK CONVENTION ON CLIMATE CHANGE (1997)

Article 1

[For the purposes of this Protocol, the definitions contained in Article 1 of the Convention shall apply ... Paragraphs 1–7 omitted.]

Article 2

1   Each Party included in Annex I, in achieving its quantified emission limitation and reduction commitments under Article 3, in order to promote sustainable development, shall:

(a) Implement and/or further elaborate policies and measures in accordance with its national circumstances, such as:

(i)   enhancement of energy efficiency in relevant sectors of the national economy;

(ii) protection and enhancement of sinks and reservoirs of greenhouse gases not controlled by the Montreal Protocol, taking into account its commitments under relevant international environmental agreements; promotion of sustainable forest management practices, afforestation and reforestation;

(iii) promotion of sustainable forms of agriculture in light of climate change considerations;

(iv) research on, and promotion, development and increased use of, new and renewable forms of energy, of carbon dioxide sequestration technologies and of advanced and innovative environmentally sound technologies;

(v)   progressive reduction or phasing out of market imperfections, fiscal incentives, tax and duty exemptions and subsidies in all greenhouse gas emitting sectors that run counter to the objective of the Convention and application of market instruments;

(vi) encouragement of appropriate reforms in relevant sectors aimed at promoting policies and measures which limit or reduce emissions of greenhouse gases not controlled by the Montreal Protocol;

(vii) measures to limit and/or reduce emissions of greenhouse gases not controlled by the Montreal Protocol in the transport sector;

(viii) limitation and/or reduction of methane emissions through recovery and use in waste management, as well as in the production, transport and distribution of energy;

(b) Co-operate with other such Parties to enhance the individual and combined effectiveness of their policies and measures adopted under this Article, pursuant to Article 4, paragraph 2(e)(i), of the Convention. To this end, these Parties shall take steps to share their experience and exchange information on such policies and measures, including developing ways of improving their comparability, transparency and effectiveness. The Conference of the Parties serving as the meeting of the Parties to this Protocol shall, at its first session or as soon as practicable thereafter, consider ways to facilitate such co-operation, taking into account all relevant information.

2   The Parties included in Annex I shall pursue limitation or reduction of emissions of greenhouse gases not controlled by the Montreal Protocol from aviation and marine

bunker fuels, working through the International Civil Aviation Organization and the International Maritime Organisation, respectively.

3   The Parties included in Annex I shall strive to implement policies and measures under this Article in such a way as to minimise adverse effects, including the adverse effects of climate change, effects on international trade, and social, environmental and economic impacts on other Parties, especially developing country Parties and in particular those identified in Article 4, paragraphs 8 and 9, of the Convention, taking into account Article 3 of the Convention. The Conference of the Parties serving as the meeting of the Parties to this Protocol may take further action, as appropriate, to promote the implementation of the provisions of this paragraph.

4   The Conference of the Parties serving as the meeting of the Parties to this Protocol, if it decides that it would be beneficial to co-ordinate any of the policies and measures in paragraph 1(a) above, taking into account different national circumstances and potential effects, shall consider ways and means to elaborate the coordination of such policies and measures.

Article 3

1   The Parties included in Annex I shall, individually or jointly, ensure that their aggregate anthropogenic carbon dioxide equivalent emissions of the greenhouse gases listed in Annex A do not exceed their assigned amounts, calculated pursuant to their quantified emission limitation and reduction commitments inscribed in Annex B and in accordance with the provisions of this Article, with a view to reducing their overall emissions of such gases by at least 5 per cent below 1990 levels in the commitment period 2008 to 2012.

2   Each Party included in Annex I shall, by 2005, have made demonstrable progress in achieving its commitments under this Protocol.

3   The net changes in greenhouse gas emissions by sources and removals by sinks resulting from direct human-induced land-use change and forestry activities, limited to afforestation, reforestation and deforestation since 1990, measured as verifiable changes in carbon stocks in each commitment period, shall be used to meet the commitments under this Article of each Party included in Annex I. The greenhouse gas emissions by sources and removals by sinks associated with those activities shall be reported in a transparent and verifiable manner and reviewed in accordance with Articles 7 and 8.

4   Prior to the first session of the Conference of the Parties serving as the meeting of the Parties to this Protocol, each Party included in Annex I shall provide, for consideration by the Subsidiary Body for Scientific and Technological Advice, data to establish its level of carbon stocks in 1990 and to enable an estimate to be made of its changes in carbon stocks in subsequent years. The Conference of the Parties serving as the meeting of the Parties to this Protocol shall, at its first session or as soon as practicable thereafter, decide upon modalities, rules and guidelines as to how, and which, additional human-induced activities related to changes in greenhouse gas emissions by sources and removals by sinks in the agricultural soils and the land-use change and forestry categories shall be added to, or subtracted from, the assigned amounts for Parties included in Annex I, taking into account uncertainties, transparency in reporting, verifiability, the methodological work of the Intergovernmental Panel on Climate Change, the advice provided by the Subsidiary Body for Scientific and Technological Advice in accordance with Article 5 and the decisions of the Conference of the Parties. Such a decision shall apply in the second and subsequent commitment periods. A Party

may choose to apply such a decision on these additional human-induced activities for its first commitment period, provided that these activities have taken place since 1990.

5   The Parties included in Annex I undergoing the process of transition to a market economy whose base year or period was established pursuant to decision 9/CP.2 of the Conference of the Parties at its second session shall use that base year or period for the implementation of their commitments under this Article. Any other Party included in Annex I undergoing the process of transition to a market economy which has not yet submitted its first national communication under Article 12 of the Convention may also notify the Conference of the Parties serving as the meeting of the Parties to this Protocol that it intends to use an historical base year or period other than 1990 for the implementation of its commitments under this Article. The Conference of the Parties serving as the meeting of the Parties to this Protocol shall decide on the acceptance of such notification.

6   Taking into account Article 4, paragraph 6, of the Convention, in the implementation of their commitments under this Protocol other than those under this Article, a certain degree of flexibility shall be allowed by the Conference of the Parties serving as the meeting of the Parties to this Protocol to the Parties included in Annex I undergoing the process of transition to a market economy.

7   In the first quantified emission limitation and reduction commitment period, from 2008 to 2012, the assigned amount for each Party included in Annex I shall be equal to the percentage inscribed for it in Annex B of its aggregate anthropogenic carbon dioxide equivalent emissions of the greenhouse gases listed in Annex A in 1990, or the base year or period determined in accordance with paragraph 5 above, multiplied by five. Those Parties included in Annex I for whom land-use change and forestry constituted a net source of greenhouse gas emissions in 1990 shall include in their 1990 emissions base year or period the aggregate anthropogenic carbon dioxide equivalent emissions by sources minus removals by sinks in 1990 from land-use change for the purposes of calculating their assigned amount.

8   Any Party included in Annex I may use 1995 as its base year for hydrofluorocarbons, perfluorocarbons and sulphur hexafluoride, for the purposes of the calculation referred to in paragraph 7 above.

9   Commitments for subsequent periods for Parties included in Annex I shall be established in amendments to Annex B to this Protocol, which shall be adopted in accordance with the provisions of Article 21, paragraph 7. The Conference of the Parties serving as the meeting of the Parties to this Protocol shall initiate the consideration of such commitments at least seven years before the end of the first commitment period referred to in paragraph 1 above.

10   Any emission reduction units, or any part of an assigned amount, which a Party acquires from another Party in accordance with the provisions of Article 6 or of Article 17 shall be added to the assigned amount for the acquiring Party.

11   Any emission reduction units, or any part of an assigned amount, which a Party transfers to another Party in accordance with the provisions of Article 6 or of Article 17 shall be subtracted from the assigned amount for the transferring Party.

12   Any certified emission reductions which a Party acquires from another Party in accordance with the provisions of Article 12 shall be added to the assigned amount for the acquiring Party.

13 If the emissions of a Party included in Annex I in a commitment period are less than its assigned amount under this Article, this difference shall, on request of that Party, be added to the assigned amount for that Party for subsequent commitment periods.

14 Each Party included in Annex I shall strive to implement the commitments mentioned in paragraph 1 above in such a way as to minimize adverse social, environmental and economic impacts on developing country Parties, particularly those identified in Article 4, paragraphs 8 and 9, of the Convention. In line with relevant decisions of the Conference of the Parties on the implementation of those paragraphs, the Conference of the Parties serving as the meeting of the Parties to this Protocol shall, at its first session, consider what actions are necessary to minimize the adverse effects of climate change and/or the impacts of response measures on Parties referred to in those paragraphs. Among the issues to be considered shall be the establishment of funding, insurance and transfer of technology.

Article 4

1 Any Parties included in Annex I that have reached an agreement to fulfil their commitments under Article 3 jointly, shall be deemed to have met those commitments provided that their total combined aggregate anthropogenic carbon dioxide equivalent emissions of the greenhouse gases listed in Annex A do not exceed their assigned amounts calculated pursuant to their quantified emission limitation and reduction commitments inscribed in Annex B and in accordance with the provisions of Article 3. The respective emission level allocated to each of the Parties to the agreement shall be set out in that agreement.

[Paragraphs 2–6 omitted.]

Article 5

1 Each Party included in Annex I shall have in place, no later than one year prior to the start of the first commitment period, a national system for the estimation of anthropogenic emissions by sources and removals by sinks of all greenhouse gases not controlled by the Montreal Protocol. Guidelines for such national systems, which shall incorporate the methodologies specified in paragraph 2 below, shall be decided upon by the Conference of the Parties serving as the meeting of the Parties to this Protocol at its first session.

2 Methodologies for estimating anthropogenic emissions by sources and removals by sinks of all greenhouse gases not controlled by the Montreal Protocol shall be those accepted by the Intergovernmental Panel on Climate Change and agreed upon by the Conference of the Parties at its third session. Where such methodologies are not used, appropriate adjustments shall be applied according to methodologies agreed upon by the Conference of the Parties serving as the meeting of the Parties to this Protocol at its first session. Based on the work of, *inter alia*, the Intergovernmental Panel on Climate Change and advice provided by the Subsidiary Body for Scientific and Technological Advice, the Conference of the Parties serving as the meeting of the Parties to this Protocol shall regularly review and, as appropriate, revise such methodologies and adjustments, taking fully into account any relevant decisions by the Conference of the Parties. Any revision to methodologies or adjustments shall be used only for the purposes of ascertaining compliance with commitments under Article 3 in respect of any commitment period adopted subsequent to that revision.

[Paragraph 3 omitted.]

Article 6

1 For the purpose of meeting its commitments under Article 3, any Party included in Annex I may transfer to, or acquire from, any other such Party emission reduction units resulting from projects aimed at reducing anthropogenic emissions by sources or enhancing anthropogenic removals by sinks of greenhouse gases in any sector of the economy, provided that:

 (a) any such project has the approval of the Parties involved;

 (b) any such project provides a reduction in emissions by sources, or an enhancement of removals by sinks, that is additional to any that would otherwise occur;

 (c) it does not acquire any emission reduction units if it is not in compliance with its obligations under Articles 5 and 7; and

 (d) the acquisition of emission reduction units shall be supplemental to domestic actions for the purposes of meeting commitments under Article 3.

2 The Conference of the Parties serving as the meeting of the Parties to this Protocol may, at its first session or as soon as practicable thereafter, further elaborate guidelines for the implementation of this Article, including for verification and reporting.

3 A Party included in Annex I may authorise legal entities to participate, under its responsibility, in actions leading to the generation, transfer or acquisition under this Article of emission reduction units.

4 If a question of implementation by a Party included in Annex I of the requirements referred to in this Article is identified in accordance with the relevant provisions of Article 8, transfers and acquisitions of emission reduction units may continue to be made after the question has been identified, provided that any such units may not be used by a Party to meet its commitments under Article 3 until any issue of compliance is resolved.

[Articles 7–8 omitted.]

Article 9

1 The Conference of the Parties serving as the meeting of the Parties to this Protocol shall periodically review this Protocol in the light of the best available scientific information and assessments on climate change and its impacts, as well as relevant technical, social and economic information. Such reviews shall be co-ordinated with pertinent reviews under the Convention, in particular those required by Article 4, paragraph 2(d), and Article 7, paragraph 2(a), of the Convention. Based on these reviews, the Conference of the Parties serving as the meeting of the Parties to this Protocol shall take appropriate action.

2 The first review shall take place at the second session of the Conference of the Parties serving as the meeting of the Parties to this Protocol. Further reviews shall take place at regular intervals and in a timely manner.

Article 10

All Parties, taking into account their common but differentiated responsibilities and their specific national and regional development priorities, objectives and circumstances, without introducing any new commitments for Parties not included in Annex I, but re-affirming existing commitments under Article 4, paragraph 1, of the Convention, and continuing to advance the implementation of these commitments in order to achieve sustainable development, taking into account Article 4, paragraphs 3, 5 and 7, of the Convention, shall:

(a) formulate, where relevant and to the extent possible, cost-effective national and, where appropriate, regional programmes to improve the quality of local emission factors, activity data and/or models which reflect the socio-economic conditions of each Party for the preparation and periodic updating of national inventories of anthropogenic emissions by sources and removals by sinks of all greenhouse gases not controlled by the Montreal Protocol, using comparable methodologies to be agreed upon by the Conference of the Parties, and consistent with the guidelines for the preparation of national communications adopted by the Conference of the Parties;

(b) formulate, implement, publish and regularly update national and, where appropriate, regional programmes containing measures to mitigate climate change and measures to facilitate adequate adaptation to climate change;

[...]

(c) co-operate in the promotion of effective modalities for the development, application and diffusion of, and take all practicable steps to promote, facilitate and finance, as appropriate, the transfer of, or access to, environmentally sound technologies, know-how, practices and processes pertinent to climate change, in particular to developing countries, including the formulation of policies and programmes for the effective transfer of environmentally sound technologies that are publicly owned or in the public domain and the creation of an enabling environment for the private sector, to promote and enhance the transfer of, and access to, environmentally sound technologies;

(d) co-operate in scientific and technical research and promote the maintenance and the development of systematic observation systems and development of data archives to reduce uncertainties related to the climate system, the adverse impacts of climate change and the economic and social consequences of various response strategies, and promote the development and strengthening of endogenous capacities and capabilities to participate in international and intergovernmental efforts, programmes and networks on research and systematic observation, taking into account Article 5 of the Convention;

(e) co-operate in and promote at the international level, and, where appropriate, using existing bodies, the development and implementation of education and training programmes, including the strengthening of national capacity building, in particular human and institutional capacities and the exchange or secondment of personnel to train experts in this field, in particular for developing countries, and facilitate at the national level public awareness of, and public access to information on, climate change. Suitable modalities should be developed to implement these activities through the relevant bodies of the Convention, taking into account Article 6 of the Convention;

(f) include in their national communications information on programmes and activities undertaken pursuant to this Article in accordance with relevant decisions of the Conference of the Parties; and

(g) give full consideration, in implementing the commitments under this Article, to Article 4, paragraph 8, of the Convention.

Article 11

1   In the implementation of Article 10, Parties shall take into account the provisions of Article 4, paragraphs 4, 5, 7, 8 and 9, of the Convention.

2   In the context of the implementation of Article 4, paragraph 1, of the Convention, in accordance with the provisions of Article 4, paragraph 3, and Article 11 of the Convention, and through the entity or entities entrusted with the operation of the financial mechanism of the Convention, the developed country Parties and other developed Parties included in Annex II to the Convention shall:

(a) provide new and additional financial resources to meet the agreed full costs incurred by developing country Parties in advancing the implementation of existing commitments under Article 4, paragraph 1(a), of the Convention that are covered in Article 10, sub-paragraph (a); and

(b) also provide such financial resources, including for the transfer of technology, needed by the developing country Parties to meet the agreed full incremental costs of advancing the implementation of existing commitments under Article 4, paragraph 1, of the Convention that are covered by Article 10 and that are agreed between a developing country Party and the international entity or entities referred to in Article 11 of the Convention, in accordance with that Article.

The implementation of these existing commitments shall take into account the need for adequacy and predictability in the flow of funds and the importance of appropriate burden sharing among developed country Parties. The guidance to the entity or entities entrusted with the operation of the financial mechanism of the Convention in relevant decisions of the Conference of the Parties, including those agreed before the adoption of this Protocol, shall apply *mutatis mutandis* to the provisions of this paragraph.

3   The developed country Parties and other developed Parties in Annex II to the Convention may also provide, and developing country Parties avail themselves of, financial resources for the implementation of Article 10, through bilateral, regional and other multilateral channels.

Article 12

1   A clean development mechanism is hereby defined.

2   The purpose of the clean development mechanism shall be to assist Parties not included in Annex I in achieving sustainable development and in contributing to the ultimate objective of the Convention, and to assist Parties included in Annex I in achieving compliance with their quantified emission limitation and reduction commitments under Article 3.

3   Under the clean development mechanism:

(a) Parties not included in Annex I will benefit from project activities resulting in certified emission reductions; and

(b) Parties included in Annex I may use the certified emission reductions accruing from such project activities to contribute to compliance with part of their quantified emission limitation and reduction commitments under Article 3, as determined by the Conference of the Parties serving as the meeting of the Parties to this Protocol.

4   The clean development mechanism shall be subject to the authority and guidance of the Conference of the Parties serving as the meeting of the Parties to this Protocol and be supervised by an executive board of the clean development mechanism.

5   Emission reductions resulting from each project activity shall be certified by operational entities to be designated by the Conference of the Parties serving as the meeting of the Parties to this Protocol, on the basis of:

    (a) voluntary participation approved by each Party involved;

    (b) real, measurable, and long-term benefits related to the mitigation of climate change; and

    (c) reductions in emissions that are additional to any that would occur in the absence of the certified project activity.

6   The clean development mechanism shall assist in arranging funding of certified project activities as necessary.

7   The Conference of the Parties serving as the meeting of the Parties to this Protocol shall, at its first session, elaborate modalities and procedures with the objective of ensuring transparency, efficiency and accountability through independent auditing and verification of project activities.

8   The Conference of the Parties serving as the meeting of the Parties to this Protocol shall ensure that a share of the proceeds from certified project activities is used to cover administrative expenses as well as to assist developing country Parties that are particularly vulnerable to the adverse effects of climate change to meet the costs of adaptation.

9   Participation under the clean development mechanism, including in activities mentioned in paragraph 3(a) above and in the acquisition of certified emission reductions, may involve private and/or public entities, and is to be subject to whatever guidance may be provided by the executive board of the clean development mechanism.

10   Certified emission reductions obtained during the period from the year 2000 up to the beginning of the first commitment period can be used to assist in achieving compliance in the first commitment period.

[Articles 13–14 omitted.]

Article 15

1   The Subsidiary Body for Scientific and Technological Advice and the Subsidiary Body for Implementation established by Articles 9 and 10 of the Convention shall serve as, respectively, the Subsidiary Body for Scientific and Technological Advice and the Subsidiary Body for Implementation of this Protocol. [...]

[Paragraphs 2–3 omitted.]

[Articles 16–28 omitted.]

Annex A

Greenhouse gases

Carbon dioxide (CO_2)

Methane (CH_4)

Nitrous oxide (N_2O)

Hydrofluorocarbons (HFCs)

Perfluorocarbons (PFCs)

Sulphur hexafluoride (SF_6)

Sectors/source categories

Energy

Fuel combustion

Energy industries

Manufacturing industries and construction

Transport

Other sectors

Other

Fugitive emissions from fuels

Solid fuels

Oil and natural gas

Other

Industrial processes

Mineral products

Chemical industry

Metal production

Other production

Production of halocarbons and sulphur hexafluoride

Consumption of halocarbons and sulphur hexafluoride

Other

Solvent and other product use

Agriculture

Enteric fermentation

Manure management

Rice cultivation

Agricultural soils

Prescribed burning of savannas

Field burning of agricultural residues

Other

Waste

Solid waste disposal on land

Wastewater handling

Waste incineration

Other

Annex B

Party Quantified emission limitation or reduction commitment

(percentage of base year or period)

Australia 108

Austria 92

Belgium 92

Bulgaria* 92

Canada 94

Croatia* 95

Czech Republic* 92

Denmark 92

Estonia* 92

European Community 92

Finland 92

France 92

Germany 92

Greece 92

Hungary* 94

Iceland 110

Ireland 92

Italy 92

Japan 94

Latvia* 92

Liechtenstein 92

Lithuania* 92

Luxembourg 92

Monaco 92

Netherlands 92

New Zealand 100

Norway 101

Poland* 94

Portugal 92

Romania* 92

Russian Federation* 100

Slovakia* 92

Slovenia* 92

Spain 92

Sweden 92

Switzerland 92

Ukraine* 100

United Kingdom of Great Britain and Northern Ireland 92

United States of America 93

*   Countries that are undergoing the process of transition to a market economy.

Convention on Long-range Transboundary Air Pollution (LRTAP) and related protocols 1979[14]

The 1979 Geneva Convention for the Control of Long-range Transboundary Air Pollution (LRTAP), which entered into force in 1983, was the outcome of protracted East-West negotiations in the wake of the environmental chapter of the Final Act of the 1975 Helsinki Conference on Security and Co-operation in Europe (CSCE). It was one of the first treaties to recognise the adverse effects of air pollution over the short and long term (Sands (1995) 248) and is still the only treaty example of major regional co-operation in the prevention and control of transboundary air pollution that results, *inter alia*, in acid rain precipitation.

This Convention was concluded within the regional framework of the UN Economic Commission for Europe (UNECE), which covers the whole of the European region from the Atlantic coast to the former Soviet Union, the Balkan States and Turkey. UNECE has 54 Member States, including the USA and Canada.

In laying down general principles for international co-operation on the abatement of air pollution LRTAP builds on both the principle laid down in the *Trail Smelter* case (mentioned above, p 94), as well as Principle 21 of the 1972 Stockholm Declaration. Since entering into force in 1983, the Convention has been supplemented by several Protocols which lay down more specific commitments:

---

14   18 ILM (1979) 1442.

- The 1984 Geneva Protocol on Long-term Financing of the Co-operative Programme for Monitoring and Evaluation of the Long-range Transmission of Air Pollutants in Europe (EMEP) (see 24 ILM (1985) 484) commits Parties to making annual contributions to the EMEP budget, *inter alia*, to support a monitoring network. The Protocol was ratified by the UK in August 1985 and entered into force on 28 January 1988.

- The 1985 Helsinki Protocol on the Reduction of Sulphur Emissions or Their Transboundary Fluxes (see 27 ILM (1988) 707) commits Parties to a 30% cut in total SO_2 emissions by 1993, using 1980 levels as a basis. The Protocol entered into force on 2 September 1987. The UK did not become a Party, although it did achieve a 37% cut in sulphur emissions by the end of 1993.

- The 1988 Sofia Protocol concerning the Control of Emissions of Nitrogen Oxides or Their Transboundary Fluxes (see 28 ILM (1989) 212) committed the Parties to a freeze of national emissions at 1987 levels by 1994, together with a package of abatement measures. The UK ratified the Protocol in October 1990 and it entered into force on 14 February 1991.

- The 1991 Geneva Protocol concerning the Control of Emissions of Volatile Organic Compounds or Their Transboundary Fluxes (see 31 ILM (1992) 568) will commit Parties to secure a 30% reduction in VOC emissions from 1988 levels by 1999. Ratified by the UK in June 1994, the Protocol came into force on 29 October 1997.

- The second Protocol on the Further Reduction of Sulphur Emissions was adopted in Oslo in 1994 (see 33 ILM (1994) 1540). This requires different percentage reductions from Parties depending in part on the quality of their emissions and takes into account the nature of the impact upon the environment, based upon the concept of critical loads. It requires the UK to make reductions in sulphur emissions of 80% of 1980 levels by 2010. The Protocol is now in force (as of 5 August 1998) with 21 States Parties as of 1999.

- Apart from the above Protocols, all of which have now entered into force, the Parties to the 1979 Convention have negotiated two other Protocols on Heavy Metals and Persistent Organic Pollutants (POPs), respectively. Both of these new Protocols were adopted on 24 June 1998 by 33 States of the UN Economic Commission for Europe (ECE) region and the European Community. The full texts of these Protocols can be found at www.unece.org/env/protocol/98hm.htm,
and www.unece.org/env/protocol/98pop.htm respectively. So far (as of 1999) only Canada has ratified these Protocols.

- The main provisions of the Heavy Metals Protocol include: (1) reduction/stabilisation of emissions with 1990 levels as the base, using mandatory emission limit values for eleven major categories of heavy metals; (2) the application of Best Available Technologies (BAT) in both new and existing installations; (3) mandatory product requirements, for example phasing out lead in petrol and mercury in batteries.

- The main provisions of the POPs Protocol include: (1) Restrictions on the use of four substances and the elimination of production and use of eleven other substances with exports allowed only for the purpose of environmentally sound destruction (see Basel Convention, 1989 in Chapter 4, below); (2) the reduction and/or stabilisation of annual emissions from individual countries at levels to be specified upon ratification; (3) the application of BAT for three substances from major source categories and/or mandatory emission limit values.

- The most recent Protocol adopted by the LRTAP Convention Parties is the Gothenburg Protocol to Abate Acidification, Eutrophication and Ground-Level Ozone. The full text of the Protocol and its Annexes can be found at www.unece.org/env/eb. Twenty-seven States have signed the Protocol, although the European Community has refrained from doing so. This Protocol aims to reduce pollutants linked to acidification, eutrophication, and ground-level ozone, namely nitrogen oxide (NOx), ammonia (NH_3) and VOCs. These pollutants have already been addressed individually under the 1988 and 1991 Protocols, respectively. The Gothenburg Protocol adopts a multi-pollutant/multi-effect approach addressing the interdependence between the three pollutants described above, as well as the extent to which sulphur (currently addressed by the 1985 and 1994 Protocols) is involved. Like the 1994 Sulphur Protocol and the 1991 VOCs Protocol, the present Protocol is based on the critical load and critical level concepts, respectively. These are further defined in an Annex to the Protocol. If successfully implemented, this Protocol could result in reduced sulphur dioxide emissions by 63%, NOx emissions by 41%, VOCs emissions by 40%, and ammonia (NH_3) by 17%, by 2010, as measured from their 1990 levels.

- Finally, an important and progressive institutional development of the LRTAP treaty structure is the establishment of an Implementation Committee whose main function is to review periodically compliance by the Parties with the reporting requirements of the Protocols.

The edited text of the Convention and further commentary on the Protocols follows below.

CONVENTION ON LONG-RANGE TRANSBOUNDARY AIR POLLUTION (1979)

Entered into force: 16 March 1983

THE PARTIES TO THE PRESENT CONVENTION,

...

Recognising the contribution of the Economic Commission for Europe to the multilateral implementation of the pertinent provisions of the Final Act of the Conference on Security and Co-operation in Europe,

Cognisant of the references in the chapter on environment of the Final Act of the Conference on Security and Co-operation in Europe calling for co-operation to control air pollution and its effects, including long-range transport of air pollutants, and to the development through international co-operation of an extensive programme for the monitoring and evaluation of long-range transport of air pollutants, starting with sulphur dioxide and with possible extension to other pollutants,

Considering the pertinent provisions of the Declaration of the United Nations Conference on the Human Environment, and in particular Principle 21, which expresses the common conviction that states have, in accordance with the Charter of the United Nations and the principles of international law, the sovereign right to exploit their own resources pursuant to their own environmental policies, and the responsibility to ensure that activities within their jurisdiction or control do not cause damage to the environment of other states or of areas beyond the limits of national jurisdiction,

Recognising the existence of possible adverse effects, in the short and long term, of air pollution including transboundary air pollution,

Concerned that a rise in the level of emission of air pollutants within the region as forecast may increase such adverse effects,

Recognising the need to study the implications of the long-range transport of air pollutants and the need to seek solutions for the problems identified,

Affirming their willingness to reinforce active international co-operation to develop appropriate national policies and by means of exchange of information, consultation, research and monitoring, to co-ordinate national action for combating air pollution including long-range transboundary air pollution,

HAVE AGREED AS FOLLOWS:

Definitions

Article 1

For the purpose of the present Convention:

(a) 'air pollution' means the introduction by man, directly or indirectly, of substances or energy into the air resulting in deleterious effects of such a nature as to endanger humans, harm living resources and eco-systems and material property and impair or interfere with amenities and other legitimate uses of the environment, and 'air pollutants' shall be construed accordingly;

Note:

It has been suggested that the definition of 'air pollution' is broad enough to include even atmospheric emissions of greenhouse gases (see Framework Convention on Climate Change 1992, above) and ozone depleting substances (covered by the 1985 Convention for the Protection of the Ozone Layer and the 1987 Protocol on Substances that Deplete the Ozone Layer) as 'air pollutants'. The word 'resulting' however suggests that actual damage or harm must have occurred before air pollution can be adjudged to have taken place. It has been argued that this appears to rule out the possibility of precautionary action or measures against any gaseous emissions, where no actual harm has occurred, on the basis that these emissions cannot be considered 'air pollutants', under the terms of this definition (Sands (1995) 249).

On the other hand, it has been noted that a much broader definition of what constitutes 'air pollution' is used, comparable to those found in marine pollution conventions, and which includes endangering human health, causing harm to living resources and eco-systems and interfering with amenities and other legitimate uses of the environment (Birnie and Boyle (1992) 398). Unlike more recent definitions of 'pollution' however this one does not include the word 'likely', thereby again precluding any interpretation that might allow the use of precautionary measures to combat such pollution, where harm is 'likely' to occur.

(b) 'long-range transboundary air pollution' means air pollution whose physical origin is situated wholly or in part within the area under the national jurisdiction of one state and which has adverse effects in the area under the jurisdiction of another state at such a distance that it is not generally possible to distinguish the contribution of individual emission sources or groups of sources.

Notes:

1   Despite the reference in the official title of the Convention to 'transboundary' air pollution, many of its provisions refer more broadly to 'air pollution, including transboundary air pollution'. Thus, these provisions are not restricted to acid rain only but also other types of widely dispersed pollutants within the region. Nor are they only confined to harm to human health or property. As Lammers notes: '(T)hey do not purport to protect merely certain specific interests against air pollution, but in fact all interests which could be detrimentally affected by such pollution' (Lammers (1991) 268). Amelioration of a wide range of potential harm is thus the treaty's basic objective (Birnie and Boyle (1992) 398).

2   The phrase 'air pollution, including transboundary air pollution' (see Art 2, below) also precludes the need to provide proof of the transboundary nature of such pollution, once it has been detected.

Fundamental Principles

Article 2

The Contracting Parties, taking due account of the facts and problems involved, are determined to protect man and his environment against air pollution and shall endeavour to limit and, as far as possible, gradually reduce and prevent air pollution including long-range transboundary air pollution.

Notes:

1   This provision has been labelled a 'soft commitment', without clear goals or objectives and detailed schedules for the reduction of various emissions contributing to air pollution (Sands (1995) 249). As Birnie and Boyle also note, '(N)o concrete commitments to specific reductions in air pollution are contained in the treaty itself' (Birnie and Boyle (1992) 398), but are set out in the Protocols referred to below, pp 131 and 140.

2   However, the provision does at least have the merit of setting down a general limitation on the right to emit atmospheric pollutants (Sands (1995) 249).

Article 3

The Contracting Parties, within the framework of the present Convention, shall by means of exchanges of information, consultation, research and monitoring, develop without undue delay policies and strategies which shall serve as a means of combating the discharge of air pollutants, taking into account efforts already made at national and international levels.

Note:

The Parties have committed themselves only to broad principles and objectives for pollution control policy in the treaty, leaving a great deal of latitude to determine what level of effort they will put into pollution control and what cost they are willing to pay in overall economic development. The Convention as a whole does however provide a framework for co-operation and development of further pollution control measures (Birnie and Boyle (1992) 398–99). This framework is being implemented through the adoption of the Protocols referred to below.

Article 4

The Contracting Parties shall exchange information on and review their policies, scientific activities and technical measures aimed at combating, as far as possible, the discharge of air pollutants, which may have adverse effects, thereby contributing to the reduction of air pollution including long-range transboundary air pollution.

Note:

> This is now almost a standard procedural requirement in many environmental treaty regimes. The duty to exchange information does not appear to extend to any requirement to harmonise policies and measures adopted by States Parties in order to fulfil their reduction targets.

Article 5

Consultations shall be held, upon request, at an early stage between, on the one hand, Contracting Parties which are actually affected by or exposed to a significant risk of long-range transboundary air pollution and, on the other hand, Contracting Parties within which and subject to whose jurisdiction a significant contribution to long-range transboundary air pollution originates, or could originate, in connexion with activities carried on or contemplated therein.

Note:

> Article 5 enshrines a duty to consult rather than merely to notify. Obligations to notify and consult are fairly common among environmental instruments attempting to regulate potentially hazardous, transboundary activities and can be traced back to the general duty owed by any State to other States under Principle 21 of Stockholm. It may be argued that the duty to consult in this case is more onerous than a duty simply to notify. This suggests that a more extended dialogue should take place with a view to mitigating the actual or potential damage caused. Here also it is important to note a precautionary element to the obligation in that the requirement to consult needs to be fulfilled even if no Contracting Party has actually been affected by transboundary air pollution, provided a 'significant' risk exists.

Air Quality Management

Article 6

Taking into account Articles 2 to 5, the ongoing research, exchange of information and monitoring and the results thereof, the cost and effectiveness of local and other remedies and, in order to combat air pollution, in particular that originating from new or rebuilt installations, each Contracting Party undertakes to develop the best policies and strategies including air quality management systems, and, as part of them, control measures compatible with balanced development, in particular by using the best available technology which is economically feasible and low and non-waste technology.

Research and Development

Article 7

The Contracting Parties, as appropriate to their needs, shall initiate and co-operate in the conduct of research into and/or development of:

(a) existing and proposed technologies for reducing emissions of sulphur compounds and other major air pollutants, including technical and economic feasibility, and environmental consequences;

(b) instrumentation and other techniques for monitoring and measuring emission rates and ambient concentrations of air pollutants;

(c) improved models for a better understanding of the transmission of long-range transboundary air pollutants;

(d) the effects of sulphur compounds and other major air pollutants on human health and the environment, including agriculture, forestry, materials, aquatic and other natural eco-systems and visibility, with a view to establishing a scientific basis for dose/effect relationships designed to protect the environment;

(e) the economic, social and environmental assessment of alternative measures for attaining environmental objectives including the reduction of long-range transboundary air pollution;

(f) education and training programmes related to the environmental aspects of pollution by sulphur compounds and other major air pollutants.

Exchange of Information

Article 8

The Contracting Parties, within the framework of the Executive Body referred to in Article 10 and bilaterally, shall, in their common interests, exchange available information on:

(a) data on emission at periods of time to be agreed upon, of agreed air pollutants, starting with sulphur dioxide, coming from grid-units of agreed size or on the fluxes of agreed air pollutants, starting with sulphur dioxide, across national borders, at distances and at periods of time to be agreed upon;

(b) major changes in national policies and in general industrial development, and their potential impact, which would be likely to cause significant changes in long-range transboundary air pollution;

(c) control technologies for reducing air pollution relevant to long-range transboundary air pollution;

(d) the projected cost of the emission control or sulphur compounds and other major air pollutants on a national scale;

(e) meteorological and physico-chemical data relating to the processes during transmission;

(f) physico-chemical and biological data relating to the effects of long-range transboundary air pollution and the extent of the damage which these data indicate can be attributed to long-range transboundary air pollution;

(g) national, sub-regional and regional policies and strategies for the control of sulphur compounds and other major oil pollutants.

Notes:

1 This treaty Article may be seen as an elaboration of the general provision for the exchange of information between Contracting Parties in Article 4. It encompasses much more than merely information on measures for combating air pollution, incorporating

emissions data, information on technological and financial cost issues in pollution control, and even major policy changes.

2. Article 8 also provides an institution within which the information exchange required between Contracting Parties can take place, namely, the Executive Body established under Article 10.

Implementation and Further Development of the Co-operative Programme for the Monitoring and Evaluation of the Long-range Transmission of Air Pollutants in Europe

Article 9

The Contracting Parties stress the need for the implementation of the existing 'Co-operative programme for the monitoring and evaluation of the long-range transmission of air pollutants in Europe' (hereinafter referred to as EMEP) and with regard to the further development of this programme, agree to emphasise:

(a) the desirability of Contracting Parties joining in and fully implementing EMEP which, as a first step, is based on the monitoring of sulphur dioxide and related substances;

(b) the need to use comparable or standardised procedures for monitoring whenever possible;

(c) the desirability of basing the monitoring programme on the framework of both national and international programmes. The establishment of monitoring stations and the collection of data shall be carried out under the national jurisdiction of the country in which the monitoring stations are located;

(d) the desirability of establishing a framework for a co-operative environmental monitoring programme, based on and taking into account present and future national, sub-regional, regional and other international programmes;

(e) the need to exchange data on emissions at periods of time to be agreed upon, of agreed air pollutants, starting with sulphur dioxide, coming from grid-units of agreed size; or on the fluxes of agreed air pollutants, starting with sulphur dioxide, across national borders, at distances and at periods of time to be agreed upon. The method, including the model, used to determine the fluxes as well as the method, including the model, used to determine the transmission of air pollutants, based on the emissions per grid-unit, shall be made available and periodically reviewed, in order to improve the methods and the models;

(f) their willingness to continue the exchange and periodic updating of national data on total emissions of agreed air pollutants, starting with sulphur dioxide;

(g) the need to provide meteorological and physico-chemical data relating to processes during transmission;

(h) the need to monitor chemical components in other media such as water, soil and vegetation, as well as a similar monitoring programme to record effects on health and environment;

(i) the desirability of extending the national EMEP networks to make them operational for control and surveillance purposes.

Note:

The provisions of this Article are also important for the future progress of this regional environmental regime. They require the Parties to continue their current co-operation in the European-wide monitoring and evaluation programme (EMEP) with a view to strengthening institutional linkages, establishing standardised monitoring procedures, and providing better, more complete data and exchanges of information as required by previous Convention Articles (Arts 3, 4, 5, 6, 7, and 8).

Executive Body

Article 10

1   The representatives of the Contracting Parties shall, within the framework of the Senior Advisers to ESE Governments on Environmental Problems, constitute the Executive Body of the present Convention, and shall meet at least annually in that capacity.

2   The Executive Body shall:

(a) review the implementation of the present Convention;

(b) establish, as appropriate, working groups to consider matters related to the implementation and development of the present Convention and to this end to prepare appropriate studies and other documentation and to submit recommendations to be considered by the Executive Body;

(c) fulfil such other functions as may be appropriate under the provisions of the present Convention.

3   The Executive Body shall utilise the Steering Body for the EMEP to play an integral part in the operation of the present Convention, in particular with regard to data collection and scientific co-operation.

4   The Executive Body, in discharging its functions, shall, when it deems appropriate, also make use of information from other relevant international organisations.

Note:

Another important facet of this Convention is in the provision of an institutional capacity, in the form of a pro-active Executive Body to review both progress in the implementation of the Convention, and facilitate proposals for recommendations to improve the operation of the Convention and its Protocols.

Secretariat

Article 11

The Executive Secretary of the Economic Commission for Europe shall carry out, for the Executive Body, the following secretariat functions:

(a) to convene and prepare the meetings of the Executive Body;

(b) to transmit to the Contracting Parties reports and other information received in accordance with the provisions of the present Convention;

(c) to discharge the functions assigned by the Executive Body.

Amendments to The Convention

Article 12

1   Any Contracting Party may propose amendments to the present convention.

2   The text of proposed amendments shall be submitted in writing to the Executive Secretary of the Economic Commission for Europe, who shall communicate them to all

Contracting Parties. The Executive Body shall discuss proposed amendments at its next annual meeting provided that such proposals have been circulated by the Executive Secretary of the Economic Commission for Europe to the Contracting Parties at least ninety days in advance.

3   An amendment to the present Convention shall be adopted by consensus of the representatives of the Contracting Parties, and shall enter into force for the Contracting Parties which have accepted it on the ninetieth day after the date on which two-thirds of the Contracting Parties have deposited their instruments of acceptance with the depositary. Thereafter, the amendment shall enter into force for any other Contracting Party on the ninetieth day after the date on which that Contracting Party deposits its instrument of acceptance of the amendment.

Settlement of Disputes

Article 13

If a dispute arises between two or more Contracting Parties to the present Convention as to the interpretation or application of the Convention, they shall seek a solution by negotiation or by any other method of dispute settlement acceptable to the Parties to the dispute.

Notes:

1   Unlike several other international environmental instruments that we shall be examining in the course of this book, the text of the Convention does not provide for an elaborate or even extended system of dispute settlement between Parties, preferring instead a general requirement that the disputing Parties resolve their disputes by negotiation or any other means acceptable to the Parties.

2   The lack of provision of specific dispute settlement mechanisms in the Convention is belied however by the relatively high level of institutionalisation, in the form of the monitoring and evaluation programme (EMEP), the Conference of the Parties (CoP) and the Executive Body that is present within this regime. Together with the extensive information exchange and consultation requirements provided in the Convention (discussed above), it may be concluded that the Parties to the Convention do not lack fora within which to voice any differences that they may have with each other. Nevertheless, the lack of formal procedures for dispute settlement in the Convention itself may prove important in the future.

3   The Protocols to the Convention however have provided for a more comprehensive system of dispute settlement between their Parties. For example, Article 9 of the 1994 Oslo Protocol on Further Reductions to Sulphur Emissions lays down several methods of dispute settlement, including submission to the International Court of Justice, arbitration and conciliation, in addition to negotiation or any other peaceful means, which are already provided for in the Convention text.

[Articles 14 (on Signature), 15 (on Ratification, Acceptance, Approval and Accession), 16 (on Entry into Force), 17 (on Withdrawal) and 18 (on Authentic Texts) omitted.]

Done at Geneva, this thirteenth day of November, one thousand nine hundred and seventy-nine.

Monitoring and Evaluation Protocol 1984

This first Protocol to the 1979 LRTAP Convention seeks to ensure the availability of adequate financial resources to implement the co-operative programme on monitoring and evaluation of transboundary air pollution in Europe (EMEP). It provides for financing the costs of the international centres co-operating within EMEP on the basis of mandatory contributions covering the annual costs of the EMEP work programme, supplemented by voluntary contributions (Arts 2 and 3). The basis for the annual contributions is set out in Art 4 and the Annex.

Sulphur Protocols 1985 and 1994

The second Protocol to the LRTAP Convention was adopted in response to evidence of widespread damage in parts of Europe and North America to natural resources, and to historical monuments and human health, caused by acidification of the environment from sulphur dioxides, nitrogen oxides and other pollutants from the combustion of fossil fuels. The 1985 Protocol established a 'Thirty Per Cent Club' by committing all Parties to a 30% reduction in their national annual sulphur emissions by 1993 at the latest, using 1980 levels as a basis. This inflexible approach to standard-setting has not been adopted in the subsequent protocols to this Convention because it fails to take account of the present and historic emissions and other differentials (Sands (1995) 251), such as local variations in pollution levels (Birnie and Boyle (1992) 400). Article 3 of the 1985 Protocol envisages further, more stringent reduction targets. These were duly introduced in the 1994 Oslo Protocol, in the form of sulphur emission percentage reductions, emission ceilings and a timetable for these objectives in Annex II (Art 2.2), as well as committing Parties to ensuring in the long term that depositions do not exceed critical loads specified in Annex I (Art 2.1). These specific standard setting measures stand in contrast to the more generally worded 'soft' obligations in the main text of the Convention itself, but may be used as evidence of the ability of a general framework type treaty regime to develop specific commitments within its terms and through the institutions it establishes (Birnie and Boyle (1992) 401).

The 1985 Protocol requires Parties to report annually to the Executive Body of the Convention on their national annual sulphur emissions (Arts 4 and 6). The Protocol also provides for the use of the institutional organs established under the Convention. For EC Member States, the 1985 Protocol has been superseded by the Large Combustion Plants Directive 88/609 (Sands (1995) 251) (see also p 155, below).

Nitrogen Oxides Protocol 1988

The third Protocol on Nitrogen Oxides is more comprehensive and flexible than the 1985 Protocol. It requires the reduction of 'total annual emissions', introducing into international law the concepts of 'national emission standards' and 'critical loads' (Sands (1995) 251). The 1988 Protocol specifically requires Parties to stabilise their nitrogen oxides emissions at the latest by 31 December 1994, using 1987 as the basis (Art 2.1). All Parties must apply national emissions standards to both major stationary sources, such as power plants and mobile sources, such as vehicle emissions (Art 2.2(a), (b) and (c)). Its approach to the co-ordination of national measures is more sophisticated than the Sulphur Protocol, however, requiring Parties to assume the use of best available technology which is economically feasible when setting national emissions standards and the eventual negotiation of internationally accepted 'critical loads' for nitrogen oxides pollution (Birnie and Boyle (1992) 401). The Parties were required to begin negotiations towards taking additional measures within six months of the Protocol entering into force. They were required to establish critical loads, reductions based on the critical loads, as well as measures to achieve these reductions and a time table for such reductions, by 1 January 1996 (Art 2.3(b)). Moreover, Parties are free to adopt more stringent measures than those required by Art 2 (Art 2(4)) (Sands (1995) 252). This approach is likely to be more suited to regional environmental protection than the flat-rate emissions reductions of the Sulphur Protocol, but whether it works in practice will depend on the ability of the Parties to reach agreement on the necessary control measures (Birnie and Boyle (1992) 401).

The Protocol is implemented under the authority of the institutions of the LRTAP Convention. This is most significant in terms of the requirement within the Protocol for Parties to report annually to the Executive Body on obligations under the Protocol, including, in particular, levels of national annual emissions, progress in applying national emission standards and introducing pollution control measures, in making unleaded fuel widely available, and in establishing critical loads (Arts 6, 7 and 8) (Sands (1995) 252).

Volatile Organic Compounds Protocol 1991

The fourth Protocol addresses the problem of volatile organic compounds (VOCs) which are mainly emitted through incomplete combustion of fossil fuels in the engines of on-road motor vehicles. In keeping with the developing complexity and sophistication of the earlier protocols, the 1991 VOC Protocol establishes specific targets and timetables committing Parties to control and reduce their emissions of VOCs. Unlike the earlier protocols, the Parties to this one have a choice of at least three ways to meet this requirement, to be specified upon signature. This reflects the realisation of the need to adopt differentiated commitments based upon a Party's emissions and particular geographic and demographic circumstances. The main target is for Parties to introduce measures to reduce their national annual emissions of VOCs by at least 30% by the year 1999, using 1988 levels as a basis (Art 2.2(a)) (Sands (1995) 253).

No later than the date when the Protocol enters into force, each Party must apply appropriate national or international emission standards to new stationary sources based on 'the best available technologies which are economically feasible', and apply national or international measures to products that contain solvents and promote the use of labelling of products specifying their VOC content (Art 2.3(a)(i) and (ii)). Within the same time frame, the Parties must 'apply appropriate national or international emission standards to new mobile sources based on best available technologies which are economically feasible', and encourage further public participation in emission control programmes, as well as the best use of all modes of transport and the promotion of traffic management schemes (Art 2.3(a)(iii) and (iv)) (Sands (1995) 254).

Within six months of the entry into force of the Protocol, the Parties are required to begin negotiations on further steps to reduce national annual emissions of VOCs. They must also co-operate to develop, *inter alia*, control strategies; ensure cost-effectiveness, possibly through the use of economic instruments; and adopt measures and a timetable for achieving such further reductions, commencing no later than 1 January 2000 (Arts 2.6 and 2.7). As in the previous protocols, Parties are free to take more stringent measures (Art 3.1). The Protocol also provides for exchange of technology, research and monitoring, regular review of its implementation in national programmes, policies and strategies (Arts 4–7). Implementation of the Protocol's obligations will be verified by the exchange of information and annual reporting requirements; alternatively the Parties undertake to establish a 'mechanism for monitoring compliance' with the Protocol (Arts 3.3 and 8). Once again, the Protocol makes use of the institutions established under the 1979 LRTAP Convention (Sands (1995) 254–55).

Vienna Convention for the Protection of the Ozone Layer 1985 and its Montreal Protocol 1987[15]

The 1985 Vienna Convention for the Protection of the Ozone Layer and its 1987 Montreal Protocol were a response to the increasing concern over the threat posed to the ozone layer due to emissions of certain chlorofluorocarbons used in aerosols and refrigeration. It was recognised that failure to protect the ozone layer posed a threat both to human health and the environment in general. The Convention has been described as an 'empty framework requiring more specific measures to deal with the problem'. (Birnie and Boyle, 211). These authors do however stress two features of the Convention. First that it is concerned with the global environment reflecting its intrinsic value independent of its utility to humans. Secondly they point out that the Convention was an early example of the precautionary approach in so far as it was adopted in advance of firm scientific proof of actual harm to the ozone layer. The Montreal Protocol sets out specific provisions for the control of ozone damaging chemicals while recognising the legitimate needs of developing States. (See further Regulation 2037/00, p 150, below.)

EUROPEAN COMMUNITY LAW

The EC is a signatory to the international treaties referred to above[16] and as such plays a major role in co-ordinating the air pollution strategies of Member States. Most EC legislation in this area dates from the 1980s and is somewhat fragmented in form, reflecting the various sources and types of pollution which affect the atmosphere. Two principal regulatory techniques are used. One focuses upon controlling emissions from particular sources, such as vehicles or industrial plants. The other sets air quality

---

15 See www.unep.org/ozone/home.htm. See also 26 ILM (1985) 1529 (Vienna) and 26 ILM (1987) 1550 (Montreal).

16 Geneva Convention on Long-range Transboundary Air Pollution (p 130, above); Vienna Convention for the Protection of the Ozone Layer and Montreal Protocol 1985; UN Framework Convention on Climate Change 1992 (pp 95, 101, above); Kyoto Protocol (pp 96, 120, above).

standards which Member States are required to meet whatever the source of the pollution. In the former case, it is relatively easy to identify and penalise those who breach emission standards. This is not so easy in the case of air quality standards which may be infringed by a combination of industrial activities and domestic fires. The only sanction is that the offending State would be answerable to the European Commission for failing to comply with EC law (see p 8, above).

Before considering the legal controls on the various types of pollutant and sources of pollution, it may be noted that by virtue of the Kyoto Protocol (above) the EC is now committed to a target of an 8% reduction in greenhouse gases by 2010. In June 1998, the Environment Council reached agreement as to how the Community is to achieve this target. Each Member State has been allocated targets under the so-called 'burden-sharing' agreement as follows:-

Belgium	-	7.5%	Italy	-	6.5%
Denmark	-	21%	Luxembourg	-	28%
Germany	-	21%	Netherlands	-	6%
Greece	+	25%	Austria	-	13%
Spain	+	15%	Portugal	+	27%
France		0%	Finland		0%
Iceland	+	13%	Sweden	+	4%
UK	-	12.5%			

Until the Kyoto Protocol comes into force this is a political agreement only, not a binding legal commitment. There is therefore no sanction against a Member State which fails to meet its target.

The following sections consider the EC Directives on Sulphur, Nitrogen Dioxide and Lead in Air. Several Directives (80/779 – Sulphur; 85/203 – Nitrogen Dioxide; and 82/884 – Lead) will be repealed in stages commencing 19 July 2001 by Art 9, Directive 99/30 (see p 170, below). The following provides commentary on these Directives, but their text is omitted.

Sulphur in air

Sulphur is a threat to human health and a major source of 'acid rain'. Several directives are aimed specifically at protecting human health and the environment by controlling levels of sulphur in the atmosphere.

The Directive on the Sulphur Content of Certain Liquid Fuels 75/716 introduced fuel composition standards for 'gas oil' which is fuel used mainly for domestic heating and cooking and for diesel engined motor vehicles. It does not cover the fuel oil which is used by industry and in power stations. The aim was to limit Sulphur pollution from this source by reducing the amount contained in the fuel in the first place, and also eliminating barriers to trade by the existence of different standards for gas oil in different States. The 1975 Directive has been amended over the years by the introduction of stricter standards. The current restrictions are now contained in the Directive on the Sulphur Content of Certain Liquid Fuels 93/12, the Directive Relating to the Quality of Petrol and

Diesel Fuels 98/70 (amending 93/12) and supplemented (in the context of heavy fuel and gas oil) by the Directive on the Reduction of the Sulphur Content of Certain Liquid Fuels 99/32. This latter Directive requires that by 1 January 2003 Member States must take all necessary steps to ensure that heavy fuel oils are not used within their territory if their Sulphur content exceeds 1% by mass.

The Directive on Air Quality Limit Values for Sulphur Dioxide and Suspended Particulates 80/779 was the first instance of community-wide legislation laying down mandatory air quality standards. The specific combination of sulphur dioxide and suspended particulates (smoke) is said to be particularly dangerous to human health[17] which explains their being dealt with in the one directive. The Directive sets 'limit' and 'guide' values for concentrations of these substances at ground level for different periods of the year in order to protect human health and the environment. The limit values for smoke (80 microgrammes per cubic metre over a year with a peak limit of 250 microgrammes) had a mandatory compliance date of 1993. The sulphur dioxide (SO_2) limits vary according to the measure of smoke – where the level of smoke is low, permitted levels of SO_2 may increase. Member States are obliged to move towards the more stringent guide values which are set out in Annex II. The Directive incorporates (Art 3) what is known as the 'standstill principle' which provides that air quality is not to be allowed to deteriorate significantly even in areas where pollution is well below the limit values.[18] In order to ensure compliance with the Directive, Member States are required to establish monitoring stations, particularly in zones where the limits are likely to be exceeded (Art 6). The Directive is to be fully repealed by January 2005 under the provisions of Directive 99/30, Art 9 (see p 170, below). Directive 99/30 will then contain the relevant law.

Nitrogen dioxide in air

Nitrogen dioxide is a primary component of acid rain. The Directive on Air Quality Standards for Nitrogen Dioxide 85/203 is intended to protect human health as well as the environment. It requires Member States to take necessary measures to ensure that concentrations of nitrogen dioxide in the atmosphere of their territories do not exceed the limit values specified in Annex I – 200 microgrammes per cubic metre. They must establish measuring stations in zones where limit values are likely to be exceeded (Art 4) and Members States may set stricter limits than those required by the Directive (Art 5). Long-term, non-obligatory guide values appear in Annex II. The Directive is to be repealed by January 2010 under the provisions of Directive 99/30, Art 9. Directive 99/30 will then contain the relevant law.

---

17 It has been linked to lung-related diseases.
18 Haigh, N, *EEC Environmental Policy and Britain*, 2nd edn, 1991, London: Longman, p 183, refers to an unpublished minute of the Council meeting declaring that this is not to be interpreted as prohibiting the siting in such areas of new plants that may be sources of smoke or sulphur dioxide.

Lead in air

Lead has been regulated in a similar way to that used for sulphur. Two regulatory measures apply.

The Directive Relating to the Quality of Petrol and Diesel Fuels 98/70 has superceded Directive 85/210 which originally established limits for the lead content of petrol. The scope of the new Directive is set out in Art 1: '[T]he Directive sets technical specifications on health and environmental grounds for fuels to be used for vehicles ...' Member States are required to prohibit the marketing of leaded petrol within their territory (from 1 January 2000, Art 3).

The Directive on the Limit Value for Lead in Air 82/884 deals with lead pollution in general[19] and is aimed purely at the protection of human health. It was preceded by a Directive on the Biological Screening of Lead 77/312 which required Member States to conduct two screening tests on a prescribed percentage of their population separated by an interval of two years[20] in order to discover the lead content of their blood. Although its purpose was to provide information rather than to change practice, it was suggested that the research might lead to the EC imposition of mandatory biological standards for lead in blood although the notion came to nought. The current Directive provides that the concentration of lead in air shall not exceed two microgrammes per cubic metre (Arts 2 and 3). It requires Member States to establish sampling stations to gather information and to draw up plans to indicate the measures being taken to achieve the necessary reductions in lead level. The Directive is to be repealed by January 2005 under the provisions of Directive 99/30, Art 9. Directive 99/30 will then contain the relevant law.

Chlorofluorocarbons and other substances which deplete the ozone layer

The 1994 Council Regulation 3093/94 on Substances that Deplete the Ozone Layer was adopted to implement the Community's obligations under the Vienna Convention for the Protection of the Ozone Layer and Montreal Protocol. It therefore places controls on the production, supply, import, export, use and recovery of various listed substances which damage the ozone layer. The manufacture of some substances within the EU has been banned outright, for example, chlorofluorocarbons, halons and carbon tetrachloride and there are provisions dealing with the recovery and recycling of ozone damaging chemicals contained in refrigeration, air conditioning and fire-fighting equipment.

New controls on the supply and use of ozone depleting substances, including HCFCs and CFCs, came into force on 1 October 2000. EC Regulation 2037/00 bans the sale and use of most of these substances (see p 150, below).

---

19 The total body burden of lead can arise from many sources, such as water and food, not just via lead in air.
20 The British screening occurred in 1979–81. See *op cit*, Haigh, fn 18, pp 213–19.

Vehicle emissions

The EC has legislated extensively in this area both to uphold the operation of the single market and to address air pollution from vehicle traffic. The first development was the Directive on Air Pollution from Motor Vehicles 70/220 (for later Directives and their implementing regulations, see p 193, below). As amended and supplemented it sets emission limits for gaseous pollutants (carbon monoxide, hydrocarbons and nitrogen oxides) for petrol and diesel engined motor vehicles up to 3.5 tonnes, that is, cars and light vehicles. Neither this Directive nor subsequent directives controlling emissions impose any obligation upon Member States to ensure that vehicles within their territories comply with directive standards. Rather, it requires Member States not to impose any stricter standards than those contained in the Directive upon vehicles being imported from another part of the EC, a technique referred to as optional harmonisation. This ensures the free movement of goods whilst encouraging car manufacturers to comply with EC standards.

The original emission limits have been tightened and extended to all vehicles since 1970 as the EC has striven to achieve cleaner cars, effectively requiring the use of catalytic converters or lean-burn technology. Directive 88/76 set emission limits for cars over 2000cc and Directive 88/77 applied limits to heavy goods vehicles (diesel engined vehicles over 3.5 tonnes). The most recent legislation on car emission standards has been Directive 94/12 which amended Directive 70/220 by requiring stricter emission standards for both petrol and diesel engines for carbon monoxide, hydrocarbons/no and particulates.[21] The new standards have required technological changes to be made to catalytic converters, particularly regarding cold start performance. The Directive also allows Member States to use tax allowances to promote the introduction of cleaner vehicles meeting the stricter standards.

It should be noted that the series of directives reducing vehicle emissions was linked to the Directive on the Lead Content of Petrol 85/210. In order to achieve these emission standards since 1990 all new cars are able to run on unleaded petrol using catalytic converters.

A further development has been the negotiation of a voluntary agreement between the Commission and the European Automobile Manufacturers Association (ACEA) to reduce CO_2 emissions from passenger cars.[22] This has now been accepted under the competition rules contained in Art 81 (which prohibit agreements between undertakings, decisions by associations and concerted practices, which might act as a distortion of the internal market). This particular agreement has been accepted, although there may be difficulties with future agreements bearing in mind that para 3 of Art 81 does not say that environmental benefits are a justification for distorting the internal market.

21	Petrol (g/km)	Diesel (g/km)
Carbon monoxide	2.2	1.0
Hydrocarbons	0.5	0.7
Particulates	N/A	0.8

22 See Commission Decision 99/59.

Emissions from industrial plants

The Directive on Air Pollution from Industrial Plants 84/360[23] (see p 151, below) was the main Community response to the problem of acid rain. Its purpose was the control of air pollution by requiring Member States to adopt a system of authorisations for industrial plants involved in the categories of activity listed in the first Annex, viz the energy industry, metal production and processing, the manufacture of non-metallic mineral products (cement, asbestos), the chemical industry, waste disposal and paper pulp manufacture (Art 3). There is a second annex containing a list of eight categories of polluting substances.

The authorisations, which must be published (Art 9), may only be granted if the conditions set out in Art 4 are complied with:

1　That all appropriate preventive measures against air pollution are taken (including the use of BATNEEC (best available technology not entailing excessive cost));

2　That emissions, particularly of those listed in the second annex, do not cause 'significant' air pollution;

3　That emission limit values must not be exceeded and air quality limit values should be taken into account.

Two points may be made here. Firstly, the Directive refers to 'significant' air pollution without providing a definition. The definition of significant air pollution is therefore left up to the Member States. Secondly, the Directive is a 'framework' directive in that it requires 'daughter' directives to set actual emission limits for particular substances.[24]

A 'daughter' directive which, in the context of combating acid rain, is more significant than its parent is the Directive on the Limitation of Emissions of Certain Pollutants into the air from Large Combustion Plants 88/609 (see p 155, below). The pollutants dealt with in the directive are sulphur dioxide and nitrogen oxides, emissions of which are to be reduced in five yearly stages culminating in 2003. In 1998 the Commission adopted a proposal to revise Directive 88/609. As required by the Directive, the Commission has proposed *inter alia* updated requirements for stricter emission limits ([1998] 4 Env Liability CS 37). Emission limit values have also been set for new municipal waste incineration plants (89/369)[25] and Hazardous Waste Incinerators (94/67).

Other air pollution initiatives

Ozone

The threat to human health posed by ground-based ozone is recognised by the 1992 Directive on Air Pollution by Ozone 92/73 which requires Member States to establish ozone measuring stations. The Directive lays down threshold amounts which are

---

23　Now replaced by the Integrated Pollution Prevention and Control Directive 96/61, see pp 538–53, below.

24　Directive 87/217 on the Prevention and Reduction of Environmental Pollution by Asbestos is such a Directive.

25　The Directive deals only with domestic, commercial and trade waste.

consistent with health and vegetation protection. If these thresholds are exceeded,[26] the public must be informed via the media.[27]

Greenhouse gases

The 1993 Council Decision on Greenhouse Gas Emissions 93/389 (see p 157, below) established an EC 'monitoring mechanism of Community CO_2 (carbon dioxide) and other greenhouse gases' and requested Member States to draw up and implement their own national programmes to meet international legal obligations. This decision has been amended by Decision 99/296 to enable the EC to monitor the burden-sharing agreement under the Kyoto Protocol to the United Nations Framework Convention on Climate Change (see p 143, above).

By virtue of this decision Member States are required to do three things: (a) to have in place national programmes for reducing CO_2 and other greenhouse gas emissions; (b) to ensure that such programmes are periodically updated; and (c) to submit annual emissions inventories to the Commission. The Commission will evaluate national programmes and assess annually whether the Community is on course to meet its commitments under the Framework Convention and the more recent Kyoto Protocol.

However, in May 1999 the Commission issued its second Strategy Communication on Climate Change (COM (99) 230) concluding that Member States' projections of greenhouse gas emissions indicate that the EC is not on track towards its 8% reduction commitment under the Kyoto Protocol. This highlights the importance of the new EC Programme on Climate Change (COM (00) 88). This Programme, published on 8 March 2000, is intended to develop a fresh EC strategy for implementing the Kyoto Protocol. This is viewed as necessary because without further measures there is likely to be a 6–8% increase in greenhouse gas emissions from 1990 levels.

In addition to the above, two further EC measures on climate change have been adopted.

1   The SAVE programme was first established by Decision 91/565 and set a Community framework for improving energy efficiency. Directive 93/76 was adopted as part of this programme with the specific aim of limiting carbon dioxide emissions by improving energy efficiency. Member States are required to adopt whatever means (laws, regulations, economic or administrative instruments) necessary to implement six programmes. They are:

    (a) energy certification of buildings;

    (b) the billing of heating, air conditioning and hot water costs on the basis of actual consumption;

    (c) third party financing of energy efficiency investment in the public sector;

    (d) thermal insulation of new buildings;

    (e) regular inspection of boilers; and

    (f) energy audits for undertakings with high energy consumption.

---

26   Uniform methods of measuring ozone are set out in the Directive.
27   See *Air Pollution by Ozone in the EU – Overview of the 1999 Summer Season* (COM (99) 125).

In April 1998 the Commission adopted a Communication (COM (98) 246), *Energy Efficiency in the European Community – Towards a Strategy for the Rational Use of Energy,* which noted that the SAVE programme had failed to meet its target of reducing energy intensity by 20% by 1995. In a bid to encourage the uptake of more energy efficient products it has suggested a review of the SAVE Directive 93/76/EEC, measures to deal with insulation levels in existing as well as new buildings and better monitoring and review arrangements for the programme as a whole ([1998] 4 Env Liability CS 37).

2   The ALTENER programme, created by Decision 93/500 was set up to promote the development and use of renewable energy sources in the Community. The Decision states that CO_2 emissions could be reduced by 180 million tonnes by the year 2005 by the realisation of three objectives:

• increasing the share of energy demand covered by renewable sources from 4% in 1991 to 8% in 2005;

• trebling the production of electricity from renewable sources;

• securing for biofuels a market share of 5% of total fuel used by motor vehicles.

A budget of 40 million ECUs over five years is available to fund various programmes, for example, studies to define technical standards or specifications, measures to support State initiatives for extending or creating infrastructures concerned with renewable energy sources.

Towards a unified framework for EC air quality law and policy

So far, this chapter has considered a variety of measures dealing with particular pollutants and sources of pollution. As mentioned above (p 142) this has led to a somewhat fragmented approach with the various directives having their own frameworks and timescales. The following Directive is a nascent example of a more unified approach.

Air Quality Framework Directive 96/62

The Directive on Ambient Air Quality Assessment and Management 96/62 aims (Art 1) at defining a common strategy to:

• define and establish objectives for ambient air quality in the community designed to avoid, prevent or reduce harmful effects on human health and the environment as a whole;

• assess the ambient air quality in Member States on the basis of common methods and criteria;

• obtain adequate information on ambient air quality and ensure that it is made available to the public, *inter alia,* by means of alert thresholds;

• maintain ambient air quality where it is good and improve it in other cases.

The Council will set limit values and alert thresholds (defined in Art 2) for the particular air pollutants referred to in Art 4 (see Annex 1). The Directive therefore requires a series of daughter directives in order to bring it into effect. The first two of these daughter directives have now appeared. The Directive Relating to Limit Values for Sulphur Dioxide, Nitrogen Dioxide etc, Particulate Matter, and Lead in Ambient Air 99/30 requires Member States to assess air quality within their territories (Art 6) and take necessary measures to improve that air quality (Art 7). Where alert threshold levels are exceeded Member States must ensure that the public are informed. The second daughter directive, the 2000 Directive Relating to Limit Values for Benzene and Carbon Monoxide in Ambient Air 00/69, adopts the same approach.

In accordance with the transitional arrangements set out in Art 9 of the Air Quality Framework Directive the following directives will be repealed: the Directive on Air Quality Limit values for Sulphur Dioxide and Suspended Particulates 80/779 (entirely by 1 January 2005); the Directive on the Limit value for lead in Air 82/884 (entirely by 1 January 2005); the Council Directive on Air Quality Standards for Nitrogen Dioxide 85/203 (entirely by 1 January 2010).

Note that from 19 July 2001, Member States must use methods of air quality assessment that comply with the daughter directives in order to assess concentrations of the various pollutants referred to.

CAFE

A recent initiative by DG XI (see Chapter 1, p 8, above) has been aimed at incorporating the various strands of EC air quality policy into a unified framework under the title 'Clean Air for Europe' (CAFE). The various areas which could be incorporated are:

(a) Air quality.

(b) Emissions from stationary sources.

(c) Fuel standards.

(d) Vehicle Emissions.

(e) Acidification and ozone strategies.

The primary aim would be to harmonise the frameworks and time scales in order to avoid conflicts between measures proposed in different areas or at different times. The CAFE proposols are now published, see COM (01) 245.

COUNCIL REGULATION

of 29 June 2000

on substances that deplete the ozone layer

(EC/2037/00)

THE EUROPEAN PARLIAMENT AND THE COUNCIL OF THE EUROPEAN UNION, Having regard to the Treaty establishing the European Community [...]

Whereas:

(1) It is established that continued emissions of ozone-depleting substances at current levels continue to cause significant damage to the ozone layer. Ozone depletion in the southern hemisphere reached unprecedented levels in 1998. In three out of four recent springs severe ozone depletion has occurred in the Arctic region. Increased UV-B radiation resulting from ozone depletion poses a significant threat to health and

environment. Further efficient measures need therefore to be taken in order to protect human health and the environment against adverse effects resulting from such emissions.

(2) In view of its responsibilities for the environment and trade, the Community, pursuant to Decision 88/540/EEC(4), has become a Party to the Vienna Convention for the Protection of the Ozone Layer and the Montreal Protocol on Substances that Deplete the Ozone Layer, as amended by the Parties to the Protocol at their second meeting in London and at their fourth meeting in Copenhagen.

(3) Additional measures for the protection of the ozone layer were adopted by the Parties to the Montreal Protocol at their seventh meeting in Vienna in December 1995 and at their ninth meeting in Montreal in September 1997, in which the Community participated.

(4) It is necessary for action to be taken at Community level to carry out the Community's obligations under the Vienna Convention and the latest amendments and adjustments to the Montreal Protocol, in particular to phase out the production and the placing on the market of methyl bromide within the Community and to provide for a system for the licensing not only of imports but also of exports of ozone-depleting substances. [...]

HAVE ADOPTED THIS REGULATION:

CHAPTER I INTRODUCTORY PROVISIONS

Article 1 Scope

This Regulation shall apply to the production, importation, exportation, placing on the market, use, recovery, recycling and reclamation and destruction of chlorofluorocarbons, other fully halogenated chlorofluorocarbons, halons, carbon tetrachloride, 1,1,1-trichloroethane, methyl bromide, hydrobromofluorocarbons and hydrochlorofluorocarbons, to the reporting of information on these substances and to the importation, exportation, placing on the market and use of products and equipment containing those substances. This Regulation shall also apply to the production, importation, placing on the market and use of substances in Annex II.

[All other provisions and Annexes omitted.]

COUNCIL DIRECTIVE

of 28 June 1984

on the combating of air pollution from industrial plants

(84/360/EEC)

(1984) OJ L188, p 20

THE COUNCIL OF THE EUROPEAN COMMUNITIES,

Having regard to the Treaty establishing the European Economic Community, and in particular Articles 100 and 235 thereof,

Whereas the 1973, 1977 and 1983 action programmes of the European Communities on the environment stress the importance of the prevention and reduction of air pollution;

Whereas the 1973 and 1977 action programmes in particular provide not only for the objective evaluation of the risks to human health and to the environment from air pollution but also for the formulation of quality objectives and the setting of quality standards, especially for a number of air pollutants regarded as the most hazardous; [...]

Whereas, moreover, under Decision 81/462/EEC ((1981) OJ L171, p 11) the Community is a party to the Convention on long-range transboundary air pollution;

Whereas the 1983 action programme, the general guidelines of which have been approved by the Council of the European Communities and by the representatives of the Member States meeting within the Council, envisages that the Commission will continue its efforts to establish air quality standards and that where appropriate emission standards for certain types of source should be laid down;

Whereas all the Member States have laws, regulations and administrative provisions concerning the combating of air pollution from stationary industrial plants; whereas several Member States are in the process of amending the existing provisions;

Whereas the disparities between the provisions concerning the combating of air pollution from industrial installations currently in force, or in the process of amendment, in the different Member States are liable to create unequal conditions of competition and thus have a direct effect on the functioning of the common market; whereas, therefore, approximation of the law in this field is required, as provided for by Article 100 of the Treaty;

Whereas one of the essential tasks of the Community is to promote throughout the Community a harmonious development of economic activities and a continuous and balanced expansion, tasks which are inconceivable in the absence of a campaign to combat pollution and nuisances or of an improvement in the quality of life and in the protection of the environment;

Whereas the Community should and must help increase the effectiveness of action undertaken by the Member States to combat air pollution from stationary industrial plants;

Whereas in order to achieve this end certain principles aiming at the implementation of a series of measures and procedures designed to prevent and reduce air pollution from industrial plants within the Community should be introduced;

Whereas the Community's endeavours to introduce these principles can be only gradual, bearing in mind the complexity of the situations and the fundamental principles on which the various national policies are based;

Whereas initially a general framework should be introduced to permit the Member States to adapt, where necessary, their existing rules to the principles adopted at Community level; whereas the Member States should therefore introduce a system of prior authorisation for the operation and substantial alteration of stationary industrial plants which can cause air pollution;

Whereas, moreover, the competent national authorities cannot grant such authorisation unless a number of conditions have been fulfilled, including the requirements that all appropriate preventive measures are taken, and that the operation of the plant does not result in a significant level of air pollution;

Whereas it should be possible to apply special provisions in particularly polluted areas and in areas in need of special protection;

Whereas the rules applicable to the authorisation procedures and to the determination of emissions must satisfy certain requirements;

Whereas in certain situations the competent authorities must explore the need to impose further requirements, which, however, must not result in excessive costs for the undertaking concerned;

Whereas the provisions taken pursuant to this Directive are to be applied gradually to existing plants, taking due account of technical factors and the economic effects;

Whereas provision must be made for co-operation between the Member States themselves and with the Commission to facilitate implementation of the measures designed to prevent and to reduce air pollution and to develop preventive technology.

HAS ADOPTED THIS DIRECTIVE:

Article 1

The purpose of this Directive is to provide for further measures and procedures designed to prevent or reduce air pollution from industrial plants within the Community, particularly those belonging to the categories set out in Annex I.

Article 2

For the purposes of this Directive:

1   'Air pollution' means the introduction by man, directly or indirectly, of substances or energy into the air resulting in deleterious effects of such a nature as to endanger human health, harm living resources and eco-systems and material property and impair or interfere with amenities and other legitimate uses of the environment.

2   'Plant' means any establishment or other stationary plant used for industrial or public utility purposes which is likely to cause air pollution.

3   'Existing plant' means a plant in operation before 1 July 1987 or built or authorised before that date.

4   'Air quality limit values' means the concentration of polluting substances in the air during a specified period which is not to be exceeded.

5   'Emission limit values' means the concentration and/or mass of polluting substances in emissions from plants during a specified period which is not to be exceeded.

Article 3

1   Member States shall take the necessary measures to ensure that the operation of plants belonging to the categories listed in Annex I requires prior authorisation by the competent authorities. The necessity to meet the requirements prescribed for such authorisation must be taken into account at the plant's design stage.

2   Authorisation is also required in the case of substantial alteration of all plants which belong to the categories listed in Annex I or which, as a result of the alteration, will fall within those categories.

3   Member States may require other categories of plants to be subject to authorisation or, where national legislation so provides, prior notification.

Article 4

Without prejudice to the requirements laid down by national and Community provisions with a purpose other than that of this Directive, an authorisation may be issued only when the competent authority is satisfied that:

1   all appropriate preventive measures against air pollution have been taken, including the application of the best available technology, provided that the application of such measures does not entail excessive costs;

2   the use of plant will not cause significant air pollution particularly from the emission of substances referred to in Annex II;

3   none of the emission limit values applicable will be exceeded;

4   all the air quality limit values applicable will be taken into account.

Article 5

Member States may:

–   define particularly polluted areas for which emission limit values more stringent than those referred to in Article 4 may be fixed;

–   define areas to be specially protected for which air quality limit values and emission limit values more stringent than those referred to in Article 4 may be fixed;

–   decide that, within the above mentioned areas, specified categories of plants set out in Annex I may not be built or operated unless special conditions are complied with.

Article 6

Applications for authorisation shall include a description of the plant containing the necessary information for the purposes of the decision whether to grant authorisation in accordance with Articles 3 and 4.

Article 7

Subject to the provisions regarding commercial secrecy, Member States shall exchange information among themselves and with the Commission regarding their experience and knowledge of measures for prevention and reduction of air pollution, as well as technical processes and equipment and air quality and emission limit values.

Article 8

1   The Council, acting unanimously on a proposal from the Commission, shall if necessary fix emission limit values based on the best available technology not entailing excessive costs, and taking into account the nature, quantities and harmfulness of the emissions concerned.

2   The Council, acting unanimously on a proposal from the Commission, shall stipulate suitable measurement and assessment techniques and methods. [...]

Article 12

The Member States shall follow developments as regards the best available technology and the environmental situation.

In the light of this examination they shall, if necessary, impose appropriate conditions on plants authorised in accordance with this Directive, on the basis both of those developments and of the desirability of avoiding excessive costs for the plants in question, having regard in particular to the economic situation of the plants belonging to the category concerned.

Article 13

In the light of an examination of developments as regards the best available technology and the environmental situation, the Member States shall implement policies and strategies, including appropriate measures, for the gradual adaptation of existing plants belonging to the categories given in Annex I to the best available technology, taking into account in particular:

–   the plant's technical characteristics,

–   its rate of utilisation and length of its remaining life,

–   the nature and volume of polluting emissions from it,

–   the desirability of not entailing excessive costs for the plant concerned, having regard in particular to the economic situation of undertakings belonging to the category in question.

Article 14

Member States may, in order to protect public health and the environment, adopt provisions stricter than those provided for in this Directive. [...]

[All other Articles and Annexes are omitted.]

COUNCIL DIRECTIVE

of 24 November 1988

on the limitation of emissions of certain pollutants into the air from large combustion plants

(88/609/EEC)

THE COUNCIL OF THE EUROPEAN COMMUNITIES,

Having regard to the Treaty establishing the European Economic Community, and in particular Article 130s thereof,

Whereas the 1973, 1977, 1983 and 1987 European Communities action programmes on the environment stress the importance of the reduction and prevention of atmosphere pollution;

Whereas in their resolution concerning the action programme on the environment 1987 to 1992, the Council and the Representatives of Governments of the Member States meeting within the Council emphasis the importance for Community action to concentrate as a priority on the reduction at source of air pollution, *inter alia*, by adopting and implementing measures concerning emissions from large combustion plants;

Whereas, moreover, under Decision 81/462/EEC, the Community became a Party to the Convention on long-range transboundary air pollution;

Whereas Council Directive 84/360/EEC of 28 June 1984 on the combating of air pollution from industrial plants provides for the introduction of certain procedures and measures aiming to prevent or reduce air pollution from industrial plants, particularly those belonging to listed categories, among which are large combustion plants;

Whereas Article 8 of the same Directive 84/360/EEC stipulates that the Council, acting unanimously on a proposal from the Commission shall, if necessary, fix emission limit values for new plants based on the best available technology not entailing excessive costs and taking into account the nature, quantities and harmfulness of the emissions concerned; whereas Article 13 thereof stipulates that Member States shall implement policies and strategies, including appropriate measures, for the gradual adaptation of existing plants belonging to listed categories to the best available technology and taking various specified matters into account;

Whereas the damage to the environment owing to air pollution makes it urgent to reduce and control emissions from new and existing large combustion plants and whereas to this end it is necessary to set overall objectives for a gradual and staged reduction of total annual emissions of sulphur dioxide and oxides of nitrogen from existing combustion plants and to fix emission limit values for sulphur dioxide, nitrogen oxides and dust in case of new plants, in accordance with the principle set out in Article 8 of the Directive 84/360/EEC;

Whereas such emission limit values for new plants will need to be reviewed in the light of technological developments and the evolution of environmental requirements, and the Commission will submit proposals to this effect;

Whereas in establishing the overall annual emission ceilings for existing large combustion plants due account has been taken of the need for comparable effort, whilst making allowance for the specific situations of Member States; whereas, in establishing the requirements for the reduction of emissions from new plants, due account has been taken of particular technical and economic constraints in order to avoid excessive costs; whereas in the case of Spain there has been granted a temporary and limited derogation from the full application of the emission limit value of sulphur dioxide fixed for new plants, since that Member State considers it needs a particularly high amount of new generating capacity to allow for its energy and industrial growth.

HAS ADOPTED THIS DIRECTIVE:

Article 2

For the purpose of this Directive:

1   'emission' means: the discharge of substances from the combustion plant into the air;

3   'emission limit value' means: the permissible quantity of a substance contained in the waste gases from the combustion plant which may be discharged into the air during a given period; it shall be calculated in terms of mass per volume of the waste gases expressed in $mg/Nm3$, assuming an oxygen content by volume in the waste gas of 3% in the case of liquid and gaseous fuels and 6% in the case of solid fuels; [...]

Article 3

1   Not later than 1 July 1990, the Member States shall draw up appropriate programmes for the progressive reduction of total annual emissions from existing plants. The programmes shall set out the timetables and the implementing procedures. [...]

Article 4

1   Member States shall take appropriate measures to ensure that all licences for the construction or, in the absence of such a procedure, for the operation of new plants contain conditions relating to compliance with the emission limit values fixed in Annexes III to VII in respect of sulphur dioxide, oxides of nitrogen and dust. [...]

[All other Articles and Annexes omitted.]

COUNCIL DECISION

of 24 June 1993

for a monitoring mechanism of Community CO_2 and other greenhouse gas emissions

(93/389/EEC)

(1993) OJ L167, p 31

THE COUNCIL OF THE EUROPEAN COMMUNITIES,

Having regard to the Treaty establishing the European Economic Community, and in particular Article 130S thereof, [...]

Whereas the 1973 [OJ C112, 20.12.1973, p 1], 1977 [OJ C139, 13.6.1977, p 1] and 1983 [OJ C46, 17.2.1983, p 1] Community action programmes on the environment stress the importance of the reduction and prevention of atmospheric pollution; whereas, in addition, the 1987 [OJ C 328, 7.12.1987, p 1] action programme emphasises the importance for Community action to concentrate as a priority on the reduction at source of such pollution; whereas the 1993 Community programme of policy and action in relation to the environment and sustainable development has as one of its principal themes climate change and outlines the need for action in the relevant economic sectors so the CO_2 and other greenhouse gas emissions are controlled; [...]

Whereas, at their meeting on 29 October 1990, the Council (Environment and Energy Ministers) agreed that the Community and Member States, assuming that other leading countries undertook similar commitments, and acknowledging the targets identified by a number of Member States for stabilising or reducing emissions by different dates, were willing to take actions aimed at reaching stabilisation of the total CO_2 emissions by 2000 at the 1990 level in the Community as a whole, and also that Member States which start from relatively low levels of energy consumption and therefore low emissions measured on a *per capita* or other appropriate basis are entitled to have CO_2 targets and/or strategies corresponding to their economic and social development, while improving the energy efficiency of their economic activities;

Whereas, at their meeting on 13 December 1991, the Council (Energy and Environment Ministers) invited the Commission to propose concrete measures arising from the Community strategy and required that such measures should take into account the concept of equitable burden sharing, according to the conclusions of the Council meeting of 29 October 1990; [...]

Whereas all Member States and the Community are signatories to the United Nations framework convention on climate change, which, when ratified, will commit the developed countries and other Parties listed in Annex I to the Convention to take measures to limit anthropogenic emissions of CO_2 and other greenhouse gases not controlled by the Montreal Protocol with the aim of returning individually or jointly to the 1990 levels these anthropogenic emissions by the end of the present decade: whereas, in this perspective, it is desirable to ensure consistency with the monitoring mechanism to be established under the Convention; whereas this is particularly relevant as regards methodologies for compiling inventories and reporting requirements; [...]

HAS ADOPTED THIS DECISION:

Article 1

A monitoring mechanism is hereby established for anthropogenic CO_2 and other greenhouse gas emissions not controlled by the Montreal Protocol in the Member States.

Article 2: National programmes

1   The Member States shall devise, publish, and implement national programmes for limiting their anthropogenic emissions of CO_2 in order to contribute to: the stabilisation of CO_2 emissions by 2000 at 1990 levels in the Community as a whole, assuming that other leading countries undertake commitments along similar lines, and on the understanding that Member States which start from relatively low levels of energy consumption and therefore low emissions measured on a per capita or other appropriate basis are entitled to have CO_2 targets and/or strategies corresponding to their economic and social development, while improving the energy efficiency of their economic activities, as agreed at the Council meetings at 29 October 1990 and 13 December 1991, and the fulfilment of the commitment relating to the limitation of CO_2 emissions in the UN Framework Convention on Climate change by the Community as a whole through action by the Community and its Member States, within their respective competences. [...]

[Articles 3–9 omitted.]

COUNCIL DIRECTIVE

of 27 September 1996

on ambient air quality assessment and management

(96/62/EC)

THE COUNCIL OF THE EUROPEAN UNION,

Having regard to the Treaty establishing the European Community, and in particular Article 130s (1) thereof, [...]

Whereas the fifth action programme of 1992 on the environment, the general approach of which was endorsed by the Council and the Representatives of the Governments of the Member States, meeting within the Council, in their Resolution 93/C 138/01 of 1 February 1993 (4), envisages amendments to existing legislation on air pollutants; whereas the said programme recommends the establishment of long term air quality objectives;

Whereas, in order to protect the environment as a whole and human health, concentrations of harmful air prevented or reduced and limit values and/or alert thresholds set for ambient air pollution levels;

Whereas, in order to take into account the specific formation mechanisms of ozone, these limit values and need to be complemented or replaced by target values;

Whereas the numerical values for limit values, alert thresholds and, as regards ozone, target values and/or limit values and alert thresholds are to be based on the findings of work carried out by international scientific groups active in the field;

Whereas the Commission is to carry out studies to analyse the effects of the combined action of various pollutants or sources of pollution and the effect of climate on the activity of the various pollutants examined in the context of this Directive;

Whereas the ambient air quality needs to be assessed against limit values and/or alert thresholds, and, as and/or limit values taking into account the size of populations and eco-systems exposed to air pollution, as well as the environment;

Whereas, in order for assessment of ambient air quality based on measurements made in Member States to be comparable, the location and number of sampling points and reference methods of measurement used should be specified when values are set for alert thresholds, limit values and target values;

Whereas, to allow for the use of other techniques of estimation of ambient air quality besides direct measurement, it is necessary to define the criteria for use and required accuracy of these techniques;

Whereas the general measures set up under this Directive have to be supplemented by others specific to individual substances covered;

Whereas these specific measures need to be adopted as soon as possible in order to fulfil the overall objectives of this Directive;

Whereas preliminary representative data on the levels of pollutants should be collected;

Whereas, in order to protect the environment as a whole and human health, it is necessary that Member States take action when limit values are exceeded in order to comply with these values within the time fixed;

Whereas the measures taken by Member States must take into account the requirements set by regulations concerning the operation of industrial installations in conformity with Community legislation in the field of integrated prevention and reduction of pollution when this legislation applies;

Whereas, because these actions require time to be implemented and become effective, temporary margins of tolerance of the limit value may need to be set;

Whereas areas may exist in Member States where pollution levels are greater than the limit value but within the allowed margin of tolerance; whereas the limit value must be complied with within the time specified;

Whereas Member States must consult with one another if the level of a pollutant exceeds, or is likely to exceed, the limit value plus the margin of tolerance or, as the case may be, the alert threshold, following significant pollution originating in another Member State;

Whereas the setting of alert thresholds at which precautionary measures should be taken will make it possible to limit the impact of pollution episodes on human health;

Whereas, in zones and agglomerations where the levels of pollutants are below the limit values, Member States must endeavour to preserve the best ambient air quality compatible with sustainable development;

Whereas, in order to facilitate the handling and comparison of data received, such data should be provided to the Commission in standardised form;

Whereas the implementation of a wide and comprehensive policy of ambient air quality assessment and management needs to be based on strong technical and scientific grounds and permanent exchange of views between the Member States;

Whereas there is a need to avoid increasing unnecessarily the amount of information to be transmitted by Member States; whereas the information gathered by the Commission pursuant to the implementation of this Directive is useful to the European Environment Agency (EEA) and may therefore be transmitted to it by the Commission;

Whereas the adaptation of criteria and techniques used for the assessment of the ambient air quality to be order to facilitate implementation of the work necessary to this end, a procedure should be set up to establish close co-operation between the Member States and the Commission within a committee;

Whereas, in order to promote the reciprocal exchange of information between Member States and the EEA, the Commission, with the assistance of the EEA, is to publish a report on ambient air quality in the Community every three years;

Whereas the substances already covered by Council Directive 80/779/EEC of 15 July 1980 on air quality limit values and guide values for sulphur dioxide and suspended particulates (1), Council Directive 82/884/EEC of 3 December 1982 on a limit value for lead in the air (2), Council Directive 85/203/EEC of 7 March 1985 on air quality standards for nitrogen dioxide (3) and Council Directive 92/72/EEC of 21 be dealt with first.

HAS ADOPTED THIS DIRECTIVE:

Article 1: Objectives

The general aim of this Directive is to define the basic principles of a common strategy to:

–   define and establish objectives for ambient air quality in the Community designed to avoid, prevent or reduce harmful effects on human health and the environment as a whole;

–   assess the ambient air quality in Member States on the basis of common methods and criteria;

–   obtain adequate information on ambient air quality and ensure that it is made available to the public, *inter alia* by means of alert thresholds;

–   maintain ambient air quality where it is good and improve it in other cases.

Article 2: Definitions

For the purposes of this Directive:

1   'ambient air' shall mean outdoor air in the troposphere, excluding work places;

2   'pollutant' shall mean any substance introduced directly or indirectly by man into the ambient air and likely to have harmful effects on human health and/or the environment as a whole;

3   'level' shall mean the concentration of a pollutant in ambient air or the deposition thereof on surfaces in a given time;

4   'assessment' shall mean any method used to measure, calculate, predict or estimate the level of a pollutant in the ambient air;

5   'limit value' shall mean a level fixed on the basis of scientific knowledge, with the aim of avoiding, preventing or reducing harmful effects on human health and/or the environment as a whole, to be attained within a given period and not to be exceeded once attained;

6   'target value' shall mean a level fixed with the aim of avoiding more long-term harmful effects on human health and/or the environment as a whole, to be attained where possible over a given period;

7　'alert threshold' shall mean a level beyond which there is a risk to human health from brief exposure and at which immediate steps shall be taken by the Member States as laid down in this Directive;

8　'margin of tolerance' shall mean the percentage of the limit value by which this value may be exceeded subject to the conditions laid down in this Directive;

9　'zone' shall mean part of their territory delimited by the Member States;

10　'agglomeration' shall mean a zone with a population concentration in excess of 250,000 inhabitants or, where the population concentration is 250,000 inhabitants or less, a population density per km^2 which for the Member States justifies the need for ambient air quality to be assessed and managed.

Article 3: Implementation and responsibilities

For the implementation of this Directive, the Member States shall designate at the appropriate levels the competent authorities and bodies responsible for:

－　implementation of this Directive,

－　assessment of ambient air quality,

－　approval of the measuring devices (methods, equipment, networks,laboratories),

－　ensuring accuracy of measurement by measuring devices and checking the maintenance of such accuracy by those devices, in particular by internal quality controls carried out in accordance, *inter alia*, with the requirements of European quality assurance standards,

－　analysis of assessment methods,

－　co-ordination on their territory of Community-wide quality assurance programmes organised by the Commission.

When they supply it to the Commission, the Member States shall make the information referred to in the first sub-paragraph available to the public.

Article 4: Setting of the limit values and alert thresholds for ambient air

1　For those pollutants listed in Annex I, the Commission shall submit to the Council proposals for the setting of limit values and, as appropriate, alert thresholds according to the following timetable:

－　no later than 31 December 1996 for pollutants 1 to 5,

－　in accordance with Article 8 of Directive 92/72/EEC for ozone,

－　no later than 31 December 1997 for pollutants 7 and 8,

－　as soon as possible, and no later than 31 December 1999, for pollutants 9 to 13.

In fixing the limit values and, as appropriate, alert thresholds, account shall be taken, by way of example, of the factors laid down in Annex II.

Regarding ozone, these proposals will take account of the specific formation mechanisms of this pollutant and, to this end, provision may be made for target values and/or limit values.

If a target value fixed for ozone is exceeded, Member States shall inform the Commission of the measures taken in order to attain that value. On the basis of this information the Commission shall evaluate whether additional measures are necessary at Community level and, should the need arise, shall submit proposals to the Council. For other pollutants, the Commission shall submit to the Council proposals for fixing limit values and, as appropriate, alert thresholds if, on the basis of scientific progress and taking into account the criteria laid down in Annex III, it appears necessary to avoid, prevent or reduce the harmful effects of such pollutants on human health and/or the environment as a whole within the Community.

2   The Commission shall be responsible, taking account of the most recent scientific-research data in the epidemiological and environmental fields concerned and of the most recent advances in metrology, for re-examining the elements on which the limit values and alert thresholds referred to in paragraph 1 are based.

3   When limit values and alert thresholds are set, criteria and techniques shall be established for:

   (a) the measurement to be used in implementing the legislation referred to in paragraph 1:

     – the location of the sampling points,

     – the minimum number of sampling points,

     – the reference measurement and sampling techniques;

   (b) the use of other techniques for assessing ambient air quality, particularly modelling:

     – spatial resolution for modelling and objective assessment methods,

     – reference modelling techniques.

These criteria and techniques shall be established in respect of each pollutant according to the size of agglomerations or to the levels of pollutants in the zones examined.

4   To take into account the actual levels of a given pollutant when setting limit values and the time needed to implement measures for improving the ambient air quality, the Council may also set a temporary margin of tolerance for the limit value. This margin shall be reduced according to procedures to be defined for each pollutant in order to attain the level of the limit value at the latest at the end of a period to be determined for each pollutant when that value is set.

5   In accordance with the Treaty, the Council shall adopt the legislation provided for in paragraph 1 and the provisions laid down in paragraphs 3 and 4.

6   When a Member State takes more stringent measures than those laid down in the provisions referred to in paragraph 5, it shall inform the Commission thereof.

7   When a Member State intends to set limit values or alert thresholds for pollutants not referred to in Annex I and not covered by Community provisions concerning ambient air quality in the Community, it shall inform the Commission thereof in sufficient time. The Commission shall be required to supply, in sufficient time, an answer to the question of the need to act at Community level following the criteria laid down in Annex III.

Article 5: Preliminary assessment of ambient air quality

Member States which do not have representative measurements of the levels of pollutants for all zones and agglomerations shall undertake series of representative measurements, surveys or assessments in order to have the data available in time for implementation of the legislation referred to in Article 4(1).

Article 6: Assessment of ambient air quality

1   Once limit values and alert thresholds have been set, ambient air quality shall be assessed throughout the territory of the Member States, in accordance with this Article.

[The rest of this Article is omitted.]

Article 7: Improvement of ambient air quality

General requirements

1   Member States shall take the necessary measures to ensure compliance with the limit values.

2   Measures taken in order to achieve the aims of this Directive shall:

   (a) take into account an integrated approach to the protection of air, water and soil;

   (b) not contravene Community legislation on the protection of safety and health of workers at work;

   (c) have no significant negative effects on the environment in the other Member States.

3   Member States shall draw up action plans indicating the measures to be taken in the short term where there is a risk of the limit values and / or alert thresholds being exceeded, in order to reduce that risk and to limit the duration of such an occurrence. Such plans may, depending on the individual case, provide for measures to control and, where necessary, suspend activities, including motor-vehicle traffic, which contribute to the limit values being exceeded.

Article 8: Measures applicable in zones where levels are higher than the limit value

1   Member States shall draw up a list of zones and agglomerations in which the levels of one or more pollutants are higher than the limit value plus the margin of tolerance.

[...]

6   When the level of a pollutant exceeds, or is likely to exceed, the limit value plus the margin of tolerance or, as the case may be, the alert threshold following significant pollution originating in another Member State, the Member States concerned shall consult with one another with a view to finding a solution. The Commission may be present at such consultations.

Article 9: Requirements in zones where the levels are lower than the limit value

Member States shall draw up a list of zones and agglomerations in which the levels of pollutants are below the limit values. Member States shall maintain the levels of pollutants in these zones and agglomerations below the limit values and shall endeavour to preserve the best ambient air quality, compatible with sustainable development.

Article 10: Measures applicable in the event of the alert thresholds being exceeded

When the alert thresholds are exceeded, Member States shall undertake to ensure that the necessary steps are taken to inform the public (for example, by means of radio, television and the press). Member States shall also forward to the Commission on a provisional basis information concerning the levels recorded and the duration of the episode(s) of pollution no later than three months following their occurrence. A list of minimum details to be supplied to the public shall be drawn up together with the alert thresholds.

[Articles 11 and 12 omitted.]

Article 13

1   Member States shall bring into force the laws, regulations and administrative provisions necessary to comply with this Directive not later than 18 months after it comes into force with regard to the provisions relating to Articles 1 to 4 and 12 and Annexes I, II, III and IV, and at the latest on the date on which the provisions referred to in Article 4(5) apply, with regard to the provisions relating to the other Articles.

[...]

[Article 14 omitted.]

[All Annexes omitted.]

COUNCIL DIRECTIVE

of 22 April 1999

relating to limit values for sulphur dioxide, nitrogen dioxide and oxides of nitrogen, particulate matter and lead in ambient air

(99/30/EC)

(1999) OJ L163, pp 0041–60

THE COUNCIL OF THE EUROPEAN UNION,

Having regard to the Treaty establishing the European Community, and in particular Article 130s(1) thereof,

Having regard to the proposal from the Commission(1),

Having regard to the opinion of the Economic and Social Committee(2),

Acting in accordance with the procedure laid down in Article 189c of the Treaty(3):

(1)   Whereas, on the basis of principles enshrined in Article 130r of the Treaty, the European Community programme of policy and action in relation to the environment and sustainable development (the fifth Environment Action Programme)(4) envisages in particular amendments to legislation on air pollutants; whereas that programme recommends the establishment of long term air-quality objectives;

(2)   Whereas Article 129 of the Treaty provides that health-protection requirements shall form a constituent part of the Community's other policies; whereas Article 3(o) of the Treaty provides that the activities of the Community shall include a contribution to the attainment of a high level of health protection;

(3)   Whereas, pursuant to Article 4(5) of Council Directive 96/62/EC of 27 September 1996 on ambient air quality assessment and management(5), the Council is to adopt the legislation provided for in paragraph 1 and the provisions laid down in paragraphs 3 and 4 of the same Article;

(4)   Whereas the limit values laid down in this Directive are minimum requirements; whereas, in accordance with Article 130t of the Treaty, Member States may maintain or introduce more stringent protective measures; whereas, in particular, stricter limit values may be introduced to protect the health of particularly vulnerable categories of the population, such as children and hospital patients; whereas a Member State may require that limit values be attained before the dates laid down in this Directive;

(5) Whereas ecosystems should be protected against the adverse effects of sulphur dioxide; whereas vegetation should be protected against the adverse effects of oxides of nitrogen;

(6) Whereas different types of particles can have different harmful effects on human health; whereas there is evidence that risks to human health associated with exposure to man-made particulate matter are higher than risks associated with exposure to naturally occurring particles in ambient air;

(7) Whereas Directive 96/62/EC requires that action plans be developed for zones within which concentrations of pollutants in ambient air exceed limit values plus any temporary margins of tolerance applicable in order to ensure compliance with limit values by the date or dates laid down; whereas insofar as they relate to particulate matter such action plans and other reduction strategies should aim to reduce concentrations of fine particles as part of the total reduction in concentrations of particulate matter;

(8) Whereas Directive 96/62/EC provides that the numerical values for limit values and alert thresholds are to be based on the findings of work carried out by international scientific groups active in the field; whereas the Commission is to take account of the most recent scientific research data in the epidemiological and environmental fields concerned and of the most recent advances in metrology for re-examining the elements on which limit values and alert thresholds are based;

(9) Whereas in order to facilitate the review of this Directive in 2003 the Commission and the Member States should consider encouraging research into the effects of the pollutants referred to herein, namely sulphur dioxide, nitrogen dioxide and oxides of nitrogen, particulate matter and lead;

(10) Whereas standardised accurate measurement techniques and common criteria for the location of measuring stations are an important element in the assessment of ambient-air quality with a view to obtaining comparable information across the Community;

(11) Whereas, in accordance with Article 12(1) of Directive 96/62/EC, the amendments necessary for adaptation to scientific and technical progress may relate solely to criteria and techniques for the assessment of concentrations of sulphur dioxide, nitrogen dioxide and oxides of nitrogen, particulate matter and lead or detailed arrangements for forwarding information to the Commission, and may not have the effect of modifying limit values or alert thresholds either directly or indirectly;

(12) Whereas up-to-date information on concentrations of sulphur dioxide, nitrogen dioxide and oxides of nitrogen, particulate matter and lead in ambient air should be readily available to the public,

HAS ADOPTED THIS DIRECTIVE:

Article 1 Objectives

The objectives of this Directive shall be to:

– establish limit values and, as appropriate, alert thresholds for concentrations of sulphur dioxide, nitrogen dioxide and oxides of nitrogen, particulate matter and lead in ambient air intended to avoid, prevent or reduce harmful effects on human health and the environment as a whole,

- assess concentrations of sulphur dioxide, nitrogen dioxide and oxides of nitrogen, particulate matter and lead in ambient air on the basis of common methods and criteria,

- obtain adequate information on concentrations of sulphur dioxide, nitrogen dioxide and oxides of nitrogen, particulate matter and lead in ambient air and ensure that it is made available to the public,

- maintain ambient-air quality where it is good and improve it in other cases with respect to sulphur dioxide, nitrogen dioxide and oxides of nitrogen, particulate matter and lead.

Article 2 Definitions

For the purposes of this Directive:

1   'ambient air' shall mean outdoor air in the troposphere, excluding work places;

2   'pollutant' shall mean any substance introduced directly or indirectly by man into the ambient air and likely to have harmful effects on human health and/or the environment as a whole;

3   'level' shall mean the concentration of a pollutant in ambient air or the deposition thereof on surfaces in a given time;

4   'assessment' shall mean any method used to measure, calculate, predict or estimate the level of a pollutant in the ambient air;

5   'limit value' shall mean a level fixed on the basis of scientific knowledge, with the aim of avoiding, preventing or reducing harmful effects on human health and/or the environment as a whole, to be attained within a given period and not to be exceeded once attained;

6   'alert threshold' shall mean a level beyond which there is a risk to human health from brief exposure and at which immediate steps shall be taken by the Member States as laid down in Directive 96/62/EC;

7   'margin of tolerance' shall mean the percentage of the limit value by which this value may be exceeded subject to the conditions laid down in Directive 96/62/EC;

8   'zone' shall mean part of their territory delimited by the Member States;

9   'agglomeration' shall mean a zone with a population concentration in excess of 250000 inhabitants or, where the population concentration is 250000 inhabitants or less, a population density per km^2 which for the Member States justifies the need for ambient air quality to be assessed and managed.

10   'oxides of nitrogen' shall mean the sum of nitric oxide and nitrogen dioxide added as parts per billion and expressed as nitrogen dioxide in micrograms per cubic meter;

11   'PM10' shall mean particulate matter which passes through a size-selective inlet with a 50 % efficiency cut-off at 10 >ISO_7>ì>ISO_1>m aerodynamic diameter;

12   'PM2,5' shall mean particulate matter which passes through a size-selective inlet with a 50 % efficiency cut-off at 2,5>ISO_7>ì>ISO_1>m aerodynamic diameter;

13   'upper assessment threshold' shall mean a level specified in Annex V, below which a combination of measurements and modelling techniques may be used to assess ambient-air quality, in accordance with Article 6(3) of Directive 96/62/EC;

14 'lower assessment threshold' shall mean a level specified in Annex V, below which modelling or objective-estimation techniques alone may be used to assess ambient-air quality in accordance with Article 6(4) of Directive 96/62/EC;

15 'natural events' shall mean volcanic eruptions, seismic activities, geothermal activities, wild-land fires, high-wind events or the atmospheric resuspension or transport of natural particles from dry regions;

16 'fixed measurements' shall mean measurements taken in accordance with Article 6(5) of Directive 96/62/EC.

Article 3 Sulphur dioxide

1 Member States shall take the measures necessary to ensure that concentrations of sulphur dioxide in ambient air, as assessed in accordance with Article 7, do not exceed the limit values laid down in Section I of Annex I from the dates specified therein.

The margins of tolerance laid down in Section I of Annex I shall apply in accordance with Article 8 of Directive 96/62/EC.

2 The alert threshold for concentrations of sulphur dioxide in ambient air shall be that laid down in Section II of Annex I.

3 In order to assist the Commission in preparing the report provided for in Article 10, until 31 December 2003 Member States shall, where practicable, record data on concentrations of sulphur dioxide averaged over ten minutes from certain measuring stations which they have selected as representative of air quality in inhabited areas close to sources and at which hourly concentrations are measured. At the same time as data are supplied on hourly concentrations in accordance with Article 11(1) of Directive 96/62/EC, Member States shall report to the Commission, for those selected measuring stations, the number of ten-minute concentrations which have exceeded 500 >ISO_7>ì>ISO_1>g/m₃, the number of days within the calendar year on which that occurred, the number of those days on which hourly concentrations of sulphur dioxide simultaneously exceeded 350 >ISO_7>ì>ISO_1>g/m^3 and the maximum ten-minute concentration recorded.

4 Member States may designate zones or agglomerations within which limit values for sulphur dioxide as laid down in Section I of Annex I are exceeded owing to concentrations of sulphur dioxide in ambient air due to natural sources. Member States shall send the Commission lists of any such zones or agglomerations together with information on concentrations and sources of sulphur dioxide therein. When informing the Commission in accordance with Article 11(1) of Directive 96/62/EC, Member States shall provide the necessary justification to demonstrate that any exceedances are due to natural sources.

Within such zones or agglomerations Member States shall be obliged to implement action plans in accordance with Article 8(3) of Directive 96/62/EC only where the limit values laid down in Section I of Annex I are exceeded owing to man-made emissions.

Article 4 Nitrogen dioxide and oxides of nitrogen

1 Member States shall take the measures necessary to ensure that concentrations of nitrogen dioxide and, where applicable, of oxides of nitrogen, in ambient air, as assessed in accordance with Article 7, do not exceed the limit values laid down in Section I of Annex II as from the dates specified therein.

The margins of tolerance laid down in Section I of Annex II shall apply in accordance with Article 8 of Directive 96/62/EC.

2   The alert threshold for concentrations of nitrogen dioxide in ambient air shall be that laid down in Section II of Annex II.

Article 5 Particulate matter

1   Member States shall take the measures necessary to ensure that concentrations of PM10 in ambient air, as assessed in accordance with Article 7, do not exceed the limit values laid down in Section I of Annex III as from the dates specified therein.

The margins of tolerance laid down in Section I of Annex III shall apply in accordance with Article 8 of Directive 96/62/EC.

2   Member States shall ensure that measuring stations to supply data on concentrations of PM2,5 are installed and operated. Each Member State shall choose the number and the siting of the stations at which PM2,5 is to be measured as representative of concentrations of PM2,5 within that Member State. Where possible sampling points for PM2,5 shall be co-located with sampling points for PM10.

Within nine months of the end of each year Member States shall send the Commission the arithmetic mean, the median, the ninety-eighth percentile and the maximum concentration calculated from measurements of PM2,5 over any twenty-four hours within that year. The ninety-eighth percentile shall be calculated in accordance with the procedure laid down in Section 4 of Annex I to Council Decision 97/101/EC of 27 January 1997 establishing a reciprocal exchange of information and data from networks and individual stations measuring ambient air pollution within the Member States(6).

3   Action plans for PM10 prepared in accordance with Article 8 of Directive 96/62/EC and general strategies for decreasing concentrations of PM10 shall also aim to reduce concentrations of PM2,5.

4   Where the limit values for PM10 laid down in Section I of Annex III are exceeded owing to concentrations of PM10 in ambient air due to natural events which result in concentrations significantly in excess of normal background levels from natural sources, Member States shall inform the Commission in accordance with Article 11(1) of Directive 96/62/EC, providing the necessary justification to demonstrate that such exceedances are due to natural events. In such cases, Member States shall be obliged to implement action plans in accordance with Article 8(3) of Directive 96/62/EC only where the limit values laid down in Section I of Annex III are exceeded owing to causes other than natural events.

5   Member States may designate zones or agglomerations within which limit values for PM10 as laid down in Section I of Annex III are exceeded owing to concentrations of PM10 in ambient air due to the resuspension of particulates following the winter sanding of roads. Member States shall send the Commission lists of any such zones or agglomerations together with information on concentrations and sources of PM10 therein. When informing the Commission in accordance with Article 11(1) of Directive 96/62/EC, Member States shall provide the necessary justification to demonstrate that any exceedances are due to such resuspended particulates, and that reasonable measures have been taken to lower the concentrations.

Within such zones or agglomerations Member States shall be obliged to implement action plans in accordance with Article 8(3) of Directive 96/62/EC only where the limit values laid down in Section I of Annex III are exceeded owing to PM10 levels other than those caused by winter road sanding.

Article 6 Lead

Member States shall take the measures necessary to ensure that concentrations of lead in ambient air, as assessed in accordance with Article 7, do not exceed the limit values laid down in Section I of Annex IV as from the dates specified therein.

The margins of tolerance laid down in Section I of Annex IV shall apply in accordance with Article 8 of Directive 96/62/EC.

Article 7 Assessment of concentrations

1   The upper and lower assessment thresholds for sulphur dioxide, nitrogen dioxide and oxides of nitrogen, particulate matter and lead for the purposes of Article 6 of Directive 96/62/EC shall be those laid down in Section I of Annex V.

   The classification of each zone or agglomeration for the purposes of the same Article 6 shall be reviewed at least every five years in accordance with the procedure laid down in Section II of Annex V. Classification shall be reviewed earlier in the event of significant changes in activities relevant to ambient concentrations of sulphur dioxide, nitrogen dioxide or, where relevant, oxides of nitrogen, particulate matter or lead.

2   The criteria for determining the location of sampling points for the measurement of sulphur dioxide, nitrogen dioxide and oxides of nitrogen, particulate matter and lead in ambient air shall be those listed in Annex VI. The minimum number of sampling points for fixed measurements of concentrations of each relevant pollutant shall be as laid down in Annex VII and they shall be installed in each zone or agglomeration within which measurement is required if fixed measurement is the sole source of data on concentrations within it.

3   For zones and agglomerations within which information from fixed measurement stations is supplemented by information from other sources, such as emission inventories, indicative measurement methods and air-quality modelling, the number of fixed measuring stations to be installed and the spatial resolution of other techniques shall be sufficient for the concentrations of air pollutants to be established in accordance with Section I of Annex VI and Section I of Annex VIII.

4   For zones and agglomerations within which measurement is not required, modelling or objective-estimation techniques may be used.

5   The reference methods for the analysis of sulphur dioxide, of nitrogen dioxide and of oxides of nitrogen and for the sampling and analysis of lead shall be as laid down in Sections I to III of Annex IX.

   The reference method for the sampling and measurement of PM10 shall be as laid down in Section IV of Annex IX.

   The provisional reference method for the sampling and measurement of PM2,5 shall be as laid down in Section V of Annex IX.

   The reference techniques for air-quality modelling shall be as laid down in Section VI of Annex IX.

6   The date by which Member States shall inform the Commission of the methods they have used for the preliminary assessment of air quality under Article 11(1)(d) of Directive 96/62/EC shall be eighteen months after the entry into force of this Directive.

7   Any amendments necessary to adapt this Article and Annexes V to IX to scientific and technical progress shall be adopted in accordance with the procedure laid down in Article 12 of Directive 96/62/EC.

Article 8 Public information

1   Member States shall ensure that up-to-date information on ambient concentrations of sulphur dioxide, nitrogen dioxide and oxides of nitrogen, particulate matter and lead is routinely made available to the public as well as to appropriate organisations such as environmental organisations, consumer organisations, organisations representing the interests of sensitive populations and other relevant health-care bodies by means, for example, of broadcast media, press, information screens or computer-network services.

Information on ambient concentrations of sulphur dioxide, nitrogen dioxide and particulate matter shall be updated on at least a daily basis, and, in the case of hourly values for sulphur dioxide and nitrogen dioxide, wherever practicable, information shall be updated on an hourly basis. Information on ambient concentrations of lead shall be updated on a three-monthly basis.

Such information shall at least indicate any exceeding of the concentrations in the limit values and alert thresholds over the averaging periods laid down in Annexes I to IV. It shall also provide a short assessment in relation to limit values and alert thresholds and appropriate information regarding effects on health.

2   When making plans or programmes available to the public under Article 8(3) of Directive 96/62/EC, including plans or programmes referred to under Articles 3(4), 5(4) and 5(5) of this Directive, Member States shall also make them available to the organisations referred to in paragraph 1.

3   When an alert threshold laid down in Annex I or II is exceeded, details made available to the public in accordance with Article 10 of Directive 96/62/EC shall at least include the items listed in Section III of the Annex in question.

4   Information made available to the public and to organisations under paragraphs 1 and 3 shall be clear, comprehensible and accessible.

Article 9 Repeals and transitional arrangements

1   Council Directive 80/779/EEC of 15 July 1980 on air-quality limit values and guide values for sulphur dioxide and suspended particulates(7) shall be repealed with effect from 19 July 2001 except that Articles 1, 2(1), 3(1), 9, 15 and 16 of Directive 80/779/EEC and Annexes I, IIIb and IV thereto shall be repealed with effect from 1 January 2005.

2   Council Directive 82/884/EEC of 3 December 1982 on a limit value for lead in the air(8) shall be repealed with effect from 19 July 2001 except that Articles 1, 2, 3(1), 7, 12 and 13 of Directive 82/884/EEC shall be repealed with effect from 1 January 2005.

3   Council Directive 85/203/EEC of 7 March 1985 on air-quality standards for nitrogen dioxide(9) shall be repealed with effect from 19 July 2001 except that Articles 1(1), first indent, and (2), 2, first indent, 3(1), 5, 9, 15 and 16 of Directive 85/203/EEC and Annex I thereto shall be repealed with effect from 1 January 2010.

4   From 19 July 2001 Member States shall employ measurement stations and other methods of air-quality assessment that comply with this Directive to assess concentrations of sulphur dioxide, nitrogen dioxide and lead in ambient air to obtain data for the purpose of demonstrating compliance with the limit values laid down in Directives 80/779/EEC, 82/884/EEC and 85/203/EEC until such time as the limit values laid down in those Directives cease to apply.

5   From 19 July 2001 Member States may employ measurement stations and other methods of air-quality assessment that comply with this Directive as regards PM10 to assess concentrations of suspended particulate matter for the purpose of demonstrating compliance with the limit values for total suspended particulates laid down in Annex IV to Directive 80/779/EEC; for the purpose of demonstrating such compliance, however, the data so collected shall be multiplied by a factor of 1.2.

6   Member States shall inform the Commission of any exceedances of the limit values laid down in Directives 80/779/EEC, 82/884/EEC and 85/203/EEC, together with the values recorded, the reasons for each recorded instance and the measures taken to prevent any recurrence, within nine months of the end of each year in accordance with the procedure laid down in Article 11 of Directive 96/62/EC until such time as the limit values laid down in those Directives cease to apply.

7   In the zones in which a Member State considers it necessary to limit or prevent a foreseeable increase in pollution by sulphur dioxide, oxides of nitrogen or suspended particulate matter it may continue to use the guide values for the protection of ecosystems laid down in Annex II to Directive 80/779/EEC and in Annex II to Directive 85/203/EEC.

[Articles 10–14 and all Annexes omitted.]

DOMESTIC LAW

The common law[28]

While, as we saw in Chapter 1, the common law is restricted principally because of its focus on private property rights, there is a long history of the common law being used to combat air pollution. McLaren, citing Blackstone, tells us that the accepted theory at the end of the 18th century was that there was a natural right to clean air.[29] During the course of the 19th century while some judges continued to follow a natural rights approach others sought to accommodate the needs of developing industries by emphasising the need to balance rights to clean air against the needs of industrial development. For example, *Hole v Barlow*[30] concerned an action brought against a landowner on the outskirts of London who was causing smoke by making bricks on his land. At the trial Byles J advised the jury that if the defendant had established his operation in a convenient and proper place no action would lie in nuisance, despite the annoyance caused. On appeal the Court of Common Pleas extended this concession to developmental interests by referring both to the reasonableness of the location and to the

---

28   See generally p 33, above.
29   McLaren, JPS, 'Nuisance and the industrial revolution' (1983) 3(2) OJLS 155–221, p 170.
30   (1858) 4 CB(NS) 334. *Ibid*, p 174.

reasonableness of the operations themselves. According to McLaren the court effectively equated liability in nuisance with the nascent action in negligence. That this 'concessionary' approach was not universally accepted by the judges can be seen in another case concerning brick-making reported just four years later, *Bamford v Turnley*.[31] Here Baron Bramwell argued that where industry damaged land belonging to others it should provide compensation and internalise the cost of the damage, or not be in business at all.

The leading case of the period was *St Helen's Smelting Co v Tipping* (1865). Mr Tipping was the owner of a 1300 acre estate in the town of St Helen's near Liverpool. He brought an action to recover damages: (a) for injuries to trees, hedges, fruit, and cattle; and (b) for substantial personal discomfort caused by the defendant's copper-smelting works. The House of Lords upheld the Exchequer Chamber's ruling that the company was liable for any physical damage it caused, but not for the deterioration of the plaintiff's comfort. In effect, the court held that since Mr Tipping lived near an industrialised area he had to expect a reduction in his personal comfort, although he could get compensation for the reduction in value to his property. This distinction between injury to property and injury to personal comfort was crude, but it was an attempt to balance rights to clean air and the needs of industry. The distinction, however, failed to recognise that property values may be adversely affected not only when the property was physically damaged, but also when pollution meant that the property could no longer be enjoyed. The principle that the level of 'comfort' that one had a right to expect depended on the location of the property also meant that legal actions based on 'comfort' were likely to be impossible in industrial areas. This provided a real obstacle to the use of nuisance to protect environmental conditions in areas where protection against pollution was most badly needed. Moreover, while the language in the case referred to 'personal comfort' implying something trivial, the reality was that air pollution was a major contributory factor to serious illness and to a short life expectancy. In the early 1840s life expectancy was calculated as being 26 years in Liverpool and 24 years in Manchester, with unusually high rates of infant death being due to lung disease.[32]

Halsey v Esso Petroleum is a more recent example of the use of nuisance and *Rylands v Fletcher* to combat air pollution. *Margereson v JR Roberts Ltd* provides an illustration of the use of negligence by victims of asbestos pollution.

Halsey v Esso Petroleum Co Ltd [1961] 1 WLR 683; [1961] 2 All ER 145; 178 EG 193

The plaintiff occupied a house in Rainville Road, Fulham, which was a road zoned for residential purposes. The defendants, Esso Petroleum Co Ltd, operated an oil distributing depot at premises adjoining Rainville Road which were situated in an area zoned for industrial purposes. The defendants' depot dealt with fuel oil in its light, medium and heavy grades, the oil being pumped from river tankers on to the depot and from the depot into road tankers. It was necessary to heat the medium and heavy grades of oil for the purpose of pumping them. The through-put of oil at the depot had increased from

---

31   [1861–73] All ER Rep 706; (1862) 3 B & S 62.

32   Brenner, J, 'Nuisance law and the industrial revolution' (1974) J of Leg 413–33, p 417.

30,414,000 gallons in 1953 to 56,607,000 gallons in 1957. In 1956 night shift working was reintroduced.

Acid smuts containing sulphate were emitted from chimneys at the depot. These smuts were visible falling outside the plaintiff's house. There was proof that the smuts had damaged clothes hung out to dry in the garden of the plaintiff's house and also paintwork of the plaintiff's car. The depot emitted a pungent and nauseating smell of oil which went beyond a background smell and was more than would affect a sensitive person but the plaintiff had not suffered any injury to health from the smell. During the night there was noise from the boilers which at its peak caused windows and doors in the plaintiff's house to vibrate and prevented the plaintiff sleeping. The defendants had attempted to reduce this noise by soundproofing, but it remained and was more than trivial.

During the night shift from 10 pm to 6 am there was noise from large road tankers which arrived at and left the depot at points close to the plaintiff's house. Up to fifteen tankers came and left the depot at different times during the night shift and sometimes up to four tankers arrived or left together. The noise from the tankers was made partly in the public highway outside the depot, as they manoeuvred on entering or leaving the depot, and partly in the depot itself.

The plaintiff brought an action for nuisance caused by the acid smuts, smell and noise.

Held: the defendants were liable to the plaintiff in the following respects and on the following grounds:

(i) for the emission of acid smuts–

   (a) under the rule in *Rylands v Fletcher* (on which see Chapter 3, p 287) in respect of the damage to clothing on the plaintiff's land and of the damage to his car while it was on the public highway since in both cases the damage was caused by the escape from the defendants' premises of a harmful substance, viz, noxious acid smuts;

   (b) as a private nuisance in respect of damage to the clothes since the damage was a material injury to the plaintiff's property resulting from trade carried on by the defendants in neighbouring property;

   St Helen's Smelting Co v Tipping (1865) 11 HL Cas 642 applied;

   (c) as a public nuisance in respect of which the plaintiff had suffered special damage by reason of the action of the noxious smuts on his car on the public highway;

(ii) in respect of nuisance by smell because the smell emanating from the defendants' premises amounted to a private nuisance, notwithstanding that there was no proof of injury to the plaintiff's health, for injury to health was not a necessary ingredient in the cause of action for nuisance by smell;

(iii) in respect of a private nuisance by noise from the boilers and the road tankers when in the depot, in either instance at night, because the noise was an inconvenience which materially interfered with the ordinary physical comfort of human existence according to plain, sober and simple notions among ordinary people, such as the plaintiff, living in this part of Fulham;

(iv) for the noise from road tankers made at night on the public highway–

(a) as a public nuisance, since the concentration of moving vehicles in a small area of the public highway, viz, outside the depot, was an unreasonable user of the highway and caused special damage to the plaintiff whom it affected more than the ordinary members of the public;

(b) as a private nuisance, since the noise was directly related to the operation of the depot and it was not a pre-requisite of private nuisance that the matter complained of emanated from the defendants' land so long as it affected the plaintiff's property, and in the present case the noise from the highway materially interfered with the plaintiff's enjoyment of his house.

[The following is an extract from the judgment of Veale J.]

Veale J: The claim is broadly put on two bases: pollution of the atmosphere and noise; but that is perhaps an over-simplification. The alleged pollution takes the form of smells (which do not cause any real injury to health unless one is allergic to such smells) and also to deposits consisting of acid smuts and oily drops which fall on washing put out to dry, on fabrics inside the house such as curtains and on paintwork, including the paintwork of a motor car. The alleged noise comprises noise from boilers, pumps and vehicles, the latter category embracing not only the noise of the vehicle itself in motion but noises caused by the driver and workmen such as shouting, slamming doors and banging pipes.

It is important that the nature of the district should be borne in mind ... There is an undoubted strip of industrial development on the river bank. This strip is zoned for industrial purposes. There are various kinds of industrial activity carried on, and the defendants' premises are not the only place where oil is dealt with. On the other hand the houses in Rainville Road and in the streets adjacent to Rainville Road are in a residential area. They are not affected by traffic in Fulham Palace Road. They are what might be described as nice small terrace houses. This area is zoned for residential purposes. In assessing the character of the neighbourhood, I have been assisted by what I have seen myself [...]

I have been referred to a very large number of authorities, but it seems to me that, save on one point to which I will refer later, there can be little dispute as to the law which has to be applied to the facts. As long ago as 1865, in *St Helen's Smelting Co v Tipping*, Lord Westbury, LC, said:

... in matters of this description it appears to me that it is a very desirable thing to mark the difference between an action brought for a nuisance upon the ground that the alleged nuisance produces material injury to the property, and an action brought for a nuisance on the ground that the thing alleged to be a nuisance is productive of sensible personal discomfort. With regard to the latter, namely, the personal inconvenience and interference with one's enjoyment, one's quiet, one's personal freedom, anything that discomposes or injuriously affects the senses or the nerves, whether that may or may not be denominated a nuisance, must undoubtedly depend greatly on the circumstances of the place where the thing complained of actually occurs. If a man lives in a town, it is necessary that he should subject himself to the consequences of those operations of trade which may be carried on in his immediate locality, which are actually necessary for trade and commerce, and also for the enjoyment of property, and for the benefit of the inhabitants of the town and of the public at large. If a man lives in a street where there are numerous shops, and a shop is opened next door to him, which is carried on in a fair and reasonable way, he has no ground for complaint, because to himself individually there may arise much discomfort from the trade carried on in that shop. But when an occupation is carried on by one person in the neighbourhood of another, and the result of that trade, or occupation, or business, is a material injury to property, then there unquestionably arises a very different consideration. I think, my Lords, that in a case of that description, the submission which is required from persons living in society to that amount of discomfort which may be necessary for the legitimate and free exercise of the trade of their neighbours, would not apply to circumstances the immediate result of which is sensible injury to the value of the property.

In this case smell and noise come into one category, actual deposits in the way of harmful smuts and oily drops come into the other. I bear in mind the observations of Lord Loreburn, LC, in *Polsue & Alfieri Ltd v Rushmer* [1907] AC 123.

Lord Loreburn, LC, said:

The law of nuisance undoubtedly is elastic, as was stated by Lord Halsbury in the case of *Colls v Home & Colonial Stores, Ltd* n(5). He said: 'What may be called the uncertainty of the test may also be described as its elasticity. A dweller in towns cannot expect to have as pure air, as free from smoke, smell, and noise as if he lived in the country, and distant from other dwellings, and yet an excess of smoke, smell, and noise may give a cause of action, but in each of such cases it becomes a question of degree, and the question is in each case whether it amounts to a nuisance which will give a right of action.'

This is a question of fact.

[...]

So far as the present case is concerned, liability for nuisance by harmful deposits could be established by proving damage by the deposits to the property in question, provided, of course, that the injury was not merely trivial. Negligence is not an ingredient of the cause of action, and the character of the neighbourhood is not a matter to be taken into consideration. On the other hand nuisance by smell or noise is something to which no absolute standard can be applied. It is always a question of degree whether the interference with comfort or convenience is sufficiently serious to constitute a nuisance. The character of the neighbourhood is very relevant and all the relevant circumstances have to be taken into account. What might be a nuisance in one area is by no means necessarily so in another. In an urban area, everyone must put up with a certain amount of discomfort and annoyance from the activities of neighbours, and the law must strike a fair and reasonable balance between the right of the plaintiff on the one hand to the undisturbed enjoyment of his property, and the right of the defendant on the other hand to use his property for his own lawful enjoyment. That is how I approach this case.

It may be possible in some cases to prove that noise or smell have in fact diminished the value of the plaintiff's property in the market. That consideration does not arise in this case, and no evidence has been called in regard to it. The standard in respect of discomfort and inconvenience from noise and smell that I have to apply is that of the ordinary reasonable and responsible person who lives in this particular area of Fulham. This is not necessarily the same as the standard which the plaintiff chooses to set up for himself. It is the standard of the ordinary man, and the ordinary man, who may well like peace and quiet, will not complain for instance of the noise of traffic if he chooses to live on a main street in an urban centre, nor of the reasonable noises of industry, if he chooses to live alongside a factory.

Nuisance is commonly regarded as a tort in respect of land. In *Read v J Lyons & Co Ltd* (9), Lord Simonds said 'only he has a lawful claim who has suffered an invasion of some proprietary or other interest in land'. In this connexion the allegation of damage to the plaintiff's motor car calls for special consideration, since the allegation is that when the offending smuts from the defendants' chimney alighted on it, the motor car was not actually on land in the plaintiff's occupation, but was on the public highway outside his door. Whether or not a claim in respect of private nuisance lies for damage to the motor car in these circumstances, in my judgment such damage is covered by the doctrine in *Rylands v Fletcher* [...] If it be the fact that harmful sulphuric acid or harmful sulphate escaped from the defendants' premises and damaged the motor car in the public highway, I am bound by the decision of the Court of Appeal in *Charing Cross Electricity Supply Co v Hydraulic Power Co* [...], and *Miles v Forest Rock Granite Co (Leicestershire), Ltd* [...] in neither of which cases was the plaintiff in occupation of land. This doctrine of *Rylands v Fletcher* [...], whether or not it is strictly based on nuisance, applies to the sulphuric acid or sulphate in smuts or oily drops wherever they alight: on washing hung out to dry, as well as on to a motor car in the street.

In my judgment the plaintiff is also right in saying that if the motor car was damaged in this way while on the public highway, it is a public nuisance in respect of which he has suffered special damage ... but even if the plaintiff was using the road as a place to garage his motor car, and he was not entitled to do so, I do not regard those facts as disentitling him to claim damages in respect of injury to the motor car.

Bearing all these considerations in mind, I turn to the facts of the case.

[His Lordship, having stated the introductory facts, went on to deal with the specific complaints. As to acid smuts, the evidence established that laundry hung out to dry in the immediate vicinity of the defendants' chimneys had been damaged by smuts causing holes in the laundry after it had been washed to remove the stains from the smuts. Black smuts up to the size of a sixpence were seen coming from the chimneys and falling in front of the plaintiff's house. The smuts when analysed showed a strong positive reaction for iron (the defendants' chimneys were iron) and for sulphuric acid, and in his Lordship's opinion this was strong evidence of pollution of the atmosphere by a harmful substance. Further tests collected from Rainville Road indicated that the pollution consisted of sulphate. His Lordship continued:]

I have no doubt at all that the defendants had been the cause of the emission into the atmosphere of noxious smuts which had caused damage to the plaintiff's washing and to his motor car. The smuts are noxious acid smuts, and it does not matter whether they contain sulphate or sulphuric acid. For this damage the defendants in my judgment are liable, both as for a nuisance and under *Rylands v Fletcher* [...]

It is not necessary for the plaintiff to prove or for me to decide precisely why this has happened. It is necessary for the plaintiff to prove the fact of it happening, and this I am satisfied that he has done. [...] This nuisance to the plaintiff may, partly at all events, be due to the shortcomings of one of the chimney stacks. I do not know and I do not have to decide. The fact is that noxious smuts have come from the defendants' depot and have done damage.

I am not impressed by any argument based on the fact that noxious smuts are to be found elsewhere and on many urban buildings. In the vast majority of such places, although they may be unsightly, they do no damage or no appreciable damage, and their origin cannot be traced. In the present case, acid smuts have done damage and their origin has been traced. There is not and cannot be any doubt that the emission of acid smuts is a well known problem. As is stated at p 23 of the 31st report of the Department of Scientific and Industrial

Research on the Investigation of Atmospheric Pollution, this is – and I quote – 'a form of pollution which is particularly troublesome in its effect'. One of the defendants' witnesses regarded it as being a particularly well known trouble in the case of metal chimneys. Wherever fuel, whether coal or oil, is burnt, sulphur dioxide is discharged into the air. This does not depend on the efficiency of the combustion. The amount of sulphur dioxide so discharged depends on the amount of sulphur in the fuel. Although fuel oil frequently contains between 3% and 4% of sulphur, the manager of the defendants' depot told me on the fourth occasion that he gave evidence, that 90% of the oil burnt by the defendants comes from Thames Haven as opposed to 10% from Purfleet. The sulphur content of Thames Haven oil is 2.2% on the average, which is low. But this case is not a complaint of damage by sulphur dioxide; it is a complaint of damage by H_2SO_4. What may happen is that the sulphur dioxide discharged up the chimney may combine with water vapour, as may very small quantities of sulphur trioxide, and it is then that sulphate or SO_4 is formed. This condenses and when in contact with particles of carbon, acid smuts may also be formed, and it is for this reason that lagging of the chimney may be important, since thereby this process is stayed and the chimney temperature is higher and above what has been called the acid dew-point.

The defendants' chimneys were lagged approximately two months after the complaint in December, 1959, by the medical officer of health, that is in approximately March, 1960. I have no details of what was done. It has certainly not stopped the emission of acid smuts, though it may have made them less frequent.

[After referring to expert evidence, His Lordship continued:]

I find as a fact that lagging has not cured the emission of acid smuts, though they may now be less frequent. There is no defence to this action so far as noxious smuts are concerned.

I find the question of oily droplets more difficult to decide – not unnaturally, because they are not visible to the naked eye and the plaintiff cannot say that he has seen them fall. No claim for damage to his curtains is included in the statement of claim. On balance, after some considerable hesitation, I do not think that I can say that the plaintiff's laundry is in real and constant danger from oily droplets as opposed to acid smuts emitted from the defendants' depot. I have no doubt that there are occasions when these oily droplets do not disperse into the atmosphere as completely as they are said to do, and I am not prepared to dismiss, as I am asked to do, the tests carried out for the plaintiff. Nevertheless, I find myself in doubt on this one point as to the frequency and extent of any oily droplets as opposed to acid smuts, and I limit my finding that the defendants are guilty of nuisance causing damage to the plaintiff to the emission of acid smuts.

I turn now to the question of smell. [...]

I turn now to the question of nuisance by noise. [...]

In my judgment, [...] the defendants are liable to the plaintiff in respect of pollution, that is both smuts as well as smell, and also in respect of noise, that is both from the plant and from the tankers. It is pleaded in para 10 of the defence that any nuisance has been legalised by prescription. There is no substance in this contention, except in so far as I have already dealt with it in relation to smell. The nuisances for which I hold the defendants liable have not continued for anything approaching 20 years, and there have been persistent complaints. No question of prescription can arise until a nuisance is first committed. The nuisances of which the defendants are guilty are all of recent origin.

The plaintiff is therefore entitled to damages. For his damaged linen he claims £5. This is a modest claim and he is entitled to it. He is also entitled, in my view, to damages in respect of his motor car, but I do not think that the alleged loss of value due to the damaged paintwork is proved. I think a new coat of paint would have maintained the value of the motor car. I have evidence as to what amount this would have been at the time the damage was sustained, and it might amount to £50. On this head I award £30. I do not think a perfect result would be necessary.

Since the end of 1956 the plaintiff has suffered very considerable discomfort. It is something which cannot easily be assessed in terms of money. I am asked by counsel for the plaintiff to award exemplary damages in view of the conduct of the defendants. I agree that there are matters in respect of which the defendants' conduct does not seem to have been satisfactory; but in my judgment this is clearly not a case for exemplary damages. Although the plaintiff fainted twice in the witness-box, there is no evidence before me of any injury to his health. I must do the best I can to award to him a sum in respect of the nuisances by noise and smell which have been inflicted on him over the last few years. On this head, which is limited to noise and smell over the past few years, I award £200. The plaintiff is therefore entitled to £235 damages.

So far as the future is concerned ... The question of remedy by injunction must be considered separately in respect of noise, smell, and smuts. As to noise [...] the plaintiff is entitled, in my judgment, to an injunction to limit it to the hours of the present night shift, namely, ten o'clock at night to six o'clock in the morning ... I am prepared to suspend the operation of this order for a reasonable time so that the defendants may make appropriate arrangements. As to smell, again I think that the plaintiff is entitled to an injunction ... I propose to grant an injunction in general terms restraining the defendants by themselves, their servants or agents from so conducting their operations at the depot as, by reason of smell, to cause a nuisance to the plaintiff. In this case there is no limitation as to the time of day or night, but again, I am prepared to suspend the operation of my order for a reasonable time if the defendants desire to make alterations or adjustments.

As to smuts [...] I do not propose either to grant an injunction or to award damages for the future. If future damage is caused by the defendants to the plaintiff, he will be able to bring a fresh action. I take this course primarily because the whole boilerhouse and the offending chimneys are to be pulled down. A new boilerhouse in a different position will be erected, and the chimney will be of brick and 65 feet high. It is to be hoped that the construction and operation of the new boilerhouse will be such that this particular nuisance will be remedied. If it is not, and this nuisance continues as it was, I have little doubt at all that an injunction could be obtained to restrain it ... In the result there will be judgment for the plaintiff for £235 and injunctions as indicated.

Margereson v JW Roberts Ltd; Hancock v JW Roberts Ltd [1996] Env LR 304

[Russell LJ read the judgment of the Court, from which the following extract is taken.]

Russell LJ: Close by the centre of the city of Leeds in Yorkshire there is a district called Armley. It was there that from the late 19th Century until 1958 the Defendants occupied a factory producing commercial products which involved in the course of their manufacture very extensive use of asbestos. This was regularly crushed and mixed, for example with cotton or cement so as to produce end products such as asbestos mattresses used in connection with heat insulation.

The factory was situated in the midst of an area which was densely populated. Aerial photographs disclose rows of terraced properties. Many were very close to the factory.

Arthur Margereson was born in 1925 and lived in a house about 200 yards or so distant from the factory. Mr Margereson spent his childhood in the property until, in 1943, he enlisted in the army. After war service he returned to Armley to the same house. He died in December 1991 from the lung disease mesothelioma.

Mrs June Marjorie Hancock was another local resident. She was born in 1936 and went to live in a house close by the factory in 1938. Although moving house she remained in the same neighbourhood close by the factory until 1951. She too contracted mesothelioma. She is still alive but sadly very gravely ill suffering from the condition.

On 18 February 1991, prior to his death, Mr Margereson issued proceedings against the Defendants. In them he claimed damages for personal injuries. He alleged that the mesothelioma from which he was suffering had been caused by asbestos dust which the Defendants negligently permitted to escape from their factory into the atmosphere surrounding it, that they had failed to take adequate steps to prevent the dust entering the atmosphere and that, further or in the alternative, the Defendants were strictly liable for the escape of the dust and/or were responsible for a nuisance. No more need be said about strict liability or nuisance for it played no further part in the proceedings. Mr Margereson was first diagnosed as suffering from an asbestos related condition in September 1990. After his death the action was continued in the name of Mr Margereson's widow as his Administratrix.

Mrs Hancock issued proceedings on 5 September 1994. She made essentially the same allegations against the Defendants as Mr Margereson. She had developed symptoms of mesothelioma from late 1992.

The two actions came on for hearing before Holland J sitting at Leeds on 20 June 1995. He had earlier heard the evidence of Mrs Hancock who by then was seriously ill. After 20 June 1995 the Judge received evidence which occupied the Court for the rest of the legal term, something like six weeks. The transcripts of evidence, the documents adduced in evidence, the pleadings and the judgment itself have generated a vast amount of paper. We are grateful to counsel for their concise submissions which have made our task less daunting than might have been the case. The judgment which runs to some 66 pages of transcript was reserved and delivered on 27 October 1995. In each case the Judge found in favour of the respective Plaintiffs on the issue of liability. Subject to those issues damages had been agreed in the case of the Margereson action in the sum of £50,000 and in the case of the Hancock action in the sum of £65,000. The Defendants appeal to this Court.

We deal now with the facts. The evidence was overwhelming to the effect that beyond the perimeters of the factory on all sides asbestos dust was deposited in enormous quantities. That dust had emanated from within the factory walls. It had escaped either through open doors and windows in the factory buildings or from open areas of the factory such as yards and loading bays of which there were eight. The dust was also extracted to an extent from within the factory itself through extraction equipment venting into the atmosphere. The dust was of blue asbestos. It was light and feathery as eiderdown in texture. The Judge found that 'at all material times a substantial emission of dust from the factory premises' took place. He also said 'yet further contributions were made by causing employees to leave for their adjacent homes covered in dust and by leaving bales of asbestos or asbestos products on loading bays for temporary storage so as to be susceptible to the dust releasing activities of playing children'.

As for the interior of the factory premises the Judge found that what might be described as their static condition involved continuing and substantial presence of visual dust which, by the end of the shift, often involved employees being so covered by dust that they acquired nicknames such as 'Abominable Snowman' or 'Feather Leg'.

It was never disputed by the Defendants that the steps taken by them to alleviate the problems of dust contamination were woefully inadequate.

The existence of the eight loading bays and the conditions prevailing there became important features of the two cases. A number of witnesses gave evidence that when they were children regular visits were paid to the loading bays of the factory, and indeed to the open yards where the children found bales of asbestos dust attractive to their childlike propensities. Witnesses, including Mrs Hancock herself, spoke of such visits. During the course of them children would jump up and down on the bales. Sometimes the bales would burst open. Dust, covering the whole of the loading bays was a common feature and doors leading to the factory interior were frequently left open. Dust fibres clung to mesh over the windows. One witness spoke of children playing 'snowballs' using dust acquired in the areas that were open to them.

The overall picture presented by the evidence relating to the areas where children regularly played was that the concentration of asbestos dust in those areas was of a very high order indeed, much higher of course than that encountered in the streets and houses surrounding the factory, although they too suffered a measure of contamination.

We take the opportunity at this stage of our judgment, to correct a misapprehension about these proceedings which gained some publicity before we embarked upon this appeal. The cases were said to be test cases, that a considerable number of other claimants were awaiting the outcome and that effectively the judgment on these appeals would determine the result of many other claims involving residents living outside the perimeters of this and other factories where asbestos dust accumulated. It is important to observe that Holland J expressly disavowed these propositions and, for our part, we confine our observations to the two cases which we are reviewing recognising that that was the approach of the trial Judge and not seeking to pre-empt in any way other claims which may or may not result in findings one way or another.

We turn now to what we regard as the only legal issue in the appeals. What was the duty owed to Mr Margereson and to Mrs Hancock? The answer is to be found almost entirely in the speech of Lord Lloyd in *Page v Smith* [1996] 1 AC 155, [1995] 2 All ER 736, at page 190 of the former report, when he said:

> The test in every case ought to be whether the Defendant can reasonably foresee that his conduct will expose the Plaintiff to the risk of personal injury. If so, then he comes under a duty of care to that Plaintiff. If a working definition of 'Personal Injury' is needed, it can be found in Section 38(1) of the Limitation Act 1980. 'Personal Injuries' includes any disease and any impairment of a person's physical or mental condition.

We add only that in the context of this case we take the view that liability only attaches to these Defendants if the evidence demonstrated that they should reasonably have foreseen a risk of some pulmonary injury, not necessarily mesothelioma.

A great deal of scientific evidence from witnesses with medical expertise as well as many published works were adduced in the court below. This judgment would become unacceptably lengthy if we were to set out extracts from the evidence led before the Judge upon this aspect of the case. We shall content ourselves by referring to the conflicting submissions made on each side before referring briefly to the burden of the evidence. Mr William Woodward QC, on behalf of the Defendants submitted that it was not until about 1933 that, on the Judge's findings, his clients could be regarded as fixed with adequate knowledge of the potentially dangerous qualities of asbestos so as to create the duty of care toward those other than employees working within the confines of the factory. The danger, submitted Mr Woodward, was confined to the condition of asbestosis which all the medical evidence indicated was a condition of gradual onset over a prolonged period of time. Mesothelioma, on the other hand, was a condition which could develop very quickly in consequence of the inhalation of asbestos dust, though the symptoms might take decades to manifest themselves. Thus, so the argument ran in the case of Mr Margereson, his Administratrix could not discount the real possibility that he acquired mesothelioma when playing as a child within the loading bays and at a time prior to 1933 when, so far as mesothelioma was concerned, there was no culpable lack of foresight on the part of the Defendants because they did not know and had no reason to believe that that particular risk as opposed to the risk of asbestosis existed.

Mr Woodward sought to derive support for these submissions from passages to be found in the Judgment of the trial Judge. At page 44 he referred to what he described as the 'seminal report' of Dr ERA Merewether and Mr CW Price. The report was published in 1930 and was entitled 'Effects of asbestos dust on the lungs and dust suppression in the asbestos industry'. [...] It was a Home Office report. Mr Woodward submitted that its real purpose was to highlight the risks of asbestosis amongst asbestos workers, whereas Mr Robin Stewart QC on behalf of Mrs Hancock referred, as did the Judge, to the first page of the report which the Judge cited. That spoke of local effects following the inhalation of dust including pulmonary and bronchial catarrh, asthma, bronchitis, fibrosis and secondary changes such as emphysema local or diffuse. The report pointed out that fibrosis was recognised to be the most important lesion and it is true to say that the Judge seemed to regard the report as the trigger for the Asbestos Industry Regulations 1931. They came into force in March 1933.

We think there is some force in Mr Woodward's submissions that the Judge regarded the Merewether and Price report as something of a watershed in relation to the fixing of a date when the Defendants were culpable and before which they lacked the necessary foresight to found a cause of action. Mr Stewart, on the other hand, drew our attention in his supplementary skeleton argument to a great deal of additional written material which the Judge considered and which ante-dated the Merewether and Price report. Indeed, so submitted Mr Stewart, there was an abundance of evidence before the Judge that prior to the turn of the century there was published material that exposure to asbestos dust could and did cause damage to the lungs of those exposed to it. Accordingly, the Plaintiffs and each of them contend that 1933 was not the year at or about which the Defendants acquired or should have acquired the requisite knowledge as to the potential danger of asbestos dust. The true date was much earlier; certainly long before Mr Margereson's birth date. His activities as a child, therefore, as well as Mrs Hancock's were at a time when the Defendants were on actual or constructive notice as to the potential pulmonary damage that exposure to asbestos dust could bring about.

We reject therefore, as did the Judge, that the Plaintiffs failed to show culpability on the part of the Defendants by virtue of their knowledge of the risk prior to 1933. The information which should have operated upon the Defendants' corporate mind was in existence long before Mr Margereson's birth date.

The final question to be posed and answered was whether any distinction could be sensibly drawn between employees working within the factory and the Plaintiffs involved in this litigation. As the Judge put it, 'did the factory wall pose such a barrier that risk of injury to persons on the further side of such arising from the emissions of asbestos dust amount at worst to no more than "a mere possibility which would never occur to the mind of a reasonable man"'.

The Judge said, 'there is nothing in the law that circumscribes the duty of care by reference to the factory wall ... if the evidence shows with respect to a person outside the factory that he or she was exposed to the knowledge of the Defendants, actual or constructive, to conditions in terms of dust emissions not materially different to those giving rise within the factory to a duty of care, then I can see no reason not to extend to that extramural neighbour a comparable duty of care'. We agree. The Judge added, 'I have no doubt that in the immediate vicinity of the premises factory conditions in terms of dust emission were at various points effectively replicated so as to give rise to like foresight of potential injury to those exposed for prolonged periods'. [...] There is in our view no warrant for interfering with [the Judge's] findings of fact. Each was open to the Judge on the material before him. Once they were made the Plaintiffs were entitled to succeed upon such elementary legal principles as we have indicated. The appeals will be dismissed.

UK legislation and policy on air pollution

The principal UK legislative schemes concerned with air pollution may be summarised as follows:

- National bodies and local authorities have powers and responsibilities in relation to the National Air Quality Strategy established by Pt IV of the Environment Act 1995.
- Integrated Pollution Control (IPC): regulation of the most complex industrial processes is the responsibility of the Environment Agency under the IPC provisions contained in Pt 1 of the Environmental Protection Act 1990. IPC is concerned not only with emissions into the air, but also with pollution of land and water. This system has partially been replaced by the Pollution Prevention and Control regime established by the Pollution Prevention and Control Act 1999. See further Chapter 5.
- Local Air Pollution Control (LAPC): less complex processes generating air pollution are regulated by local authorities (London boroughs and district councils), also under Pt 1 of the Environmental Protection Act 1990. This system has partially been replaced by the Pollution Prevention and Control regime (APC) established by the Pollution Prevention and Control Act 1999. See further Chapter 5.
- Local authorities also have powers regarding smoke pollution under the Clean Air Act 1993 (note that the provisions of Pts I–III of the Clean Air Act 1993 do not apply to any processes regulated by the LAAPC under Pt 1 of the EPA 1990 (s 41)). They may also be concerned with air pollution where activities constitute a statutory nuisance.
- Air pollution is also tackled by means of other specific provisions such as those relating to control of emissions from motor vehicles.

The Air Quality Strategy for England, Scotland, Wales and Northern Ireland

The legal basis for the National Air Quality Strategy is contained in Pt IV of the Environment Act 1995, the relevant extracts of which are set out below.

Environment Act 1995 Part IV Air Quality

Section 80: National air quality strategy

(1) The Secretary of State shall as soon as possible prepare and publish a statement (in this Part referred to as 'the strategy') containing policies with respect to the assessment or management of the quality of air.

(2) The strategy may also contain policies for implementing–

(a) obligations of the United Kingdom under the Community Treaties; or

(b) international agreements to which the United Kingdom is for the time being a party,

so far as relating to the quality of air.

(3) The strategy shall consist of or include–

(a) a statement which relates to the whole of Great Britain; or

(b) two or more statements which between them relate to every part of Great Britain.

(4) The Secretary of State–

(a) shall keep under review his policies with respect to the quality of air; and

(b) may from time to time modify the strategy.

(5) Without prejudice to the generality of what may be included in the strategy, the strategy must include statements with respect to–

(a) standards relating to the quality of air;

(b) objectives for the restriction of the levels at which particular substances are present in the air; and

(c) measures which are to be taken by local authorities and other persons for the purpose of achieving those objectives.

(6) In preparing the strategy or any modification of it, the Secretary of State shall consult–

(a) the appropriate new Agency;

(b) such bodies or persons appearing to him to be representative of the interests of local government as he may consider appropriate;

(c) such bodies or persons appearing to him to be representative of the interests of industry as he may consider appropriate; and

(d) such other bodies or persons as he may consider appropriate.

(7) Before publishing the strategy or any modification of it, the Secretary of State–

(a) shall publish a draft of the proposed strategy or modification, together with notice of a date before which, and an address at which, representations may be made to him concerning the draft so published; and

(b) shall take into account any such representations which are duly made and not withdrawn.

Note:

Section 81 requires the Environment Agency and the Scottish Environment Agency to have regard to the strategy in carrying out their functions.

The first statement of the National Air Quality Strategy was published in March 1997. The Labour government endorsed that Strategy in July 1997 but undertook a full review in

1998, a year earlier than originally planned. Following two consultations the revised *Air Quality Strategy for England, Scotland, Wales and Northern Ireland* was published in January 2000 (DETR, 2000, Cm 4548).

The primary objective of the Strategy is to 'ensure that everyone is able to enjoy a level of ambient air quality in public places[33] which poses no significant risk to his or her health and quality of life'. It seeks to map, as far as possible, the future ambient air quality policy in the UK in the medium term. It aims to provide the 'best practicable protection to human health' by setting health-based objectives for eight main air pollutants: benzene, 1,3-butadiene, carbon monoxide, lead, nitrogen dioxide, ozone, particles (PM10), and sulphur dioxide. It aims to contribute to the protection of the natural environment by setting objectives for two pollutants (nitrogen dioxide and sulphur dioxide) for the protection of vegetation and ecosystems. The Strategy is designed to enable those who contribute to air pollution, those who are involved in its abatement, and those affected by pollution to identify their role in improving air quality. It also identifies the action to be taken at international, national and local levels to achieve these objectives.

The Strategy was prepared on the basis of the following guiding principles:

- It should afford the best practical protection to human health and the environment.
- The Expert Panel on Air Quality Standard's recommendations for air quality standards should be the basis for setting the objectives, except where the objective is derived from the limit value set out in the Air Quality Daughter Directive 99/30 (see p 164, above), which is based on WHO guideline values.
- It should take full account of the need to comply with the EU Air Quality Daughter Directive 99/30 (see p 164, above), while providing the opportunity for stricter national objectives for some pollutants where this is considered appropriate.
- In addition to the health and wider environmental effects of the pollutants, objectives should take account of the practicability of abatement or mitigation measures, their costs and benefits and other social and economic factors.
- Account should be taken, as far as possible, of developments in European legislation, technological and scientific advances, improved air pollution modelling techniques and increased understanding of the economic and social issues involved.

The Strategy is said to follow an 'effects-based' approach. The eight pollutants addressed by the Strategy are all known to have adverse effects on human health. They also occur widely throughout the UK, mainly as a result of the use of motor vehicles and industry. While the Strategy is concerned with reducing damage to vegetation, ecosystems and buildings the main emphasis is upon taking targeted action to protect human health.

The Environment Act 1995 requires the Strategy to include statements on 'standards relating to the quality of air', and 'objectives for the restriction of the levels at which particular substances are present in the air'. Standards are used as benchmarks or reference points for the setting of objectives.

---

33   The Strategy is not concerned with occupational exposure to air pollution.

Standards are the concentrations of pollutants in the atmosphere which can broadly be taken to achieve a certain level of environmental quality. They are based on the assessment of the affects of each pollutant on human health.

Objectives are policy targets setting out what the Government and the devolved administrations intend should be achieved in the light of the air quality standards (see further below).

Local air quality management areas (AQMAs)[34]

The framework introduced by the Environment Act 1995 envisages that where the objectives are unlikely to be met through national action, there should be complementary action at a local level. Factors such as traffic density, topography and geography, for example, can cause local air pollution hot spots that cannot be effectively dealt with by national action. Local air quality management provides a system to enable local councils to take the lead in tackling local air pollution problems.

District Councils and unitary Councils are required to review and assess local air quality (s 82 of the Environment Act 1995). The reviews have to consider the current air quality and the likely future air quality during the 'relevant period' (a period that is prescribed by regulations). If, after undertaking such a review, it appears likely that the objectives in the Air Quality Strategy will not be met, then the council must declare an air quality management area (AQMA) and draw up an action plan explaining how it intends to ensure that the objectives will be met (ss 83 and 84 of the Environment Act 1995). Even if an AQMA is not needed, councils are encouraged to consider developing a local air quality strategy to set out its general approach to improving air quality.

The objectives set out in the Air Quality Strategy do not of themselves impose legal obligations on local authorities in respect of AQMAs. Legal obligations only arise when the objectives have been contained in regulations made under s 87 of the Environment Act 1995. The objectives contained in the first statement of the Strategy in 1997 were, with the exception of the objectives relating to Ozone,[35] included in Air Quality Regulations in 1997. The revised objectives contained in the 2000 version of the Strategy have been given legal effect by Air Quality Regulations 2000 SI 2000/928 which came in effect on 6 April 2000. The maximum levels of benzene, 1,3-butadiene, carbon monoxide, lead, nitrogen dioxide, PM 10, and sulphur dioxide in the air are to be met in accordance with a timetable, depending on the substance, ranging from 31 December 2003 to 31 December 2008 (the detailed provisions appear in Schedule 1).

---

34 The following summary of AQMAs draws on a briefing published by Friends of the Earth as part of its Atmosphere and Transport Campaign. See www.foe.uk/campaigns/atmosphere-and-transport/pubs/laqms.htm.
35 Ozone was not included because it is accepted that national rather than local action is appropriate to deal with this pollutant.

Environment Act 1995

Section 82: Local authority reviews

(1) Every local authority shall from time to time cause a review to be conducted of the quality for the time being, and the likely future quality within the relevant period, of air within the authority's area.

(2) Where a local authority causes a review under sub-section (1) above to be conducted, it shall also cause an assessment to be made of whether air quality standards and objectives are being achieved, or are likely to be achieved within the relevant period, within the authority's area.

(3) If, on an assessment under sub-section (2) above, it appears that any air quality standards or objectives are not being achieved, or are not likely within the relevant period to be achieved, within the local authority's area, the local authority shall identify any parts of its area in which it appears that those standards or objectives are not likely to be achieved within the relevant period.

Section 83: Designation of air quality management areas

(1) Where, as a result of an air quality review, it appears that any air quality standards or objectives are not being achieved, or are not likely within the relevant period to be achieved, within the area of a local authority, the local authority shall by order designate as an air quality management area (in this Part referred to as a 'designated area') any part of its area in which it appears that those standards or objectives are not being achieved, or are not likely to be achieved within the relevant period.

(2) An order under this section may, as a result of a subsequent air quality review–

    (a) be varied by a subsequent order; or

    (b) be revoked by such an order, if it appears on that subsequent air quality review that the air quality standards and objectives are being achieved, and are likely throughout the relevant period to be achieved, within the designated area.

Section 84: Duties of local authorities in relation to designated areas

(1) Where an order under s 83 above comes into operation, the local authority which made the order shall, for the purpose of supplementing such information as it has in relation to the designated area in question, cause an assessment to be made of–

    (a) the quality for the time being, and the likely future quality within the relevant period, of air within the designated area to which the order relates; and

    (b) the respects (if any) in which it appears that air quality standards or objectives are not being achieved, or are not likely within the relevant period to be achieved, within that designated area.

(2) A local authority which is required by sub-section (1) above to cause an assessment to be made shall also be under a duty–

    (a) to prepare, before the expiration of the period of 12 months beginning with the coming into operation of the order mentioned in that sub-section, a report of the results of that assessment; and

    (b) to prepare, in accordance with the following provisions of this Part, a written plan (in this Part referred to as an 'action plan') for the exercise by the authority, in pursuit of the achievement of air quality standards and objectives in the designated area, of any powers exercisable by the authority.

(3) An action plan shall include a statement of the time or times by or within which the local authority in question proposes to implement each of the proposed measures comprised in the plan.

(4) A local authority may from time to time revise an action plan.

(5) This sub-section applies in any case where the local authority preparing an action plan or a revision of an action plan is the council of a district in England which is comprised in an area for which there is a county council; and if, in a case where this sub-section applies, the county council disagrees with the authority about the contents of the proposed action plan or revision of the action plan–

(a) either of them may refer the matter to the Secretary of State;

(b) on any such reference the Secretary of State may confirm the authority's proposed action plan or revision of the action plan, with or without modifications (whether or not proposed by the county council) or reject it and, if he rejects it, he may also exercise any powers of his under section 85 below; and

(c) the authority shall not finally determine the content of the action plan, or the revision of the action plan, except in accordance with his decision on the reference or in pursuance of directions under section 85 below.

Notes:

1 Where it appears that a local authority has failed to discharge any duty imposed on it under or by virtue of this Part IV, or that its actions are inappropriate, the Secretary of State, or in Scotland SEPA, have reserve powers (s 85) to 'conduct or make, or cause to be conducted or made' a review of the air quality within the area of any local authority; to make an assessment of whether air quality standards and objectives are being achieved, or are likely to be achieved; to identify any parts of the area of a local authority in which it appears that those standards or objectives are not likely to be achieved within the relevant period; and to make an assessment of the respects (if any) in which it appears that air quality standards or objectives are not being achieved. Directions may be given to the local authority requiring it to take such steps as may be specified in the directions. These directions shall be published and copies shall be made available to the public. Local authorities have a duty to comply with any directions given.

2 Section 87 allows the making of regulations for the purposes of achieving the NAQS. The regulations must be in the form of statutory instruments and will only come into effect if a draft of the instrument has been laid before, and approved by a resolution of, each House of Parliament.

3 Section 88 empowers the Secretary of State to issue guidance to local authorities which local authorities must have regard to.

Smoke pollution and the Clean Air Act 1993

The Clean Air Act 1956 was enacted in response to mounting concern about smoke pollution generally and episodes such as the great London smog of December 1952 (see above). It introduced the current system of domestic smoke control which was amended in 1968. The Clean Air Act 1993 now consolidates the previous legislation.

Over the past 30 or 40 years problems of smoke pollution have been substantially reduced, partly due to reduction in the industrial and domestic use of coal and partly due to the legislation itself (see further the 10th Report of the Royal Commission on Environmental Pollution, 1984, Cmnd 9149). This being so, it is now widely felt that the improved regulatory system under Pt 1 of the EPA 1990 together with the statutory nuisance provisions render many of the following provisions unnecessary and powers to partially repeal the Act are contained in the Deregulation and Contracting Out Act 1994.

Clean Air Act 1993

Section 1 Prohibition of dark smoke from chimneys

(1) Dark smoke shall not be emitted from a chimney of any building, and if, on any day, dark smoke is so emitted, the occupier of the building shall be guilty of an offence.

(2) Dark smoke shall not be emitted from a chimney (not being a chimney of a building) which serves the furnace of any fixed boiler or industrial plant, and if, on any day, dark smoke is so emitted, the person having possession of the boiler or plant shall be guilty of an offence.

[Sub-sections (3)–(5) omitted.]

Notes:

1   This section covers emissions of dark smoke from chimneys of any building. It appears to create a strict liability criminal offence, although there are defences set out in sub-s (4). Conviction can lead to a fine of up to £3,000 in the case of emissions from domestic dwellings and up to £5,000 in other cases.

2   Dark smoke is defined in s 3 to mean 'smoke which, if compared in the appropriate manner with a chart of the type known on 5 July 1956 (the date of the passing of the Clean Air Act 1956) as the Ringelmann Chart, would appear to be as dark as or darker than shade 2 on the chart'. The Ringelmann Chart indicates different shades of darkness numerically categorised 0–5 with 0 being white and 5 being black. While the court must be certain that the chart was properly used to measure the density of the smoke it has been said that in practice environmental health officers do not use the Chart mechanically but rely rather on their own experience (Hughes (1996) 488).

Section 2: Prohibition of dark smoke from industrial or trade premises

(1) Dark smoke shall not be emitted from any industrial or trade premises and if, on any day, dark smoke is so emitted the occupier of the premises and any person who causes or permits the emission shall be guilty of an offence.

[Sub-sections (2)–(3) omitted.]

(4) In proceedings for an offence under this section, it shall be a defence to prove–

   (a) that the alleged emission was inadvertent; and

   (b) that all practicable steps had been taken to prevent or minimise the emission of dark smoke.

[Sub-sections (5)–(7) omitted.]

Notes:

1   Unlike s 1, this section extends to emissions of dark smoke from industrial and trade premises other than through chimneys. The section would be applied to a bonfire lit on a demolition site: see *Sheffield City Council v ADH Demolition* (1983) LGR 177. But, note

that the Clean Air (Emissions of Dark Smoke) (Exemption) Regulations SI 1969/1263 exempt from the Act the burning of certain matter, including the burning of certain waste from demolition sites; tar, pitch and asphalt in resurfacing work; and carcasses of diseased animals.

2 Section 4 requires new furnaces to be, so far as practicable, smokeless. The section does not apply to domestic furnaces nor, it seems, to furnaces used for purposes which are domestic such as heating water for central heating. Section 5 gives the Secretary of State power to make regulations prescribing limits for the emission of grit and dust from furnaces.

3 Section 12(1) provides that for the purpose of enabling local authorities properly to perform their functions under and in connection with sub-ss 5 to 11, they: '... may, by notice in writing served on the occupier of any building, require the occupier to furnish to them, within fourteen days or such longer time as may be limited by the notice, such information as to the furnaces in the building and the fuel or waste burned in those furnaces as they may reasonably require for that purpose.' Failure to comply with such a notice or to supply information which is known to be false in a material particular is an offence.

Chimneys

Section 14: Height of chimneys for furnaces

(1) This section applies to any furnace served by a chimney.

(2) An occupier of a building shall not knowingly cause or permit a furnace to be used in the building–

(a) to burn pulverised fuel;

(b) to burn, at a rate of 45.4 kilograms or more an hour, any other solid matter; or

(c) to burn, at a rate equivalent to 366.4 kilowatts or more, any liquid or gaseous matter, unless the height of the chimney serving the furnace has been approved for the purposes of this section and any conditions subject to which the approval was granted are complied with.

(3) If on any day the occupier of a building contravenes sub-section (2), he shall be guilty of an offence.

[Sub-sections (4)–(7) omitted.]

Section 15: Applications for approval of height of chimneys for furnaces

(1) This section applies to the granting of approval of the height of a chimney for the purposes of section 14.

(2) Approval [for the height of a chimney] shall not be granted by a local authority unless they are satisfied that the height of the chimney will be sufficient to prevent, so far as practicable, the smoke, grit, dust, gases or fumes emitted from the chimney from becoming prejudicial to health or a nuisance having regard to–

(a) the purpose of the chimney;

(b) the position and descriptions of buildings near it;

(c) the levels of the neighbouring ground; and

(d) any other matters requiring consideration in the circumstances.

(3) Approval may be granted without qualification or subject to conditions as to the rate or quality, or the rate and quality, of emissions from the chimney.

[Sub-section (4) omitted.]

(5) If a local authority decide not to approve the height of a chimney, or to attach conditions to their approval, they shall give the applicant a written notification of their decision which–

    (a) states their reasons for that decision; and

    (b) in the case of a decision not to approve the height of the chimney, specifies–

        (i) the lowest height (if any) which they are prepared to approve without qualification; or

        (ii) the lowest height which they are prepared to approve if approval is granted subject to any specified conditions,

    or (if they think fit) both.

Notes:

1   Applicants may within 28 days of receiving a notification under sub-section (5) appeal against the local authority's decision to the Secretary of State. The Secretary of State may confirm the decision or approve the height of the chimney without qualification or subject to conditions.

2   The above section concerns chimneys serving large industrial furnaces, s 16 deals with the height of chimneys serving other industrial plants. Chimneys serving housing, shops and offices are not covered by these provisions.

3   See also the Clean Air (Height of Chimneys) (Exemption) Regulations 1969 SI 1969/411 and the DoE Circular 25/81 'Memorandum on Chimney Heights'.

These provision are said to be based on the principle that taller chimneys enable the more effective dispersal and dilution of pollution. This legislation, however, has been insufficient to prevent pollution, either nationally or internationally.

Smoke Control Areas

Section 18: Declaration of smoke control area by local authorities

(1) A local authority may by order declare the whole or any part of the district of the authority to be a smoke control area [...].

[Sub-sections 2–4 omitted.]

Notes:

1   Local Authorities have been empowered to declare the whole or part of their areas to be smoke control areas since 1980. Previously this power was subject to confirmation by the Secretary of State.

2   The procedure for making smoke control orders is set out in Schedule 1 to the Act. This requires local authorities to publicise proposed orders and to invite objections. If objections are made they must be considered by local authorities. If no objections are received the order may be brought into effect within six months of being made.

Section 19: Power of Secretary of State to require creation of smoke control areas

(1) If, after consultation with a local authority, the Secretary of State is satisfied–

    (a) that it is expedient to abate the pollution of the air by smoke in the district or part of the district of the authority; and

    (b) that the authority have not exercised, or have not sufficiently exercised, their powers under s 18 [...] to abate the pollution, he may direct the authority to prepare and submit to him for his approval [...] proposals for making and bringing into operation one or more smoke control orders within such period or periods as the authority think fit.

[Sub-sections (2)–(3) omitted.]

(4) Where a local authority to whom a direction under sub-section (1) has been given–

    (a) fail to submit proposals to the Secretary of State within the period specified in the direction; or

    (b) submit proposals which are rejected in whole or in part, the Secretary of State may make an order declaring them to be in default and directing them for the purposes of removing the default to exercise their powers under section 18 in such manner and within such period as may be specified in the order.

[Sub-sections (5) and (6) omitted.]

[Sections 20–29 omitted.]

Notes:

1   Section 20(1) provides that 'if, on any day, smoke is emitted from a chimney of any building within a smoke control area, the occupier of the building shall be guilty of an offence'. Section 21 enables the Secretary of State to exempt any class of fireplace from the provisions of s 20 if he is satisfied that the fireplaces can be used for burning fuel other than authorised fuels without producing any smoke or a substantial quantity of smoke. A large number of Smoke Control Areas (Exempted Fireplaces) Orders have been made under these provisions exempting, for example, fireplaces designed to burn oil as well as wood and coal.

2   Section 22 gives the Secretary of State power to suspend or relax the operation of s 20 in relation to the whole or any part of a smoke control area 'if it appears to him to be necessary or expedient so to do'. This appears to be an exceptional emergency power which may be used, for example, for the duration of a temporary shortage of a particular authorised fuel.

3   Section 23 makes it an offence to acquire or sell for delivery unauthorised fuel in a smoke control area. The effect is that once a smoke control area has been established offences reach back from the production of smoke to the possession by a potential user and the sale by a retailer of unauthorised solid fuel.

4   Section 24 gives local authorities power to require occupiers or owners of private dwellings within smoke control areas to adapt fireplaces so as not to infringe s 20. Grants are payable for the work. If the building was erected before 15 August 1964 the local authority must provide a grant covering 70% of the cost and may extend the grant to cover the remaining 30% of the cost.

Road traffic pollution

Road transport is one of the major sources of air pollution, especially in urban areas. In 1997 it accounted for around two-thirds of all national emissions of four of the eight pollutants for which objectives had been set by the National Air Quality Strategy; namely, benzene, 1,3-butadiene, carbon monoxide and lead. Road transport is also responsible for a significant proportion of the pollutants for which objectives will be most difficult to meet – nitrogen dioxide and particulate matter (PM 10) (*The Environmental Impacts of Road Vehicles in Use: Air Quality, Climate Change and Noise Pollution*, August 1999). Pollution caused by road traffic is particularly severe in towns and cities. In London, traffic is said to be responsible for 99% of carbon monoxide, 76% of nitrogen oxides and 90% of hydrocarbons. Road traffic is also the main cause of ozone pollution resulting from the chemical reaction between nitrogen oxides and hydrocarbons. (Friends of the Earth, *Atmosphere and Transport Campaign, Road Transport, Air Pollution and Health* citing, The Ashden Trust, *How Vehicle Pollution Affects Our Health*, 1994).

The DETR concluded its 1999 report on the Environmental Impacts of Road Vehicles (see above) with the following summary of the way ahead.

Summary: The way forward

67 There can be no doubt that air quality and climate change are the most pressing environmental priorities in relation to road vehicles. Air pollution presents the most direct health risks, while climate change is seen as one of the most serious longer term threats facing the world. Noise too is becoming an issue of growing concern, as traffic continues to increase.

68 The key points that this document has made are:

- Road vehicles have a significant impact on the environment, although there are wide variations between the impact of different vehicles and fuels.

- Tighter emission standards have led to significant reductions in emissions of local air pollutants from road transport. Additional tightening of these standards in 2000 and beyond will achieve further improvements; however, these are unlikely to be sufficient to deliver air quality objectives in all urban areas without significant further local measures such as traffic restraint.

- Little progress has been made in average fuel consumption of new vehicles over the last decade in contrast to progress on regulated pollutants (considerable improvements in engine efficiency have been offset by additional features, and the introduction of more stringent mandatory safety and emission requirements). This has meant that the road transport sector has been one of the fastest growing sources of CO_2 emissions in the UK.

- But the voluntary agreement with motor manufacturers, as part of the EU CO_2 from cars strategy, offers an important opportunity to reduce CO_2 emissions from new cars by a quarter, especially through the development of new technology, and should stabilise CO_2 emissions from road transport by 2010, although further action will be needed.

- Cars have the most environmental impact, due to their greater number, but HGVs are a significant source of emissions and are forecast to become the primary source of both PM_{10} and NO_x emissions from road transport. The forecast growth in light goods vehicles is also of concern, particularly since they have increasingly tended to run on diesel.

- Petrol and diesel vehicles have different environmental impacts, with the former producing more CO_2 and the latter producing some of the more important pollutants that affect local air quality.

- There are clear trade-offs in tackling different environmental impacts, which need to be considered carefully – for instance some measures to tackle climate change (such as increasing the proportion of new diesel cars) may have adverse effects on air quality.

- Significant progress has been made in reducing noise emissions, but this will be largely offset by increases in traffic.

69 Government action at national and European levels has focused on improving the emissions from new vehicles and fuels, trying to persuade people to use their cars in a more environmentally friendly, and encouraging the use of forms of transport which have less impact on the environment than cars, particularly for short journeys. However, in order to reduce the environmental impact of vehicles, action needs to be taken on a wider scale. This is why the Cleaner Vehicles Task Force has been set up. However, public action is also needed. It is hoped that this document will go some way to increasing awareness of the environmental impact of road transport and provide a context in which action can take place.

Fuel standards

Emission standards for vehicles have become progressively more stringent since the 1970s. The Motor Fuel (Composition and Content) Regulations 1999 SI 1999/3107, which revoke SI 1994/2295 and implement Directive 98/70 on Petrol and Diesel Fuel, effectively bans the sale of leaded petrol (see pp 143–44, above). In addition emissions of carbon monoxide, hydrocarbons, nitrogen oxides and particles are limited for new vehicles by:

- Directive 91/441 (implemented by SI 1992/2137) which came into force from 1992 applying new limits to passenger cars and light goods vehicles from 1996;

- Directive 91/542 (implemented by SI 1992/2137) which applies to heavy duty commercial vehicles;

- Directive 93/59 (implemented by SI 1993/2201) which applied to light duty commercial vehicles; and

- Directive 94/12 (implemented by SI 1995/2210) which imposes new limits for all registrations of passenger cars from 1997. (On these Directives see p 146, above.)

These above regulations are made under Pt IV of the Clean Air Act 1993.

Clean Air Act 1993

Section 30: Regulations about motor fuel

(1) For the purpose of limiting or reducing air pollution, the Secretary of State may by regulations–

    (a) impose requirements as to the composition and contents of any fuel of a kind used in motor vehicles;

    and

(b) where such requirements are in force, prevent or restrict the production, treatment, distribution, import, sale or use of any fuel which in any respect fails to comply with the requirements, and which is for use in the United Kingdom.

(2) It shall be the duty of the Secretary of State, before he makes any regulations under this section, to consult–

(a) such persons appearing to him to represent manufacturers and users of motor vehicles;

(b) such persons appearing to him to represent the producers and users of fuel for motor vehicles; and

(c) such persons appearing to him to be conversant with problems of air pollution,

as he considers appropriate.

[Sub-section (3) omitted.]

(4) It shall be the duty of every local weights and measures authority to enforce the provisions of regulations under this section within its area [...]

[Sub-sections (5), (6) and (7) omitted.]

Notes:

1   It is under this provision that EC fuel composition standards are implemented in the UK. The current regulations are the Motor Fuel (Composition and Content) Regulations 1999 SI 1999/3107. They make it an offence to distribute non-complying motor fuels from a refinery or import terminal, and to sell such fuel at a retail filling station. See Directive 93/12 (p 143, above).

2   Section 31 permits the making of regulations imposing limits on the sulphur content of fuel oil used in furnaces or engines. See SI 1994/2249.

An interesting case involving the possible liability of oil companies for pollution caused by lead in petrol was:

Budden v BP Oil and Shell Oil; Albery-Speyer v BP Oil and Shell Oil [1980] JPL 586

The Court of Appeal upheld a decision to strike out an action in nuisance and negligence against BP Oil Ltd and Shell UK which alleged that children suffered injury as a consequence of the lead content of petrol. Responding to the argument that the oil companies could not be liable in negligence because they had complied with the relevant regulations, Megaw LJ said:

Manufacturers or suppliers of petrol could not be negligent in a matter such as this if the limit to which they adhered was a limit which they were entitled reasonably to believe to be consistent with the public interest. There is no suggestion that there was available to either of the defendants at any relevant time any relevant information which they failed properly to disclose or which would not have been available to the Secretary of State and his advisers in carrying out the task imposed on him by Parliament and in reaching his decision.

[...] This is not to say that the courts are bound to hold, where a limit has been prescribed in the interests of safety by statute or statutory regulations, that one who keeps within these limits cannot be guilty of negligence at common law. An example debated in argument before us was the speed limit for motor vehicles in built-up areas. Of course, a court may hold a motorist to have been negligent even though he was driving at less than 30 miles per hour in a built-up area. But that would be, not because his speed was 29 miles per hour, but because there were other circumstances in the particular case which made it negligent to drive at that speed.

But if Parliament had provided by statute, or by statutory regulation, that the maximum permissible speed in a built-up area was 30 miles per hour, it would, we should have thought, not have been right for a court to hold that it was *per se* negligent for anyone in any circumstances to drive at more than 20 miles per hour in a built-up area. Yet that, as we see it, is what the plaintiffs would, in substance and effect, be inviting the courts to do by their claims in these actions. For if the defendants are liable here and are subject to injunctions restricting them to some limit which would be below the limits laid down under the 1974 Act and regulations, the same would apply in all the subsequent actions which would, no doubt, perfectly properly follow against all other manufacturers and suppliers of petrol in this country. The courts would thus necessarily be, in effect, laying down a permissible limit which would be of universal application: that is, not related to, or confined to, particular areas or particular circumstances. The permissible limit thus ordained by the courts, to be enforced as being orders of the courts, would be different from, and inconsistent with, the permissible limit prescribed by the authority of Parliament. That would result in a constitutional anomaly which in our view would be wholly unacceptable. The authority of Parliament must prevail. Where Parliament has decided a matter of general policy, the courts cannot properly be asked to make decisions, by way of litigation under the adversary procedure, the effect of which would, or might, be that the courts would lay down, and require to be enforced with the authority of the courts, a different and inconsistent policy.

We stress again that this does not mean that where Parliament prescribes a limit the courts may not hold a defendant liable in negligence even though he does not go above that limit ...

Vehicle standards

Sections 41–59 of the Road Traffic Act 1988 require vehicles to conform to certain safety and environmental standards. The Road Vehicles (Construction and Use) Regulations 1986 SI 1986/1078 (as amended) continued in force under s 41 of the 1988 Act provide minimum standards for the construction and use of motor vehicles and s 42 makes non-compliance with these regulations an offence. It may be noted that catalytic converters are now fitted to all new cars. These can reduce emissions from petrol-engined vehicles by 80–90%.

Vehicle maintenance

It is recognised that emissions performance of vehicles can quickly deteriorate if vehicles are not properly maintained. Emissions are now checked as part of the annual MOT test and emissions meters have been introduced into MOT centres. More regular attention to engine maintenance is also being encouraged and the Department of Transport's Vehicle Inspectorate have introduced a programme of roadside checks to see that vehicles are complying with emissions standards and to heighten public awareness of the need to maintain vehicles properly. These now include high profile checks on cars in areas of high traffic pollution, such as major towns and cities. Local authorities have been given powers to work with the police on a trial basis enabling them to carry out checks as part of their responsibilities for Local Air Quality Management (see p 185, above). This is currently being reviewed.

Restricting the use of roads and traffic management

Sections 1 and 2 of the Road Traffic Regulation Act 1984 as amended by Sched 22, paras 36(1) and 36(2) of the Environment Act 1995 enable shire counties, unitary districts, metropolitan authorities and London boroughs to restrict the use of roads on air quality grounds. The restrictions can be permanent or limited, for example, to particular episodes of air pollution. The government has noted that such powers should be used with caution:

> ... the main ingredient of summertime smog is ozone, sometimes accompanied by a haze of fine particles. In such circumstances, pollution episodes are not localised. Whilst action to reduce traffic levels overall is desirable, action confined to a very localised area is unlikely to be effective. If a diversion is proposed on air quality or other grounds, local authorities should consider carefully whether the net effect will be to increase overall traffic levels or congestion in the area ... In wintertime the situation is different. Pollution episodes are typically complex mixtures of [emissions]. Poor air quality can be confined to pockets of still air particularly surrounding busy roads and very localised targeted action can be useful (*The National Air Quality Strategy*, Consultation Paper 1996, p 54).

In a further initiative the Transport Act 2000 gives local authorities power to reduce congestion and pollution through the introduction of road user charging and work place parking levies. The intention is that revenues raised can be recycled into local transport improvements.

R v Greenwich London Borough ex p Williams [1997] JPL 62

In the context of road management strategies to reduce traffic pollution it is pertinent to consider the decision of the High Court in CO/3160/95 *R v Greenwich London Borough ex p Williams* (1995). Here parents sought to force the Local Authority to use its powers in s 14 of the Road Traffic Regulation Act 1984 to close roads arguing that traffic pollution was a danger to health. The decision of the High Court was a disappointment, but possibly not a surprise to the applicants. The following extract is from the judgment of Macpherson J:

> Trafalgar Road is otherwise known as the A206 ... it is not one of the main Arteries of London and has been referred to as a secondary road in the hierarchy of London roads. It is however a designated road and I am prepared to accept ... that it is very busy ...

> It is apparent that it is like many roads in busy cities in that it has shops, buildings and dwellings on both sides. To that extent, I suppose, it can be described as a canyon. But, so are most of the busy roads of London. Some of course are much worse than this one in that the height of the buildings on either side must have an effect upon the accretion of pollution between the buildings ... It is a characteristic as we all know of motor vehicles that they give off polluting substances ... as everybody who lives in London knows, the level of pollution from vehicles is affected by climatic and weather conditions including what is known in the jargon of the trade as 'temperature inversion'. It has to be assumed for the purpose of the argument in this case that it is possible to identify occasions when traffic using a particular road is the cause of unacceptable air quality. In practice, apart from very special events such

as the total failure of ventilation in a tunnel, it is difficult to make the requisite measurements ...

The applicants in this case, acting through their parents, are children who live near to or in Trafalgar Road, or who use it ... [it] ... is said that in this road, from time to time, the air quality is such that it is dangerous to the children who use it. It does have to be mentioned ... that the medical report in this case prepared by Doctor Jon G Ayres, for the solicitors to the applicants, does not indicate that vehicle exhaust fumes play a great part in connection with asthma. What he said (and this is the only evidence before the court) is this:

There is overwhelming evidence that on days when air pollution is high a proportion of patients with asthma will be slightly worse. There is however no evidence that exposure to air pollution in the long term will turn an individual from a non-asthmatic to an asthmatic [...]

What happened in this case was that in May 1995 representations were made to the local authority that in certain circumstances, where there is temperature inversion and when high pollution levels are apparent, Trafalgar Road should be closed or traffic should be so restricted in it that pollution would be reduced and thus, as the applicants put it, there would be no danger to the children using the road. What was envisaged therefore was not a permanent closing of the road, nor a closing of the road for any specific event, but a temporary closure of the road while the polluting circumstances lasted ... [the judge turned to the legislation]. Section 14(2) reads as follows:

The traffic authority for a road may at any time by notice restrict or prohibit temporarily the use of the road, or of any part of it, by vehicles, or vehicles of any class, or by pedestrians, where it appears to them that it is–

(a) necessary or expedient for the reason mentioned in paragraph (a) or the purpose mentioned in paragraph (c) of sub-section (1) above; or

(b) necessary for the reason mentioned in paragraph (b) of that sub-section,

that the restriction or prohibition should come into force without delay.

[...] The argument that the applicants raise is that the words 'the likelihood of danger to the public' are wide and general and that there should be no restriction placed upon them either as a matter of construction or in common sense.

What Mr Read [for the authority] says in a nutshell is that it is not necessary to read any words of restriction into the sub-section. He says 'why should Parliament restrict what is the applicable power given to the local authority?' He says that the words must be given their ordinary and natural meaning. On the other hand when construing the section in an Act of Parliament it must be construed in the context in which it appears. This is a road traffic matter and the Section, as I have already indicated, appears (as amended) in the Road Traffic Regulation Act 1994 [sic]. Simply looking at the section and construing these words I have to say at once that I am wholly convinced that they do not cover the situation envisaged by the applicants. What is envisaged by s 14 in my judgment is a restriction upon the use of a road because of the likelihood of danger to the public from traffic ordinarily using it. Using ordinary principles of construction and indeed common sense, this section was not designed to allow local authorities temporarily to close roads because either they or somebody else concluded that the air levels were polluted by vehicles using the road. What was envisaged, simply as a matter of common sense again, was the sort of occasion mentioned by Mr Read, when for example oil upon the road made the use of the road dangerous to the public, or alternatively where pavements were out of action because of construction works so that vehicles came along the road with nowhere for the pedestrians to walk other than in the roadway itself.

It is conceded by the respondents that there may be certain extreme circumstances where s 14 may be used in order to close a road because of what they call 'environmental circumstances'. The two examples given are those of a tunnel where the ventilation system has been wholly removed so there is a risk that anybody in the tunnel may expire because of lack of air or, alternatively, in Sir George Young's letter (to which reference has been made) there is the other somewhat extreme example of closure of a road across heathland which is subject to the risk of fire when it may be possible to act to close the road because of the risk of fire and smoke. But those circumstances are so wholly different from the present that, in my judgment, the use of the relevant sections in that regard cannot indicate that the power extends to the temporary closing of a road in circumstances such as are envisaged in this case.

That is the end of the matter because if the court's view of the section is that it is incapable of meeting the circumstances envisaged in this case then, as a matter of construction, simply looking at the words themselves in their context and using a common sense application, there is no possibility of obtaining the declarations which are sought. There are other sections of this or other Acts which may deal with the situation. It may be that as time progresses people will become more aware of the risks of pollution, so that new sections or new steps may be taken by a government to give additional powers to local authorities. But at present, in my judgment, the power which the local authority has to close roads where there may be a likelihood of danger to the public does not extend to the temporary prohibition or restriction to be imposed on ordinary traffic for the purpose of removing or reducing danger to the public from air pollution. It does in my judgment require only a few moments' attention to see that any interpretation in favour of the applicants would lead to absurd results. What, for example, would happen if the alternative road to which the Trafalgar traffic was diverted reached higher levels of pollution than Trafalgar Road? What would happen in the borough in which I myself live of Islington if Essex Road and all the main arteries were polluted. Could they all become temporarily shut? Chaos would result. It does seem to me that the idea of imposing temporary restriction by notice in a city as busy as London is absurd.

It may be said that the court is unsympathetic to the position of the asthmatic children who are applicants in this case. Nobody should draw any such conclusion. I have every sympathy with them if pollution exacerbates their asthma which is very unfortunate. It may be that the remedy is to keep them away from Trafalgar Road [...]

REFERENCES AND FURTHER READING

Ashby, E and Anderson, M, *The Politics of Clean Air*, 1981, London: Clarendon

Ashden Trust, *How Vehicle Pollution Affects Our Health*, 1994

Beevers, S and Carslaw, D, *Evaluation of Local Transport Measures in Tackling National Air Quality Strategy (NAQS) Objectives*, SEIPH Report to the DETR, 1998

Bennett, G (ed), *Air Pollution Control in the European Community*, 1991, London: Graham and Trotman

Birnie, P and Boyle, A, *International Law and the Environment*, 1992, Oxford: Clarendon

Cameron, P, 'From principles to practice: the Kyoto Protocol' (2000) 18(1) Journal of Energy and Natural Resources Law 1–18

Churchill, RR and Freestone, D (eds), *International Law and Global Climate Change*, 1991, London: Graham and Trotman

Churchill, RR, Warren, L and Gibson, J, *Law, Policy and the Environment*, 1991, London: Blackwell

Climate Change: The UK programme, Cm 2427, 1994, London: HMSO

Climate Change: The UK strategy, Cm 2426, 1994, London: HMSO

Davies, PGG, 'Global warming and the Kyoto Protocol' (1998) 47(2) ICLQ 446-61

Department of Energy, *Energy Paper No 58*, 1990, London: HMSO

Department of Environment, Transport and Regional Affairs, Select Committee Report, *The UK Climate Change Programme*, Session 1999–2000, 5th Report, HC 194-I, London: HMSO

Department of Environment, Transport and Regional Affairs, *The Air Quality Strategy for England, Scotland, Wales and Northern Ireland*, Cm 4548, 2000, London: HMSO

Department of Health, *Quantification of the Effects of Air Pollution on Health in the United Kingdom*, Committee on the Medical Affects of Air Pollutants, 1998, London: DoH

Department of Trade and Industry, *CFCs and Halons*, 1990, London: HMSO

Doos, BR, 'Environmental issues requiring international action', in Lang, W, Neuhold, A and Zemanek, K (eds), *Environmental Protection and International Law*, 1991, London/Dordrecht: Graham and Trotman/Martinus Nijhoff, pp 1–54

The Effects of Acid Deposition, 1989, London: HMSO

Ellerman, AD, Jacoby, HD and Decaux, A, *The Effects on Developing Countries of the Kyoto Protocol and Carbon Dioxide Emissions Trading*, World Bank Policy Research Paper 2019, 2000, Washington DC

Elsom, DE, *Atmospheric Pollution*, 2nd edn, 1992, Oxford: Basil Blackwell

French, D, 'Developing States and international environmental law: the importance of differentiated responsibilities' (2000) 49(1) ICLQ 35–61

French, D, '1997 Kyoto Protocol to the 1992 Framework Convention on Climate Change' [1998] 10(2) JEL 227–39

Grimeaud, D, 'An overview of the policy and legal aspects of the international climate change regime Parts I and II' (2000) 2 Env Liability 39–47; 3 Env Liability 95–126

Grubb, M, *The Greenhouse Effect*, 1990, London: Royal Institute of International Affairs

Grubb, M with Vrolijk, C and Brack, D, *Kyoto Protocol: A Guide and Assessment*, 1999, London: Royal Institute of International Affairs

Haigh, N, *EEC Environmental Policy and Britain*, 2nd edn, 1991, London: Longman

House of Commons Environment Committee, *Volatile Organic Compounds*, Session 1994–95, 1st Report, HC 39–1, 1995, London: HMSO (and the government's response of 27 June 1995)

House of Commons Environment Committee, *Acid Rain*, Session 1983–84, 4th Report HC 446–1, London: HMSO

Intergovernmental Panel on Climate Change (IPCC), *Land Use, Land Use Change and Forestry*, Special Report, 2000, IPCC Secretariat, c/o World Meteorological Organization, Geneva, Switzerland, www.ipcc.ch

Johnson, S, *The Earth Summit: The United Nations Conference on Environment and Development (UNCED)*, 1993, London: Graham and Trotman

Kuik, O, Peters, P and Schrijver, N (eds), *Joint Implementation to Curb Climate Change: Legal and Economic Aspects*, 1994, Dordrecht: Kluwer

Lammers, J, 'The European approach to acid rain', in Magraw, D (ed), *International Law and Pollution*, 1991, Philadelphia: University of Pennsylvania Press

McLaren, J, 'Nuisance and the industrial revolution' (1983) 3(2) OJLS 155

National Assessment Synthesis Team, *Climate Change Impacts on the United States: The Potential Consequences of Climate Variability and Change*, 2001, Cambridge: CUP

National Assessment Synthesis Team, *Climate Change Impacts on the United States: Overview*, 2001, Cambridge: CUP

Nilsson, S and Pitt, D, *Protecting the Atmosphere: The Climate Change Convention and Its Context*, 1994, London: Earthscan

Pretty, J and Ball, A, *Agricultural Influences on Carbon Emissions and Sequestration: A Review of Evidence and the Emerging Trading Options*, Centre for Environment and Society, Occasional Paper 2001–03, 2001

Pulvenis, J-F, 'The Framework Convention on Climate Change', in Camiglio, Pineschi, Siniscalco and Treves (eds), *The Environment After Rio: International Law and Economics*, 1994, London/Dordrecht: Graham and Trotman/Martinus Nijhoff, pp 71–110

Royal Commission on Environmental Pollution, 5th Report (1976, Cmnd 6371), 9th Report (1983, Cmnd 8852), 10th Report (1984, Cmnd 9149), 15th Report (1991, Cm 1631), 18th Report (1994, Cm 2674)

Quality of Urban Air Review Group, *Diesel Vehicle Emissions and Urban Air Quality*, 1993, Birmingham: University of Birmingham

Quality of Urban Air Review Group, *Urban Air Quality in the UK*, 1993, Birmingham: University of Birmingham

Read, P, *Responding to Global Warming: The Technology, Economics and Politics of Sustainable Energy*, 1994, London: Zed Books

Sands, P, *Principles of International Environmental Law, Vol 1: Frameworks, standards and implementation*, 1995, Manchester: Manchester UP

Sebenius, J-K, 'The Law of the Sea Conference: lessons for negotiations to control global warming', in Sjostedt, G (ed), *International Environmental Negotiation*, 1993, Newbury Park, California: Sage, pp 189–216

Shaw, 'Acid-rain negotiations in North America and Europe: a study in contrast', in Sjostedt, G (ed), *International Environmental Negotiation*, 1993, Newbury Park, California: Sage

UK Climate Change Impacts Review Group, *The Potential Effects of Climate Change in the UK*, 1991, London: DoE

Victor, D, *The Collapse of the Kyoto Protocol and the Struggle to Slow Global Warming*, 2001, Princetown: Princetown UP

von Seht, H, '1999: the year in review, II. air and atmosphere, 3. global climate' (2000) 10 Yearbook of International Environmental Law 223–33

Watkins, LH (ed), *Air Pollution from Road Vehicles*, 1991, London: HMSO

Werksman, J, 'Compliance and the Kyoto Protocol: building a backbone into a "flexible" regime' (1998) 9 Yearbook of International Environmental Law 48–101

USEFUL WEBSITES

Convention on Long-range Transboundary Air Pollution: www.unece.org/env

DETR's air quality information index: www.environment.detr.gov.uk/airq/aqinfo.htm

DETR's climate change index: www.environment.detr.gov.uk/climatechange/index.htm

Framework Convention on Climate Change: www.unfcc.de/resource/convkp.html

Friends of the Earth: www.foe.uk/campaigns/atmosphere_and_transport/pubs

Intergovernmental Panel on Climate Change: www.ipcc.ch

International Energy Agency – Greenhouse Gases R & D Programme: www.seagreen. org.uk

Meteorological Office: met-office.gov.uk/research/hadleycentre/pubs

UK Climate Impacts Programme (UKCIP): www.ecu.ox.ac.uk/ukcip.html

Vienna Convention on Ozone Layer and Montreal Protocol: www.unep.org/ozone/ home.htm

For further general websites, see pp l–li, above.

CHAPTER 3

WATER AND MARINE POLLUTION

INTRODUCTION

There is now widespread concern about both the availability and the quality of water. The Water Framework Directive 00/60 describes water as 'a heritage which must be protected, defended and treated as such' (see p 237, below). A large volume of legislation exists aimed at safeguarding scarce water supplies and requiring minimum water quality standards. Over the centuries the world's rivers and seas have been used not only as a source of food, but also as a cheap and convenient repository for human and industrial waste. More recently they have become a leisure facility for bathing and water sports. Today, perhaps belatedly, they have come to be recognised as the basis of unique ecosystems worthy of protection in their own right. If the water and marine environment is to continue to perform these various roles in a sustainable manner then unrestrained disposal of materials into the aqueous environment poses an unacceptable threat.

In deciding whether water is polluted, two factors must be considered. Firstly, as Malcolm points out, pure water contains two atoms of hydrogen and one of oxygen and can only be obtained under laboratory conditions (Malcolm (1994) 169). 'Natural' water is by definition contaminated by minerals, nutrients, chemicals and bacteria but it is only where such contaminants pose a threat to human health or aquatic life that it can be described as polluted. In short the *presence* of a substance or contaminant is not indicative of pollution; it is the *effect* of the substance upon the environment which is relevant in the current context.

Secondly, whether water is polluted may well depend upon the use to which it is being put. For example, lower levels of pollution would be acceptable if a stretch of water was used as a source of drinking water, or perhaps for recreational purposes such as bathing, than if it was not used for such purposes. Acceptable measures of pollutants will therefore vary as waters are classified according to use. The combination and inter-relationship of these factors are present in all water pollution control regimes, whether they be international, European or domestic.

This chapter examines and presents the principal international, European Community and UK domestic legal instruments that currently exist to combat the threat of pollution and to satisfy our demand for clean and safe water.

INTERNATIONAL LAW

UN Convention on the Law of the Sea 1982[1]

Among the many international legal developments concerning environmental protection that have emerged in the years since the Earth Summit (United Nations Conference on the Environment and Development – UNCED) in 1992 (see Chapter 1, pp 68 *et seq*), the entry into force of the 1982 UN Convention on the Law of the Sea on 16 November 1994, is arguably the 'main event'. Part XII of UNCLOS is set out at p 214. As Nanda has put it, 'during the decade following the Stockholm Conference (on the Human Environment), the environmental provisions of the 1982 United Nations Convention on the Law of the Sea (UNCLOS) constituted the single most important step forward toward the progressive development of international environmental law' ((1995A) 257).

This is especially true in respect of the marine environment. The Convention is the only global agreement that provides comprehensive coverage of all aspects of the various uses, abuses and resources of the world's oceans (Broadus and Vartanov (1994) 223). Nanda also noted that the entry into force of UNCLOS 'represents an important step forward in international environmental law, for it raises to binding treaty status the ideals of Principle 21 of the Stockholm Declaration, and strives to balance environmental protection and resource management with the requirements of free navigation' (Nanda (1995B) 657). As Birnie and Boyle point out, '[T]he Convention thus attempts for the first time to provide a global framework for the rational exploitation and conservation of the sea's resources and the protection of the environment, which can be seen as a system for sustainable development, and as a model for the evolution of international environmental law' (Birnie and Boyle (1992) 252–53).

It is, therefore, certainly a convention which will have great impact on all human activities in the maritime sphere, both for the foreseeable future and in global terms. Indeed, it is already possible to chart the influence of the new law of the sea treaty on several different maritime activities. These include the allocation of sovereign rights and jurisdiction over natural resource exploitation activities; the regulation of the offshore installations utilised to extract the hydrocarbon resources in the continental shelf; the legal regime for the maritime transportation of the crude products of such extraction, as well as other items of international trade; the exploitation by fishing vessels of the marine living resources of the oceans; and even marine scientific research activities.

One lesson in international environmental negotiation that has been learned from the negotiation process of the 1982 Convention relates to the fact that this was the first inter-governmental negotiating conference in which many newly-independent, developing countries actively participated. Their participation was significant in two ways: first, their arrival on the international stage further upset the already uneasy balance that had hitherto obtained between the two superpowers and their allies in the immediate aftermath of the Second World War and the institution of the United Nations system. The Group of 77 – a group of developing States which now number more than 120 – constituted a majority whenever a one-State-one-vote system was utilised to resolve

---

1   21 ILM (1982) 1261.

stalemates occurring during the negotiation process.[2] Secondly, and perhaps even more importantly, these States were generally united under a shared ideological aim in demanding a New International Economic Order (NIEO), which basically called for an end to the perceived exploitative practices of the rich, developed (formerly colonial) countries to the disadvantage of the poor, developing (ex-colonial) countries, the restructuring of global economic and trade relations to reflect the above goal, and the redistribution of wealth through transfer of technology and resources.

The developing countries' participation and stance during the law of the sea treaty negotiations was a portent of things to come, especially in respect of international negotiations on environmental issues. This was the case, for example, in the UNCED negotiations, where tension was manifested in the efforts of developed and developing countries, respectively, to promote environmental versus developmental priorities. The increasingly democratic nature and consequent uncertainty, of multilateral environmental negotiations at the international level is thus an important factor to be taken into account when evaluating the international environmental legal regime evolving in the aftermath of the Rio 'Earth Summit' (Sebenius (1993) 193).

As noted above, the 1982 Convention represents the first major undertaking among States to protect the world's oceans in their entirety against all potentially polluting maritime activities, as opposed to the largely piecemeal, regional and specific activity-related international law-making processes which had previously characterised developments in this field of international environmental law. This general legal obligation of States to protect and preserve the marine environment extends throughout all maritime zones, from internal waters and coastal ports to the high seas (Broadus and Vartanov (1994) 226). Part XII of the Convention (see p 214, below), which is devoted to the protection and preservation of the marine environment, is an important advance on other conventions relating to various aspects of marine pollution since it formulates the obligation to protect the environment in terms which cover all sources of marine pollution: pollution from ships, land-based sources, sea-bed operations, dumping and the atmosphere. It also provides the framework for the series of treaties, both global and regional, which have or will be negotiated, on each of these topics (Birnie and Boyle (1992) 255).

Part XII while not providing specific rules and standards regarding the activities it aims to regulate, nevertheless lays down the broad legal framework within which all law-making on the marine environment must now take place. Article 192 sets the tone for the whole of this Part by providing, for the first time in any global convention on the law of the sea, a general legal obligation upon all States to protect and preserve the marine environment. Indeed, since the obligation to protect and preserve laid down in Art 192 is given implicit priority over the more traditional (and much abused) sovereign right of States to exploit their natural resources laid down in Art 193, it is arguable that these provisions represent a stronger statement for the sustainable development of the world's natural resources than the more widely known principles enunciated in the 1972 Stockholm and 1992 Rio Declarations (Birnie and Boyle (1992) 255). Thus, as Birnie and Boyle again note, these Articles on the protection and preservation of the marine

---

2   See Chapter 2, p 112, note 1 for website.

environment represent the culmination of a process of international law-making which has effected a number of fundamental changes in the international law of the sea.

Of these, perhaps the most important is that pollution in the form of dumping of wastes or discharges can no longer be regarded as an implicit freedom of the seas. Rather, the diligent control of all sources of pollution is now a matter of comprehensive legal obligation affecting the marine environment as a whole. This obligation no longer exists simply to safeguard the interests of other States (Birnie and Boyle (1992) 253). Article 194 elaborates the content of this obligation to show that its coverage extends not only to States and their maritime jurisdictions, but also to the marine environment as a whole, including the high seas beyond national maritime jurisdictions (Birnie and Boyle (1992) 255). Moreover, the 'marine environment' for this purpose includes 'rare and fragile ecosystems as well as the habitat of depleted, threatened or endangered species and other forms of marine life' (Art 194.5), and is thus not confined to the protection of economic interests, private property or the human use of the sea (Birnie and Boyle (1992) 255).

Part XII is strong in laying down a comprehensive framework for the taking and enforcing of measures on all the major sources of pollution but weak in indicating precisely when a violation occurs and what consequences flow from this as far as liability is concerned (Birnie (1993) 15). Part XII does not contain concrete marine pollution standards. Instead, its main objectives are to delimit States' competence pertaining to the establishment of concrete national and international rules and standards to prevent, reduce, and control pollution of the marine environment, and to ensure that its parties apply and implement these (Broadus and Vartanov (1994) 226).

At its most basic, bilateral level, the 1982 Convention provides coastal States with a formal recognition of their right, and indeed duty under international law, to protect the marine environment in the large areas of sea-bed and superjacent waters that are now within their sovereign and jurisdictional scope, if not actual territorial domain. These are the Territorial Sea (Art 3), Contiguous Zone (Art 24), Continental Shelf (Art 76) and the Exclusive Economic Zone (EEZ) (Art 57).[3] For example, while the Convention provides the coastal State with sovereign rights over the continental shelf, for the purpose of exploring and exploiting its natural resources (Art 77), nevertheless the coastal State is obliged to adopt laws and regulations to prevent, reduce and control pollution of the marine environment arising from or in connection with sea-bed activities subject to its jurisdiction (Art 208.1). Furthermore the coastal State has to ensure that such laws and regulations shall be no less effective than international rules, standards and recommended practices and procedures (Art 208.3).

The 1982 UNCLOS provides a comprehensive mechanism to prevent, reduce and control marine pollution, but its wording has been criticised as being ambiguous and generalised (Ellis (1995) 42, citing Dzidzornu and Tsamenyi (1991) 281). The standard-setting Articles dealing with operational and accidental vessel-source pollution, as well as dumping, were especially controversial during their negotiation and are extremely complex. In skeletal form, the regime has been described in this manner: first, in the

---

3   These different maritime jurisdictions are delimited according to the respective distances in nautical miles (nm) from a State's coastline. The territorial sea limit is 12 nm; the contiguous zone limit is 24 nm; and the EEZ limit is 200 nm. The Continental Shelf limit is at least 200 nm and potentially up to 350 nm.

territorial sea, coastal States may exercise their sovereignty to establish anti-pollution laws and regulations (Arts 21.1(f) and 211.4) provided that they 'shall not apply to the design, construction, manning or equipment of foreign ships unless they are giving effect to generally accepted international rules and standards' (Art 21.2). Secondly, in the exclusive economic zone, coastal States can legislate to prevent dumping (Art 210) and may establish certain other laws and regulations giving effect to generally accepted international rules and standards for ship-generated pollution (Art 211.5). Thirdly, there are certain supplementary provisions for the adoption of special mandatory measures for prevention of vessel-source pollution within particular, well-defined 'special areas' of the exclusive economic zones of coastal States due to their oceanographic and ecological conditions, as well as the protection or utilisation of their resources. These measures, which may include navigational restrictions as well as discharge standards, can only be enacted by the coastal States after consultation with other States, through the appropriate international organisation, which in this case would be International Maritime Organisation (IMO)[4] (Art 211.6) (Schneider (1981) 210).

In the area of enforcement competence, the 1982 UN Convention introduced several important jurisdictional innovations, especially related to port and coastal State enforcement. While traditionally regarded as the sole province of flag States, new enforcement powers are now recognised to lie with port and coastal States. Port States are empowered to undertake certain enforcement procedures in respect of vessel-discharge violations – even those occurring outside their internal waters, territorial seas and exclusive economic zones, when a vessel is voluntarily within a port or off-shore terminal of a State (Art 218). Also, under certain clearly delineated circumstances, coastal States will be able to cause proceedings and other measures to be taken in respect of violations of national laws and regulations, not only in their territorial sea but also in their EEZs, where these give effect to international rules and standards (Art 220). Enforcement powers are, however, subject to certain highly detailed safeguards to ensure that freedom of navigation is maintained alongside efforts to ensure environmental protection (Pt XII, s 7, Arts 223–33). These safeguards include a basic provision requiring non-discrimination against foreign vessels (Art 227), flag State pre-emption rights over enforcement proceedings in relation to violations (requiring, at the request of the flag State, suspension of proceedings that may have been initiated by other States) (Art 228), establishment of monetary penalties only for violations beyond internal waters, except in cases of 'wilful and serious' acts of pollution in the territorial sea (Art 230), and a special Article on safeguards with respect to straits used for international navigation (Art 233).

International legal regime for vessel-source marine oil pollution

The system of international legal rules governing the control of vessel-source marine oil pollution is now both well established and multifarious in terms of the number of different international instruments. As noted by one commentator, this was the first form of marine pollution to attract the attention of the world community and therefore, the first to receive concerted political and legal treatment at the international level (Rémond-

---

4   On which see p 208, below.

Gouilloud (1981) 196).[5] These international instruments range from international conventions between States governing deliberate, operational oil discharges from vessels (1973/78 MARPOL Convention, see commentary p 212, below), high seas intervention in the case of accidental oil spills from vessels in distress (1969 Intervention Convention)[6] and liability and compensation for oil pollution damage (1969 Civil Liability and 1971 Fund Conventions, replaced in 1992)[7] to voluntary international agreements between industrial participants (as opposed to States) also to provide for compensation in the event of damage sustained from such accidental spillage on the basis of strict liability, subject to previously defined limits of compensation (Tanker Owners Voluntary Agreement concerning Liability for Oil Pollution (TOVALOP) and Contract Regarding a Supplement to Tanker Liability for Oil Pollution (CRISTAL)). These latter two agreements have now lapsed in the light of the new compensation limits introduced to the 1969 Civil Liability and 1971 Fund Conventions.

The regime for vessel-source pollution has developed through a well-established international organisation with authority originally over shipping issues, primarily those concerning maritime safety, although it has subsequently greatly developed its role in the protection of the marine environment from vessel-source pollution. This is the International Maritime Organisation (IMO), a specialised agency of the United Nations, based in London.[8] The IMO Assembly is composed of all Member States, meeting every other year in plenary sessions. In 1977, the Assembly revised its constituent instrument in order to give it constitutional authority to expand its role beyond purely consultative and advisory functions. Amongst the Assembly's most important functions is the issuing of recommendations to Member State governments for the adoption of regulations and guidelines concerning maritime safety and marine pollution control. Also, by providing States with an ongoing diplomatic forum for the discussion of such issues, the IMO (previously known as the Inter-Governmental Maritime Consultative Organisation (IMCO)) has, since the 1970s, facilitated the transformation of these concerns into global agreements and has established effective equipment standards that have removed many practical and legal barriers that impeded enforcement of earlier international agreements (Mitchell (1993) 184). A great many IMO recommendations stem from authority granted to IMO under multilateral conventions dealing with these matters, complementing the Assembly's powers under the 1948 IMO Convention (Cmnd 589).

Again, as in the international negotiation process for the 1982 UNCLOS noted above, the arrival of many newly independent developing States within the ranks of the IMO during the 1970s made a substantial difference to the international regulation of this issue. Many of these countries had little domestic experience of, or concern for, marine oil pollution but supported strong controls because they expected few direct costs from such regulation and hoped that pollution controls would help establish jurisdictional precedents, especially in support of increased coastal State jurisdiction. During the then

---

5   The first instrument was the International Convention for the Prevention of Pollution of the Seas by Oil 1954 (Cmnd 395).

6   The International Convention Relating to Intervention on the High Seas in Cases of Oil Pollution Casualties 1969 (Cmnd 4403).

7   See Chapter 1, p 77, above.

8   For its website: www.imo.org.

ongoing Third UN Conference on the Law of the Sea (UNCLOS III) negotiations, which culminated in the 1982 Convention, developed States lacking strong oil and shipping interests, like Canada, Australia and New Zealand, also took environmentalist positions. Only this combination of factors allowed environmentally concerned governments to overcome the resistance of the oil and shipping interests, and the maritime governments that supported them, in order to get agreement on the expensive but effective equipment requirements necessary to reduce operational discharges, for example, to measure and collect waste oil generated by the normal operation of the ship. By 1973, the date the Third Conference was convened, these developments provided the votes needed to counter the power of maritime States and industry and to adopt international regulation that began to require real national and industrial policy responses. While the shift did not occur overnight, the international political bargaining process at the IMO was no longer weighted exclusively in favour of shipping interests (Mitchell (1993) 186 and 193). This has enabled the IMO not only to set international standards for ocean shipping, but also to attempt to ensure the efficacy of these standards through flag, coastal and port State compliance and enforcement (Kirgis, Jr (1995) 715). Having finally achieved stringent regulations on paper, especially in respect of deliberate vessel-source marine oil pollution through the 1973/78 MARPOL treaty, the IMO has in recent years sought to redirect its focus to compliance. Progress on this front however has been limited by the fact that many developing States have opened shipping registers, even though they can offer little control over the ships registered under their flag, as outlined below.

This is not to suggest, however, that the present international legal regime is a wholly successful one. As Ellis has noted, '[D]uring the last two decades, marine oil pollution has become an emotional and evocative issue as an increasing number of major oil spills have wreaked havoc on aquatic and bird life and on the fishing and tourism industries of coastal States' (Ellis (1995) 31). She cites United Nations' estimates that some 600,000 tons, approximately 4.2 million barrels, of oil spillages and seepages occur annually as a consequence of normal oceanic shipping activities. In this respect, it is important to point out that although dramatic accidental oil spills generate intense publicity, the amount of oil finding its way into the sea through such accidental oil spills is only about 12.5% of the total.[9] Indeed, as Mitchell notes, the intentional discharge of oil during tanker operations has consistently overshadowed accidents as the major source of ship-related oil pollution that soils beaches and oils sea-birds (Mitchell (1993) 183). In fact, most marine oil pollution originates either from land-based sources or through deliberate discharges by ships. Somewhat more controversially, Ellis also suggests that the use of supertankers has increased the hazard inherent in transporting oil by sea because of the far greater quantity of oil that is spilled when an accident involving a supertanker occurs (Ellis (1995) 31–32). However, the risks in using smaller less well equipped tankers may in fact be higher than using one technically advanced supertanker to transport the same amount of oil.

Despite the great number of international conventions on this issue of accidental and/or deliberate vessel-source marine oil pollution which have received broad acceptance and support in the international community, to date these conventions have proven to be inadequate for controlling this source of pollution. As Mitchell notes, for example, nations have sought international regulations to address intentional vessel-

---

9   For examples of such recent accidents, see p 211, below.

source oil pollution for more than six decades, yet it is only in the last decade and a half that oil entering the ocean from tanker operations has begun to decrease (Mitchell (1993) 183). On the other hand, the recent improvements may be an indication that international regulation is finally having effect and that the more recent instruments, such as MARPOL are more effective than their predecessors.

Two reasons have been suggested as the main causes for this delayed effect. The first and more important reason is that the concept of the national sovereignty of States over the registered vessels which fly their flags serves to prevent the successful enforcement of the current system. The primarily flag State jurisdiction over shipping is notoriously weak in this respect. Pollution controls are not easily applied on vessels of many different 'nationalities', that move almost continuously around the world, in and out of every kind of maritime jurisdictional regime, many of which seldom, if ever, return to ports or waters of their states of nationality. Even in the presence of strong evidence that an unlawful discharge has occurred, it is often easy for the suspected offender to avoid detection by an investigating port or coastal State and thus evade proceedings against it. The difficulties inherent in applying normal judicial procedures against vessels are also a function of the economic structure of the world shipping industry. Until recently, up to two-thirds of the world's merchant shipping was registered in a small number of States, many of which were more interested in protecting the commercial interests of the ships flying their flag than in protecting the marine environment. Furthermore, many of these 'flag States' were, and some still are, also 'flags of convenience' States, that is to say they maintain open registry systems, permitting the registration of almost any vessel, regardless of the nationality of its owners or operators and, more importantly for these purposes, the sea-worthiness of the vessel. Such States are often reluctant to implement any treaty-based restraints upon their registered shipping, or even to sign and ratify vessel-source pollution control treaties (Rémond-Gouilloud (1981) 196). Since the flag State itself must first consent to and then enforce any conventional obligations and take enforcement action against any breach by ships registered in that State, the national interests of the flag State in its shipping industry may prevent it from enforcing its jurisdiction over its own vessels (Ellis (1995) 33). As Mitchell notes further, 'even when domestic calls for action (in relation to the oil pollution problem) have been loud, a government's international support for strong measures depended on the level of opposition from domestic oil and shipping concerns' (Mitchell (1993) 192).

The second, longer term and more systemic-based reason for the failure of international conventions is that environmental protection generally has little value within current economic models. Mainstream economic thought has, until recently, either ignored the environment or had considerable difficulty in placing a 'value' on it. Environmental protection was 'externalised' by economists who found it either too insignificant or too difficult to include as a cost associated with human activity (Ellis (1995) 32). It is, however, only through progressive 'internalisation' of environmental costs within the overall industry cost-benefit analysis that incentives to clean-up its activities and reduce its pollution output become evident.

The economic theory requiring the internalisation of environmental externalities has manifested itself in law as the 'polluter pays' principle (Ellis (1995) 57) (see p 52, above). Applying this principle, the costs of pollution, whether damaging local, regional or global nvironments, should be borne by the producer or company that causes the pollution, ather than falling on the general community, whether local or international, to be paid hrough reduced environmental quality or increased taxation in order to mitigate the nvironmentally degrading effects of such pollution (Ellis (1995) citing Gaines (1991) 68–69 and 487). However, many commentators still contend that this is an economic rinciple for the distribution of costs rather than a legal one, although it does now appear n some treaties. For example, it is recognised in the Preamble of the 1990 Oil Pollution 'reparedness, Response and Co-operation (OPRC) Convention (Cm 2671). At the egional level, it is included in the 1992 Paris Convention for the Protection of the Marine Invironment of the North East Atlantic as a general principle to be applied, along with he 'precautionary' principle, under Art 2(2) of the Convention. Ultimately, however, the onsumer pays, rather than the polluting company, through the transferring by the latter f its costs by increasing the price of its product, even though insurance may absorb some f the burden.

Even the implementation of the polluter pays principle has not been without its roblems. This is mainly due to its assumption that everything, including the nvironment, has a market price attached to it (Ellis (1995) 57). Although this process loes provide the environment with a notional market value, the quantification of this ralue is predicated upon how much environmental damage is actually seen to affect the conomic interests of humanity or groups of individuals, rather than by how much it ffects the global ecosystem. Oil pollution of the high seas, for example, is not considered pollution damage', as defined in the 1969 Civil Liability Convention (now replaced by he 1992 Convention with the same title)[10] as no individual property interests are injured. ater Protocols to this Convention are less rigid but they only entered into force at the nd of May 1996. Although unlawful pollution occurs, ecosystems are damaged and a lelicate ecological balance adversely affected, neither the existing system nor the polluter ays concept provides a realistic or workable solution to this problem (Ellis (1995) 58).

In particular, the value of any damage to the ecological balance of the oceans per se lue to marine oil pollution is not susceptible to quantification utilising the usual nethods. While it would be preferable to focus on the overall depletion of the ecosystem nd biodiversity as a 'value' in itself, the incorporation of such an ecosystem value pproach within the usual economic cost-benefit analysis would be problematic. To deal ffectively with such global externalities requires a degree of international co-operation hat has been noticeably lacking in this sector of human activity. Current international onventions provide a weak and ineffectual regime to enforce compliance with shipping afety and environmental standards. In contrast, they provide a well-structured process or victims of oil pollution to gain compensation, albeit liability under them being limited. his too can be regarded as a reinforcement of the market-oriented economy in that it is asier and less costly to try to quantify and compensate for damage to property and conomic interests suffered by individuals (subject to limitation of liability) than it is to revent such damage from occurring in the first place (Ellis (1995) 58). The scale of some ecent spillages, however, as in the *Amoco Cadiz* [1984] 2 Lloyd's Rep 304 and *Exxon 'aldez*, not to mention the more recent *Braer* and *Sea Empress* groundings, have called this

---

0 Birnie, P and Boyle, A, *Basic Documents on International Law and the Environment*, 1995, Oxford: OUP, p 91.

system of strict but limited liability into question: *Safer Ships, Cleaner Seas* (1994) Cmnd 2560 (the Donaldson Report).

An interesting point in relation to this development is that the most progressive system of strict liability and compensation for environmental damage caused by marine oil pollution was set-up by the oil and shipping industries themselves by way of voluntary agreements in order to supplement the negotiating efforts towards a conventional regime, and in return for definitively set limits for the amounts to be compensated. As Ellis has noted above, given our current theories of economics, the polluter pays principle provides the best means to ensure that all the costs of oil production, transportation, refinement and consumption, including damage caused by it to the environment are incorporated into its price. But the problem of initiating and enforcing the polluter pays principle at the international level highlights the inadequacy of the current international legal structure.

The overall lack of success of this regime is further evidenced by the newly evolving trend involving increasing attempts by coastal States in many different regions of the world to legislate unilaterally for jurisdiction to enforce higher discharge standards and even navigational restrictions over errant vessels within their national maritime zones. This expansive jurisdictional trend is both *quantitative*, in terms of incorporating both the exclusive economic zone (EEZ), as well as the territorial waters of coastal States, and *qualitative*, in terms of providing for more stringent rules and higher standards regarding deliberate or accidental vessel source marine oil pollution. These developments pose an obvious threat for the continued freedom of navigation currently enjoyed by the maritime transport industry throughout the world's oceans.

The 1982 Convention has been criticised as being dominated by and catering to maritime commercial interests and the States in which they are located (Ellis (1995) 42 citing Stephenson (1992) 133). Despite meaningful concessions to both port and coastal States, the regime of enforcement by the 1982 UNCLOS continues to recognise the flag State as the principal repository of jurisdiction over its own vessels (Ellis (1995) 42, citing Collins (1987) 288). Although there have been moves to improve the monitoring of compliance by flag States of international discharge standards with the establishment of a new IMO body, the Flag State Compliance Sub-Committee, it is difficult to see how much this will achieve when each flag State's sovereignty continues to be jealously guarded. In an area of such economic and political importance, it is difficult to believe that this new Sub-Committee will be given sufficient authority to influence the dominant *laissez-faire* trend (Ellis (1995) 42). Indeed, it has been noted that practice by the major maritime States since the signing of the 1982 UNCLOS confirms that coastal State economic and environmental interests will remain in second place to the interests of flag States (Ellis (1995) 42, citing Dzidzornu and Tsamenyi (1991) 287).

MARPOL Convention 1973/78

The most comprehensive and important of all the conventions and the first one to provide exhaustive guidelines for ship builders and ship owners to follow in order to actively prevent marine oil pollution, is the 1973 International Convention on the Prevention of Marine Pollution from Ships, as modified by its 1978 Protocol (MARPOL

73/78).[11] The MARPOL Convention and its Annexes also provide the main source for the international rules and standards for pollution from ships referred to in Arts 194, 211, 218, and 220 of the 1982 UNCLOS (see pp 214–24, below). Under these Articles, the relevant 'international rules and standards', which in this issue area is taken to be the legal regime set-up by MARPOL, must not only be applied by flag States but may also be enforced against foreign vessels by port States, and within the territorial sea and (in certain strictly-defined circumstances) the exclusive economic zone of coastal States. Therefore, States parties to MARPOL must apply the Convention not only to their own vessels but also to violations within their maritime jurisdiction (Birnie and Boyle (1995) 189).

Under MARPOL, a ship owner is prohibited from discharging oil or oily mixtures into the sea unless certain criteria are met or an exception applies. Its main objective is to eliminate intentional pollution of the marine environment by oil and to minimise accidental discharge. The MARPOL Convention's approach relies mainly on technical measures to limit oil discharges. As Birnie and Boyle note, the discharge of small quantities of oil is still permitted, but only if it takes place *en route*, more than 50 miles from land and not in designated special areas where virtually all discharges are prohibited (Annex I, reg 10) (Birnie and Boyle (1992) 267).

MARPOL is no longer confined solely to vessel-source marine oil pollution, but also regulates other types of ship-based pollution, including the bulk carriage of noxious liquids and garbage from ships. There are five annexes which contain regulations and discharge standards governing different types of pollutant.

Annex I addresses oil pollution (entered into force on 2 October 1983), Annex II covers noxious liquid substances (entered into force on 6 April 1987), Annex III covers harmful substances in packaged form (entered into force on 1 July 1992), Annex IV covers sewage from ships (not yet in force as of 1999) and Annex V addresses garbage from ships (entered into force on 31 December 1988). Annexes I and II are binding upon the Convention's entry into force for a Party (as modified by 1978 Protocol), while Annexes III, IV and V are binding at the option of each Party (Art 14(1)). In July 1999 it was agreed that Annex IV should be revised to gain wider acceptance by Parties. Finally, air pollution from ships, including greenhouse gas emissions, is being studied with a view to making proposals for its regulation within the MARPOL 1973/78 treaty regime. The 1978 Protocol and Annexes I and II had 93 States' parties on 1 January 1995 representing 92% of the world shipping tonnage, but participation in the other Annexes varies (Birnie and Boyle (1995) 189).

Unlike the international conventions and the voluntary industrial agreements mentioned above, which are primarily concerned with compensation measures to be taken once an accident has occurred causing pollution damage, the 1973/78 MARPOL treaty includes preventative provisions relating to the design, construction and maintenance of oil tankers (Annex I). These standards are more stringent for new vessels. Once a State has adopted MARPOL, new ships constructed in that State are required to be built according to these stricter guidelines. Unfortunately, MARPOL has not been very successful in either phasing out or appropriately regulating 'ageing ships', that is, those that were built in the

---

11 IMO, *MARPOL 1973–78 Consolidated edition*, 1992, London: IMO. See also *IMO Manual on Oil Pollution*, 1983, revised edition, London: IMO, s I.

1970s or even earlier and which are still sailing under minimal safety and environmental standards (Ellis (1995) 41).

By 1992, concern was growing about the condition of some of the world's ships, especially the large number of ageing tankers and bulk carriers. It was agreed that steps had to be taken to ensure that the maintenance of such older ships should be improved and that the 'quality gap' which had arisen because of IMO's success in introducing strict standards for new ships, should be narrowed. Thus, important new measures to improve the safety of existing oil tankers have come into operation (6 July 1995). These changes were included in amendments adopted in March 1992 to MARPOL 73/78 (Annex 1). These included:

1   an enhanced programme of inspections that will apply to all oil tankers aged five years and more;

2   important new changes to the construction requirements for tankers of 25 years of age and older, including the mandatory fitting of double hulls or an equivalent design.

Other amendments adopted in March 1992 applied to all new tankers ordered after 6 July 1993. Tankers of 5000 dwt (dead-weight tonnage) and above must be fitted with double bottoms and double hulls extending along the full length of a ship's side. The 'mid-deck' design is permitted as an alternative and other designs may be allowed in due course, provided they ensure the same level of protection against pollution (Marine Pollution Bulletin, News (September (1995) 578)).

UN CONVENTION ON THE LAW OF THE SEA 1982, PART XII

Part XII Protection and Preservation of the Marine Environment

Section 1 General Provisions

Article 192 General obligation

States have the obligation to protect and preserve the marine environment.

Article 193 Sovereign right of states to exploit their natural resources

States have the sovereign right to exploit their natural resources pursuant to their environmental policies and in accordance with their duty to protect and preserve the marine environment.

Article 194 Measures to prevent, reduce and control pollution of the marine environment

1   States shall take, individually or jointly as appropriate all measures consistent with this Convention that are necessary to prevent, reduce and control pollution of the marine environment from any source, using for this purpose the best practicable means at their disposal and in accordance with their capabilities, and they shall endeavour to harmonise their policies in this connection.

2   States shall take all measures necessary to ensure that activities under their jurisdiction or control are so conducted as not to cause damage by pollution to other states and their environment, and that pollution arising from incidents or activities under their jurisdiction or control does not spread beyond the areas where they exercise sovereign rights in accordance with this Convention.

3   The measures taken pursuant to this Part shall deal with all sources of pollution of the marine environment. These measures shall include, *inter alia*, those designed to minimise to the fullest possible extent:

(a)   the release of toxic, harmful or noxious substances, especially those which are persistent, from land-based sources, from or through the atmosphere or by dumping;

(b)   pollution from vessels, in particular measures for preventing accidents and dealing with emergencies, ensuring the safety of operations at sea, preventing intentional and unintentional discharges, and regulating the design, construction, equipment, operation and manning of vessels;

(c)   pollution from installations and devices used in exploration or exploitation of the natural resources of the sea-bed and subsoil, in particular measures for preventing accidents and dealing with emergencies, ensuring the safety of operations at sea, and regulating the design, construction, equipment, operation and manning of such installations or devices;

(d)   pollution from other installations and devices operating in the marine environment, in particular measures for preventing accidents and dealing with emergencies, ensuring the safety of operations at sea, and regulating the design, construction, equipment, operation and manning of such installations or devices.

4   In taking measures to prevent, reduce or control pollution of the marine environment, states shall refrain from unjustifiable interference with activities carried out by other states in the exercise of their rights and in pursuance of their duties in conformity with this Convention.

5   The measures taken in accordance with this Part shall include those necessary to protect and preserve rare or fragile ecosystems as well as the habitat of depleted, threatened or endangered species and other forms of marine life.

Article 195 Duty not to transfer damage or hazards or transform one type of pollution into another

In taking measures to prevent, reduce and control pollution of the marine environment, states shall act so as not to transfer, directly or indirectly, damage or hazards from one area to another or transform one type of pollution into another.

Article 196 Use of technologies or introduction of alien or new species

1   States shall take all measures necessary to prevent, reduce and control pollution of the marine environment resulting from the use of technologies under their jurisdiction or control, or the intentional or accidental introduction of species, alien or new, to a particular part of the marine environment, which may cause significant and harmful changes thereto.

2   This article does not affect the application of this Convention regarding the prevention, reduction and control of pollution of the marine environment.

Section 2 Global and regional co-operation

Article 197 Co-operation on a global or regional basis

States shall co-operate on a global basis and, as appropriate, on a regional basis, directly or through competent international organisations, in formulating and elaborating international rules, standards and recommended practices and procedures consistent with this

Convention, for the protection and preservation of the marine environment, taking into account characteristic regional features.

Article 198 Notification of imminent or actual damage

When a state becomes aware of cases in which the marine environment is in imminent danger of being damaged or has been damaged by pollution, it shall immediately notify other states it deems likely to be affected by such damage, as well as the competent international organisations.

Article 199 Contingency plans against pollution

In the cases referred to in Article 198, states in the area affected, in accordance with their capabilities, and the competent international organisations shall co-operate, to the extent possible, in eliminating the effects of pollution and preventing or minimising the damage. To this end, states shall jointly develop and promote contingency plans for responding to pollution incidents in the marine environment.

Article 200 Studies, research programmes and exchange of information and data

States shall co-operate, directly or through competent international organisations, for the purpose of promoting studies, undertaking programmes of scientific research and encouraging the exchange of information and data acquired about pollution of the marine environment. They shall endeavour to participate actively in regional and global programmes to acquire knowledge for the assessment of the nature and extent of pollution, exposure to it, and its pathways, risks and remedies.

Article 201 Scientific criteria for regulations

In the light of the information and data acquired pursuant to Article 200, states shall co-operate, directly or through competent international organisations, in establishing appropriate scientific criteria for the formulation and elaboration of rules, standards and recommended practices and procedures for the prevention, reduction and control of pollution of the marine environment.

Section 3 Technical assistance

Article 202 Scientific and technical assistance to developing states

States shall, directly or through competent international organisations:

(a) promote programmes of scientific, educational, technical and other assistance to developing states for the protection and preservation of the marine environment and the prevention, reduction and control of marine pollution. Such assistance shall include, *inter alia*:

   (i) training of their scientific and technical personnel;

   (ii) facilitating their participation in relevant international programmes;

   (iii) supplying them with necessary equipment and facilities;

   (iv) enhancing their capacity to manufacture such equipment;

   (v) advice on and developing facilities for research, monitoring, educational and other programmes;

(b) provide appropriate assistance, especially to developing states, for the minimisation of the effects of major incidents which may cause serious pollution of the marine environment;

(c) provide appropriate assistance, especially to developing states, concerning the preparation of environmental assessments.

Article 203 Preferential treatment for developing states

Developing states shall, for the purposes of prevention, reduction and control of pollution of the marine environment or minimisation of its effects, be granted preference by international organisations in:

(a) the allocation of appropriate funds and technical assistance; and

(b) the utilisation of their specialised services.

Section 4 Monitoring and environmental assessment

Article 204 Monitoring of the risks or effects of pollution

1   States shall, consistent with the rights of other states, endeavour, as far as practicable, directly or through the competent international organisations, to observe, measure, evaluate and analyse, by recognised scientific methods, the risks or effects of pollution of the marine environment.

2   In particular, states shall keep under surveillance the effects of any activities which they permit or in which they engage in order to determine whether these activities are likely to pollute the marine environment.

Article 205 Publication of reports

States shall publish reports of the results obtained pursuant to Article 204 or provide such reports at appropriate intervals to the competent international organisations, which should make them available to all states.

Article 206 Assessment of potential effects of activities

When states have reasonable grounds for believing that planned activities under their jurisdiction or control may cause substantial pollution or significant and harmful changes to the marine environment, they shall, as far as practicable, assess the potential effects of such activities on the marine environment and shall communicate reports of the results of such assessments in the manner provided in Article 205.

Section 5 International Rules and National Legislation to Prevent, Reduce and Control Pollution of the Marine Environment

Article 207 Pollution from land-based sources

1   States shall adopt laws and regulations to prevent, reduce and control pollution of the marine environment from land-based sources, including rivers, estuaries, pipelines and outfall structures, taking into account internationally agreed rules, standards and recommended practices and procedures.

2   States shall take other measures as may be necessary to prevent, reduce and control such pollution.

3   States shall endeavour to harmonise their policies in this connection at the appropriate regional level.

4   States, acting especially through competent international organisations or diplomatic conference, shall endeavour to establish global and regional rules, standards and

recommended practices and procedures to prevent, reduce and control pollution of the marine environment from land-based sources, taking into account characteristic regional features, the economic capacity of developing states and their need for economic development. Such rules, standards and recommended practices and procedures shall be re-examined from time to time as necessary.

5   Laws, regulations, measures, rules, standards and recommended practices and procedures referred to in paragraphs 1, 2 and 4 shall include those designed to minimise, to the fullest extent possible, the release of toxic, harmful or noxious substances, especially those which are persistent, into the marine environment.

Article 208 Pollution from sea-bed activities subject to national jurisdiction

1   Coastal states shall adopt laws and regulations to prevent, reduce and control pollution of the marine environment arising from or in connection with sea-bed activities subject to their jurisdiction and from artificial islands, installations and structures under their jurisdiction, pursuant to Articles 60 and 80.

2   States shall take other measures as may be necessary to prevent, reduce and control such pollution.

3   Such laws, regulations and measures shall be no less effective than international rules, standards and recommended practices and procedures.

4   States shall endeavour to harmonise their policies in this connection at the appropriate regional level.

5   States, acting especially through competent international organisations or diplomatic conference, shall establish global and regional rules, standards and recommended practices and procedures to prevent, reduce and control pollution of the marine environment referred to in paragraph 1. Such rules, standards and recommended practices and procedures shall be re-examined from time to time as necessary.

[Article 209 (on Pollution from Activities in the Area) omitted.]

Article 210 Pollution by dumping

1   States shall adopt laws and regulations to prevent, reduce and control pollution of the marine environment by dumping.

2   States shall take other measures as may be necessary to prevent, reduce and control such pollution.

3   Such laws, regulations and measures shall ensure that dumping is not carried out without the permission of the competent authorities of states.

4   States, acting especially through competent international organisations or diplomatic conference, shall endeavour to establish global and regional rules, standards and recommended practices and procedures to prevent, reduce and control such pollution. Such rules, standards and recommended practices and procedures shall be re-examined from time to time as necessary.

5   Dumping within the territorial sea and the exclusive economic zone or onto the continental shelf shall not be carried out without the express prior approval of the coastal state, which has the right to permit, regulate and control such dumping after due consideration of the matter with other states which by reason of their geographical situation may be adversely affected thereby.

6   National laws, regulations and measures shall be no less effective in preventing, reducing and controlling such pollution than the global rules and standards.

Article 211 Pollution from vessels

1   States, acting through the competent international organisation or general diplomatic conference, shall establish international rules and standards to prevent, reduce and control pollution of the marine environment from vessels and promote the adoption, in the same manner, wherever appropriate, of routeing systems designed to minimise the threat of accidents which might cause pollution of the marine environment, including the coastline, and pollution damage to the related interests of coastal states. Such rules and standards shall, in the same manner, be re-examined from time to time as necessary.

2   States shall adopt laws and regulations for the prevention, reduction and control of pollution of the marine environment from vessels flying their flag or of their registry. Such laws and regulations shall at least have the same effect as that of generally accepted international rules and standards established through the competent international organisation or general diplomatic conference.

3   States which establish particular requirements for the prevention, reduction and control of pollution of the marine environment as a condition for the entry of foreign vessels into their ports or internal waters or for a call at their off-shore terminals shall give due publicity to such requirements and shall communicate them to the competent international organisation. Whenever such requirements are established in identical form by two or more coastal states in an endeavour to harmonise policy, the communication shall indicate which states are participating in such co-operative arrangements. Every state shall require the master of a vessel flying its flag or of its registry, when navigating within the territorial sea of a state participating in such co-operative arrangements, to furnish, upon the request of that state, information as to whether it is proceeding to a state of the same region participating in such co-operative arrangements and, if so, to indicate whether it complies with the port entry requirements of that state. This article is without prejudice to the continued exercise by a vessel of its right of innocent passage or to the application of Article 25, paragraph 2.

4   Coastal states may, in the exercise of their sovereignty within their territorial sea, adopt laws and regulations for the prevention, reduction and control of marine pollution from foreign vessels, including vessels exercising the right of innocent passage. Such laws and regulations shall, in accordance with Part II, s 3, not hamper innocent passage of foreign vessels.

5   Coastal states, for the purpose of enforcement as provided for in s 6, may in respect of their exclusive economic zones adopt laws and regulations for the prevention, reduction and control of pollution from vessels conforming to and giving effect to generally accepted international rules and standards established through the competent international organisation or general diplomatic conference.

6   (a) Where the international rules and standards referred to in paragraph 1 are inadequate to meet special circumstances and coastal states have reasonable grounds for believing that a particular, clearly defined area of their respective exclusive economic zones is an area where the adoption of special mandatory measures for the prevention of pollution from vessels is required for recognised technical reasons in relation to its oceanographical and ecological conditions, as well as its utilisation or the protection of its resources and the particular character

219

of its traffic, the coastal states, after appropriate consultations through the competent international organisation with any other states concerned, may, for that area, direct a communication to that organisation, submitting scientific and technical evidence in support and information on necessary reception facilities. Within 12 months after receiving such a communication, the organisation shall determine whether the conditions in that area correspond to the requirements set out above. If the organisation so determines, the coastal states may, for that area, adopt laws and regulations for the prevention, reduction and control of pollution from vessels implementing such international rules and standards or navigational practices as are made applicable, through the organisation, for special areas. These laws and regulations shall not become applicable to foreign vessels until 15 months after the submission of the communication to the organisation.

(b) The coastal states shall publish the limits of any such particular, clearly defined area.

(c) If the coastal states intend to adopt additional laws and regulations for the same area for the prevention, reduction and control of pollution from vessels, they shall, when submitting the aforesaid communication, at the same time notify the organisation thereof. Such additional laws and regulations may relate to discharges or navigational practices but shall not require foreign vessels to observe design, construction, manning or equipment standards other than generally accepted international rules and standards; they shall become applicable to foreign vessels 15 months after the submission of the communication to the organisation, provided that the organisation agrees within 12 months after the submission of the communication.

7   The international rules and standards referred to in this article should include *inter alia* those relating to prompt notification to coastal states, whose coastline or related interests may be affected by incidents, including maritime casualties, which involve discharges or probability of discharges.

Article 212 Pollution from or through the atmosphere

1   States shall adopt laws and regulations to prevent, reduce and control pollution of the marine environment from or through the atmosphere, applicable to the air space under their sovereignty and to vessels flying their flag or vessels or aircraft of their registry, taking into account internationally agreed rules, standards and recommended practices and procedures and the safety of air navigation.

2   States shall take other measures as may be necessary to prevent, reduce and control such pollution.

3   States, acting especially through competent international organisations or diplomatic conference, shall endeavour to establish global and regional rules, standards and recommended practices and procedures to prevent, reduce and control such pollution.

Section 6 Enforcement

Article 213 Enforcement with respect to pollution from land-based sources

States shall enforce their laws and regulations adopted in accordance with Article 207 and shall adopt laws and regulations and take other measures necessary to implement applicable international rules and standards established through competent international organisations or diplomatic conference to prevent, reduce and control pollution of the marine environment from land-based sources.

Article 214 Enforcement with respect to pollution from sea-bed activities

States shall enforce their laws and regulations adopted in accordance with Article 208 and shall adopt laws and regulations and take other measures necessary to implement applicable international rules and standards established through competent international organisations or diplomatic conference to prevent, reduce and control pollution of the marine environment arising from or in connection with sea-bed activities subject to their jurisdiction and from artificial islands, installations and structures under their jurisdiction, pursuant to Articles 60 and 80.

[Article 215 (on Enforcement with Respect to Pollution from Activities in the Area) omitted.]

Enforcement of international rules, regulations and procedures established in accordance with Part XI to prevent, reduce and control pollution of the marine environment from activities in the Area shall be governed by that Part.

Article 216 Enforcement with respect to pollution by dumping

1   Laws and regulations adopted in accordance with this Convention and applicable international rules and standards established through competent international organisations or diplomatic conference for the prevention, reduction and control of pollution of the marine environment by dumping shall be enforced:

(a)   by the coastal state with regard to dumping within its territorial sea or its exclusive economic zone or onto its continental shelf;

(b)   by the flag state with regard to vessels flying its flag or vessels or aircraft of its registry;

(c)   by any state with regard to acts of loading of wastes or other matter occurring within its territory or at its off-shore terminals.

2   No state shall be obliged by virtue of this article to institute proceedings when another state has already instituted proceedings in accordance with this article.

Article 217 Enforcement by flag states

1   States shall ensure compliance by vessels flying their flag or of their registry with applicable international rules and standards, established through the competent international organisation or general diplomatic conference, and with their laws and regulations adopted in accordance with this Convention for the prevention, reduction and control of pollution of the marine environment from vessels and shall accordingly adopt laws and regulations and take other measures necessary for their implementation. Flag states shall provide for the effective enforcement of such rules, standards, laws and regulations, irrespective of where a violation occurs.

2   States shall, in particular, take appropriate measures in order to ensure that vessels flying their flag or of their registry are prohibited from sailing, until they can proceed to sea in compliance with the requirements of the international rules and standards referred to in paragraph 1, including requirements in respect of design, construction, equipment and manning of vessels.

3   States shall ensure that vessels flying their flag or of their registry carry on board certificates required by and issued pursuant to international rules and standards referred to in paragraph 1. States shall ensure that vessels flying their flag are periodically inspected in order to verify that such certificates are in conformity with the

actual condition of the vessels. These certificates shall be accepted by other states as evidence of the condition of the vessels and shall be regarded as having the same force as certificates issued by them, unless there are clear grounds for believing that the condition of the vessel does not correspond substantially with the particulars of the certificates.

4   If a vessel commits a violation of rules and standards established through the competent international organisation or general diplomatic conference, the flag state, without prejudice to Articles 218, 220 and 228, shall provide for immediate investigation and where appropriate institute proceedings in respect of the alleged violation irrespective of where the violation occurred or where the pollution caused by such violation has occurred or has been spotted.

5   Flag states conducting an investigation of the violation may request the assistance of any other state whose co-operation could be useful in clarifying the circumstances of the case. States shall endeavour to meet appropriate requests of flag states.

6   States shall, at the written request of any state, investigate any violation alleged to have been committed by vessels flying their flag. If satisfied that sufficient evidence is available to enable proceedings to be brought in respect of the alleged violation, flag states shall without delay institute such proceedings in accordance with their laws.

7   Flag states shall promptly inform the requesting state and the competent international organisation of the action taken and its outcome. Such information shall be available to all states.

8   Penalties provided for by the laws and regulations of states for vessels flying their flag shall be adequate in severity to discourage violations wherever they occur.

Article 218 Enforcement by port states

1   When a vessel is voluntarily within a port or at an off-shore terminal of a state, that state may undertake investigations and, where the evidence so warrants, institute proceedings in respect of any discharge from that vessel outside the internal waters, territorial sea or exclusive economic zone of that state in violation of applicable international rules and standards established through the competent international organisation or general diplomatic conference.

2   No proceedings pursuant to paragraph 1 shall be instituted in respect of a discharge violation in the internal waters, territorial sea or exclusive economic zone of another state unless requested by that state, the flag state, or a state damaged or threatened by the discharge violation, or unless the violation has caused or is likely to cause pollution in the internal waters, territorial sea or exclusive economic zone of the state instituting the proceedings.

3   When a vessel is voluntarily within a port or at an off-shore terminal of a state, that state shall, as far as practicable, comply with requests from any state for investigation of a discharge violation referred to in paragraph 1, believed to have occurred in, caused, or threatened damage to the internal waters, territorial sea or exclusive economic zone of the requesting state. It shall likewise, as far as practicable, comply with requests from the flag state for investigation of such a violation, irrespective of where the violation occurred.

4   The records of the investigation carried out by a port state pursuant to this article shall be transmitted upon request to the flag state or to the coastal state. Any proceedings

instituted by the port state on the basis of such an investigation may, subject to s 7, be suspended at the request of the coastal state when the violation has occurred within its internal waters, territorial sea or exclusive economic zone. The evidence and records of the case, together with any bond or other financial security posted with the authorities of the port state, shall in that event be transmitted to the coastal state. Such transmittal shall preclude the continuation of proceedings in the port state.

Article 219 Measures relating to seaworthiness of vessels to avoid pollution

Subject to s 7, states which, upon request or on their own initiative, have ascertained that a vessel within one of their ports or at one of their off-shore terminals is in violation of applicable international rules and standards relating to seaworthiness of vessels and thereby threatens damage to the marine environment shall, as far as practicable, take administrative measures to prevent the vessel from sailing. Such states may permit the vessel to proceed only to the nearest appropriate repair yard and, upon removal of the causes of the violation, shall permit the vessel to continue immediately.

Article 220 Enforcement by coastal states

1   When a vessel is voluntarily within a port or at an off-shore terminal of a state, that state may, subject to s 7, institute proceedings in respect of any violation of its laws and regulations adopted in accordance with this Convention or applicable international rules and standards for the prevention, reduction and control of pollution from vessels when the violation has occurred within the territorial sea or the exclusive economic zone of that state.

2   Where there are clear grounds for believing that a vessel navigating in the territorial sea of a state has, during its passage therein, violated laws and regulations of that state adopted in accordance with this Convention or applicable international rules and standards for the prevention, reduction and control of pollution from vessels, that state, without prejudice to the application of the relevant provisions of Part II, s 3, may undertake physical inspection of the vessel relating to the violation and may, where the evidence so warrants, institute proceedings, including detention of the vessel, in accordance with its laws, subject to the provisions of s 7.

3   Where there are clear grounds for believing that a vessel navigating in the exclusive economic zone or the territorial sea of a state has, in the exclusive economic zone, committed a violation of applicable international rules and standards for the prevention, reduction and control of pollution from vessels or laws and regulations of that state conforming and giving effect to such rules and standards, that state may require the vessel to give information regarding its identity and port of registry, its last and its next port of call and other relevant information required to establish whether a violation has occurred.

4   States shall adopt laws and regulations and take other measures so that vessels flying their flag comply with requests for information pursuant to paragraph 3.

5   Where there are clear grounds for believing that a vessel navigating in the exclusive economic zone or the territorial sea of a state has, in the exclusive economic zone, committed a violation referred to in paragraph 3 resulting in a substantial discharge causing or threatening significant pollution of the marine environment, that state may undertake physical inspection of the vessel for matters relating to the violation if the vessel has refused to give information or if the information supplied by the vessel is

manifestly at variance with the evident factual situation and if the circumstances of the case justify such inspection.

6   Where there is clear objective evidence that a vessel navigating in the exclusive economic zone or the territorial sea of a state has, in the exclusive economic zone, committed a violation referred to in paragraph 3 resulting in a discharge causing major damage or threat of major damage to the coastline or related interests of the coastal state, or to any resources of its territorial sea or exclusive economic zone, that state may, subject to s 7, provided that the evidence so warrants, institute proceedings, including detention of the vessel, in accordance with its laws.

7   Notwithstanding the provisions of paragraph 6, whenever appropriate procedures have been established, either through the competent international organisation or as otherwise agreed, whereby compliance with requirements for bonding or other appropriate financial security has been assured, the coastal state if bound by such procedures shall allow the vessel to proceed.

8   The provisions of paragraphs 3, 4, 5, 6 and 7 also apply in respect of national laws and regulations adopted pursuant to Article 211, paragraph 6.

Article 221 Measures to avoid pollution arising from maritime casualties

1   Nothing in this Part shall prejudice the right of states, pursuant to international law, both customary and conventional, to take and enforce measures beyond the territorial sea proportionate to the actual or threatened damage to protect their coastline or related interests, including fishing, from pollution or threat of pollution following upon a maritime casualty or acts relating to such a casualty, which may reasonably be expected to result in major harmful consequences.

2   For the purposes of this article, 'maritime casualty' means a collision of vessels, stranding or other incident of navigation, or other occurrence on board a vessel or external to it resulting in material damage or imminent threat of material damage to a vessel or cargo.

Article 222 Enforcement with respect to pollution from or through the atmosphere

States shall enforce, within the air space under their sovereignty or with regard to vessels flying their flag or vessels or aircraft of their registry, their laws and regulations adopted in accordance with Article 212, paragraph 1, and with other provisions of this Convention and shall adopt laws and regulations and take other measures necessary to implement applicable international rules and standards established through competent international organisations or diplomatic conference to prevent, reduce and control pollution of the marine environment from or through the atmosphere, in conformity with all relevant international rules and standards concerning the safety of air navigation.

Section 7 Safeguards

Article 223 Measures to facilitate proceedings

In proceedings instituted pursuant to this Part, states shall take measures to facilitate the hearing of witnesses and the admission of evidence submitted by authorities of another state, or by the competent international organisation, and shall facilitate the attendance at such proceedings of official representatives of the competent international organisation, the flag state and any state affected by pollution arising out of any violation. The official representatives attending such proceedings shall have such rights and duties as may be provided under national laws and regulations or international law.

Article 224 Exercise of powers of enforcement

The powers of enforcement against foreign vessels under this Part may only be exercised by officials or by warships, military aircraft, or other ships or aircraft clearly marked and identifiable as being on government service and authorised to that effect.

Article 225 Duty to avoid adverse consequences in the exercise of the powers of enforcement

In the exercise under this Convention of their powers of enforcement against foreign vessels, states shall not endanger the safety of navigation or otherwise create any hazard to a vessel, or bring it to an unsafe port or anchorage, or expose the marine environment to an unreasonable risk.

Article 226 Investigation of foreign vessels

1 (a) States shall not delay a foreign vessel longer than is essential for purposes of the investigations provided for in Articles 216, 218 and 220. Any physical inspection of a foreign vessel shall be limited to an examination of such certificates, records or other documents as the vessel is required to carry by generally accepted international rules and standards or of any similar documents which it is carrying; further physical inspection of the vessel may be undertaken only after such an examination and only when:

   (i) there are clear grounds for believing that the condition of the vessel or its equipment does not correspond substantially with the particulars of those documents;

   (ii) the contents of such documents are not sufficient to confirm or verify a suspected violation; or

   (iii) the vessel is not carrying valid certificates and records.

(b) If the investigation indicates a violation of applicable laws and regulations or international rules and standards for the protection and preservation of the marine environment, release shall be made promptly subject to reasonable procedures such as bonding or other appropriate financial security.

(c) Without prejudice to applicable international rules and standards relating to the seaworthiness of vessels, the release of a vessel may, whenever it would present an unreasonable threat of damage to the marine environment, be refused or made conditional upon proceeding to the nearest appropriate repair yard. Where release has been refused or made conditional, the flag state of the vessel must be promptly notified, and may seek release of the vessel in accordance with Part XV.

2 States shall co-operate to develop procedures for the avoidance of unnecessary physical inspection of vessels at sea.

Article 227 Non-discrimination with respect to foreign vessels

In exercising their rights and performing their duties under this Part, states shall not discriminate in form or in fact against vessels of any other state.

Article 228 Suspension and restrictions on institution of proceedings

1 Proceedings to impose penalties in respect of any violation of applicable laws and regulations or international rules and standards relating to the prevention, reduction and control of pollution from vessels committed by a foreign vessel beyond the territorial sea of the state instituting proceedings shall be suspended upon the taking of

proceedings to impose penalties in respect of corresponding charges by the flag state within six months of the date on which proceedings were first instituted, unless those proceedings relate to a case of major damage to the coastal state or the flag state in question has repeatedly disregarded its obligation to enforce effectively the applicable international rules and standards in respect of violations committed by its vessels. The flag state shall in due course make available to the state previously instituting proceedings a full dossier of the case and the records of the proceedings, whenever the flag state has requested the suspension of proceedings in accordance with this article. When proceedings instituted by the flag state have been brought a conclusion, the suspended proceedings shall be terminated. Upon payment of costs incurred in respect of such proceedings, any bond posted or other financial security provided in connection with the suspended proceedings shall be released by the coastal state.

2   Proceedings to impose penalties on foreign vessels shall not be instituted after the expiry of three years from the date on which the violation was committed, and shall not be taken by any state in the event of proceedings having been instituted by another state subject to the provisions set out in paragraph 1.

3   The provisions of this article are without prejudice to the right of the flag state to take any measures, including proceedings to impose penalties, according to its laws irrespective of prior proceedings by another state.

Article 229 Institution of civil proceedings

Nothing in this Convention affects the institution of civil proceedings in respect of any claim for loss or damage resulting from pollution of the marine environment.

Article 230 Monetary penalties and the observance of recognised rights of the accused

1   Monetary penalties only may be imposed with respect to violations of national laws and regulations or applicable international rules and standards for the prevention, reduction and control of pollution of the marine environment, committed by foreign vessels beyond the territorial sea.

2   Monetary penalties only may be imposed with respect to violations of national laws and regulations or applicable international rules and standards for the prevention, reduction and control of pollution of the marine environment, committed by foreign vessels in the territorial sea, except in the case of a wilful and serious act of pollution in the territorial sea.

3   In the conduct of proceedings in respect of such violations committed by a foreign vessel which may result in the imposition of penalties, recognised rights of the accused shall be observed.

Article 231 Notification to the flag state and other states concerned

States shall promptly notify the flag state and any other state concerned of any measures taken pursuant to s 6 against foreign vessels, and shall submit to the flag state all official reports concerning such measures. However, with respect to violations committed in the territorial sea, the foregoing obligations of the coastal state apply only to such measures as are taken in proceedings. The diplomatic agents or consular officers and where possible the maritime authority of the flag state, shall be immediately informed of any such measures taken pursuant to s 6 against foreign vessels.

Article 232 Liability of states arising from enforcement measures

States shall be liable for damage or loss attributable to them arising from measures taken pursuant to s 6 when such measures are unlawful or exceed those reasonably required in the light of available information. States shall provide for recourse in their courts for actions in respect of such damage or loss.

Article 233 Safeguards with respect to straits used for international navigation

Nothing in ss 5, 6 and 7 affects the legal regime of straits used for international navigation. However, if a foreign ship other than those referred to in s 10 has committed a violation of the laws and regulations referred to in Article 42, paragraph 1(a) and (b), causing or threatening major damage to the marine environment of the straits, the states bordering the straits may take appropriate enforcement measures and if so shall respect *mutatis mutandis* the provisions of this section.

Section 8 Ice-covered areas

Article 234 Ice-covered areas

Coastal states have the right to adopt and enforce non-discriminatory laws and regulations for the prevention, reduction and control of marine pollution from vessels in ice-covered areas within the limits of the exclusive economic zone, where particularly severe climatic conditions and the presence of ice covering such areas for most of the year create obstructions or exceptional hazards to navigation, and pollution of the marine environment could cause major harm to or irreversible disturbance of the ecological balance. Such laws and regulations shall have due regard to navigation and the protection and preservation of the marine environment based on the best available scientific evidence.

Section 9 Responsibility and liability

Article 235 Responsibility and liability

1   States are responsible for the fulfilment of their international obligations concerning the protection and preservation of the marine environment. They shall be liable in accordance with international law.

2   States shall ensure that recourse is available in accordance with their legal systems for prompt and adequate compensation or other relief in respect of damage caused by pollution of the marine environment by natural or juridical persons under their jurisdiction.

3   With the objective of assuring prompt and adequate compensation in respect of all damage caused by pollution of the marine environment, states shall co-operate in the implementation of existing international law and the further development of international law relating to responsibility and liability for the assessment of and compensation for damage and the settlement of related disputes, as well as, where appropriate, development of criteria and procedures for payment of adequate compensation, such as compulsory insurance or compensation funds.

Section 10 Sovereign immunity

Article 236 Sovereign immunity

The provisions of this Convention regarding the protection and preservation of the marine environment do not apply to any warship, naval auxiliary, other vessels or aircraft owned or operated by a state and used, for the time being, only on government non-commercial service. However, each state shall ensure, by the adoption of appropriate measures not impairing operations or operational capabilities of such vessels or aircraft owned or operated by it, that such vessels or aircraft act in a manner consistent, so far as is reasonable and practicable, with this Convention.

Section 11 Obligations under other Conventions on the protection and preservation of the marine environment

Article 237 Obligations under other conventions on the protection and preservation of the marine environment

1   The provisions of this Part are without prejudice to the specific obligations assumed by states under special conventions and agreements concluded previously which relate to the protection and preservation of the marine environment and to agreements which may be concluded in furtherance of the general principles set forth in this Convention.

2   Specific obligations assumed by states under special conventions, with respect to the protection and preservation of the marine environment, should be carried out in a manner consistent with the general principles and objectives of this Convention.

EUROPEAN COMMUNITY LAW

EC legislation on water pollution

The legislation on water pollution is probably the most highly developed branch of EC environmental law and most certainly has the longest history. Approximately 30 directives concern water. The directives adopt two main approaches to pollution control (1) the imposition of limits or restrictions upon the emission or discharge of particular pollutants into the water media; and (2) the establishment of quality standards for particular designated types of water. The outcome of this dual approach has been a somewhat piecemeal body of law.

The directives on water pollution share several common features:

- The use of dual lists described as 'I' (imperative) and 'G' (guide) which require Member States to set water standards which do not fall below 'I' limits and which should aim to achieve 'G' standards.

- A requirement placed on states to designate 'types' of water for purposes of a particular directive.

- The application of a 'standstill rule' requiring states to maintain the existing quality of waters subject to a directive.

- The establishment of 'competent authorities' within Member States for purposes of inspecting relevant waters.

Perceived failures in the Member States' responses to the water pollution Directives and an overall fall in water quality throughout the EC has led to a review of EC water policy The result has been a new Framework Directive on Water Policy 00/60 (extracted below p 237). Member States have until 22 December 2003 to give effect to this important new piece of legislation. In the meantime provisions of existing Directives remain in force Before examining this Directive, the chapter will consider measures dealing with the release of dangerous substances into water, including detergents and titanium dioxide, followed by the provisions protecting particular types of water, in accordance with the dual approach referred to above.

Measures controlling the release of substances into water

Dangerous substances

The Directive on the Discharge of Dangerous Substances into Water 76/464 is a framework directive (see p 252, below) aimed at eliminating or reducing the pollution of all waters (inland, coastal and territorial waters) by particularly dangerous substances.[12] The actual standard setting for particular substances is left to a series of daughter directives referred to below. Its origins are found partly in the need to implement several international conventions concerned with water pollution, notably the Paris Convention for the Prevention of Marine Pollution from Land-based Sources 1974 (now replaced by the 1992 Paris Convention for the Protection of the Marine Environment of the North East Atlantic) and the Convention for the Protection of the Rhine against Chemical Pollution 1976. Reflecting these Conventions the Directive has a List I and a List II of various groups of substances. Substances deemed to be more dangerous (dangerousness is defined in terms of toxicity, persistence and bioaccumulation) appear in List I. List II contains less dangerous substances, although the Directive provides that any substance appearing on List I is to be treated as a List II substance until a daughter directive has been made for it.

Discharges of both List I and List II substances require prior authorisation from a 'competent authority' but the nature of this authorisation varies depending upon which list the substance appears in.[13] For List II substances, Member States must establish pollution reduction programmes[14] within set deadlines. Such programmes will set emission standards based on quality objectives laid down by existing relevant directives and all authorisations must impose such emission standards. Authorisations of discharges containing List I[15] substances can impose restrictions based on either of two alternative regimes. The 'preferred regime' (Art 3) would impose Community-set limit values (contained in daughter directives and arrived at on the basis of toxicity, bioaccumulation and persistence and taking account of the best technical means to eliminate or reduce pollution) which emission standards may not exceed. The alternative regime (preferred exclusively by the UK)[16] is to impose emission standards set by quality

---

12 For implementation of this Directive in the UK, see Department of Environment Circular 7/89.

13 For the meaning of 'discharge' under Art 1(2)(d), see Case C-232/97 *Nederhof v Dijkgraaf en Hoogheemraden van het Hoogheemraadschip Rijnland* [1999] All ER (D) 1037 (ECJ); Case 231/97 *AML van Rooij v Dagelijks Bestuur van het Waterschap de Dommel* [1999] All ER (D) 1038 (ECJ).

14 Since all List I substances are to be treated as List II substances until daughter directives are issued, all listed substances naturally require pollution reduction programmes to be drawn up.

15 The elimination of pollution by List I substances does not require zero-emissions as pollution is defined to mean the *effect* of a pollutant rather than its presence.

16 The UK opposition to centrally set fixed emission standards is due to economic cost and the fact that most UK discharges are made into estuaries and short, fast-flowing rivers where dispersal is rapid. This regime was contained in Directive 76/464, Art 6. That Article has now been repealed by Directive 2000/60, Art 22(2). It will be replaced by the combined approach set out in 2000/60, Art 10.

objectives provided for in daughter directives (see Directive on Limit Values and Quality Objectives for Discharges of Certain Dangerous Substances, included in List 1 of the Annex I, Directives 76/464, 86/280). This latter regime may only be followed provided the Member State proves to the satisfaction of the Commission that quality objectives are being met and maintained in accordance with a monitoring system established by the Council.

Directives have been issued under the parent directive as follows:

- Directive on Mercury from the Chloralkali industry 82/176.
- Directive on Mercury from other Sources 84/156.
- Directive on Cadmium 83/513.
- Directive on Hexachlorocyclohexane (Lindane) 84/491.
- Directive on Carbon Tetrachloride, DDT and Pentachlorophenol 86/280.
- Directive on Aldrin etc 88/437.

The Directive on the Protection of Groundwater against Pollution Caused by Certain Dangerous Substances 80/68 (see p 254, below) runs parallel to Directive 76/464 which does not apply to discharges into groundwater.[17] The protection of groundwater is given a particularly high priority because most of the Community's drinking water is derived from ground based sources which are very difficult to restore once pollution occurs.

The Directive's Annex contains a List I and a List II of families and groups of dangerous substances which are similar, although not identical, to those contained in Directive 76/464. Member States are required to 'prevent' the introduction into groundwater of List I substances by prohibiting all direct discharges, (direct discharges occur without percolation through the ground or subsoil: Art 3(1)). The introduction of List II substances is to be 'limited so as to avoid pollution'.[18] All such direct discharges are to be investigated before being authorised to ensure that all technical precautions for preventing groundwater pollution by these substances have been observed (Arts 3(2), 4).

Any disposal on land of either List I or List II substances which might lead to indirect discharges to groundwater is to be subject to investigation before being authorised.[19]

Detergents

The first example of EC legislation tackling pollutants in water was the Directive on Detergents 73/404. This has been amended and supplemented by four daughter Directives: 73/405, 82/242, 82/243 and 86/94.

---

17 Groundwater is defined as water which is below the surface of the ground in the saturation zone and in direct contact with the ground or subsoil.

18 Pollution is defined (Art 1) as the discharge by man, directly or indirectly, of substances or energy into groundwater, the results of which are such as to endanger human health or water supplies, harm living resources and the aquatic eco-system or interfere with the legitimate uses of water.

19 The Waste Directives will also require authorisation (see Chapter 4).

Their purpose has been to tackle the highly visible and widespread appearance of foaming in EC rivers caused by the domestic use of 'hard' detergents which cannot be broken down by sewage treatment. In addition to being aesthetically unattractive, such foaming impairs the oxygenation of water and interferes with the sewage treatment process.

Bearing in mind the main source of detergent pollution (domestic use), the directives tackle the problem by prohibiting the sale and use of particular types of detergent where the level of biodegradability of their particular constituents, the surfactants, falls below a set level, usually 90%. The daughter directives establish, *inter alia*, various acceptable methods of testing for biodegradability. The measure also ensures free trade of detergents within the EC.

Titanium dioxide

Titanium dioxide is a compound used for various purposes, particularly in the manufacture of paint. It creates particular problems because its manufacture results in a larger quantity of waste than product. The main disposal methods for this waste has either been dumping at sea or discharge into estuaries, a practice which creates the phenomenon of red mud. Responding to grave public concern (see Haigh p 113) the Directive on Waste from the Titanium Dioxide industry 78/176 now imposes a general duty on Member States to ensure that such waste is disposed of without endangering human health or harming the environment; it encourages recycling. This is to be achieved by requiring prior authorisation by a competent authority for all discharge, dumping, storage and injection of waste.

Such authorisation may only be given if the waste cannot be disposed of by more appropriate means and only after it has been determined by assessment that there will be no deleterious consequences. The ultimate aim of eliminating all pollution by waste from titanium dioxide has been furthered by Directive 92/112 which prohibits dumping of the most polluting forms of the waste (Art 4).[20]

Measures protecting designated types of water

Drinking water[21]

The quality of drinking water is the main subject of three Directives. These are primarily public health measures but they are very significant for environmental protection in that there is an obvious link between clean drinking water and pollution-free water sources.

---

[20] Directive 89/428 was an earlier measure which prohibited the dumping of titanium dioxide waste. It gave rise to an interesting case, Case C-300/89 *Commission v EC Council*, over the choice of legal basis for the Directive. The Council had chosen Art 130s whereas the Commission argued (correctly as it transpired) that the correct legal basis was Art 100a as the Directive was an environmental measure leading to the establishment of the internal market. The case also established that a directive cannot have a dual legal basis. Directive 92/112 replaced this Directive.

[21] For relevant UK law see The Surface Waters (Abstraction for Drinking Water) (Classification) Regulations 1996 SI 1996/3001 and the Water Supply (Water Quality) Regulations 1989 SI 1989/1147. See also Water Supply (Water Quality) Regulations 2000 SI 2000/3184, fully in force 1 January 2004.

The Directive on the Quality of Surface Water for Drinking 75/440 (see p 258) has two aims: (1) to ensure that surface water abstracted for use as drinking water achieves certain standards and is given appropriate treatment for use as drinking water, and (2) to improve all surface waters used as a source of drinking water.

The Directive divides surface water into three categories (A1, A2 and A3) which are potentially fit for drinking (Art 2). Annex II sets out the parameters defining the quality of A1, A2 and A3 waters which are given I (imperative values) and G (guide values) for each category. Various parameters include values for nitrates, lead and faecal coliforms.

Waters which fall within these categories must be treated in the way specified for each in Annex I to be fit for drinking. Briefly, A1 water requires only simple physical treatment, that is, filtration and disinfection. A2 requires normal physical treatment, chemical treatment and disinfection. A3 waters require intensive physical and chemical treatment plus disinfection. Water which is too poor in quality to fall within these three categories may not be used for the abstraction of drinking water.

The Directive on the Sampling and Analysis of Surface Water for Drinking 79/869 supplements Directive 75/440. It sets out 'reference methods' for measuring the parameters listed in the latter and requires them to be used 'as far as possible', but they are not mandatory. It does set minimum requirements for the frequency of testing which will be more frequent as the quality category of the surface water decreases and as the population served increases.

The Directive on the Quality of Water for Human Consumption 80/778 (see p 263) applies to water which is used for human consumption and in the manufacture or processing of foodstuffs. Annexes II and III are concerned with the water quality monitoring and methods of analysis aimed at ensuring the water quality standards set out in Annex I are achieved. Three types of standard are used: Maximum Admissible Concentration (MAC), Minimum Required Concentration (MRC) and Guide Level (GL). When the Directive only refers to a GL standard, Member States are free to decide whether to set a standard or not. For MACs and MRCs, Member States must set standards no less stringent than those which appear in the Directive. Derogation from Annex I standards is possible under Articles 9 and 10, for example, due to the nature and structure of the ground from which the supply emanates, although not if this results in the creation of a public health hazard. This Directive will be repealed and replaced by Directive 98/83 of the same name by no later than 25 December 2003. Member States are required to meet the new standards (based on the World Health Organisation's guidelines on drinking water quality, Annex 1) by that date.

In 1996 the Commission brought proceedings against the United Kingdom alleging failure to comply with the drinking water Directive. Interestingly, the Court ruled that the system of undertakings intended to ensure that water companies complied with water purity standards (as required by the Water Industry Act 1991) did not satisfy the basic requirements of the Directive (*Commission v UK* Case 340/96: see Agusten Garcia Ureta [1998] 3 Env Liability 65). Compare the decision of the Court of Appeal in *R v Secretary of State for the Environment ex p Friends of the Earth* [1996] 1 CMLR 117. Here the Court of Appeal held that acceptance by the Government of undertakings from the water suppliers that they would comply with EC standards did not breach EC law.

In addition, the 1991 Directive on the Protection of Waters against Pollution caused by Nitrates from Agricultural Sources 91/676 (see p 269, below) tackles the primary source of nitrate pollution.[22] Partly encouraged by incentives within the Common Agricultural Policy to increase productivity, farmers have increased their use of nitrate containing fertilisers which leach into sources of drinking water. The Directive requires Member States to designate vulnerable zones defined as (a) where inland or groundwater intended for drinking are likely to contain more than 50 mg/litre nitrate if protective action is not taken, or (b) where inland or coastal waters are liable to suffer from eutrophication (excessive algal growth, see Art 2(i)) if protective action is not taken (Annex I). Within such zones, detailed regulatory requirements must be taken in accordance with the Directive. The UK has been challenged for non compliance with the provisions of this Directive. In Case C-56/90 *Commission v UK* [1993] Env LR 472 the UK was found to have breached the MAC requirements for nitrates in 28 supply zones in England. More recently the UK has been held to have failed to meet other obligations under the Directive. In addition to being a year late in establishing action programmes as required by the Directive the UK has only identified water containing excessive nitrate concentrations which were intended for human consumption. The Directive requires all surface fresh water and ground water containing such concentrations to be identified (*Commission v UK*, 7 December 2000 (ECJ)).

In Case C-293/97 *R v Secretary of State for the Environment and Another ex p Standley and Others (National Farmers' Union Intervening)* (see p 272, below) the ECJ held that this Directive does not require Member States to determine precisely what proportion of the pollution in waters is attributable to nitrates of agricultural origin. It also held that States may establish action programmes regardless of the levels of pollution. Moreover, it held that the Directive only applies where the discharge of nitrogen compounds of agricultural origin make a 'significant contribution' to the pollution. Finally, it held that the Directive does not offend the right to property or the principle that the polluter pays or the principle of proportionality.

It may be noted that the report of the Commission on the measures taken pursuant to the Nitrates Directive has now been issued (COM (98) 16), although it was delayed by over a year due to the failure of Member States to submit implementation reports as required by the Directive (Art 10).

Finally, EC Decision 77/795 (see p 259, below) Establishing a Common Procedure for Exchange of Information on the Quality of Surface Fresh Water in the Community (as amended) establishes a system for monitoring the quality of fresh water within the Community. The Decision requires sampling to be done by national authorities at designated sampling points, selected by reference to physical, chemical and micro-biological parameters. The data are collated by the Commission and distributed to all Member States.

---

22 Implemented in the UK by the Protection of Water against Agricultural Nitrate Pollution (England and Wales) Regulations 1996 SI 1996/888 and the Action Programme for Nitrate Vulnerable Zones (England and Wales) Regulations 1998 SI 1998/1202.

Bathing water

The 1975 Bathing Water Directive 76/160 (see p 265, below) is concerned with protecting human health and the environment. Bathing water is defined (Art 1) as 'those fresh or sea waters in which bathing is either explicitly authorised ... or is not prohibited and is traditionally practised by large numbers of bathers'. Great care was taken in arriving at this definition, not least because Member States will be in breach of the Directive if they fail to designate bathing waters which satisfy the Directive criteria. Nonetheless, it has been accepted by the Commission that the phrase 'traditionally practised by a large number of bathers' is not easy to apply in practice. For an application of this definition see *Moase and Another v Secretary of State for the the Environment, Transport and the Regions* [2000] JPL 746 and p 336, below).

The Annex to the Directive lists 19 physical, chemical and microbiological parameters, some of which are I values and others G values. Member States must set values for bathing water which are no less stringent than the I values. The G values can be seen as desirable targets.[23] The Directive contains minimum sampling frequencies and reference methods of analysis.

Arguably, the Directive's principal effect has been to prevent, or at least minimise, the presence of sewage sludge in waters intended for bathing. A new Bathing Water Directive has been proposed which will simplify and consolidate the existing Directive and amend its provisions to take account of technical progress.[24] The existing Directive was implemented in England and Wales by the Bathing Waters (Classification) Regulations 1991 SI 1991/1597. The Commission has initiated proceedings against the UK based on the UK's continued breaches of the Bathing Water Directive, notably at Blackpool and Southend. These breaches were first established in Case C-56/90 *Commission v UK* [1993] ECR I-4109 (ECJ). The Commission has proposed a fine of 106,800 ECUs per day (£67,000 per day).

Freshwater fish and shellfish

Two Directives, which are similar in form, deal with the quality of water required for freshwater fish and shellfish. The Directive on the Quality of Fresh Waters 78/659 needed to support Fish (as amended by Directive 91/662) requires Member States to designate waters within their territories which need protection or improvement in order to support fish life (Art 1). The waters referred to are either suitable for salmonids (salmon, trout) or cyprinids (coarse fish).

Unlike the Bathing Water Directive, Member States have the final say on which waters are to be designated under the Directive and by refusing to designate waters they could avoid the financial commitments which accompany that designation. An annex lays down I and G values. Member States must set values no less stringent than the 'I' values and 'shall endeavour to respect the values laid out in Column G'. States are

---

23 See *R v National Rivers Authority ex p Moreton* [1996] Env LR 234, p 331, below for the need to set mandatory standards.

24 For further discussion, see [2001] 1 Env Liability CS 5.

required to create pollution reduction programmes so that designated waters will comply with I values within five years.

The Directive on the Quality Required of Shellfish Waters 79/923 requires Member States to designate coastal and brackish waters which need protection or improvement in order to support shellfish.[25] Again, designation is a matter for Member States who may decline to designate if they find compliance with the Directive too costly. I and G values for water quality are specified and States must introduce a programme of pollution reduction to achieve both these values within six years of designation.

The Directive was implemented in England and Wales in June 1997 by the Surface Waters (Shellfish) (Classification) Regulations 1997 and The Surface Waters (Shellfish) Directions 1997. The Regulations set mandatory minimum standards equal to the I values in the Directive. However, the Environment Agency is given the task of deciding how far it is possible to go beyond the I values towards achieving non-mandatory G values in designated waters in the light of local circumstances. In practice, the Agency will need to establish local operational standards that are at least as stringent as the Regulations' I values, while endeavouring to respect the G values in the Directions. In setting standards, the Agency must also take into account the current water quality and the principle that implementation of the Directive must not lead to increased pollution. In deriving these operational standards, the Agency will not promote expenditure which is disproportionate to the expected degree of environmental improvement.

Urban waste water

The Directive on Urban Waste Water Treatment 91/271 (see p 266, below) is concerned with the adverse effect upon the environment caused by disposal of insufficiently treated urban waste water, particularly in the North Sea. The Directive was implemented in England and Wales by the Urban Waste Water Treatment (England and Wales) Regulations 1994. The Directive requires collection systems to be in place where populations are large enough for waste water to be collected for treatment. Urban waste water is defined (Art 2) as domestic waste water (from residential settlements) and industrial waste water (from industrial premises). The waste water entering the collecting system must be subject to secondary treatment before being discharged although the actual treatment required will depend upon the type and location of the receiving waters. An annex defines 'sensitive areas' where waste waters require more stringent treatment.

Since the discharge of waste water into estuaries is subject to precise regulation, Member States are required (Art 2(12)) to define outer estuarine limits for the purpose of the Directive. The decision of the Secretary of State in relation to the Humber and Severn estuaries has been the subject of successful judicial review proceedings (*R v Secretary of State for the Environment ex p Kingston upon Hull City Council* [1996] Env LR 248). The Court held that the high cost of secondary treatment of waste water was not a relevant consideration in determining whether an area was an estuary. Following the decision, the Government restored the outer limits of the two estuaries thereby giving effect to the judgment. The Commission has published a report on the Implementation of the 1991

---

25   See Case C-225/96 *EC Commission v Italy* [1998] Env LR 370.

Urban Waste Water Treatment Directive (COM(98) 775). The report concludes that most Member States are on track to meet those requirements that have been assessed.

The Water Framework Directive 00/60

On 23 October 2000, Directive 00/60 establishing a framework for Community action in the field of water policy was finally adopted. It establishes a new approach to ensuring a sustainable water policy for both surface waters and ground water, including estuaries and coastal waters.

The purpose of the Directive (Art 1) is basically threefold: to prevent further deterioration in the condition of aquatic ecosystems as well as to better protect and enhance these ecosystems; to promote sustainable water use based on the long term protection of available water resources; to reduce discharges and emissions of particular substances (identified in Art 16).

Under the Directive (Art 3) rivers and lakes are to be managed in accordance with natural geographical boundaries rather than political or administrative boundaries. The Directive requires Member States to draw up 'river basin management plans' by 2009 (Art 13). These plans are to be based on a programme of measures aimed at achieving the environmental objectives listed in Art 4. The core objective is that Member States should 'aim to achieve good water status' by 2015. This is a notably weak obligation that has received widespread condemnation from environmental groups, particularly as the effect of the Framework Directive will be to repeal the provisions of several existing water directives.

Moreover, the phrase 'good water status' is somewhat vague and the definition provisions provide little further assistance. According to Art 2 good status for surface waters refers to their ecologic and chemical status: for ground water it refers to their quantitative and chemical status. Chemical status in this context means that concentrations of priority substances do not exceed environmental quality standards. Ecologic status means that a body of water that is demonstrated to be significantly influenced by human activity, nevertheless has a rich, balanced and sustainable ecosystem. Quantitative status means that human activities must only abstract water or interfere with the rate at which groundwater is naturally replenished in a way that is sustainable and does not lead to a loss in ecological quality.

The programme of measures set in place by Member States should reflect 'a combined approach' (Art 11). In other words, the programmes will combine both emission limit values to control discharges from particular locations (point discharges) and environmental quality standards to limit the cumulative impact of such discharges. The emission limit values will be set in accordance with best available techniques (BAT) in line with the IPPC Directive 96/61 (see Chapter 5, below). The water quality standards will be those laid down by the daughter directives made under the 1976 Directive (76/464).

Controversially, Art 9 requires Member States to incorporate the principle of 'full-recovery costs for water services' (the reference to 'full recovery' includes both environmental costs and the costs associated with providing water services). It is unclear how the costs of environmental harm will be calculated for inclusion in a State's water pricing policies prior to being passed on to the consumer.

The Directive also contains transitional measures in Art 22 setting out a timetable for the repeal of the following water directives:

Directive 75/440 will be repealed by December 2007;

Directives 78/659, 79/923, and 80/68 will be repealed by December 2013.

Directive 76/464 has been repealed with the exception of Art 6.

COUNCIL DIRECTIVE

of 23 October 2000

of the European Parliament and of the Council establishing a framework for Community action in the field of water policy

(00/60/EC)

THE EUROPEAN PARLIAMENT AND THE COUNCIL OF THE EUROPEAN UNION,

Having regard to the Treaty establishing the European Community, and in particular Article 175(1) thereof,

Having regard to the proposal from the Commission(1),

Having regard to the opinion of the Economic and Social Committee(2),

Having regard to the opinion of the Committee of the Regions(3),

Acting in accordance with the procedure laid down in Article 251 of the Treaty(4), and in the light of the joint text approved by the Conciliation Committee on 18 July 2000,

Whereas:

(1) Water is not a commercial product like any other but, rather, a heritage which must be protected, defended and treated as such.

(2) The conclusions of the Community Water Policy Ministerial Seminar in Frankfurt in 1988 highlighted the need for Community legislation covering ecological quality. The Council in its resolution of 28 June 1988(5) asked the Commission to submit proposals to improve ecological quality in Community surface waters.

(3) The declaration of the Ministerial Seminar on groundwater held at The Hague in 1991 recognised the need for action to avoid long-term deterioration of freshwater quality and quantity and called for a programme of actions to be implemented by the year 2000 aiming at sustainable management and protection of freshwater resources. In its resolutions of 25 February 1992(6), and 20 February 1995(7), the Council requested an action programme for groundwater and a revision of Council Directive 80/68/EEC of 17 December 1979 on the protection of groundwater against pollution caused by certain dangerous substances (8), as part of an overall policy on freshwater protection.

(4) Waters in the Community are under increasing pressure from the continuous growth in demand for sufficient quantities of good quality water for all purposes. On 10 November 1995, the European Environment Agency in its report 'Environment in the European Union – 1995' presented an updated State of the environment report, confirming the need for action to protect Community waters in qualitative as well as in quantitative terms.

(5) On 18 December 1995, the Council adopted conclusions requiring, *inter alia*, the drawing up of a new framework Directive establishing the basic principles of sustainable water policy in the European Union and inviting the Commission to come forward with a proposal.

(6) On 21 February 1996 the Commission adopted a communication to the European Parliament and the Council on European Community water policy setting out the principles for a Community water policy.

(7) On 9 September 1996 the Commission presented a proposal for a Decision of the European Parliament and of the Council on an action programme for integrated protection and management of groundwater(9). In that proposal the Commission pointed to the need to establish procedures for the regulation of abstraction of freshwater and for the monitoring of freshwater quality and quantity.

(8) On 29 May 1995 the Commission adopted a communication to the European Parliament and the Council on the wise use and conservation of wetlands, which recognised the important functions they perform for the protection of water resources.

(9) It is necessary to develop an integrated Community policy on water.

(10) The Council on 25 June 1996, the Committee of the Regions on 19 September 1996, the Economic and Social Committee on 26 September 1996, and the European Parliament on 23 October 1996 all requested the Commission to come forward with a proposal for a Council Directive establishing a framework for a European water policy.

(11) As set out in Article 174 of the Treaty, the Community policy on the environment is to contribute to pursuit of the objectives of preserving, protecting and improving the quality of the environment, in prudent and rational utilisation of natural resources, and to be based on the precautionary principle and on the principles that preventive action should be taken, environmental damage should, as a priority, be rectified at source and that the polluter should pay.

(12) Pursuant to Article 174 of the Treaty, in preparing its policy on the environment, the Community is to take account of available scientific and technical data, environmental conditions in the various regions of the Community, and the economic and social development of the Community as a whole and the balanced development of its regions as well as the potential benefits and costs of action or lack of action.

(13) There are diverse conditions and needs in the Community which require different specific solutions. This diversity should be taken into account in the planning and execution of measures to ensure protection and sustainable use of water in the framework of the river basin. Decisions should be taken as close as possible to the locations where water is affected or used. Priority should be given to action within the responsibility of Member States through the drawing up of programmes of measures adjusted to regional and local conditions.

(14) The success of this Directive relies on close co-operation and coherent action at Community, Member State and local level as well as on information, consultation and involvement of the public, including users.

(15) The supply of water is a service of general interest as defined in the Commission communication on services of general interest in Europe(10).

(16) Further integration of protection and sustainable management of water into other Community policy areas such as energy, transport, agriculture, fisheries, regional policy and tourism is necessary. This Directive should provide a basis for a continued dialogue and for the development of strategies towards a further integration of policy areas. This Directive can also make an important contribution to other areas of co-operation between Member States, *inter alia*, the European spatial development perspective (ESDP).

(17) An effective and coherent water policy must take account of the vulnerability of aquatic ecosystems located near the coast and estuaries or in gulfs or relatively closed seas, as their equilibrium is strongly influenced by the quality of inland waters flowing into them. Protection of water status within river basins will provide economic benefits by contributing towards the protection of fish populations, including coastal fish populations.

(18) Community water policy requires a transparent, effective and coherent legislative framework. The Community should provide common principles and the overall framework for action. This Directive should provide for such a framework and co-ordinate and integrate, and, in a longer perspective, further develop the overall principles and structures for protection and sustainable use of water in the Community in accordance with the principles of subsidiarity.

(19) This Directive aims at maintaining and improving the aquatic environment in the Community. This purpose is primarily concerned with the quality of the waters concerned. Control of quantity is an ancillary element in securing good water quality and therefore measures on quantity, serving the objective of ensuring good quality, should also be established.

(20) The quantitative status of a body of groundwater may have an impact on the ecological quality of surface waters and terrestrial ecosystems associated with that groundwater body.

(21) The Community and Member States are party to various international agreements containing important obligations on the protection of marine waters from pollution, in particular the Convention on the Protection of the Marine Environment of the Baltic Sea Area, signed in Helsinki on 9 April 1992 and approved by Council Decision 94/157/EC(11), the Convention for the Protection of the Marine Environment of the North-East Atlantic, signed in Paris on 22 September 1992 and approved by Council Decision 98/249/EC(12), and the Convention for the Protection of the Mediterranean Sea Against Pollution, signed in Barcelona on 16 February 1976 and approved by Council Decision 77/585/EEC(13), and its Protocol for the Protection of the Mediterranean Sea Against Pollution from Land-Based Sources, signed in Athens on 17 May 1980 and approved by Council Decision 83/101/EEC(14). This Directive is to make a contribution towards enabling the Community and Member States to meet those obligations.

(22) This Directive is to contribute to the progressive reduction of emissions of hazardous substances to water.

(23) Common principles are needed in order to co-ordinate Member States' efforts to improve the protection of Community waters in terms of quantity and quality, to promote sustainable water use, to contribute to the control of transboundary water problems, to protect aquatic ecosystems, and terrestrial ecosystems and wetlands

directly depending on them, and to safeguard and develop the potential uses of Community waters.

(24) Good water quality will contribute to securing the drinking water supply for the population.

(25) Common definitions of the status of water in terms of quality and, where relevant for the purpose of the environmental protection, quantity should be established. Environmental objectives should be set to ensure that good status of surface water and groundwater is achieved throughout the Community and that deterioration in the status of waters is prevented at Community level.

(26) Member States should aim to achieve the objective of at least good water status by defining and implementing the necessary measures within integrated programmes of measures, taking into account existing Community requirements. Where good water status already exists, it should be maintained. For groundwater, in addition to the requirements of good status, any significant and sustained upward trend in the concentration of any pollutant should be identified and reversed.

(27) The ultimate aim of this Directive is to achieve the elimination of priority hazardous substances and contribute to achieving concentrations in the marine environment near background values for naturally occurring substances.

(28) Surface waters and groundwaters are in principle renewable natural resources; in particular, the task of ensuring good status of groundwater requires early action and stable long-term planning of protective measures, owing to the natural time lag in its formation and renewal. Such time lag for improvement should be taken into account in timetables when establishing measures for the achievement of good status of groundwater and reversing any significant and sustained upward trend in the concentration of any pollutant in groundwater.

(29) In aiming to achieve the objectives set out in this Directive, and in establishing a programme of measures to that end, Member States may phase implementation of the programme of measures in order to spread the costs of implementation.

(30) In order to ensure a full and consistent implementation of this Directive any extensions of timescale should be made on the basis of appropriate, evident and transparent criteria and be justified by the Member States in the river basin management plans.

(31) In cases where a body of water is so affected by human activity or its natural condition is such that it may be unfeasible or unreasonably expensive to achieve good status, less stringent environmental objectives may be set on the basis of appropriate, evident and transparent criteria, and all practicable steps should be taken to prevent any further deterioration of the status of waters.

(32) There may be grounds for exemptions from the requirement to prevent further deterioration or to achieve good status under specific conditions, if the failure is the result of unforeseen or exceptional circumstances, in particular floods and droughts, or, for reasons of overriding public interest, of new modifications to the physical characteristics of a surface water body or alterations to the level of bodies of groundwater, provided that all practicable steps are taken to mitigate the adverse impact on the status of the body of water.

(33) The objective of achieving good water status should be pursued for each river basin, so that measures in respect of surface water and groundwaters belonging to the same ecological, hydrological and hydrogeological system are co-ordinated.

(34) For the purposes of environmental protection there is a need for a greater integration of qualitative and quantitative aspects of both surface waters and groundwaters, taking into account the natural flow conditions of water within the hydrological cycle.

(35) Within a river basin where use of water may have transboundary effects, the requirements for the achievement of the environmental objectives established under this Directive, and in particular all programmes of measures, should be co-ordinated for the whole of the river basin district. For river basins extending beyond the boundaries of the Community, Member States should endeavour to ensure the appropriate co-ordination with the relevant non-Member States. This Directive is to contribute to the implementation of Community obligations under international conventions on water protection and management, notably the United Nations Convention on the protection and use of transboundary water courses and international lakes, approved by Council Decision 95/308/EC(15) and any succeeding agreements on its application.

(36) It is necessary to undertake analyses of the characteristics of a river basin and the impacts of human activity as well as an economic analysis of water use. The development in water status should be monitored by Member States on a systematic and comparable basis throughout the Community. This information is necessary in order to provide a sound basis for Member States to develop programmes of measures aimed at achieving the objectives established under this Directive.

(37) Member States should identify waters used for the abstraction of drinking water and ensure compliance with Council Directive 80/778/EEC of 15 July 1980 relating to the quality of water intended for human consumption(16).

(38) The use of economic instruments by Member States may be appropriate as part of a programme of measures. The principle of recovery of the costs of water services, including environmental and resource costs associated with damage or negative impact on the aquatic environment should be taken into account in accordance with, in particular, the polluter-pays principle. An economic analysis of water services based on long-term forecasts of supply and demand for water in the river basin district will be necessary for this purpose.

(39) There is a need to prevent or reduce the impact of incidents in which water is accidentally polluted. Measures with the aim of doing so should be included in the programme of measures.

(40) With regard to pollution prevention and control, Community water policy should be based on a combined approach using control of pollution at source through the setting of emission limit values and of environmental quality standards.

(41) For water quantity, overall principles should be laid down for control on abstraction and impoundment in order to ensure the environmental sustainability of the affected water systems.

(42) Common environmental quality standards and emission limit values for certain groups or families of pollutants should be laid down as minimum requirements in Community

legislation. Provisions for the adoption of such standards at Community level should be ensured.

(43) Pollution through the discharge, emission or loss of priority hazardous substances must cease or be phased out. The European Parliament and the Council should, on a proposal from the Commission, agree on the substances to be considered for action as a priority and on specific measures to be taken against pollution of water by those substances, taking into account all significant sources and identifying the cost-effective and proportionate level and combination of controls.

(44) In identifying priority hazardous substances, account should be taken of the precautionary principle, relying in particular on the determination of any potentially adverse effects of the product and on a scientific assessment of the risk.

(45) Member States should adopt measures to eliminate pollution of surface water by the priority substances and progressively to reduce pollution by other substances which would otherwise prevent Member States from achieving the objectives for the bodies of surface water.

(46) To ensure the participation of the general public including users of water in the establishment and updating of river basin management plans, it is necessary to provide proper information of planned measures and to report on progress with their implementation with a view to the involvement of the general public before final decisions on the necessary measures are adopted.

(47) This Directive should provide mechanisms to address obstacles to progress in improving water status when these fall outside the scope of Community water legislation, with a view to developing appropriate Community strategies for overcoming them.

(48) The Commission should present annually an updated plan for any initiatives which it intends to propose for the water sector.

(49) Technical specifications should be laid down to ensure a coherent approach in the Community as part of this Directive. Criteria for evaluation of water status are an important step forward. Adaptation of certain technical elements to technical development and the standardisation of monitoring, sampling and analysis methods should be adopted by committee procedure. To promote a thorough understanding and consistent application of the criteria for characterisation of the river basin districts and evaluation of water status, the Commission may adopt guidelines on the application of these criteria.

(50) The measures necessary for the implementation of this Directive should be adopted in accordance with Council Decision 1999/468/EC of 28 June 1999 laying down the procedures for the exercise of implementing powers conferred on the Commission(17).

(51) The implementation of this Directive is to achieve a level of protection of waters at least equivalent to that provided in certain earlier acts, which should therefore be repealed once the relevant provisions of this Directive have been fully implemented.

(52) The provisions of this Directive take over the framework for control of pollution by dangerous substances established under Directive 76/464/EEC(18). That Directive should therefore be repealed once the relevant provisions of this Directive have been fully implemented.

(53) Full implementation and enforcement of existing environmental legislation for the protection of waters should be ensured. It is necessary to ensure the proper application of the provisions implementing this Directive throughout the Community by appropriate penalties provided for in Member States' legislation. Such penalties should be effective, proportionate and dissuasive,

HAVE ADOPTED THIS DIRECTIVE:

Article 1 Purpose

The purpose of this Directive is to establish a framework for the protection of inland surface waters, transitional waters, coastal waters and groundwater which:

(a) prevents further deterioration and protects and enhances the status of aquatic ecosystems and, with regard to their water needs, terrestrial ecosystems and wetlands directly depending on the aquatic ecosystems;

(b) promotes sustainable water use based on a long term protection of available water resources;

(c) aims at enhanced protection and improvement of the aquatic environment, *inter alia*, through specific measures for the progressive reduction of discharges, emissions and losses of priority substances and the cessation or phasing-out of discharges, emissions and losses of the priority hazardous substances;

(d) ensures the progressive reduction of pollution of groundwater and prevents its further pollution; and

(e) contributes to mitigating the effects of floods and droughts and thereby contributes to:

 – the provision of the sufficient supply of good quality surface water and groundwater as needed for sustainable, balanced and equitable water use,

 – a significant reduction in pollution of groundwater – the protection of territorial and marine waters, and

 – achieving the objectives of relevant international agreements, including those which aim to prevent and eliminate pollution of the marine environment, by Community action under Article 16(3) to cease or phase out discharges, emissions and losses of priority hazardous substances, with the ultimate aim of achieving concentrations in the marine environment near background values for naturally occurring substances and close to zero for man-made synthetic substances.

Article 2 Definitions

For the purposes of this Directive the following definitions shall apply:

1   'Surface water' means inland waters, except groundwater; transitional waters and coastal waters, except in respect of chemical status for which it shall also include territorial waters.

2   'Groundwater' means all water which is below the surface of the ground in the saturation zone and in direct contact with the ground or subsoil.

3   'Inland water' means all standing or flowing water on the surface of the land, and all groundwater on the landward side of the baseline from which the breadth of territorial waters is measured.

4   'River' means a body of inland water flowing for the most part on the surface of the land but which may flow underground for part of its course.

5   'Lake' means a body of standing inland surface water.

6   'Transitional waters' are bodies of surface water in the vicinity of river mouths which are partly saline in character as a result of their proximity to coastal waters but which are substantially influenced by freshwater flows.

7   'Coastal water' means surface water on the landward side of a line, every point of which is at a distance of one nautical mile on the seaward side from the nearest point of the baseline from which the breadth of territorial waters is measured, extending where appropriate up to the outer limit of transitional waters.

8   'Artificial water body' means a body of surface water created by human activity.

9   'Heavily modified water body' means a body of surface water which as a result of physical alterations by human activity is substantially changed in character, as designated by the Member State in accordance with the provisions of Annex II.

10 'Body of surface water' means a discrete and significant element of surface water such as a lake, a reservoir, a stream, river or canal, part of a stream, river or canal, a transitional water or a stretch of coastal water.

11 'Aquifer' means a sub-surface layer or layers of rock or other geological strata of sufficient porosity and permeability to allow either a significant flow of groundwater or the abstraction of significant quantities of groundwater.

12 'Body of groundwater' means a distinct volume of groundwater within an aquifer or aquifers.

13 'River basin' means the area of land from which all surface run-off flows through a sequence of streams, rivers and, possibly, lakes into the sea at a single river mouth, estuary or delta.

14 'Sub-basin' means the area of land from which all surface run-off flows through a series of streams, rivers and, possibly, lakes to a particular point in a water course (normally a lake or a river confluence).

15 'River basin district' means the area of land and sea, made up of one or more neighbouring river basins together with their associated groundwaters and coastal waters, which is identified under Article 3(1) as the main unit for management of river basins.

16 'Competent Authority' means an authority or authorities identified under Article 3(2) or 3(3).

17 'Surface water status' is the general expression of the status of a body of surface water, determined by the poorer of its ecological status and its chemical status.

18 'Good surface water status' means the status achieved by a surface water body when both its ecological status and its chemical status are at least 'good'.

19 'Groundwater status' is the general expression of the status of a body of groundwater, determined by the poorer of its quantitative status and its chemical status.

20 'Good groundwater status' means the status achieved by a groundwater body when both its quantitative status and its chemical status are at least 'good'.

21   'Ecological status' is an expression of the quality of the structure and functioning of aquatic ecosystems associated with surface waters, classified in accordance with Annex V.

22   'Good ecological status' is the status of a body of surface water, so classified in accordance with Annex V.

23   'Good ecological potential' is the status of a heavily modified or an artificial body of water, so classified in accordance with the relevant provisions of Annex V.

24   'Good surface water chemical status' means the chemical status required to meet the environmental objectives for surface waters established in Article 4(1)(a), that is the chemical status achieved by a body of surface water in which concentrations of pollutants do not exceed the environmental quality standards established in Annex IX and under Article 16(7), and under other relevant Community legislation setting environmental quality standards at Community level.

25   'Good groundwater chemical status' is the chemical status of a body of groundwater, which meets all the conditions set out in table 2.3.2 of Annex V.

26   'Quantitative status' is an expression of the degree to which a body of groundwater is affected by direct and indirect abstractions.

27   'Available groundwater resource' means the long term annual average rate of overall recharge of the body of groundwater less the long term annual rate of flow required to achieve the ecological quality objectives for associated surface waters specified under Article 4, to avoid any significant diminution in the ecological status of such waters and to avoid any significant damage to associated terrestrial ecosystems.

28   'Good quantitative status' is the status defined in table 2.1.2 of Annex V.

29   'Hazardous substances' means substances or groups of substances that are toxic, persistent and liable to bioaccumulate, and other substances or groups of substances which give rise to an equivalent level of concern.

30   'Priority substances' means substances identified in accordance with Article 16(2) and listed in Annex X. Among these substances there are 'priority hazardous substances' which means substances identified in accordance with Article 16(3) and (6) for which measures have to be taken in accordance with Article 16(1) and (8).

31   'Pollutant' means any substance liable to cause pollution, in particular those listed in Annex VIII.

32   'Direct discharge to groundwater' means discharge of pollutants into groundwater without percolation throughout the soil or subsoil.

33   'Pollution' means the direct or indirect introduction, as a result of human activity, of substances or heat into the air, water or land which may be harmful to human health or the quality of aquatic ecosystems or terrestrial ecosystems directly depending on aquatic ecosystems, which result in damage to material property, or which impair or interfere with amenities and other legitimate uses of the environment.

34   'Environmental objectives' means the objectives set out in Article 4.

35   'Environmental quality standard' means the concentration of a particular pollutant or group of pollutants in water, sediment or biota which should not be exceeded in order to protect human health and the environment.

36 'Combined approach' means the control of discharges and emissions into surface waters according to the approach set out in Article 10.

37 'Water intended for human consumption' has the same meaning as under Directive 80/778/EEC, as amended by Directive 98/83/EC.

38 'Water services' means all services which provide, for households, public institutions or any economic activity: (a) abstraction, impoundment, storage, treatment and distribution of surface water or groundwater, (b) waste-water collection and treatment facilities which subsequently discharge into surface water.

39 'Water use' means water services together with any other activity identified under Article 5 and Annex II having a significant impact on the status of water. This concept applies for the purposes of Article 1 and of the economic analysis carried out according to Article 5 and Annex III, point (b).

40 'Emission limit values' means the mass, expressed in terms of certain specific parameters, concentration and/or level of an emission, which may not be exceeded during any one or more periods of time. Emission limit values may also be laid down for certain groups, families or categories of substances, in particular for those identified under Article 16. The emission limit values for substances shall normally apply at the point where the emissions leave the installation, dilution being disregarded when determining them. With regard to indirect releases into water, the effect of a waste-water treatment plant may be taken into account when determining the emission limit values of the installations involved, provided that an equivalent level is guaranteed for protection of the environment as a whole and provided that this does not lead to higher levels of pollution in the environment.

41 'Emission controls' are controls requiring a specific emission limitation, for instance an emission limit value, or otherwise specifying limits or conditions on the effects, nature or other characteristics of an emission or operating conditions which affect emissions. Use of the term 'emission control' in this Directive in respect of the provisions of any other Directive shall not be held as reinterpreting those provisions in any respect. Article 3 Co-ordination of administrative arrangements within river basin districts 1. Member States shall identify the individual river basins lying within their national territory and, for the purposes of this Directive, shall assign them to individual river basin districts. Small river basins may be combined with larger river basins or joined with neighbouring small basins to form individual river basin districts where appropriate. Where groundwaters do not fully follow a particular river basin, they shall be identified and assigned to the nearest or most appropriate river basin district. Coastal waters shall be identified and assigned to the nearest or most appropriate river basin district or districts.

[Paragraphs 2–9 omitted.]

Article 4 Environmental objectives

1 In making operational the programmes of measures specified in the river basin management plans:

(a) for surface waters

(i) Member States shall implement the necessary measures to prevent deterioration of the status of all bodies of surface water, subject to the application of paragraphs 6 and 7 and without prejudice to paragraph 8;

(ii) Member States shall protect, enhance and restore all bodies of surface water, subject to the application of sub-paragraph (iii) for artificial and heavily modified bodies of water, with the aim of achieving good surface water status at the latest 15 years after the date of entry into force of this Directive, in accordance with the provisions laid down in Annex V, subject to the application of extensions determined in accordance with paragraph 4 and to the application of paragraphs 5, 6 and 7 without prejudice to paragraph 8;

(iii) Member States shall protect and enhance all artificial and heavily modified bodies of water, with the aim of achieving good ecological potential and good surface water chemical status at the latest 15 years from the date of entry into force of this Directive, in accordance with the provisions laid down in Annex V, subject to the application of extensions determined in accordance with paragraph 4 and to the application of paragraphs 5, 6 and 7 without prejudice to paragraph 8;

(iv) Member States shall implement the necessary measures in accordance with Article 16(1) and (8), with the aim of progressively reducing pollution from priority substances and ceasing or phasing out emissions, discharges and losses of priority hazardous substances without prejudice to the relevant international agreements referred to in Article 1 for the parties concerned;

(b) for groundwater

(i) Member States shall implement the measures necessary to prevent or limit the input of pollutants into groundwater and to prevent the deterioration of the status of all bodies of groundwater, subject to the application of paragraphs 6 and 7 and without prejudice to paragraph 8 of this Article and subject to the application of Article 11(3)(j);

(ii) Member States shall protect, enhance and restore all bodies of groundwater, ensure a balance between abstraction and recharge of groundwater, with the aim of achieving good groundwater status at the latest 15 years after the date of entry into force of this Directive, in accordance with the provisions laid down in Annex V, subject to the application of extensions determined in accordance with paragraph 4 and to the application of paragraphs 5, 6 and 7 without prejudice to paragraph 8 of this Article and subject to the application of Article 11(3)(j);

(iii) Member States shall implement the measures necessary to reverse any significant and sustained upward trend in the concentration of any pollutant resulting from the impact of human activity in order progressively to reduce pollution of groundwater. Measures to achieve trend reversal shall be implemented in accordance with paragraphs 2, 4 and 5 of Article 17, taking into account the applicable standards set out in relevant Community legislation, subject to the application of paragraphs 6 and 7 and without prejudice to paragraph 8; (c) for protected areas Member States shall achieve compliance with any standards and objectives at the latest 15 years after the date of entry into force of this Directive, unless otherwise specified in the Community legislation under which the individual protected areas have been established.

[Paragraphs 2–9 omitted.]

[Articles 5–7 omitted.]

247

Article 8 Monitoring of surface water status, groundwater status and protected areas

1   Member States shall ensure the establishment of programmes for the monitoring of water status in order to establish a coherent and comprehensive overview of water status within each river basin district:

- for surface waters such programmes shall cover:

    (i) the volume and level or rate of flow to the extent relevant for ecological and chemical status and ecological potential, and

    (ii) the ecological and chemical status and ecological potential;

- for groundwaters such programmes shall cover monitoring of the chemical and quantitative status;

- for protected areas the above programmes shall be supplemented by those specifications contained in Community legislation under which the individual protected areas have been established.

[Paragraphs 2–3 omitted.]

Article 9 Recovery of costs for water services

1   Member States shall take account of the principle of recovery of the costs of water services, including environmental and resource costs, having regard to the economic analysis conducted according to Annex III, and in accordance in particular with the polluter pays principle. Member States shall ensure by 2010:

- that water-pricing policies provide adequate incentives for users to use water resources efficiently, and thereby contribute to the environmental objectives of this Directive;

- an adequate contribution of the different water uses, disaggregated into at least industry, households and agriculture, to the recovery of the costs of water services, based on the economic analysis conducted according to Annex III and taking account of the polluter-pays principle. Member States may in so doing have regard to the social, environmental and economic effects of the recovery as well as the geographic and climatic conditions of the region or regions affected.

[Paragraphs 2–4 omitted.]

Article 10 The combined approach for point and diffuse sources

1   Member States shall ensure that all discharges referred to in paragraph 2 into surface waters are controlled according to the combined approach set out in this Article.

2   Member States shall ensure the establishment and/or implementation of:

(a) the emission controls based on best available techniques, or

(b) the relevant emission limit values, or

(c) in the case of diffuse impacts the controls including, as appropriate, best environmental practices set out in:

- Council Directive 96/61/EC of 24 September 1996 concerning integrated pollution prevention and control(19);

- Council Directive 91/271/EEC of 21 May 1991 concerning urban waste-water treatment(20);

- Council Directive 91/676/EEC of 12 December 1991 concerning the protection of waters against pollution caused by nitrates from agricultural sources(21);
- the Directives adopted pursuant to Article 16 of this Directive;
- the Directives listed in Annex IX;
- any other relevant Community legislation at the latest 12 years after the date of entry into force of this Directive, unless otherwise specified in the legislation concerned.

3   Where a quality objective or quality standard, whether established pursuant to this Directive, in the Directives listed in Annex IX, or pursuant to any other Community legislation, requires stricter conditions than those which would result from the application of paragraph 2, more stringent emission controls shall be set accordingly.

Article 11 Programme of measures

1   Each Member State shall ensure the establishment for each river basin district, or for the part of an international river basin district within its territory, of a programme of measures, taking account of the results of the analyses required under Article 5, in order to achieve the objectives established under Article 4. Such programmes of measures may make reference to measures following from legislation adopted at national level and covering the whole of the territory of a Member State. Where appropriate, a Member State may adopt measures applicable to all river basin districts and/or the portions of international river basin districts falling within its territory.

[Paragraphs 2–8 omitted.]

[Article 12 omitted.]

Article 13 River basin management plans

1   Member States shall ensure that a river basin management plan is produced for each river basin district lying entirely within their territory.

2   In the case of an international river basin district falling entirely within the Community, Member States shall ensure co-ordination with the aim of producing a single international river basin management plan. Where such an international river basin management plan is not produced, Member States shall produce river basin management plans covering at least those parts of the international river basin district falling within their territory to achieve the objectives of this Directive.

3   In the case of an international river basin district extending beyond the boundaries of the Community, Member States shall endeavour to produce a single river basin management plan, and, where this is not possible, the plan shall at least cover the portion of the international river basin district lying within the territory of the Member State concerned.

4   The river basin management plan shall include the information detailed in Annex VII.

5   River basin management plans may be supplemented by the production of more detailed programmes and management plans for sub-basin, sector, issue, or water type, to deal with particular aspects of water management. Implementation of these measures shall not exempt Member States from any of their obligations under the rest of this Directive.

6 River basin management plans shall be published at the latest nine years after the date of entry into force of this Directive.

7 River basin management plans shall be reviewed and updated at the latest 15 years after the date of entry into force of this Directive and every six years thereafter.

Article 14 Public information and consultation

1 Member States shall encourage the active involvement of all interested parties in the implementation of this Directive, in particular in the production, review and updating of the river basin management plans. Member States shall ensure that, for each river basin district, they publish and make available for comments to the public, including users:

(a) a timetable and work programme for the production of the plan, including a statement of the consultation measures to be taken, at least three years before the beginning of the period to which the plan refers;

(b) an interim overview of the significant water management issues identified in the river basin, at least two years before the beginning of the period to which the plan refers;

(c) draft copies of the river basin management plan, at least one year before the beginning of the period to which the plan refers. On request, access shall be given to background documents and information used for the development of the draft river basin management plan.

2 Member States shall allow at least six months to comment in writing on those documents in order to allow active involvement and consultation.

3 Paragraphs 1 and 2 shall apply equally to updated river basin management plans. Article 15 Reporting 1. Member States shall send copies of the river basin management plans and all subsequent updates to the Commission and to any other Member State concerned within three months of their publication:

(a) for river basin districts falling entirely within the territory of a Member State, all river management plans covering that national territory and published pursuant to Article 13;

(b for international river basin districts, at least the part of the river basin management plans covering the territory of the Member State.

[Paragraphs 2 and 3 omitted.]

Article 16 Strategies against pollution of water

1 The European Parliament and the Council shall adopt specific measures against pollution of water by individual pollutants or groups of pollutants presenting a significant risk to or via the aquatic environment, including such risks to waters used for the abstraction of drinking water. For those pollutants measures shall be aimed at the progressive reduction and, for priority hazardous substances, as defined in Article 2(30), at the cessation or phasing-out of discharges, emissions and losses. Such measures shall be adopted acting on the proposals presented by the Commission in accordance with the procedures laid down in the Treaty.

[Paragraphs 2–11 omitted.]

Article 17 Strategies to prevent and control pollution of groundwater

1   The European Parliament and the Council shall adopt specific measures to prevent and control groundwater pollution. Such measures shall be aimed at achieving the objective of good groundwater chemical status in accordance with Article 4(1)(b) and shall be adopted, acting on the proposal presented within two years after the entry into force of this Directive, by the Commission in accordance with the procedures laid down in the Treaty.

[Paragraphs 2–5 omitted.]

Article 18 Commission report

1   The Commission shall publish a report on the implementation of this Directive at the latest 12 years after the date of entry into force of this Directive and every six years thereafter, and shall submit it to the European Parliament and to the Council.

[Paragraphs 2–5 omitted.]

[Articles 19–21 omitted.]

Article 22 Repeals and transitional provisions

1   The following shall be repealed with effect from seven years after the date of entry into force of this Directive:
    – Directive 75/440/EEC of 16 June 1975 concerning the quality required of surface water intended for the abstraction of drinking water in the Member States(25);
    – Council Decision 77/795/EEC of 12 December 1977 establishing a common procedure for the exchange of information on the quality of surface freshwater in the Community(26);
    – Council Directive 79/869/EEC of 9 October 1979 concerning the methods of measurement and frequencies of sampling and analysis of surface water intended for the abstraction of drinking waters in the Member States(27).

2   The following shall be repealed with effect from 13 years after the date of entry into force of this Directive:
    – Council Directive 78/659/EEC of 18 July 1978 on the quality of freshwaters needing protection or improvement in order to support fish life(28);
    – Council Directive 79/923/EEC of 30 October 1979 on the quality required of shellfish waters(29);
    – Council Directive 80/68/EEC of 17 December 1979 on the protection of groundwater against pollution caused by certain dangerous substances;
    – Directive 76/464/EEC, with the exception of Article 6, which shall be repealed with effect from the entry into force of this Directive.

3   The following transitional provisions shall apply for Directive 76/464/EEC:
    (a) the list of priority substances adopted under Article 16 of this Directive shall replace the list of substances prioritised in the Commission communication to the Council of 22 June 1982;
    (b) for the purposes of Article 7 of Directive 76/464/EEC, Member States may apply the principles for the identification of pollution problems and the substances causing them, the establishment of quality standards, and the adoption of measures, laid down in this Directive.

4   The environmental objectives in Article 4 and environmental quality standards established in Annex IX and pursuant to Article 16(7), and by Member States under Annex V for substances not on the list of priority substances and under Article 16(8) in respect of priority substances for which Community standards have not been set, shall be regarded as environmental quality standards for the purposes of point 7 of Article 2 and Article 10 of Directive 96/61/EC.

5   Where a substance on the list of priority substances adopted under Article 16 is not included in Annex VIII to this Directive or in Annex III to Directive 96/61/EC, it shall be added thereto. 6. For bodies of surface water, environmental objectives established under the first river basin management plan required by this Directive shall, as a minimum, give effect to quality standards at least as stringent as those required to implement Directive 76/464/EEC.

[All other Articles and Annexes omitted.]

COUNCIL DIRECTIVE

of 4 May 1976

on pollution caused by certain dangerous substances discharged into the aquatic environment of the Community

(76/464/EEC)

(1976) OJ L129, p 32

THE COUNCIL OF THE EUROPEAN COMMUNITIES,

Having regard to the Treaty establishing the European Economic Community, and in particular Articles 100 and 235 thereof ...

Whereas there is an urgent need for general and simultaneous action by the Member States to protect the aquatic environment of the Community from pollution, particularly that caused by certain persistent, toxic and bioaccumulable substances;

Whereas several conventions or draft conventions, including the Convention for the prevention of marine pollution from land-based sources, the draft Convention for the protection of the Rhine against chemical pollution and the draft European Convention for the protection of international watercourses against pollution, are designed to protect international watercourses and the marine environment from pollution; whereas it is important to ensure the co-ordinated implementation of these conventions;

Whereas any disparity between the provisions on the discharge of certain dangerous substances into the aquatic environment already applicable or in preparation in the various Member States may create unequal conditions of competition and thus directly affect the functioning of the common market; whereas it is therefore necessary to approximate laws in this field, as provided for in Article 100 of the Treaty;

Whereas it seems necessary for this approximation of laws to be accompanied by Community action so that one of the aims of the Community in the sphere of protection of the environment and improvement of the quality of life can be achieved by more extensive rules; whereas certain specific provisions to this effect should therefore be laid down; whereas Article 235 of the Treaty should be invoked as the powers required for this purpose have not been provided for by the Treaty;

Whereas in order to ensure effective protection of the aquatic environment of the Community, it is necessary to establish a first list, called List I, of certain individual substances selected mainly on the basis of their toxicity persistence, and bioaccumulation, with the exception of those which are biologically harmless or which are rapidly converted into substances which are biologically harmless and a second list; called List II, containing substances which have a deleterious effect on the aquatic environment, which can, however, be confined to a given area and which depend on the characteristics and location of the water into which they are discharged; whereas any discharge of these substances should be subject to prior authorisation which specifies emission standards;

Whereas pollution through the discharge of the various dangerous substances within List I must be eliminated;

Whereas it is necessary to reduce water pollution caused by the substances within List II;

Article 1

1   Subject to Article 8, this Directive shall apply to:

–   inland surface water,

–   territorial waters,

–   internal coastal waters,

–   ground water.

2   For the purposes of this Directive:

(a) 'inland surface water' means all static or flowing fresh surface water situated in the territory of one or more Member States;

(b   'internal coastal waters' means waters on the landward side of the base line from which the breadth of territorial waters is measured, extending, in the case of watercourses, up to the fresh water limit;

(c) 'fresh water limit' means the place in the watercourse where, at low tide and in a period of low fresh water flow, there is an appreciable increase in salinity due to the presence of sea water;

(d) 'discharge' means the introduction into the waters referred to in paragraph I of any substances in List I or List II of the Annex, with the exception of:

–   discharges of dredgings,

–   operational discharges from ships in territorial waters,

–   dumping from ships in territorial waters;

(e) 'pollution' means the discharge by man, directly or indirectly, of substances or energy into the aquatic environment, the results of which are such as to cause hazards to human health, harm to living resources and to aquatic ecosystems, damage to amenities or interference with other legitimate uses of water.

Article 2

Member States shall take the appropriate steps to eliminate pollution of the waters referred to in Article I by the dangerous substances in the families and groups of substances in List I of the Annex and to reduce pollution of the said waters by the dangerous substances in the families and groups of substances in List II of the Annex, in accordance with this Directive, the provisions of which represent only a first step towards this goal.

Article 3

With regard to the substances belonging to the families and groups of substances in List I, hereinafter called 'substances' within List II:

1 all discharges into the waters referred to in Article I which are liable to contain any such substance shall require prior authorisation by the competent authority of the Member State concerned;

2 the authorisation shall lay down emission standards with regard to discharges of any such substance into the waters referred to in Article I and, where this is necessary for the implementation of this Directive, to discharges of any such substance into sewers;

3 in the case of existing discharges of any such substance into the waters referred to in Article I, the discharges must comply with the conditions laid down in the authorisation within the period stipulated therein. This period may not exceed the limits laid down in accordance with Article 6(4);

4 authorisations may be granted for a limited period only. They may be renewed, taking into account any charges in the limit values referred to in Article 6.

Article 6

Note: This Article has been repealed by the Water Framework Directive 2000/60.

Article 7

1 In order to reduce pollution of the waters referred to in Article I by the substances within List II, Member States shall establish programmes in the implementation of which they shall apply in particular the methods referred to in paragraphs 2 and 3.

2 All discharges into the waters referred to in Article 1 which are liable to contain any of the substances within List II shall require prior authorisation by the competent authority in the Member State concerned, in which emission standards shall be laid down. Such standards shall be based on the quality objectives, which shall be fixed as provided for in paragraph 3.

3 The programmes referred to in paragraph I shall include quality objectives for water; these shall be laid down in accordance with Council Directives, where they exist.

[Articles and Annexes omitted.]

COUNCIL DIRECTIVE

of 17 December 1979

on the protection of groundwater against pollution caused by certain dangerous substances

(80/68/EEC)

(1980) OJ L20, p 43

THE COUNCIL OF THE EUROPEAN COMMUNITIES,

Having regard to the Treaty establishing the European Economic Community, and in particular Articles 100 and 235 thereof ...

Whereas there is an urgent need for action to protect the groundwater of the Community from pollution, particularly that caused by certain toxic, persistent and bioaccumulable substances;

Whereas any disparity between the provisions on the discharge of certain dangerous substances into groundwater already applicable or in preparation in the Member States may create unequal conditions of competition and thus directly affect the functioning of the common market; whereas it is therefore necessary to approximate laws in this field, as provided for in Article 100 of the Treaty;

Whereas it is necessary for this approximation of laws to be accompanied by Community action in the sphere of environmental protection and improvement of the quality of life; whereas certain specific provisions to this effect should therefore be laid down; whereas Article 235 of the Treaty should be invoked as the requisite powers have not been provided for by the Treaty;

Article 1

1   The purpose of this Directive is to prevent the pollution of groundwater by substances belonging to the families and groups of substances in Lists I or II in the Annex, hereinafter referred to as 'substances in Lists I or II', and as far as possible to check or eliminate the consequences of pollution which has already occurred.

2   For the purposes of this Directive:

(a) 'groundwater' means all water which is below the surface of the ground in the saturation zone and in direct contact with the ground or subsoil;

(b) 'direct discharge' means the introduction into groundwater of substances in Lists I or II without percolation through the ground or subsoil;

(c) 'indirect discharge' means the introduction into groundwater of substances in Lists I or II after percolation through the ground or subsoil;

(d) 'pollution' means the discharge by man, directly or indirectly, of substances or energy into groundwater, the results of which are such as to endanger human health or water supplies, harm living resources and the aquatic ecosystem or interfere with other legitimate uses of water.

Article 2

This Directive shall not apply to:

(a) discharges of domestic effluents from isolated dwellings not connected to a sewage system and situated outside areas protected for the abstraction of water for human consumption;

(b) discharges which are found by the competent authority of the Member State concerned to contain substances in Lists I or II in a quantity and concentration so small as to obviate any present or future danger of deterioration in the quality of the receiving groundwater;

(c) discharges of matter containing radioactive substances.

Article 3

Member States shall take the necessary steps to:

(a) prevent the introduction into groundwater of substances in List I; and

(b) limit the introduction into groundwater of substances in List II so as to avoid pollution of this water by these substances.

Article 4

1   To comply with the obligation referred to in Article 3(a), Member States:

-   shall prohibit all direct discharge of substances in List I;
-   shall subject to prior investigation any disposal or tipping for the purpose of disposal of these substances which might lead to indirect discharge. In the light of that investigation, Member States shall prohibit such activity or shall grant authorisation provided that all the technical precautions necessary to prevent such discharge are observed;
-   shall take all appropriate measures they deem necessary to prevent any indirect discharge of substances in List I due to activities on or in the ground other than those mentioned in the second indent. They shall notify such measures to the Commission, which, in the light of this information, may submit proposals to the Council for revision of this Directive.

2   However, should prior investigation reveal that the groundwater into which the discharge of substances in List I is envisaged is permanently unsuitable for other uses, especially domestic or agricultural, the Member States may authorise the discharge of these substances provided that their presence does not impede exploitation of ground resources.

These authorisations may be granted only if all technical precautions have been taken to ensure that these substances cannot reach other aquatic systems or harm other ecosystems.

Article 5

1   To comply with the obligation referred to in Article 3(b), Member States shall make subject to prior investigation:

-   all direct discharge of substances in List II, so as to limit such discharges;
-   the disposal or tipping for the purpose of disposal of these substances which might lead to indirect discharge.

In the light of that investigation, Member States may grant an authorisation, provided that all the technical precautions for preventing groundwater pollution by these substances are observed.

2   Furthermore, Member States shall take the appropriate measures they deem necessary to limit all indirect discharge of substances in List II, due to activities on or in the ground other than those mentioned in the first paragraph.

Article 7

The prior investigations referred to in Articles 4 and 5 shall include examination of the hydrogeological conditions of the area concerned, the possible purifying powers of the soil and subsoil and the risk of pollution and alteration of the quality of the ground water from the discharge and shall establish whether the discharge of substances into groundwater is a satisfactory solution from the point of view of the environment.

Article 9

When direct discharge is authorised in accordance with Article 4(2) and (3) or Article 5, or when waste water disposal which inevitably causes indirect discharge is authorised in accordance with Article 5, the authorisation shall specify in particular:

- the place of discharge,

- the method of discharge,

- essential precautions, particular attention being paid to the nature and concentration of the substances present in the effluents, the characteristics of the receiving environment and the proximity of water catchment areas, in particular those for drinking, thermal and mineral water,

- the maximum quantity of a substance permissible in an effluent during one or more specified periods of time and the appropriate requirements as to the concentration of these substances,

- the arrangements enabling effluents discharged into groundwater to be monitored – if necessary, measures for monitoring groundwater, and in particular its quality.

Article 10

When disposal or tipping for the purpose of disposal which might lead to indirect discharge is authorised in accordance with Articles 4 or 5, authorisation shall specify in particular:

- the place where such disposal or tipping is done;

- the methods of disposal or tipping used;

- essential precautions, particular attention being paid to the nature and concentration of the substances present in the matter to be tipped or disposed of, the characteristics of the receiving environment and the proximity of water catchment areas, in particular those for drinking, thermal and mineral water;

- the maximum quantity permissible, during one or more specified periods of time, of the matter containing substances in Lists I or II and, where possible, of those substances themselves, to be tipped or disposed of and the appropriate requirements as to the concentration of those substances;

- in the cases referred to in Article 4(1) and Article 5(1) the technical precautions to be implemented to prevent any discharge into groundwater of substances in List I and any pollution of such water by substances in List II;

- if necessary, the measures for monitoring the groundwater, and in particular its quality.

Article 11

The authorisations referred to in Articles 4 and 5 may be granted for a limited period only, and will be reviewed at least every four years. They may be renewed, amended or withdrawn.

Article 13

The competent authorities of the Member States shall monitor compliance with the conditions laid down in the authorisations and the effects of discharges on groundwater.

Note: The above Directive is to be repealed by 2013 (see Water Framework Directive 2000/60).

COUNCIL DIRECTIVE

of 16 June 1975

concerning the quality required of surface water intended for the abstraction of drinking water in the Member States

(75/440/EEC)

(1975) OJ L194, p 26

THE COUNCIL OF THE EUROPEAN COMMUNITIES,

Having regard to the Treaty establishing the European Economic Community, and in particular Articles 100 and 235 thereof,

Whereas the increasing use of water resources for the abstraction of water for human consumption necessitates a reduction in the pollution of water and its protection against subsequent deterioration;

Whereas it is necessary to protect public health and, to this end, to exercise surveillance over surface water intended for the abstraction of drinking water and over the purification treatment of such water;

Whereas any disparity between the provisions on the quality required of surface water intended for the abstraction of drinking water already applicable or in preparation in the various Member States may create unequal conditions of competition and thus directly affect the functioning of the common market; whereas it is therefore necessary to approximate laws in this field as provided for in Article 100 of the Treaty;

Whereas it seems necessary for this approximation of laws to be accompanied by Community action so that one of the aims of the Community in the sphere of protection of the environment and improvement of the quality of life can be achieved by wider regulations; whereas certain specific provisions to this effect should therefore be laid down; whereas Article 235 of the Treaty should be invoked as the powers required for this purpose have not been provided by the Treaty;

Whereas the joint fixing of minimum quality requirements for surface water intended for the abstraction of drinking water precludes neither more stringent requirements in the case of such water otherwise utilised nor the requirements imposed by aquatic life;

HAS ADOPTED THIS DIRECTIVE:

Article 1

1 This Directive concerns the quality requirements which surface fresh water used or intended for use in the abstraction of drinking water, hereinafter called 'surface water', must meet after application of appropriate treatment. Ground water, brackish water and water intended to replenish water-bearing beds shall not be subject to this Directive.

2 For the purposes of applying this Directive, all surface water intended for human consumption and supplied by distribution networks for public use shall be considered to be drinking water.

Article 2

For the purposes of this Directive surface water shall be divided according to limiting values into three categories, Al, A2 and A3, which correspond to the appropriate standard methods of treatment given in Annex I. These groups correspond to three different qualities of surface water, the respective physical, chemical and microbiological characteristics of which are set out in the table given in Annex II.

Article 3

1   Member States shall set, for all sampling points, or for each individual sampling point, the values applicable to surface water for all the parameters given in Annex II.

2   The values set pursuant to paragraph 1 may not be less stringent than those given in the 'I' columns of Annex II.

3   Where values appear in the 'G' columns of Annex II, whether or not there is a corresponding value in the 'I' columns of that Annex, Member States shall endeavour to respect them as guidelines, subject to Article 6.

Article 4

1   Member States shall take all necessary measures to ensure that surface water conforms to the values laid down pursuant to Article 3. Each Member State shall apply this Directive without distinction to national waters and waters crossing its frontiers.

2   In line with the objectives of this Directive, Member States shall take the necessary measures to ensure continuing improvement of the environment. To this end, they shall draw up a systematic plan of action including a timetable for the improvement of surface water and especially that falling within category A3. In this context, considerable improvements are to be achieved under the national programmes over the next 10 years.

3   Surface water having physical, chemical and microbiological characteristics falling short of the mandatory limiting values corresponding to treatment type A3 may not be used for the abstraction of drinking water. However, such lower quality water may, in exceptional circumstances, be utilised provided suitable processes – including blending – are used to bring the quality characteristics of the water up to the level of the quality standards for drinking water.

Note: The above Directive is to be repealed by 2007 (see Water Framework Directive 000/60).

COUNCIL DECISION

of 12 December 1977

establishing a common procedure for the exchange of information on the quality of surface fresh water in the Community

(77/795/EEC)

(1977) OJ L334, p 29

THE COUNCIL OF THE EUROPEAN COMMUNITIES,

Having regard to the Treaty establishing the European Economic Community, and in particular Article 235 thereof,

Whereas the 1973 and 1977 programmes of action of the European Communities on the environment provide for the introduction of a procedure for the exchange of information between the pollution surveillance and monitoring networks;

Whereas such a procedure is necessary to determine the pollution levels of the rivers in the Community and consequently to lay down guidelines for the control of pollution and nuisances, which is one of the Community's objectives in respect of the improvement of living conditions and the harmonious development of economic activities throughout the Community; whereas no provision is made in the Treaty for the specific powers required for this purpose;

Whereas such an exchange of information on pollution levels is one of the means of monitoring the long-term trends and the improvements resulting from the application of current national and Community rules;

Whereas the exchange of information provided for in this Decision should allow for as significant a comparison as possible of the results obtained in the sampling and measuring stations;

Whereas the exchange of information provided for in this Decision would lay the foundations for a system for monitoring surface fresh-water pollution at Community level and could constitute a component of the global environment monitoring system provided for in the United Nations environment programme;

Whereas to attain these objectives the Member States must forward to the Commission data relating to certain parameters for surface fresh water; whereas the Commission will draw up a consolidated report which it will transmit to the Member States;

Whereas the list of stations in Annex I may, with advantage, be modified by the Commission at the request of the Member State concerned, provided that certain criteria are fulfilled;

Whereas technical progress requires that the technical specifications laid down in Annex II to this Decision should be adapted promptly; whereas, to facilitate the implementation of the measures required for this purpose, provision must be made for a procedure establishing close co-operation between the Member States and the Commission within the Committee for the adaptation of this Decision to technical progress.

HAS ADOPTED THIS DECISION:

Article 1

A common procedure for the exchange of information on the quality of surface fresh water in the Community is hereby established.

Article 2

1   For the purposes of this Decision 'sampling or measuring stations' means the stations listed in Annex I.

2   The information concerning the parameters listed in the first column of Annex II covered by the exchange of information shall be:

    (a) the results of the measurements carried out by the sampling or measuring stations;

    (b) a description of the sampling, sample preservation and measuring methods used and the frequency of sampling.

Article 3

1   Each Member State shall designate a central agency and inform the Commission thereof within 15 days of the notification of this Decision.

2   The information referred to in Article 2(2) shall be forwarded to the Commission through the central agency in each Member State.

3   The data referred to in Article 2(2)(a) shall be presented according to the modes of expression and with the significant figures set out in the second and third columns of Annex II. The descriptions of the methods referred to in Article 2(2)(b) may be omitted if the methods are the same as those used in previous years, provided always that an explicit reference to any such omission is made.

4   The information, covering a calendar year, shall be forwarded to the Commission before 1 October of the following year.

5   The Commission shall forward annually to the Member States which so request the information received under paragraph 2. Every three years, and for the first time in 1987, the Commission shall draw up a draft consolidated report based on the information referred to in Article 2(2). The part of this report concerning the information supplied by a Member State shall be sent to the central agency of that state for verification. Any comments on the draft shall be included in the report. The report shall include indications of the trends noted in water quality since implementation of this Decision and as much interpretative comment as possible, taking into account the objectives of the Decision.

The Commission shall publish the final version of its report and send copies to the Member States.

6   The Commission shall assess the effectiveness of the procedure for the exchange of information and shall submit proposals, where appropriate, to the Council aimed at improving the procedure and, if necessary, harmonising the methods of measurement, taking into account the provisions of Article 4.

Article 4

1   Each Member State shall organise such inter-calibration at national level amongst laboratories taking part in the collection and the analysis of data as may be necessary to ensure comparability of reference methods of measurement with those used in the laboratories of the Member States.

2   The Commission shall, if necessary, organise a comparative evaluation of nationally applied methods of measurement. This evaluation shall be the subject of a report to be transmitted to Member States.

3   On the basis of the report referred to in paragraph 2, the Commission shall, if necessary, make proposals to the Council for the inter-calibration of nationally applied methods of measurement with the reference methods of measurement listed in Annex III.

Article 4a

1   In order to implement the common procedure for the exchange of information, the Member States shall lay down a frequency for sampling and analysis, normally monthly.

2   If a Member State has established that the water quality does not display any significant variation in terms of the value of one or more parameters and if there is no risk of a deterioration of the water quality, the frequency of sampling and measurement

of that parameter or those parameters may be reduced. Such a reduction of the frequency shall not involve any risk to human beings and the environment.

Modifications to the frequency shall be explicitly mentioned in the information forwarded to the Commission under Article 3(2).

3   The reference methods of measurement for the parameters in question are set out in Annex III. Laboratories which use other methods of measurement shall satisfy themselves that the results obtained are comparable.

4   The containers used for samples, the agents or methods used to preserve part or a sample for the analysis of one or more parameters, the conveyance and storage of samples and the preparation of samples for analysis must not be such as to bring about any significant change in the results of the analysis.

5   Sampling shall take place in the same places and the sampling procedures shall be the same on each occasion.

Article 5

1   The list in Annex I may be amended by the Commission on a request from the Member State concerned.

2   The Commission shall make such amendments when it is satisfied that the following requirements are met:
   –   that the list of sampling or measuring stations for each Member State is sufficiently representative for the purposes of this Decision,
   –   that the stations are at points which are representative of water conditions in the area around and not directly and immediately influenced by a source of pollution,
   –   that they are capable of measuring at regular intervals the parameters in Annex II,
   –   that they are as a general rule not more than 100 kilometres, apart on main rivers, not including tributaries,
   –   that they are upstream of any confluences and not on tidal stretches of water.

3   The Commission shall inform the Council of any amendments which it has accepted.

4   The Commission shall submit for decision by the Council any requests for amendments which it has been unable to accept.

Article 6

Amendments necessary to adapt to technical progress the list of parameters and the modes of expression and significant figures in respect thereof set out in Annex II, as well as the reference methods of measurement, the parameters and the modes of expression set out in Annex III, shall be adopted in accordance with the procedure laid down in Article 8, provided that any additions to the list involve only parameters covered by Community rules concerned with the aquatic environment and for which data are available in all sampling and measuring stations of the Member States. Any changes in the modes of expression and significant figures must not involve changes to the methods of measurement used by the Member States in the various stations in Annex I.

Article 7

1   A Committee for the adaptation of this Decision to technical progress (hereinafter referred to as 'the Committee') is hereby set up, consisting of representatives of the Member States with a representative of the Commission as Chairman.

2   The Committee shall adopt its own rules of procedure.

Article 8

1   Where the procedure laid down in this Article is to be followed, the matter shall be referred to the Committee by its chairman, either on his own initiative or at the request of a representative of a Member State.

2   The Commission representative shall submit to the Committee a draft of the measures to be taken. The Committee shall give its opinion on the draft within a time limit set by the chairman according to the urgency of the matter. Opinions shall be delivered by a majority of 41 votes, the votes of the Member States being weighted as provided for in Article 148(2) of the Treaty. The chairman shall not vote.

3   (a) Where the measures envisaged are in accordance with the opinion of the Committee, the Commission shall adopt them.

(b) Where the measures envisaged are not in accordance with the opinion of the Committee, or if no opinion is delivered, the Commission shall without delay submit to the Council a proposal on the measures to be taken. The Council shall act by a qualified majority.

(c) If within three months of the proposal being submitted to it the Council has not acted, the proposed measures shall be adopted by the Commission.

Article 9

This Decision is addressed to the Member States.

Note: The above decision is to be repealed by 2007 (see Water Framework Directive 2000/60).

COUNCIL DIRECTIVE

of 15 July 1980

relating to the quality of water intended for human consumption

(80/778/EEC)

(1980) OJ L229, p 11

THE COUNCIL OF THE EUROPEAN COMMUNITIES,

Having regard to the Treaty establishing the European Economic Community, and in particular Articles 100 and 235 thereof,

Whereas, in view of the importance for public health of water for human consumption, it is necessary to lay down quality standards with which such water must comply;

Whereas a disparity between provisions already applicable or in the process of being drawn up in the various Member States relating to the quality of water for human consumption may create differences in the conditions of competition and, as a result, directly affect the operation of the common market; whereas laws in this sphere should therefore be approximated as provided for in Article 100 of the Treaty;

Whereas this approximation of laws should be accompanied by Community action designed to achieve, by more extensive rules concerning water for human consumption, one of the aims of the Community with regard to the improvement of living conditions, the harmonious development of economic activities throughout the Community and a continuous and balanced expansion; whereas certain specific provisions to this effect should therefore be laid down; whereas Article 235 of the Treaty should be invoked as the necessary powers have not been provided for by the Treaty.

HAS ADOPTED THIS DIRECTIVE:

Article 1

This Directive concerns standards for water intended for human consumption.

Article 2

For the purposes of this Directive, water intended for human consumption shall mean all water used for that purpose, either in its original state or after treatment, regardless of origin,

– whether supplied for consumption, or whether

– used in a food production undertaking for the manufacture, processing, preservation or marketing of products or substances intended for human consumption, and

– affecting the wholesomeness of the foodstuff in its finished form.

Article 4

This Directive shall not apply to:

1 (a) natural mineral waters recognised or defined as such by the competent national authorities;

(b) medicinal waters recognised as such by the competent national authorities.

2 Member States may not prohibit or impede the marketing of foodstuffs on grounds relating to the quality of the water used where the quality of such water meets the requirements of this Directive unless such marketing constitutes a hazard to public health.

Article 7

1 Member States shall fix values applicable to water intended for human consumption for the parameters shown in Annex I.

2 Member States may refrain from fixing, pursuant to the first paragraph, the values of parameters in respect to which no value is shown in Annex 1, as long as these values have not been determined by the Council.

3 For the parameters given in Tables A, B, C, D, and E of Annex I:

– the values to be fixed by the Member States must be less than or the same as the values shown in the 'maximum admissible concentration' column;

– in fixing the values, Member States shall take as a basis the values appearing in the 'Guide level' column.

4 For the parameters appearing in Table F of Annex I, the values to be fixed by Member States must be not lower than those given in the 'minimum required concentration' column for softened water, of the kind referred to in the first indent of Article 2.

5 In the interpretation of the values shown in Annex 1 account shall be taken of the observations.

6   Member States shall take the steps necessary to ensure that water intended for human consumption at least meets the requirements specified in Annex I.

Article 8

Member States shall take all the necessary measures to ensure that any substances used in the preparation of water for human consumption do not remain in concentrations higher than the maximum admissible concentration relating to these substances in water made available to the user and, that they do not, either directly or indirectly, constitute a public health hazard.

Article 16

Without prejudice to Article 4(2), Member States may lay down more stringent provisions than those provided for in this Directive for water intended for human consumption.

Note: This Directive is to be repealed and replaced by Council Directive on the Quality of Water Intended for Human Consumption 98/83/EC no later than 25 December 2003.

COUNCIL DIRECTIVE

of 8 December 1975

concerning the quality of bathing water

(76/160/EEC)

(1976) OJ L31, p 1

THE COUNCIL OF THE EUROPEAN COMMUNITIES,

Having regard to the Treaty establishing the European Economic Community, and in particular Articles 100 and 235 thereof ...

Whereas, in order to protect the environment and public health, it is necessary to reduce the pollution of bathing water and to protect such water against further deterioration;

Whereas surveillance of bathing water is necessary in order to attain, within the framework of the operation of the common market, the Community's objectives as regards the improvement of living conditions, the harmonious development of economic activities throughout the Community and continuous and balanced expansion;

Whereas there exist in this area certain laws, regulations or administrative provisions in Member States which directly affect the functioning of the common market whereas, however, not all the powers needed to. act in this way have been provided for in the Treaty;

Whereas the programme of action of the European Communities on the environment provides that quality objectives are to be jointly drawn up fixing the various requirements which an environment must meet inter alia the definition of parameters for water, including bathing water;

Whereas, in order to attain these quality objectives, the Member States must lay down limit values corresponding to certain parameters;

Article 1

1   This Directive concerns the quality of bathing water, with the exception of water intended for therapeutic purposes and water used in swimming pools.

2   For the purposes of this Directive:

(a) 'bathing water' means all running or still fresh waters or parts thereof and sea water, in which:

- bathing is explicitly authorised by the competent authorities of each Member State, or

- bathing is not prohibited and is traditionally practised by a large number of bathers;

(b) 'bathing area' means any place where bathing water is found;

(c) 'bathing season' means the period during which a large number of bathers can be expected, in the light of local custom, and any local rules which may exist concerning bathing and weather conditions.

Article 2

The physical, chemical and microbiological parameters applicable to bathing water are indicated in the Annex which forms an integral part of this Directive.

Article 3

1   Member States shall set, for all bathing areas or for each individual bathing area, the values applicable to bathing water for the parameters given in the Annex.

COUNCIL DIRECTIVE

of 21 May 1991

concerning urban waste water treatment

(91/271/EEC)

(1991) OJ L135, p 40

THE COUNCIL OF THE EUROPEAN COMMUNITIES,

Having regard to the Treaty establishing the European Economic Community, and in particular Article 130s thereof, ...

Whereas the Council Resolution of 28 June 1988 on the protection of the North Sea and of other waters in the Community (4) invited the Commission to submit proposals for measures required at Community level for the treatment of urban waste water;

Whereas pollution due to insufficient treatment of waste water in one Member State often influences other Member States' waters; whereas in accordance with Article 130r, action at Community level is necessary;

Whereas to prevent the environment from being adversely affected by the disposal of insufficiently-treated urban waste water, there is a general need for secondary treatment of urban waste water;

Whereas it is necessary in sensitive areas to require more stringent treatment; whereas in some less sensitive areas a primary treatment could be considered appropriate;

Whereas industrial waste water entering collecting systems as well as the discharge of waste water and disposal of sludge from urban waste water treatment plants should be subject to general rules or regulations and/or specific authorisations;

Whereas discharges from certain industrial sectors of biodegradable industrial waste water not entering urban waste water treatment plants before discharge to receiving waters should be subject to appropriate requirements;

Whereas the recycling of sludge arising from waste water treatment should be encouraged; whereas the disposal of sludge to surface waters should be phased out;

Whereas it is necessary to monitor treatment plants, receiving waters and the disposal of sludge to ensure that the environment is protected from the adverse effects of the discharge of waste waters;

Whereas it is important to ensure that information on the disposal of waste water and sludge is made available to the public in the form of periodic reports;

Whereas Member States should establish and present to the Commission national programmes for the implementation of this directive;

Whereas a Committee should be established to assist the Commission on matters relating to the implementation of this Directive and to its adaptation to technical progress.

HAS ADOPTED THIS DIRECTIVE:

Article 1

This Directive concerns the collection, treatment and discharge of urban waste water and the treatment and discharge of waste water from certain industrial sectors. The objective of the Directive is to protect the environment from the adverse effects of the above mentioned waste water discharges.

Article 2

For the purpose of this Directive:

1   'urban waste water' means domestic waste water or the mixture of domestic waste water with industrial waste water and/or run-off rain water;

2   'domestic waste water' means waste water from residential settlements and services which originates predominantly from the human metabolism and from household activities;

3   'industrial waste water' means any waste water which is discharged from premises used for carrying on any trade or industry, other than domestic waste water and run-off rain water;

4   'agglomeration' means an area where the population and/or economic activities are sufficiently concentrated for urban waste water to be collected and conducted to an urban waste water treatment plant or to a final discharge point;

5   'collecting system' means a system of conduits which collects and conducts urban waste water;

6   '1 p.e. (population equivalent)' means the organic biodegradable load having a five-day biochemical oxygen demand (BOD5) of 60g of oxygen per day;

7   'primary treatment' means treatment of urban waste water by a physical and/or chemical process involving settlement of suspended solids, or other processes in which the BOD5 of the incoming waste water is reduced by at least 20% before discharge and the total suspended solids of the incoming waste water are reduced by at least 50%;

8 'secondary treatment' means treatment of urban waste water by a process generally involving biological treatment with a secondary settlement or other process in which the requirements established in Table 1 of Annex I are respected;

9 'appropriate treatment' means treatment of urban waste water by any process and/or disposal system which after discharge allows the receiving waters to meet the relevant quality objectives and the relevant provisions of this and other Community Directives;

10 'sludge' means residual sludge, whether treated or untreated, from urban waste water treatment plants;

11 'eutrophication' means the enrichment of water by nutrients, especially compounds of nitrogen and/or phosphorus, causing an accelerated growth of algae and higher forms of plant life to produce an undesirable disturbance to the balance of organisms present in the water and to the quality of the water concerned;

12 'estuary' means the transitional area at the mouth of a river between fresh water and coastal waters. Member States shall establish the outer (seaward) limits of estuaries for the purposes of this Directive as part of the programme for implementation in accordance with the provisions of Article 17(1) and (2);

13 'coastal waters' means the waters outside the low-water line or the outer limit of an estuary.

Article 3

1 Member States shall ensure that all agglomerations are provided with collecting systems for urban waste water – at the latest by 31 December 2000 for those with a population equivalent (p.e.) of more than 15,000, and – at the latest by 31 December 2005 for those with a p.e. of between 2,000 and 15,000. For urban waste water discharging into receiving waters which are considered 'sensitive areas' as defined under Article 5, Member States shall ensure that collection systems are provided at the latest by 31 December 1998 for agglomerations of more than 10,000 p.e.

Where the establishment of a collecting system is not justified either because it would produce no environmental benefit or because it would involve excessive cost, individual systems or other appropriate systems which achieve the same level of environmental protection shall be used. [...]

Article 4

1 Member States shall ensure that urban waste water entering collecting systems shall before discharge be subject to secondary treatment or an equivalent treatment as follows: – at the latest by 31 December 2000 for all discharges from agglomerations of more than 15,000 p.e., – at the latest by 31 December 2005 for all discharges from agglomerations of between 10,000 and 15,000 p.e., – at the latest by 31 December 2005 for discharges to fresh water and estuaries from agglomerations of between 2,000 and 10,000 p.e.

[Paragraphs 2–4 omitted.]

Article 5

1 For the purposes of paragraph 2, Member States shall by 31 December 1993 identify sensitive areas according to the criteria laid down in Annex II.

2   Member States shall ensure that urban waste water entering collecting systems shall before discharge into sensitive areas be subject to more stringent treatment than that described in Article 4, by 31 December 1998 at the latest for all discharges from agglomerations of more than 10,000 p.e.

[Paragraphs 3–8 omitted.]

Article 6

1   For the purposes of paragraph 2, Member States may by 31 December 1993 identify less sensitive areas according to the criteria laid down in Annex II.

2   Urban waste water discharges from agglomerations of between 10,000 and 150,000 p.e. to coastal waters and those from agglomaterions of between 2,000 and 10,000 p.e. to estuaries situated in areas described in paragraph 1 may be subjected to treatment less stringent than that prescribed in Article 4 providing that: – such discharges receive at least primary treatment as defined in Article 2(7) in conformity with the control procedures laid down in Annex I D – comprehensive studies indicate that such discharges will not adversely affect the environment. Member States shall provide the Commission with all relevant information concerning the above mentioned studies.

[Paragraphs 3–5 omitted.]

[Articles 7–20 and annexes omitted.]

COUNCIL DIRECTIVE

of 12 December 1991

concerning the protection of waters against pollution caused by nitrates from agricultural sources

(91/676/EEC)

(1991) OJ L375, p I

THE COUNCIL OF THE EUROPEAN COMMUNITIES,

Having regard to the Treaty establishing the European Economic Community, and in particular Article 130s thereof, ...

Whereas the nitrate content of water in some areas of Member States is increasing and is already high as compared with standards laid down in Council Directive 75/440/EEC of 16 June 1975 concerning the quality required of surface water intended for the abstraction of drinking water in the Member States, as amended [...];

Whereas the fourth programme of action of the European Economic Communities on the environment ((1987) OJ C 328, p 1) indicated that the Commission intended to make a proposal for a Directive on the control and reduction of water pollution resulting from the spreading or discharge of livestock effluents and the excessive use of fertilisers;

Whereas the reform of the common agricultural policy set out in the Commission's green paper 'Perspectives for the common agricultural policy' indicated that, while the use of nitrogen-containing fertilisers and manures is necessary for Community agriculture, excessive use of fertilisers constitutes an environmental risk, that common action is needed to control the problem arising from intensive livestock production and that agricultural policy must take greater account of environmental policy;

Whereas the Council Resolution of 28 June 1988 of the protection of the North Sea and of other waters in the Community ((1988) OJ C209, p 3) invites the Commission to submit proposals for measures at Community level;

Whereas the main cause of pollution from diffuse sources affecting the Community's waters is in nitrates from agricultural sources;

Whereas it is therefore necessary, in order to protect human health and living resources and aquatic ecosystems and to safeguard other legitimate uses of water, to reduce water pollution caused or induced by nitrates from agricultural sources and to prevent further such pollution; whereas for this purpose it is important to take measures concerning the storage and the application on land of all nitrogen compounds and concerning certain land management practices;

Whereas since pollution of water due to nitrates on one Member State can influence waters in other Member States, action at Community level in accordance with Article 130r is therefore necessary;

Whereas, by encouraging good agricultural practices, Member States can provide all waters with a general level of protection against pollution in the future;

Whereas certain zones, draining into waters vulnerable to pollution from nitrogen compounds, require special protection;

Whereas it is necessary for Member States to identify vulnerable zones and to establish and implement action programmes in order to reduce water pollution from nitrogen compounds in vulnerable zones;

Whereas such action programmes should include measures to limit the land-application of all nitrogen-containing fertilisers and in particular to set specific limits for the application of livestock manure;

Whereas it is necessary to monitor waters and to apply reference methods of measurement for nitrogen compounds to ensure that measures are effective;

Whereas it is recognised that the hydrogeology in certain Member States is such that it may be many years before protection measures lead to improvements in water quality; [...]

HAS ADOPTED THIS DIRECTIVE:

Article 1

This Directive has the objective of:

reducing water pollution caused or induced by nitrates from agricultural sources and preventing further such pollution.

Article 2

For the purpose of this Directive:

(a) 'groundwater': means all water which is below the surface of the ground in the saturation zone and in direct contact with the ground or subsoil;

(b) 'freshwater': means naturally occurring water having a low concentration of salts, which is often acceptable as suitable for abstraction and treatment to produce drinking water;

(c) 'nitrogen compound': means any nitrogen-containing substance except for gaseous molecular nitrogen;

(d) 'livestock': means all animals kept for use or profit;

(e) 'fertiliser': means any substance containing a nitrogen compound or nitrogen compounds utilised on land to enhance growth of vegetation; it may include livestock manure, the residues from fish farms and sewage sludge;

(f) 'chemical fertiliser': means any fertiliser which is manufactured by an industrial process;

(g) 'livestock manure': means waste products excreted by livestock or a mixture of litter and waste products excreted by livestock, even in processed form;

(h) 'land application': means the addition of materials to land whether by spreading on the surface of the land, injection into the land, placing below the surface of the land or mixing with the surface layers of the land;

(i) 'eutrophication': means the enrichment of water by nitrogen compounds, causing an accelerated growth of algae and higher forms of plant life to produce an undesirable disturbance to the balance of organisms present in the water and to the quality of the water concerned;

(j) 'pollution': means the discharge, directly or indirectly, of nitrogen compounds from agricultural sources into the aquatic environment, the results of which are such as to cause hazards to human health, harm to living resources and to aquatic ecosystems, damage to amenities or interference with other legitimate uses of water;

(k) 'vulnerable zone': means an area of land designated according to Article 3(2).

Article 3

1   Waters affected by pollution and waters which could be affected by pollution if action pursuant to Article 5 is not taken shall be identified by the Member States in accordance with the criteria set out in Annex I.

2   Member States shall, within a two-year period following the notification of this Directive, designate as vulnerable zones all known areas of land in their territories which drain into the waters identified according to paragraph 1 and which contribute to pollution. They shall notify the Commission of this initial designation within six months [...]

Article 4

1   With the aim of providing for all waters a general level of protection against pollution, Member States shall, within a two-year period following the notification of this Directive:

(a) establish a code or codes of good agricultural practice, to be implemented by farmers on a voluntary basis, which should contain provisions covering at least the items mentioned in Annex IIA;

(b) set up where necessary a programme, including the provision of training and information for farmers, promoting the application of the code(s) of good agricultural practice [...]

Article 5

1   Within a two-year period following the initial designation referred to in Article 3(2) or within one year of each additional designation referred to in Article 3(4), Member States shall, for the purpose of realising the objectives specified in Article 1, establish action programmes in respect of designated vulnerable zones [...]

3   Action programmes shall take into account:

(a) available scientific and technical data, mainly with reference to respective nitrogen contributions originating from agricultural and other sources;

(b) environmental conditions in the relevant regions of the Member State concerned.

4   Action programmes shall be implemented within four years of their establishment and shall consist of the following mandatory measures:

(a) the measures in Annex III;

(b) those measures which Member States have prescribed in the code(s) of good agricultural practice established in accordance with Article 4, except those which have been superseded by the measures in Annex III.

5   Member States shall moreover take, in the framework of the action programmes, such additional measures or reinforced actions as they consider necessary if, at the outset or in the light of experience gained in implementing the action programmes, it becomes apparent that the measures referred to in paragraph 4 will not be sufficient for achieving the objectives specified in Article 1. In selecting these measures or actions, Member States shall take into account their effectiveness and their cost relative to other possible preventive measures [...]

7   Member States shall review and if necessary revise their action programmes, including any additional measures taken pursuant to paragraph 5, at least every four years. They shall inform the Commission of any changes to the action programmes.

[Articles 6–13 omitted. All Annexes omitted.]

Case C-293/97 R v Secretary of State for the Environment and Another ex p Standley and Others – (National Farmers' Union Intervening) [1999] QB 1279; [1999] 3 WLR 744; [1999] All ER (EC) 412; [1999] 2 CMLR 902

Headnote

The applicants sought the annulment of decisions by which the Secretary of State for the Environment and the Minister for Agriculture Fisheries and Food (i) identified surface waters, in areas where the applicants owned or farmed land, as waters which could be affected by nitrate pollution, and (ii) designated the areas of land draining into them as 'nitrate vulnerable zones' in accordance with Art 3 of Council Directive (EEC) 91/676 concerning the protection of waters against pollution caused by nitrates from agricultural sources. The applicants contended that the subsequent establishment in those areas of action programmes restricting agricultural use would cause them immediate and long term economic harm in terms of land values and farming incomes. They contended that Art 3(1) of Directive 91/676 required Member States to identify surface freshwaters as waters which were or could be affected by pollution by reason of the direct or indirect discharge, solely from agricultural sources, of a specified level of nitrogen compounds. It therefore followed that the Member States had to establish the source of the nitrates. In the alternative they contended that Directive 91/676 infringed the 'polluter pays' principle, the principle that environmental damage should as a priority be rectified at source, the principle of proportionality and the fundamental right to property. The High Court stayed the proceedings and referred to the Court of Justice of the European Communities for a preliminary ruling questions as to the interpretation and the validity of Directive 91/676.

Held

(1) Member States were not required by Art 3(1) to determine precisely what proportion of the pollution in the waters was attributable to nitrates of agricultural origin or determine that the cause was exclusively agricultural. The identification, under Art 3(1), of waters which were or might be affected by pollution formed part of a process of designating vulnerable zones and establishing action programmes.

Within the framework of that process Art 5 expressly provided that the respective nitrogen contributions originating from agricultural 'and other' sources were to be taken into account. Furthermore, Art 3(5) allowed Member States to designate the whole of their territory as a nitrate vulnerable zone instead of identifying waters affected by pollution, which meant that they could establish action programmes regardless of the levels of pollution.

(2) Directive 91/676 only applied where the discharge of nitrogen compounds of agricultural origin made a 'significant contribution' to the pollution. However, Community law could not provide precise criteria for establishing in each case whether there was such a significant contribution. Thus, in reviewing the legality of measures identifying waters affected by pollution in accordance with Art 3(1), national courts had to take account of the wide discretion enjoyed by Member States.

(3) Directive 91/676 did not offend the right to property or the principles of proportionality, polluter pays and rectification of environmental damage at source. Under Art 5, Member States were to take account of the other sources of pollution and, having regard to the circumstances, were not to impose unnecessary costs on farmers. Furthermore, although the exercise of the right to property could be restricted, any restrictions had to correspond to objectives of general interest and were not to impair the very substance of that right. In the instant case, action programmes set up under Directive 91/676 imposed conditions on the spreading of fertiliser and manure and were liable to restrict the farmers' exercise of their right. However, the system laid down by Art 5 reflected requirements relating to the protection of public health and therefore pursued an objective of general interest without impairing the substance of the right; Case C-280/93 *Germany v EU Council* Case [1994] ECR I-4973 applied.

The following is an extract from the judgment of the ECJ:

14 The applicants in the main proceedings, supported by the National Farmers' Union (the NFU), have sought annulment of the decisions by which the respondents identified surface waters comprising the Rivers Waveney, Blackwater and Chelmer and their tributaries as waters which could be affected by nitrate pollution and designated the areas of land draining into those rivers as nitrate vulnerable zones.

15 According to the applicants in the main proceedings, the establishment, in those areas where they own or farm land, of action programmes restricting agricultural use, as required by the 1996 Regulations under which the nitrate vulnerable zones have been designated, would cause them immediate and long term economic harm in terms of land values and of income from their farming businesses.

16 In their view, Art 3(1) of Directive 91/676 requires the Member States to identify surface freshwaters as waters which are or could be affected by pollution only if they exceed, or could exceed if relevant action were not taken, the threshold for nitrates of 50 mg/l by reason of the direct or indirect discharge of nitrogen compounds from agricultural sources. The Member States must therefore establish the source of the nitrates which cause that threshold to be exceeded.

17 They plead in the alternative that, if the interpretation contended for by the respondents in the main proceedings were correct, Directive 91/676 would infringe the polluter pays principle, the principle that environmental damage should as a priority be rectified at source, the principle of proportionality and the fundamental right to property.

18 According to the respondents, it follows from Art 2(j) of Directive 91/676 and para A.1 of Annex I that the term 'waters affected by pollution' in art 3(1) refers to surface freshwaters used for drinking water supplies that have a nitrate content in excess of 50 mg/l to which nitrates from agricultural sources make a significant contribution. They state that no provision of Directive 91/676 or its annexes contains even an implied obligation on the Member States to assess the concentration of nitrates attributable solely to agricultural sources of pollution when establishing whether the threshold of 50 mg/l is exceeded. The limit of 50 mg/l represents the overall concentration of nitrates, of whatever origin, in drinking water supplies above which hazards to human health arise. Moreover, it is impossible to determine accurately whether the nitrates of agricultural origin present in surface waters exceed 50 mg/l.

19 In reply to the applicants' alternative plea, the respondents point out that the measures provided for by the action programme are to take account of the quantities of nitrogen originating from agricultural and from other sources.

20 The High Court, having regard to those submissions, considered that the actions brought by the applicants in the main proceedings raised matters of general interest relevant to all farmers affected by the interpretation of Directive 91/676 and its implementation by national authorities. It therefore decided to stay proceedings and refer the following questions to the Court of Justice for a preliminary ruling:

(1) Does Council Directive 91/676/EEC of 12 December 1991 concerning the protection of waters against pollution caused by nitrates from agricultural sources ('the Nitrates Directive') require Member States, in accordance, in particular, with Articles 2(j) and 3(1) and Annex I thereof, to identify surface freshwaters as 'waters affected by pollution', and then to designate as vulnerable zones in accordance with Article 3(2) thereof all known areas of land which drain into such waters and which contribute to pollution: (i) where those waters contain a concentration of nitrates in excess of 50 mg/l (being the concentration of nitrates laid down by Annex I to the Nitrates Directive, by reference to Directive 75/440/EEC) and the Member State is satisfied that the discharge of nitrogen compounds from agricultural sources makes a 'significant contribution' to this overall concentration of nitrates and, if so, is a Member State entitled to be so satisfied if it has reason to

believe that the contribution to this overall concentration of nitrates, of nitrogen compounds discharged from agricultural sources, is greater than *de minimis* or some other amount or degree of contribution, and if the latter, what amount or degree of contribution amounts to a 'significant contribution' for these purposes; or (ii) only where the discharge of nitrogen compounds from agricultural sources itself accounts for a concentration of nitrates in those waters in excess of 50 mg/l (that is, leaving out of account any contribution from other sources); or (iii) on some other basis and, if so, what basis?

(2) If Question 1 is answered otherwise than in sense (ii) above, is the Nitrates Directive invalid (to the extent of its application to surface freshwaters) on the grounds that it infringes: (i) the principle that the polluter should pay; and/or (ii) the principle of proportionality; and/or (iii) the fundamental property rights of those owning and/or farming land draining into surface freshwaters required to be identified under Article 3(1), being areas of land which are then designated by Member States as vulnerable zones under Article 3(2)?'

Question 1

21   By its first question, the national court is essentially asking whether Arts 2(j) and 3(1) of Directive 91/676 and Annex I thereto must be interpreted as requiring the identification of surface freshwaters as 'waters affected by pollution', and therefore the designation as 'vulnerable zones' in accordance with Art 3(2) of Directive 91/676 of all known areas of land which drain into those waters and contribute to their pollution, where those waters contain a concentration of nitrates in excess of 50 mg/l and the member state concerned considers that the discharge of nitrogen compounds from agricultural sources makes a 'significant contribution' to that overall concentration of nitrates.

22   Should that question be answered in the affirmative, the national court asks what quantity of nitrates or degree of contribution to the pollution constitutes a 'significant contribution'.

23   The applicants in the main proceedings, supported by the NFU, maintain that surface freshwaters are to be identified as affected by pollution only where agricultural sources alone account for a concentration of nitrates in those waters in excess of 50 mg/l, the limit laid down in Directive 75/440.

24   That assertion, they submit, is reinforced, first, by the fact that the objective of Directive 91/676 is to protect waters from pollution due to nitrates from agricultural sources (second, third, fifth, sixth, ninth and tenth recitals in the preamble to Directive 91/676 and Art 1 thereof).

25   Secondly, the definition of the term 'pollution' set out in Art 2(j) of Directive 91/676 is expressly limited to the discharge of nitrogen compounds from agricultural sources, so that when the Member States identify waters affected by pollution under Art 3(1) of Directive 91/676 that term has an identical meaning, namely the discharge of nitrogen compounds which are exclusively agricultural in origin.

26   Thirdly, the applicants in the main proceedings contend that when the Member States apply Art 3(1) of Directive 91/676 they are to assess whether the maximum concentration of nitrates in water could be exceeded if action pursuant to Art 5 is not taken. Since such action is concerned solely with agricultural practices, the 50 mg/l limit can apply only to nitrates from agricultural sources.

27 Fourthly, while the Member States may, in accordance with Art 3(5) of Directive 91/676, establish and apply action programmes throughout their territory without designating specific vulnerable zones, a possibility which has not been taken up in this case, that does not exempt them from the obligation to determine the extent of water pollution caused by nitrates from agricultural sources.

28 Finally, as regards the 'significance' of the contribution made by agricultural sources to the level of nitrates in the waters concerned, the applicants in the main proceedings state that that concept is imprecise and does not appear anywhere in Directive 91/676. An interpretation under which the Member States may decide the level beyond which such a contribution is significant would be contrary to the principle of legal certainty and would not be justified by the impossibility of measuring the various sources of nitrates with a sufficient degree of accuracy.

29 In that regard, it should be observed that, when the Member States identify waters affected by pollution in accordance with Art 3(1) of Directive 91/676, they are to apply the criteria laid down in Annex I. Under para A.1 of that annex, surface freshwaters, in particular those used or intended for the abstraction of drinking water, must be identified as waters affected by pollution when they contain, or could contain if action pursuant to Art 5 of Directive 91/676 is not taken, more than the concentration of nitrates laid down in Directive 75/440.

30 It does not follow from the wording of that provision that the Member States are required to determine precisely what proportion of the pollution in the waters is attributable to nitrates of agricultural origin or that the cause of such pollution must be exclusively agricultural.

31 As is clear from the scheme of Directive 91/676, the identification of waters within the meaning of art 3(1) forms part of a process which also encompasses the designation of vulnerable zones and the establishment of action programmes. It would thus be incompatible with Directive 91/676 to restrict the identification of waters affected by pollution to cases where agricultural sources alone give rise to a concentration of nitrates in excess of 50 mg/1 when, within the framework of that process, Directive 91/676 expressly provides that, in establishing the action programmes under Art 5, the respective nitrogen contributions originating from agricultural and other sources are to be taken into account.

32 Similarly, art 3(5) of Directive 91/676 allows the Member States to designate the whole of their territory as a nitrate vulnerable zone instead of identifying waters affected by pollution, which means that they may establish action programmes even if the pollution caused by nitrates of exclusively agricultural origin does not exceed the threshold of 50 mg/1.

33 Finally, the interpretation put forward by the applicants in the main proceedings would lead to exclusion from the scope of Directive 91/676 of numerous cases where agricultural sources make a significant contribution to the pollution, a result which would be contrary to Directive 91/676's spirit and purpose.

34 The fact that the level for the concentration of nitrates taken into account when identifying waters was set by reference to that laid down in Directive 75/440 shows that requirements of public health protection determined the maximum concentration of nitrates, of whatever origin, permissible in water intended for human consumption, nitrate pollution being harmful to human health irrespective of whether it has been caused by agricultural or by industrial sources.

35   The question whether Directive 91/676 applies only where the discharge of nitrogen compounds of agricultural origin makes a significant contribution to the pollution must be answered in the affirmative, given the objective of the Community legislature, namely to reduce and prevent water pollution caused or induced by nitrates from agricultural sources, and the scope of the measures envisaged for that purpose by Art 5.

36   However, Directive 91/676 does not preclude the Member States, if their national law so allows, from applying the provisions of Directive 91/676 in cases not covered by it.

37   When national courts review the legality of measures identifying waters affected by pollution in accordance with Art 3(1) of Directive 91/676, as interpreted in this judgment, they must take account of the wide discretion enjoyed by the Member States which is inherent in the complexity of the assessments required of them in that context.

38   However, Community law cannot provide precise criteria for establishing in each case whether the discharge of nitrogen compounds of agricultural origin makes a significant contribution to the pollution.

39   Directive 91/676 may thus be applied by the Member States in different ways. Nevertheless, such a consequence is not incompatible with the nature of Directive 91/676, since it does not seek to harmonise the relevant national laws but to create the instruments needed in order to ensure that waters in the Community are protected against pollution caused by nitrates from agricultural sources. The Community legislature necessarily accepted that consequence when, in Annex I to Directive 91/676, it granted the Member States a wide discretion in the identification of waters covered by Art 3(1).

40   The answer to the first question must therefore be that arts 2(j) and 3(1) of Directive 91/676 and Annex I thereto must be interpreted as requiring the identification of surface freshwaters as 'waters affected by pollution', and therefore the designation as 'vulnerable zones' in accordance with art 3(2) of Directive 91/676 of all known areas of land which drain into those waters and contribute to their pollution, where those waters contain a concentration of nitrates in excess of 50 mg/l and the Member State concerned considers that the discharge of nitrogen compounds from agricultural sources makes a 'significant contribution' to that overall concentration of nitrates.

Question 2

41   By its second question, the national court asks whether the fact that the concentration of nitrates of agricultural origin in waters identified under Art 3(1) of Directive 91/676 may, in itself, not exceed 50 mg/l infringes the principle of proportionality, the polluter pays principle and the fundamental right to property of the farmers concerned, thereby rendering Directive 91/676 invalid.

42   The applicants in the main proceedings argue, first, that the identification of waters which exceed that threshold because of the presence of nitrates of non-agricultural origin (Art 3(1) of Directive 91/676), the designation as vulnerable zones of agricultural land which drains into those waters even though that land accounts for only part of the concentration of nitrates (Art 3(2)) and the establishment of an action programme which imposes on farmers alone responsibility for ensuring that the threshold is not exceeded (Art 5) give rise to disproportionate obligations on the part of the persons concerned, so that Directive 91/676 offends against the principle of proportionality.

43 Secondly, they submit that Directive 91/676 infringes the polluter pays principle laid down in Art 130r(2) of the EC Treaty, on the ground that farmers alone bear the cost of reducing the concentration of nitrates in waters to below the threshold of 50 mg/l even though agriculture is acknowledged to be only one of the sources of those nitrates, while the other sources escape all financial burden.

44 Thirdly, they maintain that Directive 91/676 is contrary to the principle under which environmental damage should as a priority be rectified at source, a principle which is to be read in conjunction with the polluter pays principle, as is clear from Art 130r(2) of the EC Treaty. Contrary to the first of those principles, the consequence of the interpretation placed on Directive 91/676 by the respondents in the main proceedings is that, instead of the nitrate pollution of waters from atmospheric deposition, which originates principally from industry and transport, being prevented or reduced at source, farmers are required to bear the entire burden of preventing or reducing nitrate pollution of surface freshwaters.

45 Finally, they submit that the right to property is infringed by imposing on farmers the entire responsibility for, and economic burden of, reducing nitrate concentrations in the waters concerned when others are the major or substantial causes of those concentrations.

46 So far as concerns the principle of proportionality, it should be observed first that, under Art 5(3) of Directive 91/676, the action programmes applicable to vulnerable zones are to take account of available scientific and technical data with reference to the respective nitrogen quantities originating from agricultural and other sources and of environmental conditions in the relevant regions.

47 Next, the mandatory measures adopted under those programmes must take into account the characteristics of the vulnerable zone concerned (para 1(3) of Annex III) and the Member States may fix amounts of livestock manure which may be spread in the vulnerable zones that differ from those specified if they are justified on the basis of objective criteria and do not prejudice the attainment of Directive 91/676's objectives (para 2(b) of Annex III).

48 Also, the Member States are required to draw up and implement suitable monitoring programmes to assess the effectiveness of the action programmes (Art 5(6) of Directive 91/676) and they are to review and, if necessary, revise their action programmes at least every four years (Art 5(7)). They can thus take account of changes of circumstance in relation to pollution from both agricultural and other sources.

49 Finally, the codes of good agricultural practice adopted by the Member States under Art 4(1)(a) of Directive 91/676 are to take account of conditions in the different regions of the Community (para A of Annex II).

50 It follows that Directive 91/676 contains flexible provisions enabling the Member States to observe the principle of proportionality in the application of the measures which they adopt. It is for the national courts to ensure that that principle is observed.

51 As regards the polluter pays principle, suffice it to state that Directive 91/676 does not mean that farmers must take on burdens for the elimination of pollution to which they have not contributed.

52 As has been pointed out in paras 46 and 48 of this judgment, the Member States are to take account of the other sources of pollution when implementing Directive 91/676

and, having regard to the circumstances, are not to impose on farmers costs of eliminating pollution that are unnecessary. Viewed in that light, the polluter pays principle reflects the principle of proportionality on which the court has already expressed its view (see paras 46–50, above).

53 The same applies to breach of the principle that environmental damage should as a priority be rectified at source, since the arguments of the applicants in the main proceedings are indissociable from their arguments relating to breach of the principle of proportionality.

54 As regards infringement of the right to property, the court has consistently held that, while the right to property forms part of the general principles of Community law, it is not an absolute right and must be viewed in relation to its social function. Consequently, its exercise may be restricted, provided that those restrictions in fact correspond to objectives of general interest pursued by the Community and do not constitute a disproportionate and intolerable interference, impairing the very substance of the rights guaranteed [...]

55 It is true that the action programmes which are provided for in Art 5 of Directive 91/676 and are to contain the mandatory measures referred to in Annex III impose certain conditions on the spreading of fertiliser and livestock manure, so that those programmes are liable to restrict the exercise by the farmers concerned of the right to property.

56 However, the system laid down in Art 5 reflects requirements relating to the protection of public health, and thus pursues an objective of general interest without the substance of the right to property being impaired.

57 While the institutions and the Member States are bound by the principle of proportionality when pursuing such an objective, Directive 91/676 does not, as has been found in paras 46 to 50 of this judgment, offend against that principle.

58 Accordingly, it must be concluded that consideration of the questions raised has disclosed no factor of such a kind as to affect the validity of Directive 91/676.

DOMESTIC LAW

Common law

With the advent of the Industrial Revolution, water pollution in England increased dramatically. Water courses had always been used as a means of disposing of waste. Demographic increases in population and its concentration in urban areas exacerbated the problem of sewage disposal. Factories used water in their industrial processes and discharged effluent into the nearest river with virtually no heed to the consequences. Although the first Act of Parliament to combat water pollution appeared in the Rivers (Pollution Prevention) Act 1876[26] the common law via the tort of nuisance remained the primary weapon against such pollution. As with all common law remedies, the main drawback was that nuisance operates mainly as a device for protecting the private rights

---

26 It created a criminal offence of polluting any British river but was totally unworkable in practice.

of landowners rather than as a protector of community rights. Despite that, the original common law remedies remain unaffected by statutory developments and are available today;[27] although statutory authority is a defence to a common law action in nuisance, at least if the statute expressly or by implication authorises the commission of the nuisance.[28] However, the inherent limitations of the common law in protecting the water environment has required more effective controls to be set by Parliament and enforced in the public interest by an independent body.[29] The bulk of this section is therefore devoted to describing the role played by the Environment Agency[30] in exercising statutory powers aimed at combating water pollution.

It is not proposed to discuss in detail the role played by the common law torts of negligence and the rule in *Rylands v Fletcher* in this context. In the light of Lord Goff's discussion of the leading authorities in his judgment in the *Cambridge Water* case (see below) we need only refer briefly to situations where the common law has been used to seek a remedy in an incident involving pollution of the water media.

A natural right to water

All riparian owners have a common law right to receive water in a stream or river coming to their property in both its natural state and natural quantity. This is a property right attaching to the freehold entitling the owner of the land to take water from the source. The owner does not acquire a proprietary right in the water itself at least until it is removed. The right to receive water is protected by the tort of nuisance. If this right is infringed, an owner would not have to prove actual harm done by the alleged pollution to himself or his property, for example, his livestock, or indeed to any consumer. The standard of water quality which he has a right to expect is a high one. As Lord MacNaghten said in *Young v Bankier Distillery* [1893] AC 691, p 698:

> The law relating to the rights of riparian proprietors is well settled. A riparian proprietor is entitled to have the water of the stream, on the banks of which his property lies, flow down as it has been accustomed to flow down to his property, subject to the ordinary use of the flowing water by upper proprietors, and to such further use, if any, on their part in connection with their property as may be reasonable under the circumstances. Every riparian proprietor is thus entitled to the water of his stream, in its natural flow, without sensible diminution or increase and without sensible alteration in its character or quality. Any invasion of this right causing actual damage or calculated to found a claim which may ripen into an adverse right entitles the party injured to the intervention of the court.

The right to unpolluted water also applies to water percolating underneath land, as was illustrated by *Ballard v Tomlinson*[31] where the defendant put sewage and waste material from his printing works into his well. This contaminated the water in a chalk aquifer so

---

27 See *AB v South West Water Services* [1993] 1 All ER 609.
28 See *Allan v Gulf Oil Refining Ltd* [1981] AC 101; Water Resources Act 1991, s 100.
29 Note the role of the local government ombudsman in combating maladministration by local authorities and water authorities. See, eg, *Restormel Borough Council and South West Water Authority* (*Complaint* Nos 89/240 and 89/8241) [1996] JPL 681.
30 On which see generally Chapter 1, pp 36 and 40, above.
31 (1885) 29 Ch D 115. Liability will attach where the defendant can be proved to have caused harm and where the type of harm is reasonably foreseeable. See the *Cambridge Water* case, pp 282–96, below.

that the plaintiff could no longer use it for his brewing process. The defendant was found liable. This case can be contrasted with *Smith v Kenrick*[32] where water percolating naturally into the defendant's mine was allowed to pass into the plaintiff's mine at a lower level. The court held that no action lay because the defendant had neither been malicious nor negligent in the way he had been working his mine. It therefore appears that a defendant will not be found liable in nuisance unless the percolating water has been used for a non-natural purpose, that is, something other than his natural right to abstract water.[33]

In the landmark case, *Cambridge Water Co v Eastern Counties Leather plc*[34] groundwater which flowed naturally below the appellant's land and which it abstracted to supply its customers, was polluted by a chemical solvent (perchloroethene) used in the respondent's tanning factory for degreasing leather. This substance had found its way into the appellant's borehole some 1.3 miles distant.[35] It was found that as a result of spillages on Eastern Counties' land, the solvent had seeped through a concrete floor, then through a layer of chalk until it reached a layer of impermeable rock. There it formed pools which gradually dissolved into the groundwater which eventually passed into the appellant's borehole. The House of Lords held that the respondent was not liable at common law for the damage done to the appellant's well which could no longer be used as it would contravene drinking water standards under Directive 80/778 which was adopted after the chemical had been escaping for many years. Although liability under the rule in *Rylands v Fletcher* is strict (the respondent could be held liable even if they had acted with reasonable care) the appellant's case could not succeed because of the remoteness of damage test. The respondent was not liable for all the natural consequences of his act but only for those which were reasonably foreseeable as established by the *Wagon Mound* case[36] in the context of negligence. The House of Lords also established that the rule in *Rylands v Fletcher* is only an application of the tort of nuisance and the reasonable foreseeability test meant that liability could not arise in nuisance either (see judgment of Lord Goff, p 282, below).

There can be no doubt that this case does restrict the usefulness of the common law as a means of combating water pollution. However, strict liability under *Rylands* will attach whenever the type of damage is reasonably foreseeable. (See Lord Goff, p 290)

Greater public awareness of pollution issues and enhanced technical knowledge of the behaviour of chemicals in underground water mean that operators of facilities akin to Eastern Counties Leather may not be able to shelter behind the test of reasonable foreseeability in the event of a similar incident arising in the future.

It may be noted in passing that although the right to sue at common law is normally exercised by a riparian owner, the right to recover damages or seek injunctions may also

---

32 [1849] 7 CB 515.

33 See *Baird v Williamson* (1863) 15 CB(NS) 376. See also Malcolm, R, *A Guidebook to Environmental Law*, 1994, London: Sweet & Maxwell, pp 39–40.

34 [1994] 1 All ER 53. See D Wilkinson (1994) 57 MLR 799.

35 Unlike *Ballard v Tomlinson* (1885) 29 Ch D 115, the litigants were not adjacent landowners and the technical problems of establishing causation were immense.

36 [1967] 1 AC 617.

be extended, for example, to the owners of fishing rights.[37] In *Cook v South West Water*[38] the plaintiffs recovered for damage to their fishing beats due to foaming caused by the discharge of sewage effluent detergent although no fish were killed.

In conclusion, it is worth pointing out that those contemplating common law action will be able to have access to information about discharges by consulting the public registers maintained under s 190 of the Water Resources Act 1991 (see p 304, below).

Cambridge Water Co v Eastern Counties Leather plc [1994] 1 All ER 53

Lord Goff of Chievely: My Lords, this appeal is concerned with the question whether the appellant company, Eastern Counties Leather plc (ECL), is liable to the respondent company, Cambridge Water Co (CWC), in damages in respect of damage suffered by reason of the contamination of water available for abstraction at CWC's borehole at Sawston Mill near Cambridge. The contamination was caused by a solvent known as perchloroethene (PCE), used by ECL in the process of degreasing pelts at its tanning works in Sawston, about 1.3 miles away from CWC's borehole, the PCE having seeped into the ground beneath ECL's works and thence having been conveyed in percolating water in the direction of the borehole. CWC's claim against ECL was based on three alternative grounds, viz negligence, nuisance and the rule in *Rylands v Fletcher* (see *Rylands v Fletcher* (1868) LR 3 HL 330; [1861–73] All ER Rep 1; affg *Fletcher v Rylands* (1866) LR 1 Ex 265). The judge, Ian Kennedy J, dismissed CWC's claim on all three grounds – on the first two grounds, because (as I will explain hereafter) he held that ECL could not reasonably have foreseen that such damage would occur, and on the third ground because he held that the use of a solvent such as PCE in ECL's tanning business constituted, in the circumstances, a natural use of ECL's land. The Court of Appeal, however, allowed CWC's appeal from the decision of the judge, on the ground that ECL was strictly liable for the contamination of the water percolating under CWC's land, on the authority of *Ballard v Tomlinson* (1885) 29 Ch D 115, and awarded damages against ECL in the sum assessed by the judge, viz £1,064,886 together with interest totalling £642,885, and costs. It is against that decision that ECL now appeals to your Lordships' House, with leave of this House.

The factual background to the case has been set out, not only in the judgments in the courts below, but also in lucid detail in the agreed statement of facts and issues helpfully prepared by counsel for the assistance of the Appellate Committee. These reveal the remarkable history of events which led to the contamination of the percolating water available at CWC's borehole, which I think it desirable that I myself should recount in some detail.

ECL was incorporated in 1879, and since that date has continued in uninterrupted business as a manufacturer of fine leather at Sawston. ECL employs about 100 people, all or whom live locally. Its present works are, as the judge found, in general modern and spacious, and admit of a good standard of housekeeping.

The tanning process requires that pelts shall be degreased; and ECL, in common with all other tanneries, has used solvents in that process since the early 1950s. It has used two types of chlorinated solvents – organochlorines known as TCE (trichloroethene) and PCE. Both solvents are cleaning and degreasing agents; and since 1950 PCE has increasingly been in

---

37 See *Pride of Derby v British Celanese Ltd* [1953] Ch 149. But see *Hunter v Canary Wharf Ltd, London Docklands Development Corp* [1997] 2 All ER 426; [1997] 2 WLR 684 where the House of Lords appears to restrict the right to sue in nuisance to those with a proprietary interest.

38   4 LMELR 99.

common, widespread and everyday use in dry-cleaning, in general industrial use (for example, as a machine cleaner or paint-thinner), domestically (for example, in 'Dab-it-off') and in tanneries. PCE is highly volatile, and so evaporates rapidly in air, but it is not readily soluble in water.

ECL began using TCE in the early 1950s and then changed over to PCE, probably sometime in the 1960s, and continued to use PCE until 1991. The amount so used varied between 50,000 and 100,000 litres per year. The solvent was introduced into what were (in effect) dry-cleaning machines. This was done in two different ways. First, from the commencement of use until 1976, the solvent was delivered in 40 gallon drums; as and when the solvent was needed, a drum was taken by forklift truck to the machine and tipped into a tank at the base of the machine. Second, from 1976 to 1991, the solvent was delivered in bulk and kept in a storage tank, from which it was piped directly to the machine.

There was no direct evidence of the actual manner in which PCE was spilled at ECL's premises. However, the judge found that the spillage took place during the period up to 1976, principally during the topping up process described above, during which there were regular spillages of relatively small amounts of PCE onto the concrete floor of the tannery. It is known that, over that period, the minimum amount which must have been spilled (or otherwise have entered the chalk aquifer below) was some 3,200 litres (1,000 gallons); it is not possible even to guess at the maximum. However, as the judge found, a reasonable supervisor at ECL would not have foreseen, in or before 1976, that such repeated spillages of small quantities of solvent would lead to any environmental hazard or damage – that is, that the solvent would enter the aquifer or that, having done so, detectable quantities would be found down-catchment. Even if he had foreseen that solvent might enter the aquifer, he would not have foreseen that such quantities would produce any sensible effect upon water taken down-catchment, or would otherwise be material or deserve the description of pollution. I understand the position to have been that any spillage would have been expected to evaporate rapidly in the air, and would not have been expected to seep through the floor of the building into the soil below. The only harm that could have been foreseen from a spillage was that somebody might have been overcome by fumes from a spillage of a significant quantity.

I turn to CWC. CWC was created under its own Act of Parliament in 1853 (the Cambridge University and Town Waterworks Act 1853 (16 & 17 Vict c xxiii), and is a licensed supplier of water following implementation of the Water Act 1989. Its function is to supply water to some 275,000 people in the Cambridge area. It takes all its water by borehole extraction from underground strata, mainly the middle and lower chalk prevalent in the area. Since 1945 public demand for water has multiplied many times, and new sources of supply have had to be found. In 1975 CWC identified the borehole at Sawston Mill as having the potential to meet a need for supply required to avert a prospective shortfall, and to form part of its long-term provision for future demand. It purchased the borehole in September 1976. Before purchase, tests were carried out on the water from the borehole; these tests indicated that, from the aspect of chemical analysis, the water was a wholesome water suitable for public supply purposes. Similar results were obtained from tests carried out during the period 1979–83. At all events CWC, having obtained the requisite statutory authority to use the borehole for public sector supply, proceeded to build a new pumping station at a cost of £184,000; and Sawston Mill water entered the main supply system in June 1979.

Meanwhile, in the later 1970s concern began to be expressed in scientific circles about the presence of organic chemicals in drinking water, and their possible effects. Furthermore, the development of, *inter alia*, high resolution gas chromatography during the 1970s enabled scientists to detect and measure organochlorine compounds (such as PCE) in water to the value of micrograms per litre (or parts per billion) expressed as 5g/litre.

In 1984 the World Health Organisation (WHO) published a Report on Guidelines for Drinking Water Quality (vol 1: recommendations). Although not published until 1984, the Report was the product of discussion and consultation during several years previously, and its recommendations appear to have formed the basis of an earlier EEC Directive, as well as of later UK Regulations. Chapter 4 of the Report is concerned with 'Chemical and Physical Aspects', and Chapter 4.3 deals with organic contaminants, three of which (including TCE and PCE) were assigned a 'Tentative Guideline Value'. The value so recommended for TCE was 305g/litre, and for PCE 105g/litre.

The EEC Directive relating to the Quality of Water intended for Human Consumption (80/778/EEC) was issued on 15 September 1980. Member States were required to bring in laws within two years of notification, and to achieve full compliance within five years. The Directive distinguished between 'Maximum Admissible Concentration' (MAC) values and 'Guide Level' (GL) values, the former being minimum standards which had to be achieved, and the latter being more stringent standards which it was desirable to achieve. TCE and PCE were assigned a GL value of only 15g/litre, ie 30 times and 10 times respectively lower than the WHO Tentative Guideline Values.

The United Kingdom responded to the Directive by Department of the Environment circular 20/82 dated 15 August 1982. The effect was that, as from 18 July 1985, drinking water containing more than 15g/litre of TCE or PCE would not be regarded as 'wholesome' water for the purpose of compliance by water authorities with their statutory obligations under the Water Act 1973. However, following a Regulation made in 1989 (SI 1989/1147) the prescribed maximum concentration values for TCE and PCE have been respectively 305g/litre and 105g/litre, so that since 1 September 1989 the United Kingdom values have been brought back into harmony with the WHO Tentative Guideline Values.

CWC employed Huntingdon Research Laboratories (HRL) to test its water for the purpose of compliance with the European Directive. In August 1983 Dr McDonald, an analytical chemist employed by HRL, decided to test tap water at his home in St Ives, Cambridge. He discovered PCE in the water. Samples then taken of his own and his neighbours' water disclosed an average PCE concentration of 38755g/litre. As a result, CWC caused investigations to be made to discover the source of the contaminant, which was identified as the Sawston Mill borehole. The borehole was taken out of commission on 13 October 1983. The Anglian Water Authority then instituted what was to become a prolonged and exhaustive programme of investigation, principally conducted by the British Geological Survey (BGS), to discover the source and path of the PCE in the borehole water. This investigation yielded, between 1987 and 1989, a number of published papers which have become the UK source material on the behaviour and characteristics of chlorinated organic industrial solvents in groundwater, and the behaviour of groundwater in a fissure-flow, anisostropic (that is, where permeability is higher in one direction rather than constant in all directions), chalk aquifer. Before publication of these papers little was known about either of these subjects.

The conclusions reached by BGS, and by the expert witnesses instructed by CWC and ECL in the present litigation, were as follows. Neat PCE had travelled down through the drift directly beneath ECL's premises, and then vertically downwards through the chalk aquifer until arrested by a relatively impermeable layer of chalk marl at a depth of about 50 metres. Thus arrested, the neat PCE had formed pools which were dissolving slowly in the groundwater and being carried down aquifer in the direction of Sawston Mill at the rate of about 8 metres per day, the travel time between pool and Sawston Mill being about nine months, and the migration of the dissolved phase PCE being along a deep, comparatively narrow, pathway or 'plume'. On the balance of probabilities, this narrow plume had reached Sawston Mill and been at least materially responsible for the PCE concentrations found there.

Sawston Mill had been taken out of supply in October 1983. As an interim measure, CWC brought forward a pre-existing proposal to construct a new pumping station at Duxford Airfield. This new source, which came on stream in the summer of 1984, made up for the loss of the Sawston supply. CWC still needed to make use of the Sawston catchment, but it rejected methods of treatment of the water there as unproven at that time. Instead it proceeded with the development of a new source of supply at Hinxton Grange. The damages assessed by the judge, and awarded by the Court of Appeal, against ECL consisted of L956,937 in respect of the development of Hinxton Grange (less L60,000, being the residual value to CWC of Sawston Mill) together with certain incidental expenses. In fact, by 1990 CWC felt sufficiently confident in carbon filtration technology to build a treatment plant at Sawston Mill, for the purpose of treating water from Duxford Airfield to remove concentrations of an organic herbicide from the water there. This plant is capable of removing PCE from Sawston Mill water as and when required.

From the foregoing history, the following relevant facts may be selected as being of particular relevance:

1   The spillage of PCE, and its seepage into the ground beneath the floor of the tannery at ECL's works, occurred during the period which ended in 1976, as a result of regular spillages of small quantities of PCE onto the floor of ECL's tannery.

2   The escape of dissolved phase PCE, from the pools of neat PCE which collected at or towards the base of the chalk aquifers beneath ECL's works, into the chalk aquifers under the adjoining land and thence in the direction of Sawston Mill, must have begun at some unspecified date well before 1976 and be still continuing to the present day.

3   As held by the judge, the seepage of the PCE beneath the floor of ECL's works down into the chalk aquifers below was not foreseeable by a reasonable supervisor employed by ECL, nor was it foreseeable by him that detectable quantities of PCE would be found down-catchment, so that he could not have foreseen, in or before 1976, that the repeated spillages would lead to any environmental hazard or damage. The only foreseeable damage from a spillage of PCE was that somebody might be overcome by fumes from a substantial spillage of PCE on the surface of the ground.

4   The water so contaminated at Sawston Mill has never been held to be dangerous to health. But under criteria laid down in the UK Regulations, issued in response to the EEC Directive, the water so contaminated was not 'wholesome' and, since 1985, could not lawfully be supplied in this country as drinking water.

The decision of Ian Kennedy J

The judge dismissed the claims against ECL in nuisance and negligence in the following passage: 'That there should now be an award of damages in respect of the 1991 impact of actions that were not actionable nuisances or negligence when they were committed 15 years before is to my mind not a proposition which the common law would entertain.'

I feel, with respect, that this passage requires some elucidation. It is not to be forgotten that both nuisance and negligence are, historically, actions on the case; and accordingly in neither case is the tort complete, so that damages are recoverable, unless and until damage has been caused to the plaintiff. It follows that, in this sense (which I understand to be the relevant sense), there could not be an actionable nuisance by virtue of the spillage of solvent on ECL's land, but only when such spillage caused damage to CWC, that is, when water available at its borehole was rendered unsaleable by reason of breach of the Regulations. It also follows that, in theory, the fact that the Regulations came into force after the relevant spillage on ECL's land, though before the relevant contamination of the water, would not of itself mean that there was no actionable nuisance committed by ECL, unless there is some applicable principle of law which would in such circumstances render the damage not actionable as a nuisance. The two possible principles are either (1) that the user of ECL's land resulting in the spillage was in the circumstances a reasonable user or (2) that ECL will not be liable in the absence of reasonable foreseeability that its action may cause damage of the relevant type to CWC. In the present case, there does not appear to have been any reliance by ECL, in its pleaded case or in argument, on the principle of reasonable user. I therefore infer that the basis upon which the judge rejected CWC's claim in nuisance must have derived from his finding of lack of reasonable foreseeability of damage of the relevant type, which is basically the same ground on which he dismissed CWC's claim in negligence. This is however a point to which I will return at a later stage, when I come to consider liability on the facts of the present case under the rule in *Rylands v Fletcher*.

The decision of the Court of Appeal: Ballard v Tomlinson

There was no appeal by CWC against the judge's conclusion on nuisance and negligence. CWC pursued its appeal to the Court of Appeal relying only on the rule in *Rylands v Fletcher*, on which point the judge had decided against it on the ground that the relevant operations of ECL constituted natural use of its land. The Court of Appeal however held ECL to be strictly liable in damages to CWC in respect of the contamination of the percolating water available for extraction by CWC from its borehole at Sawston Mill. This they did on the basis of the decision of the Court of Appeal in *Ballard v Tomlinson* (1885) 29 Ch D 115.

In that case the plaintiff and the defendant, whose properties were separated only by a highway, each had on his land a well sunk into the chalk aquifer below. The plaintiff had a brewery on his land, for the purpose of which he used water drawn from his well. A printing house was built on the defendant's land, and the defendant constructed a drain from a water closet attached to the printing house, by means of which the sewage from the closet and the refuse from the printing house found their way into the defendant's well. The sewage and refuse which entered the defendant's well polluted the common source of percolating water so that the water which the plaintiff drew from his well was unusable for brewing purposes. The Court of Appeal, reversing the decision of Pearson J (see (1884) 26 Ch D 194), held that the plaintiff was entitled to judgment against the defendant for an injunction and for damages.

The principal argument advanced by the defendant was based on the proposition that the plaintiff had no property in the water percolating beneath his land, and therefore had no cause of action for the pollution of that water. The judgments of the Court of Appeal, which were unreserved, were largely directed to the rejection of that argument. This they did on the basis that the plaintiff had a right to extract water percolating beneath his land, and the defendant had no right to contaminate what the plaintiff was entitled to get. As Brett MR said (29 Ch D 115 at 121):

... no one of those who have a right to appropriate [the water] has a right to contaminate that source so as to prevent his neighbour from having the full value of his right of appropriation.

It appears that both Brett MR and Cotton LJ considered that the plaintiff's cause of action arose under the rule in *Rylands v Fletcher*, which was the basis upon which the plaintiff's case was advanced in argument. Lindley LJ however treated the case as one of nuisance.

The Court of Appeal treated this decision as determining the present case against ECL. Mann LJ (who delivered the judgment of the court) said:

It was sufficient that the defendant's act caused the contamination. Nor do the judgments contain any warrant for attaching importance to the reasonableness of ECL's inability to foresee that spillages would have the kind of consequence which they did. It does not appear from the report whether Tomlinson either knew or ought to have known of any risk of damage attendant on his actions, but none of the judges in this court was concerned with his state of actual or imputed knowledge. The situation is one in which negligence plays no part. *Ballard v Tomlinson* decided that where the nuisance is an interference with a natural right incident to ownership then the liability is a strict one. The actor acts at his peril in that if his actions result by the operation of ordinary natural processes in an interference with the right then he is liable to compensate for any damage suffered by the owner.

In his judgment in *Ballard v Tomlinson* 29 Ch D 115 at 124 Cotton LJ spoke of the plaintiff's right to abstract percolating water beneath his land as 'a natural right incident to the ownership of his own land'. In the present context, however, this means no more than that the owner of land can, without a grant, lawfully abstract water which percolates beneath his land, his right to do so being protected by the law of tort, by means of an action for an injunction or for damages for nuisance: see Megarry and Wade, *Law of Real Property*, 1984, p 842, and Simpson, *History of Land Law*, 1986, 2nd edn, pp 263–64. There is no natural right to percolating water, as there may be to water running in a defined channel; see *Chasemore v Richards* (1859) 7 HL Cas 349 at 379; [1843–60] All ER Rep 77 at 84 *per* Lord Cranworth, and 49 *Halsbury's Laws* (4th edn) paragraph 392. In the present case Mann LJ stated that *Ballard v Tomlinson* decided that 'where the nuisance is an interference with a natural right incident to ownership then the liability is a strict one'. In my opinion, however, if in this passage Mann LJ intended to say that the defendant was held to be liable for damage which he could not reasonably have foreseen, that conclusion cannot be drawn from the judgments in the case, in which the point did not arise. As I read the judgments, they disclose no more than that, in the circumstances of the case, the defendant was liable to the plaintiff in tort for the contamination of the source of water supplying the plaintiff's well, either on the basis of the rule in *Rylands v Fletcher*, or under the law of nuisance, by reason of interference with the plaintiff's use and enjoyment of his land, including his right to extract water percolating beneath his land. It follows that the question whether such a liability may attach in any particular case must depend upon the principles governing liability under one or other of those two heads of the law. To those principles, therefore, I now turn.

Nuisance and the rule in Rylands v Fletcher

As I have already recorded, there was no appeal by CWC to the Court of Appeal against the judge's conclusion in nuisance. The question of ECL's liability in nuisance has really only arisen again because the Court of Appeal allowed CWC's appeal on the ground that ECL was liable on the basis of strict liability in nuisance on the principle laid down, as they saw it, in *Ballard v Tomlinson*. Since, for the reasons I have given, that case does not give rise to any principle of law independent of the ordinary law of nuisance or the rule in *Rylands v Fletcher*, the strict position now is that CWC, having abandoned its claim in nuisance, can only uphold the decision of the Court of Appeal on the basis of the rule in *Rylands v Fletcher*. However, one important submission advanced by ECL before the Appellate Committee was that strict liability for an escape only arises under that rule where the defendant knows or reasonably ought to have foreseen, when collecting the relevant things on his land, that those things might, if they escaped, cause damage of the relevant kind. Since there is a close relationship between nuisance and the rule in *Rylands v Fletcher*, I myself find it very difficult to form an opinion as to the validity of that submission without first considering whether foreseeability of such damage is an essential element in the law of nuisance. For that reason, therefore, I do not feel able altogether to ignore the latter question simply because it was no longer pursued by CWC before the Court of Appeal.

In order to consider the question in the present case in its proper legal context, it is desirable to look at the nature of liability in a case such as the present in relation both to the law of nuisance and the rule in *Rylands v Fletcher*, and for that purpose to consider the relationship between the two heads of liability.

I begin with the law of nuisance. Our modern understanding of the nature and scope of the law of nuisance was much enhanced by Professor Newark's seminal article 'The boundaries of nuisance' (1949) 65 LQR 480. The article is avowedly a historical analysis, in that it traces the nature of the tort of nuisance to its origins, and demonstrates how the original view of nuisance as a tort to land (or more accurately, to accommodate interference with servitudes, a tort directed against the plaintiff's enjoyment of rights over land) became distorted as the tort was extended to embrace claims for personal injuries, even where the plaintiff's injury did not occur while using land in his occupation. In Professor Newark's opinion (at p 487), this development produced adverse effects, viz that liability which should have arisen only under the law of negligence was allowed under the law of nuisance which historically was a tort of strict liability; and that there was a tendency for 'cross-infection to take place, and notions of negligence began to make an appearance in the realm of nuisance proper'. But in addition, Professor Newark considered (pp 487–88), it contributed to a misappreciation of the decision in *Rylands v Fletcher*:

This case is generally regarded as an important landmark, indeed a turning point – in the law of tort; but an examination of the judgments shows that those who decided it were quite unconscious of any revolutionary or reactionary principles implicit in the decision. They thought of it as calling for no more than a restatement of settled principles, and Lord Cairns went so far as to describe those principles as 'extremely simple'. And in fact the main principle involved was extremely simple, being no more than the principle that negligence is not an element in the tort of nuisance. It is true that Blackburn J in his great judgment in the Exchequer Chamber never once used the word 'nuisance', but three times he cited the case of fumes escaping from an alkali works – a clear case of nuisance – as an instance of liability, under the rule which he was laying down. Equally it is true that in 1866 there were a number of cases in the reports suggesting that persons who controlled dangerous things were under a strict duty to take care, but as none of these cases had anything to do with nuisance Blackburn J did not refer to them. But the profession as a whole, whose conceptions of the boundaries of nuisance were now becoming fogged, failed to see in *Rylands v Fletcher* a simple case of nuisance. They regarded it as an exceptional case – and the rule in *Rylands v Fletcher* as a generalisation of exceptional cases, where liability was to be strict on account of 'the magnitude of danger, coupled with the difficulty of proving negligence' [*Pollock on Torts* (14th edn, 1939) p 386] rather than on account of the nature of the plaintiff's interest which was invaded. They therefore jumped rashly to two conclusions: firstly, that the rule in *Rylands v Fletcher* could be extended beyond the case of neighbouring occupiers; and secondly, that the rule could be used to afford a remedy in cases of personal injury. Both these conclusions were stoutly denied by Lord Macmillan in *Read v J Lyons & Co Ltd* ([1947] AC 156; [1946] 2 All ER 471), but it remains to be seen whether the House of Lords will support his opinion when the precise point comes up for decision.

We are not concerned in the present case with the problem of personal injuries, but we are concerned with the scope of liability in nuisance and in *Rylands v Fletcher*. In my opinion it is right to take as our starting point the fact that, as Professor Newark considered, *Rylands v Fletcher* was indeed not regarded by Blackburn J as a revolutionary decision: see, for example, his observations in *Ross v Fedden* (1872) 26 LT 966, p 968. He believed himself not to be creating new law, but to be stating existing law, on the basis of existing authority; and, as is apparent from his judgment, he was concerned in particular with the situation where the defendant collects things upon his land which are likely to do mischief if they escape, in which event the defendant will be strictly liable for damage resulting from any such escape. It follows that the essential basis of liability was the collection by the defendant of such things upon his land; and the consequence was a strict liability in the event of damage caused by their escape, even if the escape was an isolated event. Seen in its context, there is no reason to suppose that Blackburn J intended to create a liability any more strict than that created by the law of nuisance; but even so he must have intended that, in the circumstances specified by him, there should be liability for damage resulting from an isolated escape.

Of course, although liability for nuisance has generally been regarded as strict, at least in the case of a defendant who has been responsible for the creation of a nuisance, even so that liability has been kept under control by the principle of reasonable user – the principle of give and take as between neighbouring occupiers of land, under which 'those acts necessary for the common and ordinary use and occupation of land and houses may be done, if conveniently done, without subjecting those who do them to an action': see *Bamford v Turnley* (1862) 3 B & S 62, p 83; [1861–73] All ER Rep 706, p 712, *per* Bramwell B. The effect is that, if the user is reasonable, the defendant will not be liable for consequent harm to his neighbour's enjoyment of his land; but if the user is not reasonable, the defendant will be liable, even though he may have exercised reasonable care and skill to avoid it. Strikingly, a comparable principle has developed which limits liability under the rule in *Rylands v Fletcher*. This is the principle of natural use of the land. I shall have to consider the principle at a later stage in this judgment. The most authoritative statement of the principle is now to be found in the advice of the Privy Council delivered by Lord Moulton in *Rickards v Lothian* [1913] AC 263, p 280; [1911–13] All ER Rep 71, p 80 when he said of the rule in *Rylands v Fletcher*:

> It is not every use to which land is put that brings into play that principle. It must be some special use bringing with it increased danger to others, and must not merely be the ordinary use of the land or such a use as is proper for the general benefit of the community.

It is not necessary for me to identify precise differences which may be drawn between this principle, and the principle of reasonable user as applied in the law of nuisance. It is enough for present purposes that I should draw attention to a similarity of function. The effect of this principle is that, where it applies, there will be no liability under the rule in *Rylands v Fletcher*; but that where it does not apply, that is, where there is a non-natural use, the defendant will be liable for harm caused to the plaintiff by the escape, notwithstanding that he has exercised all reasonable care and skill to prevent the escape from occurring.

Foreseeability of damage in nuisance

It is against this background that it is necessary to consider the question whether foreseeability of harm of the relevant type is an essential element of liability either in nuisance or under the rule in *Rylands v Fletcher*. I shall take first the case of nuisance. In the present case, as I have said, this is not strictly speaking a live issue. Even so, I propose briefly to address it, as part of the analysis of the background to the present case.

It is, of course, axiomatic that in this field we must be on our guard, when considering liability for damages in nuisance, not to draw inapposite conclusions from cases concerned only with a claim for an injunction. This is because, where an injunction is claimed, its purpose is to restrain further action by the defendant which may interfere with the plaintiff's enjoyment of his land, and *ex hypothesi* the defendant must be aware, if and when an injunction is granted, that such interference may be caused by the act which he is restrained from committing. It follows that these cases provide no guidance on the question whether foreseeability of harm of the relevant type is a pre-requisite of the recovery of damages for causing such harm to the plaintiff. In the present case, we are not concerned with liability in damages in respect of a nuisance which has arisen through natural causes, or by the act of a person for whose actions the defendant is not responsible, in which cases the applicable principles in nuisance have become closely associated with those applicable in negligence: see *Sedleigh-Denfield v O'Callagan* [1940] AC 880; [1940] 3 All ER 349 and *Goldman v Hargrave* [1967] 1 AC 645; [1966] 2 All ER 989. We are concerned with the liability of a person where a nuisance has been created by one for whose actions he is responsible. Here, as I have said, it is still the law that the fact that the defendant has taken all reasonable care will not of itself exonerate him from liability, the relevant control mechanism being found within the principle of reasonable user. But it by no means follows that the defendant should be held liable for damage of a type which he could not reasonably foresee; and the development of the law of negligence in the past 60 years points strongly towards a requirement that such foreseeability should be a pre-requisite of liability in damages for nuisance, as it is of liability in negligence. For if a plaintiff is in ordinary circumstances only able to claim damages in respect of personal injuries where he can prove such foreseeability on the part of the defendant, it is difficult to see why, in common justice, he should be in a stronger position to claim damages for interference with the enjoyment of his land where the defendant was unable to foresee such damage. Moreover, this appears to have been the conclusion of the Privy Council in *The Wagon Mound (No 2), Overseas Tankship (UK) Ltd v Miller Steamship Co Pty Ltd* [1967] 1 AC 617; [1966] 2 All ER 709. The facts of the case are too well-known to require repetition, but they gave rise to a claim for damages arising from a public nuisance caused by a spillage of oil in Sydney Harbour. Lord Reid, who delivered the advice of the Privy Council, considered that, in the class of nuisance which included the case before the Board, foreseeability is an essential element in determining liability. He then continued ([1966] 2 All ER 709, p 717, [1967] 1 AC 617, p 640):

> It could not be right to discriminate between different cases of nuisance so as to make foreseeability a necessary element in determining damages in those cases where it is a necessary element in determining liability, but not in others. So the choice is between it being a necessary element in all cases of nuisance or in none. In their Lordships' judgment the similarities between nuisance and other forms of tort to which *The Wagon Mound (No 1)* [see *Overseas Tankship (UK) Ltd v Morts Dock and Engineering Co Ltd, The Wagon Mound* [1961] AC 388; [1961] 1 All ER 404] applies far outweigh any differences,

and they must therefore hold that the judgment appealed from is wrong on this branch of the case. It is not sufficient that the injury suffered by the respondents' vessels was the direct result of the nuisance if that injury was in the relevant sense unforeseeable.

It is widely accepted that this conclusion, although not essential to the decision of the particular case, has nevertheless settled the law to the effect that foreseeability of harm is indeed a pre-requisite of the recovery of damages in private nuisance, as in the case of public nuisance. I refer in particular to the opinion expressed by Professor Fleming in his book on *Torts* 1992, 8th edn, pp 443–44. It is unnecessary in the present case to consider the precise nature of this principle; but it appears from Lord Reid's statement of the law that he regarded it essentially as one relating to remoteness of damage.

Foreseeability of damage under the rule in Rylands v Fletcher

It is against this background that I turn to the submission advanced by ECL before your Lordships that there is a similar pre-requisite of recovery of damages under the rule in *Rylands v Fletcher* (1866) LR 1 Exch 265.

I start with the judgment of Blackburn J in *Rylands v Fletcher* itself. His celebrated statement of the law is to be found where he said (pp 279–80):

> We think that the true rule of law is, that the person who for his own purposes brings on his lands and collects and keeps there anything likely to do mischief if it escapes, must keep it in at his peril, and, if he does not do so, is *prima facie* answerable for all the damage which is the natural consequence of its escape. He can excuse himself by showing that the escape was owing to the plaintiff's default; or perhaps that the escape was the consequence of *vis major*, or the act of God; but as nothing of this sort exists here, it is unnecessary to inquire what excuse would be sufficient. The general rule, as above stated, seems on principle just. The person whose grass or corn is eaten down by the escaping cattle of his neighbour, or whose mine is flooded by the water from his neighbour's reservoir, or whose cellar is invaded by the filth of his neighbour's privy, or whose habitation is made unhealthy by the fumes and noisome vapours of his neighbour's alkali works, is damnified without any fault of his own; and it seems but reasonable and just that the neighbour, who has brought something on his own property which was not naturally there, harmless to others so long as it is confined to his own property, but which he knows to be mischievous if it gets on his neighbour's, should be obliged to make good the damage which ensues if he does not succeed in confining it to his own property. But for his act in bringing it there no mischief could have accrued, and it seems but just that he should at his peril keep it there so that no mischief may accrue, or answer for the natural and anticipated consequences. And upon authority, this we think is established to be the law whether the things so brought be beasts, or water, or filth, or stenches.

In that passage Blackburn J spoke of 'anything likely to do mischief if it escapes'; and later he spoke of something 'which he knows to be mischievous if it gets on to his neighbour's [property]', and the liability to 'answer for the natural and anticipated consequences'. Furthermore, time and again he spoke of the strict liability imposed upon the defendant as being that he must keep the thing in at his peril; and, when referring to liability in actions for damage occasioned by animals, he referred (p 282) to the established principle 'that it is quite immaterial whether the escape is by negligence or not'. The general tenor of his statement of principle is therefore that knowledge, or at least foreseeability of the risk, is a pre-requisite of the recovery of damages under the principle; but that the principle is one of strict liability in the sense that the defendant may be held liable notwithstanding that he has exercised all due care to prevent the escape from occurring.

There are however early authorities in which foreseeability of damage does not appear to have been regarded as necessary.

[Lord Goff considers the decisions in *Humphries v Cousins* (1877) 2 CPD 239, [1877–80] Al ER Rep 313; *West v Bristol Tramways Co* [1908] 2 KB 14, [1908–10] All ER Rep 215; and *Rainham Chemical Works Ltd v Belvedere Fish Guano Co Ltd* [1921] 2 AC 465, [1921] All El Rep 48. He continues ...]

I feel bound to say that these two cases provide a very fragile base for any firm conclusion that foreseeability of damage has been authoritatively rejected as a pre-requisite of the recovery of damages under the rule in *Rylands v Fletcher*. Certainly, the point was not considered by this House in the *Rainham Chemicals* case. In my opinion, the matter is open for consideration by your Lordships in the present case, and, despite recent *dicta* to the contrary (see for example *Leakey v National Trust for Places of Historic Interest or Natural Beauty* [1980] 1 All ER 17 at 30, [1980] QB 485 at 519 *per* Megaw LJ), should be considered as a matter of principle. Little guidance can be derived from either of the two cases in question, save that it seems to have been assumed that the strict liability arising under the rule precluded reliance by the plaintiff on lack of knowledge or the means of knowledge of the relevant danger.

The point is one on which academic opinion appears to be divided: cf *Salmond and Heuston on Torts*, 1992, 20th edn, pp 324–25, which favours the pre-requisite of foreseeability, and *Clerk and Lindsell on Torts*, 1989, 16th edn, paragraph 25.09, which takes a different view. However, quite apart from the indications to be derived from the judgment of Blackburn J in *Fletcher v Rylands* LR 1 Exch 265 itself, to which I have already referred, the historical connection with the law of nuisance must now be regarded as pointing towards the conclusion that foreseeability of damage is a pre-requisite of the recovery of damages under the rule. I have already referred to the fact that Blackburn J himself did not regard his statement of principle as having broken new ground; furthermore, Professor Newark has convincingly shown that the rule in *Rylands v Fletcher* was essentially concerned with an extension of the law of nuisance to cases of isolated escape. Accordingly since, following the observations of Lord Reid when delivering the advice of the Privy Council in *The Wagon Mound (No 2)* [1966] 2 All ER 709 at 717, [1967] 1 AC 617, p 640, the recovery of damages in private nuisance depends on foreseeability by the defendant of the relevant type of damage, it would appear logical to extend the same requirement to liability under the rule in *Rylands v Fletcher*.

Even so, the question cannot be considered solely as a matter of history. It can be argued that the rule in *Rylands v Fletcher* should not be regarded simply as an extension of the law of nuisance, but should rather be treated as a developing principle of strict liability from which can be derived a general rule of strict liability for damage caused by ultra-hazardous operations, on the basis of which persons conducting such operations may properly be held strictly liable for the extraordinary risk to others involved in such operations. As is pointed out in Fleming on *Torts*, 1992, 8th edn, pp 327–28, this would lead to the practical result that the cost of damage resulting from such operations would have to be absorbed as part of the overheads of the relevant business rather than be borne (where there is no negligence) by the injured person or his insurers, or even by the community at large. Such a development appears to have been taking place in the United States, as can be seen from '519 of the Restatement of Torts' (2d) vol 3 (1977). The extent to which it has done so is not altogether clear; and I infer from paragraph 519, and the comment on that paragraph, that the abnormally dangerous activities there referred to are such that their ability to cause harm would be obvious to any reasonable person who carried them on.

I have to say, however, that there are serious obstacles in the way of the development of the rule in *Rylands v Fletcher* in this way. First of all, if it was so to develop, it should logically apply to liability to all persons suffering injury by reason of the ultra-hazardous operations; but the decision of this House in *Read v J Lyons & Co Ltd* [1947] AC 156; [1946] 2 All ER 471, which establishes that there can be no liability under the rule except in circumstances where the injury has been caused by an escape from land under the control of the defendant, has effectively precluded any such development. Professor Fleming has observed that 'the most damaging effect of the decision in *Read v Lyons* is that it prematurely stunted the development of a general theory of strict liability for ultra-hazardous activities' (see Fleming on *Torts*, 1992, 8th edn, p 341). Even so, there is much to be said for the view that the courts should not be proceeding down the path of developing such a general theory. In this connection, I refer in particular to the Report of the Law Commission on *Civil Liability for Dangerous Things and Activities* (Law Com No 32) 1970. In paragraphs 14–16 of the report the Law Commission expressed serious misgivings about the adoption of any test for the application of strict liability involving a general concept of 'especially dangerous' or 'ultra-hazardous' activity, having regard to the uncertainties and practical difficulties of its application. If the Law Commission is unwilling to consider statutory reform on this basis, it must follow that judges should if anything be even more reluctant to proceed down that path.

Like the judge in the present case, I incline to the opinion that, as a general rule, it is more appropriate for strict liability in respect of operations of high risk to be imposed by Parliament, than by the courts. If such liability is imposed by statute, the relevant activities can be identified, and those concerned can know where they stand. Furthermore, statute can where appropriate lay down precise criteria establishing the incidence and scope of such liability.

It is of particular relevance that the present case is concerned with environmental pollution. The protection and preservation of the environment is now perceived as being of crucial importance to the future of mankind; and public bodies, both national and international, are taking significant steps towards the establishment of legislation which will promote the protection of the environment, and make the polluter pay for damage to the environment for which he is responsible – as can be seen from the WHO, EEC and national regulations to which I have previously referred. But it does not follow from these developments that a common law principle, such as the rule in *Rylands v Fletcher*, should be developed or rendered more strict to provide for liability in respect of such pollution. On the contrary, given that so much well-informed and carefully structured legislation is now being put in place for this purpose, there is less need for the courts to develop a common law principle to achieve the same end, and indeed it may well be undesirable that they should do so.

Having regard to these considerations, and in particular to the step which this House has already taken in *Read v Lyons* to contain the scope of liability under the rule in *Rylands v Fletcher*, it appears to me to be appropriate now to take the view that foreseeability of damage of the relevant type should be regarded as a pre-requisite of liability in damages under the rule. Such a conclusion can, as I have already stated, be derived from Blackburn J's original statement of the law; and I can see no good reason why this pre-requisite should not be recognised under the rule, as it has been in the case of private nuisance. In particular, I do not regard the two authorities cited to your Lordships, *West v Bristol Tramways Co* [1908] 2 KB 14; [1908–10] All ER Rep 215 and *Rainham Chemical Works Ltd v Belvedere Fish Guano Co Ltd* [1921] 2 AC 465; [1921] All ER Rep 48, as providing any strong pointer towards a contrary conclusion. It would moreover lead to a more coherent body of common law principles if the rule were to be regarded essentially as an extension of the law of nuisance to cases of isolated escapes from land, even though the rule as established is not limited to escapes which are in fact isolated. I wish to point out, however, that in truth the escape of the PCE from ECL's land, in the form of trace elements carried in percolating water, has not been an isolated escape, but a continuing escape resulting from a state of affairs which has come into existence at the base of the chalk aquifer underneath ECL's premises. Classically, this would have been regarded as a case of nuisance; and it would seem strange if, by characterising the case as one falling under the rule in *Rylands v Fletcher*, the liability should thereby be rendered more strict in the circumstances of the present case.

The facts of the present case

Turning to the facts of the present case, it is plain that, at the time when the PCE was brought onto ECL's land, and indeed when it was used in the tanning process there, nobody at ECL could reasonably have foreseen the resultant damage which occurred at CWC's borehole at Sawston.

However, there remains for consideration a point adumbrated in the course of argument, which is relevant to liability in nuisance as well as under the rule in *Rylands v Fletcher*. It appears that, in the present case, pools of neat PCE are still in existence at the base of the chalk aquifer beneath ECL's premises, and the escape of dissolved phase PCE from ECL's land is continuing to the present day. On this basis it can be argued that, since it has become known that PCE, if it escapes, is capable of causing damage by rendering water available at boreholes unsaleable for domestic purposes, ECL could be held liable, in nuisance or under the rule in *Rylands v Fletcher*, in respect of damage caused by the continuing escape of PCE from its land occurring at any time after such damage had become foreseeable by ECL.

For my part, I do not consider that such an argument is well-founded. Here we are faced with a situation where the substance in question, PCE, has so travelled down through the drift and the chalk aquifer beneath ECL's premises that it has passed beyond the control of ECL. To impose strict liability on ECL in these circumstances, either as the creator of a nuisance or under the rule in *Rylands v Fletcher*, on the ground that it has subsequently become reasonably foreseeable that the PCE may, if it escapes, cause damage, appears to me to go beyond the scope of the regimes imposed under either of these two related heads of liability. This is because when ECL created the conditions which have ultimately led to the present state of affairs – whether by bringing the PCE in question onto its land, or by retaining it there, or by using it in its tanning process – it could not possibly have foreseen that damage of the type now complained of might be caused thereby. Indeed, long before the relevant legislation came into force, the PCE had become irretrievably lost in the ground below. In such circumstances, I do not consider that ECL should be under any greater liability than that imposed for negligence. At best, if the case is regarded as one of nuisance, it should be treated no differently from, for example, the case of the landslip in *Leakey v National Trust for Places of Historic Interest or Natural Beauty* [1980] QB 485; [1980] 1 All ER 17.

I wish to add that the present case may be regarded as one of what is nowadays called historic pollution, in the sense that the relevant occurrence (the seepage of PCE through the floor of ECL's premises) took place before the relevant legislation came into force; and it appears that, under the current philosophy, it is not envisaged that statutory liability should be imposed for historic pollution (see, for example, the Council of Europe's Draft Convention on Civil Liability for Damages Resulting from Activities Dangerous to the Environment (Strasbourg, 29 January 1993) Article 5.1, and paragraph 48 of the Explanatory Report). If so, it would be strange if liability for such pollution were to arise under a principle of common law.

In the result, since those responsible at ECL could not at the relevant time reasonably have foreseen that the damage in question might occur, the claim of CWC for damages under the rule in *Rylands v Fletcher* must fail.

Natural use of land

I turn to the question whether the use by ECL of its land in the present case constituted a natural use, with the result that ECL cannot be held liable under the rule in *Rylands v Fletcher*. In view of my conclusion on the issue of foreseeability, I can deal with this point shortly.

The judge held that it was a natural use. He said:

> In my judgment, in considering whether the storage of organochlorines as an adjunct to a manufacturing process is a non-natural use of land, I must consider whether that storage created special risks for adjacent occupiers and whether the activity was for the general benefit of the community. It seems to me inevitable that I must consider the magnitude of the storage and the geographical area in which it takes place in answering the question. Sawston is properly described as an industrial village, and the creation of employment is clearly for the benefit of that community. I do not believe that I can enter upon an assessment of the point on a scale of desirability that the manufacture of wash leathers comes, and I content myself with holding that this storage in this place is a natural use of land.

It is a commonplace that this particular exception to liability under the rule has developed and changed over the years. It seems clear that in *Rylands v Fletcher* (1866) LR 1 Ex 265 itself Blackburn J's statement of the law was limited to things which are brought by the defendant onto his land, and so did not apply to things that were naturally upon the land. Furthermore, it is doubtful whether in the House of Lords in the same case Lord Cairns, to whom we owe the expression 'non-natural use' of the land, was intending to expand the concept of natural use beyond that envisaged by Blackburn J. Even so, the law has long since departed from any such simple idea, redolent of a different age; and, at least since the advice of the Privy Council delivered by Lord Moulton in *Rickards v Lothian* [1913] AC 263 at 280, [1911–13] All ER Rep 71 at 80, natural use has been extended to embrace the ordinary use of land. I ask to be forgiven if I again quote Lord Moulton's statement of the law, which has lain at the heart of the subsequent development of this exception:

> It is not every use to which land is put that brings into play at that principle. It must be some special use bringing with it increased danger to others, and must not merely be the ordinary use of the land or such a use as is proper for the general benefit of the community.

Rickards v Lothian itself was concerned with a use of a domestic kind, viz the overflow of water from a basin whose runaway had become blocked. But over the years the concept of natural use, in the sense of ordinary use, has been extended to embrace a wide variety of uses, including not only domestic uses but also recreational uses and even some industrial uses. It is obvious that the expression 'ordinary use of the land' in Lord Moulton's statement of the law is one which is lacking in precision. There are some writers who welcome the flexibility which has thus been introduced into this branch of the law, on the ground that it enables judges to mould and adapt the principle of strict liability to the changing needs of society; whereas others regret the perceived absence of principle in so vague a concept, and fear that the whole idea of strict liability may as a result be undermined. A particular doubt is introduced by Lord Moulton's alternative criterion 'or such a use as is proper for the general benefit of the community'. If these words are understood to refer to a local community, they can be given some content as intended to refer to such matters as, for example, the provision of services; indeed the same idea can, without too much difficulty, be extended to, for example, the provision of services to industrial premises, as in a business park or an industrial estate. But if the words are extended to embrace the wider interests of the local community or the general benefit of the community at large, it is difficult to see how the exception can be kept within reasonable bounds. A notable extension was considered in your Lordships' House in *Read v J Lyons & Co Ltd* [1946] 2 All ER 471, pp 475, 478; [1947] AC 156, pp 169–70, 174, *per* Viscount Simon and Lord Macmillan, where it was suggested that, in time of war, the manufacture of explosives might be held to constitute a natural use of land, apparently on the basis that, in a country in which the greater part of the population was involved in the war effort, many otherwise exceptional uses might become 'ordinary' for the duration of the war. It is however unnecessary to consider so wide an extension as that in a case such as the present. Even so, we can see the introduction of another extension in the present case, when the judge invoked the creation of employment as clearly for the benefit of the local community, viz 'the industrial village' at Sawston. I myself, however, do not feel able to accept that the creation of employment as such, even in a small industrial complex, is sufficient of itself to establish a particular use as constituting a natural or ordinary use of land.

Fortunately, I do not think it is necessary for the purposes of the present case to attempt any redefinition of the concept of natural or ordinary use. This is because I am satisfied that the storage of chemicals in substantial quantities, and their use in the manner employed at ECL's premises, cannot fall within the exception. For the purpose of testing the point, let it be assumed that ECL was well aware of the possibility that PCE, if it escaped, could indeed cause damage, for example by contaminating any water with which it became mixed so as to render that water undrinkable by human beings. I cannot think that it would be right in such circumstances to exempt ECL from liability under the rule in *Rylands v Fletcher* on the ground that the use was natural or ordinary. The mere fact that the use is common in the tanning industry cannot, in my opinion, be enough to bring the use within the exception, nor the fact that Sawston contains a small industrial community which is worthy of encouragement or support. Indeed I feel bound to say that the storage of substantial quantities of chemicals on industrial premises should be regarded as an almost classic case of non-natural use; and I find it very difficult to think that it should be thought objectionable to impose strict liability for damage caused in the event of their escape. It may well be that, now that it is recognised that foreseeability of harm of the relevant type is a pre-requisite of liability in damages under the rule, the courts may feel less pressure to extend the concept of natural use to circumstances such as those in the present case; and in due course it may become easier to control this exception, and to ensure that it has a more recognisable basis of principle. For these reasons, I would not hold that ECL should be exempt from liability on the basis of the exception of natural use.

However, for the reasons I have already given, I would allow ECL's appeal with costs before your Lordships' House and in the courts below.

For commentary on the *Cambridge Water* case, see Driscoll J (1994) 144 NLJ 64; Cross, (1995) III LQR 421. For a recent application of the foreseeability test, see *Savage v Fairclough* [2000] Env LR 183. Here it was held that a pig farmer could not have reasonably foreseen nitrate contamination of the plaintiff's water supply.

Water pollution legislation

Prior to the Water Act 1989, water pollution was the responsibility of 10 regional water authorities who were empowered to issue discharge consents to those wishing to use watercourses as a means of disposing of waste. Three main criticisms were levelled at this system. First, the water authorities had regional jurisdiction which meant that the consents varied from region to region reflecting local needs and conditions. Secondly, because the water authorities were also responsible for sewage disposal there was an inevitable conflict of interest with the pollution control functions. Thirdly, the roles of the regional water authorities and their culture derived from a time when environmental standards and expectations were low. The result was very poor water quality.

England's current water pollution regime is principally contained in the Environment Act 1995 and the Water Resources Act (WRA) 1991. This latter Act replaced the Water Act 1989 and consolidated previous water pollution legislation. Under the WRA discharge consents are granted by the Environment Agency (EA) which has a national jurisdiction and a purely regulatory function, that is, there is no conflict of interest between the privatised water companies charged with water supply and sewage disposal and the EA. The ultimate aim of the legislation is to achieve national water quality objectives and the EA is given substantial preventive and enforcement powers to attain that end.

Although this section of the chapter is mainly concerned with the powers of the EA in relation to water pollution control, it is important to be aware that statute has imposed various other responsibilities upon the EA which have an important impact upon the aquatic environment. Similarly the role of the privatised water industry and its regulator deserves some mention.

Environment Agency

When discharging its functions the EA must bear in mind s 4 of the Environment Act 1995 which sets out its principal aim and objective. This is 'to protect or enhance the environment, taken as a whole, as to make the contribution towards the objective of achieving sustainable development'. It should also take account of its general duty which appears in s 39 to have regard to costs and benefits in exercising its powers.

Water resource management

Section 6 of the Environment Act 1995 and s 19 of the WRA 1991 impose two duties upon the EA when exercising its function of managing water resources. These are (1) to conserve, re-distribute, augment and secure the proper use of water resources in England and Wales and (2) to promote the conservation and enhancement of the natural beauty and amenity of inland and coastal waters; the conservation of flora and fauna which are dependent upon the aquatic environment and the use of such waters and land for recreational purposes taking into account the needs of chronically sick and disabled persons.

Section 20 of the WRA 1991 imposes a duty upon the EA to make water resource management schemes with water undertakers. Section 21 of the WRA 1991 empowers the

EA to submit draft minimum acceptable flow[39] statements for inland waters to the Secretary of State bearing in mind its general environmental duties and the need to attain water quality objectives.

Licences to abstract water

Chapter II, Pt II of the WRA 1991 deals with licences to abstract water. Section 24 generally prohibits the abstraction of water from any source of supply save in pursuance of a licence.

Droughts

Chapter III allows the Secretary of State to deal with droughts by issuing 'ordinary drought orders' (s 73(1)) or 'emergency drought orders' (s 73(2)) usually on the basis of a request from the EA or a water undertaker.[40] The Environment Act 1995 introduced a new system of 'drought permits' (s 79A of the WRA 1991) which are issued by the EA when there is a serious deficiency or threatened deficiency of water supplies due to an exceptional shortage of rain.

Water companies

Responsibility for the supply and quality control of water and for sewage collection and control was passed into the private sector by the Water Act 1989. The ten water and sewage companies and fifteen water only companies in England and Wales are responsible for the supply of drinking water and the collection, treatment and disposal of sewage. They are subject to the administrative control of the Water Industry Act 1991. In particular, they are regulated by the Office of Water Services (OFWAT) which is headed by the Director General of Water Services.

Director-General of Water Services

The role of the Director-General of Water Services is in essence, to ensure that water companies provide a fair and efficient service and in so doing he controls price increases and supervises their investment programmes. Since such investment is crucial in ensuring that water quality objectives are met, he plays an important environmental role. Through his price fixing role, he ensures that the water companies have available to them the funds necessary to meet water quality objectives set by the Secretary of State.

Regulation of pollution

Section 85 of the WRA 1991 contains a series of inter-related criminal offences committed by polluting 'controlled waters' which can carry a maximum sentence on indictment of

---

39   See WRA 1991, Sched 5.
40   *Ibid*, Sched 8.

two years' imprisonment and/or an unlimited fine (s 85(6)).[41] Section 85 offences only apply to discharges into 'controlled waters' as defined in s 104 to include almost all inland and coastal water and all territorial waters out to a prescribed distance. The section follows earlier statutes[42] by requiring a guilty person to have 'caused' or 'knowingly permitted' the material to have entered controlled waters.[43] In effect, the statute has created two separate offences within each sub-section; (a) causing and (b) knowingly permitting the entry.[44]

In *Empress Car Co (Abertillery) Ltd v National Rivers Authority* [1998] 1 All ER 481 (see p 308, below) Lord Hoffmann explained the difference between the two sub-sections as follows:

> Putting the matter shortly, if the charge is 'causing', the prosecution must prove that the pollution was caused by something which the defendant did, rather than merely failed to prevent. It is, however, very important to notice that this requirement is not because of anything inherent in the notion of 'causing'. It is because of the structure of the sub-section which imposes liability under two separate heads: the first limb simply for doing something which causes the pollution and the second for knowingly failing to prevent the pollution. The notion of causing is present in both limbs: under the first limb, what the defendant did must have caused the pollution and under the second limb, his omission must have caused it. The distinction in s 85(1) between acts and omissions is entirely due to the fact that Parliament has added the requirement of knowledge when the cause of the pollution is an omission. Liability under the first limb, without proof of knowledge, therefore requires that the defendant must have done something.

The offence of 'causing' pollution has been the subject of extensive judicial interpretation. In *Alphacell v Woodward*[45] Lord Wilberforce stated that the term 'cause' should be given a 'commonsense meaning'. In this case, polluted water flowed into controlled waters from a settling tank during the operation of the appellant's industrial process because pumps which would have returned the liquid to the factory for re-use became blocked by brambles, ferns and other detritus. The House of Lords took the view that 'cause' did not require proof of *mens rea*. The appellants were held liable merely because their industrial process had caused the pollution of controlled waters. The *Alphacell* approach has been followed in subsequent cases including *Southern Water Authority v Pegrum*[46] where a blocked storm drain caused water to flow into a lagoon containing effluent from a pig farm. This in turn caused seepage into a stream which led into the River Medway. Although it was suggested that ingress of water was an intervening act which broke the

---

41   The offence presently found in s 85(1) is committed when 'poisonous, noxious or polluting matter or any solid waste matter' enters controlled waters. The Act does not define these terms. In *NRA v Egger (UK)* [1992] 4 LMELR 130, polluting matter was interpreted to include matter 'capable of causing harm in that it may damage a river's potential usefulness'. 'Damage' in this context meant 'harm to animal, vegetable or other life in a river and/or aesthetic damage'.

42   Eg Rivers (Prevention of Pollution) Act 1951, s 2(1).

43   For a discussion of causation on pollution offences, see Padfield, N, 'Clear water and muddy causation: is causation a question of law or fact or just a way of allocating blame?' [1995] Crim LR 683.

44   The phrase was interpreted disjunctively in *McLeod v Buchanan* [1940] 2 All ER 179.

45   [1972] AC 824, p 834.

46   [1989] Crim LR 442.

chain of causation (an act of God) the court decided that an offence had been committed as the positive act of pig farming had 'caused' the entry into controlled waters.[47]

Some of the most difficult issues occur in situations where a third party has interfered with plant or equipment. In *National Rivers Authority v Wright Engineering Co Ltd* [1994] 4 All ER 281 vandals broke the sight gauge on a tank storing oil over the Christmas period with the result that oil escaped from the tank into a brook. On the facts, it was proved that vandalism had taken place on previous occasions at the engineering works and so the company was aware that their site was a target for vandals. Although they had taken no steps to protect the gauge from being vandalised, the chain of causation was still found to have been broken because the past acts of vandalism had been on a smaller scale and of a different type than the present incident which was therefore not reasonably foreseeable.

In *National Rivers Authority v Yorkshire Water Services* [1995] 1 All ER 225 a third party had placed a slug of iso-octonol into the sewers which had passed into controlled waters through the defendant's sewage treatment works. In the House of Lords, the defendant company was found to have 'caused' the entry even though it could not reasonably have prevented the entry of the iso-octonol into the sewers on its works and was unaware of its presence. It had 'caused' the entry merely by establishing a system whereby effluent entered controlled waters via its plant and the fact that a third party had also 'caused' the entry (and could have been prosecuted) did not mean that the defendant had not done so as well.[48] (see also *Attorney General's Reference (No 1 of 1994)* [1995] 2 All ER 1007.)

The issue was revisited by the House of Lords in the *Empress Cars* case (p 308, below). The Empress Car Co maintained a diesel tank which drained directly into a river. The tank was surrounded by a bund to contain spillage, but the company had overriden this protection by fixing an extension pipe connecting the tank to a drum situated next to the bund. The outlet from the tank was governed by a tap which had no lock. The tap was opened by a person unknown and the entire contents of the tank ran into the drum, which overflowed and passed down a drain into the river. The Company was found to have caused the pollution. They appealed unsuccessfully first to the Divisional Court and then to the House of Lords. Lord Hoffmann drew the distinction between events which are normal or familiar and events which are abnormal and extraordinary:

> The true commonsense distinction is, in my view, between acts and events which, although not necessarily foreseeable in the particular case, are in the generality a normal and familiar fact of life, and acts or events which are abnormal and extraordinary. Of course an act or event which is in general terms a normal fact of life may also have been foreseeable in the circumstances of the particular case, but the latter is not necessary for the purposes of liability. There is nothing extraordinary or abnormal about leaky pipes or lagoons as such: these things happen, even if the particular defendant could not reasonably have foreseen that it would happen to him. There is nothing unusual about people putting unlawful substances into the sewage system and the same, regrettably, is true about ordinary vandalism. So when these things happen, one does not say: that was an extraordinary coincidence, which negatived the causal connection between the original act of

---

47 See also *Wrothwell Ltd v Yorkshire Water Authority* [1984] Crim LR 43 and *Lockhart v National Coal Board* [1981] SCCR 9.

48 The House of Lords actually overturned the defendant's conviction due to the special defence available to sewerage undertakers now contained in WRA 1991, s 87(2).

accumulating the polluting substance and its escape. In the context of s 85(1), the defendant's accumulation has still caused the pollution. On the other hand, the example I gave of the terrorist attack would be something so unusual that one would not regard the defendant's conduct as having caused the escape at all.

On the facts, applying this approach, there was 'ample evidence' for finding that Empress Cars caused the pollution.[49]

Much less judicial scrutiny has been applied to the phrase 'knowingly permits'. The leading case is *Schulmans Inc v National Rivers Authority*[50] where the appellants were acquitted of knowingly permitting fuel oil from a tank on their premises to enter controlled waters on the basis that they could not have prevented the escape sooner than they did and at no point was there an escape that they could have prevented but failed to prevent. Although absence of knowledge is a defence, the case is authority for the right of the court to infer that knowledge in appropriate circumstances, that is, actual or constructive knowledge is necessary to commit the offence.[51]

Defences

Various defences to the s 85 offences appear in ss 87–89. Generally under s 88, no offence is committed if a discharge is, *inter alia*, in accordance with a permit issued by the EA under the WRA 1991. Section 89 contains a somewhat disparate list of specific defences, including discharges to avoid damage to life or health, provided reasonable steps are taken to 'minimise the extent of the entry or its polluting effect'.

Discharge consents

The issue of discharge consents is the responsibility of the EA which must act in accordance with the detailed provisions of Sched 10 of the WRA 1991. Applications are made to the EA and must contain such information as the EA may reasonably require (para 1) including the amount, location, rate of flow etc of the discharge. There is a requirement for such applications to be publicised and local authorities and water undertakers must be informed.[52] The EA must consider any written objections or representations made within six weeks of publication. It is then empowered to give consent conditionally or unconditionally or refuse it altogether whilst informing those who made representations of its decision. They are then given 21 days to request the Secretary of State to call in the application (paras 3, 4).

Any conditions attached may include those specified in para 2(5) including place of discharge, nature, temperature, volume, rate etc. The consent and the conditions

---

49 [1972] AC 824, p 834.

50 [1992] 4 LMELR 130.

51 Cf *Wing v Nuttall* (1997) *The Times*, 30 April. An employer's failure to check a tachograph could be viewed as so reckless that knowledge of an offence could be implied.

52 This publicity can be dispensed with where the EA considers that the proposed discharge will have no appreciable effect upon the waters concerned (para 1(5)). The applicant may also ask the Secretary of State for a certificate waiving the publicity requirements on the grounds of protecting a trade secret or that it would be in the public interest (para 1(7)).

attaching to the consent must be periodically reviewed by the EA (para 6(1)) although consents must specify a period during which no notice of revocation, modification or additional conditions may be served (para 7). Provision for appeal to the Secretary of State against the refusal of consent or against conditions attaching to the consent is found in s 91. The EA charges fees intended to cover the cost of issuing and monitoring discharge consents and their impact on controlled waters: an example of the polluter pays principle in operation.

A discharge consent granted to Welsh Water for the discharge of sewage from Tenby was the subject of a judicial review application in *R v National Rivers Authority ex p Moreton* (see p 331, below).[53] A new consent requiring sewage to be pumped by a pipeline to a point 2.7km from land (it had previously been discharged at a point just below low water) was challenged by a swimmer who wanted the new consent quashed and an injunction because the NRA had not required ultraviolet disinfection as a condition of consent. The application was dismissed, the court stating that it was a proper exercise of the NRA's discretion to take into account Welsh Water's financial limitations when considering the benefits of ultraviolet disinfection.

Ministerial Regulations – water quality classification and objectives

As previously discussed, the EC has established water quality criteria in respect of different water uses and this approach is reflected in the WRA 1991. Section 82 empowers the Secretary of State to prescribe a system of classifying the quality of any description of controlled waters.

The following sets of regulations have been adopted:

- Surface Waters (Dangerous Substances) (Classification) Regulations SI 1989/2286, SI 1992/337, SI 1997/2560, SI 1998/389;

- Bathing Waters (Classification) Regulations 1991 SI 1991/1597;

- Surface Waters (River ecosystem) (Classification) Regulations 1994 SI 1994/1057;

- Surface Waters (Abstraction for Drinking Water) (Classification) Regulations 1996 SI 1996/3001;

- Surface Waters (Shellfish) (Classification) Regulations 1997 SI 1997/1332;

- Surface Waters (Fishlife) (Classification) Regulations 1997 SI 1997/1331.

Section 83 allows for statutory water quality objectives (SWQOs) to be set for particular stretches of controlled waters using the water quality classifications made under s 82. It is the role of the Secretary of State to establish the SWQOs which the EA must bear in mind when issuing consents. Section 84 requires the Secretary of State and the EA when exercising their respective powers under the WRA to ensure that 'so far as practicable' the water quality of objectives specified for water under s 83 are achieved at all times. The Agency has been putting pressure on the government to establish legally binding targets for improving water quality in at least eight river catchments as a 'matter of urgency'.[54]

---

53 [1996] Env LR 234.
54 EA New releases 93–96, 1 November 1996.

The only objectives currently established partly under s 83 are the previously mentioned Surface Waters (Dangerous Substances) (Classification) Regulations 1989 and 1992 which the EA must incorporate into the discharge consents procedure.

Anti-pollution works

Section 161 empowers the EA to carry out any works/operations necessary to prevent the pollution of controlled waters where no-one can be found to be served with a works notice under s 161A. This is an important instance of the preventive principle and also the polluter pays principle in that the EA may then recover expenses 'reasonably incurred' from any person who caused or knowingly permitted the matter to enter or threaten entry into controlled waters. Such expenses are likely to be considerable and are in addition to any fine imposed for committing a s 85 offence. The current regulations are the Anti-Pollution Works Regulations 1999/1006.

Prevention of pollution

Under s 92 of the WRA 1991, the Secretary of State has power to make regulations prohibiting a person from having custody or control of any noxious, poisonous or polluting matter unless certain prescribed works are carried out to prevent or control the entry of such material into controlled waters or requiring a person already in custody or control of such matter to effect such works. The Control of Pollution (Silage, Slurry and Agricultural Fuel) Regulations S1 1991/324 have been made under s 92. The application of these regulations is entrusted to the EA. It may, for example, require action in relation to the storage of certain fuel oil to ensure controlled waters are not polluted.

Section 93 allows the Secretary of State to designate areas as Water Protection Zones (WPZ's) (after consultation with the Ministry of Agriculture, Fisheries and Food (MAFF) (now DEFRA) with a view to preventing or controlling the entry of any poisonous, noxious or polluting matter into controlled waters, or to prohibit or restrict activities within the area likely to result in such pollution. Once a WPZ designation is in place, the EA is empowered to determine the circumstances when particular activities are prohibited or when restrictions or conditions should attach to such activities. The designation procedure is set out in Sched 11 of the WRA 1991. As yet no such Zones have been designated. Section 94 provides a further power for the Secretary of State and the Minister of Agriculture, Fisheries and Foods jointly to designate an area as a nitrate sensitive area (NSA). Although this power overlaps with s 93 the proscribed activities in an NSA would be agricultural activities likely to cause nitrates to enter controlled waters – mainly the use of inorganic fertilisers. For a designation to be made, the request must be made by the EA which must be of the opinion that its other powers to prevent nitrates entering controlled waters in the area are insufficient. Orders may be voluntary or mandatory and s 95 provides for management agreements in the case of voluntary orders with provision for compensation. mandatory orders are made in accordance with the procedure set out in Sched 12 of the WRA 1991.

The Protection of Water Against Agricultural and Nitrate Pollution (England & Wales) Regulations SI 1996/888 have implemented Directive 91/676 (Nitrates Directive, see p 269, above). The Minister is required to draw up action programmes within Nitrate

Vulnerable Zones in order to achieve the aims set out in Art 1: to reduce water pollution caused or induced by nitrates and agricultural sources and to prevent further pollution.

Public registers

The EA is required to keep registers containing the prescribed particulars set out in s 190(1) of the WRA 1991. Such registers must be open to inspection free of charge by the public 'at all reasonable times' (s 190(2)). The public must be afforded reasonable facilities for obtaining copies of entries in the register on payment of a reasonable fee (s 190(3)). Persons seeking exemption from these registration requirements must apply to the Secretary of State on the grounds of public interest or protection of a trade secret (para 1(7), Sched 10). Such public registers are particularly useful to environmental groups independently monitoring water quality standards. For public registers in other contexts see Chapter 4, p 442 (waste) and Chapter 5, pp 509–10, 556 (IPC).

Quality of water supplies

Section 68 of the Water Industry Act 1991 requires water undertakers to provide wholesome water and s 70 makes it is an offence for a water undertaker to supply water that is unfit for human consumption. Sections 67 and 69 enable the Secretary of State to make regulations which prescribe the requirements for wholesomeness and set out the steps water undertakers must take to comply with the s 68 duty. The Water Supply (Water Quality) Regulations 2000 SI 2000/3184 revoke the Water Supply (Water Quality) Regulations 1989 SI 1989/1147 as from 1 January 2004, and amend them until that date. These Regulations are primarily concerned with the quality of water supplied in England for drinking, washing, cooking and food preparation. They also concern arrangements for the publication of information about water quality. The Regulations are designed to achieve the objective set out in Art 2 of Directive 98/83 (see p 232, above), namely to protect human health from the adverse effects of any contamination of water intended for human consumption by ensuring that it is wholesome and clean. In particular, they give effect (Pt III of the Regulations) to Arts 4 and 5 of the 1998 Directive which relate to the quality of water intended for human consumption and Art 7 (monitoring, Pt V of the Regulations).

Part III (reg 4) prescribes standards of wholesomeness in respect of water that is supplied by water undertakers for cooking, drinking, food preparation and washing and other domestic purposes and to premises for food production purposes (reg 4(1) purposes). Regulation 4 provides that water is to be regarded as wholesome if it contains concentrations or values in respect of various properties, elements, organisms and substances that do not contravene prescribed maximum and, in some cases, minimum concentrations or values. Some of the prescribed maximum and minimum concentrations and values are specified in reg 4, but most are included in Tables A and B which appear in Sched 1 to the Regulations. They include the values specified in Pts A and B of Annex 1 to the 1998 Directive. There are also specifications for indicator parameters in Sched 2. Part IV (regs 5 to 10) provides for the monitoring of water supplies by analysis of samples. Regulation 5 defines two monitoring regimes: 'audit' monitoring and 'check' monitoring. Regulation 6 requires water undertakers to take a minimum number of samples each year in respect of a variety of properties, elements, organisms and substances. It also makes special provision for monitoring supplies from tankers. Regulation 7 requires water undertakers to select at random the consumers' taps from which samples are to be taken. Regulation 8 authorises the taking of samples from points other than consumers' taps ('supply points') and allows the Secretary of State to authorise other supply points. Regulation 9 deals with the number of samples to be taken. Regulation 10 requires samples to be taken where water undertakers have reason to believe that the quality of the water within their water supply zone has been adversely affected by the presence of certain elements, organisms or substances. Part V (Regs 11 to 16) contains additional provisions relating to sampling. Regulations 13 and 14 require samples to be taken in respect of particular organisms and substances, at treatment works and at reservoirs which store treated water. Regulation 15 requires samples to be taken before water is supplied from new sources and from sources which have not recently been used. Regulation 16 prescribes requirements relating to the taking, handling, storage, transport and analysis of samples. Part VI (regs 17 to 24) provides for the investigation of every failure to satisfy a concentration, value or state prescribed by reg 4 and for a report to be made to the Secretary of State. Where a failure relates to a Table B parameter, and certain other conditions are met, the Secretary of State may require the water undertaker to apply to him for an authorisation allowing a departure from the requirements of Pt III, as regards that parameter. The circumstances in which such authorisations may be issued, and the conditions to which they are subject are contained in regs 21 and 22, respectively. (Article 9 of the 1998 Directive permits derogations from the parametric values.) Provision is made in reg 23 for publicising authorisations. Regulation 24 provides for the modification and withdrawal of authorisations. Part VII (regs 25 to 33) deals with the treatment of water and regulates the substances, processes and products that may be used by water undertakers in connection with the supply of water. Regulation 26 imposes requirements relating to the disinfection of water and imposes additional requirements for the treatment of surface water. Regulations 27 to 29 relate specifically to cryptosporidium. Regulation 30 makes provision for securing the elimination or reduction to a minimum of the risk that water will be contaminated after supply by excessive concentrations of copper or lead. Regulation 31 specifies the circumstances in which water undertakers may apply or introduce substances or products into water supplied for drinking, washing or cooking. Regulation 32 enables the Secretary of State to require that his approval be obtained to the use of processes. Contravention of some of the requirements of regs 28, 29, 31 and 32 is made a criminal offence by reg 33, as is the making of false statements. Part VIII deals with the provision of information by water undertakers. Regulation 34 requires water undertakers to prepare and maintain records containing information about the quality of water supplied in their water supply zones. Regulation 35 requires each water undertaker to make available for public inspection, and to supply local authorities with, information about the quality of water within its water supply zones, the extent to which Pt IV of the Regulations has been complied with, details of any departures authorised under Pt VI of the Regulations and of the action which has been taken to comply with enforcement orders. It also requires each water undertaker to provide local authorities, health authorities and customer service committees with information relating to matters that could affect the health of persons residing in the authorities' areas. Regulation 36 requires water undertakers to publish an annual report containing information about the quality of water in the area for which it is responsible. Part X (reg 39) provides that contraventions by water undertakers of duties or requirements imposed by Parts V to VIII of the Regulations are to be enforceable under s 18 of the Water Industry Act 1991 by the Secretary of State. This provision is additional to the criminal sanctions provided by reg 33 in relation to contraventions of Regs 28 and 29, 31 and 32.

Water Resources Act 1991 (c 57)

Part III Control of Pollution of Water Resources:

Chapter I Quality objectives

Section 82 Classification of quality of waters

(1) The Secretary of State may, in relation to any description of controlled waters (being a description applying to some or all of the waters of a particular class or of two or more different classes), by regulations prescribe a system of classifying the quality of those waters according to criteria specified in the regulations.

(2) The criteria specified in regulations under this section in relation to any classification shall consist of one or more of the following, that is to say–

    (a) general requirements as to the purposes for which the waters to which the classification is applied are to be suitable;

    (b) specific requirements as to the substances that are to be present in or absent from the water and as to the concentrations of substances which are or are required to be present in the water;

    (c) specific requirements as to other characteristics of those waters;

and for the purposes of any such classification regulations under this section may provide that the question whether prescribed requirements are satisfied may be determined by reference to such samples as may be prescribed.

Section 83 Water quality objectives

(1) For the purpose of maintaining and improving the quality of controlled waters the Secretary of State may, by serving a notice on the [Agency] specifying–

    (a) one or more of the classifications for the time being prescribed under s 82 above; and

    (b) in relation to each specified classification, a date, establish the water quality objectives for any waters which are, or are included in, waters of a description prescribed for the purposes of that section.

(2) The water quality objectives for any waters to which a notice under this section relates shall be the satisfaction by those waters, on and at all times after each date specified in the notice, of the requirements which at the time of the notice were the requirements for the classification in relation to which that date is so specified.

(3) Where the Secretary of State has established water quality objectives under this section for any waters he may review objectives for those waters if–

(a) five years or more have elapsed since the service of the last notice under sub-section (1) or (6) of this section to be served in respect of those waters; or

(b) the [Agency], after consultation with such water undertakers and other persons as it considers appropriate, requests a review;

and the Secretary of State shall not exercise his power to establish objectives for any waters by varying the existing objectives for those waters except in consequence of such a review.

(4) Where the Secretary of State proposes to exercise his power under this section to establish or vary the objectives for any waters he shall–

(a) give notice setting out his proposal and specifying the period (not being less than three months from the date of publication of the notice) within which representations or objections with respect to the proposal may be made; and

(b) consider any representations or objections which are duly made and not withdrawn;

and, if he decides, after considering any such representations or objections, to exercise his power to establish or vary those objectives, he may do so either in accordance with the proposal contained in the notice or in accordance with that proposal as modified in such manner as he considers appropriate.

(5) A notice under sub-section (4) above shall be given–

(a) by publishing the notice in such manner as the Secretary of State considers appropriate for bringing it to the attention of persons likely to be affected by it; and

(b) by serving a copy of the notice on the [Agency].

(6) If, on a review under this section or in consequence of any representations or objections made following such a review for the purposes of sub-section (4) above, the Secretary of State decides that the water quality objectives for any waters should remain unchanged, he shall serve notice of that decision on the [Agency].

Section 84 General duties to achieve and maintain objectives etc

(1) It shall be the duty of the Secretary of State and of the [Agency] to exercise the powers conferred on him or it by or under the water pollution provisions of this Act (other than the preceding provisions of this chapter and ss 104 and 192 below) in such manner as ensures, so far as it is practicable by the exercise of those powers to do so, that the water quality objectives specified for any waters in–

(a) a notice under s 83 above; or

(b) a notice under s 30C of the Control of Pollution Act 1974 (which makes corresponding provision for Scotland),

are achieved at all times.

(2) It shall be the duty of the [Agency], for the purposes of the carrying out of its functions under the water pollution provisions of this Act–

(a) to monitor the extent of pollution in controlled waters; and

(b) to consult, in such cases as it may consider appropriate, with [the Scottish Environment Protection Agency] in Scotland.

Section 85 Offences of polluting controlled waters

(1) A person contravenes this section if he causes or knowingly permits any poisonous, noxious or polluting matter or any solid waste matter to enter any controlled waters.

(2) A person contravenes this section if he causes or knowingly permits any matter, other than trade effluent or sewage effluent, to enter controlled waters by being discharged from a drain or sewer in contravention of a prohibition imposed under s 86 below.

(3) A person contravenes this section if he causes or knowingly permits any trade effluent or sewage effluent to be discharged–

    (a) into any controlled waters; or

    (b) from land in England and Wales, through a pipe, into the sea outside the seaward limits of controlled waters.

(4) A person contravenes this section if he causes or knowingly permits any trade effluent or sewage effluent to be discharged, in contravention of any prohibition imposed under section 86 below, from a building or from any fixed plant–

    (a) on to or into any land; or

    (b) into any waters of a lake or pond which are not inland freshwaters.

(5) A person contravenes this section if he causes or knowingly permits any matter whatever to enter any inland freshwaters so as to tend (either directly or in combination with other matter which he or another person causes or permits to enter those waters) to impede the proper flow of the waters in a manner leading, or likely to lead, to a substantial aggravation of–

    (a) pollution due to other causes; or

    (b) the consequences of such pollution.

(6) Subject to the following provisions of this chapter, a person who contravenes this section or the conditions of any consent given under this chapter for the purposes of this section shall be guilty of an offence and liable–

    (a) on summary conviction, to imprisonment for a term not exceeding three months or to a fine not exceeding 20,000 or to both;

    (b on conviction on indictment, to imprisonment for a term not exceeding two years or to a fine or to both.

Empress Car Co (Abertillery) Ltd v National Rivers Authority **[1999] 2 AC 22; [1998] 2 WLR 350 (HL); [1998] 1 All ER 481**

The following is an extract from the judgment of Lord Hoffmann [with whom Lords Brown-Wilkinson Lloyd, Nolan agreed; Lord Clyde delivered a separate concurring judgment]

My Lords, Empress Car Co (Abertillery) Ltd (the company) was convicted at the Crown Court at Newport, Gwent ... of 'causing poisonous, noxious or polluting matter or solid waste to enter controlled waters' contrary to s 85(1) of the Water Resources Act 1991 ... The company was originally convicted by the Tredegar justices and appealed to the Crown Court. Its appeal from the Crown Court to the Divisional Court by way of case stated was also dismissed. It now appeals to your Lordships' House.

The facts as found in the case stated may be summarised as follows. The company maintained a diesel tank in a yard which was drained directly into the river. The tank was surrounded by a bund to contain spillage, but the company had overridden this protection by fixing an extension pipe to the outlet of the tank so as to connect it to a drum standing outside the bund. It appears to have been more convenient to draw oil from the drum than directly from the tank. The outlet from the tank was governed by a tap which had no lock. On 20 March 1995 the tap was opened by a person unknown and the entire contents of the tank ran into the drum, overflowed into the yard and passed down the drain into the river.

The Crown Court found that there was a history of local opposition to the company's business. The tap might have been turned on by a malicious intruder, an aggrieved visitor or an upset local person. The incident coincided with a public inquiry about a disputed footpath which was to be held on the following day. But the court made no finding as to the identity of the person who turned on the tap. The evidence was consistent with it having been an employee or a stranger. The court held that it did not matter because on either view the company had 'caused' the oil to enter the river. In the case stated, the court gave the following reasons:

8   ... The Appellant had brought the oil onto the site and put it in a tank with wholly inadequate arrangements for withdrawal – outside the bund. We had regard to the nature and position of the bund, the inability of the tap to be locked and the inadequacy of the bund to contain overflow in the circumstances which happened, whether they were deliberate or negligent or careless.

9   The Appellant should have foreseen that interference with their plant and equipment was an ever-present possibility, and they failed to take the simple precaution of putting on a proper lock and a proper bund and this was a significant cause of the escape even if the major cause was third party interference.

The company's case before the Divisional Court was that if the evidence was consistent with the tap having been opened by a stranger, it should have been acquitted. The escape would have been caused by the stranger and not the company. The Divisional Court disagreed, saying that although it would be true to say that the escape had been caused by the stranger, it was open to the Crown Court to find that it had also been caused by the company. But they said that the authorities on the subject were not easy to reconcile and certified the following point of general public importance:

Whether a person can be convicted of an offence under s 85(1) of the Water Resources Act 1991 of causing polluting matter to enter controlled waters if it is proved that: (a) he held the polluting matter and contained it in such a way as it would not escape but for a positive act by himself or another; and (b) he failed to take reasonable precautions to prevent such an escape occurring as a result of an action by a third party; and it is not proved that he took any other actions which resulted in the pollution.

Before your Lordships, Mr Philpott for the company repeated his submission that the cause of the escape was not the keeping of the oil by the company but the opening of the tap by the stranger. He also said that 'causing' for the purposes of s 85(1) required some positive act and that the escape could not be said to have been caused by any such act by the company. All it had done was to create a state of affairs in which someone else could cause the oil to escape. There are accordingly two issues in the case. The first is whether there has to have been some 'positive act' by the company and, if so, whether the company did such an act. The second is whether what it did 'caused' the oil to enter the river.

(1) *Acts and omissions*

My Lords, the two limbs of s 2(1)(a) of the Rivers (Prevention of Pollution) Act 1951, which was in the same terms as s 85(1) of the 1991 Act, were analysed by Lord Wilberforce in *Alphacell Ltd v Woodward* [1972] AC 824, p 834; [1972] 2 All ER 475, p 479:

> The sub-section evidently contemplates two things – causing, which must involve some active operation or chain of operations involving as a result the pollution of the stream; knowingly permitting, which involves a failure to prevent the pollution, which failure, however, must be accompanied by knowledge.

Putting the matter shortly, if the charge is 'causing', the prosecution must prove that the pollution was caused by something which the defendant did, rather than merely failed to prevent. It is, however, very important to notice that this requirement is not because of anything inherent in the notion of 'causing'. It is because of the structure of the sub-section which imposes liability under two separate heads: the first limb simply for doing something which causes the pollution and the second for knowingly failing to prevent the pollution. The notion of causing is present in both limbs: under the first limb, what the defendant did must have caused the pollution and under the second limb, his omission must have caused it. The distinction in s 85(1) between acts and omissions is entirely due to the fact that Parliament has added the requirement of knowledge when the cause of the pollution is an omission. Liability under the first limb, without proof of knowledge, therefore requires that the defendant must have done something.

In this sense, Mr Philpott is right in saying that there must have been some 'positive act' by the company. But what counts as a positive act? We were referred to two cases in which the defendant's conduct had been held to be insufficient. In *Price v Cromack* [1975] 2 All ER 113, [1975] 1 WLR 988 the defendant maintained two lagoons on his land into which, pursuant to an agreement, the owners of adjoining land discharged effluent. The lagoons developed leaks which allowed the effluent to escape into the river. Lord Widgery CJ said that the escape had not been caused by anything which the defendant had done. There was no 'positive act' on his part. The effluent came onto the land by gravity and found its way into the stream by gravity 'with no act on his part whatever' (see [1975] 2 All ER 113 at 118, [1975] 1 WLR 988 at 994). The other case is *Wychavon DC v National Rivers Authority* [1993] 1 WLR 125; [1993] 2 All ER 440. The council maintained the sewage system in its district as agent for the statutory authority, the Severn Trent Water Authority. It operated, maintained and repaired the sewers. As sewage authority, it received raw sewage into its sewers. On the occasion in question one of the sewers became blocked. The sewage flowed into the stormwater drainage system and into the River Avon. The Divisional Court held that the council had not done any positive act which caused the pollution. If it had known of the blockage it might have been liable for 'knowingly permitting' but it could not be liable for causing.

My Lords, in my opinion these two cases take far too restrictive a view of the requirement that the defendant must have done something. They seem to require that his positive act should have been in some sense the immediate cause of the escape. But the Act contains no such requirement. It only requires a finding that something which the defendant did caused the pollution. I shall come later to the question of what amounts to causing. Assuming, for the moment, that there was a sufficient causal connection between the maintaining of the lagoons in *Price v Cromack* or the operation of the sewage system in *Wychavon DC v National Rivers Authority* and the respective escapes, I do not see why the justices were not entitled to say that the pollution was caused by something which the defendants did. Maintaining lagoons of effluent or operating the municipal sewage system is doing something.

In *National Rivers Authority v Yorkshire Water Services Ltd* [1995] 1 AC 444; [1995] 1 All ER 225 the House was invited to say that the law had 'taken a wrong turning' in the requirement of a 'positive act' as formulated in *Price v Cromack* and *Wychavon DC v National Rivers Authority*. Lord Mackay of Clashfern LC said that he regarded those cases as turning on their own facts but added that the word 'cause' should be used in its ordinary sense and that 'it is not right as a matter of law to add further requirements' (see [1995] 1 All ER 225 at 232, [1995] 1 AC 444 at 452). In *Attorney General's Reference (No 1 of 1994)* [1995] 2 All ER 1007 at 1018, [1995] 1 WLR 599 at 615 Lord Taylor of Gosforth CJ in the Court of Appeal said, in my view rightly, that the insistence in *Price v Cromack* and *Wychavon DC v National Rivers Authority* on a positive act as the immediate cause of the escape was a 'further requirement' which should not have been added. The only question was whether something which the defendant had done, whether immediately or antecedently, had caused the pollution.

In the present case, the Crown Court found that the escape was caused by the way the company maintained its tank of diesel fuel. Maintaining a tank of diesel is doing something and therefore, provided that it was open to the court to find the necessary causal connection established, they were in my view entitled to convict. It is to the notion of causing that I therefore now turn.

(2) Causing

The courts have repeatedly said that the notion of 'causing' is one of common sense. So in *Alphacell Ltd v Woodward* [1972] AC 824, p 847; [1972] 2 All ER 475, p 490 Lord Salmon said:

> ... what or who has caused a certain event to occur is essentially a practical question of fact which can best be answered by ordinary common sense rather than by abstract metaphysical theory.

I doubt whether the use of abstract metaphysical theory has ever had much serious support and I certainly agree that the notion of causation should not be overcomplicated. Neither, however, should it be oversimplified. In the *Alphacell* case [1972] 2 All ER 475 at 479; [1972] AC 824 at 834 Lord Wilberforce said in similar vein:

> In my opinion, 'causing' here must be given a common sense meaning and I deprecate the introduction of refinements, such as *causa causans*, effective cause or *novus actus*. There may be difficulties where acts of third persons or natural forces are concerned ...

The last concession was prudently made, because it is of course the causal significance of acts of third parties (as in this case) or natural forces that gives rise to almost all the problems about the notion of 'causing' and drives judges to take refuge in metaphor or Latin. I therefore propose to concentrate upon the way commonsense notions of causation treat the intervention of third parties or natural forces. The principles involved are not complicated or difficult to understand, but they do in my opinion call for some explanation. It is remarkable how many cases there are under this Act in which justices have attempted to apply common sense and found themselves reversed by the Divisional Court for error of law. More guidance is, I think, necessary.

The first point to emphasise is that commonsense answers to questions of causation will differ according to the purpose for which the question is asked. Questions of causation often arise for the purpose of attributing responsibility to someone, for example, so as to blame him for something which has happened or to make him guilty of an offence or liable in damages. In such cases, the answer will depend upon the rule by which responsibility is being attributed. Take, for example, the case of the man who forgets to take the radio out of his car and during the night someone breaks the quarterlight, enters the car and steals it. What caused the damage? If the thief is on trial, so that the question is whether he is criminally responsible, then obviously the answer is that he caused the damage. It is no answer for him to say that it was caused by the owner carelessly leaving the radio inside. On the other hand, the owner's wife, irritated at the third such occurrence in a year, might well say that it was his fault. In the context of an inquiry into the owner's blameworthiness under a non-legal, commonsense duty to take reasonable care of one's own possessions, one would say that his carelessness caused the loss of the radio.

Not only may there be different answers to questions about causation when attributing responsibility to different people under different rules (in the above example, criminal responsibility of the thief, commonsense responsibility of the owner) but there may be different answers when attributing responsibility to different people under the same rule. In *National Rivers Authority v Yorkshire Water Services Ltd* [1995] 1 AC 444; [1995] 1 All ER 225 the defendant was a sewage undertaker. It received sewage, treated it in filter beds and discharged the treated liquid into the river. One night someone unlawfully discharged a solvent called iso-octanol into the sewer. It passed through the sewage works and entered the river. The question was whether the defendant had caused the consequent pollution. Lord Mackay of Clashfern LC, with whom the other members of the House agreed, said ([1995] 1 All ER 225 at 231; [1995] 1 AC 444 at 452):

> ... I am of opinion that Yorkshire Water Services having set up a system for gathering effluent into their sewers and thence into their sewage works there to be treated, with an arrangement deliberately intended to carry the results of that treatment into controlled waters, the special circumstances surrounding the entry of iso-octanol into their sewers and works do not preclude the conclusion that Yorkshire Water Services caused the resulting poisonous, noxious and polluting matter to enter the controlled waters, notwithstanding that the constitution of the effluent so entering was affected by the presence of iso-octanol.

So in the context of attributing responsibility to Yorkshire Water Services under s 85(1) (then s 107(1)(a) of the Water Act 1989), it had caused the pollution. On the other hand, if the person who put the iso-octanol into the sewer had been prosecuted under the same sub-section, it would undoubtedly have been held that he caused the pollution.

What these examples show is that it is wrong and distracting, in the case of a prosecution under s 85(1), to ask 'What caused the pollution?' There may be a number of correct answers to a question put in those terms. The only question which has to be asked for the purposes of s 85(1) is 'Did the defendant cause the pollution?' The fact that for different purposes or even for the same purpose one could also say that someone or something else caused the pollution is not inconsistent with the defendant having caused it. The way Lord Wilberforce put it in *Alphacell Ltd v Woodward* [1972] AC 824, p 835; [1972] 2 All ER 475, p 479, was as follows:

> ... rather than say that the actions of the appellants were a cause of the pollution I think it more accurate to say that the appellants caused the polluting matter to enter the stream.

I turn next to the question of third parties and natural forces. In answering questions of causation for the purposes of holding someone responsible, both the law and common sense normally attach great significance to deliberate human acts and extraordinary natural events. A factory owner carelessly leaves a drum containing highly inflammable vapour in a place where it could easily be accidentally ignited. If a workman, thinking it is only an empty drum, throws in a cigarette butt and causes an explosion, one would have no difficulty in saying that the negligence of the owner caused the explosion. On the other hand, if the workman, knowing exactly what the drum contains, lights a match and ignites it, one would have equally little difficulty in saying that he had caused the explosion and that the carelessness of the owner had merely provided him with an occasion for what he did. One would probably say the same if the drum was struck by lightning. In both cases one would say that although the vapour-filled drum was a necessary condition for the explosion to happen, it was not caused by the owner's negligence. One might add by way of further explanation that the presence of an arsonist workman or lightning happening to strike at that time and place was a coincidence.

On the other hand, there are cases in which the duty imposed by the rule is to take precautions to prevent loss being caused by third parties or natural events. One example has already been given; the common sense rule (not legally enforceable, but neglect of which may expose one to blame from one's wife) which requires one to remove the car radio at night. A legal example is the well-known case of *Stansbie v Troman* [1948] 1 All ER 599, [1948] 2 KB 48. A decorator working alone in a house went out to buy wallpaper and left the front door unlocked. He was held liable for the loss caused by a thief who entered while he was away. For the purpose of attributing liability to the thief (for example, in a prosecution for theft) the loss was caused by his deliberate act and no one would have said that it was caused by the door being left open. But for the purpose of attributing liability to the decorator, the loss was caused by his negligence because his duty was to take reasonable care to guard against thieves entering.

These examples show that one cannot give a commonsense answer to a question of causation for the purpose of attributing responsibility under some rule without knowing the purpose and scope of the rule. Does the rule impose a duty which requires one to guard against, or makes one responsible for, the deliberate acts of third persons? If so, it will be correct to say, when loss is caused by the act of such a third person, that it was caused by the breach of duty. In *Stansbie v Troman* [1948] 2 KB 48, p 51–52; [1948] 1 All ER 599, p 600, Tucker LJ referred to a statement of Lord Sumner in *Weld-Blundell v Stephens* [1920] AC 956, p 986; [1920] All ER Rep 32, p 47, in which he had said:

> In general ... even though A is in fault, he is not responsible for injury to C which B, a stranger to him, deliberately chooses to do. Though A may have given the occasion for B's mischievous activity, B then becomes a new and independent cause ...

Tucker LJ went on to comment:

> I do not think that Lord Sumner would have intended that very general statement to apply to the facts of a case such as the present, where, as the learned judge points out, the act of negligence itself consisted in the failure to take reasonable care to guard against the very thing that in fact happened.

Before answering questions about causation, it is therefore first necessary to identify the scope of the relevant rule. This is not a question of common sense fact; it is a question of law. In *Stansbie v Troman* the law imposed a duty which included having to take precautions against burglars. Therefore breach of that duty caused the loss of the property stolen. In the example of the vapour-filled drum, the duty does not extend to taking precautions against arsonists. In other contexts there might be such a duty (compare *Mediterranean Freight Services Ltd v BP Oil International Ltd, The Fiona* [1994] 2 Lloyd's Rep 506, p 522) but the law of negligence would not impose one.

What, therefore, is the nature of the duty imposed by s 85(1)? Does it include responsibility for acts of third parties or natural events and, if so, for any such acts or only some of them? This is a question of statutory construction, having regard to the policy of the Act. It is immediately clear that the liability imposed by the sub-section is strict: it does not require *mens rea* in the sense of intention or negligence. Strict liability is imposed in the interests of protecting controlled waters from pollution. The offence is, as Lord Pearson said in *Alphacell Ltd v Woodward* [1972] AC 824, p 842; [1972] 2 All ER 475, p 486, 'in the nature of a public nuisance'. *National Rivers Authority v Yorkshire Water Services Ltd* [1995] 1 All ER 225, [1995] 1 AC 444 is a striking example of a case in which, in the context of a rule which did not apply strict liability, it would have been said that the defendant's operation of the sewage plant did not cause the pollution but merely provided the occasion for pollution to be caused by the third party who discharged the iso-octanol. And in *Alphacell Ltd v Woodward* [1972] AC 824, p 835; [1972] 2 All ER 475, p 479 Lord Wilberforce said with reference to *Impress (Worcester) Ltd v Rees* [1971] 2 All ER 357, which I shall discuss later, that:

> ... it should not be regarded as a decision that in every case the act of a third person necessarily interrupts the chain of causation initiated by the person who owns or operates the installation or plant from which the flow took place.

Clearly, therefore, the fact that a deliberate act of a third party caused the pollution does not in itself mean that the defendant's creation of a situation in which the third party could so act did not also cause the pollution for the purposes of s 85(1).

It is not easy to reconcile this proposition with the actual decision of the Divisional Court in *Impress (Worcester) Ltd v Rees*, to which I have just referred. The appellants kept a fuel oil storage tank with an unlocked valve in their yard near the river. An unauthorised person entered during the night and opened the valve. The justices convicted, but the Divisional Court allowed the appeal. Cooke J said (at 358):

> On general principles of causation, the question which the justices ought to have asked themselves was whether that intervening cause was of so powerful a nature that the conduct of the appellants was not a cause at all but was merely part of the surrounding circumstances.

That question, said the Divisional Court, was capable of only one answer, namely that 'it was not the conduct of the appellants but the intervening act of the unauthorised person which caused the oil to enter the river'. In *Alphacell Ltd v Woodward* [1972] 2 All ER 475 at 479, 490; [1972] AC 824 at 835, 847 Lord Wilberforce said that he did not 'desire to question this conclusion' and Lord Salmon said that it was an example of 'the active intervention of a stranger, the risk of which could not reasonably have been foreseen'. The difficulty is, however, that the justices said nothing about whether the risk could reasonably have been foreseen and nor did the Divisional Court. The nearest which the justices came to this question was when they said 'the valve was never locked but ... the appellants ought to have kept it closed at all material times' – a remark which rather suggests that the possibility of tampering should have been foreseen. Whether foreseeability was a relevant matter at all is a point to which I shall return later. But the actual reasoning of the Divisional Court was that the defendant was entitled to be acquitted simply because the escape had been caused by the deliberate act of a stranger. Mr Philpott urged upon us that the reasoning in *Impress (Worcester) Ltd v Rees* applied squarely to this case and I think that he is right. But in my view the case was wrongly decided. It is inconsistent with Lord Wilberforce's statement that the deliberate act of a third party does not necessarily negative causal connection and with the subsequent decision of this House in *National Rivers Authority v Yorkshire Water Services Ltd* [1995] 1 AC 444; [1995] 1 All ER 225.

While liability under s 85(1) is strict and therefore includes liability for certain deliberate acts of third parties and (by parity of reasoning) natural events, it is not an absolute liability in the sense that all that has to be shown is that the polluting matter escaped from the defendant's land, irrespective of how this happened. It must still be possible to say that the defendant caused the pollution. Take, for example, the lagoons of effluent in *Price v Cromack* [1975] 1 WLR 988; [1975] 2 All ER 113. They leaked effluent into the river and I have said that in my view the justices were entitled to hold that the pollution had been caused by the defendant maintaining leaky lagoons. But suppose that they emptied into the river because a wall had been breached by a bomb planted by terrorists. I think it would be very difficult to say, as a matter of common sense, that the defendant had caused the pollution. On what principle, therefore, will some acts of third parties (or natural events) negative causal connection for the purposes of s 85(1) and others not?

In *Alphacell Ltd v Woodward* [1972] AC 824; [1972] 2 All ER 475 Lord Salmon, as I have mentioned, suggested that the difference might depend upon whether the act of a third party or natural event was foreseeable or not. This was the approach taken by the justices in *National Rivers Authority v Wright Engineering Co Ltd* [1994] 4 All ER 281. That was another case of vandalism leading to oil escaping from a tank into a river. The justices acquitted because they said that although there had been past incidents of vandalism at the defendant's premises, 'the vandalism involved was not reasonably foreseeable because it was out of all proportion to the earlier and more minor incidents'. In the Divisional Court, Buckley J (at 285) cited with approval a remark of Lloyd LJ in the Divisional Court in *Welsh Water Authority v Williams Motors (Cymdu) Ltd* (1988) *The Times*, 5 December:

> ... the question is not what was foreseeable by the respondents or anyone else: the question is whether any act on the part of the respondents caused the pollution.

Nevertheless, said Buckley J:

> ... that does not mean that foreseeability is wholly irrelevant. It is one factor which a tribunal may properly consider in seeking to apply common sense to the question: who or what caused the result under consideration?

I have already said that I think that to frame the question as 'who or what caused the result under consideration?' is wrong and distracting, because it may have more than one right answer. The question is whether the defendant caused the pollution. How is foreseeability a relevant factor to consider in answering this question?

In the sense in which the concept of foreseeability is normally used, namely as an ingredient in the tort of negligence, in the form of the question: ought the defendant reasonably to have foreseen what happened, I do not think that it is relevant. Liability under s 85(1) is not based on negligence; it is strict. No one asked whether Yorkshire Water Services Ltd ought to have foreseen that someone would put iso-octanol in their sewage. Likewise in *CPC (UK) Ltd v National Rivers Authority* [1995] Env LR 131 the defendant operated a factory which used cleaning liquid carried through PVC piping. The piping leaked because it had been badly installed by the reputable sub-contractors employed by the previous owners of the factory. The Court of Appeal (pp 137–38) held that although the defendants were unaware of the existence of the defect and 'could not be criticised for failing to discover it', the pollution had nevertheless been caused by their operation of the factory. So the fact that the negligent installation of the pipes had been unforeseeable was no defence. I agree with Lloyd LJ that the question is not whether the consequences ought to have been foreseen; it is whether the defendant caused the pollution. And foreseeability is not the criterion for deciding whether a person caused something or not. People often cause things which they could not have foreseen.

The true commonsense distinction is, in my view, between acts and events which, although not necessarily foreseeable in the particular case, are in the generality a normal and familiar fact of life, and acts or events which are abnormal and extraordinary. Of course an act or event which is in general terms a normal fact of life may also have been foreseeable in the circumstances of the particular case, but the latter is not necessary for the purposes of liability. There is nothing extraordinary or abnormal about leaky pipes or lagoons as such: these things happen, even if the particular defendant could not reasonably have foreseen that it would happen to him. There is nothing unusual about people putting unlawful substances into the sewage system and the same, regrettably, is true about ordinary vandalism. So when these things happen, one does not say: that was an extraordinary coincidence, which negatived the causal connection between the original act of accumulating the polluting substance and its escape. In the context of s 85(1), the defendant's accumulation has still caused the pollution. On the other hand, the example I gave of the terrorist attack would be something so unusual that one would not regard the defendant's conduct as having caused the escape at all.

In the context of natural events, this distinction between normal and extraordinary events emerges in the decision of this House in *Alphacell Ltd v Woodward*. The defendant operated a paper manufacturing plant, which involved maintaining tanks of polluting liquid near the river, so that pollution would occur if they overflowed. There were pumps which ought normally to have drawn off the liquid and prevented the tanks from overflowing. But in late November the pumps became choked with brambles, ferns and long leaves: they did not function and an overflow occurred. The House found no difficulty in holding that the pollution was caused by what the defendant had done: Lord Wilberforce ([1972] 2 All ER 475 at 479, [1972] AC 824 at 834) said that the 'whole complex operation which might lead to this result was an operation deliberately conducted by the appellants'. As for 'causing', it was true that the pollution would not have happened but for a natural event, namely, the vegetation getting into the pumps, but, as Lord Pearson said that was nothing extraordinary:

> There was not even any unusual weather or freak of nature. Autumn is the season of the year in which dead leaves, ferns, pieces of bracken and pieces of brambles may be expected to fall into water and sink below the surface and, if there is a pump, to be sucked up by it. (See [1972] 2 All ER 475, p 488; [1972] AC 824, p 845.)

Lord Salmon said it would have been different if there had been an 'act of God', which I take to mean some extraordinary natural event. Likewise in the case of the acts of third parties, I think that once one accepts, as in the light of Lord Wilberforce's comments in the *Alphacell* case and the decision in *National Rivers Authority v Yorkshire Water Services Ltd* [1995] 1 AC 444; [1995] 1 All ER 225 one has to accept, that some deliberate acts of third parties will not negative causal connection, it seems to me that the distinction between ordinary and extraordinary is the only commonsense criterion by which one can distinguish those acts which will negative causal connection from those which will not.

So I think that the defendant in *Impress (Worcester) Ltd v Rees* was rightly convicted by the justices and that the defendant in *National Rivers Authority v Wright Engineering Co Ltd* [1994] 4 All ER 281 should also have been convicted. The particular form of vandalism may not have been foreseeable (someone had broken the sight gauge) but the precise details will never be foreseeable. In practical terms it was ordinary vandalism.

I shall try to summarise the effect of this discussion.

(1) Justices dealing with prosecutions for 'causing' pollution under s 85(1) should first require the prosecution to identify what it says the defendant did to cause the pollution. If the defendant cannot be said to have done anything at all, the prosecution

must fail: the defendant may have 'knowingly permitted' pollution but cannot have caused it.

(2) The prosecution need not prove that the defendant did something which was the immediate cause of the pollution: maintaining tanks, lagoons or sewage systems full of noxious liquid is doing something, even if the immediate cause of the pollution was lack of maintenance, a natural event or the act of a third party.

(3) When the prosecution has identified something which the defendant did, the justices must decide whether it caused the pollution. They should not be diverted by questions like 'What was the cause of the pollution?' or 'Did something else cause the pollution?' because to say that something else caused the pollution (like brambles clogging the pumps or vandalism by third parties) is not inconsistent with the defendant having caused it as well.

(4) If the defendant did something which produced a situation in which the polluting matter could escape but a necessary condition of the actual escape which happened was also the act of a third party or a natural event, the justices should consider whether that act or event should be regarded as a normal fact of life or something extraordinary. If it was in the general run of things a matter of ordinary occurrence, it will not negative the causal effect of the defendant's acts, even if it was not foreseeable that it would happen to that particular defendant or take that particular form. If it can be regarded as something extraordinary, it will be open to the justices to hold that the defendant did not cause the pollution.

(5) The distinction between ordinary and extraordinary is one of fact and degree to which the justices must apply their common sense and knowledge of what happens in the area.

Applying these principles, it seems to me that there was ample evidence on which the Crown Court was entitled to find that the company had caused the pollution. I would therefore dismiss the appeal.

Section 86 Prohibition of certain discharges by notice or regulations

(1) For the purposes of s 85 above a discharge of any effluent or other matter is, in relation to any person, in contravention of a prohibition imposed under this section if, subject to the following provisions of this section–

    (a) the [Agency] has given that person notice prohibiting him from making or, as the case may be, continuing the discharge; or

    (b) the [Agency] has given that person notice prohibiting him from making or, as the case may be, continuing the discharge unless specified conditions are observed, and those conditions are not observed.

(2) For the purposes of s 85 above a discharge of any effluent or other matter is also in contravention of a prohibition imposed under this section if the effluent or matter discharged–

    (a) contains a prescribed substance or a prescribed concentration of such a substance; or

    (b) derives from a prescribed process or from a process involving the use of prescribed substances or the use of such substances in quantities which exceed the prescribed amounts.

[Sub-sections (3)–(6) omitted.]

Section 88 Defence to principal offences in respect of authorised discharges

(1) Subject to the following provisions of this section, a person shall not be guilty of an offence under s 85 above in respect of the entry of any matter into any waters or any discharge if the entry occurs or the discharge is made under and in accordance with, or as a result of any act or omission and in accordance with–

   (a) a consent given under this chapter or under Part II of the Control of Pollution Act 1974 (which makes corresponding provision for Scotland);

   (b) an authorisation for a prescribed process designated for central control granted under Part I of the Environmental Protection Act 1990;

   (c) a waste management or disposal licence;

   (d) a licence granted under Part II of the Food and Environment Protection Act 1985;

   (e) s 163 below or s 165 of the Water Industry Act 1991 (discharges for works purposes);

   (f) any local statutory provision or statutory order which expressly confers power to discharge effluent into water; or

   (g) any prescribed enactment.

(2) Schedule 10 to this Act shall have effect, subject to s 91 below, with respect to the making of applications for consents under this chapter for the purposes of sub-section (1)(a) above and with respect to the giving, revocation and modification of such consents.

(3) Nothing in any disposal licence shall be treated for the purposes of sub-section (1) above as authorising–

   (a) any entry or discharge as is mentioned in sub-sections (2) to (4) of s 85 above; or

   (b) any act or omission so far as it results in any such entry or discharge.

(4)   In this section–

   'disposal licence' means a licence issued in pursuance of s 5 of the Control of Pollution Act 1974;

   'statutory order' means–

   (a) any order under s 168 below or s 167 of the Water Industry Act 1991 (compulsory works orders); or

   (b) any order, bylaw, scheme or award made under any other enactment, including an order or scheme confirmed by Parliament or brought into operation in accordance with special parliamentary procedure;

   and

   'waste management licence' means such a licence granted under Part II of the Environmental Protection Act 1990.

Section 89 Other defences to principal offences

(1) A person shall not be guilty of an offence under s 85 above in respect of the entry of any matter into any waters or any discharge if–

   (a) the entry is caused or permitted, or the discharge is made, in an emergency in order to avoid danger to life or health;

(b) that person takes all such steps as are reasonably practicable in the circumstances for minimising the extent of the entry or discharge and of its polluting effects; and

(c) particulars of the entry or discharge are furnished to the [Agency] as soon as reasonably practicable after the entry occurs.

[Sub-sections (2)–(6) omitted.]

Section 90A Applications for consent under ss 89 or 90

(1) Any application for a consent for the purposes of s 89(4)(a) or 90(1) or (2) above–

(a) must be made on a form provided for the purpose by the Agency; and

(b) must be advertised in such manner as may be required by regulations made by the Secretary of State,

except that paragraph (b) above shall not have effect in the case of an application of any class or description specified in the regulations as being exempt from the requirements of that paragraph.

(2) The applicant for such a consent must, at the time when he makes his application, provide the Agency–

(a) with all such information as it reasonably requires; and

(b) with all such information as may be prescribed for the purpose by the Secretary of State.

(3) The information required by sub-section (2) above must be provided either on, or together with, the form mentioned in sub-section (1) above.

(4) The Agency may give the applicant notice requiring him to provide it with all such further information of any description specified in the notice as it may require for the purpose of determining the application.

(5) If the applicant fails to provide the Agency with any information required under sub-section (4) above, the Agency may refuse to proceed with the application or refuse to proceed with it until the information is provided.

Section 90B Enforcement notices

(1) If the Agency is of the opinion that the holder of a relevant consent is contravening any condition of the consent, or is likely to contravene any such condition, the Agency may serve on him a notice (an 'enforcement notice').

(2) An enforcement notice shall–

(a) state that the Agency is of the said opinion;

(b) specify the matters constituting the contravention or the matters making it likely that the contravention will arise;

(c) specify the steps that must be taken to remedy the contravention or, as the case may be, to remedy the matters making it likely that the contravention will arise; and

(d) specify the period within which those steps must be taken.

(3) Any person who fails to comply with any requirement imposed by an enforcement notice shall be guilty of an offence and liable–

(a) on summary conviction, to imprisonment for a term not exceeding three months or to a fine not exceeding £20,000 or to both;

(b) on conviction on indictment, to imprisonment for a term not exceeding two years or to a fine or to both.

(4) If the Agency is of the opinion that proceedings for an offence under sub-section (3) above would afford an ineffectual remedy against a person who has failed to comply with the requirements of an enforcement notice, the Agency may take proceedings in the High Court for the purpose of securing compliance with the notice.

(5) The Secretary of State may, if he thinks fit in relation to any person, give to the Agency directions as to whether the Agency should exercise its powers under this section and as to the steps which must be taken.

(6) In this section–

'relevant consent' means–

(a) a consent for the purposes of s 89(4)(a) or 90(1) or (2) above; or

(b) a discharge consent, within the meaning of s 91 below; and

'the holder', in relation to a relevant consent, is the person who has the consent in question.

Section 91 Appeals in respect of consents under Chapter II

(1) This section applies where the [Agency], otherwise than in pursuance of a direction of the Secretary of State–

(a) on an application for a consent under this chapter for the purposes of s 88(1)(a) above, has refused a consent for any discharges;

(b) in giving a discharge consent, has made that consent subject to conditions;

(c) has revoked a discharge consent, modified the conditions of any such consent or provided that any such consent which was unconditional shall be subject to conditions;

(d) has, for the purposes of paragraph 7(1) [8(1)] or (2) of Schedule 10 to this Act, specified a period in relation to a discharge consent without the agreement of the person who proposes to make, or makes, discharges in pursuance of that consent;

(e) has refused a consent for the purposes of s 89(4)(a) above for any deposit; or

(f) has refused a consent for the purposes of s 90 above for the doing of anything by any person or, in giving any such consent, made that consent subject to conditions;

(g) has refused a person a variation of any such consent as is mentioned in paragraphs (a) to (f) above or, in allowing any such variation, has made the consent subject to conditions; or

(h) has served an enforcement notice on any person.

(2) The person, if any, who applied for the consent [or variation] in question, or any person whose deposits, discharges or other conduct is or would be authorised by the consent [or the person on whom the enforcement notice was served], may appeal against the decision to the Secretary of State.

(3) The Secretary of State may by regulations provide for the conduct and disposal of appeals under this section.

(4) Without prejudice to the generality of the power conferred by sub-section (3) above, regulations under that sub-section may, with prescribed modifications, apply any provision of paragraphs 1(3) to (6), 2(1) and 4(4) to (6) of Schedule 10 to this Act in relation to appeals under this section.

[Sub-sections (5)–(8) omitted.]

Section 92 Requirements to take precautions against pollution

(1) The Secretary of State may by regulations make provision–

    (a) for prohibiting a person from having custody or control of any poisonous, noxious or polluting matter unless prescribed works and prescribed precautions and other steps have been carried out or taken for the purpose of preventing or controlling the entry of the matter into any controlled waters;

    (b) for requiring a person who already has custody or control of, or makes use of, any such matter to carry out such works for that purpose and to take such precautions and other steps for that purpose as may be prescribed.

(2) Without prejudice to the generality of the power conferred by sub-section (1) above, regulations under that sub-section may–

    (a) confer power on the [Agency]–

        (i) to determine for the purposes of the regulations the circumstances in which a person is required to carry out works or to take any precautions or other steps; and

        (ii) by notice to that person, to impose the requirement and to specify or describe the works, precautions or other steps which that person is required to carry out or take;

    (b) provide for appeals to the Secretary of State against notices served by the [Agency] in pursuance of provision made by virtue of paragraph (a) above; and

    (c) provide that a contravention of the regulations shall be an offence the maximum penalties for which shall not exceed the penalties specified in sub-section (6) of s 85 above.

(3) This section is subject to s 114 of the 1995 Act (delegation or reference of appeals etc).

Section 93 Water protection zones

(1) Where the Secretary of State considers, after consultation (in the case of an area wholly or partly in England) with the Minister, that sub-section (2) below is satisfied in relation to any area, he may by order make provision–

    (a) designating that area as a water protection zone; and

    (b) prohibiting or restricting the carrying on in the designated area of such activities as may be specified or described in the order.

(2) For the purposes of sub-section (1) above this sub-section is satisfied in relation to any area if (subject to sub-section (3) below) it is appropriate, with a view to preventing or controlling the entry of any poisonous, noxious or polluting matter into controlled waters, to prohibit or restrict the carrying on in that area of activities which the Secretary of State considers are likely to result in the pollution of any such waters.

(3) The reference in sub-section (2) above to the entry of poisonous, noxious or polluting matter into controlled waters shall not include a reference to the entry of nitrate into

controlled waters as a result of, or of anything done in connection with, the use of any land for agricultural purposes.

(4) Without prejudice to the generality of the power conferred by virtue of sub-section (1) above, an order under this section may–

  (a) confer power on the [Agency] to determine for the purposes of the order the circumstances in which the carrying on of any activities is prohibited or restricted and to determine the activities to which any such prohibition or restriction applies;

  (b) apply a prohibition or restriction in respect of any activities to cases where the activities are carried on without the consent of the [Agency] or in contravention of any conditions subject to which any such consent is given;

  (c) provide that a contravention of a prohibition or restriction contained in the order or of a condition of a consent given for the purposes of any such prohibition or restriction shall be an offence the maximum penalties for which shall not exceed the penalties specified in sub-section (6) of s 85 above;

  (d) provide (subject to any regulations under s 96 below) for anything falling to be determined under the order by the [Agency] to be determined in accordance with such procedure and by reference to such matters and to the opinion of such persons as may be specified in the order;

  (e) make different provision for different cases, including different provision in relation to different persons, circumstances or localities; and

  (f) contain such supplemental, consequential and transitional provision as the Secretary of State considers appropriate.

(5) The power of the Secretary of State to make an order under this section shall be exercisable by statutory instrument subject to annulment in pursuance of a resolution of either House of Parliament; but the Secretary of State shall not make such an order except on an application made by the [Agency] in accordance with Schedule 11 to this Act and otherwise in accordance with that Schedule.

Section 94 Nitrate sensitive areas

(1) Where the relevant Minister considers that it is appropriate to do so with a view to achieving the purpose specified in sub-section (2) below in relation to any land, he may by order make provision designating that land, together with any other land to which he considers it appropriate to apply the designation, as a nitrate sensitive area.

(2) The purpose mentioned in sub-section (1) above is preventing or controlling the entry of nitrate into controlled waters as a result of, or of anything done in connection with, the use for agricultural purposes of any land.

(3) Where it appears to the relevant Minister, in relation to any area which is or is to be designated by an order under this section as a nitrate sensitive area, that it is appropriate for provision for the imposition of requirements, prohibitions or restrictions to be contained in an order under this section (as well as for him to be able to enter into such agreements as are mentioned in s 95 below), he may, by a subsequent order under this section or, as the case may be, by the order designating that area–

  (a) with a view to achieving the purpose specified in sub-section (2) above, require, prohibit or restrict the carrying on, either on or in relation to any agricultural land in that area, of such activities as may be specified or described in the order; and

    (b) provide for such amounts (if any) as may be specified in or determined under the order to be paid by one of the Ministers, to such persons as may be so specified or determined, in respect of the obligations imposed in relation to that area on those persons by virtue of paragraph (a) above.

(4) Without prejudice to the generality of sub-section (3) above, provision contained in an order under this section by virtue of that sub-section may–

    (a) confer power on either of the Ministers to determine for the purposes of the order the circumstances in which the carrying on of any activities is required, prohibited or restricted and to determine the activities to which any such requirement, prohibition or restriction applies;

    (b) provide for any requirement to carry on any activity not to apply in cases where one of the Ministers has consented to a failure to carry on that activity and any conditions on which the consent has been given are complied with;

    (c) apply a prohibition or restriction in respect of any activities to cases where the activities are carried on without the consent of one of the Ministers or in contravention of any conditions subject to which any such consent is given;

    (d) provide that a contravention of a requirement, prohibition or restriction contained in the order or in a condition of a consent given in relation to or for the purposes of any such requirement, prohibition or restriction shall be an offence the maximum penalties for which shall not exceed the penalties specified in sub-section (6) of s 85 above;

    (e) provide for amounts paid in pursuance of any provision contained in the order to be repaid at such times and in such circumstances, and with such interest, as may be specified in or determined under the order; and

    (f) provide (subject to any regulations under s 96 below) for anything falling to be determined under the order by any person to be determined in accordance with such procedure and by reference to such matters and to the opinion of such persons as may be specified in the order.

(5) An order under this section may–

    (a) make different provision for different cases, including different provision in relation to different persons, circumstances or localities; and

    (b) contain such supplemental, consequential and transitional provision as the relevant Minister considers appropriate.

(6) The power of the relevant Minister to make an order under this section shall be exercisable by statutory instrument subject to annulment in pursuance of a resolution of either House of Parliament; but the relevant Minister shall not make such an order except in accordance with any applicable provisions of Schedule 12 to this Act.

(7) In this section and in Schedule 12 to this Act 'the relevant Minister'–

    (a) in relation to the making of an order in relation to an area which is wholly in England or which is partly in England and partly in Wales, means the Ministers; and

    (b) in relation to the making of an order in relation to an area which is wholly in Wales, means the Secretary of State.

Section 95 Agreements in nitrate sensitive areas

(1) Where–

    (a) any area has been designated as a nitrate sensitive area by an order under s 94 above; and

    (b) the relevant Minister considers that it is appropriate to do so with a view to achieving the purpose mentioned in sub-section (2) of that section,

he may, subject to such restrictions (if any) as may be set out in the order, enter into an agreement falling within sub-section (2) below.

(2) An agreement falls within this sub-section if it is one under which, in consideration of payments to be made by the relevant Minister–

    (a) the owner of the freehold interest in any agricultural land in a nitrate sensitive area; or

    (b) where the owner of the freehold interest in any such land has given his written consent to the agreement being entered into by any person having another interest in that land, that other person,

accepts such obligations with respect to the management of that land or otherwise as may be imposed by the agreement.

(3) An agreement such as is mentioned in sub-section (2) above between the relevant Minister and a person having an interest in any land shall bind all persons deriving title from or under that person to the extent that the agreement is expressed to bind that land in relation to those persons.

(4) In this section 'the relevant Minister'–

    (a) in relation to an agreement with respect to land which is wholly in England, means the Minister;

    (b) in relation to an agreement with respect to land which is wholly in Wales, means the Secretary of State; and

    (c) in relation to an agreement with respect to land which is partly in England and partly in Wales, means either of the Ministers.

Note: See EC Regulation 2078/92 and the Nitrate Sensitive Areas Regulations 1994 SI 1994/1729, under which current Nitrate Sensitive Areas have been designated.

Section 100 Civil liability in respect of pollution and savings

Except in so far as this Part expressly otherwise provides and subject to the provisions of s 18 of the Interpretation Act 1978 (which relates to offences under two or more laws), nothing in this Part–

    (a) confers a right of action in any civil proceedings (other than proceedings for the recovery of a fine) in respect of any contravention of this Part or any subordinate legislation, consent or other instrument made, given or issued under this Part;

    (b) derogates from any right of action or other remedy (whether civil or criminal) in proceedings instituted otherwise than under this Part; or

    (c) affects any restriction imposed by or under any other enactment, whether public, local or private.

Section 102 Power to give effect to international obligations

The Secretary of State shall have power by regulations to provide that the water pollution provisions of this Act shall have effect with such modifications as may be prescribed for the purpose of enabling Her Majesty's Government in the United Kingdom to give effect–

(a) to any Community obligations; or

(b) to any international agreement to which the United Kingdom is for the time being a party.

Section 104 Meaning of 'controlled waters' etc in Part III

(1) References in this Part to controlled waters are references to waters of any of the following classes–

   (a) relevant territorial waters, that is to say, subject to sub-section (4) below, the waters which extend seaward for three miles from the baselines from which the breadth of the territorial sea adjacent to England and Wales is measured;

   (b) coastal waters, that is to say, any waters which are within the area which extends landward from those baselines as far as–

      (a) the limit of the highest tide; or

      (b) in the case of the waters of any relevant river or watercourse, the fresh-water limit of the river or watercourse,

   together with the waters of any enclosed dock which adjoins waters within that area;

   (c) inland freshwaters, that is to say, the waters of any relevant lake or pond or of so much of any relevant river or watercourse as is above the fresh-water limit;

   (d) ground waters, that is to say, any waters contained in underground strata;

and, accordingly, in this Part 'coastal waters', 'controlled waters', 'ground waters', 'inland freshwaters' and 'relevant territorial waters' have the meanings given by this sub-section.

(2) In this Part any reference to the waters of any lake or pond or of any river or watercourse includes a reference to the bottom, channel or bed of any lake, pond, river or, as the case may be, watercourse which is for the time being dry.

(3) In this section–

'fresh-water limit', in relation to any river or watercourse, means the place for the time being shown as the fresh-water limit of that river or watercourse in the latest map deposited for that river or watercourse under s 192 below;

'miles' means international nautical miles of 1,852 metres;

'lake or pond' includes a reservoir of any description;

'relevant lake or pond' means (subject to sub-section (4) below) any lake or pond which (whether it is natural or artificial or above or below ground) discharges into a relevant river or watercourse or into another lake or pond which is itself a relevant lake or pond;

'relevant river or watercourse' means (subject to sub-section (4) below) any river or watercourse (including an underground river or watercourse and an artificial river or watercourse) which is neither a public sewer nor a sewer or drain which drains into a public sewer.

(4) The Secretary of State may by order provide–

   (a) that any area of the territorial sea adjacent to England and Wales is to be treated as if it were an area of relevant territorial waters for the purposes of this Part and of any other enactment in which any expression is defined by reference to the meanings given by this section;

   (b) that any lake or pond which does not discharge into a relevant river or watercourse or into a relevant lake or pond is to be treated for those purposes as a relevant lake or pond;

   (c) that a lake or pond which does so discharge and is of a description specified in the order is to be treated for those purposes as if it were not a relevant lake or pond;

   (d) that a watercourse of a description so specified is to be treated for those purposes as if it were not a relevant river or watercourse.

(5) An order under this section may–

   (a) contain such supplemental, consequential and transitional provision as the Secretary of State considers appropriate; and

   (b) make different provision for different cases, including different provision in relation to different persons, circumstances or localities.

(6) The power of the Secretary of State to make an order under this section shall be exercisable by statutory instrument subject to annulment in pursuance of a resolution of either House of Parliament.

Section 161 Anti-pollution works and operations

(1) Subject to sub-section (2) below, subject to sub-sections (1A) and (2) below, where it appears to the Agency that any poisonous, noxious or polluting matter or any solid waste matter is likely to enter, or to be or to have been present in, any controlled waters, the Agency shall be entitled to carry out the following works and operations, that is to say–

   (a) in a case where the matter appears likely to enter any controlled waters, works and operations for the purpose of preventing it from doing so; or

   (b) in a case where the matter appears to be or to have been present in any controlled waters, works and operations for the purpose–

      (i) of removing or disposing of the matter;

      (ii) of remedying or mitigating any pollution caused by its presence in the waters; or

      (iii) so far as it is reasonably practicable to do so, of restoring the waters, including any flora and fauna dependent on the aquatic environment of the waters, to their state immediately before the matter became present in the waters.

(1A) Without prejudice to the power of the Agency to carry out investigations under sub-section (1) above, the power conferred by that sub-section to carry out works and operations shall only be exercisable in a case where–

   (a) the Agency considers it necessary to carry out forthwith any works or operations falling within paragraph (a) or (b) of that sub-section; or

   (b) it appears to the Agency, after reasonable inquiry, that no person can be found on whom to serve a works notice under s 161A below.

(2) Nothing in sub-section (1) above shall entitle the Agency to impede or prevent the making of any discharge in pursuance of a consent given under Chapter II of Part III of this Act.

(3) Where the Agency carries out any such works or operations as are mentioned in sub-section (1) above, it shall, subject to sub-section (4) below, be entitled to recover the expenses reasonably incurred in doing so from any person who, as the case may be–

(a) caused or knowingly permitted the matter in question to be present at the place from which it was likely, in the opinion of the Agency, to enter any controlled waters; or

(b) caused or knowingly permitted the matter in question to be present in any controlled waters.

(4) No such expenses shall be recoverable from a person for any works or operations in respect of water from an abandoned mine which that person permitted to reach such a place as is mentioned in sub-section (3) above or to enter any controlled waters.

(5) Nothing in this section–

(a) derogates from any right of action or other remedy (whether civil or criminal) in proceedings instituted otherwise than under this section; or

(b) affects any restriction imposed by or under any other enactment, whether public, local or private.

(6) In this section–

'controlled waters' has the same meaning as in Part III of this Act; and

'mine' has the same meaning as in the Mines and Quarries Act 1954.

Section 190 Pollution control register

(1) It shall be the duty of the [Agency] to maintain, in accordance with regulations made by the Secretary of State, registers containing prescribed particulars of [or relating to]–

(a) any notices of water quality objectives or other notices served under s 83 above;

(b) applications made for consents under Chapter II of Part III of this Act;

(c) consents given under that chapter and the conditions to which the consents are subject;

(d) certificates issued under para 1(7) of Schedule 10 to this Act;

(e) the following, that is to say–

(i) samples of water or effluent taken by the [Agency] for the purposes of any of the water pollution provisions of this Act;

(ii) information produced by analyses of those samples;

(iii) such information with respect to samples of water or effluent taken by any other person, and the analyses of those samples, as is acquired by the [Agency] from any person under arrangements made by the [Agency] for the purposes of any of those provisions; and

(iv) the steps taken in consequence of any such information as is mentioned in any of sub-paras (i) to (iii) above;

and

(f) any matter about which particulars are required to be kept in any register under s 20 of the Environmental Protection Act 1990 (particulars about authorisations for prescribed processes etc) by the Chief Inspector under Part I of that Act.

(g) applications made to the Agency for the variation of discharge consents;

(h) enforcement notices served under s 90B above;

(j) revocations, under paragraph 7 of Schedule 10 to this Act, of discharge consents;

(k) appeals under s 91 above;

(l) directions given by the Secretary of State in relation to the Agency's functions under the water pollution provisions of this Act;

(m) convictions, for offences under Part III of this Act, of persons who have the benefit of discharge consents;

(n) information obtained or furnished in pursuance of conditions of discharge consents;

(o) works notices under s 161A above;

(p) appeals under s 161C above;

(q) convictions for offences under s 161D above;

(r) such other matters relating to the quality of water or the pollution of water as may be prescribed by the Secretary of State.

(1A) Where information of any description is excluded from any register by virtue of s 191B below, a statement shall be entered in the register indicating the existence of information of that description.

(2) It shall be the duty of the [Agency]–

(a) to secure that the contents of registers maintained by the [Agency] under this section are available, at all reasonable times, for inspection by the public free of charge; and

(b) to afford members of the public reasonable facilities for obtaining from the [Agency], on payment of reasonable charges, copies of entries in any of the registers [and, for the purposes of this sub-section, places may be prescribed by the Secretary of State at which any such registers or facilities as are mentioned in paras (a) or (b) above are to be available or afforded to the public in pursuance of the paragraph in question.

(3) Section 101 above shall have effect in relation to any regulations under this section as it has effect in relation to any subordinate legislation under Part III of this Act.

(4) The Secretary of State may give to the Agency directions requiring the removal from any register maintained by it under this section of any specified information which is not prescribed for inclusion under sub-section (1) above or which, by virtue of s 191A or 191B below, ought to have been excluded from the register.

(5) In this section 'discharge consent' has the same meaning as in s 91 above.

Section 191A Exclusion from registers of information affecting national security

(1) No information shall be included in a register kept or maintained by the Agency under any provision of this Act if and so long as, in the opinion of the Secretary of State, the inclusion in such a register of that information, or information of that description, would be contrary to the interests of national security.

(2) The Secretary of State may, for the purpose of securing the exclusion from registers of information to which sub-section (1) above applies, give to the Agency directions–

(a) specifying information, or descriptions of information, to be excluded from their registers; or

(b) specifying descriptions of information to be referred to the Secretary of State for his determination;

and no information referred to the Secretary of State in pursuance of para (b) above shall be included in any such register until the Secretary of State determines that it should be so included.

(3) The Agency shall notify the Secretary of State of any information it excludes from a register in pursuance of directions under sub-section (2) above.

(4) A person may, as respects any information which appears to him to be information to which sub-section (1) above may apply, give a notice to the Secretary of State specifying the information and indicating its apparent nature; and, if he does so–

(a) he shall notify the Agency that he has done so; and

(b) no information so notified to the Secretary of State shall be included in any such register until the Secretary of State has determined that it should be so included.

Section 191B Exclusion from registers of certain confidential information

(1) No information relating to the affairs of any individual or business shall, without the consent of that individual or the person for the time being carrying on that business, be included in a register kept or maintained by the Agency under any provision of this Act, if and so long as the information–

(a) is, in relation to him, commercially confidential; and

(b) is not required to be included in the register in pursuance of directions under sub-section (7) below;

but information is not commercially confidential for the purposes of this section unless it is determined under this section to be so by the Agency or, on appeal, by the Secretary of State.

(2) Where information is furnished to the Agency for the purpose of–

(a) an application for a discharge consent or for the variation of a discharge consent;

(b) complying with any condition of a discharge consent; or

(c) complying with a notice under s 202 below,

then, if the person furnishing it applies to the Agency to have the information excluded from any register kept or maintained by the Agency under any provision of this Act, on the ground that it is commercially confidential (as regards himself or another person), the Agency shall determine whether the information is or is not commercially confidential.

(3) A determination under sub-section (2) above must be made within the period of 14 days beginning with the date of the application and if the Agency fails to make a determination within that period it shall be treated as having determined that the information is commercially confidential.

(4) Where it appears to the Agency that any information (other than information furnished in circumstances within sub-section (2) above) which has been obtained by the Agency

under or by virtue of any provision of any enactment might be commercially confidential, the Agency shall–

(a) give to the person to whom or whose business it relates notice that that information is required to be included in a register kept or maintained by the Agency under any provision of this Act, unless excluded under this section; and

(b) give him a reasonable opportunity

    (i) of objecting to the inclusion of the information on the ground that it is commercially confidential; and

    (ii) of making representations to the Agency for the purpose of justifying any such objection;

and, if any representations are made, the Agency shall, having taken the representations into account, determine whether the information is or is not commercially confidential.

(5) Where, under sub-section (2) or (4) above, the Agency determines that information is not commercially confidential–

(a) the information shall not be entered on the register until the end of the period of 21 days beginning with the date on which the determination is notified to the person concerned; and

(b) that person may appeal to the Secretary of State against the decision;

and, where an appeal is brought in respect of any information, the information shall not be entered on the register until the end of the period of seven days following the day on which the appeal is finally determined or withdrawn.

(6) Sub-sections (2A), (2C) and (2K) of s 91 above shall apply in relation to appeals under sub-section (5) above; but–

(a) sub-section (2C) of that section shall have effect for the purposes of this sub-section with the substitution for the words from '(which may)' onwards of the words '(which must be held in private)'; and

(b) sub-section (5) above is subject to s 114 of the 1995 Act (delegation or reference of appeals etc).

(7) The Secretary of State may give to the Agency directions as to specified information, or descriptions of information, which the public interest requires to be included in registers kept or maintained by the Agency under any provision of this Act notwithstanding that the information may be commercially confidential.

(8) Information excluded from a register shall be treated as ceasing to be commercially confidential for the purposes of this section at the expiry of the period of four years beginning with the date of the determination by virtue of which it was excluded; but the person who furnished it may apply to the Agency for the information to remain excluded from the register on the ground that it is still commercially confidential and the Agency shall determine whether or not that is the case.

(9) Sub-sections (5) and (6) above shall apply in relation to a determination under sub-section (8) above as they apply in relation to a determination under sub-section (2) or (4) above.

(10) The Secretary of State may by regulations substitute (whether in all cases or in such classes or descriptions of case as may be specified in the regulations) for the period for

the time being specified in sub-section (3) above such other period as he considers appropriate.

(11) Information is, for the purposes of any determination under this section, commercially confidential, in relation to any individual or person, if its being contained in the register would prejudice to an unreasonable degree the commercial interests of that individual or person.

(12) In this section 'discharge consent' has the same meaning as in s 91 above.

R v National Rivers Authority ex p Moreton [1996] Env LR 234

Harrison J: [...] This is an application for judicial review of a decision of the respondent, the National Rivers Authority (the 'NRA'), dated 5 June 1995 granting a consent to Welsh Water for discharge of sewage from the Tenby Headworks. The applicant seeks to quash that decision and she seeks an injunction to restrain the discharge of sewage pursuant to that consent.

The applicant is a regular swimmer in the sea at Tenby and she is concerned about the effect of the increased effluent discharge pursuant to the consent at the long-sea outfall at Tenby on the quality of the bathing water where she swims. Her main concern is that, in granting the discharge consent, the NRA did not impose a condition requiring ultra violet disinfection. Three submissions are made on behalf of the applicant. First, that the NRA wrongly took into account, or considered as a restriction, the investment budget of Welsh Water. Second, the NRA unlawfully failed to have regard to the EC Bathing Water Directive. Third, the NRA misunderstood the EC Urban Waste Water Treatment Directive.

The sewage at Saundersfoot is at present given primary and rudimentary secondary treatment and is then discharged into the sea just below low water mark. Under the new discharge consent it would be pumped by a pipeline, which has already been constructed, to the Tenby Headworks from where it would be discharged, together with the Tenby sewage, through the long-sea outfall at Tenby which is about 2.7 km out to sea. The transfer is proposed to commence at the end of this month, hence the urgency of this matter. Its purpose is to ensure that the quality of the water at Saundersfoot complies with the mandatory standard (the 'I' standard) of the EC Bathing Water Directive, which must be complied with by December 1995. According to the NRA, the quality of the water at Tenby complies with the mandatory standards of that Directive and would continue to do so after the increased discharge from Saundersfoot. The arrangement that I have described would be a temporary one during the 1996 bathing season, pending the completion of a new sewage treatment works at Tenby (the Gumfreston sewage treatment works) which will provide primary and secondary treatment of the Tenby and Saundersfoot sewage, together with improvements to some storm sewage overflows that presently occur at Tenby, in particular combined storm overflows into the River Ritec which itself flows via a culvert under the beach into the sea at the South Beach at Tenby. As a result of those works, it is expected by the NRA and Welsh Water, although contested by some others, that there will be compliance with the more stringent guideline standards (the 'G' standards) of the EC Bathing Water Directive and compliance with the Urban Waste Water Treatment Directive by 1997, although the requirement to comply with the latter Directive does not come into force until December 2000.

[After summarising the statutory provisions his Lordship continued ...]

Mr Saini, who appeared on behalf of the applicant, submitted first that the NRA, when considering Welsh Water's discharge consent application, wrongly had regard to Welsh

Water's investment budget known as AMP 2. Alternatively, if they were able to have regard to it, they wrongly considered themselves to be restricted by it. [...] In order to deal with that submission it is necessary to refer briefly to the exercise which culminates in the approval of AMP 2. It was helpfully described to me by Mr Bailey, who appeared on behalf of the NRA. First, the environmental quality standards are set by the Secretary of State pursuant to ss 82 and 83 of the Water Resources Act 1991 and he notifies the NRA, as the quality regulator, of the environmental qualities to be achieved. Second, the water companies, having been informed by the NRA of those mandatory standards, design the engineering solution to achieve those standards. The NRA is involved in that design process, which is an iterative process, in order to satisfy itself that the water companies' engineering solutions will achieve those standards. Third, after the NRA has signified its satisfaction, the water companies cost those engineering solutions and submit the package to the Director. Fourth, the Director, who has to assume that the solutions achieve the mandatory standards, scrutinises the costings and then sets 'K', which is the sum in percentage terms over the retail price index by which the Director will allow the water company to increase its prices. That deals with the mandatory spend.

The discretionary spend arises when water companies persuade the Director that their customers are prepared to spend more to attain a higher level of service than that achieved by the mandatory standards. The NRA draws up a prioritised list of schemes which are not required to meet mandatory standards but which are nevertheless desirable to meet environmental needs. They put that list to the Secretary of State for his approval. The Director decides on the amount of money that can be authorised out of 'K'. That amount of money is then applied to the prioritised list of schemes and it can be seen how many of them can be implemented.

Applying that process to this case, it can be seen from the documents that the need for a solution to the Tenby and Saundersfoot beach bathing water problem was identified by the NRA and Welsh Water. It featured in the iterative AMP 2 process. The need was identified to comply in due course with the EC Urban Waste Water Treatment Directive, as was the need to deal with the problem of the discharge from the River Ritec which arises both from the storm sewage overflows into that river and from the agricultural nature of its catchment. The total discretionary spend in AMP 2 was some £27 million of which £2 million was earmarked for provision of secondary treatment at the Gumfreston sewage treatment works.

[...]

In my view, it was perfectly proper for the NRA to take AMP 2 (Welsh Water's investment budget) into account. In the AMP 2 process the NRA was well aware of the Tenby/Saundersfoot problem and its solution. It was only natural that the application for the discharge consent was made later following the AMP 2 process as part of the execution of that solution. In considering that application, the NRA did consider whether to impose a condition requiring ultra violet disinfection. They concluded that the benefits would be marginal and that there was not a sufficiently pressing need for it. I quote from a part of the first Position Statement which is headed 'Disinfection':

Considerable concern has been expressed that disinfection is not currently planned as part of this scheme. Disinfection is planned at various other sites around the Welsh coastline although in these cases, it is a key element of the treatment plans to achieve the statutory standards. These standards should be readily achieved at Tenby without the need for disinfection ... The key difference at Tenby is that there is already a long-sea outfall providing high dilution and dispersion of the effluent. Therefore the benefits of disinfection at Tenby would be marginal and would not currently represent sound investment given the more pressing needs for this money to be spent elsewhere.

That seems to me to be a perfectly proper way of approaching the matter. The NRA concluded that ultraviolet disinfection was not necessary to meet the mandatory requirements of the Directive, and that otherwise the marginal benefits from imposing such a condition could not be justified bearing in mind that there were other more pressing needs. If they had concluded that the benefits were so great as to justify money being spent on it they could have imposed the condition and Welsh Water may have had to try and find the money from elsewhere. It is clear that they concluded that the benefits were only marginal. There is no suggestion that such a conclusion is Wednesbury unreasonable and, in my view, it was a perfectly proper exercise of their discretion to reach the decision which they reached. It seems to me that it is inevitable that the NRA should have regard to the priorities of environmental need and in doing so they can have regard to AMP 2. Furthermore, I am quite satisfied that the public consultation was not a sham. The evidence is that the NRA went further than they need have done and they took into account the representations that were made to them. I do not therefore accept the applicant's first submission. The second submission made by Mr Saini had two parts. First, the NRA erred in law in ignoring the mandatory requirement (the 'I' standard) relating to viruses in the EC Bathing Water Directive. Second, the NRA failed to have regard to the obligation under the Directive to endeavour to observe the guideline requirements in the Directive (the 'G' standard). His submission relating to both the 'I' standard and the 'G' standard was initially based on the requirements in the Directive itself. However, Mr Bailey drew attention to the provisions which had incorporated the Directive's requirements into the United Kingdom legislation and Mr Saini thereafter based his submissions on the domestic provisions.

The position under the Directive is that Article 3(1) requires all members to set the 'I' standards specified in the Annex to the Directive for Bathing Waters. The Annex specifies the bacterial standards and it also specifies a zero standard for entero-viruses. It does, however, provide, in relation to entero-viruses, that the concentration is to be checked when an inspection in the bathing area shows that the substance may be present or that the quality of the water has deteriorated. By notice dated 5 May 1992, the Secretary of State gave notice to the NRA under s 83 of the Water Resources Act 1991 that the water quality objectives for bathing waters including the Tenby and Saundersfoot beaches were to be satisfaction of the requirements for classification BW1 set out in the Bathing Waters (Classification) Regulations 1991. Schedule 3 of those Regulations set out the same zero standard for entero-viruses and it also provided that samples must be taken where there are grounds for suspecting that there has been a deterioration in the quality of the waters. The result of that s 83 notice is that, under s 84 of the Act, the NRA is under a duty to ensure that those standards are achieved so far as is practicable to do so.

The position relating to the 'G' standards, the guideline standards, is that by virtue of Article 3(3) of the Directive the Member States shall endeavour to observe them as guidelines. The effect of para 3 of the National Rivers Authority (Bathing Waters) Directions 1992 is that the NRA must give effect to Article 3(3) in relation to bathing waters to which the classification BW1 applies.

Thus it is that the 'I' and 'G' standards of the Directive have become incorporated into the domestic legislation. It is those provisions upon which Mr Saini relies. Dealing first with the mandatory 'I' standards, Mr Saini drew my attention to the following two passages in the NRA's first Position Statement:

The virus standards within the Directive are not considered to have any scientific basis and the government has indicated that they should not be considered in the design of schemes or the assessment of compliance with the Directive.

and,

In the case of Tenby, the minimum standards to be achieved are continued compliance with the Bathing Water Directive bacterial standards and the minimum requirements of the Urban Wastewater Treatment Directive.

Based on those passages Mr Saini submitted that it was plain that the United Kingdom government and the NRA had taken the view that they did not believe the scientific validity of the 'I' standard relating to entero-viruses and that they had decided not to apply it. There had, he said, been no monitoring since August 1991 except for one occasion this year which was after the grant of the discharge consent. He recognised, however, that the duty to monitor may not yet have been triggered in the light of Mr Brown's evidence that visual inspection had not revealed any deterioration in the water quality sufficient to trigger the virus monitoring pursuant to the Directive. He, therefore, suggested that this court should declare as part of its judgment that the stance of the NRA was unlawful, even if it did not impact on the decision in this case.

So far as the 'G' standard is concerned, Mr Saini drew my attention, *inter alia*, to the following passage in the second Position Statement which reads:

Both beaches marginally failed to achieve the much stricter guideline values with five samples exceeding the limit for faecal coliforms compared to the four exceedances permitted against this standard. It should be stressed, however, that this standard is not applied by the UK government. Details are only included on guideline compliance because of its relevance to the Blue Flag award.

Based on that passage and another passage in a letter from the NRA to the applicant's solicitor, Mr Saini submitted that the NRA had failed to have regard to the obligation to endeavour to observe the guideline standards. He urged caution in accepting Mr Brown's explanation in his affidavit that the improvements to the sewage treatment regime at Tenby should, as a matter of logic, be seen as an endeavour to comply with the guideline standards. Mr Saini pointed out that leave had been granted on the basis of the Position Statements, and that the respondent's affidavits had not dealt with the passage to which I have just referred.

Mr Bailey on behalf of the NRA dealt manfully with the contents of the Position Statements to seek to show that whatever the position of the United Kingdom government was on the virus 'I' standard, the NRA had not adopted that stance. He pointed to the data which was in the possession of the NRA which would not otherwise be in their possession if they were ignoring the mandatory virus standard. He pointed out that, although the United Kingdom government had only directed that the total coliform and faecal coliform mandatory standards of the Directive would be used, the NRA had nevertheless also monitored faecal streptococci which was required by the Directive. That showed, he said, that the NRA was not slavishly obedient to the United Kingdom government on this issue. Mr Bailey submitted that, on the evidence, the NRA did have regard to the mandatory virus standard. He referred me to the affidavits of Mr Griffiths and Mr Brown on that aspect and, in particular, to Mr Brown's evidence that at all material times visual inspection of the bathing waters had been conducted weekly and that no deterioration in the water quality sufficient to trigger virus monitoring pursuant to the Directive had been found.

I must bear in mind that the United Kingdom government is not represented in this case before this court. All I can say on the evidence before me is that it would appear that they are not implementing the mandatory virus standard as required by the Directive. However, the NRA are not the United Kingdom government. The general impression that I obtain from the documentary evidence is that the NRA are sympathetic to the stance adopted by the United Kingdom government, if that be their stance, although I do not find the evidence to be sufficiently clear to warrant a conclusion that the NRA have decided not to comply with the mandatory virus standard, although I do not discount that as a possibility.

The important point on this aspect, as I think is accepted by Mr Saini, is that the virus monitoring obligation had not yet been triggered, as was shown by Mr Brown's evidence, and there could not therefore have been a failure to comply with the Directive at the time the decision in this case was taken. For that reason alone, the applicant's point relating to the virus mandatory standard must fail.

So far as the guideline standard is concerned, Mr Bailey submitted that the statement in the second Position Statement that the guideline values are not applied by the United Kingdom government is wrong because, by the 1992 Direction made under s 5 of the Water Resources Act 1991, the Secretary of State had actually directed the NRA to give effect to the guideline standards in Article 3(3) of the Directive. He contended that the NRA had endeavoured to observe the guidelines as shown by the proposed sewage treatment improvements which are aimed at achieving the guideline standards.

I must take care to differentiate between the United Kingdom government and the NRA. There is no doubt that the Position Statement says that the guideline standard is not applied by the United Kingdom government. I find that difficult to reconcile with the direction given by the Secretary of State to the NRA to give effect to those guidelines. There is no direct evidence one way or the other as to the NRA's stance on that issue. It is true, as Mr Saini said both in relation to the mandatory and the guideline standards, that the NRA affidavits failed to deal with the point expressly. It is for the applicant to show that the NRA have failed to apply the guideline standards of the Directive and, in my view, they have failed to do so. If anything, the NRA licensing of the Gumfreston Sewage Treatment Works improvements would tend to suggest that they have taken the guideline standards of the Directive into account because the effect of that proposal is thought by the NRA and Welsh Water to achieve the guideline standard at Tenby in 1997. I, therefore, am unable to accept the applicant's second submission.

Mr Saini's third and final submission was that the NRA had misunderstood the requirements of the EC Urban Waste Water Treatment Directive. Article 6 of that Directive, which has not yet come into force, allows less stringent treatment for areas identified as less sensitive areas provided that the discharges receive primary treatment and provided that comprehensive studies indicate that such discharges will not adversely affect the environment. The coastal waters off-shore of Tenby and Saundersfoot have been designated a less sensitive area described as a 'High Natural Dispersion Area'. Mr Saini's point was that in the first Position Statement there was a passage which mentioned the proviso relating to primary treatment but failed to mention the second proviso relating to comprehensive studies and that the NRA had misunderstood the Directive and misdirected itself.

I am quite satisfied that there is nothing in that point. The mere fact that one of the provisos in Article 6 of the Directive was not mentioned in the Position Statement does not mean that the NRA misunderstood the Directive and, in any event, the Tenby and Saundersfoot sewage will receive secondary and primary treatment when the Gumfreston sewage treatment works are completed which will render the Directive, which does not come into force until 2000, irrelevant.

I, therefore, conclude, for all the reasons I have given, that this application must be dismissed.

Moase and Another v Secretary of State for the Environment, Transport and the Regions and Another CA (Civil Division) [2000] JPL 746.

The following is an extract from the judgment of the Court of Appeal read by Swinton-Thomas. The extract is limited to the aspect of the case concerned with defining 'bathing waters':

> This is an appeal against the order of Owen J dated 30 September 1999 dismissing the appellants' challenge to a compulsory purchase order ('CPO') made to acquire land at Cornborough, Devon for the purposes of constructing and operating a sewage treatment works (STW) ... The CPO was made by South West Water Services Ltd under the Water Industry Act 1991, s 155 and the Acquisition of Land Act 1981 ('the 1981 Act'), s 23. The Secretary of State for Environment, Transport and the Regions, the first respondent, appointed [an Inspector] to hold an inquiry and submit a report on the application to him by SWWS for confirmation of the order. The Inspector submitted his report to the Secretary of State who by letter dated 20 May 1998 approved the order.
>
> ...
>
> ... the waters at Abbotsham have not received classification BWI. In addition it is clear that the mandatory enterovirus standard will not be met at Abbotsham. Indeed, in a letter dated 1 July 1996 to Mr P G Scott, one of the objectors to the Cornborough STW scheme, the EA stated:
>
> > 8   Risk to bathers and surfers at the outfall point.
> >
> > Any persons bathing close to the outfall point may be bathing in waters that do not comply with the requirements of the EC Bathing Waters Directive. As these waters are not recognised as EC Bathing Waters, they are not protected by that Directive.
>
> This point is material because one of the appellants' submissions is that the waters at Abbotsham are or are likely to be 'bathing waters' for the purposes of the Bathing Waters Directive and this forms one of the grounds for their challenge to the CPO.
>
> According to the Hartland Heritage Coast draft Management Strategy, which was produced to the Inspector, Abbotsham is one of the main tourist attractions of the area and has a surfing beach. The Inspector also received a written representation from Mr C Hockin of Abbotsham and a member of the Westward Surf Club. In his representation Mr Hockin said that the discharge point for the Cornborough outfall:
>
> > ... is the exact location of the best and one of the only surf breakers that is surfable on this part of the rocky coastline. Due to the high quality of this wave, it is surfed all the year round, particularly in the winter when it is at its best. Because of the quality of this breaker not only do Westward Surf Club surf there, but it also attracts surfers from all over the South West.

The objectors at the inquiry contended that the beach at Abbotsham was also used for swimming, fishing and prawning. There is, however, no finding on this by the Inspector. The ordnance survey map shows the coastline at Abbotsham to be rocky. There is no access to the beach by road. The nearest road stops a short distance away, and thereafter it is necessary to walk. There are no facilities for users of the beach at Abbotsham.

In connection with the interpretation of Art 1.2 of the Bathing Waters Directive, the European Commission gave the following written answer in the European Parliament on 10 September 1985:

> The Commission is aware that the interpretation of the notion in Article 1 paragraph 2 second alternative of Directive 76/160/EEC, which qualifies a water as bathing water in which bathing is not prohibited and is traditionally practised by a large number of bathers is not easily practicable. The Commission believes that in order to interpret this notion, the requirement of a specific number of bathers can only be one criterion among others. Indeed the number of bathers varies according to the season, the weather, school holidays, working days and so on. Thus the number of bathers counted on a specific day cannot in itself determine the bathing water quality for a specific water. Rather some objective criteria will also have to be taken into account. Such objective criteria are amongst others:
>
> (1) facilities for access to the beach;
>
> (2) sanitary equipment;
>
> (3) facilities for changing;
>
> (4) parking space for cars;
>
> (5) life-guards on the beach;
>
> (6) first-aid service;
>
> (7) kiosks and shops (mobile shops);
>
> (8) Availability of water sport facilities;
>
> (boats, surfing, swimming lessons).
>
> Indeed, such measures of infrastructure demonstrate action of local, regional or national administration in order to promote bathing. Therefore the presence of such measures of infrastructure proves that the authorities felt induced by the great number of bathers to provide for measures to ensure safe bathing, safe access to the beach and to the waters and amenities to further increase the number of bathers.
>
> Furthermore, it is not known why persons who are on a beach abstain from bathing; they might do so in some cases also because the water is too polluted. For these reasons the Commission is of the opinion that all circumstances regarding the individual water have to be taken into consideration when assessing whether a specific water qualifies as bathing water under the second alternative of Directive 76/160/EEC Article 1 paragraph 2.
>
> (OJ Annex 2-239 Debates 1985/86, reports of proceedings 9–13 September 1985).

The criteria set out in this written answer are called 'the Prag criteria'.

[...]

We turn, then, to consider the question as to whether the Abbotsham and Cornborough waters adjacent to the outfall pipe (as opposed to the Westward Ho waters) are Bathing Waters for the purposes of the BW Directive. The relevant waters are not explicitly authorised as bathing waters with the result that in order to qualify as such under the

Regulations they would have to be waters in which bathing is 'traditionally practised by a large number of bathers'. The Inspector recorded at para 89 of his Report that the case for the objectors in relation to Abbotsham was that: 'Abbotsham beach is used throughout the year for various recreational pursuits including swimming, surfing, fishing and prawning, while the adjacent coast path is popular with walkers.' We note that in contrast in the same paragraph the objectors' case in relation to Westward Ho was: 'The golden sands of Westward Ho beach are well known to holiday makers and provide vital support to the local tourist trade.' The Inspector's conclusion at para 148 was: 'Abbotsham beach is a significant resource for various kinds of recreation. Some activities, notably bathing and surfing, involve contact with sea water.' We have seen photographs which were before the Inspector of the Abbotsham and Cornborough beach which show it to be rocky. There is no car access and access by foot is difficult. Some assistance on this issue can be derived from the *Prag* criteria. In the case of the Cornborough and Abbotsham waters none of these are fulfilled. So far as the evidence went, there were no facilities for access to the beach, no sanitary equipment, no facilities for changing, no parking space for cars, no lifeguards on the beach, no first-aid service, no kiosks or shops, and no availability of water sport facilities. There was no infrastructure to promote bathing. There was no evidence that bathing was traditionally practised by a large number of bathers. Indeed, the evidence was to the contrary, namely that the waters were to some extent used for recreational sports, not only surfing, and that there were some bathers. There was no evidence that required the Inspector to find that these particular waters were bathing waters, and, in our judgment, on the limited evidence that was available to us, it is plain that they were not. We do not consider that we are required to refer this point to the European Court of Justice.

REFERENCES AND FURTHER READING

Abecassis, DW and Jarashow, RL, *Oil Pollution from Ships*, 2nd edn, 1985, London: Stevens

Ball, S, 'Causing water pollution' [1993] 5 JEL 128

Ball, S, 'Protected nature conservation sites and the water industry' (1990) 1 Water Law 74

Bates, I, 'Causing or knowingly permitting in pollution legislation' (1977) JPL 63

Birnie, P, 'Protection of the marine environment – the public international law approach', in De La Rue, CM (ed), *Liability for Damage to the Marine Environment*, 1993, London: LLP, pp 1–22

Birnie, P, 'Protection of the marine environment in joint development', in Fox (ed), *Joint Development of Offshore Oil and Gas,* 1990, London: British Institute of International and Comparative Law, Vol II

Birnie, P and Boyle, A, *Basic Documents on International Law and the Environment*, 1995, Oxford: OUP

Birnie, P and Boyle, A, *International Law and the Environment*, 1992, Oxford: Clarendon

Bowman, M, 'Nuisance, strict liability and environmental hazards' [1995] Env Liability 105

Broadus, JM and Vartanov, RV (eds), *The Oceans and Environmental Security: Shared US and Russian Perspectives*, 1994, Washington DC: Island Press

Brubaker, D, *Marine Pollution and International Law: Principles and Practice*, 1993, London: Belhaven

Churchill, RR, Warren, C and Gibson, C, *Law, Policy and the Environment*, 1991, Oxford: Basil Blackwell, pp 95–109

Collins, DM, 'The tanker's right of harmless discharge and protection of the marine environment' (1987) 18 Journal of Maritime Law and Commerce 275

De La Rue, CM (ed), *Liability for Damage to the Marine Environment*, 1993, London: LLP

Department of Environment, *Third International Conference on the Protection of the North Sea, UK, Guidance Note on the Ministerial Declaration*, 1990, London: DoE

Dzidzornu, D and Tsamenyi, BM, 'Enhancing international control of vessel-source oil pollution under the Law of the Sea Convention 1982: a reassessment' (1991) 10 University of Tasmania L Rev 269

Ellis, EJ, 'International law and oily waters: a critical analysis' (1995) 6(1) Colorado Journal of International Environmental Law and Policy 31–60

Farmer, A, *Managing Environmental Pollution,* 1997, London: Routledge

Franckx, E, 'Coastal State jurisdiction with respect to marine pollution – some recent developments and future challenges' [1995] 10(2) International Journal of Marine and Coastal Law 253–80

Haigh, N, *Manual of Environmental Policy: The EC and Britain*, London: Longman (loose leaf)

Hawkins, K, *Environment and Enforcement*, 1984, Oxford: OUP

House of Lords Select Committee on the European Communities, *Nitrate in Water* Session 1988–89, 16th Report, HL Paper 73–1, London: HMSO

Howarth, W, 'Making water polluters pay – England and Wales' [1994] Env Liability 29

Howarth, W, 'Poisonous, noxious or polluting – contrasting approaches to environmental regulation' (1993) 56 MLR 171

Howarth, W, *Water Pollution Law*, 1988 and 1990 Supplement, London: Shaw & Sons

Howarth, W and Somsen, T, ' The EC Nitrates Directive' (1991) 2 Water Law 149

Kirgis, FL Jr, 'Shipping', in Schachter, D and Joyner, C (eds), *United Nations Legal Order* 1995, Cambridge: CUP, Vol 2, pp 715–51

Kodwo, B, 'Nature of obligations imposed by EEC clean water directives' (1991) 2 Water Law 200

Kramer, L, *EC Treaty and Environmental Law*, 4th edn, 1995, London: Sweet & Maxwell

Malcolm, R, *A Guide to Environmental Law*, 1994, London: Sweet & Maxwell

Mitchell, R, 'Intentional oil pollution of the oceans', in Haas, Keohane and Levy (eds) *Institutions for the Earth: Sources of Effective International Environmental Protection*, 1993 Cambridge, Mass: The MIT Press, pp 183–247

Nanda, P, *International Environmental Law and Policy*, 1995A, Irvington-on-Hudson, New York: Transnational

Nanda, P, 'Environment', in Schacher, O and Joyner, CC, *United Nations Legal Order* 1995B, Cambridge: CUP, Vol 2, pp 631–69

National Rivers Authority, *Bathing Water Quality in England and Wales – 1994*, NRA Water Quality Series No 22, 1995, London: HMSO

National Rivers Authority, *Pesticides in Major Aquifers*, NRA Research and Development Report No 17, 1995, London: HMSO

National Rivers Authority, *River Pollution from Farms in England*, 1995, London: National Audit Office, HMSO

National Rivers Authority, *Discharge Consents and Compliance: The NRA's Approach to Control of Discharges to Water*, NRA Water Quality Series No 17, 1994, London: HMSO

National Rivers Authority, *Implementation of the EC Freshwater Fish Directive*, NRA Water Quality Series No 20, 1994, London: HMSO

National Rivers Authority, *Water, Nature's Precious Resource, An Environmentally Sustainable Water Resources Development Strategy for England and Wales*, 1994, London: NRA, HMSO

National Rivers Authority, *Policy and Practice for the Protection of Groundwater*, 1992, London: NRA, HMSO

Nollkaemper, A and Hey, E, 'Implementation of the Law of the Sea Convention at regional level: European Community competence in regulating safety and environmental aspects of shipping' (1995) 10(2) International Journal of Marine and Coastal Law 281–300

Papworth, N, 'Causing water pollution and the acts of third parties' [1998] JPL 752–61

Rémond-Gouilloud, M, 'I. Introduction', to Chapter Three, 'Prevention and control of marine pollution', in Johnston, DM (ed), *The Environmental Law of the Sea*, 1981, IUCN Environmental Policy and Law Paper No 18, Gland, Switzerland: International Union for Conservation of Nature and Natural Resources, pp 193–202

Richardson, G, Ogus, A and Burrows, A, *Policing Pollution*, 1983, Oxford: OUP

Saetevik, S, *Environmental Co-operation Between The North Sea States*, 1988, London: Belhaven

Safer Ships, Cleaner Seas (CM 2560), *The Government's Response* (Cm 2766), London: HMSO

Schneider, J, 'II. pollution from vessels', in Chapter Three, 'Prevention and Control of Marine Pollution', in Johnston, DM (ed), *The Environmental Law of the Sea* (1981), IUCN Environmental Policy and Law Paper No 18, Gland, Switzerland: International Union for Conservation of Nature and Natural Resources, pp 203–17

Sebenius, JK, 'The Law of the Sea Conference: lessons for negotiations to control global warming', in Sjostedt, G (ed), *International Environmental Negotiation*, 1993, Newbury Park, California: Sage, pp 189–218

Simpson, AWB, 'Legal liability for bursting reservoirs: the historical context of *Rylands v Fletcher*' (1984) 13 J Leg Studies 209

Somsen, M, 'EC water directives' (1990) 1 Water Law 93

Springall, 'P & I insurance and oil pollution' (1988) 6 Journal of Energy and Natural Resources Law 25

Stephenson, MA, 'Vessel-source pollution under the Law of the Sea Convention – an analysis of the prescriptive standards' [1992] 17 University of Queensland Law Journal 117

This Common Inheritance, Cm 1200, 1990, London: HMSO, Chapter 12

Wetterstein, P, *Environmental Impairment Liability in Admiralty: A Note on Compensable Damage Under US Law*, 1992, Abo: Abo Akademi UP

White, JC, 'The Voluntary Oil Spill Compensation Agreements – TOVALOP and CRISTAL', in De La Rue, CM (ed), *Liability for Damage to the Marine Environment*, 1993, London: LLP, pp 57–69

USEFUL WEBSITES

Department of the Environment, Transport and the Regions: www.detr.gov.uk

International Maritime Organisation: www.imo.org

OFWAT: www.open.gov.uk/ofwat

The Drinking Water Inspectorate: www.detr.gov.uk

UK Rivers Network: www.abst59.care4free.net/news.html and www.abst59.care4 free.net/pollution.html. This site provides excellent further references and links

UN Law of the Sea Office homepage: www.un.org/Depts/los

Water UK: www. water.org.uk

For further general websites, see pages l–li, above.

CHAPTER 4

WASTE

INTRODUCTION TO THE LAW RELATING TO WASTE

Modern society generates enormous amounts of industrial and commercial waste, some of which is very dangerous to human health and poses a serious threat to the environment. Over one hundred million tonnes of waste is produced in England and Wales alone every year, to say nothing of the millions of tonnes of liquid waste and sewerage effluent pumped into our rivers and the marine environment (see below, *Waste Strategy 2000*, pp 431–39). The modern legal response to the problem of waste has been to adopt a holistic approach first to minimise the generation of waste by, for example, encouraging efficient technology and reducing packaging; by providing incentives for recycling and reuse of materials; and finally by setting strict environmental controls for disposing of waste. At present four main options exist for disposing of waste: dumping at sea, exporting across national boundaries, incineration and landfill. Each of these options carry adverse environmental consequences and require a balancing between environmental and economic costs taking account of what is technically feasible. The challenge confronting us is to ensure that the balance achieved is sustainable.

Most of us have no difficulty in understanding the concept of waste: waste is basically what we don't want and is usually placed in our dustbins to be collected and removed from sight. However, as we shall see later in the chapter, the legal definition of waste is far from clear. As with the previous chapters we present the principal legal materials concerned with international, European Community and UK domestic regulation of waste.

INTERNATIONAL LAW

Under public international law, the regulation of waste has focused on two main areas:

(a) waste disposal, including dumping especially but not exclusively, in areas beyond national jurisdiction, such as the high seas; and

(b) international trade in and movement of waste.

This section focuses on the Convention for the Prevention of Marine Pollution by Dumping of Waste and Other Matter 1972 and the Basel Convention on the Control of Trans-boundary Movements of Hazardous Wastes and their Disposal 1989 and the Basel Protocol 1999. A more radical regional alternative developed for the African continent, the Bamako Convention on the Ban of Imports into Africa and the Control of Trans-boundary Movement and Management of Hazardous Wastes within Africa 1991, will also be discussed, although the text of this Convention is not set out.

It is important to ask why the international legal framework on the issue of waste is focused on these two areas of dumping in the high seas and trans-boundary movements of hazardous wastes. Why, for example, are there no international treaties or other instruments regulating the movement and disposal of hazardous or toxic waste material within the land territories and internal waters of States? The main reason for the inability of international law to exert controls over domestic waste movement and disposal activities relates to the perennial issue of a State's sovereignty under international law. As frequently mentioned elsewhere in this book, the reluctance of States to countenance any constraints upon the exercise of this sovereignty has proved to be a major stumbling block to the progressive development of international law generally, and international environmental law specifically, even where uniform national controls would enhance the overall legal certainty of regimes and promote greater economic efficiency in the provision of waste disposal and transport services. For the position within the EC see the Hazardous Waste Directive 91/689, pp 381 and 396, below, and the EC Regulation on Shipments of Waste 259/93, pp 386 and 398, below.

Dumping at sea

Pollution by dumping accounts for approximately 10% of the overall pollution of the marine environment (Sands (1995) 308). It is addressed by two main international conventions of global application, the UN Convention on the Law of the Sea 1982 (UNCLOS) which establishes broad principles on this issue area, especially within Pt XII (see Chapter 3, p 214, above) and the Convention for the Prevention of Marine Pollution by Dumping 1972 (London Dumping Convention), which sets down detailed regulations at the global level (Sands (1995) 308ff). In addition, there are six regional agreements covering dumping in the North Sea, North East Atlantic, Baltic, Mediterranean and South Pacific regions.

1982 UNCLOS, Pt XII

As seen in Chapter 3, the UNCLOS lays down the framework of general obligations in respect of different types of polluting activities, including dumping, in Pt XII on the Protection and Preservation of the Marine Environment. Articles 210 and 216 require States to adopt and enforce laws and regulations and take other measures to prevent, reduce and control pollution of the marine environment by dumping, which are no less effective than the global rules and standards established for this activity by the 1972 Convention (Birnie and Boyle (1992) 320). One possibly interesting legal outcome of this provision is that it appears to bind States Parties to UNCLOS to the standards approved by the 1972 Convention even if these States are not parties to the latter Convention.

Convention for the Prevention of Marine Pollution by Dumping of Waste and Other Matter 1972

This Convention is the main international instrument on the global aspect of this problem. Its genesis was the result of initiatives developed for the 1972 Stockholm UN

Conference on the Human Environment (see Chapter 1, p 61). The Convention entered into force on 30 August 1975 and by 1999 had 77 parties, including at least 38 developing countries.[1] Its States' parties represent a wide range of interests, from industrialised States with an interest in dumping, to island States opposed to this method of waste disposal. Despite evidently conflicting interests, the Convention is widely regarded as being successful in generating an international consensus on the development of policy for dumping at sea, both at the international and national levels.

Significantly the Convention applies to all marine waters, other than internal waters (Art III(3)), thereby including within its scope the territorial waters, EEZs, and continental shelves of States' parties. This represents an extension in the reach of international law into the national maritime jurisdictions of these States in this context. The Convention obliges all States parties to 'take all practicable steps to prevent the pollution of the sea by the dumping of waste and other matter that is liable to create hazards to human health, to harm living resources and marine life, to damage amenities or to interfere with other legitimate uses of the sea' (Art I). 'Dumping' is defined as:

(i) any deliberate disposal at sea of wastes or other matter from vessels, aircraft, platforms or other man-made structures at sea;

(ii) any deliberate disposal at sea of vessels, aircraft, platforms or other man- made structures at sea (Art III(1)(a)).

Operational discharges of wastes as a result of shipping and other offshore activities are not included within the definition of 'dumping' (Art III(b) and (c)). 'Wastes or other matter' are broadly defined as 'material or substance of any kind, form or description' (Art III(4)).

The method adopted by the Convention consists mainly of rules prohibiting or regulating the dumping of wastes, which have in turn been divided into three different categories and listed in Annexes I, II and III. The dumping of highly hazardous waste substances listed in Annex I (black list) is prohibited (Art IV(1)(a)), subject only to limited exceptions covering:

(1) emergency situations where human life is threatened (Art V);

(2) warships and other vessels and aircraft entitled to sovereign immunity under international law (Art VII(4));

(3) waste substances which are rapidly rendered harmless (Annex I.8) or those containing only trace contaminants (Annex I.9).

The dumping of Annex II 'special care' substances and wastes (grey list) requires a prior 'special' permit (Art IV(1)(b)) and the dumping of all other wastes requires a prior 'general' permit (Art IV(1)(c)). Both these 'special' and 'general' permits are issued by designated national authorities of the State Party (Art VI(1)(a) and (b)), for waste matter intended for dumping which is loaded in its territory (Art VI(2)(a)), or loaded by a vessel or aircraft registered in its territory, or flying its flag when the loading occurs in the territory of a State not party to this Convention (Art VI(2)(b)).

---

1   For a full text see UKTS 43 1976; 11 ILM (1972) 1294. See also www.imo.org.

In addition to this, the designated national authorities are also required to keep records of the nature and quantities of all matter permitted to be dumped (Art VI(1)(c)), and conduct individual and collaborative monitoring operations of the condition of the seas subject to these dumping activities (Art VI(1)(d)). As Sands notes, in theory this should provide the international community with information on the dumping at sea practices of State parties. In reality however reporting requirements are not fully complied with, and there is considerable evidence of large-scale unauthorised dumping by nationals of parties in violation of the Convention (Sands (1995) 310).

The mechanism by which progress in achieving the objectives of the Convention is considered is the annual consultative meetings of the parties (Art XIV(4)). These meetings are also responsible for, *inter alia*, the review of its implementation, amendments to the Convention provisions and its Annexes, receipt of national reports, and dissemination of relevant scientific and technical information.

Amendments to the Convention are adopted by a two-thirds majority of those State parties present, and enter into force for parties accepting them 60 days after two-thirds of them have done so (Art XV(1)(a)). Amendments to Annexes are also adopted by two-thirds majority of those present, and enter into force for all parties except those which declare they are unable to accept an amendment within 100 days of the approval of the amendment (Art XV(2)). This is a subtle yet significant shift in the decision-making process which has the effect of simplifying the procedural requirement for entry into force of any amendments to the Annexes by ensuring that the States' parties that are keen to implement the proposed amendments are not held back by other parties dragging their feet in a long drawn-out approval procedure.

The simplified amendment procedure for Annexes to the Convention has been successfully utilised recently, for example, in order to prohibit all dumping of radioactive waste, ban the incineration of waste at sea and phase out the dumping of industrial waste (Birnie and Boyle (1995) 174).[2]

International trade in hazardous wastes and substances

The second area with which international law is concerned is the permissibility of international movement and trade in waste. As with dumping, the law has been driven by the need to reconcile competing interests. These include the desire among many developing countries, especially in Africa, to prohibit such trade entirely. By contrast there is opposition to such a peremptory approach by many industrialised countries wanting to keep open their waste disposal options. The middle ground is occupied by the newly-industrialising countries which alternate between viewing such trade as either an emerging market opportunity or a growing environmental threat (Birnie and Boyle (1992) 332–33 and Sands (1995) 503). As we shall see, the 1989 Basel Convention represents a compromise between these various perspectives which was ultimately not accepted by the African States. These States agreed a separate 1991 Bamako Convention which

---

2   For UK law on dumping and incineration of waste at sea, see Pt II of the Food and Environmental Protection Act 1985, which creates a licencing regime for incineration (s 6).

prohibits imports into Africa from non-parties and regulates trade in waste among African States.[3]

Basel Convention 1989[4]

The 1989 Convention on the Control of Trans-boundary Movements of Hazardous Wastes and their Disposal (28 ILM (1989) 657) is intended to establish a global regime for the control of international trade in hazardous and other wastes (see Art 1). As Sands notes, these rules are designed to regulate trade in hazardous wastes, rather than prohibit it (Sands (1995) 504). This accords with the view that in the absence of a wider consensus among exporting and importing States, it cannot be said that a policy of ending all trade in hazardous wastes has prevailed at a global level (Birnie and Boyle (1992) 333).

The Convention contains general obligations requiring all parties to ensure that the trans-boundary movements of hazardous wastes are reduced to the minimum consistent with environmentally sound and efficient management. It also reflects an approach premised upon the view that wastes should, as far as possible, be disposed of in the State where they were generated (known as the 'proximity principle') (Sands (1995) 504). What has been achieved therefore is a compromise, which places three important and far-reaching restrictions on international trade in hazardous wastes (Birnie and Boyle (1992) 333–35).

First, the Convention confirms the sovereign right to ban imports, either on an individual, bilateral or regional basis, provided the exercise of this right to prohibit trade in waste is notified to other parties through the secretariat (Preamble and Art 4(1)(a)).

Secondly, the Convention has adopted the principle of minimising the generation of hazardous waste and promoting disposal at source. Indeed, the primary obligation is to manage the trans-boundary movement of waste in an environmentally sound manner. Thus, trans-boundary movement is permitted between parties to the Basel Convention but only in circumstances where the State of export does not have the capacity or facilities to dispose of the wastes in an environmentally sound manner itself (Art 4(9)(a)), or where the wastes are intended for recycling (Art 4(9)(b)). Furthermore, recognising the importing States' responsibility under international law for the protection of their own environments, the Basel Convention places on importing States' parties an obligation of environmentally sound management (Arts 4(8) and 9(3)). However, the exporting State cannot escape its obligation to manage the wastes in an environmentally sound manner and must permit re-import if necessary (Art 4(10)).

'Environmentally sound management' is defined only in general terms in Art 2(8) (see p 398, below). More detailed guidance is given by the 1985 Cairo Guidelines and Principles of Environmentally Sound Management of Hazardous Wastes which include the use of best practicable means, approval of sites and facilities, disposal plans, monitoring, public access to information and contingency planning (see [1986] 16 EPL 5,

---

3   See also the *UK Management Plan for Exports and Imports of Waste 1996* (HMSO) which allows the export of waste for recovery as permitted under international law. The export of waste for disposal is not allowed.

4   See www.basel.int/links.htm.

p 31). Although these guidelines are 'soft law' instruments and hence not obligatory, their adoption in 1987 by the Governing Council of the UN Environment Programme (UNEP) gives them persuasive force as a basic standard for States to meet in fulfilling their obligations under the Basel Convention (Birnie and Boyle (1992) 339).

Thirdly, the Convention requires the prior, informed and written consent of both transit and import States, in the conduct of international trade in hazardous wastes (Arts 4 and 6). This is the crowning achievement of the Basel Convention. As Birnie and Boyle note, '(o)nly rarely does international law require prior consent of other States before environmentally harmful activities may be undertaken' (Birnie and Boyle (1992) 336). The basis for the requirement of prior consent is that a State's sovereignty over its territory places a duty upon other States using this territory not to cause damage or interfere with other uses of the territory.

The formulation of this requirement of prior consent, however, does not fully extend to the maritime areas of national jurisdiction such as the territorial sea or EEZs (see Chapter 3, p 206, above), through which most international movement of hazardous waste may be expected to pass. This is especially significant for transit states and constitutes one of the main weaknesses of the Basel Convention. In the territorial sea, there is a right of innocent passage, which may be qualified for ships carrying dangerous or noxious substances, but is non-suspendable. In the EEZ, foreign-flagged merchant shipping vessels have almost complete freedom of navigation. Article 4(12) appears to leave these navigational rights in the EEZ and territorial sea unaffected (Birnie and Boyle (1992) 336–37).

The Basel Convention's mechanism for ensuring effective compliance with its provisions do not differ from the method adopted by many other international environmental treaties, being composed of a Conference of Parties (Art 15) and a Secretariat (Art 16). Although the secretariat is more pro-active than most, for example in assisting with identifying illegal traffic, the role of this body in verifying alleged breaches of this Convention is confined to relaying 'all relevant information' to the parties. As Birnie and Boyle note, '[t]his allows it only a limited monitoring function ... Neither the Secretariat nor other parties are given any power of independent inspection, an omission which significantly limits the potential effectiveness of the Convention's control and supervision regime' (Birnie and Boyle (1992) 340).

The Basel Convention 1989, while laying down global standards for the transboundary movement of hazardous waste, nevertheless leaves open the possibility of national, bilateral or regional treaties incorporating stricter obligations, even amounting to total prohibitions against the imports of hazardous waste. The 1991 Bamako Convention on the Ban of Imports into Africa and the Control of Trans-boundary Movement and Management of Hazardous Wastes within Africa provides an indication of how regional instruments may give stronger protection to third world countries.

The Protocol to the Basel Convention on Liability and Compensation is discussed below (p 394) and an edited text of the Protocol is set out at pp 369–80.

Bamako Convention 1991

The Bamako Convention 1991 (30 ILM (1991) 775) establishes a regional treaty regime which prohibits trade in waste, thus giving effect to the positions adopted by many African governments in the negotiations on the Basel Convention (Sands (1995) 507). The Convention entered into force in April 1998. Although to a large extent the Bamako Convention incorporates a similar regime to the Basel Convention, there are several very important differences.

First, unlike the Basel Convention which permits trade in hazardous wastes subject to the principles of environmentally sound management and prior informed consent, the Bamako Convention prohibits the import of all hazardous wastes into Africa (Art 4(1)). Although the prohibition is restricted to non-parties, the fact that the treaty is only open for signature (Art 21), ratification (Art 22) and accession (Art 23) by Member States of the Organisation of African Unity (OAU), effectively prohibits imports from outside Africa.

Secondly, the definition of hazardous waste adopted by the Bamako Convention expands on the already wide meaning provided in the Basel Convention (Art 2(1) of Bamako cf Art 1(1) of the Basel Convention 1989). For example, category Y46 (Annex II) wastes collected from households are defined merely as 'other wastes' by Art 1(2) of the Basel Convention whereas they are regarded as 'hazardous waste' under Annex I of the Bamako Convention (Art 2(1)(a)) and include sewage and sewage sludges, which are not mentioned as part of such wastes in Annex II of the Basel Convention. In practice however there may be little difference in these definitions since the Basel Convention incorporates the phrase 'hazardous wastes and other wastes' in nearly all of its major obligations upon States' parties, thereby subjecting 'other wastes' to the same regime as 'hazardous wastes'. On the other hand, even wastes that are to be used as raw materials for recycling and recovery may not be imported. The prohibition in the Bamako Convention applies to the import of all hazardous wastes 'for any reason' (Art 4(1): see Kummer (1999) 101).

Thirdly, the Bamako Convention incorporates an express provision for the adoption of the 'precautionary principle to pollution prevention ... through the application of clean production methods, rather than ... a permissible emissions approach based on assimilative capacity assumptions' (that is, assumptions about the capacity of the environment to absorb a certain level of pollution) (Art 4(3)(f)). Although there appears to be some confusion between the meanings of the preventive and precautionary principles (see Chapter 1, p 49, above), this is still more progressive than the approach adopted by Basel which is based on scientifically proven harmful substances only.

Fourthly, the procedural requirements of notification are tighter. For example, parties must not allow the use of general notifications. A specific notification of each and every shipment is required under Bamako (Art 6(6); cf Art 6(6) of the Basel Convention). The rule requiring notification of the transit state is also stricter, disallowing without exception the commencement of trans-boundary movements until written consent has been received (Art 6(4); cf Art 6(4) of the Basel Convention), and applying to trans-boundary movements from a State Party through a State or States that are not parties to the Bamako Convention (Art 7; cf Art 7 of the Basel Convention). Where illegal trade has occurred, the Bamako Convention also places a much heavier responsibility upon the exporter, generator, and ultimately the exporting State to organise the return of the wastes in question (Art 9(3); cf Art 9(3) of the Basel Convention).

Like the Basel Convention, the Bamako Convention is administered by its own conference of parties (Art 15) and secretariat (Art 16). Significantly the Secretariat has been granted greater powers than that of the Basel Secretariat. It may carry out a verification of the substance of allegations of breach of the Convention and submit a report to all Parties (Art 19).

Basel Protocol on Liability and Compensation 1999[5]

In addition to the 1989 Basel and 1991 Bamako Conventions, the international community has focused on the increasingly worrying trend of international trade in hazardous wastes between industrialised and developing countries. The response has been the 1989 Lomé IV Convention (Cmnd 1364, entered into force 1 September 1991) between the EC and a select group of African, Caribbean, and Pacific (ACP) countries which prohibits the direct or indirect export of hazardous wastes from the EC to these countries (Art 39(1): see also Basel Convention website, p 391, above. Even more stringent is the 1991 Decision by the Organisation for Economic Co-operation and Development (OECD) Member States to ban all such trade in hazardous wastes between themselves and non-OECD countries, thereby prohibiting such OECD trade with nearly all developing countries.[6]

Finally, the Parties to the 1989 Basel Convention have recently (1999) adopted a Protocol on Liability and Compensation for damage arising from the hazardous wastes trade.[7] The text of this Protocol is included here even though it has yet to enter into force. It is one of the first international environmental instruments to address the liability and compensation aspects of hazardous international activity and therefore represents a significant progressive legal development in this respect. It also applies Principle 13 of the Rio Declaration on Environment and Development (see Chapter 1, pp 72–73, above).

The Protocol was adopted at the Fifth Conference of Parties (COP5) to the 1989 Basel Convention. It envisages both strict and fault-based liability, depending on the circumstances in which environmental damage (see Art 2(c), pp 369–70, below) arising from the international trade of hazardous wastes occurs, including illegal traffic. The Protocol negotiations were able to resolve the following issues: the focus of the strict liability concept; the Protocol's scope of application, in terms of both the definition of wastes covered and its territorial limits; the financial limits of liability; and the establishment of an international compensation fund.[8]

The person required to notify the trans-boundary movement of hazardous wastes under Art 6 of the 1989 Basel Convention is subject to strict liability under Art 4 of the Protocol for damage occurring as a result of this trans-boundary movement. This person is held liable for any damage caused until the designated waste disposer has taken

---

5 See www./basel.int/pub/Protocol; see discussion, Chapter 1, p 76, above.

6 Decision I/22 dealt with trade in waste for disposal. This has now been extended by Decision II/12 (1994) to include trade in waste for recycling and/or recovery. The Decisions are not legally binding.

7 For background to the negotiation of this Protocol, see Murphy, SD, 'Prospective liability regimes for the transboundary movement of hazardous wastes, (1994) 88 AJIL 1, pp 24–75;

8 Daniel, A, '1999: The year in review 3. Transboundary movement of hazardous wastes, (1) Basel Convention, (C) Liability Protocol', in Brunnée, J and Hey, E (eds) (2000) Yearbook of International Environmental Law 285–87, p 286.

possession of the shipment. Thereafter, strict liability attaches to the disposer of the waste shipment. While the financial limits for strict liability under Art 4 of the Protocol are left to the national laws of the parties, minimum limits were set in Annex B (Art 12(1)). Annex B in turn requires the parties to review these amounts on a regular basis, taking into account the potential environmental risks and the nature, quantity and hazardous properties of the wastes. The person designated with strict liability is required to obtain insurance (Art 14(1)). Without prejudice to the strict liability provision, any person shall be liable for causing, or contributing to damage by their lack of compliance with the Basel Convention, or through their wrongful acts or omissions, when committed intentionally, recklessly or negligently; in other words when some form of fault can be proven (Art 5 of the Protocol). Moreover, such fault-based liability is without financial limits (Art 12(2)).

In terms of the material scope of the Protocol, Art 2(2)(b) provides that hazardous wastes are included within the scope of the Protocol only if they are notified under Art 1 of the Basel Convention by either the Party of import or export, or both. A further constraint relates to the geographical scope of the Protocol, which is limited to damage arising in an 'area under the national jurisdiction' of the State that defines those wastes as hazardous (Art 3). The definition of an 'area under national jurisdiction' was already a controversial aspect of the 1989 Basel Convention. This area is defined specifically under the Convention itself as including only the land territory and territorial waters of the Party (Art 2(9)). This of course leaves out other maritime areas where States exert jurisdiction over certain, mainly resource-oriented, activities under international law.

On the other hand, Art 3(5) provides explicitly that nothing in the Protocol shall affect in any way the sovereignty of States over their territorial seas and their jurisdiction and rights in their respective exclusive economic zones (EEZs) and continental shelves in accordance with international law. This provision arguably begs the question as to whether trans-boundary shipment of hazardous wastes can take place without the consent of the coastal State in these maritime jurisdictions, especially by passage through the EEZ. If the answer to the above question is in the negative, then any damage occurring in the EEZ or continental shelf area arising from such a shipment may also not be covered by this instrument. On the other hand, Art 3(3)(c) provides that notwithstanding sub-para 3(3)(a), the Protocol shall also apply in areas beyond any national jurisdiction for damage specified in Art 2(2)(c): (i) covering loss of life or personal injury; (ii) loss of or damage to property other than property held by the person liable in accordance with the present Protocol; and (v) the costs of preventive measures, including any loss or damage caused by such measures, to the extent that the damage arises out of, or results from, the hazardous properties of the wastes involved in the trans-boundary movement.

Finally, although an international compensation fund was not established, a compromise solution was arrived at. A decision adopted at COP5 expanded the terms of reference of the existing Voluntary Technical Co-operation Trust Fund under the 1989 Basel Convention on an interim basis to provide access for Parties to the Protocol that are developing countries or economies in transition. This decision also allows the Parties to the Convention to use the fund for emergencies and capacity building.

BASEL CONVENTION ON THE CONTROL OF TRANS-BOUNDARY MOVEMENTS OF HAZARDOUS WASTES AND THEIR DISPOSAL (1989)

Entered into force: 5 May 1992

Preamble

THE PARTIES TO THIS CONVENTION,

[...]

Mindful of the growing threat to human health and the environment posed by the increased generation and complexity, and trans-boundary movement of hazardous wastes and other wastes,

Mindful also that the most effective way of protecting human health and the environment from the dangers posed by such wastes is the reduction of their generation to a minimum in terms of quantity and/or hazard potential,

Convinced that states should take necessary measures to ensure that the management of hazardous wastes and other wastes including their trans-boundary movement and disposal is consistent with the protection of human health and the environment whatever the place of their disposal,

Noting that states should ensure that the generator should carry out duties with regard to the transport and disposal of hazardous wastes and other wastes in a manner that is consistent with the protection of the environment, whatever the place of disposal,

Fully recognising that any state has the sovereign right to ban the entry or disposal of foreign hazardous wastes and other wastes in its territory,

Recognising also the increasing desire for the prohibition of trans-boundary movements of hazardous wastes and their disposal in other states, especially developing countries,

Convinced that hazardous wastes and other wastes should, as far as is compatible with environmentally sound and efficient management, be disposed of in the state where they were generated,

Aware also that trans-boundary movements of such wastes from the state of their generation to any other state should be permitted only when conducted under conditions which do not endanger human health and the environment, and under conditions in conformity with the provisions of this Convention,

Considering that enhanced control of trans-boundary movement of hazardous wastes and other wastes will act as an incentive for their environmentally sound management and for the reduction of the volume of such trans-boundary movement,

Convinced that states should take measures for the proper exchange of information on and control of the trans-boundary movement of hazardous wastes and other wastes from and to those states,

Noting that a number of international and regional agreements have addressed the issue of protection and preservation of the environment with regard to the transit of dangerous goods,

Taking into account the Declaration of the United Nations Conference on the Human Environment (Stockholm, 1972), the Cairo Guidelines and Principles for the Environmentally Sound Management of Hazardous Wastes adopted by the Governing

Council of the United Nations Environment Programme (UNEP) by Decision 14/30 of 17 June 1987, the Recommendations of the United Nations Committee of Experts on the Transport of Dangerous Goods (formulated in 1957 and updated biennially), relevant recommendations, declarations, instruments and regulations adopted within the United Nations system and the work and studies done within other international and regional organisations,

Mindful of the spirit, principles, aims and functions of the World Charter for Nature adopted by the General Assembly of the United Nations at its thirty-seventh session (1982) as the rule of ethics in respect of the protection of the human environment and the conservation of natural resources,

Affirming that states are responsible for the fulfilment of their international obligations concerning the protection of human health and protection and preservation of the environment, and are liable in accordance with international law,

Recognising that in the case of a material breach of the provisions of this Convention or any protocol thereto the relevant international law of treaties shall apply,

Aware of the need to continue the development and implementation of environmentally sound low-waste technologies, recycling options, good house-keeping and management systems with a view to reducing to a minimum the generation of hazardous wastes and other wastes,

Aware also of the growing international concern about the need for stringent control of trans-boundary movement of hazardous wastes and other wastes, and of the need as far as possible to reduce such movement to a minimum,

Concerned about the problem of illegal trans-boundary traffic in hazardous wastes and other wastes,

Taking into account also the limited capabilities of the developing countries to manage hazardous wastes and other wastes,

Recognising the need to promote the transfer of technology for the sound management of hazardous wastes and other wastes produced locally, particularly to the developing countries in accordance with the spirit of the Cairo Guidelines and Decision 14/16 of the Governing Council of UNEP on Promotion of the transfer of environmental protection technology,

Recognising also that hazardous wastes and other wastes should be transported in accordance with relevant international conventions and recommendations,

Convinced also that the trans-boundary movement of hazardous wastes and other wastes should be permitted only when the transport and the ultimate disposal of such wastes is environmentally sound, and

Determined to protect, by strict control, human health and the environment against the adverse effects which may result from the generation and management of hazardous wastes and other wastes.

HAVE AGREED AS FOLLOWS:

Article 1 Scope of the Convention

1   The following wastes that are subject to trans-boundary movement shall be 'hazardous wastes' for the purposes of this Convention:

(a) wastes that belong to any category contained in Annex I, unless they do not possess any of the characteristics contained in Annex III; and

(b) wastes that are not covered under para (a) but are defined as, or are considered to be, hazardous wastes by the domestic legislation of the Party of export, import or transit.

2   Wastes that belong to any category contained in Annex II that are subject to trans-boundary movement shall be 'other wastes' for the purposes of this Convention.

3   Wastes which, as a result of being radioactive, are subject to other international control systems, including international instruments, applying specifically to radioactive materials, are excluded from the scope of this Convention.

4   Wastes which derive from the normal operations of a ship, the discharge of which is covered by another international instrument, are excluded from the scope of this Convention.

Article 2 Definitions

For the purposes of this Convention:

1   'Wastes' are substances or objects which are disposed of or are intended to be disposed of or are required to be disposed of by the provisions of national law;

2   'Management' means the collection, transport and disposal of hazardous wastes or other wastes, including after-care of disposal sites;

3   'Trans-boundary movement' means any movement of hazardous wastes or other wastes from an area under the national jurisdiction of one state to or through an area under the national jurisdiction of another state or to or through an area not under the national jurisdiction of any state, provided at least two states are involved in the movement;

4   'Disposal' means any operation specified in Annex IV to this Convention;

5   'Approved site or facility' means a site or facility for the disposal of hazardous wastes or other wastes which is authorised or permitted to operate for this purpose by a relevant authority of the state where the site or facility is located;

6   'Competent authority' means one governmental authority designated by a Party to be responsible, within such geographical areas as the Party may think fit, for receiving the notification of a trans-boundary movement of hazardous wastes or other wastes, and any information related to it, and for responding to such a notification, as provided in Article 6;

7   'Focal point' means the entity of a Party referred to in Article 5 responsible for receiving and submitting information as provided for in Articles 13 and 16;

8   'Environmentally sound management of hazardous wastes or other wastes' means taking all practicable steps to ensure that hazardous wastes or other wastes are managed in a manner which will protect human health and the environment against the adverse effects which may result from such wastes;

9   'Area under the national jurisdiction of a state' means any land, marine area or airspace within which a state exercises administrative and regulatory responsibility in accordance with international law in regard to the protection of human health or the environment;

10 'State of export' means a Party from which a trans-boundary movement of hazardous wastes or other wastes is planned to be initiated or is initiated;

11 'State of import' means a Party to which a trans-boundary movement of hazardous wastes or other wastes is planned or takes place for the purpose of disposal therein or for the purpose of loading prior to disposal in an area not under the national jurisdiction of any state;

12 'State of transit' means any state, other than the state of export or import, through which a movement of hazardous wastes or other wastes is planned or takes place;

13 'States concerned' means Parties which are states of export or import, or transit states, whether or not Parties;

14 'Person' means any natural or legal person;

15 'Exporter' means any person under the jurisdiction of the state of export who arranges for hazardous wastes or other wastes to be exported;

16 'Importer' means any person under the jurisdiction of the state of import who arranges for hazardous wastes or other wastes to be imported;

17 'Carrier' means any person who carries out the transport of hazardous wastes or other wastes;

18 'Generator' means any person whose activity produces hazardous wastes or other wastes or, if that person is not known, the person who is in possession and/or control of those wastes;

19 'Disposer' means any person to whom hazardous wastes or other wastes are shipped and who carries out the disposal of such wastes;

20 'Political and/or economic integration organisation' means an organisation constituted by sovereign states to which its member states have transferred competence in respect of matters governed by this Convention and which has been duly authorised, in accordance with its internal procedures, to sign, ratify, accept, approve, formally confirm or accede to it;

21 'Illegal traffic' means any trans-boundary movement of hazardous wastes or other wastes as specified in Article 9.

Article 3 National definitions of hazardous wastes

1 Each Party shall, within six months of becoming a Party to this Convention, inform the Secretariat of the Convention of the wastes, other than those listed in Annexes I and II, considered or defined as hazardous under its national legislation and of any requirements concerning trans-boundary movement procedures applicable to such wastes.

2 Each Party shall subsequently inform the Secretariat of any significant changes to the information it has provided pursuant to para 1.

3 The Secretariat shall forthwith inform all Parties of the information it has received pursuant to paras 1 and 2.

4 Parties shall be responsible for making the information transmitted to them by the Secretariat under para 3 available to their exporters.

Article 4 General obligations

1   (a) Parties exercising their right to prohibit the import of hazardous wastes or other wastes for disposal shall inform the other Parties of their decision pursuant to Article 13.

   (b) Parties shall prohibit or shall not permit the export of hazardous wastes and other wastes to the Parties which have prohibited the import of such wastes, when notified pursuant to sub-para (a) above.

   (c) Parties shall prohibit or shall not permit the export of hazardous wastes and other wastes if the state of import does not consent in writing to the specific import, in the case where that state of import has not prohibited the import of such wastes.

2   Each Party shall take the appropriate measures to:

   (a) ensure that the generation of hazardous wastes and other wastes within it is reduced to a minimum, taking into account social, technological and economic aspects;

   (b) ensure the availability of adequate disposal facilities, for the environmentally sound management of hazardous wastes and other wastes, that shall be located, to the extent possible, within it, whatever the place of their disposal;

   (c) ensure that persons involved in the management of hazardous wastes or other wastes within it take such steps as are necessary to prevent pollution due to hazardous wastes and other wastes arising from such management and, if such pollution occurs, to minimise the consequences thereof for human health and the environment;

   (d) ensure that the trans-boundary movement of hazardous wastes and other wastes is reduced to the minimum consistent with the environmentally sound and efficient management of such wastes, and is conducted in a manner which will protect human health and the environment against the adverse effects which may result from such movement;

   (e) not allow the export of hazardous wastes or other wastes to a state or group of states belonging to an economic and/or political integration organisation that are Parties, particularly developing countries, which have prohibited by their legislation all imports, or if it has reason to believe that the wastes in question will not be managed in an environmentally sound manner, according to criteria to be decided on by the Parties at their first meeting;

   (f) require that information about a proposed trans-boundary movement of hazardous wastes and other wastes be provided to the states concerned, according to Annex V A, to state clearly the effects of the proposed movement on human health and the environment;

   (g) prevent the import of hazardous wastes and other wastes if it has reason to believe that the wastes in question will not be managed in an environmentally sound manner;

   (h) co-operate in activities with other Parties and interested organisations, directly and through the Secretariat, including the dissemination of information on the trans-boundary movement of hazardous wastes and other wastes, in order to improve the environmentally sound management of such wastes and to achieve the prevention of illegal traffic.

3 The Parties consider that illegal traffic in hazardous wastes or other wastes is criminal.

4 Each Party shall take appropriate legal, administrative and other measures to implement and enforce the provisions of this Convention, including measures to prevent and punish conduct in contravention of the Convention.

5 A Party shall not permit hazardous wastes or other wastes to be exported to a non-Party or to be imported from a non-Party.

6 The Parties agree not to allow the export of hazardous wastes or other wastes for disposal within the area south of 60 degrees South latitude, whether or not such wastes are subject to trans-boundary movement.

7 Furthermore, each Party shall:

(a) prohibit all persons under its national jurisdiction from transporting or disposing of hazardous wastes or other wastes unless such persons are authorised or allowed to perform such types of operations;

(b) require that hazardous wastes and other wastes that are to be the subject of a trans-boundary movement be packaged, labelled, and transported in conformity with generally accepted and recognised international rules and standards in the field of packaging, labelling, and transport, and that due account is taken of relevant internationally recognised practices;

(c) require that hazardous wastes and other wastes be accompanied by a movement document from the point at which a trans-boundary movement commences to the point of disposal.

8 Each Party shall require that hazardous wastes or other wastes, to be exported, are managed in an environmentally sound manner in the State of import or elsewhere. Technical guidelines for the environmentally sound management of wastes subject to this Convention shall be decided by the Parties at their first meeting.

9 Parties shall take the appropriate measures to ensure that the trans-boundary movement of hazardous wastes and other wastes only be allowed if:

(a) the state of export does not have the technical capacity and the necessary facilities, capacity or suitable disposal sites in order to dispose of the wastes in question in an environmentally sound and efficient manner; or

(b) the wastes in question are required as a raw material for recycling or recovery industries in the state of import; or

(c) the trans-boundary movement in question is in accordance with other criteria to be decided by the Parties, provided those criteria do not differ from the objectives of this Convention.

10 The obligation under this Convention of states in which hazardous wastes and other wastes are generated to require that those wastes are managed in an environmentally sound manner may not under any circumstances be transferred to the states of import or transit.

11 Nothing in this Convention shall prevent a Party from imposing additional requirements that are consistent with the provisions of this Convention, and are in accordance with the rules of international law, in order better to protect human health and the environment.

12 Nothing in this Convention shall affect in any way the sovereignty of states over their territorial sea established in accordance with international law, and the sovereign rights and the jurisdiction which states have in their exclusive economic zones and their continental shelves in accordance with international law, and the exercise by ships and aircraft of all states of navigational rights and freedoms as provided for in international law and as reflected in relevant international instruments.

13 Parties shall undertake to review periodically the possibilities for the reduction of the amount and / or the pollution potential of hazardous wastes and other wastes which are exported to other states, in particular to developing countries.

Article 5 Designation of competent authorities and focal point

To facilitate the implementation of this Convention, the Parties shall:

1 Designate or establish one or more competent authorities and one focal point. One competent authority shall be designated to receive the notification in case of a state of transit.

2 Inform the Secretariat, within three months of the date of the entry into force of this Convention for them, which agencies they have designated as their focal point and their competent authorities.

3 Inform the Secretariat, within one month of the date of decision, of any changes regarding the designation made by them under para 2 above.

Article 6 Trans-boundary movement between parties

1 The state of export shall notify, or shall require the generator or exporter to notify, in writing, through the channel of the competent authority of the state of export, the competent authority of the states concerned of any proposed trans-boundary movement of hazardous wastes or other wastes Such notification shall contain the declarations and information specified in Annex VA, written in a language acceptable to the state of import. Only one notification needs to be sent to each state concerned.

2 The state of import shall respond to the notifier in writing, consenting to the movement with or without conditions, denying permission for the movement, or requesting additional information. A copy of the final response of the state of import shall be sent to the competent authorities of the states concerned which are Parties.

3 The state of export shall not allow the generator or exporter to commence the trans-boundary movement until it has received written confirmation that:

(a) the notifier has received the written consent of the state of import; and

(b) the notifier has received from the state of import confirmation of the existence of a contract between the exporter and the disposer specifying environmentally sound management of the wastes in question.

4 Each state of transit which is a Party shall promptly acknowledge to the notifier receipt of the notification. It may subsequently respond to the notifier in writing, within 60 days, consenting to the movement with or without conditions, denying permission for the movement, or requesting additional information. The state of export shall not allow the trans-boundary movement to commence until it has received the written consent of the state of transit. However, if at any time a Party decides not to require prior written consent, either generally or under specific conditions, for transit trans-boundary movements of hazardous wastes or other wastes, or modifies its requirements in this

respect, it shall forthwith inform the other Parties of its decision pursuant to Article 13. In this latter case, if no response is received by the state of export within 60 days of the receipt of a given notification by the state of transit, the state of export may allow the export to proceed through the state of transit.

5   In the case of a trans-boundary movement of wastes where the wastes are legally defined as or considered to be hazardous wastes only:

 (a) by the state of export, the requirements of para 9 of this Article that apply to the importer or disposer and the state of import shall apply *mutatis mutandis* to the exporter and state of export, respectively;

 (b) by the state of import, or by the states of import and transit which are Parties, the requirements of paras 1, 3, 4 and 6 of this Article that apply to the exporter and state of export shall apply *mutatis mutandis* to the importer or disposer and state of import, respectively; or

 (c) by any state of transit which is a Party, the provisions of para 4 shall apply to such state.

6   The state of export may, subject to the written consent of the states concerned, allow the generator or the exporter to use a general notification where hazardous wastes or other wastes having the same physical and chemical characteristics are shipped regularly to the same disposer via the same customs office of exit of the state of export via the same customs office of entry of the state of import, and, in the case of transit, via the same customs office of entry and exit of the state or states of transit.

7   The states concerned may make their written consent to the use of the general notification referred to in para 6 subject to the supply of certain information, such as the exact quantities or periodical lists of hazardous wastes or other wastes to be shipped.

8   The general notification and written consent referred to in paras 6 and 7 may cover multiple shipments of hazardous wastes or other wastes during a maximum period of 12 months.

9   The Parties shall require that each person who takes charge of a trans-boundary movement of hazardous wastes or other wastes sign the movement document either upon delivery or receipt of the wastes in question. They shall also require that the disposer inform both the exporter and the competent authority of the state of export of receipt by the disposer of the wastes in question and, in due course, of the completion of disposal as specified in the notification. If no such information is received within the state of export, the competent authority of the state of export or the exporter shall so notify the state of import.

10 The notification and response required by this Article shall be transmitted to the competent authority of the Parties concerned or to such governmental authority as may be appropriate in the case of non-Parties.

11 Any trans-boundary movement of hazardous wastes or other wastes shall be covered by insurance, bond or other guarantee as may be required by the state of import or any state of transit which is a Party.

Article 7 Trans-boundary movement from a Party through states which are not Parties

Paragraph 2 of Article 6 of the Convention shall apply *mutatis mutandis* to trans-boundary movement of hazardous wastes or other wastes from a Party through a state or states which are not Parties.

Article 8 Duty to re-import

When a trans-boundary movement of hazardous wastes or other wastes to which the consent of the states concerned has been given, subject to the provisions of this Convention, cannot be completed in accordance with the terms of the contract, the state of export shall ensure that the wastes in question are taken back into the state of export, by the exporter, if alternative arrangements cannot be made for their disposal in an environmentally sound manner, within 90 days from the time that the importing state informed the state of export and the Secretariat, or such other period of time as the states concerned agree. To this end, the state of export and any Party of transit shall not oppose, hinder or prevent the return of those wastes to the state of export.

Article 9 Illegal traffic

1   For the purpose of this Convention, any trans-boundary movement of hazardous wastes or other wastes:

(a) without notification pursuant to the provisions of this Convention to all states concerned; or

(b) without the consent pursuant to the provisions of this Convention of a state concerned; or

(c) with consent obtained from states concerned through falsification, misrepresentation or fraud; or

(d) that does not conform in a material way with the documents; or

(e) that results in deliberate disposal (for example, dumping) of hazardous wastes or other wastes in contravention of this Convention and of general principles of international law, shall be deemed to be illegal traffic.

2   In case of a trans-boundary movement of hazardous wastes or other wastes deemed to be illegal traffic as the result of conduct on the part of the exporter or generator, the state of export shall ensure that the wastes in question are:

(a) taken back by the exporter or the generator or, if necessary, by itself into the state of export, or, if impracticable,

(b) are otherwise disposed of in accordance with the provisions of this Convention,

within 30 days from the time the state of export has been informed about the illegal traffic or such other period of time as states concerned may agree. To this end the Parties concerned shall not oppose, hinder or prevent the return of those wastes to the state of export.

3   In the case of a trans-boundary movement of hazardous wastes or other wastes deemed to be illegal traffic as the result of conduct on the part of the importer or disposer, the state of import shall ensure that the wastes in question are disposed of in an environmentally sound manner by the importer or disposer or, if necessary, by itself within 30 days from the time the illegal traffic has come to the attention of the state of import or such other period of time as the states concerned may agree. To this end, the Parties concerned shall co-operate, as necessary, in the disposal of the wastes in an environmentally sound manner.

4   In cases where the responsibility for the illegal traffic cannot be assigned either to the exporter or generator or to the importer or disposer, the Parties concerned or other Parties, as appropriate, shall ensure, through co-operation, that the wastes in question are disposed of as soon as possible in an environmentally sound manner either in the state of export or the state of import or elsewhere as appropriate.

5   Each Party shall introduce appropriate national/domestic legislation to prevent and punish illegal traffic. The Parties shall co-operate with a view to achieving the objects of this Article.

Article 10 International co-operation

1   The Parties shall co-operate with each other in order to improve and achieve environmentally sound management of hazardous wastes and other wastes.

2   To this end, the Parties shall:

(a) upon request, make available information, whether on a bilateral or multilateral basis, with a view to promoting the environmentally sound management of hazardous wastes and other wastes, including harmonisation of technical standards and practices for the adequate management of hazardous wastes and other wastes;

(b) co-operate in monitoring the effects of the management of hazardous wastes on human health and the environment;

(c) co-operate, subject to their national laws, regulations and policies, in the development and implementation of new environmentally sound low-waste technologies and the improvement of existing technologies with a view to eliminating, as far as practicable, the generation of hazardous wastes and other wastes and achieving more effective and efficient methods of ensuring their management in an environmentally sound manner, including the study of the economic, social and environmental effects of the adoption of such new or improved technologies;

(d) co-operate actively, subject to their national laws, regulations and policies, in the transfer of technology and management systems related to the environmentally sound management of hazardous wastes and other wastes. They shall also co-operate in developing the technical capacity among Parties, especially those which may need and request technical assistance in this field;

(e) co-operate in developing appropriate technical guidelines and/or codes of practice.

3   The Parties shall employ appropriate means to co-operate in order to assist developing countries in the implementation of sub-paras (a), (b), (c) and (d) of para 2 of Article 4.

4   Taking into account the needs of developing countries, co-operation between Parties and the competent international organisations is encouraged to promote, *inter alia*, public awareness, the development of sound management of hazardous wastes and other wastes and the adoption of new low-waste technologies.

Article 11 Bilateral, multilateral and regional agreements

1   Notwithstanding the provisions of Article 4 para 5, Parties may enter into bilateral, multilateral, or regional agreements or arrangements regarding trans-boundary movement of hazardous wastes or other wastes with Parties or non-Parties provided that such agreements or arrangements do not derogate from the environmentally sound management of hazardous wastes and other wastes as required by this Convention. These agreements or arrangements shall stipulate provisions which are not less environmentally sound than those provided for by this Convention in particular taking into account the interests of developing countries.

2   Parties shall notify the Secretariat of any bilateral, multilateral or regional agreements or arrangements referred to in para 1 and those which they have entered into prior to the entry into force of this Convention for them, for the purpose of controlling trans-boundary movements of hazardous wastes and other wastes which take place entirely among the Parties to such agreements. The provisions of this Convention shall not affect trans-boundary movements which take place pursuant to such agreements provided that such agreements are compatible with the environmentally sound management of hazardous wastes and other wastes as required by this Convention.

Article 12 Consultations on liability

The Parties shall co-operate with a view to adopting, as soon as practicable, a protocol setting out appropriate rules and procedures in the field of liability and compensation for damage resulting from the trans-boundary movement and disposal of hazardous wastes and other wastes.

Article 13 Transmission of information

1   The Parties shall, whenever it comes to their knowledge, ensure that, in the case of an accident occurring during the trans-boundary movement of hazardous wastes or other wastes or their disposal, which are likely to present risks to human health and the environment in other states, those states are immediately informed.

2   The Parties shall inform each other, through the Secretariat, of:

   (a) changes regarding the designation of competent authorities and/or focal points, pursuant to Article 5;

   (b) changes in their national definition of hazardous wastes, pursuant to Article 3; and, as soon as possible;

   (c) decisions made by them not to consent totally or partially to the import of hazardous wastes or other wastes for disposal within the area under their national jurisdiction;

   (d) decisions taken by them to limit or ban the export of hazardous wastes or other wastes;

   (e) any other information required pursuant to para 4 of this Article.

3   The Parties, consistent with national laws and regulations, shall transmit, through the Secretariat, to the Conference of the Parties established under Article 15, before the end of each calendar year, a report on the previous calendar year, containing the following information:

   (a) competent authorities and focal points that have been designated by them pursuant to Article 5;

   (b) information regarding trans-boundary movements of hazardous wastes or other wastes in which they have been involved, including:

   (i)   the amount of hazardous wastes and other wastes exported, their category, characteristics, destination, any transit country and disposal method as stated on the response to notification;

   (ii) the amount of hazardous wastes and other wastes imported, their category, characteristics, origin, and disposal methods;

   (iii) disposals which did not proceed as intended;

   (iv) efforts to achieve a reduction of the amount of hazardous wastes or other wastes subject to trans-boundary movement;

(c) information on the measures adopted by them in implementation of this Convention;

(d) information on available qualified statistics which have been compiled by them on the effects on human health and the environment of the generation, transportation and disposal of hazardous wastes or other wastes;

(e) information concerning bilateral, multilateral and regional agreements and arrangements entered into pursuant to Article 11 of this Convention;

(f) information on accidents occurring during the trans-boundary movement and disposal of hazardous wastes and other wastes and on the measures undertaken to deal with them;

(g) information on disposal options operated within the area of their national jurisdiction;

(h) information on measures undertaken for development of technologies for the reduction and/or elimination of production of hazardous wastes and other wastes; and

(i) such other matters as the Conference of the Parties shall deem relevant.

4   The Parties, consistent with national laws and regulations, shall ensure that copies of each notification concerning any given trans-boundary movement of hazardous wastes or other wastes, and the response to it, are sent to the Secretariat when a Party considers that its environment may be affected by that trans-boundary movement has requested that this should be done.

Article 14 Financial aspects

1   The Parties agree that, according to the specific needs of different regions and sub-regions, regional or sub-regional centres for training and technology transfers regarding the management of hazardous wastes and other wastes and the minimisation of their generation should be established. The Parties shall decide on the establishment of appropriate funding mechanisms of a voluntary nature.

2   The Parties shall consider the establishment of a revolving fund to assist on an interim basis in case of emergency situations to minimise damage from accidents arising from trans-boundary movements of hazardous wastes and other wastes or during the disposal of those wastes.

Article 15 Conference of the Parties

1   A Conference of the Parties is hereby established. The first meeting of the Conference of the Parties shall be convened by the Executive Director of UNEP not later than one year after the entry into force of this Convention. Thereafter, ordinary meetings of the Conference of the Parties shall be held at regular intervals to be determined by the Conference at its first meeting.

2   Extraordinary meetings of the Conference of the Parties shall be held at such other times as may be deemed necessary by the Conference, or at the written request of any Party, provided that, within six months of the request being communicated to them by the Secretariat, it is supported by at least one-third of the Parties.

3   The Conference of the Parties shall by consensus agree upon and adopt rules of procedure for itself and for any subsidiary body it may establish, as well as financial rules to determine in particular the financial participation of the Parties under this Convention.

4 The Parties at their first meeting shall consider any additional measures needed to assist them in fulfilling their responsibilities with respect to the protection and the preservation of the marine environment in the context of this Convention.

5 The Conference of the Parties shall keep under continuous review and evaluation the effective implementation of this Convention, and, in addition, shall:

(a) promote the harmonisation of appropriate policies, strategies and measures for minimising harm to human health and the environment by hazardous wastes and other wastes;

(b) consider and adopt, as required, amendments to this Convention and its annexes, taking into consideration, *inter alia*, available scientific, technical, economic and environmental information;

(c) consider and undertake any additional action that may be required for the achievement of the purposes of this Convention in the light of experience gained in its operation and in the operation of the agreements and arrangements envisaged in Article 11;

(d) consider and adopt protocols as required; and

(e) establish such subsidiary bodies as are deemed necessary for the implementation of this Convention.

6 The United Nations, its specialised agencies, as well as any state not Party to this Convention, may be represented as observers at meetings of the Conference of the Parties. Any other body or agency, whether national or international, governmental or non-governmental, qualified in fields relating to hazardous wastes or other wastes which has informed the Secretariat of its wish to be represented as an observer at a meeting of the Conference of the Parties, may be admitted unless at least one-third of the Parties present object. The admission and participation of observers shall be subject to the rules of procedure adopted by the conference of the Parties.

7 The Conference of the Parties shall undertake three years after the entry into force of this Convention, and at least every six years thereafter, an evaluation of its effectiveness and, if deemed necessary, to consider the adoption of a complete or partial ban of trans-boundary movements of hazardous wastes and other wastes in light of the latest scientific, environmental, technical and economic information.

Article 16 Secretariat

1 The functions of the Secretariat shall be:

(a) to arrange for and service meetings provided for in Articles 15 and 17;

(b) to prepare and transmit reports based upon information received in accordance with Articles 3, 4, 6, 11 and 13 as well as upon information derived from meetings of subsidiary bodies established under Article 15 as well as upon, as appropriate, information provided by relevant inter-governmental and non-governmental entities;

(c) to prepare reports on its activities carried out in implementation of its functions under this Convention and present them to the Conference of the Parties;

(d) to ensure the necessary co-ordination with relevant international bodies, and in particular to enter into such administrative and contractual arrangements as may be required for the effective discharge of its functions;

(e) to communicate with focal points and competent authorities established by the Parties in accordance with Article 5 of this Convention;

(f) to compile information concerning authorised national sites and facilities of Parties available for the disposal of their hazardous wastes and other wastes and to circulate this information among Parties;

(g) to receive and convey information from and to Parties on:

– sources of technical assistance and training;

– available technical and scientific know-how;

– sources of advice and expertise; and

– availability of resources with a view to assisting them, upon request, in such areas as:

- the handling of the notification system of this Convention;

- the management of hazardous wastes and other wastes;

- environmentally sound technologies relating to hazardous wastes and other wastes, such as low- and non-waste technology;

- the assessment of disposal capabilities and sites;

- the monitoring of hazardous wastes and other wastes; and

- emergency responses;

(h) to provide Parties, upon request, with information on consultants or consulting firms having the necessary technical competence in the field, which can assist them to examine a notification for a trans-boundary movement, the concurrence of a shipment of hazardous wastes or other wastes with the relevant notification, and/or the fact that the proposed disposal facilities for hazardous wastes or other wastes are environmentally sound, when they have reason to believe that the wastes in question will not be managed in an environmentally sound manner. Any such examination would not be at the expense of the Secretariat;

(i) to assist Parties upon request in their identification of cases of illegal traffic and to circulate immediately to the Parties concerned any information it has received regarding illegal traffic;

(j) to co-operate with Parties and with relevant and competent international organisations and agencies in the provision of experts and equipment for the purpose of rapid assistance to states in the event of an emergency situation; and

(k) to perform such other functions relevant to the purposes of this Convention as may be determined by the Conference of the Parties.

2 The secretariat functions will be carried out on an interim basis by UNEP until the completion of the first meeting of the Conference of the Parties held pursuant to Article 15.

3 At its first meeting, the Conference of the Parties shall designate the Secretariat from among those existing competent intergovernmental organisations which have signified their willingness to carry out the secretariat functions under this Convention. At this meeting, the Conference of the Parties shall also evaluate the implementation by the interim Secretariat of the functions assigned to it, in particular under para 1 above, and decide upon the structures appropriate for those functions.

Article 17 Amendment of the Convention

1   Any Party may propose amendments to this Convention and any Party to a protocol may propose amendments to that protocol. Such amendments shall take due account, *inter alia*, of relevant scientific and technical considerations.

2   Amendments to this Convention shall be adopted at a meeting of the Conference of the Parties. Amendments to any protocol shall be adopted at a meeting of the Parties to the protocol in question. The text of any proposed amendment to this Convention or to any protocol, except as may otherwise be provided in such protocol, shall be communicated to the Parties by the Secretariat at least six months before the meeting at which it is proposed for adoption. The Secretariat shall also communicate proposed amendments to the Signatories to this Convention for information.

3   The Parties shall make every effort to reach agreement on any proposed amendment to this Convention by consensus. If all efforts at consensus have been exhausted, and no agreement reached, the amendment shall as a last resort be adopted by a three-fourths majority vote of the Parties present and voting at the meeting, and shall be submitted by the Depositary to all Parties for ratification, approval, formal confirmation or acceptance.

4   The procedure mentioned in para 3 above shall apply to amendments to any protocol, except that a two-thirds majority of the Parties to that protocol present and voting at the meeting shall suffice for their adoption.

5   Instruments of ratification, approval, formal confirmation or acceptance of amendments shall be deposited with the Depositary. Amendments adopted in accordance with paras 3 or 4 above shall enter into force between Parties having accepted them on the ninetieth day after the receipt by the Depositary of their instrument of ratification, approval, formal confirmation or acceptance by at least three-fourths of the Parties who accepted the amendments to the protocol concerned, except as may otherwise be provided in such protocol. The amendments shall enter into force for any other Party on the ninetieth day after that Party deposits its instrument of ratification, approval, formal confirmation or acceptance of the amendments.

6   For the purpose of this Article, 'Parties present and voting' means Parties present and casting an affirmative or negative vote.

Article 18 Adoption and amendment of annexes

1   The annexes to this Convention or to any protocol shall form an integral part of this Convention or of such protocol, as the case may be and, unless expressly provided otherwise, a reference to this Convention or its protocols constitutes at the same time a reference to any annexes thereto. Such annexes shall be restricted to scientific, technical and administrative matters.

2   Except as may be otherwise provided in any protocol with respect to its annexes, the following procedure shall apply to the proposal, adoption and entry into force of additional annexes to this Convention or of annexes to a protocol:

   (a) annexes to this Convention and its protocols shall be proposed and adopted according to the procedure laid down in Article 17, paras 2, 3 and 4;

   (b) any Party that is unable to accept an additional annex to this Convention or an annex to any protocol to which it is Party shall so notify the Depositary, in writing, within six months from the date of the communication of the adoption by the

Depositary. The Depositary shall without delay notify all Parties of any such notification received. A Party may at any time substitute an acceptance for a previous declaration of objection and the annexes shall thereupon enter into force for that Party;

(c) on the expiry of six months from the date of the circulation of the communication by the Depositary, the annex shall become effective for all Parties to this Convention or to any protocol concerned, which have not submitted a notification in accordance with the provision of sub-para (b) above.

3   The proposal, adoption and entry into force of amendments to annexes to this Convention or to any protocol shall be subject to the same procedure as for the proposal, adoption and entry into force of annexes to the Convention or annexes to a protocol. Annexes and amendments thereto shall take due account, *inter alia*, of relevant scientific and technical considerations.

4   If an additional annex or an amendment to an annex involves an amendment to this Convention or to any protocol, the additional annex or amended annex shall not enter into force until such time as the amendment to this Convention or to the protocol enters into force.

Article 19 Verification

Any Party which has reason to believe that another Party is acting or has acted in breach of its obligations under this Convention may inform the Secretariat thereof, and in such an event, shall simultaneously and immediately inform, directly or through the Secretariat, the Party against whom the allegations are made. All relevant information should be submitted by the Secretariat to the Parties.

Article 20 Settlement of disputes

1   In case of a dispute between Parties as to the interpretation or application of, or compliance with, this Convention or any protocol thereto, they shall seek a settlement of the dispute through negotiation or any other peaceful means of their own choice.

2   If the Parties concerned cannot settle their dispute through the means mentioned in the preceding paragraph, the dispute, if the parties to the dispute agree, shall be submitted to the International Court of Justice or to arbitration under the conditions set out in Annex VI on Arbitration. However, failure to reach common agreement on submission of the dispute to the International Court of Justice or to arbitration shall not absolve the Parties from the responsibility of continuing to seek to resolve it by the means referred to in para 1.

3   When ratifying, accepting, approving, formally confirming or acceding to this Convention, or at any time thereafter, a state or political and/or economic integration organisation may declare that it recognises as compulsory *ipso facto* and without special agreement, in relation to any Party accepting the same obligation:

(a) submission of the dispute to the International Court of Justice; and/or

(b) arbitration in accordance with the procedures set out in Annex VI. Such declaration shall be notified in writing to the Secretariat which shall communicate it to the Parties.

[Articles 21 (on Signature), 22 (on Ratification, Acceptance, Formal Confirmation or Approval) and 22 (on Accession) omitted.]

Article 24 Right to vote

1   Except as provided for in para 2 below, each Contracting Party to this Convention shall have one vote.

2   Political and/or economic integration organisations, in matters within their competence, in accordance with Article 22, para 3, and Article 23, para 2, shall exercise their right to vote with a number of votes equal to the number of their Member States which are Parties to the Convention or the relevant protocol. Such organisations shall not exercise their right to vote if their member states exercise theirs, and vice versa.

Article 25 Entry into force

1   This Convention shall enter into force on the ninetieth day after the date of deposit of the twentieth instrument of ratification, acceptance, formal confirmation, approval or accession.

2   For each state or political and/or economic integration organisation which ratifies, accepts, approves or formally confirms this Convention or accedes thereto after the date of the deposit of the twentieth instrument of ratification, acceptance, approval, formal confirmation or accession, it shall enter into force on the ninetieth day after the date of deposit by such state or political and/or economic integration organisation of its instrument of ratification, acceptance, approval, formal confirmation or accession.

3   For the purposes of paras 1 and 2 above, any instrument deposited by a political and/or economic integration organisation shall not be counted as additional to those deposited by Member States of such organisation.

Article 26 Reservations and declarations

1   No reservation or exception may be made to this Convention.

2   Paragraph 1 of this Article does not preclude a state or political and/or economic integration organisations, when signing, ratifying, accepting, approving, formally confirming or acceding to this Convention, from making declarations or statements, however phrased or named, with a view, *inter alia*, to the harmonisation of its laws and regulations with the provisions of this Convention, provided that such declarations or statements do not purport to exclude or to modify the legal effects of the provisions of the Convention in their application to that state.

Article 27 Withdrawal

1   At any time after three years from the date on which this Convention has entered into force for a Party, that Party may withdraw from the Convention by giving written notification to the Depositary.

2   Withdrawal shall be effective one year from receipt of notification by the Depositary, or on such later date as may be specified in the notification.

Article 28 Depository

The Secretary-General of the United Nations shall be the Depository of this Convention and of any protocol thereto.

Article 29 Authentic texts

The original Arabic, Chinese, English, French, Russian and Spanish texts of this Convention are equally authentic.

[Annexes I to VI omitted.]

BASEL PROTOCOL ON LIABILITY AND COMPENSATION FOR DAMAGE RESULTING FROM TRANS-BOUNDARY MOVEMENTS OF HAZARDOUS WASTES AND THEIR DISPOSAL (1999)

The Parties to the Protocol,

Having taken into account the relevant provisions of Principle 13 of the 1992 Rio Declaration on Environment and Development, according to which states shall develop international and national legal instruments regarding liability and compensation for the victims of pollution and other environmental damage,

Being Parties to the Basel Convention on the Control of Trans-boundary Movements of Hazardous Wastes and their Disposal,

Mindful of their obligations under the Convention,

Aware of the risk of damage to human health, property and the environment caused by hazardous wastes and other wastes and the trans-boundary movement and disposal thereof,

Concerned about the problem of illegal trans-boundary traffic in hazardous wastes and other wastes,

Committed to Art 12 of the Convention, and emphasising the need to set out appropriate rules and procedures in the field of liability and compensation for damage resulting from the trans-boundary movement and disposal of hazardous wastes and other wastes,

Convinced of the need to provide for third Party liability and environmental liability in order to ensure that adequate and prompt compensation is available for damage resulting from the trans-boundary movement and disposal of hazardous wastes and other wastes.

HAVE AGREED AS FOLLOWS:

Article 1 Objective

The objective of the Protocol is to provide for a comprehensive regime for liability and for adequate and prompt compensation for damage resulting from the trans-boundary movement of hazardous wastes and other wastes and their disposal including illegal traffic in those wastes.

Article 2 Definitions

1   The definitions of terms contained in the Convention apply to the Protocol, unless expressly provided otherwise in the Protocol.

2   For the purposes of the Protocol:

   (a) 'the Convention' means the Basel Convention on the Control of Trans-boundary Movements of Hazardous Wastes and their Disposal;

   (b) 'hazardous wastes and other wastes' means hazardous wastes and other wastes within the meaning of Art 1 of the Convention;

   (c) 'damage' means:

      (i)   loss of life or personal injury;

      (ii) loss of or damage to property other than property held by the person liable in accordance with the present Protocol;

      (iii) loss of income directly deriving from an economic interest in any use of the environment, incurred as a result of impairment of the environment, taking into account savings and costs;

      (iv) the costs of measures of reinstatement of the impaired environment, limited to the costs of measures actually taken or to be undertaken; and

      (v) the costs of preventive measures, including any loss or damage caused by such measures, to the extent that the damage arises out of or results from hazardous properties of the wastes involved in the trans-boundary movement and disposal of hazardous wastes and other wastes subject to the Convention;

(d) 'measures of reinstatement' means any reasonable measures aiming to assess, reinstate or restore damaged or destroyed components of the environment. Domestic law may indicate who will be entitled to take such measures;

(e) 'preventive measures' means any reasonable measures taken by any person in response to an incident, to prevent, minimise, or mitigate loss or damage, or to effect environmental clean-up;

(f) 'contracting Party' means a Party to the Protocol;

(g) 'protocol' means the present Protocol;

(h) 'incident' means any occurrence, or series of occurrences having the same origin that causes damage or creates a grave and imminent threat of causing damage;

(i) 'regional economic integration organisation' means an organisation constituted by sovereign states to which its Member States have transferred competence in respect of matters governed by the Protocol and which has been duly authorised, in accordance with its internal procedures, to sign, ratify, accept, approve, formally confirm or accede to it;

(j) 'unit of account' means the Special Drawing Right as defined by the International Monetary Fund.

Article 3 Scope of application

1   The Protocol shall apply to damage due to an incident occurring during a trans-boundary movement of hazardous wastes and other wastes and their disposal, including illegal traffic, from the point where the wastes are loaded on the means of transport in an area under the national jurisdiction of a state of export. Any Contracting Party may by way of notification to the Depositary exclude the application of the Protocol, in respect of all trans-boundary movements for which it is the state of export, for such incidents which occur in an area under its national jurisdiction, as regards damage in its area of national jurisdiction. The Secretariat shall inform all Contracting Parties of notifications received in accordance with this Article.

2   The Protocol shall apply:

(a) in relation to movements destined for one of the operations specified in Annex IV to the Convention other than D13, D14, D15, R12 or R13, until the time at which the notification of completion of disposal pursuant to Art 6, para 9, of the Convention has occurred, or, where such notification has not been made, completion of disposal has occurred; and

(b) in relation to movements destined for the operations specified in D13, D14, D15, R12 or R13 of Annex IV to the Convention, until completion of the subsequent disposal operation specified in D1 to D12 and R1 to R11 of Annex IV to the Convention.

3   (a) The Protocol shall apply only to damage suffered in an area under the national jurisdiction of a Contracting Party arising from an incident as referred to in para 1;

    (b) when the State of import, but not the State of export, is a Contracting Party, the Protocol shall apply only with respect to damage arising from an incident as referred to in para 1 which takes place after the moment at which the disposer has taken possession of the hazardous wastes and other wastes. When the State of export, but not the State of import, is a Contracting Party, the Protocol shall apply only with respect to damage arising from an incident as referred to in para 1 which takes place prior to the moment at which the disposer takes possession of the hazardous wastes and other wastes. When neither the State of export nor the State of import is a Contracting Party, the Protocol shall not apply;

    (c) notwithstanding sub-para (a), the Protocol shall also apply to the damages specified in Art 2, sub-paras 2(c)(i), (ii) and (v), of the Protocol occurring in areas beyond any national jurisdiction;

    (d) notwithstanding sub-para (a), the Protocol shall, in relation to rights under the Protocol, also apply to damages suffered in an area under the national jurisdiction of a state of transit which is not a Contracting Party provided that such state appears in Annex A and has acceded to a multilateral or regional agreement concerning trans-boundary movements of hazardous waste which is in force. Sub-para (b) will apply *mutatis mutandis*.

4   Notwithstanding para 1, in case of re-importation under Art 8 or Art 9, sub-para 2(a), and Art 9, para 4, of the Convention, the provisions of the Protocol shall apply until the hazardous wastes and other wastes reach the original state of export.

5   Nothing in the Protocol shall affect in any way the sovereignty of states over their territorial seas and their jurisdiction and rights in their respective exclusive economic zones and continental shelves in accordance with international law.

6   Notwithstanding para 1 and subject to para 2 of this Article:

    (a) the Protocol shall not apply to damage that has arisen from a trans-boundary movement of hazardous wastes and other wastes that has commenced before the entry into force of the Protocol for the Contracting Party concerned;

    (b) the Protocol shall apply to damage resulting from an incident occurring during a trans-boundary movement of wastes falling under Art 1, sub-para 1(b), of the Convention only if those wastes have been notified in accordance with Art 3 of the Convention by the state of export or import, or both, and the damage arises in an area under the national jurisdiction of a state, including a state of transit, that has defined or considers those wastes as hazardous provided that the requirements of Art 3 of the Convention have been met. In this case strict liability shall be channelled in accordance with Art 4 of the Protocol.

7   (a) The Protocol shall not apply to damage due to an incident occurring during a trans-boundary movement of hazardous wastes and other wastes and their disposal pursuant to a bilateral, multilateral or regional agreement or arrangement concluded and notified in accordance with Art 11 of the Convention if:

       (i) the damage occurred in an area under the national jurisdiction of any of the Parties to the agreement or arrangement;

      (ii) there exists a liability and compensation regime, which is in force and is applicable to the damage resulting from such a trans-boundary movement or disposal provided it fully meets, or exceeds the objective of the Protocol by providing a high level of protection to persons who have suffered damage;

 (iii) the Party to the Art 11 agreement or arrangement in which the damage has occurred has previously notified the Depositary of the non-application of the Protocol to any damage occurring in an area under its national jurisdiction due to an incident resulting from movements or disposals referred to in this sub-para; and

 (iv) the Parties to the Art 11 agreement or arrangement have not declared that the Protocol shall be applicable;

(b) in order to promote transparency, a Contracting Party that has notified the Depositary of the non-application of the Protocol shall notify the Secretariat of the applicable liability and compensation regime referred to in sub-para (a)(ii) and include a description of the regime. The Secretariat shall submit to the Meeting of the Parties, on a regular basis, summary reports on the notifications received;

(c) after a notification pursuant to sub-para (a)(iii) is made, actions for compensation for damage to which sub-para (a)(i) applies may not be made under the Protocol.

8 The exclusion set out in para 7 of this Article shall neither affect any of the rights or obligations under the Protocol of a Contracting Party which is not Party to the agreement or arrangement mentioned above, nor shall it affect rights of States of transit which are not Contracting Parties.

9 Article 3, para 2, shall not affect the application of Art 16 to all Contracting Parties.

Article 4 Strict liability

1 The person who notifies in accordance with Art 6 of the Convention, shall be liable for damage until the disposer has taken possession of the hazardous wastes and other wastes. Thereafter the disposer shall be liable for damage. If the State of export is the notifier or if no notification has taken place, the exporter shall be liable for damage until the disposer has taken possession of the hazardous wastes and other wastes. With respect to Art 3, sub-para 6(b), of the Protocol, Art 6, para 5, of the Convention shall apply mutatis mutandis. Thereafter the disposer shall be liable for damage.

2 Without prejudice to para 1, with respect to wastes under Art 1, sub-para 1 (b), of the Convention that have been notified as hazardous by the state of import in accordance with Art 3 of the Convention but not by the state of export, the importer shall be liable until the disposer has taken possession of the wastes, if the state of import is the notifier or if no notification has taken place. Thereafter the disposer shall be liable for damage.

3 Should the hazardous wastes and other wastes be re-imported in accordance with Art 8 of the Convention, the person who notified shall be liable for damage from the time the hazardous wastes leave the disposal site, until the wastes are taken into possession by the exporter, if applicable, or by the alternate disposer.

4 Should the hazardous wastes and other wastes be re-imported under Art 9, sub-para 2(a), or Art 9, para 4, of the Convention, subject to Art 3 of the Protocol, the person who re-imports shall be held liable for damage until the wastes are taken into possession by the exporter if applicable, or by the alternate disposer.

5 No liability in accordance with this Article shall attach to the person referred to in paras 1 and 2 of this Article, if that person proves that the damage was:

(a) the result of an act of armed conflict, hostilities, civil war or insurrection;

(b) the result of a natural phenomenon of exceptional, inevitable, unforeseeable and irresistible character;

(c) wholly the result of compliance with a compulsory measure of a public authority of the State where the damage occurred; or

(d) wholly the result of the wrongful intentional conduct of a third party, including the person who suffered the damage.

6   If two or more persons are liable according to this Article, the claimant shall have the right to seek full compensation for the damage from any or all of the persons liable.

Article 5 Fault-based liability

Without prejudice to Art 4, any person shall be liable for damage caused or contributed to by his lack of compliance with the provisions implementing the Convention or by his wrongful intentional, reckless or negligent acts or omissions. This Article shall not affect the domestic law of the Contracting Parties governing liability of servants and agents.

Article 6 Preventive measures

1   Subject to any requirement of domestic law any person in operational control of hazardous wastes and other wastes at the time of an incident shall take all reasonable measures to mitigate damage arising therefrom.

2   Notwithstanding any other provision in the Protocol, any person in possession and/or control of hazardous wastes and other wastes for the sole purpose of taking preventive measures, provided that this person acted reasonably and in accordance with any domestic law regarding preventive measures, is not thereby subject to liability under the Protocol.

Article 7 Combined cause of the damage

1   Where damage is caused by wastes covered by the Protocol and wastes not covered by the Protocol, a person otherwise liable shall only be liable according to the Protocol in proportion to the contribution made by the wastes covered by the Protocol to the damage.

2   The proportion of the contribution to the damage of the wastes referred to in para 1 shall be determined with regard to the volume and properties of the wastes involved, and the type of damage occurring.

3   In respect of damage where it is not possible to distinguish between the contribution made by wastes covered by the Protocol and wastes not covered by the Protocol, all damage shall be considered to be covered by the Protocol.

Article 8 Right of recourse

1   Any person liable under the Protocol shall be entitled to a right of recourse in accordance with the rules of procedure of the competent court:

(a) against any other person also liable under the Protocol; and

(b) as expressly provided for in contractual arrangements.

2   Nothing in the Protocol shall prejudice any rights of recourse to which the person liable might be entitled pursuant to the law of the competent court.

Article 9 Contributory fault

Compensation may be reduced or disallowed if the person who suffered the damage, or a person for whom he is responsible under the domestic law, by his own fault, has caused or contributed to the damage having regard to all circumstances.

Article 10 Implementation

1   The Contracting Parties shall adopt the legislative, regulatory and administrative measures necessary to implement the Protocol.

2   In order to promote transparency, Contracting Parties shall inform the Secretariat of measures to implement the Protocol, including any limits of liability established pursuant to para 1 of Annex B.

3   The provisions of the Protocol shall be applied without discrimination based on nationality, domicile or residence.

Article 11 Conflicts with other liability and compensation agreements

Whenever the provisions of the Protocol and the provisions of a bilateral, multilateral or regional agreement apply to liability and compensation for damage caused by an incident arising during the same portion of a trans-boundary movement, the Protocol shall not apply provided the other agreement is in force for the party or parties concerned and had been opened for signature when the Protocol was opened for signature, even if the agreement was amended afterwards.

Article 12 Financial limits

1   Financial limits for the liability under Art 4 of the Protocol are specified in Annex B to the Protocol. Such limits shall not include any interest or costs awarded by the competent court.

2   There shall be no financial limit on liability under Art 5.

Article 13 Time limit of liability

1   Claims for compensation under the Protocol shall not be admissible unless they are brought within ten years from the date of the incident.

2   Claims for compensation under the Protocol shall not be admissible unless they are brought within five years from the date the claimant knew or ought reasonably to have known of the damage provided that the time limits established pursuant to para 1 of this Article are not exceeded.

3   Where the incident consists of a series of occurrences having the same origin, time limits established pursuant to this Article shall run from the date of the last of such occurrences. Where the incident consists of a continuous occurrence, such time limits shall run from the end of that continuous occurrence.

Article 14 Insurance and other financial guarantees

1   The persons liable under Art 4 shall establish and maintain during the period of the time limit of liability, insurance, bonds or other financial guarantees covering their liability under Art 4 of the Protocol for amounts not less than the minimum limits specified in para 2 of Annex B. States may fulfil their obligation under this paragraph by a declaration of self- insurance. Nothing in this paragraph shall prevent the use of deductibles or co-payments as between the insurer and the insured, but the failure of

the insured to pay any deductible or co-payment shall not be a defence against the person who has suffered the damage.

2   With regard to the liability of the notifier, or exporter under Art 4, para 1, or of the importer under Art 4, para 2, insurance, bonds or other financial guarantees referred to in para 1 of this article shall only be drawn upon in order to provide compensation for damage covered by Art 2 of the Protocol.

3   A document reflecting the coverage of the liability of the notifier or exporter under Art 4, para 1, or of the importer under Art 4, para 2, of the Protocol shall accompany the notification referred to in Art 6 of the Convention. Proof of coverage of the liability of the disposer shall be delivered to the competent authorities of the State of import.

4   Any claim under the Protocol may be asserted directly against any person providing insurance, bonds or other financial guarantees. The insurer or the person providing the financial guarantee shall have the right to require the person liable under Art 4 to be joined in the proceedings. Insurers and persons providing financial guarantees may invoke the defences which the person liable under Art 4 would be entitled to invoke.

5   Notwithstanding para 4, a Contracting Party shall, by notification to the Depositary at the time of signature, ratification, or approval of, or accession to the Protocol, indicate if it does not provide for a right to bring a direct action pursuant to para 4. The Secretariat shall maintain a record of the Contracting Parties who have given notification pursuant to this paragraph.

Article 15 Financial mechanism

1   Where compensation under the Protocol does not cover the costs of damage, additional and supplementary measures aimed at ensuring adequate and prompt compensation may be taken using existing mechanisms.

2   The Meeting of the Parties shall keep under review the need for and possibility of improving existing mechanisms or establishing a new mechanism.

Article 16 State responsibility

The Protocol shall not affect the rights and obligations of the Contracting Parties under the rules of general international law with respect to State responsibility.

PROCEDURES

Article 17 Competent courts

1   Claims for compensation under the Protocol may be brought in the courts of a Contracting Party only where either:

(a) the damage was suffered; or

(b) the incident occurred; or

(c) the defendant has his habitual residence, or has his principal place of business.

2   Each Contracting Party shall ensure that its courts possess the necessary competence to entertain such claims for compensation.

Article18 Related actions

1   Where related actions are brought in the courts of different Parties, any court other than the court first seized may, while the actions are pending at first instance, stay its proceedings.

2   A court may, on the application of one of the Parties, decline jurisdiction if the law of that court permits the consolidation of related actions and another court has jurisdiction over both actions.

3   For the purpose of this Article, actions are deemed to be related where they are so closely connected that it is expedient to hear and determine them together to avoid the risk of irreconcilable judgments resulting from separate proceedings.

Article 19 Applicable law

All matters of substance or procedure regarding claims before the competent court which are not specifically regulated in the Protocol shall be governed by the law of that court including any rules of such law relating to conflict of laws.

Article 20 Relation between the Protocol and the law of the competent court

1   Subject to para 2, nothing in the Protocol shall be construed as limiting or derogating from any rights of persons who have suffered damage, or as limiting the protection or reinstatement of the environment which may be provided under domestic law.

2   No claims for compensation for damage based on the strict liability of the notifier or the exporter liable under Art 4, para 1, or the importer liable under Art 4, para 2, of the Protocol, shall be made otherwise than in accordance with the Protocol.

Article 21 Mutual recognition and enforcement of judgments

1   Any judgment of a court having jurisdiction in accordance with Art 17 of the Protocol, which is enforceable in the State of origin and is no longer subject to ordinary forms of review, shall be recognised in any Contracting Party as soon as the formalities required in that Party have been completed, except:

   (a) where the judgment was obtained by fraud;

   (b) where the defendant was not given reasonable notice and a fair opportunity to present his case;

   (c) where the judgment is irreconcilable with an earlier judgment validly pronounced in another Contracting Party with regard to the same cause of action and the same parties; or

   (d) where the judgment is contrary to the public policy of the Contracting Party in which its recognition is sought.

2   A judgment recognised under para 1 of this Article shall be enforceable in each Contracting Party as soon as the formalities required in that Party have been completed. The formalities shall not permit the merits of the case to be re-opened.

3   The provisions of paras 1 and 2 of this Article shall not apply between Contracting Parties that are Parties to an agreement or arrangement in force on mutual recognition and enforcement of judgments under which the judgment would be recognisable and enforceable.

Article 22 Relationship of the Protocol with the Basel Convention

Except as otherwise provided in the Protocol, the provisions of the Convention relating to its Protocols shall apply to the Protocol.

Article 23 Amendment of Annex B

1   At its sixth meeting, the Conference of the Parties to the Basel Convention may amend para 2 of Annex B following the procedure set out in Art 18 of the Basel Convention.

2   Such an amendment may be made before the Protocol enters into force.

FINAL CLAUSES

Article 24 Meeting of the Parties

1   A Meeting of the Parties is hereby established. The Secretariat shall convene the first Meeting of the Parties in conjunction with the first meeting of the Conference of the Parties to the Convention after entry into force of the Protocol.

2   Subsequent ordinary Meetings of the Parties shall be held in conjunction with meetings of the Conference of the Parties to the Convention unless the Meeting of the Parties decides otherwise. Extraordinary Meetings of the Parties shall be held at such other times as may be deemed necessary by a Meeting of the Parties, or at the written request of any Contracting Party, provided that within six months of such a request being communicated to them by the Secretariat, it is supported by at least one third of the Contracting Parties.

3   The Contracting Parties, at their first meeting, shall adopt by consensus rules of procedure for their meetings as well as financial rules.

4   The functions of the Meeting of the Parties shall be:
   (a) to review the implementation of and compliance with the Protocol;
   (b) to provide for reporting and establish guidelines and procedures for such reporting where necessary;
   (c) to consider and adopt, where necessary, proposals for amendment of the Protocol or any annexes and for any new annexes; and
   (d) to consider and undertake any additional action that may be required for the purposes of the Protocol.

Article 25 Secretariat

1   For the purposes of the Protocol, the Secretariat shall:
   (a) arrange for and service Meetings of the Parties as provided for in Art 24;
   (b) prepare reports, including financial data, on its activities carried out in implementation of its functions under the Protocol and present them to the Meeting of the Parties;
   (c) ensure the necessary co-ordination with relevant international bodies, and in particular enter into such administrative and contractual arrangements as may be required for the effective discharge of its functions;
   (d) compile information concerning the national laws and administrative provisions of Contracting Parties implementing the Protocol;
   (e) co-operate with Contracting Parties and with relevant and competent international organisations and agencies in the provision of experts and equipment for the purpose of rapid assistance to States in the event of an emergency situation;
   (f) encourage non-parties to attend the Meetings of the Parties as observers and to act in accordance with the provisions of the Protocol; and

(g) perform such other functions for the achievement of the purposes of this Protocol as may be assigned to it by the Meetings of the Parties.

2   The secretariat functions shall be carried out by the Secretariat of the Basel Convention.

Article 26 Signature

The Protocol shall be open for signature by states and by regional economic integration organisations Parties to the Basel Convention in Berne at the Federal Department of Foreign Affairs of Switzerland from 6 to 17 March 2000 and at United Nations Headquarters in New York from 1 April 2000 to 10 December 2000.

Article 27 Ratification, acceptance, formal confirmation or approval

1   The Protocol shall be subject to ratification, acceptance or approval by states and to formal confirmation or approval by regional economic integration organisations Instruments of ratification, acceptance, formal confirmation, or approval shall be deposited with the Depositary.

2   Any organisation referred to in para 1 of this Article which becomes a Contracting Party without any of its member States being a Contracting Party shall be bound by all the obligations under the Protocol, In the case of such organisations, one or more of whose Member States is a Contracting Party, the organisation and its Member States shall decide on their respective responsibilities for the performance of their obligations under the Protocol. In such cases, the organisation and the Member States shall not be entitled to exercise rights under the Protocol concurrently.

3   In their instruments of formal confirmation or approval, the organisations referred to in para 1 of this Article shall declare the extent of their competence with respect to the matters governed by the Protocol. These organisations shall also inform the Depositary, who will inform the Contracting Parties, of any substantial modification in the extent of their competence.

Article 28 Accession

1   The Protocol shall be open for accession by any States and by any regional economic integration organisation party to the Basel Convention which has not signed the Protocol. The instruments of accession shall be deposited with the Depositary.

2   In their instruments of accession, the organisations referred to in para 1 of this Article shall declare the extent of their competence with respect to the matters governed by the Protocol. These organisations shall also inform the Depositary of any substantial modification in the extent of their competence.

3   The provisions of Art 27, para 2, shall apply to regional economic integration organisations which accede to the Protocol.

Article 29 Entry into force

1   The Protocol shall enter into force on the ninetieth day after the date of deposit of the twentieth instrument of ratification, acceptance, formal confirmation, approval or accession.

2   For each State or regional economic integration organisation which ratifies, accepts, approves or formally confirms the Protocol or accedes thereto after the date of the deposit of the 20th instrument of ratification, acceptance, approval, formal confirmation or accession, it shall enter into force on the ninetieth day after the date of deposit by

such State or regional economic integration organisation of its instrument of ratification, acceptance, approval, formal confirmation or accession.

3   For the purpose of paras 1 and 2 of this Article, any instrument deposited by a regional economic integration organisation shall not be counted as additional to those deposited by member states of such organisation.

Article 30 Reservations and declarations

1   No reservation or exception may be made to the Protocol. For the purposes of the Protocol, notifications according to Art 3, para 1, Art 3, para 6, or Art 14, para 5, shall not be regarded as reservations or exceptions.

2   Paragraph 1 of this Article does not preclude a state or a regional economic integration organisation, when signing, ratifying, accepting, approving, formally confirming or acceding to the Protocol, from making declarations or statements, however phrased or named, with a view, *inter alia*, to the harmonisation of its laws and regulations with the provisions of the Protocol, provided that such declarations or statements do not purport to exclude or to modify the legal effects of the provisions of the Protocol in their application to that state or that organisation.

Article 31 Withdrawal

1   At any time after three years from the date on which the Protocol has entered into force for a Contracting Party, that Contracting Party may withdraw from the Protocol by giving written notification to the Depositary.

2   Withdrawal shall be effective one year from receipt of notification by the Depositary, or on such later date as may be specified in the notification.

Article 32 Depositary

The Secretary-General of the United Nations shall be the Depositary of the Protocol.

Article 33 Authentic texts

The original Arabic, Chinese, English, French, Russian and Spanish texts of the Protocol are equally authentic.

Annex A

LIST OF STATES OF TRANSIT AS REFERRED TO IN ART 3(D)

1	Antigua and Barbuda	21	Micronesia (Federated States of)
2	Bahamas	22	Nauru
3	Bahrain	23	Netherlands, on behalf of Aruba
4	Barbados	24	New Zealand, on behalf of Tokelau
5	Cape Verde		and the Netherlands Antilles
6	Comoros	25	Niue
7	Cook Islands	26	Palau

8	Cuba	27	Papua New Guinea
9	Cyprus	28	Samoa
10	Dominica	29	Sao Tome and Principe
11	Dominican Republic	30	Seychelles
12	Fiji	31	Singapore
13	Grenada	32	Solomon Islands
14	Haiti	33	St Lucia
15	Jamaica	34	St Kitts and Nevis
16	Kiribati	35	St Vincent and the Grenadines
17	Maldives	36	Tonga
18	Malta	37	Trinidad and Tobago
19	Marshall Islands	38	Tuvalu
20	Mauritius	39	Vanuatu

EUROPEAN COMMUNITY LAW

Waste on land

Until the 1970s, Member States regarded waste disposal as essentially a matter for local or regional action. Greater public concern about the environmental consequences of uncontrolled waste disposal operations and an increasing shortage of waste disposal facilities led to some States deciding to adopt strategic plans for dealing with the ever-increasing bulk of industrial and domestic waste generated by modern societies. The EC has now in place a comprehensive set of measures addressing the problem of waste which apply in all Member States.

EC action in this area has taken four main approaches:

1 Measures aimed at limiting or reducing the amount of waste material generated in the first place.
2 Measures which encourage reuse or recycling of waste.
3 Controls upon waste disposal, whether through the use of landfill sites[9] or the main alternative, incineration.
4 Measures controlling or even banning the export of waste across national borders.

This last approach has seen some Member States endeavouring to restrict imports of waste unilaterally on environmental grounds. This has caused a difficulty in that the European Court of Justice has declared that waste, whether recyclable or not, is covered

---

9   Landfill accounts for around 90% of waste disposal in the UK although the Royal Commission on Environmental Pollution has advocated an increasing role for incineration in the UK national strategy – *Incineration of Waste* (1993) Cm 2181.

by the free movement of goods principle of the EC Treaty and so national measures have to be compatible with Art 28 (formerly Art 30).[10] In Case C-2/90 *Commission v Belgium* (*Walloon Waste case*) [1992] 1 ECR 4431 the Walloon Regional Executive had prohibited the disposal of waste from a foreign country in such a way as to preclude the importation of all waste from sources outside Walloonia. However, on grounds, *inter alia*, that environmental damage should be rectified at source (Art 174(2), formerly 130r(2)) and what the ECJ described as the 'particular nature of waste' the Court considered that the restrictions on imports were lawful.[11]

The meaning of waste in EC law[12]

The meaning of 'waste' in the context of EC legislation has not been easy to establish. Clearly, some means of identifying waste is necessary because the regime created by the Directives discussed below only applies to materials categorised as waste. An initial question is whether the distinction between waste and non-waste serves any useful purpose. Since the basic purpose of the waste regime is to protect human health and the environment, and since all materials pose a greater or lesser threat if disposed of or handled recklessly, then why must the regime apply only to materials which satisfy the amorphous definition of waste? The answer is that there is a tendency to deal with waste material in ways which pose an increased threat to the environment or human health precisely because the holder or producer may have no financial self-interest in ensuring that it is disposed of responsibly. Waste is therefore subject to a special regulatory regime which compensates for the possible indifference of those charged with its disposal.

Waste is defined in a very imprecise fashion in Art 1(a) of the 1975 Waste Framework Directive 75/442:

> ... any substance or object in the categories set out in Annex 1 which the holder discards or intends or is required to discard.[13]

The reference to Annex I is not particularly enlightening since the categories of waste ends with:

> ... Q16 Any materials, substances or products which are not contained in the above categories (see p 394).

Some assistance in resolving the uncertainty created by category Q16 has been provided by the list of wastes drawn up by the Commission under Art 1(a) referred to as the European Waste Catalogue (EWC – Decision 94/3).[14] However, not only does the EWC

---

10 'Quantitative restrictions on imports and all measures having equivalent effect shall be prohibited between Member States'.

11 The ECJ also referred to the Basel Convention and its principles of self sufficiency and proximity (see above, p 413) to find the prohibition on imports of waste into Walloon lawful under the EC Treaty. See also Schmidt, A, 'Transboundary movements of waste under EC law' [1992] 4 JEL 57.

12 For a more detailed discussion see Pocklington, D, 'The utility of the concept of waste' [1996] Env Liability 94; see also Salter, J, 'The meaning of waste in European Community law' [1997] EELR 14; Tromans, S, 'EC waste law – a complete mess' [2000] 13 JEL 133–56.

13 It is very odd for a directive not to specify the subjects or objects to which it applies. It makes it difficult for a Member State to know whether it has correctly implemented the directive.

14 To be replaced in 2002 by the list contained in Commission Decision 00/532.

say that the list is non-exhaustive and subject to revision (Introductory note 3 to the Decision), but the ECJ in Case C-304/94 *Tombesi* case[15] has said:

> ... the fact that a substance is mentioned on it [the EWC] does not mean that it is waste in all circumstances. An entry is only relevant when the definition of waste has been satisfied.

This rather brings us back to square one. The Directives[16] do not provide any distinctive characteristic which distinguishes waste from non-waste. We must therefore look to decisions of the ECJ for further guidance. Unfortunately, the decisions have not been very illuminating (see also discussion of UK law, p 418, below).

The ECJ in Case C-418/97 *Arco* and Case C-419/97 *Epon* said that the scope of the term waste turned on the meaning of the term 'discard'. Waste is, broadly, material which has been discarded. The term 'discard' embraces both disposal (defined as any of the operations provided for in Annex IIA) or recovery (the operations provided for in Annex IIB which are essentially concerned with recycling).[17] The meaning of the word 'discard' has given rise to controversy and academic debate (see, for example, Cheyne and Purdue (1995)).

The ECJ has emphasised that Art 1(a) covers three distinct situations. Waste is material which the holder (a) discards; (b) intends to discard; and (c) is required (by law) to discard. In *Tombesi* the Advocate General maintained that the term 'discard' had a technical (that is, non-dictionary) meaning embracing both the disposal of waste and its use in the recovery operations listed in Annexes IIA and IIB. Following this case, ECJ in *Inter-Environment Walloonie ASBL v Region Walloonie* [1998] Env LR 623 stressed that a substance could still be classed as waste under Annex IIB even if it 'directly or indirectly forms an integral part of an industrial production process'. The task, according to the ECJ, is to distinguish between waste recovery processes within the meaning of the Directive on Waste 75/442 (WFD) and normal industrial treatment of products. The latter operations would not attract the waste liability regime. Drawing this distinction, however, is likely to be extremely problematic (see further p 418, below).

In *Tombesi*, the ECJ reiterated its view that substances can be classed as being 'waste' even if they are capable of or intended for economic utilisation:

> The concept of 'waste', in Art 1 of the Council Directive 75/442/EEC of 15 July 1975 on waste, as amended by Council Directive 91/156/EEC of 18 March 1991, referred to in Art 1(3) of Council Directive 91/689/EEC of 12 December 1991 on hazardous waste and Art 2(a) of Council Regulation (EEC) No 259/93 of 1 February 1993 on the supervision and control of shipments of waste within, into and out of the European Community, is not to be understood as excluding substances and objects which are capable of economic reutilisation, even if the materials in question may be the subject of a transaction or quoted on public or private commercial lists. In particular, a deactivation process intended merely to render waste harmless, landfill tipping in hollows or embankments and waste incineration constitute disposal or recovery operations falling within the scope of the above mentioned Community rules. The fact that a substance is classified as a re-usable residue without its characteristics or purpose being defined is irrelevant in that regard. The same applies to the grinding of a waste substance.

---

15   [1997] All ER (EC) 637.

16   None of the Waste Directives referred to in this section provide a definition of 'waste' which departs from Art 1 of the 1975 Directive.

17   Although the Directive does differentiate between the two, eg a network of disposal installations must be established for waste which is to be disposed of, allowing waste to be disposed of in one of the nearest installations (Art 5). There is no such objective for waste recovery installations.

Finally, the ECJ in *Arco* and *Epon* said that whether substance is waste determined in the light of all the circumstances, having regard to Art 1(a) W , the general aim of the Directive and the 'need to ensure that its effectiveness is not undermined'. This broad interpretative approach is designed to ensure that waste is dealt with without endangering human health or the environment.

Directive on Waste 75/442 (WFD) (see p 389, below)

All Member States are required to adopt the basic framework for handling waste as follows:

1 There must be 'competent authorities' within each State responsible for organising, authorising and supervising waste disposal operations (Art 6).[18]

2 The 'competent authorities' are required to draw up waste management plans (Art 7) dealing with, *inter alia*, the type and quantity of waste to be disposed of, the general technical requirements to be met and the identification of suitable disposal sites or installations. The plans will show how the authority means to attain the objectives set out in Arts 3, 4 and 5.

3 Permits from the authorities must be secured by any undertaking carrying out waste disposal activities. The permits are required to cover the types and quantities of waste to be disposed of, technical requirements, the security precautions to be taken, the disposal site and the treatment method (Art 9).

4 The 'polluter pays' principle is to apply, meaning that the cost of disposing of waste is to be borne by the holder[19] who arranges to have the waste handled by a waste collector or by the previous holders or the producer of the product from which the waste came (Art 15).

Member States are required to encourage measures specified in Art 3. First, waste production and its harmfulness is to be prevented or reduced by, for example, encouraging clean technologies which are more sparing in their use of natural resources. Secondly, steps are to be taken to encourage reuse or recycling or the use of waste as an energy source. Thirdly, waste is to be recovered or disposed of[20] without endangering human health or harming the environment, in particular: (a) without risk to water, air, soil and plants or animals; (b) without causing a nuisance through noise or odours; and (c) without adversely affecting the countryside or places of special interest (Art 4).[21]

Article 5 requires Member States to establish an 'integrated and adequate network' of disposal installations to enable both the EC as a whole and individual Member States to be self-sufficient in waste disposal. Such disposal should take place in the nearest appropriate installation (the proximity principle) thus reducing the environmental risks inherent in waste transportation.

---

18 In England and Wales, the role of the waste regulatory authority was passed to the Environment Agency by the Environment Act 1995.

19 'Holder' is defined as 'the producer of the waste or the natural or legal person who is in possession of it' – Art 1(c).

20 'Disposal' is defined in Annexes IIA and IIB.

21 The ECJ has held that Art 4 does not have direct effect: Case C-236–92 *Comitato di Coorinamento per la Difesa della Cava v Regione Lombardia* [1999] Env LR 281.

In Case C-203/96 *Chemische AF v Alstoffen Düsseldorf BV v Minister Van Volkshuisvesting*, it was held that the principles of self-sufficiency and proximity set out in Art 5 did not apply to shipments of waste for recovery rather than disposal and Regulation 259/93 does not apply the principles to shipments of waste for recovery. Article 176 (was 130t) which permits Member States to maintain or introduce more stringent rules than those adopted by the Community cannot be used to extend the principles to waste for recovery. See Agustin, Garcia Uretin, Case Commentary [1998] 5 Env Liability 157.

Directive on the Disposal of Waste Oils 75/439

The Directive on the Disposal of Waste Oils 75/439 (amended 87/101) actually pre-dates the Framework Directive but follows its pattern of provisions. Article 2 establishes a general duty to ensure that the collection and disposal of waste oils causes no avoidable damage to man and the environment.[22] The Directive requires States to give priority to regeneration of waste oils (essentially reuse) 'where technical, economic and organisational constraints' allow, failing which burning should take place only if it can be done under 'environmentally acceptable conditions'. If not, then States must ensure their safe destruction or controlled storage (Art 3).[23]

The following are prohibited: (a) any discharge into the water media and drainage systems; (b) any deposit or discharge harmful to the soil; and (c) any processing causing pollution above the level prescribed by existing provisions (Art 4).

Directive on the Disposal of polychlorinated biphenyls and polychlorinated terphenyls 96/59 (PCB/PCT)[24]

The Directive on the Disposal of polychlorinated biphenyls and polychlorinated terphenyls 96/59 has replaced Directive 76/403 which proved insufficient and because state-of-the-art technology had evolved to the point where disposal conditions for PCBs can be improved.

Although the use of these compounds is in decline, they are still employed in some forms of closed circuit electrical equipment, including transformers and condensers. Very low concentrations of PCBs in water may prove fatal to some aquatic organisms and birdlife which feed on them. Whilst other directives restrict the sale and use of PCBs (Directives 76/769; 85/467; 89/678) the present Directive establishes a system of control over the disposal of PCBs within the framework of Directive 75/442.

The main provisions are as follows:

22　Prior to this Directive, it was reported that in some States up to 60% of all waste oil was disposed of without any controls: Haigh, M, *EEC Environmental Policy and Britain*, London: Longman, p 157.

23　See Case C-102/97 *Commission v Germany* [1999] CMLR 631 where Germany was found to be in breach of Art 3(1) by failing to give priority to the processing of waste oils by regenerating without good reason. The case also contains a discussion of the meaning of 'technical, economic and organisational constraints'. In April 2001 the UK received a formal notice from the Commission in relation to this Directive [2001] 10(5) ELM.

24　This Directive is implemented into English law by regulation – SI 2000/1043, amended by SI 2001/3359.

(1) Member States are required to take the necessary measures to ensure that used PCBs are disposed of and that PCBs and equipment containing PCBs are decontaminated or disposed of as soon as possible (Art 3).

(2) Member States must compile inventories of equipment with PCB volumes above a specified threshold. Equipment and PCBs subject to such inventories must be decontaminated or disposed of at the latest by the end of 2010 (Art 4).

(3) Until such time as they are decontaminated or disposed of, the maintenance of transformers containing PCBs may continue only if the objective is to ensure that the transformers comply with technical standards and do not leak PCBs (Art 5).

(4) Where incineration is used for disposal, Directive 94/67[25] on the Incineration of Hazardous Waste shall apply; other methods of disposing of PCBs may be accepted provided they achieve equivalent environmental safety standards and fulfil the technical requirements referred to as best available techniques (Art 8).

The EC Directive on the Incineration of Hazardous Waste 94/774 sets out special measures and procedures to prevent or reduce, as far as possible, the negative effects on the environment and human health which may arise from the incineration of hazardous waste (Art 1). To this end, it sets operating conditions and emission limit values for such incineration plants (Art 8).[26]

Directive on Hazardous Waste 91/689[27]

The Directive on Hazardous Waste 91/689 as amended by Directive 94/31 applies the framework used in Directive 75/442 but imposes more stringent controls for hazardous waste. The definition of hazardous waste is complex and recognises that some waste only becomes hazardous in particular circumstances. Article 1 defines hazardous waste as (a) waste featuring on a list now drawn up by the Commission (Decision 94/904) which is to be periodically reviewed; and (b) 'any other waste which is considered by a Member State to display any of the properties listed in Annex III'.[28]

The producers and transporters of hazardous waste must keep detailed records relating to the nature of the waste which in the case of producers must be retained for three years (Art 4). During collection, transportation and temporary storage, the waste must be properly packaged and labelled in accordance with international and community standards (Art 5). The waste must be recorded and identified at every hazardous waste tipping site (Art 2). Apart from steps taken to comply with Art 4 of the WFD (ensuring waste is disposed of without endangering human health or the environment), different categories of hazardous waste should not be mixed; nor should hazardous waste be mixed with non-hazardous waste. Categories of waste which are already mixed should be separated where technically and economically feasible (Art 2).

---

25 Supplementing Municipal Waste Incineration Plants Directive 89/369.

26 The Commission has announced enforcement action against the UK and other States (June 1998) for failing fully to transpose Directive 94/67 on the incineration of hazardous waste. The deadline for transposition was 31 December 1996.

27 For implementation in English law, see p 420, below.

28 States have latitude when classifying wastes as hazardous: see *Case* C-318/98 *Jiancarlo Fornasar*.

Council Regulation on the Shipment of Waste 259/93[29]

Council Regulation 259/93 on the supervision and control of shipments of waste within, into and out of the European Community (see p 398) takes account, *inter alia*,[30] of the Community's Decision (93/98) to become Party to the Convention on the Control of Trans-boundary Movements of Hazardous Wastes and Their Disposal – the Basel Convention 1989 (see p 352, above).

Waste is defined as in Art 1 of Directive 75/442. The Regulation establishes a complex system of different regimes, including some selective bans, for:

Shipments of waste between Member States (i) for disposal, (ii) for recovery and (iii) involving transit via third (non-EC) states (Title II);

Exports of waste outside the EC (i) for disposal, (ii) for recovery and (iii) to ACP states (African, Caribbean and Pacific) (Title IV);

Imports of waste into the EC (i) for disposal and (ii) for recovery (Title V);

Shipments of waste in transit from outside and through the EC (i) for disposal and recovery and (ii) from and to a country to which an OECD Decision applies (see Art 2(r)) (Title VI).

The basic scheme is that any person who wishes to transport waste across a frontier to which the Regulation applies must notify the competent authorities in the affected States using a standard form consignment note (Decision 94/774) which must contain specific information. Within three days the authority of destination must acknowledge receipt and send copies to other affected authorities, for example, transit states. These authorities have 20 days (if only EC States are involved) or 60 days in other cases, to object or to impose conditions on the consignment. At the end of this period, the destination authorities have 10 days in which to make a decision. If approval is given, then the other authorities must be informed. Copies of the consignment note must be sent to relevant authorities three days before waste is shipped. Receipt of the waste must be notified within three days and recovery or disposal must take place within 180 days. If an authorised shipment cannot be completed, the competent authority of despatch must ensure that the waste is returned to the State of despatch unless satisfied that the waste can be dealt with in an environmentally sound manner. All shipments must be subject to a financial guarantee or insurance to cover shipment, disposal and recovery costs in cases of illegal or incomplete shipment.

Since the Regulation permits Member States to systematically object to all imports of waste this could be viewed as a derogation from the normal free movement of goods principle (see Case C-2/90 *Commission v Belgium*, above).

At a meeting of the General Affairs Council on 20 January 1997, the EC adopted Regulation 120/97, amending Regulation 259/93. The new Regulation conforms to Decision II/12 under the Basel Convention. The effect was an immediate ban on exports

---

29 See Pocklington, D, 'The pre-treatment of wastes prior to trans-boundary movement: a European perspective' [1999] Env Liability 3. For UK implementation see also Transfrontier Shipment of Waste Regulations SI 1994/1137.

30 It also incorporates the provisions on waste exports contained in the fourth Lomé Convention and the OECD Decision (1992) on transfrontier movements of wastes destined for recovery.

of hazardous waste intended for disposal to non-OECD countries and a ban on exports of hazardous waste intended for recovery to non-OECD countries.

Directive on Sewage Sludge Directive 86/278

The aim of this Directive is twofold: (a) it aims to ensure that human beings, animals, plants and the environment are protected against possible harmful effects resulting from the uncontrolled spreading of sewage sludge on land, and (b) to promote the correct use of sewage sludge on such land (Art 1). Sewage sludge is defined in Art 2. Basically, it refers to the solid matter which remains after filtering (screening) takes place at a sewage treatment works. Although sewage can be burned or buried, it can also be sprayed on farmers' fields to improve the quality of the soil.

Sewage sludge is rich in organic matter and its use in agriculture is encouraged over other forms of disposal. However, it can pose a health hazard as it will contain a proportion of industrial residues, including some heavy metals which could ultimately pollute water courses or enter the human food chain. The Directive, therefore, provides that the use of sludge must be prohibited when heavy metal concentrations in the receiving soil exceed limit values laid down by the Directive (Art 5). The same Article requires sludge use to be regulated so that the limit values referred to in the Directive are not exceeded, either by placing a limit on the amount of sludge which may be applied per unit area per year or by imposing limit values on metal introduction per unit per year. The providers of sludge are required to keep full records of its properties, types of treatment to which it is subjected, its quantity and its ultimate destination (Art 10). It has been suggested[31] that this Directive may be the first step in creating a community policy on soil protection. Germany is particularly keen to develop soil protection as an issue for Community action: [1999] 1 Env Liability CS 2. See also *The Draft Soil Strategy for England: A Consultation Paper* (DETR, March 2001).

Directive on Packaging Waste Directive 94/62[32]

The Directive on Packaging and Packaging Waste (see p 406) has now replaced the 1985 Directive on Containers of Liquids for Human Consumption (85/339). This latter Directive was a response to the famous *Danish Bottles* case (Case C-302/86 *Commission v Denmark* [1988] ECR 460) which saw the European Court balancing the right of a Member State to enact its own environmental protection measures against the fundamental free movement of goods principle within the Treaty.

In this case, the Danish government introduced legislation making compulsory the use of standardised returnable containers for beer and soft drinks. The Commission argued that this was a form of disguised discrimination against foreign manufacturers, and so was an impediment to free trade under Art 28 (formerly Art 30). The European Court held that it was permissible to use environmental protection as a reason for such discrimination. However, the derogation from the free market had to be proportionate to the end to be achieved. Whereas the returnability requirement was acceptable, a further

---

31 *Op cit*, Haigh, fn 22, p 168.
32 For UK implementation, see p 436, below.

licensing requirement under which only a limited number of container shapes was permitted, was disproportionate and infringed EC law.

In the light of the above, the 1994 Directive has two main objectives (Art 1): (1) to prevent the production of packaging waste and ensure its reuse and recycling so as to reduce the final amount requiring disposal; and (2) to ensure the functioning of the internal market by avoiding obstacles to trade. The Directive applies to all products used to contain, protect, handle, deliver and present goods which are classed under three headings: (a) primary packaging – usually acquired by the purchaser; (b) secondary packaging – usually removed by the retailer near the point of sale; and (c) tertiary packaging – designed to facilitate handling or transportation (Art 3). Note, that on 7 October 1998 the Commission notified a reasoned opinion against Denmark saying that its ban does not comply with the Packaging Waste Directive.

As from June 1996, Member States are required to set up a system for the 'return and/or collection of used packaging and/or packaging waste from the consumer, other formal user, or from the waste stream in order to channel it to the most appropriate waste management alternatives'. The system should also provide for the 'reuse or recovery including recycling of the packaging and/or packaging waste collected' (Art 7).

To encourage recovery and recycling, the Directive has set specific recovery targets which must be met within a set timescale, for example, Art 6(1) requires States *inter alia* to ensure the recovery of 50–65% of packaging by weight within five years.

Directive on the Landfill of Waste 99/31

In order to further the aims of the Waste Framework Directive 75/442, the 1999 Directive on the Landfill of Waste imposes what are described as 'stringent operational and technical requirements' (Art 1) on landfill sites in order to prevent or reduce the possible negative effects on the environment of such sites. These measures are intended to embrace the whole life-cycle of the landfill (defined (Art 2(g)) as a waste disposal site for the deposit of waste onto or into land). Member States must apply the provisions of the Directive to landfills for hazardous, non-hazardous and inert waste (Art 4) and in order to reduce biodegradable waste (Art 2(m)) going to landfill must establish a strategy for its reduction in accordance with a timetable set out in Art 5. Such a strategy should include recycling composting, bio gas production and materials/energy recovery. 'Competent authorities' will issue permits for the operation of landfill sites containing conditions to ensure compliance with the Directive (Arts 7–9). Member States must ensure that the cost of operating landfill sites is covered by disposal charges made by the site operator (Art 10). In addition to the control and monitoring of site operations (Art 12), States must also make provision for site closure and after-care procedures (Art 13). After a landfill site has been 'definitely closed operators remain responsible for its maintenance, monitoring and control 'for as long as may be required by the competent authority, taking into account the time during which the landfill could present hazards' (Art 13c). Existing landfill sites must comply with the Directive regime by 2009 (Art 14).

Further developments

In July 1996 the Commission issued a review of the EU Waste Strategy (COM (96) 399) which sets out an agenda for future development of the EC's waste policy. The review identifies a hierarchy of principles for waste, with prevention as the preferred option, followed by increased recovery and then safe disposal. However, specific decisions on waste management choices must reflect the principle of the 'best environmental option' including economic considerations.

The Commission intends to fix targets for the reduction of waste by various means; promoting clean technologies and products; setting rules to limit dangerous substances in products; promoting reuse and recycling; economic instruments; eco-audits and life cycle analyses; increasing consumer information and awareness including eco-labelling.[33] Material recovery is preferred to energy recovery, partly on the ground that it is undesirable to base an energy strategy upon the existence of waste supplies. Also the document calls for full incorporation of EC waste definitions and threatens enforcement action against Member States which fail to fulfil this task.

In November 1996, the European Parliament sitting in plenary session signalled its dissatisfaction with progress by the Commission in relation to the above Waste Strategy. The Parliament was also critical of the strategy itself maintaining that it makes no real addition to the existing strategy and in particular does not clearly define a strategy for reducing the quantity of waste produced within the Community. The Parliament called upon the Commission to produce an Action Programme on Waste Management in 1997, laying down clear objectives and priority measures. The then Environment Commissioner, Mrs Bjerregaard told MEPs that the Commission had no plans to present such a programme. By contrast the Council by resolution of 24 February 1997 welcomed the Commission's communication and 'considers it a valuable guideline for matters to be addressed throughout the EU in the waste sector in the coming years'. The Council also invited the Commission to submit a report on progress by the end of 2000 ((1997) OJ C076).

COUNCIL DIRECTIVE

of 15 July 1975

on waste

(75/442/EEC)

(1975) OJ L194, p 39

[as amended by Council Directive 91/156/EEC of 18 March 1991]

THE COUNCIL OF THE EUROPEAN COMMUNITIES,

Having regard to the Treaty establishing the European Economic Community, and in particular Articles 100 and 235 thereof, ...

Whereas any disparity between the provisions on waste disposal already applicable or in preparation in the various Member States may create unequal conditions of competition

---

33 See Chapter 7, p 825.

and thus directly affect the functioning of the common markets; whereas it is therefore necessary to approximate laws in this field, as provided for in Article 100 of the Treaty;

Whereas it seems necessary for this approximation of laws to be accompanied by Community action so that one of the aims of the Community in the sphere of protection of the environment and improvement of the quality of life can be achieved by more extensive rules; whereas certain specific provisions to this effect should therefore be laid down; whereas Article 235 of the Treaty should be invoked as the powers required for this purpose have not been provided for by the Treaty;

Whereas the essential objective of all provisions relating to waste disposal must be the protection of human health and the environment against harmful effects caused by the collection, transport, treatment, storage and tipping of waste;

Whereas the recovery of waste and the use of recovered materials should be encouraged in order to conserve natural resources;

Whereas effective and consistent regulations on waste disposal which neither obstruct intra-Community trade nor affect conditions of competition should be applied to movable property which the owner disposes of or is required to dispose of under the provisions of national law in force, with the exception of radioactive, mining and agricultural waste, animal carcasses, waste waters, gaseous effluents and waste covered by specific Community rules;

Whereas, in order to ensure the protection of the environment, provision should be made for a system of permits for undertakings which treat, store or tip waste on behalf of third parties, for a supervisory system for undertakings which dispose of their own waste and for those which collect the waste of others, and for a plan embracing the essential factors to be taken into consideration in respect of the various waste disposal operations;

Whereas that proportion of the costs not covered by the proceeds of treating the waste must be defrayed in accordance with the 'polluter pays' principle.

HAS ADOPTED THIS DIRECTIVE:

Article 1

For the purposes of this Directive:

(a) 'waste' shall mean any substance or object in the categories set out in Annex I which the holder discards or intends or is required to discard.

The Commission, acting in accordance with the procedure laid down in Article 18, will draw up, not later than 1 April 1993, a list of wastes belonging to the categories listed in Annex I. This list will be periodically reviewed and, if necessary, revised by the same procedure;

(b) 'producer' shall mean anyone whose activities produce waste ('original producer') and/or anyone who carries out pre-processing, mixing or other operations resulting in a change in the nature or composition of this waste;

(c) 'holder' shall mean the producer of the waste or the natural or legal person who is in possession of it;

(d) 'management' shall mean the collection, transport, recovery and disposal of waste, including the supervision of such operations and after-care of disposal sites;

(e) 'disposal' shall mean any of the operations provided for in Annex II, A;

(f) 'recovery' shall mean any of the operations provided for in Annex II, B;

(g) 'collection' shall mean the gathering, sorting and/or mixing of waste for the purpose of transport.

Article 2

1   The following shall be excluded from the scope of this Directive:

(a) gaseous effluents emitted into the atmosphere;

(b) where they are already covered by other legislation:

(i)   radioactive waste;

(ii) waste resulting from prospecting, extraction, treatment and storage of mineral resources and the working of quarries;

(iii) animal carcasses and the following agricultural waste: faecal matter and other natural, non-dangerous substances used in farming;

(iv) waste waters, with the exception of waste in liquid form;

(v)   decommissioned explosives [...].

Article 3

1   Member States shall take appropriate measures to encourage:

(a) firstly, the prevention or reduction of waste production and its harmfulness, in particular by:

_   the development of clean technologies more sparing in their use of natural resources,

_   the technical development and marketing of products designed so as to make no contribution or to make the smallest possible contribution, by the nature of their manufacture, use or final disposal, to increasing the amount or harmfulness of waste and pollution hazards,

–   the development of appropriate techniques for the final disposal of dangerous substances contained in waste destined for recovery;

(b) secondly:

(i) the recovery of waste by means of recycling, reuse or reclamation or any other process with a view to extracting secondary raw materials, or

(ii) the use of waste as a source of energy.

Such permit shall cover:

–   the types and quantities of waste,

–   the technical requirements,

–   the security precautions to be taken,

–   the disposal site,

–   the treatment method.

Article 4

Member States shall take the necessary measures to ensure that waste is recovered or disposed of without endangering human health and without using processes or methods which could harm the environment, and in particular:

- without risk to water, air, soil and plants and animals,

- without causing a nuisance through noise or odours,

- without adversely affecting the countryside or places of special interest.

Member States shall also take the necessary measures to prohibit the abandonment, dumping or uncontrolled disposal of waste.

Article 5

1   Member States shall take appropriate measures, in co-operation with other Member States where this is necessary or advisable, to establish an integrated and adequate network of disposal installations, taking account of the best available technology not involving excessive costs. The network must enable the Community as a whole to become self-sufficient in waste disposal and the Member States to move towards that aim individually, taking into account geographical circumstances or the need for specialized installations for certain types of waste.

2   The network must also enable waste to be disposed of in one of the nearest appropriate installations, by means of the most appropriate methods and technologies in order to ensure a high level of protection for the environment and public health.

Article 6

Member States shall establish or designate the competent authority or authorities to be responsible for the implementation of this Directive.

Article 7

1   In order to attain the objectives referred to in Articles 3, 4 and 5, the competent authority or authorities referred to in Article 6 shall be required to draw up as soon as possible one or more waste management plans. Such plans shall relate in particular to:

- the type, quantity and origin of waste to be recovered or disposed of,

- general technical requirements,

- any special arrangements for particular wastes,

- suitable disposal sites or installations.

Such plans may, for example, cover:

- the natural or legal persons empowered to carry out the managment of waste,

- the estimated costs of the recovery and disposal operations,

- appropriate measures to encourage rationalisation of the collection, sorting and treatment of waste.

2   Member States shall collaborate as appropriate with the other Member States concerned and the Commission to draw up such plans. They shall notify the Commission thereof.

3   Member States may take the measures necessary to prevent movements of waste which are not in accordance with their waste management plans. They shall inform the Commission and the Member States of any such measures.

Article 8

Member States shall take the necessary measures to ensure that any holder of waste:

- has it handled by a private or public waste collector or by an undertaking which carries out the operations listed in Annex IIA or B, or

- recovers or disposes of it himself in accordance with the provisions of this Directive.

Article 9

1   For the purposes of implementing Articles 4, 5 and 7, any establishment or undertaking which carries out the operations specified in Annex IIA must obtain a permit from the competent authority referred to in Article 6.

Such permit shall cover:

- the types and quantities of waste,
- the technical requirements,
- the security precautions to be taken,
- the disposal site,
- the treatment method.

2   Permits may be granted for a specified period, they may be renewable, they may be subject to conditions and obligations, or, notably, if the intended method of disposal is unacceptable from the point of view of environmental protection, they may be refused.

Article 10

For the purposes of implementing Article 4, any establishment or undertaking which carries out the operations referred to in Annex II B must obtain a permit. [...]

Article 12

Establishments or undertakings which collect or transport waste on a professional basis or which arrange for the disposal or recovery of waste on behalf of others (dealers or brokers), where not subject to authorisation, shall be registered with the competent authorities.

Article 13

Establishments or undertakings which carry out the operations referred to in Articles 9 to 12 shall be subject to appropriate periodic inspections by the competent authorities.

Article 14

All establishments or undertakings referred to in Articles 9 and 10 shall:

- keep a record of the quantity, nature, origin, and, where relevant, the destination, frequency of collection, mode of transport and treatment method in respect of the waste referred to in Annex I and the operations referred to in Annex II A or B, make this information available, on request, to the competent authorities referred to in Article 6. Member States may also require producers to comply with the provisions of this Article. [...]

Article 15

In accordance with the 'polluter pays' principle, the cost of disposing of waste must be borne by:

- the holder who has waste handled by a waste collector or by an undertaking as referred to in Article 9, and / or

– the previous holders or the producer of the product from which the waste came.

Article 16

1   Every three years, and for the first time on 1 April 1995, Member States shall send the Commission a report on the measures taken to implement this Directive. […]

Article 18

The Commission shall be assisted by a committee composed of the representatives of the Member States and chaired by the representative of the Commission.

The representative of the Commission shall submit to the committee a draft of the measures to be taken. The committee shall deliver its opinion on the draft within a time limit which the Chairman may lay down according to the urgency of the matter. […]

Annex I Categories of waste

Q1   Production or consumption residues not otherwise specified below.

Q2   Off-specification products.

Q3   Products whose date for appropriate use has expired.

Q4   Materials spilled, lost or having undergone other mishap, including any materials, equipment, etc, contaminated as a result of the mishap.

Q5   Materials contaminated or soiled as a result of planned actions (for example, residues from cleaning operations, packing materials, containers, etc).

Q6   Unusable parts (for example, reject batteries, exhausted catalysts, etc).

Q7   Substances which no longer perform satisfactorily (for example, contaminated acids, contaminated solvents, exhausted tempering salts, etc).

Q8   Residues of industrial processes (for example, slags, still bottoms, etc).

Q9   Residues from pollution abatement processes (for example, scrubber sludges, baghouse dusts, spent filters, etc).

Q10 Machining/finishing residues (for example, lathe turnings, mill scales, etc).

Q11 Residues from raw materials extraction and processing (for example, mining residues, oil field slops, etc).

Q12 Adulterated materials (for example, oils contaminated with PCBs, etc).

Q13 Any materials, substances or products whose use has been banned by law.

Q14 Products for which the holder has no further use (for example, agricultural, household, office, commercial and shop discards, etc).

Q15 Contaminated materials, substances or products resulting from remedial action with respect to land.

Q16 Any materials, substances or products which are not contained in the above categories.

Annex IIA Disposal operations

NB: This Annex is intended to list disposal operations such as they occur in practice. In accordance with Article 4, waste must be disposed of without endangering human health and without the use of processes or methods likely to harm the environment.

D1 Tipping above or underground (for example, landfill, etc.).

D2 Land treatment (for example, biodegradation of liquid or sludge discards in soils, etc.).

D3 Deep injection (for example, injection of pumpable discards into wells, salt domes or naturally occurring repositories, etc.).

D4 Surface impoundment (for example, placement of liquid or sludge discards into pits, ponds or lagoons, etc.).

D5 Specially engineered landfill (for example, placement into lined discrete cells which are capped and isolated from one another and the environment, etc.).

D6 Release of solid waste into a water body except seas/oceans.

D7 Release into seas/oceans including seabed insertion.

D8 Biological treatment not specified elsewhere in this Annex which results in final compounds or mixtures which are disposed of by means of any of the operations in this Annex.

D9 Physico-chemical treatment not specified elsewhere in this Annex which results in final compounds or mixtures which are disposed of by means of any of the operations in this Annex (for example, evaporation, drying, calcination, etc.).

D10 Incineration on land.

D11 Incineration at sea.

D12 Permanent storage (for example, emplacement of containers in a mine, etc.).

D13 Blending or mixture prior to submission to any of the operations in this Annex.

D14 Re-packaging prior to submission to any of the operations in this Annex.

D15 Storage pending any of the operations in this Annex, excluding temporary storage, pending collection, on the site where it is produced.

Annex IIB Operations which may lead to recovery

NB: This Annex is intended to list recovery operations as they are carried out in practice. In accordance with Article 4, waste must be recovered without endangering human health and without the use of processes or methods likely to harm the environment.

R1 Solvent reclamation/regeneration.

R2 Recycling/reclamation of organic substances which are not used as solvents.

R3 Recycling/reclamation of metals and metal compounds.

R4 Recycling/reclamation of other inorganic materials.

R5 Regeneration of acids or bases.

R6 Recovery of components used for pollution abatement.

R7 Recovery of components from catalysts.

R8 Oil re-refining or other reuses of oil.

R9 Use principally as a fuel or other means to generate energy.

R10 Spreading on land resulting in benefit to agriculture or ecological improvement, including composting and other biological transformation processes, except in the case of waste excluded under Article 2(1)(b) (iii).

R11 Use of wastes obtained from any of the operations numbered R1–R10.

R12 Exchange of wastes for submission to any of the operations numbered R1–R11.

R13 Storage of materials intended for submission to any operation in this Annex, excluding temporary storage, pending collection, on the site where it is produced.

COUNCIL DIRECTIVE

of 12 December 1991

on hazardous waste

(91/689/EEC)

(1991) OJ L377, p 20

THE COUNCIL OF THE EUROPEAN COMMUNITIES,

Having regard to the Treaty establishing the European Economic Community, and in particular Article 103s thereof,

Whereas Council Directive 78/319/EEC of 20 March 1978 on toxic and dangerous waste established Community rules on the disposal of dangerous waste; whereas in order to take account of experience gained in the implementation of that Directive by the Member States, it is necessary to amend the rules and to replace Directive 78/319/EEC by this Directive;

Whereas the general rules applying to waste management which are laid down by Council Directive 75/442/EEC of 15 July 1975 on waste, as amended by Directive 91/156/EEC ((1991) OJ L 78, p 32), also apply to the management of hazardous waste;

Whereas the correct management of hazardous waste necessitates additional, more stringent rules to take account of the special nature of such waste;

Whereas it is necessary, in order to improve the effectiveness of the management of hazardous waste in the Community, to use a precise and uniform definition of hazardous waste based on experience;

Whereas it is necessary to ensure that disposal and recovery of hazardous waste is monitored in the fullest manner possible; [...]

HAS ADOPTED THIS DIRECTIVE:

Article 1

1   The objective of this Directive, drawn up pursuant to Article 2(2) of Directive 75/442/EEC, is to approximate the laws of the Member States on the controlled management of hazardous waste.

2   Subject to this Directive, Directive 75/442/EEC shall apply to hazardous waste.

3   The definition of 'waste' and of the other terms in this Directive shall be those in Directive 75/442/EEC.

4   For the purpose of this Directive 'hazardous waste' means:

- waste featuring on a list to be drawn up in accordance with the procedure laid down in Article 18 of Directive 75/442/EEC on the basis of Annexes I and II to this Directive, not later than six months before the date of implementation of this Directive. These wastes must have one or more of the properties listed in Annex III. The list shall take into account the origin and composition of the waste and, where necessary, limit values of concentration. This list shall be periodically reviewed and if necessary by the same procedure,

- any other waste which is considered by a Member State to display any of the properties listed in Annex III. Such cases shall be noted to the Commission and reviewed in accordance with the procedure laid down in Article 18 of Directive 75/442/EEC with a view to adaptation of the list.

5   Domestic waste shall be exempted from the provisions of this Directive. The Council shall establish, upon a proposal from the Commission, specific rules taking into consideration the particular nature of domestic waste not later than the end of 1992.

Article 2

1   Member States shall take the necessary measures to require that on every site where tipping (discharge) of hazardous waste takes place the waste is recorded and identified.

2   Member States shall take the necessary measures to require that establishment and undertaking which dispose of, recover, collect or transport hazardous waste do not mix different categories of hazardous waste or mix hazardous waste with non-hazardous waste.

3   By way of derogation from para 2, the mixing of hazardous waste with other hazardous waste or with other waste, substances or materials may be permitted only where the conditions laid down in Article 4 of Directive 75/442/EEC are complied with and in particular for the purpose of improving safety during disposal or recovery. Such an operation shall be subject to the permit requirement imposed in Articles 9, 10 and 11 of Directive 75/442/EEC.

4   Where waste is already mixed with other waste, substances or materials, separation must be effected, where technically and economically feasible, and where necessary in order to comply with Article 4 of Directive 75/442/EEC.

Article 3

1   The derogation referred to in Article 11(1)(a) of Directive 75/442/EEC from the permit requirement for establishments or undertakings which carry out their own waste disposal shall not apply to hazardous waste covered by this Directive.

2   In accordance with Article 11(1)(b) of Directive 75/442/EEC, a Member State may waive Article 10 of that Directive for establishments or undertakings which recover waste covered by the Directive:

- if the Member State adopts general rules listing the type and quantity of waste and laying down specific conditions (limit values for the content of hazardous substances in the waste, emission limit values, type of activity) and other necessary requirements for carrying out different forms of recovery, and

- if the types or quantities of waste and methods of recovery are such that the conditions laid down in Article 4 of Directive 75/442/EEC are complied with. [...]

Article 4

1   Article 13 of Directive 75/442/EEC shall also apply to producers of hazardous waste.

2   Article 14 of Directive 75/442/EEC shall also apply to producers of hazardous waste and to all establishments and undertakings transporting hazardous waste.

3   The records referred to in Article 14 of Directive 75/442/EEC must be preserved for at least three years except in the case of establishments and undertakings transporting hazardous waste which must keep such records for at least 12 months. Documentary evidence that the management operations have been carried out must be supplied at the request of the competent authorities or of a previous holder.

Article 5

1   Member States shall take the necessary measures to ensure that, in the course of collection, transport and temporary storage, waste is properly packaged and labelled in accordance with the international and Community standards in force. [...]

Article 6

1   As provided in Article 7 of Directive 75/442/EEC, the competent authorities shall draw up, either separately or in the framework of their general waste management plans, plans for the management of hazardous waste and shall make these plans public. [...]

[Articles 7–12 omitted.]

[All Annexes omitted.]

COUNCIL REGULATION

of 1 February 1993

on the supervision and control of shipments of waste within, into and out of the European Community

(EEC/259/93)

(1993) OJ L30, p 1

THE COUNCIL OF THE EUROPEAN COMMUNITIES,

Having regard to the Treaty establishing the European Economic Community, and in particular Article 130s thereof,

Whereas the Community has signed the Basel Convention of 22 March 1989 on the control of trans-boundary movements of hazardous wastes and their disposal;

Whereas provisions concerning waste are contained in Article 39 of the ACP-EEC Convention of 15 December 1989;

Whereas the Community has approved the Decision of the OECD Council of 30 March 1992 on the control of transfrontier movements of wastes destined for recovery operations;

Whereas, in the light of the foregoing, Directive 84/631/EEC, which organises the supervision and control of transfrontier shipments of hazardous waste, needs to be replaced by a Regulation;

Whereas the supervision and control of shipments of waste within a Member State is a national responsibility; whereas, however, national systems for the supervision and control of shipments of waste within a Member State should comply with minimum criteria in order to ensure a high level of protection of the environment and human health;

Whereas it is important to organise the supervision and control of shipments of wastes in a way which takes account of the need to preserve, protect and improve the quality of the environment;

Whereas Council Directive 75/442/EEC of 15 July 1975 on waste lays down in its Article 5(1) that an integrated and adequate network of waste disposal installations, to be established by Member States through appropriate measures, where necessary or advisable in co-operation with other Member States, must enable the Community as a whole to become self-sufficient in waste disposal and the Member States to move towards that aim individually, taking into account geographical circumstances or the need for specialised installations for certain types of waste; whereas Article 7 of the said Directive requests the drawing up of waste management plans, if appropriate in co-operation with the Member States concerned, which shall be notified to the Commission, and stipulates that Member States may take measures necessary to prevent movements of waste which are not in accordance with their waste management plans and that they shall inform the Commission and the other Member States of any such measures;

Whereas it is necessary to apply different procedures depending on the type of waste and its destination, including whether it is destined for disposal or recovery;

Whereas shipments of waste must be subject to prior notification to the competent authorities enabling them to be duly informed in particular of the type, movement and disposal or recovery of the waste, so that these authorities may take all necessary measures for the protection of human health and the environment, including the possibility of raising reasoned objections to the shipment;

Whereas Member States should be able to implement the principles of proximity, priority for recovery and self-sufficiency at Community and national levels – in accordance with Directive 75/442/EEC – by taking measures in accordance with the Treaty to prohibit generally or partially or to object systematically to shipments of waste for disposal, except in the case of hazardous waste produced in the Member State of dispatch in such a small quantity that the provision of new specialised disposal installations within that State would be uneconomic; whereas the specific problem of disposal of such small quantities requires co-operation between the Member States concerned and possible recourse to a Community procedure;

Whereas exports of waste for disposal to third countries must be prohibited in order to protect the environment of those countries; whereas exceptions shall apply to exports to EFTA countries which are also Parties to the Basel Convention;

Whereas exports of waste for recovery to countries to which the OECD Decision does not apply must be subject to conditions providing for environmentally sound management of waste;

Whereas agreements or arrangements on exports of waste for recovery with countries to which the OECD Decision does not apply must be subject to periodic review by the Commission leading, if appropriate, to a proposal by the Commission to reconsider the conditions under which such exports take place, including the possibility of a ban.

HAS ADOPTED THIS REGULATION:

Title I Scope and definitions

Article 1

1   This Regulation shall apply to shipments of waste within, into and out of the Community.

2   The following shall be excluded from the scope of this Regulation:

    (a) the offloading to shore of waste generated by the normal operation of ships and offshore platforms, including waste water and residues, provided that such waste is the subject of a specific binding international instrument;

    (b) shipments of civil aviation waste;

    (c) shipments of radioactive waste as defined in Article 2 of Directive 92/3/Euratom of 3 February 1992 on the supervision and control of shipments of radioactive waste between Member States and into and out of the Community;

    (d) shipments of waste mentioned in Article 2(1)(b) of Directive 75/442/EEC, where they are already covered by other relevant legislation;

    (e) shipments of waste into the Community in accordance with the requirements of the Protocol on Environmental Protection to the Antarctic Treaty. [...]

Article 2

For the purposes of this Regulation:

(a) *waste* is as defined in Article 1(a) of Directive 75/442/EEC;

(b) *competent authorities* means the competent authorities designated by either the Member States in accordance with Article 36 or non-Member States;

(c) *competent authority of dispatch* means the competent authority, designated by the Member States in accordance with Article 36, for the area from which the shipment is dispatched or designated by non-Member States;

(d) *competent authority of destination* means the competent authority, designated by the Member States in accordance with Article 36, for the area in which the shipment is received, or in which waste is loaded on board before disposal at sea without prejudice to existing conventions on disposal at sea or designated by non-Member States;

(e) *competent authority of transit* means the single authority designated by Member States in accordance with Article 36 for the state through which the shipment is in transit;

(f) *correspondent* means the central body designated by each Member State and the Commission, in accordance with Article 37;

(g) *notifier* means any natural person or corporate body to whom or to which the duty to notify is assigned, that is to say the person referred to hereinafter who proposes to ship waste or have waste shipped:

    (i) the person whose activities produced the waste (original producer); or

    (ii) where this is not possible, a collector licensed to this effect by a Member State or a registered or licensed dealer or broker who arranged for the disposal or the recovery of waste; or

    (iii) where these persons are unknown or are not licensed, the person having possession or legal control of the waste (holder); or

(iv) in the case of import or transit through the Community of waste, the person designated by the laws of the State of dispatch or, when this designation has not taken place, the person having possession or legal control of the waste (holder);

(h) *consignee* means the person or undertaking to whom or to which the waste is shipped for recovery or disposal;

(i) *disposal* is as defined in Article l(e) of Directive 75/442/EEC;

(j) *authorised centre* means any establishment or undertaking authorised or licensed pursuant to Article 6 of Directive 75/439/EEC Articles 9, 10 and 11 of Directive 75/442/EEC and Article 6 of Directive 76/403/EEC;

(k) *recovery* is as defined in Article l(j) of Directive 75/442/EEC;

(l) *state of dispatch* means any state from which a shipment of waste is planned or made;

(m) *state of destination* means any state to which a shipment of waste is planned or made for disposal or recovery, or for loading on board before disposal at sea without prejudice to existing conventions on disposal at sea;

(n) *state of transit* means any state, other than the state of dispatch or destination, through which a shipment of waste is planned or made;

(o) *consignment note* means the standard consignment note to be drawn up in accordance with Article 42;

(p) *the Basel Convention* means the Basel Convention of 22 March 1989 on the control of trans-boundary movements of hazardous wastes and their disposal;

(q) *the fourth Lomé Convention* means the Lomé Convention of 15 December 1989;

(r) *the OECD Decision* means the decision of the OECD Council of 30 March 1992 on the control of transfrontier movements of wastes destined for recovery operations.

Title II Shipments of waste between Member States

Chapter A Waste for disposal

Article 3

1   Where the notifier intends to ship waste for disposal from one Member State to another Member State and/or pass it in transit through one or several other Member States, and without prejudice to Articles 25(2) and 26(2), he shall notify the competent authority of destination and send a copy of the notification to the competent authorities of dispatch and of transit and to the consignee. [...]

Article 4

1   On receipt of the notification the competent authority of destination shall, within three working days, send an acknowledgment to the notifier and copies thereof to the other competent authorities concerned and to the consignee.

2   (a) The competent authority of destination shall have 30 days following dispatch of the acknowledgment to take its decision authorising the shipment, with or without conditions, or refusing it. It may also request additional information. [...]

   (b) The competent authorities of dispatch and transit may raise objections within 20 days following the dispatch of the acknowledgment. They may also request additional information. These objections shall be conveyed in writing to the notifier, with copies to the other competent authorities concerned. [...]

(d) The competent authorities of dispatch and transit may, within 20 days following the dispatch of the acknowledgment, lay down conditions in respect of the transport of waste within their jurisdiction. [...]

3 (a) (i) In order to implement the principles of proximity, priority for recovery and self-sufficiency at Community and national levels in accordance with Directive 75/442/EEC, Member States may take measures in accordance with the Treaty to prohibit generally or partially or to object systematically to shipments of waste. Such measures shall immediately be notified to the Commission, which will inform the other Member States. [...]

(b) The competent authorities of dispatch and destination, while taking into account geographical circumstances or the need for specialised installations for certain types of waste, may raise reasoned objections to planned shipments if they are not in accordance with Directive 75/442/EEC, especially Articles 5 and 7:

(i) in order to implement the principle of self-sufficiency at Community and national levels;

(ii) in cases where the installation has to dispose of waste from a nearer source and the competent authority has given priority to this waste;

(iii) in order to ensure that shipments are in accordance with waste management plans. [...]

Article 5

1   The shipment may be effected only after the notifier has received authorisation from the competent authority of destination. [...]

Chapter B Waste for recovery

Article 6

1   Where the notifier intends to ship waste for recovery listed in Annex III from one Member State to another Member State and/or pass it in transit through one or several other Member States, and without prejudice to Articles 25(2) and 26(2), he shall notify the competent authority of destination and send copies of the notification to the competent authorities of dispatch and transit and to the consignee. [...]

Article 7

1   On receipt of the notification the competent authority of destination shall send, within three working days, an acknowledgement to the notifier and copies thereof to the other competent authorities and to the consignee.

2   The competent authorities of destination, dispatch and transit shall have 30 days following dispatch of the acknowledgment to object to the shipment. Such objection shall be based on para 4. Any objection must be provided in writing to the notifier and to other competent authorities concerned within the 30-day period. [...]

Article 8

1   The shipment may be effected after the 30-day period has passed if no objection has been lodged. Tacit consent, however, expires within one year from that date. Where the

competent authorities decide to provide written consent, the shipment may be effected immediately after all necessary consents have been received. [...]

Title III Shipments of waste within Member States

Article 13

1   Titles II, VII and VIII shall not apply to shipments within a Member State.

2   Member States shall, however, establish an appropriate system for the supervision and control of shipments of waste within their jurisdiction. This system should take account of the need for coherence with the Community system established by this Regulation. [...]

Title IV Exports of waste

Chapter A Waste for disposal

Article 14

1   All exports of waste for disposal shall be prohibited, except those to EFTA countries which are also parties to the Basel Convention.

2   However, without prejudice to Articles 25(2), and 26(2), exports of waste for disposal to an EFTA country shall also be banned:

(a) where the EFTA country of destination prohibits imports of such wastes or where it has not given its written consent to the specific import of this waste;

(b) if the competent authority of dispatch in the Community has reason to believe that the waste will not be managed in accordance with environmentally sound methods in the EFTA country of destination concerned.

3   The competent authority of dispatch shall require that any waste for disposal authorised for export to EFTA countries be managed in an environmentally sound matter throughout the period of shipment and in the State of destination. [...]

Chapter B Waste for recovery

Article 16

1   All exports for recovery of waste listed in Annex V for recovery shall be prohibited except those to:

(a) countries to which the OECD decision applies;

(b) other countries

–   which are Parties to the Basel Convention and/or with which the Community, or the Community and its Member States, have concluded bilateral or multilateral or regional agreements or arrangements in accordance with Article 11 of the Basel Convention and para 2 of this Article. Any such exports shall however be prohibited from 1 January 1998 onwards, or

–   with which individual Member States have concluded bilateral agreements and arrangements prior to the date of application of this Regulation, in so far as these are compatible with Community legislation and in accordance with Article 11 of the Basel Convention and para 2 of this Article. [...]

Chapter C Export of waste to ACP States

Article 18

1   All exports of waste to ACP States shall be prohibited.

2   This prohibition does not prevent a Member State to which an ACP State has chosen to export waste for processing from returning the processed waste to the ACP State of origin. [...]

Title V Imports of waste into the Community

Chapter A Imports of waste for disposal

Article 19

1   All imports into the Community of waste for disposal shall be prohibited except those from:

(a) EFTA countries which are parties to the Basel Convention;

(b) other countries

–   which are Parties to the Basel Convention, or

–   with which the Community, or the Community and its Member States, have concluded bilateral or multilateral agreements or arrangements compatible with Community legislation and in accordance with Article 11 of the Basel Convention guaranteeing that the disposal operations carried out in an authorised centre and complies with the requirements for environmentally sound management, or

–   with which individual Member States have concluded bilateral agreements or arrangements prior to the date of application of this Regulation compatible with Community legislation and in accordance with Article 11 of the Basel Convention, containing the same guarantees as referred to above and guaranteeing that the waste originated in the country of dispatch and that disposal will be carried out exclusively in the Member State which has concluded the agreement or arrangement. [...]

2   The Council hereby authorises individual Member States to conclude bilateral agreements and arrangements after the date of application of this Regulation in exceptional cases for the disposal of specific waste, where such waste will not be managed in an environmentally sound manner in the country of dispatch. [...]

Chapter B Imports of waste for recovery

Article 21

1   All imports of waste for recovery into the Community shall be prohibited, except those from:

(a) countries to which the OECD decision applies;

(b) other countries

–   which are Parties to the Basel Convention and/or with which the Community, or the Community and its Member States, have concluded bilateral or multilateral or regional agreements or arrangements compatible with Community legislation and in accordance with Article 11 of the Basel Convention, guaranteeing that the recovery operation is carried out in an authorised centre and complies with the requirements for environmentally sound management, or

   – with which individual Member States have concluded bilateral agreements or arrangements prior to the date of application of this Regulation, where these are compatible with Community legislation and in accordance with Article 11 of the Basel Convention, containing the same guarantees as referred to above.

Title VI Transit of waste from outside and through the Community for disposal or recovery outside the Community

Chapter A Waste for disposal and recovery (except transit covered by Article 24)

Article 23

1   Where waste for disposal and, except in cases covered by Article 24, recovery is shipped through (a) Member State(s), notification shall be effected by means of the consignment note to the last competent authority of transit within the Community, with copies to the consignee, the other competent authorities concerned and the customs offices of entry into and departure from the Community.

2   The last competent authority of transit within the Community shall promptly inform the notifier of receipt of the notification. The other competent authorities in the Community shall, on the basis of para 5, convey their reactions to the last competent authority of transit in the Community, which shall then respond in writing to the notifier within 60 days, consenting to the shipment with or without reservations; or imposing, if appropriate, conditions laid down by the other competent authorities of transit, or withholding information. Any refusal or reservations must be justified. The competent authority shall send a certified copy of the decision to both the other competent authorities concerned and the customs offices of entry into and departure from the Community. [...]

Chapter B Transit of waste for recovery from and to a country to which the OECD Decision applies

Article 24

1   Transit of waste for recovery listed in Annexes III and IV from a country and transferred for recovery to a country to which the OECD Decision applies through (a) Member State(s) requires notification to all competent authorities of transit of the Member State(s) concerned. [...]

Title VII Common provisions

Article 25

1   Where a shipment of waste to which the competent authorities concerned have consented cannot be completed in accordance with the terms of the consignment note or the contract referred to in Articles 3 and 6, the competent authority of dispatch shall, within 90 days after it has been informed thereof, ensure that the notifier returns the waste to its area of jurisdiction or elsewhere within the state of dispatch unless it is satisfied that the waste can be disposed of or recovered in an alternative and environmentally sound manner. [...]

Article 26

1   Any shipment of waste effected:

(a) without notification to all competent authorities concerned pursuant to the provisions of this Regulation; or

(b) without the consent of the competent authorities concerned pursuant to the provisions of this Regulation; or

(c) with consent obtained from the competent authorities concerned through falsification, misrepresentation or fraud; or

(d) which is not specified in a material way in the consignment note; or

(e) which results in disposal or recovery in contravention of Community or international rules; or

(f) contrary to Articles 14, 16, 19 and 21.

2   If such illegal traffic is the responsibility of the notifier of the waste, the competent authority of dispatch shall ensure that the waste in question is:

(a) taken back by the notifier or, if necessary, by the competent authority itself, into the State of dispatch, or if impracticable;

(b) otherwise disposed of or recovered in an environmentally sound manner, within 30 days from the time when the competent authority was informed of the illegal traffic or within such other period of time as may be agreed by the competent authorities concerned. [...]

3   If such illegal traffic is the responsibility of the consignee, the competent authority of destination shall ensure that the waste in question is disposed of in an environmentally sound manner by the consignee or, if impracticable, by the competent authority itself within 30 days from the time it was informed of the illegal traffic or within any such other period of time as may be agreed by the competent authorities concerned. To this end, they shall co-operate, as necessary, in the disposal or recovery of the waste in an environmentally sound manner.

4   Where responsibility for the illegal traffic cannot be imputed to either the notifier or the consignee, the competent authorities shall co-operate to ensure that the waste in question is disposed of or recovered in an environmentally sound manner. [...]

[Articles 27–44 omitted.]

[All Annexes omitted.]

EUROPEAN PARLIAMENT AND COUNCIL DIRECTIVE

of 20 December 1994

on packaging and packaging waste

(94/62/EC)

THE EUROPEAN PARLIAMENT AND THE COUNCIL OF THE EUROPEAN UNION,

Having regard to the Treaty establishing the European Community, and in particular Article 100a thereof, [...]

Whereas the differing national measures concerning the management of packaging and packaging waste should be harmonised in order, on the one hand, to prevent any impact thereof on the environment or to reduce such impact, thus providing a high level of environmental protection, and, on the other hand, to ensure the functioning of the internal market and to avoid obstacles to trade and distortion and restriction of competition within the Community;

Whereas the best means of preventing the creation of packaging waste is to reduce the overall volume of packaging; [...]

Whereas the reduction of waste is essential for the sustainable growth specifically called for by the Treaty on European Union;

Whereas this Directive should cover all types of packaging placed on the market and all packaging waste; [...]

Whereas, in line with the Community strategy for waste management set out in Council Resolution of 7 May 1990 on waste policy, and Council Directive 75/442/EEC of 15 July 1975 on waste the management of packaging and packaging waste should include as a first priority prevention of packaging waste and, as additional fundamental principles, reuse of packaging, recycling and other forms of recovering packaging waste and, hence, reduction of the final disposal of such waste;

Whereas, until scientific and technological progress is made with regard to recovery processes, reuse and re-cycling should be considered preferable in terms of environmental impact; whereas this requires the setting up in the Member States of systems guaranteeing the return of used packaging and/or packaging waste; whereas life-cycle assessments should be completed as soon as possible to justify a clear hierarchy between re-usable, re-cyclable and recoverable packaging;

Whereas prevention of packaging waste shall be carried out through appropriate measures, including initiatives taken within the Member States in accordance with the objectives of this Directive;

Whereas Member States may encourage, in accordance with the Treaty, reuse systems of packaging which can be reused in an environmentally sound manner, in order to take advantage of the contribution of such systems to environmental protection;

Whereas from an environmental point of view, recycling should be regarded as an important part of recovery with a particular view to reducing the consumption of energy and of primary raw materials and the final disposal of waste;

Whereas energy recovery is one effective means of packaging waste recovery; [...]

Whereas it is essential that all those involved in the production, use, import and distribution of packaging and packaged products become more aware of the extent to which packaging becomes waste, and that in accordance with the polluter-pays principle they accept responsibility for such waste; [...]

HAVE ADOPTED THIS DIRECTIVE:

Article 1 Objectives

1   This Directive aims to harmonise national measures concerning the management of packaging and packaging waste in order, on the one hand, to prevent any impact thereof on the environment of all Member States as well as of third countries or to reduce such impact, thus providing a high level of environmental protection, and, on the other hand, to ensure the functioning of the internal market and to avoid obstacles to trade and distortion and restriction of competition within the Community.

2   To this end this Directive lays down measures aimed, as a first priority, at preventing the production of packaging waste and, as additional fundamental principles, at re-using packaging, at re-cycling and other forms of recovering packaging waste and, hence, at reducing the final disposal of such waste.

Article 2 Scope

1   This Directive covers all packaging placed on the market in the Community and all packaging waste, whether it is used or released at industrial, commercial, office, shop, service, household or any other level, regardless of the material used. [...]

Article 3 Definitions

For the purposes of this Directive:

1   'packaging' shall mean all products made of any materials of any nature to be used for the containment, protection, handling, delivery and presentation of goods, from raw materials to processed goods, from the producer to the user or the consumer. 'Non-returnable' items used for the same purposes shall also be considered to constitute packaging. [...]

Article 4 Prevention

1   Member States shall ensure that, in addition to the measures to prevent the formation of packaging waste taken in accordance with Article 9, other preventative measures are implemented. Such other measures may consist of national programmes or similar actions adopted, if appropriate in consultation with economic operators, and designed to collect and take advantage of the many initiatives taken within Member States as regards prevention. [...]

Article 5 Recovery and recycling

In order to comply with the objectives of this Directive, Member States shall take the necessary measures to attain the following targets covering the whole of their territory:

(a) no later than five years from the date by which this Directive must be implemented in national law, between 50% as a minimum and 65% as a maximum by weight of the packaging waste will be recovered;

(b) within this general target, and with the same time limit, between 25% as a minimum and 45% as a maximum by weight of the totality of packaging materials contained in packaging waste will be recycled with a minimum of 15% by weight for each packaging material;

(c) no later than 10 years from the date by which this Directive must be implemented in national law, a percentage of packaging waste will be recovered and recycled, which will have to be determined by the Council in accordance with para 3(b) with a view to substantially increasing the targets mentioned in paras (a) and (b). [...]

Article 7 Return, collection and recovery systems

1   Member States shall take the necessary measures to ensure that systems are set up to provide for:

(a) the return and/or collection of used packaging and/or packaging waste from the consumer, other final user, or from the waste stream in order to channel it to the most appropriate waste management alternatives;

(b) the reuse or recovery including re-cycling of the packaging and/or packaging waste collected. [...]

Article 9 Essential requirements

1 Member States shall ensure that three years from the date of the entry into force of this Directive, packaging may be placed on the market only if it complies with all essential requirements defined by this Directive including Annex II. [...]

[All other Articles/Annexes omitted.]

COUNCIL DIRECTIVE

of 26 April 1999

on the landfill of waste

(99/31/EC)

(1999) OJ L182, pp 0001–19

THE COUNCIL OF THE EUROPEAN UNION,

Having regard to the Treaty establishing the European Community, and in particular Article 130s(1) thereof,

Having regard to the proposal from the Commission(1),

Having regard to the opinion of the Economic and Social Committee(2),

Acting in accordance with the procedure laid down in Article 189c of the Treaty(3),

(1) Whereas the Council resolution of 7 May 1990(4) on waste policy welcomes and supports the Community strategy document and invites the Commission to propose criteria and standards for the disposal of waste by landfill;

(2) Whereas the Council resolution of 9 December 1996 on waste policy considers that, in the future, only safe and controlled landfill activities should be carried out throughout the Community;

(3) Whereas the prevention, re-cycling and recovery of waste should be encouraged as should the use of recovered materials and energy so as to safeguard natural resources and obviate wasteful use of land;

(4) Whereas further consideration should be given to the issues of incineration of municipal and non-hazardous waste, composting, biomethanisation, and the processing of dredging sludges;

(5) Whereas under the polluter pays principle it is necessary, *inter alia*, to take into account any damage to the environment produced by a landfill;

(6) Whereas, like any other type of waste treatment, landfill should be adequately monitored and managed to prevent or reduce potential adverse effects on the environment and risks to human health;

(7) Whereas it is necessary to take appropriate measures to avoid the abandonment, dumping or uncontrolled disposal of waste; whereas, accordingly, it must be possible to monitor landfill sites with respect to the substances contained in the waste deposited there, whereas such substances should, as far as possible, react only in foreseeable ways;

(8) Whereas both the quantity and hazardous nature of waste intended for landfill should be reduced where appropriate; whereas the handling of waste should be facilitated and its recovery enhanced; whereas the use of treatment processes should therefore be encouraged to ensure that landfill is compatible with the objectives of this Directive; whereas sorting is included in the definition of treatment;

(9) Whereas Member States should be able to apply the principles of proximity and self-sufficiency for the elimination of their waste at Community and national level, in accordance with Council Directive 75/442/EEC of 15 July 1975 on waste(5) whereas the objectives of this Directive must be pursued and clarified through the establishment of an adequate, integrated network of disposal plants based on a high level of environmental protection;

(10) Whereas disparities between technical standards for the disposal of waste by landfill and the lower costs associated with it might give rise to increased disposal of waste in facilities with low standards of environmental protection and thus create a potentially serious threat to the environment, owing to transport of waste over unnecessarily long distances as well as to inappropriate disposal practices;

(11) Whereas it is therefore necessary to lay down technical standards for the landfill of waste at Community level in order to protect, preserve and improve the quality of the environment in the Community;

(12) Whereas it is necessary to indicate clearly the requirements with which landfill sites must comply as regards location, conditioning, management, control, closure and preventive and protective measures to be taken against any threat to the environment in the short as well as in the long term perspective, and more especially against the pollution of groundwater by leachate infiltration into the soil;

(13) Whereas in view of the foregoing it is necessary to define clearly the classes of landfill to be considered and the types of waste to be accepted in the various classes of landfill;

(14) Whereas sites for temporary storage of waste should comply with the relevant requirements of Directive 75/442/EEC;

(15) Whereas the recovery, in accordance with Directive 75/442/EEC, of inert or non-hazardous waste which is suitable, through their use in redevelopment/restoration and filling-in work, or for construction purposes may not constitute a landfilling activity;

(16) Whereas measures should be taken to reduce the production of methane gas from landfills, inter alia, in order to reduce global warming, through the reduction of the landfill of biodegradable waste and the requirements to introduce landfill gas control;

(17) Whereas the measures taken to reduce the landfill of biodegradable waste should also aim at encouraging the separate collection of biodegradable waste, sorting in general, recovery and recycling;

(18) Whereas, because of the particular features of the landfill method of waste disposal, it is necessary to introduce a specific permit procedure for all classes of landfill in accordance with the general licensing requirements already set down in Directive 75/442/EEC and the general requirements of Directive 96/61/EC concerning integrated pollution prevention and control(6) whereas the landfill site's compliance with such a permit must be verified in the course of an inspection by the competent authority before the start of disposal operations;

(19) Whereas, in each case, checks should be made to establish whether the waste may be placed in the landfill for which it is intended, in particular as regards hazardous waste;

(20) Whereas, in order to prevent threats to the environment, it is necessary to introduce a uniform waste acceptance procedure on the basis of a classification procedure for waste acceptable in the different categories of landfill, including in particular standardised limit values; whereas to that end a consistent and standardised system of waste characterisation, sampling and analysis must be established in time to facilitate implementation of this Directive; whereas the acceptance criteria must be particularly specific with regard to inert waste;

(21) Whereas, pending the establishment of such methods of analysis or of the limit values necessary for characterisation, Member States may for the purposes of this Directive maintain or draw up national lists of waste which is acceptable or unacceptable for landfill, or define criteria, including limit values, similar to those laid down in this Directive for the uniform acceptance procedure;

(22) Whereas for certain hazardous waste to be accepted in landfills for non-hazardous waste acceptance criteria should be developed by the technical committee;

(23) Whereas it is necessary to establish common monitoring procedures during the operation and after-care phases of a landfill in order to identify any possible adverse environmental effect of the landfill and take the appropriate corrective measures;

(24) Whereas it is necessary to define when and how a landfill should be closed and the obligations and responsibility of the operator on the site during the after-care period;

(25) Whereas landfill sites that have been closed prior to the date of transposition of this Directive should not be subject to its provisions on closure procedure;

(26) Whereas the future conditions of operation of existing landfills should be regulated in order to take the necessary measures, within a specified period of time, for their adaptation to this Directive on the basis of a site-conditioning plan;

(27) Whereas for operators of existing landfills having, in compliance with binding national rules equivalent to those of Article 14 of this Directive, already submitted the documentation referred to in Article 14(a) of this Directive prior to its entry into force and for which the competent authority authorised the continuation of their operation, there is no need to resubmit this documentation nor for the competent authority to deliver a new authorisation;

(28) Whereas the operator should make adequate provision by way of a financial security or any other equivalent to ensure that all the obligations flowing from the permit are fulfilled, including those relating to the closure procedure and after-care of the site;

(29) Whereas measures should be taken to ensure that the price charged for waste disposal in a landfill cover all the costs involved in the setting up and operation of the facility, including as far as possible the financial security or its equivalent which the site operator must provide, and the estimated cost of closing the site including the necessary after-care;

(30) Whereas, when a competent authority considers that a landfill is unlikely to cause a hazard to the environment for longer than a certain period, the estimated costs to be included in the price to be charged by an operator may be limited to that period;

(31) Whereas it is necessary to ensure the proper application of the provisions implementing this Directive throughout the Community, and to ensure that the training and knowledge acquired by landfill operators and staff afford them the necessary skills;

(32) Whereas the Commission must establish a standard procedure for the acceptance of waste and set up a standard classification of waste acceptable in a landfill in accordance with the committee procedure laid down in Article 18 of Directive 75/442/EEC;

(33) Whereas adaptation of the Annexes to this Directive to scientific and technical progress and the standardisation of the monitoring, sampling and analysis methods must be adopted under the same committee procedure;

(34) Whereas the Member States must send regular reports to the Commission on the implementation of this Directive paying particular attention to the national strategies to be set up in pursuance of Article 5; whereas on the basis of these reports the Commission shall report to the European Parliament and the Council.

HAS ADOPTED THIS DIRECTIVE:

Article 1 Overall objective

1   With a view to meeting the requirements of Directive 75/442/EEC, and in particular Articles 3 and 4 thereof, the aim of this Directive is, by way of stringent operational and technical requirements on the waste and landfills, to provide for measures, procedures and guidance to prevent or reduce as far as possible negative effects on the environment, in particular the pollution of surface water, groundwater, soil and air, and on the global environment, including the greenhouse effect, as well as any resulting risk to human health, from landfilling of waste, during the whole life-cycle of the landfill.

2   In respect of the technical characteristics of landfills, this Directive contains, for those landfills to which Directive 96/61/EC is applicable, the relevant technical requirements in order to elaborate in concrete terms the general requirements of that Directive. The relevant requirements of Directive 96/61/EC shall be deemed to be fulfilled if the requirements of this Directive are complied with.

Article 2 Definitions

For the purposes of this Directive:

(a) 'waste' means any substance or object which is covered by Directive 75/442/EEC;

(b) 'municipal waste' means waste from households, as well as other waste which, because of its nature or composition, is similar to waste from household;

(c) 'hazardous waste' means any waste which is covered by Article 1(4) of Council Directive 91/689/EEC of 12 December 1991 on hazardous waste(7);

(d) 'non-hazardous waste' means waste which is not covered by para (c);

(e) 'inert waste' means waste that does not undergo any significant physical, chemical or biological transformations. Inert waste will not dissolve, burn or otherwise physically or chemically react, biodegrade or adversely affect other matter with which it comes into contact in a way likely to give rise to environmental pollution or harm human health. The total leachability and pollutant content of the waste and the ecotoxicity of the leachate must be insignificant, and in particular not endanger the quality of surface water and/or groundwater;

(f) 'underground storage' means a permanent waste storage facility in a deep geological cavity such as a salt or potassium mine;

(g) 'landfill' means a waste disposal site for the deposit of the waste onto or into land (that is, underground), including:

   – internal waste disposal sites (that is, landfill where a producer of waste is carrying out its own waste disposal at the place of production), and

   – a permanent site (that is, more than one year) which is used for temporary storage of waste,

   but excluding:

   – facilities where waste is unloaded in order to permit its preparation for further transport for recovery, treatment or disposal elsewhere, and

   – storage of waste prior to recovery or treatment for a period less than three years as a general rule, or

   – storage of waste prior to disposal for a period less than one year;

(h) 'treatment' means the physical, thermal, chemical or biological processes, including sorting, that change the characteristics of the waste in order to reduce its volume or hazardous nature, facilitate its handling or enhance recovery;

(i) 'leachate' means any liquid percolating through the deposited waste and emitted from or contained within a landfill;

(j) 'landfill gas' means all the gases generated from the landfilled waste;

(k) 'eluate' means the solution obtained by a laboratory leaching test;

(l) 'operator' means the natural or legal person responsible for a landfill in accordance with the internal legislation of the Member State where the landfill is located; this person may change from the preparation to the after-care phase;

(m) 'biodegradable waste' means any waste that is capable of undergoing anaerobic or aerobic decomposition, such as food and garden waste, and paper and paperboard;

(n) 'holder' means the producer of the waste or the natural or legal person who is in possession of it;

(o) 'applicant' means any person who applies for a landfill permit under this Directive;

(p) 'competent authority' means that authority which the Member States designate as responsible for performing the duties arising from this Directive;

(q) 'liquid waste' means any waste in liquid form including waste waters but excluding sludge;

(r) 'isolated settlement' means a settlement:

   – with no more than 500 inhabitants per municipality or settlement and no more than five inhabitants per square kilometre and,

   – where the distance to the nearest urban agglomeration with at least 250 inhabitants per square kilometre is not less than 50 km, or with difficult access by road to those nearest agglomerations, due to harsh meteorological conditions during a significant part of the year.

Article 3 Scope

1   Member States shall apply this Directive to any landfill as defined in Article 2(g).

2   Without prejudice to existing Community legislation, the following shall be excluded from the scope of this Directive:

–   the spreading of sludges, including sewage sludges, and sludges resulting from dredging operations, and similar matter on the soil for the purposes of fertilisation or improvement,

–   the use of inert waste which is suitable, in redevelopment/restoration and filling-in work, or for construction purposes, in landfills,

–   the deposit of non-hazardous dredging sludges alongside small waterways from where they have been dredged out and of non-hazardous sludges in surface water including the bed and its sub soil,

–   the deposit of unpolluted soil or of non-hazardous inert waste resulting from prospecting and extraction, treatment, and storage of mineral resources as well as from the operation of quarries.

3   Without prejudice to Directive 75/442/EEC Member States may declare at their own option, that the deposit of non-hazardous waste, to be defined by the committee established under Article 17 of this Directive, other than inert waste, resulting from prospecting and extraction, treatment and storage of mineral resources as well as from the operation of quarries and which are deposited in a manner preventing environmental pollution or harm to human health, can be exempted from the provisions in Annex I, points 2, 3.1, 3.2 and 3.3 of this Directive.

4   Without prejudice to Directive 75/442/EEC Member States may declare, at their own option, parts or all of Articles 6(d), 7(i), 8(a)(iv), 10, 11(1)(a), (b) and (c), 12(a) and (c), Annex I, points 3 and 4, Annex II (except point 3, level 3, and point 4) and Annex III, points 3 to 5 to this Directive not applicable to:

(a)   landfill sites for non-hazardous or inert wastes with a total capacity not exceeding 15,000 tonnes or with an annual intake not exceeding 1000 tonnes serving islands, where this is the only landfill on the island and where this is exclusively destined for the disposal of waste generated on that island. Once the total capacity of that landfill has been used, any new landfill site established on the island shall comply with the requirements of this Directive;

(b)   landfill sites for non-hazardous or inert waste in isolated settlements if the landfill site is destined for the disposal of waste generated only by that isolated settlement.

Not later than two years after the date laid down in Article 18(1), Member States shall notify the Commission of the list of islands and isolated settlements that are exempted. The Commission shall publish the list of islands and isolated settlements.

5   Without prejudice to Directive 75/442/EEC Member States may declare, at their own option, that underground storage as defined in Article 2(f) of this Directive can be exempted from the provisions in Article 13(d) and in Annex I, point 2, except first indent, points 3 to 5 and in Annex III, points 2, 3 and 5 to this Directive.

Article 4 Classes of landfill

Each landfill shall be classified in one of the following classes:

- landfill for hazardous waste,

- landfill for non-hazardous waste,

- landfill for inert waste.

Article 5 Waste and treatment not acceptable in landfills

1 Member States shall set up a national strategy for the implementation of the reduction of biodegradable waste going to landfills, not later than two years after the date laid down in Article 18(1) and notify the Commission of this strategy. This strategy should include measures to achieve the targets set out in para 2 by means of in particular, recycling, composting, biogas production or materials / energy recovery. Within 30 months of the date laid down in Article 18(1) the Commission shall provide the European Parliament and the Council with a report drawing together the national strategies.

2 This strategy shall ensure that:

(a) not later than five years after the date laid down in Article 18(1), biodegradable municipal waste going to landfills must be reduced to 75% of the total amount (by weight) of biodegradable municipal waste produced in 1995 or the latest year before 1995 for which standardised Eurostat data is available;

(b) not later than eight years after the date laid down in Article 18(1), biodegradable municipal waste going to landfills must be reduced to 50% of the total amount (by weight) of biodegradable municipal waste produced in 1995 or the latest year before 1995 for which standardised Eurostat data is available;

(c) not later than 15 years after the date laid down in Article 18(1), biodegradable municipal waste going to landfills must be reduced to 35 % of the total amount (by weight) of biodegradable municipal waste produced in 1995 or the lates year before 1995 for which standardised Eurostat data is available.

[…]

3 Member States shall take measures in order that the following wastes are not accepted in a landfill:

(a) liquid waste;

(b) waste which, in the conditions of landfill, is explosive, corrosive, oxidising, highly flammable or flammable, as defined in Annex III to Directive 91/689/EEC;

(c) hospital and other clinical wastes arising from medical or veterinary establishments, which are infectious as defined (property H9 in Annex III) by Directive 91/689/EEC and waste falling within category 14 (Annex I.A) of that Directive;

(d) whole used tyres from two years from the date laid down in Article 18(1), excluding tyres used as engineering material, and shredded used tyres five years from the date laid down in Article 18(1) (excluding in both instances bicycle tyres and tyres with an outside diameter above 1 400 mm);

(e) any other type of waste which does not fulfil the acceptance criteria determined in accordance with Annex II.

4 The dilution of mixture of waste solely in order to meet the waste acceptance criteria is prohibited.

Article 6 Waste to be accepted in the different classes of landfill

Member States shall take measures in order that:

(a) only waste that has been subject to treatment is landfilled; [...]

(b) only hazardous waste that fulfils the criteria set out in accordance with Annex II is assigned to a hazardous landfill;

(c) landfill for non-hazardous waste may be used for:

    (i) municipal waste;

    (ii) non-hazardous waste of any other origin, which fulfil the criteria for the acceptance of waste at landfill for non-hazardous waste set out in accordance with Annex II;

    (iii) stable, non-reactive hazardous wastes (for example, solidified, vitrified), with leaching behaviour equivalent to those of the non-hazardous wastes referred to in point (ii), which fulfil the relevant acceptance criteria set out in accordance with Annex II. These hazardous wastes shall not be deposited in cells destined for biodegradable non-hazardous waste;

(d) inert waste landfill sites shall be used only for inert waste.

[Articles 7 (on Application for a Permit), 8 (on Conditions of the Permit), 9 (on Content of the Permit) omitted.]

Article 10 Cost of the landfill of waste

Member States shall take measures to ensure that all of the costs involved in the setting up and operation of a landfill site, including as far as possible the cost of the financial security or its equivalent referred to in Article 8(a)(iv), and the estimated costs of the closure and after-care of the site for a period of at least 30 years shall be covered by the price to be charged by the operator for the disposal of any type of waste in that site. Subject to the requirements of Council Directive 90/313/EEC of 7 June 1990 on the freedom of access to information on the environment(9) Member States shall ensure transparency in the collection and use of any necessary cost information.

[Article 11 (on Waste Acceptance Procedures) omitted.]

Article 12 Control and monitoring procedures in the operational phase

Member States shall take measures in order that control and monitoring procedures in the operational phase meet at least the following requirements:

(a) the operator of a landfill shall carry out during the operational phase a control and monitoring programme as specified in Annex III;

(b) the operator shall notify the competent authority of any significant adverse environmental effects revealed by the control and monitoring procedures and follow the decision of the competent authority on the nature and timing of the corrective measures to be taken. These measures shall be undertaken at the expense of the operator.

At a frequency to be determined by the competent authority, and in any event at least once a year, the operator shall report, on the basis of aggregated data, all monitoring results to the competent authorities for the purpose of demonstrating compliance with permit conditions and increasing the knowledge on waste behaviour in the landfills;

(c) the quality control of the analytical operations of the control and monitoring procedures and/or of the analyses referred to in Article 11(1)(b) are carried out by competent laboratories.

Article 13 Closure and after-care procedures

Member States shall take measures in order that, in accordance, where appropriate, with the permit:

(a) a landfill or part of it shall start the closure procedure:

    (i) when the relevant conditions stated in the permit are met; or

    (ii) under the authorisation of the competent authority, at the request of the operator; or

    (iii) by reasoned decision of the competent authority;

(b) a landfill or part of it may only be considered as definitely closed after the competent authority has carried out a final on-site inspection, has assessed all the reports submitted by the operator and has communicated to the operator its approval for the closure. This shall not in any way reduce the responsibility of the operator under the conditions of the permit;

(c) after a landfill has been definitely closed, the operator shall be responsible for its maintenance, monitoring and control in the after-care phase for as long as may be required by the competent authority, taking into account the time during which the landfill could present hazards.

The operator shall notify the competent authority of any significant adverse environmental effects revealed by the control procedures and shall follow the decision of the competent authority on the nature and timing of the corrective measures to be taken;

(d) for as long as the competent authority considers that a landfill is likely to cause a hazard to the environment and without prejudice to any Community or national legislation as regards liability of the waste holder, the operator of the site shall be responsible for monitoring and analysing landfill gas and leachate from the site and the groundwater regime in the vicinity of the site in accordance with Annex III.

Article 14 Existing landfill sites

Member States shall take measures in order that landfills which have been granted a permit, or which are already in operation at the time of transposition of this Directive, may not continue to operate unless the steps outlined below are accomplished as soon as possible and within eight years after the date laid down in Article 18(1) at the latest:

(a) with a period of one year after the date laid down in Article 18(1), the operator of a landfill shall prepare and present to the competent authorities, for their approval, a conditioning plan for the site including the particulars listed in Article 8 and any corrective measures which the operator considers will be needed in order to comply with the requirements of this Directive with the exception of the requirements in Annex I, point 1;

(b) following the presentation of the conditioning plan, the competent authorities shall take a definite decision on whether operations may continue on the basis of the said conditioning plan and this Directive. Member States shall take the necessary measures to close down as soon as possible, in accordance with Article 7(g) and 13, sites which have not been granted, in accordance with Article 8, a permit to continue to operate;

(c) on the basis of the approved site-conditioning plan, the competent authority shall authorise the necessary work and shall lay down a transitional period for the completion of the plan. Any existing landfill shall comply with the requirements of this Directive with the exception of the requirements in Annex I, point 1 within eight years after the date laid down in Article 18(1);

(d) (i) within one year after the date laid down in Article 18(1), Articles 4, 5 and 11 and Annex II shall apply to landfills for hazardous waste;

(ii) within three years after the date laid down in Article 18(1), Article 6 shall apply to landfills for hazardous waste.

[Articles 15 (on Obligation to Report), 16 (on Committee), 17 (on Committee Procedure), 18 (on Transposition), 19 (on Entry into Force), and 20 (on Addressees) omitted.]

[Annex I (on General Requirements for All Classes of Landfills) and Annex II (on Waste Acceptance Criteria and Procedures) omitted.]

DOMESTIC LAW

Waste was not perceived to be a great problem until the 1970s when the Control of Pollution Act 1974 first introduced a comprehensive system of waste management. This system established a model used by other countries and by the EC in the Waste Framework Directive 75/442. The basic legislative provisions concerning waste are now contained in the 1990 Environmental Protection Act, as amended, and the key statement of policy regarding waste is set out in *Waste Strategy* 2000 (DETR, May 2000) published by virtue of Pt V Environment Act 1995 (see below).

Previous statements of general policy, and in particular – *Making Waste Work: A Strategy for Sustainable Waste Management in England and Wales* ((1995) Cm 3040) – identified the need to approach waste management having regard to a hierarchy of action (the 'waste hierarchy') which included seeking to reduce waste, reusing waste, recovering value from waste (for example, composting and energy recovery – incineration using methane from landfill sites), and disposing of waste where no benefit can be gained from materials. To achieve these objectives five complementary strategies were identified: a regulatory strategy, a market-based strategy, a land use planning strategy, a promotion strategy, and an information strategy. Despite these policy statements the domestic approach to waste management has been severely criticised as being 'characterised by inertia, careless administration and ad hoc rather than science based decisions' (House of Commons Select Committee on the Environment, Transport and Regional Affairs, 6th Report, 1998).

The meaning of waste in UK law

The statutory definition of waste in UK law is the same as it is in EC law. The statutory definition of waste is contained in s 75(2) of the EPA 1990 (as amended by the Environment Act 1995). It should be noted that the list of categories set out in Sched 2B duplicates Annex 1 of the WFD). See also the Waste Management Licensing Regulations 1994 SI 1994/1056 (Sched 4, paras 9, 2) which incorporate 'Directive Waste' into the definition of waste in domestic law (reg 1(3)). After setting out s 75 of the EPA 1990, we look at the application of the definition in some of the leading UK cases.

The statutory definition of 'waste'

Environmental Protection Act 1990, s 75

Meaning of 'waste' and household, commercial and industrial waste and special waste

(1) The following provisions apply for the interpretation of this Part [of the EPA 1990].

(2) 'Waste' means any substance or object in the categories set out in Schedule 2B to this Act which the holder discards or intends or is required to discard; and for the purposes of this definition–

'holder' means the producer of the waste or the person who is in possession of it; and

'producer' means any person whose activities produce waste or any person who carries out pre-processing, mixing or other operations resulting in a change in the nature or composition of this waste.

[*Note*: the list of categories set out in Schedule 2B duplicates Annex 1 of the Waste Framework Directive, see above p 438. Subsection 3 was repealed by the Environment Act 1995.]

(4) 'Controlled waste' means household, industrial and commercial waste or any such waste.

(5) Subject to sub-s (8) below, 'household waste' means waste from–

   (a) domestic property, that is to say, a building or self-contained part of a building which is used wholly for the purposes of living accommodation;

   (b) a caravan (as defined in s 29(1) of the Caravan Sites and Control of Development Act 1960) which usually and for the time being is situated on a caravan site (within the meaning of that Act);

   (c) a residential home;

   (d) premises forming part of a university or school or other educational establishment;

   (e) premises forming part of a hospital or nursing home.

(6) Subject to sub-s (8) below, 'industrial waste' means waste from any of the following premises:

   (a) any factory (within the meaning of the Factories Act 1961);

   (b) any premises used for the purposes of, or in connection with, the provision to the public of transport services by land, water or air;

   (c) any premises used for the purposes of, or in connection with, the supply to the public of gas, water or electricity or the provision of sewage services; or

   (d) any premises used for the purposes of, or in connection with, the provision to the public of postal or telecommunications services.

(7) Subject to sub-s (8) below, 'commercial waste' means waste from premises used wholly or mainly for the purposes of a trade or business or the purposes of sport, recreation or entertainment excluding:

    (a) household waste;

    (b) industrial waste;

    (c) waste from any mine or quarry and waste from premises used for agriculture within the meaning of the Agriculture Act 1947 or, in Scotland, the Agriculture (Scotland) Act 1948; and

    (d) waste of any other description prescribed by regulations made by the Secretary of State for the purposes of this paragraph.

(8) Regulations made by the Secretary of State may provide that waste of a description prescribed in the regulations shall be treated for the purposes of provisions of this Part prescribed in the regulations as being or not being household waste or industrial waste or commercial waste; but no regulations shall be made in respect of such waste as is mentioned in sub-s (7)(c) above and references to waste in sub-s (7) above and this sub-s do not include sewage (including matter in or from a privy) except so far as the regulations provide otherwise.

(9) 'Special waste' means controlled waste as respects which regulations are in force under s 62 above.

(10) Schedule 2B to this Act (which reproduces Annex I to the Waste Directive) shall have effect.

(11) Sub-section (2) above is substituted, and Schedule 2B to this Act is inserted, for the purpose of assigning to 'waste' in this Part the meaning which it has in the Waste Directive by virtue of paras (a) to (c) of Article 1 of, and Annex I to, that Directive, and those provisions shall be construed accordingly.

(12) In this section 'the Waste Directive' means the directive of the Council of the European Communities, dated 15 July 1975, on waste, as amended by:

    (a) the directive of that Council, dated 18 March 1991, amending Directive 75/442/EEC on waste; and

    (b) the directive of that Council, dated 23rd December 1991, standardising and rationalising reports on the implementation of certain directives relating to the environment.

Note:

The Special Waste Regulations 1996 SI 1996/972 (as amended by SI 1996/2019) came into force 1 September 1996. These substantially gave effect to the provisions of the Hazardous Waste Directive (see p 396, above). These regulations have been the subject of review by the DETR.

Applying the definition of waste

Determining whether material falls within these provisions can be extremely difficult. Essentially, the following questions must be asked. Is the material capable of being waste? If so, has the material been discarded or is there an intention or requirement to discard? If so, has the discarded material been subject to the disposal operations listed in Annex IIA of the WFD or the recovery operations in Annex IIB? If the material has been subject to these operations it will normally be treated as being waste. In the case of material undergoing a recovery operation, the material is likely to be regarded as being waste while undergoing the operation. Indeed, the material may remain waste beyond the recovery process until it is actually reused. If material can be reused without undergoing a recovery operation then it is unlikely to be treated as waste. It is important to note that the ECJ and English courts have emphasised the need to adopt a broad approach when interpreting the meaning of waste in order to ensure that the aim of the WFD and the UK provisions are not undermined (see *Castle Cement*, para 55, p 427, below).

These propositions will now be considered in more detail.

Is the material capable of being waste?

There is no exhaustive list of substances or objects that are capable of being waste. Section 75 of the EPA refers to materials that are listed in Sched 2B and this incorporates the categories of waste in Annex 1 to the WFD. As we have seen above, that list refers to 'any materials (etc) which are not contained in the above categories' (Q16). This implies that any material may be waste once it has been discarded.

Has the material been discarded?

Waste is material which has been discarded or which the holder intends or is required to discard. Whether the material has been discarded is not always clear. It may be noted that until the English definition of waste in s 75 of the EPA was amended (by s 120 of the Environment Act 1995, Sched 22, paras 88 and 95) to bring it into line with the WFD. Prior to this amendment English law used the term 'dispose' rather than 'discard'. It is now generally understood that the term 'discard' has both an ordinary (or broad) meaning and a technical (more specific) legal meaning. Its ordinary meaning is to get 'rid of' as being unwanted. However, as we have seen decisions of the ECJ have held that the term 'discard' embraces the operations listed in Annex IIA and IIB. While IIA essentially concerns methods of disposing of material that is being 'got rid of', Annex IIB deals with methods of recycling or reusing materials. Materials undergoing these operations may technically be discarded even though it is uncertain whether they have been 'got rid of' as being unwanted in the everyday sense of the term.

The judgment of Pill LJ in *Meston Technical Services and Another v Warwickshire County Council* [1995] Env LR D 36 does not deal with definition of discard as it is currently understood. The following extract does, however, help to illustrate the type of problems that this issue has given rise to. (Note that the then legislation used the term 'dispose' rather than 'discard'.)

> **Pill LJ:** ... On behalf of the Appellants, Mr Brodie ... submits that for a material to be 'waste' there has to be an intention on the part of the person or company in possession of it to dispose of or abandon it. If the material does not go out of the possession of people who want it, then it is not waste. The material in these cases was not waste because it was wanted by the Appellants.

[...] Reference has been made to the decision of this Court in *Kent County Council v Queenborough Rolling Mill Company Ltd* 89 LGR 306. In my judgment in that case (with which Woolf LJ agreed), I stated:

> In my judgment the purpose to which the material was put is irrelevant in the present situation. The nature of the material must first be considered at the time of its removal from the Stelrad site. The material had earlier been discarded and had lain on site for many years. When removed from the site it was waste within the meaning of that word in s 30. It bore the same quality when it was deposited at Coal Washer Wharf. The usefulness, if it be so, of the deposit as infill on the receiving site did not change the character of the material.

Mr Brodie also referred to the decision of this Court in *Cheshire County Council v Armstong's Transport (Wigan) Limited* ([1995] Crim LR 162; 1995 Env LR 62, p 65). In the course of her judgment in that case, Butler-Sloss LJ agreed with the statement of the law in the Kent County Council case. The first point turns upon the relevance of the state of mind of the Appellants. It is submitted that, if the material deposited was valuable to them, it was not waste within the meaning of s 30. Mr Brodie relies upon the result of the decision in the Cheshire County Council case, although he says that it was reached for the wrong reason. In that case the dismissal of information by the Magistrates was upheld in this Court on the ground that the materials concerned were not waste. Mr Brodie submits that the true basis for the decision was that the materials were valuable to the defendants.

I do not agree that that is the basis for the decision. The facts in that case arose out of the work of a housing development corporation in demolishing and rebuilding. They invited a demolition company to do preparatory work. Material was to be removed from the development site. The contractors were to crush the concrete from demolished flats so that it could be used to provide infill for the footings of a new housing development. The concrete was tipped from the demolition site onto the defendant's land for the purpose of crushing the concrete and then picking it up and returning it to the building site. In that context Butler-Sloss LJ stated at page 6 of the transcript:

> As the Magistrates said in their opinion, the concrete throughout the whole process remained the property of the housing association or the demolition contractor. The Respondents never regarded the concrete as waste to be disposed of; they could not have sold it; they could not have disposed of it in any way they chose and they were under the obligation of the contract to return it to the original site from where it had been removed. That, in my judgment, is far removed from the interpretation of 'waste' in s 30 of the Control of Pollution Act, which requires that the substance should be unwanted, to be disposed of, or to be discarded. In this particular case, quite simply, it was to be taken away, processed and returned.

It is right to say that Butler-Sloss LJ does say that the defendants (respondents) never regarded the concrete as waste to be disposed of. Reading the judgment as a whole, what the learned Lord Justice had in mind in my view was the approach to the material by the owners of it. Their state of mind, as summarised in the judgment, was such that the material did not constitute waste. I do not regard the Cheshire County Council case as authority for the proposition that, provided the depositor (the defendant) does not regard the material as waste and he proposes to make use of it by sale or in some other way, the material is taken out of the category of waste. That appears to me to be contrary to the reasoning both in the Kent County Council decision and the Cheshire County Council decision.

Not all discarded material will be waste

While materials will only be waste if they have been discarded (or if there is an intention to discard them) materials which have been discarded may not be waste if they can be reused. It appears that if material can be reused without undergoing a recovery operation it will not normally be treated as waste. In *Mayer Parry Recycling Ltd* (see below) Carnwarth J said (para 46) that:

> The general concept is now reasonably clear. The term 'discard' is used in a broad sense equivalent to 'get rid of'; but it is coloured by the examples of waste given in Annex I and the Waste Catalogue, which indicate that it is concerned generally with materials which have ceased to be required for their original purpose, normally because they are unsuitable, unwanted or surplus to requirements. That broad category is however limited by the context, which shows that the purpose is to control disposal and recovery of such materials. Accordingly, materials which are to be reused (rather than finally disposed of), but which do not require any recovery operation before being put to their new use, are not treated as waste. [...]

However, if material can only be reused following a recovery operation it will continue to be regarded as waste while it is undergoing that operation. Although the decision is now rather old, *R v Rotherham Metropolitan Borough Council and Another ex p Rankin* (1989) *The Times*, 6 November provides an interesting example of the problem of deciding whether material that is being prepared for recycling is waste. Here the basic issue was whether the local planning authority erred in law by failing to treat applications for planning permission as involving waste and therefore subject to procedures providing greater opportunities for objections by neighbours.

> Safety Kleen UK Ltd (SK) have two planning permissions each in respect of a distribution, waste extraction and recycling centre ... The applicant lives 560m away and claims he did not learn about the planning permissions until March 1989 whereupon he launched these proceedings asserting that each of the permissions was invalid because it had been insufficiently advertised and that the second permission was invalid because the relevant application was not handled as required by the Town and Country Planning (Assessment of Environmental Effects) Regulations 1988.

> ... the question which faced the authority in deciding whether or not this was an application to which s 26 applied, and thus required advertisement before it was entertained, was whether these were applications for the construction of buildings or other operations or the use of land for retaining, treating or disposing of trade waste. Before considering the legal argument further let me describe the nature of SK's business. The largest part of SK's business is their parts cleaner service and paint spray-gun cleaning service. Cellulose thinners and paraffin are widely used throughout industry for cleaning paint-spraying equipment and degreasing mechanical parts. SK provide their customers with a safe and convenient means of cleaning parts and equipment. They supply the equipment and solvent to all their customers and collect the spent solvent for recycling and reuse. All of the solvent and almost all of the equipment is leased to the customers and remains SK's property. The Dinnington centre, which is the site with which I am concerned, will recycle used paraffin and cellulose thinners returned by all the UK branches. The branches act as local distribution centres for the supply of recycled solvent to the customers and the collection of the used solvent from customers ... The relevant question was 'Is this [solvent] refuse or waste from a trade?' ... One side submitted that this material was always valuable

and could never rightly be regarded as trade waste. The other side submitted that it was useless in its present form. They submitted that the word 'waste' could perfectly properly be used of material which could usefully be incorporated in some manufacturing process [...] In principle I think that the expression 'trade waste' should be given its ordinary meaning ...

Having looked at the material before me, I am persuaded that the authority may have erred in their legal approach when deciding whether or not this application should be advertised ... they apparently proceeded on the assumption that the treatment of waste is concerned with matter which has no further use and that therefore the mere fact that a further use for the material was envisaged after recycling prevented it from being waste. Sewage remains sewage notwithstanding that the water authorities aim to treat it so as to turn it into potable water. The argument at times reminded me of those black and white lithographs by Escher which depict fishes or swallows depending on whether one is concentrating on the black or the white. Some would say the picture was of fishes; others would say it was of swallows. The right answer is that it is both fishes and swallows. Similarly here the solvents are perhaps rightly regarded as being both trade waste and raw materials ...

Mayer Parry Recycling Ltd v The Environment Agency [1999] 1 CMLR 963

A similar problem has arisen in a series of cases involving Mayer Parry Recycling Limited (MPC Ltd). Part of this company's business involves receiving scrap metal and dealing with it so that it can be used by steel manufacturers for making other items. The first case concerned the question whether MPC Ltd was managing waste and therefore required appropriate licences under the waste management regime. The issue was decided in 1998 by Carnwarth J (*Mayer Parry Recycling Limited v The Environment Agency* [1999] 1 CMLR 963; [1999] Env LR 489). Here it was held that the material remained waste until the recovery process was complete. Mayer Parry was therefore subject to the waste management regime.

Later litigation brought by the Company against the Environment Agency has raised the question whether this approach to waste also applies to the meaning of waste under the Packaging Waste Directive. Interestingly in this more recent case the Environment Agency submitted that its successful argument before Carnwarth J was wrong. Here the Environment Agency argued that the material did not cease to be waste once the recovery operations were complete, but it remained waste until actually changed into the new product.[34] As we shall see, that argument has now been accepted as being correct.

The following extract is from Carnwarth J's judgment in the 1998 case.

Carnwarth J:

(1) Mayer Parry (MPR) is one of the largest scrap metal merchants in the UK. Its turnover in 1995 exceeded L175m. It is part of the Co-Steel group of steel manufacturing companies. It operates from 19 sites in the UK, of which 17 process scrap metal, the other two being dockside sites handling exports. One of the largest is a 9 acre site at Erith ...

---

34 In September 2000 Collins J decided to refer the matter to the ECJ (CO/512/00 *R v Environment Agency* hearing date: 8 September 2000). In November 2000 he refused to grant MPC Ltd interim relief pending the decision of the ECJ.

(2) The Defendant is the Environment Agency, established by Pt I of the Environment Act 1995. It is (since 1 April 1996) the body responsible for the issuing and enforcement of waste management licences under Pt II of the Environmental Protection Act 1990; [...]

(3) The dispute between MPR and the Environment Agency (the 'Agency') concerns the scope of the definition of 'waste' in the Waste Management Regulations 1994 (the 'WMR'). They give effect in the UK to the EEC Waste Framework Directive (the 'WFD') – that is, Directive 75/442 of 15 July 1975, as amended by Directive 91/156 of 18 March 1991. The WMR introduced into English law from the WFD the concept of 'Directive waste'.

(4) For practical purposes, the principal significance of a finding whether material handled by MPR at various stages is 'waste' is in determining whether or to what extent it requires a waste management licence (under s 33 of the Environment Protection Act 1990). (MPR has in fact applied for and obtained a licence without prejudice to its contentions in this case.) It is also relevant to the application of statutory regimes governing transportation, export and brokerage of waste, as well as to the 'duty of care' applying to those handling 'waste' (under s 33 of the 1990 Act). Although the statutory regime covering such matters is complex, and much of it predates the WMR, it is common ground that (by virtue of various amending regulations) the same definition of 'Directive waste' applies throughout. [...]

The definition of waste

(12) It is common ground, for the purposes of this case, that the definition of waste as applied by the WMR is identical in effect to that in the WFD. Since the relevant European cases refer to the WFD, it will be convenient to confine references in this judgment to the WFD (with an indication, where relevant, of the corresponding provisions in the WMR). I shall refer to the WFD as amended by Directive 91/156/EEC (and with Annex IIB in its form as re-ordered by Decision 96/350/EC).

[The judge sets out the relevant legislation.]

Discussion

(42) The difference between the parties can be summarised shortly. The Agency follows the Advocate General [in the Wallonne Case, see p 381, above] in putting the emphasis not on the term 'discard', but on the description in Annex IIB of recovery operations. In this case the relevant category is 'recycling/reclamation of metals and metal compounds'. The Agency considers that this category covers all operations which have the purpose of making the metal content of substances or objects reusable as a raw material (including any measures which have the purpose of ensuring that that metal content is reusable without threat to public health or the environment). It contends accordingly that the category covers all the processes of MPR, including sorting, separating, fragmentising, cutting, shearing, crushing, compressing and baling.

(43) It agrees on the other hand that scrap metal which can be used as feedstock in a furnace without any further processing is a raw material which is not destined for a recovery operation, and that accordingly it is not waste. Furthermore, it accepts that processing solely for economic or grading reasons, as described in para 8 of Mr Crowe's second affidavit [...] does not constitute a recovery operation, and therefore that materials subject to such processing are not for that reason alone to be treated as waste.

(44) MPR by contrast treat the concept of 'discarding' as central to the interpretation of the Directive. In their submission it means 'get rid of or dispose of as unwanted and not needed'. To determine whether the definition applies in any particular case it is necessary—

... to look at all the facts in order to determine whether a discarding intention is reasonably and on objective appraisal of the surrounding circumstances to be attributed to the disposal.

They accept that the mere fact that material is sold for value to MPR does not exclude it from the definition of waste, but they ask me to find as a fact, in each of the cases referred to in the evidence, that the sale of the material is not simply discarding something unwanted (albeit for value), but that it is being dealt with in 'the mainstream of the commercial recycling industry', and as 'an integral part of the principal businesses on both supply and receipt sides'.

(45) MPR's approach would have more force if it were possible to approach the issue as purely a matter of construction of the UK regulations. However, in the light of the linguistic considerations considered above, and of the recent judgments of the European Court, I have to conclude that the Environment Agency's approach is in principle correct.

(46) The general concept is now reasonably clear. The term 'discard' is used in a broad sense equivalent to 'get rid of'; but it is coloured by the examples of waste given in Annex I and the Waste Catalogue, which indicate that it is concerned generally with materials which have ceased to be required for their original purpose, normally because they are unsuitable, unwanted or surplus to requirements. That broad category is however limited by the context, which shows that the purpose is to control disposal and recovery of such materials. Accordingly, materials which are to be reused (rather than finally disposed of), but which do not require any recovery operation before being put to their new use, are not treated as waste. Similarly, materials which are made ready for reuse by a recovery operation, cease to be waste when the recovery operation is complete.

(47) Turning to the facts of this case, all the materials referred to in the evidence are potentially within the definition of waste, in the sense that they are 'got rid of' by their original users, because they are not wanted or needed for their original purpose. Thus, manufacturers get rid of surplus material, such as borings and offcuts, because they are not needed for their primary product; materials in a building about to be demolished are no longer needed by the original owner; and the vehicle dismantler handles cars which have reached the end of their useful life for their original purpose.

(48) Accordingly, the issue in this case turns on the scope of the term 'recovery'. In so far as the discarded materials do not require any recovery operation, as the Agency concedes, they are not treated as waste at all. In so far as they do require recovery operations, they remain waste until those recovery operations are complete.

(49) The difficulty at this point is in drawing a clear line between the recovery operations, and the industrial operations for which the recycled scrap is to be used as a raw material. The Court in the *Wallonne* case affirmed the need to draw such a distinction but recognised the difficulty of doing so. Circular 11/94 tackles the problem by using the concept of 'a specialised recovery operation', defined as—

... an operation listed in (Annex IIB) which either reuses substances or objects which are waste because they have fallen out of the normal commercial cycle or chain of utility; or recycles them in a way which eliminates or diminishes sufficiently the threat posed by their original production as waste and produces a raw material which can be use in the same way as raw material of non-waste origin (para 2.31).

Accordingly, a material ceases to be waste –

... when its processing produces a material of sufficient beneficial use to eliminate or diminish sufficiently the threat posed by the original production of waste. This will generally take place when the recovered material can be used as raw material in the same way as raw materials of non-waste origin by a person other than a specialised recovery establishment or undertaking (para 2.47).

The term 'normal commercial cycle' is there used in contra-distinction to–

... the commercial cycle which exists for the purpose of collecting, transporting, storing, recovering and disposing of waste (para 2.15).

(50) This guidance seems to me in line with the approach of the European Court. However, I do not find it necessary to explore it in detail in the context of the present case. What is clear from the terms of the Directive (Annex IIB R4) is that one form of 'recovery operation' is 'recycling or reclamation of metals and metal compounds'. (It was not argued that other language versions differed materially in this respect. For example, the French text has *'recyclage ou recuperation des metaux'*.) Accordingly, so long as the materials continue to be subject to any process falling within that description they remain waste for the purpose of the definition.

(51) MPR is part of an industry which, in Mr Crowe's words, 'exists to recycle scrap metal, so that the metal content may be used in the manufacture of new products'. Thus, 'recycling/reclamation of metals' (in terms of Annex IIB) is MPR's business; the presumption, accordingly, must be that all the operations which form part of that business – from sorting to fragmentising – are recovery operations within the meaning of the directive. In particular, the mere fact that some operations do not in themselves have environmental implications is not a reason for excluding them from the definition (see *Wallonne* judgment para 30). Conversely, once MPR has restored the material to a form which is suitable for sale as raw material to steelworks or other manufacturers, the presumption is that the task of recovery is complete, and the material ceases to be waste.

[...]

Castle Cement v Environment Agency [2001] EWHC Admin 224

In *Mayer Parry*, Carnwarth J said (para 46) that: '... materials which are made ready for reuse by a recovery operation, cease to be waste when the recovery operation is complete.' This view has since been held to be incorrect and it therefore appears that some materials, at least, may remain waste even after they have been 'recovered'. As Stanley Burnton J explained in *Castle Cement v Environment Agency* [2001] EWHC Admin 224: '... whether a substance derived from waste remains waste ... depend[s] not only on the processes involved in its production, but also on the nature of the substance itself' (para 15). He gave the example of used rubber tyres which, he said, 'would not cease to be waste because they had been reduced to very small particles or powder with a view to burning them or burying them in a landfill site'.

In *Castle Cement* the question was whether a fuel used in the manufacture of cement – Cemfuel – was waste. Cemfuel is recovered from various different waste streams. Castle Cement argued that since the process of recovery has ceased by the time the fuel leaves its producer for delivery to Castle's works, the fuel is no longer waste but a raw material akin to any other fuel. The Environment Agency, on the other hand, argued that the fuel remained waste until it had been burnt. Stanley Burnton J, referring to the recent judgment of the ECJ in the conjoined decision in Case C-418/97 *Arco* and Case C-418/97 *Epon* (important parts of which he confessed to find 'Delphic' (para 45)), held that Cemfuel did remain waste until it had been burnt.

The ECJ in *Arco* and *Epon* said (paras 94–97) that the fact that a substance is the result of 'a complete recovery operation' under Annex IIB to the WFD is only one of the factors to be taken into account for the purposes of determining whether it constitutes waste. Whether the substance is waste must be determined in the light of all the circumstances, having regard to the definition in Art 1(a) of the WFD, the general aim of the directive and the 'need to ensure that its effectiveness is not undermined'. Applying this broad approach, Stanley Burnton J stressed that because Cemfuel is potentially harmful to the environment and to health its holding and use should be regulated under the WFD. If it were not regarded as being waste the effectiveness of the WFD would be undermined (*Castle Cement*, para 55).

National Waste Strategy

Environmental Protection Act 1990, s 44A National Waste Strategy: England and Wales

(1) The Secretary of State shall as soon as possible prepare a statement ('the strategy') containing his policies in relation to the recovery and disposal of waste in England and Wales.

(2) The strategy shall consist of or include–

    (a) a statement which relates to the whole of England and Wales; or

    (b) two or more statements which between them relate to the whole of England and Wales.

(3) The Secretary of State may from time to time modify the strategy.

(4) Without prejudice to the generality of what may be included in the strategy, the strategy must include–

    (a) a statement of the Secretary of State's policies for attaining the objectives specified in Schedule 2A to this Act;

    (b) provisions relating to each of the following, that is to say–

        (i) the type, quantity and origin of waste to be recovered or disposed of;

        (ii) general technical requirements; and

        (iii) any special requirements for particular wastes.

(5) In preparing the strategy or any modification of it, the Secretary of State–

    (a) shall consult the Environment Agency;

    (b) shall consult–

     (i) such bodies or persons appearing to him to be representative of the interests of local government; and

     (ii) such bodies or persons appearing to him to be representative of the interests of industry, as he may consider appropriate; and

  (c) may consult such other bodies or persons as he considers appropriate.

(6) Without prejudice to any power to give directions conferred by s 40 of the Environment Act 1995, the Secretary of State may give directions to the Environment Agency requiring it–

  (a) to advise him on the policies which are to be included in the strategy;

  (b) to carry out a survey of or investigation into–

     (i) the kinds or quantities of waste which it appears to that Agency is likely to be situated in England and Wales;

     (ii) the facilities which are or appear to that Agency likely to be available or needed in England and Wales for recovering or disposing of any such waste;

     (iii) any other matter upon which the Secretary of State wishes to be informed in connection with his preparation of the strategy or any modification of it, and to report its findings to him.

(7) A direction under sub-s (6)(b) above–

  (a) shall specify or describe the matters or the areas which are to be the subject of the survey or investigation; and

  (b) may make provision in relation to the manner in which–

     (i) the survey or investigation is to be carried out; or

     (ii) the findings are to be reported or made available to other persons.

(8) Where a direction is given under sub-s (6)(b) above, the Environment Agency shall, in accordance with any requirement of the direction–

  (a) before carrying out the survey or investigation, consult–

     (i) such bodies or persons appearing to it to be representative of local planning authorities; and

     (ii) such bodies or persons appearing to it to be representative of the interests of industry, as it may consider appropriate; and

  (b) make its findings available to those authorities.

(9) In this section–

'local planning authority' has the same meaning as in the Town and Country Planning Act 1990;

'strategy' includes the strategy as modified from time to time and 'statement' shall be construed accordingly.

(10) This section makes provision for the purpose of implementing Article 7 of the Directive of the Council of the European Communities, dated 15 July 1975, on waste, as amended by–

  (a) the Directive of that Council, dated 18 March 1991, amending Directive 75/442/EEC on waste; and

  (b) the Directive of that Council, dated 23 December 1991, standardising and rationalising reports on the implementation of certain Directives relating to the environment.

[Section 44B requires Scottish Environmental Protection Agency to prepare a waste strategy for Scotland.]

Notes:

1　The provisions in s 44A(4)(b)(i)–(iii) are essentially reproduced from Article 7(1) of the Waste Framework Directive, save for the provision in that Article relating to suitable waste disposal sites or installations. This omission was made because siting of such sites was viewed by the government as being a matter for planning authorities rather than waste regulation (see *Hansard* HL Vol 562 col 455 quoted by Tromans in his annotation to the 1995 Environment Act in Current law Statutes 25–253). However, cf the Landfill Directive 99/31 (p 453, below).

2　Section 44A(10) and s 44B(9) do not themselves implement the Directive, rather they make provision for the production of strategies which do so.

The objectives for the purposes of the National Waste Strategy

Schedule 2A of the EPA 1990 sets out the objectives for the purposes of the National Waste Strategy. They are reproduced from the Waste Framework Directive 75/442 (in particular, see Arts 3(1)(a); 3(1)(b); 4; (5)(1); and 5(2) (see p 433, below). The objectives are as follows:

1　Ensuring that waste is recovered or disposed of without endangering human health and without using processes or methods which could harm the environment and, in particular, without:

(a) risk to water, air, soil, plants or animals;

(b) causing nuisance through noise or odours; or

(c) adversely affecting the countryside or places of special interest.

2　Establishing an integrated and adequate network of waste disposal installations, taking account of the best available technology not involving excessive costs.

3　Ensuring that the network referred to in para 2 above enables:

(a) the European Community as a whole to become self-sufficient in waste disposal, and the Member States individually to move towards that aim, taking into account geographical circumstances or the need for specialised installations for certain types of waste; and

(b) waste to be disposed of in one of the nearest appropriate installations, by means of the most appropriate methods and technologies in order to ensure a high level of protection for the environment and public health.

4　Encouraging the prevention or reduction of waste production and its harmfulness, in particular by:

(a) the development of clean technologies more sparing in their use of natural resources;

(b) the technical development and marketing of products designed so as to make no contribution or to make the smallest possible contribution, by the nature of their manufacture, use or final disposal, to increasing the amount or harmfulness of waste and pollution hazards; and

(c) the development of appropriate techniques for the final disposal of dangerous substances contained in waste destined for recovery.

5   Encouraging:

(a   the recovery of waste by means of recycling, reuse or reclamation or any other process with a view to extracting secondary raw materials; and

(b) the use of waste as a source of energy.

Waste Strategy 2000[35]

The national waste strategy for England and Wales, *Waste Strategy 2000 for England and Wales*, was published by the Department of the Environment, Transport and the Regions on 25 May 2000 (Cmnd 4693). The strategy is a waste management plan for England and Wales required under the EC Waste Framework Directive 75/442, the EC Hazardous Waste Directive 91/689 and the EC Packaging Waste Directive 94/62, implemented by Section 44A of the Environment Protection Act 1990 (as amended). It is also a strategy for dealing with waste diverted from landfill in England and Wales, as required by Art 5 of the Landfill Directive 99/31. The current strategy replaces the previous statements contained in *Making Waste Work: A Strategy for Sustainable Waste Management in England and Wales* ((1995) Cm 3040) and *A Way With Waste: A Draft Waste Strategy for England and Wales* (DETR, June 1999). The strategy will be reviewed every five years. A root-and-branch review will take place in 2010. Annual monitoring of the implementation of the strategy will be undertaken by the Waste Strategy Monitoring Group sponsored by the DETR. The Group will produce an annual report.

Waste has important links with many other aspects of Government policy. This strategy has therefore been prepared in light of the policies described in other key policy statements, including:

The sustainable development strategy, *A Better Quality of Life*, Cm 4345, 1999, Climate Change: Draft UK Programme, DETR.

UK Climate Change Programme. The Government's energy policy, including sustainable energy, is set out in the DTI White Paper *Conclusions of the Review of Energy Sources for Power Generation and Government Response to Fourth and Fifth Reports of the Trade and Industry Committee*, Cm 4071, 1998.

Sustainable Business – A Consultation Paper on Sustainable Development and Business in the UK, 1998, DETR.

Building a Better Quality of Life: A Strategy for More Sustainable Construction, 2000, DETR, Product Code: 99CD1065.

New and Renewable Energy – Prospects for the 21st Century: Conclusions in Response to the Public Consultation Paper, 2000, DTI.

The Air Quality Strategy for England, Scotland, Wales and Northern Ireland, Cm 4548, 2000, DETR, SE 2000-3, NIA-7.

---

35   See also www.detr.gov.uk/wastestrategy/cm4693/index.htm.

Sustainable Production and Use of Chemicals – A Strategic Approach – The Government's Chemicals Strategy, 1999.

The Draft Soil Strategy – Published for Consultation, 2000.

White Paper on Integrated Transport, A New Deal for Transport: Better for Everyone, Cm 3950, 1998.

2000 Budget statement.

The key messages of the strategy (Chapter 1)

Chapter sets out the key messages as follows:

- we produced 106 million tonnes of commercial, industrial and municipal waste in England and Wales last year [1999], most of which was sent to landfill;

- at the heart of our strategy lies the need to tackle the growth in our waste;

- we need to maximise the amount of value we recover from waste, through increased recycling, composting and energy recovery the strategy sets challenging targets for better waste management;

  - to recover value from 45% of municipal waste by 2010, at least 30% through recycling or composting;

  - to recover value from two thirds of municipal waste by 2015, at least half of that through recycling and composting, and to go beyond this in the longer term;

  ['Recover' means obtain value from wastes through: recycling, composting, other forms of material recovery (such as anaerobic digestion), energy recovery (combustion with direct or indirect use of the energy produced).]

- we need to develop new and stronger markets for recycled materials – we will set up a major new programme, the sustainable waste action trust, to deliver more recycling and reuse, help deliver markets and end uses for secondary materials, and promote an integrated approach to resource use;

- producers must increasingly expect to arrange for recovery of their products – in particular, we will develop an initiative on junk mail;

- the amount of waste sent to landfill must be reduced substantially – we will introduce a system of tradable permits in England, restricting the amount of biodegradable municipal waste local authorities can send to landfill;

- local authorities will need to make significant strides in recycling and composting – we will set statutory performance standards for local authority recycling and composting. We will work with local authorities to pilot schemes encouraging householders to reduce waste, and to participate in recycling schemes;

- where energy recovery facilities are needed, we believe they should be appropriately sized to avoid competition with recycling, and the opportunities for incorporating Combined Heat and Power technology should always be considered.

The waste strategy summarised

Each year we produce huge quantities of waste – over 100 million tonnes from households, commerce and industry. Most of this waste is landfilled. Landfill can be a wasted opportunity, and produces greenhouse gases. We have agreed with our European partners tough targets to reduce the amount of waste sent to landfill.

This strategy describes our vision for managing waste and resources better. It sets out the changes needed to deliver more sustainable development.

We must tackle the quantity of waste produced, breaking the link between economic growth and increased waste. Household waste is growing by around 3% each year. If this growth rate continues we will need nearly twice as many new waste management facilities by 2020 as we would if the amount of waste stayed constant. This would increase pressures on the land available for development, and we do not believe it will be acceptable to the public. This is not a problem with a single, easy solution. Businesses, households, the community sector and local authorities must all play their part.

Where waste is created we must increasingly put it to good use – through recycling, composting or using it as a fuel.

Much of our waste comes from industry and commerce. Just over a third of that is already recycled or composted, and a further small proportion has energy recovered from it. But much more is possible and the Landfill Tax escalator announced last year's budget will help us achieve more in these sectors.

Our target is, by 2005, to reduce the amount of industrial and commercial waste landfilled to 85% of 1998 levels. In meeting this target we must focus on recovering value and reducing environmental impacts. This means not only putting waste materials to better use, but tackling any growth in waste.

Household waste is a relatively small part of the overall waste stream, but it is important that we make significant progress towards managing it more sustainably. At present, just 9% is recycled and a further 8% has energy recovered from it.

The Government and the National Assembly [of Wales] have set challenging targets to increase the recycling of municipal waste:

- to recycle or compost at least 25% of household waste by 2005;
- to recycle or compost at least 30% of household waste by 2010;
- to recycle or compost at least 33% of household waste by 2015.

To ensure that all local authorities contribute to achieving these targets, the Government will set statutory performance standards for local authority recycling in England. Local authorities will need to make significant strides in recycling and composting to meet these new statutory standards. The standards will be part of the existing Best Value framework which requires local authorities to set challenging targets to improve waste management services. We will work with local authorities to pilot schemes encouraging householders to reduce waste, and to participate in recycling schemes.

We have already begun putting measures in place to deliver the step change to more sustainable waste management. And we will do more. We need to develop new and stronger markets for recycled materials. We will set up a major new Waste and Resources Action Programme. The Programme will deliver more recycling and reuse, help develop markets and end-uses for secondary materials, and promote an integrated approach to resource use.

Public procurement can also play an important role in strengthening demand for recycled products. We will pilot a scheme to require public procurement of certain recycled products, initially paper goods. Increasingly, producers must expect to arrange for recovery of their products. We already have mechanisms in place to encourage the reduction and reuse of packaging, and the recycling and recovery of packaging waste. The Government has reached agreement with the Newsprint Publishers Association on target levels of recycled content of newsprint, rising to 70% by 2006. We intend to introduce producer responsibility initiatives more widely, beginning with an initiative on junk mail. Further producer responsibility proposals for end-of-life vehicles, batteries, and electrical and electronic goods are under consideration in the EU.

In his 1999 Budget Statement, the Chancellor announced that the standard rate of landfill tax would increase from £10 per tonne by £1 per year, with a review in 2004. This provides waste producers and local authorities with a strong incentive to send less waste to landfill, and provides a clear basis for planning future waste management. We propose to use the landfill tax credit scheme to help deliver an increase in recycling, particularly of household waste. We will extend the range of activities eligible for support to include recycling and reuse projects carried out by non-profit making, non-public bodies, for instance small community recycling schemes.

We will introduce tradeable permits, restricting the amount of biodegradable municipal waste local authorities can send to landfill. In some cases, authorities will need to introduce energy recovery facilities. Where energy recovery plant are needed, the Government and the National Assembly believe they should be appropriately sized to avoid competition with recycling. The opportunities for incorporating Combined Heat and Power technology should always be considered.

We will monitor progress towards the achievement of our goals and keep them under review. We will assess progress with all those – businesses, local government, community groups, the waste management industry – who have a part to play.

One of the central concerns of the strategy is the need to reduce reliance on landfill. There are several reasons for this. First, there is an acute shortage of suitable landfill sites, especially in urban areas and in the South East of England. Secondly, landfill is a major source of methane – a powerful greenhouse gas contributing to climate change. Methane is produced when biodegradable materials such as paper, food wastes and green wastes, decompose in the absence of oxygen. It is for this reason that the Landfill Directive 99/31 (see p 453) sets ambitious targets for the reduction of biodegradable municipal waste sent to landfill:

- by 2010 to reduce biodegradable municipal waste landfilled to 75% of that produced in 1995;

- by 2013 to reduce biodegradable municipal waste landfilled to 50% of that produced in 1995;

- by 2020 to reduce biodegradable municipal waste landfilled to 35% of that produced in 1995 (see Landfill Directive 99/31, Art 5, p 459, above).

The strategy recognises that (para 1.8) that '[m]eeting these targets will be a major challenge'. In particular it will bring about significant changes to the ways in which hazardous wastes are disposed of in England and Wales and might lead to a substantial reduction in the available capacity for managing hazardous wastes.

The biggest challenge, however, is identified (in para 2.5) as being to deliver better use of natural resources, through waste reduction, reuse, recycling, composting and energy recovery. Significant quantities of valuable material are currently buried in landfill sites. The strategy emphasises that 'Society cannot sensibly afford to continue wasting these resources, many of which (particularly metals and oil-based materials such as plastic) are available in limited quantities in the environment, or are difficult or environmentally damaging to extract'. Amongst the initiatives needed, the strategy calls upon business and industry to reduce waste by redesigning products and processes; and upon consumers to influence waste production through their purchasing decisions, by avoiding over-shopping and choosing products that will create less waste. It also seeks to encourage the re use of products, recycling and composting.

> 2.15 In future, we will increasingly need to rely on more cyclical production and consumption processes. Such systems enable us to cut down on our use of raw materials, and avoid the need for disposal to landfill. Wastes do not have to be recycled into the same product – we can use green glass bottles to produce fibreglass, and turn plastic drink bottles into fleece fabric. Because extraction of raw materials can use a lot of energy, recycling materials in this way can greatly reduce our consumption of energy, which in turn contributes to achieving our climate change targets.

Where it does not make sense to recycle waste, the strategy says (para 2.19) that consideration should be given to using it as a fuel. This can be done directly, in incinerators or in industrial plant such as cement kilns; or indirectly through creating refuse-derived fuel or through processes such as gasification. Not all wastes, however, are suitable for use as fuel. In particular, inorganic wastes such as glass and metals have no calorific value. Since these wastes are suitable for recycling it would only be appropriate to incinerate them in rare circumstances, for example where they cannot easily be separated from other combustible materials. The strategy notes that using waste as a fuel can reduce emissions of carbon dioxide – a greenhouse gas that contributes to climate change – by displacing the use of more polluting virgin fuels. In some cases, it can also reduce other emissions to the environment. For example burning tyres in cement kilns reduces the quantity of oxides of nitrogen released to the environment (para 2.20).

Levers of change

The strategy summarises the mechanisms for achieving the necessary changes in Chapter 3. These are summarised as follows:

- a major new Waste and Resources Action Programme, to deliver increases in reuse, recycling and use of recycled materials;

- piloting a scheme to require public procurement of certain recycled products, initially paper goods;

- tackling waste streams through producer responsibility;

- the Landfill Tax escalator;

- tradable permits limiting the amount of waste local authorities in England can send to landfill;

- using the landfill tax credit scheme to increase recycling, including extending the scheme to community reuse and recycling projects;

- waste minimisation requirements of the Integrated Pollution Prevention and Control (IPPC) regime;

- Best Practice Programmes;

- measures to encourage the recycling of waste oils;

- the 'are you doing your bit?' campaign.

The Waste and Resources Action Programme (WRAP) has now been established in order to promote the development of markets for recycled materials. Its web site is at: www.wrap.org.uk.

Public procurement: A joint Treasury/DETR note, Environmental Issues in Purchasing, explains how Government Departments can specify requirements in green terms, and that they should award contracts on the basis of value for money, namely whole life costs and quality, not simply lowest price. In the *Waste Strategy* (para 3.7) however, the Government indicated its wish to go further:

> In the United States, the Government's Comprehensive Procurement Guidelines Programme requires federal agencies to purchase certain designated products with the highest practicable level of recycled content. We are interested in exploring the impact of a similar scheme here. We will therefore pilot arrangements for a scheme under which environmental policy will require public procurement of certain recycled products, initially paper goods. These will be developed by DETR, the Office of Government Commerce, and others.

Producer responsibility.

Under the heading of producer responsibility the strategy deals with packaging, newspapers, junk mail and European initiatives concerned with end-of-life vehicles, batteries and electrical products.

Packaging: There is a statutory producer responsibility for packaging and packaging waste. The EC Directive on Packaging and Packaging Waste is implemented in England and Wales by the Producer Responsibility Obligations (Packaging Waste) Regulations 1997 SI 1997/648 and the relevant amendments, and the Packaging (Essential Requirements) Regulations 1998 SI 1998/1165. The Regulations set targets for recovery and recycling of packaging waste. Most businesses have an obligation to recover 52% packaging waste in 2001, at least half of this is to be recycled. The Packaging Directive is currently being reviewed and targets for 2006 are being considered. The DETR is considering national recycling and recovery targets for 2001–06.

Newspapers: In 1999 the estimated recycled content of newsprint stood at around 54%, up from 28% in 1991. The Government has been working with the Newspaper Publishers Association to improve this and in April 2000 reached agreement with them on future target levels of recycled content of newsprint. The newspaper publishers have agreed to commit to the following targets: 60% recycled content by end of 2001; 65% recycled content by end of 2003; 70% recycled content by end of 2006.

Direct, or 'Junk' Mail: the strategy notes (para 3.20) that junk mail can be a significant, and often unwelcome, element of the household waste stream. It is also a growing phenomenon – with the number of items sent to consumers in the UK doubling from 1.5 billion in 1990 to 3.3 billion in 1999. The government indicated that it is to develop an initiative on producer responsibility for junk mail, working with the Direct Marketing Association and other trade bodies.

European initiatives on producer responsibility

End-of-Life Vehicles: the aim of the 2000 End-of-Life Vehicle Directive 00/53 is to deliver environmental benefits by reducing the amount of waste arising from end-of-life vehicles. The proposed Directive sets targets for reuse, recycling and recovery, and introduces improved treatment standards. The proposed targets are: to increase reuse and recovery to 85% and recycling to a minimum of 80% by 1 January 2006 to increase reuse and recovery to 95% and recycling to a minimum of 85% by 1 January 2015. The Directive would also require: manufacturers to design vehicles with recyclability and reuse in mind; systems to be established to ensure that all vehicles are collected and transferred to an authorised treatment facility.

Used Tyres: the End-of-Life Vehicles Directive 00/53 is likely to apply to used tyres, where these are part of a vehicle. Together with the Landfill Directive ban on sending tyres to landfill, this will require substantial increases in recycling and recovery of used tyres.

Batteries: A proposal to replace the 1991 Directive on Batteries and Accumulators 1991/157 is currently being considered within the European Commission. An early draft indicates that the Commission is likely to: propose collection and recycling targets for spent consumer, automotive and industrial batteries and seek to restrict from 2008 the marketing of nickel cadmium batteries where suitable substitutes exist.

Waste Electrical and Electronic Goods: The European Commission is expected to make a proposal for a Directive to minimise the environmental impact of waste electrical and electronic goods. Early drafts indicate that the Commission may propose: targets for collection, reuse and recycling, specific treatment requirements, and requirements for equipment producers to meet costs of banning the use of certain hazardous substances and measures to reduce waste and improve the design and labelling of equipment to facilitate recycling.

Landfill tax

The Government introduced the Landfill Tax in October 1996. The tax has an explicit environmental objective. The strategy says (para 3.28) that the tax is already having a notable impact on waste management practices. There are two tax rates, £12 per tonne for active wastes and £2 per tonne for inactive waste. In the 1999 Budget, the Chancellor announced increases to the active rate of £1 per tonne per year, with a review in 2004. This 'ramp' will encourage greater diversion of wastes from landfill, and allow waste producers and managers to plan their future waste management options effectively. (For an assessment of the landfill tax see Patricia Park, 'An Evaluation of the Landfill Tax Two Years On' [2000] JPL 3–13.)

Landfill Tax Credit Scheme: Under the landfill tax credit scheme, landfill operators can claim up to 90% tax credit against donations they make to approved environmental bodies. These credits may not exceed 20% of an operator's annual landfill tax bill. Environmental bodies may carry out activities, defined in regulations, which include: reclamation of polluted land; research and education activities to promote reuse and recycling; provision of public parks and amenities; and restoration of historic buildings. A new category 'research and education on market development' was added in January 2000, to make explicit that funding for recycling-related research and development was eligible under the scheme.

Tradeable Permits: The strategy says that tradeable permits will be introduced by which local authorities will be able to restrict the amount of biodegradable municipal waste landfilled. It is proposed that the permits should be granted free to local authorities. Possibly allocated on the basis of a combination of population and the number of households. The permits will allow set tonnages of biodegradable municipal waste to be landfilled. The permitted tonnages will be reduced to meet the Directive's reduction targets. The reduction targets in the Landfill Directive are for the UK as a whole and will require a UK response to ensure the UK can meet them. It is intended that the permits for local authorities in England should be tradable. This is considered to have a number of advantages for both local government and the country as a whole: costs of achieving compliance can be reduced overall; authorities will have greater choice over how to meet their reduction targets in the way that best suits local needs whichever allocation method is used. Some authorities may receive more permits than they initially need and some less. A trading system will allow authorities to chose whether to landfill any additional waste (by buying extra permits from an authority that had reduced its reliance landfill further than needed) or to invest in alternative means of disposal.

IPPC and Controls on Waste Management: At present all landfill sites are subject to the waste management licensing system. However, some landfill sites will also be subject to the Regulations implementing the IPPC Directive 96/61. The Government proposes to bring the regulatory controls on all landfill sites under an integrated system under the PPC Regulations when the EC Landfill Directive is implemented in July 2001.

Thinking differently about waste

Underlying the strategy is the need for all sectors to think differently about waste. Chapter 4 of the strategy identifies, for each section of the population, the role which it will need to perform together with the policy instruments which will inform behaviour and encourage or require change (note that the government has established a new interactive website:www.useitagain.org.uk).

An indictment of the strategy

The House of Commons Select Committee on the DETR recently published a damning indictment of the above strategy, describing it as 'unimaginative and uninspiring' (see Select Committee on the DETR, Session 2000–01, 5th report, 2001). In its report the Committee claims that the strategy confirms that waste continues to be a low priority for the government. The strategy is seen to be 'woefully inadequate' to bring about the necessary changes in the way we think about and deal with waste. 'Quite simply the strategy is an awkward and underfunded compromise.' In particular, the report is severely critical about the move towards incineration. It also criticised the low level of landfill tax (currently £12.00 per tonne) which it recommends, should be increased to £25.00 per tonne by 2006. There is extreme criticism of 'convoluted and ineffective tax credit scheme' which should be radically reviewed.

Waste management in the UK

Part II of the EPA 1990 establishes the waste management system for dealing with waste on land in the UK. These provisions, as modified by reg 19 and Sched 4 of the Waste Management Licensing Regulations 1994 SI 1994/1056 are intended to comply with the Framework Directive. Section 29 contains important definitions for the purposes of this part of the Act including definitions of the 'environment' (s 29(2)), 'pollution of the environment' (s 29(3)), and 'disposal' of waste (s 29(6)). Sections 30 and 32 deal with the bodies concerned with waste regulation, collection and disposal.

Offences relating to waste: The offences established in s 33 underpin the waste licensing system. The section makes it an offence (subject to the exceptions and defences set out): to (a) deposit waste, or knowingly permit waste to be deposited in or on any land unless authorised by a waste management licence; (b) to treat, keep or dispose of waste, or knowingly cause or knowingly permit waste to be treated, kept or disposed of in or on any land except in accordance with a waste management licence; and (c) to treat, keep or dispose of waste in a manner likely to cause pollution of the environment or harm to human health (whether or not this is done in accordance with a waste management licence).[36] It is also an offence to contravene any condition of a waste management licence (sub-s (6)). Sub-section (5) also provides that 'where controlled waste is carried in and deposited from a motor vehicle, the person who controls or is in a position to control the use of the vehicle' shall be treated as knowingly causing the waste to be deposited whether or not he gave any instructions for this to be done.

The 'duty of care': Section 34 establishes the concept of the 'duty of care' regarding waste. The imposition of such a duty upon those involved at all stages in the waste chain was first recommended by the Royal Commission for Environmental Pollution in its eleventh report, *Managing Waste: The Duty of Care* ((1985) Cm 9675). In that report (paras 3.4–3.7) the Royal Commission stated that society must:

---

36 For discussion of the meaning of the terms 'deposit' and 'dispose', see *R v Met Stipendiary Magistrate ex p London Waste Regulation Authority* [1993] 3 All ER 113 and *Thames Waste Management Ltd v Surrey County Council* [1997] Env LR 148.

... identify where the responsibility lies for ensuring that wastes are properly handled and disposed of. In our judgment this must rest with the individual organisation who controls the waste. The producer incurs a duty of care which is owed to society ... we believe that the waste producer's or handler's legal obligations towards the environment need to be classified and strengthened, with particular reference to the requirement to satisfy, when passing on the waste to somebody else, that it will be correctly dealt with ...

Reflecting this idea the *duty of care* is imposed on any person who 'imports, produces, carries, keeps, treats or disposes of controlled waste or, as a broker, has control of such waste', although it does not apply to an occupier of domestic property as respects the household waste produced on the property. For discussion of the UK government's understanding of the duty of care, see *Waste Management: the Duty of Care: A Code of Practice* (HMSO, 1996). Where it exists the duty imposes the obligation to 'take all such measures applicable to him in that capacity as are reasonable in the circumstances (a) to prevent any other person contravening s 33; (b) to prevent the escape of the waste from his control or that of any other person; (c) on the transfer of the waste, to secure: (i) that the transfer is only to an authorised person or to a person for authorised transport purposes; and (ii) that there is transferred such a written description of the waste as will enable other persons to avoid a contravention of that section and to comply with the duty under this sub-s as respects the escape of waste. It is important to note that the *statutory duty* of care created by s 34 is not to be confused with the duty of care in negligence. Since the duty to take care of waste is owed to society at large, breach of the s 34 duty of care is a criminal offence.

The waste management licensing system: Sections 35–44 establish a framework for the management of waste which is far more comprehensive than previously existed under the Control of Pollution Act 1974. In particular whereas the old system focused on disposal operations, these provisions extend generally to the keeping and treatment of controlled waste (for definition, see s 75(4)), as well as its disposal. Section 35(1) provides that a waste management licence is a licence granted by the Environment Agency authorising the treatment, keeping or disposal of controlled waste in or on specified land or the treatment or disposal of controlled waste by means of a specified mobile plant. Section 35(3) gives the Environment Agency very broad powers to impose such conditions on the licence as appear to it to be appropriate. These conditions may relate (a) to the activities which the licence authorises, and (b) to the precautions to be taken and works to be carried out in connection with those activities. The conditions may (s 35(4)) require the holder of a licence to carry out works or do things even though he is not entitled to carry out the works or to do the thing. This might arise for example when a condition requires a licence holder to go onto somebody else's land to do work. The sub-s goes on to provide that 'any person whose consent would be required shall grant, or join in granting, the holder of the licence such rights in relation to the land as will enable the holder of the licence to comply with any requirements imposed on him by the licence'. The effects of this provision on third parties has been controversial and uncertain (see further Tromans (1990) 43–137). One of the main problems was the absence of any rights to compensation for the third parties. This has now been addressed by s 35A which is added by the Environment Act 1995.

Applications for waste management licences are to be made in writing to the appropriate regional office of the Environment Agency on the appropriate form providing the required information and with the necessary fees. (On the information required see further the Waste Management Regulations 1994, para 2 and Sched 1.) Licences will only be granted where planning permission has been granted (or where an established use certificate exists) and where the applicant is a 'fit and proper person'. For the definition of 'fit and proper person' see s 74 below (p 466). A 'fit and proper person' will not be refused a licence unless the Agency is satisfied that that refusal is necessary in order to prevent pollution to the environment, harm to human health or serious detriment to the amenities of the locality (however, detriment to the amenities of the locality cannot be a reason to refuse a licence where planning permission is in force) (s 36(3)). Where the Agency proposes to grant a licence it must first refer the proposal to the appropriate planning authority and the Health and Safety Executive (s 36(4)). Where any part of the land to be used is protected under s 28(1) of the Wildlife and Countryside Act 1981 the authority must also refer the application to the appropriate nature conservation body (English Nature) and consider any representations made (s 36(7)).

Revocation and suspension of licences: A licence may be revoked or suspended where it appears to the authority (a) that the holder of the licence has ceased to be a fit and proper person by reason of his having been convicted of a 'relevant offence' or (b) that the continuation of the activities authorised by the licence would cause pollution of the environment or harm to human health or would be seriously detrimental to the amenities of the locality affected; and (c) that the pollution, harm or detriment cannot be avoided by modifying the conditions of the licence (s 38(1)).

Surrenders: Licences may be surrendered, but only if the authority accepts the surrender under s 39. This provides that surrenders are only to be permitted if the authority is satisfied that the condition of the land is unlikely to cause the pollution or harm to human health. In any case where the authority proposes to accept the surrender of a site licence it must first refer the matter to the appropriate planning authority and consider any representations about the proposal made by that authority.

Transfers: licences may be transferred subject to the procedure in s 40(4) which requires the authority to be satisfied that the transferee is a fit and proper person.

Supervision of licensed activities: s 42 imposes a general duty upon the Agency to monitor and supervise licensed activities to ensure that the activities authorised by the licence do not cause pollution of the environment or harm to human health or become seriously detrimental to the amenities of the locality affected by the activities and also that the conditions of the licence are complied with. For guidance on the conducting of site inspections see: Waste Management Paper No 4A (July 2000).

Rights of appeal: s 43 provides a right of appeal to the Secretary of State where: an application for a licence is rejected; conditions are imposed or modified; a licence is suspended or revoked; an application to surrender or transfer a licence is rejected.

Clean up: under s 59 if controlled waste is deposited in or on any land in contravention of s 33(1) the authority may require the occupier to remove the waste from the land and/or take steps to eliminate or reduce the consequences of the deposit of the waste. The section provides rights of appeal.

Publicity: under s 64, the Environment Agency has a duty to maintain a public register giving particulars *inter alia* of licences granted by the authority; current or recently current applications to the authority for licences; applications to modify licences; revocations or suspensions of licences; appeals against decisions of the authority; convictions of licence holders under this part of the EPA 1990. These provisions mirror the requirements for public registers under the IPC system (see Chapter 5, pp 521–23, below, and the Water Resources Act 1991, Chapter 3, p 304, above).

Environmental Protection Act 1990 (c 43)

Part II Waste on Land

Section 29 Preliminary

(1) The following provisions have effect for the interpretation of this Part.

(2   The 'environment' consists of all, or any, of the following media, namely land, water and the air.

(3) 'Pollution of the environment' means pollution of the environment due to the release or escape (into any environmental medium) from–

   (a) the land on which controlled waste is treated,

   (b) the land on which controlled waste is kept,

   (c) the land in or on which controlled waste is deposited,

   (d) fixed plant by means of which controlled waste is treated, kept or disposed of,

   of substances or articles constituting or resulting from the waste and capable (by reason of the quantity or concentrations involved) of causing harm to man or any other living organisms supported by the environment.

(4) sub-s (3) above applies in relation to mobile plant by means of which controlled waste is treated or disposed of as it applies to plant on land by means of which controlled waste is treated or disposed of.

(5) For the purposes of sub-ss (3) and (4) above 'harm' means harm to the health of living organisms or other interference with the ecological systems of which they form part and in the case of man includes offence to any of his senses or harm to his property; and 'harmless' has a corresponding meaning.

(6) The 'disposal' of waste includes its disposal by way of deposit in or on land and, subject to sub-s (7) below, waste is 'treated' when it is subjected to any process, including making it re-usable or reclaiming substances from it and 'recycle' (and cognate expressions) shall be construed accordingly.

(7) Regulations made by the Secretary of State may prescribe activities as activities which constitute the treatment of waste for the purposes of this Part or any provision of this Part prescribed in the regulations.

[...]

Note:

In relation to Greater London, see s 360 of the Greater London Authority Act 1999

Section 30 Authorities for purposes of this Part

(1) Any reference in this Part to a waste regulation authority–

    (a) in relation to England and Wales, is a reference to the Environment Agency; and

    (b) in relation to Scotland, is a reference to the Scottish Environment Protection Agency;

    [...]

(2) For the purposes of this Part the following authorities are waste disposal authorities, namely–

    (a) for any non-metropolitan county in England, the county council;

    (b) in Greater London, the following–

        (i) for the area of a London waste disposal authority, the authority constituted as the waste disposal authority for that area;

        (ii) for the City of London, the Common Council;

        (iii) for any other London borough, the council of the borough;

    [Paragraphs (c) and (d) omitted.]

    (e) for any district in any other metropolitan county in England, the council of the district;

    (f) for any county or county borough in Wales, the council of the county or county borough;

    (g) in Scotland, a council constituted under s 2 of the Local Government etc (Scotland) Act 1994.

(3) For the purposes of this Part the following authorities are waste collection authorities–

    (a) for any district in England and Wales not within Greater London, the council of the district;

    (b) in Greater London, the following–

        (i) for any London borough, the council of the borough;

        (ii) for the City of London, the Common Council;

        [...]

    (c) in Scotland, a council constituted under s 2 of the Local Government etc (Scotland) Act 1994.

[Sub-sections (4)–(8) omitted.]

[Section 31 was repealed by EA 1995, s 120(3).]

[Section 32 (on Transition to Waste Disposal Companies etc) omitted.]

Section 33 Prohibition on unauthorised or harmful depositing, treatment or disposal etc of waste

(1) Subject to sub-ss (2) and (3) below and, in relation to Scotland, to s 54 below, a person shall not–

   (a) deposit controlled waste, or knowingly cause or knowingly permit controlled waste to be deposited in or on any land unless a waste management licence authorising the deposit is in force and the deposit is in accordance with the licence;

   (b) treat, keep or dispose of controlled waste, or knowingly cause or knowingly permit controlled waste to be treated, kept or disposed of–

      (i) in or on any land, or

      (ii) by means of any mobile plant,

     except under and in accordance with a waste management licence;

   (c) treat, keep or dispose of controlled waste in a manner likely to cause pollution of the environment or harm to human health.

(2) Sub-section (1) above does not apply in relation to household waste from a domestic property which is treated, kept or disposed of within the curtilage of the dwelling by or with the permission of the occupier of the dwelling.

(3) Sub-section (1)(a), (b) or (c) above do not apply in cases prescribed in regulations made by the Secretary of State and the regulations may make different exceptions for different areas.

[Sub-section (4) omitted.]

(5) Where controlled waste is carried in and deposited from a motor vehicle, the person who controls or is in a position to control the use of the vehicle shall, for the purposes of sub-s (1)(a) above, be treated as knowingly causing the waste to be deposited whether or not he gave any instructions for this to be done.

(6) A person who contravenes sub-s (1) above or any condition of a waste management licence commits an offence.

(7) It shall be a defence for a person charged with an offence under this section to prove–

   (a) that he took all reasonable precautions and exercised all due diligence to avoid the commission of the offence; or

   (b) that he acted under instructions from his employer and neither knew nor had reason to suppose that the acts done by him constituted a contravention of sub-s (1) above; or

   (c) that the acts alleged to constitute the contravention were done in an emergency in order to avoid danger to human health in a case where–

      (i) he took all such steps as were reasonably practicable in the circumstances for minimising pollution of the environment and harm to human health; and

      (ii) particulars of the acts were furnished to the waste regulation authority as soon as reasonably practicable after they were done.

(8) Except in a case falling within sub-s (9) below, a person who commits an offence under this section shall be liable–

   (a) on summary conviction, to imprisonment for a term not exceeding six months or a fine not exceeding £20,000 or both; and

   (b) on conviction on indictment, to imprisonment for a term not exceeding two years or a fine or both.

(9) A person who commits an offence under this section in relation to special waste shall be liable–

(a) on summary conviction, to imprisonment for a term not exceeding six months or a fine not exceeding £20,000 or both;

(b) on conviction on indictment, to imprisonment for a term not exceeding five years or a fine or both.

Note:

On the meaning of the term 'cause' see further discussion in Chapter 3, pp 299–301, above). On regulations made under sub-s (3) see below. For a recent discussion of what knowledge is required under s 33(6) see *Shanks & McEwan (Teeside) Ltd v Environment Agency* (see below). The Company argued that it was necessary to prove knowledge both of the fact of the deposit of controlled waste and that the deposit was not in accordance with the licence. It was held that 'knowingly' did not limit s 33(6) to situations in which the defendant could be shown to have knowledge that a licence had not been complied with, but only required knowledge of the deposit.

Shanks & McEwan (Teesside) Limited v The Environment Agency [1999] QB 333; [1998] 2 WLR 452; [1997] 2 All ER 332

Mance J: This is an appeal by way of case stated from a decision of the Justices of the Hartlepool Magistrates' Court convicting the Appellants on an information laid against them in terms as follows:

On 31 July 1995, at your licensed waste management facility you did knowingly cause controlled waste, namely an oil and water emulsion, to be deposited from a mobile tanker vehicle registration number G659 BAJ into the containment bund enclosing storage tanks 3A to 3D and 5A to 5C on the premises, which deposit was not in accordance with condition 27 of the Waste Management Licence CLE 226/1.

Contrary to s 33(6) of the Environmental Protection Act 1990. [The Judge set out s 33 of the EPA 1990.]

The present case relates to a waste disposal business conducted by the Appellants at a site which they occupied at Tofts Road West, Hartlepool and in respect of which they held waste disposal licence CLE 226/1. The licence was subject to conditions [...]

The circumstances as they appear from the case stated can be summarised as follows. The site was managed by a Mr Paul Blackler. Above him was an operations manager, Mr John Wood, who was absent from the site on 31 July 1995. The next in command below Mr Blackler was the site supervisor, a Mr Christopher Hanlon. He was one of the site's plant chemists and a 'technically competent person' ('TCP') and as such had delegated authority for analysing waste products brought to the site, completing the relevant inspection form and deciding where loads should be discharged. Another of the site's plant chemists and also a TCP was a Mr Leighton Evans. Under them was a Mr Julian Yuill, a 'team leader'. On the afternoon of 31 July 1995 a tanker from Leigh Environmental Limited arrived to discharge a quantity of waste water and oil. It went through the normal inspection procedure provided by condition 27, Mr Leighton Evans being the responsible TCP. He designated it for off-loading into tank 4A, and completed and initialled a corresponding waste inspection form. However, off loading into tank 4A did not take place and the material was instead discharged into the bund referred to in the information. The circumstances in which this occurred were that the bund already had a quantity of waste material in it as a result of a problem earlier that day which had necessitated the emptying of tank 5A into the bund in order to repair tank 5A. It was intended that the contents of the bund should be pumped into tank 4A. Mr Hanlon received a telephone call from Leigh Environmental Limited, requiring their tanker to be 'turned round quickly' because the vehicle was needed at another site to complete a job for a customer and conveying a sense of urgency to Mr Hanlon. Mr Hanlon did not consult Mr Blackler, but decided that the load should be discharged into the bund after going through the steps in condition 27(a) and (b) in relation to the bund. He did not however complete a new waste disposal form or advice note indicating that the load was now to be discharged into the bund. The load was being discharged into the bund when this was observed by two waste inspection officers doing a spot check at the site. Mr Hanlon was subsequently disciplined by the Appellant, with the Appellant claiming that he had no authority to make the decision he made.

The Justices found (a) that in the circumstances there was a breach of condition 27(c) of the licence, in that no new waste inspection form was completed indicating the location of the tank (that is, the bund), into which the load was deposited. They held (b) that:

> the [Appellant] company 'knowingly' caused the deposit in that it was the company's business to accept waste for storage and processing' and (c) that the company had knowledge of the breach, 'as Mr Hanlon made the decision to place the waste in the bund etc, and he was part of the directing mind and will of the company because;
>
> (i) he was acting within the scope of his authority and carrying out his ordinary duties, which had been delegated to him ...
>
> We consider that he was acting within his authority despite the fact that after the event the company disciplined him for his actions.
>
> (ii) the responsibilities delegated to Mr Hanlon as 'TCP' appear to be an intrinsic part of the appellant company's operation.

The Justices went on to hold (d) that the defence contained in s 33(7)(c) of the Act was not made out because 'the actions which contravened [sic] the breach were not done in an emergency in order to avoid danger to the public'; and (e) that, in view of their conclusions regarding Mr Hanlon's status, it was unnecessary to consider further whether a person representing the directing mind and will of the company had to know both of the fact of the deposit and that it was not in accordance with the conditions of the licence.

The Justices stated four questions of law, covering all the points in their decision as I have outlined them, save (d). They are:

(1) whether we were correct in law in holding that the deposit of the waste in question was not in accordance with condition 27 of the said Waste Management Licence;

(2) whether as a matter of law for a company to be guilty of an offence under s 33(1) and (6) of the Environmental Protection Act 1990, of knowingly causing the deposit of controlled waste in contravention of a licence condition it is necessary for the prosecution to prove that a person who comprises or is part of the directing mind and will of the company, knew both of the fact of the deposit and that such deposit was not in accordance with such condition;

(3) whether we were correct in law in holding that Mr Hanlon was part of the directing mind and will of the appellant company;

(4) whether, on the facts found, if the deposit was made not in accordance with the said condition 27, the defendant company had 'knowingly' caused controlled waste to be deposited not in accordance with condition 27 of the said licence.

The Appellant accepts that it has no basis for challenging the Justices' finding that no defence under s 33(7)(c) was made out.

The first question of law is whether it was correct in law to hold that the deposit was not in accordance with condition 27. [...]

Condition 27(c) in these circumstances clearly required issue of a fresh advice note indicating the bund as the 'tank' into which the load was to be discharged.

There having been a breach of condition, the Respondent before us sought to short-circuit matters and to avoid the Appellant's contentions under s 33(1) by simply relying on the second limb of s 33(6) – 'A person who contravenes any condition of a waste management licence commits an offence'. That on the face of it would have been a possible complaint, which might have been the subject of an appropriately worded information. The actual information, set out at the beginning of this judgment, is however clearly in terms referable to the first limb of s 33(6) – 'A person who contravenes sub-s (1) above ... commits an offence' – and was treated as such, a matter on which the manner of expression of the case stated leaves no doubt. [...] I proceed accordingly on the basis that the only matter before the Court is a conviction and appeal in respect of contravention of s 33(1)(a).

The Respondent accepted, realistically, that it could not, as a matter of law, sustain the Justices' finding that Mr Hanlon was 'part of the directing mind and will of the company'. For reasons I shall give, this way of stating the relevant issue is itself open to question. Since Mr Blackler was not in any way involved in or aware of the actual discharge into the bund, it is unnecessary to consider his position. This disposes of the third question raised by the case stated.

The second question is whether it was necessary for the prosecution to prove that a person comprising or part of the directing mind and will of the Appellant company knew both of the fact of the deposit and that such deposit was not in accordance with condition 27, and the fourth is whether, on the facts found, the Appellant company had 'knowingly' caused controlled waste to be deposited not in accordance with condition 27.

The second question assumes that under s 33(1) whatever knowledge is referred to by the word 'knowingly' must be by a person comprising or part of the directing mind and will of the company. As the case was argued before us, without objection, that was in issue. In the Respondent's submission, s 33(1) imports vicarious responsibility for the conduct and knowledge of any servant of the Appellant company acting in the course of his authority. As to what must be known, the Respondent submits that s 33(1)(a) only requires knowledge of the fact of deposit and not of the breach of condition. The Appellant submits that there must not only be knowledge of both, but that in the present case not even knowledge of the relevant deposit is established, since, in the Appellant's submission, that would have involved knowledge of the deposit into the bund on the part of the Appellant's senior management.

I take first the issue whether the knowledge required by s 33(1)(a) goes to the breach of condition as well as the deposit (however that may be identified). On this issue, the Respondent is in my judgment clearly correct. The structure of the section is that the word 'knowingly' qualifies on its face two (out of three) of the cases identified in its first part; and the exception beginning 'unless a waste management licence' appears as a separate factual qualification on all three cases, not involving any requirement of knowledge. The mitigation of the strictness of s 33(1)(a) – and indeed of s 33(1) and (6) generally – is on this basis to be found in the exceptions provided by s 33(7). Section 33(7) not only mitigates s 33(1) and (6), it indicates why it is appropriate to read those sub-ss strictly; the Appellant's submissions would in fact introduce a considerable element of overlap into the provisions of s 33(1) and (7).

For whatever reason, s 33(7) was not in fact relied on before the Justices, and Mr Lamming for the Appellant accepts that he cannot invoke it now. Some of his submissions amount in my view to attempts to repair this inability by importing into s 33(1)(a) limitations which are not actually there and for which there is also no call in view of s 33(7).

The judge followed the interpretation placed upon s 3(1) of the Control of Pollution Act 1974 (the predecessor section) in *Ashcroft v Cambro Ltd* [1981] 1 WLR 1349; [1981] 3 All ER 699. In these more environmentally conscious times it would have been strange if Parliament had wished to relax the requirements of the legislation by making prosecutions under the EPA 1990 more difficult than they had been previously.

Section 34 Duty of care etc as respects waste

(1) Subject to sub-s (2) below, it shall be the duty of any person who imports, produces, carries, keeps, treats or disposes of controlled waste or, as a broker, has control of such waste, to take all such measures applicable to him in that capacity as are reasonable in the circumstances–

    (a) to prevent any contravention by any other person of s 33 above; to prevent the escape of the waste from his control or that of any other person; and

    [Section 1(a)(a) omitted.]

    (b) to prevent the escape of the waste from his control or that of any other person; and

    (c) on the transfer of the waste, to secure–

        (i) that the transfer is only to an authorised person or to a person for authorised transport purposes; and

        (ii) that there is transferred such a written description of the waste as will enable other persons to avoid a contravention of that section and to comply with the duty under this sub-section as respects the escape of waste.

(2) The duty imposed by sub-s (1) above does not apply to an occupier of domestic property as respects the household waste produced on the property.

(3) The following are authorised persons for the purpose of sub-s (1)(c) above–

    (a) any authority which is a waste collection authority for the purposes of this Part;

    (b) any person who is the holder of a waste management licence under s 35 below or of a disposal licence under s 5 of the Control of Pollution Act 1974;

    (c) any person to whom s 33(1) above does not apply by virtue of regulations under sub-s (3) of that section;

    (d) any person registered as a carrier of controlled waste under s 2 of the Control of Pollution (Amendment) Act 1989;

    (e) any person who is not required to be so registered by virtue of regulations under s 1(3) of that Act; and

    (f) a waste disposal authority in Scotland.

(3A) The Secretary of State may by regulations amend sub-s (3) above so as to add, whether generally or in such circumstances as may be prescribed in the regulations, any person specified in the regulations, or any description of person so specified, to the persons who are authorised persons for the purposes of sub-s (1)(c) above.

(4) The following are authorised transport purposes for the purposes of sub-s (1)(c) above–

    (a) the transport of controlled waste within the same premises between different places in those premises;

    (b) the transport to a place in Great Britain of controlled waste which has been brought from a country or territory outside Great Britain not having been landed in Great Britain until it arrives at that place; and

    (c) the transport by air or sea of controlled waste from a place in Great Britain to a place outside Great Britain; and 'transport' has the same meaning in this subsection as in the Control of Pollution (Amendment) Act 1989.

(4A) For the purposes of sub-s (1)(c)(ii) above–

    (a) a transfer of waste in stages shall be treated as taking place when the first stage of the transfer takes place; and

    (b) a series of transfers between the same parties of waste of the same description shall be treated as a single transfer taking place when the first of the transfers in the series takes place.

(5) The Secretary of State may, by regulations, make provision imposing requirements on any person who is subject to the duty imposed by sub-s (1) above as respects the making and retention of documents and the furnishing of documents or copies of documents.

(6) Any person who fails to comply with the duty imposed by sub-s (1) above or with any requirement imposed under sub-s (5) above shall be liable–

    (a) on summary conviction, to a fine not exceeding the statutory maximum; and

    (b) on conviction on indictment, to a fine.

(7) The Secretary of State shall, after consultation with such persons or bodies as appear to him representative of the interests concerned, prepare and issue a code of practice for the purpose of providing to persons practical guidance on how to discharge the duty imposed on them by sub-s (1) above.

(8) The Secretary of State may from time to time revise a code of practice issued under sub-s (7) above by revoking, amending or adding to the provisions of the code.

(9) The code of practice prepared in pursuance of sub-s (7) above shall be laid before both Houses of Parliament.

(10) A code of practice issued under sub-s (7) above shall be admissible in evidence and if any provision of such a code appears to the court to be relevant to any question arising in the proceedings it shall be taken into account in determining that question.

(11) Different codes of practice may be prepared and issued under sub-s (7) above for different areas.

Note:

The provisions in s 34 are supplemented by the Environmental Protection (Duty of Care) Regulations SI 1991/2839. The Secretary of State has also issued (under s 34(7)) a Code on the duty of care: *Waste Management, The Duty of Care, A Code of Practice* (HMSO, 1996). The Code may be admitted as evidence to help determine whether there has been a breach of the duty.

Section 35 Waste management licences: general

(1) A waste management licence is a licence granted by a waste regulation authority authorising the treatment, keeping or disposal of any specified description of controlled waste in or on specified land or the treatment or disposal of any specified description of controlled waste by means of specified mobile plant.

(2) A licence shall be granted to the following person, that is to say–

    (a) in the case of a licence relating to the treatment, keeping or disposal of waste in or on land, to the person who is in occupation of the land; and

    (b) in the case of a licence relating to the treatment or disposal of waste by means of mobile plant, to the person who operates the plant.

(3) A licence shall be granted on such terms and subject to such conditions as appear to the waste regulation authority to be appropriate and the conditions may relate–

    (a) to the activities which the licence authorises; and

    (b) to the precautions to be taken and works to be carried out in connection with or in consequence of those activities; and accordingly requirements may be imposed in the licence which are to be complied with before the activities which the licence authorises have begun or after the activities which the licence authorises have ceased.

(4) Conditions may require the holder of a licence to carry out works or do other things notwithstanding that he is not entitled to carry out the works or to do the thing and any person whose consent would be required shall grant, or join in granting, the holder of the licence such rights in relation to the land as will enable the holder of the licence to comply with any requirements imposed on him by the licence.

(5) Conditions may relate, where waste other than controlled waste is to be treated, kept or disposed of, to the treatment, keeping or disposal of that other waste.

(6) The Secretary of State may, by regulations, make provision as to the conditions which are, or are not, to be included in a licence; and regulations under this sub-section may make different provision for different circumstances.

(7) The Secretary of State may, as respects any licence for which an application is made to a waste regulation authority, give to the authority directions as to the terms and conditions which are, or are not, to be included in the licence; and it shall be the duty of the authority to give effect to the directions.

(7A) In any case where–

    (a) an entry is required under this section to be made in any record as to the observance of any condition of a licence; and

    (b) the entry has not been made,

that fact shall be admissible as evidence that condition has not been observed.

(7B) Any person who–

    (a) intentionally makes a false entry in any record required to be kept under any condition of a licence; or

(b) with intent to deceive, forges or uses a licence or makes or has in his possession a document so closely resembling a licence as to be likely to deceive,

shall be guilty of an offence.

(7C) A person guilty of an offence under sub-s (7B) above shall be liable–

(a) on summary conviction, to a fine not exceeding the statutory maximum;

(b) on conviction on indictment, to a fine or to imprisonment for a term not exceeding two years, or to both.

(8) It shall be the duty of waste regulation authorities to have regard to any guidance issued to them by the Secretary of State with respect to the discharge of their functions in relation to licences.

(9) A licence may not be surrendered by the holder except in accordance with s 39 below.

(10) A licence is not transferable by the holder but the waste regulation authority may transfer it to another person under s 40 below.

(11) A licence shall continue in force until it is revoked entirely by the waste regulation authority under s 38 below or it is surrendered or its surrender is accepted under s 39 below.

(11A) A licence shall cease to have effect if and to the extent that the treatment, keeping or disposal of waste authorised by the licence is authorised by a permit granted under regulations under s 2 of the Pollution Prevention Control Act 1999.

(12) In this Part 'licence' means a waste management licence and 'site licence' and 'mobile plant licence' mean, respectively, a licence authorising the treatment, keeping or disposal of waste in or on land and a licence authorising the treatment or disposal of waste by means of mobile plant.

Notes:

1   Regulation 16 of The Waste Management Licensing Regulations 1994 SI 1994/1056 provides that certain activities are exempt from the licensing system. These principally include activities subject to other statutory controls, such as those covered by Integrated Pollution Control under Pt 1 of the EPA 1990 (see Chapter 5) and disposals of liquid waste into water which are covered by Pts I and II of the Water Resources Act 1991 (see Chapter 3).

2   It has been held that a Waste Management Licence constitutes property within the meaning of s 436 of the Insolvency Act 1986 and can be disclaimed by a liquidator as 'onerous property' under s 178 of that Act. See the following extract from *Re Celtic Extraction Ltd* which partially overruled *Re Mineral Resources Ltd, Environment Agency v Stout* [1999] 1 All ER 746. See further Carolyn Shelbourn, 'Can the insolvent polluter pay? environmental licences and the insolvent company' [2000] 12(2) JEL 217–29 and by the same author, 'Waste management and the insolvent company' [2000] JPL 134–41.

Re Celtic Extraction Ltd (In Liquidation); Re Bluestone Chemicals Ltd (In Liquidation) [2000] 2 WLR 991; [1999] 4 All ER 684; [1999] 46 EG 187; [1999] 3 EGLR 21 (CA)

Morritt LJ: [...]

37 The Official Receiver accepts that there are two possible interpretations of s 35(11). The wide one adopted by the judge so as to preclude any form of termination at all save those expressly mentioned and a narrow one which, save for those specifically mentioned, precludes termination by act of the parties but not by external statutory force. The Official Receiver contends that the court should adopt the narrower interpretation. The agency supports the judge in adopting the wider construction.

38 The agency relies on a number of indications which, it submits, show that Parliament intended the wider interpretation to apply. First is the principle of European Community law promulgated in the directive that the 'polluter pays'. If the disclaimer provisions applied then it would provide an easy escape from this obligation. Second, it is suggested that a disclaimer of the licence, or indeed of the land to which it relates, would give rise to an offence under s 33 of the 1990 Act. In the case of a disclaimer of the licence this consequence would arise from the consequential termination of the licence. Thereafter keeping the controlled waste in the land would not be under and in accordance with a waste management licence (s 33(1)(b)(i)). In the case of a disclaimer of the land there would be an offence committed under s 33(1)(b)(i) and a breach of the duty of care in s 34(1)(c) because the disclaimer would amount to a disposal of the waste in the land otherwise than in accordance with a waste management licence and to an unauthorised person. Third, as the effect of the disclaimer of the waste management licence is to terminate it the duty of the agency under s 42(1) and its emergency powers conferred by s 42(3) would terminate. I understood it to be submitted that as a consequence of the cesser of its powers and duties the agency would not be entitled to prove as a creditor pursuant to s 178(6) of the 1986 Act. [...]

39 I prefer the submissions of the Official Receiver. First, I do not accept the arguments for the agency. There is nothing in the directive to suggest that the 'polluter pays' principle is to be applied to cases where the polluter cannot pay so as to require that the unsecured creditors of the polluter should pay to the extent of the assets available for distribution among them. Yet this is the consequence of the argument for the agency that the costs of compliance have priority over provable debts and that the assets of the company must be set aside to pay for future compliance with the terms of the licence before the company is dissolved.

40 Second, I do not accept that a disclaimer of the land would constitute an offence under s 33 or a breach of duty under s 34. Though the effect of a disclaimer is to terminate leasehold interests and the obligations of landlord and tenant one to another, it does not follow that a disclaimer of either freehold or leasehold land amounts to a disposal or transfer of waste. If it did then the dissolution of the company or the death of the individual holder would do so too. Yet the agency accepts that the first is permissible and the second unavoidable. In the case of the disclaimer of the licence there would be no transfer of the waste for the purposes of either s 33 or s 34. I doubt whether for the purposes of criminal proceedings an offence would be committed under s 33 the next day by the owner of the land on the ground that he was 'keeping' waste otherwise than under a waste management licence. But even if it was, the same offence would arise on dissolution or death which, the agency accepts, terminates the licence.

41 With regard to the third point, it is true that both the duty and the emergency powers arising under s 42 are limited to the period 'while a licence is in force'. But once again that consequence will also arise on the death or dissolution of the holder of the licence ...

(Rattee J and Roch LJ agreed.)

Section 35A Compensation where rights granted pursuant to ss 35(4) or 38(9A)

(1) This section applies in any case where–

  (a) the holder of a licence is required–

    (i) by the conditions of the licence; or

    (ii) by a requirement imposed under s 38(9) below, to carry out any works or do any other thing which he is not entitled to carry out or do;

  (b) a person whose consent would be required has, pursuant to the requirements of ss 35(4) above or 38(9A) below, granted, or joined in granting, to the holder of the licence any rights in relation to any land; and

  (c) those rights, or those rights together with other rights, are such as will enable the holder of the licence to comply with any requirements imposed on him by the licence or, as the case may be, under s 38(9) below.

(2) In a case where this section applies, any person who has granted, or joined in granting, the rights in question shall be entitled to be paid compensation under this section by the holder of the licence.

(3) The Secretary of State shall by regulations provide for the descriptions of loss and damage for which compensation is payable under this section.

(4) The Secretary of State may by regulations–

  (a) provide for the basis on which any amount to be paid by way of compensation under this section is to be assessed;

  (b) without prejudice to the generality of sub-s (3) and para (a) above, provide for compensation under this section to be payable in respect of–

    (i) any effect of any rights being granted; or

    (ii) any consequence of the exercise of any rights which have been granted;

  (c) provide for the times at which any entitlement to compensation under this section is to arise or at which any such compensation is to become payable;

  (d) provide for the persons or bodies by whom, and the manner in which, any dispute–

    (i) as to whether any, and (if so) how much and when, compensation under this section is payable; or

    (ii) as to the person to or by whom it shall be paid,

    is to be determined;

  (e) provide for when or how applications may be made for compensation under this section;

  (f) without prejudice to the generality of para (d) above, provide for when or how applications may be made for the determination of any such disputes as are mentioned in that para;

  [...]

Note:

This section was added by the Environment Act 1995, s 120, Sched 22, para 67. As explained above (see p 440), it provides for the payment of compensation to third parties affected by a condition imposed under s 35(4). See also s 36(A)(3) which imposes particular consultation requirements.

Section 36 Grant of licences

(1) An application for a licence shall be made–

    (a) in the case of an application for a site licence, to the waste regulation authority in whose area the land is situated; and

    (b) in the case of an application for a mobile plant licence, to the waste regulation authority in whose area the operator of the plant has his principal place of business;

    and shall be made on a form provided for the purpose by the waste regulation authority and accompanied by such information as that authority reasonably requires and the charge prescribed for the purpose by a charging scheme under s 41 of the Environment Act 1995.

(1A) Where an applicant for a licence fails to provide the waste regulation authority with any information required under sub-s (1) above, the authority may refuse to proceed with the application, or refuse to proceed with it until the information is provided.

(2) A licence shall not be issued for a use of land for which planning permission is required in pursuance of the Town and Country Planning Act 1990 or the Town and Country Planning (Scotland) Act 1972 unless–

    (a) such planning permission is in force in relation to that use of the land; or

    (b) an established use certificate is in force under s 192 of the said Act of 1990 or s 90 of the said Act of 1972 in relation to that use of the land.

(3) Subject to sub-s (2) above and sub-s (4) below, a waste regulation authority to which an application for a licence has been duly made shall not reject the application if it is satisfied that the applicant is a fit and proper person unless it is satisfied that its rejection is necessary for the purpose of preventing–

    (a) pollution of the environment;

    (b) harm to human health; or

    (c) serious detriment to the amenities of the locality,

    but para (c) above is inapplicable where planning permission is in force in relation to the use to which the land will be put under the licence.

(4) Where the waste regulation authority proposes to issue a licence, the authority must, before it does so–

    (a) refer the proposal to the National Rivers Authority [the appropriate planning authority] and the Health and Safety Executive; and

    (b) consider any representations about the proposal which the Authority [authority] or the Executive makes to it during the allowed period.

(5), (6) ...

(7) Where any part of the land to be used is land which has been notified under s 28(1) of the Wildlife and Countryside Act 1981 (protection for certain areas) and the waste regulation authority proposes to issue a licence, the authority must, before it does so–

(a) refer the proposal to the appropriate nature conservation body; and

(b) consider any representations about the proposal which the body makes to it during the allowed period;

and in this section any reference to the appropriate nature conservation body is a reference to the Nature Conservancy Council for England, [Scottish Natural Heritage] or the Countryside Council for Wales, according as the land is situated in England, Scotland or Wales.

[...]

(9) If within the period of four months beginning with the date on which a waste regulation authority received an application for the grant of a licence, or within such longer period as the authority and the applicant may at any time agree in writing, the authority has neither granted the licence in consequence of the application nor given notice to the applicant that the authority has rejected the application, the authority shall be deemed to have rejected the application.

(9A) sub-s (9) above–

(a) shall not have effect in any case where, by virtue of sub-s (1A) above, the waste regulation authority refuses to proceed with the application in question; and

(b) shall have effect in any case where, by virtue of sub-s (1A) above, the waste regulation authority refuses to proceed with it until the required information is provided, with the substitution for the period of four months there mentioned of the period of four months beginning with the date on which the authority received the information.

(10) The period allowed to the appropriate planning authority, the Health and Safety Executive or the appropriate nature conservancy body for the making of representations under sub-s (4) or (7) above about a proposal is the period of 28 days beginning with the day on which the proposal is received by the waste regulation authority or such longer period as the waste regulation authority, the appropriate planning authority, the Executive or the body, as the case may be, agree in writing.

(11) In this section–

'the appropriate planning authority' means–

(a) where the relevant land is situated in the area of a London borough council, that London borough council;

(b) where the relevant land is situated in the City of London, the Common Council of the City of London;

(c) where the relevant land is situated in a non-metropolitan county in England, the council of that county;

(d) where the relevant land is situated in a National Park or the Broads, the National Park authority for that National Park or, as the case may be, the Broads Authority;

(e) where the relevant land is situated elsewhere in England or Wales, the council of the district or, in Wales, the county or county borough, in which the land is situated;

(f) where the relevant land is situated in Scotland, the council constituted under section 2 of the Local Government etc (Scotland) Act 1994 for the area in which the land is situated,

'the Broads' has the same meaning as in the Norfolk and Suffolk Broads Act 1988;

'National Park authority', subject to sub-s (12) below, means a National Park authority established under s 63 of the Environment Act 1995 which has become the local planning authority for the National Park in question;

'the relevant land' means–

(a) in relation to a site licence, the land to which the licence relates; and

(b) in relation to a mobile plant licence, the principal place of business of the operator of the plant to which the licence relates.

[...]

(13) The Secretary of State may by regulations amend the definition of 'appropriate planning authority' in sub-s (11) above.

(14) This section shall have effect subject to s 36A below.

Section 36A Consultation before the grant of certain licences

(1) This section applies where an application for a licence has been duly made to a waste regulation authority, and the authority proposes to issue a licence subject (by virtue of s 35(4) above) to any condition which might require the holder of the licence to–

(a) carry out any works; or

(b) do any other thing,

which he might not be entitled to carry out or do.

(2) Before issuing the licence, the waste regulation authority shall serve on every person appearing to the authority to be a person falling within sub-s (3) below a notice which complies with the requirements set out in sub-s (4) below.

(3) A person falls within this sub-s if–

(a) he is the owner, lessee or occupier of any land; and

(b) that land is land in relation to which it is likely that, as a consequence of the licence being issued subject to the condition in question, rights will have to be granted by virtue of s 35(4) above to the holder of the licence.

(4) A notice served under sub-s (2) above shall–

(a) set out the condition in question;

(b) indicate the nature of the works or other things which that condition might require the holder of the licence to carry out or do; and

(c) specify the date by which, and the manner in which, any representations relating to the condition or its possible effects are to be made to the waste regulation authority by the person on whom the notice is served.

(5) The date which, pursuant to sub-s (4)(c) above, is specified in a notice shall be a date not earlier than the date on which expires the period–

(a) beginning with the date on which the notice is served; and

(b) of such length as may be prescribed in regulations made by the Secretary of State.

(6) Before the waste regulation authority issues the licence it must, subject to sub-s (7) below, consider any representations made in relation to the condition in question, or its possible effects, by any person on whom a notice has been served under sub-s (2) above.

(7) Sub-section (6) above does not require the waste regulation authority to consider any representations made by a person after the date specified in the notice served on him under sub-s (2) above as the date by which his representations in relation to the condition or its possible effects are to be made.

(8) In sub-s (3) above–

'owner', in relation to any land in England and Wales, means the person who–

(a) is for the time being receiving the rack-rent of the land, whether on his own account or as agent or trustee for another person; or

(b) would receive the rack-rent if the land were let at a rack-rent but does not include a mortgagee not in possession; and

Note:

This section imposes specific consultation requirements where conditions imposed on a licence affect third parties under s 35(4) above.

Section 37 Variation of licences

(1) While a licence issued by a waste regulation authority is in force, the authority may, subject to regulations under s 35(6) above and to sub-s (3) below–

(a) on its own initiative, modify the conditions of the licence to any extent which, in the opinion of the authority, is desirable and is unlikely to require unreasonable expense on the part of the holder; and

(b) on the application of the licence holder accompanied by [the charge prescribed for the purpose by a charging scheme under s 41 of the Environment Act 1995, modify the conditions of his licence to the extent requested in the application.

(2) While a licence issued by a waste regulation authority is in force, the authority shall, except where it revokes the licence entirely under s 38 below, modify the conditions of the licence–

(a) to the extent which in the opinion of the authority is required for the purpose of ensuring that the activities authorised by the licence do not cause pollution of the environment or harm to human health or become seriously detrimental to the amenities of the locality affected by the activities; and

(b) to the extent required by any regulations in force under s 35(6) above.

(3) The Secretary of State may, as respects any licence issued by a waste regulation authority, give to the authority directions as to the modifications which are to be made in the conditions of the licence under sub-s (1)(a) or (2)(a) above; and it shall be the duty of the authority to give effect to the directions.

[Sub-sections (4)–(6) omitted.]

Section 37A Consultation before certain variations

(1) This section applies where–

(a) a waste regulation authority proposes to modify a licence under s 37(1) or (2)(a) above; and

(b) the licence, if modified as proposed, would be subject to a relevant new condition.

(2) For the purposes of this section, a 'relevant new condition' is any condition by virtue of which the holder of the licence might be required to carry out any works or do any other thing–

(a) which he might not be entitled to carry out or do; and

(b) which he could not be required to carry out or do by virtue of the conditions to which, prior to the modification, the licence is subject.

(3) Before modifying the licence, the waste regulation authority shall serve on every person appearing to the authority to be a person falling within sub-s (4) below a notice which complies with the requirements set out in sub-s (5) below.

(4) A person falls within this sub-section if–

(a) he is the owner, lessee or occupier of any land; and

(b) that land is land in relation to which it is likely that, as a consequence of the licence being modified so as to be subject to the relevant new condition in question, rights will have to be granted by virtue of s 35(4) above to the holder of the licence.

(5) A notice served under sub-s (3) above shall–

(a) set out the relevant new condition in question;

(b) indicate the nature of the works or other things which that condition might require the holder of the licence to carry out or do but which he could not be required to carry out or do by virtue of the conditions (if any) to which, prior to the modification, the licence is subject; and

(c) specify the date by which, and the manner in which, any representations relating to the condition or its possible effects are to be made to the waste regulation authority by the person on whom the notice is served.

(6) The date which, pursuant to sub-s (5)(c) above, is specified in a notice shall be a date not earlier than the date on which expires the period–

(a) beginning with the date on which the notice is served; and

(b) of such length as may be prescribed in regulations made by the Secretary of State.

(7) Before the waste regulation authority issues the licence it must, subject to sub-s (8) below, consider any representations made in relation to the condition in question, or its possible effects, by any person on whom a notice has been served under sub-s (3) above.

(8) Sub-section (7) above does not require the waste regulation authority to consider any representations made by a person after the date specified in the notice served on him under sub-s (3) above as the date by which his representations in relation to the condition or its possible effects are to be made.

(9) A waste regulation authority may postpone the service of any notice or the consideration of any representations required under the foregoing provisions of this section so far as the authority considers that by reason of an emergency it is appropriate to do so.

(10) In sub-s (3) above, 'owner' has the same meaning as it has in sub-s (3) of s 36A above by virtue of sub-s (8) of that section.

Section 38 Revocation and suspension of licences

(1) Where a licence granted by a waste regulation authority is in force and it appears to the authority–

    (a) that the holder of the licence has ceased to be a fit and proper person by reason of his having been convicted of a relevant offence; or

    (b) that the continuation of the activities authorised by the licence would cause pollution of the environment or harm to human health or would be seriously detrimental to the amenities of the locality affected; and

    (c) that the pollution, harm or detriment cannot be avoided by modifying the conditions of the licence,

the authority may exercise, as it thinks fit, either of the powers conferred by sub-ss (3) and (4) below.

(2) Where a licence granted by a waste regulation authority is in force and it appears to the authority that the holder of the licence has ceased to be a fit and proper person by reason of the management of the activities authorised by the licence having ceased to be in the hands of a technically competent person, the authority may exercise the power conferred by sub-s (3) below.

(3) The authority may, under this sub-section, revoke the licence so far as it authorises the carrying on of the activities specified in the licence or such of them as the authority specifies in revoking the licence.

(4) The authority may, under this sub-section, revoke the licence entirely.

(5) A licence revoked under sub-s (3) above shall cease to have effect to authorise the carrying on of the activities specified in the licence or, as the case may be, the activities specified by the authority in revoking the licence but shall not affect the requirements imposed by the licence which the authority, in revoking the licence, specify as requirements which are to continue to bind the licence holder.

(6) Where a licence granted by a waste regulation authority is in force and it appears to the authority–

    (a) that the holder of the licence has ceased to be a fit and proper person by reason of the management of the activities authorised by the licence having ceased to be in the hands of a technically competent person; or

    (b) that serious pollution of the environment or serious harm to human health has resulted from, or is about to be caused by, the activities to which the licence relates or the happening or threatened happening of an event affecting those activities; and

    (c) that the continuing to carry on those activities, or any of those activities, in the circumstances will continue or, as the case may be, cause serious pollution of the environment or serious harm to human health; the authority may suspend the licence so far as it authorises the carrying on of the activities specified in the licence or such of them as the authority specifies in suspending the licence.

(7) The Secretary of State may, if he thinks fit in relation to a licence granted by a waste regulation authority, give to the authority directions as to whether and in what manner

the authority should exercise its powers under this section; and it shall be the duty of the authority to give effect to the directions.

(8) A licence suspended under sub-s (6) above shall, while the suspension has effect, be of no effect to authorise the carrying on of the activities specified in the licence or, as the case may be, the activities specified by the authority in suspending the licence.

(9) Where a licence is suspended under sub-s (6) above, the authority, in suspending it or at any time while it is suspended, may require the holder of the licence to take such measures to deal with or avert the pollution or harm as the authority considers necessary.

(9A) A requirement imposed under sub-s (9) above may require the holder of a licence to carry out works or do other things notwithstanding that he is not entitled to carry out the works or do the thing and any person whose consent would be required shall grant, or join in granting, the holder of the licence such rights in relation to the land as will enable the holder of the licence to comply with any requirements imposed on him under that sub-section.

(9B) Sub-sections (2) to (8) of s 36A above shall, with the necessary modifications, apply where the authority proposes to impose a requirement under sub-s (9) above which may require the holder of a licence to carry out any such works or do any such thing as is mentioned in sub-s (9A) above as they apply where the authority proposes to issue a licence subject to any such condition as is mentioned in sub-s (1) of that section, but as if–

(a) the reference in sub-s (3) of that section to section 35(4) above were a reference to sub-s (9A) above; and

(b) any reference in those sub-ss–

  (i) to the condition, or the condition in question, were a reference to the requirement; and

  (ii) to issuing a licence were a reference to serving a notice, under sub-s (12) below, effecting the requirement.

(9C) The authority may postpone the service of any notice or the consideration of any representations required under s 36A above, as applied by sub-s (9B) above, so far as the authority considers that by reason of an emergency it is appropriate to do so.

(10) A person who, without reasonable excuse, fails to comply with any requirement imposed under sub-s (9) above otherwise than in relation to special waste shall be liable–

(a) on summary conviction, to a fine of an amount not exceeding the statutory maximum; and

(b) on conviction on indictment, to imprisonment for a term not exceeding two years or a fine or both.

(11) A person who, without reasonable excuse, fails to comply with any requirement imposed under sub-s (9) above in relation to special waste shall be liable–

(a) on summary conviction, to imprisonment for a term not exceeding six months or a fine not exceeding the statutory maximum or both; and

(b) on conviction on indictment, to imprisonment for a term not exceeding five years or a fine or both.

(12) Any revocation or suspension of a licence or requirement imposed during the suspension of a licence under this section shall be effected by notice served on the

holder of the licence and the notice shall state the time at which the revocation or suspension or the requirement is to take effect and, in the case of suspension, the period at the end of which, or the event on the occurrence of which, the suspension is to cease.

(13) If a waste regulation authority is of the opinion that proceedings for an offence under sub-s (10) or (11) above would afford an ineffectual remedy against a person who has failed to comply with any requirement imposed under sub-s (9) above, the authority may take proceedings in the High Court or, in Scotland, in any court of competent jurisdiction for the purpose of securing compliance with the requirement.

Section 39 Surrender of licences

(1) A licence may be surrendered by its holder to the authority which granted it but, in the case of a site licence, only if the authority accepts the surrender.

(2) The following provisions apply to the surrender and acceptance of the surrender of a site licence.

(3) The holder of a site licence who desires to surrender it shall make an application for that purpose to the authority in such form, giving such information and accompanied by such evidence as the Secretary of State prescribes by regulations and accompanied by the prescribed fee payable under s 41 below [on a form provided by the authority for the purpose, giving such information and accompanied by such evidence as the authority reasonably requires and accompanied by the charge prescribed for the purpose by a charging scheme under s 41 of the Environment Act 1995].

(4) An authority which receives an application for the surrender of a site licence–

(a) shall inspect the land to which the licence relates; and

(b) may require the holder of the licence to furnish to it further information or further evidence.

(5) The authority shall determine whether it is likely or unlikely that the condition of the land, so far as that condition is the result of the use of the land for the treatment, keeping or disposal of waste (whether or not in pursuance of the licence), will cause pollution of the environment or harm to human health.

(6) If the authority is satisfied that the condition of the land is unlikely to cause the pollution or harm mentioned in sub-s (5) above, the authority shall, subject to sub-s (7) below, accept the surrender of the licence; but otherwise the authority shall refuse to accept it.

(7) Where the authority proposes to accept the surrender of a site licence, the authority must, before it does so–

(a) refer the proposal to [the appropriate planning authority]; and

(b) consider any representations about the proposal which [the appropriate planning authority] makes to it during the allowed period;

(8) ...

(9) Where the surrender of a licence is accepted under this section the authority shall issue to the applicant, with the notice of its determination, a certificate (a 'certificate of completion') stating that it is satisfied as mentioned in sub-s (6) above and, on the issue of that certificate, the licence shall cease to have effect.

(10) If within the period of three months beginning with the date on which an authority receives an application to surrender a licence, or within such longer period as the authority and the applicant may at any time agree in writing, the authority has neither issued a certificate of completion nor given notice to the applicant that the authority has rejected the application, the authority shall be deemed to have rejected the application.

(11) Section 36(10) above applies for the interpretation of the 'allowed period' in sub-s (7) above.

[...]

Section 40 Transfer of licences

(1) A licence may be transferred to another person in accordance with sub-ss (2) to (6) below and may be so transferred whether or not the licence is partly revoked or suspended under any provision of this Part.

(2) Where the holder of a licence desires that the licence be transferred to another person ('the proposed transferee') the licence holder and the proposed transferee shall jointly make an application to the waste regulation authority which granted the licence for a transfer of it.

(3) An application under sub-s (2) above for the transfer of a licence shall be made in such form and shall include such information as the Secretary of State prescribes by regulations and shall be accompanied by the prescribed fee payable under s 41 below [on a form provided by the authority for the purpose, accompanied by such information as the authority may reasonably require, the charge prescribed for the purpose by a charging scheme under s 41 of the Environment Act 1995] and the licence.

(4) If, on such an application, the authority is satisfied that the proposed transferee is a fit and proper person the authority shall effect a transfer of the licence to the proposed transferee.

(5) The authority shall effect a transfer of a licence under the foregoing provisions of this section by causing the licence to be endorsed with the name and other particulars of the proposed transferee as the holder of the licence from such date specified in the endorsement as may be agreed with the applicants.

(6) If within the period of two months beginning with the date on which the authority receives an application for the transfer of a licence, or within such longer period as the authority and the applicants may at any time agree in writing, the authority has neither effected a transfer of the licence nor given notice to the applicants that the authority has rejected the application, the authority shall be deemed to have rejected the application.

[Section 41 repealed.]

Section 42 Supervision of licensed activities

(1) While a licence is in force it shall be the duty of the waste regulation authority which granted the licence to take the steps needed–

(a) for the purpose of ensuring that the activities authorised by the licence do not cause pollution of the environment or harm to human health or become seriously detrimental to the amenities of the locality affected by the activities; and

(b) for the purpose of ensuring that the conditions of the licence are complied with.

[(2) ...]

(3) For the purpose of performing the duty imposed on it by sub-s (1) above, any officer of the authority authorised in writing for the purpose by the authority may, if it appears to him that by reason of an emergency it is necessary to do so, carry out work on the land or in relation to plant or equipment on the land to which the licence relates or, as the case may be, in relation to the mobile plant to which the licence relates.

(4) Where a waste regulation authority incurs any expenditure by virtue of sub-s (3) above, the authority may recover the amount of the expenditure from [the holder, or (as the case may be) the former holder, of the licence], except where the holder or former holder of the licence shows that there was no emergency requiring any work or except such of the expenditure as he shows was unnecessary.

(5) Where it appears to a waste regulation authority that a condition of a licence granted by it is not being complied with [or is likely not to be complied with], then, without prejudice to any proceedings under s 33(6) above, the authority may–

    (a) serve on the holder of the licence a notice–

        (i) stating that the authority is of the opinion that a condition of the licence is not being complied with or, as the case may be, is likely not to be complied with;

        (ii) specifying the matters which constitute the non-compliance or, as the case may be, which make the anticipated non-compliance likely;

        (iii) specifying the steps which must be taken to remedy the non-compliance or, as the case may be, to prevent the anticipated non-compliance from occurring; and

        (iv) specifying the period within which those steps must be taken; and

    (b) if in the opinion of the authority the licence holder has not taken the steps specified in the notice within the period so specified, exercise any of the powers specified in sub-s (6) below.

(6) The powers which become exercisable in the event mentioned in sub-s (5)(b) above are the following–

    (a) to revoke the licence so far as it authorises the carrying on of the activities specified in the licence or such of them as the authority specifies in revoking the licence;

    (b) to revoke the licence entirely; and

    (c) to suspend the licence so far as it authorises the carrying on of the activities specified in the licence or, as the case may be, the activities specified by the authority in suspending the licence.

(6A) If a waste regulation authority is of the opinion that revocation or suspension of the licence, whether entirely or to any extent, under sub-s (6) above would afford an ineffectual remedy against a person who has failed to comply with any requirement imposed under sub-s (5)(a) above, the authority may take proceedings in the High Court or, in Scotland, in any court of competent jurisdiction for the purpose of securing compliance with the requirement.

(7) Where a licence is revoked or suspended under sub-s (6) above,

[sub-ss (5) and (12) or, as the case may be, sub-ss (8) to (12) of s 38] above shall apply with the necessary modifications as they respectively apply to revocations or suspensions of licences under that section; ...

(8) The Secretary of State may, if he thinks fit in relation to a licence granted by a waste regulation authority, give to the authority directions as to whether and in what manner the authority should exercise its powers under this section; and it shall be the duty of the authority to give effect to the directions.

Section 43 Appeals to Secretary of State from decisions with respect to licences

(1) Where, except in pursuance of a direction given by the Secretary of State–

  (a) an application for a licence or a modification of the conditions of a licence is rejected;

  (b) a licence is granted subject to conditions;

  (c) the conditions of a licence are modified;

  (d) a licence is suspended;

  (e) a licence is revoked under s 38 or 42 above;

  (f) an application to surrender a licence is rejected; or

  (g) an application for the transfer of a licence is rejected,

then, except in the case of an application for a transfer, the applicant for the licence or, as the case may be, the holder or former holder of it may appeal from the decision to the Secretary of State and, in the case of an application for a transfer, the proposed transferee may do so.

(2) Where an appeal is made to the Secretary of State–

  (a), (b) ...

  (c) if a Party to the appeal so requests, or the Secretary of State so decides, the appeal shall be or continue in the form of a hearing (which may, if the person hearing the appeal so decides, be held or held to any extent in private).

(2A) This section is subject to s 114 of the Environment Act 1995 (delegation or reference of appeals etc).

(3) Where, on such an appeal, the Secretary of State or other person determining the appeal determines that the decision of the authority shall be altered it shall be the duty of the authority to give effect to the determination.

(4) While an appeal is pending in a case falling within sub-s (1)(c) or (e) above, the decision in question shall, subject to sub-s (6) below, be ineffective; and if the appeal is dismissed or withdrawn the decision shall become effective from the end of the day on which the appeal is dismissed or withdrawn.

(5) Where an appeal is made in a case falling within sub-s (1)(d) above, the bringing of the appeal shall have no effect on the decision in question.

(6) sub-s (4) above shall not apply to a decision modifying the conditions of a licence under s 37 above or revoking a licence under s 38 or 42 above in the case of which the notice effecting the modification or revocation includes a statement that in the opinion of the authority it is necessary for the purpose of preventing or, where that is not practicable, minimising pollution of the environment or harm to human health that that sub-section should not apply.

(7) Where the decision under appeal is one falling within sub-s (6) above or is a decision to suspend a licence, if, on the application of the holder or former holder of the licence, the Secretary of State or other person determining the appeal determines that the authority

acted unreasonably in excluding the application of sub-s (4) above or, as the case may be, in suspending the licence, then–

    (a) if the appeal is still pending at the end of the day on which the determination is made, sub-s (4) above shall apply to the decision from the end of that day; and

    (b) the holder or former holder of the licence shall be entitled to recover compensation from the authority in respect of any loss suffered by him in consequence of the exclusion of the application of that sub-section or the suspension of the licence; and any dispute as to a person's entitlement to such compensation or as to the amount of it shall be determined by arbitration or in Scotland by a single arbiter appointed, in default of agreement between the parties concerned, by the Secretary of State on the application of any of the parties.

(8) Provision may be made by the Secretary of State by regulations with respect to appeals under this section [...]

    (b) as to the manner in which appeals are to be considered.

[Sections 45–48 appear below, pp 467–70.]

Section 59 Powers to require removal of waste unlawfully deposited

(1) If any controlled waste is deposited in or on any land in the area of a waste regulation authority or waste collection authority in contravention of s 33(1) above, the authority may, by notice served on him, require the occupier to do either or both of the following, that is–

    (a) to remove the waste from the land within a specified period not less than a period of 21 days beginning with the service of the notice;

    (b) to take within such a period specified steps with a view to eliminating or reducing the consequences of the deposit of the waste.

(2) A person on whom any requirements are imposed under sub-s (1) above may, within the period of 21 days mentioned in that sub-section, appeal against the requirement to a magistrates' court or, in Scotland, to the sheriff by way of summary application.

(3) On any appeal under sub-s (2) above the court shall quash the requirement if it is satisfied that–

    (a) the appellant neither deposited nor knowingly caused nor knowingly permitted the deposit of the waste; or

    (b) there is a material defect in the notice,

and in any other case shall either modify the requirement or dismiss the appeal.

(4) Where a person appeals against any requirement imposed under sub-s (1) above, the requirement shall be of no effect pending the determination of the appeal; and where the court modifies the requirement or dismisses the appeal it may extend the period specified in the notice.

(5) If a person on whom a requirement imposed under sub-s (1) above fails, without reasonable excuse, to comply with the requirement he shall be liable, on summary conviction, to a fine not exceeding level 5 on the standard scale and to a further fine of an amount equal to one-tenth of level 5 on the standard scale for each day on which the failure continues after conviction of the offence and before the authority has begun to exercise its powers under sub-s (6) below.

(6) Where a person on whom a requirement has been imposed under sub-s (1) above by an authority fails to comply with the requirement the authority may do what that person was required to do and may recover from him any expenses reasonably incurred by the authority in doing it.

(7) If it appears to a waste regulation authority or waste collection authority that waste has been deposited in or on any land in contravention of s 33(1) above and that–

(a) in order to remove or prevent pollution of land, water or air or harm to human health it is necessary that the waste be forthwith removed or other steps taken to eliminate or reduce the consequences of the deposit or both; or

(b) there is no occupier of the land; or

(c) the occupier neither made nor knowingly permitted the deposit of the waste,

the authority may remove the waste from the land or take other steps to eliminate or reduce the consequences of the deposit or, as the case may require, to remove the waste and take those steps.

(8) Where an authority exercises any of the powers conferred on it by sub-s (7) above it shall be entitled to recover the cost incurred by it in removing the waste or taking the steps or both and in disposing of the waste–

(a) in a case falling within sub-s (7)(a) above, from the occupier of the land unless he proves that he neither made nor knowingly caused nor knowingly permitted the deposit of the waste;

(b) in any case, from any person who deposited or knowingly caused or knowingly permitted the deposit of any of the waste,

except such of the cost as the occupier or that person shows was incurred unnecessarily.

(9) Any waste removed by an authority under sub-s (7) above shall belong to that authority and may be dealt with accordingly.

Section 74 Meaning of 'fit and proper person'

(1) The following provisions apply for the purposes of the discharge by a waste regulation authority of any function under this Part which requires the authority to determine whether a person is or is not a fit and proper person to hold a waste management licence.

(2) Whether a person is or is not a fit and proper person to hold a licence is to be determined by reference to the carrying on by him of the activities which are or are to be authorised by the licence and the fulfilment of the requirements of the licence.

(3) Subject to sub-s (4) below, a person shall be treated as not being a fit and proper person if it appears to the authority–

(a) that he or another relevant person has been convicted of a relevant offence;

(b) that the management of the activities which are or are to be authorised by the licence are not or will not be in the hands of a technically competent person; or

(c) that the person who holds or is to hold the licence has not made and either has no intention of making or is in no position to make financial provision adequate to discharge the obligations arising from the licence.

(4) The authority may, if it considers it proper to do so in any particular case, treat a person as a fit and proper person notwithstanding that sub-s (3)(a) above applies in his case.

(5) It shall be the duty of waste regulation authorities to have regard to any guidance issued to them by the Secretary of State with respect to the discharge of their functions of making the determinations to which this section applies.

(6) The Secretary of State may, by regulations, prescribe the offences that are relevant for the purposes of sub-s (3)(a) above and the qualifications and experience required of a person for the purposes of sub-s (3)(b) above.

(7) For the purposes of sub-s (3)(a) above, another relevant person shall be treated, in relation to the licence holder or proposed licence holder, as the case may be, as having been convicted of a relevant offence if–

    (a) any person has been convicted of a relevant offence committed by him in the course of his employment by the holder or, as the case may be, the proposed holder of the licence or in the course of the carrying on of any business by a partnership one of the members of which was the holder or, as the case may be, the proposed holder of the licence;

    (b) a body corporate has been convicted of a relevant offence committed when the holder or, as the case may be, the proposed holder of the licence was a director, manager, secretary or other similar officer of that body corporate; or

    (c) where the holder or, as the case may be, the proposed holder of the licence is a body corporate, a person who is a director, manager, secretary or other similar officer of that body corporate–

        (i) has been convicted of a relevant offence; or

        (ii) was a director, manager, secretary or other similar officer of another body corporate at a time when a relevant offence for which that other body corporate has been convicted was committed.

Waste collection and disposal

Section 45 imposes upon waste collection authorities the duty to arrange for the collection of household waste in their areas and s 46 gives power to require occupiers to place the waste for collection in a particular type of receptacle (s 47 concerns receptacles for commercial waste). Section 48 imposes a duty on waste collection authorities to deliver for disposal all waste which is collected by the authority under s 45 above to such places as the waste disposal authority for its area directs. Section 51 imposes a duty on waste disposal authorities to dispose of controlled waste collected in their area and to provide places where residents can deposit rubbish. These duties are to be performed by means of arrangements made with waste disposal contractors. The arrangements are to be regulated by s 32 of the EPA 1990 and Sched 2, Pt 1.

Section 45 Collection of controlled waste

(1) It shall be the duty of each waste collection authority–

    (a) to arrange for the collection of household waste in its area except waste–

        (i) which is situated at a place which in the opinion of the authority is so isolated or inaccessible that the cost of collecting it would be unreasonably high; and

      (ii) as to which the authority is satisfied that adequate arrangements for its disposal have been or can reasonably be expected to be made by a person who controls the waste; and

   (b) if requested by the occupier of premises in its area to collect any commercial waste from the premises, to arrange for the collection of the waste.

(2) Each waste collection authority may, if requested by the occupier of premises in its area to collect any industrial waste from the premises, arrange for the collection of the waste; but a collection authority in England and Wales shall not exercise the power except with the consent of the waste disposal authority whose area includes the area of the waste collection authority.

(3) No charge shall be made for the collection of household waste except in cases prescribed in regulations made by the Secretary of State; and in any of those cases–

   (a) the duty to arrange for the collection of the waste shall not arise until a person who controls the waste requests the authority to collect it; and

   (b) the authority may recover a reasonable charge for the collection of the waste from the person who made the request.

(4) A person at whose request waste other than household waste is collected under this section shall be liable to pay a reasonable charge for the collection and disposal of the waste to the authority which arranged for its collection; and it shall be the duty of that authority to recover the charge unless in the case of a charge in respect of commercial waste the authority considers it inappropriate to do so.

[Sub-sections (5)–(12) omitted.]

Section 46 Receptacles for household waste

(1) Where a waste collection authority has a duty by virtue of s 45(1)(a) above to arrange for the collection of household waste from any premises, the authority may, by notice served on him, require the occupier to place the waste for collection in receptacles of a kind and number specified.

(2) The kind and number of the receptacles required under sub-s (1) above to be used shall be such only as are reasonable but, subject to that, separate receptacles or compartments of receptacles may be required to be used for waste which is to be recycled and waste which is not.

(3) In making requirements under sub-s (1) above the authority may, as respects the provision of the receptacles–

   (a) determine that they be provided by the authority free of charge;

   (b) propose that they be provided, if the occupier agrees, by the authority on payment by him of such a single payment or such periodical payments as he agrees with the authority;

   (c) require the occupier to provide them if he does not enter into an agreement under para (b) above within a specified period; or

   (d) require the occupier to provide them.

(4) In making requirements as respects receptacles under sub-s (1) above, the authority may, by the notice under that sub-section, make provision with respect to–

   (a) the size, construction and maintenance of the receptacles;

(b) the placing of the receptacles for the purpose of facilitating the emptying of them, and access to the receptacles for that purpose;

(c) the placing of the receptacles for that purpose on highways or, in Scotland, roads;

(d) the substances or articles which may or may not be put into the receptacles or compartments of receptacles of any description and the precautions to be taken where particular substances or articles are put into them; and

(e) the steps to be taken by occupiers of premises to facilitate the collection of waste from the receptacles.

(5) No requirement shall be made under sub-s (1) above for receptacles to be placed on a highway or, as the case may be, road, unless–

(a) the relevant highway authority or roads authority have given their consent to their being so placed; and

(b) arrangements have been made as to the liability for any damage arising out of their being so placed.

(6) A person who fails, without reasonable excuse, to comply with any requirements imposed under sub-s (1), (3)(c) or (d) or (4) above shall be liable on summary conviction to a fine not exceeding level 3 on the standard scale.

(7) Where an occupier is required under sub-s (1) above to provide any receptacles he may, within the period allowed by sub-s (8) below, appeal to a magistrates' court or, in Scotland, to the sheriff by way of summary application against any requirement imposed under sub-s (1), sub-s (3)(c) or (d) or (4) above on the ground that–

(a) the requirement is unreasonable; or

(b) the receptacles in which household waste is placed for collection from the premises are adequate.

[Sub-sections (8)–(10) omitted.]

Section 47 Receptacles for commercial or industrial waste

(1) A waste collection authority may, at the request of any person, supply him with receptacles for commercial or industrial waste which he has requested the authority to arrange to collect and shall make a reasonable charge for any receptacle supplied unless in the case of a receptacle for commercial waste the authority considers it appropriate not to make a charge.

(2) If it appears to a waste collection authority that there is likely to be situated, on any premises in its area, commercial waste or industrial waste of a kind which, if the waste is not stored in receptacles of a particular kind, is likely to cause a nuisance or to be detrimental to the amenities of the locality, the authority may, by notice served on him, require the occupier of the premises to provide at the premises receptacles for the storage of such waste of a kind and number specified.

(3) The kind and number of the receptacles required under sub-s (2) above to be used shall be such only as are reasonable.

[Sub-sections (4)–(10) omitted.]

Section 48 Duties of waste collection authorities as respects disposal of waste collected

(1) Subject to sub-ss (2) and (6) below, it shall be the duty of each waste collection authority to deliver for disposal all waste which is collected by the authority under s 45 above to such places as the waste disposal authority for its area directs.

(2) The duty imposed on a waste collection authority by sub-s (1) above does not, except in cases falling within sub-s (4) below, apply as respects household waste or commercial waste for which the authority decides to make arrangements for recycling the waste; and the authority shall have regard, in deciding what recycling arrangements to make, to its waste recycling plan under s 49 below.

(3) A waste collection authority which decides to make arrangements under sub-s (2) above for recycling waste collected by it shall, as soon as reasonably practicable, by notice in writing, inform the waste disposal authority for the area which includes its area of the arrangements which it proposes to make.

(4) Where a waste disposal authority has made with a waste disposal contractor arrangements, as respects household waste or commercial waste in its area or any part of its area, for the contractor to recycle the waste, or any of it, the waste disposal authority may, by notice served on the waste collection authority, object to the waste collection authority having the waste recycled; and the objection may be made as respects all the waste, part only of the waste or specified descriptions of the waste.

(5) Where an objection is made under sub-s (4) above, sub-s (2) above shall not be available to the waste collection authority to the extent objected to.

[Sub-sections (6)–(9) omitted.]

Waste recycling plans[37]

Section 49 imposed a new duty on waste collection authorities to plan for waste recycling. To do so they are required to investigate what arrangements are appropriate for dealing with the waste by separating, baling or otherwise packaging it for the purpose of recycling and to prepare a plan of the arrangements being made or proposed. The plans must be kept under review. They must include information (sub-s (3)) relating *inter alia* to the kinds and quantities of controlled waste which the authority expects to collect during the period specified in the plan; the kinds and quantities of controlled waste which the authority expects to purchase during that period; the kinds and quantities of controlled waste which the authority expects to deal with during that period; and the estimated costs or savings attributable to the methods of dealing with the waste in the ways provided for in the plan. The waste collection authority, before finally determining the content of the plan or a modification, is required to send a copy of the plan in draft to the Secretary of State. He may give directions with which the authority must comply.

Section 49 Waste recycling plans by collection authorities

(1) It shall be the duty of each waste collection authority, as respects household and commercial waste arising in its area–

---

37 See *Waste Policy Guidance – Preparing and Revising Local Authority Recycling Strategies and Recycling Plans*, 1998, London: DETR.

(a) to carry out an investigation with a view to deciding what arrangements are appropriate for dealing with the waste by separating, baling or otherwise packaging it for the purpose of recycling it;

(b) to decide what arrangements are in the opinion of the authority needed for that purpose;

(c) to prepare a statement ('the plan') of the arrangements made and proposed to be made by the authority and other persons for dealing with waste in those ways;

(d) to carry out from time to time further investigations with a view to deciding what changes in the plan are needed; and

(e) to make any modification of the plan which the authority thinks appropriate in consequence of any such further investigation.

(2) In considering any arrangements or modification for the purposes of sub-s (1)(c) or (e) above it shall be the duty of the authority to have regard to the effect which the arrangements or modification would be likely to have on the amenities of any locality and the likely cost or saving to the authority attributable to the arrangements or modification.

(3) It shall be the duty of a waste collection authority to include in the plan information as to–

(a) the kinds and quantities of controlled waste which the authority expects to collect during the period specified in the plan;

(b) the kinds and quantities of controlled waste which the authority expects to purchase during that period;

(c) the kinds and quantities of controlled waste which the authority expects to deal with in the ways specified in sub-s (1)(a) above during that period;

(d) the arrangements which the authority expects to make during that period with waste disposal contractors or, in Scotland, waste disposal authorities and waste disposal contractors for them to deal with waste in those ways;

(e) the plant and equipment which the authority expects to provide under s 48(6) above or s 53 below; and

(f) the estimated costs or savings attributable to the methods of dealing with the waste in the ways provided for in the plan.

(4) It shall be the duty of a waste collection authority other than a waste collection authority in Greater London, before finally determining the content of the plan or a modification, to send a copy of it in draft to the Secretary of State for the purpose of enabling him to determine whether sub-s (3) above has been complied with; and, if the Secretary of State gives any directions to the authority for securing compliance with that sub-section, it shall be the duty of the authority to comply with the direction.

(4A) It shall be the duty of a waste collection authority in Greater London, before finally determining the content of the plan or a modification, to send a copy of it in draft to the Mayor of London.

(4B) It shall be the duty of the Mayor of London to consider the draft plan or modification sent to him under sub-s (4A) above and to give to the authority such directions as he considers necessary for securing compliance with sub-s (3) above.

(4C) Where the Mayor of London gives any direction to a waste collection authority under sub-s (4B) above, it shall be the duty of the authority to comply with the direction.

(5) When a waste collection authority has determined the content of the plan or a modification it shall be the duty of the authority–

  (a) to take such steps as in the opinion of the authority will give adequate publicity in its area to the plan or modification; and

  (b) to send to the waste disposal authority and waste regulation authority for the area which includes its area a copy of the plan or, as the case may be, particulars of the modification.

(6) It shall be the duty of each waste collection authority to keep a copy of the plan and particulars of any modifications to it available at all reasonable times at its principal offices for inspection by members of the public free of charge and to supply a copy of the plan and of the particulars of any modifications to it to any person who requests one, on payment by that person of such reasonable charge as the authority requires.

(7) The Secretary of State may give to any waste collection authority directions as to the time by which the authority is to perform any duty imposed by this section specified in the direction; and it shall be the duty of the authority to comply with the direction.

(7A) The Mayor of London may give to any waste collection authority in Greater London directions as to the time by which the authority is to perform any duty imposed by this section specified in the direction; and it shall be the duty of the authority to comply with the direction.

Note:

The above section is as amended by s 361 of the Greater London Authority Act 1999.

Section 52 Payments for recycling and disposal etc of waste

(1) Where, under s 48(2) above, a waste collection authority retains for recycling waste collected by it under s 45 above, the waste disposal authority for the area which includes the area of the waste collection authority shall make to that authority payments, in respect of the waste so retained, of such amounts representing its net saving of expenditure on the disposal of the waste as the authority determines.

(2) Where, by reason of the discharge by a waste disposal authority of its functions, waste arising in its area does not fall to be collected by a waste collection authority under s 45 above, the waste collection authority shall make to the waste disposal authority payments, in respect of the waste not falling to be so collected, of such amounts representing its net saving of expenditure on the collection of the waste as the authority determines.

(3) Where a person other than a waste collection authority, for the purpose of recycling it, collects waste arising in the area of a waste disposal authority which would fall to be collected under s 45 above, the waste disposal authority may make to that person payments, in respect of the waste so collected, of such amounts representing its net saving of expenditure on the disposal of the waste as the authority determines.

(4) Where a person other than a waste collection authority, for the purpose of recycling it, collects waste which would fall to be collected under s 45 above, the waste collection authority may make to that person payments, in respect of the waste so collected, of such amounts representing its net saving of expenditure on the collection of the waste as the authority determines.

(5) The Secretary of State may, by regulations, impose on waste disposal authorities a duty to make payments corresponding to the payments which are authorised by sub-s (3)

above to such persons in such circumstances and in respect of such descriptions or quantities of waste as are specified in the regulations.

[Sub-sections (6)–(11) omitted.]

[Section 53 (on Duties of Authorities as Respects Disposal of Waste Collected: Scotland) . omitted.]

[Section 54 (on Special Provisions for Land Occupied by Disposal Authorities: Scotland) omitted.]

Section 55 Powers for recycling waste

(1) This section has effect for conferring on waste disposal authorities and waste collection authorities powers for the purposes of recycling waste.

(2) A waste disposal authority may–

  (a) make arrangements with waste disposal contractors for them to recycle waste as respects which the authority has duties under s 51(1) above or agrees with another person for its disposal or treatment;

  (b) make arrangements with waste disposal contractors for them to use waste for the purpose of producing from it heat or electricity or both;

  (c) buy or otherwise acquire waste with a view to its being recycled;

  (d) use, sell or otherwise dispose of waste as respects which the authority has duties under s 51(1) above or anything produced from such waste.

(3) A waste collection authority may–

  (a) buy or otherwise acquire waste with a view to recycling it;

  (b) use, or dispose of by way of sale or otherwise to another person, waste belonging to the authority or anything produced from such waste.

(4) This section shall not apply to Scotland.

[Section 56 (on Powers for Recycling Waste: Scotland) omitted.]

[Section 57 (on Powers of Secretary of State to Require Waste to be Accepted, Treated, Disposed of or Delivered) omitted.]

[Section 58 (on Power of Secretary of State to Require Waste to be Accepted, Treated, Disposed of or Delivered: Scotland) omitted.]

[Section 60 (on Interference with Waste Sites and Receptacles for Waste) omitted.]

[Section 61 has been repealed.]

Special waste[38]

Section 62 Special provision with respect to certain dangerous or intractable waste

(1) If the Secretary of State considers that controlled waste of any kind is or may be so dangerous or difficult to treat, keep or dispose of that special provision is required for dealing with it he shall make provision by regulations for the treatment, keeping or disposal of waste of that kind ('special waste').

---

38 For definition, see p 420, above.

(2) Without prejudice to the generality of sub-s (1) above, the regulations may include provision–

    (a) for the giving of directions by waste regulation authorities with respect to matters connected with the treatment, keeping or disposal of special waste;

    (b) for securing that special waste is not, while awaiting treatment or disposal in pursuance of the regulations, kept at any one place in quantities greater than those which are prescribed and in circumstances which differ from those which are prescribed;

    (c) in connection with requirements imposed on consignors or consignees of special waste, imposing, in the event of non-compliance, requirements on any person carrying the consignment to re-deliver it as directed;

    (d) for requiring the occupier of premises on which special waste is situated to give notice of that fact and other prescribed information to a prescribed authority;

    (e) for the keeping of records by waste regulation authorities and by persons who import, export, produce, keep, treat or dispose of special waste or deliver it to another person for treatment or disposal, for the inspection of the records and for the furnishing by such persons to waste regulation authorities of copies of or information derived from the records;

    (f) for the keeping in the register under s 64(1) below of copies of such of those records, or such information derived from those records, as may be prescribed;

    (g) providing that a contravention of the regulations shall be an offence and prescribing the maximum penalty for the offence, which shall not exceed, on summary conviction, a fine at level 5 on the standard scale and, on conviction on indictment, imprisonment for a term of two years or a fine or both.

(3) Without prejudice to the generality of sub-s (1) above, the regulations may include provision–

    [(a) for the supervision by waste regulation authorities–

        (i) of activities authorised by virtue of the regulations or of activities by virtue of carrying on which persons are subject to provisions of the regulations; or

        (ii) of persons who carry on activities authorised by virtue of the regulations or who are subject to provisions of the regulations,and for the recovery from persons falling within sub-para (ii) above of the costs incurred by waste regulation authorities in performing functions conferred upon those authorities by the regulations;]

    (b) as to the recovery of expenses or other charges for the treatment, keeping or disposal or the re-delivery of special waste in pursuance of the regulations;

    (c) as to appeals to the Secretary of State from decisions of waste regulation authorities under the regulations.

[Sub-sections (3A)–(4) omitted.]

Note:

The current regulations made under this section are SI 1996/972. These discharge obligations under the Directive on Hazardous Waste 91/689 (p 420, above).

Section 63 Waste other than controlled waste

(1) The Secretary of State may, after consultation with such bodies as he considers appropriate, make regulations providing that prescribed provisions of this Part shall have effect in a prescribed area–

   (a) as if references in those provisions to controlled waste or controlled waste of a kind specified in the regulations included references to such waste as is mentioned in s 75(7)(c) below which is of a kind so specified; and

   (b) with such modifications as may be prescribed,

and the regulations may make such modifications of other enactments as the Secretary of State considers appropriate.

(2) A person who–

   (a) deposits any waste other than controlled waste; or

   (b) knowingly causes or knowingly permits the deposit of any waste other than controlled waste,

in a case where, if the waste were special waste and any waste management licence were not in force, he would be guilty of an offence under s 33 above shall, subject to sub-s (3) below, be guilty of that offence and punishable accordingly.

(2) A person who deposits, or knowingly causes or knowingly permits the deposit of, any waste–

   (a) which is not controlled waste; but

   (b) which, if it were controlled waste, would be special waste,

in a case where he would be guilty of an offence under s 33 above if the waste were special waste and any waste management licence were not in force, shall, subject to sub-s (3) below, be guilty of that offence and punishable as if the waste were special waste.

(3) No offence is committed by virtue of sub-s (2) above if the act charged was done under and in accordance with any consent, licence, approval or authority granted under any enactment (excluding any planning permission under the enactments relating to town and country planning).

(4) Section 45(2) and s 47(1) above shall apply to waste other than controlled waste as they apply to controlled waste.

Section 63A Power to take steps to minimise generation of controlled waste

(1) A relevant authority may do, or arrange for the doing of, or contribute towards the expenses of the doing of, anything which in its opinion is necessary or expedient for the purpose of minimising the quantities of controlled waste, or controlled waste of any description, generated in its area.

(2) Where a relevant authority in England ('the first authority') proposes to exercise any of its powers under sub-s (1), it shall before doing so consult about the proposal every other relevant authority whose area includes all or part of the area of the first authority.

(3) In this section 'relevant authority' means a waste collection authority or a waste disposal authority.

Note:

The above section was inserted by s 1 of the Waste Minimisation Act 1998 which entered into force on 19 November 1998.

Publicity

Section 64 Public registers

(1) Subject to ss 65 and 66 below, it shall be the duty of each waste regulation authority to maintain a register containing prescribed particulars of or relating to–

   (a) current or recently current licences ('licences') granted by the authority;

   (b) current or recently current applications to the authority for licences;

   (c) applications made to the authority under s 37 above for the modification of licences;

   (d notices issued by the authority under s 37 above effecting the modification of licences;

   (e) notices issued by the authority under s 38 above effecting the revocation or suspension of licences or imposing requirements on the holders of licences;

   (f) appeals under s 43 above relating to decisions of the authority;

   (g) certificates of completion issued by the authority under s 39(9) above;

   (h) notices issued by the authority imposing requirements on the holders of licences under s 42(5) above;

   (i) convictions of the holders of licences granted by the authority for any offence under this Part (whether in relation to a licence so granted or not);

   (j) the occasions on which the authority has discharged any function under s 42 or 61 above;

   (k) directions given to the authority under any provision of this Part by the Secretary of State;

   (l) ...

   (m) such matters relating to the treatment, keeping or disposal of waste in the area of the authority or any pollution of the environment caused thereby as may be prescribed,

and any other document or information required to be kept in the register under any provision of this Act.

(2) Where information of any description is excluded from any register by virtue of s 66 below, a statement shall be entered in the register indicating the existence of information of that description.

(2A) The Secretary of State may give to a waste regulation authority directions requiring the removal from any register of its of any specified information not prescribed for inclusion under sub-s (1) above or which, by virtue of s 65 or 66 below, ought to be excluded from the register.

[Sub-section (3) omitted.]

(4) It shall be the duty of each waste collection authority in England [or Wales] ... to maintain a register containing prescribed particulars of such information contained in any register maintained under sub-s (1) above as relates to the treatment, keeping or disposal of controlled waste in the area of the authority.

(5) The waste regulation authority in relation to England and Wales shall furnish any waste collection authorities in its area with the particulars necessary to enable them to discharge their duty under sub-s (4) above.

(6) Each waste regulation authority and waste collection authority–

(a) shall secure that any register maintained under this section is open to inspection ... by members of the public free of charge at all reasonable hours; and

(b) shall afford to members of the public reasonable facilities for obtaining, on payment of reasonable charges, copies of entries in the register;

and, for the purposes of this sub-section, places may be prescribed by the Secretary of State at which any such registers or facilities as are mentioned in para (a) or (b) above are to be available or afforded to the public in pursuance of the para in question.

(7) Registers under this section may be kept in any form.

(8) In this section 'prescribed' means prescribed in regulations by the Secretary of State.

Note:

The particulars to be entered into the public register are specified in regs 10 and 11 of the Waste Management Licensing Regulations 1994 SI 94/1056.

Section 65 Exclusion from registers of information affecting national security

(1) No information shall be included in a register maintained under s 64 above (a 'register') if and so long as, in the opinion of the Secretary of State, the inclusion in the register of that information, or information of that description, would be contrary to the interests of national security.

(2) The Secretary of State may, for the purpose of securing the exclusion from registers of information to which sub-s (1) above applies, give to the authorities maintaining registers directions–

(a) specifying information, or descriptions of information, to be excluded from their registers; or

(b) specifying descriptions of information to be referred to the Secretary of State for his determination,

and no information referred to the Secretary of State in pursuance of para (b) above shall be included in any such register until the Secretary of State determines that it should be so included.

(3) An authority maintaining a register shall notify the Secretary of State of any information it excludes from the register in pursuance of directions under sub-s (2) above.

(4) A person may, as respects any information which appears to him to be information to which sub-s (1) above may apply, give a notice to the Secretary of State specifying the information and indicating its apparent nature; and, if he does so–

(a) he shall notify the authority concerned that he has done so; and

(b) no information so notified to the Secretary of State shall be included in the register kept by that authority until the Secretary of State has determined that it should be so included.

Section 66 Exclusion from registers of certain confidential information

(1) No information relating to the affairs of any individual or business shall be included in a register maintained under s 64 above (a 'register'), without the consent of that individual or the person for the time being carrying on that business, if and so long as the information–

(a) is, in relation to him, commercially confidential; and

(b) is not required to be included in the register in pursuance of directions under sub-s (7) below,

but information is not commercially confidential for the purposes of this section unless it is determined under this section to be so by the authority maintaining the register or, on appeal, by the Secretary of State.

(2) Where information is furnished to an authority maintaining a register for the purpose of–

(a) an application for, or for the modification of, a licence;

(b) complying with any condition of a licence; or

(c) complying with a notice under s 71(2) below,

then, if the person furnishing it applies to the authority to have the information excluded from the register on the ground that it is commercially confidential (as regards himself or another person), the authority shall determine whether the information is or is not commercially confidential.

(3) A determination under sub-s (2) above must be made within the period of 14 days beginning with the date of the application and if the authority fails to make a determination within that period it shall be treated as having determined that the information is commercially confidential.

(4) Where it appears to an authority maintaining a register that any information (other than information furnished in circumstances within sub-s (2) above) which has been obtained by the authority under or by virtue of any provision of this Part might be commercially confidential, the authority shall–

(a) give to the person to whom or whose business it relates notice that that information is required to be included in the register unless excluded under this section; and

(b) give him a reasonable opportunity–

(i) of objecting to the inclusion of the information on the grounds that it is commercially confidential; and

(ii) of making representations to the authority for the purpose of justifying any such objection; and, if any representations are made, the authority shall, having taken the representations into account, determine whether the information is or is not commercially confidential.

(5) Where, under sub-s (2) or (4) above, an authority determines that information is not commercially confidential–

(a) the information shall not be entered in the register until the end of the period of 21 days beginning with the date on which the determination is notified to the person concerned;

(b) that person may appeal to the Secretary of State against the decision,

and, where an appeal is brought in respect of any information, the information shall not be entered in the register [until the end of the period of seven days following the day on which the appeal is finally determined or withdrawn].

(6) Sub-sections (2) and (8) of s 43 above shall apply in relation to appeals under sub-s (5) above as they apply in relation to appeals under that section; but

(a) sub-s (2)(c) of that section shall have effect for the purposes of this sub-section with the substitution for the words from 'which may' onwards of the words 'which must be held in private'; and

(b) sub-s (5) above is subject to s 114 of the Environment Act 1995 (delegation or reference of appeals etc).

(7) The Secretary of State may give to the authorities maintaining registers directions as to specified information, or descriptions of information, which the public interest requires to be included in the registers notwithstanding that the information may be commercially confidential.

(8) Information excluded from a register shall be treated as ceasing to be commercially confidential for the purposes of this section at the expiry of the period of four years beginning with the date of the determination by virtue of which it was excluded; but the person who furnished it may apply to the authority for the information to remain excluded from the register on the ground that it is still commercially confidential and the authority shall determine whether or not that is the case.

(9) Sub-sections (5) and (6) above shall apply in relation to a determination under sub-s (8) above as they apply in relation to a determination under sub-s (2) or (4) above.

(10) The Secretary of State may, by order, substitute for the period for the time being specified in sub-s (3) above such other period as he considers appropriate.

(11) Information is, for the purposes of any determination under this section, commercially confidential, in relation to any individual or person, if its being contained in the register would prejudice to an unreasonable degree the commercial interests of that individual or person.

Section 71 Obtaining of information from persons and authorities

(1) ...

(2) For the purpose of the discharge of their respective functions under this Part–

(a) the Secretary of State; and

(b) a waste regulation authority, may, by notice in writing served on him, require any person to furnish such information specified in the notice as the Secretary of State or the authority, as the case may be, reasonably considers he or it needs, in such form and within such period following service of the notice [or at such time,] as is so specified.

(3) A person who–

(a) fails, without reasonable excuse, to comply with a requirement imposed under sub-s (2) above; ...

(b) ...

shall be liable–

(i) on summary conviction, to a fine not exceeding the statutory maximum;

(ii) on conviction on indictment, to a fine or to imprisonment for a term not exceeding two years, or to both.

Note:

In *R v Hertfordshire County Council ex p Green Environmental Industries and Another* [2000] 1 All ER 773 those served with a notice seeking information under s 71(2) unsuccessfully challenged the validity of the above section on grounds that it is incompatible with the principle against self-incrimination contained in Art 6 of the European Convention for the Protection of Human Rights and Fundamental Freedoms. See further Chapter 7, pp 873–34. See also *Environment Agency v Steve Parr Haulage Ltd* [2000] Env LR 700. For a comment see: Angela Ward, 'European prohibitions on self-incrimination: can they thwart the enforcement of environmental standards?' [2000] 4 Env Liability 103–05.

Contaminated land

The DETR describes contaminated land 'as an archetypal example of our failure in the past to move towards sustainable development'. (Annex 1, para 2 of the Circular, below). The first priority of Government policy is said to be to prevent further contamination by means of regimes such as those concerned with Integrated Pollution Control, Pollution Prevention and Control and Waste Management Licensing. Land that is already contaminated must also be dealt with. It was estimated that in 1993 there were between 50,000 and 100,000 potentially contaminated sites in the UK (Parliamentary Office of Science and Technology Report, *Contaminated Land*). The Environment Agency has estimated that there may be some 300,000 hectares of land in the UK affected by contamination. Government policy is therefore: (a) to identify and remove unacceptable risks to human health and the environment; (b) to seek to bring damaged land back to beneficial use; and (c) to seek to ensure that the costs burdens are proportionate, manageable and economically sustainable. These three objectives underlie what is described as the 'suitable for use' approach. This approach recognises that risks presented by levels of contamination will vary greatly according to the use of the land and factors such as the underlying geology of the site (see further Annex 1 of the Circular, below).

New contaminated land legislation came into force in England on 1 April 2000. The new regime seeks to improve the system for the identification of contaminated land and its remediation. The regime applies to land causing unacceptable risks to human health or the wider environment, assessed in the context of the current use and circumstances of the land. The new legislation is contained in Pt 11A of the Environmental Protection Act 1990 which is inserted by s 57 of the Environment Act 1995. The DETR Circular 02/2000 (the Circular) includes a statement of government policy, a description of the new laws and the statutory guidance on their operation. The Contaminated Land (England)

Regulations 2000 SI 2000/227 (the Regulations) deal with various procedural details, remediation notices and appeals.

The new regime provides, for the first time, an explicit definition of contaminated land, focussing on risks arising from the land in the context of its current use. It places specific duties on local authorities to inspect their areas to identify contaminated land. Where such land is identified local authorities are obliged to require its remediation in line with the 'suitable for use' approach. The regime also provides rules for assigning liabilities for contaminated land, based on the 'polluter pays' principle. Local authorities are required to publish a strategy for inspecting their area by July 2001. The Environment Agency is responsible for providing advice to local authorities on specific sites, dealing with 'special sites', and monitoring and reporting on progress. Local authorities and the Environment Agency must record prescribed information about their actions on a public register.

The current provisions are the product of a review process which led to the publication in November 1994 of *Framework for Contaminated Land* (covering England & Wales) and *Contaminated Land Clean-Up and Control: Outcome of Review* (dealing with Scotland) (for a fuller discussion of the policy background to these provisions see the Commentary to the Environment Act 1995, *Current Law Statutes*, by Tromans, Nash and Poustie (1995) 25, pp 132–33).

The scheme of the provisions

The following overview draws on the above commentary. The provisions follow a sequence from identification of contaminated land through to securing its remediation. Primary responsibility for this process rests with district councils and unitary authorities, although both the Environment Agency/SEPA and the Secretary of State play important roles.

Identification of contaminated land

In s 78A(2) EPA 'contaminated land' is defined as 'any land which appears to the local authority in whose area it is situated to be in such a condition, by reason of substances in, on or under the land, that (a) significant harm is being caused or there is a significant possibility of such harm being caused; or (b) pollution of controlled waters is being, or is likely to be, caused'. Here much depends on the subjective views of the local authority. However, authorities must 'act in accordance with guidance issued by the Secretary of State' (s 78A(2)). Chapters A and B of Annex 3 to the Circular deals with the meaning and identification of contaminated land.

Local authorities are under a duty (s 78B) to inspect their area 'from time to time for the purpose (a) of identifying contaminated land; and (b) of enabling the authority to decide whether any such land is land which is required to be designated as a special site'.

Notification that land is contaminated

Once land has been identified as contaminated the local authority (s 78B(3)) 'shall give notice of that fact to (a) the appropriate Agency; (b) the owner of the land; (c) any person who appears to the authority to be in occupation of the whole or any part of the land; and (d) each person who appears to the authority to be an appropriate person (a person who is determined as being appropriate to "bear responsibility for any thing which is to be done by way of remediation in any particular case"' (ss 78A(9)and 78F).

Special sites

As well as identifying contaminated land local authorities must also decide whether the land is to be designated as a 'special site' (s 78C; for the definition of special sites, see s 78A(3)). Where land is a special site the enforcing authority is the Environment Agency/SEPA rather than the local authority. Before making this decision local authorities must seek and consider the advice of the Agency/SEPA. The Agency/SEPA may also consider that land should be a special site and may give local authorities notice of this. Disagreements between authorities and the Agency/SEPA are resolved by the Secretary of State (ss 78D, 78Q).

Duty to require remediation

Where land has been designated as a special site or as contaminated land the enforcing authority has a duty to serve on the 'appropriate person' a 'remediation notice' specifying what is to be done by way of remediation and within what period (s 78E(1)). Remediation notices cannot be served in circumstances that are covered by existing regulatory controls (s 78YB) . Thus they cannot be served where the situation is amenable to the IPPC system, where the activity is controlled by a waste management licence; covered by a discharge consent under the Water Resources Act 1991; or where the contamination is caused by radioactivity. See Chapter C of Annex 3 to the Circular.

Who is responsible for complying with a remedial notice?

Section 78F deals with the question of who has responsibility for complying with a remedial notice. This important and controversial provision places primary responsibility on those who caused or knowingly permitted the contaminating substances to be in, on or under the land (s 78F(2)). However, the current owner or occupier may also be liable where those originally responsible for the contamination cannot be found (s 78F(4) and (5)). Where a number of persons have contributed to the contamination there may be joint and several liability (s 78(F)(7)). However, the remedial action to be taken must be 'referable' to the substances that the person has contributed (s 78F(3)). Section 78K deals with situations where substances have migrated from their original source to contaminate other land. See Chapter D of Annex 3 to the Circular.

Consultation

Enforcing authorities are required to use reasonable endeavours to consult about the remediation work with the person who appears to be the responsible person and with the owner and the occupier of the land. No remediation notice may be served during a three month period from the date of the original notification that the land is regarded as being contaminated or is designated as a special site (s 78H(1)).

Appeals against remediation notices

Those served with a remediation notice may appeal. Where the notice is served by a local authority the appeal is to the magistrates' court (or in Scotland, the Sheriff). Where the notice has been served by the Agency/SEPA the appeal is to the Secretary of State (s 78L). The grounds of appeal are set out in regs 7–14 of the Contaminated Land Regulations.

Offences

Failure, without reasonable excuse, to comply with the requirements of a remediation notice is an offence (s 78M(1)). The offence is punishable on summary conviction only, by a maximum fine of £5,000 and a further fine of £500 per day for which the failure continues after conviction. Where the contaminated land in question is 'industrial, trade or business premises' the figures are £20,000 and £2,000.

Default powers

Enforcing authorities have power to carry out remediation work in certain situations. These include: where the enforcing authority considers it necessary to do the remediation work to prevent serious harm, or serious pollution of controlled waters, of which there is imminent danger; where an appropriate person has entered into a written agreement with the enforcing authority for that authority to do the work; where a person on whom the enforcing authority serves a remediation notice fails to comply with any of the requirements of the notice (s 78N).

Section 78P sets out situations where the authority is entitled to recover its reasonable costs of carrying the work. This provision is said to provide the 'teeth' to powers in s 78N (Tromans, Nash and Poustie (1995) 25–175).

Registers

Section 78R requires enforcing authorities to keep registers containing, for example, remediation notices served by the authority, appeals against these notices, convictions for failure to comply with a notice. Authorities have a duty to ensure that registers are available for public inspection at all reasonable times free of charge, and to allow copies of entries to be made on payment of reasonable charges (s 78R(8)).

Section 78A Preliminary

(1) The following provisions have effect for the interpretation of this Part.

(2) 'Contaminated land' is any land which appears to the local authority in whose area it is situated to be in such a condition, by reason of substances in, on or under the land, that–

    (a) significant harm is being caused or there is a significant possibility of such harm being caused; or

    (b) pollution of controlled waters is being, or is likely to be, caused,

and, in determining whether any land appears to be such land, a local authority shall, subject to sub-s (5) below, act in accordance with guidance issued by the Secretary of

State in accordance with s 78YA below with respect to the manner in which that determination is to be made.

(3) A 'special site' is any contaminated land–

    (a) which has been designated as such a site by virtue of s 78C(7) or 78D(6) below; and

    (b) whose designation as such has not been terminated by the appropriate Agency under s 78Q(4) below.

(4) 'Harm' means harm to the health of living organisms or other interference with the ecological systems of which they form part and, in the case of man, includes harm to his property.

(5) The questions–

    (a) what harm is to be regarded as 'significant';

    (b) whether the possibility of significant harm being caused is 'significant';

    (c) whether pollution of controlled waters is being, or is likely to be caused,

shall be determined in accordance with guidance issued for the purpose by the Secretary of State in accordance with s 78YA below.

[Sub-section (6) omitted.]

(7) 'Remediation' means–

    (a) the doing of anything for the purpose of assessing the condition of–

        (i) the contaminated land in question;

        (ii) any controlled waters affected by that land; or

        (iii) any land adjoining or adjacent to that land;

    (b) the doing of any works, the carrying out of any operations or the taking of any steps in relation to any such land or waters for the purpose–

        (i) of preventing or minimising, or remedying or mitigating the effects of, any significant harm, or any pollution of controlled waters, by reason of which the contaminated land is such land; or

        (ii) of restoring the land or waters to their former state; or

    (c) the making of subsequent inspections from time to time for the purpose of keeping under review the condition of the land or waters,

and cognate expressions shall be construed accordingly.

[Sub-section (8) omitted.]

(9) The following expressions have the meaning respectively assigned to them–

'the appropriate Agency' means–

    (a) in relation to England and Wales, the Environment Agency;

    (b) in relation to Scotland, the Scottish Environment Protection Agency;

'appropriate person' means any person who is an appropriate person, determined in accordance with s 78F below, to bear responsibility for any thing which is to be done by way of remediation in any particular case;

[...]

'enforcing authority' means–

    (a) in relation to a special site, the appropriate Agency;

(b) in relation to contaminated land other than a special site, the local authority in whose area the land is situated;

[...]

Section 78B Identification of contaminated land

(1) Every local authority shall cause its area to be inspected from time to time for the purpose–

    (a) of identifying contaminated land; and

    (b) of enabling the authority to decide whether any such land is land which is required to be designated as a special site.

(2) In performing its functions under sub-s (1) above a local authority shall act in accordance with any guidance issued for the purpose by the Secretary of State in accordance with s 78YA below.

(3) If a local authority identifies any contaminated land in its area, it shall give notice of that fact to–

    (a) the appropriate Agency;

    (b) the owner of the land;

    (c) any person who appears to the authority to be in occupation of the whole or any part of the land; and

    (d) each person who appears to the authority to be an appropriate person,

and any notice given under this sub-s shall state by virtue of which of paras (a) to (d) above it is given.

(4) If, at any time after a local authority has given any person a notice pursuant to sub-s (3)(d) above in respect of any land, it appears to the enforcing authority that another person is an appropriate person, the enforcing authority shall give notice to that other person–

    (a) of the fact that the local authority has identified the land in question as contaminated land; and

    (b) that he appears to the enforcing authority to be an appropriate person.

Section 78C Identification and designation of special sites

(1) If at any time it appears to a local authority that any contaminated land in its area might be land which is required to be designated as a special site, the authority–

    (a) shall decide whether or not the land is land which is required to be so designated; and

    (b) if the authority decides that the land is land which is required to be so designated, shall give notice of that decision to the relevant persons.

(2) For the purposes of this section, 'the relevant persons' at any time in the case of any land are the persons who at that time fall within paras (a) to (d) below, that is to say–

    (a) the appropriate Agency;

    (b) the owner of the land;

    (c) any person who appears to the local authority concerned to be in occupation of the whole or any part of the land; and

    (d) each person who appears to that authority to be an appropriate person.

(3) Before making a decision under para (a) of sub-s (1) above in any particular case, a local authority shall request the advice of the appropriate Agency, and in making its decision shall have regard to any advice given by that Agency in response to the request.

(4) If at any time the appropriate Agency considers that any contaminated land is land which is required to be designated as a special site, that Agency may give notice of that fact to the local authority in whose area the land is situated.

[Sub-sections (5)–(10) omitted.]

[Section 78D (on Referral of Special Site Decisions to the Secretary of State) omitted.]

Section 78E Duty of enforcing authority to require remediation of contaminated land etc

(1) In any case where–

 (a) any land has been designated as a special site [...]; or

 (b) a local authority has identified any contaminated land (other than a special site) in its area,

 the enforcing authority shall, in accordance with such procedure as may be prescribed and subject to the following provisions of this Part, serve on each person who is an appropriate person a notice (in this Part referred to as a 'remediation notice') specifying what that person is to do by way of remediation and the periods within which he is required to do each of the things so specified.

(2) Different remediation notices requiring the doing of different things by way of remediation may be served on different persons in consequence of the presence of different substances in, on or under any land or waters.

(3) Where two or more persons are appropriate persons in relation to any particular thing which is to be done by way of remediation, the remediation notice served on each of them shall state the proportion, determined under s 78F(7) below, of the cost of doing that thing which each of them respectively is liable to bear.

(4) The only things by way of remediation which the enforcing authority may do, or require to be done, under or by virtue of this Part are things which it considers reasonable, having regard to:

 (a) the cost which is likely to be involved; and

 (b) the seriousness of the harm, or pollution of controlled waters, in question.

(5) In determining for any purpose of this Part–

 (a) what is to be done (whether by an appropriate person, the enforcing authority or any other person) by way of remediation in any particular case;

 (b) the standard to which any land is, or waters are, to be remediated pursuant to the notice; or

 (c) what is, or is not, to be regarded as reasonable for the purposes of sub-s (4) above,

 the enforcing authority shall have regard to any guidance issued for the purpose by the Secretary of State.

(6) Regulations may make provision for or in connection with–

 (a) the form or content of remediation notices; or

 (b) any steps of a procedural nature which are to be taken in connection with, or in consequence of, the service of a remediation notice.

Section 78F Determination of the appropriate person to bear responsibility for remediation

(1) This section has effect for the purpose of determining who is the appropriate person to bear responsibility for any particular thing which the enforcing authority determines is to be done by way of remediation in any particular case.

(2) Subject to the following provisions of this section, any person, or any of the persons, who caused or knowingly permitted the substances, or any of the substances, by reason of which the contaminated land in question is such land to be in, on or under that land is an appropriate person.

(3) A person shall only be an appropriate person by virtue of sub-s (2) above in relation to things which are to be done by way of remediation which are to any extent referable to substances which he caused or knowingly permitted to be present in, on or under the contaminated land in question.

(4) If no person has, after reasonable inquiry, been found who is by virtue of sub-s (2) above an appropriate person to bear responsibility for the things which are to be done by way of remediation, the owner or occupier for the time being of the contaminated land in question is an appropriate person.

(5) If, in consequence of sub-s (3) above, there are things which are to be done by way of remediation in relation to which no person has, after reasonable inquiry, been found who is an appropriate person by virtue of sub-s (2) above, the owner or occupier for the time being of the contaminated land in question is an appropriate person in relation to those things.

(6) Where two or more persons would, apart from this sub-section, be appropriate persons in relation to any particular thing which is to be done by way of remediation, the enforcing authority shall determine in accordance with guidance issued for the purpose by the Secretary of State whether any, and if so which, of them is to be treated as not being an appropriate person in relation to that thing.

(7) Where two or more persons are appropriate persons in relation to any particular thing which is to be done by way of remediation, they shall be liable to bear the cost of doing that thing in proportions determined by the enforcing authority in accordance with guidance issued for the purpose by the Secretary of State.

(8) Any guidance issued for the purposes of sub-s (6) or (7) above shall be issued in accordance with s 78YA below.

(9) A person who has caused or knowingly permitted any substance ('substance A') to be in, on or under any land shall also be taken for the purposes of this section to have caused or knowingly permitted there to be in, on or under that land any substance which is there as a result of a chemical reaction or biological process affecting substance A.

(10) A thing which is to be done by way of remediation may be regarded for the purposes of this Part as referable to the presence of any substance notwithstanding that the thing in question would not have to be done–

(a) in consequence only of the presence of that substance in any quantity; or

(b) in consequence only of the quantity of that substance which any particular person caused or knowingly permitted to be present.

Notes:

1 On the meaning of 'caused' in s 78F(2), see discussion in Chapter 3, pp 299–301, above.

2 In their commentary to the legislation, S Tromans, M Nash and M Poustie ask: what must be known? They draw attention to the difference between knowing that a substance is present on, or is being introduced into land and in addition knowing that the substance will contaminate the land. Will a person be an 'appropriate person' if they know that a substance (which in fact is a contaminant) is being put into the land even though they do not know that it is a contaminant, or must they also know that the substance will contaminate the land? It seems that the position is as yet unclear.

3 On what constitutes 'knowledge', see *Schulmans Incorporated v National Rivers Authority* [1993] Env LRD 1 (discussed in Chapter 3, p 301, above).

Section 78G Grant of, and compensation for, rights of entry etc

(1) A remediation notice may require an appropriate person to do things by way of remediation, notwithstanding that he is not entitled to do those things.

(2) Any person whose consent is required before any thing required by a remediation notice may be done shall grant, or join in granting, such rights in relation to any of the relevant land or waters as will enable the appropriate person to comply with any requirements imposed by the remediation notice.

(3) Before serving a remediation notice, the enforcing authority shall reasonably endeavour to consult every person who appears to the authority–

(a) to be the owner or occupier of any of the relevant land or waters; and

(b) to be a person who might be required by sub-s (2) above to grant, or join in granting, any rights,

concerning the rights which that person may be so required to grant.

(4) Sub-section (3) above shall not preclude the service of a remediation notice in any case where it appears to the enforcing authority that the contaminated land in question is in such a condition, by reason of substances in, on or under the land, that there is imminent danger of serious harm, or serious pollution of controlled waters, being caused.

(5) A person who grants, or joins in granting, any rights pursuant to sub-s (2) above shall be entitled ... to be paid by the appropriate person compensation of such amount as may be determined in such manner as may be prescribed.

Sub-section (6) omitted.]

(7) In this section, 'relevant land or waters' means–

(a) the contaminated land in question;

(b) any controlled waters affected by that land; or

(c) any land adjoining or adjacent to that land or those waters.

Note:

This section concerns the situation where the appropriate person has no right to carry out the remedial work where, for example, he no longer owns the land or the works involve working on someone else's land. Those whose consent is required for the work to be done are obliged by sub-s (2) to grant such rights as are necessary. There is provision for advance consultation and for the payment of compensation by the appropriate person (sub-s (5)).

Section 78H Restrictions and prohibitions on serving remediation notices

(1) Before serving a remediation notice, the enforcing authority shall reasonably endeavour to consult–

    (a) the person on whom the notice is to be served;

    (b) the owner of any land to which the notice relates;

    (c) any person who appears to that authority to be in occupation of the whole or any part of the land; and

    (d) any person of such other description as may be prescribed,

concerning what is to be done by way of remediation.

(2) Regulations may make provision for, or in connection with, steps to be taken for the purposes of sub-s (1) above.

[Sub-sections (3) and (4) omitted. These provisions prevent the serving of a remediation notice during a period starting with the date of identification of land as contaminated until three months after notification under s 78B or notification that the land has been designated as a special site under sub-ss 78C(3) or 78D(3). These provisions apply unless it appears to the authority that the land presents a risk of imminent danger of serious land or serious water pollution.]

(5) In any case where–

    (a) a person ('person A') has caused or knowingly permitted any substances to be in, on, or under any land;

    (b) another person ('person B') who has not caused or knowingly permitted those substances to be in, on or under that land becomes the owner or occupier of that land; and

    (c) the substances, or any of the substances, mentioned in para (a) above appear to have escaped to other land,

no remediation notice shall require person B to do anything by way of remediation to that other land in consequence of the apparent acts or omissions of person A, except to the extent that person B caused or knowingly permitted the escape.

[Sub-sections (6)–(10) omitted.]

[Section 78 (on Restrictions on Liability Relating to the Pollution of Controlled Waters) omitted.]

Section 78K Liability in respect of contaminating substances which escape to other land

(1) A person who has caused or knowingly permitted any substances to be in, on or under any land shall also be taken for the purposes of this Part to have caused or, as the case

may be, knowingly permitted those substances to be in, on or under any other land to which they appear to have escaped.

(2) Sub-sections (3) and (4) below apply in any case where it appears that any substances are or have been in, on or under any land (in this section referred to as 'land A') as a result of their escape, whether directly or indirectly, from other land in, on or under which a person caused or knowingly permitted them to be.

(3) Where this sub-section applies, no remediation notice shall require a person–

  (a) who is the owner or occupier of land A; and

  (b) who has not caused or knowingly permitted the substances in question to be in, on or under that land,

to do anything by way of remediation to any land or waters (other than land or waters of which he is the owner or occupier) in consequence of land A appearing to be in such a condition, by reason of the presence of those substances in, on or under it, that significant harm is being caused, or there is a significant possibility of such harm being caused, or that pollution of controlled waters is being, or is likely to be caused.

(4) Where this sub-section applies, no remediation notice shall require a person–

  (a) who is the owner or occupier of land A; and

  (b) who has not caused or knowingly permitted the substances in question to be in, on or under that land, to do anything by way of remediation in consequence of any further land in, on or under which those substances or any of them appear to be or to have been present as a result of their escape from land A ('land B') appearing to be in such a condition; by reason of the presence of those substances in, on or under it, that significant harm is being caused, or there is a significant possibility of such harm being caused, or that pollution of controlled waters is being, or is likely to be caused, unless he is also the owner or occupier of land B.

(5) In any case where–

  (a) a person ('person A') has caused or knowingly permitted any substances to be in, on, or under any land;

  (b) another person ('person B') who has not caused or knowingly permitted those substances to be in, on or under that land becomes the owner or occupier of that land; and

  (c) the substances, or any of the substances, mentioned in para (a) above appear to have escaped to other land,

no remediation notice shall require person B to do anything by way of remediation to that other land in consequence of the apparent acts or omissions of person A, except to the extent that person B caused or knowingly permitted the escape.

(6) Nothing in sub-s (3), (4) or (5) above prevents the enforcing authority from doing anything by way of remediation under s 78N below which it could have done apart from that sub-section, but the authority shall not be entitled under s 78P below to recover from any person any part of the cost incurred by the authority in doing by way of remediation anything which it is precluded by sub-s (3), (4) or (5) above from requiring that person to do.

(7) In this section, 'appear' means appear to the enforcing authority, and cognate expressions shall be construed accordingly.

Note:

The consequence of this provision (see Hughes (1996) 437–38) is that where pollution escapes from land to other land (land A) the original polluter will be liable for all remediation costs. The innocent owners of land A (and other 'knock-on sites') will only be liable for the clean-up costs of their own sites if the original polluter cannot be found. The enforcing authority may enter land A and exercise its powers under s 78N to remediate the land.

Section 78L Appeals against remediation notices

(1) A person on whom a remediation notice is served may, within the period of 21 days beginning with the day on which the notice is served, appeal against the notice–

    (a) if it was served by a local authority, to a magistrates' court or, in Scotland, to the sheriff by way of summary application; or

    (b) if it was served by the appropriate Agency, to the Secretary of State;

    [...]

(2) On any appeal under sub-s (1) above the appellate authority–

    (a) shall quash the notice, if it is satisfied that there is a material defect in the notice; but

    (b) subject to that, may confirm the remediation notice, with or without modification, or quash it.

(3) Where an appellate authority confirms a remediation notice, with or without modification, it may extend the period specified in the notice for doing what the notice requires to be done.

[Sub-sections (4)–(6) omitted.]

[Section 78M providing that it is an offence to fail without reasonable excuse to comply with any of the requirements of a remediation notice, omitted.]

Section 78N Powers of the enforcing authority to carry out remediation

(1) Where this section applies, the enforcing authority shall itself have power, in a case falling within para (a) or (b) of s 78E(1) above, to do what is appropriate by way of remediation to the relevant land or waters.

(2) Sub-section (1) above shall not confer power on the enforcing authority to do anything by way of remediation if the authority would, in the particular case, be precluded by s 78YB below from serving a remediation notice requiring that thing to be done.

(3) This section applies in each of the following cases, that is to say–

    (a) where the enforcing authority considers it necessary to do anything itself by way of remediation for the purpose of preventing the occurrence of any serious harm, or serious pollution of controlled waters, of which there is imminent danger;

    (b) where an appropriate person has entered into a written agreement with the enforcing authority for that authority to do, at the cost of that person, that which he would otherwise be required to do under this Part by way of remediation;

    (c) where a person on whom the enforcing authority serves a remediation notice fails to comply with any of the requirements of the notice;

(d) where the enforcing authority is precluded by s78J or 78K above from including something by way of remediation in a remediation notice,

where the enforcing authority considers that, were it to do some particular thing by way of remediation, it would decide, by virtue of sub-s (2) of s 78P below or any guidance issued under that sub-s–

(i) not to seek to recover under sub-s (1) of that section any of the reasonable cost incurred by it in doing that thing; or

(ii) to seek so to recover only a portion of that cost;

(f) where no person has, after reasonable inquiry, been found who is an appropriate person in relation to any particular thing.

(4) Subject to s 78E(4) and (5) above, for the purposes of this section, the things which it is appropriate for the enforcing authority to do by way of remediation are–

(a) in a case falling within para (a) of sub-s (3) above, anything by way of remediation which the enforcing authority considers necessary for the purpose mentioned in that para;

(b) in a case falling within para (b) of that sub-s, anything specified in, or determined under, the agreement mentioned in that para;

(c) in a case falling within para (c) of that sub-s, anything which the person mentioned in that paragraph was required to do by virtue of the remediation notice;

(d) in a case falling within para (d) of that sub-section, anything by way of remediation which the enforcing authority is precluded by s 78J or 78K above from including in a remediation notice;

(e) in a case falling within para (e) or (f) of that sub-section, the particular thing mentioned in the paragraph in question.

(5) In this section 'the relevant land or waters' means–

(a) the contaminated land in question;

(b) any controlled waters affected by that land; or

(c) any land adjoining or adjacent to that land or those waters.

Section 78P Recovery of, and security for, the cost of remediation by the enforcing authority

(1) Where, by virtue of s 78N(3)(a), (c), (e) or (f) above, the enforcing authority does any particular thing by way of remediation, it shall be entitled, subject to ss 78J(7) and 78K(6) above, to recover the reasonable cost incurred in doing it from the appropriate person or, if there are two or more appropriate persons in relation to the thing in question, from those persons in proportions determined pursuant to s 78F(7) above.

(2) In deciding whether to recover the cost, and, if so, how much of the cost, which it is entitled to recover under sub-s (1) above, the enforcing authority shall have regard–

(a) to any hardship which the recovery may cause to the person from whom the cost is recoverable; and

(b) to any guidance issued by the Secretary of State for the purposes of this sub-section.

(3) Sub-section (4) below shall apply in any case where–

(a) any cost is recoverable under sub-s (1) above from a person–

(i) who is the owner of any premises which consist of or include the contaminated land in question; and

(ii) who caused or knowingly permitted the substances, or any of the substances, by reason of which the land is contaminated land to be in, on or under the land; and

(b) the enforcing authority serves a notice under this sub-section (in this Part referred to as a 'charging notice') on that person.

(4) Where this sub-section applies–

(a) the cost shall carry interest, at such reasonable rate as the enforcing authority may determine, from the date of service of the notice until the whole amount is paid; and

(b) subject to the following provisions of this section, the cost and accrued interest shall be a charge on the premises mentioned in sub-s (3)(a)(i) above.

(5) A charging notice shall–

(a) specify the amount of the cost which the enforcing authority claims is recoverable;

(b) state the effect of sub-s (4) above and the rate of interest determined by the authority under that sub-section; and

(c) state the effect of sub-ss (7) and (8) below.

(6) On the date on which an enforcing authority serves a charging notice on a person, the authority shall also serve a copy of the notice on every other person who, to the knowledge of the authority, has an interest in the premises capable of being affected by the charge.

(7) Subject to any order under sub-s (9)(b) or (c) below, the amount of any cost specified in a charging notice and the accrued interest shall be a charge on the premises–

(a) as from the end of the period of 21 days beginning with the service of the charging notice; or

(b) where an appeal is brought under sub-s (8) below, as from the final determination or (as the case may be) the withdrawal, of the appeal, until the cost and interest are recovered.

(8) A person served with a charging notice or a copy of a charging notice may appeal against the notice to a county court within the period of 21 days beginning with the date of service.

(9) On an appeal under sub-s (8) above, the court may–

(a) confirm the notice without modification;

(b) order that the notice is to have effect with the substitution of a different amount for the amount originally specified in it; or

(c) order that the notice is to be of no effect.

(10) Regulations may make provision with respect to–

(a) the grounds on which appeals under this section may be made; or

(b) the procedure on any such appeal.

(11) An enforcing authority shall, for the purpose of enforcing a charge under this section, have all the same powers and remedies under the Law of Property Act 1925, and

otherwise, as if it were a mortgagee by deed having powers of sale and lease, of accepting surrenders of leases and of appointing a receiver.

(12) Where any cost is a charge on premises under this section, the enforcing authority may by order declare the cost to be payable with interest by instalments within the specified period until the whole amount is paid.

(13) In sub-s (12) above–

'interest' means interest at the rate determined by the enforcing authority under sub-s (4) above; and

'the specified period' means such period of 30 years or less from the date of service of the charging notice as is specified in the order.

(14) Sub-sections (3) to (13) above do not extend to Scotland.

[Section 78Q which deals specifically with special sites omitted.]

Section 78R Registers

(1) Every enforcing authority shall maintain a register containing prescribed particulars of or relating to–

(a) remediation notices served by that authority;

(b) appeals against any such remediation notices;

(c) remediation statements or remediation declarations prepared and published under s 78H above;

(d) in relation to an enforcing authority in England and Wales, appeals against charging notices served by that authority;

(e) notices under sub-s (1)(b) or (5)(a) of s 78C above which have effect by virtue of sub-s (7) of that section as the designation of any land as a special site;

(f) notices under sub-s (4)(b) of section 78D above which have effect by virtue of sub-s (6) of that section as the designation of any land as a special site;

(g) notices given by or to the enforcing authority under section 78Q(4) above terminating the designation of any land as a special site;

(h) notifications given to that authority by persons–

(i) on whom a remediation notice has been served; or

(ii) who are or were required by virtue of s 78H(8)(a) above to prepare and publish a remediation statement, of what they claim has been done by them by way of remediation;

(j) notifications given to that authority by owners or occupiers of land–

(i) in respect of which a remediation notice has been served; or

(ii) in respect of which a remediation statement has been prepared and published,

of what they claim has been done on the land in question by way of remediation;

(k) convictions for such offences under s 78M above as may be prescribed;

(l) such other matters relating to contaminated land as may be prescribed;

but that duty is subject to ss 78S and 78T below.

(2) The form of, and the descriptions of information to be contained in, notifications for the purposes of sub-s (1)(h) or (j) above may be prescribed by the Secretary of State.

[Sub-sections (3)–(6) omitted.]

(7) Where information of any description is excluded by virtue of s 78T below from any register maintained under this section, a statement shall be entered in the register indicating the existence of information of that description.

(8) It shall be the duty of each enforcing authority–

(a) to secure that the registers maintained by it under this section are available, at all reasonable times, for inspection by the public free of charge; and

(b) to afford to members of the public facilities for obtaining copies of entries, on payment of reasonable charges,

and, for the purposes of this sub-section, places may be prescribed by the Secretary of State at which any such registers or facilities as are mentioned in para (a) or (b) above are to be available or afforded to the public in pursuance of the paragraph in question.

(9) Registers under this section may be kept in any form.

Section 78S Exclusion from registers of information affecting national security

(1) No information shall be included in a register maintained under section 78R above if and so long as, in the opinion of the Secretary of State, the inclusion in the register of that information, or information of that description, would be contrary to the interests of national security.

(2) The Secretary of State may, for the purpose of securing the exclusion from registers of information to which sub-s (1) above applies, give to enforcing authorities directions–

(a) specifying information, or descriptions of information, to be excluded from their registers; or

(b) specifying descriptions of information to be referred to the Secretary of State for his determination,

and no information referred to the Secretary of State in pursuance of para (b) above shall be included in any such register until the Secretary of State determines that it should be so included.

(3) The enforcing authority shall notify the Secretary of State of any information which it excludes from the register in pursuance of directions under sub-s (2) above.

(4) A person may, as respects any information which appears to him to be information to which sub-s (1) above may apply, give a notice to the Secretary of State specifying the information and indicating its apparent nature; and, if he does so–

(a) he shall notify the enforcing authority that he has done so; and

(b) no information so notified to the Secretary of State shall be included in any such register until the Secretary of State has determined that it should be so included.

Section 78T Exclusion from registers of certain confidential information

(1) No information relating to the affairs of any individual or business shall be included in a register maintained under s 78R above, without the consent of that individual or the person for the time being carrying on that business, if and so long as the information–

(a) is, in relation to him, commercially confidential; and

(b) is not required to be included in the register in pursuance of directions under sub-s (7) below; but information is not commercially confidential for the purposes of this section unless it is determined under this section to be so by the enforcing authority or, on appeal, by the Secretary of State.

(2) Where it appears to an enforcing authority that any information which has been obtained by the authority under or by virtue of any provision of this Part might be commercially confidential, the authority shall–

    (a) give to the person to whom or whose business it relates notice that that information is required to be included in the register unless excluded under this section; and

    (b) give him a reasonable opportunity–

        (i) of objecting to the inclusion of the information on the ground that it is commercially confidential; and

        (ii) of making representations to the authority for the purpose of justifying any such objection,

and, if any representations are made, the enforcing authority shall, having taken the representations into account, determine whether the information is or is not commercially confidential.

(3) Where, under sub-s (2) above, an authority determines that information is not commercially confidential–

    (a) the information shall not be entered in the register until the end of the period of 21 days beginning with the date on which the determination is notified to the person concerned;

    (b) that person may appeal to the Secretary of State against the decision,

and, where an appeal is brought in respect of any information, the information shall not be entered in the register until the end of the period of seven days following the day on which the appeal is finally determined or withdrawn.

(4) An appeal under sub-s (3) above shall, if either Party to the appeal so requests or the Secretary of State so decides, take or continue in the form of a hearing (which must be held in private).

(5) Sub-section (10) of s 15 above shall apply in relation to an appeal under sub-s (3) above as it applies in relation to an appeal under that section.

(6) Sub-section (3) above is subject to s 114 of the Environment Act 1995 (delegation or reference of appeals etc).

(7) The Secretary of State may give to the enforcing authorities directions as to specified information, or descriptions of information, which the public interest requires to be included in registers maintained under s 78R above notwithstanding that the information may be commercially confidential.

(8) Information excluded from a register shall be treated as ceasing to be commercially confidential for the purposes of this section at the expiry of the period of four years beginning with the date of the determination by virtue of which it was excluded; but the person who furnished it may apply to the authority for the information to remain excluded from the register on the ground that it is still commercially confidential and the authority shall determine whether or not that is the case.

(9) Sub-sections (3) to (6) above shall apply in relation to a determination under sub-s (8) above as they apply in relation to a determination under sub-s (2) above.

(10) Information is, for the purposes of any determination under this section, commercially confidential, in relation to any individual or person, if its being contained in the register would prejudice to an unreasonable degree the commercial interests of that individual or person.

(11) For the purposes of sub-s (10) above, there shall be disregarded any prejudice to the commercial interests of any individual or person so far as relating only to the value of the contaminated land in question or otherwise to the ownership or occupation of that land.

Note:

For discussion of the application of analogous provisions to IPC, see Chapter 5, pp 509–10.

Section 78U Reports by the appropriate Agency on the state of contaminated land

(1) The appropriate Agency shall–

    (a) from time to time; or

    (b) if the Secretary of State at any time so requests, prepare and publish a report on the state of contaminated land in England and Wales or in Scotland, as the case may be.

(2) A local authority shall, at the written request of the appropriate Agency, furnish the appropriate Agency with such information to which this sub-s applies as the appropriate Agency may require for the purpose of enabling it to perform its functions under sub-s (1) above.

(3) The information to which sub-s (2) above applies is such information as the local authority may have, or may reasonably be expected to obtain, with respect to the condition of contaminated land in its area, being information which the authority has acquired or may acquire in the exercise of its functions under this Part

[Sections 78V (on Site-Specific Guidance by the Appropriate Agency Concerning Contaminated Land) and 78W (on Giving Power to Secretary of State to Issue Guidance) omitted.]

Section 78X Supplementary provisions

(1) Where it appears to a local authority that two or more different sites, when considered together, are in such a condition, by reason of substances in, on or under the land, that–

    (a) significant harm is being caused or there is a significant possibility of such harm being caused; or

    (b) pollution of controlled waters is being, or is likely to be, caused, this Part shall apply in relation to each of those sites, whether or not the condition of the land at any of them, when considered alone, appears to the authority to be such that significant harm is being caused, or there is a significant possibility of such harm being caused, or that pollution of controlled waters is being or is likely to be caused.

(2) Where it appears to a local authority that any land outside, but adjoining or adjacent to, its area is in such a condition, by reason of substances in, on or under the land, that significant harm is being caused, or there is a significant possibility of such harm being caused, or that pollution of controlled waters is being, or is likely to be, caused within its area–

(a) the authority may, in exercising its functions under this Part, treat that land as if it were land situated within its area; and

(b) except in this sub-section, any reference–

    (i) to land within the area of a local authority; or

    (ii) to the local authority in whose area any land is situated, shall be construed accordingly; but this sub-section is without prejudice to the functions of the local authority in whose area the land is in fact situated.

(3) A person acting in a relevant capacity–

(a) shall not thereby be personally liable, under this Part, to bear the whole or any part of the cost of doing any thing by way of remediation, unless that thing is to any extent referable to substances whose presence in, on or under the contaminated land in question is a result of any act done or omission made by him which it was unreasonable for a person acting in that capacity to do or make; and

(b) shall not thereby be guilty of an offence under or by virtue of s 78M above unless the requirement which has not been complied with is a requirement to do some particular thing for which he is personally liable to bear the whole or any part of the cost.

(4) In sub-s (3) above, 'person acting in a relevant capacity' means–

(a) a person acting as an insolvency practitioner, within the meaning of s 388 of the Insolvency Act 1986 (including that section as it applies in relation to an insolvent partnership by virtue of any order made under s 421 of that Act);

(b) the official receiver acting in a capacity in which he would be regarded as acting as an insolvency practitioner within the meaning of s 388 of the Insolvency Act 1986 if sub-s (5) of that section were disregarded;

    (c) the official receiver acting as receiver or manager;

    (d) a person acting as a special manager under ss 177 or 370 of the Insolvency Act 1986;

    (e) the Accountant in Bankruptcy acting as permanent or interim trustee in a sequestration (within the meaning of the Bankruptcy (Scotland) Act 1985);

    (f) a person acting as a receiver or receiver and manager–

    (i) under or by virtue of any enactment; or

    (ii) by virtue of his appointment as such by an order of a court or by any other instrument.

(5) Regulations may make different provision for different cases or circumstances.

[Section 78Y (on Application to the Isles of Scilly) omitted.]

[Section 78YA (on Supplementary Provisions with Respect to Guidance by the Secretary of State) omitted.]

Section 78YB Interaction of this Part with other enactments

(1) A remediation notice shall not be served if and to the extent that it appears to the enforcing authority that the powers of the appropriate Agency under s 27 above may be exercised in relation to–

(a) the significant harm (if any); and

(b) the pollution of controlled waters (if any),

by reason of which the contaminated land in question is such land.

(2) Nothing in this Part shall apply in relation to any land in respect of which there is for the time being in force a site licence under Part II above, except to the extent that any significant harm, or pollution of controlled waters, by reason of which that land would otherwise fall to be regarded as contaminated land is attributable to causes other than–

(a) breach of the conditions of the licence; or

(b) the carrying on, in accordance with the conditions of the licence, of any activity authorised by the licence.

(2)(A) This Part shall not apply if and to the extent that–

(a) any significant harm, or pollution of controlled waters, by reason of which the land would otherwise fall to be regarded as contaminated, is attributable to the final disposal by deposit in or on land of controlled waste; and

(b) enforcement action may be taken in relation to that disposal.

(2)(B) A remediation notice shall not be served in respect of contaminated land if and to the extent that–

(a) the significant harm, or pollution of controlled waters, by reason of which the contaminated land is such land is attributable to an activity other than the final disposal by deposit in or on land of controlled waste; and

(b) enforcement action may be taken in relation to that activity;

(c) in sub-ss (2)(A) and (2)(b) above–

'controlled' waste has the meaning given in s 75(4) of this Act; and

'enforcement action' means action under regulation 24 (Enforcement Notices) or regulation 26(2) (Power of regulator of the Pollution Prevention and Control (England and Wales) Regulations 2000 to regulate pollution).

(3) If, in a case falling within sub-s (1) or (7) of s 59 above, the land in question is contaminated land, or becomes such land by reason of the deposit of the controlled waste in question, a remediation notice shall not be served in respect of that land by reason of that waste or any consequences of its deposit, if and to the extent that it appears to the enforcing authority that the powers of a waste regulation authority or waste collection authority under that section may be exercised in relation to that waste or the consequences of its deposit.

(4) No remediation notice shall require a person to do anything the effect of which would be to impede or prevent the making of a discharge in pursuance of a consent given under Chapter II of Part III of the Water Resources Act 1991 (pollution offences) or, in relation to Scotland, in pursuance of a consent given under Part II of the Control of Pollution Act 1974.

Note:

Where the contamination results from offences committed under Pt 1 of the EPA 1990 (IPPC and local air pollution control) action should be taken under s 27 (see Chapter 5). The above provisions generally do not apply in relation to land that is subject to a waste site licence which is in force (see p 440, above). The provisions can, however, be used where the harm or the pollution flows from causes other than a breach of licence conditions or activities carried on in accordance with a licence. Where controlled waste has been unlawfully deposited a remediation notice may not be served if and to the extent that it appears that s 59 powers may be exercised.

[Section 78 YC which provides that this Part of the Act does not apply in relation to harm or pollution attributable to radioactive substances is omitted.]

REFERENCES AND FURTHER READING

Abbot, C 'Waste management licensing: benefit or burden?' [2000] JPL 1003–10

Bates, JH, *UK Waste Law*, 2nd edn, 1997, London: Sweet & Maxwell

Cheyne, J and Purdue, M, 'Fitting definition to purpose: the search for a satisfactory definition of waste' [1995] 7 JEL 149

Coopers & Leybrand, *Landfill Costs and Prices: Correcting Possible Market Distortions*, 1993, London: HMSO

Department of the Environment, *Waste Management Planning – Principles and Practice – A Guide on Best Practice for Waste Regulators*, 1996, London: HMSO

Department of the Environment, *Draft Guidance on Whether Land is Contaminated Under Part IIA of the EPA 1990*, 1995, London: DoE

Department of the Environment, *Landfill Design, Construction and Operational Practice*, Waste Management Paper No 26B, 1995, London: HMSO

Department of the Environment, *Licensing of Metal Recycling Sites*, Waste Management Paper No 4A, 1995, London: HMSO

Department of the Environment, *Making Waste Work: Strategy for Sustainable Waste Management in England & Wales*, Cm 3040, 1995, London: HMSO

Department of the Environment, *Licensing of Waste Management Facilities*, Waste Management Paper No 4, 1994, London: HMSO

Department of the Environment, *Polychlorinated Biphenyls*, Waste Management Paper No 6, 1994, London: HMSO

Department of the Environment, *Landfill Completion*, Waste Management Paper No 26A, 1993, London: HMSO

Department of the Environment, *This Common Inheritance*, Cm 3040, 1990, London: HMSO, Chapters 14 and 15

Harris, R, 'The Environmental Protection Act 1990 – penalising the polluter' [1992] JPL 515

House of Commons Select Committee on the Environment, Session 1988–89, 2nd Report, *Hazardous Waste Disposal*, 1989, London: HMSO and Response to the Report, Cm 679, 1989, London: HMSO

House of Lords Select Committee on the European Communities, *Paying for Pollution*, Session 1989–90, 25th Report, 1990, London: HMSO

House of Lords Select Committee on Science and Technology, *Hazardous Water Disposal*, Session 1988–89, 4th Report, 1989, London: HMSO

Hughes, D, *Environmental Law*, 3rd edn, 1996, London: Butterworths

Kitson, A and Harris, R, 'A burning issue: planning controls, pollution controls and waste incineration' [1994] JPL 3

Kummer, K, *International Management of Hazardous Wastes: The Basel Convention and Related Rules*, 2nd edn, 1999, Oxford: Clarendon

Morgan, M, 'Dealing with land contamination: the latest attempt [1996] JPL 1004

Pocklington, D, 'The utility of the concept of waste' (1996) Env Liability 94

Royal Commission on Environmental Pollution, *Incineration of Waste*, 17th Report, Cm 2181, 1993, London: HMSO

Salter, JR, 'The meaning of waste in European Community law' (1997) EELR 14

Tromans, S, 'EC waste law: a complete mess' [2001] 13 JEL 133–56

Tromans, S and Turrall, R, *Contaminated Land*, 1999, London: Sweet & Maxwell

Tromans, S, 'The difficulties of enforcing waste disposal licence conditions' [1991] 3 JEL 281

Tromans, S, *Environmental Protection Act 1990: Text and Commentary*, 1990, London: Sweet & Maxwell

Tromans, S, Nash, M and Poustie, M, *Current Law Statute Annotations on the Environment Act 1995*, 1995, London: Sweet & Maxwell

Von Wilmowsky, P, 'Waste disposal in the internal markets: the state of play after the ECJ's ruling on the Walloon import ban' (1993) 30 CML Rev 541–70

USEFUL WEBSITES:

Basel convention: www.basel.int/links.htm; www.unep.ch/basel; www.lbasel.int/pub/protocol.html; www.defra.gov.uk/environment/waste/index.htm

Environment Agency (Waste): www.environment-agency.gov.uk/subjects/waste

International Maritime Organisation: www.imo.org

Waste Strategy 2000: www.detr.gov.uk/wastestrategy/cm4693/index.htm

For further general websites, see pages l–li, above.

CHAPTER 5

INTEGRATED POLLUTION CONTROL

INTRODUCTION

The system of integrated pollution control (IPC) introduced by Pt I of the Environmental Protection Act (EPA) 1990, reflected a major change in approach to controlling environmental pollution. It represented a shift from the medium-by-medium approach found in earlier legislation and discussed in the previous three chapters. As we have seen, that approach establishes separate pollution control regimes relating to air, water and land. One consequence of having different regimes with varying standards and systems of enforcement is the temptation to 'regime shop'. For example, in order to avoid air pollution controls waste may be dumped in landfill rather than incinerated. If landfill becomes uneconomic, industry may be tempted to switch to an alternative such as releasing waste into rivers and seas. Whatever option is chosen, pollution of one media is likely to affect other environmental media. Leachates from landfill sites may enter water courses; air pollution may affect soil and vegetation. The IPC regime focuses upon the effect of industrial processes upon the environment as a whole and not in relation to particular media.

The UK's IPC system was introduced in 1991 (at least for new or substantially changed processes) and similar systems operated in other European States, notably France and Denmark. The EC has adopted the long awaited Directive on Integrated Pollution Prevention and Control 96/61 which was to be transposed into Member States' legislation by 30 October 1999. Since the UK system pre-dated that of the EC this chapter will first consider the domestic regime created by Pt I of the EPA 1990. We then consider the Directive and its implementation by the Pollution Prevention and Control Act 1999 and regulations made thereunder. It should be noted that Pt I of the EPA 1990 will be repealed in 2007 when the transitional period ends. Under transitional arrangements its provisions continue to apply for periods that vary depending on the circumstances (see further below).

IPC IN THE UK

Environmental Protection Act 1990 – Pt I

The Preamble to the EPA 1990 sets out the purpose of Pt I as being: 'to make provision for the improved control of pollution arising from certain industrial and other processes'.

In order to achieve this, Pt I creates two related systems, IPC and local authority air pollution control (LAAPC). The basic mechanisms contained in Pt I, relating to authorisations, appeals, enforcement and public registers, apply to both systems as does the imposition of BATNEEC (see below). However, the two systems differ in three respects:

1   IPC applies only to the most potentially polluting or technologically complex industrial processes whereas LAAPC applies to less polluting industrial processes.

2   IPC is 'exercisable for the purpose of preventing or minimising pollution of the environment' due to the release of substances into any environmental medium (s 4(2) of the EPA 1990). LAAPC relates only to the release of substances into the air (s 4(3) of the EPA 1990).

3   The enforcement authority for IPC is the Environment Agency (formerly Her Majesty's Inspectorate of Pollution whose functions were transferred to the Environment Agency by the Environment Act 1995). The enforcement authority for LAAPC is the competent local authority, usually a district council.

Part I and the Regulations made under it are being replaced by the integrated pollution prevention and control (IPPC)/air pollution control (APC) combined regimes set up under the Pollution Prevention and Control Act 1999 (PPC Act) and the Pollution Prevention and Control (England and Wales) Regulations 2000 SI 2000/1973 (PPC Regulations). New permits are granted under the latter scheme, although existing authorisations granted under Pt I of the EPA remain in force during a transitional period ending in 2007. Part I will be repealed at the end of this period.

Prescribed processes and substances

Under the EPA 1990, carrying on a prescribed process without an authorisation from a competent enforcing authority constitutes an offence. Section 2(1) of the EPA 1990 gives the Secretary of State a wide discretion to identify prescribed processes by delegated legislation. Once prescribed the process falls under the provisions of Pt I. There are no precise criteria by which the processes subject to Pt I are to be identified but the Secretary of State may take into account the characteristics of the process and the circumstances in which it is carried on. The Environmental Protection (Prescribed Processes and Substances) Regulations 1991 SI 1991/472 (the 1991 Regulations) list the processes which are subject to IPC and Environment Agency control as well as those which fall under the LAAPC regime. Schedule 1 of the Regulations divides prescribed processes into chapters which reflect six main industry sectors: the production of fuel and power generation; metal production and processing; mineral industries; the chemical industry; waste disposal and recycling; and, other industries. Each chapter is further divided into Part A and Part B lists. The former lists processes which are potentially the most polluting (such as petroleum processing) and are subject to IPC; Part B processes are less polluting and therefore subject to LAAPC. Some processes which fall within the Sched 1 categories are nevertheless excluded from control by virtue of Reg 4. Basically, they are processes which cannot result in the release of substances listed in Scheds 4, 5 and 6 (see below) into air, into water or into land; or will result in the release of only trivial amounts of such substances.

The 1991 Regulations have been amended several times in order to include or exclude processes from IPC or LAAPC control or to move them from one category to another, for example, the Environmental Protection (Prescribed Processes and Substances, etc) (Amendment) Regulations 1994 SI 1994/1271 adopt a deregulatory approach by transferring some prescribed processes from central to local authority control and raising some of the thresholds necessary before processes would come under any control. The most recent amendments have been made by the Environmental Protection (Prescribed Process and Substances) (Amendment) (Hazardous Waste Incineration) Regulations 1998 SI 1998/767.

A process falls under Pt I of the EPA 1990 only in so far as its conduct may lead to the release of certain prescribed substances into the environment as a whole (IPC) or into the air (LAAPC).[1] Prescribed substances are those listed by the Secretary of State in Sched 4 (releases into the air), Sched 5 (releases into water) and Sched 6 (releases on to land). The Regulations require the best available technology not entailing excessive cost (BATNEEC) to be used to prevent or minimise releases of prescribed substances, or to render such releases harmless.

Authorisations and conditions

Section 6(1) of the EPA 1990 prohibits the carrying on of a prescribed process without an authorisation from the relevant enforcing authority. The Environmental Protection (Applications, Appeals and Registers) Regulations 1991 SI 1991/507 set out the procedural requirements to be followed, including a right of public participation. The enforcing authority must either grant the authorisation subject to conditions (s 7, below) or it may refuse the application. Section 6(4) stipulates that an application shall not be granted unless the enforcing authority considers that the applicant will be able to carry on the process so as to comply with the conditions to be included in the authorisation.

The case of *R v Secretary of State for the Environment ex p West Wiltshire District Council*[2] suggests that the appropriate test for deciding whether or not an application should be granted is whether the applicant (in this case an animal rendering business) is able to comply with the conditions rather than whether they are likely to comply. In *Gateshead Metropolitan Borough Council v Secretary of State for the Environment and Northumbrian Water Group*[3] the Court of Appeal considered the relationship between planning permission and IPC authorisation (see p 517, below). The Court concluded that HMIP should not:

... consider that the grant of planning permission inhibits them from refusing authorisation if they decided in their discretion that this is the proper course.[4]

This case may establish the priority power given to HMIP and now the Environment Agency over local planning authorities in pollution control matters.

Section 7 of the EPA 1990 requires certain conditions to be included in the authorisations. They are:

1   Such conditions as are necessary to achieve statutory objectives.

2   Conditions necessary to comply with directions of the Secretary of State.[5]

---

1   EPA 1990, s 2(5).

2   [1996] Env LR 312 (see p 513, below). The previous track record of the company had suggested that it was not likely to comply with conditions in the future. See also *R v Secretary of State for the Environment and Peninsular Proteins Ltd ex p Torridge District Council* [1997] JPL 1104; [1997] Env LR 557.

3   [1995] JPL 432. See also Purdue, M [1999] JPL 585.

4   *Per* Glidewell LJ.

5   For example, to comply with EC or international obligations relating to environmental protection.

3   Any other conditions deemed appropriate by the enforcing authority.

The object of these conditions is to ensure that in carrying on a prescribed process, the BATNEEC will be used: (i) for preventing the release of substances prescribed for any environmental medium into that medium or, where that is not practicable by such means, for reducing the release of such substances to a minimum and for rendering harmless any such substances which are so released; and (ii) for rendering harmless any other substances which might cause harm if released into any environmental medium (s 7(2)(a) of the EPA 1990)).

It is important to stress that the BATNEEC is required not only to prevent or reduce the emission of prescribed substances but also to render harmless substances which might cause harm if released into the environment. 'Harm' is defined to mean:

> ... harm to the health of living organisms or other interference with the ecological systems of which they form part and, in the case of man, includes offence caused to any of his senses or harm to his property (s 1(4) of the EPA 1990).

Those applying for an authorisation must pay the necessary fees (s 8 of the EPA and s 41 of the EA 1995). The basis upon which these fees are assessed is that of 'relevant expenditure attributable to authorisations'. This phrase is defined in s 8(7) of the EPA 1990 as 'expenditure incurred by the enforcing authorities in exercising their functions under this part in relation to authorisations'. This is an attempt to give effect to the polluter pays principle (see Chapter 1, p 52, above).

BATNEEC[6]

The reference to BATNEEC is fundamental to the system of authorisations underlying IPC and LAAPC. The practical interpretation of BATNEEC is to be found in the EPA itself (s 7(10) of the EPA 1990), from guidance notes issued by HMIP and the Environment Agency,[7] and the *Revised Practical Guide to Integrated Pollution Control* (1993) issued by the Department of the Environment.

The 1993 guide broke down the phrase into four elements:

(a) *Best*: means most effective in preventing, minimising or rendering harmless polluting emissions. More than one technique may be available to satisfy this criterion.

(b) *Available*: implies general accessibility. The technique must always be operable with business confidence even if only developed at a pilot scale. What is available does not have to come from sources within the UK nor does it require a competitive supply (for instance one supplier may have a monopoly over its provision).

(c) *Techniques*: is defined in s 7(10) of the EPA 1990, to include not only the technology utilised but also the numbers and qualifications of staff and the design, construction, layout and maintenance of the building.

---

6   The concept of BATNEEC (and the related concept of BPEO) has been replaced by Best Available Techniques (BAT) under IPPC (see PPC, reg 3(1), below).

7   Which are aimed at establishing consistent treatment for operators of processes in the granting of authorisations.

(d) *Not entailing excessive cost*: this varies depending on whether the process is new or already existing.

For new processes three principles must be borne in mind: (i) the cost of best available techniques must be weighed against the environmental damage from the process; the greater the environmental damage, the greater the cost of best available techniques which can be required without being considered excessive; (ii) if serious harm would still result even after best available techniques have been imposed, then the application should be refused; and (iii) the concept of cost is objective and is to be determined by considering the industry as a whole. The lack of profitability of a particular operator is not relevant.

For existing processes adaptation to the best available technology is to be gradual taking account of developments in the BAT, the general environmental situation and the desirability of avoiding excessive costs for any given plant, paying due regard to the economic circumstances within the industrial sector concerned. In particular, the following factors should be taken into account: the plant's technical characteristics; its rate of utilisation and length of its remaining life; the nature and volume of polluting emissions from it; and the desirability of avoiding excessive costs having regard to the economic situation of undertakings in the category in question.

Clearly, the BATNEEC allows for commercial considerations to be taken into account since what is excessive is judged by comparing current costs with those required by improved methods.

Best practicable environmental option (BPEO)[8]

A second key element of the original IPC system is that of the BPEO. Section 7(7) of the EPA 1990 provides that where a prescribed process is one which is likely to involve releases into more than one environmental medium, the BATNEEC is to be used to minimise the pollution which may be caused to the environment as a whole by the releases, having regard to the BPEO available in relation to the substances which will be released. The Environment Agency must therefore decide what is the least harmful allocation of emissions between the various media in order to achieve the greatest overall protection for the environment.[9]

In any particular case, it may be extremely difficult to identify the BPEO. The Environment Agency has published (1997) its guidance for operators and inspectors of IPC processes on 'Best Practicable Environmental Option Assessment for Integrated Pollution Control' (Technical Guidance Note E1) which sets out a methodology for assessing harm and comparing options for specific industrial processes to determine the BATNEEC having regard to the BPEO. The guidance also refers to the kind of economic information required to gauge the practicality of process options.

In addition, the 12th Report of the Royal Commission on Environmental Pollution ((1988) Cm 310) has suggested that process operators might consider a number of factors when selecting the BPEO. For example, they should:

---

8   Not applicable to LAAPC.

9   Attempts are being made to develop a formal system or environmental risk assessment referred to as OPRA (Operator Performance Appraisal).

1   introduce environmental considerations into project planning at the earliest possible stage;

2   identify options diligently and imaginatively in order to produce as complete a set as possible;

3   identify potential damage to the environment in such a way as to uncover the unusual as well as the familiar;

4   look at the long and short term affects of the installation's operation on the environment, whether local or remote.

Transfers, variations and enforcement

Section 9 deals with transfer of authorisations. Authorisations may be transferred to any person who proposes to carry out the process in the 'holder's place'. Consent for the transfer is not needed, although the enforcing authority must be notified in writing within 21 days of the transfer. Although in granting an authorisation the authority must have regard to the capability of the applicant (s 6(4)) the authority has no specific power to object to a transfer. But if the authority has serious doubts about the ability or intentions of the transferee to comply with the conditions of the authorisation, there is power to serve an enforcement notice (s 13), a prohibition notice (s 14) or to revoke the authorisation (s 12).

Section 10 enables enforcing authorities to vary the conditions of an authorisation if they consider that the conditions no longer comply with the legislation. Such a power enables the Environment Agency to initiate changes in an industry by ensuring authorisations are kept up to date.

Section 11 allows operators to initiate changes to the way in which they perform the process by applying to the Environment Agency which must then decide whether the proposed variation would (a) breach any conditions of the existing authorisation conditions; (b) if not, whether the Agency would be likely to vary the authorisation conditions in consequence of the change; (c) if so, whether they would consider altering conditions so that the change may be made; and (d) whether the proposal would lead to 'substantial change'[10] in the manner of carrying on the process. If *no substantial* change is involved, but where a relevant change[11] under (b) or (c) would be required, then the Agency will inform the operator of this. The operator may apply for the variation. If a substantial change is involved, then again the operator must be informed of likely changes in the authorisation. They may then apply, but the obligation to advertise and consult has to be complied with as if it were an original application. Bearing in mind the costs and delays, a system of 'envelope authorisations' has been developed. This lays down outer parameters within which changes may be made without further action.[12]

To ensure compliance with the above, inspectors from the Environment Agency are given extensive powers, including the power to enter premises and make such

---

10   Defined in EPA 1990, s 10(7), as a substantial change in the substances released from the process or in the amount or any other characteristic of any substance so released.

11   Defined in the EPA 1990, s 11(11).

12   Hughes, D, *Environmental Law*, 3rd edn, 1996, London: Butterworths, p 482. See also Environmental Protection (Applications, Appeals and Registers) Regulations 1991 SI 1991/507.

investigations as may be necessary. They also have powers to seize and render harmless any articles or substances which they have reasonable cause to believe presents an 'imminent danger of serious harm' (s 108 of the EA 1995. See pp 523–25, below).

The Environment Agency may serve 'enforcement notices' if an inspector believes that an authorisation condition has been breached or is likely to be breached (s 13 of the EPA 1990). If an inspector believes there is 'an imminent risk of serious pollution of the environment' in consequence of carrying on a prescribed process, the Environment Agency may serve a 'prohibition notice' (s 14 of the EPA 1990). The Environment Agency may ultimately revoke an authorisation 'at any time', in particular where a relevant process has not been carried on, or not for a period of 12 months (s 12 of the EPA 1990). Finally, *all* authorisations must be reviewed at least once every four years (s 6(6) of the EPA 1990) although the Secretary of State may amend the review period by regulations. It would appear that the Environment Agency intends to follow the lead set by its predecessor, the HMIP, in applying a principle of proportionality in exercising its enforcement powers, that is, the action taken will be proportionate to the environmental risks and the seriousness of breaches of the law.[13]

Access to information

Section 20 of the EPA 1990[14] obliges enforcing authorities to maintain public registers containing certain prescribed information, including details of applications for and grants of authorisation together with any variations thereof, any enforcement or prohibition notices and any appeals or relevant convictions. A major restriction on the obligation to make information publicly available relates to information which would be 'contrary to the interests of national security' (s 21(1) of the EPA 1990) or which is 'commercially confidential'. (s 22(1) of the EPA 1990). The applicant may request the enforcing authority to exclude this information. If the enforcing authority refuses, the applicant may appeal to the Secretary of State.

The Secretary of State heard two appeals in 1992 by Powergen and National Power respectively against requirements that the former should register information about the forecast schedules of emissions for 1991 and that the latter should disclose information about the future fuel consumption of its power stations. The Act states that information is commercially confidential 'if its being contained in the register would prejudice to an unreasonable degree the commercial interests of [an] individual person' (s 22(11) of the EPA 1990). The Powergen appeal was rejected on the grounds that it would not have that effect, but National Power's appeal was upheld. Mr Howard (the then Secretary of State for the Environment) took the view that the information was not directly relevant to determination of the applications for authorisations or any conditions likely to be imposed; that the information was not necessary to enable the public to comment effectively on the applications; that the information was provided in excess of HMIP's normal requirements, and was of the kind whose inclusion in the register might result in unreasonable prejudice to the company's commercial interests.[15] In this context it appears

---

13 See *op cit*, Hughes, fn 12, p 483 referring to the Agency's Enforcement Code of Practice, 14 May 1996.
14 Further details on the information to be included in the Register is contained in the Environment Protection (Applications, Appeals and Registers) Regulations 1991.
15 [1993] Env Liability CS 10.

that the Secretary of State distinguished between information about what enters a place where a prescribed process is taking place (here the fuel being consumed) and what leaves it in the form of emissions.[16] The Revised Guide to Integrated Pollution Control (1993) has changed the test on refusing disclosure of information on the grounds of commercial confidentiality to whether it:

> ... would negate or diminish a commercial advantage or produce or increase a commercial disadvantage which is unreasonable given the nature of the information and the financial effects of disclosure.

The exclusion of information only lasts for four years at which point the applicant must reapply for exclusion (s 22(8) of the EPA 1990).

Review of the operation of IPC

Studies of the workings of the IPC system[17] concluded that it was failing to force operators to comply with the aims and objectives of the legislation. It seems that the main criticisms were levied at HMIP for failing to implement the legislation. The review concluded that 'many companies have failed to fulfil their statutory duties at the first stage of the IPC process – and that HMIP has not obliged them to do so'.[18] It seems that few companies have been required to demonstrate their use of the BATNEEC or the BPEO. It is to be hoped that the new regime is more successful.

Environmental Protection Act 1990, Pt I

Section 6 Authorisations: general provisions

(1) No person shall carry on a prescribed process after the date prescribed or determined for that description of process by or under regulations under s 2(1) ... except under an authorisation granted by the enforcing authority and in accordance with the conditions to which it is subject.

[Sub-section (2) omitted.]

(3) Where an application is duly made to the enforcing authority, the authority shall either grant the authorisation subject to the conditions required or authorised to be imposed by s 7 below or refuse the application.

(4) An application shall not be granted unless the enforcing authority considers that the applicant will be able to carry on the process so as to comply with the conditions which would be included in the authorisation.

(5) The Secretary of State may, if he thinks fit in relation to any application for an authorisation, give to the enforcing authority directions as to whether or not the authority should grant the authorisation.

---

16 *Op cit*, Hughes, fn 12, p 478.
17 *Integrated Pollution Control – The First Three Years*, 1993, ENDS, p 220.
18 ENDS Report 227, 1993, p 3.

Note:

Sub-section (6) requires the enforcing authority to periodically (at least once every four years) review the conditions on which authorisations have been given.

Section 7 Conditions of authorisations

(1) There shall be included in an authorisation–

    (a) subject to para (b) below, such specific conditions as the enforcing authority considers appropriate, when taken with the general condition implied by sub-s (4) below, for achieving the objectives specified in sub-s (2) below;

    (b) such conditions as are specified in directions given by the Secretary of State under sub-s (3) below; and

    (c) such other conditions (if any) as appear to the enforcing authority to be appropriate;

    but no conditions shall be imposed for the purpose only of securing the health of persons at work (within the meaning of Part I of the Health and Safety at Work etc. Act 1974).

(2) Those objectives are–

    (a) ensuring that, in carrying on a prescribed process, the best available techniques not entailing excessive cost will be used–

        (i) for preventing the release of substances prescribed for any environmental medium into that medium or, where that is not practicable by such means, for reducing the release of such substances to a minimum and for rendering harmless any such substances which are so released; and

        (ii) for rendering harmless any other substances which might cause harm if released into any environmental medium;

    (b) compliance with any directions by the Secretary of State given for the implementation of any obligations of the United Kingdom under the Community Treaties or international law relating to environmental protection;

    (c) compliance with any limits or requirements and achievement of any quality standards or quality objectives prescribed by the Secretary of State under any of the relevant enactments;

    (d) compliance with any requirements applicable to the grant of authorisations specified by or under a plan made by the Secretary of State under s 3(5) above.

(3 Except as respects the general condition implied by sub-s (4) below, the Secretary of State may give directions to the enforcing authorities as to the conditions which are, or are not, to be included in all authorisations, in authorisations of any specified description or in any particular authorisation.

(4) Subject to sub-ss (5) and (6) below, there is implied in every authorisation a general condition that, in carrying on the process to which the authorisation applies, the person carrying it on must use the best available techniques not entailing excessive cost–

    (a) for preventing the release of substances prescribed for any environmental medium into that medium or, where that is not practicable by such means, for reducing the release of such substances to a minimum and for rendering harmless any such substances which are so released; and

(b) for rendering harmless any other substances which might cause harm if released into any environmental medium.

[Sub-section (5) provides that in sub-ss (1)–(4) in relation to authorisations granted by local authorities references to the release of substances into any environmental medium are to be read as references to the release of substances into the air.]

(6) The obligation implied by virtue of sub-s (4) above shall not apply in relation to any aspect of the process in question which is regulated by a condition imposed under sub-s (1) above.

(7) The objectives referred to in sub-s (2) above shall, where the process–

(a) is one designated for central control; and

(b) is likely to involve the release of substances into more than one environmental medium;

include the objective of ensuring that the best available techniques not entailing excessive cost will be used for minimising the pollution which may be caused to the environment taken as a whole by the releases having regard to the best practicable environmental option available as respects the substances which may be released.

(8) An authorisation for carrying on a prescribed process may, without prejudice to the generality of sub-s (1) above, include conditions–

(a) imposing limits on the amount or composition of any substance produced by or utilised in the process in any period; and

(b) requiring advance notification of any proposed change in the manner of carrying on the process.

[Sub-section (9) omitted.]

(10) References to the best available techniques not entailing excessive cost, in relation to a process, include (in addition to references to any technical means and technology) references to the number, qualifications, training and supervision of persons employed in the process and the design, construction, lay-out and maintenance of the buildings in which it is carried on.

(11) It shall be the duty of enforcing authorities to have regard to any guidance issued to them by the Secretary of State for the purposes of the application of sub-ss (2) and (7) above as to the techniques and environmental options that are appropriate for any description of prescribed process.

[Sub-section (12) omitted.]

Note:

This is a key section. As well as dealing with the conditions to be imposed when authorisations are given, it introduces the concepts of best available techniques not entailing excessive cost (BATNEEC) and best practicable environmental option (BPEO) (see pp 506–08, above). These sections are further discussed in *Ex p West Wiltshire District Council* and *Gateshead Metropolitan Borough Council v Secretary of State* which are set out below.

R v Secretary of State for the Environment & Another ex p West Wiltshire District Council [1997] JPL 210

Malcolm Spence QC (sitting as a Deputy Judge of the Queen's Bench Division): The Second Respondents, Comptons, have run a piggery and allied businesses constituting an animal by-product rendering process near Bradford-on-Avon since 1941. Over the years there have been numerous complaints about the smell thereby caused. The Environmental Protection Act was passed in 1990 and in October 1992 Comptons made an application for authorisation under the Act. The present applicants, the West Wiltshire District Council, as enforcing authority under the Act, refused it. So Comptons appealed to the Secretary of State for the Environment under s 15 of the Act. A hearing was held in August 1994 and the Inspector concluded decisively against the grant of authorisation. However, the Secretary of State disagreed with him, and by his decision letter of 22 August 1995 granted an authorisation subject to numerous conditions.

The West Wiltshire District Council applied for judicial review of this decision, and Turner J granted leave. I am told that this is the first case to reach the High Court concerning this part of the Environmental Protection Act. No point is taken as to the propriety of judicial review as the appropriate means for challenging the Secretary of State's decision, there being no statutory means provided.

The West Wiltshire District Council take three main points, together with a fourth, concerning the reasoning of the decision. However, I have only found it necessary to consider the first and main point. Mr Sullivan, who appears for the District Council, agrees with this course.

[The judge set out s 6(1), s 6(3) and s 7 and the inspector's report which concluded in para 114.]

Paragraph 114:

I consider that a clear and detailed set of costed upgrading proposals, backed by cogent evidence that the BATNEEC standard is likely to be achieved, is essential for authorisation to be granted. However, such detailed proposals are lacking; there are indications that the plant design will not facilitate observance of the objectives in s 7(2) of the Act; the plant is not complying with the BPM standard; there is an acknowledged history of problems with the management of this plant; no proposals are available to demonstrate a likelihood that these management and design shortcomings will be overcome, and this is a vulnerable and sensitive locality. I therefore conclude that the company is unlikely to be able to carry on the process in plant nos 1 and 2 so as to comply with the requirements of the Act [...]

The Secretary of State has concluded from the aforementioned documents that the conditions set out in Annex A to this letter (and as discussed further in paragraphs 18–22 below) could be included in an authorisation in order to address the evident smell problem and, in particular, to address the concerns registered in the authority's reasons for refusal which relate principally to management, operational and maintenance inadequacies. Many of the conditions in Annex A are effective either immediately or in the short term; the remainder are intended to secure completion of full upgrading in accordance with PG6/1(91) in advance of the upgrading deadline in clause 9 of that note. As to compliance with those conditions and the second question in paragraph 12 above, the Secretary of State notes the many deficiencies in operating the plant in the past and the lack of confidence expressed by the Inspector in the appellant's future operation of the process. However, the Secretary of State considers that the test provided by s 6(4) of the Act is whether a process operator is able to comply, not whether he is likely to comply. A key feature of the pollution control regime established by Part I of the Act is that explicit conditions can be imposed which are binding on the process operator and that a range of enforcement actions are available if they are breached. The Secretary of State is not persuaded that the appellant is unable to comply with the conditions which would be included in the authorisation.

[...]

17 For the reasons set out in his consideration above, the Secretary of State has decided that the authority's refusal to grant an authorisation should not be upheld and that the authority should be directed to issue an authorisation containing the conditions set out in Annex A to this letter.

Mr Sullivan's main submission is that the First Respondent misdirected himself in law, in particular, as to the meaning of s 6(4) of the Act, and (2), flowing from that misdirection, he failed to take into account relevant considerations as listed at paragraph 4.4 of the Form 86A I shall refer to some of these:

(a) The extent to which the particular Appellant has in the past been able to comply with the relevant conditions;

(b) The managerial expertise available to the particular Appellant;

(d) The extent to which proposals of the particular Appellant are available to demonstrate the means by which any past management failures or design shortcomings would be overcome.

Though I am not actually satisfied that the Secretary of State has misconstrued s 6(4), as I shall explain later, he has, in my judgment, not applied it properly, and I uphold the main thrust of Mr Sullivan's submissions for the following reasons. This was a case in which the council's main point was the poor management by the company over a period of many, many years which demonstrated, in their view, that the company did not have the ability for the future to carry on the process so as to comply with the conditions. They had put forward the conditions as part of the draft authorisation in case the Secretary of State were to grant it, but their case was that the company did not have the necessary ability to comply with them. The short point, at the end of the full consideration, is that if that case were to be rejected, then it could only be so rejected on clear and correct grounds. I am not prepared to read into the decision letter nuances of the kind which I am in effect invited to do by Mr Straker and Mr Hobson, who appear on behalf of the First and Second Respondents respectively.

This central point, the Council's contention that the company did not have the necessary ability, was reported in detail by the Inspector at paragraphs 69 to 83, dealing with inadequate record keeping, fugitive emissions from buildings, liquid effluent treatment, storage of waste products, cleaning and housekeeping, and history of emissions of offensive odours. I shall read paragraph 79:

A cycle of improvement and deterioration has been observed with the site, the improvement occurring after action by the enforcing authority which may give a short lived respite or improvement to the odour problems, but the situation deteriorates once again causing severe smell problems to the local residents. This appears to be due to a lack of preventative maintenance.

Paragraph 82:

In summary, the BATNEEC standard is unachievable because:

(a) The working methods employed are not satisfactory which includes management, housekeeping, supervision and training and buildings are poorly maintained.

(b) Access to effective techniques for minimising polluting emissions have been available to the appellants for a considerable time but have not been utilised.

Paragraph 83:

Although the scheme has been submitted by the appellants to improve the plant, the company does not have the ability to adhere to the BATNEEC standard even if the scheme were to proceed.

The Inspector made findings of fact favourable to the Council upon these matters. I have read paragraph 93. He concluded upon these – I need not read again paragraphs 106 and 107 – in paragraph 114:

the plant is not complying with the BPM standard; there is an acknowledged history of problems with the management of this plant; no proposals are available to demonstrate a likelihood that these management and design shortcomings will be overcome ...

He therefore concluded that the company was unlikely to be able to carry on the process as required. That conclusion was unambiguous, and there cannot be disagreement with it except upon cogent grounds.

However, the Secretary of State has just four sentences upon the matter as follows. The first sentence about it is in paragraph 15 and begins 'As to compliance with those conditions and the second question'. This is what the Secretary of State has called this topic. In that sentence he merely notes the Inspector's conclusion. In the next sentence he rightly says that the test is whether the process operator is able to comply, but the sentence is written as an apparent criticism of the Inspector's conclusion, as if he had based his approach upon 'whether [the applicant] is likely to comply'. The Inspector certainly did not do this. He considered in paragraph 114 whether the company was likely or not to be able to carry on the process so as to comply. However, in spite of the Secretary of State's correct approach in the first half of that sentence, he did not then, nor earlier, consider whether the process operator was able to comply. Instead, his next sentence is upon a wholly different topic, that is to point out that there is a range of enforcement actions available to deal with breaches of condition. That was not the council's nor the Inspector's point at all. The council had given evidence about the history of enforcement and how it merely gave short lived success. That showed that the company did not have the necessary ability, at any rate, not for more than short lived periods. Accordingly, the last sentence of the paragraph cannot possibly follow from what has preceded it. A proved inability to comply does not somehow in some unexplained fashion become cured by the introduction of a range of enforcement actions.

Moreover, the Secretary of State has nowhere said in his decision letter that he 'considers that the applicant will be able to carry on the process so as to comply'. Upon a matter which is so important in the present case, I refuse to make any such inference by reference to the double negatives in the last sentence of paragraph 15, nor by reference to the mere direction to grant an authorisation in paragraph 17, nor by reference to Mr Straker's 'the Secretary of State must have so decided'. That direction is given without an express conclusion upon the central issue and without consideration (other than merely 'noting') of the relevant factors, and that despite the clear findings and conclusion of the Inspector. It was not lawful to give such a direction without a finding based upon the relevant considerations, including, particularly, the three to which I have referred on Form 86A, all being points expressly mentioned by the Inspector in his concluding paragraph 114, that he considered that the applicant would be unlikely to be able to carry on the process so as to comply with the conditions.

That effectively disposes of the main point in this case, but there are various aspects with which I should also deal. Mr Hobson has addressed me concerning the exercise of discretion. He showed me, by reference to his client's affidavit, that the company had spent a great deal of money since the Inquiry carrying out various improvements. That may well be so, and I hope that it is so. However, I do not consider that the company will suffer any hardship in this regard. Indeed, I regard it as a happy outcome to this case that the quashing of the decision will result in reconsideration of the matter in the light of the up-to-date evidence. If the company have indeed effected sufficient improvements and also, most importantly, in view of the evidence, carried out proper maintenance, then they will have the opportunity of proving it during this reconsideration and may achieve an authorisation. But conversely, if this decision were not to be quashed, and if the company proved still not to have the necessary ability, then it will be wholly unsatisfactory for the local people to have to continue to endure this smell, when the Secretary of State's approach and reasoning upon the central point has been so poor.

I am gratified that there has been no dispute about the actual meaning of s 6(4). It is well stated in Mr Stephen Troman's and Professor Grant's Encyclopaedia at page D397:

> Whilst Part I does not contain any provisions equivalent in sophistication to the concept of 'fit and proper person' contained in Part II, in relation to waste management licensing, it is clear from this sub-section that the enforcing authority must have regard to characteristics of the applicant insofar as they are relevant to the applicant's ability to comply with the proposed conditions.

Mr Burdett Hall in his book says on page 342:

> In any particular case, refusal of an application will ordinarily be on the grounds that the proposed techniques are not BATNEEC. However there is an overriding provision in s 6(4) that an application shall not be granted unless the enforcing authority considers that the applicant will be able to carry on the process so as to comply with the conditions that would be included in the authorisation. Thus if the Inspector considers that an applicant simply has not got adequate financial resources or technical competence or environmental management systems, even though the applicant is willing to accept such conditions as the inspector thinks appropriate, the application must be turned down.

I consider these to be correct statements of the law, and neither Mr Straker nor Mr Hobson have sought to submit otherwise. It was unfortunate and confusing that the Secretary of State reformulated the test under s 6(4) in his paragraph 12(b) of the decision letter. 'Will be possible' is not necessarily synonymous with 'will be able'. However, I prefer to base my criticism of the decision upon the consideration which I have already set out than upon this reformulation of the test.

Gateshead Metropolitan Borough Council v Secretary of State for the Environment and Another [1995] JPL 432

Glidewell LJ: This appeal relates to an activity which, in general terms, is subject to planning control under the Town and Country Planning Act and to control as a prescribed process under Part I of the Environmental Protection Act 1990. The main issue in the appeal is, what is the proper approach for the Secretary of State for the Environment to adopt where these two statutory regimes apply and, to an extent, overlap?

Northumbrian Water Group plc ('NWG') wish to construct and operate an incinerator for the disposal of clinical waste on a site some nine acres in extent, comprising about half of the area of the disused Felling Sewage Treatment Works at Wardley, Gateshead Metropolitan Borough. Under the Town and Country Planning Act planning permission is necessary for the construction of the incinerator and for the commencement of its use thereafter. The proposed incineration is a prescribed process within s 2 of the Environmental Protection Act 1990 and Schedule 1 of the Environmental Protection (Prescribed Processes and Substances) Regulations 1991 SI 1991/472 as amended. An authorisation to carry on the process of incineration is therefore required by s 6 of the Environmental Protection Act. In this case, the enforcing authority which is responsible for granting such an authorisation is HM Inspectorate of Pollution ('HMIP').

Two applications were made to Gateshead, the local planning authority, for planning permission for the construction of the incinerator. This appeal is only concerned with the second, which was an outline application submitted on 26 October 1991. The application was refused by Gateshead by a notice dated 4 February 1991 for six reasons which I summarise as follows. The proposal is contrary to the provisions of the approved development plan, both the local plan and the county structure plan; the use of land for waste disposal purposes conflicts with the allocation of neighbouring land for industrial and/or warehousing purposes and could prejudice the development of that land; since there was no national or regional planning framework which identified the volume of clinical waste which was likely to arise, the proposal was premature; the applicants have failed to supply sufficient information that the plant could be operated without causing a nuisance to the locality; the applicants have failed to demonstrate that the overall effects on the environment, particularly in relation to health risk, have been fully investigated and taken account of. Then there was finally a ground relating to the reclamation and development of the site stating that no proposals have been submitted demonstrating how contamination arising from its previous use could be treated. That point does not arise in this appeal.

NWG appealed against the refusal to the Secretary of State for the Environment. An inquiry into the appeal was heard by an inspector of the Department of the Environment, Mr CA Jennings BSc CEng, with the assistance of Dr Waring, a chemical assessor, between 9 April and 1 May 1991. The inspector and the assessor reported to the Secretary of State on 3 August 1992. The inspector recommended that permission be refused. The Secretary of State by letter dated 24 May 1993 allowed the appeal and granted outline permission subject to conditions. Gateshead applied to the High Court under s 288 of the Town and Country Planning Act 1990 for an order that the Secretary of State's decision be quashed. On 29 September 1993 Mr Jeremy Sullivan QC, sitting as a deputy High Court judge, dismissed the application. Gateshead now appeal to this court. The relevant provision of the Town and Country Planning Act comprises ss 54A, 72(2) and 79(4). The effect of those sections is that, in determining the appeal the Secretary of State was required to decide in accordance with the provisions of the development plan unless material considerations indicated otherwise and to decide in accordance with other material considerations.

[His Lordship sets out ss 6 and 7.]

I comment first that the matters about which the inspector and his assessor expressed concern were three. First, the lack of clear information about the existing quality of the air in the vicinity of the site, which was a necessary starting point for deciding what impact the emission of any polluting substances from the stack would have. It was established that such substances would include dioxins, furans and cadmium. Second, in relation to cadmium though not in relation to the other chemicals, any increase in the quality of cadmium in the air in a rural area is contrary to the recommendations of the World Health Organisation. This, however, would not be the case in an urban area. In other words, an increase would not of itself contravene World Health Organisation recommendations relating to an urban area. Third, there is much public concern about any increase in the emission of these substances, especially dioxins, from the proposed plant. In the absence of either practical experience of the operation of a similar plant or clear information about the existing air quality, those concerns cannot be met. It was because of those concerns that the inspector recommended refusal.

I express my views as follows. Public concern is 'of course' and must be recognised by the Secretary of State to be, a material consideration for him to take into account. But if in the end that public concern is not justified, it cannot be conclusive. If it were, no industrial development – indeed very little development of any kind – would ever be permitted.

The central issue is whether the Secretary of State is correct in saying that the controls under the Environmental Pollution Act are adequate to deal with the concerns of the inspector and the assessor. The decision which was to be made on the appeal to the Secretary of State lay in the area in which the regimes of control under the Planning Act and the Environmental Pollution Act overlapped. If it had become clear at the inquiry that some of the discharges were bound to be unacceptable so that a refusal by HMIP to grant an authorisation would be the only proper course, the Secretary of State following his own express policy should have refused planning permission.

But that was not the situation. At the conclusion of the inquiry, there was no clear evidence about the quality of the air in the vicinity of the site. Moreover, for the purposes of deciding what standards or recommendations as to emissions to apply, the inspector described the site itself as 'semi-rural', while the area of maximum impact to the east he described as 'distinctly rural'.

Once the information about air quality at both those locations was obtained, it was a matter for informed judgment: (i) what, if any, increases in polluting discharges of various elements into the air were acceptable?; and (ii) whether the best available techniques, etc, would ensure that those discharges were kept within acceptable limits.

Those issues are clearly within the competence and jurisdiction of HMIP. If in the end the inspectorate conclude that the best available techniques, etc, would not achieve the results required by ss 7(2) and 7(4), it may well be that the proper course would be for them to refuse an authorisation. Certainly, in my view, since the issue has been expressly referred to them by the Secretary of State, they should not consider that the grant of planning permission inhibits them from refusing authorisation if they decide in their discretion that this is the proper course.

Thus, in my judgment, this was not a case in which it was apparent that a refusal of authorisation will, or will probably be, the only proper decision for HMIP to make. The

Secretary of State was therefore justified in concluding that the areas of concern which led to the inspector and the assessor recommending refusal were matters which could properly be decided by HMIP and that their powers were adequate to deal with those concerns.

The Secretary of State was therefore also justified in concluding that the proposed plant met, or could by conditions on an authorisation be required to meet, the third criterion in policy EN16 in the structure plan and thus accorded with that plan.

For those reasons, I conclude that the Secretary of State did not err in law nor did he reach a decision which was irrational or in any other way outside his statutory powers.

Section 13 Enforcement notices

(1) If the enforcing authority is of the opinion that the person carrying on a prescribed process under an authorisation is contravening any condition of the authorisation, or is likely to contravene any such condition, the authority may serve on him a notice ('an enforcement notice').

(2) An enforcement notice shall–

    (a) state that the authority is of the said opinion;

    (b) specify the matters constituting the contravention or the matters making it likely that the contravention will arise, as the case may be;

    (c) specify the steps that must be taken to remedy the contravention or to remedy the matters making it likely that the contravention will arise, as the case may be; and

    (d) specify the period within which those steps must be taken.

(3) The Secretary of State may, if he thinks fit in relation to the carrying on by any person of a prescribed process, give to the enforcing authority directions as to whether the authority should exercise its powers under this section and as to the steps which are to be required to be taken under this section.

(4) The enforcing authority may, as respects any enforcement notice it has issued to a person, by notice in writing served on that person, withdraw the notice.

Section 14 Prohibition notices

(1) If the enforcing authority is of the opinion [that the continued carrying on of a prescribed process under an authorisation] ... involves an imminent risk of serious pollution of the environment the authority shall serve a notice (a 'prohibition notice') on the person carrying on the process.

(2) A prohibition notice may be served whether or not the manner of carrying on the process in question contravenes a condition of the authorisation and may relate to any aspects of the process, whether regulated by the conditions of the authorisation or not.

(3) A prohibition notice shall–

    (a) state the authority's opinion;

    (b) specify the risk involved in the process;

    (c) specify the steps that must be taken to remove it and the period within which they must be taken; and

    (d) direct that the authorisation shall, until the notice is withdrawn, wholly or to the extent specified in the notice cease to have effect to authorise the carrying on of the process;

and where the direction applies to part only of the process it may impose conditions to be observed in carrying on the part which is authorised to be carried on.

(4) The Secretary of State may, if he thinks fit in relation to the carrying on by any person of a prescribed process, give to the enforcing authority directions as to–

  (a) whether the authority should perform its duties under this section; and

  (b) the matters to be specified in any prohibition notice in pursuance of sub-s (3) above which the authority is directed to issue.

(5) The enforcing authority shall, as respects any prohibition notice it has issued to any person, by notice in writing served on that person, withdraw the notice when it is satisfied that the steps required by the notice have been taken.

Section 15 Appeals as respects authorisations and against variation, enforcement and prohibition notices

(1) The following persons, namely–

  (a) a person who has been refused the grant of an authorisation under s 6 above;

  (b) a person who is aggrieved by the conditions attached, under any provision of this Part, to his authorisation;

  (c) a person who has been refused a variation of an authorisation on an application under s 11 above;

  (d) a person whose authorisation has been revoked under s 12 above;

may appeal against the decision of the enforcing authority to the Secretary of State (except where the decision implements a direction of his).

(2) A person on whom a variation notice, an enforcement notice or a prohibition notice is served may appeal against the notice to the Secretary of State.

(3) Where an appeal under this section is made to the Secretary of State–

  (a) the Secretary of State may refer any matter involved in the appeal to a person appointed by him for the purpose; or

  (b) the Secretary of State may, instead of determining the appeal himself, direct that the appeal ... shall be determined by a person appointed by him for the purpose; and a person appointed under para (b) above for the purpose of an appeal shall have the same powers under sub-s (5), (6) or (7) below as the Secretary of State.

(4) An appeal under this section shall, if and to the extent required by regulations under sub-s (10) below, be advertised in such manner as may be prescribed by regulations under that sub-section.

(5) If either party to the appeal so requests or the Secretary of State so decides, an appeal shall be or continue in the form of a hearing (which may, if the person hearing the appeal so decides, be held, or held to any extent, in private).

(6) On determining an appeal against a decision of an enforcing authority under sub-s (1) above, the Secretary of State–

  (a) may affirm the decision;

  (b) where the decision was a refusal to grant an authorisation or a variation of an authorisation, may direct the enforcing authority to grant the authorisation or to vary the authorisation, as the case may be;

(c) where the decision was as to the conditions attached to an authorisation, may quash all or any of the conditions of the authorisation;

(d) where the decision was to revoke an authorisation, may quash the decision;

and where he exercises any of the powers in paras (b), (c) or (d) above, he may give directions as to the conditions to be attached to the authorisation.

(7) On the determination of an appeal under sub-s (2) above the Secretary of State may either quash or affirm the notice and, if he affirms it, may do so either in its original form or with such modifications as he may in the circumstances think fit.

(8) Where an appeal is brought under sub-s (1) above against the revocation of an authorisation, the revocation shall not take effect pending the final determination or the withdrawal of the appeal.

(9) Where an appeal is brought under sub-s (2) above against a notice, the bringing of the appeal shall not have the effect of suspending the operation of the notice.

[Sub-section (10) enables the Secretary of State to make regulations setting out the procedure for appeals. See SI 1991/507 as amended by SI 1996/667.]

Section 20 Public registers of information

(1) It shall be the duty of each enforcing authority ... to maintain, in accordance with regulations made by the Secretary of State, a register containing prescribed particulars of or relating to–

(a) applications for authorisations made to that authority;

(b) the authorisations which have been granted by that authority ...;

(c) variation notices, enforcement notices and prohibition notices issued by that authority;

(d) revocations of authorisations effected by that authority;

(e) appeals under s 15 above;

(f) convictions for such offences under s 23(1) below as may be prescribed;

(g) information obtained or furnished in pursuance of the conditions of authorisations or under any provision of this Part;

(h) directions given to the authority under any provision of this Part by the Secretary of State; and

(i) such other matters relating to the carrying on of prescribed processes or any pollution of the environment caused thereby as may be prescribed;

but that duty is subject to ss 21 and 22 below.

[Subsection (2) omitted, sub-s (3) repealed by the EA 1995, sub-s (4) omitted.]

(5) Where information of any description is excluded from any register by virtue of s 22 below, a statement shall be entered in the register indicating the existence of information of that description.

(6) The Secretary of State may give to enforcing authorities directions requiring the removal from any register of theirs of any specified information not prescribed for inclusion under sub-s (1) or (2) above or which, by virtue of s 21 or 22 below, ought to have been excluded from the register.

(7) It shall be the duty of each enforcing authority–

    (a) to secure that the registers maintained by them under this section are available, at all reasonable times, for inspection by the public free of charge; and

    (b) to afford to members of the public facilities for obtaining copies of entries, on payment of reasonable charges.

(8) Registers under this section may be kept in any form.

[Sub-section (9) repealed by the EA 1995.]

[Sub-section (10) omitted.]

Section 21 Exclusion from registers of information affecting national security

(1) No information shall be included in a register maintained under s 20 above if and so long as, in the opinion of the Secretary of State, the inclusion in the register of that information, or information of that description, would be contrary to the interests of national security.

(2) The Secretary of State may, for the purpose of securing the exclusion from registers of information to which sub-s (1) above applies, give to enforcing authorities directions–

    (a) specifying information, or descriptions of information, to be excluded from their registers; or

    (b) specifying descriptions of information to be referred to the Secretary of State for his determination;

and no information referred to the Secretary of State in pursuance of para (b) above shall be included in any such register until the Secretary of State determines that it should be so included.

[Sub-section (3) omitted.]

(4) A person may, as respects any information which appears to him to be information to which sub-s (1) above may apply, give a notice to the Secretary of State specifying the information and indicating its apparent nature; and, if he does so–

    (a) he shall notify the enforcing authority that he has done so; and

    (b) no information so notified to the Secretary of State shall be included in any such register until the Secretary of State has determined that it should be so included.

Section 22 Exclusion from registers of certain confidential information

(1) No information relating to the affairs of any individual or business shall be included in a register maintained under s 20 above, without the consent of that individual or the person for the time being carrying on that business, if and so long as the information–

    (a) is, in relation to him, commercially confidential; and

    (b) is not required to be included in the register in pursuance of directions under sub-s (7) below;

but information is not commercially confidential for the purposes of this section unless it is determined under this section to be so by the enforcing authority or, on appeal, by the Secretary of State.

[Sub-sections (2)–(6) omitted.]

(7) The Secretary of State may give to the enforcing authorities directions as to specified information, or descriptions of information, which the public interest requires to be

included in registers maintained under s 20 above notwithstanding that the information may be commercially confidential.

[Sub-sections (8)–(10) omitted.]

(11) Information is, for the purposes of any determination under this section, commercially confidential, in relation to any individual or person, if its being contained in the register would prejudice to an unreasonable degree the commercial interests of that individual or person.

Note:

The above sections require the creation of publicly accessible registers of environment information. The provision of registers goes some way to meet the more extensive requirement on access to environmental information contained in the Directive on Freedom of Access to Environmental Information 90/313 (transposed into UK law by the Environmental Information Regulations 1992 SI 1992/3240 (p 845)). In so doing they reflect principle 10 of the Rio Declaration 1992 on access to information (see Chapter 1, p 71). For other similar registers, see for example s 64 of the EPA 1990 on waste management licences (Chapter 4, p 476, above) and s 190 of the Water Resources Act 1991 (Chapter 3, p 304, above) requiring a register of discharge consents). See further Regulation SI 1991/507 as amended by SI 1996/667.

Powers of the enforcement authorities

The following provisions are introduced by the Environment Act 1995. Tromans, in his commentary to the Act emphasises the 'great practical importance' of s 108. It 'provides a comprehensive set of powers of entry and investigation which apply to all enforcing authorities exercising pollution control functions at central and local level' (Tromans (1995) 286). The relevant authorities are the Secretary of State, the Environment Agency and the Scottish Environment Agency and local authorities. These powers are not limited to IPC, but can be used generally in relation to these authorities' pollution control functions.

Section 108 Environment Act 1995 Powers of enforcing authorities and persons authorised by them

(1) A person who appears suitable to an enforcing authority may be authorised in writing by that authority to exercise, in accordance with the terms of the authorisation, any of the powers specified in sub-s (4) below for the purpose–

  (a) of determining whether any provision of the pollution control enactments in the case of that authority is being, or has been, complied with;

  (b) of exercising or performing one or more of the pollution control functions of that authority; or

  (c) of determining whether and, if so, how such a function should be exercised or performed.

(2) A person who appears suitable to the Agency or SEPA may be authorised in writing by the Agency or, as the case may be, SEPA to exercise, in accordance with the terms of the authorisation, any of the powers specified in sub-s (4) below for the purpose of enabling the Agency or, as the case may be, SEPA to carry out any assessment or

prepare any report which the Agency or, as the case may be, SEPA is required to carry out or prepare under s 5(3) or 33(3) above.

(3 Sub-s (2) above only applies where the Minister who required the assessment to be carried out, or the report to be prepared, has, whether at the time of making the requirement or at any later time, notified the Agency or, as the case may be, SEPA that the assessment or report appears to him to relate to an incident or possible incident involving or having the potential to involve–

(a) serious pollution of the environment;

(b) serious harm to human health; or

(c) danger to life or health.

(4) The powers which a person may be authorised to exercise under sub-s (1) or (2) above are–

(a) to enter at any reasonable time (or, in an emergency, at any time and, if need be, by force) any premises which he has reason to believe it is necessary for him to enter;

(b) on entering any premises by virtue of paragraph (a) above, to take with him–

(i) any other person duly authorised by the enforcing authority and, if the authorised person has reasonable cause to apprehend any serious obstruction in the execution of his duty, a constable; and

(ii) any equipment or materials required for any purpose for which the power of entry is being exercised;

(c) to make such examination and investigation as may in any circumstances be necessary;

(d) as regards any premises which he has power to enter, to direct that those premises or any part of them, or anything in them, shall be left undisturbed (whether generally or in particular respects) for so long as is reasonably necessary for the purpose of any examination or investigation under para (c) above;

(e) to take such measurements and photographs and make such recordings as he considers necessary for the purpose of any examination or investigation under para (c) above;

(f) to take samples, or cause samples to be taken, of any articles or substances found in or on any premises which he has power to enter, and of the air, water or land in, on, or in the vicinity of, the premises;

(g) in the case of any article or substance found in or on any premises which he has power to enter, being an article or substance which appears to him to have caused or to be likely to cause pollution of the environment or harm to human health, to cause it to be dismantled or subjected to any process or test (but not so as to damage or destroy it, unless that is necessary);

(h) in the case of any such article or substance as is mentioned in para (g) above, to take possession of it and detain it for so long as is necessary for all or any of the following purposes, namely–

(i) to examine it, or cause it to be examined, and to do, or cause to be done, to it anything which he has power to do under that paragraph;

(ii) to ensure that it is not tampered with before examination of it is completed;

(iii) to ensure that it is available for use as evidence in any proceedings for an offence under the pollution control enactments in the case of the enforcing authority under whose authorisation he acts or in any other proceedings relating to a variation notice, enforcement notice or prohibition notice under those enactments;

(j) to require any person whom he has reasonable cause to believe to be able to give any information relevant to any examination or investigation under para (c) above to answer (in the absence of persons other than a person nominated by that person to be present and any persons whom the authorised person may allow to be present) such questions as the authorised person thinks fit to ask and to sign a declaration of the truth of his answers;

(k) to require the production of, or where the information is recorded in computerised form, the furnishing of extracts from, any records–

(i) which are required to be kept under the pollution control enactments for the enforcing authority under whose authorisation he acts, or

(ii) which it is necessary for him to see for the purposes of an examination or investigation under para (c) above,

and to inspect and take copies of, or of any entry in, the records;

(l) to require any person to afford him such facilities and assistance with respect to any matters or things within that person's control or in relation to which that person has responsibilities as are necessary to enable the authorised person to exercise any of the powers conferred on him by this section;

(m) any other power for–

(i) a purpose falling within any paragraph of sub-s (1) above; or

(ii) any such purpose as is mentioned in sub-s (2) above, which is conferred by regulations made by the Secretary of State.

[...]

(13) Nothing in this section shall be taken to compel the production by any person of a document of which he would on grounds of legal professional privilege be entitled to withhold production on an order for discovery in an action in the High Court or, in relation to Scotland, on an order for the production of documents in an action in the Court of Session.

[...]

(15) In this section–

[...]

'emergency' means a case in which it appears to the authorised person in question–

(a) that there is an immediate risk of serious pollution of the environment or serious harm to human health; or

(b) that circumstances exist which are likely to endanger life or health,

and that immediate entry to any premises is necessary to verify the existence of that risk or those circumstances or to ascertain the cause of that risk or those circumstances or to effect a remedy;

[...]

Section 109 Environment Act 1995 Power to deal with cause of imminent danger of serious pollution etc

(1) Where, in the case of any article or substance found by him on any premises which he has power to enter, an authorised person has reasonable cause to believe that, in the

circumstances in which he finds it, the article or substance is a cause of imminent danger of serious pollution of the environment or serious harm to human health, he may seize it and cause it to be rendered harmless (whether by destruction or otherwise).

(2) As soon as may be after any article or substance has been seized and rendered harmless under this section, the authorised person shall prepare and sign a written report giving particulars of the circumstances in which the article or substance was seized and so dealt with by him, and shall–

(a) give a signed copy of the report to a responsible person at the premises where the article or substance was found by him; and

(b) unless that person is the owner of the article or substance, also serve a signed copy of the report on the owner;

and if, where para (b) above applies, the authorised person cannot after reasonable inquiry ascertain the name or address of the owner, the copy may be served on him by giving it to the person to whom a copy was given under para (a) above.

[Sub-section (3) omitted.]

Offences

Section 23 of the EPA 1990, as amended by the Environment Act 1995, makes it an offence *inter alia* to operate a relevant process without appropriate authorisation or in breach of an enforcement or prohibition notice. Fines of up to £20,000 or terms of imprisonment of up to three months, or both may be imposed on summary conviction. On indictment unlimited fines may be imposed and periods of imprisonment up to two years.

Section 24 Enforcement by High Court

If the enforcing authority is of the opinion that proceedings for an offence under s 23(1)(c) above would afford an ineffectual remedy against a person who has failed to comply with the requirements of an enforcement notice or a prohibition notice, the authority may take proceedings in the High Court or, in Scotland, in any court of competent jurisdiction for the purpose of securing compliance with the notice.

Section 25 Onus of proof as regards techniques and evidence

(1) In any proceedings for an offence under s 23(1)(a) above consisting in a failure to comply with the general condition implied in every authorisation by s 7(4) above, it shall be for the accused to prove that there was no better available technique not entailing excessive cost than was in fact used to satisfy the condition.

[Sub-section (2) omitted.]

Section 26 Power of court to order cause of offence to be remedied

(1) Where a person is convicted of an offence under s 23(1)(a) or (c) above in respect of any matters which appear to the court to be matters which it is in his power to remedy, the court may, in addition to or instead of imposing any punishment, order him, within such time as may be fixed by the order, to take such steps as may be specified in the order for remedying those matters.

[Sub-sections (2) and (3) omitted.]

Notes:

1   Where s 26 applies the Environment Agency in England and Wales may take remedial action and recover the consequential costs from the party convicted of the offence, provided the Secretary of State has given written approval (s 27 as amended by the Environment Act 1995).

2   Section 157 provides that where an offence is committed by a body corporate 'with the consent or connivance of, or attributable to any neglect on the part of, any director, manager, secretary or similar officer of the body corporate or a person who is purporting to act in such a capacity, he as well as the body corporate shall be guilty of that offence'.

3   Section 110 of the Environment Act 1995 makes it:

   (1) [...] an offence for a person intentionally to obstruct an authorised person in the exercise or performance of his powers or duties.

   (2) It is an offence for a person, without reasonable excuse–

      (a) to fail to comply with any requirement imposed under s 108 above;

      (b) to fail or refuse to provide facilities or assistance or any information or to permit any inspection reasonably required by an authorised person in the execution of his powers or duties under or by virtue of that section; or

      (c) to prevent any other person from appearing before an authorised person, or answering any question to which an authorised person may require an answer, pursuant to sub-s (4) of that section.

   (3) It is an offence for a person falsely to pretend to be an authorised person.

[Sub-section (4) omitted.]

The Environmental Protection (Prescribed Processes and Substances) Regulations 1991 SI 1991/472

These regulations are central to an understanding and operation of the IPC scheme. Here they are extracted as amended by SI 1992/614; SI 1994/1271; SI 1993/2405; SI 1995/3247; SI 1996/2678; and SI 1998/767. Schedule 1 of the regulations establishes two lists of prescribed matters referred to as Pt A (processes subject to IPC) and Pt B (processes subject to LAAPC).

Before turning to Sched 1, note s 4(1) which provides that:

... a process shall not be taken to be a Part A process if it has the following characteristics, namely–

(i)   that it cannot result in the release into the air of any substance prescribed by Regulation 6(1) or there is no likelihood that it will result in the release into the air of any such substance except in a quantity which is so trivial that it is incapable of causing harm or its capacity to cause harm is insignificant; and

(ii) that it cannot result in the release into water of any substance prescribed by Regulation 6(2) except–

      (a) in a concentration which is no greater than the background concentration; or

(b) in a quantity which does not, in any 12 month period, exceed the background quantity by more than the amount specified in relation to the description of substance in Column 2 of Schedule 5; and

(iii) that it cannot result in the release into land of any substance prescribed by Regulation 6(3) or there is no likelihood that it will result in the release into land of any such substance except in a quantity which is so trivial that it is incapable of causing harm or its capacity to cause harm is insignificant.

(2) Subject to para (6), a process shall not be taken to be a Part B process unless it will, or there is a likelihood that it will, result in the release into the air of one or more substances prescribed by Regulation 6(1) in a quantity greater than that mentioned in para (1)(i) above.

(5) A process shall not be taken to fall within a description in Schedule 1 if it is carried on as a domestic activity in connection with a private dwelling.

[...]

Schedule 1: Descriptions of Processes

Chapter 1: Fuel production processes, combustion processes (including power generation)

Section 1.1 Gasification and associated processes

PART A

(a) Reforming natural gas.

(aa) Refining natural gas if that process is related to another Part A process or is likely to involve the use in any 12 month period of 1,000 tonnes or more of natural gas.

(b) Odorising natural gas or liquefied petroleum gas [if that process is related to another Part A process].

(c) Producing gas from coal, lignite, oil or other carbonaceous material or from mixtures thereof other than from sewage or the biological degradation of waste, unless carried on as part of a process which is a combustion process (whether or not that process falls within s 1.3 of this Schedule).

(d) Purifying or refining any product of any of the processes described in paras (a), (b) or (c) or converting it into a different product.

In this section, 'carbonaceous material' includes such materials as charcoal, coke, peat and rubber.

PART B

(a) Odorising natural gas or liquefied petroleum gas, except where that process is related to a Part A process.

(b) Blending odorant for use with natural gas or liquefied petroleum gas.

(c) Any process for refining natural gas not falling within paragraph (aa) of Part A of this section.

Section 1.2 Carbonisation and associated processes

...

Section 1.3 Combustion processes

...

Section 1.4 Petroleum processes

PART A

(a) The loading, unloading or other handling of, the storage of, or the physical, chemical or thermal treatment of–

    (i)   crude oil;

    (ii) stabilised crude petroleum;

    (iii) crude shale oil;

    (iv) if related to another process described in this paragraph, any associated gas or condensate.

...

Chapter 2: Metal production and processing

Section 2.1 Iron and steel

PART A

(a) Loading, unloading or otherwise handling or storing iron ore except in the course of mining operations.

(b) Loading, unloading or otherwise handling or storing burnt pyrites.

(c) Crushing, grading, grinding, screening, washing or drying iron ore or any mixture of iron ore and other materials.

(d) Blending or mechanically mixing grades of iron ore or iron ore with other materials but a process does full within this paragraph if–

    (i)   it is a process for heating iron, steel or any ferrous alloy in one or more furnaces or other appliances the primary combustion chambers of which have in aggregate a net rated thermal input of less than 0.2 mega watts;

    [...]

(e) Pelletising, calcining, roasting or sintering iron ore or any mixture of iron ore and other materials.

(f) Making, melting or refining iron, steel or any ferrous alloy in any furnace other than a furnace described in Part B of this section.

(g) Any process for the refining or making of iron, steel or any ferrous alloy in which air or oxygen or both are used unless related to a process described in Part B of this section.

(h) The desulphurisation of iron, steel or any ferrous alloy made by a process described in this Part of this section.

(i) Heating iron, steel or any ferrous alloy (whether in a furnace or other appliance) to remove grease, oil or any other non-metallic contaminant (including such operations as the removal by heat of plastic or rubber covering from scrap cable), if related to another process described in this Part of this section.

(j) Any foundry process (including ancillary foundry operations such as the manufacture and recovery of moulds, the reclamation of sand, fettling, grinding and shot-blasting) if related to another process described in this Part of this section.

...

(l) Handling slag in conjunction with a process described in para (f) or (g).

(m) Any process for rolling iron, steel or any ferrous alloy carried on in relation to any process described in paras (f) or (g), and any process carried on in conjunction with such rolling involving the scarfing or cutting with oxygen of iron, steel or any ferrous alloy.

Nothing in paras (a) or (b) of this Part of this section applies to the handling or storing of other minerals in association with the handling or storing of iron ore or burnt pyrites.

[...]

PART B

(a) Making, melting or refining iron, steel or any ferrous alloy in–

(i) an electric arc furnace with a designed holding capacity of less than seven tonnes; or

(ii) a cupola, crucible furnace, reverberatory furnace, rotary furnace, induction furnace or resistance furnace.

(b) Any process for the refining or making of iron, steel or any ferrous alloy in which air or oxygen or both are used, if related to a process described in this Part of this section.

(c) The desulphurisation of iron, steel or any ferrous alloy, if the process does not fall within para (h) of Part A of this section.

(d) Any such process as is described in para (i) of Part A above, if not falling within that paragraph.

(e) Any foundry process (including ancillary foundry operations such as the manufacture and recovery of moulds, the reclamation of sand, fettling, grinding, and shot-blasting) if related to another process described in this Part of this section.

(f) Any other process involving the casting of iron, steel or any ferrous alloy from deliveries of 50 tonnes or more at one time of molten metal.

Section 2.2 Non-ferrous metals

...

Chapter 3: Mineral industries

Section 3.1 Cement and lime manufacture and associated processes

...

Section 3.2 Processes involving asbestos

PART A

(a) Producing raw asbestos by extraction from the ore except where the process is directly associated with the mining of the ore.

(b) The manufacture and, where related to the manufacture, the industrial finishing of the following products where the use of asbestos is involved–

asbestos cement

asbestos cement products

asbestos fillers

asbestos filters

asbestos floor coverings

asbestos friction products

asbestos insulating board

asbestos jointing, packaging and reinforcement material

asbestos packing

asbestos paper or card

asbestos textiles.

(c) The stripping of asbestos from railway vehicles except–

(i) in the course of the repair or maintenance of the vehicle;

(ii) in the course of recovery operations following an accident; or

(iii) where the asbestos is permanently bonded in plastic, rubber or a resin [cement or in any other material (including plastic, rubber or a resin)].

(d) The destruction by burning of a railway vehicle if asbestos has been incorporated in, or sprayed on to, its structure.

PART B

The industrial finishing of any product mentioned in para (b) of Part A of this section if the process does not fall within that paragraph.

Section 3.3 Other mineral fibres

...

Section 3.4 Other mineral processes

...

Section 3.5 Glass manufacture and production

...

Section 3.6 Ceramic production

...

Chapter 4: The chemical industry

...

Section 4.1 Petrochemical processes

...

Section 4.2 The manufacture and use of organic chemicals

...

Section 4.3 Acid processes

...

Section 4.4 Processes involving halogens

...

Section 4.5 Inorganic chemical processes

PART A

(a) The manufacture of hydrogen cyanide or hydrogen sulphide other than in the course of fumigation.

(b) Any manufacturing process involving the use of hydrogen cyanide or hydrogen sulphide.

(c) Any process for the manufacture of a chemical which may result in the release into the air of hydrogen cyanide or hydrogen sulphide.

(d) The production of [any compound containing any of the following–

antimony

arsenic

beryllium

gallium

indium

lead

palladium

platinum

selenium

tellurium

thallium,

where the process may result in the release into the air of any of those elements or compounds or the release into water of any substance described in Schedule 5 ...

(e) ...

(f) ...

(g) The production or recovery of any compound of cadmium or mercury.

(h) Any process of manufacture which involves the use of cadmium or mercury or of any compound of either of those elements or which may result in the release into the air of either of those elements or any of their compounds.

[Paragraphs (i)–(p) omitted.]

PART B

Nil

Section 4.6 Chemical fertiliser production

...

Section 4.7 Pesticide production

...

Section 4.8 Pharmaceutical production

...

Section 4.9 The storage of chemicals in bulk

...

Chapter 5: Waste disposal and recycling

Section 5.1 Incineration

PART A

(a) The destruction by burning in an incinerator of any waste chemicals or waste plastic arising from the manufacture of a chemical or the manufacture of a plastic.

(b) The destruction by burning in an incinerator, other than incidentally in the course of burning other waste, of any waste chemicals being, or comprising in elemental or compound form, any of the following–

bromine

cadmium

chlorine

fluorine

iodine

lead

mercury

nitrogen

phosphorus

sulphur

zinc.

(c) The destruction by burning of any other waste, including animal remains, otherwise than by a process related to [and carried on as part of] a Part B process, on premises where there is plant designed to incinerate such waste at a rate of 1 tonne or more per hour.

(d) ...

PART B

(a) The destruction by burning in an incinerator other than an exempt incinerator of any waste, including animal remains, except where related to a Part A process.

(b) The cremation of human remains.

In this section–

...

Section 5.2 Recovery processes

...

Section 5.3 The production of fuel from waste

...

Chapter 6: Other industries

Section 6.1 Paper and pulp manufacturing processes

...

Section 6.2 Di-isocyanate processes

...

Section 6.3 Tar and bitumen processes

...

Section 6.5 Coating processes and printing

...

Section 6.6 The manufacture of dyestuffs, printing ink and coating materials

...

Section 6.7 Timber processes

...

Section 6.8 Processes involving rubber

PART A

Nil

PART B

(a) The mixing, milling or blending of–
    (i) natural rubber; or
    (ii) synthetic [organic] elastomers,
    if carbon black is used.

(b) Any process which converts the product of a process falling within para (a) into a finished product if related to a process falling within that paragraph.

Section 6.9 The treatment and processing of animal or vegetable matter

...

INTEGRATED POLLUTION PREVENTION AND CONTROL (IPPC) IN COMMUNITY LAW

Integrated Pollution Prevention and Control Directive 96/61[19]

The IPPC Directive was adopted on 30 October 1996 and Member States have three years in which to implement its provisions. There was an obvious overlap with the UK system of IPC outlined above but the Directive does contain certain unique features. The scope of the Directive is somewhat broader in that pollution[20] subject to integrated prevention and control includes noise which under the EPA is the subject of a separate system contained in Pt III (statutory nuisance). The aim is to provide protection for the environment as a whole by imposing measures to prevent or reduce emissions in the air, water and land (Art 1). The UK system of IPC required amendment in order to comply with this Directive. The legal basis for this amendment has been the Pollution Prevention and Control Act 1999.

The Directive requires Member States to take measures to ensure that operators of installations (defined to include those who have control or decisive economic power over the functioning of an installation) (Art 2(12)) comply with a number of 'general principles'. The basic obligations are:

(a) to take all appropriate preventive measures against pollution, particularly applying the best available techniques;

(b) not to cause significant pollution;

(c) to use energy efficiently;

(d) to return the site of operation to a satisfactory state when the installation is decommissioned.

The latter obligation (Art 3(f)) is not part of the IPC system and so does not form part of any application for authorisation under Pt 1 of the EPA.

As with IPC, the Directive lists the categories of industrial activity which fall within IPPC (including the chemical and energy industries, waste management, the production and processing of metals, etc) (Annex I) and achieves its aim by requiring competent authorities to issue permits to operators of such activities. In addition to compliance with the general principles outlined above, permits must incorporate any further (stricter) conditions necessary to ensure that any environmental quality standards set by Community legislation are met. If compliance with these conditions does not guarantee that Directive standards will be met, the permit is to be refused (Art 8).

---

19 See Henshawe, L, 'The EC Directive on Integrated Pollution Prevention and Control: implications for the United Kingdom' [1996] Env Liability 29.

20 Pollution is defined as 'the direct or indirect introduction as a result of human activity, of substances, vibrations, heat or noise into the air, water or land which may be harmful to human health or the quality of the environment, result in damage to material property, or impair or interfere with amenities and other legitimate uses of the environment' (Art 2(2)).

Best available techniques (BAT)

The definition of best available techniques gave rise to considerable debate during negotiations leading to the Directive. The definition is contained in Art 2(11) and Annex IV.

'*Best*' – means the most effective in achieving a 'high general level of protection of the environment as a whole'.

'*Techniques*' – include the design, maintenance and operation of an installation.

'*Available*' – means techniques which are developed on a scale which allows implementation in the relevant industrial sector, under economically and technically viable conditions, taking into consideration the costs and advantages, whether or not the techniques are used or produced inside the Member State, as long as they are reasonably accessible to the operator.

The need to take economic considerations into account when requiring the use of BAT is repeated in Annex IV. There is a requirement to weigh the principles of precaution and prevention against likely costs and benefits.

Emission limit values

Permits are to include emission limit values based on the best available techniques for those pollutants listed in Annex III which are likely to be emitted from an installation into the air or water in significant quantities (Art 9(3)). Such emissions must also be monitored (Art 9(5)). Although these limit values are to be based on best available techniques, the actual setting is to take place at national levels and shall take into account 'the technical characteristics of the installation concerned, its geographical location and the local environmental conditions' (Art 9(4)). Permits may also make provision for 'other than normal' operating conditions (Art 9(6)).

Whether the reference to geography and local conditions will amount to varying pollution control standards within the EC is open to doubt. However, as Henshawe writes:[21]

> To provide for such discretion at national level is hardly compatible with a harmonised approach to pollution control at Community level ...[22]

New and existing installations

Permits for new installations must be issued 'in accordance with the Directive' (Art 4) so the Directive's regime will apply to all installations coming into operation after the implementation of the Directive. Although some aspects of the IPPC regime will also apply to existing installations (as defined in Art 2(4)) as from the date of implementation, others will not apply for a period of eight years after that date. The provisions on public access to information (Art 15) bound existing installations as from 1999. However, other

---

21 *Op cit*, Henshawe, fn 19, p 30.
22 Note that the Directive makes no reference to the BPEO concept as contained in the IPC system. Article 1 does, however, stress the importance of achieving a high level of protection for the environment as a whole.

provisions, such as the obligation upon operators to return a site to a 'satisfactory state' after decommissioning of the installation, will not apply until 2007.

Applications etc

Article 6 specifies the information which must be contained in a permit application. Operators must also specify the measures they intend to take in order to comply with the 'general principles' referred to above including measures designed 'to avoid any pollution risk and return the site of operation to a satisfactory state' (Art 3(f)).

Once granted, operators are obliged to inform the competent authority of any changes planned to the operation of the installation which may have consequences for the environment (Art 12). No 'substantial change'[23] shall be made without the issue of a permit in accordance with the Directive (Art 12(2)). Permits are to be reviewed 'periodically' (Art 13(1)). No time-limit is set although a maximum period of 10 years has been suggested.[24] There is, however, a general obligation for competent authorities to reconsider permit conditions in the light of new Community or national legislation or where improvements in best available technology make it appropriate (Art 13(2)).

Publicity and information

The Directive contains provisions allowing for public involvement in the application procedure and for the results of the monitoring of emissions to be available for public scrutiny (Art 15). In addition, the Commission is to publish an inventory of emissions and their sources every three years. The Directive also provides for a procedure whereby every three years, Member States will provide a list of emission limit values set nationally for the various categories of industrial activities in Annex I and data on the best available techniques from which these limit values are derived. If there are wide disparities, the council may set Community emission limit values for the installations listed in Annex I and the substances listed in Annex III (Art 18).

Recent developments

The Commission has issued a consultation paper entitled *A Community Strategy for the Integrated Control of Emissions from Small Installations 1996*. The IPPC Directive 96/61 leaves most small to medium sized enterprises (SMEs) out of its scope either because their capacity falls below the relevant thresholds or because they operate in industrial sectors not covered by the Directive. Although eager to develop a regime which covers 'the totality of European industries responsible for dangerous and long-range emissions' the Commission recognises the economic difficulties faced by the SME sector in Europe and the desirability of simplifying administrative requirements for SMEs.

The factors which the Commission considers relevant affecting SME's include *inter alia*:

---

23 Defined in Art 2(10)(b) as 'a change in operation which, in the opinion of the competent authority, may have significant negative effects on human beings or the environment'.

24 The review period under the EPA 1990 is four years. See above.

- limited access to capital and to research and development, which limits the scope for significant investment in order to comply with environmental requirements;
- lower turnover than larger companies, which makes it more difficult to absorb fixed costs required by environmental regulation;
- the total number of enterprises that taken together generate serious pollution problems. A study is quoted which shows that whereas the European chlor-alkali industry releases 19 tonnes of mercury per year into the environment, 5.3–7 tonnes are released annually to sewer by dental practices.

What is proposed is a framework Directive, including the following key elements:

- only installations which release dangerous substances or have long-range effects to be covered;
- administration by a single competent authority;
- emission limit values for air and water set with reference to environmental quality standards;
- simplified authorisation procedures compared with IPPC, being sectoral rather than installation specific.
- Scope for the use of market-based or voluntary systems instead of control permits reliance upon BAT, as defined by IPPC, in determining emission limits or other controls.

The strategy is at an early stage of development.

COUNCIL DIRECTIVE

of 24 September 1996

concerning integrated pollution prevention and control

(96/61/EC)

(1996) OJ L257, p 26

THE COUNCIL OF THE EUROPEAN UNION,

Having regard to the Treaty establishing the European Community, and in particular Article 130s(1) thereof,

Having regard to the proposal from the Commission (1),

Having regard to the opinion of the Economic and Social Committee (2),

Acting in accordance with the procedure laid down in Article 189c of the Treaty (3),

Whereas the objectives and principles of the Community's environment policy, as set out in Article 130r of the Treaty, consist in particular of preventing, reducing and as far as possible eliminating pollution by giving priority to intervention at source and ensuring prudent management of natural resources, in compliance with the 'polluter pays' principle and the principle of pollution prevention;

Whereas the Fifth Environmental Action Programme, the broad outline of which was approved by the Council and the Representatives of the Governments of the Member States, meeting within the Council, in the resolution of 1 February 1993 on a Community programme of policy and action in relation to the environment and sustainable development (4), accords priority to integrated pollution control as an important part of the move towards a more sustainable balance between human activity and socio-economic development, on the one hand, and the resources and regenerative capacity of nature, on the other;

Whereas the implementation of an integrated approach to reduce pollution requires action at Community level in order to modify and supplement existing Community legislation concerning the prevention and control of pollution from industrial plants;

Whereas Council Directive 84/360/EEC of 28 June 1984 on the combating of air pollution from industrial plants (5) introduced a general framework requiring authorisation prior to any operation or substantial modification of industrial installations which may cause air pollution;

Whereas Council Directive 76/464/EEC of 4 May 1976 on pollution caused by certain dangerous substances discharged into the aquatic environment of the Community (6) introduced an authorisation requirement for the discharge of those substances;

Whereas, although Community legislation exists on the combating of air pollution and the prevention or minimisation of the discharge of dangerous substances into water, there is no comparable Community legislation aimed at preventing or minimising emissions into soil;

Whereas different approaches to controlling emissions into the air, water or soil separately may encourage the shifting of pollution between the various environmental media rather than protecting the environment as a whole;

Whereas the objective of an integrated approach to pollution control is to prevent emissions into air, water or soil wherever this is practicable, taking into account waste management, and, where it is not, to minimise them in order to achieve a high level of protection for the environment as a whole;

Whereas this Directive establishes a general framework for integrated pollution prevention and control; whereas it lays down the measures necessary to implement integrated pollution prevention and control in order to achieve a high level of protection for the environment as a whole; whereas application of the principle of sustainable development will be promoted by an integrated approach to pollution control;

Whereas the provisions of this Directive apply without prejudice to the provisions of Council Directive 85/337/EEC of 27 June 1985 on the assessment of the effects of public and private projects on the environment (7); whereas, when information or conclusions obtained further to the application of that Directive have to be taken into consideration for the granting of authorisation, this Directive does not affect the implementation of Directive 85/337/EEC;

Whereas the necessary steps must be taken by the Member States in order to ensure that the operator of the industrial activities referred to in Annex I is complying with the general principles of certain basic obligations; whereas for that purpose it would suffice for the competent authorities to take those general principles into account when laying down the authorisation conditions;

Whereas some of the provisions adopted pursuant to this Directive must be applied to existing installations after a fixed period and others as from the date of implementation of this Directive;

Whereas, in order to tackle pollution problems more effectively and efficiently, environmental aspects should be taken into consideration by the operator; whereas those aspects should be communicated to the competent authority or authorities so that they can satisfy themselves, before granting a permit, that all appropriate preventive or pollution-control measures have been laid down; whereas very different application procedures may give rise to different levels of environmental protection and public awareness; whereas, therefore, applications for permits under this Directive should include minimum data;

Whereas full co-ordination of the authorisation procedure and conditions between competent authorities will make it possible to achieve the highest practicable level of protection for the environment as a whole;

Whereas the competent authority or authorities will grant or amend a permit only when integrated environmental protection measures for air, water and land have been laid down;

Whereas the permit is to include all necessary measures to fulfil the authorisation conditions in order thus to achieve a high level of protection for the environment as a whole; whereas, without prejudice to the authorisation procedure, those measures may also be the subject of general binding requirements;

Whereas emission limit values, parameters or equivalent technical measures should be based on the best available techniques, without prescribing the use of one specific technique or technology and taking into consideration the technical characteristics of the installation concerned, its geographical location and local environmental conditions; whereas in all cases the authorisation conditions will lay down provisions on minimising long-distance or trans-frontier pollution and ensure a high level of protection for the environment as a whole;

Whereas it is for the Member States to determine how the technical characteristics of the installation concerned, its geographical location and local environmental conditions can, where appropriate, be taken into consideration;

Whereas, when an environmental quality standard requires more stringent conditions than those that can be achieved by using the best available techniques, supplementary conditions will in particular be required by the permit, without prejudice to other measures that may be taken to comply with the environmental quality standards;

Whereas, because best available techniques will change with time, particularly in the light of technical advances, the competent authorities must monitor or be informed of such progress;

Whereas, changes to an installation may give rise to pollution; whereas the competent authority or authorities must therefore be notified of any change which might affect the environment; whereas substantial changes to plant must be subject to the granting of prior authorisation in accordance with this Directive;

Whereas the authorisation conditions must be periodically reviewed and if necessary updated; whereas, under certain conditions, they will in any event be re-examined;

Whereas, in order to inform the public of the operation of installations and their potential effect on the environment, and in order to ensure the transparency of the licensing process throughout the Community, the public must have access, before any decision is taken, to information relating to applications for permits for new installations or substantial changes and to the permits themselves, their updating and the relevant monitoring data;

Whereas the establishment of an inventory of principal emissions and sources responsible may be regarded as an important instrument making it possible in particular to compare pollution activities in the Community; whereas such an inventory will be prepared by the Commission, assisted by a regulatory committee;

Whereas the development and exchange of information at Community level about best available techniques will help to redress the technological imbalances in the Community, will promote the worldwide dissemination of limit values and techniques used in the Community and will help the Member States in the efficient implementation of this Directive;

Whereas reports on the implementation and effectiveness of this Directive will have to be drawn up regularly;

Whereas this Directive is concerned with installations whose potential for pollution, and therefore trans-frontier pollution, is significant; whereas trans-boundary consultation is to be organised where applications relate to the licensing of new installations or substantial changes to installations which are likely to have significant negative environmental effects; whereas the applications relating to such proposals or substantial changes will be available to the public of the Member State likely to be affected;

Whereas the need for action may be identified at Community level to lay down emission limit values for certain categories of installation and pollutant covered by this Directive; whereas the Council will set such emission limit values in accordance with the provisions of the Treaty;

Whereas the provisions of this Directive apply without prejudice to Community provisions on health and safety at the workplace.

HAS ADOPTED THIS DIRECTIVE:

Article 1 Purpose and scope

The purpose of this Directive is to achieve integrated prevention and control of pollution arising from the activities listed in Annex I. It lays down measures designed to prevent or, where that is not practicable, to reduce emissions in the air, water and land from the above mentioned activities, including measures concerning waste, in order to achieve a high level of protection of the environment taken as a whole, without prejudice to Directive 85/337/EEC and other relevant Community provisions.

Article 2 Definitions

For the purposes of this Directive:

1   'substance' shall mean any chemical element and its compounds, with the exception of radioactive substances within the meaning of Directive 80/836/Euratom (8) and genetically modified organisms within the meaning of Directive 90/219/EEC (9) and Directive 90/220/EEC (10);

2   'pollution' shall mean the direct or indirect introduction as a result of human activity, of substances, vibrations, heat or noise into the air, water or land which may be harmful to human health or the quality of the environment, result in damage to material property, or impair or interfere with amenities and other legitimate uses of the environment;

3 'installation' shall mean a stationary technical unit where one or more activities listed in Annex I are carried out, and any other directly associated activities which have a technical connection with the activities carried out on that site and which could have an effect on emissions and pollution;

4 'existing installation' shall mean an installation in operation or, in accordance with legislation existing before the date on which this Directive is brought into effect, an installation authorised or in the view of the competent authority the subject of a full request for authorisation, provided that that installation is put into operation no later than one year after the date on which this Directive is brought into effect;

5 'emission' shall mean the direct or indirect release of substances, vibrations, heat or noise from individual or diffuse sources in the installation into the air, water or land;

6 'emission limit values' shall mean the mass, expressed in terms of certain specific parameters, concentration and/or level of an emission, which may not be exceeded during one or more periods of time. Emission limit values may also be laid down for certain groups, families or categories of substances, in particular for those listed in Annex III. The emission limit values for substances shall normally apply at the point where the emissions leave the installation, any dilution being disregarded when determining them. With regard to indirect releases into water, the effect of a water treatment plant may be taken into account when determining the emission limit values of the installation involved, provided that an equivalent level is guaranteed for the protection of the environment as a whole and provided this does not lead to higher levels of pollution in the environment, without prejudice to Directive 76/464/EEC or the Directives implementing it;

7 'environmental quality standard' shall mean the set of requirements which must be fulfilled at a given time by a given environment or particular part thereof, as set out in Community legislation;

8 'competent authority' shall mean the authority or authorities or bodies responsible under the legal provisions of the Member States for carrying out the obligations arising from this Directive;

9 'permit' shall mean that part or the whole of a written decision (or several such decisions) granting authorisation to operate all or part of an installation, subject to certain conditions which guarantee that the installation complies with the requirements of this Directive. A permit may cover one or more installations or parts of installations on the same site operated by the same operator;

10 (a) 'change in operation' shall mean a change in the nature or functioning, or an extension, of the installation which may have consequences for the environment;

(b) 'substantial change' shall mean a change in operation which, in the opinion of the competent authority, may have significant negative effects on human beings or the environment;

11 'best available techniques' shall mean the most effective and advanced stage in the development of activities and their methods of operation which indicate the practical suitability of particular techniques for providing in principle the basis for emission limit values designed to prevent and, where that is not practicable, generally to reduce emissions and the impact on the environment as a whole:

– 'techniques' shall include both the technology used and the way in which the installation is designed, built, maintained, operated and decommissioned,

- 'available' techniques shall mean those developed on a scale which allows implementation in the relevant industrial sector, under economically and technically viable conditions, taking into consideration the costs and advantages, whether or not the techniques are used or produced inside the Member State in question, as long as they are reasonably accessible to the operator,

- 'best' shall mean most effective in achieving a high general level of protection of the environment as a whole.

In determining the best available techniques, special consideration should be given to the items listed in Annex IV;

12 'operator' shall mean any natural or legal person who operates or controls the installation or, where this is provided for in national legislation, to whom decisive economic power over the technical functioning of the installation has been delegated.

Article 3 General principles governing the basic obligations of the operator

Member States shall take the necessary measures to provide that the competent authorities ensure that installations are operated in such a way that:

(a) all the appropriate preventive measures are taken against pollution, in particular through application of the best available techniques;

(b) no significant pollution is caused;

(c) waste production is avoided in accordance with Council Directive 75/442/EEC of 15 July 1975 on waste (11); where waste is produced, it is recovered or, where that is technically and economically impossible, it is disposed of while avoiding or reducing any impact on the environment;

(d) energy is used efficiently;

(e) the necessary measures are taken to prevent accidents and limit their consequences;

(f) the necessary measures are taken upon definitive cessation of activities to avoid any pollution risk and return the site of operation to a satisfactory state. For the purposes of compliance with this Article, it shall be sufficient if Member States ensure that the competent authorities take account of the general principles set out in this Article when they determine the conditions of the permit.

Article 4 Permits for new installations

Member States shall take the necessary measures to ensure that no new installation is operated without a permit issued in accordance with this Directive, without prejudice to the exceptions provided for in Council Directive 88/609/EEC of 24 November 1988 on the limitation of emissions of certain pollutants into the air from large combustion plants (12).

Article 5 Requirements for the granting of permits for existing installations

1 Member States shall take the necessary measures to ensure that the competent authorities see to it, by means of permits in accordance with Articles 6 and 8 or, as appropriate, by reconsidering and, where necessary, by updating the conditions, that existing installations operate in accordance with the requirements of Articles 3, 7, 9, 10, 13, the first and second indents of 14, and 15(2) not later than eight years after the date on which this Directive is brought into effect, without prejudice to specific Community legislation.

2   Member States shall take the necessary measures to apply the provisions of Articles 1, 2, 11, 12, 14, third indent, 15(1), (3) and (4), 16, 17 and 18(2) to existing installations as from the date on which this Directive is brought into effect.

Article 6 Applications for permits

1   Member States shall take the necessary measures to ensure that an application to the competent authority for a permit includes a description of:

- the installation and its activities,
- the raw and auxiliary materials, other substances and the energy used in or generated by the installation,
- the sources of emissions from the installation,
- the conditions of the site of the installation,
- the nature and quantities of foreseeable emissions from the installation into each medium as well as identification of significant effects of the emissions on the environment,
- the proposed technology and other techniques for preventing or, where this not possible, reducing emissions from the installation,
- where necessary, measures for the prevention and recovery of waste generated by the installation,
- further measures planned to comply with the general principles of the basic obligations of the operator as provided for in Article 3,
- measures planned to monitor emissions into the environment.

An application for a permit shall also include a non-technical summary of the details referred to in the above indents.

2   Where information supplied in accordance with the requirements provided for in Directive 85/337/EEC or a safety report prepared in accordance with Council Directive 82/501/EEC of 24 June 1982 on the major-accident hazards of certain industrial activities (13) or other information produced in response to other legislation fulfils any of the requirements of this Article, that information may be included in, or attached to, the application.

Article 7 Integrated approach to issuing permits

Member States shall take the measures necessary to ensure that the conditions of, and procedure for the grant of, the permit are fully co-ordinated where more than one competent authority is involved, in order to guarantee an effective integrated approach by all authorities competent for this procedure.

Article 8 Decisions

Without prejudice to other requirements laid down in national or Community legislation, the competent authority shall grant a permit containing conditions guaranteeing that the installation complies with the requirements of this Directive or, if it does not, shall refuse to grant the permit. All permits granted and modified permits must include details of the arrangements made for air, water and land protection as referred to in this Directive.

Article 9 Conditions of the permit

1　Member States shall ensure that the permit includes all measures necessary for compliance with the requirements of Articles 3 and 10 for the granting of permits in order to achieve a high level of protection for the environment as a whole by means of protection of the air, water and land.

2　In the case of a new installation or a substantial change where Article 4 of Directive 85/337/EEC applies, any relevant information obtained or conclusion arrived at pursuant to Articles 5, 6 and 7 of that Directive shall be taken into consideration for the purposes of granting the permit.

3　The permit shall include emission limit values for pollutants, in particular, those listed in in Annex III, likely to be emitted from the installation concerned in significant quantities, having regard to their nature and their potential to transfer pollution from one medium to another (water, air and land). If necessary, the permit shall include appropriate requirements ensuring protection of the soil and ground water and measures concerning the management of waste generated by the installation. Where appropriate, limit values may be supplemented or replaced by equivalent parameters or technical measures. For installations under sub-heading 6.6 in Annex I, emission limit values laid down in accordance with this paragraph shall take into account practical considerations appropriate to these categories of installation.

4　Without prejudice to Article 10, the emission limit values and the equivalent parameters and technical measures referred to in para 3 shall be based on the best available techniques, without prescribing the use of any technique or specific technology, but taking into account the technical characteristics of the installation concerned, its geographical location and the local environmental conditions. In all circumstances, the conditions of the permit shall contain provisions on the minimisation of long-distance or trans-boundary pollution and ensure a high level of protection for the environment as a whole.

5　The permit shall contain suitable release monitoring requirements, specifying measurement methodology and frequency, evaluation procedure and an obligation to supply the competent authority with data required for checking compliance with the permit. For installations under sub-heading 6.6 in Annex I, the measures referred to in this paragraph may take account of costs and benefits.

6　The permit shall contain measures relating to conditions other than normal operating conditions. Thus, where there is a risk that the environment may be affected, appropriate provision shall be made for start-up, leaks malfunctions, momentary stoppages and definitive cessation of operations. The permit may also contain temporary derogations from the requirements of para 4 if a rehabilitation plan approved by the competent authority ensures that these requirements will be met within six months and if the project leads to a reduction of pollution.

7　The permit may contain such other specific conditions for the purposes of this Directive as the Member State or competent authority may think fit.

8　Without prejudice to the obligation to implement a permit procedure pursuant to this Directive, Member States may prescribe certain requirements for certain categories of installations in general binding rules instead of including them in individual permit conditions, provided that an integrated approach and an equivalent high level of environmental protection as a whole are ensured.

Article 10 Best available techniques and environmental quality standards

Where an environmental quality standard requires stricter conditions than those achievable by the use of the best available techniques, additional measures shall in particular be required in the permit, without prejudice to other measures which might be taken to comply with environmental quality standards.

Article 11 Developments in best available techniques

Member States shall ensure that the competent authority follows or is informed of developments in best available techniques.

Article 12 Changes by operators to installations

1   Member States shall take the necessary measures to ensure that the operator informs the competent authorities of any changes planned in the operation of the installation as referred to in Article 2(10)(a). Where appropriate, the competent authorities shall update the permit or the conditions.

2   Member States shall take the necessary measures to ensure that no substantial change in the operation of the installation within the meaning of Article 2(10)(b) planned by the operator is made without a permit issued in accordance with this Directive. The application for a permit and the decision by the competent authority must cover those parts of the installation and those aspects listed in Article 6 that may be affected by the change. The relevant provisions of Articles 3 and 6 to 10 and Article 15(1), (2) and (4) shall apply *mutatis mutandis*.

Article 13 Reconsideration and updating of permit conditions by the competent authority

1   Member States shall take the necessary measures to ensure that competent authorities periodically reconsider and, where necessary, update permit conditions.

2   The reconsideration shall be undertaken in any event where: – the pollution caused by the installation is of such significance that the existing emission limit values of the permit need to be revised or new such values need to be included in the permit, – substantial changes in the best available techniques make it possible to reduce emissions significantly without imposing excessive costs, – the operational safety of the process or activity requires other techniques to be used, – new provisions of Community or national legislation so dictate.

Article 14 Compliance with permit conditions

Member States shall take the necessary measures to ensure that:

–   the conditions of the permit are complied with by the operator when operating the installation,

–   the operator regularly informs the competent authority of the results of the monitoring of releases and without delay of any incident or accident significantly affecting the environment,

–   operators of installations afford the representatives of the competent authority all necessary assistance to enable them to carry out any inspections within the installation, to take samples and to gather any information necessary for the performance of their duties for the purposes of this Directive.

Article 15 Access to information and public participation in the permit procedure

1   Without prejudice to Council Directive 90/313/EEC of 7 June 1990 on the freedom of access to information on the environment (14), Member States shall take the necessary measures to ensure that applications for permits for new installations or for substantial changes are made available for an appropriate period of time to the public, to enable it to comment on them before the competent authority reaches its decision. That decision, including at least a copy of the permit, and any subsequent updates, must be made available to the public.

2   The results of monitoring of releases as required under the permit conditions referred to in Article 9 and held by the competent authority must be made available to the public.

3   An inventory of the principal emissions and sources responsible shall be published every three years by the Commission on the basis of the data supplied by the Member States. The Commission shall establish the format and particulars needed for the transmission of information in accordance with the procedure laid down in Article 19. In accordance with the same procedure, the Commission may propose measures to ensure inter-comparability and complementarily between data concerning the inventory of emissions referred to in the first sub-paragraph and data from other registers and sources of data on emissions.

4   Paragraphs 1, 2 and 3 shall apply subject to the restrictions laid down in Article 3(2) and (3) of Directive 90/313/EEC.

Article 16 Exchange of information

1   With a view to exchanging information, Member States shall take the necessary measures to send the Commission every three years, and for the first time within 18 months of the date on which this Directive is brought into effect, the available representative data on the limit values laid down by specific category of activities in accordance with Annex I and, if appropriate, the best available techniques from which those values are derived in accordance with, in particular, Article 9. On subsequent occasions the data shall be supplemented in accordance with the procedures laid down in para 3 of this Article.

2   The Commission shall organise an exchange of information between Member States and the industries concerned on best available techniques, associated monitoring, and developments in them. Every three years the Commission shall publish the results of the exchanges of information.

3   Reports on the implementation of this Directive and its effectiveness compared with other Community environmental instruments shall be established in accordance with the procedure laid down in Articles 5 and 6 of Directive 91/692/EEC. The first report shall cover the three years following the date on which this present Directive is brought into effect as referred to in Article 21. The Commission shall submit the report to the Council, accompanied by proposals if necessary.

4   Member States shall establish or designate the authority or authorities which are to be responsible for the exchange of information under paras 1, 2 and 3 and shall inform the Commission accordingly.

Article 17 Trans-boundary effects

1   Where a Member State is aware that the operation of an installation is likely to have significant negative effects on the environment of another Member State, or where a Member State likely to be significantly affected so requests, the Member State in whose territory the application for a permit pursuant to Article 4 or Article 12(2) was submitted shall forward the information provided pursuant to Article 6 to the other Member State at the same time as it makes it available to its own nationals. Such information shall serve as a basis for any consultations necessary in the framework of the bilateral relations between the two Member States on a reciprocal and equivalent basis.

2   Within the framework of their bilateral relations, Member States shall see to it that in the cases referred to in para 1 the applications are also made available for an appropriate period of time to the public of the Member State likely to be affected so that it will have the right to comment on them before the competent authority reaches its decision.

Article 18 Community emission limit values

1   Acting on a proposal from the Commission, the Council will set emission limit values, in accordance with the procedures laid down in the Treaty, for:

–   the categories of installations listed in Annex I except for the landfills covered by categories 5.1 and 5.4 of that Annex, and

–   the polluting substances referred to in Annex III, for which the need for Community action has been identified, on the basis, in particular, of the exchange of information provided for in Article 16.

2   In the absence of Community emission limit values defined pursuant to this Directive, the relevant emission limit values contained in the Directives referred to in Annex II and in other Community legislation shall be applied as minimum emission limit values pursuant to this Directive for the installations listed in Annex I. Without prejudice to the requirements of this Directive, the technical requirements applicable for the landfills covered by categories 5.1 and 5.4 of Annex I, shall be fixed by the Council, acting on a proposal by the Commission, in accordance with the procedures laid down in the Treaty.

Article 19 Committee procedure referred to in Article 15(3)

The Commission shall be assisted by a committee composed of the representatives of the Member States and chaired by the representative of the Commission. The representative of the Commission shall submit to the committee a draft of the measures to be taken. The committee shall deliver its opinion on the draft within a time limit which the chairman may lay down according to the urgency of the matter. The opinion shall be delivered by the majority laid down in Article 148(2) of the Treaty in the case of decisions which the Council is required to adopt on a proposal from the Commission. The votes of the representatives of the Member States within the committee shall be weighted in the manner set out in that Article. The chairman shall not vote. The Commission shall adopt the measures envisaged if they are in accordance with the opinion of the committee. If the measures are not in accordance with the opinion of the committee, or if no opinion is delivered, the Commission shall, without delay, submit to the Council a proposal relating to the measures to be taken. The Council shall act by a qualified majority. If, on the expiry of a period of three months from the date of referral to the Council, the Council has not acted, the proposed measures shall be adopted by the Commission.

[Articles 20, 21, 22 and 23 omitted.]

Annex I Categories of industrial activities referred to in Article 1

1   Installations or parts of installations used for research, development and testing of new products and processes are not covered by this Directive.

2   The threshold values given below generally refer to production capacities or outputs. Where one operator carries out several activities falling under the same subheading in the same installation or on the same site, the capacities of such activities are added together.

1   Energy industries

1.1 Combustion installations with a rated thermal input exceeding 50 MW(1).

1.2 Mineral oil and gas refineries.

1.3 Coke ovens.

1.4 Coal gasification and liquefaction plants.

2.   Production and processing of metals

2.1 Metal ore (including sulphide ore) roasting or sintering installations.

2.2 Installations for the production of pig iron or steel (primary or secondary fusion) including continuous casting, with a capacity exceeding 2,5 tonnes per hour.

2.3 Installations for the processing of ferrous metals:
   (a) hot-rolling mills with a capacity exceeding 20 tonnes of crude steel per hour;
   (b) smitheries with hammers the energy of which exceeds 50 kilojoule per hammer, where the calorific power used exceeds 20 MW;
   (c) application of protective fused metal coats with an input exceeding 2 tonnes of crude steel per hour.

2.4 Ferrous metal foundries with a production capacity exceeding 20 tonnes per day.

2.5 Installations:
   (a) for the production of non-ferrous crude metals from ore, concentrates or secondary raw materials by metallurgical, chemical or electrolytic processes;
   (b) for the smelting, including the alloyage, of non-ferrous metals, including recovered products, (refining, foundry casting, etc) with a melting capacity exceeding 4 tonnes per day for lead and cadmium or 20 tonnes per day for all other metals.

2.6 Installations for surface treatment of metals and plastic materials using an electrolytic or chemical process where the volume of the treatment vats exceeds 30 m^3.

3   Mineral industry

3.1 Installations for the production of cement clinker in rotary kilns with a production capacity exceeding 500 tonnes per day or lime in rotary kilns with a production capacity exceeding 50 tonnes per day or in other furnaces with a production capacity exceeding 50 tonnes per day.

3.2 Installations for the production of asbestos and the manufacture of asbestos-based products.

3.3 Installations for the manufacture of glass including glass fibre with a melting capacity exceeding 20 tonnes per day.

3.4 Installations for melting mineral substances including the production of mineral fibres with a melting capacity exceeding 20 tonnes per day.

3.5 Installations for the manufacture of ceramic products by firing, in particular roofing tiles, bricks, refractory bricks, tiles, stoneware or porcelain, with a production capacity exceeding 75 tonnes per day, and/or with a kiln capacity exceeding 4 m3 and with a setting density per kiln exceeding 300 kg/m^3.

4 Chemical industry

Production within the meaning of the categories of activities contained in this section means the production on an industrial scale by chemical processing of substances or groups of substances listed in sections 4.1 to 4.6:

4.1 Chemical installations for the production of basic organic chemicals, such as:

    (a) simple hydrocarbons (linear or cyclic, saturated or unsaturated, aliphatic or aromatic);

    (b) oxygen-containing hydrocarbons such as alcohols, aldehydes, ketones, carboxylic acids, esters, acetates, ethers, peroxides, epoxy resins;

    (c) sulphurous hydrocarbons;

    (d) nitrogenous hydrocarbons such as amines, amides, nitrous compounds, nitro compounds or nitrate compounds, nitriles, cyanates, isocyanates;

    (e) phosphorus-containing hydrocarbons;

    (f) halogenic hydrocarbons;

    (g) organometallic compounds;

    (h) basic plastic materials (polymers synthetic fibres and cellulose-based fibres);

    (i) synthetic rubbers;

    (j) dyes and pigments;

    (k) surface-active agents and surfactants.

4.2 Chemical installations for the production of basic inorganic chemicals, such as:

    (a) gases, such as ammonia, chlorine or hydrogen chloride, fluorine or hydrogen fluoride, carbon oxides, sulphur compounds, nitrogen oxides, hydrogen, sulphur dioxide, carbonyl chloride;

    (b) acids, such as chromic acid, hydrofluoric acid, phosphoric acid, nitric acid, hydrochloric acid, sulphuric acid, oleum, sulphurous acids;

    (c) bases, such as ammonium hydroxide, potassium hydroxide, sodium hydroxide;

    (d) salts, such as ammonium chloride, potassium chlorate, potassium carbonate, sodium carbonate, perborate, silver nitrate;

    (e) non-metals, metal oxides or other inorganic compounds such as calcium carbide, silicon, silicon carbide.

4.3 Chemical installations for the production of phosphorous-, nitrogen- or potassium-based fertilisers (simple or compound fertilisers).

4.4 Chemical installations for the production of basic plant health products and of biocides.

4.5 Installations using a chemical or biological process for the production of basic pharmaceutical products.

4.6 Chemical installations for the production of explosives.

5 Waste management

Without prejudice of Article 11 of Directive 75/442/EEC or Article 3 of Council Directive 91/689/EEC of 12 December 1991 on hazardous waste (2):

5.1 Installations for the disposal or recovery of hazardous waste as defined in the list referred to in Article 1(4) of Directive 91/689/EEC, as defined in Annexes IIA and IIB (operations R1, R5, R6, R8 and R9) to Directive 75/442/EEC and in Council Directive 75/439/EEC of 16 June 1975 on the disposal of waste oils (3), with a capacity exceeding 10 tonnes per day.

5.2 Installations for the incineration of municipal waste as defined in Council Directive 89/369/EEC of 8 June 1989 on the prevention of air pollution from new municipal waste incineration plants (4) and Council Directive 89/429/EEC of 21 June 1989 on the reduction of air pollution from existing municipal waste-incineration plants (5) with a capacity exceeding 3 tonnes per hour.

5.3 Installations for the disposal of non-hazardous waste as defined in Annex IIA to Directive 75/442/EEC under headings D8 and D9, with a capacity exceeding 50 tonnes per day 5.4. Landfills receiving more than 10 tonnes per day or with a total capacity exceeding 25,000 tonnes, excluding landfills of inert waste.

6 Other activities

6.1 Industrial plants for the production of:

(a) pulp from timber or other fibrous materials;

(b) paper and board with a production capacity exceeding 20 tonnes per day.

6.2 Plants for the pre-treatment (operations such as washing, bleaching, mercerisation) or dyeing of fibres or textiles where the treatment capacity exceeds 10 tonnes per day.

6.3 Plants for the tanning of hides and skins where the treatment capacity exceeds 12 tonnes of finished products per day.

6.4 (a) Slaughterhouses with a carcase production capacity greater than 50 tonnes per day.

(b) Treatment and processing intended for the production of food products from:

 – animal raw materials (other than milk) with a finished product production capacity greater than 75 tonnes per day.

 – vegetable raw materials with a finished product production capacity greater than 300 tonnes per day (average value on a quarterly basis).

(c) Treatment and processing of milk, the quantity of milk received being greater than 200 tonnes per day (average value on an annual basis).

6.5 Installations for the disposal or recycling of animal carcasses and animal waste with a treatment capacity exceeding 10 tonnes per day.

6.6 Installations for the intensive rearing of poultry or pigs with more than:

(a) 40,000 places for poultry;

    (b) 2,000 places for production pigs (over 30 kg); or

    (c) 750 places for sows.

6.7 Installations for the surface treatment of substances, objects or products using organic solvents, in particular for dressing, printing, coating, degreasing, waterproofing, sising, painting, cleaning or impregnating, with a consumption capacity of more than 150 kg per hour or more than 200 tonnes per year.

6.8 Installations for the production of carbon (hard-burnt coal) or electrographite by means of incineration or graphitisation.

[Annex II omitted.]

Annex III Indicative list of the main polluting substances to be taken into account if they are relevant for fixing emission limit values

Air

1   Sulphur dioxide and other sulphur compounds.

2   Oxides of nitrogen and other nitrogen compounds.

3   Carbon monoxide.

4   Volatile organic compounds.

5   Metals and their compounds.

6   Dust.

7   Asbestos (suspended particulates, fibres).

8   Chlorine and its compounds.

9   Fluorine and its compounds.

10 Arsenic and its compounds.

11 Cyanides.

12 Substances and preparations which have been proved to possess carcinogenic or mutagenic properties or properties which may affect reproduction via the air.

13 Polychlorinated dibenzodioxins and polychlorinated dibenzofurans.

Water

1   Organohalogen compounds and substances which may form such compounds in the aquatic environment.

2   Organophosphorus compounds.

3   Organotin compounds.

4   Substances and preparations which have been proved to possess carcinogenic or mutagenic properties or properties which may affect reproduction in or via the aquatic environment.

5   Persistent hydrocarbons and persistent and bioaccumulable organic toxic substances.

6   Cyanides.

7   Metals and their compounds.

8   Arsenic and its compounds.

9   Biocides and plant health products.

10   Materials in suspension.

11   Substances which contribute to eutrophication (in particular, nitrates and phosphates).

12   Substances which have an unfavourable influence on the oxygen balance (and can be measured using parameters such as BOD, COD, etc).

Annex IV

Considerations to be taken into account generally or in specific cases when determining best available techniques, as defined in Article 2(11), bearing in mind the likely costs and benefits of a measure and the principles of precaution and prevention:

1   the use of low-waste technology;

2   the use of less hazardous substances;

3   the furthering of recovery and recycling of substances generated and used in the process and of waste, where appropriate;

4   comparable processes, facilities or methods of operation which have been tried with success on an industrial scale;

5   technological advances and changes in scientific knowledge and understanding;

6   the nature, effects and volume of the emissions concerned;

7   the commissioning dates for new or existing installations;

8   the length of time needed to introduce the best available technique;

9   the consumption and nature of raw materials (including water) used in the process and their energy efficiency;

10   the need to prevent or reduce to a minimum the overall impact of the emissions on the environment and the risks to it;

11   the need to prevent accidents and to minimise the consequences for the environment;

12   the information published by the Commission pursuant to Article 16(2) or by international organisations.

The new UK PPC regime

In order to implement Directive 96/61 on integrated pollution prevention and control, the UK has passed the Pollution Prevention and Control Act 1999. On 1 August 2000, the Pollution Prevention and Control (PPC) Regulations made under s 2 of the Act came into force establishing a new regime for integrated pollution prevention and control for England and Wales. The PPC Regulations also replaced the system of local air pollution control (LAPC) contained in Pt 1 of the EPA 1990, which is not covered by the Directive.

All new applications for permits to carry on activities subject to IPPC or APC must now be made under the PPC Regulations. Such permits will also be required for 'significant changes' in activities covered by existing authorisations. Existing authorisations under the EPA regime are allowed to continue for the time being, but must be replaced by permits under the PPC Regulations by 2007, the precise date depending upon the industry sector (see Annex IV of the Regulations).

The DETR's practical guide (*Integrated Pollution Prevention and Control: A Practical Guide*, 2000) explains the nature and purpose of IPPC as follows:

1.1 The system of Integrated Pollution and Prevention and Control (IPPC) applies an integrated environmental approach to the regulation of certain industrial activities. This means that emissions to air, water (including discharges to sewers) and land, plus a range of other environmental effects must be considered together. It also means that regulators must set permit conditions so as to achieve a high level of protection for the environment as a whole. These conditions are based on the use of the 'best available techniques' (BAT) which balances the cost to the operators against the benefits to the environment. IPPC aims to prevent emissions and waste production and where that is not practicable, reduce them to acceptable levels. IPPC also takes the integrated approach beyond the initial task of permitting, through to the restoration of sites when industrial activities cease.

2.1 The basic purpose of the IPPC regime is to introduce a more integrated approach to controlling pollution from industrial sources. It aims to achieve:

... a high level of protection of the environment taken as a whole by, in particular, preventing or, where that is not practicable, reducing emissions into the air, water and land. (Regulation 8(2)–(3).)

The main way of doing that is by determining and enforcing permit conditions based on BAT.

Like Pt I of the EPA 1990, the PPC Regulations establish two separate, albeit parallel, regulatory systems, IPPC and APC. The systems are based on common procedural provisions contained in the regulations, that is, permit applications, appeals, public registers and most features of the enforcement mechanisms. Both systems rely upon the use of BAT to achieve their ends. However, they differ in three respects: (1) IPPC applies to more serious sources of pollution, APC to less serious sources; (2) IPC controls emissions into all environmental media, APC is only concerned with emissions into the air; (3) IPC is regulated either by the Environment Agency or by local authorities, APC is regulated solely by local authorities.

It should be noted that the IPPC regime regulates installations rather than processes, as under IPC. Under the old system, Pt A processes were regulated by the Environment Agency and Pt B processes fell under local authority air pollution control. The new regulations envisage three categories of installation: Pt A1 installations are IPPC and regulated by the Environment Agency; Part B installations are subject to local air pollution control; and Pt A2 installations are IPPC controlled, but are allocated to local authority control (Pt 1, Sched 1). This changes the role of local authorities which are now charged with applying IPPC to installations which were formally subject only to APC. It was thought that transferring these installations from Pt B to Pt A was justified because of the potential for these installations to emit pollution into more than one environmental medium.

The overall effect of the new categories will be to more than double the 2,500 or so processes that were subject to IPC under the 1990 Act. When the PPC system is fully in force there will be some 6,000 installations covered, 1,500 of these being subject to Part A2 Control by local authorities. Local authorities will continue to enforce APC of some 11,500 installations (see (2000) 9(7) ELM). Many of these installations were not previously subject to BAT on any statutory basis. Permits issued under the new regime must also take into account the energy efficiency of the installation and the noise or vibration that it makes, as well as the waste, water effluent and other pollution that it generates.

The PPC Regulations apply to the operation of installations and mobile plant only in so far as they conduct activities listed in Pt 1, Sched 1 of the Regulations.[25] Part 1 identifies six main industry sectors, namely: energy industries, production and processing of metals; mineral industries; the chemical industry; waste management; and others. These activities are only covered in so far as they may lead to the release of certain prescribed substances indicated in Pt 2, Sched 1. If an activity is covered by the regulations, then it cannot be carried on in an installation or mobile plant without a permit from the competent regulator (the EA or local authority) such permits will be granted subject to such conditions as the regulator considers appropriate. The conditions must (reg 12):

(a) minimise long-distance and trans-boundary pollution;

(b) ensure protection of the soil and ground water and appropriate management of waste;

(c) relate to periods when the installation is not working normally;

(d) set out the steps to be taken prior to the commencement of operations and after their definitive cessation;

(e) set out suitable emission monitoring requirements;

(f) require the operator to supply the regulator with the results of monitoring and of any incident or accident which is causing or may cause significant pollution.

In addition, reg 11 requires that the conditions of a permit must be based on 'general principles' set out in reg 11(2), namely that an installation should be operated so that:

(a) all the appropriate preventative measures are taken against pollution, in particular through application of the best available techniques; and

(b) no significant pollution is caused.

The DETR practical guide (para 9.1) explains the basis for setting conditions as the need to ensure that operators choose the best option available to achieve a high level of protection of the environment taken as whole. This will be achieved by requiring the use of BAT which in turn will provide the main basis for setting emission limit values (ELVs). BAT is defined by reg 3(1) as follows:

---

25 Regulation 2 is an interpretation section which contains the definition of all key terms, such as 'installations', 'mobile plant' and 'activities'. There is no definition of pollution.

(a) 'available techniques' means those techniques which have been developed on a scale which allows implementation in the relevant industrial sector, under economically and technically viable conditions, taking into consideration the cost and advantages, whether or not the techniques are used or produced inside the UK, as long as they are reasonably accessible to the operator;

(b) 'best' means in relation to techniques, the most effective in achieving a high level of protection of the environment as a whole;

(c) 'techniques' includes both the technology used and the way in which the installation is designed, built, maintained, operated and decommissioned.

The practical guide (para 9.9) supplements this by stating that when determining BAT it is necessary to identify options, assess environmental effects and consider economics, bearing in mind the principles of precaution and prevention.

The concept of BAT under the new regime is to all intents the same as the concepts BATNEEC and BPEO contained in the 1990 Act.

PPC Regulations, reg 29 (see pp 521–23, above) also requires a regulator to maintain a register of prescribed information concerning the IPPC and APC regimes. There are corresponding statutory exceptions to the obligation to make information publicly available. Information relating to national security is excluded (Reg 30) as is 'commercially confidential' information, defined in reg 31(12) as follows: '... information is ... commercially confidential, in relation to any individual or person, if its being contained in the register would prejudice to an unreasonable degree the commercial interests of that individual or person.'

The applicant must ask for such information to be excluded. If the enforcing authority refuses the applicant may appeal to the Secretary of State. If the information is excluded the exclusion only lasts for up to four years, when the applicant must reapply for exclusion.

Finally, the fees and charges for applications for IPPC and APC under the PPC Regulations are in the process of being established. The government anticipates that the charges will be of a similar order to those presently charged for IPC although there may be modest increases given the wider scope of the regime.

Pollution Prevention and Control Act 1999

Chapter 24

An Act to make provision for implementing Council Directive 96/61/EC and for otherwise preventing and controlling pollution; to make provision about certain expired or expiring disposal or waste management licences; and for connected purposes.

[27 July 1999.]

BE IT ENACTED by the Queen's most Excellent Majesty, by and with the advice and consent of the Lords Spiritual and Temporal, and Commons, in this present Parliament assembled, and by the authority of the same, as follows–

General purpose of section 2 and definitions

1 (1) The purpose of section 2 is to enable provision to be made for or in connection with–

(a) implementing Council Directive 96/61/EC concerning integrated pollution prevention and control;

(b) regulating, otherwise than in pursuance of that Directive, activities which are capable of causing any environmental pollution;

(c) otherwise preventing or controlling emissions capable of causing any such pollution.

(2) In this Act–

'activities' means activities of any nature, whether–

(a) industrial or commercial or other activities, or

(b) carried on on particular premises or otherwise,

and includes (with or without other activities) the depositing, keeping or disposal of any substance;

'environmental pollution' means pollution of the air, water or land which may give rise to any harm; and for the purposes of this definition (but without prejudice to its generality)–

(a) 'pollution' includes pollution caused by noise, heat or vibrations or any other kind of release of energy, and

(b) 'air' includes air within buildings and air within other natural or man-made structures above or below ground.

(3) In the definition of 'environmental pollution' in sub-section (2), 'harm' means–

(a) harm to the health of human beings or other living organisms;

(b) harm to the quality of the environment, including–

(i) harm to the quality of the environment taken as a whole,

(ii harm to the quality of the air, water or land, and

(iii) other impairment of, or interference with, the ecological systems of which any living organisms form part;

(c) offence to the senses of human beings;

(d) damage to property; or

(e) impairment of, or interference with, amenities or other legitimate uses of the environment (expressions used in this paragraph having the same meaning as in Council Directive 96/61/EC).

Regulation of polluting activities

2 (1) The Secretary of State may by regulations make provision for any of the purposes listed in Part I of Schedule 1; and Part II of that Schedule has effect for supplementing Part I.

(2) In accordance with sub-s (1) of section 1, the provision which may be made by regulations under this section is provision for or in connection with any of the matters mentioned in paras (a) to (c) of that sub-section.

(3) Regulations under this section may–

(a) contain such consequential, incidental, supplementary, transitional or saving provisions (including provisions amending, repealing or revoking enactments) as the Secretary of State considers appropriate; and

    (b) make different provision for different cases, including different provision in relation to different persons, circumstances, areas or localities.

(4) Before making any regulations under this section, the Secretary of State shall consult–

    (a) the Environment Agency if the regulations are to apply in relation to England or Wales;

    (b) the Scottish Environment Protection Agency if the regulations are to apply in relation to Scotland;

    (c) such bodies or persons appearing to him to be representative of the interests of local government, industry, agriculture and small businesses respectively as he may consider appropriate; and

    (d) such other bodies or persons as he may consider appropriate.

(5) Consultation undertaken before the passing of this Act shall constitute as effective compliance with sub-section (4) as if undertaken after that passing.

(6) The power to make regulations under this section shall be exercised by statutory instrument.

(7) A statutory instrument containing regulations under this section, if made without a draft having been laid before, and approved by a resolution of, each House of Parliament, shall be subject to annulment in pursuance of a resolution of either House.

(8) No regulations to which this sub-section applies shall be made (whether alone or with other regulations) unless a draft of the statutory instrument containing the regulations has been laid before, and approved by a resolution of, each House of Parliament.

(9) Sub-section (8) applies to–

    (a) the first regulations to be made under this section which apply in relation to England;

    (b) the first regulations to be made under this section which apply in relation to Wales;

    (c) the first regulations to be made under this section which apply in relation to Scotland;

    (d) regulations under this section which create an offence or increase a penalty for an existing offence;

    (e) regulations under this section which amend or repeal any provision of an Act.

[Sections 3–7 omitted.]

REFERENCES AND FURTHER READING

Allot, K, *Integrated Pollution Control: The First Three Years*, 1994, Environmental Data Services Ltd

Haigh, N and Irwin, F, *Integrated Pollution Control in Europe and North America*, 1990, The Conservation Foundation

Harty, R, 'Integrated pollution control in practice' [1992] JPL 611

Henshawe, I, Aalders, M and Molander, P, 'Implementation of the EC Directive on IPPC 1996/61: a comparative study' [1998] Env Liability 39

Henshawe, I, 'The EC Directive on Integrated Pollution Prevention and Control: implications for the United Kingdom' [1996] Env Liability 29

Purdue, M, 'Integrated pollution control in the Environmental Protection Act 1990: a coming of age of environmental law?' (1991) 54 MLR 534

Tromans, S, *Encyclopaedia of Environmental Law*, 1995, London: Sweet & Maxwell (looseleaf)

Waite, A, 'Legal aspects of IPC' [1992] 4 LMELR 2

USEFUL WEBSITES

For useful general environmental websites, see pages l–li, above.

CHAPTER 6

WILDLIFE AND NATURE CONSERVATION

INTRODUCTION

States have an obvious self-interest in ensuring the prudent use of natural resources such as oil, coal and gas, not only to maintain present needs but also to protect the needs of future generations.[1] Plants and animals, on the other hand, are widely perceived as a type of natural resource which, unlike coal and gas, constitute a resource capable of self-renewal, *provided* appropriate steps are taken to conserve existing populations. It is now apparent that the conservation of living resources cannot be achieved merely by controlling their exploitation by humankind. In particular, plants and animals cannot be conserved merely by focussing on the preservation of individual species through controls over human activities impinging directly upon them. Their conservation also requires the preservation of their habitat and of related species, as well as the non-living elements of the environment on which they depend (Birnie and Boyle (1992) 419).

Threats to wildlife arise from a variety of sources. Various species have been killed throughout the centuries for food. Exploitation has taken numerous other forms, such as hunting for skins, feathers, and other products used or traded by mankind; capturing for display in zoos, for scientific research, keeping as pets, and for medicinal, cultural, religious and artistic purposes, amongst others. Although nature conservation became something of a late 20th century obsession, in the absence of any direct benefit to humankind, why should conservation measures hinder our right to use the earth's living resources as we see fit? It is common ground that conservation measures are justified to protect animals and plants which are directly useful to man as food sources, for example. Others are preserved because of aesthetic or cultural reasons such as birds or butterflies. More fundamentally, all species are part of an inter-connected eco-system and comprise an immense and diverse gene pool which is constantly evolving.[2] According to the laws of evolution it is perfectly natural for some species to die out over time and be replaced by more successful competitor species. However, the rate of species' extinctions has reached a level which is unprecedented in recorded history and science increasingly views this as a direct consequence of human activity.[3] Such a rapid and unnatural disruption of eco-systems and depletion of the gene pool carries with it unpredictable consequences for humankind and, indeed, for all life on this planet. Thus, it is now generally accepted that a holistic approach to environmental protection is required; one

---

1   Note that 'prudent and rational utilisation' is a specific objective of EC policy on the environment (Art 174(1)), see p 23, above. See also Principles 3 and 4 of the Rio Declaration 1992 in relation to sustainable development and the needs of future generations, p 70, above.

2   For a legal definition of eco-system, see Art 2 of the Biodiversity Convention 1992, p 588, below.

3   It has been reported that nearly one-quarter of the earth's biological diversity is estimated to be at risk of extinction during the next 20–30 years. See McNeely, J (ed), *Conserving the World's Biological Diversity*, 1990, IUCN (World Bank *et al*).

that encompasses both the biotic and abiotic environments[4] in which plants and animals live. The legal aspects of this approach are examined in this chapter.

INTERNATIONAL LAW

In the evolution of international environmental law, aside from the provision of rules against the pollution of media such as the atmosphere (Chapter 2), the marine environment (Chapter 3) and waste management (Chapter 4), the second main focus of international action has been upon wildlife species conservation and natural habitat preservation. An interesting point to note at the outset of this chapter is that even though these two aspects of environmental law – nature conservation and pollution controls – are connected, as part of the overall legal regime for environmental protection, they evolved separately at the international level. It was only during the late 1960s and early 1970s and especially in the run-up to the Stockholm Declaration 1972 (p 61, above) that nature conservation and pollution controls were accepted as two sides of the same coin. In particular, environmentalists were only then becoming aware that the continuing encroachment of human activities and the accumulation of wastes as a result of these activities threatened the continued existence of both individual bird and animal species, as well as their natural habitats.

Rising concern over environmental threats to whole eco-systems has been reflected in the change in emphasis of more recent international instruments which concentrate less on the protection of individual species and more on the preservation of habitats.[5] This trend is noticeable with respect to the three multilateral conventions examined in this section, namely the Convention on International Trade in Endangered Species (CITES, see p 570, below), the Rio Convention on Biological Diversity (see p 586, below) and its Protocol on Biosafety (see p 604, below), as well as the Ramsar Convention on Wetlands of International Importance 1971 (see p 625, below). Eco-system protection has become an overt objective, with many new instruments concerned with the designation and control of suitable areas for such protection. Where such eco-systems are trans-boundary in nature, in the sense of overlapping two or more different territorial jurisdictions, measures of this type require international agreement, usually in the form of binding treaty commitments.[6] Apart from such conventional obligations, there is also an evolving general principle requiring the conservation of natural resources found beyond national jurisdictions, in so-called global commons areas, such as the high seas and the atmosphere, and possibly even within national territories, thereby limiting State sovereignty.

---

4   The biotic environment includes all life forms surrounding an organism upon which its survival depends (food sources, pollinators, etc). The abiotic environment includes all non-living features, eg clean air, water and soil.

5   For example, the Berne Convention on the Conservation of European Wildlife and Natural Habitats 1982, UKTS 56, see p 630, below.

6   For example, the Convention on the Conservation of Migratory Species of Wild Animals 1979 (Bonn Convention) 19 ILM (1980) 15.

Bearing in mind the fundamental and generally accepted rule in international law which says that all States are sovereign entities able to exercise sovereign rights over all natural living and non-living resources within their land and sea territory, the notion that States are under an international legal obligation to protect certain species or habitats may seem incongruous. Indeed, notwithstanding the level of international concern expressed over endangered species of plant, bird and animal life, it is arguable that under the notion of absolute sovereignty, States have the right to conserve or exploit, exhaust, and even destroy all the natural living resources within their jurisdiction and control. This is certainly true with respect to individual animals or plants where they are situated within the territory of a State.

This absolute sovereign right is however qualified by the general rule stated in Principle 21 of the Stockholm Declaration 1972 (pp 66–67) and now Principle 2 of the Rio Declaration 1992 (pp 69–70), which provides that although States have the sovereign right to exploit their own natural resources, they also have the responsibility of ensuring that activities within their jurisdiction or control do not cause damage to the environment of other States or of areas beyond the limits of national jurisdiction. For example, allowing widespread deforestation within one State may result in biodiversity loss in other States. Terrestrial living resources will generally remain within the territory of the State or States where they are found, and their international regulation is accordingly more difficult, requiring as it does limitations on the permanent sovereignty of States over their own natural resources, and resort to concepts such as common interest, common concern, or common heritage to justify such interference, or to the language of animal rights (Birnie and Boyle (1992) 419–20).

A different problem arises with regard to sovereignty over a species as a whole. The question of whether there can be sovereignty over a species, as distinct from its individual components, is particularly acute where the range of the given species extends over the territory of more than one State, as is generally the case. Whilst each range State has sovereignty over all members of the species which happen to be under its jurisdiction at any point in time, that State cannot have sovereignty over the whole species. On the other hand, there is no principle of joint sovereignty under international law. In consequence, sovereignty can effectively only be exercised over species which are endemic to a single country (de Klemm (1993) 2).

There are also important differences in the problems affecting terrestrial and marine living resources. The latter will more often constitute common property or shared resources, and, though subject to over-exploitation, are at least in principle regulated in international law by obligations of conservation and equitable utilisation (Birnie and Boyle (1992) 419). For example, the Convention for the Conservation of Antarctic Marine Living Resources 1980 (19 ILM (1980) 841) and the Agreement for the Conservation and Management of Straddling Fish Stocks and Highly Migratory Fish Stocks 1995 (34 ILM (1995) 1542).

In the absence of any over-arching rule of international law requiring a State to conserve, rather than permitting it to destroy its natural resources, it seems to be left to individual States to voluntarily accept limitations of their sovereign rights, by the introduction of domestic conservation measures or expressing their consent to such obligations by treaty. Almost from the beginning of the 20th century, however, a consensus to conserve natural living resources was forming on the international stage. This consensus grew from the concern about the need to conserve species and natural habitats in the face of rapidly-developing threats of all kinds. There are two very different strands to this concern about the loss of biological diversity (or biodiversity as it is commonly called).[7] Firstly, the anthropocentric view is centred on the loss of such biodiversity to the advancement of scientific knowledge and possible economic exploitation, as well as a more general loss of potential benefits for both present and future generations. Secondly, what is now referred to as the 'ecocentric' view is concerned with the intrinsic value of biological diversity, which humanity may use but which it has no moral right to destroy, as well as the fundamental role played by biodiversity in maintaining the life-sustaining systems of the biosphere and the evolutionary potential of the Earth (de Klemm (1993) 2–3).

Over recent decades, therefore, the idea has taken shape that all States, and the international community in general, have at the very least an interest in the conservation of wild species and the habitats in which they live. Widespread disquiet at environmental degradation has slowly crystallised in the form of a consensus to establish rules of international law intended to achieve a better balance between the exercise of sovereign rights over natural living resources, including the right to destroy them, and the need to preserve wild species. The narrow term, 'species', was gradually changed, firstly to 'genetic resources', and still later to 'biological diversity' which encompasses the diversity of eco-systems, species and genes still found on the planet (de Klemm (1993) 3).

The realisation of the need to counter threats to individual species, followed by the recognition of the more basic need for securing their natural habitats may explain why initial treaties (for example, the Treaty for the Preservation and Protection of Fur Seals 1911) and other international instruments on this subject tended to concentrate on species protection, while later ones are focused upon the preservation of natural habitats and even eco-systems. This duality of approach is well-documented and described as the difference between species-based and area-based instruments, while noting of course that species- and area-based conservation measures are frequently combined (de Klemm (1993) 12). International law has, until recently, tended to adopt an *ad hoc* approach to wildlife protection, related to identification of 'endangered species', that is, species or discrete populations thereof, that are threatened with extinction (Birnie and Boyle (1992) 420).

The treaties that will be examined in this chapter of the book, reflect this initial disparity of treatment, with CITES focusing on control of the burgeoning international trade in individual plant, bird and animal species, and the Biodiversity Convention stressing the need for *in situ* conservation. Ramsar, on the other hand, represents an example of the combined approach. It has been described as the first wildlife convention of global application to be concerned solely with the protection of habitat (Birnie and Boyle (1992) 465). The fact remains however that it is limited to wetlands and is focused on waterfowl habitat. The CITES and Biodiversity Conventions are therefore the only two Conventions which are potentially applicable to all species in any habitat in the world (Sands (1995) 373).

---

7   Biodiversity is defined as a threefold concept embracing the diversity of eco-systems, species and genetic diversity within species: Bowman, M and Redgwell, C (eds), *International Law and the Conservation of Biological Diversity*, 1996, London: Kluwer, p 5.

Political agreement on the need to conserve biological diversity was achieved at the 1972 UN Conference on the Human Environment, which resulted in the creation of the United Nations' Environment Programme (UNEP) and the adoption of the Stockholm Declaration 1972 (Chapter 1, p 61, above). This consensus formed the foundation for the development of a number of international instruments (including the Bonn and Berne Conventions) laying down certain general conservation objectives and sometimes very specific conservation rules. The adoption of these instruments implicitly accepts that the principle of national sovereignty is not absolute and is tempered by recognition of the international community's common concern with the conservation of natural resources, even those within the jurisdiction and control of a State (de Klemm (1993) 4).

Few, if any, of these international instruments could have been developed if there had not already been a large number of national laws relating to protected species and areas in existence (such as the National Parks and Access to Countryside Act 1949). In turn, internationally agreed principles and rules constitute a basis upon which national legislation may be further developed or improved. There is therefore a process of dynamic interaction between national and international legislation which is naturally conducive to gradual changes towards better conservation standards and norms (de Klemm (1993) 4).

Stockholm Declaration 1972

The Stockholm Declaration 1972 sets out 26 Principles from which a body of international environmental law has since developed (see p 63, above). The Declaration places great emphasis on the need to protect both species and their habitats, particularly at Principles 2 and 4, which, respectively, provide for the safeguarding of representative samples of natural eco-systems for the benefit of present and future generations and humankind's responsibility to manage the heritage of wildlife and its habitat. A precursor of sustainable development may be found in the further requirement in Principle 4 that nature conservation must receive importance in planning for economic development (de Klemm (1993) 5).

World Charter for Nature 1982

Ten years after Stockholm, continuing efforts to provide a set of general rules governing the conservation of natural living resources yielded a UN General Assembly Resolution (UNGA Res 37/7 on 28 October 1982) adopting the World Charter for Nature (22 ILM (1983) 455). This 'soft law' instrument (on soft law, see pp 4–5, above) proclaims principles of conservation by which all human conduct affecting nature is to be guided and judged. It recognises the uniqueness of every form of life, regardless of its worth to man, and mankind's responsibility for all species, which should entail, at the very least, a corresponding moral duty to preserve them (de Klemm (1993) 5).

Among its General Principles are the requirement that genetic viability on the earth shall not be compromised (Art 2); that all areas of the earth, both land and sea, shall be subject to these general principles of conservation (Art 3); and that eco-systems and organisms as well as the land, marine and atmospheric resources that are utilised by man, shall be managed to achieve and maintain optimum sustainable productivity but not in such a way as to endanger the integrity of those other eco-systems with which they co-exist. (Art 4). However, although the World Charter for Nature expresses its general principles in mandatory terms, using the term 'shall' throughout, rather than 'should', they are nevertheless expressed in very general terms (Birnie and Boyle (1992) 431). Also, like other UN General Assembly Resolutions, it is difficult to argue that the Charter's provisions have any binding legal force. Nonetheless, it has been suggested that it should be regarded as an instrument having a special character, a declaration of principles after the fashion of such General Assembly Resolutions as the Universal Declaration of Human Rights 1948. The subsequent restatement of several of these principles in other international legal and policy documents shows that the World Charter for Nature does have some moral and political force.[8] Its attempt to set the equilibrium between the use of nature and its conservation accords with current goals of sustainable development and its provisions are now more likely to be influential in international policy-making (Birnie and Boyle (1992) 432).

Convention on International Trade in Endangered Species (CITES) 1973[9]

The first of the international agreements on nature conservation to be examined here is CITES. This Convention regulates the international trade in endangered species of both animal and plant life. It has been incorporated into UK law by the Endangered Species (Import and Export) Act 1976. Tens of thousands of plant and animal species are subject to its regulations. It is perhaps the most successful of all international treaties concerned with wildlife conservation, with 146 States' parties to it as of 1999. Lyster suggests that its success is mainly due to the basic principles it enunciates, which most States have proved willing to accept ((1985) 240).

CITES regulates international trade in wild plant and animal species through a permit system which is based on whether the species concerned is listed in either of three Appendices to the treaty. Appendix I species include all species threatened with extinction. Trade in such species may only be authorised in exceptional circumstances (Art II(1)). Appendix II species include all species which although not now threatened may become so if trade in them is not regulated strictly (Art II(2)(a)). Species which are similar in appearance are also included within this category (Art II(2)(b)). This is the so-called 'look-alike' provision. Trade controls therefore extend to include the 'look alike' species. Interestingly, there is no similar type provision for Appendix I species, presumably because these are defined so broadly as to include all possible look-alike species. Appendix III provides a mechanism by which States' parties that have introduced stricter domestic legislation, in terms of the export of species that are not already in either Appendix I or II, can seek the support of other parties in regulating trade in these species (Art II(3)).

---

8   For example, the Biodiversity Convention 1992 and Agenda 21 adopted at the 1992 Rio UN Conference on Environment and Development (UNCED).
9   19 ILM (1973) 1055. For latest version see www.cites.org.

A preliminary but important question that may be asked at this juncture relates to the purpose of such a Convention under international law. It is arguable that the stated aim of CITES in terms of its protection of endangered species against over-exploitation through international trade implicitly serves to legitimise such trade in fact, albeit within the strict controls of its legal regime. Wildlife conservationists in particular have long argued that the only sure way of securing what little we have left of endangered plant and animal populations is by implementing a complete prohibition of all forms of trade in wildlife species and their derivative products. As we shall see below, this view clashes with that held by many developing country governments in which these endangered species are actually located. These governments are of the opinion that first, such a trade ban would be an infringement of their sovereign right to exploit their natural resources and secondly, that trade in endangered species and their derivative products is necessary for much needed foreign currency exchange to fund development projects in their often impoverished countries. These States are keen to subject their relative wealth of biological diversity to so-called 'sustainable use' regimes in order to derive some benefit from the fact that these species are located within their territories. As Lyster notes, CITES is a protectionist treaty in the sense that it prohibits, with few exceptions, international commercial trade in species that are threatened with extinction (listed in Appendix I) and it is a trading treaty in the sense that it allows a controlled trade in species whose survival is not yet threatened but may become so (listed in Appendix II) ((1985) 240).

Therefore, it may be seen that CITES is not designed to protect or conserve endangered species by itself. Any role it may play in this respect is indirect, through the international controls it places on the commercial trade in such species. The international trade in endangered species alone is by no means the major threat to wildlife conservation generally. Loss of habitat, through land clearance for human settlement, agriculture and industry is by far the greatest danger to wildlife survival. On the other hand, the international trade in specimens of endangered species, whether alive or dead, and their derivative products, is increasing in both volume and especially value.[10] Furthermore, the growth of modern sea, air and land transport facilities have transformed international trade, making shipment of live animals and plants, as well as their derivative products, much easier (Birnie and Boyle (1992) 475).

The CITES permit system operates on a global scale and this has undoubtedly contributed to its overall success. The main reason for its effectiveness is that it combines an international export/import permit system with the establishment of national institutions to administer this system. Its main requirements provide for permit documentation between importing and exporting States in a descending order of strictness depending on whether the species involved are listed in Appendices I, II or III (Arts III, IV and V). Species listed in Appendix I are treated most strictly, in accordance with their threatened status, followed by species listed in Appendices II and III. Each party has to establish Management and Scientific Authorities (Art IX). These are responsible for ensuring that the export and import permit requirements for particular species under each Appendix as well as transport conditions for live specimens are adhered to.

---

10   The illegal trade in wildlife alone has recently been estimated to be more than $5 billion per year (Ong, DM, 'The Convention on International Trade in Endangered Species (CITES 1973: implications of recent developments in international and EC environmental law)' [1998] 10 JEL 2).

These provisions are akin to the prior informed consent procedure established for importing and exporting States under the Basel Convention on the Control of Trans-boundary Movements of Hazardous Wastes 1989 (see Chapter 4). The CITES permit system however does not extend to transit states, unlike Basel. No permits are required for the transit or trans-shipment of specimens through the territory of a State party, while the specimens remain under customs control (Art VII(1)).

For example, Art III requires that the export of specimens of species included in Appendix I be preceded by the prior presentation of an export permit. An export permit can only be issued if the Scientific Authority of the exporting State has advised that such export will not be detrimental to the survival of that species (Art III(2)(a)). Furthermore, the Management Authority has to be satisfied that the specimen was obtained lawfully (Art III(2)(b)), that the appropriate transport conditions are in place (Art III(2)(c)), and that an import permit has been obtained for the specimen (Articles III(2)(d) and III(3)). However, this last requirement is not needed for the export of specimens of Appendix II species. Indeed, Appendix III specimens do not even require a determination from the Scientific Authority of the exporting State, merely an export permit from the Management Authority (Art V(2)). Also, each consignment requires an individual permit, although individual specimens within one consignment are not required to have their own separate permits (Art VI(5)).

The major flaw in this permit system is its lack of emphasis on importing State controls, especially in the form of import permit requirements. These are not needed for Appendix II and III species, unless an importing State specifically requires such permits under its domestic legislation. This would be in exercise of its sovereign right under international law, as recognised in Art XIV(1)(a) of CITES, to adopt stricter domestic measures regarding trading conditions for Appendix I, II and III species, or even the complete prohibition thereof. International trade in endangered species is conducted mainly between the developing countries (exporters) where these species are located and developed countries (importers) where the markets for these species are located and their derivative products are destined. Therefore, it can be seen that the current emphasis in CITES on export controls places an inordinate burden on usually under-funded, ill-equipped and poorly trained implementation systems in these developing countries.

Well attended and active biennial Conferences of Parties (COPs) (Art XI) review CITES progress and discuss possible changes to the lists. A proactive Secretariat (Art XII) that monitors violations of CITES provisions effectively by relaying information on lack of implementation to the States' parties concerned, and ever vigilant NGOs, have each played important parts in the relative success of this Convention. For the remainder of this discussion we will focus on two developments: first, the implications of the downgrading of the African elephant from its Appendix I designation to Appendix II at the 10th Conference of the Parties held during June 1997 in Harare, Zimbabwe. And secondly, the promulgation of a new EC Council Regulation with regard to CITES implementation throughout the European Union member countries in response to the establishment of the European single market.

In many ways, the plight of the African elephant which is hunted in great numbers for its ivory is symbolic of the conflicting interests that are the subject of much controversy at CITES' COPs. At the Seventh Conference held in Berne in 1987, in the face of mounting evidence of elephant carnage, the parties agreed to place the African elephant on Appendix I, effectively banning all trade in it, except for explicitly non-commercial purposes (Art III(3)(c)), since when trade has declined dramatically. More effective conservation and anti-poaching measures in some African countries however have meant that the elephant population in these countries has grown substantially to the point where elephant herds are competing with local communities for the use of the land. Consequently, there has been pressure from such countries as Namibia, Tanzania, Uganda and Zambia, whose elephant populations have recovered, to be allowed to carry out limited culls and sell the resulting products to generate income for further conservation measures (Birnie and Boyle (1992) 478).

Under Art XV(1)(b), a proposed amendment to the African elephant's status under Appendix I needed a two-thirds majority of the parties present and voting. Proposals for down listing were resisted at the 8th CITES COP in Kyoto, Japan in 1992. After intensive lobbying by the three sponsoring States – Namibia, Botswana and Zimbabwe, the African elephant was moved from Appendix I to II by an overwhelming majority of the countries represented at the 10th CITES COP in Harare, with 76 countries voting in favour, 21 against and 20 abstaining. The vote effectively acknowledges that elephant numbers have grown substantially and that anti-poaching measures are strictly enforced in these countries. However, the lifting of the ban on ivory sales that this downgrading from Appendix I to II entails is subject to a special compromise agreement which allows the resumption of trade by the three countries under an international monitoring and reporting system consisting of the CITES Secretariat, the CITES Standing Committee and TRAFFIC (Trade Records Analysis of Flora and Fauna in Commerce), an international non-governmental organisation for policing plant and animal trade. It also requires that, *inter alia*, no international trade can take place within 18 months, the three countries concerned are allowed to sell only a portion of their existing stocks of ivory, not all of it, and then only to Japan. Furthermore, no ivory trade would be allowed if the COP was not satisfied with the monitoring measures proposed by Zimbabwe, Botswana, Namibia and Japan. In February 1999 the first shipment of ivory between this group of southern Africa States and Japan was allowed to proceed. This shipment occurred without incident later that year. The sale was estimated to have realised about $5 m for the African States concerned (see Favre (2000) 336).

The second important development concerns the new EC Council Regulation on the implementation of CITES which came into force 1 June 1997 (338/97). This harmonises EC Member States' legislation and policies towards imports of endangered species, especially in the light of the establishment of the European single market. It incorporates a number of changes to the legal regime implementing CITES which was based on the previous EC Regulation passed in 1982 (Council Regulation 3626/82 (as subsequently amended)). For example, a new four-annex structure (Annexes A, B, C and D) is established in order to target controls where they are most needed. A simpler text will hopefully improve implementation. External border controls will be strengthened as Customs' checks will be at the first point of entry into the Community single market. Substantively, it is difficult to say whether the new EC Regulation provides better protection for endangered species susceptible to illegal trade. Although the new Regulation continues to protect certain Appendix II and other species at Appendix I levels, other species have been downgraded, along with most Appendix III species which no longer require the presentation of import permits.

Convention on International Trade in Endangered Species of Wild Fauna and Flora (1973) (as amended)

Entered into force: 1 July 1975

THE CONTRACTING STATES,

Recognising that wild fauna and flora in their many beautiful and varied forms are an irreplaceable part of the natural systems of the earth which must be protected for this and the generations to come;

Conscious of the ever-growing value of wild fauna and flora from aesthetic, scientific, cultural, recreational and economic points of view;

Recognising that peoples and states are and should be the best protectors of their own wild fauna and flora;

Recognising, in addition, that international co operation is essential for the protection of certain species of wild fauna and flora against over exploitation through international trade;

Convinced of the urgency of taking appropriate measures to this end.

HAVE AGREED AS FOLLOWS:

Article I Definitions

For the purpose of the present Convention, unless the context otherwise requires:

(a) 'species' means any species, sub-species, or geographically separate population thereof;

(b) 'specimen' means:

    (i) an animal or plant, whether alive or dead;

    (ii) in the case of an animal: for species included in Appendices I and II, any readily recognisable part or derivative thereof; and for species included in Appendix III, any readily recognisable part or derivative thereof specified in Appendix III in relation to the species; and

    (iii) in the case of a plant: for species included in Appendix I, any readily recognisable part or derivative thereof; and for species included in Appendices II and III, any readily recognisable part or derivative thereof specified in Appendices II and III in relation to the species;

(c) 'trade' means export, re-export, import and introduction from the sea;

(d) 're-export' means export of any specimen that has previously been imported;

(e) 'Introduction from the sea' means transportation into a State of specimens of any species which were taken in the marine environment not under the jurisdiction of any state;

(f) 'Scientific Authority' means a national scientific authority designated in accordance with Article IX;

(g) 'Management Authority' means a national management authority designated in accordance with Article IX;

(h) 'Party' means a state for which the present Convention has entered into force.

Article II Fundamental principles

1   Appendix I shall include all species threatened with extinction which are or may be affected by trade. Trade in specimens of these species must be subject to particularly strict regulation in order not to endanger further their survival and must only be authorised in exceptional circumstances.

2   Appendix II shall include:

(a) all species which although not necessarily now threatened with extinction may become so unless trade in specimens of such species is subject to strict regulation in order to avoid utilisation incompatible with their survival; and

(b) other species which must be subject to regulation in order that trade in specimens of certain species referred to in sub-para (a) of this paragraph may be brought under effective control.

3   Appendix III shall include all species which any Party identifies as being subject to regulation within its jurisdiction for the purposes of preventing or restricting exploitation, and as needing the co-operation of other parties in the control of trade.

4   The Parties shall not allow trade in specimens of species included in Appendices I, II and III except in accordance with the provisions of the present Convention.

Article III Regulation of trade in specimens of species included in Appendix I

1   All trade in specimens of species included in Appendix I shall be in accordance with the provisions of this Article.

2   The export of any specimen of a species included in Appendix I shall require the prior grant and presentation of an export permit. An export permit shall only be granted when the following conditions have been met:

(a) a Scientific Authority of the state of export has advised that such export will not be detrimental to the survival of that species;

(b) a Management Authority of the state of export is satisfied that the specimen was not obtained in contravention of the laws of that state for the protection of fauna and flora;

(c) a Management Authority of the State of export is satisfied that any living specimen will be so prepared and shipped as to minimise the risk of injury, damage to health or cruel treatment; and

(d) a Management Authority of the State of export is satisfied that an import permit has been granted for the specimen.

3   The import of any specimen of a species included in Appendix I shall require the prior grant and presentation of an import permit and either an export permit or a re-export certificate. An import permit shall only be granted when the following conditions have been met:

(a) a Scientific Authority of the state of import has advised that the import will be for purposes which are not detrimental to the survival of the species involved;

(b) a Scientific Authority of the state of import is satisfied that the proposed recipient of a living specimen is suitably equipped to house and care for it; and

(c) a Management Authority of the state of import is satisfied that the specimen is not to be used for primarily commercial purposes.

4   The re-export of any specimen of a species included in Appendix I shall require the prior grant and presentation of a re-export certificate. A re-export certificate shall only be granted when the following conditions have been met:

(a) a Management Authority of the state of re-export is satisfied that the specimen was imported into that State in accordance with the provisions of the present Convention;

(b) a Management Authority of the state of re-export is satisfied that any living specimen will be so prepared and shipped as to minimise the risk of injury, damage to health or cruel treatment; and

(c) a Management Authority of the state of re-export is satisfied that an import permit has been granted for any living specimen.

5   The introduction from the sea of any specimen of a species included in Appendix I shall require the prior grant of a certificate from a Management Authority of the State of introduction. A certificate shall only be granted when the following conditions have been met:

(a) a Scientific Authority of the state of introduction advises that the introduction will not be detrimental to the survival of the species involved;

(b) a Management Authority of the state of introduction is satisfied that the proposed recipient of a living specimen is suitably equipped to house and care for it; and

(c) a Management Authority of the state of introduction is satisfied that the specimen is not to be used for primarily commercial purposes.

Article IV Regulation of trade in specimens of species included in Appendix II

1   All trade in specimens of species included in Appendix II shall be in accordance with the provisions of this Article.

2   The export of any specimen of a species included in Appendix II shall require the prior grant and presentation of an export permit. An export permit shall only be granted when the following conditions have been met:

(a) Scientific Authority of the state of export has advised that such export will not be detrimental to the survival of that species;

(b) a Management Authority of the state of export is satisfied that the specimen was not obtained in contravention of the laws of that state for the protection of fauna and flora; and

(c) a Management Authority of the state of export is satisfied that any living specimen will be so prepared and shipped as to minimise the risk of injury, damage to health or cruel treatment.

3   A Scientific Authority in each Party shall monitor both the export permits granted by that state for specimens of species included in Appendix II and the actual exports of such specimens. Whenever a Scientific Authority determines that the export of specimens of any such species should be limited in order to maintain that species throughout its range at a level consistent with its role in the eco-systems in which it

occurs and well above the level at which that species might become eligible for inclusion in Appendix I, the Scientific Authority shall advise the appropriate Management Authority of suitable measures to be taken to limit the grant of export permits for specimens of that species.

4   The import of any specimen of a species included in Appendix II shall require the prior presentation of either an export permit or a re-export certificate.

5   The re-export of any specimen of a species included in Appendix II shall require the prior grant and presentation of a re-export certificate. A re-export certificate shall only be granted when the following conditions have been met:

(a) a Management Authority of the state of re-export is satisfied that the specimen was imported into that state in accordance with the provisions of the present Convention; and

(b) a Management Authority of the state of re-export is satisfied that any living specimen will be so prepared and shipped as to minimise the risk of injury, damage to health or cruel treatment.

6   The introduction from the sea of any specimen of a species included in Appendix II shall require the prior grant of a certificate from a Management Authority of the state of introduction. A certificate shall only be granted when the following conditions have been met:

(a) a Scientific Authority of the state of introduction advises that the introduction will not be detrimental to the survival of the species involved; and

(b) a Management Authority of the state of introduction is satisfied that any living specimen will be so handled as to minimise the risk of injury, damage to health or cruel treatment.

7   Certificates referred to in para 6 of this Article may be granted on the advice of a Scientific Authority, in consultation with other national scientific authorities or, when appropriate, international scientific authorities, in respect of periods not exceeding one year for total numbers of specimens to be introduced in such periods.

Article V Regulation of trade in specimens of species included in Appendix III

1   All trade in specimens of species included in Appendix III shall be in accordance with the provisions of this Article.

2   The export of any specimen of a species included in Appendix III from any state which has included that species in Appendix III shall require the prior grant and presentation of an export permit. An export permit shall only be granted when the following conditions have been met:

(a) a Management Authority of the state of export is satisfied that the specimen was not obtained in contravention of the laws of that state for the protection of fauna and flora; and

(b) a Management Authority of the state of export is satisfied that any living specimen will be so prepared and shipped as to minimise the risk of injury, damage to health or cruel treatment.

3   The import of any specimen of a species included in Appendix III shall require, except in circumstances to which para 4 of this Article applies, the prior presentation of a certificate of origin and, where the import is from a state which has included that species in Appendix III, an export permit.

4   In the case of re-export, a certificate granted by the Management Authority of the state of re-export that the specimen was processed in that state or is being re-exported shall be accepted by the state of import as evidence that the provisions of the present Convention have been complied with in respect of the specimen concerned.

Article VI Permits and certificates

1   Permits and certificates granted under the provisions of Articles III, IV and V shall be in accordance with the provisions of this Article.

2   An export permit shall contain the information specified in the model set forth in Appendix IV, and may only be used for export within a period of six months from the date on which it was granted.

3   Each permit or certificate shall contain the title of the present Convention, the name and any identifying stamp of the Management Authority granting it and a control number assigned by the Management Authority.

4   Any copies of a permit or certificates issued by a Management Authority shall be clearly marked as copies only and no such copy may be used in place of the original, except to the extent endorsed thereon.

5   A separate permit or certificate shall be required for each consignment of specimens.

6   A Management Authority of the state of import of any specimen shall cancel and retain the export permit or re-export certificate and any corresponding import permit presented in respect of the import of that specimen.

7   Where appropriate and feasible a Management Authority may affix a mark upon any specimen to assist in identifying the specimen. For these purposes 'mark' means any indelible imprint, lead seal or other suitable means of identifying a specimen, designed in such a way as to render its imitation by unauthorised persons as difficult as possible.

Article VII Exemptions and other special provisions relating to trade

1   The provisions of Articles III, IV and V shall not apply to the transit or trans-shipment of specimens through or in the territory of a Party while the specimens remain in Customs control.

2   Where a Management Authority of the state of export or re-export is satisfied that a specimen was acquired before the provisions of the present Convention applied to that specimen, the provisions of Articles III, IV and V shall not apply to that specimen where the Management Authority issues a certificate to that effect.

3   The provisions of Articles III, IV and V shall not apply to specimens that are personal or household effects. This exemption shall not apply where:

(a) in the case of specimens of a species included in Appendix I, they were acquired by the owner outside his state of usual residence, and are being imported into that state; or

(b) in the case of specimens of species included in Appendix II:

(i) they were acquired by the owner outside his state of usual residence and in a state where removal from the wild occurred;

(ii) they are being imported into the owner's state of usual residence; and

(iii) the state where removal from the wild occurred requires the prior grant of export permits before any export of such specimens,

unless a Management Authority is satisfied that the specimens were acquired before the provisions of the present Convention applied to such specimens.

4   Specimens of an animal species included in Appendix I bred in captivity for commercial purposes, or of a plant species included in Appendix I artificially propagated for commercial purposes, shall be deemed to be specimens of species included in Appendix II.

5   Where a Management Authority of the state of export is satisfied that any specimen of an animal species was bred in captivity or any specimen of a plant species was artificially propagated, or is a part of such an animal or plant or was derived therefrom, a certificate by that Management Authority to that effect shall be accepted in lieu of any of the permits or certificates required under the provisions of Articles III, IV or V.

6   The provisions of Articles III, IV and V shall not apply to the non-commercial loan, donation or exchange between scientists or scientific institutions registered by a Management Authority of their state, of herbarium specimens, other preserved, dried or embedded museum specimens, and live plant material which carry a label Issued or approved by a Management Authority.

7   A Management Authority of any state may waive the requirements of Articles III, IV and V and allow the movement without permits or certificates of specimens which form part of a travelling zoo, circus, menagerie, plant exhibition or other travelling exhibition provided that:

(a) the exporter or importer registers full details of such specimens with that Management Authority;

(b) the specimens are in either of the categories specified in paras 2 and 5 of this Article; and

(c) the Management Authority is satisfied that any living specimen will be so transported and cared for as to minimise the risk of injury, damage to health or cruel treatment.

Article VIII Measures to be taken by the parties

1   The Parties shall take appropriate measures to enforce the provisions of the present Convention and to prohibit trade in specimens in violation thereof. These shall include measures:

(a) to penalise trade in, or possession of, such specimens, or both; and

(b) to provide for the confiscation or return to the state of export of such specimens.

2   In addition to the measures taken under para 1 of this Article a Party may, when it deems it necessary, provide for any method of internal reimbursement for expenses incurred as a result of the confiscation of a specimen traded in violation of the measures taken in the application of the provisions of the present Convention.

3   As far as possible, the Parties shall ensure that specimens shall pass through any formalities required for trade with a minimum of delay. To facilitate such passage, a Party may designate ports of exit and ports of entry at which specimens must be presented for clearance.

The Parties shall ensure further that all living specimens, during any period of transit, holding or shipment, are properly cared for so as to minimise the risk of injury, damage to health or cruel treatment.

4   Where a living specimen is confiscated as a result of measures referred to in para 1 of this Article:

(a) the specimen shall be entrusted to a Management Authority of the state of confiscation;

(b) the Management Authority shall, after consultation with the state of export, return the specimen to that state at the expense of that state, or to a rescue centre or such other place as the Management Authority deems appropriate and consistent with the purposes of the present Convention; and

(c) the Management Authority may obtain the advice of a Scientific Authority, or may, wherever it considers it desirable, consult the Secretariat in order to facilitate the decision under sub-para (b) of this paragraph, including the choice of a rescue centre or other place.

5   A rescue centre as referred to in para 4 of this Article means an institution designated by a Management Authority to look after the welfare of living specimens, particularly those that have been confiscated.

6   Each Party shall maintain records of trade in specimens of species included in Appendices I, II and III which shall cover:

(a) the names and addresses of exporters and importers; and

(b) the number and type of permits and certificates granted; the states with which such trade occurred; the numbers or quantities and types of specimens, names of species as included in Appendices I, II and III and, where applicable, the size and sex of the specimens in question.

7   Each Party shall prepare periodic reports on its implementation of the present Convention and shall transmit to the Secretariat:

(a) an annual report containing a summary of the information specified in sub-para (b) of para 6 of this Article; and

(b) a biennial report on legislative, regulatory and administrative measures taken to enforce the provisions of the present Convention.

8   The information referred to in para 7 of this Article shall be available to the public where this is not inconsistent with the law of the Party concerned.

Article IX Management and scientific authorities

1   Each Party shall designate for the purposes of the present Convention:

(a) one or more Management Authorities competent to grant permits or certificates on behalf of that Party; and

(b) one or more Scientific Authorities.

2   A state depositing an instrument of ratification, acceptance, approval or accession shall at that time inform the Depository Government of the name and address of the Management Authority authorised to communicate with other Parties and with the Secretariat.

3   Any changes in the designations or authorisations under the provisions of this Article shall be communicated by the Party concerned to the Secretariat for transmission to all other Parties.

4   Any Management Authority referred to in para 2 of this Article shall if so requested by the Secretariat or the Management Authority of another Party, communicate to it impression of stamps, seals or other devices used to authenticate permits or certificates.

Article X Trade with states not party to the Convention

Where export or re-export is to, or import is from, a state not a Party to the present Convention, comparable documentation issued by the competent authorities in that state which substantially conforms with the requirements of the present Convention for permits and certificates may be accepted in lieu thereof by any Party.

Article XI Conference of the Parties

1   The Secretariat shall call a meeting of the Conference of the Parties not later than two years after the entry into force of the present Convention.

2   Thereafter the Secretariat shall convene regular meetings at least once every two years, unless the Conference decides otherwise, and extraordinary meetings at any time on the written request of a least one-third of the Parties.

3   At meetings, whether regular or extraordinary, the Parties shall review the implementation of the present Convention and may:

(a)   make such provision as may be necessary to enable the Secretariat to carry out its duties, and adopt financial provisions;

(b)   consider and adopt amendments to Appendices I and II in accordance with Article XV;

(c)   review the progress made towards the restoration and conservation of the species included in Appendices I, II and III;

(d)   receive and consider any reports presented by the Secretariat or by any Party; and

(e)   where appropriate, make recommendations for improving the effectiveness of the present Convention.

4   At each regular meeting, the Parties may determine the time and venue of the next regular meeting to be held in accordance with the provisions of para 2 of this Article.

5   At any meeting, the Parties may determine and adopt rules of procedure for the meeting.

6   The United Nations, its Specialised Agencies and the International Atomic Energy Agency, as well as any state not a Party to the present Convention, may be represented at meetings of the Conference by observers, who shall have the right to participate but not to vote.

7   Any body or agency technically qualified in protection, conservation or management of wild fauna and flora, in the following categories, which has informed the Secretariat of its desire to be represented at meetings of the Conference by observers, shall be admitted unless at least one-third of the Parties present object:

(a)   international agencies or bodies, either governmental or non-governmental, and national governmental agencies and bodies; and

(b) national non-governmental agencies or bodies which have been approved for this purpose by the state in which they are located.

Once admitted, these observers shall have the right to participate but not to vote.

Article XII The Secretariat

1   Upon entry into force of the present Convention, a Secretariat shall be provided by the Executive Director of the United Nations Environment Programme. To the extent and in the manner he considers appropriate, he may be assisted by suitable inter-governmental or non-governmental international or national agencies and bodies technically qualified in protection, conservation and management of wild fauna and flora.

2   The functions of the Secretariat shall be:

(a) to arrange for and service meetings of the Parties;

(b) to perform the functions entrusted to it under the provisions of Articles XV and XVI of the present Convention;

(c) to undertake scientific and technical studies in accordance with programmes authorised by the Conference of the Parties as will contribute to the implementation of the present Convention, including studies concerning standards for appropriate preparation and shipment of living specimens and the means of identifying specimens;

(d) to study the reports of Parties and to request from Parties such further information with respect thereto as it deems necessary to ensure implementation of the present Convention;

(e) to invite the attention of the Parties to any matter pertaining to the aims of the present Convention;

(f) to publish periodically and distribute to the Parties current editions of Appendices I, II and III together with any information which will facilitate identification of specimens of species included in those Appendices.

(g) to prepare annual reports to the Parties on its work and on the implementation of the present Convention and such other reports as meetings of the Parties may request;

(h) to make recommendations for the implementation of the aims and provisions of the present Convention, including the exchange of information of a scientific or technical nature;

(i) to perform any other function as may be entrusted to it by the Parties.

Article XIII International measures

1   When the Secretariat in the light of information received is satisfied that any species included in Appendices I or II is being affected adversely by trade in specimens of that species or that the provisions of the present Convention are not being effectively implemented, it shall communicate such information to the authorised Management Authority of the Party or Parties concerned.

2   When any Party receives a communication as indicated in para 1 of this Article, it shall, as soon as possible, inform the Secretariat of any relevant facts insofar as its laws permit and, where appropriate, propose remedial action. Where the Party considers that an inquiry is desirable, such inquiry may be carried out by one or more persons expressly authorised by the Party.

3   The information provided by the Party or resulting from any inquiry as specified in para 2 of this Article shall be reviewed by the next Conference of the Parties which may make whatever recommendations it deems appropriate.

Article XIV Effect on domestic legislation and international conventions

1   The provisions of the present Convention shall in no way affect the right of Parties to adopt:

(a) stricter domestic measures regarding the conditions for trade, taking, possession or transport of specimens of species included in Appendices I, II and III, or the complete prohibition thereof; or

(b) domestic measures restricting or prohibiting trade, taking possession, or transport of species not included in Appendices I, II or III.

2   The provisions of the present Convention shall in no way affect the provisions of any domestic measures or the obligations of Parties deriving from any treaty, convention, or international agreement relating to other aspects of trade, taking, possession, or transport of specimens which is in force or subsequently may enter into force for any Party including any measure pertaining to the customs, public health, veterinary or plant quarantine fields.

3   The provisions of the present Convention shall in no way affect the provisions of, or the obligations deriving from, any treaty, convention or international agreement concluded or which may be concluded between states creating a union or regional trade agreement establishing or maintaining a common external customs control and removing customs controls between the parties thereto insofar as they relate to trade among the states' members of that union or agreement.

4   A State Party to the present Convention, which is also a Party to any other treaty, convention or international agreement which is in force at the time of the coming into force of the present Convention and under the provisions of which protection is afforded to marine species included in Appendix II, shall be relieved of the obligations imposed on it under the provisions of the present Convention with respect to trade in specimens of species included in Appendix II that are taken by ships registered in that state and in accordance with the provisions of such other treaty, convention or international agreement.

5   Notwithstanding the provisions of Articles III, IV and V, any export of a specimen taken in accordance with para 4 of this Article shall only require a certificate from a Management Authority of the state of introduction to the effect that the specimen was taken in accordance with the provisions of the other treaty, convention or international agreement in question.

6   Nothing in the present Convention shall prejudice the codification and development of the law of the sea by the United Nations Conference on the Law of the Sea convened pursuant to Resolution 2750 C (XXV) of the General Assembly of the United Nations nor the present or future claims and legal views of any state concerning the law of the sea and the nature and extent of coastal and flag state jurisdiction.

Article XV Amendments to Appendices I and II

1   The following provisions shall apply in relation to amendments to Appendices I and II at meetings of the Conference of the Parties:

(a) Any Party may propose an amendment to Appendix I or II for consideration at the next meeting. The text of the proposed amendment shall be communicated to the Secretariat at least 150 days before the meeting. The Secretariat shall consult the other Parties and interested bodies on the amendment in accordance with the provisions of sub-paras (b) and (c) of para 2 of this Article and shall communicate the response to all Parties not later than 30 days before the meeting.

(b) Amendments shall be adopted by a two-thirds majority of Parties present and voting. For these purposes 'Parties present and voting' means Parties present and casting an affirmative or negative vote. Parties abstaining from voting shall not be counted among the two-thirds required for adopting an amendment.

(c) Amendments adopted at a meeting shall enter into force 90 days after that meeting for all Parties except those which make a reservation in accordance with para 3 of this Article.

2   The following provisions shall apply in relation to amendments to Appendices I and II between meetings of the Conference of the Parties:

(a) Any Party may propose an amendment to Appendix I and II for consideration between meetings by the postal procedures set forth in this paragraph.

(b) For marine species, the Secretariat shall, upon receiving the text of the proposed amendment, immediately communicate it to the Parties. It shall also consult intergovernmental bodies having a function in relation to those species especially with a view to obtaining scientific data these bodies may be able to provide and to ensuring co-ordination with any conservation measures enforced by such bodies. The Secretariat shall communicate the views expressed and data provided by these bodies and its own findings and recommendations to the Parties as soon as possible.

(c) For species other than marine species, the Secretariat shall, upon receiving the text of the proposed amendments, immediately communicate it to the Parties, and, as soon as possible thereafter, its own recommendations.

(d) Any Party may, within 60 days of the date on which the Secretariat communicated its recommendations to the Parties under sub-paras (b) or (c) of this paragraph, transmit to the Secretariat any comments on the proposed amendment together with any relevant scientific data and information.

(e) The Secretariat shall communicate the replies received together with its own recommendations to the Parties as soon as possible.

(f) If no objection to the proposed amendment is received by the Secretariat within 30 days of the date the replies and recommendations were communicated under the provisions of sub-para (e) of this paragraph, the amendment shall enter into force 90 days later for all Parties except those which make a reservation in accordance with para 3 of this Article.

(g) If an objection by any Party is received by the Secretariat the proposed amendment shall be submitted to a postal vote in accordance with the provisions of sub-paras (h), (i) and (j) of this paragraph.

(h) The Secretariat shall notify the Parties that notification of objection has been received.

(i) Unless the Secretariat receives the votes for, against or in abstention from at least one-half of the Parties within 60 days of the date of notification under sub-para (h) of this para, the proposed amendment shall be referred to the next meeting of the Conference for further consideration.

(j)   Provided that votes are received from one-half of the Parties, the amendment shall be adopted by a two-thirds majority of Parties casting an affirmative or negative vote.

(k)   The Secretariat shall notify all Parties of the result of the vote.

(l)   If the proposed amendment is adopted it shall enter into force 90 days after the date of the notification by the Secretariat of its acceptance for all Parties except those which make a reservation in accordance with para 3 of this Article.

3   During the period of 90 days provided for by sub-para (c) of para 1 or sub-para (l) of para 2 of this Article any Party may by notification in writing to the Depositary Government make a reservation with respect to the amendment. Until such reservation is withdrawn the Party shall be treated as a state not a Party to the present Convention with respect to trade in the species concerned.

Article XVI Appendix III and amendments thereto

1   Any Party may at any time submit to the Secretariat a list of species which it identifies as being subject to regulation within its Jurisdiction for the purpose mentioned in para 3 of Article II. Appendix III shall include the names of the Parties submitting the species for inclusion therein, the scientific names of the species so submitted, and any parts or derivatives of the animals or plants concerned that are specified in relation to the species for the purposes of sub-para (b) of Article I.

2   Each list submitted under the provisions of para 1 of this Article shall be communicated to the Parties by the Secretariat as soon as possible after receiving it. The list shall take effect as part of Appendix III 90 days after the date of such communication. At any time after the communication of such list, any Party may by notification in writing to the Depositary Government enter a reservation with respect to any species or any parts or derivatives, and until such reservation is withdrawn, the state shall be treated as a state not a Party to the present Convention with respect to trade in the species or part or derivative concerned.

3   A Party which has submitted a species for inclusion in Appendix III may withdraw it at any time by notification to the Secretariat which shall communicate the withdrawal to all Parties. The withdrawal shall take effect 30 days after the date of such communication.

4   Any Party submitting a list under the provisions of para 1 of this Article shall submit to the Secretariat a copy of all domestic laws and regulations applicable to the protection of such species, together with any interpretations which the Party may deem appropriate or the Secretariat may request. The Party shall, for as long as the species in question is included in Appendix III, submit any amendments of such laws and regulations or any new interpretations as they are adopted.

Article XVII Amendment of the Convention

1   An extraordinary meeting of the Conference of the Parties shall be convened by the Secretariat on the written request of at least one-third of the Parties to consider and adopt amendments to the present Convention. Such amendments shall be adopted by a two-thirds majority of Parties present and voting. For these purposes 'Parties present and voting' means Parties present and casting an affirmative or negative vote. Parties

abstaining from voting shall not be counted among the two-thirds required for adopting an amendment.

2 The text of any proposed amendment shall be communicated by the Secretariat to all Parties at least 90 days before the meeting.

3 An amendment shall enter into force for the Parties which have accepted it 60 days after two-thirds of the Parties have deposited an instrument of acceptance of the amendment with the Depositary Government. Thereafter, the amendment shall enter into force for any other Party 60 days after that Party deposits its instrument of acceptance of the amendment.

Article XVIII Resolution of disputes

1 Any dispute which may arise between two or more Parties with respect to the interpretation or application of the provisions of the present Convention shall be subject to negotiation between the Parties involved in the dispute.

2 If the dispute cannot be resolved in accordance with para 1 of this Article, the Parties may, by mutual consent, submit the dispute to arbitration, in particular that of the Permanent Court of Arbitration at The Hague, and the Parties submitting the dispute shall be bound by the arbitral decision.

Article XIX Signature

The present Convention shall be open for signature at Washington until 30 April 1973 and thereafter at Berne until 31 December 1974.

Article XX Ratification, acceptance, approval

The present Convention shall be subject to ratification, acceptance or approval. Instruments of ratification, acceptance or approval shall be deposited with the government of the Swiss Confederation which shall be the Depositary Government.

Article XXI Accession

The present Convention shall be open indefinitely for accession. Instruments of accession shall be deposited with the Depositary Government.

[1 This Convention shall be open for accession by regional economic integration organisations constituted by sovereign states which have competence in respect of the negotiation, conclusion and implementation of international agreements in matters transferred to them by their Member States and covered by this Convention.

2 In their instruments of accession, such organisations shall declare the extent of their competence with respect to the matters governed by the Convention. These organisations shall also inform the Depositary Government of any substantial modification in the extent of their competence. Notifications by regional economic integration organisations concerning their competence with respect to matters governed by this Convention and modifications thereto shall be distributed to the Parties by the Depositary Government.

3 In matters within their competence, such regional integration organisations shall exercise the rights and fulfil the obligations which this Convention attributes to their Member States, which are Parties to the Convention. In such cases the Member States of the organisations shall not be entitled to exercise such rights individually.

4   In the fields of their competence, regional economic integration organisations shall exercise their right to vote with a number of votes equal to the number of their Member States which are Parties to the Convention. Such organisations shall not exercise their right to vote if their Member States exercise theirs, and *vice versa*.

5   Any reference to 'Party' in the sense used in Article I(h) of this Convention to 'state'/ 'states' or to 'state party'/ 'states' parties' to the Convention shall be construed as including a reference to any regional economic integration organisation having competence in respect of the negotiation, conclusion and application of international agreements in matters covered by this Convention.]**

** The paragraphs in square brackets are an amendment to the Convention which was adopted at an extraordinary meeting of the Conference of the Parties in Gaborone (Botswana) on 30 April 1983. The amendment is not yet in force. It will enter into force when it has been formally accepted by 54 of the 80 States which were Parties to the Convention on that date. Until the amendment is in force, the EC cannot become a party.

Article XXII Entry into force

1   The present Convention shall enter into force 90 days after the date of deposit of the tenth instrument of ratification, acceptance, approval or accession, with the Depositary Government.

2   For each state which ratifies, accepts or approves the present Convention or accedes thereto after the deposit of the tenth instrument of ratification, acceptance, approval or accession, the present Convention shall enter into force 90 days after the deposit by such state of its instrument of ratification, acceptance, approval or accession.

Article XXIII Reservations

1   The provisions of the present Convention shall not be subject to general reservations. Specific reservations may be entered in accordance with the provisions of this Article and Articles XV and XVI.

2   Any state may, on depositing its instrument of ratification, acceptance, approval or accession, enter a specific reservation with regard to:

(a) any species included in Appendix I, II, III; or

(b) any parts or derivatives specified in relation to a species included in Appendix III.

3   Until a Party withdraws its reservation entered under the provisions of this Article, it shall be treated as a state not a Party to the present Convention with respect to trade in the particular species or parts or derivatives specified in such reservation.

[Articles XXIV (on Denunciation) and XXV (on Depository) omitted.]

[Appendices omitted.]

Convention on Biological Diversity 1992[11]

The Biodiversity Convention was one of the five major international environmental instruments which came out of the 1992 Rio Earth Summit (UNCED), the others being the

---

11   31 ILM (1992) 818. For the Biodiversity Convention 1992 website see www.biodiv.org.

Rio Declaration on Environment and Development (Chapter 1), Agenda 21, the Principles for Sustainable Development of Forests and the only other multilateral convention, namely the 1992 Framework Convention on Climate Change (Chapter 2). It was signed at UNCED by 157 States and the European Community and subsequently by a further nine States. As at 12 July 2001 there were 180 States parties to the Convention, including the EC.

According to Bowman and Redgwell, the Convention is the first international treaty explicitly to address all aspects of biodiversity ranging from the conservation of biological diversity and sustainable use of biological resources to access to biotechnology and the safety of activities relating to modified living organisms (Bowman and Redgwell (1996) 1). Sands notes that the Biodiversity Convention goes beyond CITES (see p 610, above) by establishing objectives for the comprehensive preservation of biological diversity (Sands (1995) 381). However, it is important to note that the principle of biodiversity conservation is subject to the greater objective of sustainable development through the introduction of the concept of 'sustainable use' within the Convention. In other words, although the conservation of biodiversity is designated a common concern of humankind in the Preamble to the Biodiversity Convention, nevertheless the principle of sustainable development requires that such biodiversity is also subjected to sustainable use by present and future generations of humankind (Arts 1 and 6).

This brings us to the crux of the problem: should biodiversity be conserved for its intrinsic ecological value, despite the fact that this cannot easily be translated into an economic value? It has been argued that the Biodiversity Convention itself appears to answer the above question in the negative. As Boyle notes:

> Despite the Preamble's recognition of the 'intrinsic value' of biodiversity, including its ecological, cultural and aesthetic aspects, this is not a 'preservationist' convention: it assumes human use and benefit as the fundamental purpose for conserving biodiversity, limited only by the requirement of sustainability and the need to benefit future generations. Thus, references to conservation of biodiversity must be read in conjunction with the sustainable use of its components (Boyle (1994) 115).

Others have argued that the Convention tends to view the problem in terms of the need to provide a suitable international legal framework for the sustainable exploitation of a renewable natural resource, to the detriment of biological diversity and the human, social and cultural diversity that often exists alongside it (Nayar and Ong (1996) 252).

There are other differences compared with CITES. By focussing on the conservation of species diversity rather than endangered species, the Biodiversity Convention takes up the battle to protect species as a whole at a much earlier stage in the process. Conceptually, the Biodiversity Convention is also different from CITES in that although both are concerned with the protection of species, the Biodiversity Convention also attempts to conserve these species within their natural habitats as far as possible (Preamble).

This definite preference within the Convention for *in-situ* (Art 8) as opposed to *ex-situ* (Art 9) conservation measures marks another interesting aspect of this Convention. Since the Convention reaffirms the principle of States' sovereignty over their own biological resources (Preamble and Arts 3 and 15), it does not attempt to internationalise ownership over these resources. Indeed, the Convention arguably denies even a right of access to these resources for other States, requiring States which have sovereignty over biological resources merely to 'endeavour to create conditions to facilitate access to genetic resources' (Art 15). However this sovereignty is not unlimited or absolute. In particular, as Boyle notes, the acceptance of the principle of the conservation of biological resources as a common concern of humankind is significant, albeit in the much more limited sense of legitimising international interest in the conservation and use of resources which would otherwise be within the territorial sovereignty of a State. Like concern for human rights, it acknowledges that the management of a State's own environment and resources is a matter in which all States have standing, even if they are not directly injured by any specific misuse of resources. In this sense, permanent sovereignty over biological resources is no longer a basis for the exclusion of others, but entails instead 'a commitment to co-operate for the good of the international community at large' (Boyle (1994) 117–18).

This impingement on State sovereignty is also evidenced in the provision requiring environmental impact assessment (EIA) of proposed projects that are likely to have adverse impacts on biological diversity (Art 14(1)(a)). Although it has been criticised as inadequate and compares unfavourably with similar provisions in other environmental instruments, it is important to note that most EIA requirements at the international level relate to the possibility of trans-boundary environmental damage, for example, the 1995 Espoo Convention on the Environmental Impact Assessment in a Trans-boundary Context (see Chapter 7, p 795 below). The Biodiversity Convention, in contrast, requires environmental impact assessments within States' parties' territories, albeit only for projects likely to have significant adverse impacts on biodiversity. As Boyle notes, this emphasises the responsibilities now undertaken by States in the management of their own natural environments (Boyle (1994) 119).

The nature of this responsibility is outlined in Arts 6–9 of the Convention which are intended to give effect to the conservation of biodiversity. In particular, Arts 8 and 9 deal with *in-situ* and *ex-situ* conservation measures, with an emphasis on the need to protect species within their natural habitats and thus maintain eco-system integrity (Art 8(d)). As the preliminary paragraph of Art 9 makes clear, *ex-situ* conservation, for example in zoos, is predominantly for the purpose of complementing *in-situ* measures. Despite the fact that much of this is already reflected in existing, mainly regional, nature conservation instruments, the global scope of the Biodiversity Convention transcends them in providing for an overall framework for nature conservation and minimum standards of wildlife protection. A greater difficulty however relates to the generality of the wording and the qualified nature of these provisions, which are phrased in a manner that defies any imputation of legal obligation, despite the legally-binding status of the Convention itself (see, for example, Arts 6–10, 14).

The institutional arrangements put in place to oversee the implementation of the Convention's provisions comprise the Conference of Parties (Art 23), a Subsidiary Body on Scientific, Technical and Technological Advice (Art 25) and a Secretariat (Art 24). As Boyle notes, '(T)he supervisory role given to the Conference of Parties is typical of many modern environmental treaties' (Boyle (1994) 125). The parties are required *inter alia* to periodically review the implementation of the Convention (Art 23(4)), receive and consider information and reports, most notably those provided by the Subsidiary Body and the parties themselves under Art 26, adopt amendments, annexes and protocols according to the procedure set out in Arts 29 and 30, and to consider and undertake any additional action in order to achieve the purposes of the Convention (Art 23(4)(i)). These provisions cannot be considered progressive especially when the lack of any framework, not even through a proactive Secretariat as in CITES, for independent monitoring or inspection is noted. The success or otherwise of the Convention is thus dependant on the good faith of the reporting States' parties and other interested groups such as the many environmental NGOs which keep an eye on its progress. As Boyle concludes, '(O)n the spectrum of supervisory bodies this Conference of Parties thus falls closer to the weaker end' (Boyle (1994) 125–26).

Finally, this Convention is now supplemented by a Protocol on Biosafety adopted in 2000 under Art 28 of the Convention. The Biosafety Protocol establishes procedures for controlling the movement and use of living modified organisms that may adversely affect biodiversity. For further discussion of its legal implications, see p 602, below.

Convention on Biological Diversity (1992)

Entered into force: 29 December 1993

Preamble

THE CONTRACTING PARTIES,

Conscious of the intrinsic value of biological diversity and of the ecological, genetic, social, economic, scientific, educational, cultural, recreational and aesthetic values of biological diversity and its components,

Conscious also of the importance of biological diversity for evolution and for maintaining life sustaining systems of the biosphere,

Affirming that the conservation of biological diversity is a common concern of humankind, Reaffirming that states have sovereign rights over their own biological resources,

Reaffirming also that states are responsible for conserving their biological diversity and for using their biological resources in a sustainable manner,

Concerned that biological diversity is being significantly reduced by certain human activities,

Aware of the general lack of information and knowledge regarding biological diversity and of the urgent need to develop scientific, technical and institutional capacities to provide the basic understanding upon which to plan and implement appropriate measures,

Noting that it is vital to anticipate, prevent and attack the causes of significant reduction or loss of biological diversity at source,

Noting also that where there is a threat of significant reduction or loss of biological diversity, lack of full scientific certainty should not be used as a reason for postponing measures to avoid or minimise such a threat,

Noting further that the fundamental requirement for the conservation of biological diversity is the in-situ conservation of eco-systems and natural habitats and the maintenance and recovery of viable populations of species in their natural surroundings,

Noting further that *ex-situ* measures, preferably in the country of origin, also have an important role to play,

Recognising the close and traditional dependence of many indigenous and local communities embodying traditional lifestyles on biological resources, and the desirability of sharing equitably benefits arising from the use of traditional knowledge, innovations and practices relevant to the conservation of biological diversity and the sustainable use of its components,

Recognising also the vital role that women play in the conservation and sustainable use of biological diversity and affirming the need for the full participation of women at all levels of policy-making and implementation for biological diversity conservation,

Stressing the importance of, and the need to promote, international, regional and global co-operation among states and inter-governmental organisations and the non-governmental sector for the conservation of biological diversity and the sustainable use of its components,

Acknowledging that the provision of new and additional financial resources and appropriate access to relevant technologies can be expected to make a substantial difference in the world's ability to address the loss of biological diversity,

Acknowledging further that special provision is required to meet the needs of developing countries, including the provision of new and additional financial resources and appropriate access to relevant technologies,

Noting in this regard the special conditions of the least developed countries and small island states,

Acknowledging that substantial investments are required to conserve biological diversity and that there is the expectation of a broad range of environmental, economic and social benefits from those investments,

Recognising that economic and social development and poverty eradication are the first and overriding priorities of developing countries,

Aware that conservation and sustainable use of biological diversity is of critical importance for meeting the food, health and other needs of the growing world population, for which purpose access to and sharing of both genetic resources and technologies are essential,

Noting that, ultimately, the conservation and sustainable use of biological diversity will strengthen friendly relations among states and contribute to peace for humankind,

Desiring to enhance and complement existing international arrangements for the conservation of biological diversity and sustainable use of its components, and

Determined to conserve and sustainably use biological diversity for the benefit of present and future generations.

HAVE AGREED AS FOLLOWS:

Article 1 Objectives

The objectives of this Convention, to be pursued in accordance with its relevant provisions, are the conservation of biological diversity, the sustainable use of its components and the fair and equitable sharing of the benefits arising out of the utilisation of genetic resources, including by appropriate access to genetic resources and by appropriate transfer of relevant technologies, taking into account all rights over those resources and to technologies, and by appropriate funding.

Article 2 Use of terms

For the purposes of this Convention:

'Biological diversity' means the variability among living organisms from all sources including, inter alia, terrestrial, marine and other aquatic eco-systems and the ecological complexes of which they are part; this includes diversity within species, between species and of eco-systems.

'Biological resources' includes genetic resources, organisms or parts thereof, populations, or any other biotic component of eco-systems with actual or potential use or value for humanity.

'Biotechnology' means any technological application that uses biological systems, living organisms, or derivatives thereof, to make or modify products or processes for specific use.

'Country of origin of genetic resources' means the country which possesses those genetic resources in *in-situ* conditions.

'Country providing genetic resources' means the country supplying genetic resources collected from *in-situ* sources, including populations of both wild and domesticated species, or taken from *ex-situ* sources, which may or may not have originated in that country.

'Domesticated or cultivated species' means species in which the evolutionary process has been influenced by humans to meet their needs.

'Eco-system' means a dynamic complex of plant, animal and micro-organism communities and their non-living environment interacting as a functional unit.

'*Ex-situ* conservation' means the conservation of components of biological diversity outside their natural habitats.

'Genetic material' means any material of plant, animal, microbial or other origin containing functional units of heredity.

'Genetic resources' means genetic material of actual or potential value.

'Habitat' means the place or type of site where an organism or population naturally occurs.

'*In-situ* conditions' means conditions where genetic resources exist within eco-systems and natural habitats, and, in the case of domesticated or cultivated species, in the surroundings where they have developed their distinctive properties.

'*In-situ* conservation' means the conservation of eco-systems and natural habitats and the maintenance and recovery of viable populations of species in their natural surroundings and, in the case of domesticated or cultivated species, in the surroundings where they have developed their distinctive properties.

'Protected area' means a geographically defined area which is designated or regulated and managed to achieve specific conservation objectives.

'Regional economic integration organisation' means an organisation constituted by sovereign states of a given region, to which its Member States have transferred competence in respect of matters governed by this Convention and which has been duly authorised, in accordance with its internal procedures, to sign, ratify, accept, approve or accede to it.

'Sustainable use' means the use of components of biological diversity in a way and at a rate that does not lead to the long-term decline of biological diversity, thereby maintaining its potential to meet the needs and aspirations of present and future generations.

'Technology' includes biotechnology.

Article 3 Principle

States have, in accordance with the Charter of the United Nations and the principles of international law, the sovereign right to exploit their own resources pursuant to their own environmental policies, and the responsibility to ensure that activities within their jurisdiction or control do not cause damage to the environment of other states or of areas beyond the limits of national jurisdiction.

Article 4 Jurisdictional scope

Subject to the rights of other states, and except as otherwise expressly provided in this Convention, the provisions of this Convention apply, in relation to each Contracting Party:

(a) in the case of components of biological diversity, in areas within the limits of its national jurisdiction; and

(b) in the case of processes and activities, regardless of where their effects occur, carried out under its jurisdiction or control, within the area of its national jurisdiction or beyond the limits of national jurisdiction.

Article 5 Co-operation

Each Contracting Party shall, as far as possible and as appropriate, co-operate with other Contracting Parties, directly or, where appropriate, through competent international organisations, in respect of areas beyond national jurisdiction and on other matters of mutual interest, for the conservation and sustainable use of biological diversity.

Article 6 General measures for conservation and sustainable use

Each Contracting Party shall, in accordance with its particular conditions and capabilities:

(a) develop national strategies, plans or programmes for the conservation and sustainable use of biological diversity or adapt for this purpose existing strategies, plans or programmes which shall reflect, *inter alia*, the measures set out in this Convention relevant to the Contracting Party concerned; and

(b) integrate, as far as possible and as appropriate, the conservation and sustainable use of biological diversity into relevant sectoral or cross-sectoral plans, programmes and policies.

Article 7 Identification and monitoring

Each Contracting Party shall, as far as possible and as appropriate, in particular for the purposes of Articles 8 to 10:

(a) identify components of biological diversity important for its conservation and sustainable use having regard to the indicative list of categories set down in Annex I;

(b) monitor, through sampling and other techniques, the components of biological diversity identified pursuant to sub-para (a) above, paying particular attention to those requiring urgent conservation measures and those which offer the greatest potential for sustainable use;

(c) identify processes and categories of activities which have or are likely to have significant adverse impacts on the conservation and sustainable use of biological diversity, and monitor their effects through sampling and other techniques; and

(d) maintain and organise, by any mechanism data, derived from identification and monitoring activities pursuant to sub-paras (a), (b) and (c) above.

Article 8 *In-situ* conservation

Each Contracting Party shall, as far as possible and as appropriate:

(a) establish a system of protected areas or areas where special measures need to be taken to conserve biological diversity;

(b) develop, where necessary, guidelines for the selection, establishment and management of protected areas or areas where special measures need to be taken to conserve biological diversity;

(c) regulate or manage biological resources important for the conservation of biological diversity whether within or outside protected areas, with a view to ensuring their conservation and sustainable use;

(d) promote the protection of eco-systems, natural habitats and the maintenance of viable populations of species in natural surroundings;

(e) promote environmentally sound and sustainable development in areas adjacent to protected areas with a view to furthering protection of these areas;

(f) rehabilitate and restore degraded eco-systems and promote the recovery of threatened species, *inter alia*, through the development and implementation of plans or other management strategies;

(g) establish or maintain means to regulate, manage or control the risks associated with the use and release of living modified organisms resulting from biotechnology which are likely to have adverse environmental impacts that could affect the conservation and sustainable use of biological diversity, taking also into account the risks to human health;

(h) prevent the introduction of, control or eradicate those alien species which threaten eco-systems, habitats or species;

(i) endeavour to provide the conditions needed for compatibility between present uses and the conservation of biological diversity and the sustainable use of its components;

(j) subject to its national legislation, respect, preserve and maintain knowledge, innovations and practices of indigenous and local communities embodying traditional lifestyles relevant for the conservation and sustainable use of biological diversity and promote their wider application with the approval and involvement of the holders of such knowledge, innovations and practices and encourage the equitable sharing of the benefits arising from the utilisation of such knowledge, innovations and practices;

(k) develop or maintain necessary legislation and/or other regulatory provisions for the protection of threatened species and populations;

(l) where a significant adverse effect on biological diversity has been determined pursuant to Article 7, regulate or manage the relevant processes and categories of activities; and

(m) co-operate in providing financial and other support for *in-situ* conservation outlined in sub-paras (a) to (l) above, particularly to developing countries.

Article 9 *Ex-situ* conservation

Each Contracting Party shall, as far as possible and as appropriate, and predominantly for the purpose of complementing *in-situ* measures:

(a) adopt measures for the *ex-situ* conservation of components of biological diversity, preferably in the country of origin of such components;

(b) establish and maintain facilities for *ex-situ* conservation of and research on plants, animals and micro- organisms, preferably in the country of origin of genetic resources;

(c) adopt measures for the recovery and rehabilitation of threatened species and for their reintroduction into their natural habitats under appropriate conditions;

(d) regulate and manage collection of biological resources from natural habitats for *ex-situ* conservation purposes so as not to threaten eco-systems and *in-situ* populations of species, except where special temporary *ex-situ* measures are required under sub-para (c) above; and

(e) co-operate in providing financial and other support for *ex-situ* conservation outlined in sub-paras (a) to (d) above and in the establishment and maintenance of *ex-situ* conservation facilities in developing countries.

Article 10 Sustainable use of components of biological diversity

Each Contracting Party shall, as far as possible and as appropriate:

(a) integrate consideration of the conservation and sustainable use of biological resources into national decision-making;

(b) adopt measures relating to the use of biological resources to avoid or minimise adverse impacts on biological diversity;

(c) protect and encourage customary use of biological resources in accordance with traditional cultural practices that are compatible with conservation or sustainable use requirements;

(d) support local populations to develop and implement remedial action in degraded areas where biological diversity has been reduced; and

(e) encourage co-operation between its governmental authorities and its private sector in developing methods for sustainable use of biological resources.

Article 11 Incentive measures

Each Contracting Party shall, as far as possible and as appropriate, adopt economically and socially sound measures that act as incentives for the conservation and sustainable use of components of biological diversity.

Article 12 Research and training

The Contracting Parties, taking into account the special needs of developing countries, shall:

(a) establish and maintain programmes for scientific and technical education and training in measures for the identification, conservation and sustainable use of biological diversity and its components and provide support for such education and training for the specific needs of developing countries;

(b) promote and encourage research which contributes to the conservation and sustainable use of biological diversity, particularly in developing countries, *inter alia*, in accordance with decisions of the Conference of the Parties taken in consequence of recommendations of the Subsidiary Body on Scientific, Technical and Technological Advice; and

(c) in keeping with the provisions of Articles 16, 18 and 20, promote and co-operate in the use of scientific advances in biological diversity research in developing methods for conservation and sustainable use of biological resources.

Article 13 Public education and awareness

The Contracting Parties shall:

(a) promote and encourage understanding of the importance of, and the measures required for, the conservation of biological diversity, as well as its propagation through media, and the inclusion of these topics in educational programmes; and

(b) co-operate, as appropriate, with other states and international organisations in developing educational and public awareness programmes, with respect to conservation and sustainable use of biological diversity.

Article 14 Impact assessment and minimising adverse impacts

1   Each Contracting Party, as far as possible and as appropriate, shall:

(a) introduce appropriate procedures requiring environmental impact assessment of its proposed projects that are likely to have significant adverse effects on biological diversity with a view to avoiding or minimising such effects and, where appropriate, allow for public participation in such procedures;

(b) introduce appropriate arrangements to ensure that the environmental consequences of its programmes and policies that are likely to have significant adverse impacts on biological diversity are duly taken into account;

(c) promote, on the basis of reciprocity, notification, exchange of information and consultation on activities under their jurisdiction or control which are likely to significantly affect adversely the biological diversity of other states or areas beyond the limits of national jurisdiction, by encouraging the conclusion of bilateral, regional or multilateral arrangements, as appropriate;

(d) in the case of imminent or grave danger or damage, originating under its jurisdiction or control, to biological diversity within the area under jurisdiction of other states or in areas beyond the limits of national jurisdiction, notify immediately the potentially affected states of such danger or damage, as well as initiate action to prevent or minimise such danger or damage; and

(e) promote national arrangements for emergency responses to activities or events, whether caused naturally or otherwise, which present a grave and imminent danger to biological diversity and encourage international co-operation to supplement such national efforts and, where appropriate and agreed by the states or regional economic integration organisations concerned, to establish joint contingency plans.

2   The Conference of the Parties shall examine, on the basis of studies to be carried out, the issue of liability and redress, including restoration and compensation, for damage to biological diversity, except where such liability is a purely internal matter.

Article 15 Access to genetic resources

1   Recognising the sovereign rights of states over their natural resources, the authority to determine access to genetic resources rests with the national governments and is subject to national legislation.

2   Each Contracting Party shall endeavour to create conditions to facilitate access to genetic resources for environmentally sound uses by other Contracting Parties and not to impose restrictions that run counter to the objectives of this Convention.

3   For the purpose of this Convention, the genetic resources being provided by a Contracting Party, as referred to in this Article and Articles 16 and 19, are only those that are provided by Contracting Parties that are countries of origin of such resources or by the Parties that have acquired the genetic resources in accordance with this Convention.

4   Access, where granted, shall be on mutually agreed terms and subject to the provisions of this Article.

5   Access to genetic resources shall be subject to prior informed consent of the Contracting Party providing such resources, unless otherwise determined by that Party.

6   Each Contracting Party shall endeavour to develop and carry out scientific research based on genetic resources provided by other Contracting Parties with the full participation of, and where possible in, such Contracting Parties.

7   Each Contracting Party shall take legislative, administrative or policy measures, as appropriate, and in accordance with Articles 16 and 19 and, where necessary, through the financial mechanism established by Articles 20 and 21 with the aim of sharing in a fair and equitable way the results of research and development and the benefits arising from the commercial and other utilisation of genetic resources with the Contracting Party providing such resources. Such sharing shall be upon mutually agreed terms.

Article 16 Access to and transfer of technology

1   Each Contracting Party, recognising that technology includes biotechnology, and that both access to and transfer of technology among Contracting Parties are essential elements for the attainment of the objectives of this Convention, undertakes subject to the provisions of this Article to provide and/or facilitate access for and transfer to other Contracting Parties of technologies that are relevant to the conservation and sustainable use of biological diversity or make use of genetic resources and do not cause significant damage to the environment.

2   Access to and transfer of technology referred to in para 1 above to developing countries shall be provided and/or facilitated under fair and most favourable terms, including on concessional and preferential terms where mutually agreed, and, where necessary, in accordance with the financial mechanism established by Articles 20 and 21. In the case of technology subject to patents and other intellectual property rights, such access and transfer shall be provided on terms which recognise and are consistent with the adequate and effective protection of intellectual property rights. The application of this para shall be consistent with paras 3, 4 and 5 below.

3   Each Contracting Party shall take legislative, administrative or policy measures, as appropriate, with the aim that Contracting Parties, in particular those that are developing countries, which provide genetic resources are provided access to and transfer of technology which makes use of those resources, on mutually agreed terms, including technology protected by patents and other intellectual property rights, where necessary, through the provisions of Articles 20 and 21 and in accordance with international law and consistent with paras 4 and 5 below.

4   Each Contracting Party shall take legislative, administrative or policy measures, as appropriate, with the aim that the private sector facilitates access to, joint development and transfer of technology referred to in para 1 above for the benefit of both governmental institutions and the private sector of developing countries and in this regard shall abide by the obligations included in paras 1, 2 and 3 above.

5   The Contracting Parties, recognising that patents and other intellectual property rights may have an influence on the implementation of this Convention, shall co-operate in this regard subject to national legislation and international law in order to ensure that such rights are supportive of and do not run counter to its objectives.

Article 17 Exchange of information

1   The Contracting Parties shall facilitate the exchange of information, from all publicly available sources, relevant to the conservation and sustainable use of biological diversity, taking into account the special needs of developing countries.

2   Such exchange of information shall include exchange of results of technical, scientific and socio-economic research, as well as information on training and surveying programmes, specialised knowledge, indigenous and traditional knowledge as such and in combination with the technologies referred to in Article 16, para 1. It shall also, where feasible, include repatriation of information.

Article 18 Technical and scientific co-operation

1   The Contracting Parties shall promote international technical and scientific co-operation in the field of conservation and sustainable use of biological diversity, where necessary, through the appropriate international and national institutions.

2   Each Contracting Party shall promote technical and scientific co-operation with other Contracting Parties, in particular developing countries, in implementing this Convention, *inter alia*, through the development and implementation of national policies. In promoting such co-operation, special attention should be given to the development and strengthening of national capabilities, by means of human resources development and institution building.

3   The Conference of the Parties, at its first meeting, shall determine how to establish a clearing-house mechanism to promote and facilitate technical and scientific co-operation.

4   The Contracting Parties shall, in accordance with national legislation and policies, encourage and develop methods of co-operation for the development and use of technologies, including indigenous and traditional technologies, in pursuance of the objectives of this Convention. For this purpose, the Contracting Parties shall also promote co-operation in the training of personnel and exchange of experts.

5   The Contracting Parties shall, subject to mutual agreement, promote the establishment of joint research programmes and joint ventures for the development of technologies relevant to the objectives of this Convention.

Article 19 Handling of biotechnology and distribution of its benefits

1   Each Contracting Party shall take legislative, administrative or policy measures, as appropriate, to provide for the effective participation in biotechnological research activities by those Contracting Parties, especially developing countries, which provide the genetic resources for such research, and where feasible in such Contracting Parties.

2   Each Contracting Party shall take all practicable measures to promote and advance priority access on a fair and equitable basis by Contracting Parties, especially developing countries, to the results and benefits arising from biotechnologies based upon genetic resources provided by those Contracting Parties. Such access shall be on mutually agreed terms.

3   The Parties shall consider the need for and modalities of a protocol setting out appropriate procedures, including, in particular, advance informed agreement, in the field of the safe transfer, handling and use of any living modified organism resulting from biotechnology that may have adverse effect on the conservation and sustainable use of biological diversity.

4   Each Contracting Party shall, directly or by requiring any natural or legal person under its jurisdiction providing the organisms referred to in para 3 above, provide any available information about the use and safety regulations required by that Contracting Party in handling such organisms, as well as any available information on the potential adverse impact of the specific organisms concerned to the Contracting Party into which those organisms are to be introduced.

Article 20 Financial resources

1   Each Contracting Party undertakes to provide, in accordance with its capabilities, financial support and incentives in respect of those national activities which are intended to achieve the objectives of this Convention, in accordance with its national plans, priorities and programmes.

2   The developed country Parties shall provide new and additional financial resources to enable developing country Parties to meet the agreed full incremental costs to them of implementing measures which fulfil the obligations of this Convention and to benefit from its provisions and which costs are agreed between a developing country Party and the institutional structure referred to in Article 21, in accordance with policy, strategy, programme priorities and eligibility criteria and an indicative list of incremental costs established by the Conference of the Parties. Other Parties, including countries undergoing the process of transition to a market economy, may voluntarily assume the obligations of the developed country Parties. For the purpose of this Article, the Conference of the Parties, shall at its first meeting establish a list of developed country Parties and other Parties which voluntarily assume the obligations of the developed country Parties. The Conference of the Parties shall periodically review and if necessary amend the list. Contributions from other countries and sources on a voluntary basis would also be encouraged. The implementation of these commitments shall take into account the need for adequacy, predictability and timely flow of funds and the importance of burden-sharing among the contributing Parties included in the list.

3 The developed country Parties may also provide, and developing country Parties avail themselves of, financial resources related to the implementation of this Convention through bilateral, regional and other multilateral channels.

4 The extent to which developing country Parties will effectively implement their commitments under this Convention will depend on the effective implementation by developed country Parties of their commitments under this Convention related to financial resources and transfer of technology and will take fully into account the fact that economic and social development and eradication of poverty are the first and overriding priorities of the developing country Parties.

5 The Parties shall take full account of the specific needs and special situation of least developed countries in their actions with regard to funding and transfer of technology.

6 The Contracting Parties shall also take into consideration the special conditions resulting from the dependence on, distribution and location of, biological diversity within developing country Parties, in particular small island states.

7 Consideration shall also be given to the special situation of developing countries, including those that are most environmentally vulnerable, such as those with arid and semi- arid zones, coastal and mountainous areas.

Article 21 Financial mechanism

1 There shall be a mechanism for the provision of financial resources to developing country Parties for purposes of this Convention on a grant or concessional basis the essential elements of which are described in this Article. The mechanism shall function under the authority and guidance of, and be accountable to, the Conference of the Parties for purposes of this Convention. The operations of the mechanism shall be carried out by such institutional structure as may be decided upon by the Conference of the Parties at its first meeting. For purposes of this Convention, the Conference of the Parties shall determine the policy, strategy, programme priorities and eligibility criteria relating to the access to and utilisation of such resources. The contributions shall be such as to take into account the need for predictability, adequacy and timely flow of funds referred to in Article 20 in accordance with the amount of resources needed to be decided periodically by the Conference of the Parties and the importance of burden-sharing among the contributing Parties included in the list referred to in Article 20, para 2. Voluntary contributions may also be made by the developed country Parties and by other countries and sources. The mechanism shall operate within a democratic and transparent system of governance.

2 Pursuant to the objectives of this Convention, the Conference of the Parties shall at its first meeting determine the policy, strategy and programme priorities, as well as detailed criteria and guidelines for eligibility for access to and utilisation of the financial resources including monitoring and evaluation on a regular basis of such utilisation. The Conference of the Parties shall decide on the arrangements to give effect to para 1 above after consultation with the institutional structure entrusted with the operation of the financial mechanism.

3 The Conference of the Parties shall review the effectiveness of the mechanism established under this Article, including the criteria and guidelines referred to in para 2 above, not less than two years after the entry into force of this Convention and thereafter on a regular basis. Based on such review, it shall take appropriate action to improve the effectiveness of the mechanism if necessary.

4   The Contracting Parties shall consider strengthening existing financial institutions to provide financial resources for the conservation and sustainable use of biological diversity.

Article 22 Relationship with other international conventions

1   The provisions of this Convention shall not affect the rights and obligations of any Contracting Party deriving from any existing international agreement, except where the exercise of those rights and obligations would cause a serious damage or threat to biological diversity.

2   Contracting Parties shall implement this Convention with respect to the marine environment consistently with the rights and obligations of states under the law of the sea.

Article 23 Conference of the Parties

1   A Conference of the Parties is hereby established. The first meeting of the Conference of the Parties shall be convened by the Executive Director of the United Nations Environment Programme not later than one year after the entry into force of this Convention. Thereafter, ordinary meetings of the Conference of the Parties shall be held at regular intervals to be determined by the Conference at its first meeting.

2   Extraordinary meetings of the Conference of the Parties shall be held at such other times as may be deemed necessary by the Conference, or at the written request of any Party, provided that, within six months of the request being communicated to them by the Secretariat, it is supported by at least one-third of the Parties.

3   The Conference of the Parties shall by consensus agree upon and adopt rules of procedure for itself and for any subsidiary body it may establish, as well as financial rules governing the funding of the Secretariat. At each ordinary meeting, it shall adopt a budget for the financial period until the next ordinary meeting.

4   The Conference of the Parties shall keep under review the implementation of this Convention, and, for this purpose, shall:

(a)   establish the form and the intervals for transmitting the information to be submitted in accordance with Article 26 and consider such information as well as reports submitted by any subsidiary body;

(b)   review scientific, technical and technological advice on biological diversity provided in accordance with Article 25;

(c)   consider and adopt, as required, protocols in accordance with Article 28;

(d)   consider and adopt, as required, in accordance with Articles 29 and 30, amendments to this Convention and its annexes;

(e)   consider amendments to any protocol, as well as to any annexes thereto, and, if so decided, recommend their adoption to the parties to the protocol concerned;

(f)   consider and adopt, as required, in accordance with Article 30, additional annexes to this Convention;

(g)   establish such subsidiary bodies, particularly to provide scientific and technical advice, as are deemed necessary for the implementation of this Convention;

(h)   contact, through the Secretariat, the executive bodies of conventions dealing with matters covered by this Convention with a view to establishing appropriate forms of co-operation with them; and

(i) consider and undertake any additional action that may be required for the achievement of the purposes of this Convention in the light of experience gained in its operation.

5   The United Nations, its specialised agencies and the International Atomic Energy Agency, as well as any state not Party to this Convention, may be represented as observers at meetings of the Conference of the Parties. Any other body or agency, whether governmental or non-governmental, qualified in fields relating to conservation and sustainable use of biological diversity, which has informed the Secretariat of its wish to be represented as an observer at a meeting of the Conference of the Parties, may be admitted unless at least one third of the Parties present object. The admission and participation of observers shall be subject to the rules of procedure adopted by the Conference of the Parties.

Article 24 Secretariat

1   Secretariat is hereby established. Its functions shall be:

   (a) to arrange for and service meetings of the Conference of the Parties provided for in Article 23;

   (b) to perform the functions assigned to it by any protocol;

   (c) to prepare reports on the execution of its functions under this Convention and present them to the Conference of the Parties;

   (d) to co-ordinate with other relevant international bodies and, in particular to enter into such administrative and contractual arrangements as may be required for the effective discharge of its functions; and

   (e) to perform such other functions as may be determined by the Conference of the Parties.

2   At its first ordinary meeting, the Conference of the Parties shall designate the secretariat from amongst those existing competent international organisations which have signified their willingness to carry out the secretariat functions under this Convention.

Article 25 Subsidiary body on scientific, technical and technological advice

1   A subsidiary body for the provision of scientific, technical and technological advice is hereby established to provide the Conference of the Parties and, as appropriate, its other subsidiary bodies with timely advice relating to the implementation of this Convention. This body shall be open to participation by all Parties and shall be multidisciplinary. It shall comprise government representatives competent in the relevant field of expertise. It shall report regularly to the Conference of the Parties on all aspects of its work.

2   Under the authority of and in accordance with guidelines laid down by the Conference of the Parties, and upon its request, this body shall:

   (a) provide scientific and technical assessments of the status of biological diversity;

   (b) prepare scientific and technical assessments of the effects of types of measures taken in accordance with the provisions of this Convention;

   (c) identify innovative, efficient and state-of-the-art technologies and know-how relating to the conservation and sustainable use of biological diversity and advise on the ways and means of promoting development and/or transferring such technologies;

(d) provide advice on scientific programmes and international co-operation in research and development related to conservation and sustainable use of biological diversity; and

(e) respond to scientific, technical, technological and methodological questions that the Conference of the Parties and its subsidiary bodies may put to the body.

3   The functions, terms of reference, organisation and operation of this body may be further elaborated by the Conference of the Parties.

Article 26 Reports

Each Contracting Party shall, at intervals to be determined by the Conference of the Parties, present to the Conference of the Parties, reports on measures which it has taken for the implementation of the provisions of this Convention and their effectiveness in meeting the objectives of this Convention.

Article 27 Settlement of disputes

1   In the event of a dispute between Contracting Parties concerning the interpretation or application of this Convention, the parties concerned shall seek solution by negotiation.

2   If the parties concerned cannot reach agreement by negotiation, they may jointly seek the good offices of, or request mediation by, a third party.

3   When ratifying, accepting, approving or acceding to this Convention, or at any time thereafter, a state or regional economic integration organisation may declare in writing to the Depositary that for a dispute not resolved in accordance with para 1 or para 2 above, it accepts one or both of the following means of dispute settlement as compulsory:

(a) arbitration in accordance with the procedure laid down in Part 1 of Annex II;

(b) submission of the dispute to the International Court of Justice.

4   If the parties to the dispute have not, in accordance with para 3 above, accepted the same or any procedure, the dispute shall be submitted to conciliation in accordance with Part 2 of Annex II unless the parties otherwise agree.

5   The provisions of this Article shall apply with respect to any protocol except as otherwise provided in the protocol concerned.

Article 28 Adoption of protocols

1   The Contracting Parties shall co-operate in the formulation and adoption of protocols to this Convention.

2   Protocols shall be adopted at a meeting of the Conference of the Parties.

3   The text of any proposed protocol shall be communicated to the Contracting Parties by the Secretariat at least six months before such a meeting.

Article 29 Amendment of the Convention or protocols

1   Amendments to this Convention may be proposed by any Contracting Party. Amendments to any protocol may be proposed by any Party to that protocol.

2   Amendments to this Convention shall be adopted at a meeting of the Conference of the Parties. Amendments to any protocol shall be adopted at a meeting of the Parties to the Protocol in question. The text of any proposed amendment to this Convention or to any

protocol, except as may otherwise be provided in such protocol, shall be communicated to the Parties to the instrument in question by the secretariat at least six months before the meeting at which it is proposed for adoption. The secretariat shall also communicate proposed amendments to the signatories to this Convention for information.

3 The Parties shall make every effort to reach agreement on any proposed amendment to this Convention or to any protocol by consensus. If all efforts at consensus have been exhausted, and no agreement reached, the amendment shall as a last resort be adopted by a two-third majority vote of the Parties to the instrument in question present and voting at the meeting, and shall be submitted by the Depositary to all Parties for ratification, acceptance or approval.

4 Ratification, acceptance or approval of amendments shall be notified to the Depositary in writing. Amendments adopted in accordance with para 3 above shall enter into force among Parties having accepted them on the ninetieth day after the deposit of instruments of ratification, acceptance or approval by at least two-thirds of the Contracting Parties to this Convention or of the Parties to the protocol concerned, except as may otherwise be provided in such protocol. Thereafter the amendments shall enter into force for any other Party on the 90th day after that Party deposits its instrument of ratification, acceptance or approval of the amendments.

5 For the purposes of this Article, 'Parties present and voting' means Parties present and casting an affirmative or negative vote.

Article 30 Adoption and amendment of annexes

1 The annexes to this Convention or to any protocol shall form an integral part of the Convention or of such protocol, as the case may be, and, unless expressly provided otherwise, a reference to this Convention or its protocols constitutes at the same time a reference to any annexes thereto. Such annexes shall be restricted to procedural, scientific, technical and administrative matters.

2 Except as may be otherwise provided in any protocol with respect to its annexes, the following procedure shall apply to the proposal, adoption and entry into force of additional annexes to this Convention or of annexes to any protocol:

(a) annexes to this Convention or to any protocol shall be proposed and adopted according to the procedure laid down in Article 29;

(b) any Party that is unable to approve an additional annex to this Convention or an annex to any protocol to which it is Party shall so notify the Depositary, in writing, within one year from the date of the communication of the adoption by the Depositary. The Depositary shall without delay notify all Parties of any such notification received. A Party may at any time withdraw a previous declaration of objection and the annexes shall thereupon enter into force for that Party subject to sub-para (c) below;

(c) on the expiry of one year from the date of the communication of the adoption by the Depositary, the annex shall enter into force for all Parties to this Convention or to any protocol concerned which have not submitted a notification in accordance with the provisions of sub-para (b) above.

3 The proposal, adoption and entry into force of amendments to annexes to this Convention or to any protocol shall be subject to the same procedure as for the proposal, adoption and entry into force of annexes to the Convention or annexes to any protocol.

4   If an additional annex or an amendment to an annex is related to an amendment to this Convention or to any protocol, the additional annex or amendment shall not enter into force until such time as the amendment to the Convention or to the protocol concerned enters into force.

Article 31 Right to vote

1   Except as provided for in para 2 below, each Contracting Party to this Convention or to any protocol shall have one vote.

2   Regional economic integration organisations, in matters within their competence, shall exercise their right to vote with a number of votes equal to the number of their member states which are Contracting Parties to this Convention or the relevant protocol. Such organisations shall not exercise their right to vote if their member states exercise theirs, and vice versa.

Article 32 Relationship between this Convention and its protocols

1   A state or a regional economic integration organisation may not become a Party to a protocol unless it is, or becomes at the same time, a Contracting Party to this Convention.

2   Decisions under any protocol shall be taken only by the Parties to the protocol concerned. Any Contracting Party that has not ratified, accepted or approved a protocol may participate as an observer in any meeting of the parties to that protocol.

[Articles 33 (on Signature), 34 (on Ratification, Acceptance or Approval), 35 (on Accession), 36 (on Entry into Force) omitted.]

Article 37 Reservations

No reservations may be made to this Convention.

[Article 38 (on Withdrawals) omitted.]

Article 39 Financial interim arrangements

Provided that it has been fully restructured in accordance with the requirements of Article 21, the Global Environment Facility of the United Nations Development Programme, the United Nations Environment Programme and the International Bank for Reconstruction and Development shall be the institutional structure referred to in Article 21 on an interim basis, for the period between the entry into force of this Convention and the first meeting of the Conference of the Parties or until the Conference of the Parties decides which institutional structure will be designated in accordance with Article 21.

Article 40 Secretariat interim arrangements

The secretariat to be provided by the Executive Director of the United Nations Environment Programme shall be the secretariat referred to in Article 24, para 2, on an interim basis for the period between the entry into force of this Convention and the first meeting of the Conference of the Parties.

[Articles 41 (on Depository), 42 (on Authentic Texts) omitted.]

Annex I Identification and monitoring

1   Eco-systems and habitats: containing high diversity, large numbers of endemic or threatened species, or wilderness; required by migratory species; of social, economic,

cultural or scientific importance; or, which are representative, unique or associated with key evolutionary or other biological processes.

2   Species and communities which are: threatened; wild relatives of domesticated or cultivated species; of medicinal, agricultural or other economic value; or social, scientific or cultural importance; or importance for research into the conservation and sustainable use of biological diversity, such as indicator species.

3   Described genomes and genes of social, scientific or economic importance.

[Annex II, Part 1 (on Arbitration), Part 2 (on Conciliation) omitted.]

Cartagena Protocol on Biosafety 2000[12]

The Cartagena Biosafety Protocol is so named because it was intended for adoption in the eponymous city of Cartagena de Indias, Colombia sometime during February, 1999. It is a measure of the controversy surrounding almost every major aspect of this agreement that it was finally adopted (by 130 states) nearly a year later, on 29 January, 2000 in Montreal, Canada. Needless to say, the Protocol is not yet in force.[13] However, it is a very welcome international environmental instrument aimed at fleshing-out the rather vague and general provision for the environmental issues arising from the development and trade in biotechnology products in the 1992 Biodiversity Convention (Art 8(g)). The negotiations for this Protocol were presaged by Art 19(3) of the 1992 Convention which required parties to consider adopting a protocol setting out appropriate procedures for the movement and use of any living modified organisms resulting from biotechnology that may adversely affect biodiversity. Article 28 of the Convention further provides for the use of protocols as a means to co-operate on specific biodiversity issues of concern to the international community.

Generally speaking, 'biosafety' refers to regulatory measures related to human activities having adverse affects on the conservation and sustainable use of biodiversity. (Qureshi (2000) 835). More specifically, the Biosafety Protocol addresses environmental issues arising from the development of living modified organisms (LMOs), more commonly known as genetically modified organisms (GMOs). These have been defined as living organisms that contain novel combinations of genetic material as a result of the application of biotechnology (Art 3(g) of the Protocol). In particular, the Protocol seeks to control international trade in such GMOs, for example the export of genetically modified seeds for use in agriculture, thus far the principal use of such technology. Article 4 provides that the Protocol shall apply to the international trade and use of all LMOs/GMOs that may have adverse effects on the conservation and sustainable use of biological diversity, taking also into account risks to human health. While the Protocol establishes a legal regime governing such trade, it remains to be seen just how successful this regime will be in achieving its objective. The negotiations for the Protocol were dogged throughout by several outstanding issues. Indeed, the debate continues. Chief among these concerns the material scope of the Protocol and the relationship between the

---

12   See 39 ILM (2000) 1027. See also www.biodiv.org/biosafety.
13   Article 37 of the Protocol provides that it will enter into force on the 90th day after the deposit of the fiftieth (50th) instrument of ratification, acceptance, approval or accession. As of 12 July 2001, there were five parties and 103 signatory States to the Protocol.

Protocol and the now well established international trade regime centred on the World Trade Organisation (WTO).

In particular, the Biosafety Protocol covers some of the same ground as the WTO Agreement on the Application of Sanitary and Phytosanitary measures (SPS Agreement).[14] The SPS Agreement regulates trade-restricting measures for LMOs/GMOs for the purposes of protecting human, animal, or plant life, health and safety. The Biosafety Protocol meanwhile is a broader agreement governing the transboundary movement of most biotechnology products. It tries to resolve any potential dispute with the SPS regime over the scope of their respective application by providing in its Preamble that the rights and obligations under other existing international agreements are preserved. On the other hand, however, the very next recital in the Preamble emphasises that the Protocol is not intended to be subordinated to other international agreements (such as the SPS agreement). As Schoenbaum observes, this makes it difficult to resolve any conflict arising from the application of either agreement (Schoenbaum (2000) 861).

Other difficult issues are broadly concerned with the implementation of the Protocol on the transboundary movements of LMOs/GMOs. These transboundary movements are subject to an 'Advance Informed Agreement' (AIA) procedure, under which they are only allowed after advanced written consent by the competent national authority of the putative importing State party (Art 10 of the Protocol). In this respect the present regime bears a striking resemblance to the prior informed consent procedure introduced by the Basel Convention on the Control of Transboundary Movements of Hazardous Wastes 1989 (see Chapter 4, above). Like Basel's prior informed consent regime, the AIA procedure involves several distinct requirements, namely: (1) notification by the exporting Party (Art 8 of the Protocol); (2) acknowledgement of notification by the importing Party (Art 9 of the Protocol); (3) a decision-making procedure by the importing party (Art 10 of the Protocol); and (4) the right to review such decisions in the light of new scientific information (Art 12 of the Protocol). Such decisions must be arrived at using scientifically sound risk assessment techniques (Art 15 of the Protocol). Under the Protocol, however, a wide interpretation of the precautionary principle applies, providing that lack of scientific uncertainty can result in import barriers being raised against international trade in LMOs/GMOs because of their possible adverse environmental effects. Here is where potential conflict with the SPS agreement lies because the SPS agreement employs a much more restrained application of the precautionary principle (on which, see Chapter 1, p 49, above).

There are several exceptions to the AIA procedure described above. These include: (1) the transboundary movement of LMOs/GMOs that are pharmaceuticals for human consumption (Art 5 of the Protocol); (2) LMOs/GMOs that are transiting through a State Party (Art 6(1) of the Protocol), or that are destined for contained use only (Art 6(2) of the Protocol), unless the State Party involved in either of these two situations decides to regulate them for itself; and (3) LMOs/GMOs intended for direct use as food, feed, or processing (FFP) (Art 7(2) of the Protocol). LMOs/GMOs for FFP use are subject to a less rigorous regulatory regime that is also based on the national discretion of the Party involved (Art 11 of the Protocol), the only requirement being that information of any

---

14 Negotiated at the conclusion of the Uruguay Round of the General Agreement on Tariffs and Trade (GATT) in 1994.

prohibition or procedures adopted should be forwarded to the Biosafety Clearing-House, established under Art 20 of the Protocol. Finally, LMOs/GMOs deemed unlikely to have adverse effects on biodiversity may be held exempt from the AIA procedure by an express decision of the Conference of Parties, (Art 7(4) of the Protocol) as provided by Art 29(4) of the Protocol.[15]

CARTAGENA PROTOCOL ON BIOSAFETY (2000)

THE PARTIES TO THIS PROTOCOL,

Being Parties to the Convention on Biological Diversity, hereinafter referred to as 'the Convention',

Recalling Article 19, paras 3 and 4, and Articles 8(g) and 17 of the Convention,

Recalling also decision II/5 of 17 November 1995 of the Conference of the Parties to the Convention to develop a Protocol on biosafety, specifically focusing on transboundary movement of any living modified organism resulting from modern biotechnology that may have adverse effect on the conservation and sustainable use of biological diversity, setting out for consideration, in particular, appropriate procedures for advance informed agreement,

Reaffirming the precautionary approach contained in Principle 15 of the Rio Declaration on Environment and Development,

Aware of the rapid expansion of modern biotechnology and the growing public concern over its potential adverse effects on biological diversity, taking also into account risks to human health,

Recognising that modern biotechnology has great potential for human well-being if developed and used with adequate safety measures for the environment and human health,

Recognising also the crucial importance to humankind of centres of origin and centres of genetic diversity,

Taking into account the limited capabilities of many countries, particularly developing countries, to cope with the nature and scale of known and potential risks associated with living modified organisms,

Recognising that trade and environment agreements should be mutually supportive with a view to achieving sustainable development,

Emphasising that this Protocol shall not be interpreted as implying a change in the rights and obligations of a Party under any existing international agreements,

Understanding that the above recital is not intended to subordinate this Protocol to other international agreements.

HAVE AGREED AS FOLLOWS:

Article 1 Objective

In accordance with the precautionary approach contained in Principle 15 of the Rio Declaration on Environment and Development, the objective of this Protocol is to contribute

---

15 See also Hutchison, C, 'An overview of the risk analysis provisions in the Cartagena Protocol on Biosafety' [2001] 2 Env Liability 65; French, D, 'The international regulation of genetically modified organisms: synergies and tensions in world trade' [2001] 3 Env Liability 127.

to ensuring an adequate level of protection in the field of the safe transfer, handling and use of living modified organisms resulting from modern biotechnology that may have adverse effects on the conservation and sustainable use of biological diversity, taking also into account risks to human health, and specifically focusing on transboundary movements.

Article 2 General Provisions

1   Each Party shall take necessary and appropriate legal, administrative and other measures to implement its obligations under this Protocol.

2   The Parties shall ensure that the development, handling, transport, use, transfer and release of any living modified organisms are undertaken in a manner that prevents or reduces the risks to biological diversity, taking also into account risks to human health.

3   Nothing in this Protocol shall affect in any way the sovereignty of States over their territorial sea established in accordance with international law, and the sovereign rights and the jurisdiction which States have in their exclusive economic zones and their continental shelves in accordance with international law, and the exercise by ships and aircraft of all States of navigational rights and freedoms as provided for in international law and as reflected in relevant international instruments.

4   Nothing in this Protocol shall be interpreted as restricting the right of a Party to take action that is more protective of the conservation and sustainable use of biological diversity than that called for in this Protocol, provided that such action is consistent with the objective and the provisions of this Protocol and is in accordance with that Party's other obligations under international law.

5   The Parties are encouraged to take into account, as appropriate, available expertise, instruments and work undertaken in international forums with competence in the area of risks to human health.

Article 3 Use of Terms

For the purposes of this Protocol:

(a)   'Conference of the Parties' means the Conference of the Parties to the Convention;

(b)   'Contained use' means any operation, undertaken within a facility, installation or other physical structure, which involves living modified organisms that are controlled by specific measures that effectively limit their contact with, and their impact on, the external environment;

(c)   'Export' means intentional transboundary movement from one Party to another Party;

(d)   'Exporter' means any legal or natural person, under the jurisdiction of the Party of export, who arranges for a living modified organism to be exported;

(e)   'Import' means intentional transboundary movement into one Party from another Party;

(f)   'Importer' means any legal or natural person, under the jurisdiction of the Party of import, who arranges for a living modified organism to be imported;

(g)   'Living modified organism' means any living organism that possesses a novel combination of genetic material obtained through the use of modern biotechnology;

(h) 'Living organism' means any biological entity capable of transferring or replicating genetic material, including sterile organisms, viruses and viroids;

(i) 'Modern biotechnology' means the application of:

(a) in-vitro nucleic acid techniques, including recombinant deoxyribonucleic acid (DNA) and direct injection of nucleic acid into cells or organelles; or

(b) fusion of cells beyond the taxonomic family,

that overcome natural physiological reproductive or recombination barriers and that are not techniques used in traditional breeding and selection;

(j) 'Regional economic integration organisation' means an organisation constituted by sovereign States of a given region, to which its member States have transferred competence in respect of matters governed by this Protocol and which has been duly authorised, in accordance with its internal procedures, to sign, ratify, accept, approve or accede to it;

(k) 'Transboundary movement' means the movement of a living modified organism from one Party to another Party, save that for the purposes of Articles 17 and 24 transboundary movement extends to movement between Parties and non-Parties.

Article 4 Scope

This Protocol shall apply to the transboundary movement, transit, handling and use of all living modified organisms that may have adverse effects on the conservation and sustainable use of biological diversity, taking also into account risks to human health.

Article 5 Pharmaceuticals

Notwithstanding Article 4 and without prejudice to any right of a Party to subject all living modified organisms to risk assessment prior to the making of decisions on import, this Protocol shall not apply to the transboundary movement of living modified organisms which are pharmaceuticals for humans that are addressed by other relevant international agreements or organisations.

Article 6 Transit and Contained Use

1   Notwithstanding Article 4 and without prejudice to any right of a Party of transit to regulate the transport of living modified organisms through its territory and make available to the Biosafety Clearing-House, any decision of that Party, subject to Article 2, para 3, regarding the transit through its territory of a specific living modified organism, the provisions of this Protocol with respect to the advance informed agreement procedure shall not apply to living modified organisms in transit.

2   Notwithstanding Article 4 and without prejudice to any right of a Party to subject all living modified organisms to risk assessment prior to decisions on import and to set standards for contained use within its jurisdiction, the provisions of this Protocol with respect to the advance informed agreement procedure shall not apply to the transboundary movement of living modified organisms destined for contained use undertaken in accordance with the standards of the Party of import.

Article 7 Application of the Advance Informed Agreement Procedure

1   Subject to Articles 5 and 6, the advance informed agreement procedure in Articles 8 to 10 and 12 shall apply prior to the first intentional transboundary movement of living

modified organisms for intentional introduction into the environment of the Party of import.

2   'Intentional introduction into the environment' in para 1 above, does not refer to living modified organisms intended for direct use as food or feed, or for processing.

3   Article 11 shall apply prior to the first transboundary movement of living modified organisms intended for direct use as food or feed, or for processing.

4   The advance informed agreement procedure shall not apply to the intentional transboundary movement of living modified organisms identified in a decision of the Conference of the Parties serving as the meeting of the Parties to this Protocol as being not likely to have adverse effects on the conservation and sustainable use of biological diversity, taking also into account risks to human health.

Article 8 Notification

1   The Party of export shall notify, or require the exporter to ensure notification to, in writing, the competent national authority of the Party of import prior to the intentional transboundary movement of a living modified organism that falls within the scope of Article 7, para 1. The notification shall contain, at a minimum, the information specified in Annex I.

2   The Party of export shall ensure that there is a legal requirement for the accuracy of information provided by the exporter.

Article 9 Acknowledgment of Receipt of Notification

1   The Party of import shall acknowledge receipt of the notification, in writing, to the notifier within 90 days of its receipt.

2   The acknowledgment shall state:

(a) the date of receipt of the notification;

(b) whether the notification, *prima facie*, contains the information referred to in Article 8;

(c) whether to proceed according to the domestic regulatory framework of the Party of import or according to the procedure specified in Article 10.

3   The domestic regulatory framework referred to in para 2 (c) above, shall be consistent with this Protocol.

4   A failure by the Party of import to acknowledge receipt of a notification shall not imply its consent to an intentional transboundary movement.

Article 10 Decision Procedure

1   Decisions taken by the Party of import shall be in accordance with Article 15.

2   The Party of import shall, within the period of time referred to in Article 9, inform the notifier, in writing, whether the intentional transboundary movement may proceed:

(a) only after the Party of import has given its written consent; or

(b) after no less than 90 days without a subsequent written consent.

3   Within 270 days of the date of receipt of notification, the Party of import shall communicate, in writing, to the notifier and to the Biosafety Clearing-House the decision referred to in para 2 (a) above:

(a) approving the import, with or without conditions, including how the decision will apply to subsequent imports of the same living modified organism;

(b) prohibiting the import;

(c) requesting additional relevant information in accordance with its domestic regulatory framework or Annex I; in calculating the time within which the Party of import is to respond, the number of days it has to wait for additional relevant information shall not be taken into account; or

(d) informing the notifier that the period specified in this paragraph is extended by a defined period of time.

4   Except in a case in which consent is unconditional, a decision under para 3 above, shall set out the reasons on which it is based.

5   A failure by the Party of import to communicate its decision within 270 days of the date of receipt of the notification shall not imply its consent to an intentional transboundary movement.

6   Lack of scientific certainty due to insufficient relevant scientific information and knowledge regarding the extent of the potential adverse effects of a living modified organism on the conservation and sustainable use of biological diversity in the Party of import, taking also into account risks to human health, shall not prevent that Party from taking a decision, as appropriate, with regard to the import of the living modified organism in question as referred to in para 3 above, in order to avoid or minimise such potential adverse effects.

7   The Conference of the Parties serving as the meeting of the Parties shall, at its first meeting, decide upon appropriate procedures and mechanisms to facilitate decision-making by Parties of import.

Article 11 Procedure for Living Modified Organisms Intended for Direct Use as Food or Feed, or for Processing

1   A Party that makes a final decision regarding domestic use, including placing on the market, of a living modified organism that may be subject to transboundary movement for direct use as food or feed, or for processing shall, within 15 days of making that decision, inform the Parties through the Biosafety Clearing-House. This information shall contain, at a minimum, the information specified in Annex II. The Party shall provide a copy of the information, in writing, to the national focal point of each Party that informs the Secretariat in advance that it does not have access to the Biosafety Clearing-House. This provision shall not apply to decisions regarding field trials.

2   The Party making a decision under para 1 above, shall ensure that there is a legal requirement for the accuracy of information provided by the applicant.

3   Any Party may request additional information from the authority identified in para (b) of Annex II.

4   A Party may take a decision on the import of living modified organisms intended for direct use as food or feed, or for processing, under its domestic regulatory framework that is consistent with the objective of this Protocol.

5   Each Party shall make available to the Biosafety Clearing-House copies of any national laws, regulations and guidelines applicable to the import of living modified organisms intended for direct use as food or feed, or for processing, if available.

6   A developing country Party or a Party with an economy in transition may, in the absence of the domestic regulatory framework referred to in para 4 above, and in exercise of its domestic jurisdiction, declare through the Biosafety Clearing-House that its decision prior to the first import of a living modified organism intended for direct use as food or feed, or for processing, on which information has been provided under para 1 above, will be taken according to the following:

(a) a risk assessment undertaken in accordance with Annex III; and

(b) a decision made within a predictable time-frame, not exceeding 270 days.

7   Failure by a Party to communicate its decision according to para 6 above, shall not imply its consent or refusal to the import of a living modified organism intended for direct use as food or feed, or for processing, unless otherwise specified by the Party.

8   Lack of scientific certainty due to insufficient relevant scientific information and knowledge regarding the extent of the potential adverse effects of a living modified organism on the conservation and sustainable use of biological diversity in the Party of import, taking also into account risks to human health, shall not prevent that Party from taking a decision, as appropriate, with regard to the import of that living modified organism intended for direct use as food or feed, or for processing, in order to avoid or minimise such potential adverse effects.

9   A Party may indicate its needs for financial and technical assistance and capacity-building with respect to living modified organisms intended for direct use as food or feed, or for processing. Parties shall co-operate to meet these needs in accordance with Articles 22 and 28.

Article 12 Review of Decisions

1   A Party of import may, at any time, in light of new scientific information on potential adverse effects on the conservation and sustainable use of biological diversity, taking also into account the risks to human health, review and change a decision regarding an intentional transboundary movement. In such case, the Party shall, within 30 days, inform any notifier that has previously notified movements of the living modified organism referred to in such decision, as well as the Biosafety Clearing-House, and shall set out the reasons for its decision.

2   A Party of export or a notifier may request the Party of import to review a decision it has made in respect of it under Article 10 where the Party of export or the notifier considers that:

(a) a change in circumstances has occurred that may influence the outcome of the risk assessment upon which the decision was based; or

(b) additional relevant scientific or technical information has become available.

3   The Party of import shall respond in writing to such a request within ninety days and set out the reasons for its decision.

4   The Party of import may, at its discretion, require a risk assessment for subsequent imports.

Article 13 Simplified Procedure

1   A Party of import may, provided that adequate measures are applied to ensure the safe intentional transboundary movement of living modified organisms in accordance with the objective of this Protocol, specify in advance to the Biosafety Clearing-House:

(a) cases in which intentional transboundary movement to it may take place at the same time as the movement is notified to the Party of import; and

(b) imports of living modified organisms to it to be exempted from the advance informed agreement procedure.

Notifications under sub-para (a) above, may apply to subsequent similar movements to the same Party.

2   The information relating to an intentional transboundary movement that is to be provided in the notifications referred to in para 1(a) above, shall be the information specified in Annex I.

Article 14 Bilateral, Regional and Multilateral Agreements and Arrangements

1   Parties may enter into bilateral, regional and multilateral agreements and arrangements regarding intentional transboundary movements of living modified organisms, consistent with the objective of this Protocol and provided that such agreements and arrangements do not result in a lower level of protection than that provided for by the Protocol.

2   The Parties shall inform each other, through the Biosafety Clearing-House, of any such bilateral, regional and multilateral agreements and arrangements that they have entered into before or after the date of entry into force of this Protocol.

3   The provisions of this Protocol shall not affect intentional transboundary movements that take place pursuant to such agreements and arrangements as between the parties to those agreements or arrangements.

4   Any Party may determine that its domestic regulations shall apply with respect to specific imports to it and shall notify the Biosafety Clearing-House of its decision.

Article 15 Risk Assessment

1   Risk assessments undertaken pursuant to this Protocol shall be carried out in a scientifically sound manner, in accordance with Annex III and taking into account recognised risk assessment techniques. Such risk assessments shall be based, at a minimum, on information provided in accordance with Article 8 and other available scientific evidence in order to identify and evaluate the possible adverse effects of living modified organisms on the conservation and sustainable use of biological diversity, taking also into account risks to human health.

2   The Party of import shall ensure that risk assessments are carried out for decisions taken under Article 10. It may require the exporter to carry out the risk assessment.

3   The cost of risk assessment shall be borne by the notifier if the Party of import so requires.

Article 16 Risk Management

1   The Parties shall, taking into account Article 8(g) of the Convention, establish and maintain appropriate mechanisms, measures and strategies to regulate, manage and

control risks identified in the risk assessment provisions of this Protocol associated with the use, handling and transboundary movement of living modified organisms.

2   Measures based on risk assessment shall be imposed to the extent necessary to prevent adverse effects of the living modified organism on the conservation and sustainable use of biological diversity, taking also into account risks to human health, within the territory of the Party of import.

3   Each Party shall take appropriate measures to prevent unintentional transboundary movements of living modified organisms, including such measures as requiring a risk assessment to be carried out prior to the first release of a living modified organism.

4   Without prejudice to para 2 above, each Party shall endeavour to ensure that any living modified organism, whether imported or locally developed, has undergone an appropriate period of observation that is commensurate with its life-cycle or generation time before it is put to its intended use.

5   Parties shall co-operate with a view to:

    (a) identifying living modified organisms or specific traits of living modified organisms that may have adverse effects on the conservation and sustainable use of biological diversity, taking also into account risks to human health; and

    (b) taking appropriate measures regarding the treatment of such living modified organisms or specific traits.

Article 17 Unintentional Transboundary Movements and Emergency Measures

1   Each Party shall take appropriate measures to notify affected or potentially affected States, the Biosafety Clearing-House and, where appropriate, relevant international organisations, when it knows of an occurrence under its jurisdiction resulting in a release that leads, or may lead, to an unintentional transboundary movement of a living modified organism that is likely to have significant adverse effects on the conservation and sustainable use of biological diversity, taking also into account risks to human health in such States. The notification shall be provided as soon as the Party knows of the above situation.

2   Each Party shall, no later than the date of entry into force of this Protocol for it, make available to the Biosafety Clearing-House the relevant details setting out its point of contact for the purposes of receiving notifications under this Article.

3   Any notification arising from para 1 above, should include:

    (a) available relevant information on the estimated quantities and relevant characteristics and/or traits of the living modified organism;

    (b) information on the circumstances and estimated date of the release, and on the use of the living modified organism in the originating Party;

    (c) any available information about the possible adverse effects on the conservation and sustainable use of biological diversity, taking also into account risks to human health, as well as available information about possible risk management measures;

    (d) any other relevant information; and

    (e) a point of contact for further information.

4   In order to minimise any significant adverse effects on the conservation and sustainable use of biological diversity, taking also into account risks to human health, each Party, under whose jurisdiction the release of the living modified organism referred to in

para 1 above, occurs, shall immediately consult the affected or potentially affected States to enable them to determine appropriate responses and initiate necessary action, including emergency measures.

Article 18 Handling Transport, Packaging and Identification

1   In order to avoid adverse effects on the conservation and sustainable use of biological diversity, taking also into account risks to human health, each Party shall take necessary measures to require that living modified organisms that are subject to intentional transboundary movement within the scope of this Protocol are handled, packaged and transported under conditions of safety, taking into consideration relevant international rules and standards.

2   Each Party shall take measures to require that documentation accompanying:

(a) living modified organisms that are intended for direct use as food or feed, or for processing, clearly identifies that they 'may contain' living modified organisms and are not intended for intentional introduction into the environment, as well as a contact point for further information. The Conference of the Parties serving as the meeting of the Parties to this Protocol shall take a decision on the detailed requirements for this purpose, including specification of their identity and any unique identification, no later than two years after the date of entry into force of this Protocol;

(b) living modified organisms that are destined for contained use clearly identifies them as living modified organisms; and specifies any requirements for the safe handling, storage, transport and use, the contact point for further information, including the name and address of the individual and institution to whom the living modified organisms are consigned; and

(c) living modified organisms that are intended for intentional introduction into the environment of the Party of import and any other living modified organisms within the scope of the Protocol, clearly identifies them as living modified organisms; specifies the identity and relevant traits and/or characteristics, any requirements for the safe handling, storage, transport and use, the contact point for further information and, as appropriate, the name and address of the importer and exporter; and contains a declaration that the movement is in conformity with the requirements of this Protocol applicable to the exporter.

3   The Conference of the Parties serving as the meeting of the Parties to this Protocol shall consider the need for and modalities of developing standards with regard to identification, handling, packaging and transport practices, in consultation with other relevant international bodies.

Article 19 Competent National Authorities and National Focal Points

1   Each Party shall designate one national focal point to be responsible on its behalf for liaison with the Secretariat. Each Party shall also designate one or more competent national authorities, which shall be responsible for performing the administrative functions required by this Protocol and which shall be authorised to act on its behalf with respect to those functions. A Party may designate a single entity to fulfil the functions of both focal point and competent national authority.

2   Each Party shall, no later than the date of entry into force of this Protocol for it, notify the Secretariat of the names and addresses of its focal point and its competent national authority or authorities. Where a Party designates more than one competent national

authority, it shall convey to the Secretariat, with its notification thereof, relevant information on the respective responsibilities of those authorities. Where applicable, such information shall, at a minimum, specify which competent authority is responsible for which type of living modified organism. Each Party shall forthwith notify the Secretariat of any changes in the designation of its national focal point or in the name and address or responsibilities of its competent national authority or authorities.

3   The Secretariat shall forthwith inform the Parties of the notifications it receives under para 2 above, and shall also make such information available through the Biosafety Clearing-House.

Article 20 Informational Sharing and the Biosafety Clearing-House

1   A Biosafety Clearing-House is hereby established as part of the clearing-house mechanism under Article 18, para 3, of the Convention, in order to:

(a) facilitate the exchange of scientific, technical, environmental and legal information on, and experience with, living modified organisms; and

(b) assist Parties to implement the Protocol, taking into account the special needs of developing country Parties, in particular the least developed and small island developing States among them, and countries with economies in transition as well as countries that are centres of origin and centres of genetic diversity.

2   The Biosafety Clearing-House shall serve as a means through which information is made available for the purposes of para 1 above. It shall provide access to information made available by the Parties relevant to the implementation of the Protocol. It shall also provide access, where possible, to other international biosafety information exchange mechanisms.

3   Without prejudice to the protection of confidential information, each Party shall make available to the Biosafety Clearing-House any information required to be made available to the Biosafety Clearing-House under this Protocol, and:

(a) any existing laws, regulations and guidelines for implementation of the Protocol, as well as information required by the Parties for the advance informed agreement procedure;

(b) any bilateral, regional and multilateral agreements and arrangements;

(c) summaries of its risk assessments or environmental reviews of living modified organisms generated by its regulatory process, and carried out in accordance with Article 15, including, where appropriate, relevant information regarding products thereof, namely, processed materials that are of living modified organism origin, containing detectable novel combinations of replicable genetic material obtained through the use of modern biotechnology;

(d) its final decisions regarding the importation or release of living modified organisms; and

(e) reports submitted by it pursuant to Article 33, including those on implementation of the advance informed agreement procedure.

4   The modalities of the operation of the Biosafety Clearing-House, including reports on its activities, shall be considered and decided upon by the Conference of the Parties serving as the meeting of the Parties to this Protocol at its first meeting, and kept under review thereafter.

Article 21 Confidential Information

1 The Party of import shall permit the notifier to identify information submitted under the procedures of this Protocol or required by the Party of import as part of the advance informed agreement procedure of the Protocol that is to be treated as confidential. Justification shall be given in such cases upon request.

2 The Party of import shall consult the notifier if it decides that information identified by the notifier as confidential does not qualify for such treatment and shall, prior to any disclosure, inform the notifier of its decision, providing reasons on request, as well as an opportunity for consultation and for an internal review of the decision prior to disclosure.

3 Each Party shall protect confidential information received under this Protocol, including any confidential information received in the context of the advance informed agreement procedure of the Protocol. Each Party shall ensure that it has procedures to protect such information and shall protect the confidentiality of such information in a manner no less favourable than its treatment of confidential information in connection with domestically produced living modified organisms.

4 The Party of import shall not use such information for a commercial purpose, except with the written consent of the notifier.

5 If a notifier withdraws or has withdrawn a notification, the Party of import shall respect the confidentiality of commercial and industrial information, including research and development information as well as information on which the Party and the notifier disagree as to its confidentiality.

6 Without prejudice to para 5 above, the following information shall not be considered confidential:

(a) the name and address of the notifier;

(b) a general description of the living modified organism or organisms;

(c) a summary of the risk assessment of the effects on the conservation and sustainable use of biological diversity, taking also into account risks to human health; and

(d) any methods and plans for emergency response.

Article 22 Capacity-Building

1 The Parties shall co-operate in the development and/or strengthening of human resources and institutional capacities in biosafety, including biotechnology to the extent that it is required for biosafety, for the purpose of the effective implementation of this Protocol, in developing country Parties, in particular the least developed and small island developing States among them, and in Parties with economies in transition, including through existing global, regional, sub-regional and national institutions and organisations and, as appropriate, through facilitating private sector involvement.

2 For the purposes of implementing para 1 above, in relation to co-operation, the needs of developing country Parties, in particular the least developed and small island developing States among them, for financial resources and access to and transfer of technology and know-how in accordance with the relevant provisions of the Convention, shall be taken fully into account for capacity-building in biosafety. Co-operation in capacity-building shall, subject to the different situation, capabilities and

requirements of each Party, include scientific and technical training in the proper and safe management of biotechnology, and in the use of risk assessment and risk management for biosafety, and the enhancement of technological and institutional capacities in biosafety. The needs of Parties with economies in transition shall also be taken fully into account for such capacity-building in biosafety.

Article 23 Public Awareness and Participation

1   The Parties shall:

(a) promote and facilitate public awareness, education and participation concerning the safe transfer, handling and use of living modified organisms in relation to the conservation and sustainable use of biological diversity, taking also into account risks to human health. In doing so, the Parties shall co-operate, as appropriate, with other States and international bodies;

(b) endeavour to ensure that public awareness and education encompass access to information on living modified organisms identified in accordance with this Protocol that may be imported.

2   The Parties shall, in accordance with their respective laws and regulations, consult the public in the decision-making process regarding living modified organisms and shall make the results of such decisions available to the public, while respecting confidential information in accordance with Article 21.

3   Each Party shall endeavour to inform its public about the means of public access to the Biosafety Clearing-House.

Article 24 Non-Parties

1   Transboundary movements of living modified organisms between Parties and non-Parties shall be consistent with the objective of this Protocol. The Parties may enter into bilateral, regional and multilateral agreements and arrangements with non-Parties regarding such transboundary movements.

2   The Parties shall encourage non-Parties to adhere to this Protocol and to contribute appropriate information to the Biosafety Clearing-House on living modified organisms released in, or moved into or out of, areas within their national jurisdictions.

Article 25 Illegal Transboundary Movements

1   Each Party shall adopt appropriate domestic measures aimed at preventing and, if appropriate, penalising transboundary movements of living modified organisms carried out in contravention of its domestic measures to implement this Protocol. Such movements shall be deemed illegal transboundary movements.

2   In the case of an illegal transboundary movement, the affected Party may request the Party of origin to dispose, at its own expense, of the living modified organism in question by repatriation or destruction, as appropriate.

3   Each Party shall make available to the Biosafety Clearing-House information concerning cases of illegal transboundary movements pertaining to it.

Article 26 Socio-Economic Considerations

1   The Parties, in reaching a decision on import under this Protocol or under its domestic measures implementing the Protocol, may take into account, consistent with their international obligations, socio-economic considerations arising from the impact of

living modified organisms on the conservation and sustainable use of biological diversity, especially with regard to the value of biological diversity to indigenous and local communities.

2   The Parties are encouraged to co-operate on research and information exchange on any socio-economic impacts of living modified organisms, especially on indigenous and local communities.

Article 27 Liability and Redress

The Conference of the Parties serving as the meeting of the Parties to this Protocol shall, at its first meeting, adopt a process with respect to the appropriate elaboration of international rules and procedures in the field of liability and redress for damage resulting from transboundary movements of living modified organisms, analysing and taking due account of the ongoing processes in international law on these matters, and shall endeavour to complete this process within four years.

Article 28 Financial Mechanism and Resources

1   In considering financial resources for the implementation of this Protocol, the Parties shall take into account the provisions of Article 20 of the Convention.

2   The financial mechanism established in Article 21 of the Convention shall, through the institutional structure entrusted with its operation, be the financial mechanism for this Protocol.

3   Regarding the capacity-building referred to in Article 22 of this Protocol, the Conference of the Parties serving as the meeting of the Parties to this Protocol, in providing guidance with respect to the financial mechanism referred to in para 2 above, for consideration by the Conference of the Parties, shall take into account the need for financial resources by developing country Parties, in particular the least developed and the small island developing States among them.

4   In the context of para 1 above, the Parties shall also take into account the needs of the developing country Parties, in particular the least developed and the small island developing States among them, and of the Parties with economies in transition, in their efforts to identify and implement their capacity-building requirements for the purposes of the implementation of this Protocol.

5   The guidance to the financial mechanism of the Convention in relevant decisions of the Conference of the Parties, including those agreed before the adoption of this Protocol, shall apply, *mutatis mutandis*, to the provisions of this Article.

6   The developed country Parties may also provide, and the developing country Parties and the Parties with economies in transition avail themselves of, financial and technological resources for the implementation of the provisions of this Protocol through bilateral, regional and multilateral channels.

Article 29 Conference of the Parties serving as the Meeting of the Parties to this Protocol

1   The Conference of the Parties shall serve as the meeting of the Parties to this Protocol.

2   Parties to the Convention that are not Parties to this Protocol may participate as observers in the proceedings of any meeting of the Conference of the Parties serving as the meeting of the Parties to this Protocol. When the Conference of the Parties serves as the meeting of the Parties to this Protocol, decisions under this Protocol shall be taken only by those that are Parties to it.

3   When the Conference of the Parties serves as the meeting of the Parties to this Protocol, any member of the bureau of the Conference of the Parties representing a Party to the Convention but, at that time, not a Party to this Protocol, shall be substituted by a member to be elected by and from among the Parties to this Protocol.

4   The Conference of the Parties serving as the meeting of the Parties to this Protocol shall keep under regular review the implementation of this Protocol and shall make, within its mandate, the decisions necessary to promote its effective implementation. It shall perform the functions assigned to it by this Protocol and shall:

(a) make recommendations on any matters necessary for the implementation of this Protocol;

(b) establish such subsidiary bodies as are deemed necessary for the implementation of this Protocol;

(c) seek and utilise, where appropriate, the services and co-operation of, and information provided by, competent international organisations and intergovernmental and non-governmental bodies;

(d) establish the form and the intervals for transmitting the information to be submitted in accordance with Article 33 of this Protocol and consider such information as well as reports submitted by any subsidiary body;

(e) consider and adopt, as required, amendments to this Protocol and its annexes, as well as any additional annexes to this Protocol, that are deemed necessary for the implementation of this Protocol; and

(f) exercise such other functions as may be required for the implementation of this Protocol.

5   The rules of procedure of the Conference of the Parties and financial rules of the Convention shall be applied, *mutatis mutandis*, under this Protocol, except as may be otherwise decided by consensus by the Conference of the Parties serving as the meeting of the Parties to this Protocol.

6   The first meeting of the Conference of the Parties serving as the meeting of the Parties to this Protocol shall be convened by the Secretariat in conjunction with the first meeting of the Conference of the Parties that is scheduled after the date of the entry into force of this Protocol. Subsequent ordinary meetings of the Conference of the Parties serving as the meeting of the Parties to this Protocol shall be held in conjunction with ordinary meetings of the Conference of the Parties, unless otherwise decided by the Conference of the Parties serving as the meeting of the Parties to this Protocol.

7   Extraordinary meetings of the Conference of the Parties serving as the meeting of the Parties to this Protocol shall be held at such other times as may be deemed necessary by the Conference of the Parties serving as the meeting of the Parties to this Protocol, or at the written request of any Party, provided that, within six months of the request being communicated to the Parties by the Secretariat, it is supported by at least one-third of the Parties.

8   The United Nations, its specialised agencies and the International Atomic Energy Agency, as well as any State member thereof or observers thereto not party to the Convention, may be represented as observers at meetings of the Conference of the Parties serving as the meeting of the Parties to this Protocol. Any body or agency, whether national or international, governmental or non-governmental, that is qualified in matters covered by this Protocol and that has informed the Secretariat of its wish to

be represented at a meeting of the Conference of the Parties serving as a meeting of the Parties to this Protocol as an observer, may be so admitted, unless at least one-third of the Parties present object. Except as otherwise provided in this Article, the admission and participation of observers shall be subject to the rules of procedure, as referred to in para 5 above.

Article 30 Subsidiary Bodies

1   Any subsidiary body established by or under the Convention may, upon a decision by the Conference of the Parties serving as the meeting of the Parties to this Protocol, serve the Protocol, in which case the meeting of the Parties shall specify which functions that body shall exercise.

2   Parties to the Convention that are not Parties to this Protocol may participate as observers in the proceedings of any meeting of any such subsidiary bodies. When a subsidiary body of the Convention serves as a subsidiary body to this Protocol, decisions under the Protocol shall be taken only by the Parties to the Protocol.

3   When a subsidiary body of the Convention exercises its functions with regard to matters concerning this Protocol, any member of the bureau of that subsidiary body representing a Party to the Convention but, at that time, not a Party to the Protocol, shall be substituted by a member to be elected by and from among the Parties to the Protocol.

Article 31 Secretariat

1   The Secretariat established by Article 24 of the Convention shall serve as the secretariat to this Protocol.

2   Article 24, para 1, of the Convention on the functions of the Secretariat shall apply, *mutatis mutandis*, to this Protocol.

3   To the extent that they are distinct, the costs of the secretariat services for this Protocol shall be met by the Parties hereto. The Conference of the Parties serving as the meeting of the Parties to this Protocol shall, at its first meeting, decide on the necessary budgetary arrangements to this end.

Article 32 Relationship with the Convention

Except as otherwise provided in this Protocol, the provisions of the Convention relating to its protocols shall apply to this Protocol.

Article 33 Monitoring and Reporting

Each Party shall monitor the implementation of its obligations under this Protocol, and shall, at intervals to be determined by the Conference of the Parties serving as the meeting of the Parties to this Protocol, report to the Conference of the Parties serving as the meeting of the Parties to this Protocol on measures that it has taken to implement the Protocol.

Article 34 Compliance

The Conference of the Parties serving as the meeting of the Parties to this Protocol shall, at its first meeting, consider and approve co-operative procedures and institutional mechanisms to promote compliance with the provisions of this Protocol and to address cases of non-compliance. These procedures and mechanisms shall include provisions to offer advice or assistance, where appropriate. They shall be separate from, and without prejudice to, the dispute settlement procedures and mechanisms established by Article 27 of the Convention.

Article 35 Assessment and Review

The Conference of the Parties serving as the meeting of the Parties to this Protocol shall undertake, five years after the entry into force of this Protocol and at least every five years thereafter, an evaluation of the effectiveness of the Protocol, including an assessment of its procedures and annexes.

Article 36 Signature

This Protocol shall be open for signature at the United Nations Office at Nairobi by States and regional economic integration organisations from 15 to 26 May 2000, and at United Nations Headquarters in New York from 5 June 2000 to 4 June 2001.

Article 37 Entry into Force

1   This Protocol shall enter into force on the 19th day after the date of deposit of the 50th instrument of ratification, acceptance, approval or accession by States or regional economic integration organisations that are Parties to the Convention.

2   This Protocol shall enter into force for a State or regional economic integration organisation that ratifies, accepts or approves this Protocol or accedes thereto after its entry into force pursuant to para 1 above, on the 19th day after the date on which that State or regional economic integration organisation deposits its instrument of ratification, acceptance, approval or accession, or on the date on which the Convention enters into force for that State or regional economic integration organisation, whichever shall be the later.

3   For the purposes of paras 1 and 2 above, any instrument deposited by a regional economic integration organisation shall not be counted as additional to those deposited by member States of such organisation.

Article 38 Reservations

No reservations may be made to this Protocol.

Article 39 Withdrawal

1   At any time after two years from the date on which this Protocol has entered into force for a Party, that Party may withdraw from the Protocol by giving written notification to the Depositary.

2   Any such withdrawal shall take place upon expiry of one year after the date of its receipt by the Depositary, or on such later date as may be specified in the notification of the withdrawal.

Article 40 Authentic Texts

The original of this Protocol, of which the Arabic, Chinese, English, French, Russian and Spanish texts are equally authentic, shall be deposited with the Secretary-General of the United Nations.

IN WITNESS WHEREOF the undersigned, being duly authorised to that effect, have signed this Protocol.

DONE at Montreal on this twenty-ninth day of January, two thousand.

Annex I Information Required in Notifications Under Articles 8, 10 and 13

(a) Name, address and contact details of the exporter.

(b) Name, address and contact details of the importer.

(c) Name and identity of the living modified organism, as well as the domestic classification, if any, of the biosafety level of the living modified organism in the State of export.

(d) Intended date or dates of the transboundary movement, if known.

(e) Taxonomic status, common name, point of collection or acquisition, and characteristics of recipient organism or parental organisms related to biosafety.

(f) Centres of origin and centres of genetic diversity, if known, of the recipient organism and/or the parental organisms and a description of the habitats where the organisms may persist or proliferate.

(g) Taxonomic status, common name, point of collection or acquisition, and characteristics of the donor organism or organisms related to biosafety.

(h) Description of the nucleic acid or the modification introduced, the technique used, and the resulting characteristics of the living modified organism.

(i) Intended use of the living modified organism or products thereof, namely, processed materials that are of living modified organism origin, containing detectable novel combinations of replicable genetic material obtained through the use of modern biotechnology.

(j) Quantity or volume of the living modified organism to be transferred.

(k) A previous and existing risk assessment report consistent with Annex III.

(l) Suggested methods for the safe handling, storage, transport and use, including packaging, labelling, documentation, disposal and contingency procedures, where appropriate.

(m) Regulatory status of the living modified organism within the State of export (for example, whether it is prohibited in the State of export, whether there are other restrictions, or whether it has been approved for general release) and, if the living modified organism is banned in the State of export, the reason or reasons for the ban.

(n) Result and purpose of any notification by the exporter to other States regarding the living modified organism to be transferred.

(o) A declaration that the above-mentioned information is factually correct.

Annex II Information Required Concerning Living Modified Organisms Intended for Direct Use as Food or Feed or for Processing Under Article 11

(a) The name and contact details of the applicant for a decision for domestic use.

(b) The name and contact details of the authority responsible for the decision.

(c) Name and identity of the living modified organism.

(d) Description of the gene modification, the technique used, and the resulting characteristics of the living modified organism.

(e) Any unique identification of the living modified organism.

(f) Taxonomic status, common name, point of collection or acquisition, and characteristics of recipient organism or parental organisms related to biosafety.

(g) Centres of origin and centres of genetic diversity, if known, of the recipient organism and/or the parental organisms and a description of the habitats where the organisms may persist or proliferate.

(h) Taxonomic status, common name, point of collection or acquisition, and characteristics of the donor organism or organisms related to biosafety.

(i) Approved uses of the living modified organism.

(j) A risk assessment report consistent with Annex III.

(k) Suggested methods for the safe handling, storage, transport and use, including packaging, labelling, documentation, disposal and contingency procedures, where appropriate.

Annex III Risk Assessment

Objective

1   The objective of risk assessment, under this Protocol, is to identify and evaluate the potential adverse effects of living modified organisms on the conservation and sustainable use of biological diversity in the likely potential receiving environment, taking also into account risks to human health.

Use of Risk Assessment

2   Risk assessment is, inter alia, used by competent authorities to make informed decisions regarding living modified organisms.

General principles

3   Risk assessment should be carried out in a scientifically sound and transparent manner, and can take into account expert advice of, and guidelines developed by, relevant international organisations.

4   Lack of scientific knowledge or scientific consensus should not necessarily be interpreted as indicating a particular level of risk, an absence of risk, or an acceptable risk.

5   Risks associated with living modified organisms or products thereof, namely, processed materials that are of living modified organism origin, containing detectable novel combinations of replicable genetic material obtained through the use of modern biotechnology, should be considered in the context of the risks posed by the non-modified recipients or parental organisms in the likely potential receiving environment.

6   Risk assessment should be carried out on a case-by-case basis. The required information may vary in nature and level of detail from case to case, depending on the living modified organism concerned, its intended use and the likely potential receiving environment.

Methodology

7   The process of risk assessment may on the one hand give rise to a need for further information about specific subjects, which may be identified and requested during the

assessment process, while on the other hand information on other subjects may not be relevant in some instances.

8   To fulfil its objective, risk assessment entails, as appropriate, the following steps:

(a) an identification of any novel genotypic and phenotypic characteristics associated with the living modified organism that may have adverse effects on biological diversity in the likely potential receiving environment, taking also into account risks to human health;

(b) an evaluation of the likelihood of these adverse effects being realised, taking into account the level and kind of exposure of the likely potential receiving environment to the living modified organism;

(c) an evaluation of the consequences should these adverse effects be realised;

(d) an estimation of the overall risk posed by the living modified organism based on the evaluation of the likelihood and consequences of the identified adverse effects being realised;

(e) a recommendation as to whether or not the risks are acceptable or manageable, including, where necessary, identification of strategies to manage these risks; and

(f) where there is uncertainty regarding the level of risk, it may be addressed by requesting further information on the specific issues of concern or by implementing appropriate risk management strategies and/or monitoring the living modified organism in the receiving environment.

Points to consider

9   Depending on the case, risk assessment takes into account the relevant technical and scientific details regarding the characteristics of the following subjects:

(a) *Recipient organism or parental organisms.* The biological characteristics of the recipient organism or parental organisms, including information on taxonomic status, common name, origin, centres of origin and centres of genetic diversity, if known, and a description of the habitat where the organisms may persist or proliferate.

(b) *Donor organism or organisms.* Taxonomic status and common name, source, and the relevant biological characteristics of the donor organisms;

(c) *Vector.* Characteristics of the vector, including its identity, if any, and its source or origin, and its host range.

(d) *Insert or inserts and/or characteristics of modification.* Genetic characteristics of the inserted nucleic acid and the function it specifies, and/or characteristics of the modification introduced.

(e) *Living modified organism.* Identity of the living modified organism, and the differences between the biological characteristics of the living modified organism and those of the recipient organism or parental organisms.

(f) *Detection and identification of the living modified organism.* Suggested detection and identification methods and their specificity, sensitivity and reliability.

(g) *Information relating to the intended use.* Information relating to the intended use of the living modified organism, including new or changed use compared to the recipient organism or parental organisms.

(h) *Receiving environment.* Information on the location, geographical, climatic and ecological characteristics, including relevant information on biological diversity and centres of origin of the likely potential receiving environment.

Convention on Wetlands of International Importance, especially as Waterfowl Habitat 1971 (Ramsar Convention)[16]

This multilateral convention was the first global attempt to regulate the conservation of a particular type of habitat, namely wetlands, as opposed to the species-based approach to wildlife protection (Sands (1995) 404 and Birnie and Boyle (1992) 465) (for UK domestic response, see s 37A of the Wildlife and Countryside Act 1981, pp 707–08, below). 'Wetlands' are defined in Art 1(1) of the Convention (see p 625, below). Although Lyster notes that the definition is suitably broad (Lyster (1985) 184), Sands argues that it does not reflect the enormous variety of wetland types or the fact that they are dynamic, capable of changing with the seasons and over longer periods of time, and that accordingly their boundaries are often difficult to define with any degree of precision (Sands (1995) 404). Their importance as wildlife habitats, especially in respect of waterfowl species is well-documented (Lyster (1985) 183), as is their rapid deterioration from various threats such as human settlement, degradation of the watershed, soil erosion, siltation, diversion of water supplies, pollution, hunting, fishing and agricultural drainage (Sands (1995) 404).

As of 13 July 2001, the Convention had 124 States' parties, including an increasing number of developing country parties. This follows a recommendation adopted in 1987 to make participation in the Convention more attractive for them by stressing the value of wetlands and the need for wise use; rather than emphasising the need for conservation measures as such. The establishment in 1990 of the Small Wetlands Conservation Fund to assist conservation of listed wetlands has also helped in this respect.

Each State Party shall designate at least one wetland for inclusion in a List of Wetlands of International Importance upon joining the Convention (Art 2(1)). These should be precisely described and delimited on a map (Art 2(4)). Wetlands should be selected for the list on account of their international significance in terms of ecology, botany, zoology, limnology or hydrology (Art 2(2)). The addition of further wetlands, or the enlargement of listed wetlands, is up to the discretion of the State Party concerned. The withdrawal of a listed wetland or the restriction of its boundaries may only be done because of 'urgent national interests' (Art 2(5)). Where this occurs, the State Party concerned is required as far as possible to compensate for any loss of wetland resources either by creating additional waterfowl nature reserves or by protecting in the same area or elsewhere an adequate portion of the original habitat (Art 4(2)).

Rather incongruously, the inclusion of a wetland in the List is not supposed to prejudice the exclusive sovereign rights of the Party in whose territory the wetland is situated (Art 2(3)). By joining the Convention and designating wetland(s) on the List, however, a State Party is surely accepting a limitation of sorts upon its 'exclusive' sovereignty to do as it will, at least in respect of its designated and listed wetland(s). This much is clear from the requirement that States' parties formulate and implement their

---

16 11 ILM (1972) 963; 22 ILM (1983) 698. See also www.ramsar.org.

planning so as to promote the conservation of listed wetlands and as far as possible, the wise use of wetlands in their territory (Art 3(1)). It is unclear however from the first part of the provision whether parties have an obligation to promote the conservation of listed sites in all States' parties or only of their own sites (Lyster (1985) 195 and Birnie and Boyle (1992) 465). Other basic commitments are the establishment of nature reserves, whether they are listed or not (Art 4(1)); endeavouring to increase waterfowl populations (Art 4(4)); and ensuring that it is informed of any actual or likely change in the ecological character of any of its listed wetlands, which information is to be passed on to the Ramsar Bureau (Art 3(2)). The Convention also encourages research, the exchange of data, training of personnel, and consultation between parties about implementing their obligations (Arts 4(3), 4(5) and 5). On the other hand, Birnie and Boyle note that the taking of species for any purpose is neither forbidden nor required to be regulated, although any such use must not affect the ecological characteristics of the wetland (Birnie and Boyle (1992) 465).

The original Ramsar Convention 1971 was blighted with ambiguities and gaps in its provisions, among the most crucial being the fact that initially no amendment procedure was included within it, leaving the Conference of Parties to issue non-binding interpretative recommendations in lieu of this inadequacy at its three yearly meetings to review the implementation of the Convention. Indeed, even the regular, three-yearly timing of the Conference of Parties and permanent secretariat were not explicitly provided for in the original Convention text (see the amended Art 6(1)). A system of national financial contributions to the work of the Convention was also not forthcoming. As Birnie and Boyle note, the lack of amendment procedure was a serious defect for a wildlife conservation treaty as it inhibited flexibility in adapting the instrument to different priorities, such flexibility being considered vital to successful conservation ((1992) 467).

The Conferences of Parties (as well as Extraordinary Conferences) were therefore utilised to address these various procedural difficulties. Through these meetings, the Convention has been amended twice: first, by a Protocol to provide for an amendment procedure and approve equally authentic, different language versions of the Convention. This entered into force on 1 October 1986. Secondly, by using the amendment procedure above to establish an independent secretariat called the Ramsar Bureau and to enable it to convene a regular Conference of the Parties to review and promote the Convention (Art 6(1) as amended). These amendments entered into force on 1 May 1994 (Birnie and Boyle (1995) 447–48).

Apart from the procedural gaps in the original Convention, there have been substantive problems too. For example, the Convention's 'wise use' of wetlands requirement (Art 6(3)) was not defined initially. This term was defined in the first Conference of the Parties (Cagliari, 1980) but then subsequently redefined at the 1987 Regina Conference as 'their sustainable utilisation for the benefit of human kind in a way that is compatible with the maintenance of the natural properties of the eco-system'. Overall, the strengthening of the procedural and substantive weaknesses of the Convention through the introduction of an amendment procedure, the establishment of an independent and permanent Secretariat, a Standing Committee, a financial regime of State Party contributions and the increased authority of the Conference of Parties should all enhance the effectiveness of this Convention. Increasing co-operation with other wildlife conventions such as the Bonn Convention 1979 (see p 562, note 6, above) and the Biodiversity Convention 1992 (see p 586, above) have undoubtedly assisted in this respect. For example, Ramsar COP 7 (1999) endorsed a joint work plan with the latter Convention for areas of high coastal and marine biodiversity as well as inland water eco-systems.

CONVENTION ON WETLANDS OF INTERNATIONAL IMPORTANCE ESPECIALLY AS WATERFOWL HABITAT (1971) (AS AMENDED)

Entered into force: 21 December 1975

THE CONTRACTING PARTIES,

Recognising the interdependence of man and his environment;

Considering the fundamental ecological functions of wetlands as regulators of water regimes and as habitats supporting a characteristic flora and fauna, especially waterfowl;

Being convinced that wetlands constitute a resource of great economic, cultural, scientific and recreational value, the loss of which would be irreparable;

Desiring to stem the progressive encroachment on and loss of wetlands now and in the future;

Recognising that waterfowl in their seasonal migrations may transcend frontiers and so should be regarded as an international resource;

Being confident that the conservation of wetlands and their flora and fauna can be ensured by combining far-sighted national policies with co-ordinated international action;

HAVE AGREED AS FOLLOWS:

Article 1

1   For the purpose of this Convention wetlands are areas of marsh, fen, peatland or water, whether natural or artificial, permanent or temporary, with water that is static or flowing, fresh, brackish or salt, including areas of marine water the depth of which at low tide does not exceed six metres.

2   For the purpose of this Convention waterfowl are birds ecologically dependent on wetlands.

Article 2

1   Each Contracting Party shall designate suitable wetlands within its territory for inclusion in a List of Wetlands of International Importance, hereinafter referred to as 'the List' which is maintained by the bureau established under Article 8. The boundaries of each wetland shall be precisely described and also delimited on a map and they may incorporate riparian and coastal zones adjacent to the wetlands, and islands or bodies of marine water deeper than six metres at low tide lying within the wetlands, especially where these have importance as waterfowl habitat.

2   Wetlands should be selected for the List on account of their international significance in terms of ecology, botany, zoology, limnology or hydrology. In the first instance wetlands of international importance to waterfowl at any season should be included.

3 The inclusion of a wetland in the List does not prejudice the exclusive sovereign rights of the Contracting Party in whose territory the wetland is situated.

4 Each Contracting Party shall designate at least one wetland to be included in the List when signing this Convention or when depositing its instrument of ratification or accession, as provided in Article 9.

5 Any Contracting Party shall have the right to add to the List further wetlands situated within its territory, to extend the boundaries of those wetlands already included by it in the List, or, because of its urgent national interests, to delete or restrict the boundaries of wetlands already included by it in the List and shall, at the earliest possible time, inform the organisation or government responsible for the continuing bureau duties specified in Article 8 of any such changes.

6 Each Contracting Party shall consider its international responsibilities for the conservation, management and wise use of migratory stocks of waterfowl, both when designating entries for the List and when exercising its right to change entries in the List relating to wetlands within its territory.

Article 3

1 The Contracting Parties shall formulate and implement their planning so as to promote the conservation of the wetlands included in the List, and as far as possible the wise use of wetlands in their territory.

2 Each Contracting Party shall arrange to be informed at the earliest possible time if the ecological character of any wetland in its territory and included in the List has changed, is changing or is likely to change as the result of technological developments, pollution or other human interference. Information on such changes shall be passed without delay to the organisation or government responsible for the continuing bureau duties specified in Article 8.

Article 4

1 Each Contracting Party shall promote the conservation of wetlands and waterfowl by establishing nature reserves on wetlands, whether they are included in the List or not, and provide adequately for their wardening.

2 Where a Contracting Party in its urgent national interest, deletes or restricts the boundaries of a wetland included in the List, it should as far as possible compensate for any loss of wetland resources, and in particular it should create additional nature reserves for waterfowl and for the protection, either in the same area or elsewhere, of an adequate portion of the original habitat.

3 The Contracting Parties shall encourage research and the exchange of data and publications regarding wetlands and their flora and fauna.

4 The Contracting Parties shall endeavour through management to increase waterfowl populations on appropriate wetlands.

5 The Contracting Parties shall promote the training of personnel competent in the fields of wetland research, management and wardening.

Article 5

The Contracting Parties shall consult with each other about implementing obligations arising from the Convention especially in the case of a wetland extending over the territories of more than one Contracting Party or where a water system is shared by Contracting Parties.

They shall at the same time endeavour to co-ordinate and support present and future policies and regulations concerning the conservation of wetlands and their flora and fauna.

Article 6[17]

1   There shall be established a Conference of the Contracting Parties to review and promote the implementation of this Convention. The bureau referred to in Article 8, para 1, shall convene ordinary meetings of the Conference of the Contracting Parties at intervals of not more than three years, unless the Conference decides otherwise, and extraordinary meetings at the written request of at least one third of the Contracting Parties. Each ordinary meeting of the Conference of the Contracting Parties shall determine the time and venue of the next ordinary meeting.

2   These Conferences of the Contracting Parties shall be competent:

(a) to discuss the implementation of this Convention;

(b) to discuss additions to and changes in the List;

(c) to consider information regarding changes in the ecological character of wetlands included in the List provided in accordance with para 2 of Article 3;

(d) to make general or specific recommendations to the Contracting Parties regarding the conservation, management and wise use of wetlands and their flora and fauna;

(e) to request relevant international bodies to prepare reports and statistics on matters which are essentially international in character affecting wetlands;

(f) to adopt other recommendations, or resolutions, to promote the functioning of this Convention.

3   The Contracting Parties shall ensure that those responsible at all levels for wetlands management shall be informed of, and take into consideration, recommendations of such Conferences concerning the conservation, management and wise use of wetlands and their flora and fauna.

4   The Conference of the Contracting Parties shall adopt rules of procedure for each of its meetings.

5   The Conference of the Contracting Parties shall establish and keep under review the financial regulations of this Convention. At each of its ordinary meetings, it shall adopt the budget for the next financial period by a two-thirds majority of Contracting Parties present and voting.

6   Each Contracting Party shall contribute to the budget according to a scale of contributions adopted by unanimity of the Contracting Parties present and voting at a meeting of the ordinary Conference of the Contracting Parties.

Article 7

1   The representatives of the Contracting Parties at such Conferences should include persons who are experts on wetlands or waterfowl by reason of knowledge and experience gained in scientific, administrative or other appropriate capacities.

---

17   As amended by Extraordinary Conference of the Parties done at Regina on 3 June 1987. These amendments entered into force on 1 May 1994.

2   Each of the Contracting Parties represented at a Conference shall have one vote, recommendations being adopted by a simple majority of the votes cast, provided that not less than half the Contracting Parties cast votes.

Article 8

1   The International Union for the Conservation of Nature and Natural Resources shall perform the continuing bureau duties under this Convention until such time as another organisation or government is appointed by a majority of two-thirds of all Contracting Parties.

2   The continuing bureau duties shall be, *inter alia*:

   (a) to assist in the convening and organising of Conferences specified in Article 6;

   (b) to maintain the List of Wetlands of International Importance and to be informed by the Contracting Parties of any additions, extensions, deletions or restrictions concerning wetlands included in the List provided in accordance with para 5 of Article 2;

   (c) to be informed by the Contracting Parties of any changes in the ecological character of wetlands included in the List provided in accordance with para 2 of Article 3;

   (d) to forward notification of any alterations to the List, or changes in character of wetlands included therein, to all Contracting Parties and to arrange for these matters to be discussed at the next Conference;

   (e) to make known to the Contracting Party concerned, the recommendations of the Conferences in respect of such alterations to the List or of changes in the character of wetlands included therein.

Article 9

1   This Convention shall remain open for signature indefinitely.

2   Any member of the United Nations or of one of the Specialised Agencies or of the International Atomic Energy Agency or Party to the Statute of the International Court of Justice may become a Party to this Convention by:

   (a) signature without reservation as to ratification;

   (b) signature subject to ratification followed by ratification;

   (c) accession.

3   Ratification or accession shall be effected by the deposit of an instrument of ratification or accession with the Director-General of the United Nations Educational, Scientific and Cultural Organisation (hereinafter referred to as 'the Depository').

Article 10

1   This Convention shall enter into force four months after seven states have become Parties to this Convention in accordance with para 2 of Article 9.

2   Thereafter this Convention shall enter into force for each Contracting Party four months after the day of its signature without reservation as to ratification, or its deposit of an instrument of ratification or accession.

Article 10 bis[18]

1   This Convention may be amended at a meeting of the Contracting Parties convened for that purpose in accordance with this Article.

2   Proposals for amendment may be made by any Contracting Party.

3   The text of any proposed amendment and the reasons for it shall be communicated to the organisation or government performing the continuing bureau duties under the Convention (hereinafter referred to as 'the Bureau') and shall promptly be communicated by the Bureau to all Contracting Parties. Any comments on the text by the Contracting Parties shall be communicated to the Bureau within three months of the date on which amendments were communicated to the Contracting Parties by the Bureau. The Bureau shall, immediately after the last day for submission of comments, communicate to the Contracting Parties all comments submitted by that day.

4   A meeting of Contacting Parties to consider an amendment communicated in accordance with para 3 shall be convened by the Bureau upon the written request of one third of the Contracting Parties. The Bureau shall consult the Parties concerning the time and venue of the meeting.

5   Amendments shall be adopted by a two-thirds majority of the Contracting Parties present and voting.

6   An amendment adopted shall enter into force for the Contracting Parties which have accepted it on the first day of the fourth month following the date on which two-thirds of the Contracting Parties have deposited an instrument of acceptance with the Depository. For each Contracting Party which deposits an instrument of acceptance after the date on which two-thirds of the Contracting Parties have deposited an instrument of acceptance, the amendment shall enter into force on the first day of the fourth month following the date of the deposit of its instrument of acceptance.

Article 11

1   This Convention shall continue in force for an indefinite period.

2   Any Contracting Party may denounce this Convention after a period of five years from the date on which it entered into force for that Party by giving written notice thereof to the Depository. Denunciation shall take effect four months after the day on which notice thereof is received by the Depository.

Article 12

1   The Depository shall inform all states that have signed and acceded to this Convention as soon as possible of:

(a) signatures to the Convention;

(b) deposits of instruments of ratification of this Convention;

(c) deposits of instruments of accession to this Convention;

(d) the date of entry into force of this Convention;

(e) notifications of denunciation of this Convention.

---

18   This provision was included by Art 1 of the Protocol of Amendment to the Convention on Wetlands of International Importance done at Paris on 3 December 1982. It entered into force on 1 October 1986.

2 When this Convention has entered into force, the Depository shall have it registered with the Secretariat of the United Nations in accordance with Article 102 of the Charter.

Convention on the Conservation of European Wildlife and Natural Habitats 1979 (Berne Convention)[19]

This Convention was negotiated under the auspices of the Council of Europe Although its text is not included, it is discussed here in order to show the link between the various multilateral conventions of global application such as CITES and the Convention on Biological Diversity and regionally-based instruments which are focused on the conservation of regionally-occurring wild flora and fauna. The Convention itself operates on a regionally-inclusive basis, being open for signature by the Member States of the Council of Europe and non-Member States that participated in its elaboration, as well as the European Community (Art 19). It was concluded in Berne, Switzerland on 19 September 1979 and entered into force on 1 June 1982. As at 13 July 2001 it had 45 parties, including the EC. The Convention has been implemented by the European Community through the EC Directives on the Conservation of Natural Habitats of Wild Fauna and Flora 92/43 (the Habitats Directive 92/43, see pp 635 and 642, below), and on Conservation of Wild Birds 79/409, (the Birds Directive 79/409, see pp 632 and 639, below).

The Convention was one of the earliest to recognise the principle of inter-generational equity in terms of the need to preserve the natural heritage of wild flora and fauna for future generations (Preamble). It was also innovative in its awareness of the importance of natural habitats for the conservation of wild flora and fauna (Preamble and Chapter II, Art 4). The aim of wildlife and natural habitat conservation embraces migratory species and trans-boundary habitats, requiring co-operation among two or more States (Art 1(1)). In order to achieve its objectives of conserving wild flora and fauna and their natural habitats, especially endangered and vulnerable migratory species (Art 1(2)), the Convention provides for the conservation of wildlife in general, including species not included in the Appendices (Arts 2 and 3(1)) and for special protection of species listed in Appendix I (strictly protected plants), Appendix II (strictly protected animals) and Appendix III (protected animals) of the Convention (Chapter III, Arts 5, 6 and 7).

Article 2 which is almost identical to Art 2 of the EEC Directive on the conservation of wild birds 79/409 (see p 640, below), requires Parties to maintain wildlife populations primarily according to ecological, scientific and cultural criteria. While economic and recreational criteria may also be taken into account, these cannot be given priority over the former criteria. Article 2 therefore provides an early example of the eco-system approach to wildlife conservation which recognises the intrinsic value of maintaining eco-systems, quite apart from the economic value that may be derived from the exploitation of significant components of these eco-systems.

It is also interesting to note that the Berne Convention is one of the few nature conservation treaties to emphasise and explicitly prioritise the protection of flora. It imposes a clear obligation on Parties to prohibit the picking, collecting, cutting, or

---

19 UKTS 56 (1982); Cmnd 8738.

uprooting of plant species listed in Appendix I (Art 5). An equally clear obligation to protect animal species listed in Appendix II (Art 6), including prohibiting damage or disturbance of their breeding and resting sites (Art 6(b) and (c)) is also imposed. However, exceptions are allowed (Art 9(1)), and States' parties may lodge reservations upon ratification regarding particular species listed in the Appendices (Art 22(1)).

According to Lyster, the Berne Convention is an extremely important wildlife conservation treaty for two main reasons: first, the mandatory nature of its provisions is a departure from the hortatory language utilised by most environmental and especially wildlife treaties. Rather than encouraging parties to implement conservation measures, the Convention almost always requires them to do so. Secondly, the administrative system created by the Convention to promote and oversee implementation of its provisions represents a major advance on previous instruments. The full range of mechanisms including *inter alia* a Secretariat (provided by the Council of Europe), regular meetings of the Standing Committee at which all Parties are represented, attendance by non-governmental observers at these meetings, and reporting requirements, to ensure effective enforcement of obligations are all provided for (Lyster (1985) 130–31).

EUROPEAN COMMUNITY LAW

Measures promoting nature conservation within EC law are primarily based upon two directives, the Directive on the Conservation of Birds 79/409 and the Directive on the Conservation of Natural Habitats and of Wild Fauna and Flora 92/43.

Although this section will deal exclusively with these directives, it is appropriate to note here that the general activities of the EC in promoting regional development, and in particular through operating the Common Agricultural Policy, have had a profound impact upon the countryside. Although some farming policy initiatives such as the system of Environmentally Sensitive Area (ESA)[20] designation and the 'set-aside' scheme[21] undoubtedly assist wildlife to survive, they are not drafted with that aim in mind and are not discussed further in this section. It is also apparent that nature conservation does not operate in isolation and its aims of species protection and habitat conservation would not be achieved without enforcement of the EC pollution control regimes discussed in the previous chapters.

Also, The European Commission has adopted the EC Biodiversity Strategy (COM (98) 42) in order to fulfil its obligations arising under Art 6 of the Biodiversity Convention (see p 589, above). The strategy is to be implemented by the development of sectoral and cross-sectoral Action Plans. (See [1998] 1 Env Liability CS 4.)[22]

---

20 Introduced by 1985 Regulation on improving the efficiency of agricultural structures 797/85 – implemented by the Agriculture Act 1986.

21 Under which farmers receive payments for taking 15% of their land out of cultivation and so reducing 'food mountains' and 'wine lakes'. The scheme was originally introduced by EC Regulations 1765/92 and 2293/93.

22 Thereby upholding EC Treaty, Art 6, which calls for environmental protection requirements to be integrated into Community policies and activities.

These plans known as biodiversity action plans (BAPs) covering agriculture, fisheries, economic development cooperation and natural resources, plus a cross sectoral plan, were adopted by the Commission on 28 March 2001 (see COM (01) 162). The plans set out methods of meeting the objectives of the strategy, in particular how to reverse the current losses of wildlife, ecosystems, crop and domestic animal varieties and fish stocks.

Birds Directive 79/409

Although bird conservation has always had an influential following in the UK that is not the case in all parts of Europe. In some countries the traditional right to hunt birds for sport is fiercely defended and is by no means an insignificant political force. It was indeed wide-spread revulsion at the indiscriminate killing of migratory birds in some Mediterranean States that led to the passing of the Birds Directive. It was also accepted that the protection of migratory species of birds is typically a trans-frontier environmental problem requiring the assumption of common responsibilities by Member States. National legislation cannot in itself provide complete or effective protection for wild birds.

The Directive's aim is to set up a scheme to protect populations of wild birds in Europe 'at a level which corresponds in particular to ecological, scientific and cultural requirements, while taking account of economic and recreational requirements' (Art 2). It aims to achieve this by two methods: firstly by controlling the hunting and killing of birds and protecting their nests and eggs; and secondly by requiring the provision of habitats so as to maintain the populations of species.

Hunting and killing[23]

The Directive's system of protection has three elements:

1   It imposes a general prohibition against the killing, capturing, disturbing, keeping or marketing of birds as well as the destruction, damage or removal of nests and eggs (Articles 5, 6(1)). Article 8 prohibits the use of all means, arrangements or methods used for large-scale or non-selective capture or killing of birds, particularly those listed in Annex IV(a). These include snares, explosives, nets, the use of blind or mutilated birds as decoys and types of semi-automatic or automatic weapons.

2   Subject to conditions and limitations, Member States may authorise the marketing of the species listed in Annex III and the hunting of those in Annex II (Art 6(2)–(4), Art 7). Member States must ensure that hunting complies with the principles of wise use and the ecologically balanced control of the species concerned. States must ensure in particular that birds are not hunted during the rearing season nor during various

---

23   In a number of cases, the European Court of Justice has had to consider whether Member States have altered their domestic laws on hunting wild birds so as to comply with the Directive. See, eg, Case C-262/85 *Commission v Italy* [1987] ECR 3073; Case C-252/85 *Commission v France* [1988] ECR 2243. See most recently Case C-38/99 *Commission v France*. The relationship between the Birds Directive 79/409 and Arts 28 and 30 of the EC Treaty (free circulation of goods) was discussed in Case C-169/89 *Gourmetrie Van Den Burg* [1990] ECR 2143.

stages of reproduction. Migratory birds should not be hunted during their return to their rearing grounds.

3   Article 9 permits Member States to adopt a general derogation from the Directive provided three conditions are satisfied:

(a) The derogation must be restricted to cases in which there is no other satisfactory solution.

(b) The derogation must be based on at least one of the reasons listed in Article 9(1) as follows:

– in the interests of public health and safety including the interests of air safety;

– to prevent serious damage to crops, livestock, forests, fisheries and water;

– for the protection of flora and fauna;

– for the purposes of research and teaching;

– for repopulation or reintroduction;

– to permit, under strictly supervised conditions and on a selective basis the capture, keeping or other judicious use of certain birds in small numbers.

(c) The derogation must comply with the formal conditions set out in Article 9(2).

Habitat protection

Annex I[24] contains a list of bird species which are to be the subject of special conservation measures regarding their habitat in order to ensure their survival and reproduction. *Member States* (that is, not the European Commission) are to classify the most suitable territories (both at land and sea) as Special Protection Areas (SPAs) for the conservation of these species (Art 4). Similar measures must be taken for regularly occurring migratory species not listed in Annex I. Particular attention must be paid to the protection of wetlands.

Member States are under a general duty to avoid pollution or the deterioration of habitats. When an SPA has been declared, however, Member States must take appropriate steps both to avoid pollution and deterioration of such habitats, *and* any disturbances affecting the birds, insofar as they are significant to the objectives of habitat protection (Art 4(4)).

Habitat protection under the Birds Directive 79/409 has been the subject of several cases before the European Court of Justice. The three leading cases are discussed here and set out later in the chapter.

The Leybucht Dykes case – EC Commission v Germany[25]

The Leybucht (Eastern Friesland, Germany) is an important wetland area for both resident and migratory birds and a particularly important nesting area for avocets (a bird listed in Annex I of the Directive). The German government classified the Leybucht as an

---

24   Directive 85/411 replaced the original list.
25   See p 652, below.

SPA during the 1980s. In 1985 Germany decided to sanction coastal defence works involving the Leybucht which were said to be necessary in order to protect the land and its inhabitants from flooding due to high storm tides. In 1987 the Commission began proceedings against the German government under Art 169 of the EC Treaty for failure on the part of the German authorities to prohibit the deterioration of habitats or any disturbances affecting birds in an SPA as required by Art 4(4) of the Directive. The Court took the view that:

> Although the Member States do have a certain discretion with regard to the choice of territories which are most suitable for classification as special protection areas pursuant to Article 4(1) of the Directive, they do not have the same discretion under Article 4(4) of the directive in modifying or reducing the extent of the areas, since they have themselves acknowledged in their declarations that those areas contain the most suitable environments for the species listed in Annex I to the directive ... It follows that the power of the Member States to reduce the extent of a special protection area can be justified only on exceptional grounds. These grounds must correspond to a general interest which is superior to the general interest represented by the ecological objective of the Directive. In that context the interests referred to in Article 2 of the directive, namely economic and recreational requirements, do not enter into consideration.

The court concluded that public interest in protecting against the danger of flood and the protection of the coastline was, when taken together, an 'exceptional ground' upon which a State could rely when reducing the area of an SPA. However, such measures had to be confined to a strict minimum involving the smallest possible reduction of an SPA. Applying the above to the Leybucht project, the court found that there had been no breach of the Directive.

The Marismas de Santoña case[26]

The Marismas de Santoña is an estuarial wetland area on the Cantabrian coast of Spain which provides a habitat for 15,000–20,000 birds, including some species, notably the spoonbill, listed in Annex I. It is also visited by around 40 species of migratory birds. These two facts meant that the area met the criteria for designation as an SPA but the area had not been so designated by the Spanish government. During the 1980s, complaints were made to the Commission regarding various matters and activities (including land reclamation projects, industrial zoning, waste disposal and road-building schemes) which were thought likely to lead to pollution and the deterioration of the area and which would affect the conservation of the bird species. The Commission commenced formal proceedings against Spain in 1988 alleging, *inter alia*, that Spain was in breach of Art 4(1) and (2) by failing to classify the Marismas de Santoña as an SPA and that the various matters and activities referred to were a violation of Art 4(4).

As regards the failure to designate the area as an SPA, the Spanish government argued that national governments retained discretion in relation to choice as well as the possible delimitation of SPAs, including the time at which they were to be designated. The ECJ agreed that Member States did have some discretion as to the choice of SPAs, but that choice had to be based on ornithological grounds. Because of the importance of the

---

26 See p 657, below.

Marismas de Santoña for water birds and endangered migratory birds, the Spanish government was found to have breached Arts 4(1) and 4(2) by failing to classify it as an SPA. Spain was also found to be in breach of Art 4(4) for not taking appropriate measures to prevent the deterioration of the area.

The RSPB (Lappel Bank) case[27]

The case concerned the decision of the United Kingdom government to exclude an area called Lappel Bank from an SPA designation in the Medway estuary on the ground that the area was needed by the Port of Sheerness for expansion. Lappel Bank is an area of inter-tidal mud flat used by wildfowl and waders on migration which also supports breeding populations of avocet and little tern, both listed in Annex I. The decision was challenged by the Royal Society for the Protection of Birds on the ground that taking economic and social factors (Art 2) into account at the stage of designating an SPA under Art 4 was an incorrect interpretation of the directive and a breach of ECJ case law. The House of Lords felt the need for clarification from the ECJ on two points: (a) whether Member States are entitled to take account of the provisions of Art 2 when classifying an area as an SPA and/or defining its boundary; and (b) if the answer to (a) is no, then whether a Member State may still take account of economic considerations (Art 2) in the classification process if 'they amount to a general interest which is superior to the general interest which is represented by the ecological objective of the Directive' or if they amount to 'imperative reasons of overriding public interest' as set out in Art 6(4) of the Habitats Directive 92/43.[28]

The ECJ ruled that when designating an SPA Member States are 'not authorised' to take account of economic requirements. The court reasoned that Art 2 does not constitute a 'derogation' from the general system of protection established by the Directive and therefore the 'ecological requirements' laid down by Art 4 'do not have to be balanced against the interests listed' in Art 2. For the first part of the second question, the Court simply reiterated its judgments in the *Leybucht* and *Marismas de Santoña* cases, that economic requirements cannot be invoked in that context.

Habitats Directive 92/43

The Directive, which was progressing through the Community legislative process at the time of the *Leybucht Dykes* decision,[29] is similar in form to the Birds Directive 79/409. Its aim (Art 2) is 'to contribute towards ensuring biodiversity through the conservation of natural habitats and of wild fauna and flora in the European territory of the Member States to which the Treaty applies'. It will achieve this aim by establishing a system which (a) protects species of plants and animals and (b) protects types of natural habitat and the habitats where species live.

---

27 See p 646, below.
28 See p 645, below.
29 The effect of the decision can be seen in the provisions of the Directive, eg Arts 6(4), 7.

Protection of species

The system of species protection (like the Birds Directive of 1979)[30] has three elements. Firstly, there is a general prohibition (Art 12) against the capture, killing, keeping, transport or marketing of the animal species listed in Annex IV as well as the taking of eggs or the destruction of breeding sites. Provisions protecting those plant species listed in Annex IV(b) from picking, collecting, cutting, uprooting and marketing appear in Art 13.

Secondly, Art 14 allows Member States to permit the taking in the wild of specimens of species of wild fauna and flora listed in Annex V as well as their exploitation, if this is 'compatible with their being maintained at a favourable conservation status'. Indiscriminate means of killing or capturing species of wild fauna which are capable of causing the local disappearance of, or serious disturbance to populations of species are prohibited, particularly those means listed in Annex VI(a).

Thirdly, Member States may derogate from the Directive species protection provisions if (a) there is no satisfactory alternative and the derogation is not detrimental to the maintenance of the populations of the species concerned at a favourable conservation status in their natural range and (b) one of the reasons for derogation listed in Art 16 applies:

- it is in the interest of protecting wild fauna and flora and conserving natural habitats;
- to prevent serious damage to crops, livestock, forests, fisheries, water and other types of property;
- it is in the interests of public health and public safety or for other imperative reasons of overriding public interest, including those of a social or economic nature and beneficial consequences of primary importance for the environment;
- for the purpose of research and education, including repopulating or re-introducing species;
- to allow the taking or keeping of specimens of species listed in Annex IV,

and (c) the procedural requirements of Art 16(2) and (3) are complied with.

Conservation of natural habitats and habitats of species

In order to enable natural habitat types (listed in Annex I) and species' habitats (listed in Annex II) to be maintained or restored at a favourable conservation status, Art 3 requires a 'coherent European ecological network of special areas of conservation' (SACs) to be set up under the title Natura 2000. In addition, in order to improve the ecological coherence of the Natura 2000 network, Member States are under a general duty (Art 10) to encourage the management of landscape features which are of major importance for wild fauna or flora (such as ponds which can function as stepping stones for wildlife) in their land-use planning and development policies.

Although Member States (rather than the Commission) are to designate the sites which are to become SACs, there is a procedure (Art 5) under which (in 'exceptional cases') the Commission may ask the Council to designate a site even against the wishes of

---

30   The Birds Directive 79/409 applies to all wild birds. The 1992 Directive only applies to listed species.

a Member State where it is deemed essential for the maintenance or the survival of a priority natural habitat type or a priority species.[31] Member States and the Commission were to agree the sites of Community importance to become designated SACs by June 1998. (Member States have not as yet met this deadline.) Once designated an SAC, Member States must take appropriate steps to avoid the deterioration of habitat as well as the disturbance of the species for which the areas have been designated. Article 6 requires States to draw up appropriate management plans to conserve the SAC. Significantly, however, Art 6(4) would allow damage to an SAC in circumstances which would be outlawed by the decision in *Leybucht Dykes* when 'plans or projects must be carried out for imperative reasons of overriding public interest, including those of a social or economic nature'. This provision does not apply to sites which host a priority natural habitat type and/or a priority species[32] where 'the only considerations which may be raised are those relating to human health or public safety, to beneficial consequences of primary importance for the environment, or, further to an opinion from the Commission, to other imperative reasons of overriding public interest'.

Although similar, it is apparent that there are differences in substance between the regimes created by the Wild Birds Directive 79/409 and the Habitats Directive 92/43. Unfortunately, the relationship between the two Directives is not altogether clear. Habitats Directive Art 3(1) says that Bird Directive SPAs are to be included in the Natura 2000 network. Article 7 of the Habitats Directive states that 'the obligations arising under Art 6(2), (3) and (4) of this Directive shall replace any obligations arising under the first sentence of Art 4(4) of [the Birds Directive] in respect of areas classified pursuant to Art 4(1) or similarly recognised under Art 4(2) thereof as from the date of this Directive or the date of classification or recognition by a Member State under the [Birds Directive] where the latter date is later'. On this basis it would appear that SPAs will simply become SACs subject to the protection criteria of Art 6(4).[33] However, Art 6(4) was considered in the *Lappel Bank* case where the court ruled that Art 6(4) applies only to sites once they have been designated as an SAC and as a result, economic considerations cannot be considered as 'imperative reasons of overriding public interest' when a Member State is designating an SPA. Although the Habitats Directive was not in force at the time of the designation, this finding sets a precedent for future SAC designations.

The ECJ has considered the Directive in three recent cases. In Case 3/96 *Commission of the European Communities v Kingdom of the Netherlands* [1999] Env LR 147 the ECJ examined the obligation of Member States to designate Special Protection Areas (SPAs) and the criteria to be used for this purpose. This is the first case in which the Court examined the question whether a Member State had designated a sufficient number of SPAs under the Habitats Directive.

In 1996 the Commission brought an action before the ECJ alleging that the Kingdom of the Netherlands had not designated a sufficient number of SPAs as required by Art 4(1). The following main issues were decided: First, was there a failure to designate a sufficient number of SPAs? The Dutch Government maintained that States could have recourse to other conservation measures in order to comply with Art 4(1) and designation

---

31 As defined Art 1.
32 Defined in Art 1.
33 Replacing the criteria set by the European Court in the Case C-57/89 *Leybucht Dykes* case [1991] ECR I-883; [1991] 3 LMELR 97.

of an SPA was not necessary. The ECJ held that designation of SPAs could not be avoided by resorting to other special conservation measures.

> ... if Member States could escape the obligation to classify SPAs if they considered that other special conservation measures were sufficient to ensure survival and reproduction of the species mentioned in Annex I, the objective of creating a coherent network of SPAs referred to in Art 4(3) of the Directive 92/43 on the protection of habitats' would be frustrated, because it is an express objective to create a coherent network including both SPAs and special conservation areas (Art 3).

Secondly, what margin of discretion do Member States' have when establishing SPAs? This point was already discussed in the *Marismas de Santoña* and *Lappel Bank* cases (see pp 690 and 701). If an area complies with the ornithological criteria set out in Art 4(1) via the existence of Annex I birds or migratory birds, then the Member State is obliged to designate these areas. The court went on:

> ... where it appears that a Member State has classified as SPA sites, the number and total area of which are marginally less than the number and total area of the sites considered to be the most suitable for conservation of the species in question, it will be possible to find that the Member State has failed to fulfil its obligation under Art 4(1) of the Directive'. (Paragraph 63.)

Economic and recreational requirements are not to be taken into account for the designation of SPA's.

Finally, the ECJ ruled that the Inventory of Important Bird Areas in the European Community (IBA 89) prepared for the Commission by the Eurogroup for the Conservation of Birds and Habitats in conjunction with the International Council of Bird Preservation in co-operation with Commission experts, although having no binding legal force, can be used to assess whether a member State has fulfilled its obligations as to the designation of SPAs.

Case C-166/97 *Commission v France* concerned the Seine Estuary. In 1990 the French authorities designated 2,750 hectares in the Seine Estuary as an SPA. However, the ornithological inventory, 'Important Bird Areas in Europe' (IBA 1989) included an area of 78,000 hectares. The Commission maintained that the SPA designated by the French authorities was too small to comply with the requirements of the Directive. The Court took the view that it was 'common ground' that the French authorities had failed to classify a sufficiently large area of the estuary as an SPA. However, the court did not refer to the extent the area should have covered, as it did in the *Marismas de Santoña* case. Nor did it examine the regime which the French Government had adopted to protect the SPA designated in 1990. This had taken the form of an agreement between the Ministry of the Environment and the Autonomous Port of Le Havre & Rouen and was regarded as inadequate by the Commission in the light of the Directive. It seems that the form the regime takes is a matter for Member States, provided the regime ensures the survival and reproduction of Annex I species and other migratory species. It would appear that merely classifying land as 'State-owned' would not, in itself, amount to compliance with the Directive. Finally, the Commission alleged that the construction of a plant for the deposit of Titanogypsum close to the SPA was incompatible with Art 4(4). Although the Court accepted that the site of this plant was the feeding and resting area of a member of species listed in Annex I, it took the view that because the plant only covered a small part of the area, the Commission had not satisfied the burden of proof required by Art 169 of the EC Treaty and therefore that Art 4(4) had been breached by the French authorities. As Agustin Garcia Ureta writes (*Commission v France,* Case Note [1999] 1 Env Liability 16, p 21) 'reliance on strong scientific evidence is very important in order to sustain a breach of the Directive'.

In Case C-371/98 R *(On the Application of First Corporate Shipping Ltd) v Secretary of State for the Environment, Transport and the Regions (World Wide Fund for Nature UK and Another Intervening)* [2001] 1 All ER (EC) 177, Bristol Port Authority sought judicial review to challenge the Secretary of States decision to propose to the European Commission that the Severn Estuary be designated as an SAC under the Habitats Directive 92/43. On a referral to the ECJ, the Port argued that the Secretary of State was obliged to take account of economic and cultural requirements when deciding to designate. The ECJ held that under Art 4 a Member State could not take account of such considerations or regional and local characteristics when selecting and defining the boundaries of the proposed site.

COUNCIL DIRECTIVE

of 2 April 1979

on the conservation of wild birds

(79/409/EEC)

THE COUNCIL OF THE EUROPEAN COMMUNITIES,

Having regard to the Treaty establishing the European Economic Community, and in particular Article 235 thereof, [...]

Whereas the Council declaration of 22 November 1973 on the programme of action of the European Communities on the environment calls for specific action to protect birds, supplemented by the resolution of the Council of the European Communities and of the representatives of the Governments of the Member States meeting within the Council of 17 May 1977 on the continuation and implementation of a European Community policy and action programme on the environment;

Whereas a large number of species of wild birds naturally occurring in the European territory of the Member States are declining in number, very rapidly in some cases; whereas this decline represents a serious threat to the conservation of the natural environment, particularly because of the biological balances threatened thereby;

Whereas the species of wild birds naturally occurring in the European territory of the Member States are mainly migratory species; whereas such species constitute a common heritage and whereas effective bird protection is typically a trans-frontier environment problem entailing common responsibilities; [...]

Whereas the preservation, maintenance or restoration of a sufficient diversity and area of habitats is essential to the conservation of all species of birds; whereas certain species of birds should be the subject of special conservation measures concerning their habitats in order to ensure their survival and reproduction in their area of distribution; whereas such measures must also take account of migratory species and be co-ordinated with a view to setting up a coherent whole; [...]

Whereas, because of their high population level, geographical distribution and reproductive rate in the Community as a whole, certain species may be hunted, which constitutes acceptable exploitation; where certain limits are established and respected, such hunting must be compatible with maintenance of the population of these species at a satisfactory level;

Whereas the various means, devices or methods of large-scale or non-selective capture or killing and hunting with certain forms of transport must be banned because of the excessive pressure which they exert or may exert on the numbers of the species concerned;

Whereas, because of the importance which may be attached to certain specific situations, provision should be made for the possibility of derogations on certain conditions and subject to monitoring by the Commission; [...]

HAS ADOPTED THIS DIRECTIVE:

Article 1

1   This Directive relates to the conservation of all species of naturally occurring birds in the wild state in the European territory of the Member States to which the Treaty applies. It covers the protection, management and control of these species and lays down rules for their exploitation.

2   It shall apply to birds, their eggs, nests and habitats. [...]

Article 2

Member States shall take the requisite measures to maintain the population of the species referred to in Article 1 at a level which corresponds in particular to ecological, scientific and cultural requirements, while taking account of economic and recreational requirements, or to adapt the population of these species to that level.

Article 3

1   In the light of the requirements referred to in Article 2, member states shall take the requisite measures to preserve, maintain or re-establish a sufficient diversity and area of habitats for all the species of birds referred to in Article 1.

2   The preservation, maintenance and re-establishment of biotopes and habitats shall include primarily the following measures:

   (a) creation of protected areas;

   (b) upkeep and management in accordance with the ecological needs of habitats inside and outside the protected zones;

   (c) re-establishment of destroyed biotopes;

   (d) creation of biotopes.

Article 4

1   The species mentioned in Annex I shall be the subject of special conservation measures concerning their habitat in order to ensure their survival and reproduction in their area of distribution. In this connection, account shall be taken of:

   (a) species in danger of extinction;

   (b) species vulnerable to specific changes in their habitat;

(c) species considered rare because of small populations or restricted local distribution;

(d) other species requiring particular attention for reasons of the specific nature of their habitat.

Trends and variations in population levels shall be taken into account as a background for evaluations. Member States shall classify in particular the most suitable territories in number and size as special protection areas for the conservation of these species, taking into account their protection requirements in the geographical sea and land area where this directive applies.

2 Member States shall take similar measures for regularly occurring migratory species not listed in Annex I, bearing in mind their need for protection in the geographical sea and land area where this directive applies, as regards their breeding, moulting and wintering areas and staging posts along their migration routes. To this end, Member States shall pay particular attention to the protection of wetlands and particularly to wetlands of international importance

3 Member States shall send the commission all relevant information so that it may take appropriate initiatives with a view to the co-ordination necessary to ensure that the areas provided for in paras 1 and 2 above form a coherent whole which meets the protection requirements of these species in the geographical sea and land area where this directive applies.

4 In respect of the protection areas referred to in paras 1 and 2 above, Member States shall take appropriate steps to avoid pollution or deterioration of habitats or any disturbances affecting the birds, in so far as these would be significant having regard to the objectives of this article. Outside these protection areas, Member States shall also strive to avoid pollution or deterioration of habitats.

Article 5

Without prejudice to Articles 7 and 9, Member States shall take the requisite measures to establish a general system of protection for all species of birds referred to in Article 1, prohibiting in particular:

(a) deliberate killing or capture by any method;

(b) deliberate destruction of, or damage to, their nests and eggs or removal of their nests;

(c) taking their eggs in the wild and keeping these eggs even if empty;

(d) deliberate disturbance of these birds particularly during the period of breeding and rearing, in so far as disturbance would be significant having regard to the objectives of this directive;

(e) keeping birds of species the hunting and capture of which is prohibited.

Article 6

1 Without prejudice to the provisions of paras 2 and 3, Member States shall prohibit, for all the bird species referred to in Article 1, the sale, transport for sale, keeping for sale and the offering for sale of live or dead birds and of any readily recognisable parts or derivatives of such birds.

Article 7

Owing to their population level, geographical distribution and reproductive rate throughout the Community, the species listed in Annex II may be hunted under national legislation. Member States shall ensure that the hunting of these species does not jeopardise conservation efforts in their distribution area. [...]

Article 8

In respect of the hunting, capture or killing of birds under this Directive, Member States shall prohibit the use of all means, arrangements or methods used for the large-scale or non-selective capture or killing of birds or capable of causing the local disappearance of a species, in particular the use of those listed in Annex IV(a). [...]

Article 9

1   Member States may derogate from the provisions of Articles 5, 6, 7 and 8, where there is no other satisfactory solution, for the following reasons:

    (a) in the interests of public health and safety;

        –   in the interests of air safety;

        –   to prevent serious damage to crops, livestock, forests, fisheries and water,

        –   for the protection of flora and fauna;

    (b) for the purposes of research and teaching, of re-population, of re-introduction and for the breeding necessary for these purposes;

    (c) to permit, under strictly supervised conditions and on a selective basis, the capture, keeping or other judicious use of certain birds in small numbers. [...]

Article 13

Application of the measures taken pursuant to this directive may not lead to deterioration in the present situation as regards the conservation of species of birds referred to in Article 1.

Article 14

Member States may introduce stricter protective measures than those provided for under this directive.

[All other Articles and Annexes omitted.]

COUNCIL DIRECTIVE

of 21 May 1992

on the conservation of natural habitats and of wild fauna and flora

(92/43/EEC)

THE COUNCIL OF THE EUROPEAN COMMUNITIES,

Having regard to the Treaty establishing the European Economic Community, and in particular Article 130s thereof, [...]

Whereas the preservation, protection and improvement of the quality of the environment, including the conservation of natural habitats and of wild fauna and flora, are an essential objective of general interest pursued by the Community, as stated in Article 130r of the Treaty;

Whereas the European Community policy and action programme on the environment (1987 to 1992) makes provision for measures regarding the conservation of nature and natural resources;

Whereas, the main aim of this Directive being to promote the maintenance of biodiversity, taking account of economic, social, cultural and regional requirements, this Directive makes a contribution to the general objective of sustainable development; whereas the maintenance of such biodiversity may in certain cases require the maintenance, or indeed the encouragement, of human activities;

Whereas, in the European territory of the Member States, natural habitats are continuing to deteriorate and an increasing number of wild species are seriously threatened; whereas given that the threatened habitats and species form part of the Community's natural heritage and the threats to them are often of a trans-boundary nature, it is necessary to take measures at Community level in order to conserve them;

Whereas, in view of the threats to certain types of natural habitat and certain species, it is necessary to define them as having priority in order to favour the early implementation of measures to conserve them;

Whereas, in order to ensure the restoration or maintenance of natural habitats and species of Community interest at a favourable conservation status, it is necessary to designate special areas of conservation in order to create a coherent European ecological network according to a specified timetable; [...]

Whereas sites eligible for designation as special areas of conservation are proposed by the Member States but whereas a procedure must nevertheless be laid down to allow the designation in exceptional cases of a site which has not been proposed by a Member State but which the Community considers essential for either the maintenance or the survival of a priority natural habitat type or a priority species; [...]

Whereas it is recognised that the adoption measures intended to promote the conservation of priority natural habitats and priority species of Community interest is a common responsibility of all Member States; whereas this may, however, impose an excessive financial burden on certain Member States given, on the one hand, the uneven distribution of such habitats and species throughout the Community and, on the other hand, the fact that the 'polluter pays' principle can have only limited application in the special case of nature conservation;

Whereas it is therefore agreed that, in this exceptional case, a contribution by means of Community co-financing should be provided for within the limits of the resources made available under the Community's decisions; [...]

HAS ADOPTED THIS DIRECTIVE:

Definitions

Article 1

For the purpose of this Directive:

- (a) *conservation* means a series of measures required to maintain or restore the natural habitats and the populations of species of wild fauna and flora at a favourable status as defined in (e) and (i);
- (b) *natural habitats* means terrestrial or aquatic areas distinguished by geographic, abiotic and biotic features, whether entirely natural or semi-natural;

(c) *natural habitat types of Community interest* means those which, within the territory referred to in Article 2:

    (i) are in danger of disappearance in their natural range; or

    (ii) have a small natural range following their regression or by reason of their intrinsically restricted area; or

    (iii) present outstanding examples of typical characteristics of one or more of the five following biogeographical regions: Alpine, Atlantic, Continental, Macaronesian and Mediterranean.

Such habitat types are listed or may be listed in Annex I;

(l) 'special area of conservation' means a site of Community importance designated by the Member States through a statutory, administrative and/or contractual act where the necessary conservation measures are applied for the maintenance or restoration, at a favourable conservation status, of the natural habitats and/or the populations of the species for which the site is designated; [...]

Article 2

The aim of this Directive shall be to contribute towards ensuring biodiversity through the conservation of natural habitats and of wild fauna and flora in the European territory of the Member States to which the Treaty applies. [...]

Conservation of natural habitats and habitats of species

Article 3

A coherent European ecological network of special areas of conservation shall be set up under the title Natura 2000. This network, composed of sites hosting the natural habitat types listed in Annex I and habitats of the species listed in Annex II, shall enable the natural habitat types and the species' habitats concerned to be maintained or, where appropriate, restored at a favourable conservation status in their natural range. [...]

Article 4

2   On the basis of the criteria set out in Annex III (Stage 2) and in the framework both of each of the five biogeographical regions referred to in Article 1(c)(iii) and of the whole of the territory referred to in Article 2(1), the Commission shall establish, in agreement with each Member State, a draft list of sites of Community importance drawn from the Member States' lists identifying those which lost one or more priority natural habitat types or priority species.

4   Once a site of Community importance has been adopted in accordance with the procedure laid down in para 2, the Member State concerned shall designate that site as a special area of conservation as soon as possible and within six years at most, establishing priorities in the light of the importance of the sites for the maintenance or restoration, at a favourable conservation status, of a natural habitat type in Annex I or a species in Annex II and for the coherence of Natura 2000, and in the light of the threats of degradation or destruction to which those sites are exposed. [...]

Article 6

2   Member States shall take appropriate steps to avoid, in the special areas of conservation, the deterioration of natural habitats and the habitats of species as well as

disturbance of the species for which the areas have been designated, in so far as such disturbance could be significant in relation to the objectives of this Directive.

4   If, in spite of a negative assessment of the implications for the site and in the absence of alternative solutions, a plan or project must nevertheless be carried out for imperative reasons of overriding public interest, including those of a social or economic nature, the Member State shall take all compensatory measures necessary to ensure that the overall coherence of Natura 2000 is protected. It shall inform the Commission of the compensatory measures adopted.

Where the site concerned hosts a priority natural habitat type and/or a priority species, the only considerations which may be raised are those relating to human health or public safety, to beneficial consequences of primary importance for the environment or, further to an opinion from the Commission, to other imperative reasons of overriding public interest.

Protection of species

Article 12

1   Member States shall take the requisite measures to establish a system of strict protection for the animal species listed in Annex IV(a) in their natural range, prohibiting:

   (a) all forms of deliberate capture or killing of specimens of these species in the wild;

   (b) deliberate disturbance of these species, particularly during the period of breeding, rearing, hibernation and migration;

   (c) deliberate destruction or taking of eggs from the wild;

   (d) deterioration or destruction of breeding sites or resting places. [...]

Note: For a recent interpretation of this Article by a UK court, see *R v Secretary of State for Trade and Industry ex p Greenpeace* [2000] Env LR 221, p 732, below.

Article 13

1   Member States shall take the requisite measures to establish a system of strict protection for the plant species listed in Annex IV(b), prohibiting:

   (a) the deliberate picking, collecting, cutting, uprooting or destruction of such plants in their natural range in the wild;

   (b) the keeping, transport and sale or exchange and offering for sale or exchange of specimens of such species taken in the wild, except for those taken legally before this Directive is implemented. [...]

Article 16

1   Provided that there is no satisfactory alternative and the derogation is not detrimental to the maintenance of the populations of the species concerned at a favourable conservation status in their natural range, Member States may derogate from the provisions of Articles 12, 13, 14 and 15(a) and (b):

   (a) in the interest of protecting wild fauna and flora and conserving natural habitats;

   (b) to prevent serious damage, in particular to crops, livestock, forests, fisheries and water and other types of property;

(c) in the interests of public health and public safety, or for other imperative reasons of overriding public interest, including those of a social or economic nature and beneficial consequences of primary importance for the environment;

(d) for the purpose of research and education, of repopulating and re-introducing these species and for the breedings operations necessary for these purposes, including the artificial propagation of plants;

(e) to allow, under strictly supervised conditions, on a selective basis and to a limited extent, the taking or keeping of certain specimens of the species listed in Annex IV in limited numbers specified by the competent national authorities. [...]

[All other Articles and Annexes omitted.]

Case C-44/95 *R v Secretary of State for the Environment ex p Royal Society for the Protection of Birds* [1997] QB 206; [1996] ECR I-3805

Summary:

Article 4(1) or Art 4(2) of Directive 79/409 on the conservation of wild birds, which requires the Member States to take special conservation measures for certain species, and in particular to designate as Special Protection Areas (SPAs) the most suitable territories for their conservation, must be interpreted as meaning that a Member State is not authorised to take account of the economic requirements mentioned in Art 2 of the Directive when choosing and defining the boundaries of a Special Protection Area or even to take account of economic requirements constituting a general interest superior to that represented by the ecological objective of that directive. Similarly, a Member State may not take account of economic requirements in so far as they amount to imperative reasons of overriding public interest of the kind referred to in Art 6(4) of Directive 92/43 on the conservation of the natural habitats of wild fauna and flora, as inserted in Directive 79/409. Although the latter provision widened the range of grounds on which it may be justified to encroach upon SPAs already designated as such, by expressly including therein reasons of a social or economic nature, it nevertheless did not make any change regarding the initial stage of classification referred to in Art 4(1) and (2) of Directive 79/409, and therefore the classification of sites as SPAs must in all circumstances be carried out in accordance with the criteria accepted by those provisions.

Grounds:

1   By order of 9 February 1995, received at the Court on 24 February 1995, the House of Lords referred to the Court of Justice for a preliminary ruling under Art 177 of the EC Treaty two questions on the interpretation of Arts 2 and 4 of Directive 79/409 of 2 April 1979 on the conservation of wild birds ((1979) OJ L103, p 1, hereinafter 'the Birds Directive').

2   Those questions were raised in proceedings between an association for the protection of birds, the Royal Society for the Protection of Birds (hereinafter 'the RSPB'), and the Secretary of State for the Environment (hereinafter 'the Secretary of State') concerning a decision designating a special protection area for the protection of wild birds.

3   The Birds Directive, which covers all species of birds naturally occurring in the wild in the European territory of the Member States to which the Treaty applies, provides, in Art 2, that the Member States are to take all necessary measures to maintain the population of all those species of birds at a level which corresponds in particular to ecological, scientific and cultural requirements, while taking account of economic and recreational requirements.

4   According to Art 3 of the Birds Directive, the Member States, having regard to the requirements mentioned in Art 2, are to take all necessary measures to preserve, maintain or re-establish a sufficient diversity and area of habitats for all the protected species.

5   Pursuant to Art 4(1) of that directive, the species mentioned in Annex I are to be the subject of special conservation measures concerning their habitat in order to ensure their survival and reproduction in their area of distribution. In particular, the Member States are to classify the most suitable territories in terms of number and size as Special Protection Areas for the conservation of those species in the geographical sea and land area where the Directive applies.

6   According to Art 4(2), 'Member States shall take similar measures for regularly occurring migratory species not listed in Annex I, bearing in mind their need for protection in the geographical sea and land area where this directive applies, as regards their breeding, moulting and wintering areas and staging posts along their migration routes. To this end, Member States shall pay particular attention to the protection of wetlands and particularly to wetlands of international importance'.

7   Finally, according to Article 4(4), '[I]n respect of the areas referred to in paras 1 and 2 above, Member States shall take appropriate steps to avoid pollution or deterioration of habitats or any disturbances affecting the birds, in so far as these would be significant having regard to the objectives of this Article. Outside these protection areas, Member States shall also strive to avoid pollution or deterioration of habitats'.

8   Directive 92/43 of 21 May 1992 on the conservation of the natural habitats of wild fauna and flora ((1992) OJ L206, p 7, hereinafter 'the Habitats Directive'), to be implemented in the United Kingdom by June 1994, provides in Art 7 that the obligations under Art 6(2), (3) and (4) are to replace any obligations arising under the first sentence of Art 4(4) of the Birds Directive in respect of areas classified pursuant to Art 4(1) or similarly recognised under Art 4(2) of that directive. Article 6(2), (3) and (4) of the Habitats Directive is worded as follows:

   2   Member States shall take appropriate steps to avoid, in the special areas of conservation, the deterioration of natural habitats and the habitats of species as well as disturbance of the species for which the areas have been designated, in so far as such disturbance could be significant in relation to the objectives of this Directive.

   3   Any plan or project not directly connected with or necessary to the management of the site but likely to have a significant effect thereon, either individually or in combination with other plans or projects, shall be subject to appropriate assessment of its implications for the site in view of the site's conservation objectives. In the light of the conclusions of the assessment of the implications for the site and subject to the provisions of this paragraph.

647

4   The competent national authorities shall agree to the plan or project only after having ascertained that it will not adversely affect the integrity of the site concerned and, if appropriate, after having obtained the opinion of the general public.

5   If, in spite of a negative assessment of the implications for the site and in the absence of alternative solutions, a plan or project must nevertheless be carried out for imperative reasons of overriding public interest, including those of a social or economic nature, the Member State shall take all compensatory measures necessary to ensure that the overall coherence of Natura 2000 is protected. It shall inform the Commission of the compensatory measures adopted. Where the site concerned hosts a priority natural habitat type and/or a priority species, the only considerations which may be raised are those relating to human health or public safety, to beneficial consequences of primary importance for the environment or, further to an opinion from the Commission, to other imperative reasons of overriding public interest.

9   The United Kingdom did not transpose the Habitats Directive until October 1994.

10 On 15 December 1993, the Secretary of State decided to designate the Medway Estuary and Marshes as a Special Protection Area (hereinafter 'SPA'). At the same time, he decided to exclude from it an area of about 22 hectares known as Lappel Bank.

11 According to the order for reference, the Medway Estuary and Marshes are an area of wetland of international importance covering 4681 hectares on the north coast of Kent and listed under the Ramsar Convention. They are used by a number of wildfowl and wader species as a breeding and wintering area and as a staging post during spring and autumn migration. The site also supports breeding populations of the avocet and the little tern, which are listed in Annex I to the Birds Directive.

12 Lappel Bank is an area of inter-tidal mudflat immediately adjoining, at its northern end, the Port of Sheerness and falling geographically within the bounds of the Medway Estuary and Marshes. Lappel Bank shares several of the important ornithological qualities of the area as a whole. Although it does not support any of the species referred to in Art 4(1) of the Birds Directive, some of the bird species of the area are represented in significantly greater numbers than elsewhere in the Medway SPA. Lappel Bank is an important component of the overall estuarine eco-system and the loss of that inter-tidal area would probably result in a reduction in the wader and wildfowl populations of the Medway Estuary and Marshes.

13 The Port of Sheerness is at present the fifth largest in the United Kingdom for cargo and freight handling. It is a flourishing commercial undertaking, well located for sea traffic and access to its main domestic markets. The port, which is also a significant employer in an area with a serious unemployment problem, plans extended facilities for car storage and value added activities on vehicles and in the fruit and paper product market, in order better to compete with continental ports offering similar facilities. Lappel Bank is the only area into which the Port of Sheerness can realistically envisage expanding.

14 Accordingly, taking the view that the need not to inhibit the viability of the port and the significant contribution that expansion into the area of Lappel Bank would make to the local and national economy outweighed its nature conservation value, the Secretary of State decided to exclude that area from the Medway SPA.

15 The RSPB applied to the Divisional Court of the Queen's Bench Division to have the Secretary of State's decision quashed on the ground that he was not entitled, by virtue of the Birds Directive, to have regard to economic considerations when classifying an SPA. The Divisional Court found against the RSPB. On appeal by the RSPB, the Court of Appeal upheld that judgement. The RSPB therefore appealed to the House of Lords.

16 Uncertain as to how the Directive should be interpreted, the House of Lords stayed proceedings pending a preliminary ruling from the Court of Justice on the following questions:

1 Is a Member State entitled to take account of the considerations mentioned in Art 2 of Directive 79/409/EEC of 2 April 1979 on the conservation of wild birds in classification of an area as a Special Protection Area and/or in defining the boundaries of such an area pursuant to Art 4(1) and/or 4(2) of that Directive?

2 If the answer to Question 1 is 'no', may a Member State nevertheless take account of Art 2 considerations in the classification process in so far as:

(a) they amount to a general interest which is superior to the general interest which is represented by the ecological objective of the Directive (that is, the test which the European Court has laid down in, for example, Case 57/89 *Commission v Germany* ('*Leybucht Dykes*'), for derogation from the requirements of Art 4(4)); or

(b) they amount to imperative reasons of overriding public interest such as might be taken into account under Art 6(4) of Directive 92/43/EEC of 21 May 1992 on the conservation of natural habitats and of wild fauna and flora?

17 The point of this question is whether Art 4(1) or (2) of the Birds Directive is to be interpreted as meaning that a Member State is authorised to take account of the economic requirements mentioned in Art 2 thereof when designating an SPA and defining its boundaries.

18 As a preliminary point, it must be borne in mind that, according to the ninth recital in the Preamble to the Birds Directive, 'the preservation, maintenance or restoration of a sufficient diversity and area of habitats is essential to the conservation of all species of birds [covered by the directive]', that 'certain species of birds should be the subject of special conservation measures concerning their habitats in order to ensure their survival and reproduction in their area of distribution', and, finally, that 'such measures must also take account of migratory species'.

19 That recital is formally reflected in Arts 3 and 4 of the directive. In para 23 of its judgment in Case C-355/90 *Commission v Spain* [1993] ECR I–4221 (hereinafter 'Santoña Marshes') the court pointed out that the first of those provisions imposes obligations of a general character, namely the obligation to ensure a sufficient diversity and area of habitats for all the birds referred to in the directive, while the second contains specific obligations with regard to the species of birds listed in Annex I and the migratory species not listed in that annex.

20 According to the United Kingdom government and the Port of Sheerness Limited, Art 4 cannot be considered in isolation from Art 3. They state that Art 4 provides, in relation to certain species of particular interest, for the specific application of the

general obligation imposed by Art 3. Since the latter provision allows account to be taken of economic requirements, the same should apply to Art 4(1) and (2).

21 The French government reaches the same conclusion, observing that, when an SPA is created, the Member States take account of all the criteria mentioned in Art 2 of the Birds Directive, which is general in scope, and, therefore, *inter alia*, of economic requirements.

22 Those arguments cannot be upheld.

23 It must be noted first that Art 4 of the Birds Directive lays down a protection regime which is specifically targeted and reinforced both for the species listed in Annex I and for migratory species, an approach justified by the fact that they are, respectively, the most endangered species and the species constituting a common heritage of the Community (see Case C-169/89 *Gourmetrie Van den Burg Case* [1990] ECR I-2143, para 11).

24 Whilst Art 3 of the Birds Directive provides for account to be taken of the requirements mentioned in Art 2 for the implementation of general conservation measures, including the creation of protection areas, Art 4 makes no such reference for the implementation of special conservation measures, in particular the creation of SPAs.

25 Consequently, having regard to the aim of special protection pursued by Art 4 and the fact that, according to settled case-law (see in particular Case C-435/92 *APAS v Préfets de Maine-et-Loire and de la Loire Atlantique* [1994] ECR I-67, para 20), Art 2 does not constitute an autonomous derogation from the general system of protection established by the Directive, it must be held (see paras 17 and 18 of *Santoña Marshes*) that the ecological requirements laid down by the former provision do not have to be balanced against the interests listed in the latter, in particular economic requirements.

26 It is the criteria laid down in paras (1) and (2) of Art 4 which are to guide the Member States in designating and defining the boundaries of SPAs. It is clear from paras 26 and 27 of *Santoña Marshes* that, notwithstanding the divergences between the various language versions of the last sub-paragraph of Art 4(1), the criteria in question are ornithological criteria.

27 In view of the foregoing, the answer to the first question must be that Art 4(1) or (2) of the Birds Directive is to be interpreted as meaning that a Member State is not authorised to take account of the economic requirements mentioned in Art 2 thereof when designating an SPA and defining its boundaries.

28 By the first part of the second question, the national court seeks to ascertain whether Art 4(1) or (2) of the Birds Directive must be interpreted as allowing a Member State, when designating an SPA and defining its boundaries, to take account of economic requirements as constituting a general interest superior to that represented by the ecological objective of that Directive.

29 In its judgment in Case C-57/89 *Commission v Germany* [1991] ECR I-883, paras 21 and 22 (hereinafter '*Leybucht Dykes*'), the Court held that the Member States may, in the context of Art 4(4) of the Birds Directive, reduce the extent of a SPA only on exceptional grounds, being grounds corresponding to a general interest superior to the general interest represented by the ecological objective of the Directive. It was held that economic requirements cannot be invoked in that context.

30 It is also clear from para 19 of *Santoña Marshes* that, in the context of Art 4 of that Directive, considered as a whole, economic requirements cannot on any view correspond to a general interest superior to that represented by the ecological objective of the Directive.

31 Accordingly, without it being necessary to rule on the possible relevance of the grounds corresponding to a superior general interest for the purpose of classifying an SPA, the answer to the first part of the second question must be that Art 4(1) or (2) of the Birds Directive is to be interpreted as meaning that a Member State may not, when designating an SPA and defining its boundaries, take account of economic requirements as constituting a general interest superior to that represented by the ecological objective of that Directive.

32 By the second part of the second question, the House of Lords asks essentially whether Art 4(1) or (2) of the Birds Directive is to be interpreted as meaning that a Member State may, when designating an SPA and defining its boundaries, take account of economic requirements to the extent that they reflect imperative reasons of overriding public interest of the kind referred to in Art 6(4) of the Habitats Directive.

33 The United Kingdom government considers that that question is relevant only to cases of classification decisions made after the expiry of the period for transposition of the Habitats Directive. Since that is not the case in the main proceedings, it considers that it is unnecessary to answer the question.

34 It is well settled that it is for the national courts alone, before which the proceedings are pending and which will be responsible for the eventual judgment, to determine, having regard to the particular features of each case, both the need for a preliminary ruling to enable them to give judgment and the relevance of the questions which they refer to the court. A request for a preliminary ruling from a national court may be rejected only if it is clear that the interpretation of Community law requested bears no relation to the true nature of the case or the subject matter of the main action (see in particular Case C-129/94 *Ruiz Barnáldez* [1996] 1 ECR 1829, para 7). That is, however, not the case in the main proceedings.

35 Consequently, it is necessary to examine the second part of the second question submitted by the national court.

36 It is important first to bear in mind that Art 7 of the Habitats Directive provides in particular that the obligations arising under Art 6(4) thereof are to apply, in place of any obligations arising under the first sentence of Art 4(4) of the Birds Directive, to the areas classified under Art 4(1) or similarly recognised under Art 4(2) of that Directive as from the date of implementation of the Habitats Directive or the date of classification or recognition by a Member State under the Birds Directive, whichever is the later.

37 As the Commission submits in its observations, Art 6(4) of the Habitats Directive, as inserted in the Birds Directive, has, following *Leybucht Dykes* where the point in issue was the reduction of an area already classified, widened the range of grounds justifying encroachment upon SPAs by expressly including therein reasons of a social or economic nature.

38 Thus, the imperative reasons of overriding public interest which may, pursuant to Art 6(4) of the Habitats Directive, justify a plan or project which would significantly affect an SPA in any event include grounds relating to a superior general interest of the kind identified in *Leybucht Dykes* and may where appropriate include grounds of a social or economic nature.

39 Next, although Art 6(3) and (4) of the Habitats Directive, in so far as it amended the first sentence of Art 4(4) of the Birds Directive, established a procedure enabling the Member States to adopt, for imperative reasons of overriding public interest and subject to certain conditions, a plan or a project adversely affecting an SPA and so made it possible to go back on a decision classifying such an area by reducing its extent, it nevertheless did not make any amendments regarding the initial stage of classification of an area as an SPA referred to in Art 4(1) and (2) of the Birds Directive.

40 It follows that, even under the Habitats Directive, the classification of sites as SPAs must in all circumstances be carried out in accordance with the criteria permitted under Art 4(1) and (2) of the Birds Directive.

41 Economic requirements, as an imperative reason of overriding public interest allowing a derogation from the obligation to classify a site according to its ecological value, cannot enter into consideration at that stage. But that does not, as the Commission has rightly pointed out, mean that they cannot be taken into account at a later stage under the procedure provided for by Art 6(3) and (4) of the Habitats Directive.

42 The answer to the second part of the second question must therefore be that Art 4(1) or (2) of the Birds Directive is to be interpreted as meaning that a Member State may not, when designating an SPA and defining its boundaries, take account of economic requirements which may constitute imperative reasons of overriding public interest of the kind referred to in Art 6(4) of the Habitats Directive.

Case C-57/89 *Commission of the European Communities v Federal Republic of Germany* [1991] ECR I-0883

Summary:

Although the Member States do have a certain discretion with regard to the choice of the territories which are most suitable for classification as special protection areas pursuant to Art 4(4) of Directive 79/409 on the conservation of wild birds, they do not have the same discretion to modify or reduce the extent of such areas, which contain the most suitable environments for the species listed in Annex I, and thus unilaterally escape from the obligations imposed on them by Art 4(4) of the Directive. The power of the Member States to reduce the extent of special protection areas can be justified only on exceptional grounds corresponding to a general interest which is superior to the general interest represented by the ecological objective of the Directive. In that context the economic and recreational requirements referred to in Art 2 of the Directive do not enter into consideration, since that provision does not constitute an autonomous derogation from the system of protection established by the Directive.

Grounds:

1   By application lodged at the Court Registry on 28 February 1989, the Commission of the European Communities brought an action under Art 169 of the EEC Treaty for a declaration that by planning or undertaking works detrimental to the habitat of protected birds in special protection areas, contrary to Art 4 of Directive 79/409/EEC of 2 April 1979 on the conservation of wild birds ((1979) OJ L103, p 1, hereinafter referred to as 'the Directive'), the Federal Republic of Germany has failed to fulfil its obligations under the EEC Treaty.

2   Art 4 of the Directive is worded as follows:

    1   The species mentioned in Annex I shall be the subject of special conservation measures concerning their habitat in order to ensure their survival and reproduction in their area of distribution. Member States shall classify in particular the most suitable territories in number and size as special protection areas for the conservation of these species, taking into account their protection requirements in the geographical sea and land area where this Directive applies.

    2   Member States shall take similar measures for regularly occurring migratory species not listed in Annex I, bearing in mind their need for protection in the geographical sea and land area where this Directive applies, as regards their breeding, moulting and wintering areas and staging posts along their migration routes. To this end, Member States shall pay particular attention to the protection of wetlands and particularly to wetlands of international importance.

    3   Member States shall send the Commission all relevant information so that it may take appropriate initiatives with a view to the co-ordination necessary to ensure that the areas provided for in paras 1 and 2 above form a coherent whole which meets the protection requirements of these species in the geographical sea and land area where this Directive applies.

    4   In respect of the protection areas referred to in paras 1 and 2 above, Member States shall take appropriate steps to avoid pollution or deterioration of habitats or any disturbances affecting the birds, in so far as these would be significant having regard to the objectives of this Art. Outside these protection areas, Member States shall also strive to avoid pollution or deterioration of habitats.

3   The application initially comprised two claims, the first concerning dredging and filling operations in the Rysumer Nacken, and the second concerning dyke-building operations carried out in the Leybucht.

4   With regard to the first claim, the Commission, at the hearing, formally acknowledged that the Rysumer Nacken is not covered by the regulation of the Land of Lower Saxony of 13 December 1985 creating the Niedersaechisches Wattenmeer National Park and that, consequently, the Rysumer Nacken is not designated as a special protection area. However, the Commission argues that that is a new argument put forward by the defendant in its rejoinder, so that the defendant must bear the costs relating to that point.

5   The German government replies that the Commission was aware, even before the commencement of proceedings before the Court, of all the information concerning the legal status of the Rysumer Nacken, in particular of maps showing the boundaries of the national park. It is clear from those maps that the Rysumer Nacken is not

designated as a special protection area. According to the German government, the details it provided in its rejoinder do not therefore constitute a new argument.

6   The information regarding the extent of the protected areas in the Wattenmeer was supplied by the German government in its letter of 6 September 1988 sent pursuant to Art 4(3) of the Directive. At the time it lodged its application, the Commission had at its disposal, *inter alia*, the maps appended to the above mentioned regulation, defining the boundaries of the protected area. It is evident from that information that the Rysumer Nacken is not one of the sites designated as a special protection area. Consequently, since the withdrawal of this part of the application is not the consequence of the conduct of the German government, the Commission must bear the costs relating thereto.

7   With regard to the dyke-building operations in the Leybucht, the Commission claims that they disturb birds which enjoy special protection under the provisions of Art 4(1) of the Directive, in conjunction with Annex I, and damage the habitat of the birds, which is designated as a special protection area. The Commission emphasises that the first sentence of Art 4(4) of the Directive requires Member States to take positive steps to avoid any deterioration or pollution of habitats as part of the management of special protection areas.

8   The Commission states that coastal defence measures such as the strengthening of a dyke are acceptable in the case of a threat to human life, but only on condition that the necessary measures are restricted to those which cause only the minimum necessary deterioration of the special protection area in question

9   According to the Commission, those conditions have not been fulfilled in the present case. It is of the opinion that both the construction work in the Leybucht and its results entail deterioration in the living conditions of protected birds and the loss of land areas of considerable ecological importance, thereby leading to lower population densities for some of the species of birds listed in Annex I to the Directive, in particular the avocet.

10 The German government observes that according to the information sent to the Commission pursuant to Art 4(3) of the Directive, the new line of the dyke in the Leybucht and the areas located on the landward side of the dyke are excluded from the special protection area. It states that the boundaries of the area in question are defined in the regulation creating the national park in such a way that the protected area extends only to the foot of the dyke, in the form it will have once the construction work in question has been completed.

11 According to the German government, the sole purpose of the operations is to secure the safety of the dyke. It emphasises that during the planning stage of the project at issue the competent authorities took account of all bird conservation requirements and balanced them against the requirements of coastal protection. The German government states that the new line of the dyke and the temporary disturbances caused by the works constitute the smallest possible interference for bird life in the Leybucht. It adds that the Commission has not furnished any evidence at all that the measures at issue significantly impair the protection of those birds.

12 With regard to the interpretation of Art 4(4) of the Directive, the German government claims that that provision requires a balance to be struck between the various public interests likely to be affected by the management of a special protection area, so that the Member States must have a wide discretionary power in this field.

13 The United Kingdom considers that the Commission has not established that the project at issue has a significant effect within the meaning of the first sentence of Art 4(4) of the Directive. It states that that condition must be interpreted as meaning that the deterioration of a special protection area must be such as to threaten the survival or reproduction of protected species within their area of distribution. In the United Kingdom's view, the material supplied by the Commission does not appear sufficient to support the conclusion that the operations in the Leybucht involve such deterioration.

14 The United Kingdom emphasises the importance of the evidence supplied by the defendant which shows that the works at issue will significantly improve ecological conditions in the Leybucht. It considers that it is legitimate, when assessing whether a particular project will cause deterioration to a special protection area and whether any such deterioration will be significant, to consider whether the works will at the same time bring compensatory ecological improvements.

15 In the submission of the United Kingdom, within the context of Art 4(4) of the Directive account can be taken of other important public interest considerations, including those referred to in Art 2 of the Directive. It considers that the Member States must be able to take into account the interests of persons living in or around a special protection area.

16 Reference is made to the Report for the Hearing for a fuller account of the facts of the case, the course of the procedure and the submissions and arguments of the parties, which are mentioned or discussed hereinafter only in so far as is necessary for the reasoning of the Court.

17 With regard to the boundaries of the special protection area in question, it must be pointed out that the boundary of the Leybucht is defined by the regulation creating the national park and the maps appended thereto. Although the plan of the area does include a reference to the regional planning scheme, the legal measure designating the special protection area nevertheless sets out its precise territorial delimitation, constituted by the present line of the dyke. The displacement of the dyke towards the sea as part of the coastal defence project thus entails a reduction in the protected area.

18 Consequently, in order to resolve this dispute it is necessary to settle a number of questions of principle concerning the obligations of the Member States under Art 4(4) of the Directive in relation to the management of the special protection areas. It must be determined whether – and if so, under what conditions – the Member States are authorised to reduce the size of a special protection area and to what extent other interests may be taken into account.

19 With regard to the powers of the Member States to review in that way a decision to classify an area as a special protection area, it must be stated that a reduction in the geographical extent of a protected area is not expressly envisaged by the terms of the Directive.

20   Although the Member States do have a certain discretion with regard to the choice of the territories which are most suitable for classification as special protection areas pursuant to Art 4(1) of the Directive, they do not have the same discretion under Art 4(4) of the Directive in modifying or reducing the extent of the areas, since they have themselves acknowledged in their declarations that those areas contain the most suitable environments for the species listed in Annex I to the Directive. If that were not so, the Member States could unilaterally escape from the obligations imposed on them by Art 4(4) of the Directive with regard to special protection areas.

21   That interpretation of Art 4(4) of the Directive is borne out, moreover, by the ninth recital in the Preamble, which underlines the special importance which the directive attaches to special conservation measures concerning the habitats of the birds listed in Annex I in order to ensure their survival and reproduction in their area of distribution. It follows that the power of the Member States to reduce the extent of a special protection area can be justified only on exceptional grounds.

22   Those grounds must correspond to a general interest which is superior to the general interest represented by the ecological objective of the Directive. In that context the interests referred to in Art 2 of the Directive, namely economic and recreational requirements, do not enter into consideration. As the Court pointed out in its judgments in Case 247/85 *Commission v Belgium* [1987] ECR 3029 and Case 262/85 *Commission v Italy* [1987] ECR 3073, that provision does not constitute an autonomous derogation from the general system of protection established by the Directive.

23   With regard to the reason put forward in this case, it must be stated that the danger of flooding and the protection of the coast constitute sufficiently serious reasons to justify the dyke works and the strengthening of coastal structures as long as those measures are confined to a strict minimum and involve only the smallest possible reduction of the special protection area.

24   With regard to the part of the project concerning the Leyhoern area, the line of the dyke was influenced by considerations relating not only to coastal protection but also to the concern to ensure that fishing vessels from Greetsiel had access to the harbour. In the light of the principles for the interpretation of Art 4(4) of the Directive set out above, to take account of such an interest is in principle incompatible with the requirements of the provision.

25   However, that part of the project has at the same time specific positive consequences for the habitat of birds. Once the works are completed it will be possible to close two navigation channels which cross the Leybucht, with the result that the Leybucht will be left in absolute peace. Moreover, the decision approving the proposed works envisages a strict protection scheme for the Leyhoern area. The dyke which previously protected the Hauener Hooge site will be opened, thus once more exposing an extensive area to tidal movements and allowing the formation of salt meadows of considerable ecological importance.

26 The desire to ensure the survival of the fishing port of Greetsiel could thus be taken into account in order to justify the decision on the line of the new dyke because there were the above mentioned offsetting ecological benefits, and solely for that reason.

27 Finally, the disturbance arising from the construction work itself does not exceed what is necessary to carry it out. The information concerning the number of avocets in that sector of the Wattenmeer shows, moreover, that during the period in question there was no significant change, within the meaning of Art 4(4) of the Directive, in population trends for that species. Furthermore, the Commission has not supplied any other evidence relating to population trends for protected species.

28 It follows from the foregoing that the application must be dismissed.

Case C-355/90 *Commission of the European Communities v Kingdom of Spain* [1993] ECR I-4221

Summary:

1 Articles 3 and 4 of Directive 79/409 on the conservation of wild birds require Member States to preserve, maintain and re-establish the habitats of the said birds as such, because of their ecological value. The obligations on Member States under those Articles exist even before any reduction is observed in the number of birds or any risk of a protected species becoming extinct has materialised.

2 In implementing Directive 79/409 on the conservation of wild birds, Member States are not authorised to invoke, at their option, grounds of derogation based on taking other interests into account. With respect, more specifically, to the obligation to take special conservation measures for certain species under Art 4 of the Directive, such grounds must, in order to be acceptable, correspond to a general interest which is superior to the general interest represented by the ecological objective of the Directive. In particular, the interests referred to in Art 2 of the Directive, namely economic and recreational requirements, do not enter into consideration, as that provision does not constitute an autonomous derogation from the general system of protection established by the Directive.

3 In choosing the territories which are most suitable for classification as special protection areas pursuant to Art 4(1) of Directive 79/409 on the conservation of wild birds, Member States have a certain discretion which is limited by the fact that the classification of those areas is subject to certain ornithological criteria determined by the directive, such as the presence of birds listed in Annex I to the Directive, on the one hand, and the designation of a habitat as a wetland area, on the other. However, Member States do not have the same discretion under Art 4(4) of the directive to modify or reduce the extent of such areas.

Grounds:

1 By application lodged at the Court Registry on 30 November 1990, the Commission of the European Communities brought an action under Art 169 of the EEC Treaty for a declaration that, by failing to take upkeep and management measures, in accordance

with the ecological needs of habitats, or measures to re-establish biotopes which have been destroyed in the Santoña marshes in the Autonomous Community of Cantabria, by not classifying those marshes as a special protection area and by not taking appropriate steps to avoid pollution or deterioration of habitats in that area, the Kingdom of Spain has failed to fulfil its obligations under Arts 3 and 4 of Council Directive 79/409 of 2 April 1979 on the conservation of wild birds ((1979) OJ L103, p 1, hereinafter 'the Directive').

2   Article 3(1) of the Directive provides that, in the light of economic and recreational requirements, Member States shall take the requisite measures to preserve, maintain or re-establish a sufficient diversity and area of habitats for all the species of birds referred to in Art 1.

3   Article 4(1) of the Directive provides that the species mentioned in Annex I shall be the subject of special conservation measures concerning their habitat in order to ensure their survival and reproduction in their area of distribution. Member States are required to classify in particular the most suitable territories in number and size as special protection areas for the conservation of these species of birds.

4   Article 4(2) of the Directive provides that Member States shall take similar measures for regularly occurring migratory species not listed in Annex I, as regards their breeding, moulting and wintering areas and staging posts along their migration routes. To this end, Member States are required to pay particular attention to the protection of wetlands and particularly to wetlands of international importance.

5   Lastly, Art 4(4) of the Directive provides that, in respect of the protection areas referred to in paras 1 and 2 of that Article, Member States are to take appropriate steps to avoid pollution or deterioration of habitats or any disturbances affecting the birds, in so far as these would be significant having regard to the objectives of that art.

6   The Commission considers that, as a result of a number of actions in the Santoña marshes, the Kingdom of Spain has failed to fulfil the obligations of protection arising under Arts 3 and 4 of the Directive.

7   The Spanish government rejects the Commission's allegations on both legal and factual grounds.

8   Reference is made to the Report for the Hearing for a fuller account of the facts, the procedure and the pleas and arguments of the parties, which are mentioned or discussed hereinafter only in so far as is necessary for the reasoning of the Court.

I   **The interpretation of Arts 3 and 4 of the Directive**

9   In the first place, the Commission considers that the Kingdom of Spain was under an obligation to comply with the provisions of the Directive from 1 January 1986.

10 The Spanish government contends that the obligations laid down in Arts 3 and 4 of the Directive can, by their nature, be fulfilled only gradually, not immediately.

11 That argument must be rejected. In the first place, the Act concerning the conditions of accession of the Kingdom of Spain to the European Communities contains no specific provision on the applicability of the Directive in that Member State, which was required under Art 395 of that Act to put into effect the measures necessary for it to comply with the Directive from the date of accession. Moreover, the Directive itself contains no indication of any specific time being allowed for the national authorities

to fulfil the obligations laid down in Arts 3 and 4, for which, in common with all the provisions of the Directive, the necessary transposition measures had to be taken within the two year period prescribed by Art 18 of the Directive.

12 Furthermore, the Commission gave the Spanish government a considerable amount of time to fulfil those obligations. It did not bring the action until more than two years after the letter before action and almost five years after the Kingdom of Spain joined the Communities.

13 In the second place, the Commission claims that, as a result of the obligations arising under Arts 3 and 4 of the Directive, specific measures must be taken to conserve the habitats of wild birds.

14 The Spanish government contends, on the contrary, that those provisions merely impose an obligation to achieve a result, namely to secure the conservation of wild birds.

15 The Commission's view must be upheld on this point. Arts 3 and 4 of the Directive require Member States to preserve, maintain and re-establish habitats as such, because of their ecological value. Moreover, it follows from the ninth recital in the Preamble to the Directive that the preservation, maintenance or restoration of a sufficient diversity and area of habitats is essential to the conservation of all species of birds. The obligations on Member States under Arts 3 and 4 of the Directive therefore exist before any reduction is observed in the number of birds or any risk of a protected species becoming extinct has materialised.

16 In the third place, the Commission claims that the obligations imposed by Art 4 of the Directive are imperative.

17 The Spanish government takes the view that the ecological requirements laid down in that provision must be subordinate to other interests, such as social and economic interests, or must at the very least be balanced against them.

18 That argument cannot be accepted. It is clear from the court's judgment in Case C-57/89 *Commission v Germany* [1991] ECR I-883 that, in implementing the Directive, Member States are not authorised to invoke, at their option, grounds of derogation based on taking other interests into account.

19 With respect more specifically to Art 4 of the Directive, the Court held in that judgment that, in order to be acceptable, such grounds must correspond to a general interest which is superior to the general interest represented by the ecological objective of the Directive. In particular, the interests referred to in Art 2 of the Directive, namely economic and recreational requirements, do not enter into consideration. In this connection, the Court held in Case 247/85 *Commission v Belgium* [1987] ECR 3029 and Case 262/85 *Commission v Italy* [1987] ECR 3073 that that provision does not constitute an autonomous derogation from the general system of protection established by the Directive.

20 In the fourth place, the Commission claims that it is possible for a Member State to infringe both Art 4(1) and (2), relating to the classification of a territory as a special protection area, and Art 4(4) of the Directive, which concerns the protection measures relating to such an area.

21 According to the Spanish government, a Member State cannot be accused of having infringed both those provisions at the same time, because the protection measures cannot be implemented until the decision has been taken to classify a territory as a special protection area.

22 That line of reasoning must be rejected. The objectives of protection set out in the Directive, as expressed in the ninth recital in its Preamble, could not be achieved if Member States had to comply with the obligations arising under Art 4(4) only in cases where a special protection area had previously been established.

23 Lastly, with respect to the relationship between Arts 3 and 4 of the directive, it must be borne in mind that the first of those provisions imposes obligations of a general nature, namely the obligation to ensure a sufficient diversity and area of habitats for all the birds referred to in the directive, while the second contains specific obligations with regard to the species of birds listed in Annex I and migratory species not listed in that annex. As it is undisputed that both categories of birds are found in the Santoña marshes, it will be sufficient to consider the Commission's complaints in the light of the provisions of Art 4 of the Directive.

II The obligation to classify the Santoña marshes as a special protection area pursuant to Art 4(1) and (2) of the Directive

24 The Commission claims that the Santoña marshes are not only a habitat that is essential for the survival of several species in danger of extinction within the meaning of Art 4(1) of the Directive but also wetlands of international importance for regularly occurring migratory species in that area within the meaning of Art 4(2).

25 The Spanish government recognises the ecological value of the area. It points out that the Santoña and Noja marshes were classified as nature reserves by Law No 6 of 27 March 1992, because of the importance of those wetlands as habitats for many species of animals. However, it considers that the national authorities have a margin of discretion with regard to the choice and delimitation of special protection areas and the timing of their classification as such.

26 That argument cannot be accepted. Although Member States do have a certain margin of discretion with regard to the choice of special protection areas, the classification of those areas is nevertheless subject to certain ornithological criteria determined by the Directive, such as the presence of birds listed in Annex I, on the one hand, and the designation of a habitat as a wetland area, on the other.

27 In this connection, it is common ground that the Santoña marshes are one of the most important eco-systems in the Iberian peninsula for many aquatic birds. The marshes serve as a wintering area or staging post for many birds on their migrations from European countries to the southern latitudes of Africa and the Iberian peninsula itself. The birds observed in the area include various species that are becoming extinct, in particular the spoonbill, which feeds and rests in the Santoña marshes in the course of its migrations. Moreover, it emerged from the case file and at the hearing before the court that the area in question is regularly visited by 19 of the species listed in Annex I to the Directive and at least 14 species of migratory birds.

28 As to the classification of the Santoña marshes as a nature reserve by Law No 6 of 27 March 1992, this cannot be regarded as satisfying the requirements laid down in the

directive, either in respect of the territorial extent of the area or as regards its legal status as a protected area.

29 In this connection, it must be observed first of all that the nature reserve does not cover the whole of the marshes, since an area of 40,000 square metres is excluded. Yet that land is of particular importance for aquatic birds in danger of extinction within the meaning of Art 4(1)(a) of the Directive, since a steady reduction in the space available for nesting has been observed in the other marshland areas close to the coast.

30 Next the necessary protection measures have not been defined even for the marshes within the classified area. Indeed, it appears from the case file that the plan for the management of nature reserves provided for in Art 4 of the Law has not been approved by the competent authorities. Yet that plan is of the utmost importance for the protection of wild birds because it intended to identify activities which will give rise to a change in the eco-systems of the area.

31 Since measures as essential as those determining the management of the area or governing the use of the marshes and the activities carried out there have not been adopted, the requirements of the Directive cannot be held to have been satisfied.

32 It must therefore be held that the Kingdom of Spain has failed to fulfil its obligations under Art 4(1) and (2) of the Directive by not classifying the Santoña marshes as a special protection area.

III The obligation to protect the Santoña marshes pursuant to Art 4(4) of the Directive

A The second section of the road between Argoños and Santoña

33 The Commission claims that the new route followed by the Case C-629 road between Argoños and Santoña results not only in a considerable reduction in the surface area of the Santoña marshes but also in disturbances affecting the peaceful nature of the area and consequently the wild birds protected by the provisions of the Directive.

34 The Spanish Government explains that the new road is necessary to improve access to the town of Santoña. Also, the new route is the best of various possible alternatives, mainly because it affects only a small proportion of the total surface area of the marshes.

35 These explanations cannot be accepted. As the Court stressed in Case C-57/89 *Commission v Germany* [1991] ECR I-883, although Member States do have a certain discretion with regard to the choice of the territories which are most suitable for classification as special protection areas, they do not have the same discretion under Art 4(4) of the Directive in modifying or reducing the extent of those areas.

36 The Court finds in this connection that the construction of the new section of road Case C-629 between Argoños and Santoña involves a reduction in the surface area of the marshland, an effect that, moreover, is aggravated by the erection of a number of new buildings near this new section of road. These operations have resulted in the loss of refuge, rest and nesting areas for birds. In addition to the disturbances caused by the road works, the action in question has modified the ebb and flow of the tide, causing this part of the marshland to silt up.

37 Since, regard being had to the considerations of principle set out above, such action cannot be justified by the need to improve access to the municipality of Santoña, the complaint must be upheld.

B   The industrial estates at Laredo and Colindres

38 The Commission considers that the establishment of industrial estates at Laredo and Colindres is resulting in the disappearance of a substantial part of the marshland, namely the area adjoining the ... Treto estuary. The filling-in of land adjoining these sites is also alleged to affect the ebb and flow of the tide in the bay.

39 The Spanish government explains that the competent authorities have abandoned the idea of establishing these industrial estates as they were originally planned.

40 The Court takes note of the written and oral statements of the Spanish government to the effect that the industrial estates at Laredo and Colindres have not been established and the municipalities concerned have abandoned the idea of carrying out those two projects as they were originally planned.

41 Although it is no longer proposed to carry out those projects, the fact remains that, after the Kingdom of Spain joined the Communities, the local authorities re-sealed the dykes previously built round the land earmarked for the industrial estates. Nor is it disputed that no steps have so far been taken to demolish those dykes, even though the local authorities have acknowledged their harmful impact on the aquatic environment and have undertaken to demolish them. Accordingly, it must be held that there has been a failure to fulfil obligations in this respect.

C   The aquaculture facilities

42 The Commission takes issue with the granting of authorisation by the Spanish authorities to a fishermen's association to farm clams in the middle of the marshes, as well as the projects for other aquaculture operations in the estuary.

43 The Spanish government emphasises the economic interest of this activity and contends that it has only a small impact on the ecological situation of the marshes.

44 In this connection, it should be stressed that the installation of aquaculture facilities, which not only reduce the surface area of the marshland and cause variations in the natural sedimentation processes there, but also modify the structure of the existing marsh bed, has the effect of destroying the particular vegetation of those areas, which is an important source of food for the birds.

45 As has already been observed, considerations relating to the economic problems caused by the decline in the industrial and fishery sectors in the region, which are, moreover, contradicted by the fact that other projects have been abandoned because they were not profitable, cannot justify a derogation from the protection requirements laid down in Art 4(4) of the Directive.

46 As the area affected by the activity in question is by no means negligible and the activity in question has caused a significant deterioration in the habitat and the quality of the living conditions of the birds in the middle of the Santoña marshes, it must be concluded that the complaint is well founded.

D   The tipping of solid waste

47 The Commission claims that the tipping of solid waste affects the currents produced by the interaction of the tides and the waters from the rivers and consequently causes a significant change in the physical and chemical parameters of the marshes.

48 The Spanish government explains that the problem was solved in 1988. It claims that measures were taken under the plan for the management of urban solid waste from the municipalities in the Santoña bay area. Only a small amount of illegal tipping took place until 1990.

49 It emerged during the hearing before the Court that authorised tipping of waste ceased in 1988, that is to say before the Commission delivered its reasoned opinion. The complaint must therefore be rejected as inadmissible.

E **The discharge of waste water**

50 The Commission claims that the discharge of untreated waste water, has had detrimental effects on the quality of the water in Santoña bay.

51 The Spanish government does not deny that untreated waste water from the municipalities in the Santoña bay area has been discharged into the Santoña marshes. However, it claims that the Directive does not contain any provision obliging Member States to equip themselves with systems for treating waste in order to preserve the quality of the water in a special protection area.

52 That argument must be rejected. The discharge of waste water containing dangerous toxic substances is highly detrimental to the ecological conditions in the Santoña marshes and has a significant effect on the quality of the water in the area.

53 In view of the fundamental importance of the quality of that water to the marshlands, the Kingdom of Spain is under a duty, where necessary, to provide systems for treating waste in order to prevent pollution of those habitats. The failure to fulfil obligations in this respect is therefore made out.

F **The in-filling works at Escalante and the activities of the Montehano quarry**

54 The Commission claims that the in-filling operations carried out on marshland by the municipality of Escalante, together with the exploitation of the quarry and the tipping of unused material into the marshes, have reduced the extent of the protected area.

55 The Spanish government observes that these allegations refer to facts that occurred before Spain joined the Community. The tipping of this material into the marshes was prohibited in 1986 and is therefore now illegal.

56 It must be noted that neither the time nor the extent of the contested operations at the edge of the marshland were clarified at the hearing before the court. It is consequently impossible to determine whether and to what extent in-filling works and tipping of material from the quarry in question into the marshland have taken place since 1986. However, it is not disputed, on the one hand, that the works carried out by the municipality of Escalante were completed in 1986 and no authorisation has been granted for any further work and, on the other, that the activities of the Montehano quarry are controlled and the tipping of dry matter into the marshes has been definitively prohibited. This complaint must therefore be rejected.

G **All the complaints under III**

57 It follows from the foregoing considerations that, as a result of the above mentioned actions, with the exception of those described in the allegations under III D and F, the Kingdom of Spain has failed to fulfil its obligations under Art 4(4) of the Directive by not taking appropriate steps to avoid pollution or deterioration of habitats in the Santoña marshes.

58 It must therefore be held that, by not classifying the Santoña marshes as a special protection area and by not taking appropriate steps to avoid pollution or deterioration of habitats in that area, contrary to the provisions of Art 4 of the Directive, the Kingdom of Spain has failed to fulfil its obligations under the Treaty.

DOMESTIC LAW

British law on wildlife protection and nature conservation is mainly found in the Wildlife and Countryside Act 1981 and the Conservation (Natural Habitats, etc) Regulations 1994 SI 1994/2716 both of which were responses to EC Directive 79/409 and 92/43 discussed above.[34] Important amendments to the former were made by the Countryside and Rights of Way Act 2000. The protection offered by these enactments falls into two main categories: measures protecting individual plants and animals by imposing criminal penalties upon those who interfere with particular species; and habitat designation schemes, particularly the system of National Nature Reserves (NNRs) and Sites of Special Scientific Interest (SSSIs). Although this section will focus exclusively upon these two categories of measure, it should be noted that there exists a host of legal provisions which protect wildlife indirectly. It has long been accepted that nature conservation requirements should be incorporated into general rural and farming policy. Under the Agriculture Act 1986 (s 17), ministers have a duty to seek a balance between the interests of agriculture, the economic and social needs of rural communities and the conservation of the countryside. A range of grants and incentives for environmentally friendly farming is currently available.[35] In addition there are numerous pieces of legislation relating to hunted species, such as game birds and wildfowl, which are aimed primarily at protecting hunting interests rather than the species themselves. The recent Wild Mammals (Protection) Act 1996 may be mentioned, although this is an animal welfare/cruelty provision, rather than a nature conservation measure.

The nature conservancy councils

Between 1949 and 1 April 1991 there was a single national body responsible for nature conservation matters in the UK, the Nature Conservancy Council (NCC).[36] From that date, under the EPA, Pt VII, the NCC was split into three bodies: an NCC England (called English Nature,[37] s 73 Countryside and Rights of Way Act 2000), a Countryside Council for Wales, combining the functions of the NCC and the Countryside Commission in

---

34 That is not to say that wildlife in the UK had no statutory protection prior to these enactments. The 1981 Act consolidated with amendments the Protection of Birds Acts 1954–67 and the Conservation of Wild Creatures and Wild Plants Act 1975. The provisions on habitat designation originally appeared in the National Parks and Access to the Countryside Act 1949.

35 Agriculture Act 1986, s 18 allows for the designation of Environmentally Sensitive Areas. Payments are available in return for the adoption of agreed agricultural practices. Twenty-two ESAs covering 1.1m hectares have been designated in England.

36 Originally named, Nature Conservancy.

37 For home page see www.english-nature.org.uk.

Wales, and an NCC Scotland.[38] The national NCCs are now the government's statutory advisers on all nature conservation issues, including giving advice on species and habitat protection. In particular, they are responsible for the selection and management of NNRs and for the designation and safeguarding of SSSIs. A Joint Nature Conservation Committee of the new bodies was established (s 128(4) of the EPA 1990) which assumes the role of the old NCC in giving effect to the UK's international responsibilities. It endeavours to ensure that uniform standards are used by the national bodies in key areas of activity, such as selecting the criteria for designating SSSIs.[39]

Species protection

The Wildlife and Countryside Act 1981 (WCA) reflects traditional public priorities by providing blanket protection for all wild birds. It is an offence (s 1(1)) to kill, injure or take any wild bird or to take, damage or destroy a nest while it is in use or being built or to destroy eggs. It is also an offence to possess a wild bird (dead or alive) or its eggs (s 1(2)), or to sell or to advertise for sale such birds (s 6). The Act lists rarer birds in Schedule 1 and those committing an offence against these species will be subject to a 'special' (heavier) penalty. Part 1 of the WCA was amended by the Countryside and Rights of Way Act 2000 to create new offences of reckless disturbance of birds and animals listed in Scheds 1 and 5 (see ss 1(5), 9(4A) of the WCA 1981, pp 715 and 721, below).

The Act qualifies the above by allowing certain wild bird species to be killed or taken but some methods of killing are prohibited (s 5). Game birds (defined in s 27) are not protected by the Act apart from the provisions of s 5 which outlaws certain methods of killing or capture. Pest species listed in Sched 2, Pt II may be killed or taken and their nests and eggs destroyed but only by the owner or occupier of land or an 'authorised person' (s 2(2)).

Section 4 lists various defences, such as killing an already injured bird. Acts which would otherwise be illegal will be exempt where they are 'an incidental result of a lawful operation and could not reasonably have been avoided' (s 4(2)(c)). Killing or injuring wild birds (other than those listed in Sched 1) is not an offence if the 'authorised person' can show that his action was necessary for one of three purposes set out in s 4(3):

(a) preserving public health or public or air safety;

(b) preventing the spread of disease;

(c) preventing serious damage to livestock, foodstuffs for livestock, crops, vegetables, fruit, growing timber, fisheries or inland waters.

As far as (c) is concerned, the authorised person must, in addition, show that there was no other satisfactory solution (s 4(4)) if he is not to commit an offence. Section 16 allows for exceptions from the criminal provisions of the Act if a licence has been obtained from the 'appropriate authority'.

38 Now Scottish Natural Heritage, combining the functions of NCC Scotland and the Countryside Commission for Scotland: the Natural Heritage (Scotland) Act 1991.
39 See further Bell and McGillivray, *Environmental Law*, 5th edn, 2000, London: Blackstone.

All wild birds are protected by the above provisions unless expressly excluded. Only the animals listed in Sched 5[40] (bats, reptiles, amphibians but only very rare mammals, fish and butterflies) are protected by the legislation. The offences, defences and exceptions covering these creatures are similar to those for wild birds.[41]

Wild plants are protected by s 13. It is an offence for anyone other than the owner, occupier or other authorised person to intentionally uproot any wild plant. In addition, it is an offence for anyone to intentionally pick, uproot or destroy any wild plant included in Sched 8 or to sell or advertise for sale any such plant. It would be a defence to show that the act was an incidental result of a lawful operation and could not reasonably have been avoided.

The provisions of the EC Habitats Directive 92/43 relating to the protection of species (animals and plants) (see p 636, above) are implemented by Pt III of the Conservation (Natural Habitats, etc) Regulations 1994. The basic effect of the Regulations is to extend the species protection regime set up by the WCA to the European protected species of plants and animals whose natural range includes Great Britain and which are listed in Annex IV(a) and IV(b) of the Habitats Directive.

Habitat protection

The United Kingdom is fortunate in having a large number of well-funded private charitable organisations able and willing to buy and manage land for its nature conservation value. Each county in England has a wildlife trust affiliated to the Royal Society for Nature Conservation whose task is primarily to acquire and manage nature reserves. On a national scale, organisations such as the Royal Society for the Protection of Birds, the Woodland Trust and the National Trust also acquire land which conforms to the respective remits. Once the land is purchased, these various organisations can exercise property rights to preserve its wildlife value, such as the law relating to trespass or interference with property.[42]

Alongside the efforts of the voluntary conservation organisations stands the system of habitat designation created by statute and administered by the appropriate nature conservation body. The two principal designations are Sites of Special Scientific Interest (SSSIs) and National Nature Reserves (NNRs).

Sites of special scientific interest (SSSIs)

SSSIs, of which there are over 6,400 in Great Britain covering approximately 8% of the area of England,[43] are intended to comprise a representative sample of British habitats aimed at maintaining the present diversity of wild animals and plants in Great Britain. As the name suggests, selection is made on scientific grounds in order to preserve the best

---

40 Schedules 5 and 8 are reviewed every five years by the Joint Nature Conservation Committee. Note, some species are protected by specific pieces of legislation: the Conservation of Seals Act 1970 and the Protection of Badgers Act 1992, see *Green and Others v DPP* (2000) 9(7) ELM on the meaning of 'badger set'.

41 Sections 9, 10, 11 and 16.

42 As can any private individual, of course.

43 English Nature home page: www.english-nature.org.uk.

examples of various habitat types. SSSIs may also be notified for their geological interest, the aim being to conserve sites viewed as essential for research and education. Section 28 of the WCA (now amended by the Countryside and Rights of Way Act 2000) gives English Nature a wide discretion to formulate criteria for designation and to apply that criteria in particular cases. The section states:

> Where the Nature Conservancy Council are of the opinion that any area of land is of special interest by reason of any of its flora, fauna or geological or physiographical features, it shall be the duty of the council to notify that fact:
>
> (a) to the local planning authority in whose area the land is situated;
>
> (b) to every owner or occupier of any of that land; and
>
> (c) to the Secretary of State.

Two points may be highlighted. Firstly, the list of SSSIs will be extended as new information about the importance of habitats becomes available. Similarly, if one SSSI is damaged or its scientific value is lost (see below), this may make the notification of new sites all the more essential. English Nature will denotify a site which has lost its scientific value (s 28(D)).

Secondly, s 28 refers to the *duty* of English Nature to notify sites, that is, English Nature would be acting illegally if it refused to designate a site for any reason outside s 28. The nature of the duty to notify (and confirm) a site as an SSSI was discussed in *R v Nature Conservancy Council ex p London Brick Company Limited* [1996] Env LR 1 (see p 700, below).

The boundaries of an SSSI are a matter for English Nature who may draw them wide enough to encompass land of lesser scientific interest if it forms part of the same environmental unit as the land which is of interest (see now s 28B). SSSIs cannot extend below the low water mark. This effectively excludes at least part of estuarial and coastal sites from protection.

When notifying the site as an SSSI (which has immediate interim effect, Wildlife and Countryside (Amendment) Act 1985) English Nature must identify the features which make the land of specific interest and must specify those operations which might damage those features. Such 'potentially damaging operations' were given a very broad interpretation in *Sweet v Secretary of State and Nature Conservancy Council* [1989] 1 JEL 245:

> ... cultivation, including ploughing, rotovating, harrowing and reseeding; growing, mowing or other methods of cutting vegetation; application of manure, fertilisers and lime; burning; the release into the site of any wild, feral or domestic animal, reptile, amphibian, bird, fish or invertebrate, or any plant or seed; the storage of materials; the use of materials; the use of vehicles or craft likely to damage or disturb features of interest.

The notification must also contain a statement of the Council's views about the management of the land, including its views about the positive measures necessary to conserve and enhance flora or fauna or the other features by reason of which the land is of special interest.

Two main changes to the SSSI regime were made by the 2000 Act. Firstly, once notified, English Nature can impose permanent restrictions upon operations which might damage SSSIs (s 28(E)), rather than the temporary four-month restriction which applied previously. The owner or occupier may seek permission from English Nature to carry out any such operations but can only do so if English Nature provides written consent (which may be for a limited period and/or subject to conditions) or the operation may be permitted to proceed under a management scheme or notice under ss 28(J) or 28(K). Owners or occupiers may appeal to the Secretary of State in accordance with s 28(F). It would be an offence without reasonable excuse to carry out a potentially damaging operation without the required consents. An unlimited fine can be imposed on indictment. Two specific defences are available: (a) that the operation was authorised by planning permission or (b) that it was carried out in an emergency.

Secondly, s 28(J) allows English Nature to formulate a management scheme for SSSIs, which would conserve and restore the features for which the land is of special interest. Owners and occupiers are given three months from notification to make representations or objections. English Nature then have nine months to decide whether the confirm the notification. Where it appears to English Nature that the owner or occupier of land is not giving effect to the provisions of a management scheme and as a result the features for which the land is of interest are not being restored, they may serve a management notice upon him, if they cannot secure his voluntary agreement to abide by the management scheme (s 28(K)). The notice will set a time table for compliance. If there is no compliance then English Nature is empowered to enter the land and carry out the work, recovering 'reasonably incurred expenses' from the owner or occupier. This is subject to a right of appeal to the Secretary of State (s 28(L)).

Powers of compulsory purchase appear in s 28(N) when English Nature is unable to conclude an agreement, on reasonable terms as to the management of the land. Such powers may also be used if the agreement is breached (s 28(N)).

The new regime represents a significant improvement on the previous scheme which was castigated by Lord Mustill as being 'toothless' and providing 'little more than a breathing space to the [then] NCC in which to apply moral pressure' (see *Southern Water Authority v Nature Conservancy Council* [1993] 5 JEL 109).

National nature reserves (NNRs)

English Nature has power under the National Parks and Access to the Countryside Act (NPA) 1949 to declare an area as an NNR provided it is expedient in the national interest to do so. Section 15 of the NPA 1949 defines an NNR as an area managed for study or research into flora, fauna or geological or physiographical interest, or for preserving such features which are of special interest.[44] In order to manage these sites, the NCCE must have control over them which it achieves either by buying the land, leasing it or entering into a nature reserve agreement with the owner under s 16 of the NPA 1949. The NCCE

---

44 Wildlife and Countryside Act 1981, s 35 allows English Nature to declare an NNR on land which is of national importance and is being managed by an approved body, see p 704, below.

has compulsory purchase powers if it cannot conclude an agreement with the owner or if such an agreement is breached (s 17). In addition to any nature reserve agreement, the NCCE may make bylaws for the protection of the reserve (s 20 of the NPA 1949). As at March 2000 there were 200 NNRs in England.[45]

Marine nature reserves

MNRs are the marine equivalents of NNRs and are provided for by s 36 of the WCA 1981. The basis for designation is the same as for NNRs and they may cover any area of land or water from the high tide mark to a line three miles from the baselines used for measuring the territorial sea.[46] The procedure for designation is also similar to that used for NNRs (Schedule 12) with a requirement for wide publicity. Once designated by the Secretary of State, the NCC is empowered to make bylaws within the limits set by s 37, subject to confirmation by the Secretary of State. Only two MNRs have so far been designated (off Skomer and Lundy).

Other habitat designation provisions

Three other provisions in the legislation ought to be noted. Section 3 of the WCA 1981 permits the Secretary of State to designate land as bird sanctuaries provided he has the consent of the owners or occupiers. Bylaws may then be made for the site, including limitations on access.

Section 21 of the National Parks and Access to the Countryside Act 1949 allows local authorities to designate and manage local nature reserves on the same basis as the NCC does for NNRs. The basis for designation is that the site is of local (rather than national) importance and local authorities are obliged to consult with the NCC. There are currently over 600 such sites in England.[47]

Finally, bearing in mind their importance for wildlife, the Secretary of State has now promulgated the Hedgerows Regulations 1997 SI 1997/1160 under powers granted by s 97 of the Environment Act 1995. The regulations are intended to protect important hedgerows in England and Wales by making it an offence to remove them except in prescribed cases.[48]

SPAs and SACs in the UK

The Birds Directive 79/409 and Habitats Directive 92/43 (discussed above) lay down specific objectives to be achieved in terms of habitat protection but leaves it to Member States to decide how these objectives are to be achieved in practice. Alongside the planning system, the UK has implemented its obligations under both Directives by using the SSSI designation scheme under the Wildlife and Countryside Act 1981.

---

45   English Nature website: www.english-nature.org.uk.

46   Territorial Sea Act 1987.

47   English Nature: www.english-nature.org.uk.

48   See Holder, J, 'Law and landscape: the legal constriction and protection of hedgerows' (1999) MLR 100.

Until the introduction of the new provisions concerning SSSIs by virtue of Sched 9 of the Countryside and Rights of Way Act 2000 (see p 685, below), it could have been argued that the UK was in breach of its EC obligations. Prior to reform, the protection offered by SSSIs only provided legal protection for a four-month period and so failed to satisfy the requirement for permanent protection in both the Birds and Habitats Directives. The new provision (see the new s 28 Wildlife and Countryside Act 1981, below p 685) imposes permanent restrictions upon operations that might damage an SSSI.

However, there remains a further potential problem. Despite *R v Secretary of State for Trade and Industry ex p Greenpeace (No 2)* [2000] Env LR 221 (see p 732, below) in which a declaration was obtained that the Habitats Directive 92/43 extends to the Continental Shelf (see Chapter 3, p 206, note 3), the Conservation (Natural Habitats etc) Regulations 1994 (see below p 709) only apply to the territorial sea (see s 2(5), pp 710–11, below). This appears to be inconsistent with the judgment. Moreover, SSSIs cannot extend beyond the low water mark, thus excluding significant sections of estuarial and coastal sites which ought to fall within the scope of the Directives. Since the UK has only two MNRs at present it does not appear that marine nature reserves are being used to remedy this significant omission.

WILDLIFE AND COUNTRYSIDE ACT 1981 (C 69)

[as amended by the Countryside and Rights of Way Act 2000]

Section 1 Protection of wild birds, their nests and eggs

(1) Subject to the provisions of this Part, if any person intentionally–

    (a) kills, injures or takes any wild bird;

    (b) takes, damages or destroys the nest of any wild bird while that nest is in use or being built; or

    (c) takes or destroys an egg of any wild bird,

he shall be guilty of an offence.

(2) Subject to the provisions of this Part, if any person has in his possession or control–

    (a) any live or dead wild bird or any part of, or anything derived from, such a bird; or

    (b) an egg of a wild bird or any part of such an egg,

he shall be guilty of an offence.

(3) A person shall not be guilty of an offence under subsection (2) if he shows that–

    (a) the bird or egg had not been killed or taken, or had been killed or taken otherwise than in contravention of the relevant provisions; or

    (b) the bird, egg or other thing in his possession or control had been sold (whether to him or any other person) otherwise than in contravention of those provisions,

and in this subsection 'the relevant provisions' means the provisions of this Part and of orders made under it and, in the case of a bird or other thing falling within subsection (2)(a), the provisions of the Protection of Birds Acts 1954 to 1967 and of orders made under those Acts.

(4) Any person convicted of an offence under sub-ss (1) or (2) in respect of–

    (a) a bird included in Schedule 1 or any part of, or anything derived from, such a bird;

(b) the nest of such a bird; or

(c) an egg of such a bird or any part of such an egg.

(5) Subject to the provisions of this Part, if any person intentionally or recklessly –

(a) disturbs any wild bird included in Schedule 1 while it is building a nest or is in, on or near a nest containing eggs or young; or

(b) disturbs dependent young of such a bird, he shall be guilty of an offence.

(6) In this section 'wild bird' does not include any bird which is shown to have been bred in captivity.

(7) Any reference in this Part to any bird included in Schedule 1 is a reference to any bird included in Part I and, during the close season for the bird in question, any bird included in Part II of that Schedule.

Section 2 Exceptions to s 1

(1) Subject to the provisions of this section, a person shall not be guilty of an offence under section 1 by reason of the killing or taking of a bird included in Part I of Schedule 2 outside the close season for that bird, or the injuring of such a bird outside that season in the course of an attempt to kill it.

(2) Subject to the provisions of this section, an authorised person shall not be guilty of an offence under section 1 by reason of–

(a) the killing or taking of a bird included in Part II of Schedule 2, or the injuring of such a bird in the course of an attempt to kill it;

(b) the taking, damaging or destruction of a nest of such a bird; or

(c) the taking or destruction of an egg of such a bird.

(3) Sub-sections (1) and (2) shall not apply in Scotland on Sundays or on Christmas Day; and sub-s (1) shall not apply on Sundays in any area of England and Wales which the Secretary of State may by order prescribe for the purposes of that sub-section.

(4) In this section and s 1 'close season' means–

(a) in the case of capercaillie and (except in Scotland) woodcock, the period in any year commencing with 1 February and ending with 30 September;

(b) in the case of snipe, the period in any year commencing with 1 February and ending with 11 August;

(c) in the case of wild duck and wild geese in or over any area below high-water mark of ordinary spring tides, the period in any year commencing with 21 February and ending with 31 August;

(d) in any other case, subject to the provisions of this Part, the period in any year commencing with 1 February and ending with 31 August.

(5) The Secretary of State may by order made with respect to the whole or any specified part of Great Britain vary the close season for any wild bird specified in the order.

(6) If it appears to the Secretary of State expedient that any wild birds included in Part II of Schedule 1 or Part I of Schedule 2 should be protected during any period outside the close season for those birds, he may by order made with respect to the whole or any specified part of Great Britain declare any period (which shall not in the case of any order exceed 14 days) as a period of special protection for those birds; and this section

and s 1 shall have effect as if any period of special protection declared under this subsection for any birds formed part of the close season for those birds.

(7) Before making an order under sub-s (6) the Secretary of State shall consult a person appearing to him to be a representative of persons interested in the shooting of birds of the kind proposed to be protected by the order.

Section 3 Areas of special protection

(1) The Secretary of State may by order make provision with respect to any area specified in the order providing for all or any of the following matters, that is to say–

   (a) that any person who, within that area or any part of it specified in the order, at any time or during any period so specified, intentionally–

   (i) kills, injures or takes any wild bird or any wild bird so specified;

   (ii) takes, damages or destroys the nest of such a bird while that nest is in use or being built;

   (iii) takes or destroys an egg of such a bird;

   (iv) disturbs such a bird while it is building a nest or is in, on or near a nest containing eggs or young; or

   (v) disturbs dependent young of such a bird,

   shall be guilty of an offence under this section;

   (b) that any person who, except as may be provided in the order, enters into that area or any part of it specified in the order at any time or during any period so specified shall be guilty of an offence under this section;

   (c) that where any offence under this Part, or any such offence under this Part as may be specified in the order, is committed within that area the offence shall be treated as falling within s 7(3A).

(2) An authorised person shall not by virtue of any such order be guilty of an offence by reason of–

   (a) the killing or taking of a bird included in Part II of Schedule 2, or the injuring of such a bird in the course of an attempt to kill it;

   (b) the taking, damaging or destruction of the nest of such a bird;

   (c) the taking or destruction of an egg of such a bird; or

   (d) the disturbance of such a bird or dependent young of such a bird.

(3) The making of any order under this section with respect to any area shall not affect the exercise by any person of any right vested in him, whether as owner, lessee or occupier of any land in that area or by virtue of a licence or agreement.

(4) Before making any order under this section the Secretary of State shall give particulars of the intended order either by notice in writing to every owner and every occupier of any land included in the area with respect to which the order is to be made or, where the giving of such a notice is in his opinion impracticable, by advertisement in a newspaper circulating in the [locality] in which that area is situated.

(5) The Secretary of State shall not make an order under this section unless–

   (a) all the owners and occupiers aforesaid have consented thereto;

(b) no objections thereto have been made by any of those owners or occupiers before the expiration of a period of three months from the date of the giving of the notice or the publication of the advertisement; or

(c) any such objections so made have been withdrawn.

Section 4 Exceptions to ss 1 and 3

(1) Nothing in s 1 or in any order made under s 3 shall make unlawful–

    (a) anything done in pursuance of a requirement by the Minister of Agriculture, Fisheries and Food or the Secretary of State under s 98 of the Agriculture Act 1947, or by the Secretary of State under s 39 of the Agriculture (Scotland) Act 1948;

    (b) anything done under, or in pursuance of an order made under, ss 21 or 22 of the Animal Health Act 1981; or

    (c) except in the case of a wild bird included in Sched 1 or the nest or egg of such a bird, anything done under, or in pursuance of an order made under, any other provision of the said Act of 1981.

(2) Notwithstanding anything in the provisions of s 1 or any order made under s 3, a person shall not be guilty of an offence by reason of–

    (a) the taking of any wild bird if he shows that the bird had been disabled otherwise than by his unlawful act and was taken solely for the purpose of tending it and releasing it when no longer disabled;

    (b) the killing of any wild bird if he shows that the bird had been so seriously disabled otherwise than by his unlawful act that there was no reasonable chance of its recovering; or

    (c) any act made unlawful by those provisions if he shows that the act was the incidental result of a lawful operation and could not reasonably have been avoided.

(3) Notwithstanding anything in the provisions of s 1 or any order made under s 3, an authorised person shall not be guilty of an offence by reason of the killing or injuring of any wild bird, other than a bird included in Sched 1, if he shows that his action was necessary for the purpose of–

    (a) preserving public health or public or air safety;

    (b) preventing the spread of disease; or

    (c) preventing serious damage to livestock, foodstuffs for livestock, crops, vegetables, fruit, growing timber[, fisheries or inland waters.

(4) An authorised person shall not be regarded as showing that any action of his was necessary for a purpose mentioned in sub-s (3)(c) unless he shows that as regards that purpose, there was no other satisfactory solution.

(5) An authorised person shall not be entitled to rely on the defence provided by sub-s (3)(c) as respects any action taken at any time for any purpose mentioned in that paragraph if it had become apparent, before that time, that that action would prove necessary for that purpose and either–

    (a) a licence under s 16 authorising that action had not been applied for by him as soon as reasonably practicable after that fact had become apparent; or

    (b) an application by him for such a licence had been determined.

(6) An authorised person shall not be entitled to rely on the defence provided by sub-s (3)(c) as respects any action taken at any time unless he notified the agriculture Minister as soon as reasonably practicable after that time that he had taken the action.

Section 5 Prohibition of certain methods of killing or taking wild birds

(1) Subject to the provisions of this Part, if any person–

   (a) sets in position any of the following arts, being an art which is of such a nature and is so placed as to be calculated to cause bodily injury to any wild bird coming into contact therewith, that is to say, any springe, trap, gin, snare, hook and line, any electrical device for killing, stunning or frightening or any poisonous, poisoned or stupefying substance;

   (b) uses for the purpose of killing or taking any wild bird any such art as aforesaid, whether or not of such a nature and so placed as aforesaid, or any net, baited board, bird-lime or substance of a like nature to bird-lime;

   (c) uses for the purpose of killing or taking any wild bird–

      (i) any bow or crossbow;

      (ii) any explosive other than ammunition for a firearm;

      (iii) any automatic or semi-automatic weapon;

      (iv) any shot-gun of which the barrel has an internal diameter at the muzzle of more than one and three-quarter inches;

      (v) any device for illuminating a target or any sighting device for night shooting;

      (vi) any form of artificial lighting or any mirror or other dazzling device;

      (vii) any gas or smoke not falling within paras (a) and (b); or

      (viii) any chemical wetting agent;

   (d) uses as a decoy, for the purpose of killing or taking any wild bird, any sound recording or any live bird or other animal whatever which is tethered, or which is secured by means of braces or other similar appliances, or which is blind, maimed or injured; ...

   (e) uses any mechanically propelled vehicle in immediate pursuit of a wild bird for the purpose of killing or taking that bird; or

   (f) knowingly causes or permits to be done an act which is mentioned in the foregoing provisions of this subsection and which is not lawful under sub-s (5),

   he shall be guilty of an offence and be liable to a special penalty.

(2) Subject to sub-s (3), the Secretary of State may by order, either generally or in relation to any kind of wild bird specified in the order, amend sub-s (1) by adding any method of killing or taking wild birds or by omitting any such method which is mentioned in that subsection.

(3) The power conferred by sub-s (2) shall not be exercisable, except for the purpose of complying with an international obligation, in relation to any method of killing or taking wild birds which involves the use of a firearm.

(4) In any proceedings under sub-s (1)(a) it shall be a defence to show that the art was set in position for the purpose of killing or taking, in the interests of public health, agriculture, forestry, fisheries or nature conservation, any wild animals which could be lawfully killed or taken by those means and that he took all reasonable precautions to prevent injury thereby to wild birds.

(4A) In any proceedings under sub-s (1)(f) relating to an act which is mentioned in sub-s (1)(a) it shall be a defence to show that the art was set in position for the purpose of killing or taking, in the interests of public health, agriculture, forestry, fisheries or nature conservation, any wild animals which could be lawfully killed or taken by those means and that he took or caused to be taken all reasonable precautions to prevent injury thereby to wild birds.

(5) Nothing in sub-s (1) shall make unlawful–

    (a) the use of a cage-trap or net by an authorised person for the purpose of taking a bird included in Part II of Sched 2;

    (b) the use of nets for the purpose of taking wild duck in a duck decoy which is shown to have been in use immediately before the passing of the Protection of Birds Act 1954; or

    (c) the use of a cage-trap or net for the purpose of taking any game bird if it is shown that the taking of the bird is solely for the purpose of breeding,

but nothing in this subsection shall make lawful the use of any net for taking birds in flight or the use for taking birds on the ground of any net which is projected or propelled otherwise than by hand.

Section 6 Sale etc of live or dead wild birds, eggs etc

(1) Subject to the provisions of this Part, if any person–

    (a) sells, offers or exposes for sale, or has in his possession or transports for the purpose of sale, any live wild bird other than a bird included in Part I of Sched 3, or an egg of a wild bird or any part of such an egg; or

    (b) publishes or causes to be published any advertisement likely to be understood as conveying that he buys or sells, or intends to buy or sell, any of those things, he shall be guilty of an offence.

(2) Subject to the provisions of this Part, if any person–

    (a) sells, offers or exposes for sale, or has in his possession or transports for the purpose of sale, any dead wild bird other than a bird included in Part II or III of Sched 3, or any part of, or anything derived from, such a wild bird; or

    (b) publishes or causes to be published any advertisement likely to be understood as conveying that he buys or sells, or intends to buy or sell, any of those things,

he shall be guilty of an offence.

(3) Subject to the provisions of this Part, if any person shows or causes or permits to be shown for the purposes of any competition or in any premises in which a competition is being held–

    (a) any live wild bird other than a bird included in Part I of Sched 3; or

    (b) any live bird one of whose parents was such a wild bird,

he shall be guilty of an offence.

(4) Any person convicted of an offence under this section in respect of–

    (a) a bird included in Sched 1 or any part of, or anything derived from, such a bird; or

    (b) an egg of such bird or any part of such an egg,

shall be liable to a special penalty.

(5) Any reference in this section to any bird included in Part I of Sched 3 is a reference to any bird included in that Part which was bred in captivity and has been ringed or marked in accordance with regulations made by the Secretary of State; and regulations so made may make different provision for different birds or different provisions of this section.

(6) Any reference in this section to any bird included in Part II or III of Sched 3 is a reference to any bird included in Part II and, during the period commencing with 1 September in any year and ending with 28 February of the following year, any bird included in Part III of that Schedule.

(7) The power of the Secretary of State to make regulations under sub-s (2) shall include power–

(a) to impose requirements as to the carrying out by a person registered in accordance with the regulations of any act which, apart from the registration, would constitute an offence under this section; and

(b) to provide that any contravention of the regulations shall constitute such an offence.

(8) Regulations under sub-s (2) shall secure that no person shall become or remain registered–

(a) within five years of his having been convicted of an offence under this Part for which a special penalty is provided; or

(b) within three years of his having been convicted of any other offence under this Part so far as it relates to the protection of birds or other animals or any offence involving their ill-treatment,

no account being taken for this purpose of a conviction which has become spent by virtue of the Rehabilitation of Offenders Act 1974.

(9) Any person authorised in writing by the Secretary of State may, at any reasonable time and (if required to do so) upon producing evidence that he is authorised, enter and inspect any premises where a registered person keeps any wild birds for the purpose of ascertaining whether an offence under this section is being, or has been, committed on those premises.

(10) Any person who intentionally obstructs a person acting in the exercise of the power conferred by sub-s (9) shall be guilty of an offence.

Section 9 Protection of certain wild animals

(1) Subject to the provisions of this Part, if any person intentionally kills, injures or takes any wild animal included in Sched 5, he shall be guilty of an offence.

(2) Subject to the provisions of this Part, if any person has in his possession or control any live or dead wild animal included in Sched 5 or any part of, or anything derived from, such an animal, he shall be guilty of an offence.

(3) A person shall not be guilty of an offence under sub-s (2) if he shows that–

(a) the animal had not been killed or taken, or had been killed or taken otherwise than in contravention of the relevant provisions; or

(b) the animal or other thing in his possession or control had been sold (whether to him or any other person) otherwise than in contravention of those provisions;

and in this subsection 'the relevant provisions' means the provisions of this Part and of the Conservation of Wild Creatures and Wild Plants Act 1975.

(4) Subject to the provisions of this Part, if any person intentionally or recklessly–

    (a) damages or destroys, or obstructs access to, any structure or place which any wild animal included in Sched 5 uses for shelter or protection; or

    (b) disturbs any such animal while it is occupying a structure or place which it uses for that purpose,

he shall be guilty of an offence.

4A Subject to the provisions of this Part, if any person intentionally or recklessly disturbs any wild animal included in Sched 5 as–

    (a) a dolphin or whale (*cetacea*), or

    (b) a basking shark (*cetorhinus maximus*),

he shall be guilty of an offence.

(5) Subject to the provisions of this Part, if any person–

    (a) sells, offers or exposes for sale, or has in his possession or transports for the purpose of sale, any live or dead wild animal included in Sched 5, or any part of, or anything derived from, such an animal; or

    (b) publishes or causes to be published any advertisement likely to be understood as conveying that he buys or sells, or intends to buy or sell, any of those things,

he shall be guilty of an offence.

(6) In any proceedings for an offence under sub-s (1), (2) or (5)(a), the animal in question shall be presumed to have been a wild animal unless the contrary is shown.

Note: The above section is as amended by Countryside and Rights of Way Act 2000 which added s 9(4A).

Section 10 Exceptions to s 9

(1) Nothing in s 9 shall make unlawful–

    (a) anything done in pursuance of a requirement by the Minister of Agriculture, Fisheries and Food or the Secretary of State under s 98 of the Agriculture Act 1947, or by the Secretary of State under s 39 of the Agriculture (Scotland) Act 1948; or

    (b) anything done under, or in pursuance of an order made under, the Animal Health Act 1981.

(2) Nothing in sub-s (4) of s 9 shall make unlawful anything done within a dwelling-house.

(3) Notwithstanding anything in s 9, a person shall not be guilty of an offence by reason of–

    (a) the taking of any such animal if he shows that the animal had been disabled otherwise than by his unlawful act and was taken solely for the purpose of tending it and releasing it when no longer disabled;

    (b) the killing of any such animal if he shows that the animal had been so seriously disabled otherwise than by his unlawful act that there was no reasonable chance of its recovering; or

(c) any act made unlawful by that section if he shows that the act was the incidental result of a lawful operation and could not reasonably have been avoided.

(4) Notwithstanding anything in s 9, an authorised person shall not be guilty of an offence by reason of the killing or injuring of a wild animal included in Sched 5 if he shows that his action was necessary for the purpose of preventing serious damage to livestock, foodstuffs for livestock, crops, vegetables, fruit, growing timber or any other form of property or to fisheries.

(5) A person shall not be entitled to rely on the defence provided by sub-s (2) or (3)(c) as respects anything done in relation to a bat otherwise than in the living area of a dwelling house unless he had notified the Nature Conservancy Council [for the area in which the house is situated or, as the case may be, the act is to take place] of the proposed action or operation and allowed them a reasonable time to advise him as to whether it should be carried out and, if so, the method to be used.

(6) An authorised person shall not be entitled to rely on the defence provided by sub-s (4) as respects any action taken at any time if it had become apparent, before that time, that that action would prove necessary for the purpose mentioned in that subsection and either–

(a) a licence under s 16 authorising that action had not been applied for as soon as reasonably practicable after that fact had become apparent; or

(b) an application for such a licence had been determined.

Section 11 Prohibition of certain methods of killing or taking wild animals

(1) Subject to the provisions of this Part, if any person–

(a) sets in position any self-locking snare which is of such a nature and so placed as to be calculated to cause bodily injury to any wild animal coming into contact therewith;

(b) uses for the purpose of killing or taking any wild animal any self-locking snare, whether or not of such a nature or so placed as aforesaid, any bow or crossbow or any explosive other than ammunition for a firearm; ...

(c) uses as a decoy, for the purpose of killing or taking any wild animal, any live mammal or bird whatever; or

(d) knowingly causes or permits to be done an act which is mentioned in the foregoing provisions of this section,

he shall be guilty of an offence.

(2) Subject to the provisions of this Part, if any person–

(a) sets in position any of the following arts, being an art which is of such a nature and so placed as to be calculated to cause bodily injury to any wild animal included in Sched 6 which comes into contact therewith, that is to say, any trap or snare, any electrical device for killing or stunning or any poisonous, poisoned or stupefying substance;

(b) uses for the purpose of killing or taking any such wild animal any such art as aforesaid, whether or not of such a nature and so placed as aforesaid, or any net;

(c) uses for the purpose of killing or taking any such wild animal–

(i) any automatic or semi-automatic weapon;

(ii) any device for illuminating a target or sighting device for night shooting;

(iii) any form of artificial light or any mirror or other dazzling device; or

(iv) any gas or smoke not falling within paras (a) and (b);

(d) uses as a decoy, for the purpose of killing or taking any such wild animal, any sound recording; ...

(e) uses any mechanically propelled vehicle in immediate pursuit of any such wild animal for the purpose of driving, killing or taking that animal; or

(f) knowingly causes or permits to be done an act which is mentioned in the foregoing provisions of this subsection,

he shall be guilty of an offence.

(3) Subject to the provisions of this Part, if any person–

(a) sets in position [or knowingly causes or permits to be set in position] any snare which is of such a nature and so placed as to be calculated to cause bodily injury to any wild animal coming into contact therewith; and

(b) while the snare remains in position fails, without reasonable excuse, to inspect it, or cause it to be inspected, at least once every day,

he shall be guilty of an offence.

(4) The Secretary of State may, for the purpose of complying with an international obligation, by order, either generally or in relation to any kind of wild animal specified in the order, amend sub-s (1) or (2) by adding any method of killing or taking wild animals or by omitting any such method as is mentioned in that sub-section.

(5) In any proceedings for an offence under sub-ss (1)(b) or (c) or (2)(b), (c), (d) or (e) [and in any proceedings for an offence under sub-ss (1)(d) or (2)(f) relating to an act which is mentioned in any of those paragraphs], the animal in question shall be presumed to have been a wild animal unless the contrary is shown.

(6) In any proceedings for an offence under sub-s (2)(a) it shall be a defence to show that the art was set in position by the accused for the purpose of killing or taking, in the interests of public health, agriculture, forestry, fisheries or nature conservation, any wild animals which could be lawfully killed or taken by those means and that he took all reasonable precautions to prevent injury thereby to any wild animals included in Sched 6.

(7) In any proceedings for an offence under sub-s (2)(f) relating to an act which is mentioned in sub-s (2)(a) it shall be a defence to show that the art was set in position for the purpose of killing or taking, in the interests of public health, agriculture, forestry, fisheries or nature conservation, any wild animals which could be lawfully killed or taken by those means and that he took or caused to be taken all reasonable precautions to prevent injury thereby to any wild animals included in Sched 6.

Section 12 Protection of certain mammals

Schedule 7, which amends the law relating to the protection of certain mammals, shall have effect.

Section 13 Protection of wild plants

(1) Subject to the provisions of this Part, if any person–

(a) intentionally picks, uproots or destroys any wild plant included in Sched 8; or

    (b) not being an authorised person, intentionally uproots any wild plant not included in that Schedule,

he shall be guilty of an offence.

(2) Subject to the provisions of this Part, if any person–

    (a) sells, offers or exposes for sale, or has in his possession or transports for the purpose of sale, any live or dead wild plant included in Sched 8, or any part of, or anything derived from, such a plant; or

    (b) publishes or causes to be published any advertisement likely to be understood as conveying that he buys or sells, or intends to buy or sell, any of those things,

he shall be guilty of an offence.

(3) Notwithstanding anything in sub-s (1), a person shall not be guilty of an offence by reason of any act made unlawful by that subsection if he shows that the act was an incidental result of a lawful operation and could not reasonably have been avoided.

(4) In any proceedings for an offence under sub-s (2)(a), the plant in question shall be presumed to have been a wild plant unless the contrary is shown.

Section 16 Power to grant licences

(1) Sections 1, 5, 6(3), 7 and 8 and orders under s 3 do not apply to anything done:

    (a) for scientific, research or educational purposes;

    (b) for the purpose of ringing or marking, or examining any ring or mark on, wild birds;

    (c) for the purpose of conserving wild birds;

    (ca) for the purposes of the re-population of an area with, or the re-introduction into an area of, wild birds, including any breeding necessary for those purposes;

    (cb) for the purpose of conserving flora or fauna;

    (d) for the purpose of protecting any collection of wild birds;

    (e) for the purposes of falconry or aviculture;

    (f) for the purposes of any public exhibition or competition;

    (g) for the purposes of taxidermy;

    (h) for the purpose of photography;

    (i) for the purposes of preserving public health or public or air safety;

    (j) for the purpose of preventing the spread of disease; or

    (k) for the purposes of preventing serious damage to livestock, foodstuffs for livestock, crops, vegetables, fruit, growing timber, fisheries or inland waters,

if it is done under and in accordance with the terms of a licence granted by the appropriate authority.

(1A) The appropriate authority–

    (a) shall not grant a licence for any purpose mentioned in sub-s (1) unless it is satisfied that, as regards that purpose, there is no other satisfactory solution; and

    (b) shall not grant a licence for any purpose mentioned in paras (e) to (h) of that subsection otherwise than on a selective basis and in respect of a small number of birds.

(2) Section 1 and orders under s 3 do not apply to anything done for the purpose of providing food for human consumption in relation to–

   (a) a gannet on the island of Sula Sgeir; or

   (b) a gull's egg or, at any time before 15 April in any year, a lapwing's egg, if it is done under and in accordance with the terms of a licence granted by the appropriate authority.

(3) Sections 9(1), (2), (4) and (4A), 11(1) and (2) and 13(1) do not apply to anything done–

   (a) for scientific or educational purposes;

   (b) for the purpose of ringing or marking, or examining any ring or mark on, wild animals;

   (c) for the purpose of conserving wild animals or wild plants or introducing them to particular areas;

   (d) for the purpose of protecting any zoological or botanical collection;

   (e) for the purpose of photography;

   (f) for the purpose of preserving public health or public safety;

   (g) for the purpose of preventing the spread of disease; or

   (h) for the purpose of preventing serious damage to livestock, foodstuffs for livestock, crops, vegetables, fruit, growing timber or any other form of property or to fisheries,

   if it is done under and in accordance with the terms of a licence granted by the appropriate authority.

(4) The following provisions, namely–

   (a) section 6(1) and (2);

   (b) sections 9(5) and 13(2); and

   (c) section 14,

   do not apply to anything done under and in accordance with the terms of a licence granted by the appropriate authority.

(5) Subject to sub-ss (5A) and (6), a licence under the foregoing provisions of this section–

   (a) may be, to any degree, general or specific;

   (b) may be granted either to persons of a class or to a particular person;

   (c) may be subject to compliance with any specified conditions;

   (d) may be modified or revoked at any time by the appropriate authority; and

   (e) subject to para (d), shall be valid for the period stated in the licence,

   and the appropriate authority may charge therefor such reasonable sum (if any) as they may determine.

(5A) A licence under sub-s (1) which authorises any action in respect of wild birds–

   (a) shall specify the species of wild birds in respect of which, the circumstances in which, and the conditions subject to which, the action may be taken;

   (b) shall specify the methods, means or arrangements which are authorised or required for the taking of the action; and

   (c) subject to sub-s (5)(d), shall be valid for the period, not exceeding two years, stated in the licence.

(6) A licence under sub-s (2) or (3) which authorises any person to kill wild birds or wild animals—

    (a) shall specify the area within which, and the methods by which the wild birds or wild animals may be killed; and

    (b) subject to sub-s (5)(d), shall be valid for the period, not exceeding two years, stated in the licence.

(7) It shall be a defence in proceedings for an offence under s 8(b) of the Protection of Animals Act 1911 or s 7(b) of the Protection of Animals (Scotland) Act 1912 (which restrict the placing on land of poison and poisonous substances) to show that–

    (a) the act alleged to constitute the offence was done under and in accordance with the terms of a licence issued under sub-s (1) or (3); and

    (b) any conditions specified in the licence were complied with.

(8) For the purposes of a licence granted under the foregoing provisions of this section, the definition of a class of persons may be framed by reference to any circumstances whatever including, in particular, their being authorised by any other person.

(9) In this section 'the appropriate authority' means–

    (a) in the case of a licence under any of paras (a) to (cb) of sub-s (1), either the Secretary of State after consultation with whichever one of the advisory bodies he considers is best able to advise him as to whether the licence should be granted, or the relevant Nature Conservancy Council;

    (b) in the case of a licence under any of paras (d) to (g) of sub-s (1), sub-s (2) or para (a) or (b) of sub-s (4), the Secretary of State after such consultation as aforesaid;

    (c) in the case of a licence under para (h) of sub-s (1) or any of paras (a) to (e) of subsection (3), the relevant Nature Conservancy Council;

    (d) in the case of a licence under para (i), (j) or (k) of sub-s (1) or para (f), (g) or (h) of sub-s (3) or a licence under para (c) of sub-s (4) which authorises anything to be done in relation to fish or shellfish, the agriculture Minister; and

    (e) in the case of any other licence under para (c) of sub-s (4), the Secretary of State.

(9A) In this section 're-population' and 're-introduction', in relation to wild birds, have the same meaning as in the Directive of the Council of the European Communities dated 2 April 1979 (79/409/EEC) on the conservation of wild birds.

(10) The Agricultural Minister–

    (a) shall from time to time consult with each of the Nature Conservancy Councils as to the exercise in the area of that Council of his functions under this section; and

    (b) shall not grant a licence of any description unless he has been advised by the relevant Nature Conservancy Council as to the circumstances in which, in their opinion, licences of that description should be granted.

(11) For the purposes of this section a reference to a relevant Nature Conservancy Council is a reference to the Nature Conservancy Council for the area in which it is proposed to carry on the activity requiring a licence.

Section 21 Penalties, forfeitures etc

(1) Subject to sub-s (5), a person guilty of an offence under ss 1, 3, 5, 6, 7 or 8 shall be liable on summary conviction–

(a) in a case where this Part or any order made under it provides that he shall be liable to a special penalty, to a fine not exceeding level 5 on the standard scale;

(b) in any other case, to a fine not exceeding level 3 on the standard scale.

(2) Subject to sub-s (5), a person guilty of an offence under s 9 or 11(1) or (2) shall be liable on summary conviction to a fine not exceeding level 5 on the standard scale.

(3) Subject to sub-s (5), a person guilty of an offence under s 11(3), 13 or 17 shall be liable on summary conviction to a fine not exceeding level 4 on the standard scale.

(4) A person guilty of an offence under s 14 shall be liable–

(a) on summary conviction, to a fine not exceeding the statutory maximum;

(b) conviction on indictment, to a fine.

(5) Where an offence to which sub-s (1) applies was committed in respect of more than one bird, nest, egg, other animal, plant or other thing, the maximum fine which may be imposed under that subsection shall be determined as if the person convicted had been convicted of a separate offence in respect of each bird, nest, egg, animal, plant or thing.

(6) The court by which any person is convicted of an offence under this Part–

(a) shall order the forfeiture of any bird, nest, egg, other animal, plant or other thing in respect of which the offence was committed; and

(b) may order the forfeiture of any vehicle, animal, weapon or other thing which was used to commit the offence and, in the case of an offence under s 14, any animal or plant which is of the same kind as that in respect of which the offence was committed and was found in his possession.

(7) Any offence under this Part shall, for the purpose of conferring jurisdiction, be deemed to have been committed in any place where the offender is found or to which he is first brought after the commission of the offence.

Section 27 Interpretation of Pt I

(1) In this Part, unless the context otherwise requires–

'advertisement' includes a catalogue, a circular and a price list;

'advisory body' has the meaning given by s 23;

'agriculture Minister' means the Minister of Agriculture, Fisheries and Food or the Secretary of State;

'authorised person' means–

(a) the owner or occupier, or any person authorised by the owner or occupier, of the land on which the action authorised is taken;

(b) any person authorised in writing by the local authority for the area within which the action authorised is taken;

(c) as respects anything done in relation to wild birds, any person authorised in writing by any of the following bodies, that is to say, [any of the Nature Conservancy Councils, ... a district board for a fishery district within the meaning of the Salmon Fisheries (Scotland) Act 1862 or a local fisheries committee constituted under the Sea Fisheries Regulation Act 1966];

(d) any person authorised in writing by the Environment Agency, a water undertakers or a sewerage undertaker;

so, however, that the authorisation of any person for the purposes of this definition shall not confer any right of entry upon any land;

'automatic weapon' and 'semi-automatic weapon' do not include any weapon the magazine of which is incapable of holding more than two rounds;

'aviculture' means the breeding and rearing of birds in captivity;

'destroy', in relation to an egg, includes doing anything to the egg which is calculated to prevent it from hatching, and 'destruction' shall be construed accordingly;

'domestic duck' means any domestic form of duck;

'domestic goose' means any domestic form of goose;

'firearm' has the same meaning as in the Firearms Act 1968;

'game bird' means any pheasant, partridge, grouse (or moor game), black (or heath) game or ptarmigan;

'inland waters' means–

(a) inland waters within the meaning of the Water Resources Act 1991;

(b) any waters not falling within para (a) above which are within the seaward limits of the territorial sea;

(c) controlled waters within the meaning of Part II of the Control of Pollution Act 1974 other than ground waters as defined in s 30A(1)(d) of that Act.

'livestock' includes any animal which is kept–

(a) for the provision of food, wool, skins or fur;

(b) for the purpose of its use in the carrying on of any agricultural activity; or

(c) for the provision or improvement of shooting or fishing;

'local authority' means–

(a) in relation to England ... , a county, district or London borough council ...;

(aa) in relation to Wales, a county council or county borough council;

(b) in relation to Scotland, a council constituted under s 2 of the Local Government etc (Scotland) Act 1994;

'occupier', in relation to any land other than the foreshore, includes any person having any right of hunting, shooting, fishing or taking game or fish;

'pick', in relation to a plant, means gather or pluck any part of the plant without uprooting it;

'poultry' means domestic fowls, geese, ducks, guinea-fowls, pigeons and quails, and turkeys;

'sale' includes hire, barter and exchange and cognate expressions shall be construed accordingly;

'uproot', in relation to a plant, means dig up or otherwise remove the plant from the land on which it is growing;

'vehicle' includes aircraft, hovercraft and boat;

'water authority', in relation to Scotland, has the same meaning as in the Water (Scotland) Act 1980;

'wild animal' means any animal (other than a bird) which is or (before it was killed or taken) was living wild;

'wild bird' means any bird of a kind which is ordinarily resident in or is a visitor to Great Britain in a wild state but does not include poultry or, except in ss 5 and 16, any game bird;

'wild plant' means any plant which is or (before it was picked, uprooted or destroyed) was growing wild and is of a kind which ordinarily grows in Great Britain in a wild state.

'Wildlife inspector' has the meaning given by section 19(ZA)(1).

(2) A bird shall not be treated as bred in captivity for the purposes of this Part unless its parents were lawfully in captivity when the egg was laid.

(3) Any reference in this Part to an animal of any kind includes, unless the context otherwise requires, a reference to an egg, larva, pupa, or other immature stage of an animal of that kind.

(3A) Any reference in this Part to the Nature Conservancy Councils is a reference to the Nature Conservancy Council for England, Scottish Natural Heritage and the Countryside Council for Wales.

(4) This Part shall apply to the Isles of Scilly as if the Isles were a county and as if the Council of the Isles were a county council.

(5) This Part extends to the territorial waters adjacent to Great Britain, and for the purposes of this Part any part of Great Britain which is bounded by territorial waters shall be taken to include the territorial waters adjacent to that part.

Section 28 Sites of special scientific interest

(1) Where the Nature Conservancy Council are of the opinion that any area of land is of special interest by reason of any of its flora, fauna, or geological or physiographical features, it shall be the duty of the Council to notify that fact–

(a) to the local planning authority in whose area the land is situated;

(b) to every owner and occupier of any of that land; and

(c) to the Secretary of State.

(2) The Council shall also publish a notification of that fact in at least one local newspaper circulating in the area in which the land is situated.

(3) A notification under sub-s (1) shall specify the time (not being less than three months from the date of the giving of the notification) within which, and the manner in which, representations or objections with respect to it may be made; and the Council shall consider any representation or objection duly made.

(4) A notification under sub-s (1)(b) shall also specify–

(a) the flora, fauna, or geological or physiographical features by reason of which the land is of special interest; and

(b) any operations appearing to the Council to be likely to damage that flora or fauna or those features,

and shall contain a statement of the Council's views about the management of the land (including any views the Council may have about the conservation and enhancement of that flora or fauna or those features).

(5) Where a notification under sub-s (1) has been given, the Council may within the period of nine months beginning with the date on which the notification was served on the Secretary of State either–

(a) give notice to the persons mentioned in sub-s (1) withdrawing the notification; or

(b) give notice to those persons confirming the notification (with or without modifications).

(6) A notification shall cease to have effect–

(a) on the giving of notice of its withdrawal under sub-s (5)(a) to any of the persons mentioned in sub-s (1); or

(b) if not withdrawn or confirmed by notice under sub-s (5) within the period of nine months referred to there, at the end of that period.

(7) The Council's power under sub-s (5)(b) to confirm a notification under sub-s (1) with modifications shall not be exercised so as to add to the operations specified in the notification or extend the area to which it applies.

(8) As from the time when there is served on the owner or occupier of any land which has been notified under sub-s (1)(b) a notice under sub-s (5)(b) confirming the notification with modifications, the notification shall have effect in its modified form in relation to so much (if any) of that land as remains subject to it.

(9) A notification under sub-s (1)(b) of land in England and Wales shall be a local land charge.

(10) For the purposes of this section and ss 28A to 28D, 'local planning authority', in relation to land within the Broads, includes the Broads Authority.

Variation of notification under s 28.

A(1) At any time after notice has been given under s 28(5)(b) confirming a notification (with or without modifications), the Nature Conservancy Council may by notice vary the matters specified or stated in the confirmed notification (whether by adding to them, changing them, or removing matter from them).

(2) The area of land cannot be varied under this section.

(3) The Council shall give notice setting out the variation to–

(a) the local planning authority in whose area the land is situated,

(b) every owner and occupier of any of the land who in the opinion of the Council may be affected by the variation; and

(c) the Secretary of State,

and after service of a notice under para (b) the notification under s 28(1)(b) shall have effect in its varied form.

(4) Section 28(3) shall apply to such a notice as it applies to a notification under s 28(1).

(5) Where a notice under sub-s (3) has been given, the Council may within the period of nine months beginning with the date the last of the owners and occupiers referred to in sub-s (3)(b) was served with the notice either–

(a) give notice to the persons mentioned in sub-s (3) withdrawing the notice; or

(b) give notice to them confirming the notice (with or without modifications).

(6) A notice under sub-s (3) shall cease to have effect–

   (a) on the giving of notice of its withdrawal under sub-s (5)(a) to any of the persons mentioned in sub-s (3); or

   (b) if not withdrawn or confirmed by notice under sub-s (5) within the period of nine months referred to in that sub-section, at the end of that period.

(7) As from the time when there is served on the owner or occupier of any land a notice under sub-s (5)(b) confirming a notice of variation with modifications, the notification under s 28(1)(b) shall have effect as so varied.

(8) A local land charge existing by virtue of s 28(9) shall be varied in accordance with a notice under sub-s (3) or (5)(b).

Notification of additional land

B(1) Where the Nature Conservancy Council are of the opinion that if land adjacent to a site of special scientific interest ('the extra land') were combined with the site of special scientific interest ('the SSSI'), the combined area of land would be of special interest by reason of any of its flora, fauna, or geological or physiographical features, the Council may decide to notify that fact.

(2) If they do so decide, the persons whom they must notify are–

   (a) the local planning authority in whose area the extra land is situated;

   (b) every owner and occupier of any of that extra land; and

   (c) the Secretary of State.

(3) No such notification may be given until after notice has been given under s 28(5)(b) confirming (with or without modifications) the notification under s 28(1) relating to the SSSI.

(4) Sub-sections (2) and (3) of s 28 shall apply for the purposes of this section as they apply for the purposes of that section.

(5) A notification under sub-s (2)(b) shall also specify–

   (a) the area of land constituting the SSSI;

   (b) what (as at the date of the notification under sub-s (2)(b)) is specified or contained in the notification under s 28(1)(b) relating to the SSSI by virtue of s 28(4); and

   (c) the reasons why the Council is of the opinion referred to in sub-s (1).

(6) In addition, the notification under sub-s (2)(b) shall include a statement–

   (a) saying whether or not anything among the matters specified in the notification by virtue of sub-s (5)(c) is particularly relevant to the extra land; and

   (b) if any such thing is of particular relevance, specifying which.

(7) Sub-sections (5) to (7) of s 28 apply in relation to a notification under sub-s (2) of this section as they apply in relation to a notification under sub-s (1) of that section, as if references to 'sub-s (1)' in s 28(5) to (7) were references to sub-s (2) of this section.

(8) As from the time when a notification under sub-s (2)(b) is served on the owner or occupier of any land, the notification under s 28(1)(b) shall have effect as if it included the notification under sub-s (2)(b).

(9) As from the time when there is served on the owner or occupier of any land which has been notified under sub-s (2)(b) a notice under s 28(5)(b) (as applied by sub-s (7) of this section) confirming the notification under sub-s (2)(b) with modifications, the notification under s 28(1)(b) (as extended by virtue of sub-s (8) of this section) shall have effect in its modified form.

(10) A local land charge existing by virtue of s 28(9) shall be varied in accordance with a notification under sub-s (2) or under s 28(5)(b) as applied by sub-s (7) of this section.

Enlargement of SSSI

C(1) Where the Nature Conservancy Council are of the opinion that any area of land which includes, but also extends beyond, a site of special scientific interest ('the SSSI') is of special interest by reason of any of its flora, fauna, or geological or physiographical features, the Council may decide to notify that fact.

(2) If they do so decide, the persons whom they must notify are–

    (a) the local planning authority in whose area the land (including the SSSI) is situated;

    (b) every owner and occupier of any of that land (including the SSSI); and

    (c) the Secretary of State.

(3) Sub-ss (2) to (8) of s 28 apply to a notification under sub-s (2) of this section as they apply to a notification under sub-s (1) of that section, as if references to 'sub-s (1)' and 'sub-s (1)(b)' in s 28(2) to (8) were references to sub-s (2) and sub-s (2)(b) of this section respectively.

(4) No notification may be given under sub-s (2) until after notice has been given under s 28(5)(b) (or s 28(5)(b) as applied by sub-s (3)) confirming (with or without modifications) the notification under s 28(1) (or sub-s (2)) relating to the SSSI.

(5) As from the time when a notification under sub-s (2) is served on the owner or occupier of any land included in the SSSI, the notification in relation to that land which had effect immediately before the service of the notification under sub-s (2) shall cease to have effect.

(6) A notification under sub-s (2)(b) of land in England and Wales shall be a local land charge; and, to the extent that any such land was the subject of a local land charge by virtue of s 28(9), that local land charge shall be discharged.

(7) A notice under section 28E(1)(a) and a consent under s 28E(3)(a) given before a notification under sub-s (2)(b) continue to have effect.

(8) The enlargement of a site of special scientific interest under this section does not affect anything done under s 28J to 28L.

(9) Any reference to–

    (a) a notification under s 28(1) (or any of its paragraphs) shall be construed as including the corresponding notification under sub-s (2);

    (b) a notification under s 28(5)(b) shall be construed as including a notification under that provision as applied by sub-s (3); and

(c) a local land charge existing by virtue of s 28(9) shall be treated as including one existing by virtue of sub-s (6).

Denotification

D(1) Where the Nature Conservancy Council are of the opinion that all or part of a site of special scientific interest is no longer of special interest by reason of any of the matters mentioned in s 28(1), they may decide to notify that fact.

(2) If they do so decide, the persons whom they must notify are–

(a) the local planning authority in whose area the land which the Council no longer consider to be of special interest is situated;

(b) every owner and occupier of any of that land;

(c) the Secretary of State;

(d) the Environment Agency; and

(e) every relevant undertaker (within the meaning of s 4(1) of the Water Industry Act 1991) and every internal drainage board (within the meaning of s 61C(1) of the Land Drainage Act 1991) whose works, operations or activities may affect the land.

(3) The Council shall also publish a notification of that fact in at least one local newspaper circulating in the area in which the land referred to in sub-s (2)(a) is situated.

(4) Section 28(3) shall apply to a notification under sub-s (2) or (3) as it applies to a notification under s 28(1).

(5) Where a notification under sub-s (2) has been given, the Council may within the period of nine months beginning with the date on which the notification was served on the Secretary of State either–

(a) give notice to the persons mentioned in sub-s (2) withdrawing the notification, or

(b) give notice to those persons confirming the notification, or confirming it in relation to an area of land specified in the notice which is smaller than that specified in the notification under sub-s (2),

but if they do neither the notification shall cease to have effect.

(6) A notification under sub-s (2) shall have effect in relation to any land as from the time a notice under sub-s (5)(b) is served on its owner or occupier, and from that time a notification under s 28(1)(b) in relation to that land shall cease to have effect.

(7) A local land charge existing by virtue of s 28(9) shall be discharged in relation to land which is the subject of a notice under sub-s (5)(b).

Duties in relation to sites of special scientific interest

E(1) The owner or occupier of any land included in a site of special scientific interest shall not while the notification under s 28(1)(b) remains in force carry out, or cause or permit to be carried out, on that land any operation specified in the notification unless–

(a) one of them has, after service of the notification, given the Nature Conservancy Council notice of a proposal to carry out the operation specifying its nature and the land on which it is proposed to carry it out; and

(b) one of the conditions specified in sub-s (3) is fulfilled.

(2) Sub-section (1) does not apply to an owner or occupier being an authority to which s 28G applies acting in the exercise of its functions.

(3) The conditions are–

    (a) that the operation is carried out with the Council's written consent;

    (b) that the operation is carried out in accordance with the terms of an agreement under s 16 of the 1949 Act or s 15 of the 1968 Act;

    (c) that the operation is carried out in accordance with a management scheme under s 28J or a management notice under s 28K.

(4) A consent under sub-s (3)(a) may be given–

    (a) subject to conditions; and

    (b) for a limited period,

as specified in the consent.

(5) If the Council do not consent, they shall give notice saying so to the person who gave the notice under sub-s (1).

(6) The Council may, by notice given to every owner and occupier of any of the land included in the site of special scientific interest, or the part of it to which the consent relates–

    (a) withdraw the consent; or

    (b) modify it (or further modify it) in any way.

(7) The following–

    (a a consent under sub-s (3)(a) granting consent subject to conditions or for a limited period; and

    (b) a notice under sub-s (5) or (6),

must include a notice of the Council's reasons for imposing the conditions, for the limitation of the period, for refusing consent, or for withdrawing or modifying the consent, and also a notice of the matters set out in sub-s (8).

(8) The matters referred to in sub-s (7) are–

    (a) the rights of appeal under s 28F;

    (b) the effect of sub-s (9); and

    (c) in the case of a notice under sub-s (6), the effect of s 28M.

(9) A withdrawal or modification of a consent is not to take effect until–

    (a) the expiry of the period for appealing against it; or

    (b) if an appeal is brought, its withdrawal or final determination.

(10) The Council shall have power to enforce the provisions of this section.

Appeals in connection with consents

F(1) The following persons–

    (a) an owner or occupier who has been refused a consent under s 28E(3)(a);

    (b) an owner or occupier who has been granted such a consent but who is aggrieved by conditions attached to it, or by the fact that it is for a limited period, or by the length of that period;

    (c) an owner or occupier who is aggrieved by the modification of a consent;

    (d) an owner or occupier who is aggrieved by the withdrawal of a consent,

may by notice appeal to the Secretary of State against the relevant decision.

(2) If the Nature Conservancy Council neither give consent nor refuse it within the period of four months beginning with the date on which the notice referred to in s 28E(1)(a) was sent, the person who gave that notice may for the purposes of sub-s (1) treat the Council as having refused consent (and his appeal is to be determined on that basis).

(3) Notice of an appeal must reach the Secretary of State–

    (a) except in a case falling within sub-s (2), within the period of two months beginning with the date of the notice giving consent or the notice under s 28E(5) or (6); or

    (b) in a case falling within sub-s (2), within the period of two months beginning immediately after the expiry of the four-month period referred to there,

or, in either case, within such longer period as is agreed in writing between the Council and the appellant.

(4) Before determining an appeal, the Secretary of State may, if he thinks fit–

    (a) cause the appeal to take, or continue in, the form of a hearing (which may be held wholly or partly in private if the appellant so requests and the person hearing the appeal agrees); or

    (b) cause a local inquiry to be held,

and he must act as mentioned in para (a) or (b) if either party to the appeal asks to be heard in connection with the appeal.

(5) On determining an appeal against a decision, the Secretary of State may–

    (a) affirm the decision;

    (b) where the decision was a refusal of consent, direct the Council to give consent;

    (c) where the decision was as to the terms of a consent (whether the original or a modified one), quash all or any of those terms;

    (d) where the decision was a withdrawal or modification of consent, quash the decision,

and where he exercises any of the powers in paras (b), (c) or (d) he may give directions to the Council as to the terms on which they are to give consent.

(6) The Secretary of State may by regulations made by statutory instrument make provision about appeals under this section, and in particular about–

    (a) notices of appeal and supporting documentation required; and

    (b) how appeals are to be brought and considered,

and any such regulations may make different provision for different cases and circumstances.

(7) A statutory instrument containing regulations under sub-s (6) shall be subject to annulment in pursuance of a resolution of either House of Parliament.

(8) The Secretary of State may appoint any person to exercise on his behalf, with or without payment, his function of determining an appeal under this section or any matter involved in such an appeal.

(9) Schedule 10A shall have effect with respect to appointments under sub-s (8).

(10) Sub-sections (2) to (5) of s 250 of the Local Government Act 1972 (local inquiries: evidence and costs) apply in relation to hearings or local inquiries under this section as they apply in relation to local inquiries under that section, but as if the reference there–

(a) to the person appointed to hold the inquiry were a reference to the Secretary of State or to the person appointed to conduct the hearing or hold the inquiry under this section; and

(b) to the Minister causing an inquiry to be held were to the Secretary of State.

(11) Section 322A of the Town and Country Planning Act 1990 (orders as to costs where no hearing or inquiry takes place) applies in relation to a hearing or local inquiry under this section as it applies in relation to a hearing or local inquiry referred to in that section.

Statutory undertakers, etc: general duty

G(1) An authority to which this section applies (referred to in this section and in ss 28H and 28I as 'a section 28G authority') shall have the duty set out in sub-s (2) in exercising its functions so far as their exercise is likely to affect the flora, fauna or geological or physiographical features by reason of which a site of special scientific interest is of special interest.

(2) The duty is to take reasonable steps, consistent with the proper exercise of the authority's functions, to further the conservation and enhancement of the flora, fauna or geological or physiographical features by reason of which the site is of special scientific interest.

(3) The following are section 28G authorities–

(a) a Minister of the Crown (within the meaning of the Ministers of the Crown Act 1975) or a Government department;

(b) the National Assembly for Wales;

(c) a local authority;

(d) a person holding an office–

(i) under the Crown;

(ii) created or continued in existence by a public general Act of Parliament; or

(iii) the remuneration in respect of which is paid out of money provided by Parliament;

(e) a statutory undertaker (meaning the persons referred to in s 262(1), (3) and (6) of the Town and Country Planning Act 1990); and

(f) any other public body of any description.

Statutory undertakers, etc: duty in relation to carrying out operations

H(1) A section 28G authority shall give notice to the Nature Conservancy Council before carrying out, in the exercise of its functions, operations likely to damage any of the flora, fauna or geological or physiographical features by reason of which a site of special scientific interest is of special interest.

(2) Sub-section (1) applies even if the operations would not take place on land included in a site of special scientific interest.

(3) In response to the notice referred to in sub-s (1), the Council may send a notice–

(a) saying that they do not assent to the proposed operations; or

(b) assenting to them (with or without conditions),

but if they do not send a notice under para (b) within the period of 28 days beginning with the date of the notice under sub-s (1) they shall be treated as having declined to assent.

(4) If the Council do not assent, or if the authority proposes to carry out the operations otherwise than in accordance with the terms of the Council's assent, the authority–

    (a) shall not carry out the operations unless the condition set out in sub-s (5) is satisfied; and

    (b) shall comply with the requirements set out in sub-s (6) when carrying them out.

(5) The condition is that the authority has, after the expiry of the period of 28 days beginning with the date of the notice under sub-s (1), notified the Council of–

    (a) the date on which it proposes to start the operations (which must be after the expiry of the period of 28 days beginning with the date of the notification under this paragraph); and

    (b) how (if at all) it has taken account of any written advice it received from the Council, before the date of the notification under this paragraph, in response to the notice under sub-s (1).

(6) The requirements are–

    (a) that the authority carry out the operations in such a way as to give rise to as little damage as is reasonably practicable in all the circumstances to the flora, fauna or geological or physiographical features by reason of which the site is of special interest (taking account, in particular, of any such advice as is referred to in sub-s (5)(b)); and

    (b) that the authority restore the site to its former condition, so far as is reasonably practicable, if any such damage does occur.

Statutory undertakers, etc: duty in relation to authorising operations

I(1) This section applies where the permission of a section 28G authority is needed before operations may be carried out.

(2) Before permitting the carrying out of operations likely to damage any of the flora, fauna or geological or physiographical features by reason of which a site of special scientific interest is of special interest, a section 28G authority shall give notice of the proposed operations to the Nature Conservancy Council.

(3) Sub-section (2) applies even if the operations would not take place on land included in a site of special scientific interest.

(4) The authority shall wait until the expiry of the period of 28 days beginning with the date of the notice under sub-s (2) before deciding whether to give its permission, unless the Nature Conservancy Council have notified the authority that it need not wait until then.

(5) The authority shall take any advice received from the Council into account–

    (a) in deciding whether or not to permit the proposed operations; and

    (b) if it does decide to do so, in deciding what (if any) conditions are to be attached to the permission.

(6) If the Council advise against permitting the operations, or advise that certain conditions should be attached, but the section 28G authority does not follow that advice, the authority–

   (a) shall give notice of the permission, and of its terms, to the Council, the notice to include a statement of how (if at all) the authority has taken account of the Council's advice; and

   (b) shall not grant a permission which would allow the operations to start before the end of the period of 21 days beginning with the date of that notice.

(7) In this section 'permission', in relation to any operations, includes authorisation, consent, and any other type of permission (and 'permit' and 'permitting' are to be construed accordingly).

Management schemes

J(1) The Nature Conservancy Council may formulate a management scheme for all or part of a site of special scientific interest.

(2) A management scheme is a scheme for–

   (a) conserving the flora, fauna, or geological or physiographical features by reason of which the land (or the part of it to which the scheme relates) is of special interest; or

   (b) restoring them; or

   (c) both.

(3) The Council shall serve notice of a proposed management scheme on every owner and occupier of any of the land (or the part of it to which the scheme would relate); but it may be served on them only after they have been consulted about the proposed management scheme.

(4) The notice may be served with the notification referred to in s 28(1)(b) or afterwards.

(5) The owners and occupiers upon whom the notice must be served (referred to in this section as 'the relevant owners and occupiers') are–

   (a) if it is served with the notification under s 28(1)(b), or later but before the notification referred to in s 28(5)(b), the owners and occupiers referred to in s 28(1)(b);

   (b) if it is served with the notification under s 28(5)(b) or later, the owners and occupiers of such of the land as remains subject to the notification.

(6) The notice of a proposed management scheme must include a copy of the proposed scheme.

(7) The notice must specify the time (not being less than three months from the date of the giving of the notice) within which, and the manner in which, representations or objections with respect to the proposed management scheme may be made; and the Council shall consider any representation or objection duly made.

(8) Where a notice under sub-s (3) has been given, the Council may within the period of nine months beginning with the date on which the notice was served on the last of the relevant owners and occupiers either–

   (a) give notice to the relevant owners and occupiers withdrawing the notice; or

(b) give notice to them confirming the management scheme (with or without modifications),

and if notice under para (b) is given, the management scheme shall have effect from the time the notice is served on all of the relevant owners or occupiers.

(9) A notice under sub-s (3) shall cease to have effect–

(a) on the giving of a notice of withdrawal under sub-s (8)(a) to any of the relevant owners and occupiers; or

(b) if not withdrawn or confirmed by notice under sub-s (8) within the period of nine months referred to there, at the end of that period.

(10) The Council's power under sub-s (8)(b) to confirm a management scheme with modifications shall not be exercised so as to make complying with it more onerous.

(11) The Council may at any time cancel or propose the modification of a management scheme.

(12) In relation to–

(a) the cancellation of a management scheme, sub-ss (3) to (5) apply; and

(b) a proposal to modify a management scheme, sub-ss (3) to (10) apply,

as they apply in relation to a proposal for a management scheme.

(13) An agreement under s 16 of the 1949 Act or s 15 of the 1968 Act relating to a site of special scientific interest may provide for any matter for which a management scheme relating to that site provides (or could provide).

Management notices

K(1) Where it appears to the Nature Conservancy Council that–

(a) an owner or occupier of land is not giving effect to a provision of a management scheme; and

(b) as a result any flora, fauna or geological or physiographical features by reason of which the land is of special interest are being inadequately conserved or restored,

they may if they think fit serve a notice on him (a 'management notice').

(2) They may not serve a management notice unless they are satisfied that they are unable to conclude, on reasonable terms, an agreement with the owner or occupier as to the management of the land in accordance with the management scheme.

(3) A management notice is a notice requiring the owner or occupier to–

(a) carry out such work on the land; and

(b) do such other things with respect to it,

as are specified in the notice, and to do so before the dates or within the periods so specified.

(4) The work and other things specified in the notice must appear to the Council to be measures which it is reasonable to require in order to ensure that the land is managed in accordance with the management scheme.

(5) The management notice must explain the effect of sub-s (7) and (8) and of ss 28L and 28M(2)–(4).

(6) A copy of the management notice must be served on every other owner and occupier of the land.

(7) If any of the work or other things required by a management notice have not been done within the period or by the date specified in it, the Council may–

    (a) enter the land, and any other land, and carry out the work, or do the other things; and

    (b) recover from the owner or occupier upon whom the notice was served any expenses reasonably incurred by them in carrying out the work or doing the other things.

(8) If an appeal is brought against the management notice, and upon the final determination of the appeal the notice is affirmed (with or without modifications), sub-s (7) applies as if the references there to the management notice were to the notice as affirmed.

Appeals against management notices

L(1) A person who is served with a management notice may appeal against its requirements to the Secretary of State; and a management notice does not take effect until–

    (a) the expiry of the period for appealing against it; or

    (b) if an appeal is brought, its withdrawal or final determination.

(2) An appeal may be on the ground that some other owner or occupier of the land should take all or any of the measures specified in the management notice, or should pay all or part of their cost.

(3) Where the grounds of appeal are, or include, that mentioned in sub-s (2), the appellant must serve a copy of his notice of appeal on each other person referred to.

(4) Before determining an appeal, the Secretary of State may, if he thinks fit–

    (a) cause the appeal to take, or continue in, the form of a hearing (which may be held wholly or partly in private if the appellant so requests and the person hearing the appeal agrees); or

    (b) cause a local inquiry to be held,

and he must act as mentioned in para (a) or (b) if either party to the appeal (or, in a case falling within sub-s (2), any of the other persons mentioned there) asks to be heard in connection with the appeal.

(5) On determining the appeal, the Secretary of State may quash or affirm the management notice; and if he affirms it, he may do so either in its original form or with such modifications as he thinks fit.

(6) In particular, on determining an appeal whose grounds are, or include, those mentioned in sub-s (2), the Secretary of State may–

    (a) vary the management notice so as to impose its requirements (or some of them) upon any such other person as is referred to in the grounds; or

    (b) determine that a payment is to be made by any such other person to the appellant.

(7) In exercising his powers under sub-s (6), the Secretary of State must take into account, as between the appellant and any of the other people referred to in sub-s (2)–

(a) their relative interests in the land (considering both the nature of the interests and the rights and obligations arising under or by virtue of them);

(b) their relative responsibility for the state of the land which gives rise to the requirements of the management notice; and

(c) the relative degree of benefit to be derived from carrying out the requirements of the management notice.

(8) The Secretary of State may by regulations made by statutory instrument make provision about appeals under this section, and in particular about–

(a) the period within which and the manner in which appeals are to be brought; and

(b) the manner in which they are to be considered,

and any such regulations may make different provision for different cases or circumstances.

(9) A statutory instrument containing regulations under sub-s (8) shall be subject to annulment in pursuance of a resolution of either House of Parliament.

(10) The Secretary of State may appoint any person to exercise on his behalf, with or without payment, his function of determining an appeal under this section or any matter involved in such an appeal.

(11) Schedule 10A shall have effect with respect to appointments under sub-s (10).

(12) Sub-sections (2) to (5) of s 250 of the Local Government Act 1972 (local inquiries: evidence and costs) apply in relation to hearings or local inquiries under this section as they apply in relation to local inquiries under that section, but as if the reference there–

(a) to the person appointed to hold the inquiry were a reference to the Secretary of State or to the person appointed to conduct the hearing or hold the inquiry under this section; and

(b) to the Minister causing an inquiry to be held were to the Secretary of State.

(13) Section 322A of the Town and Country Planning Act 1990 (orders as to costs where no hearing or inquiry takes place) applies in relation to a hearing or local inquiry under this section as it applies in relation to a hearing or local inquiry referred to in that section.

Payments

M(1) Where the Council, under s 28E(6), modify or withdraw a consent, they shall make a payment to any owner or occupier of the land who suffers loss because of the modification or withdrawal.

(2) The Council may, if they think fit, make one or more payments to any owner or occupier of land in relation to which a management scheme under s 28J is in force.

(3) The amount of a payment under this section is to be determined by the Council in accordance with guidance given and published by the Ministers.

(4) Section 50(3) applies to the determination of the amount of payments under this section as it applies to the determination of the amount of payments under that section.

Compulsory purchase

N(1) The Nature Conservancy Council may in circumstances set out in sub-s (2) acquire compulsorily all or any part of a site of special scientific interest.

(2) The circumstances are–

(a) that the Council are satisfied that they are unable to conclude, on reasonable terms, an agreement with the owner or occupier as to the management of the land; or

(b) that the Council have entered into such an agreement, but they are satisfied that it has been breached in such a way that the land is not being managed satisfactorily.

(3) A dispute about whether or not there has been a breach of the agreement for the purposes of sub-s (2)(b) is to be determined by an arbitrator appointed by the Lord Chancellor.

(4) Where the Council have acquired land compulsorily under this section, they may–

(a) manage it themselves; or

(b) dispose of it, or of any interest in it, on terms designed to secure that the land is managed satisfactorily.

(5) Section 103 of the 1949 Act (general provisions as to acquisition of land) applies for the purposes of this section as it applies for the purposes of that Act.

Offences

P(1) A person who, without reasonable excuse, contravenes s 28E(1) is guilty of an offence and is liable on summary conviction to a fine not exceeding £20,000 or on conviction on indictment to a fine.

(2) A s 28G authority which, in the exercise of its functions, carries out an operation which damages any of the flora, fauna or geological or physiographical features by reason of which a site of special scientific interest is of special interest–

(a) without first complying with s 28H(1); or

(b) (if it has complied with s 28H(1)) without first complying with s 28H(4)(a),

is, unless there was a reasonable excuse for carrying out the operation without complying, guilty of an offence and is liable on summary conviction to a fine not exceeding £20,000 or on conviction on indictment to a fine.

(3) A s 28G authority acting in the exercise of its functions which, having complied with s 28H(1), fails without reasonable excuse to comply with s 28H(4)(b) is guilty of an offence and is liable on summary conviction to a fine not exceeding £20,000 or on conviction on indictment to a fine.

(4) For the purposes of sub-ss (1), (2) and (3), it is a reasonable excuse in any event for a person to carry out an operation (or to fail to comply with a requirement to send a notice about it) if–

(a) subject to sub-s (5), the operation in question was authorised by a planning permission granted on an application under Part III of the Town and Country Planning Act 1990 or permitted by a section 28G authority which has acted in accordance with s 28I; or

(b) the operation in question was an emergency operation particulars of which (including details of the emergency) were notified to the Nature Conservancy Council as soon as practicable after the commencement of the operation.

(5) If an operation needs both a planning permission and the permission of a s 28G authority, sub-s (4)(a) does not provide reasonable excuse unless both have been obtained.

(6) A person (other than a s 28G authority acting in the exercise of its functions) who without reasonable excuse–

    (a) intentionally or recklessly destroys or damages any of the flora, fauna, or geological or physiographical features by reason of which land is of special interest, or intentionally or recklessly disturbs any of those fauna; and

    (b) knew that what he destroyed, damaged or disturbed was within a site of special scientific interest,

is guilty of an offence and is liable on summary conviction to a fine not exceeding £20,000 or on conviction on indictment to a fine.

(7) It is a reasonable excuse in any event for a person to do what is mentioned in sub-s (6) if–

    (a) para (a) or (b) of sub-s (4) is satisfied in relation to what was done (reading references there to an operation as references to the destruction, damage or disturbance referred to in sub-s (6)); and

    (b) where appropriate, sub-s (5) is also satisfied, reading the reference there to an operation in the same way.

(8) A person who without reasonable excuse fails to comply with a requirement of a management notice is guilty of an offence and is liable on summary conviction to a fine not exceeding the statutory maximum or on conviction on indictment to a fine.

(9) In determining the amount of any fine to be imposed on a person convicted of an offence under this section, the court shall in particular have regard to any financial benefit which has accrued or appears likely to accrue to him in consequence of the offence.

(10) Proceedings in England and Wales for an offence under this section shall not, without the consent of the Director of Public Prosecutions, be taken by a person other than the Council.

(11) In this section, 'a section 28G authority' means an authority to which s 28G applies.

Change of owner or occupier

Q(1) This section applies where the owner of land included in a site of special scientific interest–

    (a) disposes of any interest of his in the land; or

    (b) becomes aware that it is occupied by an additional or a different occupier.

(2) If this section applies, the owner shall send a notice to the Nature Conservancy Council before the end of the period of 28 days beginning with the date on which he disposed of the interest or became aware of the change in occupation.

(3) The notice is to specify the land concerned and–

    (a) in a sub-s (1)(a) case, the date on which the owner disposed of the interest in the land, and the name and address of the person to whom he disposed of the interest; or

(b) in a sub-s (1)(b) case, the date on which the change of occupation took place (or, if the owner does not know the exact date, an indication of when to the best of the owner's knowledge it took place), and, as far as the owner knows them, the name and address of the additional or different occupier.

(4) A person who fails without reasonable excuse to comply with the requirements of this section is guilty of an offence and is liable on summary conviction to a fine not exceeding level 1 on the standard scale.

(5) For the purposes of sub-s (1), an owner 'disposes of' an interest in land if he disposes of it by way of sale, exchange or lease, or by way of the creation of any easement, right or privilege, or in any other way except by way of mortgage.

Bylaws

R(1) The Nature Conservancy Council may make bylaws for the protection of a site of special scientific interest.

(2) The following provisions of the 1949 Act apply in relation to bylaws under this section as they apply in relation to bylaws under s 20 of that Act–

(a) sub-ss (2) and (3) of s 20 (reading references there to nature reserves as references to sites of special scientific interest); and

(b) ss 106 and 107.

Note: The current version of s 28 was inserted by Sched 9 to the Countryside and Rights of Way Act 2000.

R v Nature Conservancy Council ex p London Brick Property Ltd [1996] JPL 227

May J: This case concerns the attempted conservation of a number of scarce species of water beetle at a clay pit, known as Star Pit, near the applicants' Dogsthorpe Brickworks, Peterborough, Northamptonshire. The Nature Conservancy Council ('English Nature') have powers and duties under the Wildlife and Countryside Act 1981 (as amended). It is accepted that the applicants, London Brick Property Limited, have a sufficient interest for the purpose of these proceedings for judicial review which has been prejudiced by the facts which I shall shortly state.

Pill J initially refused leave to move on 1 March 1994 because the then evidence did not sufficiently establish the applicant's interest. Potts J granted leave on 13 May 1994 upon a renewed and amended application ...

The parties are agreed that there are two outstanding issues. It now being accepted by English Nature that the applicants had demonstrated a sufficient interest and prejudice to sustain this application, the first agreed issue is this: Did English Nature, in resolving to confirm its notification of Star Pit as a site of special scientific interest, misdirect itself by failing to have regard to considerations fundamentally material to its decision whether or not to confirm the notification? The second issue is agreed to be: Did English Nature, in resolving to confirm the notification, act perversely as nobody in its position, properly informing itself of the relevant material, would have acted? The applicants contend that the answer to each of these questions should be 'yes'. The respondents contend that the answers should be 'no'.

The applicants' essential submissions on issue 1 are that English Nature misdirected itself in two ways; first, that it failed to address, fairly and afresh, in the light of the applicants' objections, the question whether the site in fact remained a site of special scientific interest when pumping had ceased and the water levels were rising and were likely to rise further. The applicants had challenged the basis of notification in March 1993 upon grounds which are not the concern of this court, but pumping had ceased just before the original notification and the contention is that a fundamental reassessment was necessary in the changed circumstances to determine if the interest which pertained in March still pertained in November. The lists which existed of species which were relevant to the notification essentially ante-date the cessation of pumping. It is submitted that Mr Idle and Miss Pugsley must have been quite unable to make any sensible judgment about whether the special interest still existed in the change of circumstances.

The second contention is that English Nature failed to have proper regard to whether, and if so, how, the conditions necessary for the continuance of special interest were to be maintained, failing which the interest would predictably come to an end. English Nature, as is now conceded, had no power under s 28, short of a compulsory purchase order, to compel the applicants to resume the pumping which was necessary to maintain the artificial conditions necessary for the survival of the water beetles. This could only be achieved by a management agreement. Such an agreement was against the applicants' interest. They were not likely to enter into such an agreement and did not do so when they were subsequently invited to. It is submitted English Nature did not properly consider before confirming the notification whether or how such an agreement could be achieved.

English Nature submit on the first of these two points that they did sufficiently consider for the purpose of confirmation the continued existence of the special interest. They knew that pumping had ceased but, first, the applicants did not contend under this ground of objection that the interest had ceased only that in time the pit would become typical of its environment and an inland freshwater body. Secondly, the water level had only risen slightly. Thirdly, they had received and considered Dr Drake's report on the applicants' objection which addressed the matter, and whilst accepting that the current aquatic interest was likely to diminish if the water continued to rise, provided sufficient material and advice for English Nature properly to be able to conclude that the special interest remained at the date of confirmation. Fourthly, Mr Idle and Miss Pugsley had viewed the site on 16 November 1993, shortly before confirmation, and were able to see what they reported about water levels.

In my judgment, this first contention fails. I consider that English Nature both had and considered material from which it was open to them to conclude that the special interest still existed at the date of the confirmation.

English Nature's submission on the second point starts with the argument that they had a duty under s 28 of the 1981 Act to confirm the notification once they concluded that the site was of special interest, that is, that the duty under sub-s (1) persists as a duty under sub-s (4)(a). I reject that stark contention, which does not, in my view, accord with the language or sense of the sub-sections. I agree with Mr Lindblom that it is a discretion which has to be exercised in accordance with what the Master of the Rolls, Lord Green, said in the Wednesbury case, *Associated Provincial Picture Houses v Wednesbury Corporation* [1948] I KB 223; [1947] 2 All ER 680.

In reaching the conclusion that I have just expressed, I take into account the form of this legislation, in particular s 28, before it was amended in 1985.

Having said, however, that I reject the stark contention, it is nevertheless necessary to consider the policy of the legislation to determine what the matters are which the section requires to be taken into consideration. It is, I think, plain that the first and most important consideration is the existence, or otherwise, of the special interest. If such an interest does exist, that in itself will be a strong reason for confirmation. I agree with Mr Lindblom to the extent that another consideration will be to have regard to the future conservation of the interest, but I do not agree with his further submission which in effect requires that future conservation should be assured, or perhaps he would say 'reasonably assured', before English Nature could properly proceed to confirmation.

In his affidavit in these proceedings, Lord Cranbrook, the Chairman English Nature, says this: 'It must always be remembered that the Council's statutory duty under s 28(1) of the 1981 Act is to notify when members *are of opinion that any area of land is of special interest by reason of any of its flora, fauna, or geographical or physiographical features* (my emphasis). There must be special interest at notification and, in practice, at confirmation. If there is, we have a duty to notify, notwithstanding fears about, or even threats to, the maintenance of the interest in future. If we are satisfied of special interest at the time confirmation is considered, we only withhold confirmation if we can see a certainty that such interest will soon be eliminated by some unavoidable cause. In the present case, management of water level by pumping is a straightforward process.'

Here, Lord Cranbrook is, in my view, recognising a duty to notify with which Mr Lindblom does not, I think, quarrel, and a policy to confirm (a) if the special interest exists at confirmation and (b) unless the continued existence of the special interest is doomed. As a policy, in my judgment, this is both reasonable and in conformity with the legislation which I have sought to set out. Further, in my judgment, the policy was in fact applied in this case.

Lord Cranbrook said, at an earlier point in his affidavit:

> I chaired the meeting of the Council on 23 November 1993. English Nature's Director dealing with SSSIs, Mr Idle, was in attendance, and had viewed the site a week previously. He reported his visit to Council, and told us that water on the Site was generally very shallow and he was satisfied that the nature conservation interest had not been materially affected by changes in water level.
>
> After discussing the submission Council considered that the objection was not made out, that the Site was of special scientific interest, and that notification should be confirmed, with no change of boundary or change in the list of potentially damaging operations.

In addition to this the meeting had before it the report from the meeting of 1 September 1993 and papers which included Dr Drake's September report. The September meeting with the applicants had considered management and its costs. The report for the meeting recognised that some management costs for pumping would be necessary in the future to retain the special interest. A management agreement was not in place, nor had one been specifically asked for, but it was not in my view unreasonable nor a failure to have regard to a relevant matter, to apply a policy which identified the site and gave such powers of persuasion as Lord Mustill recognised, within the limit of this toothless section, in the hope that the applicants would co-operate with the conservation of the special interest.

Accordingly, my answer to both limbs of the first issue is 'no'. In resolving to confirm its notification of a site of special scientific interest, English Nature did not misdirect itself by failing to have regard to considerations fundamentally material to its decision whether or not to confirm the notification.

I move to the second issue. The applicants' essential arguments on issue 2 are that it was irrational or perverse to confirm the notification, first, when the maintenance of the conditions for the survival of the water beetle probably could not be achieved, that is, for the reasons advanced in support of issue 1; secondly, because they confirmed the inclusion in the list of operations under s 28(4) (that is, operations which the applicants were by sub-s (5) restricted from performing on pain of a criminal sanction). The very operation, that is, drainage, which was necessary to maintain the conditions necessary for survival of the water beetles. I have already found against the applicants on issue 1and I proceed to consider the second limb of this submission.

It is superficially attractive to say that, since drainage in the form of pumping was necessary for the continuance of the special interest, to place a restriction on drainage was irrational. But drainage which, for example, wholly drained the pit so that it was dry would plainly be likely to damage the water beetles, I imagine, to extinction. Thus drainage was an operation which was capable of coming within sub-s 4. Mr Lindblom objects that to include drainage and changing the water levels, unqualified by a provision such as to maintain the water level at such and such a level, was nevertheless irrational because it imposed a restriction on the very thing which the water beetles needed. I am unpersuaded by this submission. Unlimited drainage was likely to damage the beetles. Sub-section (6) enables English Nature to consent to controlled drainage. There was, in my view, nothing irrational in a notification of drainage and changing water levels in the terms in which they were notified, thereby achieving such measure of control as the toothless section affords over drainage. I accordingly answer issue 2 'no'. In resolving to confirm the notification, English Nature did not act perversely and as nobody in its position properly informed of relevant material would have acted. For these reasons, the application fails.

[Sections 29 and 30 were repealed by Sched 9 to the Countryside and Rights of Way Act 2000. The Schedule inserted the current version of s 31(1).]

Section 31

(1) Where–

  (a) the operation in respect of which a person is convicted of an offence under s 28P(1), (2) or (3) has destroyed or damaged any of the flora, fauna or geological or physiographical features by reason of which a site of special scientific interest is of special interest; or

  (b) a person is convicted of an offence under s 28P(6),

  the court by which he is convicted, in addition to dealing with him in any other way, may make an order requiring him to carry out, within such period as may be specified in the order, such operations (whether on land included in the site of special scientific interest or not) as may be so specified for the purpose of restoring the site of special scientific interest to its former condition.

(2) An order under this section made on conviction on indictment shall be treated for the purposes of ss 30 and 42(1) and (2) of the Criminal Appeal Act 1968 (effect of appeals on orders for the restitution of property) as an order for the restitution of property; and where by reason of the quashing by the Court of Appeal of a person's conviction any such order does not take effect, and on appeal to the House of Lords the conviction is restored by that House, the House may make any order under this section which could be made on his conviction by the court which convicted him.

(3) In the case of an order under this section made by a magistrates' court the period specified in the order shall not begin to run–

(a) in any case until the expiration of the period for the time being prescribed by law for the giving of notice of appeal against a decision of a magistrates' court;

(b) where notice of appeal is given within the period so prescribed, until determination of the appeal.

(4) At any time before an order under this section has been complied with or fully complied with, the court by which it was made may, on the application of the person against whom it was made, discharge or vary the order if it appears to the court that a change in circumstances has made compliance or full compliance with the order impracticable or unnecessary.

(5) If, within the period specified in an order under this section, the person against whom it was made fails, without reasonable excuse, to comply with it, he shall be liable on summary conviction–

(a) to a fine not exceeding level 5 on the standard scale; and

(b) in the case of a continuing offence, to a further fine not exceeding 100 for each day during which the offence continues after conviction.

(6) If, within the period specified in an order under this section, any operations specified in the order have not been carried out, the Nature Conservancy Council may enter the land and carry out those operations and recover from the person against whom the order was made any expenses reasonably incurred by them in doing so.

(7) In the application of this section to Scotland–

(a) sub-ss (2) and (3) shall not apply; and

(b) for the purposes of any appeal or review, an order under this section is a sentence.

Section 35 National nature reserves

(1) Where the Nature Conservancy Council are satisfied that any land which–

(a) is being managed as a nature reserve under an agreement entered into with the Council;

(b) is held by the Council and is being managed by them as a nature reserve; or

(c) is held by an approved body and is being managed by that body as a nature reserve, is of national importance, they may declare that land to be a national nature reserve.

(2) A declaration by the Council that any land is a national nature reserve shall be conclusive of the matters declared; and sub-ss (4) and (5) of s 19 of the 1949 Act shall apply in relation to any such declaration as they apply in relation to a declaration under that section.

(3) On the application of the approved body concerned, the Council may, as respects any land which is declared to be a national nature reserve under sub-s (1)(c), make bylaws for the protection of the reserve.

(4) Sub-sections (2) and (3) of s 20 and s 106 of the 1949 Act shall apply in relation to bylaws under this section as they apply in relation to bylaws under the said s 20.

(5) In this section–

'approved body' means a body approved by the Council for the purposes of this section;

'nature reserve' has the same meaning as in Part III of the 1949 Act.

Section 36 Marine nature reserves

(1) Where, in the case of any land covered (continuously or intermittently) by tidal waters or parts of the sea which are landward of the baselines from which the breadth of the territorial sea adjacent to Great Britain is measured or are seaward of those baselines up to a distance of three nautical miles, it appears to the Secretary of State expedient, on an application made by the Nature Conservancy Council, that the land and waters covering it should be managed by the Council for the purpose of–

    (a) conserving marine flora or fauna or geological or physiographical features of special interest in the area; or

    (b) providing, under suitable conditions and control, special opportunities for the study of, and research into, matters relating to marine flora and fauna and the physical conditions in which they live, or for the study of geological and physiographical features of special interest in the area,

he may by order designate the area comprising that land and those waters as a marine nature reserve; and the Council shall manage any area so designated for either or both of those purposes.

(2) An application for an order under this section shall be accompanied by–

    (a) a copy of the bylaws which, if an order is made, the Council propose making under s 37 for the protection of the area specified in the application; and

    (b) a copy of any bylaws made or proposed to be made for the protection of that area by a relevant authority,

and an order made on the application shall authorise the making under that section of such of the bylaws proposed to be made by the Council as may be set out in the order with or without modifications.

(3) Bylaws the making of which is so authorised–

    (a) shall not require the Secretary of State's consent under sub-s (1) of s 37; and

    (b) notwithstanding anything in the provisions applied by sub-s (4) of that section, shall take effect on their being made.

(4) The provisions of Sched 12 shall have effect as to the making, validity and date of coming into operation of orders under this section; and an order made under this section may be amended or revoked by a subsequent order so made.

(5) The powers exercisable by the Council for the purpose of managing an area designated as a marine nature reserve under this section shall include power to install markers indicating the existence and extent of the reserve.

(6) Nothing in this section or in bylaws made under s 37 shall interfere with the exercise of any functions of a relevant authority, any functions conferred by or under an enactment (whenever passed) or any right of any person (whenever vested).

(7) In this section–

'enactment' includes an enactment contained in a local Act;

'local authority' means–

    (a) in relation to England and Wales, a county council, a county borough council, a district council ... or a London borough council;

(b) in relation to Scotland, a council constituted under s 2 of the Local Government etc (Scotland) Act 1994;

'nautical miles' means international nautical miles of 1,852 metres;

'relevant authority' means a local authority, the Environment Agency, a water undertaker, a sewerage undertaker, an internal drainage board, a navigation authority, a harbour authority ... a lighthouse authority, a conservancy authority, the Scottish Environment Protection Agency, a district board for a fishery district within the meaning of the Salmon Fisheries (Scotland) Act 1862, or a local fisheries committee constituted under the Sea Fisheries Regulation Act 1966.

Section 37 Bylaws for protection of marine nature reserves

(1) The Nature Conservancy Council may, with the consent of the Secretary of State make bylaws for the protection of any area designated as a marine nature reserve under s 36.

(2) Without prejudice to the generality of sub-s (1), bylaws made under this section as respects a marine nature reserve–

    (a) may provide for prohibiting or restricting, either absolutely or subject to any exceptions–

        (i) the entry into, or movement within, the reserve of persons and vessels;

        (ii) the killing, taking, destruction, molestation or disturbance of animals or plants of any description in the reserve, or the doing of anything therein which will interfere with the sea bed or damage or disturb any object in the reserve; or

        (iii) the depositing of rubbish in the reserve;

    (b) may provide for the issue, on such terms and subject to such conditions as may be specified in the bylaws, of permits authorising entry into the reserve or the doing of anything which would otherwise be unlawful under the bylaws; and

    (c) may be so made as to apply either generally or with respect to particular parts of the reserve or particular times of the year.

(3) Nothing in bylaws made under this section shall–

    (a) prohibit or restrict the exercise of any right of passage by a vessel other than a pleasure boat; or

    (b) prohibit, except with respect to particular parts of the reserve at particular times of the year, the exercise of any such right by a pleasure boat.

(4) Nothing in bylaws so made shall make unlawful–

    (a) anything done for the purpose of securing the safety of any vessel, or of preventing damage to any vessel or cargo, or of saving life;

    (b) the discharge of any substance from a vessel; or

    (c) anything done more than 30 metres below the sea bed.

(5) Sections 236 to 238 of the Local Government Act 1972 or ss 202 to 204 of the Local Government (Scotland) Act 1973 (which relate to the procedure for making bylaws, authorise bylaws to impose fines not exceeding the amount there specified and provide for the proof of bylaws in legal proceedings) shall apply to bylaws under this section as if the Council were a local authority within the meaning of the said Act of 1972 or the said Act of 1973, so however that in relation to such bylaws the said sections shall apply subject to such modifications (including modifications increasing the maximum fines

which the bylaws may impose) as may be prescribed by regulations made by the Secretary of State.

Regulations under this sub-s shall be made by statutory instrument which shall be subject to annulment in pursuance of a resolution of either House of Parliament.

(6) In relation to bylaws under this section the confirming authority for the purposes of the said s 236 or the said s 202 shall be the Secretary of State.

(7) The Secretary of State may, after consultation with the Council, direct them–

(a) to revoke any bylaws previously made under this section; or

(b) to make any such amendments of any bylaws so made as may be specified in the direction.

(8) The Council shall have power to enforce bylaws made under this section; but nothing in this sub-section shall be construed as authorising the Council to institute proceedings in Scotland for an offence.

(9) Proceedings in England and Wales for an offence under bylaws made under this section shall not, without the consent of the Director of Public Prosecutions, be taken by a person other than the Council.

(10) In this section 'vessel' includes a hovercraft and any aircraft capable of landing on water and 'pleasure boat' shall be construed accordingly.

(11) References in this section to animals or plants of any description include references to eggs, seeds, spores, larvae or other immature stages of animals or plants of that description.

Ramsar sites

37A(1) Where a wetland in Great Britain has been designated under para 1 of Art 2 of the Ramsar Convention for inclusion in the list of wetlands of international importance referred to in that article, the Secretary of State shall–

(a) notify English Nature if all or part of the wetland is in England;

(b) notify the Countryside Council for Wales if it is in Wales; or

(c) notify both of them if it is partly in England and partly in Wales.

(2) Subject to sub-s (3), upon receipt of a notification under sub-s (1), each body notified shall, in turn, notify–

(a) the local planning authority in whose area the wetland is situated;

(b) every owner and occupier of any of that wetland;

(c) the Environment Agency; and

(d) every relevant undertaker (within the meaning of s 4(1) of the Water Industry Act 1991) and every internal drainage board (within the meaning of s 61C(1) of the Land Drainage Act 1991) whose works, operations or activities may affect the wetland.

(3) English Nature and the Countryside Council for Wales may agree that in a case where the Secretary of State notifies both of them under sub-s (1)(c), any notice under sub-s (2) is to be sent by one or the other of them (and not both), so as to avoid duplicate notices under that sub-section.

(4) Subject to sub-s (5), the 'Ramsar Convention' is the Convention on Wetlands of International Importance especially as Waterfowl Habitat signed at Ramsar on 2 February 1971, as amended by–

   (a) the Protocol known as the Paris Protocol done at Paris on 3 December 1982; and

   (b) the amendments known as the Regina Amendments adopted at the Extraordinary Conference of the Contracting Parties held at Regina, Saskatchewan, Canada, between 28 May and 3 June 1987.

(5) If the Ramsar Convention is further amended after the passing of the Countryside and Rights of Way Act 2000, the reference to the Ramsar Convention in sub-s (1) is to be taken after the entry into force of the further amendments as referring to that Convention as further amended (and the reference to para 1 of Art 2 is, if necessary, to be taken as referring to the appropriate successor provision).

Note: the above section was introduced by s 77 of the Countryside and Rights of Way Act 2000.

Section 39 Management agreements with owners and occupiers of land

(1) A relevant authority may, for the purpose of conserving or enhancing the natural beauty or amenity of any land which is within their area or promoting its enjoyment by the public, make an agreement (in this section referred to as a 'management agreement') with any person having an interest in the land with respect to the management of the land during a specified term or without limitation of the duration of the agreement.

(2) Without prejudice to the generality of sub-s (1), a management agreement–

   (a) may impose on the person having an interest in the land restrictions as respects the method of cultivating the land, its use for agricultural purposes or the exercise of rights over the land and may impose obligations on that person to carry out works or agricultural or forestry operations or do other things on the land;

   (b) may confer on the relevant authority power to carry out works for the purpose of performing their functions under the 1949 Act and the 1968 Act; and

   (c) may contain such incidental and consequential provisions (including provisions for the making of payments by either party to the other) as appear to the relevant authority to be necessary or expedient for the purposes of the agreement.

(3) The provisions of a management agreement with any person interested in the land shall, unless the agreement otherwise provides, be binding on persons deriving title under or from that person and be enforceable by the relevant authority against those persons accordingly.

(4) Schedule 2 to the Forestry Act 1967 (power for tenant for life and others to enter into forestry dedication covenants) shall apply to management agreements as it applies to forestry dedication covenants.

(5) In this section 'the relevant authority' means–

   (a) as respects land in England which is not in an area for which a National Park authority is the local planning authority but is in a National Park and outside a metropolitan county, the county planning authority;

(aa) as respects land within the Broads, the Broads Authority;

(b) ...;

(c) as respects any other land, the local planning authority.

(6) The powers conferred by this section on a relevant authority shall be in addition to and not in derogation of any powers conferred on such an authority by or under any enactment.

Note: The above section is as amended by the Countryside and Rights of Way Act 2000.

CONSERVATION (NATURAL HABITATS, ETC) REGULATIONS 1994 SI 1994/2716 20 OCTOBER 1994

Regulation 1 Citation and commencement

(1) These regulations may be cited as the Conservation (Natural Habitats, etc) Regulations 1994.

(2) These regulations shall come into force on the tenth day after that on which they are made.

Regulation 2 Interpretation and application

(1) In these regulations—

'agriculture Minister' means the Minister of Agriculture, Fisheries and Food or the Secretary of State;

'competent authority' shall be construed in accordance with Regulation 6;

'destroy', in relation to an egg, includes doing anything to the egg which is calculated to prevent it from hatching, and 'destruction' shall be construed accordingly;

'enactment' includes a local enactment and an enactment contained in subordinate legislation within the meaning of the Interpretation Act 1978;

'European site' has the meaning given by Regulation 10 and 'European marine site' means a European site which consists of, or so far as it consists of, marine areas;

'functions' includes powers and duties;

'the Habitats Directive' means Council Directive 92/43/EEC on the Conservation of Natural Habitats and of Wild Fauna and Flora as amended by the Act of Accession to the EU by Austria, Finland and Sweden and by Council Directive 97/62/EC;

'land' includes land covered by water and as respects Scotland includes salmon fishings;

'livestock' includes any animal which is kept–

(a) for the provision of food, skins or fur;

(b) for the purpose of its use in the carrying on of any agricultural activity; or

(c) for the provision or improvement of shooting or fishing;

'local planning authority' means–

(a) in England and Wales, except as otherwise provided, any authority having any function as a local planning authority or mineral planning authority under the Town and Country Planning Act 1990; and

(b) in Scotland, a planning authority within the meaning of s 172(1) of the Local Government (Scotland) Act 1973;

'management agreement' means an agreement entered into, or having effect as if entered into, under Regulation 16;

'marine area' means any land covered (continuously or intermittently) by tidal waters or any part of the sea in or adjacent to Great Britain up to the seaward limit of territorial waters;

'Natura 2000' means the European network of special areas of conservation, and special protection areas under the Wild Birds Directive, provided for by Art 3(1) of the Habitats Directive;

'nature conservation body', and 'appropriate nature conservation body' in relation to England, Wales or Scotland, have the meaning given by Regulation 4;

'occupier', for the purposes of Part III (protection of species), includes, in relation to any land other than the foreshore, any person having any right of hunting, shooting, fishing or taking game or fish;

'planning authority', in Scotland, means a planning authority within the meaning of s 172(1) of the Local Government (Scotland) Act 1973;

'the register' means the register of European sites in Great Britain provided for by Regulation 11;

'relevant authorities', in relation to marine areas and European marine sites, shall be construed in accordance with Regulation 5;

'statutory undertaker' has the same meaning as in the National Parks and Access to the Countryside Act 1949;

'the Wild Birds Directive' means Council Directive 79/409/EEC on the conservation of wild birds.

(2) Unless the context otherwise requires, expressions used in these regulations and in the Habitats Directive have the same meaning as in that Directive.

The following expressions, in particular, are defined in Art 1 of that Directive–

'priority natural habitat types' and 'priority species';

'site' and 'site of Community importance'; and

'special area of conservation'.

(3) In these regulations, unless otherwise indicated–

(a) any reference to a numbered regulation or Schedule is to the regulation or Schedule in these regulations which bears that number; and

(b) any reference in a regulation or Schedule to a numbered paragraph is to the paragraph of that regulation or Schedule which bears that number.

(4) Subject to Regulation 68 (which provides for Part IV to be construed as one with the Town and Country Planning Act 1990), these regulations apply to the Isles of Scilly as if the Isles were a county and the Council of the Isles were a county council.

(5) For the purposes of these regulations the territorial waters of the United Kingdom adjacent to Great Britain shall be treated as part of Great Britain and references to England, Wales and Scotland shall be construed as including the adjacent territorial waters. For the purposes of this paragraph–

(a) territorial waters include any waters landward of the baselines from which the breadth of the territorial sea is measured; and

(b) any question as to whether territorial waters are to be treated as adjacent to England, Wales or Scotland shall be determined by the Secretary of State or, for any purpose in relation to which the Minister of Agriculture, Fisheries and Food has responsibility, by the Secretary of State and that Minister acting jointly.

Regulation 3 Implementation of Directive

(1) These regulations make provision for the purpose of implementing, for Great Britain, the 'Habitats Directive'.

(2) The Secretary of State, the Minister of Agriculture, Fisheries and Food and the nature conservation bodies shall exercise their functions under the enactments relating to nature conservation so as to secure compliance with the requirements of the Habitats Directive.

Those enactments include–

Part III of the National Parks and Access to the Countryside Act 1949;

Section 49A of the Countryside (Scotland) Act 1967 (management agreements);

Section 15 of the Countryside Act 1968 (areas of special scientific interest);

Part I and ss 28 to 38 of the Wildlife and Countryside Act 1981;

Sections 131 to 134 of the Environmental Protection Act 1990;

Sections 2, 3, 5, 6, 7 and 11 of the Natural Heritage (Scotland) Act 1991, and

these regulations.

(3) In relation to marine areas any competent authority having functions relevant to marine conservation shall exercise those functions so as to secure compliance with the requirements of the Habitats Directive.

This applies, in particular, to functions under the following enactments–

the Sea Fisheries Acts within the meaning of s 1 of the Sea Fisheries (Wildlife Conservation) Act 1992;

the Dockyard Ports Regulation Act 1865;

Section 2(2) of the Military Lands Act 1900 (provisions as to use of sea, tidal water or shore);

the Harbours Act 1964;

Part II of the Control of Pollution Act 1974;

Sections 36 and 37 of the Wildlife and Countryside Act 1981 (marine nature reserves);

Sections 120 to 122 of the Civic Government (Scotland) Act 1982 (control of the seashore, adjacent waters and inland waters);

the Water Resources Act 1991;

the Land Drainage Act 1991;

and these regulations.

(4) Without prejudice to the preceding provisions, every competent authority in the exercise of any of their functions, shall have regard to the requirements of the Habitats Directive so far as they may be affected by the exercise of those functions.

Regulation 4 Nature conservation bodies

In these regulations 'nature conservation body' means the Nature Conservancy Council for England, the Countryside Council for Wales or Scottish Natural Heritage; and references to 'the appropriate nature conservation body', in relation to England, Wales or Scotland, shall be construed accordingly.

Regulation 5 Relevant authorities in relation to marine areas and European marine sites

For the purposes of these regulations the relevant authorities, in relation to a marine area or European marine site, are such of the following as have functions in relation to land or waters within or adjacent to that area or site–

(a) a nature conservation body;

(b) county council, county council borough, district council, London borough council or, in Scotland, a regional, islands or district council;

(c) the Environment Agency, a water undertaker or sewerage undertaker, or an internal drainage board;

(d) a navigation authority within the meaning of the Water Resources Act 1991;

(e) a harbour authority within the meaning of the Harbours Act 1964;

(f) a lighthouse authority;

(g) the Scottish Environment Protection Agency or a district salmon fishery board;

(h) a local fisheries committee constituted under the Sea Fisheries Regulation Act 1966 or any authority exercising the powers of such a committee.

Regulation 6 Competent authorities generally

(1) For the purposes of these regulations the expression 'competent authority' includes any Minister, government department, public or statutory undertaker, public body of any description or person holding a public office.

The expression also includes any person exercising any function of a competent authority in the United Kingdom.

(2) In para (1)–

(a) 'public body' includes any local authority, joint board or joint committee; and

(b) 'public office' means–

(i) an office under Her Majesty;

(ii) an office created or continued in existence by a public general Act of Parliament; or

(iii) an office the remuneration in respect of which is paid out of money provided by Parliament.

(3) In para (2)(a)–

'local authority'–

(a) in relation to England, means a county council, district council or London borough council, the Common Council of the City of London, the sub-treasurer of the Inner Temple, the under treasurer of the Middle Temple or a parish council;

(b) in relation to Wales, means a county council, county borough council or community council; and

(c) in relation to Scotland, means a regional, islands or district council;

'joint board' and 'joint committee' in relation to England and Wales mean–

(a) a joint or special planning board constituted for a National Park by order under para 1 or 3 of Schedule 17 to the Local Government Act 1972, or a joint planning board within the meaning of s 2 of the Town and Country Planning Act 1990; and

(b) a joint committee appointed under s 102(1)(b) of the Local Government Act 1972,

and in relation to Scotland have the same meaning as in the Local Government (Scotland) Act 1973.

Regulation 7 Selection of sites eligible for identification as of Community importance

(1) On the basis of the criteria set out in Annex III (Stage 1) to the Habitats Directive, and relevant scientific information, the Secretary of State shall propose a list of sites indicating with respect to each site–

(a) which natural habitat types in Annex I to the Directive the site hosts; and

(b) which species in Annex II to the Directive that are native to Great Britain the site hosts.

(2) For animal species ranging over wide areas these sites shall correspond to the places within the natural range of such species which present the physical or biological factors essential to their life and reproduction.

For aquatic species which range over wide areas, such sites shall be proposed only where there is a clearly identifiable area representing the physical and biological factors essential to their life and reproduction.

(3) Where appropriate the Secretary of State may propose modification of the list in the light of the results of the surveillance referred to in Art 11 of the Habitats Directive.

(4) The list shall be transmitted to the Commission on or before 5 June 1995, together with information on each site including–

(a) a map of the site;

(b) its name, location and extent; and

(c) the data resulting from application of the criteria specified in Annex III (Stage 1),

provided in a format established by the Commission.

Regulation 8 Adoption of list of sites: designation of special areas of conservation

(1) Once a site of Community importance in Great Britain has been adopted in accordance with the procedure laid down in para 2 of Art 4 of the Habitats Directive, the Secretary of State shall designate that site as a special area of conservation as soon as possible and within six years at most.

(2) The Secretary of State shall establish priorities for the designation of sites in the light of–

(a) the importance of the sites for the maintenance or restoration at a favourable conservation status of–

(i) a natural habitat type in Annex I to the Habitats Directive; or

(ii) a species in Annex II to the Directive,

and for the coherence of Natura 2000; and

(b) the threats of degradation or destruction to which those sites are exposed.

Regulation 9 Consultation as to inclusion of site omitted from the list

If consultation is initiated by the Commission in accordance with Art 5(1) of the Habitats Directive with respect to a site in Great Britain hosting a priority natural habitat type or priority species and–

(a) the Secretary of State agrees that the site should be added to the list transmitted in accordance with Regulation 7; or

(b) the Council, acting on a proposal from the Commission in pursuance of para 2 of Art 5 of the Habitats Directive, so decides,

the site shall be treated as added to the list as from the date of that agreement or decision.

Regulation 10 Meaning of 'European site' in these regulations

(1) In these Regulations a 'European site' means–

    (a) a special area of conservation;

    (b) a site of Community importance which has been placed on the list referred to in the third sub-para of Art 4(2) of the Habitats Directive;

    (c) a site hosting a priority natural habitat type or priority species in respect of which consultation has been initiated under Art 5(1) of the Habitats Directive, during the consultation period or pending a decision of the Council under Art 5(3); or

    (d) an area classified pursuant to Art 4(1) or (2) of the Wild Birds Directive; or

    (e) a site in England included in the list of sites which has been proposed by the Secretary of State and transmitted to the Commission under Regulation 7 until such time as–

        (i) the draft list of sites of Community importance is established under the first sub-paragraph of Art 4(2) of the Habitats Directive where in any case the site is not included in that list; or

        (ii) the list of sites referred to in the third sub-paragraph of Art 4(2) of the Habitats Directive is adopted by the Commission in accordance with that sub-paragraph.

(2) Sites which are European sites by virtue only of para (1)(c) are not within Regulations 20(1) and (2), 24 and 48 (which relate to the approval of certain plans and projects); but this is without prejudice to their protection under other provisions of these regulations.

Regulation 11 Duty to compile and maintain register of European sites

(1) The Secretary of State shall compile and maintain, in such form as he thinks fit, a register of European sites in Great Britain.

(2) He shall include in the register–

    (a) special areas of conservation, as soon as they are designated by him;

    (b) sites of Community importance as soon as they are placed on the list referred to in the third sub-paragraph of Art 4(2) of the Habitats Directive, until they are designated as special areas of conservation;

(c) any site hosting a priority natural habitat type or priority species in respect of which consultation is initiated under Art 5(1) of the Habitats Directive, during the consultation period or pending a Council decision under Art 5(3); and

(d) areas classified by him pursuant to Art 4(1) or (2) of the Wild Birds Directive, as soon as they are so classified or, if they have been classified before the commencement of these Regulations, as soon as practicable after commencement; and

(e) any site in England included in the list of sites which has been proposed by the Secretary of State and transmitted to the Commission under Regulation 7 until such time as para (i) or para (ii) of Regulation 10(1)(e) applies.

(3) He may, if appropriate, amend the entry in the register relating to a European site.

(4) He shall remove the relevant entry–

(a) if a special area of conservation is declassified by the Commission under Art 9 of the Habitats Directive; or

(b) if a site otherwise ceases to fall within any of the categories listed in para (2) above.

(5) He shall keep a copy of the register available for public inspection at all reasonable hours and free of charge.

Regulation 12 Notification to appropriate nature conservation body

(1) The Secretary of State shall notify the appropriate nature conservation body as soon as may be after including a site in the register, amending an entry in the register or removing an entry from the register.

(2) Notification of the inclusion of a site in the register shall be accompanied by a copy of the register entry.

(3) Notification of the amendment of an entry in the register shall be accompanied by a copy of the amended entry.

(4) Each nature conservation body shall keep copies of the register entries relating to European sites in their area available for public inspection at all reasonable hours and free of charge.

Regulation 13 Notice to landowners, relevant authorities, etc

(1) As soon as practicable after a nature conservation body receive notification under regulation 12 they shall give notice to–

(a) every owner or occupier of land within the site;

(b) every local planning authority in whose area the site, or any part of it, is situated; and

(c) such other persons or bodies as the Secretary of State may direct.

(2) Notice of the inclusion of a site in the register, or of the amendment of an entry in the register, shall be accompanied by a copy of so much of the relevant register entry as relates to land owned or occupied by or, as the case may be, to land within the area of, the person or authority to whom the notice is given.

(3) The Secretary of State may give directions as to the form and content of notices to be given under this regulation.

Regulation 14 Local registration: England and Wales

An entry in the register relating to a European site in England and Wales is a local land charge.

[Section 15 omitted.]

Regulation 16 Management agreements

(1) The appropriate nature conservation body may enter into an agreement (a 'management agreement') with every owner, lessee and occupier of land forming part of a European site, or land adjacent to such a site, for the management, conservation, restoration or protection of the site, or any part of it.

(2) A management agreement may impose such restrictions as may be expedient for the purposes of the agreement on the exercise of rights over the land by the persons who can be bound by the agreement.

(3) A management agreement–

   (a) may provide for the management of the land in such manner, the carrying out thereon of such work and the doing thereon of such other things as may be expedient for the purposes of the agreement;

   (b) may provide for any of the matters mentioned in sub-para (a) being carried out, or for the costs thereof being defrayed, either by the said owner or other persons or by the appropriate nature conservation body, or partly in one way and partly in another;

   (c) may contain such other provisions as to the making of payments by the appropriate nature conservation body, and in particular for the payment by them of compensation for the effect of the restrictions mentioned in para (2), as may be specified in the agreement.

(4) Where land in England and Wales is subject to a management agreement, the appropriate nature conservation body shall, as respects the enforcement of the agreement against persons other than the original contracting party, have the like rights as if–

   (a) they had at all material times been the absolute owners in possession of ascertained land adjacent to the land subject to the agreement and capable of being benefited by the agreement; and

   (b) the management agreement had been expressed to be for the benefit of that adjacent land,

and s 84 of the Law of Property Act 1925 (which enables the Lands Tribunal to discharge or modify restrictive covenants) shall not apply to the agreement.

(5) A management agreement affecting land in Scotland may be registered either–

   (a) in a case where the land affected by the agreement is registered in that register, in the Land Register of Scotland; or

   (b) in any other case, in the General Register of Sasines,

   and, on being so recorded, it shall be enforceable at the instance of the appropriate nature conservation body against any person having an interest in the land and against any person deriving title from him: Provided that a management agreement shall not be so enforceable against a third party who has *bona fide* onerously acquired right (whether completed by infeftment or not) to his interest in the land prior to the agreement being recorded as aforesaid, or against any person deriving title from such third party.

Regulation 17 Continuation in force of existing agreement, etc

(1) Any agreement previously entered into under–

   (a) section 16 of the National Parks and Access to the Countryside Act 1949 (nature reserves);

   (b) section 15 of the Countryside Act 1968 (areas of special scientific interest); or

   (c) section 49A of the Countryside (Scotland) Act 1967 (management agreements),

   in relation to land which on or after the commencement of these regulations becomes land within a European site, or adjacent to such a site, shall have effect as if entered into under Regulation 16 above.

   Regulation 32(1)(b) (power of compulsory acquisition in case of breach of agreement) shall apply accordingly.

(2) Any other thing done or deemed to have been done under any provision of Parts III or VI of the National Parks and Access to the Countryside Act 1949, or under s 49A of the Countryside (Scotland) Act 1967, in respect of any land prior to that land becoming land within a European site, or adjacent to such a site, shall continue to have effect as if done under the corresponding provision of these regulations.

   For the purposes of this para Part III of the 1949 Act shall be deemed to include s 15 of the Countryside Act 1968 and anything done or deemed to be done under that section and to which this para applies shall have effect as if done or deemed to be done under s 16 of the 1949 Act.

(3) Any reference in an outlying enactment to a nature reserve within the meaning of s 15 of the National Parks and Access to the Countryside Act 1949 shall be construed as including a European site.

   For this purpose an 'outlying enactment' means an enactment not contained in, or in an instrument made under, the National Parks and Access to the Countryside Act 1949 or the Wildlife and Countryside Act 1981.

Regulation 18 Notification of potentially damaging operations

(1) Any notification in force in relation to a European site under s 28 of the Wildlife and Countryside Act 1981 (areas of special scientific interest) specifying–

   (a) the flora, fauna, or geological or physiographical features by reason of which the land is of special interest; and

   (b) any operations appearing to the appropriate nature conservation body to be likely to damage that flora or fauna or those features,

   shall have effect for the purposes of these regulations.

(2) The appropriate nature conservation body may, for the purpose of securing compliance with the requirements of the Habitats Directive, at any time amend the notification with respect to any of the matters mentioned in para (1)(a) or (b).

(3) Notice of any amendment shall be given–

   (a) to every owner and occupier of land within the site who in the opinion of the appropriate nature conservation body may be affected by the amendment; and

(b) to the local planning authority,

and the amendment shall come into force in relation to an owner or occupier upon such notice being given to him.

(4) The provisions of–

   (a) s 28(11) of the Wildlife and Countryside Act 1981 (notification to be local land charge in England and Wales); and

   (b) s 28(12) to (12B) of that Act (local registration of notification in Scotland),

apply, with the necessary modifications, in relation to an amendment of a notification under this regulation as in relation to the original notification.

Regulation 19 Restriction on carrying out operations specified in notification

(1) The owner or occupier of any land within a European site shall not carry out, or cause or permit to be carried out, on that land any operation specified in a notification in force in relation to the site under Regulation 18, unless–

   (a) one of them has given the appropriate nature conservation body written notice of a proposal to carry out the operation, specifying its nature and the land on which it is proposed to carry it out; and

   (b) one of the conditions specified in para (2) is fulfilled.

(2) Those conditions are–

   (a) that the operation is carried out with the written consent of the appropriate nature conservation body;

   (b) that the operation is carried out in accordance with the terms of a management agreement;

   (c) that four months have expired from the giving of the notice under para (1)(a).

(3) A person who, without reasonable excuse, contravenes para (1) commits an offence and is liable on summary conviction to a fine not exceeding level 4 on the standard scale.

(4) For the purposes of para (3) it is a reasonable excuse for a person to carry out an operation–

   (a) that the operation was an emergency operation particulars of which (including details of the emergency) were notified to the appropriate nature conservation body as soon as practicable after the commencement of the operation; or

   (b) that the operation was authorised by a planning permission granted on an application under Part III of the Town and Country Planning Act 1990 or Part III of the Town and Country Planning (Scotland) Act 1972.

(5) The appropriate nature conservation body has power to enforce this regulation; but nothing in this paragraph shall be construed as authorising the institution of proceedings in Scotland for an offence.

(6) Proceedings in England and Wales for an offence under this regulation shall not, without the consent of the Director of Public Prosecutions, be taken by a person other than the appropriate nature conservation body.

Regulation 20 Supplementary provisions as to consents

(1) Where it appears to the appropriate nature conservation body that an application for consent under Regulation 19(2)(a) relates to an operation which is or forms part of a plan or project which–

(a) is not directly connected with or necessary to the management of the site; and

(b) is likely to have a significant effect on the site (either alone or in combination with other plans or projects), they shall make an appropriate assessment of the implications for the site in view of that site's conservation objectives.

(2) In the light of the conclusions of life assessment, they may give consent for the operation only after having ascertained that the plan or project will not adversely affect the integrity of the site.

(3) The above provisions do not apply in relation to a site which is a European site by reason only of Regulation 10(1)(c) (site protected in accordance with Art 5(4) [of the Habitats Directive]).

(4) Where in any case, whether in pursuance of this regulation or otherwise, the appropriate nature conservation body have not given consent for an operation, but they consider that there is a risk that the operation may nevertheless be carried out, they shall notify the Secretary of State.

(5) They shall take such steps as are requisite to secure that any such notification is given at least one month before the expiry of the period mentioned in Regulation 19(2)(c) (period after which operation may be carried out in absence of consent).

Regulation 21 Provision as to existing notices and consents

(1) Any notice or consent previously given under s 28(5)(a) or (6)(a) of the Wildlife and Countryside Act 1981 in relation to land which on or after the commencement of these regulations becomes land within a European site shall have effect, subject as follows, as if given under Regulation 19(1)(a) or (2)(a) above.

(2) The appropriate nature conservation body shall review any such consent as regards its compatibility with the conservation objectives of the site, and may modify or withdraw it.

(3) Notice of any such modification or withdrawal of consent shall be given to every owner and occupier of land within the site who in the opinion of the appropriate nature conservation body may be affected by it; and the modification or withdrawal shall come into force in relation to an owner or occupier upon such notice being given to him.

(4) The modification or withdrawal of a consent shall not affect anything done in reliance on the consent before the modification or withdrawal takes effect.

(5) Where or to the extent that an operation ceases to be covered by a consent by reason of the consent being modified or withdrawn, the period after which in accordance with Regulation 19(2)(c) the operation may be carried out in the absence of consent shall be four months from the giving of notice of the modification or withdrawal under para (3) above.

(6) Regulation 20(4) and (5) (provisions as to notification of Secretary of State) apply in such a case, with the following modifications–

(a) for the reference to consent not having been given substitute a reference to consent being modified or withdrawn;

(b) for the reference to the period specified in Regulation 19(2)(c) substitute a reference to the period specified in para (5) above.

Regulation 22 Power to make special nature conservation order

(1) The Secretary of State may, after consultation with the appropriate nature conservation body, make in respect of any land within a European site an order (a 'special nature conservation order') specifying operations which appear to him to be likely to destroy or damage the flora, fauna, or geological or physiographical features by reason of which the land is a European site.

(2) A special nature conservation order may be amended or revoked by a further order.

(3) Schedule 1 has effect with respect to the making, confirmation and coming into operation of special nature conservation orders and amending or revoking orders.

(4) A special nature conservation order in relation to land in England and Wales is a local land charge.

(5) A special nature conservation order in relation to land in Scotland shall be registered either–

   (a) in a case where the land affected by the order is registered in that Register, in the Land Register of Scotland; or

   (b) in any other case, in the appropriate Division of the General Register of Sasines.

(6) A report submitted by a nature conservation body to the Secretary of State under para 20 of Schedule 6 to the Environmental Protection Act 1990 or s 10(2) of the Natural Heritage (Scotland) Act 1991 shall set out particulars of any land in their area as respects which a special nature conservation order has come into operation during the year to which the report relates.

Regulation 23 Restriction on carrying out operations specified in order

(1) No person shall carry out on any land within a European site in respect of which a special nature conservation order is in force any operation specified in the order, unless the operation is carried out, or caused or permitted to be carried out, by the owner or occupier of the land and–

   (a) one of them has, after the making of the order, given the appropriate nature conservation body written notice of a proposal to carry out the operation, specifying its nature and the land on which it is proposed to carry it out; and

   (b) one of the conditions specified in para (2) is fulfilled.

(2) Those conditions are–

   (a) that the operation is carried out with the written consent of the appropriate nature conservation body;

   (b) that the operation is carried out in accordance with the terms of a management agreement.

(3) A person who, without reasonable excuse, contravenes para (1) commits an offence and is liable–

   (a) on summary conviction, to a fine not exceeding the statutory maximum;

   (b) on conviction on indictment, to a fine.

(4) For the purposes of para (3) it is a reasonable excuse for a person to carry out an operation–

    (a) that the operation was an emergency operation particulars of which (including details of the emergency) were notified to the appropriate nature conservation body as soon as practicable after the commencement of the operation; or

    (b) that the operation was authorised by a planning permission granted on an application under Part III of the Town and Country Planning Act 1990 or Part III of the Town and Country Planning (Scotland) Act 1972.

Regulation 24 Supplementary provisions as to consents

(1) Where it appears to the appropriate nature conservation body that an application for consent under Regulation 23(2)(a) relates to an operation which is or forms part of a plan or project which–

    (a) is not directly connected with or necessary to the management of the site; and

    (b) is likely to have a significant effect on the site (either alone or in combination with other plans or projects),

they shall make an appropriate assessment of the implications for the site in view of that site's conservation objectives.

(2) In the light of the conclusions of the assessment, they may give consent for the operation only after having ascertained that the plan or project will not adversely affect the integrity of the site.

(3) Where the appropriate nature conservation body refuse consent in accordance with para (2) they shall give reasons for their decision.

(4) The owner or occupier of the land in question may–

    (a) within two months of receiving notice of the refusal of consent; or

    (b) if no notice of a decision is received by him within three months of an application for consent being made,

by notice in writing to the appropriate nature conservation body require them to refer the matter forthwith to the Secretary of State.

(5) If on the matter being referred to the Secretary of State he is satisfied that, there being no alternative solutions, the plan or project must be carried out for imperative reasons of overriding public interest (which, subject to para (6), may be of a social or economic nature), he may direct the appropriate nature conservation body to give consent to the operation.

(6) Where the site concerned hosts a priority natural habitat type or a priority species the reasons referred to in para (5) must be either–

    (a) reasons relating to human health, public safety or beneficial consequences of primary importance to the environment; or

    (b) other reasons which in the opinion of the European Commission are imperative reasons of overriding public interest.

(7) Where the Secretary of State directs the appropriate nature conservation body to give consent under this regulation, he shall secure that such compensatory measures are taken as are necessary to ensure that the overall coherence of Natura 2000 is protected.

(8) This regulation does not apply in relation to a site which is a European site by reason only of Regulation 10(1)(c) (site protected in accordance with Art 5(4)).

Regulation 25 Compensation for effect of order

(1) Where a special nature conservation order is made, the appropriate nature conservation body shall pay compensation to any person having at the time of the making of the order an interest in land comprised in an agricultural unit comprising land to which the order relates who, on a claim made to the appropriate nature conservation body within the time and in the manner prescribed by regulations, shows that the value of his interest is less than it would have been if the order had not been made.

(2) For this purpose an 'agricultural unit' means land which is occupied as a unit for agricultural purposes, including any dwelling-house or other building occupied by the same person for the purpose of farming the land.

(3) No claim for compensation shall be made under this regulation in respect of an order unless the Secretary of State has given notice under para 6(1) or (2) of Schedule 1 of his decision in respect of the order.

Regulation 26 Restoration where order contravened

(1) Where a person is convicted of an offence under Regulation 23, the court by which he is convicted may, in addition to dealing with him in any other way, make an order requiring him to carry out, within such period as may be specified in the order, such operations for the purpose of restoring the land to its former condition as may be so specified.

(2) An order under this regulation made on conviction on indictment shall be treated for the purposes of s 30 of the Criminal Appeal Act 1968 (effect of appeals on orders for the restitution of property) as an order for the restitution of property.

(3) In the case of an order under this regulation made by a magistrates' court the period specified in the order shall not begin to run–

    (a) in any case until the expiration of the period for the time being prescribed by law for the giving of notice of appeal against a decision of a magistrates' court;

    (b) where notice of appeal is given within the period so prescribed, until determination of the appeal.

(4) At any time before an order under this regulation has been complied with or fully complied with, the court by which it was made may, on the application of the person against whom it was made, discharge or vary the order if it appears to the court that a change in circumstances has made compliance or full compliance with the order impracticable or unnecessary.

(5) If a person fails without reasonable excuse to comply with an order under this regulation, he commits an offence and is liable on summary conviction to a fine not exceeding level 5 on the standard scale; and if the failure continues after conviction, he may be proceeded against for a further offence from time to time until the order is complied with.

(6) If, within the period specified in an order under this regulation, any operations specified in the order have not been carried out, the appropriate nature conservation body may enter the land and carry out those operations and recover from the person against whom the order was made any expenses reasonably incurred by them in doing so.

(7) In the application of this regulation to Scotland–

   (a) paras (2) and (3) shall not apply; and

   (b) for the purposes of any appeal or review, an order under this regulation is a sentence.

Regulation 27 Continuation in force of existing orders, etc

(1) Where an order is in force under s 29 of the Wildlife and Countryside Act 1981 (special protection for certain areas of special scientific interest) in relation to land which on or after the commencement of these regulations becomes land within a European site, the order shall have effect as if made under Regulation 22 above.

(2) Any notice previously given under s 29(4)(a) (notice by owner or occupier of proposal to carry out operation) shall have effect as if given under Regulation 23(1)(a) and, if the appropriate nature conservation body have neither given nor refused consent, shall be dealt with under these regulations.

(3) Any consent previously given under s 29(5)(a) shall be reviewed by the appropriate nature conservation body as regards its compatibility with the conservation objectives of the site, and may be modified or withdrawn.

(4) Notice of any such modification or withdrawal of consent shall be given to every owner and occupier of land within the site who in the opinion of the appropriate nature conservation body may be affected by it; and the modification or withdrawal shall come into force in relation to an owner or occupier upon such notice being given to him.

(5) The modification or withdrawal of a consent shall not affect anything done in reliance on the consent before the modification or withdrawal takes effect.

(6) Section 29(5)(c), (6) and (7) shall cease to apply and the carrying out, or continuation, of any operation on land within a European site which is not otherwise authorised in accordance with these regulations shall be subject to the prohibition in Regulation 23(1).

Regulation 28 Power to make bylaws

(1) The appropriate nature conservation body may make bylaws for the protection of a European site under s 20 of the National Parks and Access to the Countryside Act 1949 (bylaws for protection of nature reserves).

(2) Without prejudice to the generality of para (1), bylaws under that section as it applies by virtue of this regulation may make provision of any of the following kinds.

(3) They may–

   (a) provide for prohibiting or restricting the entry into, or movement within, the site of persons, vehicles, boats and animals;

   (b) prohibit or restrict the killing, taking, molesting or disturbance of living creatures of any description in the site, the taking, destruction or disturbance of eggs of any such creature, the taking of, or interference with, vegetation of any description in the site, or the doing of anything in the site which will interfere with the soil or damage any object in the site;

   (c) contain provisions prohibiting the depositing of rubbish and the leaving of litter in the site;

(d) prohibit or restrict, or provide for prohibiting or restricting, the lighting of fires in the site or the doing of anything likely to cause a fire in the site.

(4) They may prohibit or restrict any activity referred to in para (3) within such area surrounding or adjoining the site as appears to the appropriate nature conservation body requisite for the protection of the site.

(5) They may provide for the issue, on such terms and subject to such conditions as may be specified in the bylaws, of permits authorising—

(a) entry into the site or any such surrounding or adjoining area as is mentioned in para (4); or

(b) the doing of anything within the site, or any such surrounding or adjoining area,

where such entry, or doing that thing, would otherwise be unlawful under the bylaws.

(6) They may be made so as to relate either to the whole or to any part of the site, or of any such surrounding or adjoining area as is mentioned in para (4), and may make different provision for different parts thereof.

(7) This regulation does not apply in relation to a European marine site (but see Regulation 36).

Regulation 29 Bylaws: limitation on effect

Bylaws under s 20 of the National Parks and Access to the Countryside Act 1949 as it applies by virtue of Regulation 28 shall not interfere with—

(a) the exercise by any person of a right vested in him as owner, lessee or occupier of land in the European site, or in any such surrounding or adjoining area as is mentioned in para (4) of that regulation;

(b) the exercise of any public right of way;

(c) the exercise of any functions of statutory undertakers;

(d) the exercise of any functions of an internal drainage board, a district salmon fishery board or the Commissioners appointed under the Tweed Fisheries Act 1969; or

(e) the running of a telecommunications code system or the exercise of any right conferred by or in accordance with the telecommunications code on the operator of any such system.

Regulation 30 Compensation for effect of bylaws

Where the exercise of any right vested in a person, whether by reason of his being entitled to any interest in land or by virtue of a licence or agreement, is prevented or hindered by the coming into operation of bylaws under s 20 of the National Parks and Access to the Countryside Act 1949 as it applies by virtue of Regulation 28, he shall be entitled to receive from the appropriate nature conservation body compensation in respect thereof.

Regulation 31 Continuation in force of existing bylaws

Any bylaws in force under s 20 of the National Parks and Access to the Countryside Act 1949 in relation to land which on or after the commencement of these regulations becomes land within a European site, or adjacent to such a site, shall have effect as if made under the said s 20 as it applies by virtue of Regulation 28 and shall be construed as if originally so made.

Regulation 32 Powers of compulsory acquisition

(1) Where the appropriate nature conservation body are satisfied–

    (a) that they are unable, as respects any interest in land within a European site, to conclude a management agreement on terms appearing to them to be reasonable; or

    (b) where they have entered into a management agreement as respects such an interest, that a breach of the agreement has occurred which prevents or impairs the satisfactory management of the European site, they may acquire that interest compulsorily.

(2) Such a breach as is mentioned in para (1)(b) shall not be treated as having occurred by virtue of any act or omission capable of remedy unless there has been default in remedying it within a reasonable time after notice given by the appropriate nature conservation body requiring the remedying thereof.

(3) Any dispute arising whether there has been such a breach of a management agreement shall be determined–

    (a) in the case of land in England and Wales, by an arbitrator appointed by the Lord Chancellor;

    (b) in the case of land in Scotland, by an arbiter appointed by the Lord President of the Court of Session.

Regulation 33 Marking of site and advice by nature conservation bodies

(1) The appropriate nature conservation body may install markers indicating the existence and extent of a European marine site.

This power is exercisable subject to the obtaining of any necessary consent under s 34 of the Coast Protection Act 1949 (restriction of works detrimental to navigation).

(2) As soon as possible after a site becomes a European marine site, the appropriate nature conservation body shall advise other relevant authorities as to–

    (a) the conservation objectives for that site; and

    (b) any operations which may cause deterioration of natural habitats or the habitats of species, or disturbance of species, for which the site has been designated.

Regulation 34 Management scheme for European marine site

(1) The relevant authorities, or any of them, may establish for a European marine site a management scheme under which their functions (including any power to make bylaws) shall be exercised so as to secure in relation to that site compliance with the requirements of the Habitats Directive.

(2) Only one management scheme may be made for each European marine site.

(3) A management scheme may be amended from time to time.

(4) As soon as a management scheme has been established, or is amended, a copy of it shall be sent by the relevant authority or authorities concerned to the appropriate nature conservation body.

Regulation 35 Direction to establish or amend management scheme

(1) The relevant Minister may give directions to the relevant authorities, or any of them, as to the establishment of a management scheme for a European marine site.

(2) Directions may, in particular–

    (a) require conservation measures specified in the direction to be included in the scheme;

    (b) appoint one of the relevant authorities to co-ordinate the establishment of the scheme;

    (c) set time limits within which any steps are to be taken;

    (d) provide that the approval of the Minister is required before the scheme is established; and

    (e) require any relevant authority to supply to the Minister such information concerning the establishment of the scheme as may be specified in the direction.

(3) The relevant Minister may give directions to the relevant authorities, or any of them, as to the amendment of a management scheme for a European marine site, either generally or in any particular respect.

(4) Any direction under this regulation shall be in writing and may be varied or revoked by a further direction.

(5) In this regulation 'the relevant Minister' means, in relation to a site in England, the Secretary of State and the Minister of Agriculture, Fisheries and Food acting jointly and in any other case the Secretary of State.

Regulation 36 Bylaws for protection of European marine site

(1) The appropriate nature conservation body may make bylaws for the protection of a European marine site under s 37 of the Wildlife and Countryside Act 1981 (bylaws for protection of marine nature reserves).

(2) The provisions of sub-ss (2) to (11) of that section apply in relation to bylaws made by virtue of this regulation with the substitution for the references to marine nature reserves of references to European marine sites.

(3) Nothing in bylaws made by virtue of this regulation shall interfere with the exercise of any functions of a relevant authority, any functions conferred by or under an enactment (whenever passed) or any right of any person (whenever vested).

Regulation 37 Nature conservation policy in planning contexts

(1) For the purposes of the planning enactments mentioned below, policies in respect of the conservation of the natural beauty and amenity of the land shall be taken to include policies encouraging the management of features of the landscape which are of major importance for wild flora and fauna.

Such features are those which, by virtue of their linear and continuous structure (such as rivers with their banks or the traditional systems of marking field boundaries) or their function as stepping stones (such as ponds or small woods), are essential for the migration, dispersal and genetic exchange of wild species.

(2) The enactments referred to in para (1) are–

(a) in the Town and Country Planning Act 1990, s 12(3A) (unitary development plans), s 31(3) (structure plans) and s 36(3) (local plans);

(b) in the Town and Country Planning (Scotland) Act 1972, s 5(3)(a) (structure plans) and s 9(3)(a) (local plans).

Part II Protection of species: protection of animals

Regulation 38 European protected species of animals

The species of animals listed in Annex IV(a) to the Habitats Directive whose natural range includes any area in Great Britain are listed in Schedule 2 to these regulations.

References in these regulations to a 'European protected species' of animal are to any of those species.

Regulation 39 Protection of wild animals of European protected species

(1) It is an offence–

   (a) deliberately to capture or kill a wild animal of a European protected species;

   (b) deliberately to disturb any such animal;

   (c) deliberately to take or destroy the eggs of such an animal; or

   (d) to damage or destroy a breeding site or resting place of such an animal.

(2) It is an offence to keep, transport, sell or exchange, or offer for sale or exchange, any live or dead wild animal of a European protected species, or any part of, or anything derived from, such an animal.

(3) Paras (1) and (2) apply to all stages of the life of the animals to which they apply.

(4) A person shall not be guilty of an offence under para (2) if he shows–

   (a) that the animal had not been taken or killed, or had been lawfully taken or killed, or

   (b) that the animal or other thing in question had been lawfully sold (whether to him or any other person).

   For this purpose 'lawfully' means without any contravention of these regulations or Part I of the Wildlife and Countryside Act 1981.

(5) In any proceedings for an offence under this regulation, the animal in question shall be presumed to have been a wild animal unless the contrary is shown.

(6) A person guilty of an offence under this regulation is liable on summary conviction to a fine not exceeding level 5 on the standard scale.

Regulation 40 Exceptions from Regulation 39

(1) Nothing in Regulation 39 shall make unlawful–

   (a) anything done in pursuance of a requirement by the agriculture Minister under s 98 of the Agriculture Act 1947 or s 39 of the Agriculture (Scotland) Act 1948 (prevention of damage by pests); or

   (b) anything done under, or in pursuance of an order made under, the Animal Health Act 1981.

(2) Nothing in Regulation 39(1)(b) or (d) shall make unlawful anything done within a dwelling-house.

(3) Notwithstanding anything in Regulation 39, a person shall not be guilty of an offence by reason of—

    (a) the taking of a wild animal of a European protected species if he shows that the animal had been disabled otherwise than by his unlawful act and was taken solely for the purpose of tending it and releasing it when no longer disabled;

    (b) the killing of such an animal if he shows that the animal has been so seriously disabled otherwise than by his unlawful act that there was no reasonable chance of its recovering; or

    (c) any act made unlawful by that regulation if he shows that the act was the incidental result of a lawful operation and could not reasonably have been avoided.

(4) A person shall not be entitled to rely on the defence provided by para (2) or (3)(c) as respects anything done in relation to a bat otherwise than in the living area of a dwelling-house unless he had notified the appropriate nature conservation body of the proposed action or operation and allowed them a reasonable time to advise him as to whether it should be carried out and, if so, the method to be used.

(5) Notwithstanding anything in Regulation 39 a person—

    (a) being the owner or occupier, or any person authorised by the owner or occupier, of the land on which the action authorised is taken; or

    (b) authorised by the local authority for the area within which the action authorised is taken,

shall not be guilty of an offence by reason of the killing or disturbing of an animal of a European protected species if he shows that his action was necessary for the purpose of preventing serious damage to livestock, foodstuffs, crops, vegetables, fruit, growing timber or any other form of property or fisheries.

(6) A person may not rely on the defence provided by para (5) as respects action taken at any time if it had become apparent before that time that the action would prove necessary for the purpose mentioned in that paragraph and either—

    (a) a licence under Regulation 44 authorising that action had not been applied for as soon as reasonably practicable after that fact had become apparent; or

    (b) an application for such a licence had been determined.

(7) In para (5) 'local authority' means—

    (a) in relation to England and Wales, a county, county borough, district or London borough council and includes the Common Council of the City of London; and

    (b) in Scotland, a regional, islands or district council.

Note: In *R v Secretary of State for Trade and Industry ex p Greenpeace (No 2)* (2000) Env LR 221 (see p 776, below) the High Court rejected the argument that reg 40(3)(c) was inconsistent with the obligation to provide strict protection for animals under Habitats Directive 1992, Art 12.

Regulation 41 Prohibition of certain methods of taking or killing wild animals

(1) This regulation applies in relation to the taking or killing of a wild animal—

    (a) of any of the species listed in Sched 3 to these regulations (which shows the species listed in Annex V(a) to the Habitats Directive, and to which Art 15 applies, whose natural range includes any area of Great Britain); or

    (b) of a European protected species, where the taking or killing of such animals is permitted in accordance with these regulations.

(2) It is an offence to use for the purpose of taking or killing any such wild animal–

    (a) any of the means listed in para (3) or (4) below; or

    (b) any form of taking or killing from the modes of transport listed in para (5) below.

(3)   The prohibited means of taking or killing of mammals are–

    (a) blind or mutilated animals used as live decoys;

    (b) tape recorders;

    (c) electrical and electronic devices capable of killing or stunning;

    (d) artificial light sources;

    (e) mirrors and other dazzling devices;

    (f) devices for illuminating targets;

    (g) sighting devices for night shooting comprising an electronic image magnifier or image converter;

    (h) explosives;

    (i) nets which are non-selective according to their principle or their conditions of use;

    (j) traps which are non-selective according to their principle or their conditions of use;

    (k) crossbows;

    (l) poisons and poisoned or anaesthetic bait;

    (m) gassing or smoking out;

    (n) semi-automatic or automatic weapons with a magazine capable of holding more than two rounds of ammunition.

(4) The prohibited means of taking or killing fish are–

    (a) poison;

    (b) explosives.

(5) The prohibited modes of transport are–

    (a) aircraft;

    (b) moving motor vehicles.

(6) A person guilty of an offence under this regulation is liable on summary conviction to a fine not exceeding level 5 on the standard scale.

Part III Protection of Species: Protection of plants

Regulation 42 European protected species of plants

The species of plants listed in Annex IV(b) to the Habitats Directive whose natural range includes any area in Great Britain are listed in Schedule 4 to these regulations.

References in these regulations to a 'European protected species' of plant are to any of those species.

Regulation 43 Protection of wild plants of European protected species

(1) It is an offence deliberately to pick, collect, cut, uproot or destroy a wild plant of a European protected species.

(2) It is an offence to keep, transport, sell or exchange, or offer for sale or exchange, any live or dead wild plant of a European protected species, or any part of, or anything derived from, such a plant.

(3) Paragraphs (1) and (2) apply to all stages of the biological cycle of the plants to which they apply.

(4) A person shall not be guilty of an offence under para (1), by reason of any act made unlawful by that paragraph if he shows that the act was an incidental result of a lawful operation and could not reasonably have been avoided.

(5) A person shall not be guilty of an offence under para (2) if he shows that the plant or other thing in question had been lawfully sold (whether to him or any other person).

For this purpose 'lawfully' means without any contravention of these regulations or Part I of the Wildlife and Countryside Act 1981.

(6) In any proceedings for an offence under this regulation, the plant in question shall be presumed to have been a wild plant unless the contrary is shown.

(7) A person guilty of an offence under this section is liable on summary conviction to a fine not exceeding level 4 on the standard scale.

Regulation 44 Grant of licences for certain purposes

(1) Regulations 39, 41 and 43 do not apply to anything done for any of the following purposes under and in accordance with the terms of a licence granted by the appropriate authority.

(2) The purposes referred to in para (1) are–

(a) scientific or educational purposes;

(b) ringing or marking, or examining any ring or mark on, wild animals;

(c) conserving wild animals or wild plants or introducing them to particular areas;

(d) protecting any zoological or botanical collection;

(e) preserving public health or public safety or other imperative reasons of overriding public interest including those of a social or economic nature and beneficial consequences of primary importance for the environment;

(f) preventing the spread of disease; or

(g) preventing serious damage to livestock, foodstuffs for livestock, crops, vegetables, fruit, growing timber or any other form of property or to fisheries.

(3) The appropriate authority shall not grant a licence under this regulation unless they are satisfied–

(a) that there is no satisfactory alternative; and

(b) that the action authorised will not be detrimental to the maintenance of the population of the species concerned at a favourable conservation status in their natural range.

(4) For the purposes of this regulation 'the appropriate authority' means–

(a) in the case of a licence under any of sub-paras (a) to (d) of para (2), the appropriate nature conservation body; and

(b) in the case of a licence under any of sub-paras (e) to (g) of that paragraph, the agriculture Minister.

(5) The agriculture Minister shall from time to time consult with the nature conservation bodies as to the exercise of his functions under this regulation; and he shall not grant a licence of any description unless he has been advised by the appropriate nature conservation body as to the circumstances in which, in their opinion, licences of that description should be granted.

Regulation 45 Licences: supplementary provisions

(1) A licence under Regulation 44–

(a) may be, to any degree, general or specific;

(b) may be granted either to persons of a class or to a particular person; and

(c) may be subject to compliance with any specified conditions.

(2) For the purposes of a licence under Regulation 44 the definition of a class of persons may be framed by reference to any circumstances whatever including, in particular, their being authorised by any other person.

(3) A licence under Regulation 44 may be modified or revoked at any time by the appropriate authority; but otherwise shall be valid for the period stated in the licence.

(4) A licence under Regulation 44 which authorises any person to kill wild animals shall specify the area within which and the methods by which the wild animals may be killed and shall not be granted for a period of more than two years.

(5) It shall be a defence in proceedings for an offence under s 8(b) of the Protection of Animals Act 1911 or s 7(b) of the Protection of Animals (Scotland) Act 1912 (which restrict the placing on land of poison and poisonous substances) to show that–

(a) the act alleged to constitute the offence was done under and in accordance with the terms of a licence under Regulation 44; and

(b) any conditions specified in the licence were complied with.

(6) The appropriate authority may charge for a licence under Regulation 44 such reasonable sum (if any) as they may determine.

Regulation 46 False statements made for obtaining licence

(1) A person commits an offence who, for the purposes of obtaining, whether for himself or another, the grant of a licence under Regulation 44–

(a) makes a statement or representation, or furnishes a document or information, which he knows to be false in a material particular; or

(b) recklessly makes a statement or representation, or furnishes a document or information, which is false in a material particular.

(2) A person guilty of an offence under this regulation is liable on summary conviction to a fine not exceeding level 4 on the standard scale.

R v Secretary of State for Trade and Industry ex p Greenpeace Ltd (No 2) [2000] Env LR 221

Maurice Kay J: This is an application by Greenpeace Limited, the corporate identity of Greenpeace UK, which is part of Greenpeace International. I shall refer to the Applicant as 'Greenpeace'. It is a well known campaigning body, the prime object of which relates to the protection of the natural environment. Its legal standing to bring proceedings such as the present application is well established.

[...]

The case is concerned with an area in the North East Atlantic which has become known as the Atlantic Frontier. In broad terms it lies to the North and the West of the Hebrides, Orkney and Shetland. The Secretary of State has the power to grant licences to companies who wish to search and bore for oil in the area. Licensing takes place through a series of 'rounds' which commenced some time ago and which it is intended should continue in the years to come. Licences are generally granted in respect of 'tranches', each tranche relating to a number of 'blocks'. A licence is granted for different stages. The first stage involves exploration which is a process of appraisal of the blocks in question. It involves seismic testing of the seabed and, where appropriate, the drilling of exploratory wells. The second stage involves extraction. The licences require the licensee to obtain the consent of the Secretary of State before proceeding from the first stage to the second stage.

On 7 April 1997 the Secretary of State granted licences in the Seventeenth Round. Greenpeace applied for leave to move for judicial review of that decision but were refused leave by Laws J on 14 October 1997 by reason of delay. (*R v Secretary of State for Trade and Industry ex p Greenpeace* [1988] Env LR 415). I shall adopt the language of counsel and refer to that case as Greenpeace 1. In December 1998 the Secretary of State granted licences in the Eighteenth Round and a few other licences have been granted 'out of round', without further challenge by Greenpeace.

The present case is concerned with the Nineteenth Round. On 30 July 1997 the Secretary of State publicised outline plans for future 'oil and gas exploration opportunities around the United Kingdom in a five-year programme of offshore licensing rounds held under new environmental regulations'.

The plans referred to six rounds, from the Eighteenth to the Twenty-third, and indicated the general areas but not the precise locations of the blocks. As far as the Nineteenth Round is concerned the Secretary of State has not yet granted licences and the precise locations remain uncertain. Greenpeace issued the present application on 1 April 1999.

The basis of the present application

In a nutshell Greenpeace's challenge may be described as follows. The areas to be licensed in the Nineteenth Round lie outside the 12-mile limit of United Kingdom Territorial waters but within the area of the United Kingdom Continental Shelf (UKCS). Council Directive 92/43/EEC on the conservation of natural habitats and of wild fauna and flora (the Habitats Directive) which was issued on 21 May 1992 obliged Member States to legislate. The domestic legislation which ensued, in particular the Conservation (National Habitats etc) Regulations 1994, is expressly stated to apply only up to the 12-mile limit.

The Secretary of State contends that the Regulations are a proper implementation of the Habitats Directive which did not impose obligations beyond the 12-mile limit. Accordingly, he does not consider the Regulations or the Habitats Directive in the course of his licensing function, although he does have due regard to various other environmental obligations. Greenpeace contends that the Secretary of State has fallen into fundamental legal error in that the Habitats Directive, properly construed, required the domestic legislation which implemented it to extend to the UKCS and the waters above; that the Secretary of State is obliged to carry out his licensing function in accordance with the Habitats Directive; and that, on that basis, he has particular responsibilities in the Nineteenth Round towards cetaceans (whales, porpoises and dolphins) and lophelia pertusa. There are many substantive issues in the case but at the forefront of them all is the issue as to the territorial scope of the Habitats Directive.

The Legal context: international, European and domestic

The United Kingdom, the Member States of the European Community and the Community itself are all parties to the United Nations Convention on the Law of the Sea (UNCLOS).

Art 2 of UNCLOS provides:

1   The sovereignty of a coastal State extends beyond its land territory and internal waters ... to an adjacent belt of sea, described as the territorial sea.

2   This sovereignty extends to the air space over the territorial sea as well as to its bed and subsoil.

By Art 3:

Every State has the right to establish the breadth of its territorial sea up to a limit not exceeding 12 nautical miles, measured from baselines determined in accordance with this Convention.

UNCLOS also recognises two further concepts, namely the exclusive economic zone (EEZ) and the continental shelf. The EEZ is:

... an area beyond and adjacent to the territorial sea, subject to the specific legal regime established in this Part, under which the rights and jurisdiction of the coastal State and the rights and freedoms of other States are governed by the relevant provisions of this Convention (Art 55).

In an EEZ the coastal State has, *inter alia*:

... sovereign rights for the purpose of exploring and exploiting, conserving and managing the natural resources, whether living or non-living, of the waters superjacent to the seabed and of the seabed and its subsoil ... and jurisdiction with regard to 'the protection and preservation of the marine environment' (Art 56.1).

The continental shelf of a coastal State comprises:

... the seabed and subsoil of the submarine areas that extend beyond its territorial sea throughout the natural prolongation of its land territory to the outer edge of the continental margin, or to a distance of 200 nautical miles from the baselines from which the breadth of the territorial sea is measured where the outer edge of the continental margin does not extend up to that distance (Art 76).

The coastal State exercises over the continental shelf:

... sovereign rights for the purpose of exploring it and exploiting its natural resources (Art 77.1).

So far as the United Kingdom is concerned, it has not formally declared an EEZ but it has declared a 200 nautical miles exclusive fishery zone (EFZ) pursuant to section 1(1) of the

Fishery Limits Act 1976. Also, as regards the continental shelf, by section 1(1) of the Continental Shelf Act 1964, any rights exercisable outside territorial waters with respect to the seabed and subsoil and their natural resources (except in relation to coal) are vested in the Crown. Section 1(7) enables areas of the continental shelf to be prescribed by Order in Council for the purposes of exploitation and this has occurred or will occur in relation to those areas which are to be subject to the Nineteenth Round. Thus it is common ground that the Nineteenth Round is concerned with areas outside the UK territorial sea but within the UKCS and its EFZ, and in respect of which the UK exercises sovereign rights.

Art 174 (formerly 130r) of the EC Treaty defines the objectives of Community policy on the environment and states:

> Community policy on the environment shall aim at a high level of protection taking into account the diversity of situations in the various regions of the Community. It shall be based on the precautionary principle and on the principles that preventive action should be taken, that environmental damage should as a priority be rectified at source and that the polluter should pay.

This is the provision upon which the Habitats Directive was expressly based.

The aim of the Habitats Directive is set out in Art 2 in the following terms:

> 1   The aim of this Directive shall be to contribute towards ensuring biodiversity through the conservation of natural habitats and of wild fauna and flora in the European territory of the Member States to which the Treaty applies.

I shall have to return to several other parts of the Habitats Directive in some detail but the words I have emphasised in Art 2(1) are at the heart of the issue about its geographical scope. So far as the structure of the Directive is concerned, Arts 3 to 11 are headed 'Conservation of natural habitats and habitats of species' and they are concerned with the setting up of 'Natura 2000' a coherent European network of special areas of conservation (SACs). Article 12, the first of five arts headed 'Protection of species', requires Member States to 'take the requisite measures to establish a system of strict protection for the animal species listed in Annex IV(a) in their natural range'. That list refers to all species of cetaceans.

The Government of the United Kingdom sought to transpose the requirements of the Habitats Directive into domestic law in the Conservation (Natural Habitats etc) Regulations 1994 ('the 1994 Regulations') which came into force on 30 October 1994. Their scope extends to any 'European marine site', that is, a European site which consists of, or so far as it consists of, 'marine areas' and 'marine area' is defined as: '... any land covered (continuously or intermittently) by tidal waters or any part of the sea in or adjacent to Great Britain up to the seaward limit of territorial waters.' (Regulation 2(1)). In other words, up to 12 nautical miles.

The issues

At the commencement of his submissions, Mr Pleming QC on behalf of Greenpeace, identified the issues in the application in a list. Although other counsel put forward other items or the same items but in a different form or sequence, I propose to approach the application initially by reference to Mr Pleming's list. It is as follows:

1   Does the geographical reach of Arts 4 and 12 of the Habitats Directive extend beyond a Member State's land, internal and territorial waters, to apply to areas over which a

Member State exercises sovereign rights, viz the continental shelf and superjacent waters?

2   If so, do those provisions of the Habitats Directive apply to the area of the UKCS which the Secretary of State intends to offer for oil exploration in the Nineteenth Round?

3   Is there evidence to show that natural habitats of Community interest (reefs of lophelia pertusa) are likely to be found in those areas of the UKCS which the Secretary of State intends to offer for oil exploration in the Nineteenth Round or to be affected by licensed activities in those areas?

4   Are there species of Community interest (cetaceans) within Annex IV(a) of the Habitats Directive which have their natural range within the area of the UKCS and superjacent waters which the Secretary of State intends to offer for oil exploration in the Nineteenth Round?

5   Are the natural habitats and species referred to in 3 and 4, above, likely to be adversely affected by the proposed activities (oil exploration) in the area of the UKCS covered by the Nineteenth Round?

6   In forming his proposals for the Nineteenth Round, has the Secretary of State complied with the requirements of the Habitats Directive?

7   Has the Government correctly transposed the requirements of Art 12 to the protected species within any waters over which it has sovereignty or exercises sovereign rights? [Dealt with as issue 6.]

8   Should Greenpeace be refused permission to apply for judicial review or be refused the relief which it seeks on the basis of delay?

[This extract only deals with aspects of the argument in relation to issues 1 and 6 (issue 6 is listed above as issue 7).]

Issue 1: the geographical scope of the Habitats Directive

What is meant by 'the European territory of the Member States' in Art 2(1) of the Habitats Directive? The words are not the subject of express definition in the Directive. As a matter of history, when the Commission first put forward the text of a proposed Directive, the words were: the European territory of the Member States, including maritime areas under the sovereignty or jurisdiction of the Member States but the additional words were omitted from the final version. It is suggested on behalf of the Secretary of State and the Oil Companies that this illustrates an intention on the part of the Council to limit the Directive to land and the territorial sea, whilst the case for Greenpeace is that the omission was for the purpose of bringing the Habitats Directive in line with the earlier Directive on the Conservation of Wild Birds (79/409/EEC), Art 1 of which uses the same wording as Art 2(1)of the Habitats Directive. Indeed the EC treaty itself applies its provisions to 'the European territories for whose external relations a Member State is responsible' (Art 299(4)), without further definition of 'European territories'. Mr Pleming seeks to attach significance to this formulation and submits that it is not restricted to 'sovereignty' in the strict sense and that Community Law must apply to activities in and over areas such as the Continental Shelf because otherwise they would be, in Community Law terms, 'lawless zones'. In this regard, he refers to *Halsbury's Laws of England*, 4th edn, Vol 51, paras 1–53:

Community law should apply to areas such as the continental shelf and the contiguous zone which, although not 'territory' in the strict sense of the term, are, under the rules of international law, subject to the limited jurisdiction of the coastal state. Therefore the national control, particularly relevant to the exporation and exploitation of oil and mineral wealth, must be exercised subject to Community rules.

Clearly these submissions on behalf of Greenpeace are intended to reflect the purposive or teleological approach to construction with which we are all now familiar and which require no citation of authority at this stage. They are also a prelude to eight headings or propositions which, Mr Pleming submits, all point to the geographical scope for which Greenpeace contends. It is to them that I now turn.

(1) Consistency with the object and purpose of the Habitats Directive

In the Preamble to the Habitats Directive, its 'main aim' is referred to as being:

> ... to promote the maintenance of biodiversity, taking account of economic, social, cultural and regional requirements,

and it is stated that the Directive:

> ... makes a contribution to the general objective of sustainable development.

I have already set out 'the aim of this Directive' as defined in Art 2(1). It is submitted on behalf of Greenpeace that these objectives are more likely to be achieved if the geographical scope extends to the continental shelf and its superjacent waters. Cetaceans spend only a limited amount of time in territorial waters and, like lophelia pertusa, are generally found beyond those limits. Cetaceans are specifically listed in Annex IV(a) and the purpose of the Directive in relation to them (and in relation to lophelia pertusa which is not specifically listed) is more likely to be achieved if the geographical scope is liberally construed.

[...]

Conclusion on geographical scope

My task is to concentrate on the text of the Habitats Directive, bringing to it where necessary the purposive or teleological approach to which I have referred. In my judgment the wider scope contended for by Greenpeace is correct. It seems to me that a Directive which includes in its aims the protection of *inter alia*, lophelia pertusa and cetaceans will only achieve those aims, on a purposive construction, if it extends beyond territorial waters. Although much of the concern of the Directive and some of its language can properly be described as 'land-based', it also deals specifically with some habitats and species which are sea-based and, to a large extent, flourish beyond territorial waters [...]

Issue 6: Art 12 of the Habitats Directive

Greenpeace's case in relation to cetaceans is based on Art 12 which provides:

1 Member States shall take the requisite measures to establish a system of strict protection for the animal species listed in Annex IV(a) in their natural range, prohibiting:

   (a) all forms of deliberate capture or killing of specimens of these species in the wild;

   (b) deliberate disturbance of these species, particularly during the period of breeding, rearing and hibernation and migration;

   (c) deliberate destruction or taking of eggs from the wild;

   (d) deterioration or destruction of breeding sites or resting places.

Greenpeace does not rely on (a) or (c) but I include them because of the construction issues which arise. The transposition of these requirements into the 1994 Regulations took the following form:

39 (1) It is an offence:

(a) deliberately to capture or kill a wild animal of a European protected species;

(b) deliberately to disturb any such animal;

(c) deliberately to take or destroy the eggs of such an animal;

(d) to damage or destroy a breeding site or resting place of such an animal.

Regulation 40(3) provides certain defences, the most relevant one being that a person is not guilty by reason of:

(c) any act made unlawful by that regulation if he shows that the act was the incidental result of a lawful operation and could not reasonably have been avoided.

These Regulations are, of course, applicable only up to the seaward limit of territorial waters (reg 2(1)). Several sub-issues arise in relation to Art 12 and regs 39 and 40.

(1) What does Art 12 mean?

Greenpeace contends for a wide construction of Art 12(1). In making his submissions, Mr Pleming puts Art 12 in the context of the aim of the Habitats Directive as set out in Art 2 (to which I have already referred) as providing the basis for a purposive construction. He also refers to the 'precautionary principle' referred to in Art 174 (formerly Art 130r) of the EC Treaty which I set out earlier. Thus, it is submitted, Art 12(1) provides for a duty not only in relation to the prohibitions listed as (a) to (d) but also in relation to a free-standing duty to establish a system of strict protection. As against this, Miss Sharpston (supported by Mr Ouseley) submits that there is no free-standing duty to establish a system of strict protection. The words 'a system of strict protection' are not defined in the Directive and so, it is submitted, the prohibitions listed as (a) to (d) are, in effect, the definition. The key word is 'prohibiting', which indicates that the following provisions are an exhaustive code so far as the requirement to establish a system of strict protection is concerned. In my judgment, Miss Sharpston and Mr Ouseley are right. Their construction is the more attractive from a literal standpoint and a purposive approach does not justify a construction of the width contended for by Mr Pleming. It would lead to a system of protection on land and at sea of a degree which cannot have been contemplated.

The next point of construction relates to the meaning of the word 'deliberate' in the context of deliberate disturbance (Art 12(1)(b)). The assumed factual matrix is that oil exploration activities of the type contemplated will or are likely to or may disturb cetaceans particularly during breeding, rearing, hibernation and migration. Mr Pleming submits that when an operator conducts an activity in the knowledge that such disturbance will result or knowing that it is likely or possible that it will result, he is 'deliberately' disturbing. It does not require an intention or desire to disturb, simply that the consequence is known or foreseen or foreseeable. Miss Sharpston and Mr Ouseley submit that that is an erroneous construction of 'deliberate' which, it is suggested, is the antithesis of 'incidental'. On their, narrower, construction 'deliberate disturbance' connotes a specific aim of disturbing a species. They also point to Art 12(4) which provides:

Member States shall establish a system to monitor the incidental capture and killing of the animal species listed in Annex IV(a). In the light of the information gathered,

Member States shall take further research on conservation measures as required to ensure that incidental capture and killing does not have a significant negative effect on the species concerned.

The word 'deliberate' is not commonly used in our domestic criminal law to prescribe the mental element of an offence. When we use it, it tends to be in contradiction to 'accidental' and to relate to an act rather than to its consequences, in respect of which we tend to resort to concepts of 'intention' and 'recklessness'. This no doubt explains why counsel, in this impressively prepared case, have been unable to cite authority from our criminal jurisprudence on the meaning of 'deliberate'. However, Mr Pleming did refer to *Marcel Beller Ltd v Hayden* [1978] QB 694; [1978] 3 All ER 111 where the subject matter was an exception in an insurance policy in relation to death resulting from 'deliberate exposure to exceptional danger'. The danger in question was that involved in driving when drunk. It was held that the words meant conscious exposure to such danger. There was no evidence that the deceased had deliberately chosen to take the risk. His driving, although negligent, did not amount to a deliberate exposure to exceptional danger. Assuming that that case was correctly decided on this point, I do not find it to be of much assistance in the present context.

In my judgment, the submissions of Miss Sharpston and Mr Ouseley and the antithesis of 'deliberate' and 'incidental' are correct. I do not consider that it could properly be said that the Oil Companies engage in the deliberate disturbance of cetaceans. However, whilst that may put an end to Greenpeace's reliance on para (b), it does not deal with para (d) where the word 'deliberate' is absent. Mr Ouseley submits that, since para (d) relates only to destruction or deterioration of breeding sites or resting places and not to species or specimens, it presupposes some permanent and/or physical damage to a site and that, as cetaceans do not have anything comparable with, say, a badger sett, they fall outside the ambit of para (d). That is a submission of typical ingenuity but it is difficult to accept or reject it on the evidence. I have already referred to reg 40(3)(c) and the defence of 'incidental result of a lawful activity' which 'could not reasonably have been avoided'.

This provision has polarised the parties. To Greenpeace it is a wholly unwarranted and unlawful derogation from Art 12 but it is nevertheless a useful aid to construction. To the Secretary of State and the Oil Companies it is justifiable, lawful and, as an aid to the proper construction of Art 12, it does nothing to assist Greenpeace. I shall have to return to the question whether Mr Pleming's primary submission is correct. For the moment, I am concerned with its potential as an aid to construction. Mr Pleming submits that reg 40(3)(c) presupposes that, in the absence of the defence which it purports to provide, the act in question would fall foul of reg 39(1) – and therefore Art 12. In other words, 'incidental' disturbance or deterioration would come within the prohibition. I do not consider this approach to be correct because Regulations which are intended to transpose the requirements of a Directive are of limited value in the construction of the Directive itself. At the highest, all that can be said is that the point is indicative of the Government holding a different view on the issue of construction at the time of transposition from the one they now postulate.

The next question is whether reg 40(3)(c) can live in harmony with the Habitats Directive. Mr Pleming submits that it cannot because it has no basis in the Directive and it has the effect of an impermissible derogation from the Directive. As the Regulations apply only to the limit of territorial waters, the transposition of Art 12 is deficient even there. Miss Sharpston submits that reg 40(3)(c) is entirely compatible with Art 12. She relies on the antithesis between 'deliberate' in Art 12(1) and 'incidental' in Art 12(4). And, although 'deliberate' is absent from Art 12(1)(d) which does not cross-refer to Art 12(4), it is, she submits, open to a Member State to transpose Art 12(1)(d) with a defence of the kind found in reg 40(3)(c). In other words, it falls within the margin of appreciation or discretion. She refers to *Ministero delle Finanze v Philip Morris (Belgium) SA* [1993] ECR I-3469 and *R v Secretary of State for Health ex p Gallaher Ltd* [1993] ECR I-3545. In a different context (tobacco advertising), those cases illustrate how some Directive provisions admit of a degree of discretion in Member States when transposing but others do not. In the final analysis it is a matter of interpretation. So far as Art 12 of the Habitats Directive is concerned, I can see no reason why a Member State should not include in its transposition a defence of the kind found in reg 40(3)(c). It is significant, as Mr Ouseley points out, that Art 12, while expressed in terms of 'prohibition', does not in terms require the creation of criminal offences. This Member State has chosen to express the prohibition in the form of criminal offence. In the circumstances, it is entirely natural, reasonable and within the degree of discretion, that the criminal offences are defined (whether by reference to a defence or otherwise) in a manner which is clear and consistent with the style and ethos of our criminal law. Moreover, without reg 40(3)(c), the range of criminality which might arise in the course of carrying out activities which are in other respects lawful would be intolerable, especially if Art 12(1)(d) were allowed to create a crime of virtually strict liability.

In my judgment there is great force in the submissions of Miss Sharpston and Mr Ouseley in relation to reg 40(3). I do not consider it to be an unlawful derogation from the requirements of Art 12 and, accordingly, I do not find the transposition to be deficient as regards territorial waters. It follows from all that I have said in relation to Art 12 that I am deciding the construction points in favour of the Secretary of State (and the Oil Companies) and against Greenpeace.

[...]

Conclusions

It follows from what I have said that I grant permission to apply for judicial review. To the extent that I have indicated, I find that the challenge succeeds. As to relief, I propose to make declaration in the form of the first one sought, namely a declaration that the Habitats Directive applies to the UKCS and to the superjacent waters up to a limit of 200 nautical miles from the baseline from which the territorial sea is measured. [...]

REFERENCES AND FURTHER READING

Baldock, D, 'The status of special protection areas for the protection of wild birds' [1999] JEL 39

Baldock, D et al, 'Environmental sensitive areas: incrementalism or reform?' (1990) 6 J of Rural Studies 143

Birnie, P and Boyle, A, Basic Documents on International Law and the Environment, 1995, Oxford: Clarendon

Birnie, P and Boyle, A, International Law and the Environment, 1992, Oxford: OUP

Boyle, A, 'The Convention on Biological Diversity', in Campiglio et al (eds), The Environment After Rio: International Law and Economics, 1994, London/Dordrecht: Graham and Trotman/Martinus Nijhoff, pp 111–27

Bowman, M and Redgwell, C (eds), International Law and the Conservation of Biological Diversity, 1996, London: Kluwer

Centre for Agriculture and Environment, Greening the CAP, Report 1995, London: IEEP; Netherlands: CLM

Cheyne, I, 'Law and ethics in the trade and environment debate: tuna, dolphins and turtles' [2000] 12 JEL 3

Farrier, D and Tucker, L, 'Wise use of wetlands under the Ramsar Convention: a challenge for meaningful implementation of international Law' [2000] JEL 27–42

Favre, D, 'Trade in endangered species, VIII Natural resource management and conservation', 1999: The Year in Review (2000) 10 Yearbook of International Environmental Law 336

Garner, J and Jones, B, Countryside Law, 3rd edn, 1997, Crayford: Shaw

Gibson, J, 'Marine nature reserves' [1984] JPL 699

Handl, G, 'Environmental security and global change: the challenge to international law', in Handl, G (ed), Yearbook of International Environmental Law, 1991, London/Dordrecht: Graham and Trotman/Martinus Nijhoff

Johnston, S, '1999: The year in review, VIII. Natural resource management and conservation, B. Convention on Biological Diversity' (2000) 10 Yearbook of International Environmental Law 323–31

de Klemm, C (with Shine, C), Biological Diversity Conservation and the Law: Legal Mechanisms for Conserving Species and Eco-systems, IUCN Environmental Policy and Law Paper No 29, 1993, Gland, Switzerland: IUCN – The World Conservation Union

Lyster, S, International Wildlife Law, 1985, Cambridge: Grotius

Matthews, G, The Ramsar Convention on Wetlands: Its History and Development, 1993, Gland, Switzerland: Gland International Water Fowl and Wetlands Conservation Bureau

Nayar, J, and Ong, DM, 'Developing countries, "development" and the conservation of biological diversity', in Bowman, M and Redgwell, C (eds), *International Law and the Conservation of Biological Diversity*, 1996, London: Kluwer, pp 235–53

Ong, DM, 'The Convention on International Trade in Endangered Species (CITES 1973: implications of recent developments in international and EC environmental law)' [1998] 10 JEL 2

Qureshi, AH, 'The Cartagena Protocol on Biosafety and the WTO – co-existence or incoherence?' (2000) 49(4) ICLQ 835-55

Reid, C, *Nature Conservation Law*, 1994, Edinburgh: W Green/Sweet & Maxwell

Sands, D, *Principles of International Environmental Law*, 1995, Manchester: MUP, Vol I

Schoenbaum, Thomas J, 'International trade in living modified organisms: the new regimes' (2000) 49(4) ICLQ 856–67

Tuddenham, *Report on the Application of Directive 79/409/EEC on the Conservation of Wild Birds (1981–92)*, 1993, Paris: IPEE

USEFUL WEBSITES:

Biodiversity Convention: www.biodiv.org

Biosafety Protocol: www.biodiv.org/biosafety

Cites Convention: www.cites.org

English Nature: www.english-nature.org.uk

Marine Conservation Society: www.mcsuk.org/home.html

Ramsar Convention: www.ramsar.org

Royal Society for Nature Conservation: www.rsnc.org

Royal Society for the Protection of Birds: www.rspb.org.uk

Woodland Trust: www.woodland-trust.org.uk

World Wide Fund for Nature – WWF global network: www.panda.org

For further general websites, see pages l–li, above.

CHAPTER 7

HUMAN RIGHTS, PARTICIPATION AND ACCESS TO JUSTICE IN ENVIRONMENTAL LAW

INTRODUCTION

We saw in Chapter 1 that Principle 10 of the Rio Declaration 1992 enshrines the principle of citizen participation in environmental decision-making. This principle is based on the premise that participation is necessary for effective implementation of environmental laws at all levels. The White Paper, *This Common Inheritance*,[1] explains the importance of participation in terms of responsibility: 'The responsibility for our environment is shared. It is not a duty for government alone. It is an obligation on us all (para 1.38).' To be effective participants, however, citizens must be well-informed and have access to accurate and reliable information as well as opportunities to present their views and to question and challenge decisions which have adverse environmental impacts. In order to exercise this responsibility citizens must therefore be granted certain rights, including access to information, the right to participate in environmental decision making and access to tribunals in order to challenge environmental decisions.

The various advantages of conferring such rights may be summarised as follows:[2]

- it is likely to improve confidence in environmental decision-making (public reassurance);

- it will better inform consumer choice. For example, eco-labelling will enable people to make environmentally responsible purchasing decisions;

- in turn, informed consumer choices may stimulate industry to take environmental protection seriously;

- knowledge that their decisions will come under scrutiny and may be challenged will improve accountability of public agencies and may also improve the quality of their decision-taking;

- the democratic process will be advanced by enabling the public to participate more effectively both in policy formulation and decision-taking on environmental issues.

As Ebbesson explains, these advantages of conferring rights of participation in environmental decision-making rest on three categories of argument. First is the straightforward argument that participation is good for environmental protection and effective implementation of the law. It improves the quality of decisions taken. The second argument links participation with international human rights concepts. Participation is an important element in protecting and promoting human rights, both in a procedural sense and in a substantive sense. The third argument is that rights to

---

1   (1990) Cm 1200.
2   See Royal Commission 10th Report, *Tackling Pollution – Experience and Prospects*, Cmnd 9149 discussed by Rowan-Robinson, J *et al*, 'Public access to environmental information: a means to what end?' [1996] 8(1) JEL 19–42.

participate confer legitimacy upon decisions by public bodies affecting the environment (Ebbesson (1997) 62).

This chapter considers the principal international, EC and UK domestic law directly concerned with rights and the environment. In particular it covers: access to environmental information; environmental impact assessment; access to justice in environmental matters; and human rights and the environment, particularly in relation to the European Convention on Human Rights and Fundamental Freedoms (ECHR) (UKTS 71 (1953)).

INTERNATIONAL LAW

On the international stage the combined issues of access to environmental information and provisions enabling consultation or participation in environmental decision-making processes are addressed at two levels. First, at the inter-State level, both general and specific international environmental instruments have laid down, with varying degrees of strictness, requirements to exchange relevant environmental information and to consult each other on potentially hazardous activities conducted within their territorial jurisdictions or under their control.[3] These obligations to notify and consult other States may be regarded as partly fulfilling a duty of due diligence under international law.[4] Secondly, recent international agreements are arguably more progressive in calling for the provision of environmental rights by States to their citizens and others. This reflects trends at the domestic and regional levels towards greater provision of substantive and procedural rights in order to promote environmental protection. Inter-State obligations and the obligation to confer rights upon individuals will be discussed in turn.

When introducing the international legal framework of rules for the protection of the environment (Chapter 1, p 2), we noted that the concept of State sovereignty requires State consent to be bound by international law. Consent to international legal obligations by States is manifested by the signature and ratification of international conventions in accordance with the law of treaties and recognition of State practice as evidence of *opinio juris*, that is, acceptance as law under customary international law. However, the evolution of specific customary rules of international law relating to the environment has been hampered by the rapid pace of technological development and progress in scientific understanding of environmental problems. The specific and technical nature of many of these problems and the complexity of proposed solutions also mitigate against the formation of general customary rules of international law. Thus, progress in the evolution of international environmental law has been, and will continue to be achieved mainly by the development of treaty regimes.

---

3   See, eg, UN/ECE Convention on the Transboundary Effects of Industrial Accidents 1992 (Art 9) and the UN/ECE Convention on the Protection and Use of Transboundary Water Courses and International Lakes 1999 (31 ILM (1992) 312): www.unece.org/env.

4   This due diligence duty can in turn be traced from the general duty to ensure that activities within national jurisdictions do not cause damage to other States (see Principle 21 of the Stockholm Declaration 1972 and Principle 2 of the Rio Declaration 1992, Chapter 1, pp 66–67 and 69–70, above).

On the other hand, certain basic international obligations in relation to the environment have been included within the customary rules of international law which are generally applicable to all States. This is especially true in the case of rules relating to State responsibility and liability over trans-boundary environmental damage caused by activities within the jurisdiction or control of any State. These general rules in turn give rise to a specific duty of due diligence on the part of the State in which the activity is taking place. Many questions arise in relation to the due diligence requirement, not least among them being the standard of behaviour that it obliges States to attain in order to fulfil this requirement.

As a consequence of this concern, however, it is possible to discern within specific environmental treaty regimes, efforts by the international community to prescribe some form of standard behaviour in order to meet the due diligence requirement imposed by general customary international law. The evolving standards of State behaviour have focused upon requirements of prior notification and consultation with respect to hazardous activities conducted within their territories which may cause damage, either to other States' territories or areas beyond national jurisdiction. These duties of prior notification and consultation may be seen as imperative in order to discharge the more generally applicable obligation of due diligence imputed upon all States as a result of their international responsibility for trans-boundary environmental damage.

In this chapter, we will discuss the international legal precedents for such requirements of prior notification and consultation in respect of hazardous activities occurring within a State's jurisdiction or control. We will also be examining their inclusion in two international conventions; the first of which is sectoral in terms of the nature of the activity involved but global in terms of its geographical application, while the second is universal in terms of the activities involved but limited in its application to a specific geographical region. These treaties are respectively, the 1986 Convention on Early Notification of a Nuclear Accident (see commentary, p 749, below) and the 1991 UN Economic Commission for Europe (ECE) Convention on Environmental Impact Assessment in a Trans-boundary Context (see commentary and text, p 751, below). In addition, the system of prior informed consent established for the international movement of hazardous wastes between exporting, importing and transit states under the 1989 Basel Convention on the Control of Trans-boundary Movements of Hazardous Wastes and Their Disposal will also be referred to. These treaties will be analysed in respect of their contribution to the articulation of the standard of State behaviour required to fulfil the duty of due diligence under international law for hazardous activities undertaken within a State's jurisdiction or control.

Before we begin our discussion of the duty of due diligence owed between States, it is important to analyse the other main strand of the evolving legal regime for ensuring environmental protection. This second equally important trend involves the recognition by States of a duty to inform, consult and possibly even allow certain rights of participation to their citizens in environmental decision-making matters, especially when these involve their local environments. The overall scope of this duty is yet to be properly defined at the international level but the range of possibilities that it encompasses is extremely wide. These include: the rights of individuals or local communities to be consulted within local environmental decision-making processes (such as planning inquiries); their input in environmental impact assessment exercises; standing before courts of law in order to challenge environmental laws and policies which may affect them negatively, and the legal remedies they may be able to rely upon, ranging from injunctions against certain activities to a right to recover civil damages and even protection by criminal sanctions. The nature and extent of the recognition of this right at the international level will be discussed below. For a recent articulation of these rights in a regional context, see the Aarhus Convention 1998 p 808, below. See also Lugano Convention on Civil Liability for Damage Resulting from Activities Dangerous to the Environment 1993 (32 ILM (1993) 1228).

On an even broader front, the question of whether similar types of rights may be enjoyed by different constituencies such as ethnic minority groups, indigenous peoples, future generations of peoples, animals, plants, and the natural environment *per se*, is one which will be noted but not discussed here due to the constraints of space.[5] Suffice to note, as Birnie and Boyle do, that '(C)laims of this kind are usually intended to effect a reorientation of the relationship between man and the environment, through broader participation in the process of law enforcement, dispute resolution, and environmental guardianship' (Birnie and Boyle (1992) 188).

It is clear from the above points that even an accepted definition of the term 'environmental right' has yet to be recognised under international law. Among the many unanswered questions concerning this right are whether it is a substantive new right, or merely a reinterpretation of an existing right; is it a procedural rather than a substantive right? Who has the right to exercise it? At what stage in any environmental decision-making process can they exercise this right? And, what remedies can they request in the exercise of this right? These issues have only recently been addressed by international lawyers as part of a general trend towards realising the extent of limitations placed upon the doctrine of State sovereignty by international human rights and environmental law (Anderson (1996) 1–3).

Without entering into a detailed discussion on exactly what an 'environmental right' entails and to whom it should be made available, the focus here will be on the extent to which certain formulations of environmental rights have been recognised under international law, especially in the aftermath of the Rio 'Earth Summit' (see Chapter 1, pp 53–54, 63 and 68–69, above). The conclusion arrived at through such an analysis is that autonomous and explicit environmental rights, which would legitimise international supervision of the whole range of a State's domestic environmental policies and allow individual claimants access to human rights or environmental institutions, are currently lacking in international law (Boyle (1996) 44 and Birnie and Boyle (1992) 190–91). Such environmental rights as do exist are either derived from other existing treaty rights such as the right to life, health or ownership of property (Birnie and Boyle (1992) 192), or of a much more general nature, in the sense of the right to an environment of quality suitable for the enjoyment of all other human rights (Boyle (1996) 57).

In the absence of a well-defined and fully-accepted catalogue of 'environmental rights' that States agree are owed to their citizens, this leaves environmental rights to be

---

5   See, eg, Stone, C, *Should Trees have Standing?: And Other Essays on Law, Morals and the Environment*, 1996, Dobbs Ferry: Oceana.

protected only in a procedural sense. In other words, this means that the protection of environmental rights can proceed only on the basis of an exercise of procedural rights in order to ensure access to environmental information, allowing participation in environmental decision-making and providing administrative and judicial remedies for cases of environmental injustice (Birnie and Boyle (1992) 194).

The prevailing ambivalence among States as to the provision of substantive as opposed to procedural rights to environmental protection may be discerned from an examination of the relevant provisions on this subject in the general standard setting international environmental instruments such as the Stockholm Declaration 1972 on the human environment and the Rio Declaration 1992 on environment and development (see Chapter 1, pp 63 and 69 *et seq*). Although Principle 1 of the Stockholm Declaration arguably provides for individual and collective rights to an environment of such quality as to permit a life of dignity and well-being, it is significant that no other treaty refers explicitly to the right to a decent environment in these terms (Birnie and Boyle (1992) 191). Where environmental rights are mentioned at all, they are usually phrased in collective terms (peoples' as opposed to individual's rights), as in Art 24 of the African Charter on Human and Peoples' Rights, or as a right to a healthy, as opposed to decent, environment such as in Art 12 of the UN Covenant on Economic and Social Rights 1966. Even these weaker formulations of substantive environmental rights have yet to be fully accepted by States[6] (Birnie and Boyle (1992) 192–93).

The Rio Declaration contains no explicit human right to a decent environment. Indeed, by placing human beings at the centre of concerns for sustainable development in Principle 1, albeit 'in harmony with nature', the Declaration appears to have laid down an explicitly anthropocentric approach that views the environment and its natural resources as existing only for human benefit, with no intrinsic value in themselves (Birnie and Boyle (1992) 193). Principle 10 of the Rio Declaration however does give substantial support in mandatory language for participatory environmental rights of an individualistic and fairly comprehensive nature (Boyle (1996) 61). As Boyle notes, this formulation of participatory rights is distinguishable from other such rights found in the context of human rights instruments due to its focus on environmental matters and its emphasis on participation rights throughout the environmental decision-making process, from 'appropriate' access to information to effective access to administrative and judicial remedies (Boyle (1996) 60–61). The accompanying para in Chapter 23 of Agenda 21 elaborating this broad right of participation also emphasises the need for individual, group and organisational inputs to the environmental impact assessment procedures (para 23.2).

This emphasis on participation rights is maintained by the UN/ECE Convention on Access to Information, Public Participation in Decision-making and Access to Justice in Environmental Matters (the Aarhus Convention 1998, which is the first binding international treaty to recognise 'the right of every person of present and future generations to live in an environment adequate to his or her health and well being' (Art 1) (see further, below).

---

6   See, however, 1990 UN General Assembly (UNGA) Resolution 45/94 which provides that 'individuals are entitled to have an environment adequate for their health and well-being'. Also Aarhus Convention 1998, Preamble and Art 1, p 810, below.

Aspects of Principle 10 of the Rio Declaration 1992 can also be found in Principle 23 of the World Charter for Nature 1982 (see commentary, Chapter 6, pp 565–66, above), Arts 2(6) and 3(8) of the ECE Convention on Environmental Impact Assessment 1991 (see pp 751 *et seq* below), Art 14 of the Biodiversity Convention 1992 (see commentary and text, Chapter 6, p 583, above), and in respect of access to environmental information, in EC Directives 85/337 and 90/313 (see pp 782 and 804, below). The inclusion of provisions relating to participatory rights in environmental decision-making processes within these global as well as regional instruments reflects significant international support among States for procedural as opposed to substantive environmental rights (Boyle (1996) 61).

Returning to the obligations owed between States under the duty of due diligence, a short discussion of the position under customary international law will be followed by an analysis of the treaty regimes that provide explicit requirements of notification and consultation for hazardous activities conducted within a State's jurisdiction or control.

Customary international law

In formulating the duty of due diligence under customary international law, reference must be made to the *Trail Smelter Arbitration (US v Canada)*[7] and the *Corfu Channel Case (UK v Albania)*[8] in order to distil the substance of the obligations that it entails.

In *Trail Smelter Arbitration* (see Chapter 2, p 94, above), once the question of Canada's responsibility and consequent liability under international law for damage caused by sulphur dioxide fumes carrying over the border to the United States had been resolved, a second question arose, as to whether the Trail Smelter company that was actually responsible for the production of the said fumes should be required to refrain from causing further damage in the future and, if so, to what extent? The Arbitration Tribunal held that Trail Smelter was to be required to refrain from causing any further damage and that a new operational system be introduced in order to reduce the pollution to an acceptable level. The principle enunciated by the Tribunal as the basis for this decision, namely that no State has the right to use or permit the use of its territory in such a manner as to cause injury to the territory of another State apparently binds the offending State both presently and for the future.

In the *Corfu Channel* case, the question arose as to whether mere knowledge on the part of the Albanian authorities of the laying of a minefield within the territorial waters of Albania gave rise to an international legal obligation to warn ships reported to be near the danger zone. Here the International Court of Justice reached the conclusion that despite the fact that there was insufficient evidence of connivance by the Albanian government with the (unknown) mine-layers, the mine-laying operation itself could not have taken place without the knowledge of the Albanian authorities. The court held that the failure of these authorities to warn approaching British warships of the danger, which resulted in damage to two warships and loss of human life, gave rise to the international responsibility of Albania. The relevant international obligation which was found to have

---

7   Reports of International Arbitration Awards, RIAA (1938 and 1941), p 1905.
8   (1949) ICJ Rep 4.

been breached in this case was formulated in these terms: every State has an obligation not to knowingly allow its territory to be used for acts contrary to the rights of other States.

In summary, the duty of due diligence as owed between States under customary international law appears to be neither temporal in the sense that it is not limited to the present time but extends into the future, nor is it especially fault-based in terms of requiring some evidence of malice or negligence before it may be deemed to have been breached (cf Higgins (1994) 160–61). These general criteria of the due diligence requirement have been supplemented and arguably strengthened by further treaty obligations of notification and consultation in cases of hazardous activities conducted within States' territories or under their control. The question remains whether these additional criteria for the fulfilment of the due diligence duty have transcended the treaty instruments in which they are found and become part of general customary international law as well?

Convention on Early Notification of a Nuclear Accident 1986[9]

The Notification Convention, along with the Convention on Assistance in the Case of a Nuclear Accident or Radiological Emergency (hereafter Assistance Convention), both of which are global in scope, were negotiated, adopted, and entered into force within months of the Chernobyl nuclear reactor accident in the former Union of Soviet Socialist Republics (USSR). They were adopted on 26 September 1986 and entered into force on 27 October 1986, no doubt helped by the minimal requirement that only three States parties' consent to be bound were needed for each Convention. The swiftness of their entry into force is in itself of great significance in terms of the evolution and progress of international environmental law. It is clear that despite the much-criticised protracted nature of most international negotiations leading towards the adoption of multilateral conventions, including environmental treaties, where the issue is of sufficient concern to governments, especially when they are galvanised by a strong tide of public opinion, agreement can be reached at an impressive speed.

On closer inspection however it may be argued that at least one reason why governments felt able to adopt the Notification Convention so readily is the fact that it does little more than clarify in treaty or conventional terms what most commentators would argue already exists under customary international law, namely that all States owe a duty to other States to notify them as soon as is feasible of possible trans-boundary damage due to activities under their jurisdiction or control. As Birnie and Boyle note, '(D)espite the looseness of its terminology and the range of excluded occurrences, the Convention does seem to justify the conclusion that the principle of timely notification is a customary obligation' (Birnie and Boyle (1992) 300).

In other words, there was a consensus among States on the need to elaborate upon the content of the duty of due diligence owed by nuclear operating States to other States, especially neighbouring States, in terms of the prevention and mitigation of trans-boundary nuclear damage. As Politi notes however this consensus was in stark contrast

---

9   25 ILM (1986) 1370.

to the lack of agreement on the vexed issue of assigning responsibility and liability as well as determining the value of compensation to be paid as a result of trans-boundary nuclear damage, which accounts for its absence in either of the Chernobyl-spawned Conventions ((1991) 475).

The Notification Convention created a mechanism for the provision of information as early as possible in order to minimise the trans-boundary environmental, health and economic consequences of a nuclear accident. It imposes on parties a duty to notify the International Atomic Energy Agency (IAEA) and other States (Art 2(a) and (b)) of incidences in which the release of radioactive material has or is likely to occur, and which has or is likely to result in an international trans-boundary release that could be of radiological safety significance to those other States (Arts 1(1)). An element of the precautionary principle (see p 49, above) may be discerned in the use of the term 'likely' in respect of the release of radioactive material that triggers the mandatory obligation to notify both the IAEA and other States. This is mitigated though by the lack of a definition of the phrase 'radiological safety significance'. As Birnie and Boyle note, 'this provision deliberately avoids objective definition, and thus leaves substantial discretion to States where incidents occur' (Birnie and Boyle (1992) 365).

The Convention lays down very specific obligations of information provision, including information on the exact circumstances of the incident (Arts 2(a) and 5(1)(a)), the means of minimising its radiological consequences in other States (Art 2(b)), the cause (Art 5(1)(c)), characteristics (Art 5(1)(d)) and predicted behaviour of any trans-boundary release of radioactive materials (Art 5(1)(h)), as well as information on the meteorological and hydrological conditions (Art 5(1)(e)), results of environmental monitoring relevant to the trans-boundary release (Art 5(1)(f)), and protective measures taken or planned (Art 5(1)(g)). These particular requirements arguably go a long way towards establishing a very clear set of criteria that need to be fulfilled in order for States to be able to discharge their duty of due diligence in respect of nuclear accidents within their jurisdiction or control. Conversely, a State which shows that it has indeed fulfilled all these requirements of early notification and information may argue that it should be able to avoid inter-State claims of responsibility and liability for consequent environmental and other damage to other States caused by an accidental trans-boundary release.

Quite apart from the above requirements which are specifically directed at nuclear activities, several more general questions may be asked concerning the extent of the due diligence requirement under general customary international law. For example, should the rather specific criteria outlined in relation to international trans-boundary releases of radiological safety significance be limited in their application to similar types of hazardous activities such as those involving nuclear-powered merchant shipping vessels or spacecraft, or the carriage of other hazardous and noxious substances? Or should this enhanced set of obligations be extended to include all activities capable of posing an environmental threat?

It would seem that the international community of States is beginning to identify and define the types of hazardous activities that it needs to regulate under international environmental law, at least in terms of setting-out the standards and criteria that need to be fulfilled in order to satisfy the duty of due diligence owed to other States in respect of such activities. In light of this, reference may be made to the Basel Convention 1989 (see also discussion in Chapter 4, p 347, above).

Basel Convention on the Control of Trans-boundary Movements of Hazardous Wastes and their Disposal 1989

Basel arguably raises the due diligence requirement for the trans-boundary movement of hazardous wastes in two ways. First, through the prior informed consent procedure between exporting, transit and importing States (Art 6), so that failure to secure the consent of either the transit or importing States according to the rules laid down by the Convention may be interpreted as falling short of the accepted due diligence standard should environmental damage occur, quite apart from being in breach of a treaty obligation. Secondly, by the imposition of the requirement that all hazardous wastes to be exported are managed in an environmentally sound manner (Art 4(8)), along with other similar requirements such as waste minimisation (Arts 4(2)(a) and (d)) and the provision of adequate waste disposal facilities (Art 4(2)(b)), the failure of which may also be interpreted negatively in terms of the due diligence duty.

More recent evidence of the efforts of the international community to regulate potentially hazardous activities, such as the movement of hazardous wastes by sea, more strictly, arguably enhancing the requirements of due diligence in respect of these activities, comes in the form of the adoption on 9 May 1996 of the International Convention on Liability and Compensation for Damage in Connection with the Carriage of Hazardous and Noxious Substances by Sea. The provisions of this Convention have been implemented in the UK by ss 182A–C Merchant Shipping Act 1995.

Convention on Environmental Impact Assessment in a Trans-boundary Context 1991 (Espoo)[10]

The Espoo Convention is the first multilateral agreement to lay down detailed rules, procedures, and practices for trans-boundary environmental impact assessment, albeit on a regional basis. It was negotiated under the auspices of the UN Economic Commission for Europe (ECE) and is open to all UN ECE Member States and the European Community. The Convention entered into force on 10 September 1997 and as of 4 May 2001 has 36 parties, including the EC. Other instances of environmental impact assessment requirements are confined to individual obligations in major treaties such as Art 206 in Pt XII of the 1982 UN Convention on the Law of the Sea (UNCLOS) (see Chapter 3, p 217). An increasing number of national legal systems also make provision for such assessments, irrespective of whether the effects are domestic or trans-boundary, as does the EC (see below, Directive 85/337, Art 7, p 830).

The Espoo Convention provides for detailed procedural requirements for a range of proposed activities that are 'likely to cause significant adverse trans-boundary impact' (Art 2(1)), the definition of which is not to be found within the text of the Convention. A similar omission is the failure to define 'an international trans-boundary release of radiological safety significance' in Art 1(1) of the 1986 Early Notification Convention (p 793, above). These procedural obligations include the notification of other 'affected' States parties of proposed activities listed in Appendix I that are likely to cause a

---

10   30 ILM (1991) 802; www.unece.org/env/eia.

significant adverse trans-boundary impact (Art 2(4)) and participation by an 'affected' State (defined in Art 1(iii)) in the environmental impact assessment procedure for the proposed activity (Arts 3 and 5), as well as public participatory rights in environmental impact assessment procedures in a trans-boundary area likely to be affected by the proposed activities, on an equal access, non-discriminatory basis (Arts 2(6) and 3(8)). Espoo therefore applies both aspects of the developing international environmental law on this issue: first, it contributes to the notification and consultation criteria to be fulfilled in order to discharge the duty of due diligence owed between States for potentially hazardous activities within their jurisdiction or control; and secondly, it provides the public with procedural rights in the environmental decision-making process through participation in the environmental impact assessment procedure.

CONVENTION ON ENVIRONMENTAL IMPACT ASSESSMENT IN A TRANS-BOUNDARY CONTEXT (1991)

THE PARTIES TO THIS CONVENTION,

Aware of the interrelationship between economic activities and their environmental consequences,

Affirming the need to ensure environmentally sound and sustainable development,

Determined to enhance international co-operation in assessing environmental impact in particular in a trans-boundary context,

Mindful of the need and importance to develop anticipatory policies and of preventing, mitigating and monitoring significant adverse environmental impact in general and more specifically in a trans-boundary context,

Recalling the relevant provisions of the Charter of the United Nations, the Declaration of the Stockholm Conference on the Human Environment, the Final Act of the Conference on Security and Co-operation in Europe (CSCE) and the Concluding Documents of the Madrid and Vienna Meetings of Representatives of the Participating States of the CSCE,

Commending the ongoing activities of states to ensure that, through their national legal and administrative provisions and their national policies, environmental impact assessment is carried out,

Conscious of the need to give explicit consideration to environmental factors at an early stage in the decision-making process by applying environmental impact assessment, at all appropriate administrative levels, as a necessary tool to improve the quality of information presented to decision-makers so that environmentally sound decisions can be made paying careful attention to minimising significant adverse impact, particularly in a trans-boundary context,

Mindful of the efforts of international organisations to promote the use of environmental impact assessment both at the national and international levels, and taking into account work on environmental impact assessment carried out under the auspices of the United Nations Economic Commission for Europe, in particular results achieved by the Seminar on Environmental Impact Assessment (September 1987, Warsaw, Poland) as well as noting the Goals and Principles on environmental impact assessment adopted by the Governing Council of the United Nations Environment Programme, and the Ministerial Declaration on Sustainable Development (May 1990, Bergen, Norway).

HAVE AGREED AS FOLLOWS:

Article 1 Definitions

For the purposes of this Convention,

(i) 'Parties' means, unless the text otherwise indicates, the Contracting Parties to this Convention;

(ii) 'Party of origin' means the Contracting Party or Parties to this Convention under whose jurisdiction a proposed activity is envisaged to take place;

(iii) 'Affected Party' means the Contracting Party or Parties to this Convention likely to be affected by the trans-boundary impact of a proposed activity;

(iv) 'Concerned Parties' means the Party of origin and the affected Party of an environmental impact assessment pursuant to this Convention;

(v) 'Proposed activity' means any activity or any major change to an activity subject to a decision of a competent authority in accordance with an applicable national procedure;

(vi) 'Environmental impact assessment' means a national procedure for evaluating the likely impact of a proposed activity on the environment;

(vii) 'Impact' means any effect caused by a proposed activity on the environment including human health and safety, flora, fauna, soil, air, water, climate, landscape and historical monuments or other physical structures or the interaction among these factors; it also includes effects on cultural heritage or socio-economic conditions resulting from alterations to those factors;

(viii) 'Trans-boundary impact' means any impact, not exclusively of a global nature, within an area under the jurisdiction of a Party caused by a proposed activity the physical origin of which is situated wholly or in part within the area under the jurisdiction of another Party;

(ix) 'Competent authority' means the national authority or authorities designated by a Party as responsible for performing the tasks covered by this Convention and/or the authority or authorities entrusted by a Party with decision-making powers regarding a proposed activity;

(x) 'The Public' means one or more natural or legal persons.

Article 2 General provisions

1 The Parties shall, either individually or jointly, take all appropriate and effective measures to prevent, reduce and control significant adverse trans-boundary environmental impact from proposed activities.

2 Each Party shall take the necessary legal, administrative or other measures to implement the provisions of this Convention, including, with respect to proposed activities listed in Appendix I that are likely to cause significant adverse trans-boundary impact, the establishment of an environmental impact assessment procedure that permits public participation and preparation of the environmental impact assessment documentation described in Appendix II.

3 The Party of origin shall ensure that in accordance with the provisions of this Convention an environmental impact assessment is undertaken prior to a decision to

authorise or undertake a proposed activity listed in Appendix I that is likely to cause a significant adverse trans-boundary impact.

4   The Party of origin shall, consistent with the provisions of this Convention, ensure that affected Parties are notified of a proposed activity listed in Appendix I that is likely to cause a significant adverse trans-boundary impact.

5   Concerned Parties shall, at the initiative of any such Party, enter into discussions on whether one or more proposed activities not listed in Appendix I is or are likely to cause a significant adverse trans-boundary impact and thus should be treated as if it or they were so listed. Where those Parties so agree, the activity or activities shall be thus treated. General guidance for identifying criteria to determine significant adverse impact is set forth in Appendix III.

6   The Party of origin shall provide, in accordance with the provisions of this Convention, an opportunity to the public in the areas likely to be affected to participate in relevant environmental impact assessment procedures regarding proposed activities and shall ensure that the opportunity provided to the public of the affected Party is equivalent to that provided to the public of the Party of origin.

7   Environmental impact assessments as required by this Convention shall, as a minimum requirement, be undertaken at the project level of the proposed activity. To the extent appropriate, the Parties shall endeavour to apply the principles of environmental impact assessment to policies, plans and programmes.

8   The provisions of this Convention shall not affect the right of Parties to implement national laws, regulations, administrative provisions or accepted legal practices protecting information the supply of which would be prejudicial to industrial and commercial secrecy or national security.

9   The provisions of this Convention shall not affect the right of particular Parties to implement, by bilateral or multilateral agreement where appropriate, more stringent measures than those of this Convention.

10 The provisions of this Convention shall not prejudice any obligations of the Parties under international law with regard to activities having or likely to have a trans-boundary impact.

Article 3 Notification

1   For a proposed activity listed in Appendix I that is likely to cause a significant adverse trans-boundary impact, the Party of origin shall, for the purposes of ensuring adequate and effective consultations under Art 5, notify any Party which it considers may be an affected Party as early as possible and no later than when informing its own public about that proposed activity.

2   This notification shall contain, *inter alia*:

(a) information on the proposed activity, including any available information on its possible trans-boundary impact;

(b) the nature of the possible decision; and

(c) an indication of a reasonable time within which a response under para 3 of this Art is required, taking into account the nature of the proposed activity,

and may include the information set out in para 5 of this Article.

3   The affected Party shall respond to the Party of origin within the time specified in the notification, acknowledging receipt of the notification, and shall indicate whether it intends to participate in the environmental impact assessment procedure.

4   If the affected Party indicates that it does not intend to participate in the environmental impact assessment procedure, or if it does not respond within the time specified in the notification, the provisions in paras 5, 6, 7 and 8 of this Article and in Arts 4 to 7 will not apply. In such circumstances the right of a Party of origin to determine whether to carry out an environmental impact assessment on the basis of its national law and practice is not prejudiced.

5   Upon receipt of a response from the affected Party indicating its desire to participate in the environmental impact assessment procedure, the Party of origin shall, if it has not already done so, provide to the affected Party:

   (a) relevant information regarding the environmental impact assessment procedure, including an indication of the time schedule for transmittal of comments; and

   (b) relevant information on the proposed activity and its possible significant adverse trans-boundary impact.

6   An affected Party shall, at the request of the Party of origin, provide the latter with reasonably obtainable information relating to the potentially affected environment under the jurisdiction of the affected Party, where such information is necessary for the preparation of the environmental impact assessment documentation. The information shall be furnished promptly and, as appropriate, through a joint body where one exists.

7   When a Party considers that it would be affected by a significant adverse trans-boundary impact of a proposed activity listed in Appendix I, and when no notification has taken place in accordance with para 1 of this Article, the concerned Parties shall, at the request of the affected Party, exchange sufficient information for the purposes of holding discussions on whether there is likely to be a significant adverse trans-boundary impact. If those Parties agree that there is likely to be a significant adverse trans-boundary impact, the provisions of this Convention shall apply accordingly. If those Parties cannot agree whether there is likely to be a significant adverse trans-boundary impact, any such Party may submit that question to an inquiry commission in accordance with the provisions of Appendix IV to advise on the likelihood of significant adverse trans-boundary impact, unless they agree on another method of settling this question.

8   The concerned Parties shall ensure that the public of the affected Party in the areas likely to be affected be informed of, and be provided with possibilities for making comments or objections on, the proposed activity, and for the transmittal of these comments or objections to the competent authority of the Party of origin, either directly to this authority or, where appropriate, through the Party of origin.

Article 4 Preparation of the environmental impact assessment documentation

1   The environmental impact assessment documentation to be submitted to the competent authority of the Party of origin shall contain, as a minimum, the information described in Appendix II.

2   The Party of origin shall furnish the affected Party, as appropriate through a joint body where one exists, with the environmental impact assessment documentation. The concerned Parties shall arrange for distribution of the documentation to the authorities

and the public of the affected Party in the areas likely to be affected and for the submission of comments to the competent authority of the Party of origin, either directly to this authority or, where appropriate, through the Party of origin within a reasonable time before the final decision is taken on the proposed activity.

Article 5 Consultations on the basis of the environmental impact assessment documentation

The Party of origin shall, after completion of the environmental impact assessment documentation, without undue delay enter into consultations with the affected Party concerning, *inter alia*, the potential trans-boundary impact of the proposed activity and measures to reduce or eliminate its impact. Consultations may relate to:

(a) possible alternatives to the proposed activity, including the no-action alternative and possible measures to mitigate significant adverse trans-boundary impact and to monitor the effects of such measures at the expense of the Party of origin;

(b) other forms of possible mutual assistance in reducing any significant adverse trans-boundary impact of the proposed activity; and

(c) any other appropriate matters relating to the proposed activity.

The Parties shall agree, at the commencement of such consultations, on a reasonable time-frame for the duration of the consultation period. Any such consultations may be conducted through an appropriate joint body, where one exists.

Article 6 Final decision

1   The Parties shall ensure that, in the final decision on the proposed activity, due account is taken of the outcome of the environmental impact assessment, including the environmental impact assessment documentation, as well as the comments thereon received pursuant to Art 3, para 8 and Art 4, para 2, and the outcome of the consultations as referred to in Art 5.

2   The Party of origin shall provide to the affected Party the final decision on the proposed activity along with the reasons and considerations on which it was based.

3   If additional information on the significant trans-boundary impact of a proposed activity, which was not available at the time a decision was made with respect to that activity and which could have materially affected the decision, becomes available to a concerned Party before work on that activity commences, that Party shall immediately inform the other concerned Party or Parties. If one of the concerned Parties so requests, consultations shall be held as to whether the decision needs to be revised.

Article 7 Post-project analysis

1   The concerned Parties, at the request of any such Party, shall determine whether, and if so to what extent, a post-project analysis shall be carried out, taking into account the likely significant adverse trans-boundary impact of the activity for which an environmental impact assessment has been undertaken pursuant to this Convention. Any post-project analysis undertaken shall include, in particular, the surveillance of the activity and the determination of any adverse trans-boundary impact. Such surveillance and determination may be undertaken with a view to achieving the objectives listed in Appendix V.

2   When, as a result of post-project analysis, the Party of origin or the affected Party has reasonable grounds for concluding that there is a significant adverse trans-boundary impact or factors have been discovered which may result in such an impact, it shall immediately inform the other Party. The concerned Parties shall then consult on necessary measures to reduce or eliminate the impact.

Article 8 Bilateral and multilateral co-operation

The Parties may continue existing or enter into new bilateral or multilateral agreements or other arrangements in order to implement their obligations under this Convention. Such agreements or other arrangements may be based on the elements listed in Appendix VI.

Article 9 Research programmes

The Parties shall give special consideration to the setting up, or intensification of, specific research programmes aimed at:

(a) improving existing qualitative and quantitative methods for assessing the impacts of proposed activities;

(b) achieving a better understanding of cause-effect relationships and their role in integrated environmental management;

(c) analysing and monitoring the efficient implementation of decisions on proposed activities with the intention of minimising or preventing impacts;

(d) developing methods to stimulate creative approaches in the search for environmentally sound alternatives to proposed activities, production and consumption patterns;

(e) developing methodologies for the application of the principles of environmental impact assessment at the macro-economic level.

The results of the programmes listed above shall be exchanged by the Parties.

Article 10 Status of the appendices

The Appendices attached to this Convention form an integral part of the Convention.

Article 11 Meeting of parties

1   The Parties shall meet, so far as possible, in connection with the annual sessions of the Senior Advisers to ECE Governments on Environmental and Water Problems. The first meeting of the Parties shall be convened not later than one year after the date of the entry into force of this Convention. Thereafter, meetings of the Parties shall be held at such other times as may be deemed necessary by a meeting of the Parties, or at the written request of any Party; provided that, within six months of the request being communicated to them by the secretariat, it is supported by at least one third of the Parties.

2   The Parties shall keep under continuous review the implementation of this Convention, and, with this purpose in mind, shall:

(a) review the policies and methodological approaches to environmental impact assessment by the Parties with a view to further improving environmental impact assessment procedures in a trans-boundary context;

(b) exchange information regarding experience gained in concluding and implementing bilateral and multilateral agreements or other arrangements regarding the use of environmental impact assessment in a trans-boundary context to which one or more of the Parties are party;

(c) seek, where appropriate, the services of competent international bodies and scientific committees in methodological and technical aspects pertinent to the achievement of the purposes of this Convention;

(d) at their first meeting, consider and by consensus adopt rules of procedure for their meetings;

(e) consider and, where necessary, adopt proposals for amendments to this Convention;

(f) consider and undertake any additional action that may be required for the achievement of the purposes of this Convention.

Article 12 Right to vote

1   Each Party to this Convention shall have one vote.

2   Except as provided for in para 1 of this Article, regional economic integration organisations, in matters within their competence, shall exercise their right to vote with a number of votes equal to the number of their Member States which are Parties to this Convention. Such organisations shall not exercise their right to vote if their Member States exercise theirs, and vice versa.

Article 13 Secretariat

The Executive Secretary of the Economic Commission for Europe shall carry out the following secretariat functions:

(a) the convening and preparing of meetings of the Parties;

(b) the transmission of reports and other information received in accordance with the provisions of this Convention to the Parties; and

(c) the performance of other functions as may be provided for in this Convention or as may be determined by the Parties.

Article 14 Amendments to the Convention

1   Any Party may propose amendments to this Convention.

2   Proposed amendments shall be submitted in writing to the secretariat, which shall communicate them to all Parties. The proposed amendments shall be discussed at the next meeting of the Parties, provided these proposals have been circulated by the secretariat to the Parties at least 90 days in advance.

3   The Parties shall make every effort to reach agreement on any proposed amendment to this Convention by consensus. If all efforts at consensus have been exhausted, and no agreement reached, the amendment shall as a last resort be adopted by a three-fourths majority vote of the Parties present and voting at the meeting.

4   Amendments to this Convention adopted in accordance with para 3 of this Article shall be submitted by the Depositary to all Parties for ratification, approval or acceptance. They shall enter into force for Parties having ratified, approved or accepted them on the ninetieth day after the receipt by the Depositary of notification of their ratification, approval or acceptance by at least three-fourths of these Parties. Thereafter they shall

enter into force for any other Party on the ninetieth day after that Party deposits its instrument of ratification, approval or acceptance of the amendments.

5   For the purpose of this Article, 'Parties present and voting' means Parties present and casting an affirmative or negative vote.

6   The voting procedure set forth in para 3 of this Article is not intended to constitute a precedent for future agreements negotiated within the Economic Commission for Europe.

Article 15 Settlement of disputes

1   If a dispute arises between two or more Parties about the interpretation or application of this Convention, they shall seek a solution by negotiation or by any other method of dispute settlement acceptable to the parties to the dispute.

2   When signing, ratifying, accepting, approving or acceding to this Convention, or at any time thereafter, a Party may declare in writing to the Depositary that for a dispute not resolved in accordance with para 1 of this Article, it accepts one or both of the following means of dispute settlement as compulsory in relation to any Party accepting the same obligations:

(a) submission of the dispute to the International Court of Justice;

(b) arbitration in accordance with the procedure set out in Appendix VII.

3   If the parties to the dispute have accepted both means of dispute settlement referred to in para 2 of this Article, the dispute may be submitted only to the International Court of Justice, unless the parties agree otherwise.

[Articles 16 (on Signature), 17 (on Ratification, Acceptance, Approval and Accession), 18 (on Entry Into Force), 19 (on Withdrawal) and 20 (on Authentic Texts) omitted.]

Appendix I List of activities

1   Crude oil refineries (excluding undertakings manufacturing only lubricants from crude oil) and installations for the gasification and liquefaction of 500 tonnes or more of coal or bituminous shale per day.

2   Thermal power stations and other combustion installations with a heat output of 300 megawatts or more and nuclear power stations and other nuclear reactors (except research installations for the production and conversion of fissionable and fertile materials, whose maximum power does not exceed 1 kilowatt continuous thermal load).

3   Installations solely designed for the production or enrichment of nuclear fuels, for the reprocessing of irradiated nuclear fuels or for the storage, disposal and processing of radioactive waste.

4   Major installations for the initial smelting of cast-iron and steel and for the production of non-ferrous metals.

5   Installations for the extraction of asbestos and for the processing and transformation of asbestos and products containing asbestos: for asbestos-cement products, with an

annual production of more than 20,000 tonnes finished product; for friction material, with an annual production of more than 50 tonnes finished product; and for other asbestos utilisation of more than 200 tonnes per year.

6   Integrated chemical installations.

7   Construction of motorways, express roads[11] and lines for long-distance railway traffic and of airports with a basic runway length of 2,100 metres or more.

8   Large-diameter oil and gas pipelines.

9   Trading ports and also inland waterways and ports for inland-waterway traffic which permit the passage of vessels of over 1,350 tonnes.

10   Waste-disposal installations for the incineration, chemical treatment or landfill of toxic and dangerous wastes.

11   Large dams and reservoirs.

12   Groundwater abstraction activities in cases where the annual volume of water to be abstracted amounts to 10 million cubic metres or more.

13   Pulp and paper manufacturing of 200 air-dried metric tonnes or more per day.

14   Major mining, on-site extraction and processing of metal ores or coal.

15   Offshore hydrocarbon production.

16   Major storage facilities for petroleum, petrochemical and chemical products.

17   Deforestation of large areas.

Appendix II Content of the environmental impact assessment documentation

Information to be included in the environmental impact assessment documentation shall, as a minimum, contain, in accordance with Art 4:

(a)   a description of the proposed activity and its purpose;

(b)   a description, where appropriate, of reasonable alternatives (for example, locational or technological) to the proposed activity and also the no-action alternative;

(c)   a description of the environment likely to be significantly affected by the proposed activity and its alternatives;

(d)   a description of the potential environmental impact of the proposed activity and its alternatives and an estimation of its significance;

---

11   For the purposes of this Convention:

'Motorway' means a road specially designed and built for motor traffic, which does not serve properties bordering on it, and which:

(a)   is provided, except at special points or temporarily, with separate carriageways for the two directions of traffic, separated from each other by a dividing strip not intended for traffic or, exceptionally, by other means;

(b)   does not cross at level with any road, railway or tramway track, or footpath; and

(c)   is specially sign-posted as a motorway.

'Express road' means a road reserved for motor traffic accessible only from interchanges or controlled junctions and on which, in particular, stopping and parking are prohibited on the running carriageway(s).

(e) a description of mitigation measures to keep adverse environmental impact to a minimum;

(f) an explicit indication of predictive methods and underlying assumptions as well as the relevant environmental data used;

(g) an identification of gaps in knowledge and uncertainties encountered in compiling the required information;

(h) where appropriate, an outline for monitoring and management programmes and any plans for post-project analysis; and

(i) a non-technical summary including a visual presentation as appropriate (maps, graphs, etc).

Appendix III General criteria to assist in the determination of the environmental significance of activities not listed in Appendix I

1   In considering proposed activities to which Art 2, para 5, applies, the concerned Parties may consider whether the activity is likely to have a significant adverse trans-boundary impact in particular by virtue of one or more of the following criteria:

(a) size: proposed activities which are large for the type of the activity;

(b) location: proposed activities which are located in or close to an area of special environmental sensitivity or importance (such as wetlands designated under the Ramsar Convention, national parks, nature reserves, sites of special scientific interest, or sites of archaeological, cultural or historical importance); also, proposed activities in locations where the characteristics of proposed development would be likely to have significant effects on the population;

(c) effects: proposed activities with particularly complex and potentially adverse effects, including those giving rise to serious effects on humans or on valued species or organisms, those which threaten the existing or potential use of an affected area and those causing additional loading which cannot be sustained by the carrying capacity of the environment.

2   The concerned Parties shall consider for this purpose proposed activities which are located close to an international frontier as well as more remote proposed activities which could give rise to significant trans-boundary effects far removed from the site of development.

Appendix IV Inquiry procedure

1   The requesting Party or Parties shall notify the secretariat that it or they submit(s) the question of whether a proposed activity listed in Appendix I is likely to have a significant adverse trans-boundary impact to an inquiry commission established in accordance with the provisions of this Appendix. This notification shall state the subject-matter of the inquiry. The secretariat shall notify immediately all Parties to this Convention of this submission.

2   The inquiry commission shall consist of three members. Both the requesting party and the other party to the inquiry procedure shall appoint a scientific or technical expert, and the two experts so appointed shall designate by common agreement the third expert, who shall be the president of the inquiry commission. The latter shall not be a national of one of the parties to the inquiry procedure, nor have his or her usual place

of residence in the territory of one of these parties, nor be employed by any of them, nor have dealt with the matter in any other capacity.

3 If the president of the inquiry commission has not been designated within two months of the appointment of the second expert, the Executive Secretary of the Economic Commission for Europe shall, at the request of either party, designate the president within a further two-month period.

4 If one of the parties to the inquiry procedure does not appoint an expert within one month of its receipt of the notification by the secretariat, the other party may inform the Executive Secretary of the Economic Commission for Europe, who shall designate the president of the inquiry commission within a further two-month period. Upon designation, the president of the inquiry commission shall request the party which has not appointed an expert to do so within one month. After such a period, the president shall inform the Executive Secretary of the Economic Commission for Europe, who shall make this appointment within a further two-month period.

5 The inquiry commission shall adopt its own rules of procedure.

6 The inquiry commission may take all appropriate measures in order to carry out its functions.

7 The parties to the inquiry procedure shall facilitate the work of the inquiry commission and, in particular, using all means at their disposal, shall:

(a) provide it with all relevant documents, facilities and information; and

(b) enable it, where necessary, to call witnesses or experts and receive their evidence.

8 The parties and the experts shall protect the confidentiality of any information they receive in confidence during the work of the inquiry commission.

9 If one of the parties to the inquiry procedure does not appear before the inquiry commission or fails to present its case, the other party may request the inquiry commission to continue the proceedings and to complete its work. Absence of a party or failure of a party to present its case shall not constitute a bar to the continuation and completion of the work of the inquiry commission.

10 Unless the inquiry commission determines otherwise because of the particular circumstances of the matter, the expenses of the inquiry commission, including the remuneration of its members, shall be borne by the parties to the inquiry procedure in equal shares. The inquiry commission shall keep a record of all its expenses, and shall furnish a final statement thereof to the parties.

11 Any Party having an interest of a factual nature in the subject matter of the inquiry procedure, and which may be affected by an opinion in the matter, may intervene in the proceedings with the consent of the inquiry commission.

12 The decisions of the inquiry commission on matters of procedure shall be taken by majority vote of its members. The final opinion of the inquiry commission shall reflect the view of the majority of its members and shall include any dissenting view.

13 The inquiry commission shall present its final opinion within two months of the date on which it was established unless it finds it necessary to extend this time limit for a period which should not exceed two months.

14 The final opinion of the inquiry commission shall be based on accepted scientific principles. The final opinion shall be transmitted by the inquiry commission to the parties to the inquiry procedure and to the secretariat.

Appendix V Post-project analysis

Objectives include:

(a) monitoring compliance with the conditions as set out in the authorisation or approval of the activity and the effectiveness of mitigation measures;

(b) review of an impact for proper management and in order to cope with uncertainties;

(c) verification of past predictions in order to transfer experience to future activities of the same type.

Appendix VI Elements for bilateral and multilateral co-operation

1 Concerned Parties may set up, where appropriate, institutional arrangements or enlarge the mandate of existing institutional arrangements within the framework of bilateral and multilateral agreements in order to give full effect to this Convention.

2 Bilateral and multilateral agreements or other arrangements may include:

(a) any additional requirements for the implementation of this Convention, taking into account the specific conditions of the subregion concerned;

(b) institutional, administrative and other arrangements, to be made on a reciprocal and equivalent basis;

(c) harmonisation of their policies and measures for the protection of the environment in order to attain the greatest possible similarity in standards and methods related to the implementation of environmental impact assessment;

(d) developing, improving, and/or harmonising methods for the identification, measurement, prediction and assessment of impacts, and for post-project analysis;

(e) developing and/or improving methods and programmes for the collection, analysis, storage and timely dissemination of comparable data regarding environmental quality in order to provide input into environmental impact assessment;

(f) the establishment of threshold levels and more specified criteria for defining the significance of trans-boundary impacts related to the location, nature or size of proposed activities, for which environmental impact assessment in accordance with the provisions of this Convention shall be applied; and the establishment of critical loads of trans-boundary pollution;

(g) undertaking, where appropriate, joint environmental impact assessment, development of joint monitoring programmes, intercalibration of monitoring devices and harmonisation of methodologies with a view to rendering the data and information obtained compatible.

[Appendix VII (on Arbitration) omitted.]

Convention on Access to Information, Public Participation in Decision-Making and Access to Justice in Environmental Matters (Aarhus Convention)[12]

The Aarhus Convention is regarded as being the most advanced international treaty on public participation concluded so far (Ebbesson (1997) 96). The Convention was adopted on 25 June 1998 and at 3 July 2001 has 14 parties. It requires 16 parties to enter into force (Art 20). The Convention provides a comprehensive right to public participation in environmental decision-making, particularly in relation to specific activities (Art 6). In addition it provides for a right of access to environmental information (note the breadth of the definition of environmental information in Art 2(3)). This right is defined in terms of a right to request and obtain information (Art 4) and an obligation upon States to collect and disseminate information (Art 5). Important as these provisions are, they have been criticised on the grounds that States are given broad discretion to refuse access (Art 5(3)). Moreover, Ebbesson says that 'the obligation to establish systems for the collection of environmental information fails to provide a firm basis for a right to know' and thereby easy access for individuals to information on any harmful activity and on the pollutants and risks involved (Ebbesson (1997) 96).[13]

The third aspect of Aarhus is the right of access to the courts in environmental matters (Art 9). This right ensures that decisions relating to participation and access to information may be challenged in the courts. It also encompasses 'the right to challenge the substantive legality of decisions' (Ebbesson (1997) 96). This link between procedural rights and substantive decisions is also recognised in the context of broader human rights issues. In the Preamble to the Convention, for example, it is recognised that every person has the 'right to live in an environment adequate to his or her health and well being' and that in order to be able to assert this right citizens 'must have' access to information, entitlements to participate in decision-making and access to justice.

One of the most important features of the Convention is the explicit assertion of the interests of Non-Governmental Organisations (NGOs). In most cases, they are entitled to participate in decision-making on behalf of public interests, to require the disclosure of environmental information, and to litigate.

Ebbesson points to the methods for ensuring compliance as being the weakest aspect of the Convention ((1997) 96). The parties were unable to agree on a compliance mechanism through which individuals and other non-State actors could complain or communicate to an international body in respect of alleged breaches.

---

12 For full text, see UN Doc ECE/CEP/43/(1998); see also www.unece.org/env/pp/etreaty.htm.
13 See also Kramer, L, 'The citizen in the environment: access to justice [2000] 5 Env Liability 127; Jendroska, J and Stec, S, 'The Aarhus Convention: towards a new era in environmental democracy' [2001] 3 Env Liability 140.

CONVENTION ON ACCESS TO INFORMATION, PUBLIC PARTICIPATION

IN DECISION-MAKING AND ACCESS TO JUSTICE IN ENVIRONMENTAL MATTERS (1998)

THE PARTIES TO THIS CONVENTION,

Recalling principle 1 of the Stockholm Declaration on the Human Environment,

Recalling also Principle 10 of the Rio Declaration on Environment and Development,

Recalling further General Assembly resolutions 37/7 of 28 October 1982 on the World Charter for Nature and 45/94 of 14 December 1990 on the need to ensure a healthy environment for the well-being of individuals,

Recalling the European Charter on Environment and Health adopted at the First European Conference on Environment and Health of the World Health Organisation in Frankfurt-am-Main, Germany, on 8 December 1989,

Affirming the need to protect, preserve and improve the state of the environment and to ensure sustainable and environmentally sound development,

Recognising that adequate protection of the environment is essential to human well-being and the enjoyment of basic human rights, including the right to life itself,

Recognising also that every person has the right to live in an environment adequate to his or her health and well-being, and the duty, both individually and in association with others, to protect and improve the environment for the benefit of present and future generations,

Considering that, to be able to assert this right and observe this duty, citizens must have access to information, be entitled to participate in decision-making and have access to justice in environmental matters, and acknowledging in this regard that citizens may need assistance in order to exercise their rights,

Recognising that, in the field of the environment, improved access to information and public participation in decision-making enhance the quality and the implementation of decisions, contribute to public awareness of environmental issues, give the public the opportunity to express its concerns and enable public authorities to take due account of such concerns,

Aiming thereby to further the accountability of and transparency in decision-making and to strengthen public support for decisions on the environment,

Recognising the desirability of transparency in all branches of government and inviting legislative bodies to implement the principles of this Convention in their proceedings,

Recognising also that the public needs to be aware of the procedures for participation in environmental decision-making, have free access to them and know how to use them,

Recognising further the importance of the respective roles that individual citizens, non-governmental organisations and the private sector can play in environmental protection,

Desiring to promote environmental education to further the understanding of the environment and sustainable development and to encourage widespread public awareness of, and participation in, decisions affecting the environment and sustainable development,

Noting, in this context, the importance of making use of the media and of electronic or other, future forms of communication,

Recognising the importance of fully integrating environmental considerations in governmental decision-making and the consequent need for public authorities to be in possession of accurate, comprehensive and up-to-date environmental information,

Acknowledging that public authorities hold environmental information in the public interest,

Concerned that effective judicial mechanisms should be accessible to the public, including organisations, so that its legitimate interests are protected and the law is enforced,

Noting the importance of adequate product information being provided to consumers to enable them to make informed environmental choices,

Recognising the concern of the public about the deliberate release of genetically modified organisms into the environment and the need for increased transparency and greater public participation in decision-making in this field,

Convinced that the implementation of this Convention will contribute to strengthening democracy in the region of the United Nations Economic Commission for Europe (ECE),

Conscious of the role played in this respect by ECE and recalling, *inter alia*, the ECE Guidelines on Access to Environmental Information and Public Participation in Environmental Decision-making endorsed in the Ministerial Declaration adopted at the Third Ministerial Conference 'Environment for Europe' in Sofia, Bulgaria, on 25 October 1995,

Bearing in mind the relevant provisions in the Convention on Environmental Impact Assessment in a Transboundary Context, done at Espoo, Finland, on 25 February 1991, and the Convention on the Trans-boundary Effects of Industrial Accidents and the Convention on the Protection and Use of Trans-boundary Watercourses and International Lakes, both done at Helsinki on 17 March 1992, and other regional conventions,

Conscious that the adoption of this Convention will have contributed to the further strengthening of the 'Environment for Europe' process and to the results of the Fourth Ministerial Conference in Aarhus, Denmark, in June 1998.

HAVE AGREED AS FOLLOWS:

Article 1 Objective

In order to contribute to the protection of the right of every person of present and future generations to live in an environment adequate to his or her health and well-being, each Party shall guarantee the rights of access to information, public participation in decision-making, and access to justice in environmental matters in accordance with the provisions of this Convention.

Article 2 Definitions

For the purposes of this Convention,

1   'Party' means, unless the text otherwise indicates, a Contracting Party to this Convention.

2   'Public authority' means:

    (a) Government at national, regional and other level;

    (b) natural or legal persons performing public administrative functions under national law, including specific duties, activities or services in relation to the environment;

(c) any other natural or legal persons having public responsibilities or functions, or providing public services, in relation to the environment, under the control of a body or person falling within sub-paras (a) or (b) above;

(d) the institutions of any regional economic integration organisation referred to in Art 17 which is a Party to this Convention.

This definition does not include bodies or institutions acting in a judicial or legislative capacity.

3   'Environmental information' means any information in written, visual, aural, electronic or any other material form on:

(a) the state of elements of the environment, such as air and atmosphere, water, soil, land, landscape and natural sites, biological diversity and its components, including genetically modified organisms, and the interaction among these elements;

(b) factors, such as substances, energy, noise and radiation, and activities or measures, including administrative measures, environmental agreements, policies, legislation, plans and programmes, affecting or likely to affect the elements of the environment within the scope of sub-para (a) above, and cost-benefit and other economic analyses and assumptions used in environmental decision-making;

(c) the state of human health and safety, conditions of human life, cultural sites and built structures, inasmuch as they are or may be affected by the state of the elements of the environment or, through these elements, by the factors, activities or measures referred to in sub-para (b) above.

4   'The public' means one or more natural or legal persons, and, in accordance with national legislation or practice, their associations, organisations or groups.

5   'The public concerned' means the public affected or likely to be affected by, or having an interest in, the environmental decision-making; for the purposes of this definition, non-governmental organisations promoting environmental protection and meeting any requirements under national law shall be deemed to have an interest.

Article 3 General Provisions

1   Each Party shall take the necessary legislative, regulatory and other measures, including measures to achieve compatibility between the provisions implementing the information, public participation and access-to-justice provisions in this Convention, as well as proper enforcement measures, to establish and maintain a clear, transparent and consistent framework to implement the provisions of this Convention.

2   Each Party shall endeavour to ensure that officials and authorities assist and provide guidance to the public in seeking access to information, in facilitating participation in decision-making and in seeking access to justice in environmental matters.

3   Each Party shall promote environmental education and environmental awareness among the public, especially on how to obtain access to information, to participate in decision-making and to obtain access to justice in environmental matters.

4   Each Party shall provide for appropriate recognition of and support to associations, organisations or groups promoting environmental protection and ensure that its national legal system is consistent with this obligation.

5   The provisions of this Convention shall not affect the right of a Party to maintain or introduce measures providing for broader access to information, more extensive public participation in decision-making and wider access to justice in environmental matters than required by this Convention.

6   This Convention shall not require any derogation from existing rights of access to information, public participation in decision-making and access to justice in environmental matters.

7   Each Party shall promote the application of the principles of this Convention in international environmental decision-making processes and within the framework of international organisations in matters relating to the environment.

8   Each Party shall ensure that persons exercising their rights in conformity with the provisions of this Convention shall not be penalised, persecuted or harassed in any way for their involvement. This provision shall not affect the powers of national courts to award reasonable costs in judicial proceedings.

9   Within the scope of the relevant provisions of this Convention, the public shall have access to information, have the possibility to participate in decision-making and have access to justice in environmental matters without discrimination as to citizenship, nationality or domicile and, in the case of a legal person, without discrimination as to where it has its registered seat or an effective centre of its activities.

Note: Referring to the obligation (Art 3(7)) upon parties to promote application of the principles of this Convention in international environmental decision-making processes, Ebbesson notes that this is particularly to be welcomed as such procedures are 'traditionally obscure and restricted' ((1997) 93).

Article 4 Access to Environmental Information

1   Each Party shall ensure that, subject to the following paragraphs of this article, public authorities, in response to a request for environmental information, make such information available to the public, within the framework of national legislation, including, where requested and subject to sub-para (b) below, copies of the actual documentation containing or comprising such information:

(a) without an interest having to be stated;

(b) in the form requested unless:

(i) it is reasonable for the public authority to make it available in another form, in which case reasons shall be given for making it available in that form; or

(ii) the information is already publicly available in another form.

2   The environmental information referred to in para 1 above shall be made available as soon as possible and at the latest within one month after the request has been submitted, unless the volume and the complexity of the information justify an extension of this period up to two months after the request. The applicant shall be informed of any extension and of the reasons justifying it.

3   A request for environmental information may be refused if:

  (a) the public authority to which the request is addressed does not hold the environmental information requested;

  (b) the request is manifestly unreasonable or formulated in too general a manner; or

  (c) the request concerns material in the course of completion or concerns internal communications of public authorities where such an exemption is provided for in national law or customary practice, taking into account the public interest served by disclosure.

4   A request for environmental information may be refused if the disclosure would adversely affect:

  (a) the confidentiality of the proceedings of public authorities, where such confidentiality is provided for under national law;

  (b) international relations, national defence or public security;

  (c) the course of justice, the ability of a person to receive a fair trial or the ability of a public authority to conduct an enquiry of a criminal or disciplinary nature;

  (d) the confidentiality of commercial and industrial information, where such confidentiality is protected by law in order to protect a legitimate economic interest. Within this framework, information on emissions which is relevant for the protection of the environment shall be disclosed;

  (e) intellectual property rights;

  (f) the confidentiality of personal data and/or files relating to a natural person where that person has not consented to the disclosure of the information to the public, where such confidentiality is provided for in national law;

  (g) the interests of a third party which has supplied the information requested without that party being under or capable of being put under a legal obligation to do so, and where that party does not consent to the release of the material; or

  (h) the environment to which the information relates, such as the breeding sites of rare species.

The aforementioned grounds for refusal shall be interpreted in a restrictive way, taking into account the public interest served by disclosure and taking into account whether the information requested relates to emissions into the environment.

5   Where a public authority does not hold the environmental information requested, this public authority shall, as promptly as possible, inform the applicant of the public authority to which it believes it is possible to apply for the information requested or transfer the request to that authority and inform the applicant accordingly.

6   Each Party shall ensure that, if information exempted from disclosure under paras 3(c) and 4 above can be separated out without prejudice to the confidentiality of the information exempted, public authorities make available the remainder of the environmental information that has been requested.

7   A refusal of a request shall be in writing if the request was in writing or the applicant so requests. A refusal shall state the reasons for the refusal and give information on access to the review procedure provided for in accordance with Art 9. The refusal shall be

made as soon as possible and at the latest within one month, unless the complexity of the information justifies an extension of this period up to two months after the request. The applicant shall be informed of any extension and of the reasons justifying it.

8   Each Party may allow its public authorities to make a charge for supplying information, but such charge shall not exceed a reasonable amount. [...]

Notes:

1   The traditional human rights approach to information is to provide a right to seek, receive, and impart information as part of the freedom of expression. See, for example, Art 10 of the European Convention for the Protection of Human Rights and Fundamental Freedoms 1953 and Art 19 of the UN Covenant on Civil and Political Rights 1966 (UKTS 6 (1977); 6 ILM 368). This right does not result in a duty upon the State to take positive action to keep specific information and provide it to the public, although such a right may exist under other provisions of the ECHR: see *Guerra & Others v Italy* (1998) 26 EHRR 357 (p 919, below).

2   The requirement that the grounds for refusing information that are listed in Art 4(3) and (4) be 'interpreted in a restrictive way' emphasises the importance of access to the courts in this context, see Art 9.

Article 5 Collection and Dissemination of Environmental Information

1   Each Party shall ensure that:

   (a) public authorities possess and update environmental information which is relevant to their functions;

   (b) mandatory systems are established so that there is an adequate flow of information to public authorities about proposed and existing activities which may significantly affect the environment;

   (c) in the event of any imminent threat to human health or the environment, whether caused by human activities or due to natural causes, all information which could enable the public to take measures to prevent or mitigate harm arising from the threat and is held by a public authority is disseminated immediately and without delay to members of the public who may be affected.

2   Each Party shall ensure that, within the framework of national legislation, the way in which public authorities make environmental information available to the public is transparent and that environmental information is effectively accessible, *inter alia*, by:

   (a) providing sufficient information to the public about the type and scope of environmental information held by the relevant public authorities, the basic terms and conditions under which such information is made available and accessible, and the process by which it can be obtained;

   (b) establishing and maintaining practical arrangements, such as:

      (i)   publicly accessible lists, registers or files;

      (ii) requiring officials to support the public in seeking access to information under this Convention; and

      (iii) the identification of points of contact; and

   (c) providing access to the environmental information contained in lists, registers or files as referred to in sub-para (b) (i) above free of charge.

3   Each Party shall ensure that environmental information progressively becomes available in electronic databases which are easily accessible to the public through public telecommunications networks. Information accessible in this form should include:

(a) reports on the state of the environment, as referred to in para 4 below;

(b) texts of legislation on or relating to the environment;

(c) as appropriate, policies, plans and programmes on or relating to the environment, and environmental agreements; and

(d) other information, to the extent that the availability of such information in this form would facilitate the application of national law implementing this Convention,

provided that such information is already available in electronic form.

4   Each Party shall, at regular intervals not exceeding three or four years, publish and disseminate a national report on the state of the environment, including information on the quality of the environment and information on pressures on the environment.

5   Each Party shall take measures within the framework of its legislation for the purpose of disseminating, *inter alia*:

(a) legislation and policy documents such as documents on strategies, policies, programmes and action plans relating to the environment, and progress reports on their implementation, prepared at various levels of government;

(b) international treaties, conventions and agreements on environmental issues; and

(c) other significant international documents on environmental issues, as appropriate.

6   Each Party shall encourage operators whose activities have a significant impact on the environment to inform the public regularly of the environmental impact of their activities and products, where appropriate within the framework of voluntary eco-labelling or eco-auditing schemes or by other means.

7   Each Party shall:

(a) publish the facts and analyses of facts which it considers relevant and important in framing major environmental policy proposals;

(b) publish, or otherwise make accessible, available explanatory material on its dealings with the public in matters falling within the scope of this Convention; and

(c) provide in an appropriate form information on the performance of public functions or the provision of public services relating to the environment by government at all levels.

8   Each Party shall develop mechanisms with a view to ensuring that sufficient product information is made available to the public in a manner which enables consumers to make informed environmental choices.

9   Each Party shall take steps to establish progressively, taking into account international processes where appropriate, a coherent, nationwide system of pollution inventories or registers on a structured, computerised and publicly accessible database compiled through standardised reporting. Such a system may include inputs, releases and transfers of a specified range of substances and products, including water, energy and resource use, from a specified range of activities to environmental media and to on-site and off-site treatment and disposal sites.

10   Nothing in this article may prejudice the right of Parties to refuse to disclose certain environmental information in accordance with Art 4, paras 3 and 4.

Note:

1   Ebbesson regards the provisions in Art 5 as coming close to the notion of an environmental right-to-know. However, he draws attention to discretion that is left to the parties. In particular, Art 5(9) only requires States to 'take steps to establish progressively'. It also says that systems *'may* include inputs, releases' ((1997) 93).

2   The wording in Art 5(1)(c) may be compared with the wording used by the European Court of Human Rights in *Guerra and Others v Italy* (1998) 26 EHRR 357(on which see p 857, below).

Article 6 Public Participation in Decisions on Specific Activities

1   Each Party:

(a) shall apply the provisions of this article with respect to decisions on whether to permit proposed activities listed in annex I;

(b) shall, in accordance with its national law, also apply the provisions of this article to decisions on proposed activities not listed in annex I which may have a significant effect on the environment. To this end, Parties shall determine whether such a proposed activity is subject to these provisions; and

(c) may decide, on a case-by-case basis if so provided under national law, not to apply the provisions of this article to proposed activities serving national defence purposes, if that Party deems that such application would have an adverse effect on these purposes.

2   The public concerned shall be informed, either by public notice or individually as appropriate, early in an environmental decision-making procedure, and in an adequate, timely and effective manner, *inter alia,* of:

(a) the proposed activity and the application on which a decision will be taken;

(b) the nature of possible decisions or the draft decision;

(c) the public authority responsible for making the decision;

(d) the envisaged procedure, including, as and when this information can be provided:

(i)   the commencement of the procedure;

(ii) the opportunities for the public to participate;

(iii) the time and venue of any envisaged public hearing;

(iv) an indication of the public authority from which relevant information can be obtained and where the relevant information has been deposited for examination by the public;

(v)   an indication of the relevant public authority or any other official body to which comments or questions can be submitted and of the time schedule for transmittal of comments or questions; and

(vi) an indication of what environmental information relevant to the proposed activity is available; and

(e) The fact that the activity is subject to a national or trans-boundary environmental impact assessment procedure.

3   The public participation procedures shall include reasonable time-frames for the different phases, allowing sufficient time for informing the public in accordance with para 2 above and for the public to prepare and participate effectively during the environmental decision-making.

4   Each Party shall provide for early public participation, when all options are open and effective public participation can take place.

5   Each Party should, where appropriate, encourage prospective applicants to identify the public concerned, to enter into discussions, and to provide information regarding the objectives of their application before applying for a permit.

6   Each Party shall require the competent public authorities to give the public concerned access for examination, upon request where so required under national law, free of charge and as soon as it becomes available, to all information relevant to the decision-making referred to in this article that is available at the time of the public participation procedure, without prejudice to the right of Parties to refuse to disclose certain information in accordance with Art 4, paras 3 and 4. The relevant information shall include at least, and without prejudice to the provisions of Art 4:

     (a) a description of the site and the physical and technical characteristics of the proposed activity, including an estimate of the expected residues and emissions;

     (b) a description of the significant effects of the proposed activity on the environment;

     (c) a description of the measures envisaged to prevent and/or reduce the effects, including emissions;

     (d) a non-technical summary of the above;

     (e) an outline of the main alternatives studied by the applicant; and

     (f) in accordance with national legislation, the main reports and advice issued to the public authority at the time when the public concerned shall be informed in accordance with para 2 above.

7   Procedures for public participation shall allow the public to submit, in writing or, as appropriate, at a public hearing or inquiry with the applicant, any comments, information, analyses or opinions that it considers relevant to the proposed activity.

8   Each Party shall ensure that in the decision due account is taken of the outcome of the public participation.

9   Each Party shall ensure that, when the decision has been taken by the public authority, the public is promptly informed of the decision in accordance with the appropriate procedures. Each Party shall make accessible to the public the text of the decision along with the reasons and considerations on which the decision is based.

10   Each Party shall ensure that, when a public authority reconsiders or updates the operating conditions for an activity referred to in para 1, the provisions of paras 2 to 9 of this article are applied *mutatis mutandis*, and where appropriate.

11   Each Party shall, within the framework of its national law, apply, to the extent feasible and appropriate, provisions of this article to decisions on whether to permit the deliberate release of genetically modified organisms into the environment.

Article 7 Public Participation Concerning Plans, Programmes and Policies Relating to the Environment

Each Party shall make appropriate practical and/or other provisions for the public to participate during the preparation of plans and programmes relating to the environment, within a transparent and fair framework, having provided the necessary information to the public. Within this framework, Art 6, paras 3, 4 and 8, shall be applied. The public which may participate shall be identified by the relevant public authority, taking into account the objectives of this Convention. To the extent appropriate, each Party shall endeavour to provide opportunities for public participation in the preparation of policies relating to the environment.

Article 8 Public Participation During the Preparation of Executive Regulations and/or Generally Applicable Legally Binding Normative Instruments

Each Party shall strive to promote effective public participation at an appropriate stage, and while options are still open, during the preparation by public authorities of executive regulations and other generally applicable legally binding rules that may have a significant effect on the environment. To this end, the following steps should be taken:

(a) time-frames sufficient for effective participation should be fixed;

(b) draft rules should be published or otherwise made publicly available; and

(c) the public should be given the opportunity to comment, directly or through representative consultative bodies.

The result of the public participation shall be taken into account as far as possible.

Article 9 Access to Justice

1   Each Party shall, within the framework of its national legislation, ensure that any person who considers that his or her request for information under Art 4 has been ignored, wrongfully refused, whether in part or in full, inadequately answered, or otherwise not dealt with in accordance with the provisions of that art, has access to a review procedure before a court of law or another independent and impartial body established by law.

In the circumstances where a Party provides for such a review by a court of law, it shall ensure that such a person also has access to an expeditious procedure established by law that is free of charge or inexpensive for reconsideration by a public authority or review by an independent and impartial body other than a court of law.

Final decisions under para 1 shall be binding on the public authority holding the information. Reasons shall be stated in writing, at least where access to information is refused under this paragraph.

2   Each Party shall, within the framework of its national legislation, ensure that members of the public concerned:

(a) having a sufficient interest;

or, alternatively,

(b) maintaining impairment of a right, where the administrative procedural law of a Party requires this as a precondition,

have access to a review procedure before a court of law and/or another independent and impartial body established by law, to challenge the substantive and procedural legality of any decision, act or omission subject to the provisions of Art 6 and, where so provided for under national law and without prejudice to para 3 below, of other relevant provisions of this Convention.

What constitutes a sufficient interest and impairment of a right shall be determined in accordance with the requirements of national law and consistently with the objective of giving the public concerned wide access to justice within the scope of this Convention. To this end, the interest of any non-governmental organisation meeting the requirements referred to in Art 2, para 5, shall be deemed sufficient for the purpose of sub-para (a) above. Such organisations shall also be deemed to have rights capable of being impaired for the purpose of sub-para (b) above.

The provisions of this para 2 shall not exclude the possibility of a preliminary review procedure before an administrative authority and shall not affect the requirement of exhaustion of administrative review procedures prior to recourse to judicial review procedures, where such a requirement exists under national law.

3   In addition and without prejudice to the review procedures referred to in paras 1 and 2 above, each Party shall ensure that, where they meet the criteria, if any, laid down in its national law, members of the public have access to administrative or judicial procedures to challenge acts and omissions by private persons and public authorities which contravene provisions of its national law relating to the environment.

4   In addition and without prejudice to para 1 above, the procedures referred to in paras 1, 2 and 3 above shall provide adequate and effective remedies, including injunctive relief as appropriate, and be fair, equitable, timely and not prohibitively expensive. Decisions under this article shall be given or recorded in writing. Decisions of courts, and whenever possible of other bodies, shall be publicly accessible.

5   In order to further the effectiveness of the provisions of this article, each Party shall ensure that information is provided to the public on access to administrative and judicial review procedures and shall consider the establishment of appropriate assistance mechanisms to remove or reduce financial and other barriers to access to justice.

Note:

The requirement that 'sufficient interest and impairment of a right' (Art 9(2)(a) and (b)) be determined 'consistently with the objective of giving the public concerned wide access to justice' and that NGOs shall be deemed to have a sufficient interest should be examined in the light of decisions of the UK courts on standing, particular the *Greenpeace* case, the *World Development Movement* case and Sedley J's judgment in *ex p Dixon* on the one hand and the restrictive approach taken by the ECJ to standing of NGOs on the other. On this see further p 837, below. The reference to 'impairment of a right' should also be considered in the light of the ECHR, and in particular Art 6(1), on which see p 873, below).

Article 10 Meeting of the Parties

1   The first meeting of the Parties shall be convened no later than one year after the date of the entry into force of this Convention. Thereafter, an ordinary meeting of the Parties shall be held at least once every two years, unless otherwise decided by the Parties, or at the written request of any Party, provided that, within six months of the request being communicated to all Parties by the Executive Secretary of the Economic

Commission for Europe, the said request is supported by at least one-third of the Parties.

2   At their meetings, the Parties shall keep under continuous review the implementation of this Convention on the basis of regular reporting by the Parties, and, with this purpose in mind, shall:

   (a) review the policies for and legal and methodological approaches to access to information, public participation in decision-making and access to justice in environmental matters, with a view to further improving them;

   (b) exchange information regarding experience gained in concluding and implementing bilateral and multilateral agreements or other arrangements having relevance to the purposes of this Convention and to which one or more of the Parties are a party;

   (c) seek, where appropriate, the services of relevant ECE bodies and other competent international bodies and specific committees in all aspects pertinent to the achievement of the purposes of this Convention;

   (d) establish any subsidiary bodies as they deem necessary;

   (e) prepare, where appropriate, protocols to this Convention;

   (f) consider and adopt proposals for amendments to this Convention in accordance with the provisions of Art 14;

   (g) consider and undertake any additional action that may be required for the achievement of the purposes of this Convention;

   (h) at their first meeting, consider and by consensus adopt rules of procedure for their meetings and the meetings of subsidiary bodies;

   (i) at their first meeting, review their experience in implementing the provisions of Art 5, para 9, and consider what steps are necessary to develop further the system referred to in that paragraph, taking into account international processes and developments, including the elaboration of an appropriate instrument concerning pollution release and transfer registers or inventories which could be annexed to this Convention.

3   The Meeting of the Parties may, as necessary, consider establishing financial arrangements on a consensus basis.

4   The United Nations, its specialised agencies and the International Atomic Energy Agency, as well as any State or regional economic integration organisation entitled under Art 17 to sign this Convention but which is not a Party to this Convention, and any intergovernmental organisation qualified in the fields to which this Convention relates, shall be entitled to participate as observers in the meetings of the Parties.

5   Any non-governmental organisation, qualified in the fields to which this Convention relates, which has informed the Executive Secretary of the Economic Commission for Europe of its wish to be represented at a meeting of the Parties shall be entitled to participate as an observer unless at least one-third of the Parties present in the meeting raise objections.

6   For the purposes of paras 4 and 5 above, the rules of procedure referred to in para 2 (h) above shall provide for practical arrangements for the admittance procedure and other relevant terms.

[Articles 11 (on Right of Parties to Vote), 12 (on Secretariat), 13 (on Annexes) and 14 (on Amendments to the Convention) omitted.]

Article 15 Review of Compliance

The Meeting of the Parties shall establish, on a consensus basis, optional arrangements of a non-confrontational, non-judicial and consultative nature for reviewing compliance with the provisions of this Convention. These arrangements shall allow for appropriate public involvement and may include the option of considering communications from members of the public on matters related to this Convention.

[Articles 16 (on Settlement of Disputes), 17 (on Signature), 18 (on Depository) and 19 (on Ratification, Acceptance, Approval and Accession) omitted.]

Article 20 Entry into Force

1   This Convention shall enter into force on the ninetieth day after the date of deposit of the sixteenth instrument of ratification, acceptance, approval or accession.

[Paragraphs 2 and 3 omitted.]

[Articles 21 (on Withdrawal) and 22 (on Authentic Texts) omitted.]

[Annex I (which lists activities referred to in Art 6, para 1(a)) and Annex II (on Arbitration) omitted.]

THE RIGHT TO PARTICIPATE IN ENVIRONMENTAL DECISION-MAKING IN EC AND UK LAW

The right of the public to participate in environmental decision-making has been given tangible expression in three main areas: environmental impact assessment; access to environmental information; and eco-labelling. The relevant EC and UK instruments are examined in turn.

EC – environmental impact assessment

Applying the preventive approach to environmental protection (see Chapter 1, p 49, above), the Directive on the Assessment of the Effects of Certain Public and Private Projects on the Environment 85/337 came into force on 3 July 1988. The first example of EC involvement in the planning process, the Directive requires specific environmental information to be considered by those involved in the process of project authorisation; in particular it requires Member States to ensure that the effect of certain proposed projects upon human beings and the environment is assessed before permission for them is granted. As such, it is a means of integrating environmental concerns into the planning process in cases where such issues were not already considered.[14] The Directive has now been amended by Directive 97/11 primarily because of inconsistencies amongst Member States in its application, particularly in relation to Annex II projects (see below).

---

14   The UK government originally opposed this Directive on the grounds that the existing planning process was already sufficient: see Haigh, N, *Manual of Environmental Policy: The EC and Britain,* London: Longman (loose leaf), pp 352–54.

The Directive provides (Art 2) that projects likely to have significant effects on the environment by virtue of their nature, size or location are to be made subject to an assessment of their effects before consent is given. Projects listed in Annex I *must* be subject to assessment; such projects include oil refineries, power stations, installations for disposal of radioactive waste, iron and steel works, asbestos works, chemical works, motorways, ports and waste-disposal installations. The projects which appear in Annex II are to be subject to assessment where Member States consider that their characteristics so require. The Annex lists classes of project under 13 headings: agriculture, silviculture and aquaculture; extractive industry; energy industry; production and processing of metals; mineral industry; chemical industry; food industry; textile, leather, wood and paper industry; rubber industry; infrastructure projects; other projects; tourism and leisure; and change or extension of projects listed in Annex I or II. Within the confines of Annex II, Member States are free to establish criteria or thresholds (or determine through a case by case examination) for deciding when assessment is necessary (Art 4(2)). (See cases, p 780, below.)

The effect of the project on four factors (listed in Art 3) are to be identified, described and assessed by the environmental impact assessment:

• human beings, flora and fauna;

• soil, water, air, climate and the landscape;

• material assets and the cultural heritage;

• the interaction between the factors mentioned in the above bullet points.

It is the responsibility of the developer to provide at least the information prescribed in Art 5(3), viz:

• a description of the project comprising information on its site, design and size;

• measures intended to avoid, reduce or remedy significant adverse effects;

• the data required to identify and assess the main environmental effects;

• an outline of the main alternatives studied by the developer and an indication of the main reasons for its choice;

• a non-technical summary of the above four.

Annex IV provides a more specific statement of the information which the developer must supply. However, the developer is required to supply this information only in so far as the Member State considers it relevant to a given stage of the consent procedure; to the specific characteristics of a particular project or type of projects; to the environmental features likely to be affected; and where it is reasonable having regard to current knowledge (Art 5(1)).

Although the detailed arrangements for public consultation are a matter for Member States (Art 6(3)), Art 6(2) requires that any request for development consent and the information supplied by the developer must be made public. Those concerned must also be given the opportunity to express an opinion before the development consent is granted. Similarly, authorities with specific environmental responsibilities likely to be concerned by a project must be given the opportunity to express an opinion on the request for development consent (Art 6(1)). If the project is likely to have significant effects in another Member State, a description of the project combined with any available information on its possible trans-boundary impact and information on the nature of the decision which may be taken, should be sent to that Member State. The Member State may then indicate that it wishes to participate in the environmental impact assessment procedure (Art 7). This requirement gives better effect to the Espoo provisions than did the previous version of the Directive (see, p 751, above).

The information supplied by the developer and gathered from consultation must then be taken into account in the development consent procedure. The public must be informed of: (1) the decision and any conditions attached to it; (2) the main reasons and considerations on which the decision is based; (3) a description where necessary of the main measures taken to avoid, reduce and offset the major adverse effects of the project (Art 9). This requirement to provide reasons fills an important gap in the original version of the Directive.

Projects, the details of which are adopted by a specific act of national legislation, are not covered by the Directive (Art 1).[15] Nor are projects serving national defence purposes. In addition, provided the procedure laid down in Art 2(3) is followed, a Member State may exempt any project from the requirements of the Directive.

The European Court of Justice has had to consider the EIA Directive on several occasions, partly due to its somewhat vague and unclear drafting. Please note, particularly when reading the cases, that all decisions to date concern the provisions of the original version of the EIA Directive.

One initial point which required clarification was whether the Directive required Member States as from 3 July 1988, to subject to environmental assessment all non-previously approved projects or whether Member States were obliged to submit to environmental assessment only projects where the consent procedure was initiated after this date. It is clear that whenever the consent procedure begins after 3 July 1988, projects must be subject to environmental assessment provided they fulfil the criteria set out in Arts 2 and 4. The ECJ has clarified the issue for projects whose consent procedure began before the Directive's entry into force but were finally approved after that date.[16] In Case C-81/96 *Burgemeester en Wethouders van Haarlemerliede en Paarnwoude v Gede Puteerde Staten van Noord-Holland* the ECJ stressed that the EIA Directive does not apply to consent procedures launched before 3 July 1988. The Court explained:

> The reason for that is that the Directive is primarily designed to cover large-scale projects which will most often require a long time to complete. It would therefore not be appropriate for the relevant procedures, which are already complex at national level and which were formally initiated prior to the date of the expiry of the period for transposing the directive, to be made more cumbersome and time-consuming by the specific requirements imposed by the Directive, and for situations already established to those affected by it.

---

15   See also Case C-287/98 *Luxembourg v Linster* (2000) *The Times*, 30 October.
16   See Case C-396/2 *Bund Naturschutz in Bayern Ev v Stahsdorf* [1994] ECR 1-3717; Case C-431/92 *Commission v Germany* [1995] ECR 1-2192.

A second issue which has troubled the ECJ is whether the Directive could have direct effect (see Chapter 1). In Case C-431/92 *Commission v Germany* [1995] ECR I-2192, the German government argued that Arts 2, 3 and 8 were not so clear and precise as unequivocally to lay down a specific obligation so that their application by national authorities would be mandatory. The ECJ disagreed and held that the provisions of the Directive did impose an obligation on the national authorities which did have direct effect. Referring to Arts 2, 3 and 8 the court held:

> Regardless of their details, those provisions therefore unequivocally impose on the national authorities responsible for granting consent an obligation to carry out an assessment of the effects of certain projects on the environment.

In *Aannemersbedrijf PK Kraaijeveld BV v Gedeputeerde-Staten van Zuid Holland* [1997] All ER (EC) 134 (hereafter the *Dutch Dykes* case which is extracted below) the court took it as settled law that the Directive could have direct effect (see also Case C-435/97 *World Wildlife Fund* [1999] All ER (D) 1016, below). Although there has been some doubt on this matter, the House of Lords in *R v North Yorkshire Council ex p Brown and Cartwright* [1998] Env LR 393 held it to be 'common ground' that the Directive has direct effect.

A third issue considered by the ECJ concerned the confusing wording of Arts 2(1), 4(2) and Annex II. Article 2 provides that Member States shall adopt all measures necessary to ensure that, before consent is given, projects likely to have significant effects on the environment by virtue, *inter alia*, of their nature, size or location, are made subject to an assessment with regard to their effects. According to Art 4(2) projects listed in Annex II are to be made subject to an assessment 'where Member States so require'. To this end, Member States may specify certain types of project as being subject to an assessment or may establish the criteria and/or thresholds necessary to determine which of the projects of the classes listed in Annex II are to be subject to an assessment in accordance with the provisions of the Directive.

The unclear wording of Art 4 made it uncertain whether Member States were entirely free to determine which projects were to be subject to environmental assessment. Could all of them be excluded or were they obliged to consider under what circumstances the projects listed in Annex II required an assessment?

In the *Dutch Dykes* case the ECJ, following its decision in Case C-133/94 *Commission v Belgium* [1996] 1 ECR 2323 held that, although Art 4(2) confers on Member States a measure of discretion, the limits of the discretion are set out in Art 2(1) which require all projects likely to have significant effects on the environment to be subject to assessment. The Community legislature felt that all projects listed in Annex II may possibly have significant effects on the environment and so Member States cannot exclude generally and definitely from possible assessment any class of project mentioned in Annex II. So any Member State which established criteria or thresholds at a level so high that in practice all projects of that type would be exempted in advance would exceed the limits of its discretion, unless all the projects excluded could, when viewed as a whole, be regarded as unlikely to have significant effects. This view has been reinforced by Case C-435/97 *World Wild Life Fund v Autonome Provinz Bozen* [1999] All ER (D) 1016. The ECJ reiterated that Art 4(2) does not allow States a discretion to exempt from the Directive procedures whole classes of projects listed in Annex II. An exemption is only permitted after consideration of the facts of each project. The Italian Government was proposing to exclude from the requirements of the Directive all projects involving the construction of small airports with runways less than 2,100 metres in length. However, Art 2 would allow an assessment procedure other than that found in the Directive provided: (a) it does not undermine the purpose of the Directive, namely to ensure that no project likely to have a significant impact on the environment is exempt from assessment; and (b) it satisfied the Directive's various requirements such as the need for public participation. The procedure under Italian law did not meet the requirements of the Directive.

That the discretion of a State under Art 4(2) to set criteria for the assessment of Annex II projects is limited by the requirements of Art 2(1) was yet again confirmed by the ECJ in Case C-392/96 *Commission v Ireland* [1999] 3 CMLR 727. Here it was deemed unacceptable to set a threshold simply by reference to the size of the project.

Recent developments

The law on environmental impact assessment has to date focused solely on the impact of individual projects, rather than on the plans or programmes that give rise to such projects. For example, on the construction of a power station rather than on the government's policy relating to energy. For some time concerns have been expressed that the existing form of assessment occurred too late in the planning process. Commentators argued that the assessment should take place when plans, programmes and policies were being considered, rather than when the resultant projects implementing those plans were put forward. In 1991 the first proposal for a draft directive on Strategic Environmental Assessment (SEA) was made. Over the years that proposal has been subject to considerable discussion and change. The Council has now adopted a *Common Position* (Com (99) 73) which proposes that an SEA be undertaken for plans and programmes which impact upon the environment. Significantly, following pressure from Member States, the Council has dropped the proposal for SEAs to be undertaken in relation to policies.

Under the proposed Directive, SEA will apply, *inter alia*, to all plans and programmes which are prepared for the following sectors: agriculture, forestry, fisheries, energy, industry, transport, waste management, water management, telecommunications, tourism, town and country planning or land use, and those plans and programmes which set a framework for future development consents for projects listed in Annexes I and II to the EIA Directive. Basically, Member States should assess any plans or programmes which provide a framework for any future development consents and which are likely to have significant environmental effects.

The Directive will require 'an environmental report' containing specified information on the effects of implementing the plan or programme including:

- existing problems relevant to the plan or programme;
- environmental characteristics of the area affected;
- environmental obligations imposed to meet international, European and national objectives;
- the likely environmental effects of implementing the plan or programme;

- any envisaged mitigating measures;
- and, perhaps significantly, consideration of any reasonable alternatives and the reasons for not adopting the alternatives considered (for example, consideration of alternative sites).

Once an environmental report is prepared the public must be given 'an early and effective opportunity' to comment upon it.

It is hoped that the overall effect of the proposal will be to incorporate environmental considerations into the wider decision-making process and so reflect the principle of integration (see Art 6 of the EC Treaty, Chapter 1, p 54, above).

Agreement has now been reached between Council and Parliament within the Conciliation Committee on a final text of the SEA Directive (April 2001). The Directive will come into effect before 31 December 2001. Amongst the changes made at this stage are: (1) a detailed list of the types of environmental impacts to be assessed is now provided; and (2) there now appears a broader definition of who has the right to be consulted, namely any person or organisation affected or likely to be affected by, or having an interest in, the decision including relevant NGOs. Finally, note that in response to Aarhus the Commission has produced a new proposal 'providing for public participation in respect of the drawing up of certain plans and programmes relating to the environment' (COM (00) 331). The plans referred to are contained in specific items of EC legislation, such as the WFD and the Air Quality Directive, rather than allowing participation in the development of EC environmental law in general.

COUNCIL DIRECTIVE

of 27 June 1985

on the assessment of the effects of certain public and private projects on the environment

(85/337/EEC)

(1985) OJ L175, p 40

[as amended by Directive 97/11/EC]

THE COUNCIL OF THE EUROPEAN COMMUNITIES,

Having regard to the Treaty establishing the European Economic Community, and in particular Arts 100 and 235 thereof, [...]

Whereas the 1973 and 1977 action programmes of the European Communities on the environment, as well as the 1983 action programme, the main outlines of which have been approved by the Council of the European Communities and the representatives of the governments of the Member States, stress that the best environmental policy consists in preventing the creation of pollution or nuisances at source, rather than subsequently trying to counteract their effects; whereas they affirm the need to take effects on the environment into account at the earliest possible stage in all the technical planning and decision-making processes; whereas to that end, they provide for the implementation of procedures to evaluate such effects;

Whereas the disparities between the laws in force in the various Member States with regard to the assessment of the environmental effects of public and private projects may create unfavourable competitive conditions and thereby directly affect the functioning of the common market; whereas, therefore, it is necessary to approximate national laws in this field pursuant to Art 100 of the Treaty;

Whereas, in addition, it is necessary to achieve one of the Community's objectives in the sphere of the protection of the environment and the quality of life;

Whereas, since the Treaty has not provided the powers required for this end, recourse should be had to Art 235 of the Treaty;

Whereas general principles for the assessment of environmental effects should be introduced with a view to supplementing and co-ordinating development consent procedures governing public and private projects likely to have a major effect on the environment;

Whereas development consent for public and private projects which are likely to have significant effects on the environment should be granted only after prior assessment of the likely significant environmental effects of these projects has been carried out; whereas this assessment must be conducted on the basis of the appropriate information supplied by the developer, which may be supplemented by the authorities and by the people who may be concerned by the project in question;

Whereas the principles of the assessment of environmental effects should be harmonised, in particular with reference to the projects which should be subject to assessment, the main obligations of the developers and the content of the assessment;

Whereas projects belonging to certain types have significant effects on the environment and these projects must as a rule be subject to systematic assessment;

Whereas projects of other types may not have significant effects on the environment in every case and whereas these projects should be assessed where the Member States consider that their characteristics so require;

Whereas, for projects which are subject to assessment, a certain minimal amount of information must be supplied, concerning the project and its effects;

Whereas the effects of a project on the environment must be assessed in order to take account of concerns to protect human health, to contribute by means of a better environment to the quality of life, to ensure maintenance of the diversity of species and to maintain the reproductive capacity of the eco-system as a basic resource for life;

Whereas, however, this Directive should not be applied to projects the details of which are adopted by a specific act of national legislation, since the objectives of this Directive, including that of supplying information, are achieved through the legislative process;

Whereas, furthermore, it may be appropriate in exceptional cases to exempt a specific project from the assessment procedures laid down by this Directive, subject to appropriate information being supplied to the Commission.

HAS ADOPTED THIS DIRECTIVE:

Article 1

1   This Directive shall apply to the assessment of the environmental effects of those public and private projects which are likely to have significant effects on the environment.

2   For the purposes of this Directive:

'project' means:

the execution of construction works or of other installations or schemes, other interventions in the natural surroundings and landscape including those involving the extraction of mineral resources;

'developer' means:

the applicant for authorisation for a private project or the public authority which initiates a project;

'development consent' means:

the decision of the competent authority or authorities which entitles the developer to proceed with the project.

3   The competent authority or authorities shall be that or those which the Member States designate as responsible for performing the duties arising from this Directive.

4   Projects serving national defence purposes are not covered by this Directive.

5   This Directive shall not apply to projects the details of which are adopted by a specific act of national legislation, since the objectives of this Directive, including that of supplying information, are achieved through the legislative process.

Article 2

1   Member States shall adopt all measures necessary to ensure that, before consent is given, projects likely to have significant effects on the environment by virtue, *inter alia*, of their nature, size or location are made subject to a requirement for development consent and an assessment with regard to their effects. These projects are defined in Art 4.

2   The environmental impact assessment may be integrated into the existing procedures for consent to projects in the Member States, or, failing this, into other procedures or into procedures to be established to comply with the aims of this Directive.

2a   Member States may provide for a single procedure in order to fulfil the requirements of this Directive and the requirements of Council Directive 96/61/EC of 24 September 1996 on integrated pollution prevention and control.

3   Without prejudice to Art 7, Member States may, in exceptional cases, exempt a specific project in whole or in part from the provisions laid down in this Directive [...].

Article 3

The environmental impact assessment shall identify, describe and assess in an appropriate manner, in the light of each individual case and in accordance with Arts 4 to 11, the direct and indirect effects of a project on the following factors:

–   human beings, fauna and flora;

–   soil, water, air, climate and the landscape;

–   material assets and the cultural heritage;

–   the interaction between the factors mentioned in the first, and second and third indents.

Article 4

1   Subject to Art 2(3), projects listed in Annex I shall be made subject to an assessment in accordance with Arts 5 to 10.

2   Subject to Art 2(3), for projects listed in Annex II, the Member States shall determine through:

(a) a case-by-case examination; or

(b) thresholds or criteria set by the Member State whether the project shall be made subject to an assessment in accordance with Arts 5 to 10.

Member States may decide to apply both procedures referred to in (a) and (b).

3   When a case-by-case examination is carried out or thresholds or criteria are set for the purpose of para 2, the relevant selection criteria set out in Annex III shall be taken into account.

4   Member States shall ensure that the determination made by the competent authorities under para 2 is made available to the public.

Article 5

1   In the case of projects which, pursuant to Art 4, must be subjected to an environmental impact assessment in accordance with Arts 5 to 10, Member States shall adopt the necessary measures to ensure that the developer supplies in an appropriate form the information specified in Annex IV inasmuch as:

(a) the Member States consider that the information is relevant to a given stage of the consent procedure and to the specific characteristics of a particular project or type of project and of the environmental features likely to be affected;

(b) the Member States consider that a developer may reasonably be required to compile this information having regard *inter alia* to current knowledge and methods of assessment.

2   Member States shall take the necessary measures to ensure that, if the developer so requests before submitting an application for development consent, the competent authority shall give an opinion on the information to be supplied by the developer in accordance with para 1. The competent authority shall consult the developer and authorities referred to in Art 6(1) before it gives its opinion. The fact that the authority has given an opinion under this paragraph shall not preclude it from subsequently requiring the developer to submit further information. Member States may require the competent authorities to give such an opinion, irrespective of whether the developer so requests.

3   The information to be provided by the developer in accordance with para 1 shall include at least:

–   a description of the project comprising information on the site, design and size of the project;

–   a description of the measures envisaged in order to avoid, reduce and, if possible, remedy significant adverse effects;

–   the data required to identify and assess the main effects which the project is likely to have on the environment;

–   an outline of the main alternatives studied by the developer and an indication of the main reasons for his choice, taking into account the environmental effects;

–   a non-technical summary of the information mentioned in the previous indents.

4 Member States shall, if necessary, ensure that any authorities holding relevant information, with particular reference to Art 3, shall make this information available to the developer.

Article 6

1 Member States shall take the measures necessary to ensure that the authorities likely to be concerned by the project by reason of their specific environmental responsibilities are given an opportunity to express their opinion on the information supplied by the developer and on the request for development consent [...].

2 Member States shall ensure that:
   – any request for development consent and any information gathered pursuant to Art 5 are made available to the public within a reasonable time in order to give the public concerned the opportunity to express an opinion before the development consent is granted.

Article 7

1 Where a Member State is aware that a project is likely to have significant effects on the environment in another Member State or where a Member State likely to be significantly affected so requests, the Member State in whose territory the project is intended to be carried out shall send to the affected Member State as soon as possible and no later than when informing its own public, *inter alia*:
   (a) a description of the project, together with any available information on its possible trans-boundary impact;
   (b) information on the nature of the decision which may be taken, and shall give the other Member State a reasonable time in which to indicate whether it wishes to participate in the Environmental Impact Assessment procedure, and may include the information referred to in para 2.

2 If a Member State which receives information pursuant to para 1 indicates that it intends to participate in the Environmental Impact Assessment procedure, the Member State in whose territory the project is intended to be carried out shall, if it has not already done so, send to the affected Member State the information gathered pursuant to Art 5 and relevant information regarding the said procedure, including the request for development consent.

3 The Member States concerned, each insofar as it is concerned, shall also:
   (a) arrange for the information referred to in paras 1 and 2 to be made available, within a reasonable time, to the authorities referred to in Art 6(1) and the public concerned in the territory of the Member State likely to be significantly affected; and
   (b) ensure that those authorities and the public concerned are given an opportunity, before development consent for the project is granted, to forward their opinion within a reasonable time on the information supplied to the competent authority in the Member State in whose territory the project is intended to be carried out.

4   The Member States concerned shall enter into consultations regarding, *inter alia*, the potential trans-boundary effects of the project and the measures envisaged to reduce or eliminate such effects and shall agree on a reasonable time frame for the duration of the consultation period.

5   The detailed arrangements for implementing the provisions of this Article may be determined by the Member States concerned.

Article 8

The results of consultations and the information gathered pursuant to Arts 5, 6 and 7 must be taken into consideration in the development consent procedure.

Article 9

1   When a decision to grant or refuse development consent has been taken, the competent authority or authorities shall inform the public thereof in accordance with the appropriate procedures and shall make available to the public the following information:

- the content of the decision and any conditions attached thereto;
- the main reasons and considerations on which the decision is based;
- a description, where necessary, of the main measures to avoid, reduce and, if possible, offset the major adverse effects.

2   The competent authority or authorities shall inform any Member State which has been consulted pursuant to Art 7, forwarding to it the information referred to in para 1.

Article 10

The provisions of this Directive shall not affect the obligation on the competent authorities to respect the limitations imposed by national regulations and administrative provisions and accepted legal practices with regard to commercial and industrial confidentiality, including intellectual property, and the safeguarding of the public interest.

Where Art 7 applies, the transmission of information to another Member State and the receipt of information by another Member State shall be subject to the limitations in force in the Member State in which the project is proposed.

[All other Articles omitted.]

[Annex I, II and III omitted.]

Annex IV Information referred to in Article 5(1)

1   Description of the project, including in particular:

- a description of the physical characteristics of the whole project and the land-use requirements during the construction and operational phases;
- a description of the main characteristics of the production processes, for instance, nature and quantity of the materials used;
- an estimate, by type and quantity, of expected residues and emissions (water, air and soil pollution, noise, vibration, light, heat, radiation, etc) resulting from the operation of the proposed project.

2   An outline of the main alternatives studied by the developer and an indication of the main reasons for his choice, taking into account the environmental effect.

3   A description of the aspects of the environment likely to be significantly affected by the proposed project, including, in particular, population, fauna, flora, soil, water, air, climatic factors, material assets, including the architectural and archaeological heritage, landscape and the inter-relationship between the above factors.

4   A description of the likely significant effects of the proposed project on the environment resulting from: the existence of the project, the use of natural resources, the emission of pollutants, the creation of nuisances and the elimination of waste; and the description by the developer of the forecasting methods used to assess the effects on the environment.

5   A description of the measures envisaged to prevent, reduce and where possible offset any significant adverse effects on the environment.

6   A non-technical summary of the information provided under the above headings.

7   An indication of any difficulties (technical deficiencies or lack of know-how) encountered by the developer in compiling the required information.

This description should cover the direct effects and any indirect, secondary, cumulative, short, medium and long term, permanent and temporary, positive and negative effects of the project.

Case C-72/95 *Aannemersbedrijf PK Kraaijeveld BV and Others v Gedeputeerde Staten van Zuid-Holland (Dutch Dykes case)* [1997] All ER (EC) 134

Headnote

A Dutch local authority adopted a plan to reinforce the dykes in its area which was later approved by the Provincial Executive without any consideration of the environmental effects of the constructional work involved. Under the proposed modifications, the waterway to which the plaintiff company had access and which was vital to its business activities would no longer be linked to navigable waterways. The plaintiff therefore brought an action before the Netherlands State Council, seeking an annulment of the Provincial Executive's decision to approve the plan on the ground that that decision had not been prepared with the necessary care. The State Council observed that no environmental impact assessment of the plan had been made pursuant to Art 2(1) of Council Directive (EEC) 85/337 on the assessment of the effects of certain public and private projects on the environment, which obliged Member States to make projects likely to have significant effects on the environment by virtue of their nature, size or location subject to such an assessment, since the size of the works was such as to exclude it from the requirement under the national legislation implementing the Directive. It was further observed that the minimum size of project laid down by the national legislation pursuant to Art 4(2) of the Directive was fixed at a level which excluded the majority of dyke reinforcement projects from the assessment requirement. In particular, Art 4(2) provided that for certain classes of project listed in Annex II (which included 'canalisation and flood relief') Member States could establish criteria and/or thresholds to determine whether relevant projects should be subject to prior assessment. The State Council therefore stayed the proceedings and referred to the Court of Justice of the European Communities for a preliminary ruling questions regarding: (i) the interpretation of Arts 2(1) and 4(2) of the Directive and (ii) whether the obligation to make an environmental impact assessment of the project had direct effect and whether it had to be applied by the national court even if it had not been invoked in the main proceedings.

Held

(1) Although Art 4(2) of Directive 85/337 conferred on Member States a discretion to specify certain types of project which would be subject to an assessment or to establish criteria and/or thresholds for that purpose, that discretion was limited by the obligation set out in Art 2(1) that projects likely, by virtue of their nature, size or location, to have significant effects on the environment were subject to an impact assessment. The criteria/thresholds referred to in Art 4(2) were designed to facilitate the examination of individual projects in order to determine whether an assessment was required and not to exempt, in advance, certain classes of projects from assessment. Further, the question whether a Member State exceeded the limits of its discretion in setting such criteria could not be determined in relation to the characteristics of a single project, but depended on an overall assessment of the characteristics of projects of that nature which could be envisaged in the Member State. Thus a Member State which established criteria or thresholds at a level such that, in practice, all projects relating to dykes would be exempted in advance from an impact assessment would exceed the limits of its discretion under Arts 2(1) and 4(2) unless all projects excluded could, when viewed as a whole, be regarded as not being likely to have significant effects on the environment: Case C-133/94 *Commission v Belgium* (1996) ECJ Transcript, 2 May, applied.

(2) Where a court was entitled under national law to raise, of its own motion, pleas in law based on a binding national rule which had not been put forward by the parties, it had to examine, in relation to matters within its jurisdiction, whether the legislative or administrative authorities of the Member State were within the limits of their discretion under the Directive and take account thereof when examining the application for annulment. If that discretion had been exceeded so that national provisions had to be set aside, it was for the authorities of the Member State, according to their respective powers, to take all the measures necessary to ensure that projects were examined to determine whether they were likely to have significant effects on the environment and, if so, to ensure that they were subject to an impact assessment.

Opinion

The Court of Justice delivered the following judgment:

1   By judgment of 8 March 1995, received at the Court of Justice of the European Communities on 14 March 1995, the Nederlandse Raad van State (the Netherlands State Council) referred to the Court of Justice for a preliminary ruling under Art 177 of the EC Treaty four questions on the interpretation of Council Directive (EEC) 85/337 on the assessment of the effects of certain public and private projects on the environment and on the duty of national courts to ensure that a directive having direct effect is complied with although no individual has invoked it.

[...]

20 By judgment of 8 March 1995 the Nederlandse Raad van State decided to refer to the Court of Justice for a preliminary ruling the following four questions:

(1) Must the expression 'canalisation and flood-relief works' in Annex II to Directive 85/337/EEC be interpreted as including certain types of work on a dyke running alongside waterways?

(2) Having regard in particular to the terms 'projects' and 'modifications to development projects' employed in the directive, does it make any difference to the answer to Question 1 whether what is involved is:

   (a) the construction of a new dyke;

   (b) the relocation of an existing dyke;

   (c) the reinforcement and/or widening of an existing dyke;

   (d) the replacement *in situ* of a dyke whether or not the new dyke is stronger and/or wider than the old one; or

   (e) a combination of two or more of (a) to (d) above?

(3) Must Art 2(1) and Art 4(2) of the Directive be interpreted as meaning that where a Member State in its national implementing legislation has laid down specifications, criteria or thresholds for a particular project covered by Annex II in accordance with Art 4(2) of the Directive, but those specifications, criteria or thresholds are incorrect, Art 2(1) requires that an environmental impact assessment be made if the project is likely to have 'significant effects on the environment by virtue *inter alia* of [its] nature, size or location' within the meaning of that provision?

(4) If Question 3 is answered in the affirmative, does that obligation have direct effect, that is to say, may it be relied upon by an individual before a national court and must it be applied by the national court even if it was not in fact invoked in the matter pending before that court?

[...]

[The judgment of the European Court of Justice in relation to Questions 1 and 2 is omitted.]

Questions (3) and (4)

43 By these questions, which will be examined together, the national court asks whether Arts 2(1) and 4(2) of the Directive should be interpreted as meaning that where a Member State in its national implementing legislation has laid down specifications, criteria or thresholds for a particular project covered by Annex II in accordance with Art 4(2) of the Directive, but those specifications, criteria or thresholds are incorrect, Art 2(1) requires that an environmental impact assessment be made if the project is likely to have 'significant effects on the environment by virtue *inter alia* of [its] nature, size or location' within the meaning of that provision. If that question is answered in the affirmative, the national court asks whether that obligation to make an environmental impact assessment of the project has direct effect, so that it may be relied upon by an individual before a national court, and whether it must be applied by the national court even if it was not in fact invoked in the matter pending before that court.

44 Referring to Case C-355/90 *Commission v Spain* [1993] ECR I-4221, the Nederlandse Raad van State states that it is possible to argue that the measure of discretion which Art 4(2) allows the Member States in establishing the specifications, criteria or thresholds is limited by the expression 'likely to have significant effects on the environment by virtue *inter alia* of their nature, size or location' in Art 2(1).

45 Kraaijeveld and the Commission put forward a similar argument. The Commission states that the specifications, criteria or thresholds established by the Member States are primarily designed to facilitate examination of projects in order to determine whether

they should undergo an impact assessment, but that the existence of those specifications, criteria or thresholds does not exempt the Member States from undertaking an actual examination of the project in order to verify that it satisfies the criteria in Art 2(1) of the Directive. Both consider that the Netherlands has not properly performed its obligation to implement the Directive since the minimum size criteria laid down by the national legislation on dykes was fixed at a level such that no river dyke projects met the criteria and hence all dyke reinforcement projects remained outside the ambit of impact assessments. On this issue Kraaijeveld produced a decision of a Netherlands court supporting its argument.

46 According to the government of the Netherlands, however, the discretion allowed to the Member States is not limited in a precise manner in the Directive. Moreover, the choice of thresholds for dyke length and cross-section measurements was made with due account taken of the impact of such work on the environment. The fact that, in practice, the Netherlands legislation transposing the directive left numerous projects free of the requirement of an assessment is wholly immaterial, since those projects had no harmful effects. It therefore considers that it did not go beyond the limits of its discretion in establishing those thresholds.

47 As regards the direct effect of the obligation to make impact assessments for some projects, the national court considers that that obligation may be regarded as resulting from a precise and unconditional provision of the directive. Kraaijeveld and the Commission have submitted observations to that effect, and the Commission adds that since the rules are of a procedural nature they leave no latitude as far as the result to be achieved is concerned. Conversely, the Netherlands and UK governments consider that Art 2(1), read in conjunction with Art 4(2), of the Directive is not sufficiently precise and unconditional to have direct effect, in view of the discretion conferred on Member States with regard to establishing thresholds and criteria or the procedure for consulting the public.

48 It should be noted that Art 2(1) of the Directive refers to Art 4 for the definition of projects which must undergo an assessment of their effects. Art 4(2) allows Member States a certain discretion, since it states that projects of the classes listed in Annex II are to be subject to an assessment 'where Member States consider that their characteristics so require' and that, to that end, Member States may *inter alia* specify certain types of projects as being subject to an assessment or may establish the criteria or thresholds necessary to determine which projects are to be subject to an assessment.

49 The interpretation put forward by the Commission – namely that the existence of specifications, criteria and thresholds does not remove the need for an actual examination of each project in order to verify that it fulfils the criteria of Art 2(1) – would deprive Art 4(2) of any point. A Member State would have no interest in fixing specifications, thresholds and criteria if, in any case, every project had to undergo an individual examination with respect to the criteria in Art 2(1).

50 However, although the second paragraph of Art 4(2) of the Directive confers on Member States a measure of discretion to specify certain types of projects which will be subject to an assessment or to establish the criteria or thresholds applicable, the limits of that discretion are to be found in the obligation set out in Art 2(1) that projects likely, by virtue *inter alia* of their nature, size or location, to have significant effects on the environment are to be subject to an impact assessment.

51 Thus, ruling on the legislation of a Member State in terms of which certain entire classes of projects included in Annex II were excluded from the obligation of an impact

assessment, the court held in its judgment in Case C-133/94 *Commission v Belgium* (1996) ECJ Transcript, 2 May (para 42), that the criteria and/or the thresholds mentioned in Art 4(2) are designed to facilitate examination of the actual characteristics of any given project in order to determine whether it is subject to the requirement of assessment, not to exempt in advance from that obligation certain whole classes of projects listed in Annex II which may be envisaged as taking place on the territory of a Member State.

52 In a situation such as the present, it must be accepted that the Member State concerned was entitled to fix criteria relating to the size of dykes in order to establish which dyke projects had to undergo an impact assessment. The question whether, in laying down such criteria, the Member State went beyond the limits of its discretion cannot be determined in relation to the characteristics of a single project. It depends on an overall assessment of the characteristics of projects of that nature which could be envisaged in the Member State.

53 Thus a Member State which established criteria or thresholds at a level such that, in practice, all projects relating to dykes would be exempted in advance from the requirement of an impact assessment would exceed the limits of its discretion under Arts 2(1) and 4(2) of the Directive unless all projects excluded could, when viewed as a whole, be regarded as not being likely to have significant effects on the environment.

54 Lastly, as regards more particularly the fourth question, it appears from the order for reference that in its action Kraaijeveld did not raise the question whether an environmental impact assessment ought to have been made. In order to reply to the question, it must therefore be considered whether the national court hearing an action for annulment of a decision approving a zoning plan is required to raise of its own motion the question whether an environmental impact assessment should have been carried out pursuant to Art 2(1) and Art 4(2) of the Directive.

55 First of all it should be recalled that the obligation of a Member State to take all the measures necessary to achieve the result prescribed by a directive is a binding obligation imposed by the third paragraph of Art 189 of the EC Treaty and by the Directive itself (see the judgments in Case 51/76 *Verbond van Nederlandse Ondernemingen v Inspecteur der Invoerrechten en Accijzen* [1977] ECR 113 (para 22) and Case 152/84 *Marshall v Southampton and South West Hampshire Health Authority (Teaching)* [1986] 2 All ER 584; [1986] ECR 723 (para 48)).That duty to take all appropriate measures, whether general or particular, is binding on all the authorities of Member States including, for matters within their jurisdiction, the courts (see the judgment in Case C-106/89 *Marleasing SA v La Comercial Internacional de Alimentacisn SA* [1990] ECR I-4135 (para 8)).

56 As regards the right of an individual to invoke a Directive and of the national court to take it into consideration, the court has already held that it would be incompatible with the binding effect attributed to a Directive by Art 189 to exclude, in principle, the possibility that the obligation which it imposes may be invoked by those concerned. In particular, where the Community authorities have, by Directive, imposed on Member States the obligation to pursue a particular course of conduct, the useful effect of such an act would be weakened if individuals were prevented from relying on it before their national courts, and if the latter were prevented from taking it into consideration as an element of Community law in order to rule whether the national legislature, in exercising the choice open to it as to the form and methods for implementation, has

kept within the limits of its discretion set out in the Directive (see the judgment in *Verbond van Nederlandse Ondernemingen* [1977] ECR 113 (paras 22–24)).

57　Secondly, where, by virtue of national law, courts or tribunals must, of their own motion, raise points of law based on binding domestic rules which have not been raised by the parties, such an obligation also exists where binding Community rules are concerned (see especially the judgment in Joined Cases C-430–431/93 *Van Schijndel v Stichting Pensioenfonds voor Fysiotherapeuten* [1996] All ER (EC) 259; [1995] ECR I-4705 (para 13)).

58　The position is the same if national law confers on courts and tribunals a discretion to apply of their own motion binding rules of law. Indeed, pursuant to the principle of co-operation laid down in Art 5 of the Treaty, it is for national courts to ensure the legal protection which persons derive from the direct effect of provisions of Community law (see especially the judgments in Case C-213/89 *R v Secretary of State for Transport ex p Factortame Ltd (No 2)* [1991] 1 All ER 70; [1990] ECR I-2433 (para 19) and *Van Schijndel* [1996] All ER (EC) 259; [1995] ECR I-4705 (para 14)).

59　The fact that in this case the Member States have a discretion under Arts 2(1) and 4(2) of the Directive does not preclude judicial review of the question whether the national authorities exceeded their discretion (see especially the judgment in *Verbond van Nederlandse Ondernemingen* [1977] ECR 113 (paras 27–29)).

60　Consequently where, pursuant to national law, a court must or may raise of its own motion pleas in law based on a binding national rule which were not put forward by the parties, it must, for matters within its jurisdiction, examine of its own motion whether the legislative or administrative authorities of the Member State remained within the limits of their discretion under Arts 2(1) and 4(2) of the Directive, and take account thereof when examining the action for annulment.

61　If that discretion has been exceeded and consequently the national provisions must be set aside in that respect, it is for the authorities of the Member State, according to their respective powers, to take all the general or particular measures necessary to ensure that projects are examined in order to determine whether they are likely to have significant effects on the environment and, if so, to ensure that they are subject to an impact assessment.

62　Consequently, the replies to the third and fourth questions must be that: Art 4(2) of the Directive and point 10(e) of Annex II must be interpreted as meaning that a Member State which establishes the criteria or thresholds necessary to classify projects relating to dykes at a level such that, in practice, all such projects are exempted in advance from the requirement of an impact assessment exceeds the limits of its discretion under Arts 2(1) and 4(2) of the Directive unless all projects excluded could, when viewed as a whole, be regarded as not being likely to have significant effects on the environment. Where under national law a court must or may raise of its own motion pleas in law based on a binding national rule which have not been put forward by the parties, it must, for matters within its jurisdiction, examine of its own motion whether the legislative or administrative authorities of the Member State have remained within the limits of their discretion under Arts 2(1) and 4(2) of the Directive, and take account thereof when examining the action for annulment. Where that discretion has been exceeded and consequently the national provisions must be set aside in that respect, it is for the authorities of the Member State, according to their respective powers, to take all the general or particular measures necessary to ensure that projects are examined in order to determine whether they are likely to have significant effects on the environment and, if so, to ensure that they are subject to an impact assessment.

UK – environmental impact assessment (EIA)

EC Directive 85/337 was implemented in the UK mostly within the existing framework of land-use planning laws. The additional procedural requirements imposed by the Directive relating to the consideration of planning applications are now set out in the Town and Country Planning (Environmental Impact Assessment) (England and Wales) Regulations 1999 SI 1999/293. (Note also, the Transport and Works (Applications and Objections) Regulations 2000 SI 2000/2190). There are also several supplementary statutory instruments which implement the Directive in respect of projects which are not subject to planning laws.[17]

Guidance on the application of EIA has been provided by the courts, notably in the judgment of Simon Brown J in *R v Swale Borough Council ex p Royal Society for the Protection of Birds* [1991] JPL 39 (see p 795, below). The case concerned the 1989 grant of planning permission for the reclamation of the Medway mud flats. The evidence was that this grant was actually part of a much larger development.[18] The RSPB opposed the grant of planning permission because the area was important for migratory birds and there was a proposal to designate the mudflats as an SSSI. They maintained that an EIA should have taken place and the Local Planning Authority had erred in not requiring it. They argued that either the aim was to provide a trading port (which fell within Sched I of the 1988 Regulations 1988 SI 1988/1199 and would therefore require mandatory EIA) or the project fell within Schedule II because the development would have significant environmental effects.

In finding against the RSPB, Simon Brown J stated that whether a development falls within the regulations and if so, which Schedule, was a matter for the relevant planning authority and one which was a question of fact, not law.[19] Generally the authority's decision must be made in relation to the development applied for rather than any contemplated future development. However, this must be qualified if the application relates to a Sched 2 matter and in reality the application project is part of a greater development. In such a case, the authority should consider the wider issues as otherwise developers could avoid the regulations by submitting piecemeal development proposals.

The House of Lords has recently considered environmental impact assessment in *R v North Yorkshire County Council ex p Brown* [1998] Env LR 393. The case concerned an interim development order made in 1947 authorising mineral extraction. There are no

---

17 *Inter alia* Environmental Assessment (Afforestation) Regulations 1988 SI 1988/1207; the Land Drainage Improvement Works (Assessment of Environmental Effects) Regulations 1988 SI 1988/1217; the Highways (Assessment of Environmental Effects) Regulations 1988 SI 1988/1241; the Harbour Works (Assessment of Environmental Effects) Regulations 1988 SI 1988/1336.

18 Sometimes referred to as 'salami-slicing': Hughes, D, *Environmental Law*, 3rd edn, 1996, London: Butterworths, p 354.

19 Note the limitations imposed on planning authority discretion at EC level by the *Dutch Dykes* case [1997] All ER (EC) 134 and *WWF v Bozen* [1999] All ER (D) 1016 (see p 824, above). Simon Brown J's approach seems to have been followed in *R v Metropolitan Borough of Wirral and Another ex p Gray* [1998] Env LR D 13; *R v St Edmundsbury Borough Council ex p Walton* [1999] JPL 805.

time restrictions on such orders but the Planning and Compensation Act 1991 provided that if works covered by such orders were not commenced by 1993, then the holder of the consent must apply to the Mineral Planning Authority for registration and the determination of conditions. When the holder of the consent followed this procedure the Council imposed new conditions upon the operation, but it did not undertake an environmental impact assessment before doing so. Local householders applied for judicial review challenging the Council's action on the ground that such an assessment should have been undertaken. The Council argued that there was no need to carry out an environmental impact assessment because under the Directive this is only required where 'development consent' is granted; consent was originally granted in 1947, not when the new conditions were imposed. The House of Lords rejected this argument and held that an environmental impact assessment should have been undertaken. Lord Hoffmann said that:

> The principle in this and similar cases seems to me to be clear: the Directive does not apply to decisions which involve merely the detailed regulation of activities for which the principal consent, raising the substantial environmental issues, has already been given ... It seems to me clear ... that it can have no application to this one. The procedure created by the Act of 1991 was not merely a detailed regulation of a project in respect of which the substantial environmental issues had already been considered. The purpose of the procedure was to give the mineral planning authority a power to assess the likely environmental effects of old mining permissions which had been granted without, to modern ways of thinking, any serious consideration of the environment at all. It is true that the power to deal with these effects was limited to the imposition of conditions rather than complete prohibition. But the procedure was nevertheless a new and freestanding examination of the issues and could therefore, in my opinion, require the information provided by an environmental impact assessment.

The strict application of the (original) 1988 Regulations transposing the 1985 EIA Directive into English Law was reaffirmed by Lord Hoffmann in the recent decision of the House of Lords in *Berkeley v Secretary of State for the Environment and Others* [2000] 3 All ER 897.[20] In this case the House unanimously overturned both the Court of Appeal and the first instance decision. The House rejected a contention that where it could be shown that substantial compliance with the EIA requirements had occurred, the fact that no EIA had actually been requested did not justify quashing a grant of planning permission. Citing *ex p Brown* (above) Lord Hoffmann said that even if information amounting to an environmental statement was available to the general public as a result of a public inquiry into the proposed development, this was not sufficient to comply with the terms of the Directive.

R v Swale Borough Council and another ex p Royal Society for the Protection of Birds [1991] 1 PLR 6

Simon Brown J: Lappel Bank is an area of intertidal mud flats near the mouth of the River Medway. It lies at the north-western edge of the Isle of Sheppey and stretches southwards from Sheerness Docks to Queenborough at the mouth of the River Swale. Opposite the

---

20 See Upton, W, 'The EIA process and the directly enforceable rights of citizens' – *Berkeley v Secretary of State for the Environment and Others*' [2001] 13(1) JEL 89–105.

bank, across the River Medway, lies the Isle of Grain. The Medway estuary is an important nature conservation area recognised both nationally and internationally for supporting migratory wader birds: shelduck, ringed plover, dunlin, curlew and redshank.

Although the environmental significance of Lappel Bank itself was not at first recognised, the applicants, the Royal Society for the Protection of Birds, came to regard it as such, certainly before August 1989, and in November 1989 both it and the River Medway were proposed for addition to the two existing sites of special scientific interest in the region (Medway Marshes SSSI and Swale SSSI). The whole area is also now already either designated or, in so far as not, a candidate for designation both under the Ramsar Convention on wetlands of international importance and as a special protection area under the EC Directive on the conservation of wild birds, a directive implemented by ministerial circular in the UK.

The applicants are, of course, well known. They are the largest conservation charity in the United Kingdom, with over half a million members.

That is the broad environmental background against which this challenge lies: a challenge to the grant of planning permission on August 16 1989 by Swale Borough Council (SBC) to the Medway Ports Authority (MPA) for 'land reclamation' of 125 acres of Lappel Bank.

That very act of reclamation will, assert the applicants, greatly damage the prospects for wintering birds irrespective of what, if any, further development is carried out on the reclaimed land.

It is the mud flats themselves which are the feeding grounds of the bird population. The act of reclamation, I should say, is already in progress. A total of 2m m/3 (nearly 3m tonnes) of material is to be dredged from the main Medway approach channel and deposited behind a retaining bund so as to raise the bank permanently above high-water level. Very approximately a quarter of that material has thus far been deposited on the bank and about a third of its area thus far covered. From an environmental standpoint the point of no return will, I was informed during the hearing, shortly arrive.

The essential grounds of challenge are twofold. It is said, first, that the applicants were not consulted on the planning application despite an express written assurance that they would be. That is a challenge based on legitimate expectation. Second, it is said that SBC, in granting the planning permission without first requiring an environmental statement, breached the Town and Country Planning (Assessment of Environmental Effects) Regulations 1988 SI 1988/1199 (the 1988 Regulations), introduced as they were to give effect to another EC Directive 85/337/EEC and to ensure that the environmental effects of certain specified categories of development are considered at the planning stage.

[The judge considers the issue of planning permission and the applicant's legitimate expectation of being consulted.]

Environmental assessment

I pass to the next issue, which is that of environmental assessment under the 1988 Regulations. SBC regarded, indeed still regard, the MPA development as falling outside these regulations. What, then, do the 1988 Regulations provide? Essentially, that no planning application which falls within the schedules to the regulations can be granted unless the planning authority has 'first taken the environmental information into consideration' (see Regulation 4). Environmental information is defined in Regulation 2 to mean: the environmental statement prepared by the applicant ... any representations made by anybody required by these regulations to be invited to make representations or to be consulted and any representations duly made by any other person about the likely environmental effects of the proposed development.

A Schedule 1 application, so far as material, means an application for planning permission for carrying out a development of any description mentioned in that schedule. A Schedule 2 application is defined to mean an application for planning permission for development of any description mentioned in that schedule 'and which would be likely to have significant effects on the environment by virtue of factors such as its nature, size or location'. The contents of the schedules will sufficiently appear in a moment.

I do not propose to burden this judgment further with the detailed rival arguments about whether the MPA development should or should not be found to fall within any of the categories described in the schedules. Rather, I shall seek to state my broad conclusions upon this aspect of the case:

1   The decision whether any particular development is or is not within the scheduled descriptions is exclusively for the planning authority in question, subject only to Wednesbury challenge. Questions of classification are essentially questions of fact and degree, not of law. I reject Mr Cran's submission that only one possible view was open to SBC. I accordingly decline now to take the decision myself. Even less am I persuaded that this court is entitled upon judicial review to act effectively as an appeal court and to reach its own decision so as to ensure that our EC Treaty obligations are properly discharged.

2   The question falls strictly to be asked in relation to the planning application rather than the permission being granted, assuming the latter to be materially different (see Regulation 9). SBC were here granting a more restricted permission than was being sought. Since, however, they regarded neither as falling within the regulations, that matters not. It would always be open to a planning authority to invite the applicants to submit a lesser application if that was all they were minded to grant and if that would then make an environmental assessment unnecessary.

3   The question whether the development is of a category described in either schedule must be answered strictly in relation to the development applied for, not any development contemplated beyond that. But the further question arising in respect of a Schedule 2 development, the question whether it 'would be likely to have significant effects on the environment by virtue of factors such as its nature, size or location' should, in my judgment, be answered rather differently. The proposal should not then be considered in isolation if in reality it is properly to be regarded as an integral part of an inevitably more substantial development. This approach appears to me appropriate on the language of the regulations, the existence of the smaller development of itself promoting the larger development and thereby likely to carry in its wake the environmental effects of the latter. In common sense, moreover, developers could otherwise defeat the object of the regulations by piecemeal development proposals.

Mr Harman may well, therefore, have been asking the wrong question as to environmental significance through considering the issue in relation to Lappel Bank alone. But I would certainly not regard the planning permission as flawed on that basis. In the first place, SBC did not regard the development in any event as falling within a Schedule 2 description and, second, it is, of course, the applicants' own case that it is in fact the bank's reclamation alone rather than any subsequent development that will have the significant environmental effects here. Once the bank is reclaimed, the essential damage will have been done.

4   Although Mr Cran contends that this development is an operation 'to provide ... a trading port' within para 1.8 of Schedule 1, that seems to me a very difficult proposition. I should have thought that at most it constitutes the 'modification of a development ... within a description mentioned in Schedule 1' – namely the modification of a trading port – given that that dichotomy is specifically introduced by the regulations themselves. As stated, I conclude that for the purposes of classification the development must be looked at in isolation.

The other candidate categories in Schedule 2 are, first, within para 10(a) 'an industrial estate development project' and, second, within para 11(e) as 'a site for depositing sludge'. I am bound to say that this latter description of the development seems to me to be the applicants' best bet given the *Oxford English Dictionary* definition of 'sludge', *inter alia*, as 'mud, mire, or ooze ... forming a deposit at the bottom of rivers'.

5   Although Mr Cran urges me to regard this development as falling within para 1(f) of Schedule 2, that paragraph expressly refers to 'the reclamation of land from the sea' for the 'purposes of agriculture'. Although Mr Cran submits that the reference there to agriculture makes a nonsense of the underlying object of these regulations and that it should, therefore, be ignored, this seems to me an impossible contention, torturing the construction of these regulations beyond breaking point. The curious fact is that the draftsman appears specifically to have omitted from Schedule 2 'land reclamation for the purposes of conversion to another type of land use', that is, apart from the purposes of agriculture, even although the former also is expressly envisaged in the European Directive itself.

6   I am quite satisfied that on the information then before them SBC were well entitled to regard this development, for one reason or another, as falling outside either schedule. Even, moreover, had they categorised it as being *prima facie* within Schedule 2, they cannot be faulted for concluding that it would not have a significant environmental effect on the environment. After all, not only had such reclamation work not previously given rise to environmental concern on anyone's part, but NCC themselves in their letter of 25 July responded to express consultation about it by advising that they had no objection.

7   Were I to quash this planning permission and remit the matter to SBC for redetermination they would, of course, have regard to these observations, albeit, as I repeat, the decision whether an environmental assessment is here required would necessarily remain with them. Importantly, however, the applicants would then have the opportunity, as previously they have not, to seek to influence that decision both as to the appropriate categorisation of the development and as to its environmental significance. Indeed, they would also have the opportunity of inviting the Secretary of State to exercise his s 35 [of the Town and Country Planning Act 1990] call-in power to determine this planning application himself.

[Simon Brown J decided against the RSPB however.]

ACCESS TO ENVIRONMENTAL INFORMATION IN EC AND UK LAW

Freedom of Access to Information on the Environment Directive 90/313

The provision of public access to environmental information has been a declared aim of EC Environmental policy for a number of years. In 1987 the Fourth Action Programme on the Environment[21] stated that better access to information on the environment was a priority area and the current action programme[22] stresses the role of the general public in ensuring environmental protection. It declares that individuals must have access to information to ensure that they play their part in achieving sustainable development.

The Directive on the Freedom of Access to Information on the Environment 90/313 requires Member States to ensure that public authorities make available information relating to the environment, to any natural or legal person at his request and without his having to declare an interest (Art 3). Furthermore, 'bodies with public responsibilities for the environment and under the control of public authorities' are required to make any relevant information they hold available to the public (Art 6). At least some provisions of the Directive are likely to have 'direct effect'.[23]

'Public authorities' are defined in Art 2(b) as meaning any public administration at national, regional or local level which has responsibilities for and possesses information relating to the environment apart from bodies acting in a judicial or legislative capacity.

'Information relating to the environment' means (Art 2(a)) any available information in written, visual, aural or database form on the state of water, air, soil, fauna, flora, land and natural sites and on activities (including those which give rise to nuisances) or measures adversely affecting these natural resources or likely to so affect them, and on activities or measures designed to protect them, including administrative measures and environmental management programmes.

In Case C-321/96 *Mecklenberg v Kreis Pinneberg-Der Landrat* (extracted below, p 811) the ECJ held that the concept of 'information relating to the environment' contained in Art 2(a) is a broad one covering any activities engaged in by public authorities. This approach by the ECJ is particularly significant in that virtually all actions adopted by public authorities could be said to have an impact on the environment and thus fall within the Directive. (See also the approach taken by UK courts in *ex p Ibstock Building Products* and the *Birmingham Northern Relief Road* case (extracted at pp 862 and 865 respectively). The ECJ also considered the concept of 'preliminary investigation proceedings' contained in Art 3(2).

The Directive permits a request for such information to be refused for certain reasons, including commercial and industrial confidentiality and public security (Art 3(2)), but the reasons for a refusal must be given within two months. A person who feels that his request for information has been unreasonably refused or ignored or that it has been

---

21 (1987) OJ C328.
22 *Fifth Action Programme on the Environment – Towards Sustainability;* see Chapter 1, p 46.
23 Including Art 3. See Rose, I, 'Industry and access to information on the environment', in Somsen, H (ed), *Protecting the European Environment: Enforcing EC Environmental Law*, 1996, London: Blackstone, pp 255–56.

inadequately answered by a public authority, is given the right to seek judicial or administrative review in accordance with his national legal system (Art 4). These provisions may be compared with Art 4(4) of the Aarhus Convention 1998 where there is a specific statement that the grounds for refusal are to be 'interpreted in a restrictive way' (see p 813, above). This point was stressed by the ECJ in *Mecklenberg* in relation to Arts 3(2) and 3(3).

In Case C-217/97 *Commission v Germany* (1999), the ECJ held that Germany had failed to fulfil its obligations under the Directive (i) by failing to provide for access to be given to information during administrative proceedings where the public authorities have received information in the course of those proceedings; (ii) by failing to provide for information to be supplied in part where it is possible to separate out information concerning the interests referred to in Art 3(2) of the directive; and (iii) by failing to provide that a charge is to be made only where information is in fact supplied.

The Directive will require amendment in several significant aspects to bring it in line with the Aarhus Convention. In particular:

* the definition of 'environmental information' must be amended to include explicit reference to biological diversity and GMOs.

* Public bodies must respond to information requests within one month rather than two months, unless the volume and complexity of information justify an extension to two months.

* The grounds for with holding information will need revision and reduction.

* There will be a need to strengthen the procedures for reviewing decisions not to grant information.

* Most significantly, the access to information requirement will apply to EC Institutions for the first time (Art 2(d)).

It may be noted that the Convention also has provisions on public participation which reflect those found in the EIA and IPPC Directives. Note that the public participation procedure in the IPPC Directive (Art 15, see p 591) will need revision in the light of the more detailed provision in the Directive. See [1998] 4 Env Liability CS 39.

Access to information from community institutions

It is interesting to note that although the Directive requires Member States to ensure that their public authorities make environmental information available, it does not apply to the institutions of the European Union. Although a 'right of access to information' does not exist, Art 255 of the EC Treaty enshrines a right of access to documents held by the European Parliament, Council and Commission.[24] There are also some legislative provisions reflecting this move towards 'transparency' in government at the European level. For example, Regulation 1210/90 which established the European Environment Agency, provides in Art 6:

---

24 See also the very recent Council and European Parliament Regulation 1049/01; adopted 30 May 2001. See generally Birkinshaw, P, *Freedom of Information*, 3rd edn, 2001, London: Butterworths, pp 369–74.

> Environmental data supplied or emanating from the Agency may be published and shall be accessible to the public, subject to compliance with the rules of the Commission and the Member States on the dissemination of information, particularly as regards confidentiality.

More generally, even before the introduction of Art 255 the Council and Commission had committed themselves to transparency in the code of conduct attached to Decision 93/731[25] which states:

> ... the public will have the widest possible access to the documents held by the Commission and the Council.

The actual Decision 93/731 relating to Council documents qualifies the reference to wide access. It states:

> ... access to a Council document may be refused in order to protect the confidentiality of the Council's proceedings.

In 1994 the Commission adopted Decision 94/90[26] on public access to Commission documents. The general right of access is subject to a number of exceptions allowing the institutions to refuse access in some circumstances. These circumstances have been the subject of a recent legal challenge: *WWF UK (Sweden Intervening) v European Commission (France and Another Intervening)* [1997] All ER (EC) 300 (extracted at p 850, below) before the EC's Court of First Instance. This challenge may pave the way for more challenges in the future. The case involved a plan to build a visitors' centre at Mullaghmore in the Burren National Park in Ireland, with funding from EC Structural Funds. Worldwide Fund for Nature (WWF), with others, objected to the project on the basis that it would infringe EC environmental law and therefore result in a wrongful application of the Structural Funds. The Commission investigated, but eventually (in 1992) allowed the project to proceed. WWF sought access to the documents surrounding the investigation on the basis of Decision 94/90 but were refused on the grounds that the application fell within two exceptions contained in the Decision – (a) the protection of the public interest and (b) to protect the institution's interest in the confidentiality of its proceedings.

WWF brought an action to annul the Commission's decision denying access. The court ruled that the Commission was justified in relying upon the two exceptions. However, because the Commission had refused to give any reason for invoking these exceptions, the court annulled the Commission's decision. The court suggested that when exercising its discretion in relation to the confidentiality of its own proceedings, a genuine balance should be struck between the interests of citizens in gaining access to documents and the interests of the Commission in protecting confidentiality.

Given the principle of transparency (Art 1, Title I of the Treaty of European Union), the impact of Aarhus (which is binding on EU Institutions, Art 2(2)(d)), and the impact of Art 255 and Regulation 1049/01 made thereunder, it is clear that the interests of citizens in gaining access to documents is likely to prevail.

---

25 (1993) OJ L340.
26 (1994) OJ L46.

Environmental Information Regulations 1992 SI 1992/3240

Directive 90/313 has been implemented in Great Britain by the Environmental Information Regulations 1992 SI 1992/3240, as amended by the Environmental Information (Amendment) Regulations 1998 SI 1998/1447. The regulations apply to environmental information which is not already subject to a statutory obligation of disclosure. In previous chapters we have seen that various provisions require environmental information to be made available to the public, for example, s 190 of the Water Resources Act (Chapter 3); s 64 (Chapter 4 on waste) and s 20 of the Environmental Protection Act 1990 and reg 29, PPC Regulations (Chapter 5 on IPC) require information be placed on public registers. Where these specific provisions apply the regulations do not.

There are also miscellaneous provisions contained in diverse pieces of legislation which prescribe the circumstances when documents or information must be provided to interested parties. The case of *R v Rochdale MBC ex p Brown* [1997] Env LR 100 involved the right of an objector to copies of documents relating to a planning control matter under the Local Government Act 1972. In another recent case, *R v Hertfordshire County Council ex p Green Environmental Industries Ltd* [2000] 1 All ER 773 a company unsuccessfully argued that it could refuse to answer a request for information under s 71 and s 34 of the EPA 1990 on the grounds of self-incrimination. The court ruled that self-incrimination was not a justification for a refusal to answer (see Chapter 4, p 523).

Environmental information must be made available by 'relevant persons'. 'Environmental information' is defined (reg 2(2)) in terms similar to Art 2(a) of the Directive (see p 849). The regulations apply to information held 'in an accessible form' (reg 2(1)(b)) without defining what is meant by the phrase. It has been suggested (by Rose (1996) 258) that this might exclude information held which has not been collated, or is difficult to track down.

'Relevant persons' are defined (reg 2(3)) as Ministers of the Crown, central and local government authorities and administrators together with any body with public responsibilities for the environment controlled by them. The definition does not make the position of privatised utilities under the regulation very clear and the water companies do not regard themselves as subject to its provisions. Hughes ((1996) 29) maintains that because they have been described as 'emanations of the state' (*Griffin v South West Water* [1995] IRLR 15) they do fall within the scope of the regulations. The guidance on the regulations produced by the Department of the Environment is unhelpful:[27]

> ... the government is unable to give a definitive list of organisations subject to the requirements of the regulations. So organisations will need to take a view themselves as to whether they fall into any of the categories and thus become a relevant person. In cases of dispute, it will be for the Courts to decide.

---

27 Guidance on the Implementation of the Environmental Information Regulations 1992 in Great Britain (1992). See also Birtles, W, 'A right to know: the Environmental Information Regulations 1992' [1993] JPL 615.

Relevant persons must respond to requests for information promptly, at least within two months,[28] and when a request is refused, they must give reasons for the refusal. The regulations exempt information which is held for the purpose of 'any judicial or legislative functions' (reg 2(1)(b)). Regulation 4 contains an exhaustive list of exceptions including information which must be treated as confidential (Art 4(3)) and information which is capable of being treated as confidential (Art 4(2)). Information falls under Art 4(2) 'if and only if' it (a) relates to a matter of national defence or public security; (b) relates to matters which have been the subject of actual or prospective legal proceedings; (c) the confidential deliberations of any relevant persons or the contents of the internal communications of bodies corporate etc; (d) information in records still in the course of completion; and (e) information relating to matters of commercial or industrial confidentiality or affecting intellectual property.

Regulation 3(3) allows relevant persons to refuse manifestly unreasonable requests or requests formulated in too general a manner. The regulations do not contain an appeal mechanism against a refusal to disclose information. However, decisions to refuse access to information may be challenged by judicial review. The operation of the regulations has been discussed in *R v British Coal Corp ex p Ibstock Building Products Ltd*[29] (see p 818, below) and *R v Secretary of State for the Environment, Transport and Regions and Another ex p Alliance Against the Birmingham Northern Relief Road and Others* [1999] JPL 231 (p 821, below).

Future developments on access to environmental information

Currently the two principal instruments dealing with access to environmental information are the 1990 EC Directive 93/313 and the Environmental Information Regulations 1992. Both these instruments are to be revised in the light of the Aarhus Convention provisions on access to information. Accordingly, The Department of the Environment, Transport and the Regions have recently undertaken a consultation on proposals for a revised public access to information regime to include new regulations implementing Aarhus. The period of consultation closed on 5 January 2001: a summary of responses can be found via the internet at: www.environment.detr. gov.uk/consult/pubaccess/response/index.htm. The European Commission is also revising the Directive. On 29 June 2000 it adopted a proposal in Commission Document COM (00) 402 Final. This is available via the internet at: http://europa.eu.int/comm/ environment/ docum/00402-en.pdf.

Perhaps the most significant change in what will be a new Directive is the establishment of a 'right to access' rather than 'freedom of access' to environmental information. The main differences to be introduced by the new Directive will be: (i) the public interest served by disclosure is to be weighed by the interest served by refusal; (ii) there is to be a wider definition of environmental information, encompassing information on policies; (iii) there is a more detailed definition of 'environmental authorities'; and (iv)

---

28 The Environment Agency has revised its policy for processing public registers and environmental information requests from 1 April 1997. The Agency will endeavour to reply to all requests for information within three or four weeks. A charge of £35 + VAT is imposed for a single residential site; £50 + VAT for a non-residential site.

29 [1995] JPL 40 (QBD).

the Directive establishes the requirements to be satisfied by review procedures for challenging decisions on access to information.

These reforms will have to operate alongside the Freedom of Information Act 2000, when in force. Broadly speaking, it is intended that access to environmental information will form a distinct regime. The provisions of the Freedom of Information Act 2000 system will, however, be available should requests for information be refused under the environmental information regime. Note in this context that under Pt II, s 39, Environmental Information is 'exempt information' under the Freedom of Information Act 2000. Section 74, however, confers power to make regulations implementing the information provisions of the Aarhus Convention.

COUNCIL DIRECTIVE

of 7 June 1990

on the freedom of access to information on the environment

(90/313/EEC)

THE COUNCIL OF THE EUROPEAN COMMUNITIES,

Having regard to the Treaty establishing the European Economic Community, and in particular Art 130s thereof, [...]

Considering the principles and objectives defined by the action programmes of the European Communities on the environment of 1973, 1977 and 1983, and more particularly the action programme of 1987, which calls, in particular, for devising 'ways of improving public access to information held by environmental authorities'; [...]

Whereas the European Parliament stressed, in its opinion on the fourth action programme of the European Communities on the environment that 'access to information for all must be made possible by a specific Community programme';

Whereas access to information on the environment held by public authorities will improve environmental protection;

Whereas the disparities between the laws in force in the Member States concerning access to information on the environment held by public authorities can create inequality within the Community as regards access to information and/or as regards conditions of competition;

Whereas it is necessary to guarantee to any natural or legal person throughout the Community free access to available information on the environment in written, visual, aural or data-base form held by public authorities, concerning the state of the environment, activities or measures adversely affecting, or likely so to affect the environment, and those designed to protect it;

Whereas, in certain specific and clearly defined cases, it may be justified to refuse a request for information relating to the environment;

Whereas a refusal by a public authority to forward the information requested must be justified;

Whereas it must be possible for the applicant to appeal against the public authority's decision;

Whereas access to information relating to the environment held by bodies with public responsibilities for the environment and under the control of public authorities should also be ensured;

Whereas, as part of an overall strategy to disseminate information on the environment, general information should actively be provided to the public on the state of the environment; [...]

HAS ADOPTED THIS DIRECTIVE

Article 1

The object of this Directive is to ensure freedom of access to, and dissemination of, information on the environment held by public authorities and to set out the basic terms and conditions on which such information should be made available.

Article 2

For the purposes of this Directive:

(a) 'information relating to the environment' shall mean any available information in written, visual, aural or data-base form on the state of water, air, soil, fauna, flora, land and natural sites, and on activities (including those which give rise to nuisances such as noise) or measures adversely affecting, or likely so to affect these, and on activities or measures designed to protect these, including administrative measures and environmental management programmes;

(b) 'public authorities' shall mean any public administration at national, regional or local level with responsibilities, and possessing information, relating to the environment with the exception of bodies acting in a judicial or legislative capacity.

Article 3

1 Save as provided in this Article, Member States shall ensure that public authorities are required to make available information relating to the environment to any natural or legal person at his request and without his having to prove an interest.

   Member States shall define the practical arrangements under which such information is effectively made available.

2 Member States may provide for a request for such information to be refused where it affects:

   – the confidentiality of the proceedings of public authorities, international relations and national defence,

   – public security,

   – matters which are, or have been, judice, or under enquiry (including disciplinary enquiries), or which are the subject of preliminary investigation proceedings,

   – commercial and industrial confidentiality, including intellectual property,

   – the confidentiality of personal data and/or files,

- material supplied by a third party without that party being under a legal obligation to do so;

- material, the disclosure of which would make it more likely that the environment to which such material related would be damaged.

Information held by public authorities shall be supplied in part where it is possible to separate out information on items concerning the interests referred to above.

3   A request for information may be refused where it would involve the supply of unfinished documents or data or internal communications, or where the request is manifestly unreasonable or formulated in too general a manner.

4   A public authority shall respond to a person requesting information as soon as possible and at the latest within two months. The reasons for a refusal to provide the information requested must be given.

Article 4

A person who considers that his request for information has been unreasonably refused or ignored, or has been inadequately answered by a public authority, may seek a judicial or administrative review of the decision in accordance with the relevant national legal system.

Article 5

Member States may make a change for supplying the information, but such change may not exceed a reasonable cost.

Article 6

Member States shall take the necessary steps to ensure that information relating to the environment held by bodies with public responsibilities for the environment and under the control of public authorities is made available on the same terms and conditions as those set out in Arts 3, 4 and 5 either via the competent public authority or directly by the body itself.

[Articles 7–10 omitted.]

Case T-105/95 WWF UK (Sweden Intervening) v European Commission (France and Another Intervening) [1997] All ER (EC) 300

Headnote

In 1991 the Irish authorities announced a plan to build a visitors' centre in an Irish national park using Community structural funds. WWF, an English trust, complained to the European Commission, contending that the project would infringe Community environmental law and involve a wrongful application of structural funds. The Commission investigated the project and decided not to initiate infringement proceedings against Ireland because the project did not infringe the relevant provisions. Following an unsuccessful action for annulment of that decision, WWF requested access to all documents held by Directorates General XI (Environment) and XVI (Regional Policy) which related to the investigation of the project. The directorates refused WWF's request, on the ground that the requested documents all related to the investigation of complaints and/or to the Commission's internal deliberations and therefore fell under the public interest and/or confidentiality exceptions to access set out in the code of conduct annexed to Commission Decision (ECSC, EC, Euratom) 94/90 on public access to Commission documents. The Secretary General of the Commission subsequently confirmed those refusals and the directorates' reasoning. Thereafter the WWF applied to the Court of First Instance of the

European Communities seeking annulment of the Secretary General's decision. WWF contended that Decision 94/90 and the code of conduct were legally binding on the Commission and conferred on the public rights of access to documents 'to the widest extent possible' and further that the Commission had interpreted the public interest exception too widely, had failed to meet the conditions for application of the confidentiality exception and had also failed to give sufficient reasons for its decision, thereby infringing both Decision 94/90 and Art 190 of the EC Treaty.

Held

The Secretary General's decision would be annulled for the following reasons–

(1) The code of conduct contained in Decision 94/90 set out the general principle that the public should have the widest possible access to documents held by the Commission and conferred on third parties legal rights which the Commission was obliged to respect. The code contained two categories of exception to the general principle which were either mandatory or discretionary. The discretionary exception was designed to protect the Commission's interest in the confidentiality of its proceedings; and, in deciding whether to refuse access to requested documents the Commission should strike a genuine balance between the interest of the citizen in obtaining access and its own interest in protecting the confidentiality of its deliberations. The mandatory exceptions were designed to protect the interests of third parties or the public in cases where disclosure would risk causing harm to persons who could legitimately refuse access to the documents if held in their own possession. The confidentiality which Member States were entitled to expect of the Commission when investigating possible Treaty infringements warranted, under the public interest heading, a refusal of access to documents relating to those investigations, even where a period of time had elapsed since the closure of the investigation. However, the Commission was required to indicate, at least by reference to categories of documents, the reasons for which it considered the sought-after documents to be related to the possible opening of an infringement procedure, the subject matter to which the documents related and whether they involved inspections or investigations relating to a possible infringement procedure – Case T-194/94 *Carvel v EU Council* [1996] All ER (EC) 53, applied.

(2) The contested decision, read in conjunction with the two decisions which it confirmed, did not indicate (a) that the Commission had undertaken a genuine balancing of the interests involved in relation to the documents refused under the discretionary exception, or (b) the Commission's reasons for considering that the documents refused under the mandatory category related to possible infringement proceedings and therefore came under the public interest heading. It followed that the Commission had not met the requirements to state reasons laid down in Art 190.

[Paragraphs 1–52 omitted.]

Findings of the court

53 It seems necessary to consider, in the first place, the legal force to be attributed to Decision 94/90, Art 1 of which adopted the code of conduct, and, secondly, the scope of the exceptions provided for in the code.

54 It is clear, first of all, that the decision constitutes the Commission's response to the calls made by the European Council to reflect at Community level the right of citizens to have access to documents held by public authorities, a right which is recognised in the domestic legislation of most of the Member States. So long as the Community

legislature has not adopted general rules on the right of public access to documents held by the Community institutions, it falls to those institutions themselves to take measures within their powers of internal organisation to enable them to respond to and to process such requests for access in a manner commensurate with the interests of good administration in respect of the corresponding decision – Council Decision (EC) 93/731 on public access to Council documents (see the judgment in Case C-58/94 *Netherlands v EU Council* [1996] ECR I-2169 (paras 34–37)).

55 By adopting the decision, the Commission has indicated to citizens who wish to gain access to documents which it holds that their requests will be dealt with according to the procedures, conditions and exceptions laid down for the purpose. Although the decision is, in effect, a series of obligations which the Commission has voluntarily assumed for itself as a measure of internal organisation, it is nevertheless capable of conferring on third parties legal rights which the Commission is obliged to respect.

56 Next, it is necessary to consider the scope to be given to the exceptions contained in the code of conduct. In that regard, it is important to note that where a general principle is established and exceptions to that principle are then laid down, the exceptions should be construed and applied strictly, in a manner which does not defeat the application of the general rule. In particular, the grounds for refusing a request for access to Commission documents, set out in the code of conduct as exceptions, should be construed in a manner which will not render it impossible to attain the objective of transparency expressed in the response of the Commission to the calls of the European Council (see paras 2 and 54, above).

57 The court considers that the code of conduct contains two categories of exception to the general principle of citizens' access to Commission documents and these correspond to the provisions of Art 4 of Decision 93/731.

58 According to the wording of the first category, drafted in mandatory terms:

> ... the institutions will refuse access to any document where disclosure could undermine [in particular] the protection of the public interest (public security, international relations, monetary stability, court proceedings and investigations).

It follows that the Commission is obliged to refuse access to documents falling under any one of the exceptions contained in this category once the relevant circumstances are shown to exist (see in relation to the corresponding provisions of Decision 93/731, Case T-194/94 *Carvel v EU Council* [1996] All ER (EC) 53; [1995] ECR II-2765 (para 64)).

59 By way of contrast, the wording of the second category, drafted in discretionary terms, provides that the Commission 'may also refuse access in order to protect the institution's interest in the confidentiality of its proceedings'. It follows, accordingly, that the Commission enjoys a margin of discretion which enables it, if need be, to refuse a request for access to documents which touch upon its deliberations. The Commission must nevertheless exercise this discretion by striking a genuine balance between, on the one hand, the interest of the citizen in obtaining access to those documents and, on the other, its own interest in protecting the confidentiality of its deliberations (see, in relation to the corresponding provisions of Decision 93/731, the judgment in Case T-194/94 *Carvel* [1996] All ER (EC) 53; [1995] ECR II-2765 (paras 64–65)).

60 The court considers that the distinction between these two categories of exception in the code of conduct is explained by the nature of the interest which the categories seek respectively to protect. The first category, comprising the 'mandatory exceptions',

effectively protects the interest of third parties or of the general public in cases where disclosure of particular documents by the institution concerned would risk causing harm to persons who could legitimately refuse access to the documents if held in their own possession. On the other hand, in the second category, relating to the internal deliberations of the institution, it is the interest of the institution alone which is at stake.

61 The Commission is, however, entitled to invoke jointly an exception within the first category and one within the second in order to refuse access to documents which it holds, since no provision of Decision 94/90 precludes it from doing so. In effect, the possibility cannot be ruled out that the disclosure of particular documents by the Commission could cause damage both to interests protected by the exceptions of the first category and to the Commission's interest in maintaining the confidentiality of its deliberations.

62 Having regard to these factors, it is necessary to consider, secondly, whether the documents relating to an investigation into a possible breach of Community law, leading potentially to the opening of a procedure under Art 169 of the Treaty, satisfy the conditions which must be met for the Commission to be able to rely upon the public interest exception, which is one of the exceptions within the first category provided for in the code of conduct.

63 In this regard, the court considers that the confidentiality which the Member States are entitled to expect of the Commission in such circumstances warrants, under the heading of protection of the public interest, a refusal of access to documents relating to investigations which may lead to an infringement procedure, even where a period of time has elapsed since the closure of the investigation.

64 It is important, nevertheless, to point out that the Commission cannot confine itself to invoking the possible opening of an infringement procedure as justification, under the heading of protecting the public interest, for refusing access to the entirety of the documents identified in a request made by a citizen. The court considers, in effect, that the Commission is required to indicate, at the very least by reference to categories of documents, the reasons for which it considers that the documents detailed in the request which it received are related to the possible opening of an infringement procedure. It should indicate to which subject matter the documents relate and particularly whether they involve inspections or investigations relating to a possible procedure for infringement of Community law.

65 The duty identified in the preceding paragraph does not, however, mean that the Commission is obliged in all cases to furnish, in respect of each document, 'imperative reasons' in order to justify the application of the public interest exception and thereby risk jeopardising the essential function of the exception in question, which follows from the very nature of the public interest to be protected and the mandatory character of the exception. It would be impossible, in practical terms, to give reasons justifying the need for confidentiality in respect of each individual document without disclosing the content of the document and, thereby, depriving the exception of its very purpose.

66 Thirdly, it is necessary to consider whether the contested decision meets the requirement to state reasons which flows from Art 190 of the Treaty. In that connection, it should be noted that the duty to give reasons for every decision has a twofold purpose, namely, on the one hand, to permit interested parties to know the justification for the measure in order to enable them to protect their rights; and, on the other, to enable the Community judicature to exercise its power to review the legality of the

decision (see especially the judgments of the Court of Justice in Case C-350/88 *Société Française des Biscuits Delacre v EC Commission* [1990] ECR I-395 (para 15) and of the Court of First Instance in Case T-85/94 *Eugenio Branco Lda v European Commission* [1995] ECR II-45 (para 32)).

67 The court next notes that in the contested decision, the Secretary General of the Commission relied simultaneously both on the confidentiality exception and on the public interest exception in justifying his decision to refuse access to the entirety of the documents identified in the applicant's request, in relation both to DG XVI and to DG XI, without making any distinction between the documents held by those Directorates General respectively. In the contested decision, the Secretary General also confirmed the refusal which had been given to the applicant, on the one hand by DG XVI on the basis of the confidentiality exception alone (see para 16 above), and, on the other hand, by DG XI on the dual basis of the public interest exception and the confidentiality exception (see para 15 above). In order to assess the adequacy of the reasons given in the contested decision for the purposes of Art 190 of the Treaty, it is therefore necessary to examine the terms of the contested decision together with those of the letters from DG XVI and DG XI on 24 and 17 November 1994 respectively (see paras 16–15 above).

68 So far as concerns the refusal of the applicant's request for access to the documents held by DG XVI, it is to be noted that the contested decision, apart from its general reference to the public interest exception, confirms the terms of the letter of 24 November 1994 from DG XVI. In this letter, DG XVI had relied solely on the confidentiality exception.

69 Given that the Commission confined itself in the contested decision to confirming the terms of the letter of 24 November 1994 from DG XVI without indicating either that the reference to the public interest exception applied equally to the documents covered by the applicant's request to DG XVI or that a connection existed between the documents held by that Directorate General and the possible commencement of an infringement proceeding, it necessarily follows that the contested decision confined its reasons for refusing that request solely to the confidentiality exception, as had been indicated in the letter of 24 November 1994.

70 It does not appear from the letter of 24 November 1994 from DG XVI or from the contested decision that the Commission had fulfilled its duty to undertake a genuine balancing of the interests involved as required by the code of conduct (see para 59 above) because both the contested decision and the letter from DG XVI of 24 November confined themselves to mention of the confidentiality exception in order to refuse the applicant's request, and made no mention of any balancing of the interests involved.

71 Furthermore, it is not now open to the Commission to claim before the court, as it did in its letter of 18 July 1996 in response to a question from the court (see para 24 above), that all of the documents in question, including those held by DG XVI, are covered by the public interest exception, since the contested decision refers expressly to the letter of 24 November 1994 from DG XVI, which makes no reference to the public interest exception.

72 It follows that, in so far as it deals with the request of the applicant in relation to the documents held by DG XVI, the contested decision does not meet the requirement to state reasons laid down in Art 190 of the Treaty, and must therefore be annulled to that extent.

73 In so far as concerns the refusal of the applicant's request for access to the documents held by DG XI, inasmuch as the contested decision confirmed the terms of the letter of

DG XI of 17 November 1994 (see para 20 above), invoking jointly the public interest exception and the confidentiality exception, it cannot be held incompatible with the provisions of the code of conduct (see para 61 above).

74 The court also notes that even though, in the contested decision, the Commission sets out in general terms the reasons for which it considers that the public interest exception ought to be applied to documents relating to investigations into a possible infringement of Community law, leading potentially to the opening of an infringement procedure under Art 169 of the Treaty, it has given no indication, even by reference to categories of documents, of its reasons for considering that the documents covered by the request to DG XI were all related to a possible infringement proceeding (see para 64 above).

75 Furthermore, it is also clear that in its letter of 17 November 1994 DG XI had not indicated either, even by reference to categories of documents, the reasons for which the requested documents were in its view all covered by the public interest exception. It confined itself to the explanation that:

> ... the relevant exemptions in the case of the documents you have requested are the protection of the public interest (in particular, inspections and investigations) and the protection of the Commission's interest in the confidentiality of its own proceedings. The documents you have requested relate to the investigation of complaints, as well as to the Commission's internal deliberations.

76 Thus, as the Commission refrained both in the contested decision and in the letter of 17 November 1994 from DG XI from indicating that all the documents requested from DG XI were covered by the public interest exception and simultaneously relied upon the confidentiality exception, the applicant could not have ruled out the possibility that some of the documents held by DG XI were refused to it because they were covered by the confidentiality exception alone. Neither the terms of the contested decision nor those of the letter of 17 November 1994 from DG XI enable the applicant and, therefore, the court to ascertain whether the Commission fulfilled its obligation to undertake a genuine balancing of the interests involved as required by the code of conduct (see para 59 above), given that they both rely upon the confidentiality exception and make no mention of any balancing of the interests involved.

77 It follows that, in so far as the contested decision deals with the request made by the applicant to DG XI, it again fails to meet the requirements to state reasons which it laid down in Art 190 of the Treaty and must therefore be annulled to that extent.

78 For all of these reasons, the court considers that the application is well-founded and that the contested decision must be annulled.

Case C-321/96 *Mecklenburg v Kreis Pinneberg-Der Landrat (Der Vertreter des offentlichen Interesses) (Kiel Intervening)* [1999] All ER 166; [1999] 2 CMLR 418

Headnote

The applicant requested the municipality of Kreis Pinneberg to send him a copy of the statement of views submitted by the competent countryside protection authority in connection with planning approval for the construction of a road. By virtue of Art 2 of Council Directive (EEC) 90/313 on the freedom of access to information on the environment, 'information relating to the environment' included administrative measures; however, Art 3 provided that member states could refuse a request for such information where it affected matters which were, or had been, *sub judice*, or under inquiry, or which were the subject of 'preliminary investigation proceedings'. Kreis Pinneberg rejected the request on the grounds that the authority's statement of views was not 'information relating to the environment' within the meaning of Art 2(a) because it was merely an assessment of information already available to the applicant and, in any event, the criteria for refusal set out in Art 3 applied, since a development consent procedure constituted 'preliminary investigation proceedings'. Kreis Pinneberg rejected the applicant's appeal and he brought an action against those decisions before the Schleswig-Holsteinisches Verwaltungsgericht, contending that the authority's statement of views constituted an administrative measure and that, in any event, its evaluation of the information in its possession did not detract from its nature as 'information relating to the environment'. The Verwaltungsgericht dismissed the action on the ground that the information sought was covered by the confidentiality of the proceedings of public authorities within the meaning of para 7(1) of the German Law on information on the environment. The applicant appealed to the Oberverwaltungsgericht, which stayed the proceedings and referred to the Court of Justice of the European Communities for a preliminary ruling on questions on the interpretation of Arts 2 and 3 of Directive 90/313.

Held

(1) On a proper construction of Art 2(a) the concept of 'information relating to the environment' was intended to be a broad one: the Community legislature had purposely avoided giving any definition of the term which could lead to the exclusion of any of the activities engaged in by the public authorities and the term 'measures' served merely to make it clear that the acts governed by the Directive included all forms of administrative activity. Thus, in order to constitute such information, it was sufficient for a statement of views put forward by an authority to be an act capable of adversely affecting or protecting the State of one of the sectors of the environment covered by the Directive. Accordingly, the Directive covered a statement of views given by a countryside protection authority in development consent proceedings if that statement was capable of influencing the outcome of the development consent proceedings in relation to interests pertaining to the protection of the environment.

(2) The exception in Art 3(2) covered exclusively proceedings of a judicial or quasi-judicial nature, or at least proceedings which would inevitably lead to the imposition of a penalty if the offence was established. It followed that the term 'preliminary investigation proceedings' included an administrative procedure, such as that referred to in para 7(1)(2) of the German Law on Information and the Environment, which merely prepared the way for an administrative measure, only if it immediately preceded a contentious or quasi-contentious procedure and arose from the need to obtain proof or to investigate a matter prior to the opening of the actual procedure.

[The following is an extract from the judgment of the ECJ:]

First question

16 The first question asks in essence whether Art 2(a) of the Directive is to be interpreted as covering a statement of views given in development consent proceedings by a countryside protection authority participating in those proceedings.

17 The Commission has pointed out that for the purposes of defining the scope of the Directive the phrase 'environmental management' (zum Umweltschutz) used in Art 2(a) of the Directive applies solely to 'programmes', so that it is not correct to speak, as the referring court has done, of 'an administrative measure for

environmental management'. However, it considers that the statement of views provided by the countryside protection authority must be understood as being an 'administrative measure designed to protect the environment' within the meaning of the Directive.

18 The parties to the main proceedings both proceed to analyse the term 'measure' in the light of German law, and disagree as to whether a statement of views by an administrative authority, such as that at issue in the main proceedings, is an act linked to an individual case directed towards a specific aim and having determinative effects, the conditions to be satisfied in order for the term to apply in national law.

19 It must be noted in the first place that Art 2(a) of the Directive includes under 'information relating to the environment' any information on the state of the various aspects of the environment mentioned therein as well as on activities or measures which may adversely affect or protect those aspects, 'including administrative measures and environmental management programmes'. The wording of the provision makes it clear that the Community legislature intended to make that concept a broad one, embracing both information and activities relating to the state of those aspects.

20 Secondly, the use in Art 2(a) of the Directive of the term 'including' indicates that 'administrative measures' is merely an example of the 'activities' or 'measures' covered by the Directive. As the Advocate General pointed out in paragraph 15 of his opinion, above, the Community legislature purposely avoided giving any definition of 'information relating to the environment' which could lead to the exclusion of any of the activities engaged in by the public authorities, the term 'measures' serving merely to make it clear that the acts governed by the directive included all forms of administrative activity.

21 In order to constitute 'information relating to the environment for the purposes of the Directive', it is sufficient for the statement of views put forward by an authority, such as the statement concerned in the main proceedings, to be an act capable of adversely affecting or protecting the state of one of the sectors of the environment covered by the Directive. That is the case, as the referring court mentioned, where the statement of views is capable of influencing the outcome of the development consent proceedings as regards interests pertaining to the protection of the environment.

22 Accordingly, the reply to the first question is that Art 2(a) of the Directive is to be interpreted as covering a statement of views given by a countryside protection authority in development consent proceedings if that statement is capable of influencing the outcome of those proceedings as regards interests pertaining to the protection of the environment.

Second question

23 The second question asks in essence whether the phrase 'preliminary investigation proceedings' in Art 3(2), third indent, of the Directive is to be interpreted as including the proceedings of an administrative authority, such as those referred to in para 7(1)(2) of the UIG, which is restricted to preparing the way for an administrative measure.

24 It should be noted that under the third indent of Art 3(2) of the Directive national law may permit requests for information relating to–

matters which are, or have been, *sub judice*, or under enquiry (including disciplinary enquiries), or which are the subject of preliminary investigation proceedings.

25 Since that is a derogation from the general rules laid down by the Directive, Art 3(2), third indent, may not be interpreted in such a way as to extend its effects beyond what is necessary to safeguard the interests which it seeks to secure. Furthermore, the scope of the derogations which it lays down must be determined in the light of the aims pursued by the Directive (see the judgment in Case C-335/94 *Mrozek (Action Challenging an Administrative Fee)* [1996] ECR I-1573 (para 9)).

26 As far as the aims of the directive are concerned, the principle of freedom of access to information is laid down in Art 1 thereof. The seventh recital in the preamble to the directive emphasises the fact that the refusal to comply with a request for information relating to the environment may, however, be justified 'in certain specific and clearly defined cases'.

27 As regards the interests the protection of which the third indent of Art 3(2) of the Directive serves to secure, the exceptions provided for therein relate to information held by a public authority relating, first, to matters which are the subject of legal proceedings, next, to matters which are the subject of enquiries (including disciplinary enquiries) and, lastly, to matters which are the subject of 'preliminary investigation proceedings'. It is thus clear, as the Advocate-General pointed out in paragraph 23 of his opinion, above, that that exception covers exclusively proceedings of a judicial or quasi-judicial nature, or at least proceedings which will inevitably lead to the imposition of a penalty if the offence (administrative or criminal) is established. Viewed in that context, therefore, 'preliminary investigation proceedings' must refer to the stage immediately prior to the judicial proceedings or the enquiry.

28 That interpretation is borne out by the history of the Directive. Article 8(1) of the proposal for a directive submitted by the Commission on 31 October 1988 ((1988) OJ C335, p 5) allowed for an exception to the right of access to information where exercise of that right might be prejudicial 'to the secrecy of procedures brought before the courts'. It was as a result of the opinion given by the Economic and Social Committee on 31 March 1989 ((1989) OJ C139, p 47, point 2.6.1), which proposed the inclusion of a reference to the confidentiality of 'investigative proceedings', that the term 'preliminary investigation proceedings' was added to the proposal for a directive.

29 Lastly, it is settled case law that the need for a uniform interpretation of Community directives makes it impossible for the text of a provision to be considered, in case of doubt, in isolation; on the contrary, it requires that it be interpreted and applied in the light of the versions existing in the other official languages (see, to that effect, *R v Customs and Excise Comrs ex p EMU Tabac SARL* (1998) ECJ Transcript, 4 April (para 36)). The German word at issue, *Vorverfahren*, should therefore be compared, not only with the terms *instruction preliminaire*, *azione investigativa preliminare*, *investigacion preliminar* and *investigagco preliminar* in French, Italian, Spanish and Portuguese, but also with 'preliminary investigation proceedings' in the English version, *opsporingsonderzoeken* in Dutch and *indledende undersøgelser* in Danish. As the Advocate-General pointed out in paragraph 25 of his opinion ... comparison of the various language versions shows that the 'preliminary investigation proceedings' referred to by the Directive must be linked to the activities which precede contentious or quasi-contentious proceedings and

which arise from the need to obtain proof or to investigate a matter before the procedural phase properly so-called has even begun. However, 'preliminary investigation proceedings' does not cover all acts of the administration which are open to challenge in the courts.

30 In the light of those considerations the reply to the second question is that the term 'preliminary investigation proceedings' in the third indent of Art 3(2) of the Directive must be interpreted as including an administrative procedure such as that referred to in para 7(1)(2) of the UIG, which merely prepares the way for an administrative measure, only if it immediately precedes a contentious or quasi-contentious procedure and arises from the need to obtain proof or to investigate a matter prior to the opening of the actual procedure.

ENVIRONMENTAL INFORMATION REGULATIONS 1992 SI 1992/3240

[as amended by SI 1998/1447]

Regulation 1 Citation, commencement and extent

(1) These regulations may be cited as the Environmental Information Regulations 1992.

(2) These regulations shall come into force on 31 December 1992.

(3) These regulations shall extend to Great Britain only.

Regulation 2 Construction of regulations

(1) These regulations apply to any information which–

   (a) relates to the environment;

   (b) is held by a relevant person in an accessible form and otherwise than for the purposes of any judicial or legislative functions; and

   (c) is not (apart from these regulations) either–

      (i) information which is required, in accordance with any statutory provision, to be provided on request to every person who makes a request; or

      (ii) information contained in records which are required, in accordance with any statutory provision, to be made available for inspection by every person who wishes to inspect them.

(2) For the purposes of these regulations information relates to the environment if, and only if, it relates to any of the following, that is to say–

   (a) the state of any water or air, the state of any flora or fauna, the state of any soil or the state of any natural site or other land;

   (b) any activities or measures (including activities giving rise to noise or any other nuisance) which adversely affect anything mentioned in sub-para (a) above or are likely adversely to affect anything so mentioned;

   (c) any activities or administrative or other measures (including any environmental management programmes) which are designed to protect anything so mentioned.

(3) For the purposes of these regulations the following are relevant persons, that is to say–

   (a) all such Ministers of the Crown, government departments, local authorities and other persons carrying out functions of public administration at a national, regional or local level as, for the purposes of or in connection with their functions, have responsibilities in relation to the environment; and

(b) any body with public responsibilities for the environment which does not fall within sub-para (a) above but is under the control of a person falling within that sub-paragraph.

(4) In these regulations–

'information' includes anything contained in any records;

'records' includes registers, reports and returns, as well as computer records and other records kept otherwise than in a document; and

'statutory provision' means any provision made by or under any enactment.

Regulation 3 Obligation to make environmental information available

(1) Subject to the following provisions of these regulations, a relevant person who holds any information to which these regulations apply shall make that information available to every person who requests it.

(2) It shall be the duty of every relevant person who holds information to which these regulations apply to make such arrangements for giving effect to para (1) above as secure–

(a) that every request made for the purposes of that paragraph is responded to as soon as possible;

(b) that no such request is responded to more than two months after it is made; and

(c) that, where the response to such a request contains a refusal to make information available, the refusal is in writing and specifies the reasons for the refusal.

(3) Arrangements made by a relevant person for giving effect to para (1) above may include provision entitling that person to refuse a request for information in cases where a request is manifestly unreasonable or is formulated in too general a manner.

(4) The arrangements made by a relevant person for giving effect to para (1) above may–

(a) include provision for the imposition of a charge on any person in respect of the costs reasonably attributable to the supply of information to that person in pursuance of that paragraph; and

(b) make the supply of any information in pursuance of that paragraph conditional on the payment of such a charge.

(5) The obligation of a relevant person to make information available in pursuance of para (1) above shall not require him to make it available except in such form, and at such times and places, as may be reasonable.

(6) Without prejudice to any remedies available apart from by virtue of this paragraph in respect of any failure by a relevant person to comply with the requirements of these regulations, the obligation of such a person to make information available in pursuance of para (1) above shall be a duty owed to the person who has requested the information.

(7) Subject to Regulation 4 below, where any statutory provision or rule of law imposes any restriction or prohibition on the disclosure of information by any person, that restriction or prohibition shall not apply to any disclosure of information in pursuance of these regulations.

Regulation 4 Exceptions to right to information

(1) Nothing in these regulations shall–

    (a) require the disclosure of any information which is capable of being treated as confidential; or

    (b) authorise or require the disclosure of any information which must be so treated.

(2) For the purposes of these regulations, information is to be capable of being treated as confidential if, and only if, it is information the disclosure of which–

    (a) would affect international relations, national defence or public security;

    (b) would affect matters which are, or have been, an issue in any legal proceedings or in any enquiry (including any disciplinary enquiry), or are the subject-matter of any investigation undertaken with a view to any such proceedings or enquiry;

    (c) would affect the confidentiality of the deliberations of any relevant person;

    (d) would involve the supply of a document or other record which is still in the course of completion, or of any internal communication of a relevant person;

    (e) would affect the confidentiality of matters to which any commercial or industrial confidentiality attaches, including intellectual property.

(3) For the purposes of these regulations information must be treated as confidential if, and only if, in the case of any request made to a relevant person under Regulation 3 above–

    (a) it is capable of being so treated and its disclosure in response to that request would (apart from Regulation 3(7) above) contravene any statutory provision or rule of law or would involve a breach of any agreement;

    (b) the information is personal information contained in records held in relation to an individual who has not given his consent to its disclosure;

    (c) the information is held by the relevant person in consequence of having been supplied by a person who–

        (i) was not under, and could not have been put under, any legal obligation to supply it to the relevant person;

        (ii) did not supply it in circumstances such that the relevant person is entitled apart from these regulations to disclose it; and

        (iii) has not consented to its disclosure; or

    (d) the disclosure of the information in response to that request would, in the circumstances, increase the likelihood of damage to the environment affecting anything to which the information relates.

(4) Nothing in this regulation shall authorise a refusal to make available any information contained in the same record as, or otherwise held with, other information which is withheld by virtue of this regulation unless it is incapable of being separated from the other information for the purpose of making it available.

Notes:

1   The current version of reg 4(2) was inserted by the Environmental Information (Amendment) Regulations 1998. The previous rule was incompatible with the Directive and said that information is capable of being treated as confidential if it merely 'related' to particular matters. The new rule requires such information to 'affect' the matters listed.

2   Section 4(5) was deleted by the Environmental Information (Amendment) Regulations 1998.

Regulation 5 Existing rights to information

Where any information which is not information to which these regulations apply is required under any statutory provision to be made available to any person, the arrangements made by any relevant person for giving effect to the requirements of that provision shall be such as to secure–

(a) that every request for information relating to the environment which is made for the purposes of that provision is responded to as soon as possible;

(b) that no such request is responded to more than two months after it is made;

(c) that, where the response to such a request contains a refusal to make information available, the refusal is in writing and specifies the reasons for the refusal; and

(d) that no charge that exceeds a reasonable amount is made for making information relating to the environment available in accordance with that provision.

R v British Coal Corporation ex p Ibstock Building Products Limited [1995] JPL 836

Harrison J: This is an application for judicial review of what was described in Form 86A as the continuing refusal of the respondent, the British Coal Corporation, to disclose information in its possession relating to the alleged dumping of naval munitions in 1947 down mine shafts beneath the applicant's land, known as Ibstock Brick Works. The real information that was required by the applicant was the identity of the person who had informed British Coal that the dumping had occurred. On 21 June 1993 leave was granted by Macpherson J to enable the applicant to apply for an Order of Mandamus requiring British Coal to supply that information to the applicant. On 7 July 1993 British Coal disclosed the identity of the informant to the applicant. The applicant has thereby obtained the information which it needed. As a result, the sole issue before the court is who should pay for the costs of this action?

The applicant company says that it should be entitled to its costs because British Coal had previously refused to supply the name of the informant and that they only did so after leave to move for judicial review had been obtained. The respondent contends that the action should not have been brought. They seek an order that the costs of the action should be paid by the applicant. They base that contention on The Environmental Information Regulations 1992. Whilst they do not accept that the regulations apply to British Coal, they do not pursue that contention, simply to assist in shortening the length of this hearing. They do, however, contend that they are not obliged under the regulations to disclose the information sought for four reasons, to which I will return.

[Harrison J then summarised both submissions and continued:]

I turn, first, to the submissions that have been made relating to the applicability of the Environmental Information Regulations 1992. I am told that this is the first time that the question of interpretation of the regulations has been considered by the courts, albeit that it is in the context of an application relating to costs.

The first issue is whether the identity of the informant is information relating to the environment within the meaning of reg 2.

Regulation 2(1)(a) provides:

These regulations apply to any information which–

(a) relates to the environment.

Regulation 2(2) provides:

For the purposes of these regulations information relates to the environment if, and only if, it relates to any of the following, that is to say–

(a) the state of any land;

(b) any activities which adversely affect anything mentioned in sub-para (a) above or are likely adversely to affect anything so mentioned.

Regulation 2(4), states that:

'Information' includes anything contained in any records.

It is accepted by both parties that the presence of munitions in the mineshafts is information relating to the state of the land within reg 2(2). The point in dispute is whether the name of the informant is information relating to the state of the land. Mr Hobson submits that the source of the information is part of the information because it is required so that an assessment can be made of the credibility and weight to be accorded to that information. He stressed the word 'any' information in reg 2(1). He said that a broad interpretation should be given to the words in reg 2 in order to give effect to the purpose of EEC Council Directive 90/313. He also referred to Art 2 of that Directive, which defines information relating to the environment as meaning:

Any information in written ... form on the state of ... land.

Mr Corner, on behalf of the respondent, contended for a narrow interpretation of the regulation. He stressed that the provisions of reg 2(2) are exclusive, rather than inclusive. He submitted that the regulation applies to information which itself relates to the state of the land, not to matters which may lead to such information. He said that the name of the informant did not relate to the state of the land.

Whilst I acknowledge that this is an arguable point, I prefer the broader interpretation of reg 2. The source of the information relating to the dumping of the munitions can be said to 'relate to' the state of the land because it directly affects the quality of that information. It is necessary to know the source of the information in order to assess the credibility of the information and to assess how much weight can be attached to it. The purpose of the legislation, it seems to me, is to provide for freedom of access to information on the environment. It would be strange if the legislature had intended that only the bare information itself should be disclosed, without it being possible to ascertain whether it was right, wrong or indifferent. Any questions of confidentiality that may arise from such an interpretation of the regulation are safeguarded by reg 4. I therefore conclude that the source of the information which relates to the state of the land is capable of being information which 'relates to' the state of the land.

The second issue is whether the name of the informant is exempted from disclosure under reg 4(2)(a). Regulation 4(1) provides:

Nothing in these regulations shall–

(a) require the disclosure of any information which is capable of being treated as confidential; or

(b) authorise or require the disclosure of any information which must be so treated.

Regulation 4(2) provides:

> For the purposes of these regulations information is to be capable of being treated as confidential if, and only if, it is–
>
> (a) information relating to matters affecting international relations, national defence or public security.

Mr Corner submitted that the information relating to the dumping of naval ordnance secretly by night down the mineshafts, involving as it does, ammunition for the Navy, is information relating to matters affecting national defence or public security within the meaning of reg 4(2)(a). Mr Hobson stressed that, for the information to come within that provision, the information has to relate to a matter which actually affects national defence or public security, not which is merely capable of affecting it.

It is noteworthy that Mr Corner's submission is based on the information relating to the dumping of the munitions, rather than to the identity of the informant. However, dealing with it on that basis, there is no evidence in this case that the dumping of the munitions in the mineshafts in about 1947 is a matter which affects national defence or public security now in 1994. Indeed, such evidence as there is, is to the contrary, in that when the Ministry of Defence were consulted on this matter in April 1993, they did not take any point on national defence or public security. I therefore conclude that the information in this case is not exempted by reg 4(2)(a).

The third issue is whether the name of the informant is exempted from disclosure under reg 4(2)(b), which provides as follows:

> For the purposes of these regulations information is to be capable of being treated as confidential if, and only if, it is–
>
> (b) information relating to, or to anything which is or has been the subject matter of, any legal or other proceedings (whether actual or prospective).

Regulation 4(5) defines 'legal or other proceedings' as including:

> The proceedings at any local or other public inquiry.

Mr Hobson submits that reg 4(2)(b) should be interpreted as applying only to legal proceedings in respect of the matter to which the information relates, that is to say, legal proceedings relating to the dumping of munitions in the mineshafts. He referred to Art 3(2) of the Directive in support of that contention. To hold otherwise, he said, would be to nullify the effect of the Directive and of the regulations wherever there was a planning application which might lead to an appeal. Alternatively, he said, if the regulation does apply to a planning appeal, it is not applicable when only a planning application was being considered.

Mr Corner submitted that the plain words of reg 4(5) include a public inquiry within the definition of 'legal proceedings' and that there is a prospective public inquiry where a planning application is submitted, because there does not have to be any certainty that there would be an appeal.

I must confess to having some difficulty with this point because, on the face of it, reg 4(5) does appear to include a public inquiry for a planning appeal, whereas one of the plain purposes of the planning inquiry is to determine the effect of a development on the environment. It is therefore a situation where one would think that the regulations would be intended to bite. Be that as it may, I do not have to decide that point because the circumstances of this case relate only to a planning application. Regulation 4(2)(b) applies to 'prospective' legal proceedings, but in my view the mere existence of a planning application does not mean that there is a prospective appeal. The application may be granted or it may be refused without an appeal. In this case the application still remained to be determined. In those circumstances, I do not consider that it can be said that there were 'prospective' legal proceedings within the meaning of reg 4(2)(b).

The fourth issue is whether the name of the informant is exempted from disclosure by reg 4(3)(b) which reads as follows:

For the purposes of these regulations information must be treated as confidential if, and only if, in the case of any request made to a relevant person under reg 3 above–

    (b) the information is personal information contained in records held in relation to an individual who has not given his consent to its disclosure.

Mr Corner submitted that the identity of Dr Farley comes within the terms of that regulation and that Dr Farley did not give his consent to the disclosure of his identity until 2 July 1993, namely, after the date of the commencement of these proceedings. Mr Hobson submitted that the letter written by Dr Farley is not information that can be said to be contained in records held in relation to an individual within the meaning of the regulation.

I have no doubt that reg 4(3)(b) is not applicable to the circumstances of this case. The regulation applies to personal information contained in records held in relation to an individual. The name of Dr Farley as the writer of a letter, held by the respondent, dealing with the dumping of munitions is not, in my view, personal information contained in records held by them relating to Dr Farley.

For all those reasons, I therefore conclude that the respondent was obliged to give the identity of their informant. Even if that had not been, so far as I am aware, no reason was given by the respondent for not disclosing the name of their informant at the relevant time. No doubt the lack of justification put forward by the respondent would have contributed to the applicant's decision to commence proceedings. As a responsible corporation, one would have expected British Coal to have given the information in the potentially serious circumstances of this case, unless they put forward some reason for not doing so, even if the reason was that they were not obliged to do so. Their refusal to give the information without giving any reason led the applicant to commence judicial review proceedings. In my view, they were justified in doing so in those circumstances and that is confirmed by the fact that leave to move was granted. It was not until leave was granted that British Coal gave the information that had been requested. Even if I were wrong on the issues arising under the regulations, those are matters which would entitle the court to exercise its discretion so as to award costs against the respondent. My decision, therefore, is that the applicants should have their costs.

R v Secretary of State for the Environment, Transport and Regions and Another ex p Alliance Against the Birmingham Northern Relief Road and Others [1999] JPL 231; [1999] Env LR 447

This decision concerned the controversial decision to construct the first private toll motorway in this country. The motorway is intended to be some 44 kilometres long and to go around the northern and eastern side of the West Midlands conurbation. The intention is that it would be designed, built, financed and operated by Midland Expressway Limited ('MEL') under the terms of a concession agreement which was entered into in 1992 by the Secretary of State with MEL. The decision to proceed with the motorway was made following a lengthy public enquiry which sat for over 200 days between 21 June 1994 and 4 October 1995. In this case the applicants, an alliance formed from some 20 groups, including Parish Councils and Residents Associations, who are opposed to the BNRR, and residents who live between 300 m–12 km. from the route of the proposed motorway challenged the department's refusal to disclose the Concession Agreement by way of judicial review. A parallel challenge was made to the decision to proceed with the motorway: see *Alliance Against the Birmingham Northern Relief Road and others v Secretary of State for the Environment, Transport and the Regions and Another*, 23 March 1999 (CA).

Sullivan J having set out the background and the relevant law continued:

There was broad agreement between the parties as to the questions which have to be answered. I find it helpful to group the parties submissions, and my answers to the list of issues, under the following headings.

(1) What is the basis upon which questions arising under the regulations should be determined by the Court?

Mr Howell QC for the Applicants submits that where issues arise as to whether information relates to the environment, and if it does whether any of the exceptions set out in reg 4 are applicable, those questions fall to be determined by the court, upon the basis of the facts as found by the Court itself. The Court is not limited to reviewing the Secretary of State's view of the facts to see if that view is Wednesbury perverse ...

He points to the language of the regulations which is couched in objective terms. The regulations apply to any information which relates to the environment, not to information which in the opinion of the relevant person relates to the environment. The exception relates to information which is capable of being treated as confidential, not information which is confidential in the opinion of the relevant person.

In *R v British Coal Corporation ex p Ibstock Building Products Ltd* [1995] JPL 836, Harrison J having set out the factual material before him reached his own conclusions as to whether the information sought from the respondents related to the environment, and whether it was exempt from disclosure under reg 4(2)(a). Question (1) (above) does not appear to have been raised before Harrison J.

Regulation 3(6) imposes a duty upon the relevant person which shall be a duty owed to the person who has requested the information. Thus, it is submitted that the individual making the request may commence ordinary civil proceedings if his request is refused in breach of that duty. In such proceedings the Court would have to reach its own view upon the evidence ...

Recital 13 to the Directive requires that there should be an appeal against the public authority's decision. That means an effective appeal, on both fact and law, and the reference to seeking a judicial or administrative review of the decision in Art 4 of the Directive must be read in that context. Confining any challenge to a review of the relevant body's decision on *Wednesbury* grounds would make it virtually impossible or excessively difficult for the individual seeking environmental information to challenge a refusal, because the Court could not review the merits of the refusal in the light of the evidence. This, submits Mr Howell, would be in breach of Community Law ...

Mr Howell accepts that the regulations do confer an element of discretion upon the relevant person (in this case the Secretary of State) if the information which is requested falls within reg 4(1)(a). Whether it falls within that regulation is for the Court to decide, but if it does, then the Secretary of State has a discretion as to whether to disclose. In exercising that discretion he would, no doubt, bear in mind the guidance given by his department in 1992.

Mr Sales, on behalf of the Secretary of State, accepts that whether the Agreement contains information which relates to the environment, and whether it may, or must be treated as confidential are to be determined, on an objective basis, by the Court. Mr Pleming QC on behalf of MEL did not go so far. He submitted that an individual whose request for information was refused was limited to a challenge by way of judicial review, and in such a challenge the Court should not engage, as in an ordinary writ action, in the ascertainment of the primary facts. He submitted that since para (a) of reg 4(1) conferred a discretion upon the Secretary of State, which was reviewable only on Wednesbury grounds, it was unlikely that a refusal to disclose information under para (b) could be challenged on any wider basis.

I accept Mr Howells submissions in answer to question (1). The language used in the regulations is clear: whether information relates to the environment, is capable of being treated as confidential, and if so, whether it falls within any of the categories in reg 4(3) are all factual questions, to be determined in an objective manner. It would have been possible to incorporate a subjective element into the regulations [...]

There is a clear distinction between resolving the primary issues of fact, whether the information sought does relate to the environment, and whether it is capable of being treated as confidential, and deciding, if the information falls within para (a) of reg 4(1), whether it should be disclosed. The latter is a discretionary decision, reviewable only on Wednesbury grounds.

Whilst it is unusual for the court to have to resolve disputed factual issues in applications for judicial review, questions of precedent fact can arise: see the discussion on page 252 of De Smith Woolf and Jowells *Judicial Review of Administrative Action*, 5th ed, and in an immigration context the decision of the House of Lords in *R v Secretary of State for the Home Department ex p Khawaja* [1984] 1 AC 74; [1983] 1 All ER 765, *per* Lord Fraser, p 97D of the former report. In my view this is a precedent fact case, for the reasons advanced by Mr Howell.

(2) Should the Secretary of State's decision be quashed in any event because the reasons given were inaccurate and/or inadequate?

Regulation 3(2)(c) provides that a refusal to make information available must be in writing and must specify the reasons for the refusal. Mr Howell submits that Mrs Dixon's letter dated 23 September, 1997 (above) does not comply with reg 3 because it is:

(a) inaccurate, in that it relies on reg 4(1)(a), but we know from her affidavit that this was an error, and that the Secretary of State now contends that reg 4(1)(b) applies; and

(b) inadequate, in that it is not sufficient merely to identify a regulation upon which the refusal is based without any explanation as to why the information falls within that regulation.

[...]

If information is refused on grounds of confidentiality it may be difficult to amplify the reasoning without breaching the confidentiality.

[...]

... the issue is not whether the Secretary of State is satisfied that the agreement contains information relating to the environment, and whether that information may, or must be treated as confidential, but whether those conditions are, in fact, established. The Secretary of State's reasoning, whilst it may well be persuasive, is not decisive. Moreover, I agree with the respondents' submission that if information does, in fact, fall within reg 4(3) the Secretary of State has no power to disclose it, and cannot confer power upon himself by an erroneous reference to reg 4(1)(a), instead of reg 4(1)(b) in his refusal letter. For these reasons I consider that the evidence in Mrs Dixon's affidavit as to the grounds of refusal is admissible.

That said, I accept Mr Howell's submission that the reason given in Mrs Dixon's letter dated 23 September 1997, if accurate, would have been inadequate. The purpose of Art 3.4 of the Directive, as reflected in reg 3(2)(c) of the regulations, is to enable an individual who is refused information to ascertain whether the refusal is well founded in fact and law, or whether it is susceptible to challenge. That purpose is not fulfilled by the bare assertion that the Agreement is confidential under a particular regulation. It should be possible to provide some, albeit brief explanation as to why the information sought is confidential, without breaching that confidentiality.

[...]

(3) Does the Agreement fall within the description of any information which relates to the environment?

[...] The fact that the Agreement can be described as a commercial document does not mean that it does not contain information which relates to the environment. It simply means that if such information is contained in the Agreement it may fall within one of the exceptions in reg 4 ...

[...]

The definition of information relating to the environment in Art 2 of the Directive is very broad, in my view deliberately so, and this broad definition has been carried through into the regulations. It would have been possible to define more narrowly the obligation to disclose environmental information, but that was not the intention of either the Council of the European Communities, or Parliament. In the *British Coal Corporation* case [1995] JPL 836 Harrison J adopted a broad interpretation of the scope of reg 2. I respectfully agree with his approach. The fact that, upon such an approach, reg 2 may cover a large range of documentation, is not a valid argument for a narrow interpretation. The obligation to disclose information relating to the environment is subject to the exceptions contained in reg 4, and reg 3(3) gives the relevant body power to refuse requests which are manifestly unreasonable or formulated in too general a manner.

(4) Is the Agreement capable of being treated as confidential under reg 4(2)(e), and if so must it be treated as confidential under reg 4(3)(a)?

Mr Howell submitted that the Secretary of State had not established that the Agreement, or any part of it fell within reg 4(2)(e), thus it could not fall within reg 4(3)(a). Underlying his approach was the proposition that commercial or industrial confidentiality in reg 4(2)(e) means specific information which a business needs to keep confidential in order to protect its competitive position, technological know-how, or production methods. There has to be clear evidence of the need for protection, and there is none here.

The respondents contended that the Agreement as a whole fell within reg 4(2)(e) by virtue of its very nature as a commercial document which contained a bundle of rights and obligations, which would have financial implications for the parties, and which the parties had agreed should be treated as confidential. It was unnecessary for there to be evidence of specific harm, as required by Mr Howell; it was enough that the Agreement embodied the terms on which MEL was prepared to construct the BNRR. MEL was entitled to keep those terms confidential in order to protect its position against rivals in the field of private finance initiatives.

It would have been possible to decide between these two all-or-nothing approaches without looking at the Agreement itself, but having heard Mr Howell's opening submission and the respondents' arguments, I provisionally concluded that there might be a middle path: some parts of the Agreement might fall within reg 4(2)(e), whilst others might not.

[In the event, Sullivan J inspected the agreement and ordered that parts of it be disclosed.]

Eco-labelling

Council Regulation 880/92 established a Community eco-label award scheme to enable consumers to make environmentally-informed choices when making purchases. To obtain the eco-label, manufacturers or importers into the Community must apply to the competent body[30] designated by the Member State in which the product is manufactured, first placed on the market, or imported. This body would decide whether to award the label to the product after assessing its environmental performance with reference to the general principles set out in the regulation (Art 4) and criteria established for product groups (Art 5). The Regulation did not apply to food, drink or pharmaceuticals.

The Commission has acknowledged that the procedure for the award of the eco-label was complex and 'did not constitute a good framework for the long term development of the system'. Regulation 880/92 has now been replaced by Regulation 1980/00. The regulation has established an EC Eco-Labelling Board (EUEB) which is required to draft criteria for the award of the eco-label to particular product groups. The scheme has been extended to include service providers, traders and retailers, as well as manufacturers and importers. It does not apply to food, drink, pharmaceuticals or medical devices.

---

30 In the UK this body was the United Kingdom Eco-Labelling Board for the UK. See Nelson, E, 'Eco-labelling' [1993] Env Liability 16–19. This body was abolished by the UK Eco-labelling Board (Abolition) Regulations 1999 SI 1999/931. Its functions have been taken over by the Secretary of State (reg 4). The UK government no longer regards eco-labelling as the main plank in its approach to limiting the environmental impact of consumer products.

COUNCIL REGULATION

of 17 July 2000

on a revised Community eco-label award scheme

(EC/1980/00)

THE EUROPEAN PARLIAMENT AND THE COUNCIL OF THE EUROPEAN UNION,

Having regard to the Treaty establishing the European Community and in particular Art 175(1) thereof,

Having regard to the proposal from the Commission,

Having regard to the opinion of the Economic and Social Committee,

After consulting the Committee of the Regions,

Acting in accordance with the procedure laid down in Art 251 of the Treaty,

Whereas:

(1) The aims of Council Regulation (EEC) No 880/92 of 23 March 1992 on a Community eco-label award scheme were to establish a voluntary Community eco-label scheme intended to promote products with a reduced environmental impact during their entire life-cycle and to provide consumers with accurate, non-deceptive and scientifically based information on the environmental impact of products.

(2) Art 18 of Regulation (EEC) No 880/92 provides that within five years from its entry into force the Commission should review the scheme in the light of the experience gained during its operation and should propose any appropriate amendments to the regulation.

(3) The experience gained during the implementation of the regulation has shown the need to amend the scheme in order to increase its effectiveness, improve its planning and streamline its operation.

(4) The basic aims for a voluntary and selective Community eco-label award scheme are still valid; in particular such an award scheme should provide guidance to consumers on products with a potential for reducing environmental impact when viewed through its entire life-cycle, and should provide information on the environmental characteristics of labelled products.

(5) For the acceptance by the general public of the Community eco-label award system it is essential that environmental NGOs and consumer organisations play an important role and are actively involved in the development and setting of criteria for Community eco-labels.

(6) It is necessary to explain to consumers that the eco-label represents those products which have the potential to reduce certain negative environmental impacts, as compared with other products in the same product group, without prejudice to regulatory requirements applicable to products at a Community or a national level.

(7) The scope of the Scheme should include products and environmental factors which are of interest from the point of view both of the internal market and of the environment; for the purpose of this regulation, products should also include services.

(8) The procedural and methodological approach for setting eco-label criteria should be updated in the light of scientific and technical progress and of the experience gained in this area, to ensure consistency with relevant internationally recognised standards which are evolving in this area.

(9) The principles for establishing the selectivity level of the eco-label should be clarified, in order to facilitate consistent and effective implementation of the Scheme.

(10) The eco-label should include simple, accurate, non-deceptive and scientifically based information on the key environmental aspects which are considered in the award of the label, in order to enable consumers to make informed choices.

(11) In the various stages of the award of an eco-label, efforts must be made to ensure the efficient use of resources and a high level of environmental protection.

(12) It is necessary to provide more information on the label about the reasons for the award in order to assist consumers in understanding the significance of the award.

(13) The eco-label scheme should in the long term be mainly self-financing. Financial contributions from the Member States should not increase.

(14) It is necessary to assign the task of contributing to setting and reviewing eco-label criteria as well as assessment and verification requirements to an appropriate body, the European Union Eco-Labelling Board (EUEB), in order to achieve an efficient and neutral implementation of the scheme; the EUEB should be composed of the competent bodies already designated by the Member States under Art 9 of Regulation (EEC) No 880/92, and of a consultation forum which should provide for a balanced participation of all relevant interested parties.

(15) It is necessary to ensure that the Community eco-label award scheme is consistent and co-ordinated with the priorities of the Community environmental policy and with other Community labelling or quality-certification schemes such as those established by Council Directive 92/75/EEC of 22 September 1992 on the indication by labelling and standard product information of the consumption of energy and other resources by household appliances and by Council Regulation (EEC) No 2092/91 of 24 June 1991 on organic production of agricultural products and indications referring thereto on agricultural products and foodstuffs.

(16) While existing, as well as new eco-label schemes in the Member States may continue to exist, provision should be made to ensure co-ordination between the Community eco-label and other eco-label schemes in the Community, in order to promote the common objectives of sustainable consumption.

(17) It is necessary to guarantee transparency in the implementation of the scheme and to ensure consistency with relevant international standards in order to facilitate access to, and participation in, the Scheme by manufacturers and exporters of countries outside the Community.

(18) The measures necessary for the implementation of this regulation should be adopted in accordance with Council Decision 1999/468/EC of 28 June 1999 laying down the procedures for the exercise of implementing powers conferred to the Commission.

(19) Regulation (EEC) No 880/92 should be replaced by this regulation in order to introduce in the most effective way the necessary revised provisions for the reasons

mentioned above, while appropriate transitional provisions ensure continuity and smooth transition between the two regulations,

HAVE ADOPTED THIS REGULATION:

Article 1 Objectives and principles

1   The objective of the Community eco-label award scheme (hereafter referred to as the Scheme) is to promote products which have the potential to reduce negative environmental impacts, as compared with the other products in the same product group, thus contributing to the efficient use of resources and a high level of environmental protection. This objective shall be pursued through the provision of guidance and accurate, non-deceptive and scientifically based information to consumers on such products.

For the purpose of this Regulation:

–   the term 'product' is taken to include any goods or services,

–   the term 'consumer' is taken to include professional purchasers.

2   The environmental impacts shall be identified on the basis of examination of the interactions of products with the environment, including the use of energy and natural resources, during the life cycle of the product.

3   Participation in the Scheme shall be without prejudice to environmental or other regulatory requirements of Community or national law applicable to the various life stages of goods, and where appropriate to a service.

4   The implementation of the Scheme shall comply with the provisions of the Treaties, including the precautionary principle, with the instruments adopted pursuant thereto and the Community environmental policy, as specified in the Community Programme of Policy and Action in relation to the Environment and Sustainable Development Fifth Action Programme established by the Resolution of 1 February 1993, and shall be co-ordinated with other labelling or quality certification arrangements as well as schemes such as, in particular, the Community Energy Labelling Scheme established by Directive 92/75/EEC and the Organic Agriculture Scheme established by Regulation (EEC) No 2092/91.

ACCESS TO JUSTICE IN ENVIRONMENTAL MATTERS

Throughout the book we have seen examples of the way courts are being used to adjudicate upon environmental issues. It is widely predicted that the volume of environmental litigation will continue to grow, particularly in the light of developments in environmental impact assessment (see pp 777–81, above) and the greater access to environmental information (see p 799, above).[31] The European Commission in its report, *Implementing Community Environmental Law*[32] has recognised that it is an important characteristic of environmental law that private interests frequently do not exist to drive its enforcement. The environment is often characterised as being our 'common heritage':

---

31   Grosz, S, 'Access to environmental justice in public law', in Robinson, D and Dunkley, J (eds) *Public Interest Perspectives in Environmental Law*, 1995.

32   COM (96) 500 Final.

Therefore, it is often the case that deterioration of the environment does not cause immediate reaction, and even if a problem does arise, there is no means by which individuals can use the law to remedy the problem, or there are no appropriate legal remedies available. Even for Community environmental law, it can be the case that important general principles cannot be enforced by individuals (for example, polluter pays, preventive and precautionary principles).[33]

The importance of access to justice in environmental law has now been reinforced by the Aarhus Convention discussed above and by the European Commission in its recent White Paper on *Environmental Liability* (see the discussion in Chapter 1, and in particular the proposed two-tier approach to litigation).

Partly because private interests are so frequently absent environmental litigation often involves the use of public law procedures, such as judicial review to challenge decisions of the various public authorities which have responsibilities for environmental matters. Much of this litigation has been spearheaded by groups such as WWF, Friends of the Earth and Greenpeace which have seen litigation as being a useful vehicle for their own campaigning strategies. In recent years, in the UK, their involvement has been encouraged by the liberalisation of rules on standing evident in decisions such as the *Greenpeace* and *World Development Movement* cases (see below).

Despite the liberalisation of standing, access to justice remains a problem for many potential litigants. Litigation, for instance, is often prohibitively costly, even for relatively well-funded organisations. One reason is that civil legal aid is now only available to help the poorest. In an attempt to provide support for litigation which affects public interests, under the Access to Justice Act (which came into force on 1 April 2000), the Legal Services Commission has the power to fund a claim on the ground that it raises public interest, although a means test applies (*The Funding Code: A New Approach to Funding Civil Cases*, report to the Lord Chancellor following consultation: Legal Aid Board). The notorious reg 32 of the Civil Legal Aid (General) Regulations 1989, enabled the legal aid authorities to refuse funding to individuals because others, who would benefit from the litigation, could afford to pay or contribute towards the costs. The effect of this was illustrated by Grosz using the experience of two of the Oxleas 9.[34] The Oxleas 9 were part of a campaign against the proposal to construct part of the East London River Crossing (this was a major road construction project) through Oxleas Wood in Greenwich, South London. The wood was described as ancient woodland and was in 1984 designated as a Site of Special Scientific Interest under s 28 of the Wildlife and Countryside Act 1981 (see Chapter 6, pp 666 and 685). In litigation seeking to challenge decisions relating to the road, legal aid was refused to two of the nine who were themselves eligible for funding because others were considered able to pay.

Regulation 32 no longer exists. Section 5.4.2 of the Funding Code now covers situations where alternative funding might exist for litigation, for example, where the litigant may obtain funding from insurance or where there are other persons or bodies, including those who might be expected to benefit from the proceedings, who can reasonably be expected to bring or fund the case. Because the Funding Code recognises

---

33 Paragraph 38.
34 *Mayor and Burgesses of the London Borough of Greenwich and Yates v Secretaries of State for Transport and the Environment* (1993) unreported, 19 February; *op cit*, Grosz, fn 31, p 205.

that public interest litigation – litigation that benefits a wider group of persons than the applicant – may be funded where the applicant satisfies a means test, the implication is that legal aid should not be refused in public interest cases solely because alternative means of funding appear to exist. Indeed, the Legal Services Commission has indicated that they would not require a contribution from an interest group or refuse legal aid because such a contribution could be made (see *A New Approach to Funding Civil Cases*, above). On paper, therefore, if the Legal Services Commission is prepared to use its powers to support public interest cases, the situation in the Oxleas 9 case should not arise.

One further point should be noted in this context. Whenever parties are not supported by legal aid they may be ordered to pay the other side's costs if they lose. As Grosz observes: '... [t]he combination of one's own legal costs and the risk of having to foot the opposition's bill can act as a serious deterrent to bringing proceedings at all.'[35] The Law Commission has now recognised that where public interests are involved the courts should be able to order costs to be paid from central funds (the public purse) rather than by individual parties. This would be a much needed reform.[36] The Bowman Committee (*Review of the Crown Office List*, March 2000, paras 73–76) recently added its weight to this proposal and called upon judges in public interest cases to carefully examine whether to make an order for costs.

Standing in EC law

C-321/95P *Stichting Greenpeace Council (Greenpeace International) & Others v European Commission* [1998] All ER (EC) 620

This case deals with the question whether private individuals and environmental associations have *locus standi* before the Court of First Instance and the European Court of Justice in Art 173 (now Art 230) proceedings. The case arose out of a decision by the Commission to grant financial assistance to Spain from the European Regional Development Fund for the construction of two power stations in the Canary Islands. A number of persons, 16 private individuals plus Greenpeace, sought to challenge the Commission's decision to pay an instalment of this assistance on various grounds, notably that the funded projects were being carried out contrary to Community law and that work on the projects had commenced without a proper environmental impact assessment, contrary to the EC Directive 85/337 on Environmental Impact Assessment. This action was brought before the Court of First Instance (CFI) under Art 173 by which Community acts can be annulled by the Court. Under the Article, privileged persons (Member states, the Council and the Commission) may challenge any binding act as of right; non-privileged applicants are entitled to challenge only if the Community act in question is addressed to him or her, or if the decision (in the form of a regulation or a decision) is addressed to someone else, and is of 'direct and individual concern'. The Commission lodged an objection based on admissibility claiming that the applicants lacked *locus standi*.

---

35 *Op cit*, Grosz, fn 31, p 206.
36 Law Commission, *Administrative Law: Judicial Review and Statutory Appeals*, Law Com No 226 (1994) para 10.6.

The Court of First Instance dealt with the standing of private individuals and associations separately. Focusing upon the fourth paragraph of Art 173 the Court applied previous case law *Plaumann v Commission* [1963] ECR 95, *Spijker v Commission* [1983] ECR 2559 in finding that the 16 individuals were not possessed of any attribute which would set them apart from all the people in the area and as such could not establish the 'direct and individual concern' required by the Article.

The Court dismissed the argument that the existing case law on *locus standi* was too restrictive when the case was brought to protect environment interests rather than economic interests. It maintained that the impact of harmful environmental effects attributable to the Commission's decision would be felt generally 'by a large number of persons who cannot be determined in advance which has distinguished them individually in the same way as the addressee of a decision'. In so doing, the Court of First Instance stressed that the 'direct and individual concern' requirement in Art 173 would deny standing to individuals who might satisfy the requirements of national law, where it might only be necessary to show 'sufficient' interest.

Turning to the *locus standi* of an association (including Greenpeace in this case) the Court of First Instance again applied previous case law (Case 282/85 *DEFI v Commission* [1986] ECR 2469 and Case 72/74 *Union Syndicale – Service Public European and Others v Council* [1975] ECR 401), under which associations which existed to protect the interests of a category of people who would not be regarded as 'directly and individually concerned' by a measure which affected the general interests of that category where the members of the association did not have standing as individuals in their own right. The Court had already established that the private individuals lacked standing and so the members of the associations also lacked standing.[37]

The opinion of the Advocate General in this case is instructive. Whilst expressing his support for the existing case law followed by the court he did express support for recognising *locus standi* in Art 173 proceedings for some private individuals:

> ... persons close to the construction works suffer its consequences in a different, more intense manner than persons farther away, the latter being at a greater radius from the epicentre of the intervention in the environment. By way of logical extension, it may be argued that persons near the epicentre comprise a particularly closed and deferred 'class' who find themselves in a situation which differentiates them from any other person. By logical extension, persons within that class should be regarded as having *locus standi* to bring an action against the decision occasioning consequences for the environment.

In his view the private individuals in this case had not met the above criteria. Nor did he feel that the express wording of Art 173 would permit the award of *locus standi* to an environmental association concerned about the impact on the environment of a contested measure.

The applicant appealed against the order of the Court of First Instance, maintaining that the application of existing case law on *locus standi* was inappropriate in cases involving environmental issues. The ECJ held that the CFI had not erred in law by

---

37 The court did refer to 'special circumstances' where the association had played a role in the procedure leading to the adoption of an Act within the meaning of Art 173. In such a case an associations standing could be recognised even though its members were not directly and individually concerned. Greenpeace involvement did not amount to special circumstances (see *Van der Kooj and Others v Commission* [1988] ECR 219).

denying the applicant's *locus standi* and interestingly made no reference to the suggestion made by the Advocate-General to relax the *locus standi* rules.

The following judgment of the ECJ confirms the narrow approach taken in regard to standing and in this regard may be contrasted with the far more liberal attitude of UK national courts, displayed in *ex p Greenpeace* (see below at p 895) and *ex p The World Development Movement* (see p 891, below). Compare also the 'victim' requirement under the European Convention on Human Rights incorporated into UK domestic law by the Human Rights Act 1998; see generally, p 852, below.

Judgment of the Court in Stichting Greenpeace

2 April 1998

[The Court set out the background and continued:]

7   As regards, first, the *locus standi* of the applicants who are private individuals, the Court of First Instance, in para 48, referred first to the settled case-law of the Court of Justice according to which persons other than the addressees may claim that a decision is of direct concern to them only if that decision affects them by reason of certain attributes which are peculiar to them, or by reason of factual circumstances which differentiate them from all other persons and thereby distinguish them individually in the same way as the person addressed (Case 25/62 *Plaumann v Commission* [1963] ECR 95; Case 231/82 *Spijker v Commission* [1983] ECR 2559; Case 97/85 *Deutsche Lebensmittelwerke and Others v Commission* [1987] ECR 2265; Case C-198/91 *Cook v Commission* [1993] ECR I-2487; Case C-225/91 *Matra v Commission* [1993] ECR I-3203; Case T-2/93 *Air France v Commission* [1994] ECR II-323 and Case T-465/93 *Consorzio Gruppo di Azione Locale 'Murgia Messapica' v Commission* [1994] ECR II-361).

8   The Court of First Instance then decided to examine, at para 49, the applicants' argument that the Court should not be constrained by the limits imposed by that case-law and should concentrate on the sole fact that third-party applicants had suffered or would potentially suffer loss or detriment from the harmful environmental effects arising out of unlawful conduct on the part of the Community institutions.

9   In that regard, the Court of First Instance held, at para 50, that whilst the settled case-law of the Court of Justice concerned essentially cases involving economic interests, the essential criterion which it applied (namely, a combination of circumstances sufficient for the third-party applicant to be able to claim to be affected by the contested decision in a manner which differentiated him from all other persons) remained applicable whatever the nature, economic or otherwise, of the applicants' interests which were affected.

10   The Court of First Instance accordingly held, at para 51, that the criterion proposed by the applicants for appraising their *locus standi*, namely the existence of harm suffered or to be suffered, was not in itself sufficient to confer *locus standi* on an applicant; this was because such harm might affect, in a general abstract way, a large number of persons who could not be determined in advance in such a way as to distinguish them individually just like the addressee of a decision, as required under the case-law cited above. The Court of First Instance added that, in view of the conditions laid down in the fourth paragraph of Art 173 of the Treaty, that conclusion could not be affected by the practice of national courts whereby *locus standi* might depend merely on applicants having a 'sufficient' interest.

11 The Court of First Instance therefore concluded, at para 52, that the applicants' argument that the question of their *locus standi* in this case should be determined in the light of criteria other than those already laid down in the case-law could not be accepted, and went on to hold, at para 53, that their *locus standi* had to be assessed in the light of the criteria laid down in that case-law.

12 In this regard, the Court of First Instance stated first of all, at paras 54 and 55, that the objective status of 'local resident', 'fisherman' or 'farmer' or of persons concerned by the impact which the building of two power stations might have on local tourism, on the health of Canary Island residents and on the environment, relied on by the applicants, did not differ from that of all the people living or pursuing an activity in the areas concerned and that the applicants thus could not be affected by the contested decision otherwise than in the same manner as any other local resident, fisherman, farmer or tourist who was, or might be in the future, in the same situation.

13 Finally, at para 56, the Court of First Instance held that the fact that certain of the applicants had submitted a complaint to the Commission could not confer *locus standi* under Art 173 of the Treaty, since no specific procedures were provided for whereby individuals might be associated with the adoption, implementation and monitoring of decisions taken in the field of financial assistance granted by the ERDF. The Court of Justice had held that, although a person who asked an institution not to take a decision in respect of him, but to open an inquiry with regard to third parties, might be considered to have an indirect interest, such a person was nevertheless not in the precise legal position of the actual or potential addressee of a measure which might be annulled under Art 173 of the Treaty (Case 246/81 *Lord Bethell v Commission* [1982] ECR 2277).

14 Second, as regards the *locus standi* of the applicant associations, the Court of First Instance recalled, at para 59, that it had consistently been held that an association formed for the protection of the collective interests of a category of persons could not be considered to be directly and individually concerned, for the purposes of the fourth paragraph of Art 173 of the Treaty, by a measure affecting the general interests of that category, and was therefore not entitled to bring an action for annulment where its members could not do so individually (Joined Cases 19/62 to 22/62 *Fédération Nationale de la Boucherie en Gros et du Commerce en Gros des Viandes and Others v Council* [1962] ECR 491; Case 72/74 *Union Syndicale – Service Public Européen and Others v Council* [1975] ECR 401; Case 60/79 *Féderation Nationale des Producteurs de Vins de Table et Vins de Pays v Commission* [1979] ECR 2429; Case 282/85 *DEFI v Commission* [1986] ECR 2469; Case 117/86 *UFADE v Council and Commission* [1986] ECR 3255, para 12; and Joined Cases T-447/93, T-448/93 and T-449/93 *AITEC and Others v Commission* [1995] ECR II-1971, paras 58 and 59). Since the Court of First Instance had held that the applicants who were private individuals could not be considered to be individually concerned by the contested decision, it therefore concluded, at para 60, that the members of the applicant associations, as local residents of Gran Canaria and Tenerife, likewise could not be considered to be individually concerned.

15 The Court of First Instance went on to observe, at para 59, that special circumstances, such as the role played by an association in a procedure which led to the adoption of an act within the meaning of Art 173 of the Treaty, might justify treating as admissible an action brought by an association whose members were not directly and individually concerned by the contested measure (Joined Cases 67/85, 68/85 and 70/85 *Van der Kooj*

and Others v Commission [1988] ECR 219 and Case C-313/90 *CIRFS and Others v Commission* [1993] ECR I-1125).

16 However, at para 62 of its judgment, the Court of First Instance came to the conclusion that the exchange of correspondence and the discussions which Greenpeace had with the Commission concerning the financing of the project for the construction of two power stations in the Canary Islands did not constitute special circumstances of that kind since the Commission did not, prior to the adoption of the contested decision, initiate any procedure in which Greenpeace participated. Nor was Greenpeace in any way the interlocutor of the Commission with regard to the adoption of the basic Decision C (91) 440 and/or of the contested decision.

17 In their appeal the appellants submit that, in determining whether they were individually concerned by the contested decision within the meaning of Art 173 of the Treaty, the Court of First Instance erred in its interpretation and application of that provision and that, by applying the case-law developed by the Court of Justice in relation to economic issues and economic rights, according to which an individual must belong to a 'closed class' in order to be individually concerned by a Community act, the Court of First Instance failed to take account of the nature and specific character of the environmental interests underpinning their action.

18 In particular, the appellants argue, first, that the approach adopted by the Court of First Instance creates a legal vacuum in ensuring compliance with Community environmental legislation, since in this area the interests are, by their very nature, common and shared, and the rights relating to those interests are liable to be held by a potentially large number of individuals so that there could never be a closed class of applicants satisfying the criteria adopted by the Court of First Instance.

19 Nor can that legal vacuum be filled by the possibility of bringing proceedings before the national courts. According to the appellants, such proceedings have in fact been brought in the present case, but they concern the Spanish authorities' failure to comply with their obligations under Council Directive 85/337/EEC, and not the legality of the Commission measure, that is to say the lawfulness under Community law of the Commission's disbursement of structural funds on the ground that that disbursement is in violation of an obligation for protecting the environment.

20 Second, the appellants submit that the Court of First Instance was wrong to take the view, at para 51 of the contested order, that reference to national laws on *locus standi* was irrelevant for the purposes of Art 173. The solution adopted by the Court of First Instance appears to conflict with that required by national judicial decisions and legislation as well as by developments in international law. According to the appellants, it is clear from the Final Report on Access to Justice (1992), prepared by the ÖKO-Institut for the Commission, which describes the position concerning *locus standi* on environmental issues, that, if they had been required to bring proceedings before a court of a Member State, actions brought by some or all of the applicants would have been declared admissible. The appellants add that the above mentioned developments have been influenced by American law, the Supreme Court holding in 1972 in *Sierra Club v Morton* 405 US 727 (1972), 31 Led 2d 636 (1972), p 643 that:

> Aesthetic and environmental well-being, like economic well-being, are important ingredients of the quality of life in our society, and the fact that particular environmental interests are shared by the many rather than the few does not make them less deserving of legal protection through the judicial process.

21 Third, the appellants submit that the approach adopted by the Court of First Instance in the contested order is at odds with both the case-law of the Court of Justice and declarations of the Community institutions and governments of the Member States on environmental matters. As regards case-law, they rely on the holding that environmental protection is 'one of the Community's essential objectives' (judgments in Case 240/83 *Procureur de la République v Association de Défense des Brûleurs d'Huiles Usagées* [1985] ECR 531, para 13, and Case 302/86 *Commission v Denmark* [1988] ECR 4607, para 8) and submit that Community environmental legislation can create rights and obligations for individuals (judgments in Case C-131/88 *Commission v Germany* [1991] ECR I-825, para 7, and Case C-361/88 *Commission v Germany* [1991] ECR I-2567, paras 15 and 16). Furthermore, in the present case, the appellants submit that their arguments relating to individual concern are based essentially on their individual rights conferred by Directive 85/337, Arts 6(2) and 8 which provide for participation in the environmental impact assessment procedure in relation to certain projects (judgment in Case C-431/92 *Commission v Germany* [1995] ECR I-2189, paras 37–40), and that they are singled out by virtue of those rights which are recognised and protected in Commission Decision C (91) 440.

22 The appellants go on to refer to the Fifth Environmental Action Programme ((1993) OJ C138, p 1), to Principle 10 of the Rio Declaration, ratified by the Community at the United Nations Conference of 1992 on Environment and Development, to Agenda 21, adopted at the same conference, to the Council of Europe Convention on Civil Liability for Damage resulting from Activities Dangerous to the Environment, and to the system of administrative review introduced by the World Bank to allow review of its acts where they have negative effects on the environment (World Bank, Resolution 93-10, Resolution IDA93-6, 22 September 1993, para 12).

23 Fourth, the appellants propose a different interpretation of the fourth paragraph of Art 173 of the Treaty. In order to determine whether a particular applicant is individually concerned by a Community act involving violations of Community environmental obligations, that applicant should be required to demonstrate that:

(a) he has personally suffered (or is likely personally to suffer) some actual or threatened detriment as a result of the allegedly illegal conduct of the Community institution concerned, such as a violation of his environmental rights or interference with his environmental interests;

(b) the detriment can be traced to the act challenged; and

(c) the detriment is capable of being redressed by a favourable judgment.

24 The appellants contend that they satisfy those three conditions. As regards the first condition, they state that they submitted statements describing the detriment which they have suffered as a result of the Commission's acts. As regards the second condition, they point out that, by disbursing to the Kingdom of Spain the funds granted under Decision C (91) 440 for the construction of projects carried out in breach of Community environmental law, the Commission directly contributed to the detriment caused to their interests since the Spanish authorities had no discretion as to the use to which those funds were to be put. As regards the third condition, the appellants consider that, if the Court of First Instance had annulled the contested decision, the Commission would not have continued to finance work on construction of the power stations which would then have probably been suspended until completion of the environmental impact procedure.

25   The appellants submit further that environmental associations should be recognised as having *locus standi* where their objectives concern chiefly environmental protection and one or more of their members are individually concerned by the contested Community decision, but also where, independently, their primary objective is environmental protection and they can demonstrate a specific interest in the question at issue.

26   Referring to the judgment in *Plaumann v Commission*, cited above, the appellants conclude that Art 173 must not be interpreted restrictively; its wording does not expressly require an approach based on the idea of a 'closed class', as affirmed in the case-law of the Court of Justice and the Court of First Instance (judgments in Case 11/82 *Piraiki-Patraiki and Others v Commission* [1985] ECR 207; Case C-358/89 *Extramet Industrie v Council* [1991] ECR I-2501; Case C-309/89 *Codorniu v Council* [1994] ECR I-1853; and Joined Cases T-480/93 and T-483/93 *Antillean Rice Mills and Others v Commission* [1995] ECR II-2305). Rather, it must be interpreted in such a way as to safeguard fundamental environmental interests and protect individual environmental rights effectively (judgments in *Procureur de la République v Association de Défense des Brûleurs d'Huiles Usagées*, cited above, para 13; Case 222/84 *Johnston v Chief Constable of the Royal Ulster Constabulary* [1986] ECR 1651, paras 13 to 21; and Case 222/86 *UNECTEF v Heylens and Others* [1987] ECR 4097, para 14).

Findings of the Court

27   The interpretation of the fourth paragraph of Art 173 of the Treaty that the Court of First Instance applied in concluding that the appellants did not have *locus standi* is consonant with the settled case-law of the Court of Justice.

28   As far as natural persons are concerned, it follows from the case-law, cited at both para 48 of the contested order and at para 7 of this judgment, that where, as in the present case, the specific situation of the applicant was not taken into consideration in the adoption of the act, which concerns him in a general and abstract fashion and, in fact, like any other person in the same situation, the applicant is not individually concerned by the act.

29   The same applies to associations which claim to have *locus standi* on the basis of the fact that the persons whom they represent are individually concerned by the contested decision. For the reasons given in the preceding paragraph, that is not the case.

30   In appraising the appellants' arguments purporting to demonstrate that the case-law of the Court of Justice, as applied by the Court of First Instance, takes no account of the nature and specific characteristics of the environmental interests underpinning their action, it should be emphasised that it is the decision to build the two power stations in question which is liable to affect the environmental rights arising under Directive 85/337 that the appellants seek to invoke.

31   In those circumstances, the contested decision, which concerns the Community financing of those power stations, can affect those rights only indirectly.

32   As regards the appellants' argument that application of the Court's case-law would mean that, in the present case, the rights which they derive from Directive 85/337 would have no effective judicial protection at all, it must be noted that, as is clear from the file, Greenpeace brought proceedings before the national courts challenging the administrative authorisations issued to Unelco concerning the construction of those power stations. TEA and CIC also lodged appeals against CUMAC's declaration of environmental impact relating to the two construction projects (see paras 6 and 7 of the contested order, reproduced at para 2 of this judgment).

33   Although the subject-matter of those proceedings and of the action brought before the Court of First Instance is different, both actions are based on the same rights afforded to individuals by Directive 85/337, so that in the circumstances of the present case those rights are fully protected by the national courts which may, if need be, refer a question to this Court for a preliminary ruling under Art 177 of the Treaty.

34   The Court of First Instance did not therefore err in law in determining the question of the appellants' *locus standi* in the light of the criteria developed by the Court of Justice in the case-law set out at para 7 of this judgment.

35   In those circumstances the appeal must be dismissed.

For a critique of the decision see Ward, A, 'Judicial review of environmental misconduct in the European Community: problems, prospects, and strategies' (2000) 1 Yearbook of European Environmental Law 137–59, p 150.

Standing in the UK law[38]

Applicants will have standing to seek judicial review if they have a 'sufficient interest in the matter to which the application relates'.[39] What constitutes a sufficient interest is essentially a matter for judicial discretion. The most straightforward situation is where applicants can show that they have been personally adversely affected by the action being challenged. Examples might include a situation where a landowner is challenging the decision to construct a motorway crossing his or her property, or where an applicant for a waste management licence seeks to challenge a decision relating to that licence. In such cases standing will rarely be a problem today.

Likewise, problems ought not to arise where the applicant is a group or an organisation which can show that its own interests have been directly adversely affected by official action. It was, for example, accepted that the Child Poverty Action Group (CPAG) had standing to challenge the manner in which the Secretary of State for Social Services administered social security payments partly because delayed payments to claimants meant that the CPAG was having to expend its resources advising greater numbers of claimants.[40] In *R v Poole Borough Council ex p Beebee and Others* [1991] 2 PLR 27; [1991] JPL 643; [1991] 3 LMELR 60 (see p 840, below) the British Herpetological Society and the Worldwide Fund for Nature sought to challenge a grant of planning permission for development on land designated as an SSSI. The court held that the British Herpetological Society had standing because it had been closely associated with the particular site, but would have denied standing to the Worldwide Fund for Nature to litigate on its own because it had failed to show a close connection and its interest was too general.

---

38   For discussions of standing see, in particular: Schiemann, Sir K, '*Locus Standi*' [1990] PL 342; Feldman, D, 'Public interest litigation and constitutional theory in comparative perspective' (1992) 55 MLR 44; Cane, P, 'Standing, representation and the environment', in Loveland, I (ed), *A Special Relationship? American Influences on Public Law in the UK* (1995) and 'Standing up for the public' [1995] PL 276; Robinson, D and Dunkley, J (eds), *Public Interest Perspectives in Environmental Law*, 1995, Chapters 3, 10, and 11; Hilson, C, and Cram, I, 'Judicial review and environmental law – is there a coherent view of standing?' (1996) 16 Legal Studies 1, p 1.

39   Supreme Court Act 1981, s 31(2).

40   *R v Secretary of State for Social Services ex p CPAG* [1990] 2 QB 540.

In the above situations the applicant is claiming standing on the basis that their own interests are at stake. Applicants, whether individual or more usually organisations, may also seek judicial review on behalf of others, a section of the community or the public in general.[41] Generally speaking, the courts will allow a representative application if those being represented would have standing had they litigated. The most difficult cases are those in which the applicant seeks to represent, not individuals or the interests of identifiable groups, but wider public interests. In the past the courts have adopted a restrictive approach in such cases. *R v Secretary of State for the Environment ex p Rose Theatre Trust Co Ltd* [1990] 1 QB 504 is an example. Construction work in London had revealed the remains of the Elizabethan Rose Theatre. A number of people interested in protecting these remains and in securing public access to them requested the Secretary of State to list the remains under the Ancient Monuments and Archaeological Areas Act 1979. The Secretary of State accepted that the remains were of national importance but refused to list them. The objectors then formed a company which applied for judicial review challenging this refusal. Schiemann J decided that the Secretary of State had acted within his powers but that, in any case, the company lacked standing. He accepted that this could mean that unlawful decisions made by the Secretary of State might be unchallengeable. But, in his view:

> ... the law does not see it as the function of the courts to be there for every individual who is interested in having the legality of an administrative action litigated. Parliament could have given such a wide right of access to the court but it has not done so ... We all expect our decision-makers to act lawfully. We are not all given by Parliament the right to apply for judicial review.

More recently this narrow approach has not been followed. Two decisions are of particular importance.

The first is Otton J's judgment in the *Greenpeace* case[42] (see p 842, below). Greenpeace UK challenged the decision of Her Majesty's Inspector of Pollution (HMIP) and the Minister of Agriculture Fisheries and Food (MAFF) to allow British Nuclear Fuels to test its new thermal oxide reprocessing plant (THORP) at Cumbria. In making the application Greenpeace claimed to represent 2,500 of its members who live in the Cumbrian region where THORP is situated and who are concerned about the health risks associated with radioactive pollution. They also sought to represent the wider public interest in preventing such pollution. Greenpeace was granted leave to seek judicial review. However, British Nuclear Fuels (BNFL) (who were to operate the plant but were not respondents in the case) were permitted to join the litigation and argue that leave should be set aside because Greenpeace had failed to establish a sufficient interest. Otton J rejected this argument. After applauding the integrity of Greenpeace and its genuine concern for the environment he went on to say that he would be ignoring the blindingly obvious if he were to disregard the genuine concern of its 2,500 members who lived near the site. He also had no doubt that the issues raised by the application were serious and worthy of determination and that if he were to deny standing to Greenpeace 'those they

---

41   A third situation is where public bodies are given authority to bring proceedings by statute, eg local authorities under s 222 of the Local Government Act 1972. Also the Attorney General has standing to bring legal proceedings in the public interest.

42   *R v HM Inspectorate of Pollution ex p Greenpeace Ltd (No 2)* [1994] 4 All ER 329.

represent might not have an effective way to bring the issues before the court'. He was, moreover, particularly impressed by the competence and expertise of Greenpeace, saying that if Greenpeace were unable to make the application:[43]

> ... a less well-informed challenge might be mounted which could stretch unnecessarily the courts resources and which would not afford the court the assistance it requires in order to do justice between the parties ... because of its access to experts in the relevant realms of science and technology (not to mention the law) it is able to mount a carefully selected, focused, relevant and well argued challenge.

The second case is *R v Secretary of State for Foreign Affairs ex p World Development Movement Ltd* (*Pergau Dam* case).[44] Here the World Development Movement (WDM), a pressure group which campaigns to improve the quality of British aid to the Third World, challenged the Foreign Secretary's decision to help fund the Pergau Dam project in Malaysia. Unlike Greenpeace the WDM did not claim to represent members who were directly adversely affected by the decision, but based its application on wider public interests and in particular on the public interest in ensuring that ministers comply with the law. The court held both that the Foreign Secretary had exceeded his powers and that the WDM had standing. As in the *Greenpeace* case, Rose LJ acknowledged the reputation, status and expertise of the applicants. He also emphasised the importance of vindicating the rule of law; the importance of the issue raised; the likely absence of any other responsible challenger; the nature of the breach of duty against which relief is sought; and the prominent role of the WDM in giving advice, guidance and assistance with regard to aid issues. All of these factors, he said, pointed to the conclusion that the WDM had a sufficient interest in the matter.

Sedley J reinforced the desirability of adopting a liberal approach to standing in *R v Somerset County Council and ARC Southern Ltd ex p Dixon* [1997] JPL 1030. Conditional planning permission was given to ARC Southern Ltd to extend a limestone quarry at Whatley in Somerset. Dixon applied for judicial review to challenge the grant of permission. He was a local resident, Parish Councillor in the Whatley area, member of the Executive Committee of the Somerset Association of Local Councils and a candidate for election to the District Council covering the Whatley area. He was also a member of several other local organisations concerned with the environment. Although Sedley J dismissed the application on its merits, he held that Dixon was plainly neither a busybody nor a mere troublemaker and was perfectly entitled as a citizen to draw the attention of the Court to what he argued was an unlawful granting of planning permission that was bound to have an impact on the natural environment. Aware that Popplewell J had shortly before this decision denied standing to an applicant in very similar circumstances (*Ex p Garnett* [1997] JPL 1015), Sedley J undertook a thorough review of the law on standing. He concluded by saying:

> I have taken some time on this issue because I am concerned to see that even the clear decision in the *World Development Movement* case, affirming as it does a strong line of modern authority and restoring ... a powerful line of older authority, does not appear to have stopped attempts, some of them successful, to elevate the question of standing at the

---

43 See p 845, below.
44 See p 847, below.

leave stage above the elementary level of excluding busybodies and troublemakers and to demand something akin to a special private interest in the subject matter. Such an argument may – depending on the issue – be insufficient even at the substantive hearing to exclude an applicant. At the leave stage it is, in my respectful view, entirely misconceived.

Public law is not at base about rights, even though abuses of power may and often do invade private rights; it is about wrongs – that is to say misuses of public power; and the courts have always been alive to the fact that a person or organisation with no particular stake in the issue or the outcome may, without in any sense being a mere meddler, wish and be well placed to call the attention of the court to the apparent misuse of public power ...

It may be noted that the Law Commission has recommended that there should be a 'two-track' approach to standing. Those who are personally adversely affected should normally be given standing as a matter of course. Other applicants, including public interest litigants, should be granted standing as a matter of discretion.[45] This discretionary approach appears to be incompatible with developments in European Community law where the movement seems to be towards the encouragement of Member States to confer rights to litigate upon non governmental organisations. The European Commission, for example, recognising that non-governmental organisations should have better access to the courts has recommended that such organisations should be given standing to bring judicial review actions against public authorities in Member States.[46] A broader proposal to give, 'environmental associations' access before domestic courts to secure a wide range of remedies in respect of 'harmful environmental activities', including damages has been suggested.[47] See now Art 9(2) of the Aarhus Convention 1998, p 818, above.

R v Poole Borough Council ex p Beebee and Others [1991] 2 PLR 27; [1991] JPL 643

Schiemann J: This is an application for judicial review of what in substance is a grant on 6 April 1989 by Poole Borough Council to themselves of planning permission for housing development of some land which is part of Canford Heath and to which I shall refer as the subject sites. The subject sites have a long history of being seen as appropriate for development of this kind. They used not to be part of a site of special scientific interest ('SSSI') under the terms of the Wildlife and Countryside Act of 1981, although much of Canford Heath was such a site.

However, on 7 November 1988 the Nature Conservancy Council (NCC) notified the Council that they had revised the boundaries of the SSSI so as to include the subject sites. The main reason for the revision of the boundaries was that the sites support a number of protected species, including smooth snakes, sand lizards, the Dartford warbler, the nightjar and the hobby.

The effect of this notification in broad terms was to oblige the council to consult the NCC before doing anything in respect of the subject sites which might harm the protected species. This the Council did. The NCC objected to the housing proposal and asked the Secretary of State for the Environment to call it in for his decision. The Secretary of State

---

45 Law Com No 226, para 5.20.
46 *Implementing Community Environmental Law* (COM (96) 500 Final), para 40.
47 The proposal was suggested by the Institute for Applied Ecology, Germany and the Foundation for International Environmental Law and Development (FIELD). See *op cit*, Robinson and Dunkley, Chapter 3.

refused to do so, and so the council made the planning decision themselves and in effect granted themselves planning permission.

Standing

The applicants tried to persuade the NCC to apply for leave to move for judicial review of the Council's decision but the NCC was not prepared to act. So the appellants applied instead. Pursuant to s 31(3) of the Supreme Court Act 1981, I have considered whether the applicants have a sufficient interest in the matter to which the application relates. The applicants are two pairs of individuals, one pair claiming to represent the Worldwide Fund for Nature (UK) and the other the British Herpetological Society (BHS), both unincorporated associations.

The BHS has a long-established association with the subject sites; much of its work in the field has been funded by the NCC and it has carried out work at Canford Heath. It has had a continuing and genuine interest in the subject sites for years, which has been recognised by the Council. Indeed the sixth condition of the planning permission which the Council granted themselves provides 'that prior to any development starting on the site a full season's notice shall be given to the BHS to enable the catching and relocation of rare species known to inhabit the site'. This is a condition said to be imposed in the interests of conservation and to conform with the Wildlife and Countryside Act. The position of the Worldwide Fund for Nature (the current name for the World Wildlife Fund) is that it had been involved in the conservation of the Dorset heathlands for over 15 years, has made grants to the BHS since 1971 to assist them in carrying out their work on habitats for sand lizards and smooth snakes, and is an accredited participant at meetings of the contracting parties to the Berne Convention since 1986.

Mr Sullivan QC, who appears on behalf of the respondents, submits that neither of these associations has a sufficient interest. He relies on the fact that they have no legal interest in the land, or in any neighbouring land, and on the fact that the NCC has been given a role by Parliament to play in relation to SSSIs. He submits that where, as here, Parliament has set up a body such as the NCC specifically to protect the interest which is sought to be protected by the application, the court ought to be slow to find that others have a sufficient interest. I have some sympathy with this submission.

Further, he relies on the approach which I adopted in *R v Secretary of State for the Environment ex p Rose Theatre Trust Co* [1990] 1 QB 504 p 518. My decision in that case has not escaped academic criticism (see for instance [1990] Public Law 307 and [1990] Cambridge Law Journal 189) and the question of *locus standi* is something of a legal minefield following the five separate judgments on the point delivered in the House of Lords in *R v Inland Revenue Commissioners ex p National Federation of Self-Employed and Small Businesses Ltd* [1982] AC 617.

The Worldwide Fund for Nature made no representations in relation to the grant of planning permission and indeed were not a party to the original application for leave to move for judicial review. They were joined by consent on 16 July 1990 upon giving an undertaking to pay the respondents' costs in the event of the applicants being ordered to do so. It seems to me that the BHS, with its long association with this site, its financial input into the site and its connection with the planning permission by being named therein, has sufficient interest for me to be entitled to look at its application on its merits. This I now do. Had the Worldwide Fund for Nature stood on their own, or had there been no consent order, I would not have considered them to have had a sufficient interest, but in the circumstances I do.

R v Inspectorate of Pollution and Another ex p Greenpeace Ltd (No 2) [1994] 4 All ER 329

Otton J: This is an application by Greenpeace Ltd for judicial review of a decision by HM Inspectorate of Pollution (HMIP) and the Minister of Agriculture, Fisheries and Food (MAFF) dated 25 August 1993 to grant applications by British Nuclear Fuels plc (BNFL) for variations of authorisations under the Radioactive Substances Act 1960 (as amended) to discharge radioactive waste from BNFL's premises at Sellafield, Cumbria, in order to test BNFL's (new) thermal oxide processing plant (THORP) [the judge dealt with the merits, deciding against Greenpeace and then dealt with the standing issue].

Mr G Newman QC, leading counsel for BNFL, the party directly affected by the decision under review, submits that in principle and on authority Greenpeace has failed to establish a sufficient interest in the matter to which the application relates and that accordingly the grant of leave should be set aside and in the exercise of my discretion I should disallow the application on that ground, however I may have found on the merits of the case.

In advancing this argument Mr Newman was careful to preface his submissions by emphasising that this issue does not question the sincerity of Greenpeace and its supporters for the causes it supports. BNFL do not seek to question the legitimacy of Greenpeace's objectives and views. The question at issue is not the extent of its reputation and the extent to which it is known nationally and internationally or the integrity of its aims.

Mr Newman took me through an extensive and helpful review of the authorities on the point, which included: *Covent Garden Community Association Ltd v Greater London Council* [1981] JPL 183; *R v Stroud DC ex p Goodenough* (1982) 43 P & CR 59; *IRC v National Federation of Self-Employed and Small Businesses Ltd* [1981] 2 All ER 93, [1982] AC 617; *R v Hammersmith and Fulham London Borough Council ex p People before Profit Ltd* (1981) 80 LGR 322; *R v Secretary of State for Social Services ex p Child Poverty Action Group* (1984) *The Times*, 16 August; rvsd (1985) *The Times*, 8 August, *R v Chief Adjudication Officer ex p Bland* (1985) *The Times*, 6 February; *R v Secretary of State for Social Services ex p Child Poverty Action Group* [1989] 1 All ER 1047, [1990] 2 QB 540 and *R v Secretary of State for the Environment ex p Rose Theatre Trust Co* [1990] 1 All ER 754, [1990] 1 QB 504, a decision of Schiemann J. I do not need to explore that decision in any great detail.

In particular he relied upon the speeches in the House of Lords in *IRC v National Federation of Self-Employed and Small Businesses Ltd*. This concerned a decision by the Inland Revenue Commissioners in respect of the tax affairs of the 'Fleet Street casuals' not to investigate tax lost in earlier periods. The applicants were a federation representing the self-employed and small businesses. It was held that the applicants did not have a sufficient interest in the matter to which the application related. The federation was merely a body of taxpayers which had shown no sufficient interest in that matter to justify their application for relief and the federation had completely failed to show any conduct of the revenue which was *ultra vires* or unlawful. In particular he relied upon extracts from three of the speeches. Lord Wilberforce said ([1981] 2 All ER 93, p 96, [1982] AC 617, p 630):

> ... it will be necessary to consider the powers or the duties in law of those against whom the relief is asked, the position of the applicant in relation to those powers or duties, and the breach of those said to have been committed.

From Lord Diplock ([1981] 2 All ER 93, p 101, [1982] AC 617, p 636):

> ... the questions (1) what was the public duty of the Board of Inland Revenue of which it was alleged to be in breach? and (2) what was the nature of the breaches that were

relied on by the federation? ... need to be answered in the instant case before it is possible to say whether the federation has 'a sufficient interest in the matter to which the application relates'.

and *per* Lord Fraser ([1981] 2 All ER 93, p 108, [1982] AC 617, p 646):

The correct approach is to look at the statute under which the duty arises, and to see whether it gives any express or implied right to persons in the position of the applicant to complain of the alleged unlawful act or omission.

He also submitted that the analysis of Schiemann J in *Ex p Rose Theatre Trust Co* was a correct statement in principle, notably where he set out the following propositions ([1990] 1 All ER 754, p 766, [1990] 1 QB 504, p 520):

1   Once leave has been given to move for judicial review, the court which hears the application ought still to examine whether the applicant has a sufficient interest.

2   Whether an applicant has a sufficient interest is not purely a matter of discretion in the court.

3   Not every member of the public can complain of every breach of statutory duty by a person empowered to come to a decision by that statute. To rule otherwise would be to deprive the phrase 'a sufficient interest' of all meaning.

4   However, a direct financial or legal interest is not required.

5   Where one is examining an alleged failure to perform a duty imposed by statute it is useful to look at the statute to see whether it gives an applicant a right enabling him to have that duty performed.

6   Merely to assert that one has an interest does not give one an interest.

7   The fact that some thousands of people join together and assert that they have an interest does not create an interest if the individuals did not have an interest.

8   The fact that those without an interest incorporate themselves and give the company in its memorandum power to pursue a particular object does not give the company an interest.

Mr Newman takes as his starting point the context of the 1960 Act. He submits that Parliament's purpose in passing the statute is to permit such activities subject to regulation by the designated statutory authorities, not to forbid them altogether. There are built into the statutory framework provisions for consultation in respect of new authorisations and even variations. Thus, there is no express or implied right to persons in the position of Greenpeace to complain of the alleged unlawful act or omission. He analysed the position of Greenpeace in relation to the statutory duties and powers. He emphasised that Greenpeace's primary object is:

In the United Kingdom and internationally to promote, encourage, further, establish, procure and achieve the protection of wildlife and the elimination of threats and damage to the environment or the global environment of the earth.

Thus Greenpeace asserts that it represents a wider public interest. This demonstrates that the complaint is in furtherance of Greenpeace's general campaign against the use of radioactive material and the disposal of radioactive waste. Greenpeace merely subscribes to a different view as to the risks associated with such activities from that formed by the authorities charged by statute to regulate and control these activities. Thus Greenpeace's complete opposition to authorising the disposal of radioactive waste is fundamentally incompatible with the statutory scheme adopted by Parliament in the 1960 Act. The fact that an individual or a pressure group has commented on a proposed decision and those comments have been considered by the statutory authorities does not confer on the individual or pressure group a sufficient interest in the decision to challenge the decision by proceedings for judicial review. To hold otherwise, he submits, would be to discourage the statutory authorities from inviting or considering comments from the public beyond their statutory obligations to do so.

He further analyses the challenge to the lawfulness of the procedure and comments:

> This is the classic case of the busybody. The nub of Greenpeace's complaint is that, although it has itself the opportunity to make comments the decision is flawed because some person or body should have been consulted. Allegations that procedural rights have not been respected are properly vindicated by those entitled to those rights and not by a pressure group which itself has no practical complaint.

In any event, he submits the case does not fall within the exceptional category envisaged by the House of Lords of 'flagrant and serious breaches of the law' or 'exceptionally grave or widespread illegality' or 'a most extreme case' which would justify an exceptional approach to the question of 'sufficient interest' (see *IRC v National Federation of Self-Employed and Small Businesses Ltd* [1981] 2 All ER 93, pp 104, 108, 120, 99, [1982] AC 617, pp 641, 647, 662, 633 *per* Lord Diplock, Lord Fraser of Tullybelton, Lord Roskill and Lord Wilberforce).

Conclusions

The requirement of a sufficient interest emerges from s 31(3) of the Supreme Court Act 1981:

> No application for judicial review shall be made unless the leave of the High Court has been obtained in accordance with rules of court; and the court shall not grant leave to make such an application unless it considers that the applicant has a sufficient interest in the matter to which the application relates.

RSC Ord 53, r 3 (7) provides:

> The Court shall not grant leave unless it considers that the applicant has a sufficient interest in the matter to which the application relates.

In reaching my conclusions I adopt the approach indicated by Lord Donaldson MR in *R v Monopolies and Mergers Commission ex p Argyll Group plc* [1986] 1 WLR 763, p 773; [1986] 2 All ER 257, p 265:

> The first stage test, which is applied on the application for leave, will lead to a refusal if the applicant has no interest whatsoever and is, in truth, no more than a meddlesome busybody. If, however, the application appears to be otherwise arguable and there is no other discretionary bar, such as dilatoriness on the part of the applicant, the applicant may expect to get leave to apply, leaving the test of interest or standing to be reapplied as a matter of discretion on the hearing of the substantive application. At this second stage, the strength of the applicant's interest is one of the factors to be weighed in the balance.

This approach was followed and developed by Purchas LJ in *R v Dept of Transport ex p Presvac Engineering Ltd* (1989) *The Times*, 4 April when, after considering the decision of the House of Lords in *IRC v National Federation of Self-Employed and Small Businesses Ltd*, he said:

> Personally I would prefer to restrict the use of the expression *locus standi* to the threshold exercise and to describe the decision at the ultimate stage as an exercise of

discretion not to grant relief as the applicant has not established that he had been or would be sufficiently affected.

Thus I approach this matter primarily as one of discretion. I consider it appropriate to take into account the nature of Greenpeace and the extent of its interest in the issues raised, the remedy Greenpeace seeks to achieve and the nature of the relief sought.

In doing so I take into account the very nature of Greenpeace. Lord Melchett has affirmed thus:

> Greenpeace International has nearly five million supporters worldwide; Greenpeace UK has over 400,000 supporters in the United Kingdom and about 2,500 of them are in the Cumbria region, where the BNFL plant is situated. Greenpeace is a campaigning organisation which has as its prime object the protection of the natural environment.

Greenpeace International has also been accredited with consultative status with the United Nations Economic and Social Council (including United Nations General Assembly). It has accreditation status with the United Nations Conference on Environment and Development. They have observer status or the right to attend meetings of 17 named bodies including Parcom (Paris Convention for the Prevention of Marine Pollution from Land Based Sources).

BNFL rightly acknowledges the national and international standing of Greenpeace and its integrity. So must I. I have not the slightest reservation that Greenpeace is an entirely responsible and respected body with a genuine concern for the environment. That concern naturally leads to a *bona fide* interest in the activities carried on by BNFL at Sellafield and in particular the discharge and disposal of radioactive waste from its premises and to which the respondents' decision to vary relates. The fact that there are 400,000 supporters in the United Kingdom carries less weight than the fact that 2,500 of them come from the Cumbria region. I would be ignoring the blindingly obvious if I were to disregard the fact that those persons are inevitably concerned about (and have a genuine perception that there is) a danger to their health and safety from any additional discharge of radioactive waste even from testing. I have no doubt that the issues raised by this application are serious and worthy of determination by this court.

It seems to me that if I were to deny standing to Greenpeace, those it represents might not have an effective way to bring the issues before the court. There would have to be an application either by an individual employee of BNFL or a near neighbour. In this case it is unlikely that either would be able to command the expertise which is at the disposal of Greenpeace. Consequently, a less well informed challenge might be mounted which would stretch unnecessarily the court's resources and which would not afford the court the assistance it requires in order to do justice between the parties. Further, if the unsuccessful applicant had the benefit of legal aid it might leave the respondents and BNFL without an effective remedy in costs. Alternatively, the individual (or Greenpeace) might seek to persuade Her Majesty's Attorney General to commence a relator action which (as a matter of policy or practice) he may be reluctant to undertake against a government department (see the learned commentary by Schiemann J on *'locus Standi'* [1990] Pub L 342). Neither of these courses of action would have the advantage of an application by Greenpeace, who, with its particular experience in environmental matters, its access to experts in the relevant realms of science and technology (not to mention the law), is able to mount a carefully selected, focused, relevant and well argued challenge. It is not without significance that in this case the form 86 contains six grounds of challenge but by the time it came to the substantive hearing before me, the Greenpeace 'team' (if I may call them that) had been able to evaluate the respondents' and BNFL's evidence and were able to jettison four grounds and concentrate on two. This responsible approach undoubtedly had the advantage of sparing scarce court resources, ensuring an expedited substantive hearing and an early result (which it transpires is helpful to the respondents and to BNFL). This line of reasoning has some support from the approach to be found in a line of cases in the Supreme Court of Canada (see *Thorson v Attorney General of Canada* [1975] 1 SCR 138; *McNeil v Nova Scotia Board of Censors* [1976] 2 SCR 265; *Borowski v Minister of Justice of Canada* [1981] 2 SCR 575 and *Finlay v Minister of Finance of Canada* [1986] 2 SCR 607 especially the judgment of Le Dain J; see also the helpful and imaginative commentary of the authors Supperstone and Goudie, *Judicial Review* (1992) 335–56 and 338–40).

I also take into account the nature of the relief sought. In *IRC v National Federation of Self-Employed and Small Businesses Ltd* the House of Lords expressed the view that if *mandamus* were sought that would be a reason to decline jurisdiction. Here, the primary relief sought is *certiorari* (less stringent) and, if granted, the question of an injunction to stop the testing pending determination of the main applications would still be in the discretion of the court. I also take into account the fact that Greenpeace has been treated as one of the consultees during the consultation process and that they were invited (albeit with other non-consultees) to comment on the 'minded to vary' letter.

It follows that I reject the argument that Greenpeace is a 'mere' or 'meddlesome busybody'. I regard the applicant as eminently respectable and responsible and its genuine interest in the issues raised is sufficient for it to be granted *locus standi*.

I should add that Lord Roskill in *IRC v National Federation of Self-Employed and Small Businesses Ltd* [1982] AC 617, p 659; [1981] 2 All ER 93, p 117 approved the commentary to Ord 53 in The Supreme Court Practice 1989 (see now The Supreme Court Practice 1993, Vol 1, para 53/1-14/11) that the question of whether the applicant has a sufficient interest appears to be:

> ... a mixed question of fact and law; a question of fact and degree and the relationship between the applicant and the matter to which the application relates, having regard to all the circumstances of the case.

Thus it must not be assumed that Greenpeace (or any other interest group) will automatically be afforded standing in any subsequent application for judicial review in whatever field it (and its members) may have an interest. This will have to be a matter to be considered on a case by case basis at the leave stage and if the threshold is crossed again at the substantive hearing as a matter of discretion.

I also bear this consideration in mind when I respectfully decline to follow the decision of Schiemann J in *R v Secretary of State for the Environment ex p Rose Theatre Trust Co* [1990] 1 QB 504; [1990] 1 All ER 754. Suffice it to say that the circumstances were different, the interest group had been formed for the exclusive purpose of saving the Rose Theatre site and no individual member could show any personal interest in the outcome. In any event his decision on the *locus standi* point (as indeed is mine) was not central to his decision.

In exercising my discretion I would grant Greenpeace standing in this case. If I had found in their favour on the grounds advanced, the question of what relief would have been appropriate would still have been within my discretion. Although I would probably have granted an order of *certiorari* to strike down the decision, it would have been a matter of considerable argument and further representation before I would have taken the further step of granting an injunction to end the testing. In case this case goes any further, I say no more on that particular point.

In the event, having granted in my discretion Greenpeace leave to make this application on behalf of its members on these matters of considerable interest to the public, I cannot find for Greenpeace on the merits of the application. It must therefore be refused.

R v Secretary of State for Foreign Affairs ex p World Development Movement Ltd [1995] 1 WLR 386; [1995] 1 All ER 611

Rose LJ: There is before the court an application by World Development Movement Ltd for judicial review of two decisions of the Secretary of State for Foreign Affairs in relation to aid to fund the Pergau dam in Malaysia. The initial decision to grant aid was made on or shortly before 8 July 1991. The application refers to 15 July, which was the date of a press release in relation to the matter, but nothing turns on the precise date. In early 1994 there were proceedings in public before the House of Commons Public Accounts Committee and the Foreign Affairs Committee which led the applicants' solicitors to seek an assurance from the Secretary of State that no further funds would be furnished. On 29 April 1994 the Foreign Secretary refused to give such an assurance, and that is the second decision which is challenged.

By the notice of motion the applicants seek to have both decisions quashed and an order preventing further payments from being made. But it may be that the applicants will be content with a declaration that the July 1991 decision to make a grant was unlawful.

In the course of the hearing before this court there have been four issues: first, whether the applicants have standing to make the application; secondly, whether disclosure should be ordered of two minutes from Sir Tim Lankester, Permanent Secretary in the Overseas Development Administration (the ODA) to Baroness Chalker, the Minister of Overseas Development, dated 5 and 7 February 1991; thirdly, whether the July 1991 decision was lawful; fourthly, what is the appropriate relief, if any, taking delay into account? As to the second issue, the court refused disclosure during the hearing and indicated that reasons would be given later.

As to standing, s 31(3) of the Supreme Court Act 1981 provides:

> No application for judicial review shall be made unless the leave of the High Court has been obtained in accordance with rules of court; and the court shall not grant leave to make such an application unless it considers that the applicant has a sufficient interest in the matter to which the application relates.

RSC Ord 53, r 3(7) provides:

> The Court shall not grant leave unless it considers that the applicant has a sufficient interest in the matter to which the application relates.

The affidavit of Mr Jackson, the applicants' campaign co-ordinator, describes the applicant company. It is a non-partisan pressure group, over 20 years old and limited by guarantee. It has an associated charity which receives financial support from all the main United Kingdom development charities, the churches, the European Community and a range of other trusts. About 60% of its total income comes from members and supporters. The council of the applicants has cross-political party membership, and, indeed, historically, a Member of Parliament from each of the three main political parties has sat on the council. There are 7,000 full voting members throughout the United Kingdom with a total supporter base of some 13,000. There are 200 local groups whose supporters actively campaign through letter-writing, lobbying and other democratic means to improve the quantity and quality of British aid to other countries. It conducts research and analysis in relation to aid.

It is a founder member of the Independent Group on British Aid, which brings academics and campaigners together. It has pressed the British government, the European Union, the banks and other businesses for better trade access for developing countries. It is in regular contact with the ODA and has regular meetings with the minister of that department, and it makes written and oral submissions to a range of select committees in both Houses of Parliament. It has run all-party campaigns against aid cuts in 1987 and 1992.

Internationally, it has official consultative status with UNESCO and has promoted international conferences. It has brought together development groups within the OECD. It tends to attract citizens of the United Kingdom concerned about the role of the United Kingdom government in relation to the development of countries abroad and the relief of poverty abroad.

Its supporters have a direct interest in ensuring that funds furnished by the United Kingdom are used for genuine purposes, and it seeks to ensure that disbursement of aid budgets is made where that aid is most needed. It seeks, by this application, to represent the interests of people in developing countries who might benefit from funds which otherwise might go elsewhere. If the applicants have no standing, it is said that no person or body would ensure that powers under the 1980 Act are exercised lawfully. For the applicants Mr Pleming QC submitted that the Foreign Secretary himself, in a written statement of 2 March 1994, has expressly accepted that the matter is 'clearly of public and Parliamentary interest'. It cannot be said that the applicants are 'busybodies', 'cranks' or 'mischief-makers'. They are a non-partisan pressure group concerned with the misuse of aid money. If there is a public law error, it is difficult to see how else it could be challenged and corrected except by such an applicant. He referred the court to a number of authorities: *IRC v National Federation of Self-Employed and Small Businesses Ltd* [1982] AC 617; [1981] 2 All ER 93, in particular the speech of Lord Wilberforce ([1982] AC 617, p 630; [1981] 2 All ER 93, p 96) and the speech of Lord Diplock, where there appears this passage:

> It would, in my view, be a grave lacuna in our system of public law if a pressure group, like the federation, or even a single public-spirited taxpayer, were prevented by outdated technical rules of *locus standi* from bringing the matter to the attention of the court to vindicate the rule of law and get the unlawful conduct stopped. The Attorney General, although he occasionally applies for prerogative orders against public authorities that do not form part of central government, in practice never does so against government departments. It is not, in my view, a sufficient answer to say that judicial review of the actions of officers or departments of central government is unnecessary because they are accountable to Parliament for the way in which they carry out their functions. They are accountable to Parliament for what they do so far as regards efficiency and policy, and of that Parliament is the only judge; they are responsible to a court of justice for the lawfulness of what they do, and of that the court is the only judge (see [1981] 2 All ER 93 at 107, [1982] AC 617 at 644).

Mr Pleming also referred to *R v Monopolies and Mergers Commission ex p Argyll Group plc* [1986] 2 All ER 257, [1986] 1 WLR 763. Donaldson MR, when referring to the provision of Ord 53, r 3(7), said this ([1986] 1 WLR 763, p 773; [1986] 2 All ER 257, p 265):

> The first stage test, which is applied on the application for leave, will lead to a refusal if the applicant has no interest whatsoever and is, in truth, no more than a meddlesome busybody. If, however, the application appears to be otherwise arguable and there is no other discretionary bar, such as dilatoriness on the part of the applicant, the applicant may expect to get leave to apply, leaving the test of interest or standing to be re-applied as a matter of discretion on the hearing of the substantive application. At this second

stage, the strength of the applicant's interest is one of the factors to be weighed in the balance.

There is a reference to Professor Wade's work on *Administrative Law*, to which I shall come later.

Mr Pleming also referred to *R v Secretary of State for Social Services ex p Child Poverty Action Group* [1990] 2 QB 540; [1989] 1 All ER 1047, where that group was held to have a sufficient interest or standing. He referred also to *R v Inspectorate of Pollution ex p Greenpeace Ltd (No 2)* [1994] 4 All ER 329, in particular to passages in the judgment of Otton J, which it is unnecessary to read (see [1994] 4 All ER 329, pp 350, 351). Finally on this aspect, he invited the court's attention to *R v Secretary of State for Foreign and Commonwealth Affairs ex p Rees-Mogg* [1994] QB 552, p 562; [1994] 1 All ER 457, p 461, where Lloyd LJ, delivering the judgment of the Divisional Court (comprised of himself, Mann LJ and Auld J), accepted that the applicant had standing 'because of his sincere concern for constitutional issues'. The question of lawfulness being for the court, Mr Pleming submitted that the court in its discretion should accept the standing of the applicants. If they cannot seek relief, he said, who can? Neither a government nor citizen of a foreign country denied aid is, in practical terms, likely to be able to bring such a challenge.

For the Foreign Secretary, there is no evidential challenge to the applicants' standing. Mr Richards made submissions on sufficiency of interest, not with a view to preventing the court from considering the substantive issue as to the validity of the decision, but because sufficiency of interest goes to the court's jurisdiction (see *Ex p Child Poverty Action Group* [1990] 2 QB 540, p 556, *per* Woolf LJ; [1989] 1 All ER 1047, p 1056). The applicants, Mr Richards submitted, are at the outer limits of standing. He submitted, and indeed Mr Pleming accepted, that neither the applicants nor any of the individual members have any direct personal interest in funding under the 1980 Act, but they seek to act in the interest of potential recipients of aid overseas. Mr Richards submitted that this is too remote an interest to be sufficient, and he contrasted Greenpeace members, some of whom, as Otton J pointed out, were liable to be personally directly affected by radioactive discharge.

Mr Richards accepted that the requirements of standing will vary from case to case and that the court may accord standing to someone who would not otherwise qualify where exceptionally grave or widespread illegality is alleged. He referred to that part of Lord Diplock's speech in *IRC v National Federation of Self-Employed and Small Businesses Ltd* [1982] AC 617, p 637; [1981] 2 All ER 93, p 101, which shows that his comments which I have read are obiter. He referred to the speeches of both Lord Wilberforce and Lord Fraser, to the effect that a United Kingdom taxpayer's interest, which is no more than that of taxpayers in general, is insufficient to confer standing, save in an extreme case (see [1982] AC 617, pp 633, 646; [1981] 2 All ER 93, pp 98–99, 108). If no United Kingdom taxpayer could raise the matter, this not being an exceptional case, the applicants, submitted Mr Richards, cannot be in a better position.

It is to be observed, in passing, that there are *dicta* since *IRC v National Federation of Self-Employed and Small Businesses Ltd* which are in favour of according standing to a single taxpayer in an appropriate case (see *R v HM Treasury ex p Smedley* [1985] QB 657, pp 670, 667, *per* Slade LJ and Donaldson MR; [1985] 1 All ER 589, pp 595, 594). There is, submitted Mr Richards, 'a certain tension' between what Lloyd LJ said in *Ex p Rees-Mogg* [1994] QB 552, p 562; [1994] 1 All ER 457, p 461, and what Donaldson MR said in *Ex p Argyll Group plc* [1986] 1 WLR 763, p 774; [1986] 2 All ER 257, pp 265–66. The rules of standing should not, submitted Mr Richards, be allowed to evolve further so as to embrace the applicants.

For my part, I accept that standing (albeit decided in the exercise of the court's discretion, as Donaldson MR said) goes to jurisdiction, as Woolf LJ said. But I find nothing in *IRC v National Federation of Self-Employed and Small Businesses Ltd* to deny standing to these applicants. The authorities referred to seem to me to indicate an increasingly liberal approach to standing on the part of the courts during the last 12 years. It is also clear from *IRC v National Federation of Self-Employed and Small Businesses Ltd* that standing should not be treated as a preliminary issue, but must be taken in the legal and factual context of the whole case (see [1982] AC 617, pp 630, 649, 653, *per* Lord Wilberforce, Lord Fraser and Lord Scarman; [1981] 2 All ER 93, pp 96, 110, 113).

Furthermore, the merits of the challenge are an important, if not dominant, factor when considering standing. In Professor Sir William Wade's words in *Administrative Law* (7th edn, 1994), p 712:

... the real question is whether the applicant can show some substantial default or abuse, and not whether his personal rights or interests are involved.

Leaving merits aside for a moment, there seem to me to be a number of factors of significance in the present case: the importance of vindicating the rule of law, as Lord Diplock emphasised in *IRC v National Federation of Self-Employed and Small Businesses Ltd* [1982] AC 617, p 644; [1981] 2 All ER 93, p 107; the importance of the issue raised, as in *Ex p Child Poverty Action Group*; the likely absence of any other responsible challenger, as in *Ex p Child Poverty Action Group* and *Ex p Greenpeace Ltd*; the nature of the breach of duty against which relief is sought (see *IRC v National Federation of Self-Employed and Small Businesses Ltd* [1982] AC 617, p 630, *per* Lord Wilberforce; [1981] 2 All ER 93, p 96); and the prominent role of these applicants in giving advice, guidance and assistance with regard to aid (see *Ex p Child Poverty Action Group* [1990] 2 QB 540, p 546; [1989] 1 All ER 1047, p 1048). All, in my judgment, point, in the present case, to the conclusion that the applicants here do have a sufficient interest in the matter to which the application relates within s 31(3) of the 1981 Act and Ord 53, r 3(7).

It seems pertinent to add this, that if the Divisional Court in *Ex p Rees-Mogg* eight years after *Ex p Argyll Group* was able to accept that the applicant in that case had standing in the light of his 'sincere concern for constitutional issues', *a fortiori*, it seems to me that the present applicants, with their national and international expertise and interest in promoting and protecting aid to underdeveloped nations, should have standing in the present application.

The above decisions may be compared with the recent US decision in *Friends of the Earth Incorporated v Laidlaw Environmental Services* (120 US Supreme Ct 693 (2000); full text at: http://supct.law.cornell.edu/supct). For an analysis, see JG Miller and Hilson in the *Journal of Environmental Law* (Vol 12, No 3) pp 370–84. Here the authors comment that *Laidlaw* should make American environmentalists dance in the streets. The Court held that a pressure group whose members' aesthetic and recreational interests were injured by the defendant's discharge of mercury into the North Tyger River in North Carolina in violation of a permit issued under the Clean Water Act had standing under the Act to seek assessment of civil penalties for the violations.

HUMAN RIGHTS AND THE ENVIRONMENT IN EUROPEAN AND UK DOMESTIC LAW

European Union law

The Treaties do not expressly provide for a right to a healthy environment or quality of life. However, fundamental rights form an integral part of the general principles of community law. In safeguarding these rights the ECJ draws inspiration from constitutional traditions common to the Member States as well as international treaties on which Member States have collaborated or have signed. The key treaty for these purposes is the European Convention for the Protection of Human Rights and Fundamental Freedoms (see *Nold KG v Commission* [1974] ECR 491). The obligation of the European Union to respect human rights is enshrined in Art 6, Title I, of the Maastricht Treaty. This provides:

> The Union shall respect fundamental rights, as guaranteed by the European Convention for the Protection of Human Rights and Fundamental Freedoms ... and as they result from the constitutional traditions common to the Member States, as general principles of Community law.

More recently the Charter of Fundamental Rights of the European Union ((2001) OJ C364, p 1) states in Art 37 (Environmental Protection) that:

> A high level of environmental protection and the improvement of the quality of the environment must be integrated into the policies of the Union and ensured in accordance with the principle of sustainable development.

This provision has been criticised by the European Parliament on the grounds that it fails to bestow upon individuals an enforceable right to a clean environment, even to the extent contained in Principle 1 of the Stockholm Declaration 1972 (see p 63, above). (See also [2000] 6 Env Liability CS 57).

European Convention for the Protection of Human Rights and Fundamental Freedoms (ECHR)[48]

The ECHR is an international regional treaty that was adopted in 1950 and ratified by the UK in 1951. It came into force in 1953. Under the treaty States parties may claim that other States have violated the Convention. States may also agree to permit individuals to complain that breaches have occurred. The UK has permitted the right of individual petition since 1966. Because the ECHR is an international treaty, until the Human Rights Act 1998 came into effect in October 2000 the rights established by the ECHR were not part of domestic law. However, they could be relied on to indicate how ambiguous legislative provisions and ambiguous aspects of the common law should be interpreted. The Human Rights Act 1998 effectively incorporates certain of the rights contained in the ECHR into UK domestic law. For more detailed consideration of these issues reference

---

48   UKTS 71 (1953).

may be made to a number of specialised texts, including: Starmer, K, *European Human Rights Law* (LAG, 1999); Clayton, R and Tomlinson, H, *The Law of Human Rights* (Oxford, 2000).

The institutional structure of the ECHR

Before November 1998 complaints were first taken to the European Commission on Human Rights. The Commission would investigate the matter and decide whether the complaint was admissible and, if so, it would give its opinion on the merits. If there was no friendly settlement, the Commission or the State (but not the individual) could refer the matter to the European Court of Human Rights. The Court would make a final and binding determination on whether there was a violation of the Convention, and if so, whether compensation should be paid. Protocol 11, which came into force on the 1 November 1998, abolished the European Commission on Human Rights and reformed the Court. Complaints now go direct to the Court. A committee of three judges of the Court will determine whether the complaint is admissible. If admissible, the case will normally be dealt with by a court of seven judges. Cases that involve a serious question of interpretation are dealt with by a Grand Chamber of eleven judges.

The rights and freedoms protected by the ECHR

In summary the ECHR protects the following rights and freedoms:

Right to life (Art 2).

Prohibition of torture (Art 3).

Prohibition of slavery and forced labour (Art 4).

Right to liberty and security (Art 5).

Right to a fair trial (Art 6).

No punishment without law (Art 7).

Right to respect for private and family life (Art 8).

Freedom of thought, conscience and religion (Art 9).

Freedom of expression (Art 10).

Freedom of assembly and association (Art 11).

Right to marry (Art 12).

Right to an effective remedy (Art 13).

Prohibition of discrimination (Art14).

Right to Property (Art 1 of the First Protocol).

The Human Rights Act 1998

The Human Rights Act 1998 gives domestic effect to certain of the rights in the ECHR. These 'Convention Rights' are those set out in Arts 2–12, and 14, as well as Arts 1–3 of the First Protocol and Arts 1 and 2 of the Sixth Protocol. The main omission is the Art 13 right to an 'effective remedy before a national authority'.

The following are the principal ways in which the Human Rights Act 1998 gives effect to these rights.

- There is a general obligation upon courts and tribunals, when determining a question involving Convention rights, to take account of decisions made by the European Court of Human Rights, the European Commission of Human Rights and the Committee of Ministers of the Council of Europe concerning the Convention (s 2).

- Primary and secondary legislation must be interpreted, so far as it is possible to do so, in a way which is compatible with Convention rights (s 3).

- It is unlawful for any public authority to act in a way which is incompatible with a Convention right, unless primary legislation prevents the authority acting differently (s 6(1) and (2)). In this context 'public authority' includes a court or tribunal and 'any person certain of whose functions are functions of a public nature' (s 6(3)).

- The High Court, Court of Appeal, House of Lords and Judicial Committee of the Privy Council have the power to declare primary legislation incompatible with Convention rights (s 4).

- Where the court finds that a public authority has acted, or proposes, to act contrary to Convention rights the court may grant such relief or remedies within its powers as it considers just and appropriate (s 8(1)). However, damages or compensation may only be awarded where the court has power to make the award in civil proceedings (s 8(2)).

- Note also that only 'victims' of the unlawful act are able to bring proceedings under the Act or rely on Convention rights (s 7(1)). In judicial review proceedings an applicant will only have a sufficient interest to claim that a public authority has acted contrary to Convention rights if the applicant is, or would be, a victim (s 7(3)).

The Convention rights and the environment

The list of rights and freedoms set out in the ECHR does not include specific reference to environmental rights. This means that in order to use the Convention in environmental matters, either domestically or as a basis for a complaint to the European Court of Human Rights, it is necessary to bring claims within the scope of one or more of those rights and freedoms that are set out. From an environmental law perspective the most important substantive rights are the right to life (Art 2); the right to private, home and family life (Art 8); the right to property (Art 1 of the first Protocol); and the prohibition against discrimination (Art 14). The right to a fair trial (Art 6) and the freedom of expression, including the right to receive information (Art 10) are the principal provisions providing procedural rights relevant to environmental claims. Other rights, such as the freedom of association (Art 11) and the prohibition of degrading treatment (Art 3) may also be relevant. It is crucial to remember that human rights law is far from static and that the jurisprudence is developing very rapidly, particularly in contexts such as environmental protection. The inter-relationship between rights (such as the link between non-discrimination and the right to property) and the notion of implied rights (such is the implied right to access to justice within the concept of a fair trial) are likely to provide particularly fertile fields for legal development. The following discussion owes much to the following Articles: Thornton, J and Tromans, S, 'Human rights and environmental wrongs: incorporating the European Convention on Human Rights: some thoughts on the consequences for UK environmental law' [1999] 11(1) JEL 35–57; Hart, D, 'The impact of the European Convention on Human Rights on planning & environmental law' [2000] JPL 117–33: an updated and revised version of this Article appears as Chapter 10 in English and Havers (2000).

The 'victim' requirement

Only those who are 'victims' of an alleged violation are protected by the ECHR machinery (Art 34). Likewise only 'victims' can bring proceedings under or rely on Convention rights under the Human Rights Act 1998 (s 7(1). The term 'victim' is not defined. As a general rule victims are those who are 'directly affected' by acts or omissions of public bodies. This phrase extends to those who are at risk of being affected by such actions or omissions as well as those who are indirectly affected by violations of the rights of others (for example, *McCann v UK* (1995) 21 EHRR 97 where relatives of three IRA suspects killed by members of the SAS in Gibralter brought claims under Art 2 (right to life)) . However, residents of Tahiti were unable to claim that nuclear testing by France violated Arts 2, 3, 8 and 14 of the Convention. The Commission held that the applicants had not established that they were victims because they lived over 1000 km from the test site and had not produced sufficient evidence to show that future tests would affect them personally.

A similar approach was taken by the European Court of Human Rights in *Asselbourg and 78 Others and Greenpeace Luxemburg v Luxemburg* (29 June 1999). In the following extract the Court considers the 'victim' test in the context of Art 8 and Art 6 claims brought by individuals and Greenpeace (Luxemburg). The decision considers whether an association can claim to be a victim under Art 8. In relation to Art 6, the decision provides an interesting example of the relationship between standing requirements before national courts and the 'victim' test.

Asselbourg and 78 Others and Greenpeace Luxemburg v Luxemburg (29 June 1999)[49]

The application was lodged by 78 individuals, the majority of whom reside in the local authorities of Esch-sur-Alzette and Schifflange in Luxembourg, and the association Greenpeace, which has its registered office in Esch-sur-Alzette. All the applicants, who either own or rent their homes, are Luxembourg nationals.

A The circumstances of the case

Since the end of the Second World War, Luxembourg ... has concentrated the country's steelworks on three major sites (Esch-Schifflange, Differdange and Esch-Belval), passing legislation where possible, especially since 1990, to reduce air and water pollution and the quantity of waste products. The solution chosen was not to adapt the existing plants but

---

49   Application No 00029121/95; Hudoc ref: 00006033 (ECHR).

rather to change the production methods from traditional processes to electrically-fired steelworks, which were considered to be less polluting.

Accordingly, the ARBED SA company ... decided to change its production methods and to produce steel from scrap instead of iron ore. With a view to building a new electrically-fired steelworks on the boundary between the local authorities of Esch-Alzette and Schifflange, the company applied for licences to the Minister of Labour and the Minister of the Environment, in accordance with the Act of 9 May 1990 on dangerous, unhealthy and offensive establishments ... The company was granted the licences, to which a number of conditions were attached, in ... February 1993 ...

On 8 April 1993 the applicants lodged an application to set aside the two ministerial decisions coupled with an application to vary them, in which they requested modification of the qualifying conditions for the licence concerning, in particular, emissions of gas and dust, including emissions of dioxin and furan, reduction of pollutant waste and noise abatement.

They argued in particular that the authorities responsible for granting the operating licence had not required the use of the best possible technology to avoid the risk of air pollution, and criticised the impact studies made in 1992 by the Institute for Environmental Protection and Energy Technology in Cologne (TÜV Rheinland).

Since the joint application did not have suspensive effect, the new electrically-fired steelworks was brought into production in late 1993.

In 1994 various newspaper arts reported nauseating and intolerable smells around the steelworks. Others stated that the inhabitants of Esch-Schifflange had to throw away their vegetables, which had been contaminated by heavy metals.

In a judgment of 3 May 1995 the Conseil d'Etat ruled [*inter alia* that the applicants lacked standing to challenge the decisions] ...

1   The applicants complained of a violation of Art 8 of the Convention. They submitted that because the conditions attached to the operating licences for electrically-fired steelworks were inadequate, their right to respect for their homes and private and family life ... had been infringed, on the ground that since the steelworks in question had started operating nuisances had arisen.

2   The applicants further complained that the Conseil d'Etat had rejected their application to vary the decisions for lack of standing. They argued on that basis that their right of access to a tribunal had been infringed because, as the merits of their appeal had not been examined, they had been unable to obtain more stringent conditions for the operation of the steelworks so as to protect the environment and local residents. They relied on Art 6, § 1 of the Convention.

    [...]

The Law

The Court must first examine whether the applicants can claim to be the 'victims' of a violation of Art 8 of the Convention, within the meaning of Art 34 of the Convention.

[...]

With regard to the association Greenpeace-Luxembourg, the Court considers that a non-governmental organisation cannot claim to be the victim of an infringement of the right to respect for its 'home', within the meaning of Art 8 of the Convention, merely because it has its registered office close to the steelworks that it is criticising, where the infringement of the right to respect for the home results, as alleged in this case, from nuisances or problems which can be encountered only by natural persons. In so far as Greenpeace-Luxembourg sought to rely on the difficulties suffered by its members or employees working or spending time at its registered office in Esch-sur-Alzette, the Court considers that the association may only act as a representative of its members or employees, in the same way as, for example, a lawyer represents his client, but it cannot itself claim to be the victim of a violation of Art 8 (see *X v France*, Application No 9939/82, Commission Decision of 4 July 1983, Decisions and Reports (DR) 34, p 213).

As for the other applicants, some of whom, moreover, do not live within the boundaries of the local authorities of Esch or Schifflange, the Court notes that the application to vary an administrative decision lodged by the applicants in April 1993 was directed against the operating licences of an electrically-fired steelworks which had not yet been built. It was therefore not a matter of the applicants putting an end to a violation of Art 8 of the Convention, but rather trying, by obtaining stricter operating conditions, to prevent it.

From the terms 'victim' and 'violation' in Art 34 of the Convention, like the underlying philosophy of the obligation to exhaust all domestic remedies imposed by Art 35, it can be deduced that, in the system for the protection of human rights as envisaged by the framers of the Convention, exercise of the right of individual petition cannot have the aim of preventing a violation of the Convention. It is only in wholly exceptional circumstances that the risk of a future violation may nevertheless confer the status of 'victim' on an individual applicant, and only then if he or she produces reasonable and convincing evidence of the probability of the occurrence of a violation concerning him or her personally: mere suspicions or conjectures are not enough in that respect.

In the instant case, the Court considers that the mere mention of the pollution risks inherent in the production of steel from scrap iron is not enough to justify the applicants' assertion that they are the victims of a violation of the Convention. They must be able to assert, arguably and in a detailed manner, that for lack of adequate precautions taken by the authorities the degree of probability of the occurrence of damage is such that it can be considered to constitute a violation, on condition that the consequences of the act complained of are not too remote (see, *mutatis mutandis*, the *Soering v the United Kingdom* (1989) judgment of 7 July, Series A No 161, p 33, § 85). In the Court's opinion, it is not evident from the file that the conditions of operation imposed by the Luxembourg authorities and in particular the norms dealing with the discharge of air-polluting wastes were so inadequate as to constitute a serious infringement of the principle of precaution.

[...]

[The Court then considered whether there had been an infringement of the right of access to justice under Art 6.]

The case-law of the Convention institutions has always affirmed the autonomous scope of the concept of 'victim' in Art 34 of the Convention, particularly in relation to concepts under internal law such as standing or capacity to take part in legal proceedings. As to the right of access to a tribunal, it cannot be taken to mean, as the applicants would have it, that when a tribunal with the fullest possible jurisdiction, as in the instant case, dismisses an application for lack of standing it thereby denies the individual litigant access to a tribunal with jurisdiction to examine an alleged infringement of his substantive rights.

There are some situations where even though under internal law a person has the standing or capacity to undertake legal proceedings, he will not necessarily be considered a 'victim', within the meaning of Art 34 of the Convention, in the absence of a sufficiently direct link between the applicant and the prejudice he thinks he has suffered (see *Tauira and 18 Others v France*, Application No 28204/95, Commission Decision of 4 December 1995, DR 83-B, p 112). The Court reiterates in that connection that the Convention does not allow an *actio popularis* but requires as a condition for exercise of the right of individual petition that an applicant must be able to claim on arguable grounds that he himself has been a direct or indirect victim of a violation of the Convention resulting from an act or omission which can be attributed to a contracting state.

In the instant case, the Court considers that the dismissal of the applicants' appeal for lack of standing did not restrict their access to a tribunal [...].

For these reasons, the Court unanimously

Declares the application inadmissible.

The principal substantive Convention rights affecting the environment

Article 2 – Right to life

1 Everyone's right to life shall be protected by law. No one shall be deprived of his life intentionally save in the execution of a sentence of a court following his conviction of a crime for which this penalty is provided by law.

While this right is directed at protecting life itself, there is support for the view that the right to life may be infringed when circumstances such as pollution endanger health. The Article requires States to take positive action in order to safeguard the lives of those within its jurisdiction (see *LCB v UK* (1998) 27 EHRR 212, below). In his judgment in *Guerra v Italy*, Judge Jambrek argues that States may violate Art 2 by witholding information about circumstances which foreseeably present a real risk of danger to health and the physical integrity of people (even where these circumstances are created by private commercial activities). He also called for the development of implied rights associated with the right to life. Such implied rights might include the right to an environment free from health-threatening pollution. Liability might be imposed upon the State where a threat to life or the health of people arises from the actions of a private body and public bodies have taken inadequate steps to prevent or stop the threat.

Guerra and Others v Italy (1998) 26 EHRR 357

The population of an Italian village successfully complained about the local government's maladministration in relation to a nearby chemical works. There had been a history of incidents at the works, including an explosion in 1976 which led to local people being hospitalised with acute arsenic poisoning. The applicants in this case, however, could not show that they had been directly and physically injured by the acts or omissions of the local authorities. The judgment of the Court concentrated on breaches of Art 8 and the obligations arising from Art 10 (see further, below). However, the application of the right to life was considered by two concurring members of the Court: Jambrek and Walsh JJ.

Judge Jambrek

In their memorial the applicants also expressly complained of a violation of Art 2 of the Convention. The Court held that it was not necessary to consider the case under that Article given that it had found a violation of Art 8. I wish, nevertheless, to make some observations on the possible applicability of Art 2 in this case.

... The protection of health and physical integrity is, in my view, as closely associated with the 'right to life' as with the 'respect for private and family life'. An analogy may be made with the Court's case-law on Art 3 concerning the existence of 'foreseeable consequences'; where – *mutatis mutandis* – substantial grounds can be shown for believing that the person(s) concerned face a real risk of being subjected to circumstances which endanger their health and physical integrity, and thereby put at serious risk their right to life, protected by law. If information is withheld by a government about circumstances which foreseeably, and on substantial grounds, present a real risk of danger to health and physical integrity, then such a situation may also be protected by Art 2 ...

It may therefore be time for the Court's case-law on Art 2 ... to start evolving, to develop the respective implied rights, articulate situations of real and serious risk to life, or different aspects of the right to life. Article 2 also appears relevant and applicable to the facts of the instant case in that 150 people were taken to hospital with severe arsenic poisoning. Through the release of harmful substances into the atmosphere, the activity carried on at the factory thus constituted a 'major-accident hazard dangerous to the environment'.

These remarks have been contrasted with those of the Human Rights Committee of the United Nations when considering a claim by two Pacific Islanders that France's intention to test nuclear weapons at Murora Atoll threatened their right to life. Although the committee said that nuclear weapons constituted one of the gravest threats to the right to life, the case was dismissed because the applicants were not considered to be 'victims'. See Christopher Miller referring to *Bordes and Temeharov France*, UN Doc CCPR/C/57/D/645/1995 in 'The European Convention on Human Rights: another weapon in the environmentalist's armoury' [1999] 11(1) JEL 169–76, p 173.

LCB v UK (1998) 27 EHRR 212

In *LCB v UK* (1998) 27 EHRR 212 the applicant's father served on Christmas Island during testing of nuclear weapons during 1957 and 1958. The applicant was born in 1966 and was diagnosed as suffering from leukaemia in 1970. Her records of admission to hospital stated, under the heading 'Summary of Possible Causative Factors: Father – Radiation Exposure'. The applicant complained to the Commission *inter alia* under Arts 2 and 3 of the Convention that she had not been warned of the effects of her father's alleged exposure to radiation, which prevented pre- and post-natal monitoring that would have led to earlier diagnosis and treatment of her illness. Although it declared these complaints admissible it found that there was no breach of the convention.

The case was referred to the Court. The principal issue before the Court was whether the UK's failure to warn and advise her parents or monitor her health prior to her diagnosis in 1970 had given rise to a violation of Art 2 of the Convention.

2   Assessment of the complaint concerning failure to take measures in respect of the applicant

1   The applicant complained in addition that the respondent state's failure to warn and advise her parents or monitor her health prior to her diagnosis with leukaemia in October 1970 had given rise to a violation of Art 2 of the Convention.

In this connection, the Court considers that the first sentence of Art 2 § 1 enjoins the state not only to refrain from the intentional and unlawful taking of life, but also to take appropriate steps to safeguard the lives of those within its jurisdiction (cf the Court's reasoning in respect of Art 8 in the *Guerra and Others v Italy* judgment of 19 February 1998, Reports 1998-I, p 227, § 58, and see also the decision of the Commission on the admissibility of Application No 7154/75 of 12 July 1978, Decisions and Reports 14, p 31). It has not been suggested that the respondent state intentionally sought to deprive the applicant of her life. The Court's task is, therefore, to determine whether, given the circumstances of the case, the State did all that could have been required of it to prevent the applicant's life from being avoidably put at risk.

2   The Court notes that the applicant's father was serving as a catering assistant on Christmas Island at the time of the United Kingdom's nuclear tests there ... In the absence of individual dose measurements, it cannot be known with any certainty whether, in the course of his duties, he was exposed to dangerous levels of radiation. However, the Court observes that it has not been provided with any evidence to prove that he ever reported any symptoms indicative of the fact that he had been exposed to above-average levels of radiation.

The Court has examined the voluminous evidence submitted by both sides relating to the question whether or not he was so exposed. It notes in particular that records of contemporaneous measurements of radiation on Christmas Island ... indicate that radiation did not reach dangerous levels in the areas in which ordinary servicemen were stationed. Perhaps more importantly for the issues under Art 2, these records provide a basis to believe that the state authorities, during the period between the United Kingdom's recognition of the competence of the Commission to receive applications on 14 January 1966 and the applicant's diagnosis with leukaemia in October 1970, could reasonably have been confident that her father had not been dangerously irradiated.

3   Nonetheless, in view of the lack of certainty on this point, the Court will also examine the question whether, in the event that there was information available to the authorities which should have given them cause to fear that the applicant's father had been exposed to radiation, they could reasonably have been expected, during the period in question, to provide advice to her parents and to monitor her health.

The Court considers that the state could only have been required of its own motion to take these steps in relation to the applicant if it had appeared likely at that time that any such exposure of her father to radiation might have engendered a real risk to her health.

4   Having examined the expert evidence submitted to it, the Court is not satisfied that it has been established that there is a causal link between the exposure of a father to radiation and leukaemia in a child subsequently conceived. As recently as 1993, the High Court judge sitting in the cases of *Reay and Hope v British Nuclear Fuels plc*, having examined a considerable amount of expert evidence, found that 'the scales

tilt[ed] decisively' in favour of a finding that there was no such causal link ... The Court could not reasonably hold, therefore, that, in the late 1960s, the United Kingdom authorities could or should, on the basis of this unsubstantiated link, have taken action in respect of the applicant.

5   Finally, in the light of the conflicting evidence of Dr Bross and Professor Eden ... and as the Commission also found ... it is clearly uncertain whether monitoring of the applicant's health *in utero* and from birth would have led to earlier diagnosis and medical intervention such as to diminish the severity of her disease. It is perhaps arguable that, had there been reason to believe that she was in danger of contracting a life-threatening disease owing to her father's presence on Christmas Island, the state authorities would have been under a duty to have made this known to her parents whether or not they considered that the information would assist the applicant. However, this is not a matter which the Court is required to decide in view of its above findings ...

6   In conclusion, the Court does not find it established that, given the information available to the state at the relevant time (see para 37 above) concerning the likelihood of the applicant's father having been exposed to dangerous levels of radiation and of this having created a risk to her health, it could have been expected to act of its own motion to notify her parents of these matters or to take any other special action in relation to her.

It follows that there has been no violation of Art 2.

In *McGinley & Egan v UK* (1998) 27 EHRR 1 the Court held that where a government undertakes hazardous activities, which might have hidden adverse effects on the health of those involved in the activities, the obligation to provide essential information extends beyond ensuring the provision of particular documents. It requires the existence of effective and accessible procedures by which information may be obtained. In this case the procedures that existed were found to be adequate.

These decisions show that Art 2 might be used to force environmental enforcement bodies who are aware of the existence of significant hazards either to take steps within their powers to stop such hazards or to make those likely to be affected aware of the risks (Hart in English and Havers (2000) 163). See in this context the obligation under Art 5(1)(c) of the Aarhus Convention 1998, p 814, above.

Article 8 – Right to respect for private life and home

1   Everyone has the right to respect for his private and family life, his home and his correspondence.

2   There shall be no interference by a public authority with the exercise of this right except such as is in accordance with the law and is necessary in a democratic society in the interests of national security, public safety or the economic well-being of the country, for the prevention of disorder or crime, for the protection of health or morals, or for the protection of the rights and freedoms of others.

It is established both that the effects of pollution can interfere with the right to a private life and a home. In this context the respect for a home extends beyond the physical to cover factors associated with the quality of life. In *López Ostra v Spain* (1995) 20 EHRR 277; (1994) EHRR A 303-C (see below) the Court said that '[n]aturally, severe environmental pollution may affect individuals' well-being and prevent them from enjoying their homes in such a way as to affect their private and family life adversely, without however, seriously endangering their health (para 51)'. See also *Guerra v Italy* (1998) 26 EHRR 357, below. Moreover, the concept of a home has been interpreted broadly. In *G & E v Norway* (1983) 35 D & R 30, for example, the Commission held that a proposal to flood the hunting grounds of Laplanders infringed Art 8(1), although the interference was found to be justified under Art 8(2). In *Buckley v UK* (1996) 23 EHRR 101 an enforcement notice against a gypsy family was held to be an infringement of Art 8(1) and in *Coster, Beard et al v UK* (1998) 25 EHRR claims that the traditional lifestyle of gypsies fall within Art 8 were declared admissible.

Obligations under Art 8 may be both negative and positive. States, for example, may be under positive obligations to take action to prevent a person's private life, family and home being interfered with by commercial concerns, by for example, failing to provide: '... essential information that would have entitled [local people] to assess the risks they and they families might run if they continued to live at Mafredonia (*Guerra v Italy*, para 60).' This failure, however, did not constitute a breach of Art 10, despite the fact that this Art icle expressly includes a right to receive information. On this see the discussion of Art 10, p 919.

Article 8(2) – Justifying an infringement of the right to a home

As can be seen from Art 8(2), circumstances may exist to justify interference with the rights in Art 8(1). In *López Ostra* (see extract below) the Court was not satisfied that the State had properly balanced the general economic needs of the community against the specific interests of the individual. In its earlier decision in *Powell and Rayner* (1990) 12 EHRR 345 (see p 866, below), by contrast, the Court decided that while the noise caused by planes using the runways at Heathrow did interfere with the applicants' enjoyment of their home, the interference was justified by the importance of the airport to the British economy. It also said that the steps taken to deal with noise pollution resulting from the use of the airport were within the UK's margin of appreciation (see the following extract from the Judgment of the Court). In *S v France* (1990) 65 D & R 250 a similar approach was taken in relation to a nuclear power station that was located close to an 18th century chateau. Hart (Hart in English and Havers (2000) 169) notes that Art 8(2) may allow greater scope for interfering with rights than is traditionally permitted by analogous common law principles in domestic law. He considers, for example, the Docklands litigation, contrasting the House of Lord's decision in *Hunter v Canary Wharf Ltd* [1997] AC 655 (see Chapter 1, p 34, above) and the decision on admissibility in *Khatun v UK* (26 EHRR CD 212) where the infringement of Art 8(1) rights was found to be justified within Art 8(2) by the legitimate aim of regenerating the Docklands region.

López Ostra v Spain (1995) 20 EHRR 277

In *López Ostra v Spain* a treatment plant for liquid and solid waste was built with a State subsidy on municipal land 12 metres away from the applicant's home. The plant released fumes, smells and contamination which caused health problems and nuisance to the local people. The town council evacuated local residents and rehoused them for several months before closing down one of the plant's activities. This did not solve all the problems. The applicant claimed that she was a victim of a breach of Art 8(1) as her private and family life had become impossible. She also claimed to be a victim of Art 3 (degrading treatment). The Court held that there had been a breach of Art 8, but not of Art 3. In reaching this decision the Court accepted that under Art 8(2) it was necessary to balance the interests of the town authorities in improving economic well being and the applicant's right to a home life under Art 8(1). While the authorities had a margin of appreciation, in this case the balance had not been fairly struck. The following is an extract from the Court's judgment.

34   The applicant alleged that there had been a violation of Arts 8 and 3 ... of the Convention on account of the smells, noise and polluting fumes caused by a plant for the treatment of liquid and solid waste sited a few metres away from her home. She held the Spanish authorities responsible, alleging that they had adopted a passive attitude.

[The Court rejected the Government's preliminary objection that there had been a failure to exhaust domestic remedies and went on to consider its objection that the applicant was not a 'victim'.]

B   The objection that the applicant was not a victim

40   The Government raised a second objection already advanced before the Commission. They acknowledged that Mrs López Ostra – like, for that matter, the other residents of Lorca – had been caused serious nuisance by the plant until 9 September 1988, when part of its activities ceased ... However, even supposing that smells or noise – which would not have been excessive – had continued after that date, the applicant had in the meantime ceased to be a victim. From February 1992 the López Ostra family were rehoused in a flat in the town centre at the municipality's expense, and in February 1993 they moved into a house they had purchased ... In any case, the closure of the plant in October 1993 brought all nuisance to an end, with the result that neither the applicant nor her family now suffered the alleged undesirable effects of its operation.

41   At the hearing the Delegate of the Commission pointed out that the investigating judge's decision of 27 October 1993 ... did not mean that someone who had been forced by environmental conditions to abandon her home and subsequently to buy another house had ceased to be a victim.

42   The Court shares this opinion. Neither Mrs López Ostra's move nor the waste-treatment plant's closure, which was moreover temporary ... alters the fact that the applicant and her family lived for years only 12 metres away from a source of smells, noise and fumes.

At all events, if the applicant could now return to her former home following the decision to close the plant, this would be a factor to be taken into account in assessing the damage she sustained but would not mean that she ceased to be a victim ...

43   The objection is therefore unfounded.

II   ALLEGED VIOLATION OF ARTICLE 8 OF THE CONVENTION

44   Mrs López Ostra first contended that there had been a violation of Art 8 of the Convention ...

The Commission subscribed to this view, while the Government contested it.

45   The Government said that the complaint made to the Commission and declared admissible by it ... was not the same as the one that the Spanish courts had considered

in the application for protection of fundamental rights since it appeared to be based on statements, medical reports and technical experts' opinions of later date than that application and wholly unconnected with it.

46 This argument does not persuade the Court. The applicant had complained of a situation which had been prolonged by the municipality's and the relevant authorities' failure to act. This inaction was one of the fundamental points both in the complaints made to the Commission and in the application to the Murcia Audiencia Territorial ... The fact that it continued after the application to the Commission and the decision on admissibility cannot be held against the applicant. Where a situation under consideration is a persisting one, the Court may take into account facts occurring after the application has been lodged and even after the decision on admissibility has been adopted (see, as the earliest authority, the *Neumeister v Austria* judgment of 27 June 1968, Series A No 8, p 21, para 28, and p 38, para 7).

47 Mrs López Ostra maintained that, despite its partial shutdown on 9 September 1988, the plant continued to emit fumes, repetitive noise and strong smells, which made her family's living conditions unbearable and caused both her and them serious health problems. She alleged in this connection that her right to respect for her home had been infringed.

48 The Government disputed that the situation was really as described and as serious ...

[...]

51 Naturally, severe environmental pollution may affect individuals' well-being and prevent them from enjoying their homes in such a way as to affect their private and family life adversely, without, however, seriously endangering their health.

Whether the question is analysed in terms of a positive duty on the state – to take reasonable and appropriate measures to secure the applicant's rights under para 1 of Art 8 (Art 8-1) –, as the applicant wishes in her case, or in terms of an 'interference by a public authority' to be justified in accordance with para 2 (Art 8-2), the applicable principles are broadly similar. In both contexts regard must be had to the fair balance that has to be struck between the competing interests of the individual and of the community as a whole, and in any case the state enjoys a certain margin of appreciation. Furthermore, even in relation to the positive obligations flowing from the first paragraph of Art 8 (Art 8-1), in striking the required balance the aims mentioned in the second paragraph (Art 8-2) may be of a certain relevance (see, in particular, the *Rees v the United Kingdom* judgment of 17 October 1986, Series A No 106, p 15, para 37, and the *Powell and Rayner v the United Kingdom* (1990) judgment of 21 February, Series A No 172, p 18, para 41).

52 It appears from the evidence that the waste-treatment plant in issue was built by SACURSA in July 1988 to solve a serious pollution problem in Lorca due to the concentration of tanneries. Yet as soon as it started up, the plant caused nuisance and health problems to many local people ...

Admittedly, the Spanish authorities, and in particular the Lorca municipality, were theoretically not directly responsible for the emissions in question. However, as the Commission pointed out, the town allowed the plant to be built on its land and the state subsidised the plant's construction ...

53 The town council reacted promptly by re-housing the residents affected, free of charge, in the town centre for the months of July, August and September 1988 and then by stopping one of the plant's activities from 9 September ... However, the council's members could not be unaware that the environmental problems continued after this partial shutdown (see paras 9 and 11 above) [...]).

54 Mrs López Ostra submitted that by virtue of the general supervisory powers conferred on the municipality by the 1961 regulations the municipality had a duty to act. In addition, the plant did not satisfy the legal requirements, in particular as regards its location and the failure to obtain a municipal licence ...

55 On this issue the Court points out that the question of the lawfulness of the building and operation of the plant has been pending in the Supreme Court since 1991 ... The Court has consistently held that it is primarily for the national authorities, notably the courts, to interpret and apply domestic law ...

At all events, the Court considers that in the present case, even supposing that the municipality did fulfil the functions assigned to it by domestic law ... it need only establish whether the national authorities took the measures necessary for protecting the applicant's right to respect for her home and for her private and family life under Art 8 ...

56 It has to be noted that the municipality not only failed to take steps to that end after 9 September 1988 but also resisted judicial decisions to that effect. In the ordinary administrative proceedings instituted by Mrs López Ostra's sisters-in-law it appealed against the Murcia High Court's decision of 18 September 1991 ordering temporary closure of the plant, and that measure was suspended as a result ...

Other state authorities also contributed to prolonging the situation. On 19 November 1991 Crown Counsel appealed against the Lorca investigating judge's decision of 15 November temporarily to close the plant in the prosecution for an environmental health offence ... with the result that the order was not enforced until 27 October 1993 ...

57 The Government drew attention to the fact that the town had borne the expense of renting a flat in the centre of Lorca, in which the applicant and her family lived from 1 February 1992 to February 1993 ...

The Court notes, however, that the family had to bear the nuisance caused by the plant for over three years before moving house with all the attendant inconveniences. They moved only when it became apparent that the situation could continue indefinitely and when Mrs López Ostra's daughter's paediatrician recommended that they do so ... Under these circumstances, the municipality's offer could not afford complete redress for the nuisance and inconveniences to which they had been subjected.

58 Having regard to the foregoing, and despite the margin of appreciation left to the respondent state, the Court considers that the state did not succeed in striking a fair balance between the interest of the town's economic well-being – that of having a waste-treatment plant – and the applicant's effective enjoyment of her right to respect for her home and her private and family life.

There has accordingly been a violation of Art 8.

[The Court went on to hold that there was no violation of Art 3. It held that that Spain should pay 4 million pesetas for damage and 1.5 million pesetas, less 9,700 French francs, costs and expenses.

Guerra and Others v Italy (1998) 26 EHRR 357

For a summary of the facts see p 901, above. The following extract from the Judgment of the European Court of Human Rights deals with Art 8. For the Court's consideration of Art 10, see p 919, below.

III ALLEGED VIOLATION OF ARTICLE 8 OF THE CONVENTION

7   The applicants ... maintained before the Court that they had been the victims of a violation of Art 8 of the Convention ...

8   The Court's task is to determine whether Art 8 is applicable and, if so, whether it has been infringed.

The Court notes, firstly, that all the applicants live at Manfredonia, approximately 1 kilometre away from the factory, which, owing to its production of fertilisers and caprolactam, was classified as being high-risk in 1988, pursuant to the criteria laid down in DPR 175/88.

In the course of its production cycle the factory released large quantities of inflammable gas and other toxic substances, including arsenic trioxide. Moreover, in 1976, following the explosion of the scrubbing tower for the ammonia synthesis gases, several tonnes of potassium carbonate and bicarbonate solution, containing arsenic trioxide, escaped and 150 people had to be hospitalised on account of acute arsenic poisoning.

In addition, in its report of 8 December 1988, a committee of technical experts appointed by the Manfredonia District Council said in particular that because of the factory's geographical position, emissions from it into the atmosphere were often channelled towards Manfredonia ...

The direct effect of the toxic emissions on the applicants' right to respect for their private and family life means that Art 8 is applicable.

9   The Court considers that Italy cannot be said to have 'interfered' with the applicants' private or family life; they complained not of an act by the state but of its failure to act. However, although the object of Art 8 is essentially that of protecting the individual against arbitrary interference by the public authorities, it does not merely compel the state to abstain from such interference: in addition to this primarily negative undertaking, there may be positive obligations inherent in effective respect for private or family life (see the *Airey v Ireland* (1979) judgment of 9 October, Series A No 32, p 17, § 32).

In the present case it need only be ascertained whether the national authorities took the necessary steps to ensure effective protection of the applicants' right to respect for their private and family life as guaranteed by Art 8 (see the *López Ostra v Spain* (1994) judgment of 9 December, Series A No 303-C, p 55, § 55).

10   On 14 September 1993, pursuant to Art 19 of DPR 175/88, the Ministry for the Environment and the Ministry of Health jointly adopted conclusions on the safety report submitted by the factory in July 1989. Those conclusions prescribed improvements to be made to the installations, both in relation to current fertiliser production and in the event of resumed caprolactam production, and provided the prefect with instructions as to the emergency plan – that he had drawn up in 1992 – and the measures required for informing the local population under Art 17 of DPR 175/88.

In a letter of 7 December 1995 to the European Commission of Human Rights, however, the mayor of Monte Sant'Angelo indicated that the investigation for the purpose of drawing up conclusions under Art 19 was still continuing and that he had not received any documents relating to them. He pointed out that the District Council was still awaiting direction from the Civil Defence Department before deciding what safety measures should be taken and what procedures should be followed in the event of an accident and communicated to the public. He said that if the factory resumed production, the measures for informing the public would be taken as soon as the conclusions based on the investigation were available ...

11 The Court reiterates that severe environmental pollution may affect individuals' well-being and prevent them from enjoying their homes in such a way as to affect their private and family life adversely (see, *mutatis mutandis*, the López Ostra judgment cited above, p 54, § 51). In the instant case the applicants waited, right up until the production of fertilisers ceased in 1994, for essential information that would have enabled them to assess the risks they and their families might run if they continued to live at Manfredonia, a town particularly exposed to danger in the event of an accident at the factory.

The Court holds, therefore, that the respondent state did not fulfil its obligation to secure the applicants' right to respect for their private and family life, in breach of Art 8 of the Convention.

There has consequently been a violation of that provision.

Powell and Rayner v UK (1990) 12 EHRR 345

C The claim under Article 8

37 The applicants also maintained that, as a result of excessive noise generated by air traffic in and out of Heathrow Airport, they had each been a victim of an unjustified interference by the United Kingdom with the right guaranteed to them under Art 8.

[...]

40 In each case, albeit to greatly differing degrees, the quality of the applicant's private life and the scope for enjoying the amenities of his home have been adversely affected by the noise generated by aircraft using Heathrow Airport ... Art 8 is therefore a material provision in relation to both Mr Powell and Mr Rayner.

41 Whether the present case be analysed in terms of a positive duty on the state to take reasonable and appropriate measures to secure the applicants' rights under para 1 of Art 8 or in terms of an 'interference by a public authority' to be justified in accordance with para 2, the applicable principles are broadly similar. In both contexts regard must be had to the fair balance that has to be struck between the competing interests of the individual and of the community as a whole; and in both contexts the state enjoys a certain margin of appreciation in determining the steps to be taken to ensure compliance with the Convention ...

42 As the Commission pointed out in its admissibility decisions, the existence of large international airports, even in densely populated urban areas, and the increasing use of jet aircraft have without question become necessary in the interests of a country's economic well-being. According to the uncontested figures supplied by the Government, Heathrow Airport, which is one of the busiest airports in the world, occupies a position of central importance in international trade and communications and in the economy of the United Kingdom ... The applicants themselves conceded that

the operation of a major international airport pursued a legitimate aim and that the consequential negative impact on the environment could not be entirely eliminated.

43 A number of measures have been introduced by the responsible authorities to control, abate and compensate for aircraft noise at and around Heathrow Airport, including aircraft noise certification, restrictions on night jet movements, noise monitoring, the introduction of noise preferential routes, runway alternation, noise-related landing charges, the revocation of the licence for the Gatwick/Heathrow helicopter link, a noise insulation grant scheme, and a scheme for the purchase of noise-blighted properties close to the Airport ... These measures, adopted progressively as a result of consultation of the different interests and people concerned, have taken due account of international standards established, developments in aircraft technology, and the varying levels of disturbance suffered by those living around Heathrow Airport.

44 On the other hand, section 76(1) of the Civil Aviation Act 1982 limits the possibilities of legal redress open to the aggrieved person ... However, it is to be noted that the exclusion of liability in nuisance is not absolute: it applies only in respect of aircraft flying at a reasonable height and in accordance with the relevant regulatory provisions, including the Air Navigation (Noise Certification) Order 1987 ...

Since a forerunner of s 76(1) was enacted in 1949, successive Governments in the United Kingdom have proceeded on the view that the problems posed by aircraft noise are in general better dealt with by taking and enforcing specific regulatory measures to ensure that disturbance caused by aircraft noise is minimised, to the exclusion of having the matter settled by the case-law of the courts on the general criterion of reasonableness in any actions for nuisance which might be brought at common law. It is certainly not for the Commission or the Court to substitute for the assessment of the national authorities any other assessment of what might be the best policy in this difficult social and technical sphere. This is an area where the contracting states are to be recognised as enjoying a wide margin of appreciation ...

45 In view of the foregoing, there is no serious ground for maintaining that either the policy approach to the problem or the content of the particular regulatory measures adopted by the United Kingdom authorities gives rise to violation of Art 8, whether under its positive or negative head. In forming a judgment as to the proper scope of the noise abatement measures for aircraft arriving at and departing from Heathrow Airport, the United Kingdom Government cannot arguably be said to have exceeded the margin of appreciation afforded to them or upset the fair balance required to be struck under Art 8 ...

Article 1 of the First Protocol – Peaceful enjoyment of possessions and property

Every natural or legal person is entitled to the peaceful enjoyment of his possessions. No-one shall be deprived of his possessions except in the public interest and subject to the conditions provided by law and by the general principles of international law.

The proceeding provisions shall not, however, in any way impair the right of a state to enforce such laws as it deems necessary to control property in accordance with the general interest or to secure the payment of taxes or other contributions or penalties.

This Article comprises three distinct rules. The first rule is of a general nature. It enounces the principle of *peaceful enjoyment of property*. The second rule covers *deprivation of possessions* and subjects it to certain conditions. The third rule recognises that the states are entitled, amongst other things, to control *the use of property* in accordance with the general interest, by enforcing such laws as they deem necessary for the purpose; it is contained in the second paragraph (see *Sporrong and Lonnroth*, the ECHR (Series A No 52 (1982), para 61).

The rights set out in this provision are potentially very important in the context of environmental law, where legal regulation is often directed at controlling the way property, including land, is used.[50] In practice, however, the ability of public authorities to take action which affects property in the general public interest operates as a considerable limitation on the use of this Article by claimants and a breach of the Article will only be found in exceptional circumstances. In this context it may be noted that the 'public interest' may include environmental protection. The revocation of a permit to extract gravel in the interests of nature conservancy, for example, was held to constitute a justified interference with property in *Fredin v Sweden* (1990) 13 EHRR 784.

The following two decisions illustrate how courts approach the argument that that there is a right to compensation when official action interferes with property rights. In these cases the property rights concern cheese and fish and the interference occurred in the interests of food safety and public health. The extract from the *Booker Aquaculture* case is also of interest for the way the court deals with the relationship between EU law and the ECHR.

R v Secretary of State for Health ex p Eastside Cheese Co (1999) 55 BMLR 38; [1999] 3 CMLR 12

The case followed the serious illness of a 12-year old boy suffering from e-coli 0157. It was believed that the infection could be traced to cheese produced by RA Duckett & Co. The Secretary of State for Health made an emergency control order under s 13 of the Food Safety Act 1990 prohibiting the carrying out of any commercial operation in relation to cheese originating from RA Duckett & Co. The order paralysed the business of cheese processors such as the Eastside Cheese Company (the applicant). Under the provisions of s 13 no compensation was payable to those in the applicant's position. The applicant obtained leave to seek judicial review of the order which was held to be unlawful by Moses J on 13 November 1998 ((1998) 47 BMLR 1). The Court allowed the appeal.

In the Court of Appeal the applicant unsuccessfully argued that the failure to pay compensation for the commercial losses caused by the emergency control order and the inability to use or sell the cheese in question was contrary to Art 1 of Protocol 1 of the European Convention on Human Rights. The following is an extract from the judgment.

> ... it would seem clear that the effect of the s 13 order made in this case was to interfere with the peaceful enjoyment by Ducketts and Eastside of the cheeses which belonged to them. We are doubtful whether the present case is one in which the effect of the order was to deprive them of their possessions: there was no transfer of ownership from them to the state or any other party; the s 13 order could have been revoked at any time, and if revoked could have ceased to have any effect; and it was always open to Ducketts and Eastside to seek the Minister's consent under s 13(3) of the Act. In a deprivation case the availability of compensation is a relevant consideration. In *Holy Monasteries v Greece* (1994) 20 EHRR 1, p 48, para 71, the European Court said:

---

50 Note that a waste management licence is 'property' for the purposes of s 436 of the Insolvency Act 1986, see Chapter 4, p 484.

In this connection, the taking of property without payment of an amount reasonably related to its value will normally constitute a disproportionate interference and a total lack of compensation can be considered justifiable under Art 1 only in exceptional circumstances.

Such a rule is readily understandable where the state is itself assuming ownership of property belonging to another, or where property is being transferred from one citizen to another. It appears to us to have very much less force where, in a case such as the present, the object of the measure is to restrain the use of property in the public interest. If, however, the general rule stated by the court concerning compensation has any application to a situation such as faced the Secretary of State, we would have little hesitation in holding that the circumstances were sufficiently exceptional to displace it.

The present case is, in our judgment, much more appropriately regarded as one in which the state deemed it necessary to control the use of property in accordance with the general interest. Although the *Holy Monasteries* case was concerned with deprivation, it would seem to us that the observations of the court ((1994) 20 EHRR 1, p 48 (para 70)) are relevant:

> 70 An interference with peaceful enjoyment of possessions must strike a 'fair balance' between the demands of the general interests of the community and the requirements of the protection of the individual's fundamental rights. The concern to achieve this balance is reflected in the structure of Art 1 as a whole, including therefore the second sentence, which is to be read in the light of the general principle enunciated in the first sentence. In particular, there must be a reasonable relationship of proportionality between the means employed and the aim sought to be realised by any measure depriving a person of his possessions.

Thus there must be proportionality between the means employed and the ends sought to be achieved, and a fair balancing of the interests of the public and those of private individuals. While the court must never abdicate its duty of review, it will accord a margin of appreciation to the decision-making authority. Particularly must this be true, in our view, where the decision-making authority is responding to what it reasonably regards as an imminent threat to the life or health of the public.

No doubt the Secretary of State appreciated, when making the s 13 order, that its effect might well be to lead to the destruction of cheeses held by Ducketts and Eastside and others in the same position. These cheeses were, however, reasonably regarded as unsafe. Had they ceased to be so regarded, the order would, we assume, have been revoked. On the present facts we can see no room for an argument that the emergency action taken by the Secretary of State involved an unjustified violation of fundamental human rights on the part of Ducketts and Eastside.

Booker Aquaculture Ltd v Secretary of State for Scotland [1999] Inner House Cases

McConnell Salmon Ltd (MSL) leased a site rearing turbot. MSL came to suspect that some of the turbot might be infected with viral haemorrhagic septicaemia (VHS) and, as required by reg 11 of the Fish Health Regulations 1992 SI 1992/3300, MSL informed the Secretary of State of their suspicion. In September 1994 the Secretary of State served a notice on MSL under reg 7 of the Diseases of Fish (Control) Regulations 1994 SI 1994/1447 requiring MSL *inter alia* to destroy all eggs, dead fish and fish which in the opinion of an inspector showed clinical signs of disease and to kill all fish and destroy their carcasses, with the exception of fish of commercial size. Fish of commercial size could be slaughtered for marketing or processing for human consumption, subject to a number of conditions, in particular that in the opinion of the inspector they showed no clinical signs of disease. In practice these fish of commercial size were to be kept for a period during which any traces of antibiotics would be eliminated from their systems and they were then to be slaughtered. MSL complied with the notice.

On 13 December 1994 MSL wrote to the Secretary of State seeking compensation for the losses which they said they had suffered as a result of complying with the notice. The claim was for over £ 600,000. The Secretary of State replied that:

> After careful consideration it has been concluded that your legal claim for compensation cannot be accepted. In addition, in line with the Government's long-established policy of non-payment of compensation for fish diseases, an *ex-gratia* payment would not be appropriate.

On 23 December 1996 MSL assigned to Booker Aquaculture Limited all claims and rights competent to them to sue or raise any court proceedings in respect of losses incurred by them arising *inter alia* out of the service on them of the notice under reg 7. In January 1997 Booker Aquaculture Ltd lodged a petition for judicial review of the 1994 Regulations and of the Secretary of State's decision. The petition was successful at first instance. The Secretary of State appealed. The following is an extract from the judgment of the Lord President.

> In the case of the slaughter of animals in relation to certain diseases, compensation is payable under s 31 of, and Sched 3 to, the Animal Health Act 1981. It would have been open to the Minister and to the Secretary of State, by virtue of s 87(3), to extend the definition of animals to include 'fish' and so to give themselves the power to pay compensation for the slaughter of fish under s 32(3) of the same Act. But they have not done so and, as the letter to MSL indicated, this is because of 'the Government's long-established policy of non-payment of compensation for fish diseases'. The situation therefore is that reg 7 was introduced into our law in a situation where our law deliberately excludes any right on the part of those whose fish are killed and destroyed to claim compensation from the Scottish Executive.

> [...]

> Counsel for both parties were agreed that ... in implementing the 1993 Directive the United Kingdom had been subject to the general rules of the treaty and in particular to the general principles of Community law, including the fundamental rights enshrined in Community law. That approach is fully vouched by the observations of Advocate General Jacobs in *Wachauf v Bundesamt für Ernahrung und Forstwirtschaft* [1989] ECR 2609, p 2629 where he says that:

>> It appears to me self-evident that when acting in pursuance of powers granted under Community law, Member States must be subject to the same constraints, in any event in relation to the principle of respect for fundamental rights, as the Community legislator.

> This approach was adopted by the Court of Justice in para 19 of their judgment in the same case where they stated that, since the requirements of the protection of fundamental rights in the Community legal order:

>> ... are also binding on the Member States when they implement Community rules, the Member States must, as far as possible, apply those rules in accordance with those requirements.

Although there was therefore no dispute between the parties that in principle the fundamental rights would apply when a Member State implemented Community rules, there is, as will be seen below, an issue between the parties as to whether, in determining compensation arising out of the application of the national measures implementing Community rules, the Member State is acting within the scope of Community law or within the area of its own competence.

The Right to Property

Counsel for the respondent did not seek to question the existence of the fundamental right to property with which these proceedings are concerned. A convenient statement of the general approach to fundamental rights in Community law is to be found in *Nold KG v Commission* [1974] ECR 491 in para 13 of the judgment of the Court:

> As the Court has already stated, fundamental rights form an integral part of the general principles of law, the observance of which it ensures.
>
> In safeguarding these rights, the Court is bound to draw inspiration from constitutional traditions common to the Member States, and it cannot therefore uphold measures which are incompatible with fundamental rights recognised and protected by the Constitutions of those states.
>
> Similarly, international treaties for the protection of human rights on which the Member States have collaborated or of which they are signatories, can supply guidelines which should be followed within the framework of Community law.

More particularly, as the Court made clear, for instance, in *Hauer v Land Rheinland-Pfalz* [1979] ECR 3727, para 17 of its judgment, the right to property as guaranteed in the Community legal order is in accordance with the ideas which are reflected in the terms of the first Protocol to the European Convention for the Protection of Human Rights.

[...]

The preceding provisions shall not, however, in any way impair the right of a state to enforce such laws as it deems necessary to control the use of property in accordance with the general interest or to secure the payment of taxes or other contributions or penalties.

[...]

In the present case it appears that a notice under reg 7 of the 1994 Regulations would impair an owner's right of property in his fish in two ways. First, as counsel for the respondent accepted, in so far as the Secretary of State's notice required him to kill and destroy fish, it would deprive him of his property in the fish ... Secondly, in so far as it permitted him to slaughter fish of commercial size for marketing or processing for human consumption, but only subject to certain conditions, then it would restrict the owner's exercise of his right of property in those fish ...

So far as concerned the deprivation of their property by the compulsory killing and destruction of MSL's fish, counsel for the petitioners accepted, of course, that deprivation of property was permissible 'in the public interest' (Art 1, second sentence) ... In these circumstances counsel for the petitioners did not argue that a requirement on a fish farmer, whether in terms of a direct transposition of Art 9 or in terms of a more stringent regime imposed by the United Kingdom in reg 7, to destroy turbot where there had been an outbreak of VHS could not be justified in the public interest. Rather, they argued that, even though in these circumstances the deprivation of the owner's property might be justified in the public interest, the absence of any possibility of the owner recovering compensation meant that reg 7 was nonetheless in breach of the right of property as that right was to be understood in Community law.

In this connexion counsel for the petitioners referred in particular to the approach of the European Court of Human Rights in interpreting Art 1 of the First Protocol. In *Sporrong and Lonnroth,* para 69, when discussing the rule contained in the first sentence of the first paragraph of the Article, the Court said:

> For the purposes of the latter provision, the Court must determine whether a fair balance was struck between the demands of the general interest of the community and the requirements of the protection of the individual's fundamental rights ... The search for this balance is inherent in the whole of the Convention and is also reflected in the structure of Art 1.

In *Lithgow v United Kingdom* (1986) Series A No 102, in para 120 of the judgment the Court confirmed that these observations were applicable also in a case of deprivation under the second sentence in the first paragraph of Art 1:

> The question remains whether the availability and amount of compensation are material considerations under the second sentence of the first paragraph of Art 1, the text of the provision being silent on the point. The Commission, with whom both the Government and the applicants agreed, read Art 1 as in general impliedly requiring the payment of compensation as a necessary condition for the taking of property of anyone within the jurisdiction of a Contracting State. Like the Commission, the Court observes that under the legal systems of the Contracting States, the taking of property in the public interest without payment of compensation is treated as justifiable only in exceptional circumstances not relevant for present purposes. As far as Art 1 is concerned, the protection of the right of property it affords would be largely illusory and ineffective in the absence of any equivalent principle.
>
> In this connection, the Court recalls that not only must a measure depriving a person of his property pursue, on the facts as well as in principle, a legitimate aim 'in the public interest', but there must also be a reasonable relationship of proportionality between the means employed and the aim sought to be realised. This latter requirement was expressed in other terms in the above-mentioned *Sporrong and Lonnroth* judgment by the notion of the 'fair balance' that must be struck between the demands of the general interest of the community and the requirements of the protection of the individual's fundamental rights (Series A No 52, p 26, § 69). The requisite balance will not be found if the person concerned has had to bear 'an individual and excessive burden' (*ibid*, p 28, § 73). Although the Court was speaking in that judgment in the context of the general rule of peaceful enjoyment of property enunciated in the first sentence of the first paragraph, it pointed out that 'the search for this balance is ... reflected in the structure of Art 1' as a whole (*ibid*, p 26, § 69).
>
> Clearly, compensation terms are material to the assessment whether a fair balance has been struck between the various interests at stake and, notably, whether or not a disproportionate burden has been imposed on the person who has been deprived of his possessions.

[...]

In the light of these authorities I am satisfied that the right to property is recognised as a fundamental right under Community law and that the availability of compensation is relevant to any consideration of whether the right has been respected. Moreover, the right pervades the Community legal order and (as was said in *Wachauf* and other cases) will fall to be taken into account by any Member State when implementing the obligations placed on it by a directive.

[...]

The fundamental question in this case ... [is] ... whether the matter of compensation for fish which are killed and destroyed or whose use is controlled by virtue of reg 7 is governed by Community or national law [in January 2000 a reference was made to the ECJ on this point].

Article 14 – Prohibition of discrimination

The enjoyment of the rights and freedoms set forth in this Convention shall be secured without discrimination on any ground such as sex, race, colour, language, religion, political or other opinion, national or social origin, association with a national minority, property, birth or other status.

This provision does not protect against discrimination *per se*, rather it seeks to prevent discrimination in relation to one of the other rights. Note, however, that Art 14 may be used even when the right to which it has been attached has not been breached. This may be illustrated by *Pine Valley Developments v Ireland* (1991) 14 EHRR 319. The applicants had been granted outline planning consent and expended significant sums on the site. The permission was later declared to be a nullity by the Supreme Court. Legislation was passed giving compensation in relation to all other consents affected by this decision, but not the applicants'. The applicants argued that the failure to compensate them constituted a breach of the right to enjoyment of property under Art 1 of the First Protocol. Although this claim failed, it was held that there was no objective justification for treating the applicants differently from those who had been awarded compensation. They were therefore victims of a breach of Art 14 in relation to Art 1 of the First Protocol.

The principal process-based Convention rights affecting the environment

Article 6 – Right to a fair trial

1   In the determination of his civil rights and obligations or of any criminal charge against him, everyone is entitled to a fair and public hearing within a reasonable time by an independent and impartial tribunal established by law.

The procedural rights associated with obtaining a fair hearing are of considerable importance in the context of environmental law. The concept of civil rights and obligations has been given an 'autonomous' meaning in ECHR jurisprudence that extends beyond rights in contract or tort. In *Zander v Sweden* (1993) 18 EHRR 175, for example, applicants were able to use Art 6 to challenge a decision to permit the dumping of waste on nearby land despite the call for the imposition of conditions requiring the company to supply free drinking water as a precautionary measure in case the waste caused cyanide pollution. The decision affected the applicants' civil rights because it was likely to adversely affect the value of their property and because it was arguable that Swedish law provided protection against water pollution (see also *Ortenburg v Austria* (1994) 19 EHRR 524).

This case may be contrasted with the more recent decision of the European Court of Human Rights in *Balmer-Schafroth v Switzerland* (1998) EHRR 598. Here people living within 5 km of a nuclear power station opposed the decision to extend the plant on safety grounds. The Federal Government dismissed these objections and there was no opportunity for further domestic appeal or judicial review. The European Commission on Human Rights (by 16 votes to 12) was of the opinion that there was a breach of Art 6(1). The Court by 12 to 8 disagreed. The majority said that the applicants' 'civil rights' were not affected because they had failed to show that the proposed extension of the plant would expose them to a danger that was specific and imminent. Hart (Hart in English and Havers (2000) 177) notes that the minority objected to this conclusion on the ground that to say that 'civil rights' were not involved begged the question. As the minority put it: 'Does the local population have to be irradiated before being able to exercise a remedy?' (See also *Greenpeace Schweiz v Switzerland* (1977) 23 EHRR 116.)

The right to a fair trial implies certain rights which are not specifically referred to in Art 6, including a right of access to the courts (*Golder v UK* (1975) Series A No 18). This right is breached, for example, by the existence of an immunity protecting the police from being sued in negligence for the way they investigate crimes (*Osman v UK* (2000) 29 EHRR 245). The privilege against self-incrimination is also an aspect of the right to a fair trial. In *R v Hertfordshire County Council ex p Green Environmental Industries Ltd and Another* [2000] 2 WLR 373 (HL); [2000] 1 All ER 773, this privilege was relied on in an attempt to thwart environmental protection proceedings. The Company argued that s 71(2) of the EPA 1990 (under which the company was compelled, on pain of criminal sanctions, to provide information to the local authority prior to being prosecuted under s 33(1) of that Act, see Chapter 4, p 439 is invalid because it conflicts with the privilege against self-incrimination which is implied in the Art 6(1) notion of a fair trial. The argument failed at first instance, in the Court of Appeal and, on further appeal, in the House of Lords.

In the Lords it was accepted that since the EPA 1990 gave effect to the European Waste Framework Directive (Directive 91/156: see p 389, above) it must be interpreted in accordance with Community law, including the general principles of human rights which form part of Community jurisprudence. These principles include the provisions and jurisprudence of the European Convention of Human Rights. However, in the leading case on the privilege against self-incrimination, *Saunders v UK* (1997) 23, the European Court of Human Rights said that the privilege did not extend to the giving of information to extra-judicial inquiries. Although the local authority had power to prosecute in criminal proceedings, a request for information under s 71(2) was not part of an adjudication and was not therefore covered. This meant that the company could not refuse to provide answers to the questions asked by the local authority. As Angela Ward has commented: '... a finding in favour of the appellants would have drastically impaired the capacity of local authorities to collect the threshold of evidence necessary to mount prosecutions for environmental crimes.' (Ward, A, 'European prohibitions on self-incrimination: can they thwart the enforcement of environmental standards?' [2000] 4 Env Liability 103–05, p 105.)

Independent and impartial tribunal

The requirement that decisions affecting civil rights be taken by an independent tribunal has potentially significant implications for UK planning and environmental law where administrative bodies and ministers are often charged with taking decisions potentially affecting rights. In *Bryan v UK* (1996) 21 EHRR 342 the Court held that UK procedures by which individuals can challenge planning decisions accord with Art 6(1) when taken as a whole. However, while the totality of the procedures were held compatible with Art 6, particular stages, and in particular proceedings before planning inspectors, were said to lack a sufficient degree of independence from government (see also *Benthem v Netherlands* (1985) EHRR l; *Fredin v Sweden* (1990) 13 EHRR 784). More recently, the Divisional Court's decision in *R (On the Application of Holding and Barnes plc) v Secretary of State for the Environment, Transport and the Regions* (13 December 2000) raised a question mark over whether the Minister's role in planning appeals and related procedures is, in view of his policy role, compatible with Art 6. The House of Lords has now overturned this decision, holding that the Minister's role in these procedures is not incompatible with Art 6 ([2001] 2 All ER 929).

Article 10 – Freedom of expression

1   Everyone has the right to freedom of expression. This right shall include freedom to hold opinions and to receive and impart information and ideas without interference by public authority and regardless of frontiers. This article shall not prevent States from requiring the licensing of broadcasting, television or cinema enterprises.

2   The exercise of these freedoms, since it carries with it duties and responsibilities, may be subject to such formalities, conditions, restrictions or penalties as are prescribed by law and are necessary in a democratic society, in the interests of national security, territorial integrity or public safety, for the prevention of disorder or crime, for the protection of health or morals, for the protection of the reputation or rights of others, for preventing the disclosure of information received in confidence, or for maintaining the authority and impartiality of the judiciary.

Despite the recognised importance of public access to environmental information Art 10 has been interpreted narrowly by the European Court of Human Rights. In particular, the right to 'receive information' has been held to create no more than a negative obligation on the State to refrain from action restricting the freedom of individuals to publish information or to prevent individuals obtaining access to information that they request. It imposes no positive obligation to provide information. This was confirmed in *Guerra v Italy* (1998) 26 EHRR 357(see the extract set out below).

While Art 10 is limited in this way, as we have seen above, obligations to provide information may exist in particular circumstances covered by other provisions of the Convention and in particular Arts 2 and 8.

Guerra and Others v Italy (1998) 26 EHRR 357

[See above for the facts and the Court's consideration of Art 8.]

II ALLEGED VIOLATION OF ARTICLE 10 OF THE CONVENTION

B Merits of the complaint

12 It remains to be determined whether Art 10 of the Convention is applicable and, if so, whether it has been infringed.

13 In the Government's submission, that provision merely guaranteed freedom to receive information without hindrance by states; it did not impose any positive obligation. That was shown by the fact that Resolution 1087 (1996) of the Council of Europe's Parliamentary Assembly and Directive 90/313/EEC of the Council of the European Communities on freedom of access to information on the environment spoke merely of access, not a right, to information. If a positive obligation to provide information existed, it would be 'extremely difficult to implement' because of the need to determine how and when the information was to be disclosed, which authorities were responsible for disclosing it and who was to receive it.

14 Like the applicants, the Commission was of the opinion that the provision of information to the public was now one of the essential means of protecting the well-being and health of the local population in situations in which the environment was at risk. Consequently, the words: 'This right shall include freedom ... to receive ... information...' in para 1 of Art 10 had to be construed as conferring an actual right to receive information, in particular from the relevant authorities, on members of local populations who had been or might be affected by an industrial or other activity representing a threat to the environment.

Article 10 imposed on states not just a duty to make available information to the public on environmental matters, a requirement with which Italian law already appeared to comply, by virtue of section 14(3) of Law No 349 in particular, but also a positive obligation to collect, process and disseminate such information, which by its nature could not otherwise come to the knowledge of the public. The protection afforded by Art 10 therefore had a preventive function with respect to potential violations of the Convention in the event of serious damage to the environment and Art 10 came into play even before any direct infringement of other fundamental rights, such as the right to life or to respect for private and family life, occurred.

15 The Court does not subscribe to that view. In cases concerning restrictions on freedom of the press it has on a number of occasions recognised that the public has a right to receive information as a corollary of the specific function of journalists, which is to impart information and ideas on matters of public interest (see, among other authorities, the *Observer and Guardian v the United Kingdom* (1991) judgment of 26 November, Series A No 216, p 30, § 59 (b), and the *Thorgeir Thorgeirson v Iceland* (1992) judgment of 25 June, Series A No 239, p 27, § 63). The facts of the present case are, however, clearly distinguishable from those of the aforementioned cases since the applicants complained of a failure in the system set up pursuant to *DPR* 175/88, which had transposed into Italian law Directive 82/501/EEC of the Council of the European Communities (the 'Seveso' directive) on the major-accident hazards of certain industrial activities dangerous to the environment and the well-being of the local population. Although the prefect of Foggia prepared the emergency plan on the basis of the report

submitted by the factory and the plan was sent to the Civil Defence Department on 3 August 1993, the applicants have yet to receive the relevant information (see paras 26 and 27, above).

The Court reiterates that freedom to receive information, referred to in para 2 of Art 10 of the Convention, 'basically prohibits a government from restricting a person from receiving information that others wish or may be willing to impart to him' (see the *Leander v Sweden* (1987) judgment of 26 March, Series A No 116, p 29, § 74). That freedom cannot be construed as imposing on a State, in circumstances such as those of the present case, positive obligations to collect and disseminate information of its own motion.

16   In conclusion, Art 10 is not applicable in the instant case.

REFERENCES AND FURTHER READING

Anderson, M, 'Human rights approaches to environmental protection: an overview', in Boyle, A and Anderson, M (eds), *Human Rights Approaches to Environmental Protection*, 1996, Oxford: Clarendon, pp 1–23

Birnie, P and Boyle, A, *International Law and the Environment*, 1992, Oxford: OUP

Boyle, A, 'The role of international human rights law in the protection of the environment', in Boyle, A and Anderson, M (eds) *Human Rights Approaches to Environmental Protection*, 1996, Oxford: Clarendon, pp 43–69

Birtles, W, 'A right to know: the Environmental Information Regulations 1992' [1993] JPL 615

Cane, P, 'Standing, representation and the environment', in Loveland, I (ed), *A Special Relationship? American Influences on Public Law in the UK*, 1995, Oxford: Clarendon

Cane, P, 'Standing up for the public' [1995] PL 276

De Merieux, M, 'Deriving environmental rights from the ECHR' (2001) 21(3) OJLS 521

Ebbesson, J, 'The notion of public participation in international environmental law' (1997) 8 Yearbook of International Environmental Law 51–97

Eleftheriadis, PZ, 'The future of environmental rights in the European Union', in Alston, P (ed), *The EU and Human Rights*, 1999, Oxford: Clarendon

English, R and Havers, P (eds), *An Introduction to Human Rights and the Common Law*, 2000, London: Hart

Feldman, D, 'Public interest litigation and constitutional theory in comparative perspective' (1992) 55 MLR 44

Ureta, G, 'The EC Environmental Impact Assessment Directive before the European Court of Justice' [1997] Env Liability 1

Ureta, G, 'Prevention rather than cure: the EC Environmental Assessment Directive and its impact in Spain and the UK' [1993] Env Liability 61

Hart, D, 'The impact of the European Convention on Human Rights on planning and environmental law' [2000] JPL 117–33

Hart, D, 'Environmental rights', in English, R and Havers, P (eds), *An Introduction to Human Rights and the Common Law*, 2000, London: Hart

Higgins, R, *Problems and Process: International Law and How We Use It*, 1994 Oxford: OUP

Hilson, C and Cram, I, 'Judicial review and environmental law – is there a coherent view of standing?' (1996) 16 Legal Studies 1

Hughes, D, *Environmental Law*, 3rd edn, 1996, London: Butterworths

McGoldrick, D, 'Sustainable development and human rights – an integrated conception' (1996) 45 ICLQ 796

Miller, C, *Environmental Rights: Critical Perspectives*, 1998, London: Routledge

Mowbray, A, *'Guerra and Others v Italy*: the right to environmental information under the European Convention on Human Rights' [1998] 3 Env Liability 81

Mowbray, A, 'The greening of human rights law' [1995] Solicitors Journal 994

Mowbray, A, 'A new European Court of Human Rights' [1994] PL S40

Nelson, E, 'Eco-labelling' [1993] Env Liability 16

Politi, M, 'The impact of the Chernobyl accident on the States' perception of international responsibility for nuclear damage', in Francioni, F and Scovazzi, T (eds), *International Responsibility for Environmental Harm*, 1991, London/Dordrecht: Graham and Trotman/Martinus Nijhoff, pp 473–90

Reid, C, 'Judicial review and the environment', in Hadfield, B (ed), *Judicial Review: A Thematic Approach*, 1995, London: Macmillan

Robinson, D and Dunkley, J (eds), *Public Interest Perspectives in Environmental Law*, 1995, Chichester: Chancery, Chapters 3, 10 and 11

Rose, I, 'Industry and access to information on the environment', in Somsen, H (ed), *Protecting the European Environment: Enforcing EC Environmental Law*, 1996, London: Blackstone

Salter, J, 'Environmental assessment: the challenge from Brussels' [1992] JPL 14

Salter, J, 'Environmental assessment: the question of implementation' [1992] JPL 214

Salter, J, 'Environmental assessment: the needs for transparency' [1992] JPL 313

Schiemann, K, *'Locus standi'* [1990] PL 342

Sheat, W, *Making an Impact – A Guide to EIA Law and Policy*, 1994, London: Cameron May

Steele, J, 'Participation and deliberation in environmental law: Exploring a problem-solving approach' (2001) 21(3) OJLS 415

Thornton, J and Tromans, S, 'Human rights and environmental wrongs incorporating the ECHR: some thoughts on the consequences for UK environmental law ' [1999] 11 JEL 35

Trindale, A, 'Human rights and the environment', in Symonides, J (ed), *Human Rights – New Dimensions and Challenges*, 1998, Aldershot: Ashgate

Ward, A, 'The right to an effective remedy in European Community law – environmental protection: a case study of UK judicial decisions concerning the Environmental Assessment Directive' [1993] 5 JEL 221

Ward, A, 'Judicial review of environmental misconduct in the European Community: problems, prospects, and strategies' (2000) 1 Yearbook of European Environmental Law 137–59

Williams, R, 'Direct effect of EC Directive on Impact Assessment' [1991] CLJ 382

USEFUL WEBSITES

Aarhus Convention: www.unece.org/env/pp/etreaty.htm

Access to Environmental Information: www.environment.detre.gov.uk/consult/pub access-response-index.htm

www.europa.eu.int/comm/environment/docum/00402-en.pdf

Espoo Convention: www.unece.org/env/eia

European Court of Human Rights: www.echr.coe.int

UN Economic Commission for Europe: www.unece.org/env

For further general websites, see pages l–li, above.